LAW

OF

MASS COMMUNICATIONS

FREEDOM AND CONTROL OF PRINT AND BROADCAST MEDIA

By

HAROLD L. NELSON, Ph.D.

Professor Emeritus, Journalism
University of Wisconsin—Madison

and

DWIGHT L. TEETER, JR., Ph.D.

William P. Hobby Centennial Professor of Communication
Department of Journalism
The University of Texas at Austin

FIFTH EDITION

Mineola, New York
THE FOUNDATION PRESS, INC.
1986

Library of Congress Cataloging in Publication Data

Nelson, Harold L.
  Law of mass communications.

  Bibliography: p.
  1. Press law—United States. 2. Telecommunication—
Law and legislation—United States. I. Teeter, Dwight L.
II. Title.
KF2750.N4 1986   343.73'099   85–27438
ISBN 0–88277–319–4   347.30399

Nelson & Teeter Mass.Comm. 5th Ed.–FP

FOR ANN AND TISH

*

PREFACE TO FIFTH EDITION

When we began work on the first edition of Law of Mass Communications in the mid-1960s, we had heard of that formidable Chinese curse, "May you live in interesting times!" Although uncursed personally, we—like many concerned with the First Amendment—have been afflicted by its terms: "Interesting times" equals "changing times." But there are worse curses.

Recall just a few of the changes, and count us all blessed for the stimulation and excitement (and exhilaration and dismay) that they have brought: New York Times v. United States (the "Pentagon Papers" case, 1971); Red Lion Broadcasting Co. v. FCC (the right of the audience, not of broadcasters, is paramount, 1969); Miller v. California (local, not national, standards for obscenity, 1973); Branzburg v. Hayes (shielding sources limited, 1972); Gertz v. Robert Welch and its progeny (lessening Sullivan's protection in libel, 1974ff); Tornillo v. Miami Herald (the First Amendment prohibits government coercion of newspapers by a "right of reply", 1974); Herbert v. Lando (libel plaintiffs may inquire into editorial processes, 1979); Richmond Newspapers v. Virginia (there is a First Amendment right to attend criminal trials, 1980); Chandler v. Florida (states may permit television coverage of trials, 1981). Passage of the Copyright Act of 1976, of the Cable Communications Act of 1984, broadcast deregulation. Or list your own dozen favorites.

More recently, we hear of a Gypsy curse: "May you have a lawsuit you believe in!" That goes hand in hand with the folk saying, "put one lawyer in a town; that lawyer will starve. Put two in a town and they'll get rich." As for the folk saying, it stands to reason: Two-thirds of all lawyers in the world in the mid-1980s are in the United States. At least arguably, the biggest change we've seen in three decades with communications law is the increase in volume of legal activity affecting the media. Ponder these items:

- Ours is a litigious society. During the years from 1960 to 1980, new lawsuits filed in federal district courts more than doubled, from 86,000 to more than 179,000. That's a 108% increase. Meanwhile, U.S. population increased from 181 million to 227 million, an increase of 25%.

- In 1985, there were roughly 650,000 lawyers in the United States, or one lawyer for every 388 persons. By the year 2000, there could be more than one million lawyers in the United States.

Shakespeare's Dick in Henry VI has a famous line, "The first thing we do, let's kill all the lawyers." We protest more mildly. We merely want to take issue with lawyers who advise that media codes of ethics and procedural manuals be locked away as legally dangerous. We believe that kind of advice should be resisted, however much occasional sense it makes in this time when codes and manuals are factored into jury struggles such as those over "reasonable" journalism compared with "negligent" journalism.

At every hand, media leaders are searching souls over Americans' disenchantment with media performance. Ethics is central to that public temper. Consider the recent, most-publicized-of-all libel case, brought against CBS News by General William Westmoreland for the documentary, "The Uncounted Enemy." After charges surfaced that the documentary had significant errors and was in real ways unfair, CBS Senior Producer Burton Benjamin performed an internal investigation to evaluate the documentary. His conclusions in "The Benjamin Report" contained strong criticisms of some aspects of the documentary and the way it was made.

The judge ordered that "The Benjamin Report" be made available to Westmoreland's lawyers. Quickly, the notion spread among many journalists and lawyers that news organizations should henceforth avoid making such candid internal probes, lest they fall into the hands of the enemy for use in a lawsuit.

Floyd Abrams, perhaps the best-known First Amendment lawyer of the 1980s, has said: "CBS ought to have gotten a little more praise than it did for the Benjamin Report." He declared that such an internal investigation "is precisely what I think most people would want a news organization to do." Similarly, Boston Globe Editor Robert Phelps has suggested that it is better to have ethical goals to shoot at (even if sometimes missed) than to have no such goals. We agree, and have added Appendix D offering approaches to ethical newsgathering.

We are grateful for the generosity of The Dallas Morning News in allowing us to reprint its "Advertising Standards of Acceptability in The Dallas Morning News." Special thanks are due to Vice President Harry M. Stanley, Jr.

Colleagues in the study of communications law who helped us include Professor David A. Anderson, School of Law, The University of Texas at Austin, Professor Emeritus Hillier Krieghbaum of New York University, and Dr. Sallie Martin Sharp, Ph.D. and J.D., of Austin. Teeter was aided by the helpful research specialists of the Tarlton Law Library of The University of Texas at Austin, and thanks Professor Roy M. Mersky, J.D., Law Librarian, Daniel P. Dabney, J.D., Eleanor H. Delashmitt, J.D., and Mickie Voges (now Librarian, School of Law, University of Oklahoma).

We again thank the persons whose forbearance and hard work got us through our fifth edition: Ann S. Nelson and Letitia T. Teeter.

Chapters 1 through 5, 9, 10 and 12 were written by Nelson; chapters 6 through 8, 11 and 13 through 15 were written by Teeter.

HAROLD L. NELSON
DWIGHT L. TEETER, JR.

November, 1985

*

SUMMARY OF CONTENTS

APPENDICES

TABLE OF CONTENTS

Part III

FACT GATHERING AND CITIZENS' RIGHTS

Part IV

MEDIA INSTITUTIONS AND THE ADMINISTRATIVE AGENCIES

TABLE OF CONTENTS

*

LAW

OF

MASS COMMUNICATIONS

FREEDOM AND CONTROL OF PRINT
AND BROADCAST MEDIA

*

Part I

PRINCIPLES AND DEVELOPMENT OF FREEDOM OF EXPRESSION

Chapter 1

FREEDOM AND CONTROL

Sec.
1. The Worth of Freedom.
2. The Constitutional Guarantees.
3. Legal Boundaries for Speech and Press.
4. Prior Restraint.

A major test of a nation's freedom is the degree of liberty its people have in speaking, writing, and publishing. Seventeenth and Eighteenth Century thought in much of Western Europe and America turned to faith in man's reason as the safest basis for government. And if man was rational, indeed, he needed access to a maximum flow of information and opinion as a basis for making decisions. Leaders of Enlightenment thought considered freedom of speech and press indispensable to the life of a public capable of self-government. In addition, it was widely considered that this freedom was essential to the individual's own development and realization, a "natural right" to which every person had claim in exploiting his faculties.

Even the age of faith in pure reason and natural rights, however, stopped short of granting perfect freedom in all that people did or said. Citizens turned over to government the powers and rights which it needed in order to protect them in the enjoyment of their rights, in Lockean theory. Furthermore, though the outer boundaries of the freedoms enjoyed might be few and indistinct, some boundaries existed. To the late Twentieth Century, which grants at most that man possesses some elements of reason in his complex makeup, and which is skeptical indeed about the existence of "natural rights," boundaries continue to exist.

The hand of authority rests lightly on speech and press at some places and times, heavily at others. But its presence is felt everywhere, including the nations of the western world which generally consider themselves the most freedom-loving of all. Some degree of legal control over expression has been sought or permitted by the freest societies through history; for although the

1

values of free speech and press may be considered paramount and be exalted, there are circumstances where other values may take priority and win in a conflict over rights. The individual's right to his good reputation limits verbal attacks through the penalties of the civil libel law; society's interest in morality denies legal protection to the obscene; a host of laws regulating business, industry, and trade applies fully to the commercial press and broadcasting.

SEC. 1. THE WORTH OF FREEDOM

Major values underlying free speech and press are society's need for maximum flow of information and opinion, and the individual's right to fulfillment.

It is not always easy to separate society's need and the individual's right as the two grounds for freedom of expression. If the individual's right is thoroughly protected, the social good in confrontation of ideas presumably follows. John Locke, often called the philosophical father of the American Revolution, in the Seventeenth Century argued the individual's rights—the "natural right" of every person to life, liberty, and property. His ideological descendants included speech and press as one of these liberties, equally applicable to all men in all times and situations, they held.[1]

Almost half a century earlier, John Milton's seminal *Areopagitica* went straighter to the social good as the justification for expression. Arguing against pre-publication censorship in 1644, he cast his case in the religious context, and said that religious truth—so ubiquitously sought or asserted in that century when strife centered upon whose god should prevail—was so essential to the fate of mankind that authority should open up the arena for debate. Truth was the only safe basis for a society's life, he said: [2]

> And though all the winds of doctrine were let loose to play upon the earth, so Truth be in the field, we do injuriously, by licensing and prohibiting, to misdoubt her strength. Let her and Falsehood grapple; who ever knew Truth put to the worse, in a free and open encounter?

There are those who would rather talk than live, no doubt, and without the protection of their individual right to do so, life would be empty to them. Human beings are fulfilled in many

---

[1] John Locke, Second Treatise of Government, ed. Thomas P. Peardon (N.Y., 1952); Leo Strauss, Natural Right and History (Chicago, 1953).

[2] John Milton, Areopagitica (Chicago, 1953). See Thomas I. Emerson, The System of Freedom of Expression (New York: Random House, 1970), Chap. 1, for discussion of social and individual goods. Also Vincent Blasi, The Checking Value in First Amendment Theory, 1977 Am.Bar Foundation Res.J. 523.

ways, and for many none is more important than making their views known and felt. To be allowed to express is central to the right to use one's faculties and to develop one's personality—one way of defining liberty. There are many who would deny that this freedom, or any other, constitutes a "natural right" as defined by the Enlightenment. But that it is real, important to human dignity, and worthy of far-reaching protection under law is widely agreed upon by societies of the West.[3]

The social good has been more compelling to the Twentieth Century as a basis for freedom and control of expression than has natural right. Society's stake in free speech and press is plain in the structure and functioning of a self-governing people: Only through a "clash of ideas in the open marketplace" can working truths be arrived at; the widest diversity of opinion and information must course through the channels of debate and discussion in arriving at solutions to problems and sound public policy. If Milton found freer debate essential to religious "truth," modern theorists find the confrontation of one idea with another, one set of facts with others, essential to all kinds of "truth," in social relations, politics, economics or art.

The individual and the society benefit alike, of course, in the rationale of the western world's practice of open debate. Whether the goal is sound public policy, the news media's serving as an external check on government, human beings' fulfillment of their potentialities, maintaining the kind of community where people do not need to live in suspicion and distrust of each other, or the fulfilling of the "duty of the thinker to his thought," free expression is held as crucial.[4]

Jurists and lawyers alike have based their cases for freedom on both the social and the individual good. Barrister Francis L. Holt, whose early Nineteenth-Century work on libel was one of the English texts heavily relied on by American law, put primary emphasis on freedom of the press as one of the "rights of nature * * * that is to say, of the free exercise of our faculties"; but at the same time saw the common good in England's "system of liberty, equally remote from feudal anarchy, and monarchial despotism" as being "the fruit of a free press."[5]

---

[3] Morris R. Cohen, Reason and Nature (Glencoe, Ill., 1953), 2d ed., Ch. 4.

[4] For the range of values making up the worth of freedom of expression, see Blasi, 544–567.

[5] Francis L. Holt, The Law of Libel * * * in the Law of England, ed. Anthony Bleecker (New York, 1818), quoted in H.L. Nelson, Freedom of the Press from Hamilton to the Warren Court (New York, 1967), pp. 19–20. The individual right claimed emphasis anew in the 1970s: Thomas I. Emerson, First Amendment Doctrine and the Burger Court, 68 Calif.Law Rev. 422, 424–7; Ronald Dworkin, Is the Press Losing the First Amendment?, New York Review, Dec. 4, 1980, 49–57.

Twentieth-Century jurists speak similarly. The late Justice Hugo Black of the United States Supreme Court pointed out in Braden v. U.S. that "There are grim reminders all around this world that the distance between individual liberty and firing squads is not always as far as it seems." [6] And in Bridges v. California, he wrote of society's stake: contempt of court citations for newspaper comment about a trial in progress, he warned, "produce their restrictive results at the precise time when public interest in the matters discussed would naturally be at its height." [7]

Yet to suggest that the worth of freedom to the individual and the society goes unchallenged, even in western democracies, is misleading. In any society, some hate and fear the expression of ideas contrary to their own. Is it permissible to denigrate races, nationalities or religions or for pornographers to "subordinate" women in demeaning or violent depiction? To permit a socialist newspaper to publish in times of threat from "alien ideologies"? Even today, after almost two centuries in which the First Amendment to the Constitution has proclaimed free speech and press as a central American value, some Americans answer "no." [8]

One doubt expressed about free speech is that, for all its supposed power to bring about understanding and agreement, it really accomplishes little. Widespread discussion, freely engaged in, may in this view lead to no settlement of issues. Even scholars and social scientists, supposedly trained in coming to conclusions on the basis of evidence, find it hard to get agreement among themselves. And as for human beings in general, the argument continues, they are not really disposed to engage in the difficult process of hammering out serious issues, for they find mental effort the most onerous of work.[9]

There is also the position that true "liberation" of societies cannot come about as long as toleration of aggression in national policies is practiced, or if racial, religious, or class hatred may be propounded. Some ideas and policies must be forbidden in this

---

[6] 365 U.S. 431, 445–446, 81 S.Ct. 584, 593 (1961). And see Branzburg v. Hayes, 408 U.S. 665, 92 S.Ct. 2646, 2668 (1972).

[7] 314 U.S. 252, 268, 62 S.Ct. 190, 196 (1941).

[8] Robert O'Neil, Second Thoughts on the First Amendment, 13 N.Mex.L.Rev. 577, Summer 1983. A Gallup poll of 1979–80 found that Americans favored 2 to 1, stricter control of the press: 5 Med.L.Rptr. 1/29/80, News Notes. Charles E. Swanson, "Midcity Daily: What the People Think a Newspaper Should Be," 26 Journalism Quarterly 173 (June 1949); Hadley Cantril, ed., Public Opinion 1935–1946 (Princeton, 1949), pp. 244–245.

[9] Frank Knight, Ethics of Competition and Other Essays (New York: Harper & Brothers, 1935), pp. 302, 304, 353.

view, for to permit them free rein is to tolerate conditions that perpetuate servitude and unhappiness.[10]

The right to challenge or denounce the principle and worth of free expression is itself, of course, a rough measure of the extent of freedom in a society. "* * * [M]an can *seem* to be free in any society, no matter how authoritarian, as long as he accepts the postulates of the society, but he can only *be* free in a society that is willing to allow its basic postulates to be questioned." [11]

Protection, for the dissenters who challenge the worth of free expression as for those who cherish it, forms its front line in the organic law of the United States. The Federal and State constitutions unanimously give free expression a position of prime value.

SEC. 2.　THE CONSTITUTIONAL GUARANTEES

Federal and State Constitutions unanimously guarantee freedom of expression; most State Constitutions declare that citizens are responsible for the abuse of the right.

The Americans who wrote and in 1791 adopted the Bill of Rights of the United States Constitution served a theme in Anglo-American liberty that had surged to recurrent apogee. They wrought in the line of Englishmen who forced the Magna Charta from King John in 1215, dared to sign the Petition of Right in 1628, passed the Habeas Corpus Act in 1679 and the Bill of Rights in 1689, and in 1776 broke the bands connecting them with motherland by adopting the Declaration of Independence. The first provision in the 1791 Bill of Rights provided freedom of speech and press, and this First Amendment to the Constitution has since been the basic legal framework for protecting liberty of expression in the United States: [12]

> Congress shall make no law respecting an establishment of religion, or prohibiting the free exercise thereof; or abridging the freedom of speech, or of the press; or the right of the people peaceably to assemble, and to petition the government for a redress of grievances.

The framers did not say precisely what they meant by "freedom of speech and press"—an ill-defined and much-debated concept in England and America at the time. But however unsettled the nation's Founders were about expanding the reach of free expression beyond that of their erstwhile motherland, they stated

[10] Robert P. Wolff, Barrington Moore, Jr., Herbert Marcuse, A Critique of Pure Tolerance (Boston, 1965), pp. 87–ff; Davis, "Free Speech for the Klan Is Fraud, not a Right," Progressive, July 1983, p. 22.

[11] John B. Wolfe, in Wilbur Schramm, Responsibility in Mass Communication (New York, 1957), 106.

[12] U.S. Constitution, Amendment 1.

a broad principle in firmly protective terms, and left it to future generations to interpret.[13]

As the states adopted their own constitutions, each included a provision for freedom of expression. A few made spare, unelaborated statements such as that of Massachusetts: "The liberty of the press is essential to the security of freedom in a state: it ought not, therefore, to be restrained in this commonwealth. The right of free speech shall not be abridged." [14]

Many states, deeply aware of dangers in the old doctrine of seditious libel which governments had used to silence their critics, added further provisions. They denied to their governments the use of two legal instruments that they considered especially hateful. One was based on the Eighteenth Century reasoning that statements critical of government were only aggravated if they were true. On this basis, the English common law had ruled that the accused was not to be permitted to try to defend himself by pleading that his offensive words were true.

The second instrument barred to government was the practice of giving judges, rather than juries, the power to decide whether the particular criticism of government amounted to a crime—was libelous. Juries in seditious libel cases had been restricted to deciding whether the accused had, indeed, printed the illegal statement—to deciding "the fact" of printing, but not "the law." The overwhelming majority of state constitutions came to bar these instruments to government's use. New York, an early one, did so first with a law of 1805, and later placed the principles in its Constitution: [15]

> Every citizen may freely speak, write and publish his sentiments on all subjects, being responsible for the abuse of that right; and no law shall be passed to restrain or abridge the liberty of speech or of the press. In all criminal prosecutions or indictments for libels, the truth may be given in evidence to the jury; and if it shall appear to the jury that the matter charged as libelous is true, and was published with good motives and for justifiable ends, the party shall be acquitted; and the jury shall have the right to determine the law and the fact.

Denying governments the use of these instruments implied that speech and press might be limited in some ways—although not these. The freedoms were not "absolutes." This was recognized by most states' constitutions. Nearly all agreed that freedom of expression could be "abused," although they did not say

---

[13] Leonard Levy, *Emergence of a Free Press* (New York, 1985), 348–9.

[14] Constitution of Massachusetts, Part I, Art. XVI.

[15] Constitution of New York, Art. 1, § 8.

what "abuse" meant. Typically, the sentence in the state constitution that started with the guarantee of free expression, ended with the qualification, as in Pennsylvania's: "The free communication of thoughts and opinions is one of the invaluable rights of man, and every citizen may freely speak, write and print on any subject, being responsible for the abuse of that liberty." [16]

As the Federal Constitution's First Amendment left the "freedom of speech and press" to future interpretation, the state constitutions left "abuse" of free speech and press to future interpretation. The principle resembled that expressed by Sir William Blackstone, prestigious English legal authority whose famous *Commentaries,* published in 1765–1769, influenced American law heavily. He had said: [17]

> The liberty of the press is indeed essential to the nature of a free state: but this consists in laying no *previous* restraints upon publications, and not in freedom from censure for criminal matter when published. Every freeman has an undoubted right to lay what sentiments he pleases before the public: to forbid this, is to destroy the freedom of the press: but if he publishes what is improper, mischievous, or illegal, he must take the consequences of his own temerity.

America was to part company with Blackstone not on the principle that "abuse" was possible, but on what would be considered "improper, mischievous or illegal * * *." His ideas of sedition and contempt of court, for example, although they at times enjoyed strong and active lives in the United States, ultimately were widely rejected.

Each state's power to define what it considered abuse of free expression long went unchallenged by the Federal courts. But in 1925, the United States Supreme Court changed this situation. It said that the Fourteenth Amendment to the U.S. Constitution protected freedom of speech and press from invasion by the states. The amendment, which became effective in 1868, declares that no state shall "deprive any person of life, liberty or property, without due process of law * * *." [18] The "liberty" was not, until Gitlow v. New York, interpreted to include liberty of speech and press, and state courts' rulings on expression before that decision were allowed to stand without review by the U.S. Supreme Court. In the Gitlow decision, however, the Court said: [19]

[16] Constitution of Pennsylvania, Art. 1, § 7.

[17] 4 Blackstone Commentaries 151, 152.

[18] U.S. Constitution, Amendment 14.

[19] 268 U.S. 652, 666, 45 S.Ct. 625, 630 (1925).

* * * we may and do assume that freedom of speech and of the press—which are protected by the First Amendment from abridgment by Congress—are among the fundamental personal rights and "liberties" protected by the due process clause of the Fourteenth Amendment from impairment by the States.

Thereafter, states' punishment of expression that they considered abuse of freedom was subject to review by the U.S. Supreme Court. The Fourteenth Amendment took its place with the First as a major protection for expression.

One other amendment to the Federal Constitution applies to expression. This is the Fifth Amendment, which bars the Federal government from certain acts against expression in language similar to that of the Fourteenth: "No person * * * shall be compelled in any criminal case to be witness against himself, nor be deprived of life, liberty, or property, without due process of law." [20]

While the last part guarantees the liberty to speak or write, the first protects the right to silence, not only in criminal cases but also, by extension, in such encounters with government as appearances before committees of Congress. It is protection for a witness against self-incrimination. Its origins lie in the revulsion against the practice of forcing people to testify against themselves. The practice was commonplace until the Seventeenth Century in England. With it was associated torture to wring confessions from the accused. "Freeborn John" Lilburne, one of the most contentious figures in the history of England's freedoms, won the day for the right "not to accuse oneself" in 1641. Whipped and pilloried because he refused to take an oath before the Star Chamber to answer questions truly about his alleged importing of seditious and heretical books, he petitioned Parliament for redress. Parliament declared the sentence "illegal and against the liberty of the subject," and voted him indemnity of 3,000 pounds.[21]

The Fifth and Fourteenth Amendments and the state constitutions hold at bay government's acts against the freedoms of speech and press. Yet the two amendments concede that persons may be deprived of liberty through due process of law. The state constitutions widely agree that the right of free expression can be abused. While the First Amendment contains no such specific limiting phrase, the courts have held consistently that even its sweeping command against suppression does not promise an "absolute" freedom of expression. The Constitutional imperatives, lib-

---

[20] U.S. Constitution, Amendment 5.

[21] Erwin N. Griswold, The Fifth Amendment Today (Cambridge, 1955), pp. 3, 4.

ertarian in spirit and voice, yet provide certain boundaries to speech and press.

SEC. 3. LEGAL BOUNDARIES FOR SPEECH AND PRESS

Although a few voices have urged an "absolute" freedom for speech and press, legislatures and courts have limited the freedom through various formulations.

Even in stating that "Congress shall make no law ＊ ＊ ＊ abridging freedom of speech, or of the press ＊ ＊ ＊.", the First Amendment draws no exact, ruler-straight line between the permissible and the punishable. American theorists, courts, legislators, and laymen have stated the boundaries of expression in various ways. If a scale could be made with "freedom" at one end and "restraint" at the other, most American spokesmen would be found well toward the "liberty" pole. Yet while clustering in that sector, they would insist on various ways of describing their positions. Of all American spokesmen, the late Supreme Court Justice Hugo Black most flatly stated the position for the right of unlimited expression, for interpreting the First Amendment as an "absolute" command forbidding any restraint on speech and press: [22]

> It is my belief that there *are* "absolutes" in our Bill of Rights, and that they were put there on purpose by men who knew what words meant and meant their prohibitions to be "absolutes."
>
> ＊   ＊   ＊
>
> I believe when our Founding Fathers ＊ ＊ ＊ wrote this [First] Amendment they ＊ ＊ ＊ knew what history was behind them and they wanted to ordain in this country that Congress ＊ ＊ ＊ should not tell the people what religion they should have or what they should believe or say or publish, and that is about it. It [the First Amendment] says "no law," and that is what I believe it means.
>
> ＊   ＊   ＊
>
> I have no doubt myself that the provision, as written and adopted, intended that there should be no libel or defamation law in the United States. ＊ ＊ ＊

The late philosopher Alexander Meiklejohn, speaking of the realm of political affairs only, urged a similar absolute freedom of expression. Speaking at a time when fear of domestic Commu-

---

[22] Anon., Justice Black and First Amendment "Absolutes": a Public Interview, 37 N.Y.U.L.Rev. 548 (1962).

nism was at its height in the nation and tendencies to curb Communists' freedom were strong, Meiklejohn declared: [23]

> The first amendment seems to me a very uncompromising statement. It admits of no exceptions. It tells us that the Congress, and by implication, all other agencies of the Government are denied any authority whatever to limit the political freedom of the citizens of the United States. It declares that with respect to political discussion, political advocacy, political planning, our citizens are sovereign, and the Congress is their subordinate agent
>
>   *   *   *   *   *.*

But the "absolute freedom" position, theoretically appealing to some, has not found official acceptance or support. Three centuries ago, John Milton's extraordinary plea for expanded freedom yet drew the line when it came to those whose religion and morals he could not accept; and though religious toleration has long since dissolved the religious barriers he supported, the case for freedom in England and America ever since has been qualified in various ways in the attempt to state principles, rules and aphorisms that would confine or enlarge the boundaries of legal control.

William Blackstone's Eighteenth-Century formula was adhered to for long periods of time in England and America: government shall lay no restraint on writers *in advance* of publication, but may punish them *after* publication of anything that violates the law. Sweeping in its restrictions as it was, his rule has long since disappeared as a guide in American courts, although in the early Twentieth Century, the United States Supreme Court quoted it with approval.[24]

An old dividing-line that rolls easily off the tongue but has little operational content is stated as this: "Liberty is not the same as licentiousness." It is impossible to say where one begins and the other leaves off.

In the law of criminal defamation of individuals, the rule was laid down in state after state that the defendant could not have protection from punishment unless he could prove that his words were the truth, and spoken with "good motives and for justifiable ends."

[23] Alexander Meiklejohn, Testimony of Nov. 14, 1955, U.S. Senate, Committee on Judiciary, Sub-Committee on Constitutional Rights, "Security and Constitutional Rights," pp. 14–15. For those who would give expression broad freedom in the politico/governmental sphere, but less elsewhere, see Emerson, First Amendment Doctrine, 428.

[24] Patterson v. State of Colo. ex rel. Attorney General, 205 U.S. 454, 462, 27 S.Ct. 556, 558 (1907).

The intent of the writer—justifiable or malicious—was and is used as a gauge for testing the degree of culpability of one accused of defamation. The "tendency" of words to cause a breach of the peace, or to undermine government, or thwart the process of justice in the courts, was for centuries a judgment to be made by the courts in deciding whether words were criminal.

One formula which some have recommended is that freedom of speech and press should be denied only to those who would deny it to others. The principle was urged by some Americans in the mid-Twentieth Century years when domestic Communists were identified as those who demanded free speech but presumably would crush it if they came to power.[25]

Do the demands of freedom give First-Amendment protection to advertising? Is the salesman's "pitch" to be given the same protection afforded the aggrieved citizen who seeks political or social change, or the candidate for office who assails the incumbent?[26] Is there a freedom *not* to speak when government demands testimony?[27]

Two famous formulations of Supreme Court justices attempt to state broad rules that may be applied to many situations. One is the test that was laid out by Justice Oliver Wendell Holmes, Jr.—the clear and present danger test. First articulated in Schenck v. U.S. in 1919,[28] the rule was an attempt, in part, to afford much greater freedom than the old "tendency" rule. Under it, before words can be punished it must be shown that they present a "clear and present danger," rather than merely a tendency, to bring about a serious evil.

The second, propounded in the 1930's by various justices, speaks for a "preferred position" for First-Amendment freedoms of speech and press. The reasoning assumes that these are the paramount freedoms among all, the "indispensable condition of liberty." Therefore, where a law on its face restricts these freedoms, the Court should not grant it the normal presumption that laws reaching the Court for its scrutiny are valid. The government must prove that the law under question is constitutional, and that the speech or print under challenge by the prosecution endangers a major social interest.[29]

[25] Max Eastman, Freedom Must Defend Itself, in H.M. Bishop and Samuel Hendel, Basic Issues of American Democracy (New York, 1948), pp. 89–92.

[26] Bigelow v. Virginia, 421 U.S. 809, 95 S.Ct. 2222 (1975).

[27] U.S. v. Rumley, 345 U.S. 1, 73 S.Ct. 543 (1953); West Virginia State Board of Education v. Barnette, 319 U.S. 624, 63 S.Ct. 1178 (1943).

[28] 249 U.S. 47, 39 S.Ct. 247 (1919).

[29] West Virginia State Board of Education v. Barnette, 319 U.S. 624, 63 S.Ct. 1178 (1943); Thomas v. Collins, 323 U.S. 516, 530, 65 S.Ct. 315 (1945).

For radio and television broadcasting, legal formulas and principles have been based considerably upon the limited capacity of the air waves—the nature of the physical universe—for establishing areas of freedom and control. Deciding who will be given access to frequencies, and under what conditions, was assigned to government by the Federal Radio Act of 1927 and the Communications Act of 1934. The Federal Communications Commission licenses broadcasters, choosing one rather than another, deciding whether a station will be re-licensed each five years, and occasionally rescinding a license. Thus while First Amendment protection is provided for broadcast as well as for printed communication, special conditions for broadcasting qualify the right in special ways.[30]

A major formulation by Thomas I. Emerson, one of the nation's foremost First Amendment scholars, is stated this way: "The central idea of a system of freedom of expression is that a fundamental distinction must be drawn between conduct which consists of 'expression' and conduct which consists of 'action.' 'Expression' must be freely allowed and encouraged. 'Action' can be controlled ∗ ∗ ∗."[31] Among insistent questions of the 1970s and 1980s are these: Does the press deserve rights under the First Amendment superior to rights of other institutions and people?[32] Can press freedom be divided into clear categories of that which deserves absolute protection and that which deserves only qualified? Is there a "people's right to know" in the Constitution? Should government be disqualified from acting as critic of the mass media? Does news gathering deserve to be granted First Amendment protection, along with printing and distribution? Has the formula devised by courts as a constitutional protection for media against libel suits proved inadequate?

Salient and persistent is a view articulated most fully by Jerome A. Barron:[33] In an age of mass communication, the members of the public must have access to the columns and airwaves of the mass media if their voices are to be heard. Barron elaborated the position that for many decades the high cost of ownership of media had barred countless voices from a part in the "marketplace of ideas." The media—giant in size and cost; relatively few in number and owned by largely like-minded entrepreneurs devoted to the economic and political *status quo;* possessed

[30] Walter B. Emery, Broadcasting and Government (East Lansing, Mich., 1961) Ch. 3.

[31] Emerson, The System of Freedom of Expression, p. 17.

[32] Former U.S. Supreme Court Justice Potter Stewart has said "yes," in a famous article: Or of the Press, 26 Hastings L.Journ. 633 (Jan.1975).

[33] Access to the Press—a New First Amendment Right, 80 Harv.L.Rev. 1641 (1967).

of the power to deny the citizen the right to have his message communicated widely—are themselves, in this view, a crucial barrier to diversity of opinion and fact in the marketplace. And diversity is one of the central features sought under the liberal view of free expression. "At the very minimum," Barron wrote, "the creation of two remedies is essential—(1) a nondiscriminatory right to purchase editorial advertisements in daily newspapers, and (2) a right of reply for public figures and public officers defamed in newspapers." [34]

A decision by the Supreme Court of Florida in mid-1973 told newspapers that a right of public access to their columns existed under a Florida statute. In Tornillo v. Miami Herald,[35] the Florida Court declared the statute constitutional in requiring newspapers which criticized political candidates, in news or editorial columns, to print the candidates' replies. The Herald had refused to print a reply by Pat L. Tornillo, Jr., to an editorial critical of him in his unsuccessful race for the Florida Legislature in 1972. Thus a state supreme court upheld a right of reply in print media similar to the right granted under the equal opportunities and fairness doctrines to persons attacked by broadcast media and cable (see Chap. 12). The First Amendment, said the Florida Court, "is not for the benefit of the press so much as for the benefit of us all," and it added: [36]

> The right of the public to know all sides of a controversy and from such information to be able to make an enlightened choice is being jeopardized by the growing concentration of the ownership of the mass media into fewer and fewer hands, resulting ultimately in a form of private censorship.

The *Miami Herald* appealed the decision to the Supreme Court of the United States. The Supreme Court reversed the Florida court.[37] It reviewed in outline the dangers of concentration of media ownership, cross-channel ownership, chains, syndicates and the focusing in the hands of a few, the power to inform and influence public opinion. However valid the arguments are that these phenomena threaten the free marketplace of ideas, the Court said, governmental coercion of remedies such as right of reply "at once brings about a confrontation with the express provisions of the First Amendment." Beginning with Associated

[34] Jerome A. Barron, Freedom of the Press for Whom? (Bloomington, Ind., 1973), p. 6.

[35] 287 So.2d 78 (Fla.1973).

[36] Ibid.

[37] Miami Herald Pub. Co. v. Tornillo, 418 U.S. 241, 94 S.Ct. 2831 (1974).

Press v. U.S.[38] in 1945 and running through other decisions since, Chief Justice Warren Burger wrote for a unanimous Court: [39]

> * * * the Court has expressed sensitivity as to whether a restriction or requirement constituted the compulsion exerted by government on a newspaper to print that which it would not otherwise print. The clear implication has been that any such compulsion to publish that which " 'reason' tells them should not be published" is unconstitutional. A responsible press is an undoubtedly desirable goal, but press responsibility is not mandated by the Constitution and like many other virtues it cannot be legislated.

While Tornillo argued that the Florida statute did not prevent the *Miami Herald* from printing anything it wished, that missed the core question:

> Compelling editors or publishers to publish that which " 'reason' tells them should not be published" is what is at issue in this case. The Florida statute operates as a command in the same sense as a statute or regulation forbidding appellant from publishing specified matter.

The Florida statute, the Court said, penalizes on the basis of the content of a newspaper. The penalty is increased cost of production, and taking up space that could go to other material the paper may have preferred to print. Infinite expansion of its size to accommodate replies that a statute might require is not to be expected of a newspaper.

But cost aside, the Florida statute failed "to clear the barriers of the First Amendment because of its intrusion into the function of editors." This function—choosing content, determining size of the paper, treatment of public issues—may be fair or unfair, said Justice Burger, but "It has yet to be demonstrated how governmental regulation of this crucial process can be exercised consistent with First Amendment guarantees of a free press as they have evolved to this time."

The decision developed no reasoning as to why newspapers were exempt but broadcasting was not, from the requirements of furnishing the opportunity to reply. Once again, as in other circumstances previously, the First Amendment's shield proved stronger for printed journalism than for broadcast.[40]

---

[38] 326 U.S. 1, 65 S.Ct. 1416 (1945).

[39] Miami Herald Pub. Co. v. Tornillo, 418 U.S. 241, 94 S.Ct. 2831 (1974). All quotes are from Chief Justice Burger's majority opinion at 2838–2840.

[40] See below, Chap. 12.

SEC. 4. PRIOR RESTRAINT

Despite authoritative statements that the chief purpose of the First Amendment guarantee is to prevent previous restraints upon publication, various arguments and instruments continue to give force to licensing, deletions, prohibitions and injunctions in the late Twentieth Century.

In one of the most famous and influential First Amendment decisions by the United States Supreme Court, Chief Justice Charles Evans Hughes wrote that "it has been generally, if not universally, considered that it is the chief purpose of the [First Amendment] guarantee to prevent previous restraints upon publication." [41] Journalists and libertarians have long counted the term and the concept "previous restraint" as the most despised in the annals of control of publication. The somewhat slippery term refers, in common usage, to the practice common to the Sixteenth and Seventeenth Centuries of requiring printers to get permission or license from government to publish, and the actual censoring by authority of parts or all of a piece of writing, with punishment for violation. [42] There are no boundaries to authority's inventiveness in fashioning the devices of prior restraint. Nowhere in the journalist's tradition has repetition less dulled the edge of aphorism:

> "Liberty is always unfinished business."

> "Eternal vigilance is the price of liberty."

The power in government to approve who might publish, or to order non-publication or a halt to publication, under threat of punishment, had a long and oppressive history; and revolutionary America's leaders and printers considered that whatever freedom of the press meant, it meant an end to prior restraint. [43] If the press were to act as a check on government and as a means of aiding the spread of all kinds of knowledge and opinion in a self-governing society, government could not count suppression as one of its instruments of power. Society's chief weapon against the institution which possessed the power of guns and police was words.

[41] Near v. Minnesota, 283 U.S. 697, 713, 51 S.Ct. 625 (1931).

[42] While restraint in advance of publication or distribution plainly exists in the threat of penalty or punishment *after* publication (e.g., libel, invasion of privacy, obscenity), that is not the consideration here. As the U.S. Supreme Court has said: "If it can be said that a threat of criminal or civil sanctions after publication 'chills' speech, prior restraint 'freezes' it at least for the time." Nebraska Press Ass'n v. Stuart, 427 U.S. 539, 559, 96 S.Ct. 2791 (1976), 1 Med.L.Rptr. 1064.

[43] Levy, Chaps. 6, 8.

Strong as the conviction was, certain exceptions appeared in the Nineteenth Century. The South employed the weapon regularly in its attempts to shield its "peculiar institution" of slavery before the Civil War, its postmasters as a matter of course refusing to deliver the publications of northern anti-slavery societies. During the Civil War, northern generals occasionally closed down the newspapers of "Copperhead" publishers, and President Lincoln himself ordered the closing of newspapers on one occasion. Heavy restrictions on the publishing and distribution of the materials of sex arose in the last quarter of the century, and prior restraint was part of the control. Postal and customs officials' employment of the instrument in peace and war, to control that which was considered obscene or seditious, was vigorous and frequent through the first third of the Twentieth Century, modifying later.[44]

And the arena of prior restraint was to grow in the Twentieth Century in matters not related to government's acts of self-protection. Sanctioned most thoroughly—and presumably ordained by the limited number of frequencies available—is the licensing by government of all broadcasters to prevent the overcrowding of the airwaves (Chap. 12). Courts and lawyers find real problems in defining precisely what prior restraint means.[45] Not only licensing and ordering deletions from publications, but also the court injunction (the "enjoining" of a person) against speaking, publishing, or distributing words or symbols, is a restraint in advance of a communication act—a prior restraint.[46] For example, the Federal Trade Commission has power to issue "cease and desist" orders and to seek court injunctions against advertising which restrains trade or is false and deceptive, and to require advertisers to correct misinterpretations.[47] Copyright law (Chap. 7) provides for injunctions to prevent or restrain illegal use of copyrighted materials.[48] A book detailing psychiatric case histories has been enjoined under an action claiming violation of right to privacy, even though the book contained no names of persons treated.[49] Various states have permitted the abatement of movies and books under public nuisance statutes where the materials

[44] Nelson, Parts 4–6.

[45] Vincent Blasi, Toward a Theory of Prior Restraint, 66 Minn.L.Rev. 11, 14–15, Nov. 1981.

[46] Ibid., 92–93.

[47] Glen O. Robinson and Ernest Gellhorn, The Administrative Process (St. Paul: West Pub. Co., 1974), pp. 501–21; Anon., The FTC's Injunctive Authority Against False Advertising of Food and Drugs, 75 Mich.L.Rev. 745 (March 1977).

[48] 17 U.S.C.A. §§ 502, 503. Meredith Corp. v. Harper & Row Publishers, Inc., 378 F.Supp. 686 (S.D.N.Y.1974); Robert Stigwood Group Ltd. v. O'Reilly, 346 F.Supp. 376 (D.C.Conn.1972).

[49] Roe v. Doe, 345 N.Y.S.2d 560, 42 A.D.2d 559 (1973).

shown or sold have been found obscene, and the principle of censorship ordinances for screening of movies before public showing has been approved.[50]

The United States Supreme Court has approved the prohibition of newspaper publication of material from "discovery" (pretrial) proceedings.[51] A newspaper has been enjoined from publishing an advertising "shopper." [52] Under the federal Securities Acts, the Securities and Exchange Commission has long had power to enjoin financial news letters, its actions that involve "commercial speech" doctrine having recently raised serious First Amendment questions.[53]

In the 1970s, a striking extension of prior restraint burst out of courts across the nation as they attempted to forbid news media's publishing accounts of parts or all of the record in trials and hearings (Chap. 11). No phase of prior restraint has proved more alarming to news media than this, although few aspects of the use of the instrument have escaped a drumfire of attack from media, commentators on the law, social critics and others.

Subsequent chapters will detail aspects of prior restraint. In this chapter, the special concern goes to the state's claims to suppress, on its own behalf, attacks on government personnel and words alleged to constitute danger to national security or confidence in national security programs.

Mr. Chief Justice Hughes' majority opinion in Near v. Minnesota, a case of 1931, establishes groundwork that may be seen as a watershed which turned United States Supreme Court majorities in the direction of expanded press freedom.[54]

That decision grew out of scruffy origins. Howard Guilford and J.M. Near were publishing partners in producing *The Saturday Press,* a Minneapolis "smear sheet" which charged that gangsters were in control of Minneapolis gambling, bootlegging and racketeering, and that the city law enforcement and government agencies and officers were derelict in their duties. It vilified Jews and Catholics. And it published the articles that eventually required the Supreme Court of the United States to make one of

[50] Pamela Chappelle, Can an Adult Theater or Bookstore Be Abated as a Public Nuisance in California? 10 U.San Francisco L.Rev. 115, 128 (Summer 1975); Times Film Corp. v. Chicago, 365 U.S. 43, 81 S.Ct. 391 (1961); Chateau-X v. North Carolina (N.C.Sup.Ct.1971) 7 Med.L.Rptr. 1279.

[51] Seattle Times v. Rinehart, 10 Med.L.Rptr. 1705 (1984).

[52] Advantage Pubs. v. Daily Press (D.C.E.Va.1983), 9 Med.L.Rptr. 1761.

[53] James C. Goodale, The First Amendment and Securities Act: a Collision Course?, N.Y.L.Journ., April 8, 1983, p. 1.

[54] Near v. Minnesota ex rel. Olson, 283 U.S. 697, 51 S.Ct. 625 (1931); Paul L. Murphy, Near v. Minnesota in the Context of Historical Developments, 66 Minn.L. Rev. 95 (Nov.1981); Fred W. Friendly, Minnesota Rag (N.Y., 1981).

its most notable descriptions of the extent of freedom of the press in America.

Publication of *The Saturday Press* was halted when a Minnesota statute authorizing prior restraint of "nuisance" or "undesirable" publications was invoked. That statute declared that any person publishing a "malicious, scandalous and defamatory newspaper, magazine or other periodical" could be found guilty of creating a nuisance and could be enjoined from future wrongdoing.[55] Near and Guilford were indeed brought into court after a temporary injunction ordered cessation of all activity by their paper. After the hearing, the injunction was made permanent by a judge, but with the provision that *The Saturday Press* could resume publication if the publishers could persuade the court that they would run a newspaper without objectionable content described in the Minnesota "gag law" statute.[56]

Near and Guilford appealed to the Supreme Court, which found in their favor by the margin of five votes to four. Speaking for the Court, Chief Justice Charles Evans Hughes noted the importance of this case: "This statute, for the suppression as a public nuisance of a newspaper or periodical, is unusual, if not unique, and raises questions of grave importance transcending the local interest involved in the particular action." Hughes declared: [57]

> If we cut through mere details of procedure, the operation and effect of the statute in substance is that public authorities may bring the owner or publisher of a newspaper or periodical before a judge upon a charge of conducting a business publishing scandalous and defamatory matter—in particular that the matter consists of charges against public officers of official dereliction—and, unless the owner or publisher is able and disposed to bring competent evidence to satisfy the judge that the charges are true and are published for good motives and for justifiable ends, his newspaper or periodical is suppressed and further publication is made punishable as a contempt. This is the essence of censorship.

Hughes then turned to history-as-precedent to answer the question of whether a statute authorizing such proceedings in restraint of publication was consistent with the concept of liberty

[55] Chapter 285, Minn.Sess.Laws 1925, in Mason's Minn.Stats., 1927, Secs. 10123–1 to 10123–3.

[56] Near v. Minnesota ex rel. Olson, 283 U.S. 697, 702–707, 51 S.Ct. 625, 628 (1931).

[57] Ibid., 707, 713.

of the press, declaring here that the chief purpose of the constitutional guaranty is to prevent previous restraints.

He embarked upon a two-fold modification of the old English authority, Blackstone. Blackstone would have had *no prior restraint*, period. The Chief Justice, however, conceded that such a prohibition against all prior restraint might be "stated too broadly," and said that "* * * the protection even as to previous restraint is not absolutely unlimited." In a few exceptional cases, limitation of the principle of "no prior restraint" could be recognized: [58]

> No one would question but that a government might prevent actual obstruction to its recruiting service or the publication of sailing dates of transports or the number and location of troops. On similar grounds, the primary requirements of decency may be enforced against obscene publications. The security of the community life may be protected against incitements to acts of violence and the overthrow by force of orderly government. The constitutional guaranty of free speech does not "protect a man from an injunction against uttering words that may have all the effect of force."

Although Blackstone's "no prior restraint" was thus modified, another aspect of Blackstone was liberalized. Blackstone had approved punishing the publication of criticisms of government or government officials. But Hughes said that the press had a right—and perhaps even a duty—to discuss and debate the character and conduct of public officers.[59]

> While reckless assaults upon public men, and efforts to bring obloquy upon those who are endeavoring faithfully to discharge official duties, exert a baleful influence and deserve the severest condemnation in public opinion, it cannot be said that this abuse is greater, and it is believed to be less, than that which characterized the period in which our institutions took shape. Meanwhile, the administration of government has become more complex, the opportunities for malfeasance and corruption have multiplied, crime has grown to most serious proportions, and the danger of its protection by unfaithful officials and of the impairment of the fundamental security of life and property by criminal alliances and official neglect, emphasizes the primary need of a vigilant and courageous press, especially in great cities.

[58] Ibid., 716.

[59] Ibid., 719–720.

The fact that the liberty of the press may be abused by miscreant purveyors of scandal does not make any the less necessary the immunity of the press from previous restraint in dealing with official misconduct. Subsequent punishment for such abuses as may exist is the appropriate remedy, consistent with constitutional privilege.

Despite the four dissenting votes, Near v. Minnesota has stood since 1931 as one of the most important decisions of the Supreme Court. *Near* was the first case involving newspapers in which the Court applied the provisions of the First Amendment against states through the language of the Fourteenth Amendment.[60] And it was to serve as important precedent for protecting the press against government's demands for suppression.

It was 40 years before the press again collided with government bent on protecting its own interest and functions through prior restraint. On June 30, 1971, the United States Supreme court cleared the confrontation with a decision hailed by many news media with such headlines as "VICTORY FOR THE PRESS" and "The Press Wins and the Presses Roll." [61] These triumphant headlines were tied to the "Pentagon Papers" case. Early in 1971, *New York Times* reporter Neil Sheehan was given photocopies of a 47-volume study of the United States involvement in Vietnam titled *History of the United States Decision-Making Process on Vietnam Policy.* On Sunday, June 13, 1971, the *New York Times*—after a team of reporters had worked with the documents for three months—published a story headlined: "Vietnam Archive: Pentagon Study Traces 3 Decades of Growing U.S. Involvement." Within 48 hours after publication, Attorney General John Mitchell sent a telegram to the Times, urging that no more articles based on the documents be published, charging that the series would bring about "irreparable injury to the defense interests of the United States." [62] The Times chose to ignore Attorney General Mitchell's plea, and columnist James Reston angrily wrote: "For the first time in the history of the Republic, the Attorney General of the United States has tried to suppress documents he hasn't read about a war that hasn't been declared." [63]

After the Times' refusal to stop the series of articles, the Department of Justice asked U.S. District Court Judge Murray I.

---

[60] William A. Hachten, The Supreme Court on Freedom of the Press: Decisions and Dissents (Ames, Ia.: Iowa State Univ. Press, 1968), p. 43.

[61] Newsweek, Time, July 12, 1971.

[62] Don R. Pember, "The Pentagon Papers Decision: More Questions Than Answers," Journalism Quarterly 48:3 (Autumn, 1971) p. 404; New York Times, June 15, 1971, p. 1.

[63] New York Times, June 16, 1971, p. 1.

Gurfein to halt publication of the stories. Judge Gurfein, who was serving his first day as a federal judge, issued a temporary injunction on June 15, putting a stop to the Times' publication of the articles. But silencing the Times did not halt all publication of the "Pentagon Papers." *The Washington Post* —and a number of other major journals—also weighed in with excerpts from the secret report. The Justice Department likewise applied for—and was granted—a temporary restraining order against *The Washington Post*.[64]

After two weeks of uncertainty, the decision by the Supreme Court of the United States cleared the papers for publication. *New York Times* Managing Editor A.M. Rosenthal was jubilant: "This is a joyous day for the press—and for American society." *Time* added, "Certainly the Justice Department was slapped down in its efforts to ask the courts to enjoin newspapers, and will not likely take that route again." [65] Despite such optimism, some observers within the press were disturbed by the outcome of the *"Pentagon Papers"* case. Not only were there three dissents against lifting the injunction among the nine justices, there was also deep reluctance to do so on the part of two of the majority justices. Furthermore, federal court injunctions had now, for the first time in American history, been employed to impose prior restraint upon newspapers, and the courts had preserved those injunctions intact for two weeks.

The Court's decision was short. It refused to leave in effect the injunctions which the Justice Department had secured against the Times and the Post, and quoted Bantam Books v. Sullivan: [66]

> "Any system of prior restraints of expression comes to this Court bearing a heavy presumption against its constitutional validity." Bantam Books, Inc. v. Sullivan, 372 U.S. 58, 83 S.Ct. 631 * * * (1963); see also Near v. Minnesota ex rel. Olson, 283 U.S. 697, 51 S.Ct. 625 * * * (1931). The Government "thus carries a heavy burden of showing justification for the imposition of such a restraint." Organization for a Better Austin v. Keefe, 402 U.S. 415, 91 S.Ct. 1575, 1578 (1971).

With those words, a six-member majority of the Court ruled that the government had not shown sufficient reason to impose prior restraint. Of the six, four found nothing in the facts of the case to qualify their positions. Justices Hugo L. Black and William O. Douglas expressed abhorrence for prior restraint, Douglas

---

[64] For a clear account of the cases' journeys through the courts, see Pember, pp. 404–405.

[65] Time, July 12, 1971, p. 10.

[66] New York Times Co. v. United States, 403 U.S. 713, 714, 91 S.Ct. 2140 (1971).

saying "uninhibited, robust and wide-open debate" on public questions was essential, and "The stays in these cases that have been in effect for more than a week constitute a flouting of the principles of the First Amendment as interpreted in Near v. Minnesota * * *." [67]

Justice William J. Brennan, Jr., although not subscribing to an absolutist position about prior restraint, nevertheless declared that it was permissible in only a "single, extremely narrow" class of cases, as when the nation was at war or when troop movements might be endangered. For all the government's alarms as to possible dangers of nuclear holocaust if secrecy were breached, it had not presented a case that publication of the Pentagon Papers would cause such an event. Therefore: [68]

> * * * every restraint issued in this case, whatever its form, has violated the First Amendment—and none the less so because the restraint was justified as necessary to examine the claim more thoroughly. Unless and until the government has clearly made out its case, the First Amendment commands that no injunction may issue.

With reluctance, Justices Byron White and Potter Stewart joined the majority. Stewart approved secrecy in some contexts, and said he was convinced that the Executive branch of government was correct in attempting to suppress publication of some of the documents here. But he voted with the majority, he said, because he could not say that disclosure of any of the Pentagon Papers "will surely result in direct, immediate, or irreparable damage to our Nation * * *." [69] White said that if any of the published material proved, after publication, to be punishable under the Espionage Act of 1917, the newspapers now stood warned: "I would have no difficulty in sustaining convictions under [the Espionage Act] on facts that would not justify * * * the imposition of a prior restraint." [70]

Justice Marshall declared that Congress had twice rejected proposed legislation that would have given the President war-time powers to prohibit some kinds of publication. And, he said, it would be inconsistent within the concept of separation of powers for the Court to use its contempt power to prevent behavior that Congress had specifically declined to prohibit. [71]

Dissenting, Justice Harlan thought that dispute about matters so grave as the alleged contempt and publication of the Pentagon

[67] Ibid., 724.
[68] Ibid., 727.
[69] Ibid., 730.
[70] Ibid., 735–738.
[71] Ibid., 746.

Papers needed more time to resolve, and he voted to support the injunctions.[72] He found that the Court had been almost "irresponsibly feverish in dealing with these cases" of such high national importance in only a few days' time. Justice Blackmun agreed with Harlan, and added in a shrill indictment of the press: [73]

> If, however, damage has been done, and if, with the Court's action today, these newspapers proceed to publish the critical documents and there results therefrom "the death of soldiers, the destruction of alliances, the greatly increased difficulty of negotiation with our enemies, the inability of our diplomats to negotiate," to which list I might add the factors of prolongation of the war and of further delay in the freeing of United States prisoners, then the Nation's people will know where the responsibility for these sad consequences rests.

It should be recognized that no new legal course was charted by the *Pentagon Papers* case. After a delay of two weeks—a prior restraint imposed by lower federal courts at the insistence of the Department of Justice—the Supreme Court allowed the press to resume publication of the documents. By a 6–to–3 margin, the Supreme Court adhered to Near v. Minnesota, that classic case which, by a 5–to–4 margin, forbade prior restraint except in time of war, or when the materials involved were obscene, or when there was incitement to violence or to the overthrow of the Government.

The *Pentagon Papers* case underlines an important truth, that no freedom is ever won, once and for all. Consider this statement:

> Some people may think that leaders of the free press would perhaps accomplish more if their claims of constitutional right were less expansive. I do not agree with this. I say it is their duty to fight like tigers right down to the line and not give an inch. This is the way our freedoms have been preserved in the past, and it is the way they will be preserved in the future.

No editor, publisher, or reporter said that. The quotation is from a statement by U.S. Senior Circuit Judge for the Second Circuit Harold R. Medina. Judge Medina's words emphasize an obvious but necessary history lesson. Each freedom has to be rewon by each succeeding generation. And sometimes, as is apparently true during the latter third of the Twentieth Century,

---

[72] Ibid., 753.

[73] Ibid., 763. Blackmun was quoting the dissent of Judge Wilkey in the Pentagon Papers case involving the Washington Post in the Court of Appeals for the Second Circuit, United States v. Washington Post Co., 446 F.2d 1327 (D.C.Cir.1971).

freedom has to be fought for again and again within one generation.

Doom for the national security had been forecast by officials of the State Department as they testified against permitting the Times to continue publishing the Pentagon Papers, one of them declaring that further publication would "irreparably harm the United States." But, as Times columnist Anthony Lewis remarked some five years later, "the Republic still stands," and "Today, hardly anyone can remember a single item of the papers that caused all the fuss." [74]

A multi-volume history of policy-making in the Vietnam War was not the publication at issue, however, when at the end of the decade the federal government learned that *The Progressive,* a magazine of Madison, Wis., was about to print an article titled "The H-Bomb Secret: How We Got It, Why We're Telling It." The manuscript, the U.S. Attorney charged, carried the deepest of technical secrets relating to the security of our weapons. Publication would endanger national security and that of the world, and in the process would violate the U.S. Atomic Energy Act of 1954 by making public "restricted data" about thermonuclear weapons. The government sought and got a temporary injunction against publication of the article by journalist Howard Morland.[75]

Morland swore that everything in the article was in the public domain, that he had in no way been forced to secret sources for the information; the government denied that this was the case. While the trial was in mid-stream, it also came to light that similar information had been available to the public by accident, for a time, in a government science laboratory.[76] Federal District Judge Robert Warren was fully aware of the Supreme Court's rule that "any prior restraint on publication comes into court under a heavy presumption against its constitutional validity." Warren found the revelation of secret technical details about the H-bomb quite different, however, from revealing a secret history of war-policy making. He found that publication offered the possibility of "grave, direct, immediate and irreparable harm to the United States," and said: [77]

> * * * because the government has met its heavy burden of showing justification for the imposition of a

[74] "Congress Shall Make No Law," New York Times, Sept. 16, 1976, p. 39.

[75] United States v. Progressive, 467 F.Supp. 990 (D.C.W.Wis.1979), 4 Med.L.Rptr. 2377. Major prior restraint cases are discussed by U.S. Circuit Judge J.L. Oakes in "The Doctrine of Prior Restraint Since the Pentagon Papers," 15 U.Mich.Journ.L. Reform 497 (Spring, 1982).

[76] United States v. Progressive, (D.C.W.Wis.1980), 5 Med.L.Rptr. 2441.

[77] United States v. Progressive, 467 F.Supp. 990 (D.C.W.Wis.1979), 4 Med.L.Rptr. 2377, 2380.

prior restraint on publication of the objected-to technical portions of the Morland article, and because the Court is unconvinced that suppression of the objected-to technical portions of the Morland article would in any plausible fashion impede the defendants in their laudable crusade to stimulate public knowledge of nuclear armament and bring about enlightened debate on national policy questions, the Court finds that the objected-to portions of the article fall within the narrow area recognized by the Court in Near v. Minnesota in which a prior restraint on publication is appropriate.

Yet Warren's deep concern at the possible outcome of publication ("I'd want to think a long, hard time before I'd give a hydrogen bomb to Idi Amin.") was questioned in the national debate and discussion which surged over the case. The government, it was asserted, had not shown that publication would result in "direct, immediate, or irreparable damage to the Nation" that the Pentagon Papers decision had insisted was necessary to justify prior restraint. The field of journalism was divided in its support.[78]

The Progressive and Morland, seizing on implications of the Atomic Energy Act that conceivably rendered even innocent conversations about nuclear weapons subject to classification ("classified at birth") insisted that no real secrets had been told. They appealed, and prior restraint held through six months of court process. Suddenly intruding into the matter was the publication on Sept. 16, 1979, of a long letter in the Madison, Wis. *Press Connection,* a daily of 11,000 circulation, from an amateur student of the nuclear bomb. A copy of a letter from computer programmer Charles Hansen to Sen. Charles Percy of Illinois, it included a diagram and list of key components of an H-bomb. Other newspapers which had received copies had not yet published it when, on the following day, the government moved to drop its court action to bar publication of the Morland article. A U.S. Justice Department spokesman said that the Hansen letter had exposed three "crucial concepts" that the government was trying to protect from publication.

Morland's article was published. *The Progressive* set about trying to raise $200,000 from the public, which was the cost, it said, of defending. No prosecution of the *Press Connection* or other newspapers that published the Hansen letter materialized.

---

[78] Civil Liberties, No. 328, June 1979, p. 1; Ben Bagdikian, "A Most Insidious Case," Quill, 67:6, June 1979, pp. 21, 22; "Editors and Lawyers Share Mixed Views on Story Ban," Editor & Publisher, March 17, 1979, p. 13.

Judge Warren dismissed the case against *The Progressive* on Sept. 4, 1980.[79]

Not only the security of the United States' war effort and the provisions of the Atomic Energy Act have made a groundwork for the government's demand for prior restraint. Rules of administrative agencies can furnish the same.[80] The CIA is experienced in the matter. Its employee Victor L. Marchetti resigned from the agency and, with John Marks, wrote *The CIA and the Cult of Intelligence.* This, the CIA charged upon learning of its existence in manuscript form, violated the secrecy contract Marchetti had signed when first employed, promising not to divulge any classified information without specific permission from the CIA.[81] It obtained an injunction in federal district court, the judge ordering Marchetti to submit all writings about the CIA or intelligence work to the Agency for review as to whether it contained classified information that had not been released to the public. As the case proceeded (the Supreme Court of the United States denied certiorari),[82] the CIA's scrutiny of the manuscript resulted in its demand that 339 deletions be performed. "It was the Devil's work we did that day," said Marchetti's attorney, Melvin L. Wulf, after he and the authors spent hours literally cutting out passages of the manuscript—perhaps as much as 20 per cent.[83] Resisting all the way, Marchetti finally won agreement from the court that all but 27 of the 339 deletions would be restored.[84] The book was finally published with blank spaces and the prominent, repeated notation: DELETED.

Frank Snepp, strategy analyst for the CIA in Vietnam, succeeded in getting his case against the CIA to the Supreme Court. He, too, had resigned from the agency and written a book—*Decent Interval* —about his experiences. He, too, had signed an agreement not to publish without first submitting the manuscript to the CIA, and the agency brought legal action. The Supreme Court, by a 6–3 vote, ruled that Snepp had broken his contract, approved an injunction requiring Snepp to submit future writings for publication review, and ruled that he must give all profits from the sale of the book to the CIA through a "constructive trust" imposed on

[79] Milwaukee Journal, Sept. 4, 1980, Part 2, pp. 1, 10.

[80] Ithiel de Sola Pool, "Prior Restraint," New York Times, Dec. 16, 1979, p. E19, portrays unintended prior restraint on research publication through elaborate funding rules of the U.S. Dept. of Health, Education, and Welfare—"a nightmare of bureaucracy run wild, producing results that no one intended."

[81] United States v. Marchetti, 466 F.2d 1309 (4th Cir.1972).

[82] 409 U.S. 1063, 93 S.Ct. 553 (1972).

[83] Melvin D. Wulf, Introduction to Victor Marchetti and John D. Marks, The CIA and the Cult of Intelligence (New York: Alfred A. Knopf, 1974), p. xxv.

[84] Ibid., p. xxiv.

him by the court.[85]　He had a fiduciary obligation to the CIA and had breached his trust by publishing.

The government had not alleged that classified or confidential information was revealed by the Snepp book.　Rather, it alleged "irreparable harm" in his failure to clear the material with the CIA, and the Supreme Court approved the lower courts' finding that publication of unreviewed material "can be detrimental to vital national interests even if the published information is unclassified." [86]

> Undisputed evidence in this case shows that a CIA agent's violation of his obligation to submit writings about the Agency for prepublication review impairs the CIA's ability to perform its statutory duties.　Admiral Turner, Director of the CIA, testified without contradiction that Snepp's book and others like it have seriously impaired the effectiveness of American intelligence operations. "Over the last six to nine months," he said, "we have had a number of sources discontinue work with us.　We have had more sources tell us that they are very nervous about continuing work with us.　We have had very strong complaints from a number of foreign intelligence services with whom we conduct liaison, who have questioned whether they should continue exchanging information with us, for fear it will not remain secret." ＊ ＊ ＊

If the agent published unreviewed material in violation of his fiduciary and contractual obligation, said the court, the constructive trust remedy simply "required him to disgorge the benefits of his faithlessness ＊ ＊ ＊." Snepp "disgorged" about $138,000, the proceeds from *Decent Interval.* [87]

The Snepp case was more than just a case of prior restraint applied through the administrative machinery, law reporter Anthony Lewis of the *New York Times* found.　For the fiduciary, constructive-trust formulation was a far-reaching legal theory: [88]

> ＊ ＊ ＊ one that could apply to hundreds of thousands of federal government employees.　For Snepp ＊ ＊ ＊ had no greater access to secrets than do vast numbers of people in the State and Defense Departments ＊ ＊ ＊.　Any one of them, under the theory of the Snepp case, can now be enjoined from talking to a reporter—or have his profits seized if he writes a book.

[85] Snepp v. United States, 5 Media L.Rptr. 2409 (1980).

[86] Ibid., 2411.

[87] Herbert Mitgang, "Royalties to the Treasury," New York Times Book Review, Aug. 31, 1980.

[88] New York Times, Feb. 25, 1980.

Non-disclosure agreements similar to that which Snepp and Marchetti had signed so appealed to President Ronald Reagan that in 1983, he issued a directive requiring them of all persons who had access to classified government information, numbering—declared protesting media—more than 100,000 employees. The President withdrew the directive in the face of congressional and media protest.[89]

If the emergence of non-disclosure agreements in the decade beginning with Marchetti appeared as one more example of government creativity in devising prior restraints in the name of national security, predictably enough that newly minted instrument was not the end of invention in prior restraint. In 1982, the Secretary of State's denial of a passport to former CIA agent Philip Agee was upheld by the United States Supreme Court: Agee had asserted his purpose of exposing CIA agents abroad, driving them out of the countries where they operated, and obstructing the operations and recruitment efforts of the CIA, and had taken measures to do so. These statements and actions, the Court said, were no more protected by the First Amendment than those proscribed in Near v. Minnesota half a century earlier.[90] By 1982, Congress and the President had effected a law making it a crime for news media to make public the names of secret U.S. intelligence agents or their sources.[91]

[89] Directive on Safeguarding National Security Information, 9 Med.L.Rptr. 1759 (1983).

[90] Haig v. Agee, 453 U.S. 280, 101 S.Ct. 2766 (1981), 7 Med.L.Rptr. 1545.

[91] News Media and the Law, Sept./Oct. 1982, 39.

Chapter 2

HISTORICAL BACKGROUND: CRIMINAL WORDS

The delicate balance between control and freedom of expression under the law has been most violently disrupted, over the centuries, when government has sought to arm or protect itself against attack by the press. Libertarians have viewed struggles for freedom of expression as crucial when government, acting in its own interest, has been the press' adversary and in its own behalf has brought criminal actions against critics. This is not to minimize struggles over control stemming from sources other than government's acting to protect its repute or legitimacy against critical words. Major confrontations have occurred where government has accused the press of damaging official procedures shaped long ago to protect individual citizens against harm or unfairness. Major battles have involved civil suits for damages brought by citizens against the media. Major contests have settled principles of freedom and control where government has taken the part of the public against the press as in prosecutions of the media for monopolizing and restraint of trade.

Elemental aspects of the fortunes of political liberty are accentuated in the story of the collision between freedom and control in its most basic and often most dramatic form—when government has felt threatened by its critics and acted to bring them in check. Equally instructive is the long unfolding of growth and retreat in government's power to control its critics, and the substantial eclipse of that power in the mid- to late-twentieth century. Today's legal controls over the mass media have their own shape and characteristics; journalists still feel the force of government. But the word crimes with which their forerunners could be charged exist today as hardly more than the shadow of threat. The historical context develops the story best.

29

SEC. 5.　SEVENTEENTH–CENTURY ENGLAND

John Milton's thought and contentious martyrs' action helped unshackle printing; insistent printers' economic demands were the main factor in the death of licensing and censorship.

Stephen Daye, the first American colonial printer, pulled his first impressions from a hand press while the authoritarianism of divine right monarchy was still strong in the mother country. The year was 1638, the place was Harvard College, and the work was "The Freeman's Oath," approved for printing by the theocracy of Massachusetts Bay colony which had no more concept of freedom of the press than did Charles I who ruled in London. Yet by the time the first colonial newspaper appeared some 65 years later, major battles and major ideas had intruded upon the intricate network of press control in England, and the American printers whose numbers grew substantially after 1700 owed much to their brothers of the press and to contentious speakers across the Atlantic. Advance toward freedom of the press, unthinkable in Seventeenth-Century America, had occurred in England and had saved the Eighteenth-Century colonial printers some of the hard work and pain of breaking free of authority.

The ingenious system of control established in the Sixteenth Century by the Tudor monarchs, Henry VIII and Elizabeth I, and perpetuated by the Stuart kings of the Seventeenth Century, had largely disappeared by the close of England's Glorious Revolution of 1689. Gone was the Stationers Company policing of the printers of England, first required by Elizabeth in return for economic protection, monopolies, and privileges for this printing guild's members. The arbitrary Courts of the Star Chamber and the High Commission had died amid rejoicing. Torture for criminal offenses, officially at least, was over. Weakened and about to collapse was the system of licensing and censorship in advance of publication; the demands of business-oriented printers for release from its strictures, and the impossibility of managing the surveillance as the number of printers and the reading needs of the public grew, had more to do with the death of the system than did the high principle of Milton's *Areopagitica.* Licensing and censorship in England died in 1695 when the House of Commons refused to renew the law for it.[1]

There was much left in the art and craft of government to overcome before a broad liberty would be accomplished. Criminal

---

[1] Fredrick S. Siebert, Freedom of the Press in England 1476–1776 (Urbana: Univ. of Ill. Press, 1952). This is the fullest and best-ordered treatment of the instruments of control. See especially parts 2 and 4.

prosecutions for sedition would thrive through the next century and beyond. Control of newspapers and magazines through taxes would be tried repeatedly by Queen Anne and her successors. Parliament would punish speakers and printers for contempt of its august stature, and would continue to refuse access to newsmen seeking to report it. Yet this robust and oppressive body of restrictive instruments, available to the law for keeping printers in line, was hardly the equal of its predecessors. American colonial printers would face all these remaining controls, and also, for a time, the persistence in the colonial setting of some of those that England had shed. They would also be spared many of the grim restrictions of absolute monarchy.

A detailed account of the advance toward the relative freedom of the Eighteenth Century in England is beyond the scope of this work. But some Seventeenth Century English names, some ideas and drifts in government and society, must be accounted for. America took her law and her ideas of government largely from England.

The base of the national authority was broadened somewhat when Parliament asserted its supremacy over the power residing in the individual monarch, with the Glorious Revolution and its Bill of Rights. William and Mary came to the throne of England in a position subordinate to Parliament; their predecessors for two centuries had acknowledged themselves subordinate only to God. Representing a few people who elected them, members of the Commons had some responsibility to a constituency, even though universal suffrage was centuries away. The Commons, thus, held new power and responsibility in relation to a segment of the public that chose it.[2] This may be seen as a step on the way to the ascendancy of the public in a self-governing society. A century or more later, the constituency—the public—would hold the position of ascendancy. The relationship may be seen in terms of a people's right of expression as well as in their power to elect and remove their officials:[3]

> Two different views may be taken of the relation between rulers and their subjects. If the ruler is regarded as the superior of the subject, as being by the nature of his position presumably wise and good, the rightful ruler and guide of the whole population, it must necessarily follow that it is wrong to censure him openly; that even if he is mistaken his mistakes should be pointed out with the utmost respect, and that whether mistaken or not no

[2] T.P. Taswell-Langmead, English Constitutional History (London: Street & Maxwell, Limited, 1929), 9th ed. by A.L. Poole, pp. 594–599.

[3] Sir James Fitzjames Stephen, History of the Criminal Law of England (London: Macmillan, 1883), II, p. 299.

censure should be cast upon him likely or designed to diminish his authority.

If on the other hand the ruler is regarded as the agent and servant, and the subject as the wise and good master who is obliged to delegate his power to the so-called ruler because being a multitude he cannot use it himself, it is obvious that this sentiment must be reversed. Every member of the public who censures the ruler for the time being exercises in his own person the right which belongs to the whole of which he forms a part.

He is finding fault with his servant. If others think differently they can take the other side of the dispute, and the utmost that can happen is that the servant will be dismissed and another put in his place, or perhaps that the arrangements of the household will be modified.

The new structure of government, then, implied that behind the supremacy of Parliament lay at least a segment of the public, empowered to choose new governors in the Commons if it wished. And thorny, difficult men had been pressing throughout the Seventeenth Century—and indeed before—for recognition that members of the public ought to have this kind of power as well as its necessary concomitant, freedom of expression. It was part of the widespread recasting of thought in the Western world that came to be known as the Enlightenment and the age of faith in man's reason.

John Milton's matchless prose is a starting point in the thinking of Seventeenth Century England about increased freedom of expression. Others of his time, less known today, sought a wider freedom than he; others never violated that which they advocated as he did in accepting a position as a censor of the printed word. Others' actions were more important than his arguments in bringing the death of censorship in 1695.[4] Yet Milton's *Areopagitica,* written in 1644, was to serve as a standard and banner for centuries to come in England's and America's annals of free expression.

Milton wrote just after Charles I had been driven from his throne in England's Civil War. He wanted a divorce, and had written a tract that he hoped would lead to authority's relaxing of the strict legal barriers forbidding it. Under deep official disapproval for publishing it without license, Milton addressed to Parliament a plea for unlicensed printing, the *Areopagitica.* Wide in its sweep, it argued that licensing was unworkable, was an indignity to those engaged in it, and was socially undesirable because of

[4] Siebert, pp. 195–197, 260–263.

its strictures on the spread of truth. Let falsehood grapple with truth, he argued: "Who ever knew Truth put to the worse in a free and open encounter?" [5]

Milton's position on any scale measuring freedom today would be far from liberal. His argument was made within the framework of religious freedom; he was a Puritan, and religion was a central issue in the nation's Civil War. He would not tolerate Catholicism in his argument for freedom of expression. Nor would he permit atheism to have the freedom he sought. Yet viewed in the light of his time, his work was a clear advance over the prevailing authoritarianism of the Stuarts and over that of Parliament as well. Licensing, of course, was perpetuated through the life of the Long Parliament and Cromwell's reign, and lasted with short interruption from the Stuart Restoration of 1660 to 1695.

While Milton pleaded, others in England defied authority in their insistence on speaking. Most of them sectarians of Protestant stripe, their troubles stemmed from their intransigence in attacking the Romanism of which they suspected the Stuart kings and in propagating their own faiths. The law of seditious libel, the law of treason, and the procedures of the arbitrary Court of the Star Chamber were used against them, and some suffered maiming and torture.

William Prynn's book, *Histrio-Mastix,* propounded a strict Puritanism in behavior: he execrated such pastimes of people as dancing, play-going, hunting, Christmas-keeping and dressing up the house with green-ivy, and public festivals. He was brought before the Star Chamber on charges of seditious libel, his attack on government being inferred from Prynn's writing, shortly after the Queen had taken part in a pastoral play at Somerset House, that lewd women and whores were accustomed to act in plays. He was fined £ 10,000 and given life imprisonment, in addition to being pilloried, and having his ears cropped off.[6] During the year 1637, two other men, Dr. John Bastwick and Henry Burton, were handled similarly by the Star Chamber for their attacks on the Pope. Mob demonstrations against authority followed a public sentencing; Prynn was released by the Long Parliament on the ground that his trial had been illegal, after the abolition in 1641 of the Court of the Star Chamber.[7]

Treason in England had been defined by law since 1352, in Edward III's time. It included "compassing" or imagining the king's death, levying war against the king or giving aid and

---

[5] John Milton, Areopagitica (Chicago: Henry Regnery Co., 1949), p. 58.

[6] 3 Howell's State Trials 561 (1632–3).

[7] Siebert, pp. 123–125.

comfort to his enemies. Writing was included as part of compassing the king's death, and in 1663 at the session of Old Bailey, printer Twyn was indicted and tried for this crime by printing a book called *A Treatise on the Execution of Justice.* The book held to the view that the ruler is accountable to the people, and that the people may take up arms against a king and his family and put the king to death if he refuses accountability. John Twyn did not write the book, but he refused to say who did. The court's vengeance and the law's brutality were in the pronouncement of sentence: [8]

> [T]he country have found you guilty; therefore the judgment of the court is, and the court doth award, "that you be led back to the place from whence you came and from thence to be drawn upon an hurdle to the place of execution; and there you shall be hanged by the neck, and being alive, shall be cut down, and your privy-members shall be cut off, your entrails shall be taken out of your body, and you living, the same to be burnt before your eyes; your head to be cut off, your body to be divided into four quarters and your head and quarters to be disposed of at the pleasure of the king's majesty. And the Lord have mercy upon your soul."

Thirty years later, William Anderton printed books that were called treasonable in their intent to incite rebellion and the return to the throne of James II. Anderton refused to name the author, and was hanged in 1693.[9]

Martyrs to the principle of free expression had their impact and spokesmen for a new philosophy such as Milton and John Locke had theirs. Yet it was the independent printing and bookselling trade itself, according to the scholar Fredrick S. Siebert, that forced the end of licensing and censorship. Economic goals and profit were the central interest of the growing numbers of these tradesmen in the late Seventeenth Century; hedged and bound by the Regulation of Printing Act, cut out of the privileges still granted guild printers of the Stationers Company, they sought relief from Parliament. Unsuccessful in 1692, they continued pressing, and with help from people of power including philosopher John Locke, won their way in 1695. The House of Commons, offering a long list of reasons for its refusal to renew the Printing Act, focused on the restraint of the trades as the main factor, saying nothing about the principles of freedom of the press.[10] The classic instrument for press control was dead in England.

[8] Howell's State Trials 513 (1663).

[9] Howell's State Trials 1246 (1693).

[10] Siebert, pp. 260–263.

SEC. 6. EIGHTEENTH–CENTURY AMERICA

Colonial assemblies' control of the press persisted after governors' and courts' control was neutralized; in spite of the adoption of the First Amendment to the Constitution by the new nation, prosecutions for seditious libel rose again under the Alien and Sedition Acts.

American colonial printers never had to contend with the searches and seizures of a Stationers Company empowered with police functions. The courts they faced were scarcely the sinister and threatening bodies that the Courts of the Star Chamber and the High Commission were in the homeland. The punishments they received for illegal printing were far short of mutilation, life imprisonment, or hanging. Yet the first newspaper printers had to contend with licensing and censorship as a remnant of the English system, for some 30 years after the Commons rejected its renewal in 1695.

Newsman Benjamin Harris of Boston managed in 1690 to print his single, famous issue of *Publick Occurrences, Both Foreign and Domestick* without the authorities' stopping him. But the licensing power of the Massachusetts Bay authorities prevented another issue, and it was not until 1704 that there was a second attempt at a newspaper. This, by John Campbell also of Boston, was licensed, subsidized, sterilized, and blessed by the colonial government, and Campbell never offended. Governors licensed by order of their monarch in England, who was supreme in colonial affairs, and not until the 1720's did they yield the power in the face of reality: There had been no Regulation of Printing Act in England for about 30 years, and there was no power in the monarch to enforce the observance of licensing.[11] Barring Ben Harris, it was the first bold newspaperman in the colonies, James Franklin, who defied the demand that he submit to licensing. Though this printer of the *New England Courant* was made to suffer twice in jail for his belittling of authority, licensing had to be acknowledged dead after his release in 1723. The direct power over print held by the Governor and his council was neutralized.[12]

Next in order to face the challenge of a contentious printer was the power of the courts to try for seditious libel, the crime of criticizing government. This instrument for control had advanced

[11] Clyde A. Duniway, The Development of Freedom of the Press in Massachusetts (Cambridge: Harvard Univ.Press, 1906), pp. 104–105. For the influence of changing socio-political conditions that facilitated growing press freedom in the Eighteenth Century, see Richard Buel, Jr., "Freedom of the Press in Revolutionary America * * *," Bernard Bailyn and John B. Hench, eds., The Press & the American Revolution. Worcester, Mass. 1980, pp. 59, 62–68.

[12] Ibid.

to major proportions in England in the late Seventeenth and early Eighteenth Centuries. At least four colonial Americans faced sedition actions for printed words before the most celebrated criminal trial in the colonial period occurred in 1735. This was the trial of John Peter Zenger, printer of the *New York Weekly Journal* whose work was given much to the cause of undermining Governor William Cosby. Courage was the ingredient that Zenger brought to the attack; he had neither the schooling nor the knowledge to launch and sustain the political assault planned and executed by James Alexander of the powerful Lewis Morris faction which opposed the grasping and autocratic Cosby.[13] What Zenger had to fear was going to jail for the attacks that labeled Cosby a tyrant and oppressor of the colony.

And to jail Zenger went in late 1734, under an information filed by the governor's attorney general after fruitless efforts to get a grand jury to indict the printer. For eight months he awaited trial for seditious libel, while Alexander managed to keep the Journal printing and the campaign against Cosby simmering. And Alexander, disbarred by Chief Justice De Lancey (a Cosby appointee), turned to lawyer Andrew Hamilton of Philadelphia as the best man to plead Zenger's case.

The original "Philadelphia lawyer," Hamilton had built a reputation as the ablest attorney in the colonies. The dignity of age, his utter confidence, and his bold advocacy that the court discard old patterns of thinking about sedition came to bear in an irresistible way with jurors already sympathetic to Zenger's cause. The law of sedition had long held that the defendant was not to be permitted to plead that his offending words against government were true; the truth, it was held, only aggravated the offense, for it was more likely than falsehood to cause the target to seek violent revenge and breach the community's peace. Furthermore, the law had given the jury only a minor role in a sedition trial: its job was to decide whether the accused had, indeed, printed the words; it was up to the court to decide whether they were illegal words.

Jockeying with De Lancey, Hamilton urged the jury to recognize truth as a defense for Zenger, and argued that the jury should decide "the law"—the libelousness of the words—as well as the fact of printing. Blocked by the judge from pursuing these points far, he shifted his tactic and went to the importance of permitting men to criticize their governments: [14]

---

[13] Stanley Katz (ed.), A Brief Narrative of the Case and Trial of John Peter Zenger (Cambridge: Harvard Univ.Press, 1963), pp. 2–9.

[14] Ibid., p. 99.

Men who injure and oppress the people under their administration provoke them to cry out and complain, and then make that very complaint the foundation for new oppressions and prosecutions. I wish I could say there were no instances of this kind. But to conclude, the question before the Court and you, gentlemen of the jury, is not of small or private concern; it is not the cause of a poor printer, nor of New York alone, which you are trying. No! it may, in its consequences, affect every freeman that lives under a British government, on the main of America. It is the best cause; it is the cause of liberty; and I make no doubt but your upright conduct, this day, will not only entitle you to the love and esteem of your fellow citizens, but every man who prefers freedom to a life of slavery, will bless and honor you as men who have baffled the attempts of tyranny; and by an impartial and uncorrupt verdict, have laid a noble foundation for securing to ourselves, our posterity, and our neighbors, that to which nature and the laws of our country have given us a right—the liberty—both of exposing and opposing arbitrary power in these parts of the world at least, by speaking and writing truth.

Hamilton ended his plea in an emotion-charged courtroom; De Lancey delivered a confusing charge to the jury, which retired to deliberate; and in a short time the jury emerged with the "not guilty" verdict. There were celebrations in the streets that night; there were printings and re-printings of the Hamilton plea for years to come, more even in England than in the colonies; and the court trial for seditious libel was finished for the colonial period as an instrument for control of the press. Not for 40 years or more would it be used again in America.[15]

It was the elected Assembly, or lower house of the colonial legislature, that was the most successful and most active force in official control of Eighteenth Century colonial printers. Jealous of its powers under the view that it was Parliament in miniature, and unwilling to have its acts criticized, this agency of government disciplined printer after printer. Even as it emerged as the main check on the powers of the Crown's governors, even as it showed itself as the seat of government support for the movement for independence, the Assembly demonstrated its aversion to popular criticism. Its instrument for control was the citation for contempt ("breach of privilege"), and it haled a long line of printers before it for their "seditious" attacks on its performance. The legislative contempt citation was a legislative sedition action.

[15] Harold L. Nelson, Seditious Libel in Colonial America, 3 Am.Journ.Legal History 160 (1959).

Levy has demonstrated the relative power and activity of the Assemblies in respect to the press. Up and down the seaboard, printers were brought to the legislative bar and there were forced to kneel and beg the pardon of the stern law-makers, swear that they meant no harm by their writings, and accept rebuke or imprisonment. James Franklin's irony put him in jail; he had speculated that the Massachusetts government might get around to outfitting a ship to pursue a pirate "sometime this month, wind and weather permitting." New Yorkers James Parker and William Weyman were jailed for an article on the poverty of Orange and Ulster counties; the Assembly construed it as a reflection upon their stewardship. These were only a few actions among many, and they continued to the eve of the Revolutionary War in some colonies.[16]

The great article of faith that heads America's commitment to free expression was written in 1791 by men who had not yet thought through all that "free speech and press" implies. The founders stated in the First Amendment to the Constitution that "Congress shall make no law *   *   * abridging freedom of speech, or of the press *   *   *." while still arguing over precisely what they meant by the words. None spoke doubts about the importance of the principle. They were deeply aware of the lasting symbolic power of the courageous Zenger in accepting prison in the cause of free press. They were possessed of the spirited, soaring arguments for free press by England's famed "Cato," printed and re-printed in the little colonial newspapers. Behind them lay the great pamphleteering and newspapering that had raised sedition to an art in bringing the colonies to revolt against the Mother country, printed words indispensable in bringing down the most powerful nation on earth.

Yet in the searing newspaper debates of the early Independence, with Federalists and anti-Federalists indulging political vitriol seen by many as seditious and thus criminal, the axioms of centuries were with them. It still seemed to many that no government could stand if it could not at some point punish its critics, and their new government was meant to last. Some words surely were illegal. Not, perhaps, in the realm of religion, where James Madison, among others, argued an unlimited freedom to

---

[16] Leonard W. Levy, Emergence of a Free Press (N.Y., 1985), 71–84. No other historian has stimulated others to study 18th-Century American press freedom as has Levy, whose thesis that the First Amendment was not intended by the Framers to end the British common law of seditious libel in America has aroused many to dissent. Revising his early, provocative Legacy of Suppression (1960) in Emergence of a Free Press (1985), and conceding some errors and misinterpretations in Legacy, he responds directly to many of the protestors but concedes nothing central to his main thesis. See Emergence of a Free Press, passim, for many of the confrontations.

speak and write; but could sedition be given such scope? It was the party of Thomas Jefferson that gave an answer, in the debates and sequel of the Alien and Sedition Acts of 1798–1800.

SEC. 7.   SEDITION

Attacks on the form of government, its laws, its institutions, and its individual officers have been made punishable as sedition by laws of both the federal and state governments.

In the complex story about the reluctant retreat of the crime of sedition through more than 150 years of American history, no episode stands out more than the controversy of 1798–1800 over the Alien and Sedition Acts. It was only seven years after the adoption of the Bill of Rights and its First Amendment that the Acts were written, at a time of high public and official alarm. With France and England in conflict through the 1790s, America had been pulled by both toward war. The Republicans—Jefferson's party—had favored France, while the Federalists sided with England. Angered at Jay's Treaty of 1794 with England, which she felt placed America on the side of her enemy, France had undertaken the raiding of American shipping. America's envoys, sent to France to negotiate a settlement, were faced with a demand for an American war loan to France, and a bribe of a quarter-million dollars. This unofficial demand as a price for negotiations was revealed to Americans as the famous "X, Y, Z Affair." Now most of America was incensed; President John Adams called for war preparation, which his Federalist Congress set about furnishing in 1797.[17]

The Republicans, though suffering heavy political losses in the nation's war fever, did not abandon their support of France. Stigmatized in the refusal to do so, associated by the Federalists with the recent French Revolution and its Terror, and beleaguered on all sides for their continued opposition to Britain, the Republicans were in deep trouble. And in this context, the Federalist Congress passed the Alien and Sedition Acts as measures to control opposition to America's war policy and to the Federalist majority party.

It was the Sedition Act that struck most lethally at opposition and at the Republicans. The Act made it a crime to publish or utter false, scandalous, and malicious criticism of the President, Congress, or the government with the intent to defame them or bring them into disrepute.[18]

[17] James M. Smith, Freedom's Fetters (Ithaca: Cornell Univ.Press, 1956), Chap. 2. This is the leading work on the Alien and Sedition Acts.

[18] Ibid., Chap. 6.

Fourteen indictments were brought under the Act, all against Republican newspapermen and publicists, and all 14 resulted in convictions.[19]   The first action put Rep. Matthew Lyon in jail for four months and cost him a fine of $1,000.   He had implied that under President Adams, the Executive Branch showed "an unbounded thirst for ridiculous pomp, foolish adulation, and selfish avarice," and that the public welfare was "swallowed up in a continual grasp for power."   Anthony Haswell, Republican editor of the (Bennington) *Vermont Gazette,* came to Lyon's defense while the latter was in prison.   He wrote that Lyon was held by "the oppressive hand of usurped power," and said that the federal marshal who held him had subjected him to indignities that might be expected of a "hard-hearted savage."   Haswell's fine was $200 and his term in federal prison two months.[20]

Its back to the wall under the attempt of the Federalists to proscribe it as a party of disloyalty and subversion, the Republican Party put forth spokesmen who declared that the idea of sedition was odious to a self-governing society, and denied that the federal government had any kind of power over the press.   The Acts, they said, were unconstitutional in making it a crime to criticize the President and government.   No matter that the Acts permitted the defenses for which Andrew Hamilton had argued in defending Zenger: truth was of little use in defending opinions (how prove the truth of an opinion?); and jury power to find the law could be circumvented by judges in various ways.   A people, they argued, cannot call itself free unless it is superior to its government, unless it can have unrestricted right of discussion.   No natural right of the individual, they contended in the Lockean framework, can be more important than free expression.   They rested their case on their belief in reason as the central characteristic of men, and on the people's position of ascendancy over government.[21] The radical Thomas Cooper, friend of Joseph Priestley, dissected one by one the arguments for permitting a sedition power in government.[22]   Calmly and systematically, lawyer Tunis Wortman worked out philosophical ground for freedom in the fullest statement of the group.[23]   Madison, St. George Tucker, and others drove home the arguments.

The unpopularity of the Alien and Sedition Acts and outrage at the prosecutions of Republican printers helped defeat the Fed-

[19] Ibid., p. 185.

[20] Each trial is treated in Smith, Chaps. 11–17.

[21] Levy, Chap. 10. And see Chap. 9 for evidence that several Jeffersonians had no objection to a sedition power in *state* governments.

[22] Political Essays (Phila.: Printed for R. Campbell, 1800), pp. 71–88.

[23] Treatise Concerning Political Enquiry, and the Liberty of the Press (New York: Printed by George Forman, 1800).

eralist Party and President John Adams in 1800. President Jefferson was committed to letting the Acts lapse, and they died in early 1801. The nation would see no federal peacetime sedition act again for 140 years. Furthermore, the alternative route of using the common law as a basis for federal sedition actions was closed to the government only a few years later. The Supreme Court ruled in cases of 1812 and 1816 that federal courts had been given no authority over common-law crimes by the Constitution, and that whatever question there had been about the matter had been settled by public opposition to such jurisdiction.[24]

The fear and hatred of French revolutionary doctrine had been real factors in the passage of the Alien and Sedition Acts. Different fears, different hatreds led to suppressive laws in the South about a generation later, when states began passing laws to silence Abolitionists. The anti-slavery drive, coupled with incidents such as Nat Turner's slave rebellion, caused paroxysms of fear among Southerners that their "peculiar institution" and the shape of society and government would be subverted and destroyed. Laws were passed—sedition laws, though not labeled as such in statute books—making it a crime to advocate the abolition of slavery or to argue that owners "have no property" in slaves, and denying abolitionist literature access to the mails.[25] The suppression of anti-slavery argument became almost total in most of the South by 1850.

Sedition actions emerged uncloaked again at their next time of strength, in the early Twentieth Century when both state and federal lawmakers acted to check criticism of government in response to alarm at the rise of socio-political protest. Prosecutions to punish verbal attacks on the form of government, on laws, and on government's conduct, found new life at the federal level some 100 years after they had been discredited by the Alien and Sedition Act prosecutions of 1798–1800. The actions focused on a new radicalism, flourishing in the poverty and sweat-shop conditions of industrial cities and in the lumber and mining camps of the West. Whether seeking an improved life for the deprived, driving for power, or fostering revolution, socialists, anarchists, and syndicalists advocated drastic change in the economic and political system. Laws and criminal prosecutions rose to check their words.[26]

[24] United States v. Hudson and Goodwin, 11 U.S. (7 Cranch.) 32 (1812); United States v. Coolidge, 14 U.S. (1 Wheat.) 415 (1816).

[25] Three Virginia laws passed between 1832 and 1848 are in Nelson, Freedom of the Press from Hamilton to the Warren Court, pp. 173–178.

[26] William Preston, Jr., Aliens and Dissenters, Federal Suppression of Radicals, 1903–1933 (Cambridge: Harvard Univ.Press, 1963).

In the aftermath of the assassination of President William McKinley in 1901, the states of New York, New Jersey and Wisconsin passed laws against anarchists' advocating the destruction of existing government. Congress passed the Immigration Act of 1903, barring from the country those who believed in or advocated the overthrow of the United States government by violence. Industrial turbulence, the growth of the Industrial Workers of the World, the surge of right- and left-wing socialism, contributed to alarm in the nation. And as the varied voices of drastic reform and radical change rose loud in the land, the coming of World War I increased their stridency: This, they insisted, was a "Capitalists' war," fostered and furthered for industrial profit. By 1918, national alarm was increased by the victory of revolutionary communism in Russia.[27]

World War I brought a wave of legislation across the states to make criminal the advocacy of violent overthrow of government. Yet it was the federal government's Espionage Act of 1917 and its amendment of 1918 to include sedition that put most muscle into prosecution for criminal words. Foremost among proscribed and prosecuted statements were those that were construed to cause insubordination or disloyalty in the armed forces, or to obstruct enlistment or recruiting.[28] Some 1,900 persons were prosecuted for speech, and possibly 100 newspapers and periodicals were barred from the mails.[29] Polemics in pamphlet form, as well as books, also were the cause of prosecutions.

The best-known of the Socialist newspapers prosecuted under the Espionage Act were the *New York Call,* the *Masses,* also of New York, and the *Milwaukee Leader.* In the last of these, editor Victor Berger had denounced the war, the United States government, and munitions makers. Postmaster General Albert Burleson considered this the kind of opposition to the war forbidden by the Espionage Act, and excluded it from the mails as the Act provided. Further, he said, the repeated attacks on the war effort in the Leader were evidence that it would continue doing the same in the future, and on these grounds, the Leader's second-class mail permit should be revoked. He was upheld in his revocation of the permit by the United States Supreme Court, and

[27] Ibid.; Paul L. Murphy, World War I and the Origins of Civil Liberties in the United States (New York, 1979); H.C. Peterson and Gilbert C. Fite, Opponents of War, 1917–1918 (Madison: Univ. of Wis.Press, 1957).

[28] 40 U.S. Statutes 217. For state laws, see Zechariah Chafee, Jr., Free Speech in the United States (Boston, 1941), pp. 575–597.

[29] Chafee, p. 52.

the Leader was thus denied the low-rate mailing privilege from 1917 until after the war.[30]

Pamphleteers of the left were convicted under the Espionage Act and under state anarchy and sedition acts. The famous case of Schenck v. U.S., in which Schenck was prosecuted for polemics that actually went to the matter of resisting the draft, brought Justice Oliver Wendell Holmes' articulation of the famous clear and present danger test: [31]

> We admit that in many places and in ordinary times the defendants in saying all that was said in the circular would have been within their constitutional rights. But the character of every act depends upon the circumstances in which it was done * * *. The question in every case is whether the words used are used in such circumstances and are of such a nature as to create a clear and present danger that they will bring about the substantive evils that Congress has a right to prevent. It is a question of proximity and degree. When a nation is at war many things that might be said in time of peace are such a hindrance to its effort that their utterance will not be endured * * *.

The new test did not free Schenck, nor was it to be used by Supreme Court majorities in support of free expression for two decades to come. Its plain implications, however, were that old tests were too restrictive for the demands of freedom under the First Amendment. As elaborated and developed in subsequent opinions by Holmes and Justice Brandeis against restrictive interpretations of free expression,[32] the test helped force the Court to think through the meaning of the First and Fourteenth Amendments, and served as a rallying-point for libertarians for decades to come.

Another milestone in the Supreme Court's consideration of sedition cases was reached in a post-war case, Gitlow v. People of New York.[33] Here the 1902 New York statute on anarchy was invoked against the publication of the "left Wing Manifesto" in a radical paper called *Revolutionary Age*. It advocated and forecast mass struggle, mass strikes, and the overthrow of the bourgeoisie after a long revolutionary period. Convicted, business manager

---

[30] United States ex rel. Milwaukee Social Democratic Pub. Co. v. Burleson, 255 U.S. 407, 41 S.Ct. 352 (1921).

[31] 249 U.S. 47, 39 S.Ct. 247 (1919).

[32] Notably Abrams v. United States, 250 U.S. 616, 40 S.Ct. 17 (1919); Gilbert v. State of Minn., 254 U.S. 325, 41 S.Ct. 125 (1920); Gitlow v. People of State of New York, 268 U.S. 652, 45 S.Ct. 625 (1925); Whitney v. People of State of California, 274 U.S. 357, 47 S.Ct. 641 (1927).

[33] 268 U.S. 652, 45 S.Ct. 625 (1925).

Benjamin Gitlow appealed to the Supreme Court. It upheld his conviction under an old test of criminality in words—whether the words have a tendency to imperil or subvert government.

But even as it upheld conviction, the Court wrote a single short paragraph accepting a principle long sought by libertarians: It said that the Fourteenth Amendment's barrier to states' depriving citizens of life, liberty, or property without due process of law protected liberty of speech and press against invasion by the states. Heretofore, the Supreme Court had tightly restricted the scope of the "liberty" protected by the Fourteenth Amendment; it had left it up to each state to say what liberty of speech and press was. Henceforth, the Supreme Court would review state laws and decisions on free expressions, under the Gitlow case pronouncement that read: [34]

> [W]e may and do assume that freedom of speech and of the press—which are protected by the First Amendment from abridgment by Congress—are among the fundamental personal rights and "liberties" protected by the due process clause of the Fourteenth Amendment from impairment by the States.

Although Gitlow went to jail, his case had brought acceptance of a principle of high importance. The confining interpretation of free expression fostered in many states over many decades now would be brought to the scrutiny of the United States Supreme Court.

Immediately after World War I, the thrust of revolutionary communism had spurred the Attorney General of the United States to urge the passage of a federal peacetime sedition act. His call for such a peacetime measure (the Espionage Act of 1917 had applied only to war) brought concerted opposition; the move was stopped although widespread deportation of Russians and other aliens for their ideas and words was accomplished. But 20 years later, similar fears engendered with the coming of World War II and the activity of domestic communists brought success for a similar bill. This was the Alien Registration Act of 1940, known as the Smith Act for Rep. Howard W. Smith of Virginia who introduced it.[35] For the first time since the Alien and Sedition Acts of 1798, America had a federal peacetime sedition law. The heart of its provisions, under Section 2, made it a crime to advocate forcible or violent overthrow of government, or to publish or distribute material advocating violence with the intent to overthrow government.

Upon the mass media of general circulation, the Act was to have little or no impact; they advocated the *status quo*, not radical

---

[34] Ibid., 268 U.S. 652, 666, 45 S.Ct. 625, 630 (1925).

[35] 54 U.S. Statutes 670.

change or revolution. But for speakers, teachers, and pamphleteers of the Communist Party, the Smith Act came to mean a great deal. Fewer than 20 persons had been punished under the Alien and Sedition Acts of 1798–1801; it is estimated that approximately 100 persons were fined or imprisoned under the Smith Act between 1940 and 1960.[36] In a real sense, however, the Smith Act was less suppressive than its ancestor: The Alien and Sedition Acts had punished criticism of government officials, Congress, and the laws, an everyday exercise of the press, but the Smith Act limited the ban to advocating violent overthrow.

The government made its first move in 1943. Leaders of a revolutionary splinter, the Socialist Workers Party which followed Russia's banished Trotsky, were the target. They were brought to trial in Minneapolis and convicted for the advocacy of violent overthrow in their printed polemics. The Court of Appeals sustained the conviction, and the United States Supreme Court refused to review the case.[37]

But the Communist Party was much more the target of government prosecution than the little group of Trotskyites. In the context of the cold war between the United States and the U.S.S.R. following World War II, almost 10 years of prosecution took place. The first case, Dennis v. United States, brought major figures in the Communist Party to trial and convicted 11 of them.[38] The charges were that they had reconstituted the American Communist Party in 1945, and conspired to advocate violent overthrow of the government.

For almost nine months the trial went on in federal district court under Judge Harold Medina. The nation was fascinated and bored in turn as the defense introduced complex legal challenges to the trial and the prosecution introduced exhibit after exhibit. Newspapers, pamphlets, and books were employed as evidence of the defendants' intent, from the *Daily Worker* to *The Communist Manifesto*. Scores of pages were read into the record, as the government sought to show conspiracy by publishing and circulating the literature of revolutionary force. Judge Medina followed the doctrine of the *Gitlow* case in instructing the jury that advocacy or teaching of violent overthrow of the government was not illegal if it were only "abstract doctrine." What the law forbade was teaching or advocating "action" to overthrow the

---

[36] Don R. Pember, The Smith Act as a Restraint of the Press, Journalism Monographs # 10, May 1969; Zechariah Chafee, Jr., The Blessings of Liberty (Phila., N.Y.: J.B. Lippincott Co., 1954), p. 22.

[37] Dunne v. United States, 138 F.2d 137 (8th Cir.1943).

[38] 341 U.S. 494, 71 S.Ct. 857 (1951).

government.[39] The jury found that the 11 did, indeed, conspire to advocate forcible overthrow. The Court of Appeals upheld the conviction and the case was accepted for review by the Supreme Court of the United States.

The justices wrote five opinions, three opinions concurring in conviction and two dissenting. Chief Justice Vinson wrote the opinion that carried the most names (three besides his). He said that free expression is not an unlimited or unqualified right, and that "the societal value of speech must, on occasion, be subordinated to other values and considerations." [40] But a conviction for violation of a statute limiting speech, he said, must rest on the showing that the words created a "clear and present danger" that a crime would be attempted or accomplished. Thus he went to the famous Holmes rule first expressed in the *Schenck* case in 1919, and interpreted it as follows: [41]

> In this case we are squarely presented with the application of the "clear and present danger" test, and must decide what that phrase imports. We first note that many of the cases in which this Court has reversed convictions by use of this or similar tests have been based on the fact that the interest which the State was attempting to protect was too insubstantial to warrant restriction of speech * * *. Overthrow of the government by force and violence is certainly a substantial enough interest for the government to limit speech. Indeed, this is the ultimate value of any society, for if a society cannot protect its very structure from armed internal attack, it must follow that no subordinate value can be protected. If, then, this interest may be protected, the literal problem which is presented is what has been meant by the use of the utterances bringing about the evil within the power of Congress to punish. Obviously, the words cannot mean that before the Government may act, it must wait until the *putsch* is about to be executed, the plans have been laid and the signal is awaited. If Government is aware that a group aiming at its overthrow is attempting to indoctrinate its members and to commit them to a course whereby they will strike when the leaders feel the circumstances permit, action by the government is required * * *. Certainly an attempt to overthrow the Government by force, even though doomed from the outset be-

---

[39] United States v. Foster, 80 F.Supp. 479 (D.C.N.Y.1949). Upon appeal, this case became United States v. Dennis et al., 183 F.2d 201 (2d Cir.1950).

[40] Dennis v. United States, 341 U.S. 494, 71 S.Ct. 857 (1951).

[41] Ibid., 508–509.

cause of inadequate numbers or power of the revolution-
ists, is a sufficient evil for Congress to prevent.

Having thus rejected the position that likelihood of success in
committing the criminal act is the criterion for restricting speech,
Chief Justice Vinson adopted the statement of the Court of Appeals in interpreting the clear and present danger test. Chief
Judge Hand had written: "In each case [courts] must ask whether
the gravity of the 'evil,' discounted by its improbability justifies
such invasion of free speech as is necessary to avoid the danger." [42]
Vinson was arguing that the danger need not be immediate when
the interest (here, self-preservation of government) is important
enough.

Deep disagreement in the Court over thus limiting the scope
of free expression appeared in the dissents of Justices Black and
Douglas. The latter could see no clear and present danger to the
government and state in the words and papers of the 11 Communists. Neither as a political force nor as a disciplined corps of
poised saboteurs did Justice Douglas see them as a threat: [43]

> Communists in this country have never made a re-
> spectable or serious showing in any election * * *.
> Communism has been so thoroughly exposed in this coun-
> try that it has been crippled as a political force. Free
> speech has destroyed it as an effective political party. It
> is inconceivable that those who went up and down this
> country preaching the doctrine of revolution which peti-
> tioners espouse would have any success.
>
> *   *   *
>
> How it can be said that there is a clear and present
> danger that this advocacy will succeed is, therefore, a
> mystery. Some nations less resilient than the United
> States, where illiteracy is high and where democratic
> traditions are only budding, might have to take drastic
> steps and jail these men for merely speaking their creed.
> But in America they are miserable merchants of unwant-
> ed ideas; their wares remain unsold. The fact that their
> ideas are abhorrent does not make them powerful.
>
> *   *   *
>
> * * * Free speech—the glory of our system of gov-
> ernment—should not be sacrificed on anything less than
> plain and objective proof of danger that the evil advocated
> is imminent.

Through most of the 1950's, cases under the Smith Act continued to move through the courts. But in the wake of the decision

---

[42] Ibid., 510.

[43] Dennis v. United States, 341 U.S. 494, 71 S.Ct. 857 (1951).

in Yates v. United States in 1957, prosecutions dwindled and died out. In this case, the Supreme Court reversed the conviction of 14 Communist Party leaders under the Smith Act. Its decision turned in large part on the difference between teaching the need for violent overthrow as an abstract theory or doctrine, and teaching it as a spur to action. The Court said: [44]

> We are * * * faced with the question whether the Smith Act prohibits advocacy and teaching of forcible overthrow as an abstract principle, divorced from any effort to instigate action to that end, so long as such advocacy or teaching is engaged in with evil intent. We hold that it does not.

> The distinction between advocacy of abstract doctrine and advocacy directed at promoting unlawful action is one that has been consistently recognized in the opinions of this Court * * *.

> * * *

> * * * The legislative history of the Smith Act and related bills shows beyond all question that Congress was aware of the distinction between the advocacy or teaching of abstract doctrine and the advocacy or teaching of action, and that it did not intend to disregard it. The statute was aimed at the advocacy and teaching of concrete action for the forcible overthrow of the Government, and not of principles divorced from action.

Since the trial court had not required the jury which found the defendant guilty to make the distinction, the conviction was reversed. There was no reference to the famous clear and present danger doctrine.

The Warren Court—so called for chief Justice Earl Warren who had been appointed in 1953—had grown less and less willing to uphold convictions under the Smith Act, and with the *Yates* decision, charges against many other defendants in pending cases were dismissed in lower courts. The Smith Act soon lapsed into disuse, and in the several versions of a bill for the broad reform of the federal Criminal Code that labored toward adoption by Congress beginning in 1977, the Act was omitted and thus scheduled for repeal.[45]

Yates had found that the trial judge's instructions had allowed conviction for mere advocacy without reference to its tendency to bring about forcible action, and overturned the convictions. In 1969, the Supreme Court was presented with the appeal of a Ku

---

[44] Yates v. United States, 354 U.S. 298, 77 S.Ct. 1064 (1957).

[45] For other controls on news media embraced by the Act (S.1437), see Reporters Committee for Freedom of the Press, News Media Alert, Aug. 1977, pp. 4–5.

Klux Klan leader who had been convicted under the Ohio Criminal Syndicalism statute for advocating the duty or necessity of crime, violence or unlawful methods of terrorism to accomplish political reform. The leader, Brandenburg, had been televised as he made a speech in which he said the Klan was "not a revengent [sic] organization, but if our President, our Congress, our Supreme Court, continues to suppress the white, Caucasian race, it's possible that there might have to be some revengeance taken." He added that "We are marching on Congress * * * four hundred thousand strong."

The Supreme Court reversed the conviction. Citing precedent since *Dennis,* it said: [46]

> These later decisions have fashioned the principle that the constitutional guarantees of free speech and free press do not permit a State to forbid or proscribe advocacy of the use of force or of law violation except where such advocacy is directed to inciting or producing imminent lawless action and is likely to incite or produce such action. * * * A statute which fails to draw this distinction impermissibly intrudes upon the freedoms guaranteed by the First and Fourteenth Amendments.

The "inciting" or producing imminent lawless action clause has been called merely a version of the "clear and present danger" test. But it also must be considered that "An incitement-nonincitement distinction had only fragmentary and ambiguous antecedents in the pre-Brandenburg era; it was Brandenburg that really 'established' it * * *." [47] It has continued to serve a protective role. Words challenging the authority of the state have brought criminal conviction at trial, but under the test have continued to find protection upon appeal to the Supreme Court. [48] Less than an absolute barrier to government's control of expression, the *Brandenburg* test yet takes its place as a strong element in the heavy crippling of the sedition action. [49]

---

[46] Brandenburg v. Ohio, 395 U.S. 444, 89 S.Ct. 1827 (1969).

[47] Gerald Gunther, Cases and Materials on Constitutional Law, 9th ed., Mineola, N.Y. 1975, p. 1128; Thomas I. Emerson, "First Amendment Doctrine and the Burger Court," 68 Univ. of Calif.L.Rev. 422, 445–46, feels the "incitement" test is subject to "serious objections," including its permitting government to interfere with expression "at too early a state."

[48] Hess v. Indiana, 414 U.S. 105, 94 S.Ct. 326 (1973); Healy v. James, 408 U.S. 169, 92 S.Ct. 2338 (1972).

[49] See Harry Kalven, "The New York Times Case: a Note on 'The Central Meaning of the First Amendment'", 1964 Sup.Ct.Rev. 191.

SEC. 8. CRIMINAL LIBEL

Control of words critical of officials and other citizens was provided by criminal libel law in the states, beginning in the nation's early years, building to strength between 1880 and 1920, and dying out in the period after World War II.

The same sedition that made it a crime to attack verbally the form of government or the laws, applied also to words that assailed government officials, as we saw in the story of the Alien and Sedition Acts. However, when the target of verbal attack was an official, the offense and its details were in effect embraced in the law of criminal libel—defamation, which brings one into hatred, ridicule, disgrace, or causes one to be shunned, or damages one in business. And after the death of the Alien and Sedition Acts in 1801, statutes making libel a crime began to proliferate in the states.

The Jeffersonians had in varying degree accepted this power when held by the states.[50] Supposedly, citizens could control their local, state affairs and check tendencies toward oppression within that sphere much more easily than they could check a remote, centralized national government. Under the common law and under statutes, the new states provided that libel could be a crime whether it was aimed at plain citizens or government men. That the laws went under the name "criminal libel" laws instead of under the rubric of the hated "seditious libel" made them no less effective as tools for prosecution of those who attacked officials.

The states drew up safeguards against some of the harshest features of the old English law of libel. The principles that Andrew Hamilton pleaded for in defending Zenger, and that the Alien and Sedition Acts had provided, emerged as important ones early in the Nineteenth Century as states embarked upon prosecutions. Truth slowly was established as a defense in criminal libel actions, and juries were permitted to find the law under growing numbers of state constitutions and statutes as the century progressed. A celebrated early case in New York encouraged the spread. It stemmed from a paragraph reprinted by Federalist editor Harry Croswell from the *New York Evening Post* attacking President Thomas Jefferson:[51]

> Jefferson paid Callender [a Republican editor] for calling Washington a traitor, a robber, and a perjurer; for calling Adams a hoary-headed old incendiary, and for

[50] Levy, Chap. 9; Berns, pp. 89–119.

[51] People v. Croswell, 3 Johnson's Cases 337 (N.Y.1804).

most grossly slandering the private characters of men who he well knew to be virtuous.

The great Federalist leader, Alexander Hamilton, in 1804 took up Croswell's case after he had been convicted of criminal libel in a jury trial in which he had not been permitted to show the truth of his charge. Hamilton argued that "the liberty of the press consists of the right to publish with impunity truth with good motives for justifiable ends though reflecting on government, magistracy, or individuals." This, of course, made the intent of the publisher crucial. He also urged that the jury be allowed to find both the law and the facts of the case. He lost, the appeals court being evenly divided; but the result was so repugnant to people and lawmakers that the New York Legislature in 1805 passed a law embracing the principles that Hamilton urged.[52]

In the states' adoption of Hamilton's formula (a few, indeed, made truth a defense no matter what the motives of the writer) there was an implied rejection of an ancient justification for punishing libel as a crime against the state. The old reasoning was that the truer the disparaging words, the more likely the insulted person to seek violent revenge, breaching the peace. If the words were false, the logic ran, they could be demonstrated as such, and the defamed would be more easily mollified. Thus the legal aphorism of the Eighteenth Century: "the greater the truth, the greater the libel."

But courts were reluctant to permit truth a protected position in the law, even though statutes seemed to endorse the position that the public needs to know the truth. As legislatures adopted truth as a defense in libel statutes through the Nineteenth Century, courts nevertheless clung tenaciously to breach of the peace as an overriding excuse for punishing libel.[53] While few statutes or constitutions retained words' "tendency to breach the peace" as a basis for criminality in libel in the Twentieth Century, judges who wanted to employ it found it readily accessible in common law principles.

Criminal libel actions were few through most of the Nineteenth Century. They surged in number in the 1880s and held at some 100 reported cases per decade for 30 years or more. Not all, by any means, were brought for defamation of public officials in the pattern of seditious libel actions.[54] But criticism of police,

---

[52] An Act Concerning Libels, Laws of the State of New York, Albany, 1805.

[53] Elizabeth Goepel, "The Breach of the Peace Provision in Nineteenth Century Criminal Libel Law," (Univ. of Wis.1981), unpublished Master's thesis.

[54] John D. Stevens, et al., Criminal Libel as Seditious Libel, 43 Journalism Quar. 110 (1966); Robert A. Leflar, The Social Utility of the Criminal Law of Defamation, 34 Texas L.Rev. 984 (1956). Stevens et al. finds that about one-fifth (31) of the 148

governors, mayors, judges, prosecutors, sheriffs, and other government officials was the offense in scores of criminal libel cases.

Of all of them, the most famous was that stemming from the abortive attempt of President Theodore Roosevelt to punish the *New York World* and the *Indianapolis News* for charging deep corruption in the nation's purchase of the title to the Panama Canal from France. Enraged especially by the World and its publisher, Joseph Pulitzer, President Roosevelt delivered a special message to Congress. He charged that Pulitzer was responsible for libeling the United States Government, individuals in the government, and the "good name of the American people." He called it "criminal libel," but his angry words carried his accusation deep into various realms of sedition. He said of the articles and editorials: [55]

> In form, they are in part libels upon individuals * * *. But they are in fact wholly, and in form partly, a libel upon the United States Government. I do not believe we should concern ourselves with the particular individuals who wrote the lying and libelous editorials * * * or articles in the news columns. The real offender is Mr. Joseph Pulitzer, editor and proprietor of the World. While the criminal offense of which Mr. Pulitzer has been guilty is in form a libel upon individuals, the great injury done is in blackening the good name of the American people * * *. He should be prosecuted for libel by the governmental authorities * * *. The Attorney-General has under consideration the form in which the proceedings against Mr. Pulitzer shall be brought * * *.

For charges brought against Pulitzer in federal court in New York, the indictment was quashed on grounds that the federal government did not have jurisdiction. The action was upheld by the United States Supreme Court. Charges against the *Indianapolis News,* also pushing the attack on the Panama Canal purchase, were brought before Judge A.B. Anderson who decided the case on its merits. The government sought to have News officials sent to Washington for trial. Judge Anderson said he had deep doubts that the newspaper articles were libelous, and thought they might be privileged as well as non-libelous. But it was on other grounds that he refused to send journalists to Washington for trial. He

criminal libel cases reported in the half-century after World War I grew out of charges made against officials.

[55] House of Rep.Docs., 60 Cong., 2 Sess., § 1213 (Dec. 15, 1908), pp. 3–5.

said that the Sixth Amendment governed, in guaranteeing trial in the state or district where the alleged crime was committed: [56]

> To my mind that man has read the history of our institutions to little purpose who does not look with grave apprehension upon the possibility of the success of a proceeding such as this. If the history of liberty means anything, if constitutional guaranties are worth anything, this proceeding must fail.

> If the prosecuting officers have the authority to select the tribunal, if there be more than one tribunal to select from, if the government has that power, and can drag citizens from distant states to the capital of the nation, there to be tried, then, as Judge Cooley says, this is a strange result of a revolution where one of the grievances complained of was the assertion of the right to send parties abroad for trial.

> The defendants will be discharged.

There is little indication that the failure of Roosevelt's action deterred lesser officials at lower levels of government from instituting criminal libel actions. Not until more than a decade later, after World War I, did a sharp decline in the number of actions set in, dropping from approximately 100 per decade to far smaller numbers.[57] Courts increasingly came to take the position that civil libel suits to recover damages were much to be preferred to criminal libel prosecutions, which more and more seemed inappropriate to personal squabbles between citizens. Furthermore, violent revenge—breach of the peace—was rarely to be seen in connection with defamation. No longer were the evils of duelling as a way of avenging verbal insults part of life, real though they had been to the Seventeenth and Eighteenth Centuries. Also, the defamed ordinarily had more to gain through a civil judgment for money damages than through a criminal conviction that helps only in the sense that it is a "moral victory."

Yet as the number of cases retreated—to about 15 in the decade of the 1940s—the tendency of harsh words to cause breach of the peace clung to the law's provisions and reasoning in several states. Thus this test was applied to a newspaper article about the police chief of New Britain, Conn., which charged him and his family with bootlegging. "The gist of the crime is, not the injury to the reputation of the person libeled, but that the publication affects injuriously the peace and good order of society," said the Connecticut Supreme Court in upholding the conviction of the

---

[56] United States v. Smith, 173 F. 227 (D.C.Ind.1909).

[57] Stevens, op. cit.

newspaper.[58] And as late as 1961 in the same state, it was made plain that the law still held—and that the crime lay in the mere *tendency* of the words to create a breach of the peace, and that "it is immaterial that no one was incited to commit any act by reason of the libel * * *." [59]

Perhaps adding tenacity to the shrinking offense of criminal libel was a highly unusual case of 1952 that claimed the attention of much of the world of civil liberties. It involved a special and rarely employed version of the ancient criminal libel law—that under some circumstances, *groups* could be libeled and the state could bring criminal action against the libeler. Beauharnais v. Illinois was decided in 1952 with a finding of "guilty." [60] It involved a leaflet attack on the Negro race in Chicago, at a time when the memory of Hitler Germany's proscription, ostracism, and mass killing of Jews was fresh in the minds of the nation. Migration of Negroes from the south into northern cities was swelling. Beauharnais, president of the White Circle League, had organized his group to distribute the leaflets, and they did so in downtown Chicago. Among other things the leaflet called for city officials to stop "the further encroachment, harassment, and invasion of the white people * * * by the Negro * * *", and predicted that "rapes, robberies, knives, guns, and marijuana of the negro" surely would unite Chicago whites against blacks.

Beauharnais was prosecuted and convicted under an Illinois law making it unlawful to exhibit a publication which "portrays depravity, criminality, unchastity, or lack of virtue of a class of citizens, of any race, color, creed or religion which said publication * * * exposes the citizens of any race, color, creed or religion to contempt, derision, or obloquy or which is productive of breach of the peace or riots." [61]

The charges against Negroes, said the Court, were unquestionably libelous; and the central question became whether the "liberty" of the Fourteenth Amendment prevents a state from punishing such libels when they are directed not at an individual, but at "designated collectivities." The Court said that only if the law were a "wilful and purposeless restriction unrelated to the peace

---

[58] State v. Gardner, 112 Conn. 121, 124, 151 A. 349, 350 (1930).

[59] State v. Whiteside, 148 Conn. 208, 169 A.2d 260 (1961).

[60] 343 U.S. 250, 72 S.Ct. 725 (1952). See also People v. Spielman, 318 Ill. 482, 149 N.E. 466 (1925). Also "Knights of Columbus" cases: People v. Turner, 28 Cal.App. 766, 154 P. 34 (1914); People v. Gordon, 63 Cal.App. 62, 219 P. 486 (1923); Crane v. State, 14 Okl.Cr. 30, 166 P. 1110 (1917); Alumbaugh v. State, 39 Ga.App. 599, 147 S.E. 714 (1929). And see Joseph Tannehaus, Group Libel, 35 Cornell L.Q. 261 (1950).

[61] Beauharnais v. Illinois, 343 U.S. 250, 251, 72 S.Ct. 725, 728 (1952).

and well-being of the State," could the Court deny a state power to punish utterances directed at a defined group.

Justice Frankfurter found that for more than a century, Illinois had been "the scene of exacerbated tension between races, often flaring into violence and destruction." He cited the murder of abolitionist Elijah Lovejoy in 1837, the "first northern race riot"—in Chicago in 1908—in which six persons were killed, and subsequent violence in the state of Illinois down to the Cicero, Ill. race riot of 1951. He concluded that "In the face of this history and its frequent obligato of extreme racial and religious propaganda, we would deny experience to say that the Illinois legislature was without reason in seeking ways to curb false or malicious defamation of racial and religious groups." [62]

Four members of the court delivered strong dissents to the majority opinion that sustained Beauharnais' conviction. Justice Hugo Black stated much of the case against the concept of group libel as an offense acceptable to American freedom. Calling the law a "state censorship" instrument, Black said that permitting states to experiment in curbing freedom of expression "is startling and frightening doctrine in a country dedicated to self-government by its people." He said that criminal libel as "constitutionally recognized" has provided for punishment of false, malicious, scurrilous charges against individuals, not against huge groups. [63]

Beauharnais v. Illinois had almost no progeny, [64] and neither group libel nor garden-variety criminal libel of individuals showed signs of revival in its wake. Indeed, in revising its code of criminal law in 1961, Illinois did not re-enact the group libel statute despite its recent success. In the 1960s, two decisions of the United States Supreme Court dealt the finish to criminal libel as a threat to the media of any but the most negligible proportion.

In 1966, the Court focused on breach of the peace in common law criminal libel, and found that it did not square with the First Amendment. Merely to say that words which tend to cause breach of the peace are criminal, is too indefinite to be understandable, the court said. The case, Ashton v. Kentucky, [65] involved a pamphlet in which Ashton charged a police chief with law-breaking during a strike of miners, a sheriff with attempts to buy off a prosecution, and a newspaper owner with diverting food and clothing collected for strikers, to anti-strike workers. Ashton

[62] Ibid., 258–261.

[63] Ibid., 270, 272, 273.

[64] But see Hadley Arkes, "Civility and Restriction of Speech: Rediscovering the Defamation of Groups," 1974 Sup.Ct.Rev. 281–335; Chicago v. Lambert, 47 Ill.App. 2d 151 (1964).

[65] 384 U.S. 195, 86 S.Ct. 1407 (1966).

was convicted under a definition of criminal libel given, in part, by the judge as "any writing calculated to create disturbances of the peace." The Supreme Court said that without specification that was too vague an offense to be constitutional: [66]

> * * * to make an offense of conduct which is "calculated to create disturbances of the peace" leaves wide open the standard of responsibility. It involves calculations as to the boiling point of a particular person or a particular group, not an appraisal of the comments *per se.* This kind of criminal libel "makes a man a criminal simply because his neighbors have no self-control and cannot refrain from violence." Chafee, Free Speech in the United States 151 (1954).

> Here * * * we deal with First Amendment rights. Vague laws in any area suffer a constitutional infirmity. When First Amendment rights are involved, we look even more closely lest, under the guise of regulating conduct that is reachable by the police power, freedom of speech or of the press suffer.

> Reversed.

In the second case, the Supreme Court's 1964 ruling in the civil libel action New York Times Co. v. Sullivan produced a heavy impact on the decaying bastions of criminal libel as applied to criticism of public officials. The *Sullivan* decision said that critical words must be made with actual malice if they were to be the object of a *civil* libel action against officials, and now the Supreme Court moved the same rule into the field of *criminal* libel. The case was Garrison v. Louisiana.[67] Here Garrison, a prosecuting attorney for the State of Louisiana, gave out a statement at a press conference attacking several judges of his parish (county) for laziness and inattention to their official duties. He was convicted of criminal libel, and his case ultimately reached the Supreme Court.

The Court cited the Times v. Sullivan rule defining actual malice—that a public official might recover damages as a remedy for civil libel only "if he establishes that the utterance was false and that it was made with knowledge of its falsity or in reckless disregard of whether it was false or true." [68]

> The reasons which led us so to hold * * * apply with no less force merely because the remedy is criminal. The constitutional guarantees of freedom of expression

[66] Ibid., 384 U.S. 195, 198, 86 S.Ct. 1407, 1409–1411.

[67] 379 U.S. 64, 85 S.Ct. 209 (1964); Harry Kalven, "The New York Times Case: a Note on the Central Meaning of the First Amendment," 1964 Sup.Ct.Rev. 191.

[68] Ibid., 74; 215.

compel application of the same standard to the criminal remedy. Truth may not be the subject of either civil or criminal sanctions where discussion of public affairs is concerned. And since "*　*　* erroneous statement is inevitable in free debate *　*　*" only those false statements made with the high degree of awareness of their probable falsity demanded by New York Times may be the subject of either civil or criminal sanctions. For speech concerning public affairs is more than self-expression; it is the essence of self-government.

The Louisiana court's ruling that Garrison's criticism of the judges constituted an attack on the personal integrity of the judges, rather than on their official conduct, was not accepted. The state court had said that Garrison had imputed fraud, deceit, and dishonesty to the judges; violation of Louisiana's "deadhead" statute; and malfeasance in office. But, said the United States Supreme Court: [69]

> Of course, any criticism of the manner in which a public official performs his duties will tend to affect his private, as well as his public, reputation. The New York Times rule is not rendered inapplicable merely because an official's private reputation, as well as his public reputation, is harmed. The public official rule protects the paramount public interest in a free flow of information to the people concerning public officials, their servants. To this end, anything which might touch on an official's fitness for office is relevant. Few personal attributes are more germane to fitness for office than dishonesty, malfeasance, or improper motivation *　*　*.

As criminal libel cases arose on rare occasions during the decade after *Garrison,* several state statutes were found in violation of the Constitution—Pennsylvania's,[70] Arkansas',[71] and in 1976, California's. In the last of these, an action was brought against the publisher of the *L.A. Star,* a weekly tabloid of southern California, by the Los Angeles city attorney. The Star had published a photo superimposing a picture of a well-known actress' face on an unidentified nude female body in "a sexually explicit pose."[72] At trial and on appeal, the California criminal libel statute was held unconstitutional. For one thing, it provided that truth was a defense to a charge of criminal libel only if it were

[69] Ibid., 77; 217.

[70] Commonwealth v. Armao, 446 Pa. 325, 286 A.2d 626 (1972).

[71] Weston v. State, 258 Ark. 707, 528 S.W.2d 412 (1975). See also Williamson v. Georgia, 249 Ga. 851, 295 S.E.2d 305 (1982), 9 Med.L.Rptr. 1703, striking down the state's criminal libel statute.

[72] Press Censorship Newsletter No. VI, Dec.-Jan. 1974–75, p. 31.

published with good motives and for justifiable ends, and since the *Sullivan* case, that had been an unconstitutional limitation on the truth defense. Further, the law provided that an injurious publication is presumed to be malicious if no justifiable motive is shown, and malice may not be presumed but must be alleged and proved. Burdened with these rules out of the past which now were rejected under an outlook in the Supreme Court of the United States that over a 50-year period had slowly freed the press from ancient restrictions of English origin and American adoption, the criminal libel statute of California was shredded by the decision. The Supreme Court of the state said that "any attempt at draftmanship on the part of the court to save the remainder of the statute would transgress both the legislative intent and the judicial function and would be a flagrant breach of the doctrine of separation of powers." [73] Broken and impotent, the law was an unlikely candidate for salvage by the state's legislature.

SEC. 9.   CRITICIZING COURTS

Criticism of judges while cases were pending before them was long considered an interference with justice, and was punishable as contempt of court.

Besides sedition and criminal libel, the offense against government known as constructive contempt of court—notably, contempt shown toward judges in newspaper criticism—lived a separate, long, and sometimes robust life in the United States. The nation was more than 150 years old before this word crime met its challenge in the United States Supreme Court and was almost demolished.

This control of the press lay in the power of judges to punish their critics while cases were pending in court. Masters over all that occurred in their court rooms, there was no question that judges might cite, try, and convict for interference with the administration of justice within the court itself. And despite weak English precedent for punishing out-of-court ("constructive") contempt, much of the American judiciary successfully asserted this extended authority.[74]

Before 1800, a few state-court cases had brought home to newspapermen the danger of attacking judges. Soon after 1800, both Pennsylvania and New York passed laws curbing their judg-

---

[73] Eberle v. Municipal Court, Los Angeles Judicial District, 55 Cal.App.3d 423, 127 Cal.Rptr. 594, 600 (1976). For a suggestion that criminal libel may not be dead, see Keeton v. Hustler Magazine, 465 U.S. 770, 104 S.Ct. 1473 (1984) fn. 6, 10 Med.L.Rptr. 1405.

[74] Walter Nelles and Carol Weiss King, Contempt by Publication in the United States, 28 Col.Law.R. 401–431, 525–562 (1928).

es' contempt power over printed criticism. In 1831, Congress followed suit. The impetus for its action came from a determined attorney, Luke Lawless, who sought for four years the impeachment of Federal Judge James H. Peck. With deep financial interests in questionable claims of speculators to lands once part of Spain's Upper Louisiana, Lawless had attacked Peck in newspaper articles for the judge's decision placing the claims in doubt. He delineated at length "some of the principal errors" of Peck's decision. The judge cited him for contempt, tried him, and punished him by suspending him from practice for eighteen months. Lawless asked Congress to impeach Peck, and though it took years to accomplish the impeachment, he succeeded. Almost endless debate in the Senate aired every phase of the subject of punishment for constructive contempt. Its resemblance to sedition actions, in the eyes of many of the senators, was striking. Finally the Senate voted, exonerating Peck by the narrowest of margins.[75]

But Congress wanted no more punishment of the press for criticism of federal judges. Only a month after the impeachment, it passed an act which said that federal judges might punish only for that misbehavior which took place "in the presence of the * * * courts, or so near thereto as to obstruct the administration of justice." [76]

Many states' judges were far less ready to permit criticism. The main line of cases from the mid-Nineteenth Century until 1941 found judges asserting their "immemorial power" to cite and try for newspaper criticism that took place far from their courtrooms, as well as for misbehavior in the courtroom.[77]

It became axiomatic that courts could not function properly, that the administration of justice would be harmed, that the scales of justice would be joggled, if news media were freely allowed to publish criticisms of judges while cases were pending, or to attempt to influence judges or participants in pending cases, or to publish grossly false or inaccurate reports of court trials. "When a case is finished," said Justice Oliver Wendell Holmes, Jr., in a federal decision of 1907, "courts are subject to the same criticism as other people, but the propriety and necessity of preventing interference with the course of justice by premature statement, argument or intimidation hardly can be denied." [78] Eleven years later, the Supreme Court in upholding another conviction of a newspaper that had commented freely on a case pending in court,

[75] Arthur J. Stansbury, Report of the Trial of James H. Peck (Boston: Hilliard Gray and Company, 1833).

[76] 4 U.S. Statutes 487.

[77] Ronald L. Goldfarb, The Contempt Power, New York, 1963.

[78] Patterson v. State of Colorado ex rel. Attorney General, 205 U.S. 454, 27 S.Ct. 556 (1907).

relied on the "reasonable tendency" rule: "Not the influence upon the mind of the particular judge is the criterion [of the offensiveness of newspaper comment] but the reasonable tendency of the acts done to influence or bring about the baleful result is the test." [79]

But the reasonable tendency formulation—which critics of the law had decried for generations as an arrogantly restrictive device of courts attempting to preserve the status quo against critics of government—finally gave way. So did the "pending case" doctrine. And, importantly, the courts restored the force of the federal contempt statute of 1831, which had said punishment for contempts does not extend to any cases "except the misbehavior of any person or persons in the presence of said courts, or so near thereto as to obstruct the administration of justice"—a law seemingly ignored in the Supreme Court's decisions of 1907 and 1918 which had punished critical publications by newspapers.

Justice Holmes, who wrote the decision in the 1907 case that upheld a contempt finding, dissented in the 1918 case that did the same: "so near thereto," he said, means so near as actually to obstruct justice, and misbehavior means more than unfavorable comment or even disrespect.[80] In 1941, the Supreme Court majority agreed, and held that "so near thereto" means physical proximity and that punishment by summary contempt proceedings for published criticism is precluded.[81]

Then in a series of decisions in quick succession during the 1940s, the United States Supreme Court engaged in a remarkable release of its long-standing power, telling the entire judicial branch to do the same. In Bridges v. California,[82] both the pending case rule and the reasonable tendency test gave way under the majority opinion written by Justice Hugo Black. In two differing cases, combined under the *Bridges* title, trial-court judges had convicted Californians for contempt by publications that had admonished authorities about decisions in pending cases. In one case, the *Los Angeles Times* had warned a judge not to give probation to two convicts; in the other, labor leader Harry Bridges had threatened to tie up the entire west coast with a longshoreman's strike if a judge's ruling in a case were enforced.

Black said in addressing the pending case rule that contempt judgments punishing publications made during the pendency of a case [83]

[79] Toledo Newspaper Co. v. United States, 247 U.S. 402, 421, 38 S.Ct. 560 (1918).

[80] Ibid., at 422.

[81] Nye v. United States, 313 U.S. 33, 61 S.Ct. 810 (1941).

[82] 314 U.S. 252, 62 S.Ct. 190 (1941).

[83] Ibid., at 268–269.

* * * produce their restrictive results at the precise time when public interest in the matters discussed would naturally be in its height. * * * An endless series of moratoria on public discussion, even if each were very short, could hardly be dismissed as an insignificant abridgement of freedom of expression. And to assume that each would be short is to overlook the fact that the "pendency" of a case is frequently a matter of months or even years rather than days or weeks.

As for the rule that the publication, to be contempt, need present only a reasonable tendency to interfere with the orderly administration of justice, he denied it and applied a different test: whether the publication presented an immediate likelihood that justice would be thwarted—whether there were a "clear and present danger" that the publication would obstruct justice. The famous rule, expressed first in 1919 by Justice Holmes in Schenck v. United States [84] (a case involving seditious, rather than contemptuous expression), now was expanded to embrace alleged contempt of court. Neither a reasonable tendency nor an inherent tendency of words to interfere with the orderly administration of justice was sufficient to justify restriction of publication, said Black. Instead, there must be a clear and present danger that the substantive evil would come about. The use of the test was continued in Pennekamp v. Florida,[85] Craig v. Harney,[86] and Wood v. Georgia,[87] in all of which convictions were overturned. Courts since then have found it largely fruitless to levy contempt charges for publication of criticism.

The clear and present danger rule had served as the instrument for freeing voices that had been muffled in commenting on courts of law. Contempt for publishing criticism of the judiciary, which was in effect the power to punish for the ancient, odious, and discredited crime of sedition, was all but dead. The rare contempt citation and conviction for publishing criticism of the lower court that occurs today is overruled on appeal.[88]

[84] 249 U.S. 47, 39 S.Ct. 247 (1919).

[85] 328 U.S. 331, 66 S.Ct. 1029 (1946).

[86] 331 U.S. 367, 67 S.Ct. 1249 (1947).

[87] 370 U.S. 375, 82 S.Ct. 1364 (1962).

[88] E.g., Cooper v. Rockford Newspapers, 34 Ill.App.3d 645, 339 N.E.2d 477 (1977), 2 Med.L.Rptr. 2288.

Part II

FREE EXPRESSION AND CITIZENS' RIGHTS

Chapter 3

DEFAMATION: LIBEL AND SLANDER

SEC. 10.   DEFAMATION DEFINED

Defamation is communication which exposes a person to hatred, ridicule, or contempt, lowers him in the esteem of his fellows, causes him to be shunned, or injures him in his business or calling. Its categories are libel—broadly, printed, written or broadcast material—and slander— broadly, spoken words of limited reach.

The legal hazard that lurks most unfailingly in reporters' and editors' employment of words and pictures lies in the damage that these basic "tools of the trade" may do to the reputations of individuals in the news. The damage is libel, which with slander makes up the "twin torts" of defamation. The law classifies defamation as a tort, a civil wrong other than breach of contract for which the legal remedy is a court action for damages.[1] Under various circumstances, one citizen may recover money from another who harms his reputation with the symbols of communication.

Protecting one's reputation and society's strong interest in providing such protection justify the suit for libel. As Supreme Court Justice Potter Stewart said, an individual's right to the

---

[1] William Prosser, Law of Torts (St. Paul: West Publishing Co., 1964) 3rd ed., 2. For a recent, authoritative, and book-length work on defamation, see Robert Sack, Libel, Slander, and Related Problems (New York, 1980).

protection and comfort of his own good name "reflects no more than our basic concept of the essential dignity and worth of every human being—a concept at the root of any decent system of ordered liberty." [2] At the same time, First Amendment values of freedom, an informed citizenry, and media that serve as a check on government, justify strong defenses against the suit. "It is important to safeguard First Amendment rights; it is also important to give protection to a person who is defamed, and to discourage * * * defamation in the future. A balance must be struck." [3]

A great new protection against libel judgments opened for the mass media in the decision in New York Times Co. v. Sullivan in 1964. Here for the first time, the United States Supreme Court ruled that, where public officials in their public work are reported on by media, the First Amendment clears a broad path for expression through the thickets and jungles of centuries-old libel law. The protection was provided in response to an explosion of libel suits that sought damages of many millions of dollars from mass media, and that thus posed a financial threat to vigorous and aggressive reporting of news. The court said that "a profound national commitment to the principle that debate on public issues should be uninhibited, robust and wide-open * * *" [4] prevents recovery for libel in words about the public acts of public officials unless actual malice is present. Later, courts required that the same actual malice be proved not only by public officials but also by "public figures"—persons who thrust themselves into debate on public issues in an effort to resolve controversies or those who have general fame or notoriety in the community.

Broad shield for journalists that these decisions are, they have not decreased the number of libel suits by public officials and figures, nor eliminated the threat. Media must face very large expenses for defense attorneys and drawn-out court process, even in making a successful defense against a libel action. Libel suits are many, and although few libel suits result, on appeal, in awards for plaintiffs, some judgments continue to be won by public officials and figures, with courts finding various circumstances where the *Sullivan* rule does not protect media. And for persons whom the courts judge to be private people, barriers to suits are lower. Such persons ordinarily need prove only "negligence" by the publisher, instead of the more stringent "actual malice."

Damages justly termed "staggering" by the Libel Defense Resource Center, are commonly returned by juries, whose multi-

[2] Rosenblatt v. Baer, 383 U.S. 75, 92, 86 S.Ct. 669, 679 (1966).

[3] Maheu v. Hughes Tool Co., 569 F.2d 459, 480 (9th Cir.1977).

[4] New York Times Co. v. Sullivan, 376 U.S. 254, 84 S.Ct. 710 (1964).

million-dollar awards to plaintiffs ($40 million in one case) are nearly always drastically reduced by judges, but which, nevertheless, in one case finally totalled $600,000.[5] In addition, attorneys' fees may be even greater than such an award. In one extraordinary case of 1985, costs to *Time* magazine were estimated as $3 million for its successful defense; and in another—arguably the most-publicized libel case in the nation's history—one estimate was $8 million in legal costs for both sides, although the plaintiff dropped his suit before it reached the jury. Such prospects may lead media to avoid the huge costs of defending a drawn-out trial by settling out of court—for $800,000 in case of a 1984 agreement by the *Wall Street Journal.*[6]

The Times v. Sullivan decision brought its own problems of interpretation, but it also cut through the confusion of centuries of development in the law of libel and slander. Defamation traced a tortuous course through the medieval and early modern courts of England. Feudal and then ecclesiastical courts had jurisdiction over the offense before it moved haltingly into the common law courts. The Court of the Star Chamber took part during the first half of the Seventeenth Century, until it was dissolved during the Civil War, by punishing libel of political figures as a crime in its arbitrary, sometimes secret, and widely hated procedures. Difficulties arose when printing became common, for some distinction seemed important to separate damage done by the spoken word, which was fleeting, from damage by the printed word, which might be more harmful because it was permanent and much more widely diffused than speech. Rules resulted which, if once appropriate, became confounding anachronisms that persisted into the age of television and communication satellites.[7]

In bringing defamation substantially under the U.S. Constitution, the *Sullivan* decision was one factor that tended to wipe out a major complicating element in the law as applied to media: the division of defamation into libel (written defamation) and slander (spoken). Because radio broadcasting was speech, some states considered broadcast defamation to be slander; because it relied on written scripts, other states called it libel; because in combin-

[5] Libel Defense Resource Center Bulletin # 11, Summer-Fall 1984, 1, 2; Fleming v. Moore, 221 Va. 884, 275 S.E.2d 632 (1981), 7 Med.L.Rptr. 1313 remanding case for re-trial, upon which jury awarded $350,000 plus interest from date of publication, totaling $600,000, for libel by Moore in newspaper advertisements. Certiorari denied by Va. and U.S. Supreme Courts, 10 Med.L.Rptr. # 44, 11/6/84, News Notes.

[6] Sharon v. Time, Inc., Time, Feb. 4, 1985, 64; Westmoreland v. CBS, New York Times, Feb. 19, 1985, 1, Feb. 20, 1985, 13; 10 Med.L.Rptr. # 25, 6/19/84, News Notes, citing LDRC Report of July 29, 1984.

[7] Prosser, 754, 769; John Kelly, "Criminal Libel and Free Speech," 6 Kans.L.Rev. 295 (1958); Anon., "Developments in the Law, Defamation," 69 Harv.L.Rev. 875 (1956).

ing slander and libel rules for broadcasting, one court was persuaded that a new name was called for, a judicial flyer into creative linguistics produced the name "defamacast"—by which, it was suggested, the tort of defamation had been defamed.[8] *Sullivan* treated the matter as libel, and where *Sullivan* applied, states were to follow suit.

Meanwhile, the American Law Institute resolved the question for its followers by emphasizing the extensive harm that a defamatory broadcast to thousands or millions could do to a reputation. It followed, said ALI, that the more severe penalties of libel should result from broadcast defamation, rather than the lesser ones of slander which had been shaped centuries before to compensate for unenhanced oral denigration to small audiences. Thus the ALI says: "* * * defamation by any form of communication that has the potentially harmful qualities characteristic of written or printed words is to be treated as libel."[9]

The ALI pronouncement that libel should encompass broadcasting was by no means the first time that adjustments in the law had attached "libel" to varied media of communication. Before broadcasting, the Twentieth Century had produced motion pictures, and they had rather early been ruled to be libelous, if defamatory. Long before movies arrived—at least as early as the celebrated case of People v. Croswell in 1804—pictures and signs were included in the embrace of libel.[10]

The most-used definition of libel is that it is a false statement about an individual which exposes him to "hatred, ridicule, or contempt, or which causes him to be shunned, or avoided, or which has a tendency to injure him in his office, profession or trade."[11] While that definition takes in a wide reach of words, it is nevertheless probably too narrow. Courts recognize mental anguish and personal humiliation as the bases of libel; Prosser points out that words which would cause most people to sympathize with the target have been held defamatory, such as an imputation of poverty, or the statement that a woman has been raped.[12] If a

[8] D.H. Remmers, "Recent Legislative Trends in Defamation by Radio," 64 Harv. L.Rev. 727, 1951; Prosser, 754, 769–81; Grein v. La Poma, 54 Wash.2d 844, 340 P.2d 766 (1959); American Broadcasting-Paramount Theaters, Inc. v. Simpson, 106 Ga.App. 230, 126 S.E.2d 873 (1962).

[9] Restatement, Second, Torts, Vol. 3, 182. Some states have abolished the distinction between libel and slander, e.g. Illinois: Brown & Williamson v. Jacobson, 713 F.2d 262 (7th Cir.1983), 9 Med.L.Rptr. 1936, 1939. But see Nevada Broadcasting Co. v. Allen (Nev.Sup.Ct.1982) 9 Med.L.Rptr. 1770.

[10] Movies: Youssoupoff v. Metro-Goldwyn-Mayer Pictures, 51 L.Q.Rev. 281, 99 A.L.R. 864 (1934); Pictures: People v. Croswell, 3 Johns Cases 337 (N.Y.1804).

[11] Sir Hugh Fraser, Libel and Slander (London: 1936), 7th ed., p. 3; Perry v. Columbia Broadcasting System, Inc., 499 F.2d 797 (7th Cir.1974).

[12] Time, Inc. v. Firestone, 424 U.S. 448, 96 S.Ct. 958 (1976); Prosser, p. 756.

person is lowered in the estimation or respect of the community, he is not necessarily hated, held in contempt, or shunned.

To have definitions such as the above is by no means always to be able to predict what will be held libelous. The legal axiom which says that "every definition in the law is dangerous" most certainly applies to defamation. Whether words are defamatory depends, in part, on the temper of the times and current public opinion; "words harmless in one age, in one community, may be highly damaging to reputation at another time or * * * place." [13] While it was probably not defamation to falsely call one a Communist in the 1930s, several subsequent cases have found the appellation libelous.[14] In the North it is not defamatory to call a white person a Negro, but southern courts long recognized the social prejudices of centuries and considered it defamation.[15]

It must be understood that in a suit where false defamation is found—that is, where it is shown that the plaintiff has been libeled—money damages are not necessarily awarded. There are various circumstances in which the law protects media against liability for libeling. Chapters 4 and 5 below are largely devoted to the defenses that furnish these protections.

Anyone who is living may be defamed—unless he is so notorious as a criminal that he is "libel-proof" and courts will not accept his libel action—[16] and so may a corporation or partnership where its business standing or practices are impugned. A voluntary association organized for purposes not connected with profit or the self-interest of the organizers has been defamed.[17] However, it is not possible for one to be defamed through an insult or slur upon someone close to him, such as a member of his family.[18] Nor can a

[13] Mencher v. Chesley, 297 N.Y. 94, 75 N.E.2d 257 (1947).

[14] Spanel v. Pegler, 160 F.2d 619 (7th Cir.1947); Levy v. Gelber, 175 Misc. 746, 25 N.Y.S.2d 148 (1941); Gertz v. Robert Welch, Inc., 418 U.S. 323, 94 S.Ct. 2997 (1974).

[15] Natchez Times Pub. Co. v. Dunigan, 221 Miss. 320, 72 So.2d 681 (1954); Strauder v. State of West Virginia, 100 U.S. 303 (1880).

[16] Cardillo v. Doubleday & Co., 518 F.2d 638 (2d Cir.1975).

[17] Americans for Democratic Action v. Meade, 72 Pa.D. & C. 306 (1951); New York Society for the Suppression of Vice v. MacFadden Publications, 129 Misc. 408, 221 N.Y.S. 563 (1927), affirmed 222 App.Div. 739, 226 N.Y.S. 870 (1928); Mullins v. Brando, 13 Cal.App.3d 409, 91 Cal.Rptr. 796 (1970); Friends of Animals v. Associated Fur Manufacturers, 46 N.Y.2d 1065, 416 N.Y.S.2d 790, 390 N.E.2d 298 (1979), 4 Med.L.Rptr. 2503.

[18] Gonzales v. Times-Herald Printing Co., 513 S.W.2d 124 (Tex.Civ.App.1974); Wildstein v. New York Post Corp., 40 Misc.2d 586, 243 N.Y.S.2d 386 (1963); Security Sales Agency v. A.S. Abell Co., 205 F. 941 (D.C.Md.1913); but "daughter of a murderer" has been held libelous: Van Wiginton v. Pulitzer Pub. Co., 218 F. 795 (8th Cir.1914).

dead person be defamed,[19] nor in most circumstances a group. A government entity, such as the city of Philadelphia, cannot bring a civil libel action.[20]

Large groups such as businessmen in general, or labor, or a political party, or all the Muslims of the world, or an ethnic group of a large city, cannot sue for libel.[21] When, however, a charge is leveled against a small group, each member may be considered by the law to be libeled, and the individuals may bring separate suits even though no one has been named or singled out. It is by no means clear what the upper limit of a "small group" that warrants such treatment is; twenty-five has been suggested.[22] Courts have held that each member of a jury can be defamed,[23] or all four officers of a labor union,[24] or all salesmen in a force of 25 employed by a department store.[25] But an action for libel would not lie against a magazine, brought in the name of all distributors (unnamed) of laetrile,[26] nor against a newspaper by 21 officers of a town police department following a printed rumor about one unidentified officer.[27]

SEC. 11. LIBELOUS WORDS CLASSIFIED

Five categories or kinds of words may be identified in organizing the field of libel. Libel may also be classified according to libel *per se,* or words defamatory on their face; and libel *per quod,* or words defamatory when facts extrinsic to the story make them damaging.

Danger signals to help journalists avoid libel can be raised by grouping the kinds of statements and the circumstances which

[19] McBeth v. United Press International, Inc., 505 F.2d 959 (5th Cir.1974). But see Camino v. New York News, 10 Med.L.Rptr. 1852 (N.J.Sup.Ct.1984), where a libel action filed before death did not abate at death.

[20] Philadelphia v. Washington Post, 482 F.Supp. 897 (D.C.E.Pa.1979), 5 Med.L. Rptr. 2221.

[21] Exner v. American Medical Association, 12 Wash.App. 215, 529 P.2d 863, 867 (1974); Webb v. Sessions, 531 S.W.2d 211 (Tex.Civ.App.1975); Mansour v. Fanning, 6 Med.L.Rptr. 2055 (D.C.N.Cal.1980).

[22] Prosser, p. 768; Schutzman & Schutzman v. News Syndicate Co., 60 Misc.2d 827, 304 N.Y.S.2d 167 (1969). For the logic and many citations, see Michigan United Conservation Clubs v. CBS, 485 F.Supp. 893 (D.C.Mich., 1980), 5 Med.L. Rptr. 2566. And see Brady v. Ottaway Newspapers, 84 A.D.2d 226, 445 N.Y.S.2d 786 (1981), 8 Med.L.Rptr. 1671 where a plaintiff policeman who was a member of a group of 53 unnamed policemen was not barred from bringing a libel suit.

[23] Byers v. Martin, 2 Colo. 605 (1875).

[24] DeWitte v. Kearney & Trecker Corp., 265 Wis. 132, 60 N.W.2d 748 (1953).

[25] Neiman-Marcus Co. v. Lait, 13 F.R.D. 311 (D.C.N.Y.1952).

[26] Schuster v. U.S. News & World Report, 602 F.2d 850 (8th Cir.1980), 5 Med.L. Rptr. 1773.

[27] Arcand v. Evening Call Pub. Co., 567 F.2d 1163 (1st Cir.1977).

have brought suits into classes. A study of reported libel cases in a three-and-one-half-year period from 1976 to 1979 found that the large majority of accusations by plaintiffs were that they had been falsely accused of "crime, moral failings, and incompetence in trade or profession." [28] In the following pages, five categories are used to help clarify that which can bring hatred, ridicule, contempt, loss of esteem, humiliation, or damage in one's trade or profession.

Damage to the Esteem or Social Standing in Which One Is Held

Of the various ways in which a person may be lowered in the estimation in which he is held, none has brought as many libel suits as a false charge of crime. The news media cover the police and crime beat daily; the persistent possibility of a mistake in names and addresses is never absent. And the courts hold everywhere that it is libel to charge one erroneously with a crime. It is easy to get a libel case based on such a charge into court, even though it has become harder to win it under court doctrine of the 1960s, 1970s, and 1980s.

Thus to print falsely that a person is held in jail on a forgery charge,[29] or to say incorrectly that one has illicitly sold or distributed narcotics,[30] is libelous on its face. To say without legal excuse that one made "shakedown attempts" on elected officers,[31] or committed bigamy,[32] perjury,[33] or murder [34] is libelous.

There is no substitute as a protection against libel suits for the ancient admonition to the reporter: "Accuracy always." [35] Failure to check one more source of information before writing a story based upon a plausible source has brought many libel suits.

The *Saturday Evening Post* published a story titled "They Call Me Tiger Lil" in its Oct. 26, 1963 issue. The subject was Lillian Reis Corabi, a Philadelphia night club owner and entertainer.

[28] Marc Franklin, Winners and Losers and Why: a Study of Defamation Litigation, Am. Bar Foundation Research Journ. 1980, Summer, 499.

[29] Oklahoma Pub. Co. v. Givens, 67 F.2d 62 (10th Cir.1933); Barnett v. Schumacher, 453 S.W.2d 934 (Mo.1970).

[30] Snowden v. Pearl River Broadcasting Co., 251 So.2d 405 (La.App.1971).

[31] Bianco v. Palm Beach Newspapers, 381 So.2d 371 (Fla.App.1980), 6 Med.L. Rptr. 1485.

[32] Taylor v. Tribune Pub. Co., 67 Fla. 361, 65 So. 3 (1914); Pitts v. Spokane Chronicle Co., 63 Wash.2d 763, 388 P.2d 976 (1964).

[33] Milan v. Long, 78 W.Va. 102, 88 S.E. 618 (1916); Riss v. Anderson, 304 F.2d 188 (8th Cir.1962).

[34] Shiell v. Metropolis Co., 102 Fla. 794, 136 So. 537 (1931); Frechette v. Special Magazines, 285 App.Div. 174, 136 N.Y.S.2d 448 (1954).

[35] For a classic mixup in names: Francis v. Lake Charles American Press, 262 La. 875, 265 So.2d 206 (1972).

The article connected her in various ways with murder and theft, quoting a police captain as saying she and others were responsible for a death by dynamite, and in other ways connecting her with burglary and an apparent drowning. The *Post* argued that the words complained of were not defamatory, but the Pennsylvania Supreme Court upheld the trial judge in his finding some 18 paragraphs of the article "capable of defamatory meaning." It defined defamation as that which "tends so to harm the reputation of another as to lower him in the estimation of the community * * *." [36] The court's decision thus found the elements of libel present in the story, although it agreed with the lower court that because of a grossly excessive award of damages by the jury—[37] $250,000 in compensating and $500,000 in punitive damages— there should be a new trial.

Nor was the *Post* successful in arguing that libel was not present in a story on Mafia activities on Grand Bahama Island, in which it carried a photo of a group of people including Holmes, a tourist. The photo caption referred to "High-Rollers at the Monte Carlo club," and said that the club's casino grossed $20 million a year with a third "skimmed off for American Mafia 'families'." Holmes, the focal point of the picture and a man in no way connected with Mafia, sued for libel. The *Post*, saying the story was not defamatory, moved for a judgment on the pleadings; but the court held that a jury case was called for and that a jury might find libel.[38]

The failure of a reporter to check the proper source for an address caused an error in identities in a story about a man who pleaded guilty to breaking into business establishments—and the result was a $60,000 libel judgment against a newspaper company. In taking the details of the trial for "breaking" from the court records, the reporter omitted the address of Anthony Liquori of Springfield, the convicted man, and later extracted an address from a telephone book. Unfortunately, the telephone-book address was for a different man of the same name, and, using it, the reporter wrote that Anthony Liquori of 658 Cooper St., Agawam, Mass., had been convicted. The innocent Liquori brought a libel action. The Massachusetts Appeals Court said that there was negligence in not checking the address with court personnel or the attorney for the accused, and also that the story did not deserve privilege (see below, Sec. 25) because it was not fair and accurate. The court upheld the jury award of damages.[39]

[36] Corabi v. Curtis Pub. Co., 441 Pa. 432, 273 A.2d 899, 904 (1971).

[37] Corabi v. Curtis Pub. Co., 437 Pa. 143, 262 A.2d 665, 670 (1970).

[38] Holmes v. Curtis Pub. Co., 303 F.Supp. 522 (D.C.S.C.1969).

[39] Liquori v. Republican Co., 8 Mass.App.Ct. 671, 396 N.E.2d 726 (1979), 5 Med.L. Rptr. 2180.

The news story which states incorrectly that a person has been *convicted* of a crime, as in the Liquori case, may be more dangerous than the one which wrongly suggests or states that he is *accused* of crime. But whatever the difference, the latter can cause libel suits, as we have seen above in the suggestion that Corabi was associated with major crimes.

Not every suggestion of liability, however, has resulted in judgment against the defending news medium. This story, for example, was held by the court to contain nothing defamatory and capable of meaning that a fire was of incendiary origin and set by the owner of the burned building: [40]

THRICE BURNED

The Daniels & Cornell Block Again Visited by Fire— Damage Largely by Water, and Estimated at $70,000, Covered by Insurance

At 10:15 o'clock last night R.A. Reid, of the printer's firm of J.A. & R.A. Reid, while working at his desk on the top floor of the tall Daniels & Cornell Building on Customhouse street, discovered smoke and flame issuing from the composing room in the rear of the office * * *. The fiery element completely invaded the entire fifth floor, which was all occupied by the Messrs. Reid, who claim complete loss from fire and water. They were insured for $55,000 * * *. The fire is the third to have occurred in this building in the past thirteen years * * *. Every fire in this building has started on the upper floor, and twice in Reid's printing establishment.

Sometimes but not always involving crime are words imputing to women sexual acts outside prevailing moral codes, or that falsely state that a woman has been raped. Esteem and social standing, it is plain, are at stake. Courts everywhere regard written or printed statements charging without foundation that a woman is immoral as actionable libel. The charge of indiscretion need not be pronounced; any statement fairly imputing immoral conduct is actionable. [41]

Pat Montandon, author of *How To Be a Party Girl*, was to discuss her book on the Pat Michaels "Discussion" show. *TV Guide* received the show producer's advance release, which said that Montandon and a masked, anonymous prostitute would discuss "From Party-Girl to Call-Girl?" and "How far can the 'party-

[40] Reid v. Providence Journal Co., 20 R.I. 120, 37 A. 637 (1897).

[41] Baird v. Dun & Bradstreet, 446 Pa. 266, 285 A.2d 166 (1971); Wildstein v. New York Post Corp., 40 Misc.2d 586, 243 N.Y.S.2d 386 (1963); Youssoupoff v. Metro-Goldwyn-Mayer, 50 Times L.R. 581, 99 A.L.R. 864 (1934).

girl' go until she becomes a 'call-girl'." *TV Guide* ineptly edited the release, deleting reference to the prostitute and publishing this: "10:30 Pat Michaels—*Discussion* 'From Party Girl to Call Girl.' Scheduled guest: TV Personality Pat Montandon and author of 'How to Be a Party Girl'." Montandon sued for libel and won $150,000 in damages. On appeal, the court noted that *TV Guide* editors had testified that they did not believe the average reader would interpret the program note in the magazine as relating Montandon to a call girl or labeling her as a call girl. The appeals court said that that testimony "flies in the face of reason" and upheld the libel judgment.[42]

On the other hand, a woman who posed in the nude for a film maker but later got his agreement not to show the film, was unsuccessful in a libel action following his breaking of the agreement. She charged that his showing of the film to people who knew her caused her shame, disgrace and embarrassment. But the court said that "a film strip which includes a scene of plaintiff posing in the nude does not necessarily impute unchastity", and that it was not libel *per se.*[43]

Esteem and social standing can be lowered in the eyes of others by statements concerning race and political belief, as well as by those grouped under crime and under sexual immorality in the preceding pages. To take political belief first, the salient cases since the late 1940's have largely involved false charges of "Communist" or "Red" or some variant of these words indicating that one subscribes to a generally hated political doctrine. But before these, a line of cases since the 1890's produced libel convictions against those who had anathematized others as anarchists, socialists, or fascists.

In the days of Emma Goldman and Big Bill Haywood, it was laid down by the courts that to call one "anarchist" falsely was libelous;[44] when socialism protested capitalism and America's involvement in World War I, "red-tinted agitator" and "Socialist" were words for which a wronged citizen could recover;[45] in the revulsion against Nazi Germany and Japan during World War II,

---

[42] Montandon v. Triangle Pubs., Inc., 45 Cal.App.3d 938, 120 Cal.Rptr. 186 (1975).

[43] McGraw v. Watkins, 49 A.D.2d 958, 373 N.Y.S.2d 663 (1975). But contra, see Clifford v. Hollander, (N.Y.Civ.1980), 6 Med.L.Rptr. 2201, where a photo of a nude woman, identified falsely as that of a woman journalist, was held libelous.

[44] Cerveny v. Chicago Daily News Co., 139 Ill. 345, 28 N.E. 692 (1891); Wilkes v. Shields, 62 Minn. 426, 64 N.W. 921 (1895).

[45] Wells v. Times Printing Co., 77 Wash. 171, 137 P. 457 (1913); Ogren v. Rockford Star Printing Co., 288 Ill. 405, 123 N.E. 587 (1919).

false accusations of "Fascist" and "pro-Jap" brought libel judgments.[46]

Magazines, columnists, newspapers, and corporations have paid for carelessness indulged in by charging others as "Communist" or "representative for the Communist Party." The "basis for reproach is a belief that such political affiliations constitute a threat to our institutions * * *." [47]

The decisions holding false charges of communism as libelous largely began as America and the USSR entered the "cold war" period following World War II. One of the early cases stemmed from an article in the *Reader's Digest,* in which the author charged that the Political Action Committee of his union had hired Sidney S. Grant, "who but recently was a legislative representative for the Massachusetts Communist Party." Grant sued for libel, saying that the article was false. The magazine was unable to convince the court that "representative for the Communist Party" was not in the same category as a flat charge of "Communist," and Grant won the suit.[48]

In the famous case of Gertz v. Robert Welch, Inc.,[49] the trial court found that the publication of the John Birch Society had libeled Chicago Attorney Elmer Gertz in charging falsely that he was a "Leninist," a "Communist-fronter," and a member of the "Marxist League for Industrial Democracy." In another case, where one organization called another "communist dominated" and failed to prove the charge in court, $25,000 was awarded to the plaintiff organization.[50]

Not every insinuation that a person is less than American, however, is libelous. Goodman, a selectman of Ware, Mass., phoned a call-in radio talk-show of the Central Broadcasting Corp. station, WARE, to deliver his opposition to a proposed contract for the local police union, at issue in the town prior to a citizen vote on the matter. During his extended and agitated discussion, he said that " * * * if we do not get together and stop the inroad of communism, something will happen." A libel suit was brought by the police local's parent union against Central Broadcasting, and the Massachusetts Supreme Judicial Court held that this fragment

[46] Hartley v. Newark Morning Ledger Co., 134 N.J.L. 217, 46 A.2d 777 (1946); Hryhorijiv v. Winchell, 180 Misc. 574, 45 N.Y.S.2d 31 (1943).

[47] Anon., "Supplement," 171 A.L.R. 709, 712 (1947).

[48] Grant v. Reader's Digest Ass'n, 151 F.2d 733 (2d Cir.1945). And see Wright v. Farm Journal, 158 F.2d 976 (2d Cir.1947); Spanel v. Pegler, 160 F.2d 619 (7th Cir. 1947); MacLeod v. Tribune Pub. Co., 52 Cal.2d 536, 343 P.2d 36 (1959).

[49] 306 F.Supp. 310 (N.D.Ill.1969); 418 U.S. 323, 94 S.Ct. 2997 (1974).

[50] Utah State Farm Bureau Federation v. National Farmers Union Service Corp., 198 F.2d 20 (10th Cir.1952). See also Cahill v. Hawaiian Paradise Park Corp., 56 Hawaii 522, 543 P.2d 1356 (1975).

of Goodman's statement was "mere pejorative rhetoric," and an "unamiable but nonlibelous utterance." [51]

Where the courts hold an incorrect racial identification as libelous in America, the word at issue usually is "Negro" and the locale is below the Mason-Dixon line. The slur on Negroes inherent in a decision which says a white man can recover for being identified as a Negro has been no barrier to these decisions. At least as far back as 1791 and as recently as 1957, cases in the South have asserted inferiority in the Negro race, and judgments have been upheld in which whites called Negro have been awarded damages.[52]

Under the heading "Negro News" and a picture of a Negro soldier, the *Anderson (S.C.) Daily Mail* printed an item saying that the son of a Mrs. Bowen had been transferred to a government hospital. Mrs. Bowen brought a libel suit, saying she had been named in the story as the mother, and that she was white. The newspaper asked the trial court for a directed verdict, arguing that it was not libel on its face to call a white person a Negro. The trial court gave the newspaper the verdict, Mrs. Bowen appealed, and the South Carolina Supreme Court reversed the verdict. It cited a line of South Carolina cases going back to 1791, and said: [53]

> The earlier cases were decided at a time when slavery existed, and since then great changes have taken place in the legal and political status of the colored race. However, there is still to be considered the social distinction existing between the races, since libel may be based upon social status.
>
> *   *   *
>
> Although to publish in a newspaper of a white woman that she is a Negro imputes no mental, moral or physical fault for which she may justly be held accountable to public opinion, yet in view of the social habits and customs deep-rooted in this State, such publication is calculated to affect her standing in society and to injure her in the estimation of her friends and acquaintances.

[51] National Ass'n of Government Employees v. Central Broadcasting Corp., 379 Mass. 220, 396 N.E.2d 996 (1979). Also McAuliffe v. Local Union No. 3, 29 N.Y.S.2d 963 (Sup.1941); McGraw v. Webster, 79 N.M. 104, 440 P.2d 296 (1968); "pro-Castro," Menendez v. Key West Newspaper Corp., 293 So.2d 751 (Fla.App. 1974).

[52] Eden v. Legare, 1 Bay 171 (1791); Strauder v. West Virginia, 100 U.S. 303 (1880); Jones v. R.L. Polk & Co., 190 Ala. 243, 67 So. 577 (1915).

[53] Bowen v. Independent Pub. Co., 230 S.C. 509, 512–513, 96 S.E.2d 564, 565–566 (1957); Natchez Times Pub. Co. v. Dunigan, 221 Miss. 320, 72 So.2d 681 (1954).

Finally, there are many words among those lowering esteem or social standing that defy classifying. Appellations that may be common enough in the excited conversation of neighborhood gossips can turn to actionable libel when reduced to print or writing. It has been held actionable on its face to print and publish that one is "a liar," [54] "a skunk," [55] or "a scandalmonger"; [56] "a drunkard," [57] "a hypocrite," [58] or "a hog"; [59] or to call one heartless and neglectful of his family.[60] Name-calling where private citizens are concerned is occasionally the kind of news that makes a lively paragraph, but the alert as well as the responsible reporter recognizes it for what it is and decides whether to use it on better grounds than its titillation value.

Damage Through Ridicule

It is fruitless to try to draw too narrow a line between words that ridicule and those treated previously, that lower esteem and social standing. That which ridicules may at times have the effect of damaging social standing. Yet that which attempts to satirize, or which makes an individual appear uncommonly foolish, or makes fun of misfortune has a quality distinct enough to serve as its own warning signal.

Ridicule must be more than a simple joke at another's expense, for life cannot be so grim that the thin-skinned, the solemn, and the self-important may demand to go entirely unharried. But when the good-humored barb penetrates too deeply or carries too sharp a sting, or when a picture can be interpreted in a deeply derogatory manner, ridicule amounting to actionable libel may have occurred.

Mary and Letitia Megarry objected to the repeated parking of a car in violation of parking rules near their business. They wrote a note and placed it on the car, saying that they'd call the matter to the attention of the police unless the practice were stopped. James Norton, the owner of the car, hung a sign in public view saying "Nuts to You—You Old Witch." The Megarrys

[54] Melton v. Bow, 241 Ga. 629, 247 S.E.2d 100 (1978); Paxton v. Woodward, 31 Mont. 195, 78 P. 215 (1904); Smith v. Lyons, 142 La. 975, 77 So. 896 (1918); contra, Bennett v. Transamerican Press, 298 F.Supp. 1013 (D.C.Iowa 1969); Calloway v. Central Charge Service, 142 U.S.App.D.C. 259, 440 F.2d 287 (1971).

[55] Massuere v. Dickens, 70 Wis. 83, 35 N.W. 349 (1887).

[56] Patton v. Cruce, 72 Ark. 421, 81 S.W. 380 (1904).

[57] Giles v. State, 6 Ga. 276 (1848); cf. Smith v. Fielden, 205 Tenn. 313, 326 S.W.2d 476 (1959).

[58] Overstreet v. New Nonpareil Co., 184 Iowa 485, 167 N.W. 669 (1918).

[59] Solverson v. Peterson, 64 Wis. 198, 25 N.W. 14 (1885).

[60] Brown v. Du Frey, 1 N.Y.2d 649, 151 N.Y.S.2d 649, 134 N.E.2d 469 (1956).

sued for $5,000, and on appeal their suit was upheld.[61] The court said that the sign "was intended to subject appellants to contempt and ridicule," and that the words could not fairly be read to have an innocent interpretation. This was libel.

To sensationalize the poverty of a woman so as to bring her into ridicule and contempt, and to make a joke out of the desertion of a bride on her wedding day [62] have been held libelous. A famed case arose from a picture that accidentally showed a "fantastic and lewd deformity" of a steeplechaser.[63]

Yet there is room for satire, burlesque and exaggeration. *Boston Magazine* published a page titled "Best and Worst Sports," including the categories "sports announcer," "local ski slopes," and "sexy athlete," some categories plainly waggish, some straightforward and complimentary. Under "sports announcer," the best was named and given kudos; and then appeared: "*Worst:* Jimmy Myers, Channel 4. The only newscaster in town who is enrolled in a course for remedial speaking." Myers sued, lost at trial for failure to establish defamation, and appealed.[64]

The Massachusetts Supreme Judicial Court described the appearance of the magazine's page, with its title, lampooning cartoons, and a mood of rough humor in the words, including "one-liners" and preposterous propositions under such titles as "Sports Groupie." It ruled that the statement about Myers made on such a page would not reasonably be understood by a reader to be an assertion of fact. "Taken in context, it can reasonably be considered to suggest that Myers should have been so enrolled," even though the words read "is enrolled." The words stated "a critical judgment, an opinion." And since Myers was himself available to the critic's audience, being often on view, his performances were in line with the rule that facts underlying opinions could be assumed—the performances "furnished the assumed facts from which the critic fashioned his barb." The court said that words such as these are meant to "sting and be quickly forgotten"; and that while, for the plaintiff who "is the victim of ridicule, the forgetting may not be easy," the law refuses to find a statement of fact where none has been uttered. This was opinion, and if such

---

[61] Megarry v. Norton, 137 Cal.App.2d 581, 290 P.2d 571 (1955).

[62] Moffatt v. Cauldwell, 3 Hun. 26, 5 Thomp. & C. 256 (N.Y.1874), but "poverty" and "unemployment" have been held not actionable words: Sousa v. Davenport, 3 Mass.App. 715, 328 N.E.2d 910 (1975); Kirman v. Sun Printing & Pub. Ass'n, 99 App.Div. 367, 91 N.Y.S. 193 (1904).

[63] Burton v. Crowell Pub. Co., 82 F.2d 154 (1st Cir.1936).

[64] Myers v. Boston Magazine, (Mass.Sup.Jud.Ct.1980), 6 Med.L.Rptr. 1241.

"is based on assumed, nondefamatory facts, the First Amendment forbids the law of libel from redressing the injury." [65]

The columnist Jimmy Breslin of the former *New York Herald Tribune* has a fine talent for satire, and a libel suit based on his account of barkeep Hyman Cohen's encounter with murder was not successful. Cohen was a witness to the murder of one Munos at the Vivere Lounge in New York City, and fearing for his life if he talked to authorities about the killers, he denied for a time that the murder had happened at the Lounge or that he had witnessed it. He also fled the city. Breslin's column about Cohen was written after he had interviewed police, the district attorney and Cohen's employer, and had read about and inspected the scene of the murder. The column began:

> Among New Yorkers out of town for the week end, and out of town for a lot of week ends to come if he has his way, is Mr. Hyman Cohen, of the Bronx. His friends say that he went to the Catskills for the rest of the summer, but there is a feeling that the Catskills are not quite far enough away for Hy at present.
>
> "The last time I saw Hy he asked me about the Italian Alps," a detective was saying the other night.
>
> Hy is a man who once liked this city very much. Particularly, he liked the part of the city they make television shows about. Gunmen, action guys; they were Hy's idea of people. Then a couple of weeks ago, this little corner of life in our town grew too big for Hy to handle. He had a change of heart. A heart 'attack' might be a better word for it. And he left town thoroughly disillusioned.
>
> Hy is a bartender, and it all started a couple of summers ago when he worked at a hotel in the Catskills and found himself pouring drinks for some underworld notables. He never really got over this. When the summer ended, Hy came back to New York and he was no longer Hy Cohen of the Bronx. He was Hy Cohen of the Rackets. He wore a big, snap-brim extortionist's hat, white on white shirts and a white tie. And when he would talk, especially if there were only a few people at the bar and they all could listen, Hy would begin talking about all the tough guys he knew. This was Hy's field.

The court held that though the article was not literally true in every detail, "it presented a fair sketch of a confident talkative bartender who was reduced to speechlessness, self-effacement and

65 Ibid., 1243, 1245. See below, Chap. 5, Sec. 29.

flight by gangsters * * *." [66]   It explained why it was not libelous: [67]

> With sardonic humor Breslin described Cohen's frantic flight to avoid the murderous gangsters as well as to escape the police who were hot on the killer's trail. The humor was not funny, except on the surface. Murder and terror are * * * the subjects of satire which superficially conceals a tragic or solemn happening. Our courts have held that mere exaggeration, irony or wit does not make a writing libelous unless the article would be libelous without the exaggeration, irony or wit.

While a living man whose obituary has mistakenly been printed may feel annoyed and injured, and may attract unusual attention and perhaps a rough joke or two as he walks into his office the next morning, he has not been libeled. As one court said, death "is looked for in the history of every man," and where there is notice of a death that has not occurred, "Prematurity is the sole peculiarity." [68] Yet an erroneous report of death has been held to be the cause of an action for "negligent infliction of emotional distress"—an injury closely related to defamation.[69]

Damage Through Words Imputing Disease or Mental Illness

The law has long held that diseases which may be termed "loathsome, infectious, or contagious" may be libelous when falsely attributed to an individual. That which is "loathsome" may change with time and changing mores, of course, but venereal disease, the plague, leprosy, and small pox seem to fit this description. Anyone alleged to be at present suffering from any of these diseases is likely to be shunned by his fellows. And if the disease carries the stigma of immorality, such as venereal disease or alcoholism or addiction, it may be libelous to say of a person that he formerly had it, although he has since been cured.

To charge without legal excuse that one has leprosy was held libelous in Lewis v. Hayes; the imputation of venereal disease was held libelous in King v. Pillsbury.[70] As for an incorrect assignment of mental impairment or of mental illness to a person, it is

[66] Cohen v. New York Herald Tribune, Inc., 63 Misc.2d 87, 310 N.Y.S.2d 709, 725 (1970).

[67] Ibid., 724. See also Sellers v. Time, Inc., 299 F.Supp. 582 (D.C.Pa.1969); Fram v. Yellow Cab Co. of Pittsburgh, 380 F.Supp. 1314 (D.C.Pa.1974).

[68] Cohen v. New York Times Co., 153 App.Div. 242, 138 N.Y.S. 206 (1912); Cardiff v. Brooklyn Eagle, Inc., 190 Misc. 730, 75 N.Y.S.2d 222 (1948).

[69] Rubinstein v. New York Post, (N.Y.Sup.Ct.1983) 9 Med.L.Rptr. 1581. Emotional distress is treated in Sec. 13, below.

[70] 165 Cal. 527, 132 P. 1022 (1913); King v. Pillsbury, 115 Me. 528, 99 A. 513 (1918); Sally v. Brown, 220 Ky. 576, 295 S.W. 890 (1927).

libel on its face.[71] The magazine *Fact* published in its September-October issue of 1964, an article billed as "The Unconscious of a Conservative: A Special Issue on the Mind of Barry Goldwater." Goldwater was the Republican Party's candidate for president and a senator from Arizona at the time. He was portrayed in one of two articles as "paranoid," his attacks on other politicians stemming from a conviction that "everybody hates him, and it is better to attack them first." A *Fact* poll of psychiatrists, asked to judge whether Goldwater was psychologically fit to serve as president, also was reported on. A jury found libel and awarded Goldwater $1.00 in compensatory damages and $75,000 in punitive damages.[72]

Damaging One in His Trade, Occupation, or Profession

So long as one follows a legal calling, he has a claim not to be traduced unfairly in the performance of it. The possibilities are rich for damaging one through words that impugn his honesty, skill, fitness, ethical standards, or financial capacity in his chosen work, whether it be banking or basket-weaving. Observe some of the possibilities: that a University was a "degree mill";[73] that a contractor engaged in unethical trade;[74] that a clergyman was "an interloper, a meddler, a spreader of distrust";[75] that a schoolmaster kept girls after school so that he could court them;[76] that a jockey rode horses unfairly and dishonestly;[77] that an attorney was incompetent;[78] that a corporation director embezzled.[79]

By no means every statement to which a businessman, tradesman or professional takes exception, however, is libelous. Thus Frederick D. Washington, a church bishop, sued the *New York Daily News* and columnist Robert Sylvester for his printed statement that Washington had attended a nightclub performance at which a choir member of his church sang. The bishop argued that his church did not approve of its spiritual leaders' attending nightclubs, and that he had been damaged. The court said the account was not, on its face, an attack on the plaintiff's integrity,

[71] Cowper v. Vannier, 20 Ill.App.2d 499, 156 N.E.2d 761 (1959); Kenney v. Hatfield, 351 Mich. 498, 88 N.W.2d 535 (1958). But not in Virginia: Mills v. Kingsport Times-News, 475 F.Supp. 1005 (D.C.W.Va.1979), 5 Med.L.Rptr. 2288.

[72] Goldwater v. Ginzburg, 414 F.2d 324 (2d Cir.1969).

[73] Laurence University v. State, 68 Misc.2d 408, 326 N.Y.S.2d 617 (1971). Reversed on grounds that State official's words were absolutely privileged, 41 A.D.2d 463, 344 N.Y.S.2d 183 (1973).

[74] Greenbelt Co-op Pub. Ass'n v. Bresler, 253 Md. 324, 252 A.2d 755 (1969), reversed on other grounds 398 U.S. 6, 90 S.Ct. 1537 (1970).

[75] Van Lonkhuyzen v. Daily News Co., 195 Mich. 283, 161 N.W. 979 (1917).

[76] Spears v. McCoy, 155 Ky. 1, 159 S.W. 610 (1913).

[77] Wood v. Earl of Durham, 21 Q.B. 501 (1888).

[78] Hahn v. Andrello, 44 A.D.2d 501, 355 N.Y.S.2d 850 (1974).

[79] Weenig v. Wood, 169 Ind.App. 413, 349 N.E.2d 235 (1976).

and called the item a "warm human interest story" in which there was general interest. This was not libel on its face and the court upheld dismissal of Bishop Washington's complaint.[80]

Nor did David Brown convince the court that there was libel in a pamphlet that opposed his attempt to get a zoning change from the City Council of Knoxville, Tenn. The pamphlet attacked a change that would have permitted Brown to build apartments in a residential district, and asked the question: "Have the 'Skids Been Greased' at City Council?" Brown sued for libel, arguing that the question suggested he had bribed the City Council and that it had accepted the bribe. But the court held that the question was clearly unambiguous and did not suggest bribery in its reasonable and obvious meaning; but rather, that pressure in the form of political influence had been brought to bear on certain Council members to expedite matters. This was not libel. Had the pamphlet said that "palms are greased at the City Council," that would have been libel on its face and actionable.[81]

A margin of protection also exists in the occasional finding by a court that mistakenly attributing a single instance of clumsiness or error to a professional man is not enough to damage him. Rather, such cases have held, there must be a suggestion of more general incompetency or lack of quality before a libel charge will hold. One court said: [82]

> To charge a professional man with negligence or unskillfulness in the management or treatment of an individual case, is no more than to impute to him the mistakes and errors incident to fallible human nature. The most eminent and skillful physician or surgeon may mistake the symptoms of a particular case without detracting from his general professional skill or learning. To say of him, therefore, that he was mistaken in that case would not be calculated to impair the confidence of the community in his general professional competency.

The "single instance" rule, however, does nothing to protect printed material that generalizes about one's questionable ethics or business practices. The *Bristow Record* carried a story saying

---

[80] Washington v. New York News, 37 A.D.2d 557, 322 N.Y.S.2d 896 (1971).

[81] Brown v. Newman, 224 Tenn. 297, 454 S.W.2d 120 (1970). An official who resigned from a "financially troubled bank" was not libeled: Bordoni v. New York Times Co., 400 F.Supp. 1223 (D.C.N.Y.1975).

[82] Blende v. Hearst Publications, 200 Wash. 426, 93 P.2d 733 (1939); November v. Time, Inc., 13 N.Y.2d 175, 244 N.Y.S.2d 309, 194 N.E.2d 126 (1963); Holder Constr. Co. v. Ed Smith & Sons, Inc., 124 Ga.App. 89, 182 S.E.2d 919 (1971). But see Cohn v. Am-Law, (N.Y.Sup.Ct.1980), 5 Med.L.Rptr. 2367, where defamation was found in a magazine story saying an attorney went "unprepared" to a single hearing.

that L.M. Nichols had sold a building. While he owned it, the Record said,

> Nichols used the building for the purpose of attempting to destroy the value of the Record-Citizen publishing plant after he had sold that plant and collected the money from the sale.

> However, he later discovered that * * * business firms in the city * * * did not enjoy doing business with organizations that openly operate with shady ethics. In recent years his publishing activities have been maintained on a sneak basis.

Nichols sued for libel, and though he lost his case at trial, he won it on appeal. The Supreme Court of Oklahoma said that an article accusing one of "shady ethics" and of operating on a "sneak basis" tends "to deprive that person of public confidence, and tends to injure him in his occupation." [83]

Damage to a Corporation's Integrity, Credit, or Ability to Carry on Business

Finally, it is possible to damage the reputation of a corporation or partnership by defamation that reflects on the conduct, management, or financial condition of the corporation.[84] To say falsely that a company is in shaky financial condition, or that it cannot pay its debts, would be libelous, as would the imputation that it has engaged in dishonest practices. While a corporation is an entity quite different from the individuals that head it or staff it, there is no doubt that it has a reputation, an "image" to protect.

Cosgrove Studio and Camera Shop, Inc., advertised in two community newspapers that it would offer a free roll of film for every roll brought to it for developing and printing. The next day its business competitor, Cal R. Pane, advertised in one of the same newspapers, in part as follows:

USE COMMON SENSE * * *
You Get NOTHING for NOTHING!
WE WILL NOT!

1. Inflate the prices of your developing to give you a new roll free!

[83] Nichols v. Bristow Pub. Co., 330 P.2d 1044 (Okl.1957).

[84] Dupont Engineering Co. v. Nashville Banner Pub. Co., 13 F.2d 186 (D.C.Tenn. 1925); Electric Furnace Corp. v. Deering Milliken Research Corp., 325 F.2d 761 (6th Cir.1963); Golden Palace, Inc. v. National Broadcasting Co., 386 F.Supp. 107 (D.D.C.1974).

2. Print the blurred negatives to inflate the price of your shapshots!

Cosgrove brought a suit for libel, alleging that Pane's advertisement was by implication a response to its advertisements to give free film, and implied that Cosgrove was dishonest in business practices and inflated its prices. The trial court said that the words of Pane's advertisement were not libelous in themselves, and found for Pane. Cosgrove appealed and the appeals court reversed the judgment, saying that Cosgrove did indeed have a cause of action. The words, it said, were libelous on their faces. Any language which "unequivocally, maliciously, and falsely imputes to an individual or corporation want of integrity in the conduct of his or its business is actionable," it held.

In arriving at this decision, the appeals court made a point important in many cases: that identification of the defamed need not be by name—as indeed it was not in this case. "The fact that the plaintiff is not specifically named in the advertisement is not controlling. A party need not be specifically named, if pointed to by description or circumstances tending to identify him," it ruled.[85]

SEC. 12. OPINION AND RHETORICAL HYPERBOLE

In defining "libel," many abusive words arising in heated controversies are treated as statements of opinion, or rhetorical hyperbole, and as such are not libelous.

Courts have increasingly come to rule that the agitated, heated dialogue of encounters such as political controversy and labor dispute deserve strong protection against libel actions when it is reported in the media. Rich name-calling that grows out of spirited and hot argument is protected because it is essentially opinion, or it is "rhetorical hyperbole"—extravagant or fanciful exaggeration. We have already seen above (p. 72–73) in the *National Ass'n of Government Employees* case, that in one such circumstance, "communism" was not libelous when spoken of a union.

As for opinion, the rule takes force from the Supreme Court's statement in Gertz v. Robert Welch in 1974:[86] "Under the First Amendment there is no such thing as a false idea. However

---

[85] Cosgrove Studio and Camera Shop, Inc. v. Pane, 408 Pa. 314, 319, 182 A.2d 751, 753 (1962). Also, Grove v. Dun & Bradstreet, Inc., 438 F.2d 433 (3rd Cir.1971). Also, Dictaphone v. Sloves, (N.Y.Sup.Ct.1980) 6 Med.L.Rptr. 1114, where an advertising agency executive said that a firm "was going out of business when they came to us."

[86] 418 U.S. 323, 339–40, 94 S.Ct. 2997, 3007 (1974). Opinion is treated in detail in Sec. 29, Chap. 5, below.

pernicious an opinion may seem, we depend for its correction not on the conscience of judges and juries but on the competition of other ideas."

In the *Old Dominion* case of 1974,[87] shortly after *Gertz* was decided, the Supreme Court found that the word "scabs" applied by publications of union letter-carriers against named, non-union letter-carriers was opinion, and not libel. The publications were used in on-going efforts to organize remaining non-union people. In a long statement accompanying the names, the publication used many pejorative terms in defining "scab," including "traitor." The named non-union people brought a libel action and were awarded damages which were upheld by the Virginia Supreme Court. The union appealed, and the United States Supreme Court reversed the verdict, 6–3, Justice Marshall writing the majority opinion. He reviewed the verbal rough-and-tumble of labor organizing dispute, and cited precedent that had refused to consider this language libel. Speaking of the union publication's definition of the word "scab," derived partly from an old description of scabs by the novelist Jack London, he said: [88]

> The definition's use of words like "traitor" cannot be construed as representations of fact. As the Court said * * * in reversing a state court injunction of union picketing, "to use loose language or undefined slogans that are part of the conventional give-and-take in our economic and political controversies—like 'unfair' or 'fascist'—is not to falsify facts" * * * Cafeteria Employees Local 302 v. Tsakires, 320 U.S. 293, 295, 64 S.Ct. 126, 127 (1943). Such words were obviously used here in a loose, figurative sense to demonstrate the union's strong disagreement with the views of those workers who oppose unionization. Expression of such an opinion, even in the most pejorative terms is protected * * *.

It was considerably opinion that brought a libel suit against reporter Jack Newfield and his publisher, for charges against New York Judge Dominic Rinaldi in Newfield's Book, *Cruel and Unusual Justice.* Newfield called Rinaldi one of New York's 10 worst judges, and in detailed, illustrative cases about the judge's work, said that large-scale heroin dealers and people close to organized crime got lenient treatment from the judge, while blacks and Puerto Ricans received long sentences. Newfield called for Rinaldi's removal from the bench. Rinaldi sued. Newfield and his publisher asked for summary judgment (i.e., a decision in their

---

[87] Old Dominion Branch No. 496, National Ass'n of Letter Carriers, AFL–CIO v. Austin, 418 U.S. 264, 94 S.Ct. 2770 (1974).

[88] Ibid., 2781.

favor without going to trial), were denied it by the trial court, and appealed the case to a higher court and won.[89]

Newfield's attacks on Rinaldi were largely opinion, the New York Court of Appeals found, and the facts supporting them were set forth in the book. The court quoted *Gertz* (above, p. 72, "there is no such thing as a false idea"), and added that opinions "false or not, libelous or not, are constitutionally privileged and may not be the subject of private damage actions provided that the facts supporting the opinion are set forth." The free flow of information to the people concerning the performance of their public officials is essential. "Erroneous opinion must be protected so that debate on public issues may remain robust and unfettered." [90]

At the same time that Justice Marshall ruled in *Letter Carriers* (above, p. 82) that statements of opinion in such agitated circumstances were not to be held libelous, he also characterized the words as no more than "rhetorical hyperbole": " * * * Jack London's 'definition of a scab' is merely rhetorical hyperbole, a hasty and imaginative expression of the contempt felt by union members toward those who refuse to join." [91] Hyperbole earlier had been emphasized as not libelous in the *Greenbelt* case, decided in 1970 by the Supreme Court.[92] Here, real estate developer Charles Bresler was petitioning the Greenbelt, Md., City Council for certain zoning changes that would allow him to build high-density housing on some of his land. Simultaneously, the city was trying to buy a tract of Bresler's land on which to build a school. As the Supreme Court said, the situation provided Bresler and the council with much bargaining leverage against each other. Community controversy arose over the matter, and several tumultuous city council meetings were held at which citizens emphatically spoke their minds. The *Greenbelt News Review*, a small weekly newspaper, reported the meetings at length, including charges by citizens that Bresler's negotiating position was "blackmail," and a case of "unethical trade." Bresler sued and a jury awarded him a total of $17,000 in compensatory and punitive damages. The Maryland Court of Appeals upheld the judgment, and the newspaper took its case to the United States Supreme Court, which reversed the lower courts. The *News Review*, it said, was performing its function as a community newspaper when it published the

[89] Rinaldi v. Holt, Rinehart & Winston, Inc., 42 N.Y.2d 369, 397 N.Y.S.2d 943, 366 N.E.2d 1299 (1975), certiorari denied 98 S.Ct. 514, 434 U.S. 969 (1977), 2 Med.L. Rptr. 2169.

[90] Ibid., 380; 2173.

[91] Old Dominion Branch No. 496, National Ass'n of Letter Carriers, AFL–CIO v. Austin, 418 U.S. 264, 94 S.Ct. 2770, 2782 (1974).

[92] Greenbelt Cooperative Pub. Ass'n v. Bresler, 398 U.S. 6, 90 S.Ct. 1537 (1970).

reports. The reports were accurate, full and fair, with Bresler's proposal given proper coverage. The court said: [93]

> It is simply impossible to believe that a reader who reached the word "blackmail" in either article would not have understood exactly what was meant: it was Bresler's public and wholly legal negotiating proposals that were being criticized. No reader could have thought that either the speakers at the meeting or the newspaper articles reporting their words were charging Bresler with the commission of a criminal offense. On the contrary, even the most careless reader would have perceived that the word was no more than rhetorical hyperbole, a vigorous epithet used by those who considered Bresler's negotiating position extremely unreasonable.

To find libel for such rhetorical hyperbole, the Court said, would "subvert the most fundamental meaning of a free press, protected by the First and Fourteenth Amendments."

Numerous decisions following *Greenbelt* and *Letter Carriers* have found words in similar settings to be matters of opinion or hyperbole, and sometimes both as Justice Marshall did in the latter. In the *Myers* decision (above, p. 75), "the only sports announcer enrolled in a course for remedial speaking" was ruled to be opinion and "rhetorical license." In a Delaware case, Alfred Pierce had business dealings with the Port Authority of which he had once been a commissioner, and a television station used his name in a news report titled "Public Bridges and Private Riches," the story suggesting that some commissioners had seen opportunity for "enormous profits" in a bridge project. Pierce sued, saying that the broadcast suggested that he had acted in "abuse of his public trust." But the court said that a libel case would not stand against publication of hyperbole, if reasonable viewers would understand the statement as such.[94] In a Missouri case, the Court of Appeals has ruled that "sleazy sleight-of-hand" written by a newspaper of an attorney was opinion and not libelous.[95]

In other cases, however, defendants have asserted that their words were hyperbole or opinion without success. The United States Labor Party published a leaflet opposing a candidate for the Baltimore City Council, charging him with a "SS [Nazi] background" and asserting that he had had associations with the Gestapo—charges which, in a libel suit, won $30,000 for the plaintiff. On appeal, the Labor Party argued that its words were

---

[93] Ibid.

[94] Pierce v. Capital Cities Communication, Inc., 576 F.2d 495 (3d Cir.1978), certiorari denied 439 U.S. 861, 99 S.Ct. 181 (1978).

[95] Anton v. St. Louis Suburban Newspapers, Inc., 598 S.W.2d 493 (Mo.App.1980).

merely "rhetorical hyperbole" and so not libelous. But the Maryland Supreme Court said no: Rhetorical hyperbole exists only when a reader could not possibly understand the statement to be a fact—and the general public which saw the leaflet had nothing to prevent its understanding that the words did not mean what they said.[96] Similarly, a California court refused to agree that it was either opinion or hyperbole where the newsletter of a citizens' group charged a councilman with "outright extortion" and "blackmail." [97]

SEC. 13.   EMOTIONAL DISTRESS AND MENTAL ANGUISH

Attending libel's damage to reputation is a kind of handmaiden whose presence in recent years has become a disagreeable reality for libel defendants, even though it remains an infrequent visitor.[98] Widely termed intentional or negligent "infliction of emotional distress," it refers to the power of words and pictures to carry psychological, rather than reputational harm. A tort separate from defamation in many states, it exists in other states as part of the law of defamation. Thus Justice Powell of the United States Supreme Court said, in discussing harmful components of defamatory falsehood in the *Gertz* case, that among them are "personal humiliation, and mental anguish and suffering." [99]

Under that *Gertz* rule, Mary Alice Firestone's suit for libel—against *Time* magazine for an erroneous report that her exhusband had won his divorce action on grounds of adultery—was held permissible despite the fact that she had withdrawn her claim for harm to reputation before trial.[1] The much-publicized case of Carol Burnett followed, in which she recovered damages in a libel suit against the *National Inquirer,* almost entirely for emotional distress over the magazine's portrayal of her as "drunk, rude, uncaring and abusive" at a restaurant.[2] A jury awarded the Rev. Jerry Falwell $200,000 for emotional distress in his libel suit

---

[96] U.S. Labor Party v. Whitman, (Md.Ct.App.1979).

[97] Good Government Group of Seal Beach v. Superior Court, 22 Cal.3d 672, 150 Cal.Rptr. 258, 586 P.2d 572 (1978); McManus v. Doubleday, 513 F.Supp. 1383 (D.C. S.D.N.Y.1981), 7 Med.L.Rptr. 1475.

[98] Terrance C. Mead, "Suing Media for Emotional Distress," 23 Washburn Law Journ. 24, Fall 1983. Mead found only 18 cases in which emotional distress was part of libel actions, out of 484 against media defendants between 1977 and 1981. See David A. Anderson, Reputation, Compensation, and Proof, 25 William and Mary L.Rev. # 5, 1983–84, 747, 756–64.

[99] Gertz v. Robert Welch, Inc., 418 U.S. 323, 94 S.Ct. 2997, 3011–12 (1974).

[1] Time, Inc. v. Firestone, 424 U.S. 448, 460, 96 S.Ct. 958, 968 (1976).

[2] Burnett v. National Inquirer, (Cal.Sup.Ct.1981) 7 Med.L.Rptr. 1321.

against *Hustler* magazine for portraying him in a parody as an incestuous drunkard.[3]

As a separate tort, negligent infliction of emotional distress as a valid cause of action is illustrated by Rubinstein in his suit to recover from the *New York Post* for an erroneous report of his death.[4] And as part of a libel suit, infliction of emotional distress in some states is "parasitic" upon a finding of harm to reputation—it will not be recognized until harm to reputation has first been demonstrated.[5] A 1983 case in Maryland, however, held that a libel plaintiff could recover damages for emotional distress without also showing actual impairment of reputation.[6]

SEC. 14. THE FORM OF THE LIBEL

Damage may be caused by any part of the medium's content, including headlines, pictures and advertisements.

Whatever is printed is printed at the peril of the publisher. A picture may be as libelous as words; a headline, in some states, may be libelous even though modified or negated by the story that follows; libelous copy in an advertisement leaves the publisher liable along with the merchant or advertising agency that furnished it.

A 1956 decision explains how headlines and closing "tag-lines" of a news story can be libelous (even though in this case the newspaper defended itself successfully). One story in a series published by the *Las Vegas Sun* brought a libel suit because of its headline and closing tag-line advertising the next article in the series. The headline read "Babies for Sale. Franklin Black Market Trade of Child Told." The tag-line promoting the story to appear the next day read "Tomorrow—Blackmail by Franklin." The body of the story told factually the way in which attorney Franklin had obtained a mother's release of her child for adoption. Franklin sued for libel and won. But the *Sun* appealed, claiming among other things that the trial judge had erred in instructing the jury that the words were libelous. The *Sun* said that the language was ambiguous, and susceptible of more than one interpretuon.

---

[3] 11 Med.L.Rptr. # 3, 12/18/84, News Notes. The judge threw out the verdict, saying statements too incredible to believe are not actionable: LDRC Bulletin # 13, Spring 1985, 47.

[4] Rubinstein v. New York Post, (N.Y.Sup.Ct.1983) 9 Med.L.Rptr. 1581.

[5] France v. St. Clare's Hospital, 82 A.D.2d 1, 441 N.Y.S.2d 79 (1981), 7 Med.L. Rptr. 2242, 2244; Gobin v. Globe Pub. Co., 232 Kan. 1, 649 P.2d 1239 (1982); Little Rock Newspapers v. Dodrill, 281 Ark. 25, 660 S.W.2d 933 (1983), 10 Med.L.Rptr. 1063.

[6] Hearst Corp. v. Hughes, 297 Md. 112, 466 A.2d 486 (1983), 9 Med.L.Rptr. 2504.

But the Nevada Supreme Court[7] said that the headline and tagline were indeed libelous. Under any reasonable definition, it said, "black market sale" and "blackmail" "would tend to lower the subject in the estimation of the community and to excite derogatory opinions against him and hold him up to contempt." Then it explained the part that the headline had in creating a libel:[8]

> Appellants * * * contend, the headline must be qualified by and read in the light of the article to which it referred and the tag-line must be qualified by and read in the light of the subsequent article to which it referred.

> This is not so. The text of a newspaper article is not ordinarily the context of its headline, since the public frequently reads only the headline * * *. The same is true of a tag-line or leader, since the public frequently reads only the leader without reading the subsequent article to which it refers. The defamation of Franklin contained in the headline was complete upon its face * * *. The same is true of the tag-line.

The dangers of libel in advertisements, of course, have already been illustrated in the case of Cosgrove Studio and Camera Shop, Inc. v. Pane.[9] As for pictures, pictures standing alone, without caption or story with them, would rarely pose danger of defamation, but almost invariably in the mass media, illustration is accompanied by words, and it is almost always the combination that carries the damaging impact. In an issue of *Tan*, a story titled "Man Hungry" was accompanied by a picture taken several years earlier in connection with a woman's work as a professional model for a dress designer. With it were the words "She had a good man—but he wasn't enough. So she picked a bad one!" On the cover of the magazine was the title, "Shameless Love."

The woman sued for libel, and the court granted her claim for $3,000. "There is no doubt in this court's mind that the publication libeled plaintiff," the judge wrote. "A publication must be

---

[7] Las Vegas Sun, Inc. v. Franklin, 74 Nev. 282, 329 P.2d 867 (1958). The *Sun* won the appeal on other grounds.

[8] Ibid. at 869. New York and Louisiana follow the same rule: Schermerhorn v. Rosenberg, 73 A.D.2d 276, 426 N.Y.S.2d 274 (1980), 6 Med.L.Rptr. 1376, Forrest v. Lynch, 347 So.2d 1255 (La.App.1977) 3 Med.L.Rptr. 1187. But in some states, the meaning of headline and story *taken together* govern the finding: Ross v. Columbia Newspapers, Inc., 266 S.C. 75, 221 S.E.2d 770 (1976); Sprouse v. Clay Communication, Inc., 211 S.E.2d 674 (W.Va.1975); Andreani v. Hansen, (Ill.App.1980) 6 Med.L. Rptr. 1015.

[9] 408 Pa. 314, 182 A.2d 751 (1962).

considered in its entirety, both the picture and the story which it illustrates." [10]

During a program broadcast in Albuquerque, N.M., over station KGGM–TV, the secretary of a Better Business Bureau was speaking about dishonest television repairmen. He held up to the camera a newspaper advertisement of the Day and Night Television Service Company, which offered low-cost service through long hours of each day. In making his point, the speaker said that some television servicemen were cheating the public:

> This is what has been referred to in the trade as the ransom. Ransom, the ransom racket. The technique of taking up the stuff after first assuring the set owner that the charges would only be nominal, and then holding the set for ransom * * *.

The New Mexico Supreme Court pointed up the effect of combining the picture and the words: "Standing alone, neither the advertisement nor the words used by Luttbeg could be construed as libel. But the two combined impute fraud and dishonesty to the company and its operators." [11]

The use of the wrong picture in an advertisement gives the foundation for actionable libel, as decided in Peck v. Tribune Co. [12] The use of false or unauthorized testimonials in advertisements may constitute libel according to decisions in Pavesich v. New England Life Ins. Co. [13] and Foster Milburn Co. v. Chinn. [14]

SEC. 15. BROADCAST DEFAMATION

Broadcasting's vast audience gives vast potential for harm in defamation, and it is now treated as libel instead of the lesser wrong of slander. Special problems arise in broadcast libel uttered without advance warning by participants in programs.

While defamation suits during the early decades of radio were sometimes brought under the rules of slander [15]—spoken defamation—the offense today is handled as libel. The American Law Institute finds that "defamation by any form of communication

[10] Martin v. Johnson Pub. Co., 157 N.Y.S.2d 409, 411 (1956). See also Farrington v. Star Co., 244 N.Y. 585, 155 N.E. 906 (1927) (wrong picture); Wasserman v. Time, Inc., 138 U.S.App.D.C. 7, 424 F.2d 920 (1970), certiorari denied 398 U.S. 940, 90 S.Ct. 1844 (1970).

[11] Young v. New Mexico Broadcasting Co., 60 N.M. 475, 292 P.2d 776 (1956); Central Arizona Light & Power Co. v. Akers, 45 Ariz. 526, 46 P.2d 126 (1935).

[12] 214 U.S. 185, 29 S.Ct. 554 (1909).

[13] 122 Ga. 190, 50 S.E. 68 (1905).

[14] 134 Ky. 424, 120 S.W. 364 (1909).

[15] See footnote 8, above.

that has the potentially harmful qualities characteristic of written or printed words is to be treated as libel." [16]   Broadcasting's wide diffusion of its programs to millions, and its prestige and impact among audiences, makes it potentially much more damaging than the slanderous speech of one to another in a neighborhood gathering, or of one to an audience in a lecture hall.   *Media Law Reporter,* the publication that gathers and reprints court decisions from all jurisdictions in the nation, has no "Slander" subtitle in its classification guide.

If there were a rare case in which broadcasting defamation might still be ruled slander, it would be somewhat harder for the offended person to get his case into court than if his case were libel.   Ancient rules persist that protect spoken defamation more than written.   Thus slander plaintiffs must show precise, special damages of a pecuniary kind to get many cases into court—in fact, all cases except those arising from offending words that impute crime, loathsome or contagious disease, or unchastity or immorality in a female, or injure one in business or calling.   And special damages are very hard to establish at trial.[17]

That is not to say that broadcasting presents no special circumstances in the libel peril—circumstances different from those of the printed media.   For one thing, a study [18] of a recent three-and-one-half-year period of all defamation decisions reported among the official published court cases, showed that radio and television were the defendants in 32 cases (26 television, 6 radio), compared to 94 for newspapers, 25 for magazines, and 12 for books.   For whatever reasons, thus, the raw numbers of reported cases suggest that broadcasters are much less frequently confronted with the libel peril than are newspapers.[19]

Yet if broadcasters are favored in that respect, in another the tools of their trade often present an uncomfortable problem: When will some participant in an untaped, live broadcast fire off a defamatory statement?   Is the station to be liable for a defamation suit rising out of the spontaneously articulated wit of a gifted comedian in the middle of a broadcast program?   Is the careless slur of an insensitive entertainer or interviewee, injected without warning into the flow of his talk, to be the basis for libel action against the station that is powerless to prevent the misfortune?   Or the sudden burst of invective from an unknown caller on a call-in talk-show?

[16] Restatement Second, Torts, Vol. 3 p. 182.

[17] Prosser, 754, 769–781.

[18] Franklin, 479.

[19] Ibid., 488.

Before the 1930's were out, one answer had been provided by the Pennsylvania court in the famous case of Summit Hotel Co. v. National Broadcasting Co.[20] Here the great entertainer, Al Jolson, appeared on an NBC Program under the sponsorship of Shell Eastern Petroleum Products, Inc. He was paid by the advertising agency which Shell had hired, J. Walter Thompson. A golf champion appearing on Jolson's show mentioned that his first professional golf job was with the Summit Hotel. Jolson blurted out an unscripted ad lib: "That's a rotten hotel." Summit sued NBC.

Was NBC to be held to strict accountability for the words, as a newspaper is held strictly accountable for anything it publishes? Or would the nature of the communication process by radio, incompatible with total advance control by the broadcast company, permit a different treatment? The court took into account the special character of broadcasting, and held that the rule of strict accountability did not apply: [21]

> Publication by radio has physical aspects entirely different from those attending the publication of a libel or a slander as the law understands them. The danger of attempting to apply the fixed principles of law governing either libel or slander to this new medium of communication is obvious * * *.

> * * *

> A rule unalterably imposing liability without fault on the broadcasting company under any circumstances is manifestly unjust, unfair and contrary to every principle of morals * * *.

> * * *

> We * * * conclude that a broadcasting company that leases its time and facilities to another, whose agents carry on the program, is not liable for an interjected defamatory remark where it appears that it exercised due care in the selection of the lessee, and, having inspected and edited the script, had no reason to believe an extemporaneous defamatory remark would be made. Where the broadcasting station's employe or agent makes the defamatory remark, it is liable, unless the remarks are privileged and there is no malice.

The popular radio format of the call-in talk-show presents a similar problem. Louisiana and Wyoming courts have settled actions against telephoned libel in diametrically opposed ways. The announcer for the call-in program of station WBOX of Boga-

[20] 336 Pa. 182, 8 A.2d 302 (1939).

[21] Ibid., 336 Pa. 182, 185–205, 8 A.2d 302, 310, 312 (1939).

lusa, La., asked call-ins not to use specific names and places unless they were willing to identify themselves, in fairness to all people. On April 2, 1968, a call-in by an unidentified person associated the Pizza Shanty with narcotics, and said that Dr. Newman "is writing those prescriptions," and "Guerry Snowden [manager of a drug store] is filling them and they are selling them down there." The announcer broke in repeatedly, trying to get the name of the caller, but did not succeed. Snowden, Newman and Blackwell of the Pizza Shanty sued, and a jury awarded them $4,000, $5,000, and $2,500 respectively. The station appealed, and in upholding the judgments, the Louisiana Appeals Court explained in detail why the station's behavior was reckless disregard of truth or falsity: [22]

> We would have no difficulty in finding a station liable, if it received defamatory material from an anonymous source, and broadcast the report without attempting verification. The direct broadcast of such anonymous defamatory material, without the use of any monitoring or delay device, is no less reprehensible in our judgment. The publication, in either event, is done by the station, and we find that there is the same reckless disregard for the truth in each instance.
>
> The procedure employed amounted to an open invitation to make any statement a listener desired, regardless of how untrue or defamatory it might be, about any person or establishment, provided only that the declarer identify himself. * * * We find that the style utilized encouraged the utterance of defamatory statements with utter disregard of their truth or falsity. Appellant placed itself in a position fraught with the imminent danger of broadcasting anonymous unverified, slanderous remarks based on sheer rumor, speculation and hearsay, and just such a result actually occurred. Such an eventuality was easily foreseeable and likely to occur, as it in fact did. In our judgment, the First Amendment does not protect a publisher against such utter recklessness.

The vastly different outlook of the Wyoming courts was delivered in the case Adams v. Frontier Broadcasting Co., 1976.[23] Here a caller to a talk-show charged falsely that businessman Adams (a former state official) "had been discharged as Insurance Commissioner for dishonesty," and Adams sued. The trial court ruled that he did not have a suit, because the station did not have "reckless disregard" for truth or falsity in failing to use a delay

---

[22] Snowden v. Pearl River Broadcasting Corp., 251 So.2d 405 (La.App.1971).

[23] 555 P.2d 556 (Wyo.1976), 2 Med.L.Rptr. 1166.

device to cut dangerous words off the air. Adams appealed, and the Wyoming Supreme Court upheld the trial court. It said that requiring stations to use the delay system would mean that [24]

> * * * broadcasters, to protect themselves from judgments for damages, would feel compelled to adopt and regularly use one of the tools of censorship, an electronic delay system. While using such a system a broadcaster would be charged with the responsibility of concluding that some comments should be edited or not broadcast at all. Furthermore, we must recognize the possibility that the requirement for the use of such equipment might, on occasion, tempt the broadcaster to screen out the comments of those with whom the broadcaster * * * did not agree and then broadcast only the comments of those with whom the broadcaster did agree.

The court said that uninhibited, robust, wide-open debate "must, in the balance, outweigh the * * * right of an * * * official or public figure to be free from defamatory remarks." Reports such as the call-ins, the court added, are a modern version of the town meeting, and give every citizen a chance to speak his mind on issues.

The Candidate for Public Office

A special problem in broadcast defamation grew in the special relationship of the political candidates and the broadcast media. The famous Section 315 of the federal Communications Act of 1934 [25] says that if a station decides to carry one political candidate's message on the air, it must carry those of any of his political opponents who may seek air time. The station is specifically barred from censoring the candidate's copy.

For decades, this put the station in a difficult position. If it refused air time to all candidates, it could be criticized for refusing to aid the democratic political process, even though it was within the law in so doing. But suppose that it accepted the responsibility of carrying campaign talks: Then, if it spotted possible defamation in the prepared script of the candidate about to go on the air, it had no way of denying him access to its microphone and no power to censor. The law in effect forced the station to carry material that might very well damage it.

---

[24] Ibid., 564–67; 1173–75.

[25] 48 Stat. 1088, as amended, 47 U.S.C.A. § 315(a).

Several cases arose in which campaign talk produced defamation for which stations were held liable.[26] But in 1959, a case from North Dakota reached the Supreme Court of the United States and the problem was settled in favor of the beleaguered broadcasters. A.C. Townley, some 30 years after he had been a major political figure in upper midwest states, returned to the political arena in 1956. He ran for the U.S. Senate in North Dakota. Under the requirements of Section 315, radio station WDAY of Fargo, N.D., permitted Townley to broadcast a speech in reply to two other candidates. In it, Townley accused the Farmers Educational and Cooperative Union of America of conspiring to "establish a Communist Farmers Union Soviet right here in North Dakota." The FECUA sued Townley and WDAY for libel. The North Dakota courts ruled that WDAY was not liable and FECUA appealed.[27]

The Supreme Court held that stations did not have power to censor the speeches of political candidates. For with that power, it said, "Quite possibly if a station were held responsible for the broadcast of libelous material, all remarks evenly [sic] faintly objectionable would be excluded out of an excess of caution," and further, a station could intentionally edit a candidate's "legitimate presentation under the guise of lawful censorship of libelous matter." [28] The Court was confident that Congress had intended no such result when it wrote Section 315.

FECUA also argued that Section 315 gave no immunity to a station from liability for defamation spoken during a political broadcast even though censorship of possibly libelous matter was not permitted. The court said: [29]

> Again, we cannot agree. For under this interpretation, unless a licensee refuses to permit any candidate to talk at all, the section would sanction the unconscionable result of permitting civil and perhaps criminal liability to be imposed for the very conduct the statute demands of the licensee.

In ruling that WDAY was not liable for defamation in campaign broadcasts under Section 315, the Supreme Court gave great weight to the principle of maximum broadcast participation in the political process. And it relieved stations of an onerous burden

---

[26] Houston Post Co. v. United States, 79 F.Supp. 199 (S.D.Tex.1948); Sorensen v. Wood, 123 Neb. 348, 243 N.W. 82 (1932); Daniell v. Voice of New Hampshire, Inc., 10 Pike & Fischer Radio Reg. 2045.

[27] Farmers Educational and Cooperative Union of America v. WDAY, Inc., 360 U.S. 525, 79 S.Ct. 1302 (1959).

[28] Ibid., 530.

[29] Ibid., 531.

that they had formerly carried in the furtherance of that participation.

SEC. 16. EXTRINSIC CIRCUMSTANCES, LIBEL PER SE, AND LIBEL PER QUOD

Facts extrinsic to the story itself sometimes are necessary to make out a defamatory meaning; such "libel per quod" is distinguished from "libel per se" which ordinarily means that the words are defamatory on their face.

In most cases of libel, the hard words that cause a suit are plain to see or hear in the written word or broadcast. They carry the derogatory meaning in themselves: "thief" or "swindler" or "whore" or "communist" is defamatory on its face if falsely applied to a person. Words that are libelous on their face are called libel *per se*.[30]

But on some occasions, words that have no apparent derogatory meaning turn out to be libelous because circumstances outside the words of the story itself become involved. In the classic case, there was no apparent derogatory meaning in a brief but erroneous story saying that a married woman had given birth to twins. But many people who read the story knew that the woman had been married only a month.[31] Facts extrinsic to the story itself gave the words of the story a libelous meaning. Where extrinsic facts turn an apparently harmless story into defamation, it is called by many American courts libel *per quod*.[32]

In a vital column in the *Spokane Chronicle,* this entry appeared on April 21, 1961: "Divorce Granted Hazel M. Pitts from Philip Pitts." In these words alone there was no defamation. But the divorce had taken place on Feb. 2, 1960, 14 months earlier, and now Pitts had been married to another woman for several months. Some of his acquaintances and neighbors concluded that Pitts had been married to two women at once and was a bigamist. Extrinsic facts made the story libelous, and the Pittses were awarded $2,000.[33]

In some jurisdictions it is held that where extrinsic facts are involved in making out a libel, the plaintiff must plead and prove special damages. These damages are specific amounts of pecuniary loss that one suffers as a result of libel, such as cancelled contracts or lost wages.

[30] 33 Am.Jur. Libel and Slander § 5; Martin v. Outboard Marine Corp., 15 Wis. 2d 452, 113 N.W.2d 135, 138 (1962); Prosser, p. 782.

[31] Morrison v. Ritchie & Co., 39 Scot.L.R. 432 (1902).

[32] 53 C.J.S. Libel and Slander § 8a; Prosser, p. 781; Electric Furnace Corp. v. Deering Milliken Research Corp., 325 F.2d 761, 764–765 (6th Cir.1963).

[33] Pitts v. Spokane Chronicle Co., 63 Wash.2d 763, 388 P.2d 976 (1964).

Where the defamatory nature of the writing does not appear upon the face of the writing, but rather appears only when all of the circumstances are known, it is said to be libel per quod, as distinguished from libel per se, and in such cases damages are not presumed but must be proven before the plaintiff can recover.[34]

The magazine *Life* published a story on May 20, 1966, dealing with electronic eavesdropping. With it was a picture of Mary Alice Firestone, her estranged husband, and Jack Harwood who had a business in electronic "snooping," especially in connection with divorce suits. The story read:[35]

> TWO-WAY SNOOP. In Florida, where electronic eavesdropping is frequently employed in divorce suits, private eyes like Jack Harwood of Palm Beach shown above with some of his gear, do a thriving business. Harwood, who boasts, "I'm a fantastic wire man," was hired by tire heir Russell Firestone to keep tabs on his estranged wife, Mary Alice. * * * She in turn got one of Harwood's assistants to sell out and work for her and, says Harwood "He plays just as rough with the bugs as I do." * * * A court recently ordered Russell and Mary to stop spying on each other.

Mrs. Firestone brought suit for libel per quod, saying that the story injured her in her pending marital litigation. The trial court dismissed her complaint, but the U.S. Circuit Court of Appeals ruled that she had a case, reversing the trial court. It said:[36]

> We are of the opinion that appellant's allegations of injury to her pending marital litigation constitute allegations of "special damages" for libel per quod which are sufficient to withstand a motion to dismiss. While it may be difficult indeed [for Mrs. Firestone] to prove these damages, we are not convinced that they are so speculative that she could not prove them under any circumstances.

For the mass media, the "special damage" requirement is the much more favorable rule; it is seldom easy for a plaintiff to

---

[34] Electric Furnace Corp. v. Deering Milliken Research Corp., 325 F.2d 761, 764–765 (6th Cir.1963); see also Solotaire v. Cowles Magazines, Inc., 107 N.Y.S.2d 798 (Sup.1951); Moore v. P.W. Pub. Co., 3 Ohio St.2d 183, 209 N.E.2d 412 (1965); Campbell v. Post Pub. Co., 94 Mont. 12, 20 P.2d 1063 (1933). For other uses of *"per quod"* see Developments in the Law of Defamation, 69 Harv.L.Rev. 375, 889 (1956).

[35] Firestone v. Time, Inc., 414 F.2d 790, 791 (5th Cir.1969).

[36] Ibid.

demonstrate specific money loss as a result of derogatory words.[37] Some courts have in recent decades accepted the position that the plaintiff must show special damage if he is to recover for libel involving extrinsic facts; others hold that "all libels are actionable without proof of special damages." [38]

SEC. 17. BRINGING A LIBEL ACTION

The plaintiff in a libel suit must plead that there was publication, identification, defamation, injury, and fault.

Having taken care to meet the deadline set by his state's statute of limitations—in most, one year after publication and in others two or three—the party filing a libel suit must make five allegations.[39] These are that the derogatory statement was published, that the statement identified the plaintiff, that the statement was defamatory, that it actually injured the plaintiff, and that there was fault on the part of the publisher.

To start with publication, the statement may of course be printed or written or, in the case of movies and broadcasting, oral.[40] It must be made not only to the defamed, for a communicator cannot blacken a reputation unless he spreads the charge to at least one person besides the target. Although those in the mass media ordinarily publish to huge audiences, it is worth remembering that no more than a "third person" need be involved for publication to take place. In Ostrowe v. Lee,[41] a man dictated a letter to his secretary accusing the addressee of grand larceny. The stenographer typed the letter and it was sent through the mail. The accused brought a libel suit and the court held that publication took place at the time the stenographic notes were read and transcribed.

For the printed media, courts of most states call the entire edition carrying the alleged libel one publication; an over-the-counter sale of back copies of a newspaper weeks or months after they were printed does not constitute a further publication. The

---

[37] Laurence H. Eldredge, The Spurious Rule of Libel Per Quod, 79 Harv.L.Rev. 733, 755 (1966).

[38] Martin v. Outboard Marine Corp., 15 Wis.2d 452, 113 N.W.2d 135, 139 (1962). For two interpretations of recent trends, see Eldredge, op. cit., and William L. Prosser, More Libel Per Quod, 79 Harv.L.Rev. 1629 (1966).

[39] See Sec. 10 for who may bring a libel action. New Hampshire is unusual in having a six-year statute of limitations, and Florida has a four-year statute. See above, Sec. 10, for who may bring a libel action.

[40] Signs, statutes, effigies, and other communications that may carry libel are in Sec. 11, supra.

[41] 256 N.Y. 36, 175 N.E. 505 (1931). See also Arvey Corp. v. Peterson, 178 F.Supp. 132 (E.D.Pa.1959); Gambrill v. Schooley, 93 Md. 48, 48 A. 730 (1901).

rule is known as the "single publication rule." [42]   Where this is not the rule, there is a chance that a plaintiff can stretch the statute of limitations indefinitely, perhaps by claiming a separate publication in a newspaper's selling a February issue the following December. In Tocco v. Time, Inc., it was held that the publication takes place at the time a magazine is mailed to subscribers, or put in the hands of those who will ship the edition to wholesale distributors.[43] This rule has not been universally accepted; Osmers v. Parade Publications, Inc., rejected it and stated this as its rule for publication date:[44]

> * * * what is really determinative is the earliest date on which the libel was substantially and effectively communicated to a meaningful mass of readers—the public for which the publication was intended, not some small segment of it.

Publication established, the plaintiff must also demonstrate that he was identified in the alleged libel—that the statement he complains of referred to him. In most cases, this presents little problem to the plaintiff. His name and the derogatory words are there, and one or more readers or listeners attach the name to the person. Yet as we have seen in the Cosgrove Studio case above (p. 80), a successful libel suit was brought by a merchant against a competitor who charged "dishonesty" in such a way as to identify the Cosgrove shop without naming it.

It is not uncommon for identification of a totally unintended kind to occur in the mass media. A typographical error, wrong initials, the incorrect address, the careless work of a reporter or editor—and an innocent person may have been linked with a crime, immorality, unethical business conduct, or another activity that is a basis for a libel suit. The law has modified the old "strict liability" rules in libel (p. 157), but innocent error in identification can still bring libel actions.[45]

In a celebrated English case, E. Hulton & Co. v. Jones,[46] the *Sunday Chronicle* had published a story from a correspondent in France concerning a supposedly fictitious person named Artemus Jones. He had been seen, the story said, in the company of a woman who was not his wife. The Chronicle soon learned, with the filing of a libel action, that a real Artemus Jones did, indeed,

---

[42] Robert Leflar, The Single Publication Rule, 25 Rocky Mt.Law R. 263, 1953; Wheeler v. Dell Pub. Co., 300 F.2d 372 (7th Cir.1962). Restatement of Torts, § 578, Comment (b) does not accept the single publication rule.

[43] 195 F.Supp. 410 (E.D.Mich.1961).

[44] 234 F.Supp. 924, 927 (D.C.N.Y.1964).

[45] See Chap. 3, Sec. 15.

[46] (1910) A.C. 20, 1909, 2 K.B. 444.

exist, and that he said that some of his friends believed that the story referred to him. The courts held that the identification was sufficient and awarded Jones, a lawyer, £ 1750 in damages.

Plaintiffs may, of course, allege identification but fail to establish it at trial. Harry Landau operated a business known as Credit Consultants. He brought a libel suit based on a television show titled "The Easy Way." The plot involved a newspaper photographer's attempt to expose a book-making ring headed by a character named Sam Henderson, whose private office door carried the printed legend, "Credit Consultant, Inc." Landau contended that the use of that name identified him as Sam Henderson, the head of an unlawful gambling syndicate. But the court held that there was no identification of Landau in the television drama. There was no resemblance between Landau and Henderson, or between the televised office and Landau's office. The fictional Henderson was killed at the end of the play, and Landau was alive and suing. The defendant Columbia Broadcasting System, Inc., was given the judgment.[47]

Springer sued Viking Press for libel, complaining that she was identifiable to friends as the model for a prostitute in a novel written by Tine, a former friend. The book, Springer alleged, portrayed the prostitute's physical characteristics as highly similar to her own. Both Springer and the fictional prostitute lived on the same street in Manhattan, she said, both received gifts of a diamond and a necklace from a boy friend, both spoke fluent French and dated men of Iranian heritage. The New York Court said that there was sufficient connection between Springer and the prostitute to indicate that the characterization of the prostitute could be "of and concerning" Springer. It refused to grant Viking's motion to dismiss the libel action.[48]

Identification cannot be established by a person who says that an attack upon a large heterogeneous group libels him because he happens to belong to it. Derogatory statements about a political party, an international labor union, the Presbyterian church, the American Legion, for example, do not identify individuals so as to permit them to bring a libel action.

However, if the attack is on a small group such as the officers of a local post of the American Legion, or the presiding elders of a local church, or the directors of the Smith County Democratic Party, each individual of the group may be able to establish

---

[47] Landau v. Columbia Broadcasting System, Inc., 205 Misc. 357, 128 N.Y.S.2d 254 (1954). See also Summerlin v. Washington Star, (D.D.C.1981) 7 Med.L.Rptr. 2460.

[48] Springer v. Viking Press, (N.Y.Sup.Ct.1981) 7 Med.L.Rptr. 2040.

identification and bring suit.[49]   One of a group of 53 unnamed policemen said by a newspaper to have "guilty knowledge of misconduct" by 18 other policemen was not barred from pressing a libel suit despite the fact that his group numbered more than 25.[50]

The case of Neiman-Marcus Co. v. Lait [51] involved the portion of a book entitled *U.S.A. Confidential* about a well-known department store in Dallas and its employees.   An action for libel was brought by the Neiman-Marcus Co., operator of the store, nine individual models who were the entire group of models employed by the store, 15 salesmen of a total of 25 salesmen employed, and 30 saleswomen of a total of 382.   The defendants moved to dismiss the complaint on the grounds that the individual plaintiffs were not capable of identification from the alleged libelous words.   The court stated that the following rules were applicable:

(1) Where the group or class libeled is large, none can sue even though the language used is inclusive.

(2) When the group or class libeled is small, and each and every member of the group or class is referred to, then any individual member can sue.

(3) That while there is a conflict in authorities where the publication complained of libeled some or less than all of a designated small group, it would permit such an action.

In applying these rules to the facts, the court dismissed the suits of the saleswomen, but allowed the suits of the models and salesmen.

Identity may be in reference to a member of a board although no specific member of the board or no director is actually named,[52] to a "city hall ring," [53] or to a radio editor when there are only a few to whom the libel could refer.[54]

The third necessary allegation, that the statement was defamatory, says in effect that the words injured reputation, or, in some circumstances, caused emotional distress.   The allegation of defamation must be made in bringing the suit, although it, like publication and identification, can fail of proof at trial.   The court decides whether a publication is libelous *per se;* but when the words complained of are susceptible of two meanings, one innocent and the other damaging, it is for the jury to decide in what sense

---

[49] Above, Chap. 3, Sec. 10.

[50] Brady v. Ottaway Newspapers, 84 A.D.2d 226, 445 N.Y.S.2d 786 (1981), 8 Med. L.Rptr. 1671.

[51] 107 F.Supp. 96 (S.D.N.Y.1952); 13 F.R.D. 311 (1952).

[52] Children v. Shinn, 168 Iowa 531, 150 N.W. 864 (1915).

[53] Petsch v. St. Paul Dispatch Printing Co., 40 Minn. 291, 41 N.W. 1034 (1889).

[54] Gross v. Cantor, 270 N.Y. 93, 200 N.E. 592 (1936).

the words were understood by the audience. Both court and jury, in their interpretation of the alleged defamatory statement, should give the language its common and ordinary meaning.[55]

> What sense will be given to them by a reader of ordinary intelligence? Will the natural and proximate consequence be to injure the person about whom they have been published? Will such words tend to bring a person into public hatred, contempt or ridicule? If the words are plain, and unambiguous and susceptible of but one meaning, it is the duty of the court to determine from the face of the writing without reference to innuendo, whether the same are actionable *per se.*

A fourth element necessary for the aggrieved person to allege and persuasively demonstrate as he brings a libel action is "fault" on the part of the publisher or broadcaster. A public official or public figure must show evidence that the fault of the news medium amounted to *actual malice:* knowledge that the communication was false, or reckless disregard for its truth or falsity. A private individual who sues for libel must bring evidence that the fault amounted at least to *negligence* by the news medium. In the absence of some evidence of the appropriate level of fault, a libel suit will no more "stick" (be accepted for trial) than if there is no publication, identification, or defamation. Many courts have rejected libel suits and discharged them without trial (granted "summary judgment" to the defendant) for this defect. Fault and summary judgment will be treated at length in Chapter 4.

Finally, there is the fifth element—"actual injury." The private-person plaintiff must demonstrate loss of some kind. Actual injury includes out-of-pocket money loss, impairment of reputation and standing in the community, personal humiliation, and mental anguish and suffering, as the United States Supreme Court said in Gertz v. Robert Welch.[56]

SEC. 18.   DAMAGES

Compensatory or general damages are granted for injury to reputation, special damages for specific pecuniary loss, and punitive damages as punishment for malicious or extremely careless libel.

Courts and statutes are not entirely consistent in their labeling of the kinds of damages that may be awarded to a person who

---

[55] Peck v. Coos Bay Times Pub. Co., 122 Or. 408, 259 P. 307, 311 (1927); Prosser, 765.

[56] 418 U.S. 323, 94 S.Ct. 2997, 3011–12 (1974).

is libeled. Generally, however, three bases exist for compensating the injured person.

The first is that injuring reputation or causing humiliation ought to be recognized as real injury, even though it is impossible to make a scale of values and fix exact amounts due the injured for various kinds of slurs. If such injury is proved, "general" or "compensatory" damages are awarded.

There is also harm of a more definable kind—actual pecuniary loss that a person may suffer as a result of a libel. It may be the loss of a contract or of a job, and if it can be shown that the loss is associated with the libel, the defamed may recover "special" damages—the cost to him. It is plain, however, that some states use the term "actual damages" to cover both pecuniary loss and damaged reputations. Thus it was held in Miami Herald Pub. Co. v. Brown:[57]

> Actual damages are compensatory damages and include (1) pecuniary loss, direct or indirect, or special damages; (2) damages for physical pain and inconvenience; (3) damages for mental suffering; and (4) damages for injury to reputation.

The third basis for awarding damages is public policy—that persons who maliciously libel others ought to be punished for the harm they cause. Damages above and beyond general and actual damages may be awarded in this case, and are called punitive or exemplary damages. Some states deny punitive damages, having decided long ago that they are not justified. For almost a century, Massachusetts, for example, has rejected punitive damages, under a statement by the famed Oliver Wendell Holmes, Jr., then judge of the Massachusetts high court: "The damages are measured in all cases by the injury caused. Vindictive or punitive damages are never allowed in this State. Therefore, any amount of malevolence on the defendant's part in and of itself would not enhance the amount the plaintiff recovered by a penny ＊   ＊   ＊."[58]

Huge amounts of damage are often claimed, and sometimes awarded although juries' judgments of such astronomical sums as $5,000,000 or $25,000,000 are invariably cut back by trial judges or by appeals courts. Thus not only "private" persons, but also public officials and public figures, even under the requirements of proving actual malice, have in recent years won such amounts as $114,000 compensatory plus $100,000 punitive damages (charge of

---

[57] 66 So.2d 679, 680 (Fla.1953). See, also, Ellis v. Brockton Pub. Co., 198 Mass. 538, 84 N.E. 1018 (1908); Osborn v. Leach, 135 N.C. 628, 47 S.E. 811 (1904).

[58] Burt v. Advertiser Newspaper Co., 154 Mass. 238, 245, 28 N.E. 1 (1891).

soliciting bribes);[59] $250,000 plus interest (dishonest practices in real estate);[60] $85,000 (sadistic, paranoid);[61] $450,000 (fixed a football game);[62] $350,000 plus possible $50,000 court costs (connections with underworld);[63] $50,000 (judge put drug pushers back on the street—settled out of court);[64] $400,000, of which $300,000 was punitive damages (false charge of "Communist").[65]

A California court jury in 1981 awarded $1.6 million to America's beloved comedienne, Carol Burnett, who was falsely portrayed by the *National Enquirer,* said the judge in the case, as "drunk, rude, uncaring and abusive" in the Rive Gauche restaurant, Los Angeles.[66] The judge disagreed with the jury only in the amount of damages, which he cut in half to $50,000 compensatory plus $750,000 punitive, and the punitive total was cut to $150,000 by the California Court of Appeal more than two years after the jury trial.[67]

"Miss Wyoming" of 1978, Kimberli Jayne Pring, won a jury award of $25 million in punitive damages plus $1.5 million in compensatory damages from *Penthouse* magazine in 1981. She alleged that a *Penthouse* story falsely implied that she was sexually promiscuous and immoral. The staggering punitive award was quickly halved by Federal District Court Judge Clarence C. Brimmer, who said that the reduced figure must be one that would exceed *Penthouse's* libel insurance protection of $10 million if the magazine were to be punished. *Penthouse,* of course, appealed the enormous remainder, and after another year received the judgment: the article could be reasonably understood by readers as only a "pure fantasy," not as defamation of Pring.[68]

One of the largest libel judgments on record against a newspaper is $9.2 million granted in 1980 by an Illinois circuit court jury to a builder for words that the *Alton Telegraph* never published.

[59] Cape Publications, Inc. v. Adams, 336 So.2d 1197 (Fla.App.1976), certiorari denied 348 So.2d 945 (1977).

[60] Sprouse v. Clay Communication, Inc., 211 S.E.2d 674 (1975).

[61] Goldwater v. Ginzburg, 414 F.2d 324 (2d Cir.1969).

[62] Curtis Pub. Co. v. Butts, 388 U.S. 130, 87 S.Ct. 1975 (1967).

[63] Alioto v. Cowles Communications, Inc., 430 F.Supp. 1363 (N.D.Cal.1977). Four trials were conducted over eight years before ex-Mayor Alioto of San Francisco won the judgment.

[64] Editor & Publisher, Feb. 26, 1977, p. 24 (Village Voice and its advertising agency Scali, McCabe, Sloves paid New York Supreme Court Justice Dominick Rinaldi). And see C. David Rambo, "Wave of Expensive Libel Awards * * *," Presstime, May 1981, p. 10.

[65] Gertz v. Welch, 680 F.2d 527 (7th Cir.1982), 8 Med.L.Rptr. 1769.

[66] 7 Med.L.Rptr. 1321, 1323 (Cal.Super.Ct. 5/31/81).

[67] Burnett v. National Enquirer, 9 Med.L.Rptr. 1921 (Cal.App.1983) appeal dismissed ___ U.S. ___, 104 S.Ct. 1260 (1984).

[68] Pring v. Penthouse, 695 F.2d 438 (10th Cir.1982), 8 Med.L.Rptr. 2409.

The offending words were in a memo from two Telegraph reporters to a Justice Department task force on crime, alleging connections of Alton citizens with organized crime.   The paper filed for
bankruptcy to delay the force of the judgment until the outcome of
its appeal was known, and in May 1982, the U.S. Bankruptcy
Court for the Southern District of Illinois approved a settlement
reported to be $1.4 million between the Telegraph and the central
complainant, relator James Green.[69]   The "chill" induced upon
future investigative reporting by a newspaper of modest size by
such an award takes meaning from the Telegraph's publisher, who
said: "Let someone else stick their neck out next time." [70]

Courts—as well as media and their attorneys—find evidence
in such astronomical awards of hatred and resentment of media by
juries.   Widespread anti-media attitudes in the public of recent
decades [71] are likely to be represented among the cross-section of
people that comprises a jury: attitudes that media are over-
powerful, arrogant, unfair, immoral, inaccurate, and invaders of
privacy.   In Guccione v. Hustler [72] the Ohio Court of Appeals
looked at a jury award of some $40 million to Guccione.   Even
though the trial judge had reduced it to about $1/13$ of that amount,
the Appeals Court said, the jury award was so influenced by
passion and prejudice and was so grossly excessive as to indicate
the jury's intent to drive *Hustler* out of business.   The Court
ordered a new trial on the issue of damages.

[69] News Media & the Law, June/July 1982, p. 20.

[70] Carley, How Libel Suit Sapped the Crusading Spirit of a Small Newspaper,
Wall St. Journal, Sept. 29, 1983, p. 1; Marc Franklin, What Does "Negligence"
Mean in Defamation Cases?   6 Comm/Ent 259, 277 (Winter 1984).

[71] Max McCombs, Opinion Surveys Offer Conflicting Views as to How Public
Views Press, presstime, Feb. 1983, p. 4; "The Media's Credibility Gap," Washington Post National Weekly, April 29, 1985, 38.

[72] 7 Med.L.Rptr. 2077 (1981).

Chapter 4

THE CONSTITUTIONAL DEFENSE AGAINST LIBEL SUITS

SEC. 19.   THE PUBLIC PRINCIPLE

News media defend against libel suits on grounds of their service to the public interest.

The American Constitution was nearing two centuries in age before courts, attorneys, and journalists divined that it ought to protect speech and press against libel actions. It was in 1964 that the Supreme Court of the United States ruled in New York Times Co. v. Sullivan that public officials who sued for libel would have to clear a First Amendment barrier rather than the long-used lesser barriers of state laws and precedents. The emergence of multiple suits claiming formerly unheard-of amounts of damages threatened losses so high as to turn "watchdog" media into sheep. The public interest in vigorous, unintimidated reporting of the news was endangered. The society could not accept self-censorship on the part of media "chilled" by fear of libel awards. The United States Constitution itself, through the First Amendment, would provide the shield for discussion of public matters that the crabbed vagaries of many state libel laws denied and that the public welfare demanded.

Striking as the new application of the Constitution was, it really amounted to an extension of the "public principle" inherent in centuries-old defenses against libel suits. Defenses had grown in the context of the need of an open society for information and discussion in media if its citizens are to participate in decisions that affect their lives, are to have the opportunity to choose, are to maintain ultimate control over government. Those who claimed harm to their reputations might find their suits unavailing if certain public concerns and values were furthered by the publication: Where the hard words were the truth, or were privileged as

104

in news of court proceedings, or were fair criticism of performances by artists and others, the public had a real stake in receiving those words. Media, which pursued their own self-interest in
defending against libel awards, made their claims on the basis of
the public interest. State libel laws that honored this principle in
the Nineteenth Century remain in effect today (Chap. 5).

The First Amendment protection raised by the Supreme Court
in the 1964 *Sullivan* case told public officials they would have to
accept more fully the verbal rough-and-tumble of political life.
They would have to live by the warning metaphor that the late
President Harry Truman delivered to aspirants in politics: "If you
can't stand the heat, stay out of the kitchen!" They would succeed
in libel suits only by clearing new legal hurdles. Most notably,
they would have to show that the news medium published the
offending words with *actual malice*—knowledge of falsity, or reckless disregard for falsity.

As we have seen above (pp. 63–64), however, and as we shall
see in this and the next chapter, libel suits remain at the forefront
of media's legal encounters. Suits do not drop in number, jury
awards to plaintiffs are often astronomical and are sometimes
found by courts to reflect deep jury prejudice against media,
defense attorneys' fees may reach six or seven figures, public
hostility toward media is widespread and intense. The self-censorship and "chill" that the *Sullivan* decision was intended to avert
unquestionably has penetrated some newsrooms, diluting investigative reporting. Journalists, legal scholars, the American Civil
Liberties Union, and others have urged strengthening of the
Sullivan doctrine.[1] They are of course opposed by some who feel
that *Sullivan* has been too protective of media.[2]

[1] Anthony Lewis, The Sullivan Case, The New Yorker, Nov. 5, 1984, 52; Marc
Franklin, Good Names and Bad Law: a Critique of Libel Law and a Proposal, 18
Univ.S.F.L.Rev. 1, Fall 1983; Symposium, Defamation and the First Amendment:
New Perspectives, 25 William & Mary L.Rev. 1983–1984, Special Issue; Michael
Massing, The Libel Chill: How Cold Is It Out There?, Columbia Journ. Rev., May/
June, 1985, 31; Gilbert Cranberg, ACLU Moves to Protect All Speech on Public
Issues from Libel Suits, Civil Liberties, Feb. 1983, 2.

[2] Jan Greene, Libel Plaintiffs Organize Against Media, 1985 Report of Society of
Professional Journalists, Sigma Delta Chi, Freedom of Information '84–'85, 4;
Bruce E. Fein, New York Times v. Sullivan: an Obstacle to Enlightened Public
Discourse * * *, quoted in 11 Med.L.Rptr. # 3, 12/18/84, News Notes.

SEC. 20. DEFENSE AGAINST PUBLIC OFFICIALS' SUITS

Under the doctrine of New York Times Co. v. Sullivan, the First Amendment broadly protects the news media from judgments for defamation of public officials.

The Supreme Court of the United States handed down a decision in 1964 that added a great new dimension of protection to news media in the field of libel. It said that news media are not liable for defamatory words about the public acts of public officials unless the words are published with malice. It defined the word "malice" with a rigor and preciseness that had been lacking for centuries and in a way that gave broad protection to publication. Public officials, it said, must live with the risks of a political system in which there is "a profound national commitment to the principle that debate on public issues should be uninhibited, robust, and wide-open * * *." Even the factual error, it said, will not make one liable for libel in words about the public acts of public officials unless malice is present.

The case was New York Times Co. v. Sullivan.[3] It stemmed from an "editorial advertisement" in the Times, written and paid for by a group intensely involved in the struggle for equality and civil liberties for the American Negro. Suit was brought by L. B. Sullivan, Commissioner of Public Affairs for the city of Montgomery, Ala., against the Times and four Negro clergymen who were among the 64 persons whose names were attached to the advertisement.

The since-famous advertisement, titled "Heed Their Rising Voices," recounted the efforts of southern Negro students to affirm their rights at Alabama State College in Montgomery and told of a "wave of terror" that met them. It spoke of violence against the Reverend Martin Luther King, Jr. in his leadership of the civil rights movement:[4]

Heed Their Rising Voices

As the whole world knows by now, thousands of Southern Negro students are engaged in wide-spread, nonviolent demonstrations in positive affirmation of the right to live in human dignity as guaranteed by the U.S. Constitution and the Bill of Rights. In their effort to uphold these guarantees, they are being met by an unprecedented wave of terror by those who would deny and

---

[3] 376 U.S. 254, 84 S.Ct. 710 (1964).

[4] Ibid., facing 292.

negate that document which the whole world looks upon
as setting the pattern for modern freedom ＊ ＊ ＊.

＊ ＊ ＊

In Montgomery, Alabama, after students sang "My
Country, 'Tis of Thee" on the State Capitol steps, their
leaders were expelled from school, and truck-loads of
police armed with shotguns and tear-gas ringed the Alabama State College Campus. When the entire student
body protested to state authorities by refusing to re-
register, their dining hall was padlocked in an attempt to
starve them into submission.

＊ ＊ ＊

Again and again the Southern violators have answered Dr. King's protests with intimidation and violence.
They have bombed his home almost killing his wife and
child. They have assaulted his person. They have arrested him seven times—for "speeding," "loitering" and similar "offenses." And now they have charged him with
"perjury"—a *felony* under which they could imprison him
for *ten years*. Obviously, their real purpose is to remove
him physically as the leader to whom the students and
millions of others—look for guidance and support, and
thereby to intimidate *all* leaders who may rise in the
South ＊ ＊ ＊. The defense of Martin Luther King, spiritual leader of the student sit-in movement, clearly, therefore, is an integral part of the total struggle for freedom
in the South.

Sullivan was not named in the advertisement, but claimed
that because he was Commissioner who had supervision of the
Montgomery police department, people would identify him as the
person responsible for police action at the State College campus.
He said also that actions against the Rev. King would be attributed to him by association. Libel law, of course, does not require
that identification be by name.

It was asserted by Sullivan, and not disputed, that there were
errors in the advertisement. Police had not "ringed" the campus
although they had been there in large numbers. Students sang
the National Anthem, not "My Country, 'Tis of Thee." The
expulsion had not been protested by the entire student body, but
by a large part of it. They had not refused to register, but had
boycotted classes for a day. The campus dining hall was not
padlocked. The manager of the Times Advertising Acceptability
Department said that he had not checked the copy for accuracy
because he had no cause to believe it false, and some of the signers
were well-known persons whose reputation he had no reason to
question.

The trial jury ruled that Sullivan had been libeled and awarded him $500,000, the full amount of his claim. The Supreme Court of Alabama upheld the finding and judgment. But the Supreme Court of the United States reversed the decision, holding that the Alabama rule of law was "constitutionally deficient for failure to provide the safeguards for freedom of speech and of the press that are required by the First and Fourteenth Amendments * * *."

The Court said there was no merit to the claim of Sullivan that a paid, commercial advertisement does not ever deserve constitutional protection. Of this advertisement is said:[5]

> It communicated information, expressed opinion, recited grievances, protested claimed abuses, and sought financial support on behalf of a movement whose existence and objectives are matters of the highest public concern * * *. That the Times was paid for publishing the advertisement is as immaterial in this connection as is the fact that newspapers and books are sold * * *. Any other conclusion would discourage newspapers from carrying "editorial advertisements" of this type, and so might shut off an important outlet for the promulgation of information and ideas by persons who do not themselves have access to publishing facilities—who wish to exercise their freedom of speech even though they are not members of the press. The effect would be to shackle the First Amendment * * *.

The Court said that the question about the advertisement was whether it forfeited constitutional protection "by the falsity of some of its factual statements and by its alleged defamation of respondent".

The Court rejected the position that the falsity of some of the factual statements in the advertisement destroyed constitutional protection for the Times and the clergymen. "[E]rroneous statement is inevitable in free debate, and * * * it must be protected if the freedoms of expression are to have the 'breathing space' that they 'need to survive,' * * *" it ruled. Quoting the decision in Sweeney v. Patterson,[6] it added that " 'Cases which impose liability for erroneous reports of the political conduct of officials reflect the obsolete doctrine that the governed must not criticize their governors * * *. Whatever is added to the field of libel is taken from the field of free debate.' "

Elaborating the matter of truth and error, it said that it is not enough for a state to provide in its law that the defendant may

---

[5] Ibid., 266.

[6] 76 U.S.App.D.C. 23, 128 F.2d 457, 458 (1952).

plead the truth of his words, although that has long been considered a bulwark for protection of expression:[7]

> A rule compelling the critic of official conduct to guarantee the truth of all his factual assertions—and to do so on pain of libel judgments virtually unlimited in amount—leads to a * * * "self-censorship." Allowance of the defense of truth, with the burden of proving it on the defendant, does not mean that only false speech will be deterred. Even courts accepting this defense as an adequate safeguard have recognized the difficulties of adducing legal proofs that the alleged libel was true in all its factual particulars * * *. Under such a rule, would-be critics of official conduct may be deterred from voicing their criticism, even though it is believed to be true and even though it is in fact true, because of doubt whether it can be proved in court or fear of the expense of having to do so * * *. The rule thus dampens the vigor and limits the variety of public debate.

This was the end for Alabama's rule that "the defendant has no defense as to stated facts unless he can persuade the jury that they were true in all their particulars." But the decision reached much farther than to Alabama: most states had similar rules under which public officials had successfully brought libel suits for decades. In holding that the Constitution protects even erroneous statements about public officials in their public acts, the Court was providing protection that only a minority of states had previously provided.

Having decided that the constitutional protection was not destroyed by the falsity of factual statements in the advertisement, the Court added that the protection was not lost through defamation of an official. "Criticism of their official conduct," the Court held, "does not lose its constitutional protection merely because it is effective criticism and hence diminishes their official reputations." [8]

Then Mr. Justice Brennan, who wrote the majority decision, stated the circumstances under which a public official could recover damages for false defamation: Only if malice were present in the publication:[9]

> The constitutional guarantees require, we think, a federal rule that prohibits a public official from recovering damages for a defamatory falsehood relating to his official conduct unless he proves that the statement was

---

[7] New York Times Co. v. Sullivan, 376 U.S. 254, 279, 84 S.Ct. 710, 725 (1964).
[8] Ibid., 273.
[9] Ibid., 279–280.

made with "actual malice"—that is, with knowledge that it was false or with reckless disregard of whether it was false or not.

That statement of the court not only gave the broadest protection to publications critical of public officials that had been granted by the "minority rule" states which had held similarly for almost 50 years. It also defined "malice" with a rigor and preciseness that it had seldom been given. Malice was not the vague, shifting concept of ancient convenience for judges who had been shocked or angered by words harshly critical of public officials. It was not the oft-used "evidence of ill-will" on the part of the publisher; it was not "hatred" of the publisher for the defamed; it was not "intent to harm" the defamed; it was not to be found in "attributing bad motives" to the defamed. Rather, the malice which the plaintiff would have to plead and prove lay in the publisher's knowledge that what he printed was false, or else disregard on the part of the publisher as to whether it was false or not.

The old, tort-based libel requirement that the publisher would have to prove the truth of his words disappeared in Brennan's formulation: No longer would the publisher carry the burden; instead, the plaintiff official would have to prove falsity. Further, it would not be enough for the plaintiff to prove knowing or reckless falsity by "the preponderance of evidence"; instead, he would have to prove it "with convincing clarity." Also, to learn whether the trial court had properly applied the law in this important case over how expression might be regulated, the appellate courts were to independently review the trial record itself to make sure that there had been no forbidden intrusion on free expression.[10]

As court interpretation and litigation proceeded after these drastic revisions of the libel law of centuries, New York Times Co. v. Sullivan came to be recognized as the most important First Amendment case for decades. Attorney Floyd Abrams, a true "heavyweight" among leading media attorneys of the nation, termed the decision "majestic," and "one of the most far reaching, extraordinary, and beautiful decisions in American history." [11]

---

[10] Ibid., 285. Reaffirmed 20 years later by the Supreme Court in Bose Corp. v. Consumers Union, 466 U.S. 485, 104 S.Ct. 1949 (1984), 10 Med.L.Rptr. 1625, 1636–9, this rule was held to govern all appellate courts in the determination of actual malice under *Sullivan,* rather than a lesser legal standard which provides that trial-court findings of fact are not to be set aside by appellate courts unless they are "clearly erroneous." Appeals courts have usually practiced independent review: LDRC Bulletin # 13, Spring 1985, 2.

[11] 10 Med.L.Rptr. # 17, 4/24/84, News Notes.

The United States Constitution's guarantee of freedom of speech and press—which of course rules in all states as well as in federal courts [12]—thus protects all that is said about a public official in his public conduct except the malicious. But did "public official" mean every person who is employed by government at any level? Justice Brennan foresaw that this question would arise, but said in a footnote in the *Sullivan* case: "It is enough for the present case that respondent's position as an elected city commissioner clearly made him a public official * * *." [13]

In 1966, Rosenblatt v. Baer helped the definition. Newspaper columnist Alfred D. Rosenblatt wrote in the *Laconia Evening Citizen* that a public ski area which in previous years had been a financially shaky operation, now was doing "hundreds of percent" better. He asked, "What happened to all the money last year? And every other year?" Baer, who had been dismissed from his county post as ski area supervisor the year before, brought a suit charging that the column libeled him. The New Hampshire court upheld his complaint and awarded him $31,500. But when the case reached the United States Supreme Court, it reversed and remanded the case. It said that Baer did indeed come within the "public official" category:[14]

> Criticism of government is at the very center of the constitutionally protected area of free discussion. Criticism of those responsible for government operations must be free, lest criticism of government be penalized. It is clear, therefore, that the "public official" designation applies at the very least to those among the hierarchy of government employees who have, or appear to the public to have, substantial responsibility for or control over the conduct of governmental affairs.

The Court also said that the *Sullivan* rule may apply to a person who has left public office, as Baer had, where public interest in the matter at issue is still substantial.

Meanwhile, cases that did not reach the United States Supreme Court were working their way through state courts. During 1964, the Pennsylvania court applied the rule to a senator who was candidate for re-election.[15] Shortly, state legislators were included,[16] a former mayor,[17] a deputy sheriff,[18] a school board

[12] Dodd v. Pearson, 277 F.Supp. 469 (D.D.C.1967); Beckley Newspapers Corp. v. Hanks, 389 U.S. 81, 88 S.Ct. 197 (1967).

[13] New York Times Co. v. Sullivan, 376 U.S. 254, 84 S.Ct. 710, fn. 23 (1964).

[14] Rosenblatt v. Baer, 383 U.S. 75, 86 S.Ct. 669 (1966).

[15] Clark v. Allen, 415 Pa. 484, 204 A.2d 42 (1964).

[16] Washington Post Co. v. Keogh, 125 U.S.App.D.C. 32, 365 F.2d 965 (1966); Rose v. Koch and Christian Research, Inc., 278 Minn. 235, 154 N.W.2d 409 (1967).

member,[19] an appointed city tax assessor,[20] and a police sergeant.[21] A state legislative clerk was ruled a public official, in his suit against a former state senator who accused the clerk of wiretapping when he was actually doing his clerk's duty in trying to identify a telephone caller of obscenities.[22]

In some cases, it has been held that one retains public-official status despite lapse of time: A former federal narcotics agent was designated "public official" in his libel suit for a story about his official misconduct, despite the fact that he had left office six years earlier.[23] And since 1971, the Supreme Court's rule has been that a charge of criminal conduct against a present official, no matter how remote in time or place the conduct was, is always "relevant to his fitness for office," and that he must prove actual malice in a libel suit.[24]

Although "public official" would seem to be readily identifiable, questions remain. Courts and commentators have long taken the view that holding a government position almost automatically gives one the status of public official. But in a case of 1979, Hutchinson v. Proxmire, the Supreme Court said in a footnote that "public official" is not synonymous with "public employee"; that matter remains unsettled.[25] In a Texas case, a county surveyor who brought a libel suit against a newspaper for its criticism of his work as an engineering consultant to a municipality was ruled not to be a public official but a private person in his consultant's work.[26] And in a federal case of 1980, the Court of Appeals for the Fourth Circuit ruled that the Iroquois Research Institute, employed by the Fairfax County (Va.) Water Authority as a research consultant in a county project, was not a public official. Relying on the Rosenblatt v. Baer decision (above, p. 111), the court said that Iroquois was in the sole role of a scientific factfinder, merely

---

[17] Lundstrom v. Winnebago Newspapers, Inc., 58 Ill.App.2d 33, 206 N.E.2d 525 (1965).

[18] St. Amant v. Thompson, 390 U.S. 727, 88 S.Ct. 1323 (1968).

[19] Cabin v. Community Newspapers, Inc., 50 Misc.2d 574, 270 N.Y.S.2d 913 (1966).

[20] Eadie v. Pole, 91 N.J.Super. 504, 221 A.2d 547 (1966).

[21] Suchomel v. Suburban Life Newspapers, Inc., 84 Ill.App.2d 239, 228 N.E.2d 172 (1967).

[22] Martonik v. Durkan, 23 Wash.App. 47, 596 P.2d 1054 (1979), 5 Med.L.Rptr. 1266.

[23] Hart v. Playboy Enterprises, (D.C.Kan.) 5 Med.L.Rptr. 1811 (1979).

[24] Monitor Patriot Co. v. Roy, 401 U.S. 265, 91 S.Ct. 621 (1971).

[25] 443 U.S. 111, 99 S.Ct. 2675 (1979), footnote # 8. See David A. Elder, "The Supreme Court and Defamation: a Relaxation of Constitutional Standards," Kentucky Bench and Bar, Jan. 1980, pp. 38–39.

[26] Laredo Newspapers v. Foster, 541 S.W.2d 809 (Tex.1976), certiorari denied 429 U.S. 1123, 97 S.Ct. 1160.

reporting the facts it found to the Water Authority. It had no control over the conduct of government affairs, made no recommendations, was little known to the public, and exercised no discretion.[27] It was private.

Nine major media organizations unsuccessfully urged the United States Supreme Court to review the appeals court decision for Iroquois, asserting that the case "presents perhaps the most significant unresolved issue in the constitutional law of defamation * * *." They said that the appeals court decision might lead "elected officials [to] avoid public scrutiny or chill criticism simply by delegating their public responsibilities to contractors and consultants." [28] The Supreme Court denied review and the case went back to trial court with Iroquois confirmed for trial as a private agency.

SEC. 21. DEFENSE WHERE PUBLIC FIGURES AND PUBLIC ISSUES ARE CONCERNED

The doctrine of New York Times Co. v. Sullivan extends the requirement of proving actual malice to public figures, such as non-official persons who involve themselves in the resolution of public questions; but the Court has rejected requiring this proof from private persons libeled in news stories on matters of public interest.

In the *Rosenblatt* case treated above, Justice William O. Douglas of the Supreme Court wrote a separate concurring opinion. In it he raised the question of what persons and what issues might call for an extension of the *Sullivan* doctrine beyond "public officials." He said:[29]

> * * * I see no way to draw lines that exclude the night watchman, the file clerk, the typist, or, for that matter, anyone on the public payroll. And how about those who contract to carry out governmental missions? Some of them are as much in the public domain as any so-called officeholder. And how about the dollar-a-year man * * *? And the industrialists who raise the price of a basic commodity? Are not steel and aluminum in the public domain? And the labor leader who combines trade unionism with bribery and racketeering? Surely the public importance of collective bargaining puts labor as well as management into the public arena so far as the present

[27] Arctic Co. v. Loudoun Times Mirror et al., 624 F.2d 518 (4th Cir.1980), 6 Med.L. Rptr. 1433, 1435.

[28] 6 Med.L.Rptr. # 31 (Dec. 9, 1980), News Notes; John Consoli, "Consultants to Gov't. Aren't Public Figures," Editor & Publisher, Jan. 17, 1981, 9.

[29] Rosenblatt v. Baer, 383 U.S. 75, 89, 86 S.Ct. 669, 678 (1966).

constitutional issue is concerned ∗ ∗ ∗. [T]he question is whether a public *issue* not a public official, is involved.

And in 1966, the decision in a suit brought by the noted scientist and Nobel Prize winner, Dr. Linus Pauling, indeed said that not only "public officials" would have to prove malice if they were to succeed with libel suits.

Pauling sued the *St. Louis Globe-Democrat* for alleged libel in an editorial entitled "Glorification of Deceit." It referred to an appearance by Pauling before a subcommittee of the United States Senate, in connection with Pauling's attempts to promote a nuclear test ban treaty. It read in part: "Pauling contemptuously refused to testify and was cited for contempt of Congress. He appealed to the United States District Court to rid him of the contempt citation, which that Court refused to do." Bringing libel suit, Pauling said that he had not been cited for contempt, that he had not appealed to any court to rid himself of any contempt citation, and that no appeal was expected.

The federal court conceded that Pauling was not a "public official" such as the plaintiff in New York Times Co. v. Sullivan. But it added: [30]

> We feel, however, that the implications of the Supreme Court's majority opinions are clear. Professor Pauling, by his public statements and actions, was projecting himself into the arena of public controversy and into the very "vortex of the discussion of a question of pressing public concern". He was attempting to influence the resolution of an issue which was important, which was of profound effect, which was public and which was internationally controversial ∗ ∗ ∗.
>
> ∗ ∗ ∗
>
> We ∗ ∗ ∗ feel that a rational distinction cannot be founded on assumption that criticism of private citizens who seek to lead in the determination of national policy will be less important to the public interest than will criticism of government officials. A lobbyist, a person dominant in a political party, the head of any pressure group, or any significant leader may possess a capacity for influencing public policy as great or greater than that of a comparatively minor public official who is clearly subject to *New York Times*. It would seem, therefore, that if such a person seeks to realize upon his capacity to guide public policy and in the process is criticized, he should have no greater remedy than does his counterpart in public office.

[30] Pauling v. Globe-Democrat Pub. Co., 362 F.2d 188, 195–196 (8th Cir.1966).

Pauling took his case to the United States Supreme Court, but that court denied certiorari, and the lower court's decision stood.[31]

While public figure Linus Pauling was thus being embraced within the *Sullivan* rules, another man who had formerly been a general in the United States Army was undertaking a set of "chain" libel suits. This was retired Maj. Gen. Edwin A. Walker, who after a storm of controversy over his troop-indoctrination program had resigned from the Army in 1961. Opposed to the integration of the University of Mississippi, he had in 1962 appeared on the scene there when rioting took place over the enrollment of Negro James H. Meredith. An Associated Press dispatch, circulated to member newspapers around the nation, said that Walker had taken command of a violent crowd and had personally led a charge against federal marshals. Further, it described Walker as encouraging rioters to use violence.

Walker's chain libel suits totalled $23,000,000 against the *Louisville Courier-Journal* and *Louisville Times* and their radio station; against *Atlanta Newspapers Inc.* and publisher Ralph McGill; against the Associated Press, the *Denver Post,* the *Fort Worth Star-Telegram* and its publisher, Amon G. Carter, Jr.; against *Newsweek,* the Pulitzer Publishing Co. (*St. Louis Post-Dispatch*), and against the *Delta* (Miss.) *Democrat-Times* and its editor, Hodding Carter.[32]

Walker's case for recovery reached the Supreme Court of the United States through a suit against the Associated Press which he filed in Texas. He had been awarded $500,000 by the trial court. The Texas Court of Civil Appeals upheld the judgment, and stated without elaboration that the Times v. Sullivan rule was not applicable. The Supreme Court of Texas denied a writ of error,[33] and the United States Supreme Court granted certiorari.

The U.S. Supreme Court decided Associated Press v. Walker and Curtis Publishing Co. v. Butts in the same opinion.[34] Wallace Butts was former athletic director of the University of Georgia, and had brought suit against Curtis for a story in the *Saturday Evening Post* that had accused him of conspiring to "fix" a football game between Georgia and the University of Alabama. Neither Walker nor Butts was a "public official" and the late Justice John M. Harlan's opinion said explicitly that the Court took up the two cases to consider the impact of the Times v. Sullivan rule "on libel actions instituted by persons who are not public officials, but who

---

[31] Pauling v. National Review, Inc., 49 Misc.2d 975, 269 N.Y.S.2d 11 (1966).

[32] Editor & Publisher, Oct. 5, 1963, p. 10.

[33] Associated Press v. Walker, 393 S.W.2d 671 (Tex.Civ.App.1965).

[34] Curtis Pub. Co. v. Butts, 388 U.S. 130, 87 S.Ct. 1975 (1967).

are 'public figures' and involved in issues in which the public has a justified and important interest." [35]

Four opinions were delivered by the Court. All agreed that a publication about a "public figure" deserves First Amendment protection. All agreed that both men were public figures. All agreed that Walker should not recover damages against the AP, and most agreed that Butts should recover.

Walker was a "public figure," said Justice John Harlan in writing for four members of the Court, "by his purposeful activity amounting to a thrusting of his personality into the 'vortex' of an important public controversy." Agreeing, in writing for three members, Chief Justice Earl Warren said that "Under any reasoning, General Walker was a public man" in whose conduct society had a substantial interest. Warren said that giving a public figure, such as Walker, an easier burden to meet than a public official in recovering damages for libel [36]

> * * * has no basis in law, logic or First Amendment Amendment policy. Increasingly in this country, the distinction between governmental and private sectors are blurred * * *.

This blending of positions and power has * * * occurred in the case of individuals so that many who do not hold public office at the moment are nevertheless intimately involved in the resolution of important public questions, or by reason of their fame, shape events in areas of concern to society at large.

> Viewed in this context then, it is plain that although they are not subject to the restraints of the political process, "public figures" like "public officials," often play an influential role in ordering society * * *. Our citizenry has a legitimate and substantial interest in the conduct of such persons, and freedom of the press to engage in uninhibited debate about their involvement in public issues and events is as crucial as it is in the case of "public officials."

> *   *   *

> [T]he *New York Times* standard is an important safeguard for the rights of the press and public to inform and be informed on matters of legitimate interest. Evenly applied to cases involving "public men"—whether they be "public officials" or "public figures"—it will afford the

[35] Ibid., 134.

[36] Ibid., 163–165.

necessary insulation for the fundamental interests which
the first Amendment was designed to protect.

*   *   *

Under any reasoning, General Walker was a public
man in whose public conduct society and the press had a
legitimate and substantial interest.

Harlan argued that the public figure should not have to meet
as difficult a standard of proof as the public official. He articulated a lower barrier for the former: [37]

> We consider and would hold that a "public figure" who is
> not a public official may * * * recover damages for a
> defamatory falsehood whose substance makes substantial
> danger to reputation apparent, on a showing of highly
> unreasonable conduct constituting an extreme departure
> from the standards of investigation and reporting ordina-
> rily adhered to by responsible publishers.

Then he examined AP's reporting in the Walker case and found no
such departure from responsible reporting standards: The AP
story was news which required immediate dissemination, the
correspondent was competent and his dispatches were internally
consistent with a single exception.[38]

So public figure Walker lost his case because Harlan found no
"extreme departure from responsible reporting" by the Post and
Warren found no "actual malice." But public figure Butts, according to both opinions, should win his case against the *Saturday
Evening Post,* and keep the $460,000 that he had been awarded at
trial. The Post had stated that Butts had revealed his school's
football secrets to Alabama coach Paul Bryant just before a game
between the schools. The article said that one George Burnett
had accidentally been connected, in using the telephone, to the
conversation between the two in which Butts told Bryant the
secrets. According to the article, Burnett made notes of the
conversation as he listened, and the Post obtained his story.
Justice Harlan's analysis of the Post's methods of investigation—
analysis that was noted with approval in the separate opinion of
chief Justice Warren—found the Post wanting. He said, in part: [39]

> The evidence showed that the Butts story was in no
> sense "hot news" and the editors of the magazine recog-
> nized the need for a thorough investigation of the serious
> charges. Elementary precautions were, nevertheless, ig-
> nored. The Saturday Evening Post knew that Burnett

[37] Ibid., 155.

[38] Ibid., 158–9.

[39] Ibid., 157.

had been placed on probation in connection with bad check charges, but proceeded to publish the story on the basis of his affidavit without substantial independent support. Burnett's notes were not even viewed by any of the magazine personnel prior to publication. John Carmichael who was supposed to have been with Burnett when the phone call was overheard was not interviewed. No attempt was made to screen the films of the game to see if Burnett's information was accurate, and no attempt was made to find out whether Alabama had adjusted its plans after the alleged divulgence of information.

Again, there was the application of different standards by Harlan and Warren. Harlan found this kind of reporting to be "highly unreasonable conduct constituting an extreme departure from the standards of investigation and reporting ordinarily adhered to by responsible publishers." And in Chief Justice Warren's opinion, it was evidence of "reckless disregard" of whether the statement were false or not.

Justices Black and Douglas joined the three who endorsed Warren's opinion on a single matter—applying the same actual malice requirement to public figures as to public officials. Thus five justices provided a majority for this standard to prevail over Harlan's "extreme departure" standard. Further, Warren had said he could not believe that "a standard which is based on such an unusual and uncertain formulation" as Harlan's could either guide a jury or afford "the protection for speech and debate that is fundamental to our society and guaranteed by the First Amendment." [40] While Justice Harlan's attempt to place an easier burden upon public figures than public officials through his "extreme departure" standard was persuasive for a few lower courts,[41] his formulation came ultimately to be flatly rejected as a rule for public persons' libel suits.[42]

In an evolving sphere of the law, lower courts seek guidance not only in rules endorsed by a majority of the Supreme Court but also in opinions embraced by fewer than five justices. That search, apparent in lower courts' occasional use of Justice

[40] Ibid., 163.

[41] Cerrito v. Time, Inc., 302 F.Supp. 1071 (D.C.Cal.1969); Fotochrome Inc. v. New York Herald Tribune, Inc., 61 Misc.2d 226, 305 N.Y.S.2d 168 (1969); Holmes v. Curtis Pub. Co., 303 F.Supp. 522, 525 (D.C.S.C.1969); Buckley v. Vidal, 50 F.R.D. 271 (D.C.N.Y.1970); Cervantes v. Time, Inc., 330 F.Supp. 936 (D.C.Mo.1971). See esp. Chapadeau v. Utica Observer-Dispatch, 38 N.Y.2d 196, 379 N.Y.S.2d 61, 341 N.E.2d 569 (1975) for the New York courts' development of a "fault" standard in libel cases brought by private persons under Gertz v. Robert Welch, Inc., 418 U.S. 323, 94 S.Ct. 2997 (1974).

[42] Hunt v. Liberty Lobby, 720 F.2d 631 (11th Cir.1983), 10 Med.L.Rptr. 1097, 1109.

Harlan's "extreme departure" standard, was vastly more prominent in their employment and elaboration of Justice Douglas'
reasoning in Rosenblatt v. Baer, 1966.[43] Pointing out first, in his
concurring opinion, why public figures as well as public officials
should be required to prove actual malice in libel suits, Douglas
then went further and said it really didn't matter much whether
the *people* involved were public or private: The heart of the
matter was " *   *   * whether a public *issue* not a public official, is
involved." For the next eight years, courts struggled with varia-
tions on this theme before a majority of the Supreme Court ruled
in Gertz v. Robert Welch, Inc.,[44] and rejected it.

During this period 1967–1974, private persons involved in
matters of public interest (Douglas' "public issues") were often
faced with proving *New York Times* malice in their libel suits, no
matter that many were unwilling participants in public events.
Not only Douglas' reasoning supported the extension of the rule to
private persons. A 1967 decision of the U.S. Supreme Court in the
realm of privacy—Time, Inc. v. Hill—did also.[45]

Life magazine had published an article about a play based on
a book about a family held hostage in its home by convicts. The
article said that the novel was "inspired" by the true-life ordeal of
the James Hill family. Hill sued, saying the article gave the
impression that the play "mirrored the Hill family's experience"
and referred to the play as a re-enactment of the Hills' ordeal,
whereas *Life* knew this to be false. Hill won at trial, *Life*
appealed, and the Supreme Court brought the Times v. Sullivan
rule to bear against Hill. It said that a play is a matter of public
interest, and even though Hill was a private citizen, he would
have to prove that *Life* published the report with knowledge of
falsity or reckless disregard of the truth—the new actual malice of
Times v. Sullivan.[46] (The case is discussed in Chap. 6.)

Having borrowed the malice rule from libel to apply it in
privacy, the law now reversed the flow: Lower courts took the new
"matter of public interest" interpretation—the broadest possible
application of the public principle—from the Time v. Hill privacy
case and began applying it in libel. The private individual who
believed he was defamed would have to prove actual malice if the
damaging news story concerned any matter of public interest.
Now lower courts put this rule to work in libel suits brought by a
mail-order medical testing laboratory against CBS and Walter

[43] 383 U.S. 75, 86 S.Ct. 669 (1966).

[44] 418 U.S. 323, 94 S.Ct. 2997 (1974).

[45] 385 U.S. 374, 87 S.Ct. 534 (1967).

[46] Ibid., 388.

Cronkite; [47] by a man who said he had been identified incorrectly by NBC as a homosexual who had involved himself in the defense of Lee Harvey Oswald, accused assassin of Pres. John F. Kennedy; [48] by taxicab firm owners who said they were falsely charged in a newspaper with furnishing liquor to minors; [49] by a basketball player of whom a magazine said he was "destroyed" professionally by the skill of another. [50]

Then in the famous case of Rosenbloom v. Metromedia, Inc., [51] in 1971, a plurality of three justices of the U.S. Supreme Court approved extending the actual malice requirement in libel whenever the news was a "matter of public interest." It denied recovery for libel to George Rosenbloom, distributor of nudist magazines in Philadelphia, a private citizen involved in a matter of public interest. Metromedia radio station WIP had said Rosenbloom had been arrested on charges of possessing obscene literature, and linked him to the "smut literature rackets." Later acquitted of obscenity charges, Rosenbloom sued for libel in the WIP broadcasts, and won $275,000 in trial court before losing upon the station's appeal. In the U.S. Supreme Court, five justices agreed that Rosenbloom should not recover. Three of them endorsed the "matter of public interest" rationale, laid out in Justice William J. Brennan's plurality opinion: [52]

> If a matter is a subject of public or general interest, it cannot suddenly become less so merely because a private individual is involved, or because in some sense the individual did not "voluntarily" choose to become involved. The public's primary interest is in the event * * *. We honor the commitment to robust debate on public issues, which is embodied in the First Amendment, by extending constitutional protection to all discussion and communication involving matters of public or general concern, without regard to whether the persons involved are famous or anonymous.

Lower courts accepted the plurality opinion as ruling. The sweep of "matter of public or general interest" was so powerful that few libel suits, whether by public or private persons, were won. Commentators on press law forecast the disappearance of libel suits. But in mid-1974, hardly three years after *Rosenbloom,*

[47] United Medical Laboratories, Inc., v. Columbia Broadcasting System, Inc., 404 F.2d 706 (9th Cir.1968), certiorari denied 394 U.S. 921, 89 S.Ct. 1197 (1969).

[48] Davis v. National Broadcasting Co., 320 F.Supp. 1070 (D.C.La.1970).

[49] West v. Northern Pub. Co., 487 P.2d 1304 (Alaska 1971).

[50] Time, Inc. v. Johnston, 448 F.2d 378 (4th Cir.1971).

[51] 403 U.S. 29, 91 S.Ct. 1811 (1971).

[52] Ibid., at 1824.

the support of a three-justice plurality in that decision for the "matter of public interest" interpretation revealed itself as a shaky foundation. A five-man majority of the U.S. Supreme Court rejected it as a rule in Gertz v. Robert Welch, Inc.: [53] Requiring private persons libeled in stories that were "matters of public interest" to prove actual malice was not required by the Constitution. The *Rosenbloom* standard had focused on the *topic* or *subject matter* ("Was it a topic of general or public interest?")—and it would not do. The standard would have to focus instead on the plaintiff ("Is he or she a public figure? "). Several years of judicial experimenting had ended, although much remained to be settled.

SEC. 22. DEFINING "PUBLIC FIGURE"

**Distinguishing a public from a private person under *Gertz*
rests on either of two bases—fame, notoriety, power or
influence that render one a public figure for all purposes,
and the status that makes one a public figure only for a
limited range of issues. In either case, the person assumes special prominence in the resolution of public
controversy.**

Elmer Gertz, a Chicago lawyer, was retained by a family to bring a civil action against Policeman Nuccio who had shot and killed their son and had been convicted of second degree murder. *American Opinion,* a monthly publication given to the views of the John Birch Society, carried an article saying that Gertz was an architect of a "frame-up" of Nuccio, that he was part of a communist conspiracy to discredit local police, and that he was a Leninist and a "Communist-fronter." Gertz, who was none of these things, brought a libel suit, and for six years battled the shifting uncertainties of the courts' attitudes toward "public official," "public figure," and "matter of public interest" for the purposes of libel. A jury found libel *per se* and awarded Gertz $50,000 in damages, disallowed by the trial judge and also by the Seventh Circuit Court of Appeals: [54] Because the *American Opinion* story concerned a matter of public interest, Gertz would have to show actual malice on its part, even though he might be a private citizen. Objecting, Gertz appealed to the U.S. Supreme Court.

[53] 418 U.S. 323, 94 S.Ct. 2997 (1974). For the position that the "public interest" criterion sould be the rule, see Anthony Lewis, New York Times v. Sullivan Reconsidered * * *, 83 Columbia L.Rev. 603 (1983).

[54] Gertz v. Robert Welch, Inc., 471 F.2d 801 (7th Cir.1972). A dozen years after Gertz brought his first action, a federal jury awarded him $400,000 upon re-trial, and the Seventh Circuit Court of Appeals upheld the award: Gertz v. Welch, 680 F.2d 527 (7th Cir.1982), 8 Med.L.Rptr. 1769.

Private Individuals Exempted From Actual Malice Rule

With four other justices agreeing, Justice Powell wrote for the majority.[55] The plurality opinion in Rosenbloom v. Metromedia, relied on by the Circuit Court, should not stand. Justice Powell had no quarrel with requiring public officials and public figures to prove actual malice in their libel suits. But he reasoned that the legitimate state interest in compensating injury to the reputation of private individuals—of whom, it was found, Gertz was one—requires that such persons be held to less demanding proof of fault by the offending news medium—only "negligence," rather than the stern actual malice. (See Chap. 5 for this new standard.) They are at a disadvantage, compared with public officials and public figures, where they are defamed: [56]

Public officials and public figures usually enjoy significantly greater access to the channels of effective communication and hence have a more realistic opportunity to counteract false statements than private individuals normally enjoy. Private individuals are therefore more vulnerable to injury, and the state interest in protecting them is correspondingly greater.

More important than the likelihood that private individuals will lack effective opportunities for rebuttal, there is a compelling normative consideration underlying the distinction between public and private defamation plaintiffs. An individual who decides to seek governmental office must accept certain necessary consequences of that involvement in public affairs. He runs the risk of closer public scrutiny than might otherwise be the case.

* * *

Those classed as public figures stand in a similar position. Hypothetically, it may be possible for someone to become a public figure through no purposeful action of his own, but the instances of truly involuntary public figures must be exceedingly rare. For the most part those who attain this status have assumed roles of special prominence in the affairs of society.

* * * the communications media are entitled to act on the assumption that public officials and public figures have voluntarily exposed themselves to increased risk of injury from defamatory falsehoods concerning them. No such assumption is justified with respect to a private individual. He has not accepted public office nor assumed an "influential role in ordering society." * * *

[55] Gertz v. Robert Welch, Inc., 418 U.S. 323, 94 S.Ct. 2997 (1974).
[56] Ibid., 3009–10.

He has relinquished no part of his interest in the protection of his own good name, and consequently he has a more compelling call on the courts for redress of injury inflicted by defamatory falsehood.

The various new rules that were to change the face of libel law for private plaintiffs as much as Times v. Sullivan had changed it for public persons will be taken up in Chapter 5. Here our concern is with defining "public figures" and elaborating further constitutional requirements under Times v. Sullivan for libel suits of those found to be "public."

Dissenting Justices Douglas and Brennan wanted to affirm the Court of Appeals finding that anyone—including Gertz—would have to prove actual malice in offending words from a story of general or public interest. Brennan felt that the *Gertz* decision damaged the protection which mass media ought to have under the First Amendment. Douglas repeated his view that the First Amendment would bar Congress from passing any libel law; and like Congress, "States are without power 'to use a civil libel law or any other law to impose damages for merely discussing public affairs'." [57]

Brennan, who had written the plurality opinion in *Rosenbloom,* reiterated his point there: "Matters of public or general interest do not 'suddenly become less so merely because a private individual is involved, or because in some sense the individual did not "voluntarily" choose to become involved'." [58] He found unconvincing the majority's reasoning that the private individual deserves a more lenient rule in libel than the public official or public figure. As to their comparative ability to respond through the media to defamation, he said it is unproved and highly improbable that the public figure will have better access to the media. The ability of all to get access will depend on the "same complex factor * * *: the unpredictable event of the media's continuing interest in the story." As to the assumption that private people deserve special treatment because they do not assume the risk of defamation by freely entering the public arena, he relied on Time, Inc. v. Hill which had developed the reasoning that " * * * voluntarily or not, we are all 'public' men to some degree." [59]

Gertz Is Not a "Public" Person

Returning, now, to Gertz and the finding that he was a private individual rather than a public person: The Supreme

[57] Ibid., 3015.

[58] Ibid., 3018.

[59] Ibid., 3019.

Court majority first brushed off the notion that he might be considered a public *official.*

He'd never had a remunerative government position, and his only "office" had been as a member of mayor's housing committees years before. As for the suggestion that he was a "de facto public official" because he had appeared at the coroner's inquest into the murder (incidental to his representing the family in civil litigation): If that made him a "public official," the court said, all lawyers would become such in their status as "officers of the court," and that would distort the plain meaning of the "public official" category beyond all recognition.[60]

But the thorny possibility that Gertz was a public *figure* remained. Because lower courts have so frequently drawn on the Supreme Court's treatment of the matter in *Gertz,* detail is called for here.

To start with, the court said, persons in either of two cases "assume special prominence in the resolution of public questions."[61] In either case, "they invite attention and comment."

> [Public figure] designation may rest on either of two alternative bases. In some instances an individual may achieve such pervasive fame or notoriety that he becomes a public figure for all purposes and contexts. More commonly, an individual voluntarily injects himself or is drawn into a particular public controversy and thereby becomes a public figure for a limited range of issues. In either case such persons assume special prominence in the resolution of public questions.

1. The first of the two—deemed a public figure for all purposes and in all contexts: One should not be deemed a public personality for all aspects of his life, "absent clear evidence of general fame or notoriety in the community and pervasive involvement in the affairs of society."

Gertz was not a public figure under this first rubric. He had, indeed, been active in community and professional affairs, serving as an officer of local civil groups and various legal agencies. He had published several works on law. Thus he was well-known in some circles. But he had "achieved no general fame or notoriety in the community." No member of the jury panel, for example, had ever heard of him.

2. The second of the two—where "an individual voluntarily injects himself * * * into a particular public controversy and

---

[60] Ibid., 3012.

[61] Ibid., 3013. Succeeding definitions and procedure in determining "public figure" are taken from *Gertz,* pp. 3009 and 3013.

thereby becomes a public figure for a limited range of issues."
Alternative wording used by the court was that "commonly, those
classed as public figures have thrust themselves to the forefront of
particular public controversies in order to influence the resolution
of the issues involved." [62]

In determining the status of this person who has no general
fame or notoriety in the community, the court said the procedure
should be one of "looking to the nature and extent of an individual's participation in the particular controversy giving rise to the
defamation." In this statement, the Court was rejecting the trend
under *Rosenbloom* to examine the *topic* of the news to determine
whether the public principle held, and instead to examine the
individual and his role in public life. Doing this for Attorney
Gertz, the court found again that he was not a public figure: He
had played only a minimal role at the coroner's inquest, and only
as the representative of a private client; he had had no part in the
criminal prosecution of Officer Nuccio; he had never discussed the
case with the press; and he "did not thrust himself into the vortex
of this public issue * * *" nor "engage the public's attention in
an attempt to influence its outcome." Gertz was not, by this
second basis, a public figure, and he would not, consequently, have
to prove that *American Opinion* libeled him with actual malice.
The Supreme Court ordered a new trial.

The modification of *Sullivan* and *Rosenbloom* by *Gertz* was a
damaging retreat in protection, in the eyes of media commentators. Justice White, vigorously dissenting in *Gertz,* predicted that
the decision would be popular with media, but only opposition was
to be found in professional journalism publications.[63] Even in the
years of maximum protection, when lower courts—on their own at
first and later under the *Rosenbloom* plurality—were requiring
private persons to prove actual malice in their libel suits, it was
not clear that there was any reduction in the number of suits
brought (although the number of judgments won on appeal had
dropped sharply). Now, journalists suspected that although there
were gains for the media under *Gertz*—in requiring plaintiffs to
show fault and in limiting the reach of punitive damages—it was
on the whole a great door-opener for libel suits by private plaintiffs who no longer had to prove actual malice.

---

[62] As a variant of the "limited range of issues" public figure, the Court identified
the person who has not *voluntarily* entered a public controversy, but is *drawn* into
it. Subsequent decisions have heavily vitiated this concept. See M.L. Rosen,
"Media Lament: the Rise and Fall of Involuntary Public Figures," 54 St. John's
L.Rev. 487, Spring 1980.

[63] Press Censorship Newsletter No. V, Aug.-Sept. 1974, p. 6. D. Charles Whitney,
"Libel * * *," Quill, Aug. 1974, pp. 22–25.

David A. Anderson, legal scholar and former journalist, argues that even under the protection of the *Rosenbloom* interpretation, the self-censorship by the press which *Sullivan* had sought to minimize in establishing the malice rule and other safeguards, was real.[64] Not exclusively, but particularly, he finds, the unconventional, non-established media, sometimes known as the "alternative" press, and the world of magazines, are forced to self-censorship under *Gertz*. The people about whom the alternative press writes are frequently from spheres of life not much handled by the established newspaper media, and thus not established as "public figures." Often financially marginal, the unconventional media face a further problem in the high cost of legal defense. Anderson's worry over self-censorship, whether under *Gertz* or under Draconian jury awards even where the greater protection of *Sullivan* applies, runs strongly through the world of the media.[65]

Courts Determine the "Public" and the "Private" under *Gertz*

Whatever the level of press self-censorship under *Gertz* may be, subsequent cases show that media need to be discriminating. Sometimes, distinguishing the "public" from the "private" is not easy, even for the judge, who makes the decision before the case goes to the jury. One judge has said that the two concepts are "nebulous," and "Defining public figures is much like trying to nail a jellyfish to the wall."[66] Nevertheless, many findings seem straightforward in the facts and in the decisions.

The first of the two *Gertz* categories of public figures is those who "occupy positions of such persuasive power and influence they are deemed public figures for all purposes." This was the case with Myron Steere, attorney for Nellie Schoonover in her trial and conviction for first degree murder. Some time after the trial, an Associated Press story said that the Kansas State Board of Law Examiners had recommended to the Kansas Supreme Court that it publicly censure Steere for his conduct of the defense. The examiners found, among other things, that Steere had entered into a "contingency agreement" with Mrs. Schoonover, providing that he would get all but $10,000 of her late husband's estate if she was acquitted. Steere sued broadcasters and newspapers for libel, charging inaccuracies in the stories.[67] The trial court held

---

[64] David A. Anderson, Libel and Press Self-Censorship, 53 Tex.L.Rev. 422 (1975).

[65] 10 Med.L.Rptr. # 13, 3/27/84, News Notes; 10 Med.L.Rptr. # 34, 8/21/84, News Notes.

[66] Rosanova v. Playboy Enterprises, Inc., 411 F.Supp. 440, 443 (S.D.Ga.1976).

[67] Steere v. Cupp, 226 Kan. 556, 602 P.2d 1267 (1979), 5 Med.L.Rptr. 2046. And see Sprouse v. Clay Communication, 158 W.Va. 427, 211 S.E.2d 674 (1975), 1 Med.L. Rptr. 1695, 1704.

that he would have to prove actual malice, for he was a public figure for all purposes, and the Kansas Supreme Court agreed, finding that "appellant was a public figure for all purposes by virtue of his general fame and notoriety in the community." Then it described the reach and breadth of Steere's involvement in the life of the community: [68]

> Myron Steere has been practicing law for 32 years in Franklin County. For 8 of those years he was the county attorney. He was well known in the community for the publicity he received in that capacity. After Steere ended his service as county attorney, he served as special counsel for the board of county commissioners in a controversial dispute over the construction of a new courthouse. During plaintiff's 32 years in Franklin County, he was a prominent participant in numerous social activities and served as an officer and representative for many professional, fraternal and social activities. He was well known to the public prior to his defense of Nellie Schoonover. * * * He has achieved a position of some influence in local affairs capped by his representation of Nellie Schoonover in her well publicized, famous murder trial. We find the totality of his experience in Franklin County gave Myron Steere the requisite fame and notoriety in his community to be declared a public figure for all purposes.

Not only a *person* may be a "public figure." In Ithaca College v. Yale Daily News, the facts started with the publication of "The Insider's Guide to the Colleges 1978–79," 404 pages of material compiled and edited by the *Yale Daily News*. Through stringers, the editors obtained information on many colleges, and published of Ithaca College such statements as "Sex, drugs, and booze are the staples of life." Ithaca College sued for libel, charging falsity and damage to its business and academic reputation. While Ithaca terms itself a "private" college, the New York Supreme Court said it could not be such in a libel suit.[69] The college assumes a role as a qualified educator of many students, serves the public good, is responsible for fair dealing with its students, the court ruled. It is recognized to be of "general fame or notoriety in the community [with] pervasive involvement in the affairs of society." The court decided that the college was a "public figure for all purposes."

Far more common than the person of general fame or notoriety who is a public figure for all purposes is the individual who is

[68] Ibid., 573–74, 1273–74, 2050–51. Note, General Public Figures Since Gertz v. Welch, 58 St. John's L.Rev. 355 (Winter 1984).

[69] (N.Y.Sup.Ct. 11/3 1980) 6 Med.L.Rptr. 2180.

such for a "limited range of issues." Thus Dr. Frederick Exner for two decades and more had been "injecting" and "thrusting" himself into the fluoridation-of-water controversy through speeches, litigation, books, and articles. When he brought a libel suit for a magazine's criticism of his position, he was adjudged a public figure for "the limited issue of fluoridation" by having assumed leadership and by having attempted to influence the outcome of the issue. He had taken the role of "attempting to order society" in its concern with fluoridation.[70]

Harry Buchanan and his firm were retained to perform accounting services for the Finance Committee to Re-elect the President in 1971. Common Cause brought suit in 1972 to force the Committee to report transactions, and Buchanan's deposition was taken in the matter. In reporting the suit, Associated Press compared matters involving Buchanan with the handling of money by convicted Watergate conspirator Bernard L. Barker. Buchanan sued AP for libel, and on the question whether he was a public figure, the court said "yes." There was intense interest in campaign finances at the time Buchanan was working for the Committee. The system he helped set up for the Committee and the cash transactions in which he took part, were legitimate matters of public scrutiny and concern. Buchanan was a key person for attempts to investigate. He was an agent of the committee who voluntarily accepted his role, and as such a public figure.[71]

A businessman-president of a state bailbond underwriters' association attacked a Pennsylvania state commission's report on bailbond abuses and attempted to have the commission dissolved; he had injected himself into controversy and was a public figure.[72] The United States Labor Party is a public political organization actively engaged in publishing articles, magazines, and books, and is a public figure "at least in regard to those areas of public controversy *   *   * in which [it has] participated.[73] The Church of Scientology seeks to play an influential role in ordering society, has thrust itself onto the public scene, and is a public figure.[74] So is a Roman Catholic priest who has actively involved himself in

[70] Exner v. American Medical Ass'n, 12 Wash.App. 215, 529 P.2d 863 (1974).

[71] Buchanan v. Associated Press, 398 F.Supp. 1196 (D.D.C.1975).

[72] Childs v. Sharon Herald, (Pa.Ct.Com.Pls.1979) 5 Med.L.Rptr. 1597.

[73] U.S. Labor Party v. Anti-Defamation League, (N.Y.Sup.Ct.1980) 6 Med.L.Rptr. 2209.

[74] Church of Scientology v. Siegelman, 475 F.Supp. 950 (D.C.S.D.N.Y.1979), 5 Med.L.Rptr. 2021.

the debate over the independence of Northern Ireland, through radio, television, and speeches.[75]

If the above persons and organizations strike one as plainly appropriate public figures, where does the problem arise? What of the above-quoted comment by a judge: "Defining public figures is much like trying to nail a jellyfish to the wall."? The fact is that there have been hard cases—occasionally notorious, and often deeply disturbing to media people who express dismay at courts' finding certain individuals to be private even though in the public eye. Two circumstances illustrate problems:

First: Not rarely, citizens who become involved in any of myriad proceedings of government turn out to be "private" under new rules, whereas journalists' long-standing presumption has been that government proceedings are public and almost inevitably make public figures out of participants. Alas for the presumption.

We may start with the most spectacular, notorious case in the line of separating "private" from "public" persons since *Gertz*. Mary Alice Firestone—wife of a prominent member of the wealthy industrial family and member of the "society" elite of Palm Beach, Fla. (the "sporting set," as U.S. Supreme Court Justice Marshall called it)—went to court to seek separate maintenance from her husband, Russell. He counterclaimed for divorce on grounds of adultery and extreme cruelty. The trial covered 17 months, both parties charging extramarital escapades ("that would curl Dr. Freud's hair," the trial judge said). Several times during the 17 months, Mrs. Firestone held press conferences. She subscribed to a clipping service. *Time* magazine reported the trial's outcome: Russell Firestone was granted a divorce on grounds of extreme cruelty and adultery, *Time* said. But the trial judge had not, technically, found adultery, and Mrs. Firestone sued *Time* for libel.[76] A jury awarded her $100,000 and *Time* appealed, arguing that Mrs. Firestone was a public figure and as such would have to prove actual malice in *Time's* story.

Justice Rehnquist, writing for the majority of five of the U.S. Supreme Court, said "no" to *Time's* appeal. He quoted various passages from the *Gertz* definition of "public figure" which he said did not fit Mrs. Firestone: "special prominence in the resolution of public questions," "persuasive power and influence," "thrust themselves to the forefront of particular public controversies in

[75] McManus v. Doubleday & Co., Inc., 513 F.Supp. 1383 (S.D.N.Y.1981), 7 Med.L. Rptr. 1475.

[76] Time, Inc. v. Firestone, 424 U.S. 448, 96 S.Ct. 958 (1976).

order to influence the resolution of the issues involved." The crux of the matter was that, for all the publicity involved: [77]

> Dissolution of marriage through judicial proceedings is not the sort of "public controversy" referred to in *Gertz,* even though the marital difficulties of extremely wealthy individuals may be of interest to some portion of the reading public.

In spite of her position in the "Palm Beach 400," her press conferences, and her clipping service, Mrs. Firestone was a "private" individual, and her "private" marital affairs did not "become public for the purposes of libel law solely because they are aired in a public forum."

Predictably, news media were outraged at the designation of Mrs. Firestone as "private." Accustomed to thinking of official proceedings including divorce trials as public matters which could be reported without fear of injuring the privacy of the participants, journalists had to make a conscious effort to think of Mrs. Firestone as in some sense private. Their effort was made more difficult in that her position in society had for years before the divorce placed her among the "newsworthy," and in the public eye. And with her use of clipping services and press conferences during the drawn-out divorce trial, her "public" character had seemed confirmed. What might the decision mean for future cases?

Three years after *Firestone,* the Supreme Court took up another case whose background was also a public court proceeding. And again, the fact that a libel plaintiff's suit arose from his involvement in an official public matter did not destroy private status for his libel suit. Ilya Wolston had been summoned in 1958 to appear before a grand jury that was investigating espionage, but failed to appear. Later, he pleaded guilty to a charge of criminal contempt for failing to respond to the summons and accepted conviction. Sixteen years later, *Reader's Digest* published a book by John Barron on Soviet espionage in the U.S. The book said that the FBI had identified Wolston as a Soviet intelligence agent. Wolston sued for libel. He asserted that he had been out of the lime-light for many years, and that if he had been a public figure during the investigations, he now deserved to be considered private. The lower courts disagreed, saying the long lapse of time was immaterial, that Soviet espionage of 1958 continued to be a subject of importance, and that Wolston thus remained a public figure. He appealed to the Supreme Court, which by a vote of 8–1 reversed the lower courts and determined that Wolston was a private person who would not have to prove

[77] Ibid., 965.

actual malice in his libel suit against the *Reader's Digest.*   Justice
Rehnquist wrote: [78]

> We do not agree with respondents and the lower
> courts that petitioner can be classed as such a limited-
> purpose public figure.   First, the undisputed facts do not
> justify the conclusion of the District Court and the Court
> of Appeals that petitioner "voluntarily thrust" or "inject-
> ed" himself into the forefront of the public controversy
> surrounding the investigation of Soviet espionage.
> *   *   * It would be more accurate to say that petitioner
> was dragged unwillingly into the controversy.   The gov-
> ernment pursued him in its investigation.   Petitioner did
> fail to respond to a grand jury subpoena, and this failure,
> as well as his subsequent citation for contempt, did at-
> tract media attention.   But the mere fact that petitioner
> voluntarily chose not to appear before the grand jury,
> knowing that his action might be attended by publicity, is
> not decisive on the question of public figure status.   In
> Gertz, we *   *   * emphasized that a court must focus on
> the "nature and extent of an individual's participation in
> the particular controversy giving rise to the defamation."
> *   *   * [Wolston] never discussed this matter with the
> press and limited his involvement to that necessary to
> defend himself on the contempt charge.   It is clear that
> petitioner played only a minor role in whatever public
> controversy there may have been concerning the investi-
> gation of Soviet espionage.   We decline to hold that his
> mere citation for contempt rendered him a public figure
> for purposes of comment on the investigation of Soviet
> espionage.
>
> Petitioner's failure to appear before the grand jury
> and his citation for contempt were no doubt "news-
> worthy," but the simple fact that these events attracted
> media attention is also not conclusive of the public figure
> issue.   A private individual is not automatically trans-
> formed into a public figure just by becoming involved in
> or associated with a matter that attracts public attention
> *   *   *.   A libel defendant must show more than mere
> newsworthiness to justify application of the demanding
> burden of *New York Times.*   *   *   *
>
> Nor do we think that petitioner engaged the atten-
> tion of the public in an attempt to influence the resolu-
> tion of the issues involved *   *   *.   His failure to respond
> to the grand jury's subpoena was in no way calculated to

[78] Wolston v. Reader's Digest Ass'n, 443 U.S. 157, 99 S.Ct. 2701 (1979).

draw attention to himself in order to invite public comment or influence the public with respect to any issue * * *. [P]etitioner's failure to appear before the grand jury appears simply to have been the result of his poor health * * *. In short, we find no basis whatever for concluding that petitioner relinquished, to any degree, his interest in the protection of his own name.

This reasoning leads us to reject the further contention of respondents that any person who engages in criminal conduct automatically becomes a public figure for purposes of comment on a limited range of issues related to his conviction.

Rehnquist's last paragraph quoted above is a particularly sobering note for media accustomed to consider criminal trials to be intensely "public" affairs, and participants in them more inescapably "public" than, say, Mrs. Firestone in her civil marital action. And, indeed, within two months after the *Wolston* decision, the federal district court for the Western District of Virginia held that the defendant in a murder trial was a private person, not a public figure, for purposes of her libel case. She had not "assumed a role of special prominence as a result of the [murder] charge," and she "did not inject herself into the homicide trial to attract attention or influence a public controversy," but rather was dragged unwillingly into the controversy.[79] The district court relied extensively on the *Wolston* decision, and the Rehnquist paragraphs pointed out above.

On the date of the *Wolston* decision, another Supreme Court ruling on the definition of public figure was handed down, and again the decision cast the public figure into a narrower light than a host of journalists felt warranted. This time, the Court said that researcher Ronald Hutchinson, who had received some $500,000 in federal government grants for his experiments, including some on monkeys' response to aggravating stimuli, was a private figure.[80] He would not have to prove actual malice in his libel suit against Sen. William Proxmire of Wisconsin, who had labeled Hutchinson's work "monkey business" and had given a "Golden Fleece of the Month Award" to government funding agencies which he ridiculed for wasting public money on grants to Hutchinson. A Proxmire press release, a newsletter, and a television appearance were involved, all following Proxmire's announcement of the Award on the senate floor.

[79] Mills v. Kingsport Times-News, 475 F.Supp. 1005 (D.C.W.D.Va.1979), 5 Med.L. Rptr. 2288.

[80] Hutchinson v. Proxmire, 443 U.S. 111, 99 S.Ct. 2675 (1979).

Concerned about the narrowing of the definition of "public figure," media attorney James C. Goodale had reasoned in advance of the decision that the lower courts' holding that Hutchinson was, indeed, a public figure deserved to be upheld in the Supreme Court. "Clearly information about how our government grants money and who gets it," he said, "should be the subject of unlimited comment by anyone—especially by a U.S. Senator." [81]

The Supreme Court, however, did not see it that way. It reversed the lower courts, saying that their conclusion that Hutchinson was a public figure was erroneously based upon two factors: one, his success in getting federal grants and newspaper reports about the grants, and two, his access to media as represented by news stories that reported his response to the Golden Fleece Award. But: [82]

> Neither of those factors demonstrates that Hutchinson was a public figure prior to the controversy engendered by the Golden Fleece Award; his access, such as it was, came after the alleged libel.
>
> * * * Hutchinson's activities and public profile are much like those of countless members of his profession. His published writings reach a relatively small category of professionals concerned with research in human behavior. To the extent the subject of his published writings became a matter of controversy it was a consequence of the Golden Fleece Award. Clearly those charged with defamation cannot, by their own conduct, create their own defense by making the claimant a public figure.
>
> * * *
>
> Hutchinson did not thrust himself or his views into public controversy to influence others. Respondents have not identified such a particular controversy; at most, they point to concern about general public expenditures. But that concern is shared by most and relates to most public expenditures; it is not sufficient to make Hutchinson a public figure. If it were, everyone who received or benefited from the myriad public grants for research could be classified as a public figure.

"Subject-matter classifications"—such as general public expenditures—had been rejected in *Gertz* as the touchstone for deciding

---

[81] "Court Again to Consider Who Is A Public Figure," National Law Journal, Feb. 8, 1979, 23.

[82] Hutchinson v. Proxmire, 443 U.S. 111, 134–5; 99 S.Ct. 2675, 2688 (1979). Proxmire was reported to have settled the suit out of court for $10,000, and the Senate was reported to have assumed his trial costs of more than $100,000. D.S. Greenberg, "Press Was a Co-Villain in Proxmire's Golden Gimmick," Chicago Tribune, April 17, 1980.

who would have to prove actual malice, the Court said: instead, the person and his activities must be the basis. And, finally, the Court said it could not agree that Hutchinson had such access to the media that he should be classified as a public figure; his access was limited to responding to the announcement of the Golden Fleece Award.

Second: Other circumstances complicate the defining of public figures. Justice Powell's definition in *Gertz* and various courts' since (as in *Firestone, Wolston,* and *Hutchinson*), make it crucial to decide whether the person has voluntarily injected himself into a matter of public controversy to help resolve that controversy. Yet it is plain that there are many public figures besides those who voluntarily seek to help resolve public issues. Longstanding tort libel law has provided the defense of "fair comment" for media that are sued by persons who are involved in matters of public concern (Chap. 5, Sec. 29).[83] Thus celebrities and public entertainers of all kinds, such as actors, artists, writers, and musicians are public figures whom the media may criticize and evaluate, as are schools, hospitals, public utilities, and other institutions whose work affects the welfare of the community.[84] These may or may not inject themselves into public controversy.

In this framework, recent decisions have defined the following as public figures: a credit union corporation chartered under law, in whose financial condition the general public has "a vital interest";[85] an insurance company which, in view of the insurance business's power and influence, invites attention and comment from media;[86] a sportswriter who actively sought publicity for his views and his extensive writing and thrust himself into the public eye;[87] a nude dancer, who is "an entertainer and therefore subject to 'Public Figure Rule'" in libel actions;[88] entertainer Carol Burnett.[89] Of these kinds of entities and persons, the most troublesome for definition have been corporations, sometimes found by courts to be public and sometimes private.[90]

[83] Prosser, 812–813.

[84] Cepeda v. Cowles Magazines, 392 F.2d 417, 419 (9th Cir.1968); James v. Gannett Co., 40 N.Y.2d 415, 422, 386 N.Y.S.2d 871, 876, 353 N.E.2d 834 (1976).

[85] Coronado Credit Union v. KOAT, 99 N.M. 233, 656 P.2d 896 (App.1982), 9 Med. L.Rptr. 1031.

[86] American Benefit Life Co. v. McIntyre, 375 So.2d 239 (Ala.1979), 5 Med.L.Rptr. 1124.

[87] Maule v. Nym Corp., (N.Y.App.Div.1982) 7 Med.L.Rptr. 2092.

[88] Griffin v. Kentucky Post, (6th Cir.1983) 10 Med.L.Rptr. 1159, 1160.

[89] Burnett v. National Enquirer, (Cal.1981) 7 Med.L.Rptr. 1321.

[90] Robert Drechsler and Deborah Moon, Corporate Libel Plaintiffs and the News Media, 21 Am.Bus.L.Journ. 127 (Summer, 1983).

SEC. 23.   ACTUAL MALICE

Courts examine reporting procedures in testing for actual malice, and find reckless disregard for falsity much more often than knowledge of falsity.

If a libel plaintiff is found by the judge to be a public official or public figure, his next move is to try to show that the offending words were published with actual malice. This term, as we have seen, is defined by the Supreme Court as reckless disregard for falsity in the words, or as knowledge that the publication is false. The burden is on the plaintiff to prove falsity, although the defendant may well undertake to demonstrate truth—a complete defense.

It is worth remembering that, as was said earlier (p. 110), the actual malice of *Sullivan* is quite different from the concept "malice" as it is usually understood. The word ordinarily has to do with hostility, ill will, spite, intent to harm—as, indeed, it was defined in libel law for generations before *Sullivan,* and as it continues to be defined in its tort-related sense in state libel law where the constitutional standard does not apply (see Chap. 5). The Supreme Court has said that "actual malice" is a "term of art, created to provide a convenient shorthand expression for the standard of liability that must be established" [91] where public persons bring libel suits. The court that is trying the libel issue must direct itself to the factual issue as to the defendant's subjective knowledge of actual falsity or his high degree of awareness of probable falsity before publishing.[92]

Very soon after *Sullivan* had established the new definition of actual malice, the Supreme Court began the process of defining "reckless disregard." In Garrison v. Louisiana,[93] a criminal libel action, it said that reckless disregard means a "high degree of awareness of probable falsity" of the publication, and in 1968 in St. Amant v. Thompson, it said that for reckless disregard to be found, "There must be sufficient evidence to permit the conclusion that the defendant in fact entertained serious doubts as to the truth of his publication.[94]

St. Amant read, in a televised political campaign speech, the accusation by one Albin that Herman Thompson had had money dealings with another man accused of nefarious activities in labor union affairs. Thompson sued for defamation, and the Supreme

[91] Cantrell v. Forest City Pub. Co., 419 U.S. 245, 95 S.Ct. 465 (1974).

[92] Orr v. Argus-Press Co., 586 F.2d 1108 (6th Cir.1978).

[93] 379 U.S. 64, 74, 85 S.Ct. 209, 216 (1964).

[94] St. Amant v. Thompson, 390 U.S. 727, 731, 88 S.Ct. 1323, 1325 (1968).

Court of Louisiana upheld a judgment in his favor. It said there was sufficient evidence that St. Amant recklessly disregarded whether the statements about Thompson were true or false. The United States Supreme Court reversed the decision.

Reviewing decisions since New York Times Co. v. Sullivan, it said: [95]

> These cases are clear that reckless conduct is not measured by whether a reasonably prudent man would have published, or would have investigated before publishing. There must be sufficient evidence to permit the conclusion that the defendant in fact entertained serious doubts as to the truth of his publication. Publishing with such doubts shows reckless disregard for truth or falsity and demonstrates actual malice.

In this case, the Supreme Court found, there was no evidence that St. Amant was aware of the probable falsity of Albin's statement about Thompson. Albin had sworn to his statements and St. Amant had verified some of them, and Thompson's evidence had failed to demonstrate "a low community assessment of Albin's trustworthiness."

As for the specifying of reckless disregard in Garrison v. Louisiana: Garrison, a Louisiana prosecuting attorney, had attacked several judges during a press conference, for laziness and inattention to duty. He was convicted of criminal libel, and the Supreme Court of the United States reversed the conviction. It said that the fact that the case was a criminal case made no difference to the principles of the Times v. Sullivan rule, and that malice would have to be shown. And the "reckless disregard" of truth or falsity in malice, it said, lies in a "high degree of awareness of probable falsity" on the part of the publisher. Nothing indicated that Garrison had this awareness of falsity when he castigated the Louisiana judges.[96]

Since the first case providing the constitutional protection in libel, the courts have been at pains to distinguish between "reckless disregard of truth" and "negligence." [97] The latter is not enough to sustain a finding of actual malice. In the leading case, the Court went to this point. Errors in the famous advertisement, "Heed Their Rising Voices," could have been discovered by the *New York Times* advertising staff had it taken an elevator up a floor to the morgue and checked earlier stories on file. Failure to make this check, the Supreme Court said, did not constitute

---

[95] Ibid., 1325.

[96] 379 U.S. 64, 85 S.Ct. 209 (1964).

[97] Priestely v. Hastings & Sons Pub. Co. of Lynn, 360 Mass. 118, 271 N.E.2d 628 (1971); A.S. Abell Co. v. Barnes, 258 Md. 56, 265 A.2d 207 (1970).

"reckless disregard"; at the worst it was negligence, and negligence is not enough to indicate malice.[98] (In Chapter 5, we shall examine other situations in which negligence does apply.)

In another case, a New York congressman sued the *Washington Post* for a story by columnist Drew Pearson which the Post carried. The story accused the congressman of bribe-splitting. The Post did not check the accuracy of the columnist's charges. The Federal Court of Appeals held that the Post showed no reckless disregard in not verifying Pearson's charge, regardless of Pearson's reputation for accuracy. The court held that to require such checking by the Post would be to burden it with greater responsibilities of verification than the Supreme Court required of the *New York Times* in the landmark case. It said: [99]

> Verification is * * * a costly process, and the newspaper business is one in which survival has become a major problem. * * * We should be hesitant to impose responsibilities upon newspapers which can be met only through costly procedures or through self-censorship designed to avoid risks of publishing controversial material. The costliness of this process would especially deter less established publishers from taking chances and, since columns such as Pearson's are highly popular attractions, competition with publishers who can afford to verify or to litigate, would become even more difficult.

In the foregoing decisions in *Garrison, St. Amant,* and *Keogh,* courts defined reckless disregard by saying what it is *not.* Subsequent decisions have held that "internal inconsistencies" in a reporter's story do not make reckless disregard; [1] nor does the possibility that the reporter harbored "animosity", or a "grudge" or "ill will" toward the plaintiff; [2] nor does a combination of a reporter's failure to investigate, plus his possession (but omission from the story) of material contradictory to the hard words, plus the fact that the material was not "hot news" and so could have been further checked.[3] And to repeat, reckless disregard is not carelessness or negligence, which are flaws found often enough in news stories but which must be accepted in news of public persons if freedom is to have the "breathing space" it requires to survive.

---

[98] New York Times Co. v. Sullivan, 376 U.S. 254, 288, 84 S.Ct. 710, 730 (1964).

[99] Washington Post Co. v. Keogh, 125 U.S.App.D.C. 32, 365 F.2d 965, 972–973 (1966).

[1] Foster v. Upchurch, 624 S.W.2d 564 (Tex.1981), 7 Med.L.Rptr. 2533.

[2] Lancaster v. Daily Banner-News, 274 Ark. 145, 622 S.W.2d 671 (1981), 8 Med.L. Rptr. 1093; Curtis v. Southwestern Newspapers, 677 F.2d 115 (5th Cir.1982), 8 Med. L.Rptr. 1651.

[3] McNabb v. Oregonian Pub. Co., 69 Or.App. 136, 685 P.2d 458 (1984), 10 Med.L. Rptr. 2181.

Recently and prominently, the jury recognized this in the case of Ariel Sharon v. Time, Inc.: While it found *Time* magazine's story about public official Sharon to be false defamation, it said specifically that *Time* was negligent and careless, but not possessed of reckless disregard. *Time* had erred but not lied, and was not liable for any of the $50 million that Sharon sought.[4]

The cases of public-person plaintiffs who must accept without compensation the negligent, the careless—indeed the "irresponsible" and the "unreasonable"—[5] sometimes warrant the journalist's reflection: Floyd Rood, a tireless worker and publicist in youth assistance efforts including drug rehabilitation, was said in a news story to have begun a money-raising project "to help solve his drug addiction problem." The word "his" was wrong; it had accidentally been changed from "the" in wire transmission. He lost his suit.[6] Alderwoman Glover, said erroneously by a newspaper to have had abortions, could not recover for libel, for the newspaper had been no more than negligent in its mistake.[7] In deciding a case brought by a school superintendent against a newspaper for a long series of critical articles, the Florida Supreme Court said it could find no actual malice in the stories or cartoons even though most of them could "fairly be described as slanted, mean, vicious, and substantially below the level of objectivity that one would expect of responsible journalism * * *."[8]

Turning now to cases where reckless disregard *was* found in news: The earliest was the 1967 case, Curtis Publishing Co. v. Butts, treated above, in which the former athletic director of the University of Georgia sued for a *Saturday Evening Post* story accusing him of conspiring to "fix" a football game between Georgia and Alabama. The Post had relied on the story of Burnett, a man serving on probation in connection with bad check charges, had not seen Burnett's notes about the alleged telephone conversation he said he had overheard, had not interviewed a man supposedly in the company of Burnett at the time of the phone conversation. Furthermore, the story was not "hot news" that demanded immediate publication. In the words of Chief Justice Earl Warren, this was reckless disregard of whether the statements were true or false.[9]

---

[4] Time, Feb. 4, 1985, 64.

[5] Lawrence v. Bauer Pub. & Printing Ltd., 89 N.J. 451, 446 A.2d 469 (1982), 8 Med.L.Rptr. 1536, 1543.

[6] Rood v. Finney, 418 So.2d 1 (La.App.1982), 8 Med.L.Rptr. 2047.

[7] Glover v. Herald Co., 549 S.W.2d 858 (1977), 2 Med.L.Rptr. 1846.

[8] Early v. Palm Beach Newspapers, 354 So.2d 351 (1977), 3 Med.L.Rptr. 2183.

[9] Curtis Pub. Co. v. Butts, 388 U.S. 130, 155, 87 S.Ct. 1975 (1967). Supra, fn. 41 for subsequent cases employing "extreme departure" standard.

Journalistic practices and attitudes that could indicate reckless disregard to courts multiplied in the wake of those which the Supreme Court used in early cases: *Butts* (story was not "hot news" and should have been checked further), *St. Amant* (obvious reasons to doubt the veracity of sources), and *Garrison* (high degree of awareness of probable falsity of the story).[10] Further, journalists' practices could evoke opposite conclusions as between a trial court and appeals court. One of the most prominent of these was a 1984–85 case, Tavoulareas v. Washington Post. William Tavoulareas, president of Mobil Oil Corp., sued the Post for a story saying that he had "set up" his son to head a London shipping firm, and implying misuse of his corporate position. A public figure, he charged false defamation and actual malice by the Post.[11] The jury agreed and awarded him $250,000 compensatory and $1.8 million punitive damages. But after reviewing the facts at length, the judge threw out the jury award (rendered a "judgment n.o.v."). He said that while the story in question was far short of being a model of fair, unbiased investigative journalism, there was "no evidence in the record * * * to show that it contained knowing lies or statements made in reckless disregard of the truth," and no evidence to support the jury's verdict.[12]

The U.S. Court of Appeals, District of Columbia Circuit, reversed the trial judge on a 2–1 vote, and reinstated the jury verdict of $2.05 million.[13] The majority found clear and convincing evidence of reckless disregard under the rules of *Butts, St. Amant,* and *Garrison* (above paragraph)—and added these other indicators of fault in the story: (1) The story carried on its face the warning to the newspaper that it had high potential for harm to Tavoulareas' reputation; (2) the journalists "were motivated by a plan to 'get' the plaintiffs, and deliberately slanted, rejected and ignored evidence contrary to the false premise of the story"; (3) the reporter's interview notes "reflect exactly the opposite of what he was told by the interviewees"; (4) the newspaper refused to retract the story or to print Tavoulareas' letter to the paper.[14]

In elaborating, Judge George MacKinnon (joined by Judge Antonin Scalia) raised an alarm among journalists. The Post's policy of exposing wrongdoing in public life might be characterized

[10] The three cases are treated above, respectively, at pp. 117, 135–136.

[11] Tavoulareas v. Washington Post, 567 F.Supp. 651 (D.C.D.C.1983), 9 Med.L.Rptr. 1553.

[12] Ibid., 1555, 1561.

[13] Tavoulareas v. Washington Post, 759 F.2d 90 (D.C.Cir.1985), 11 Med.L.Rptr. 1777. The same judges denied a petition of the Post to re-hear the case on another 2–1 vote, 763 F.2d 1472 (D.C.Cir. 1985); but the 3-member panel's decision was vacated by the full Circuit Court (10 judges), which voted to hear the case *en banc*: Ibid., 1481.

[14] Ibid., 1809–1810.

as "hard hitting investigative journalism" or as "sophisticated muckraking," the Court said, and either "certainly is relevant to the inquiry of whether a newspaper employee acted in reckless disregard of whether a statement is false or not." [15]   The suggestion that a newspaper's devotion to these two honored traditions in journalism might be evidence of reckless disregard of falsity shocked the field.

Judge J. Skelly Wright, at almost total odds with the court majority, spoke for countless journalists in his long, ranging dissent that rejected MacKinnon's analysis. Holding that a newspaper policy of investigative journalism and muckraking could be evidence of reporters' acting in reckless disregard of falsity, Wright declared,[16]

> represents a sharp departure from the principles of free and vigorous discussion that have been the touchstone of First Amendment jurisprudence. It is a conclusion fraught with the potential to shrink the First Amendment's "majestic protection" * * *. In our society speech may be controversial and contentious; words may be intended to arouse, disturb, provoke, and upset * * *. [Free speech] "may indeed serve its high purpose when it induces a condition of unrest, creates, dissatisfaction with things as they are * * *."
>
> Muckraking—a term developed when writers like Lincoln Steffens, Ida Tarbell, and Upton Sinclair relentlessly exposed pervasive corruption—may be seen to serve that high purpose even if it offends and startles * * *.

Wright found in the majority opinion "deep hostility to an aggressive press" that "is directly contrary to the mandates of the Supreme Court and the spirit of a free press," and concluded that "neither a newspaper's muckraking policy nor its hard-hitting investigative journalism should *ever* be considered probative of actual malice."

Court-determined indicators of "reckless disregard" (which amount to court-determined standards of news reporting) do not end with those used in *Tavoulareas*. They include: where a reporter did not make personal contact with anyone involved in the event before writing; [17] where a publication relied on an obviously biased source, was advised of the falsity of information,

---

[15] Ibid., 1798.

[16] Ibid., 1821–22. For similar reactions from journalists, see Peter Prichard, Tavoulareas Case Returns—with Bite, Quill, May 1985, 25; Anthony Lewis, Getting Even, New York Times, 4/11/85, A27; Anon., Press Must Be Tough, but Fair, Milwaukee Journal, 4/12/85, 14.

[17] Akins v. Altus Newspapers, Inc., 609 P.2d 1263 (Okl.1977).

and published with no further investigation of the story; [18] where the publication printed although the story was inherently improbable.[19] Ill will of the reporter toward the subject of the story may in some cases contribute to a finding of reckless disregard.[20]

The "reckless disregard" aspect of actual malice, then, is shown rather often in libel suits. But the second aspect—knowing falsehood—is far less frequently found. One case involved a suit by State Sen. Richard Schermerhorn of New York. He was interviewed by reporter Ron Rosenberg of the Middletown *Times Herald Record* about the senator's proposal for the redevelopment plan (the NDDC) in Newburgh. They discussed community controversy about whether minorities' chances for benefiting from NDDC were sufficient. Rosenberg wrote a story which was published under the headline SCHERMERHORN SAYS NDDC CAN DO WITHOUT BLACKS. There was no reference to this in the story. A storm of protest against the senator arose, and Senators Beatty and von Luther proposed a resolution of censure in the Senate against Schermerhorn. In a later story, Beatty was quoted as saying that he had access to tapes in which Schermerhorn made subtle anti-black and anti-Semitic statements.

Schermerhorn denied making the headline statement and told his Senate colleagues that if there were tapes showing he had made such statements, he would be unfit to serve in the Senate and would resign. He brought a libel suit, and charged knowing falsehood.[21] At trial, Rosenberg agreed that Schermerhorn had not told him what the headline reported, and that a copy editor— who was never produced at the trial—had written it. But both von Luther and Beatty testified, that, in telephone calls to them, Rosenberg had assured them that Schermerhorn had said that the NDDC could do without blacks, and von Luther added that Rosenberg volunteered that he had a tape in which Schermerhorn made racial and ethnic slurs. The tape was never produced, although both senators testified that they made repeated requests for it.

The jury was unconvinced that a copy editor who never showed up for Rosenberg's trial had written the headline, and in addition, the jury had von Luther's and Beatty's testimony that Rosenberg assured them the headline was accurate. The jury brought in a verdict of $36,000 in damages for Schermerhorn. The New York Supreme Court, Appellate Division, upheld the

---

[18] Stevens v. Sun Pub. Co., 270 S.C. 65, 240 S.E.2d 812 (1978).

[19] Hunt v. Liberty Lobby, 720 F.2d 631 (11th Cir.1983), 10 Med.L.Rptr. 1097, 1107.

[20] Cochran v. Indianapolis Newspapers, 175 Ind.App. 548, 372 N.E.2d 1211 (1978), 3 Med.L.Rptr. 2131; Tavoulareas v. Washington Post, 759 F.2d 90, 114 (D.C.Cir. 1985), 11 Med.L.Rptr. 1777, 1820.

[21] Schermerhorn v. Rosenberg, (N.Y.S.Ct.App.Div. 3/17/80), 6 Med.L.Rptr. 1376.

verdict on three of four counts saying "In our view, then, the evidence was sufficient to sustain the jury's determination that Rosenberg * * * had composed a defamatory headline with actual knowledge that the matter asserted therein was false." [22]

Dun & Bradstreet, in a credit report to subscribers, linked Joseph F. Morgan to his brother, Claude B., in a scheme of incorporating retail stores and defaulting on obligations due suppliers. The publication implied that Joseph F. was a deadbeat and fraud, and as a result his credit was terminated and finally his drug business was destroyed. Despite notices from Joseph to Dun & Bradstreet that he had not since 1959 associated with his brother in business, and responsible third parties' similar notices, the company republished the report in November 1965 and March 1966, "in the teeth of findings by [its own] agent Olney that there was no business connection between the Morgan brothers in 1965." The Court of Appeals held that "The subsequent publication of a libel with knowledge of its falsity is proof of malice." [23] Morgan's recovery included $25,000 punitive damages.

SEC. 24. SPECIAL ISSUES: JURIES, SUMMARY JUDGMENT, NEUTRAL REPORTING, DISCOVERY

Juries

If "actual malice" leaves journalists uncertain in the fine distinctions and contradictions among courts, it presents a broader problem for juries called upon to analyze and employ it in deciding libel suits.[24] Jurors' minds must be cleared of predispositions to consider that the ill will or spite associated in plain English with "malice" is not really at issue, but rather, knowing or reckless falsehood by the publisher. This may involve a difficult "turn-around" in jurors' thought processes, and possibly resentment at the idea that a writer/publisher who harbors spite, hatred, or ill will against the plaintiff nevertheless may be legally immune from a libel judgment. Justice Potter Stewart said, after 15 years' experience with the Times v. Sullivan actual malice, that he "came greatly to regret" the Court's employment of that term: [25]

---

[22] Ibid., 1381.

[23] Morgan v. Dun & Bradstreet, Inc., 421 F.2d 1241, 1242 (5th Cir.1970). See also Sprouse v. Clay Communication, 158 W.Va. 427, 211 S.E.2d 674 (1975), 1 Med.L. Rptr. 1695, 1704.

[24] Marc Franklin, "Good Government and Bad Law * * *," 18 Univ.S.F.L.Rev. 1, 8 (1983); 10 Med.L.Rptr. # 12, 3/20/84, News Notes, 8 Ibid. # 39, 11/30/82, News Notes.

[25] Herbert v. Lando, 441 U.S. 153, 199, 99 S.Ct. 1635, 1661 (1979).

For the fact of the matter is that "malice" as used in the New York Times opinion simply does not mean malice as the word is commonly understood. In common understanding, malice means ill will or hostility ∗ ∗ ∗. As part of the ∗ ∗ ∗ standard enunciated in the New York Times case, however, "actual malice" has nothing to do with hostility or ill will ∗ ∗ ∗.

And if judge and attorneys in the case succeed in making the legal definition clear to the jury, there remains another problem for jurors enmeshed in libel law: That harsh words are proved false may be almost insurmountable evidence of media liability for some jurors, but that, of course, is not the case, for the falsity must be knowing or reckless. Justice Goldberg of the United States Supreme Court warned of problems for juries in New York Times Co. v. Sullivan: [26] "The requirement of proving actual malice ∗ ∗ ∗ may, in the mind of the jury, add little to the requirement of proving falsity, a requirement which the Court recognizes not to be an adequate standard."

After trial Judge Gasch in *Tavoulareas* found the jury's verdict of some $2 million unsupportable and disallowed it, Attorney Steven Brill interviewed five of the six jurors.[27] He found that they did not understand that falsity must be knowing or reckless to justify an award. One juror said that, if their task had been to decide "whether the *Post* had been recklessly or deliberately inaccurate," they would not have given Tavoulareas the judgment.[28] They further believed that the *Post* was required to show the truth of its charges, whereas, of course, the rule actually was that Tavoulareas was required to show falsity.

Brill asserts that the *Post* attorneys did not drum these points into the jury's minds, and talked to the jury of ordinary citizens in language appropriate to lawyers not laymen.[29] As for Judge Gasch, his instructions to the jury consisted of almost two hours of review of legal points involved, bound to be difficult for jurors despite the fact that on the matter of finding "actual malice," his charge to the jury was correct.[30]

Judge James L. Oakes of the federal bench has said that he finds persuasive the argument that "the judge's charge has only a

[26] 376 U.S. 254, 299, 84 S.Ct. 710, 736 (1964).

[27] Steven Brill, "Inside the Jury Room at the Washington Post Libel Trial," *American Lawyer*, Nov. 1982, 1, 93, 94.

[28] Ibid.

[29] Ibid., 1, 90.

[30] Ibid., 92. The Libel Defense Resource Center is preparing a manual of jury instructions on libel: LDRC Bulletin # 10, Spring 1984, 1–2.

slight practical effect upon a jury." [31]   He has cited the late
Supreme Court Justice Robert Jackson upon the matter, Jackson
saying in a conspiracy case that "The naive assumption that
prejudicial effects can be overcome by instructions to the jury
* * *, all practicing lawyers know to be unmitigated fiction." [32]
And the late Justice Hugo Black, concurring in New York Times
Co. v. Sullivan, said of the jury verdict against the *Times,* overturned by the U.S. Supreme Court: [33]

> The record certainly does not indicate that any different
> verdict would have been rendered here whatever the
> [trial] court had charged the jury about "malice," "truth,"
> "good motives," "justifiable ends," or any other legal
> formulas which in theory would protect the press.

As for Tavoulareas' case, Brill reported, four jurors whom he
interviewed told him that they had not understood Judge Gasch's
instructions.[34]

A procedure widely praised as a clarification of its task for a
jury was initiated in 1985 by Federal Judge Abraham Sofaer.
Ariel Sharon, former defense minister of Israel, brought a libel
suit for $50 million against *Time* magazine for its report that
Sharon had discussed with Christian Phalangists of Lebanon the
need for them to take revenge against assassins, just before the
massacre of hundreds of Palestinians by Phalangists.   In his
instructions, Judge Sofaer had the jury take up three questions,
one at a time, and report its finding on each before proceeding.
First, he asked the jury, was the story defamatory? ("Yes," the
jury found.) Next, was it false? ("Yes," the jury found.) Finally,
was it done with actual malice? ("No," the jury found, and thus,
Time was not liable for damages.) [35]   Whether courts will generally follow this procedure remains to be seen.

In the libel case brought by Gen. William C. Westmoreland
against CBS in 1985—perhaps unequalled in the publicity attending it and costliness to the participants— [36] Judge Pierre Laval
used another device to aid the jury: He simply barred the use of
the confounding term "actual malice" during the trial, substitut-

[31] Proof of Actual Malice in Defamation Actions: an Unsolved Dilemma, 7
Hofstra L.Rev. 655, 701.

[32] Krulewitch v. United States, 336 U.S. 440, 453, 69 S.Ct. 716, 723 (1949).

[33] 376 U.S. 254, 295, 84 S.Ct. 710, 734 (1964).

[34] Brill, 93; James Goodale, "The Tavoulareas Jury Verdict Provides a Chilling
Lesson for the Press," Communications Lawyer, Summer 1983, p. 1.

[35] Time, Feb. 4, 1985, 64, 66.

[36] The 18-week trial may have cost the parties $10 million in expenses, New York
Times, Feb. 19, 1985, 10, 26; and see Ibid., from mid-October 8, 1984, to Feb. 19,
1985, for the extent of coverage.

ing the "state of mind" of the journalists as a clearer criterion.[37] Westmoreland, who sued for "CBS Reports'" accusation that he engaged in a "conspiracy" to understate enemy troop strength when he was Commander of United States forces during the Vietnam War, withdrew his suit after 18 weeks of testimony. The jury was never put to the test of grappling with "actual malice" and "state of mind."

The troubling problem of legal technicalities' confronting lay juries by no means ends the question of how media faced with libel suits need to cope with the jury setting.[38] For example, widespread anti-media attitudes of recent decades are likely to be represented among the cross-section of people that often comprises a jury. A juror's support for media's rights to publish may be qualified by resentment and lack of trust in media for what the juror considers arrogance, inaccuracy, and invasion of privacy by media. (Brill, however, found no such anti-media attitude among the jurors whom he interviewed.)[39] The many awards by juries of enormous judgments for libel—particularly punitive damages (above, pp. 63–64)—suggest powerfully that jurors often are disposed to punish media. Jurors often, also, tend to sympathize with the individual whose reputation, feelings, and status among his friends seem tarnished by the rich media corporation, seen by the jury as callous and careless. Where unfairness in media stories is at issue in libel trials, such proclivities may heavily qualify the rights of free expression and jurors' understanding of the open society's need for uninhibited, robust, wide-open discussion in the columns and broadcasts of the mass media.

Summary Judgment

If a judge at the threshold of a libel trial finds that a plaintiff is a public figure or public official, the case moves at once to a second pretrial consideration, of first importance to the defending news media and the plaintiff. The plaintiff alleges actual malice, and the defendant ordinarily denies it and moves that the judge dismiss the case in a "summary judgment" for the defendant. Winning such a motion forestalls trial, with its frequently heavy expenses and extended distraction—a threat to vigorous reporting. The importance of summary judgment to the media's defense and to the public need for robust, uninhibited, wide-open reporting was laid out in the decision in Washington Post Co. v. Keogh,[40] an early case that interpreted the import of Times v. Sullivan:

[37] Washington Post National Weekly Edition, March 11, 1985, 28.

[38] See James J. Brosnahan, First Amendment Jury Trials, 6 Litigation 4, 28 (Summer 1980).

[39] Brill, 94.

[40] 125 U.S.App.D.C. 32, 365 F.2d 965, 968 (1966).

In the First Amendment area, summary procedures are * * * essential. For the stake here, if harassment succeeds, is free debate. One of the purposes of the *Times* principle, in addition to protecting persons from being cast in damages in libel suits filed by public officials, is to prevent persons from being discouraged in the full and free exercise of their First Amendment rights with respect to the conduct of their government. The threat of being put to the defense of a lawsuit brought by a popular public official may be as chilling to the exercise of First Amendment freedoms as fear of the outcome of the lawsuit itself, especially to advocates of unpopular causes.

In ruling on the motion for summary judgment by the defendant, the judge must make a decision: Is there a "genuine issue of material fact"—a substantial claim by the plaintiff supported by evidence—that there was knowing or reckless falsity in the publication? [41] While it is plain that it is not enough for the plaintiff merely to allege actual malice without giving evidence of it, courts have taken different positions on just what the judge's role should be in this pretrial motion in a libel case. One position is that the trial judge is to take the responsibility of finding whether there is actual knowledge of falsity or reckless disregard of the truth by the publication. "Unless the court finds, on the basis of pretrial * * * documentary evidence, that the plaintiff can prove actual malice in the *Times* sense, it should grant summary judgment for the defendant." [42] This takes the jury out of its normal role of finding the facts—in public-person libel, of deciding whether the facts show actual malice.

The more usual position of courts is that the judge takes a lesser role in deciding the question of actual malice: [43]

> The question to be resolved at summary judgment is whether plaintiff's proof is sufficient such that a reasonable jury could find malice with convincing clarity, *and not whether the trial judge is convinced of the existence of actual malice.* [emphasis in original]

---

[41] Restatement, Second, Torts, Vol. 3, p. 220. Cerrito v. Time, Inc., 449 F.2d 306 (9th Cir.1971); Hayes v. Booth Newspapers, 97 Mich.App. 758, 295 N.W.2d 858, (1980) 6 Med.L.Rptr. 2319.

[42] Wasserman v. Time, Inc., 138 U.S.App.D.C. 7, 424 F.2d 920, 922–23 (1970). The opinion, by Circuit Judge J. Skelly Wright, is considered the leading opinion for this position.

[43] Nader v. de Toledano, 408 A.2d 31 (D.C.App.1979), certiorari denied 444 U.S. 1078, 100 S.Ct. 1028 (1980), 5 Med.L.Rptr. 1550, 1563. See also Yiamouyiannis v. Consumers Union, 619 F.2d 932 (2d Cir.1980), 6 Med.L.Rptr. 1065, 1071.

In other words, the Appellate Court said, "a libel plaintiff need not prove malice twice—first to the judge, then to the jury." [44]

The judge is to look at all the evidence, and resolve all permissible inferences in the evidence in favor of the plaintiff. After doing this, the judge may find that there are no disputed facts remaining that would establish actual malice, or that any remaining disputed facts are too trivial for the jury to determine that actual malice of convincing clarity exists. If so, he is to grant summary judgment to the publisher. [45]

Chief Justice Warren Burger of the United States Supreme Court in 1979 wrote a famous footnote—number 9 in Hutchinson v. Proxmire—casting doubt on the appropriateness of summary judgment in libel cases. [46] Lower courts take his admonition into account and sometimes have found it a basis for denial of summary judgment, but summary judgment is granted defendants far more often in libel suits brought by public people than it is denied. [47]

Police Chief Prease alleged in a suit that stories in the Akron, (O.) *Beacon Journal* libeled him. Assistant Managing Editor Timothy Smith said that all statements in the stories were made in good faith with no serious doubts about their accuracy, and the Chief did not refute Smith. Thus the judge found that there was no issue between them about actual malice—no "genuine issue of material fact" that would have to be argued before a jury for decision. He granted summary judgment for the newspaper. [48]

But the United States Court of Appeals, Fourth District, found such an issue in Fitzgerald v. Penthouse, [49] and reversed a trial court's grant of summary judgment to *Penthouse*. Fitzgerald, a specialist in the use of dolphins as military weapons, sued *Penthouse* for an article about his work that might have been construed as an allegation of espionage—selling dolphins trained as "torpedoes" to other nations, for "fast bucks." The Court found that *Penthouse* relied almost exclusively for its story upon a questionable source, and detailed his "many bold assertions about the United States intelligence community" which in some cases "invite skepticism." It quoted St. Amant v. Thompson: [50] Reck-

[44] Ibid., 1561.

[45] Ibid., 1563.

[46] Hutchinson v. Proxmire, 443 U.S. 111, 99 S.Ct. 2675 (1979).

[47] Yiamouyiannis v. Consumers Union, 619 F.2d 932 (2d Cir.1980), 6 Med.L.Rptr. 1065. Defendants' motions for summary judgment in the 1980s have been successful about 75% of the time, and Burger's "footnote 9" has been used rarely: Libel Defense Resource Center Bulletin # 13, Spring 1985, 10.

[48] Prease v. Poorman, (Ohio Com.Pls.1981) 7 Med.L.Rptr. 2378.

[49] 691 F.2d 666 (4th Cir.1982), 8 Med.L.Rptr. 2340.

[50] 390 U.S. 727, 732, 88 S.Ct. 1323, 1326 (1968).

lessness may be found "where there are obvious reasons to doubt the veracity of the informant or the accuracy of his reports." Fitzgerald had presented a factual question about whether *Penthouse* had "obvious reasons to doubt" its source; *Penthouse* would have to go to trial on the matter of actual malice.

Neutral Reporting

A new doctrine in libel, termed the privilege of "neutral reportage" or "neutral reporting," emerged in 1977 from the U.S. Court of Appeals, Second Circuit, in Edwards v. National Audubon Society.[51] It raised the possibility that requiring plaintiffs to prove actual malice might become seriously weakened or even damaged beyond repair. The court, Judge Irving Kaufman writing, found that the Constitution protects accurate, disinterested news reporting of accusations made against public figures regardless of the reporter's view of their truth. It is related to the long-standing common-law and statutory doctrine of qualified privilege—immunity from successful libel suit for fair and accurate reports without comments, of official proceedings (see Chap. 5): The society needs an unvarnished and accurate account of its public figures, *Edwards* says, even as it needs the same of official public proceedings.

The New York Times carried a story reporting accurately a National Audubon Society spokeman's written statement that some scientists were paid to lie about the effects of the insecticide DDT upon birds. Outraged scientists who were implicated brought libel suit against the Society and the Times. A jury returned a verdict for the scientists, and the case was appealed. Judge Kaufman wrote for the Court of Appeals that " * * * a libel judgment against the *Times,* in face of this finding of fact, is constitutionally impermissible." He reasoned: [52]

> At stake in this case is a fundamental principle. Succinctly stated, when a responsible, prominent organization like the National Audubon Society makes serious charges against a public figure, the First Amendment protects the accurate and disinterested reporting of those charges, regardless of the reporter's private views regarding their validity. See Time, Inc. v. Pape, 401 U.S. 279, 91 S.Ct. 633 (1971) * * *. What is newsworthy about such accusations is that they were made. We do not believe that the press may be required under the First Amendment to suppress newsworthy statements merely

[51] 556 F.2d 113 (2d Cir.1977). See Kathryn D. Sowle, "Defamation and the First Amendment: The Case for a Constitutional Privilege of Fair Report," 54 NYU L.Rev. 469, June 1979.

[52] Edwards v. National Audubon Society, 556 F.2d 113, 120 (2d Cir.1977).

because it has serious doubts regarding their truth. Nor must the press take up cudgels against dubious charges in order to publish them without fear of liability for defamation * * *. The public interest in being fully informed about controversies that often rage around sensitive issues demands that the press be afforded the freedom to report such charges without assuming responsibility for them.

> The contours of the press's right of neutral reportage are, of course, defined by the principle that gives life to it. Literal accuracy is not a prerequisite; if we are to enjoy the blessings of a robust and unintimidated press, we must provide immunity from defamation suits where the journalist believes, reasonably and in good faith, that his report accurately conveys the charges made.

Kaufman limited the reach of the doctrine in somewhat the same way that the old protection of qualified privilege does. He said that a publisher who "in fact espouses or concurs in the charges made by others, or who deliberately distorts these statements to launch a personal attack of his own on a public figure, cannot rely on a privilege of neutral reportage. In such instances he assumes responsibility for the underlying accusations." But in this case, Kaufman said, reporter John Devlin wrote an accurate account, did not espouse the Society's position, and included the indignant scientists' reactions to the charge in the article. "The *Times* article, in short, was the exemplar of fair and dispassionate reporting of an unfortunate but newsworthy contretemps. Accordingly, we hold that it was privileged under the First Amendment." [53]

Welcome as the new protection was in media circles, it quickly was met by an opposing view—from the U.S. Court of Appeals, Third Circuit. Writing in Dickey v. CBS, Judge Hunder ruled for the court that "no constitutional privilege of neutral reportage exists." The case involved a libel action resulting from a television broadcast of a pretaped talk show in which an incumbent Pennsylvania congressman accused a public figure of accepting payoffs. Although CBS won the case, it was not on "neutral reportage" ground, which Hunder said flies in the face of the much-cited decision of 1964 in St. Amant v. Thompson (above, p. 135).[54]

> The apparent holding of *Edwards*—that whenever remarks are judged by the press to be "newsworthy," * * * they may be published without fear of a libel suit

[53] Ibid., 120.

[54] Dickey v. CBS, 583 F.2d 1221, 1225–1226 (3d Cir.1978).

even if the publisher "has serious doubts regarding their truth," * * *—is contrary to the Supreme Court's ruling in *St. Amant.* While the Second Circuit found that there can be no liability despite the publisher's "serious doubts" as to truthfulness, *St. Amant* holds that for libel against a public figure to be proved, "[t]here must be sufficient evidence to permit the conclusion that the defendant in fact entertained *serious doubts* as to the truth of his publication. Publishing with such doubts shows reckless disregard for truth or falsity and demonstrates actual malice." 390 U.S. at 731, 88 S.Ct. at 1325 (emphasis added).

* * *

We therefore conclude that a constitutional privilege of neutral reportage is not created * * * merely because an individual newspaper or television or radio station decides that a particular statement is newsworthy.

A subsequent decision of the Second Circuit (the enunciator of the *Edwards* doctrine) flatly denied its protection to the *New Times,* whose story (suggesting that a mayor had once been a rapist) violated many of the qualifications limiting the privilege as expressed by Kaufman (fair and accurate report without "espousal"; charges made by a "responsible and well-noted organization like the National Audubon Society.") [55] Several states have accepted the *Edwards* doctrine, including Florida, Ohio, and perhaps Washington.[56] Among those that have examined and rejected it are New York, Kentucky, and Michigan.[57] Illinois is of two minds, the districts of its Appellate Court being split between approval and disapproval, and its Supreme Court having expressly refused to address the issue.[58] The United States Supreme Court has not ruled, although it denied review of *Edwards.*[59]

[55] Cianci v. New Times Pub. Co., (2d Cir.1980) 6 Med.L.Rptr. 1625.

[56] El Amin v. Miami Herald, (Fla.1983) 9 Med.L.Rptr. 1079; Horvath v. Ashtabula Telegraph, (Ohio App., 1982) 8 Med.L.Rptr. 1657; Senear v. Daily Journal-American, 97 Wash.2d 148, 641 P.2d 1180 (1982), 8 Med.L.Rptr. 2489, 2493.

[57] Hogan v. Herald Co., 84 A.D.2d 470, 446 N.Y.S.2d 836 (1982), 8 Med.L.Rptr. 1137, 1141 affirmed 58 N.Y.2d 630, 458 N.Y.S.2d 538, 444 N.E.2d 1002 (1982), 8 Med.L.Rptr. 2567; McCall v. Courier-Journal, 7 Med.L.Rptr. 2118 (Ky.Sup.Ct., 1981); Postill v. Booth Newspapers, 118 Mich.App. 608, 325 N.W.2d 511 (1982), 8 Med.L.Rptr. 2222.

[58] Fogus v. Capital Cities Media, Inc., 111 Ill.App.3d 1060, 67 Ill.Dec. 616, 444 N.E.2d 1100 (1982), 9 Med.L.Rptr. 1141, 1143.

[59] Certiorari denied Edwards v. New York Times Co., 434 U.S. 1002, 98 S.Ct. 647 (1977).

Discovery

The libel plaintiff knows that he will be faced at the outset of his action with a motion for summary judgment by the defendant, and seeks evidence in advance of the trial to counter the motion he knows will come. Often using "discovery proceedings," his attorney confronts the defendant with questions aimed at helping prepare the case. Meanwhile, the defendant news medium is interrogating the plaintiff in similar discovery. Plaintiffs commonly seek evidence, during discovery, of actual malice on the part of the journalist, for their "threshold" showing of this essential ingredient at the outset of the trial. Another element often sought is the identity of confidential sources of the reporter's information—persons quoted in a story, but not named. Refusal by the journalist to testify in discovery proceedings can result in citation for contempt of court.

In one of the most celebrated media cases of the 1970s, Barry Lando and Mike Wallace of CBS' "60 Minutes" refused to answer questions in discovery proceedings that sought to probe their "state of mind" in preparing a segment on one Col. Anthony Herbert. Herbert, a public figure, was suing for words in the broadcast which, he said, portrayed him as a liar in his accusations that his superiors covered up reports of Vietnam War crimes. He was seeking evidence of actual malice on the part of Lando and Wallace. Confronted in discovery proceedings that lasted a year and produced almost 3,000 pages of Lando's testimony alone, Lando refused to respond when it came to inquiries into his state of mind in editing and producing the program, and into the editorial process in general. He said this was a realm of journalistic work that must not be intruded upon for fear of its chilling effect on expression protected by the First Amendment.

While the Court of Appeals, Second District, held on a 2–1 vote that First Amendment interests warranted an absolute evidentiary privilege for Lando, the U.S. Supreme Court reversed, saying that the First Amendment does not prohibit plaintiffs from directly inquiring into the editorial processes of those whom they accuse of defamation.[60] Journalists in libel cases had been testifying as to their motives, discussions, and thoughts relating to their copy, for a century and more before Times v. Sullivan without objecting to the process, said Justice White in writing the majority opinion; and Times v. Sullivan "made it essential to proving liability that plaintiffs focus on the conduct and state of mind of the defendant." He elaborated: [61]

[60] Herbert v. Lando, 441 U.S. 153, 99 S.Ct. 1635 (1979), 4 Med.L.Rptr. 2575.

[61] Ibid., 160; 1641; 2578.

To be liable, the alleged defamer of public officials or of public figures must know or have reason to suspect that his publication is false. In other cases proof of some kind of fault, negligence perhaps, is essential to recovery. Inevitably, unless liability is to be completely foreclosed, the thoughts and editorial processes of the alleged defamer would be open to examination.

A few newspaper editorials and media voices recognized that the *Herbert* decision had broken no new ground and presented no fresh menace to the First Amendment, but attacking of the Supreme Court was far more common as media took the view that the justices had violated the integrity of the "editorial process" and the First Amendment.[62] The response of those dismayed was an example of the historical reaction of journalists to various decisions on First Amendment questions that had never before the 1970s reached the Supreme Court. Alarmed reactions of shock over presumed new damage by the Court to the First Amendment were often without understanding that what the Court was finding was in line with what lower courts had found for decades or for a century. The press reaction spoke eloquently to journalists' superficial education in the history of press freedom, and to their necessary occupational fix upon the world's current "hot scoop," unalloyed by knowledge of the history in which their own First Amendment roots were embedded.

Discovery in libel had arrived to stay, the *Herbert* case confirming its applicability. Said one media attorney:[63] "While there was an outcry from some representatives of the press at the time, it now seems unlikely that the opinion will have any dramatic effect. Before *Herbert* journalists had routinely testified about the editorial process in establishing their freedom from 'actual malice' or 'fault.' As a result of *Herbert,* they will continue to do so."

[62] Editorials on File, April 16–30, 1979, pp. 437–446.

[63] Robert D. Sack, "Special Discovery Problems in Media Cases," Communications Law 1980, I, 235, 242 (Practicing Law Institute 1980).

Chapter 5

DEFENDING AGAINST LIBEL SUITS
UNDER STATE LAW

Sec.

25. Determining Who Is "Private".
26. Ending Strict Liability in Libel.
27. Qualified Privilege as a Defense.
28. Truth as a Defense.
29. Opinion and Fair Comment as Defenses.
30. Retraction.

SEC. 25. DETERMINING WHO IS "PRIVATE"

Since the 1974 decision in Gertz v. Robert Welch, Inc. provided that private persons' libel suits have a lower barrier to clear than public persons', determining who is "private" has been of first importance in defamation actions.

We have seen that news media invoke the United States Constitution and its First Amendment when they defend against libel suits brought by public people. As we shall see in this chapter, when private persons bring libel actions, news media ordinarily invoke state statutes and state constitutions as their defenses.[1] This is the result of the important decision in Gertz v. Robert Welch, Inc., announced by the United States Supreme Court in 1974.[2] Here the Court said that society's stake in getting news reports of private persons does not warrant the full degree of First Amendment protection in libel suits provided for media where public persons are involved. Society's stake in providing protection against libel to private people is also high, and such people may meet a somewhat less stern test than the constitutional barrier of proving actual malice.

The reasons for this were covered in an earlier treatment of *Gertz* (above, p. 121). Briefly, the Court said that private people have not accepted the risk of exposing themselves to the rough-and-tumble give-and-take of public scrutiny and controversy associated with public life. Further, it said, private people do not have the access to media that public people do, to refute false and disparaging news. Another reason that is sometimes given is that

---

[1] Comment, "The Impending Federalization of Missouri Defamation Law," 43 Mo.L.Rev. 270 (1978). Discusses relationships of traditional and constitutional principles in the law of defamation.

[2] 418 U.S. 323, 94 S.Ct. 2997 (1974).

private people do not have the immunity from successful libel suits that public officials have in making statements from the platform of libel-proof official proceedings.[3]

To begin, then, who is a private person? A central test, we learned earlier, is that one is private unless he voluntarily thrusts himself into the "vortex" of public controversy in order to influence the outcome of that controversy. It is worth repeating earlier points: One, of course, is that a person's presence in an official proceeding which is open to the public does not automatically destroy his private status (as with Ilya Wolston, Attorney Gertz, Mrs. Firestone, above).

Another is that the media cannot make a private person public merely by bringing the person into the news. That is illustrated by Hutchinson, of course, and also by Mrs. Mary Troman.[4] Mrs. Troman was drawn into a public controversy by a newspaper which, she said, implied that her home was a gang headquarters when it was no such thing. The court ruled that she was private. She had not in any way "injected" herself into a public controversy, nor had she invited public attention or comment.[5]

We have seen also that the United States Supreme Court said in *Gertz* that *the individual's own status as private or public* is the key in deciding whether he must prove actual malice. This is the case where the story is one of public interest or concern. Thus, although efficiency and honesty in the practice of the professions such as law and medicine may be topics of deep public concern, a news story does not automatically get *Sullivan* protection in reporting on the individuals in those professions; they are not necessarily public figures.

For example, in Chapter 4 we saw an attorney declared a public figure for all purposes (p. 127): Myron Steere had been county attorney for eight years, with substantial attending publicity; he had been special counsel for the board of county commissioners in a controversy over a new courthouse; had been prominent in numerous social activities and was an officer and representative for many professional, fraternal and social activities; had achieved influence in local affairs; and his 32-year

[3] Ibid., 344–45, 3009–10.

[4] Troman v. Wood, 62 Ill.2d 184, 340 N.E.2d 292 (1975).

[5] Ibid.

career in law practice in the county was now capped by representing a woman in her well-publicized, famous murder trial.

Yet attorney Paul Littlefield was not a public figure even though involved in a topic of public interest—his own disciplinary proceedings by the Iowa State Bar Association and the Iowa Supreme Court for practicing law while he was on probation. He brought a libel suit for an erroneous news story about the proceedings, and was declared a public figure by the trial court, which said he was drawn into a public forum and debate as a result of his "purposeful act of practicing law in Iowa in direct contravention of his probation." But the U.S. Court of Appeals for the 8th district did not agree. It was Littlefield's status as a person, not the high public interest in his story, that was crucial: [6]

> We fail to see anything in Littlefield's status indicating that he has ready access to effective means of self-help or that he has voluntarily assumed the risks of public exposure by thrusting himself into a public controversy with a view toward influencing its resolution. While it is true that he "voluntarily" practiced law in violation of his probation, there is no indication that he did so out of a desire to influence any public controversy * * *. Furthermore, the public's interest should not be considered in making the public figure/private individual determination. * * * the status of the person allegedly defamed is the controlling factor.

A segment of CBS' "60 Minutes" dealt with the abuse of amphetamine drugs. One Barbara Goldstein was interviewed by Mike Wallace. She said that a Dr. Greenberg had prescribed drugs for her obesity, that under his direction she was taking 80 pills of various kinds a day, that for two years she had bizarre physical symptoms ("I could not determine where I ended and you began * * *."), and that she associated the drugs with physical birth defects of her child. Greenberg sued for libel, and his status as "public figure" was an issue: CBS argued that Greenberg thrust himself into controversy surrounding amphetamines by prescribing "amphetamine-type" drugs to Goldstein. The New York Supreme Court, Appellate Division, ruled that Greenberg's prescribing the drugs did not make him a public figure: [7]

> Goldstein's short period of treatment under Greenberg care terminated more than ten years prior to the telecast

[6] Littlefield v. Fort Dodge Messenger, 614 F.2d 581, 584 (8th Cir.1980), certiorari denied 445 U.S. 945, 100 S.Ct. 1342, 5 Med.L.Rptr. 2325 (1980). See also Little Rock Newspapers, Inc. v. Dodrill, 265 Ark. 628, 590 S.W.2d 840 (1979), certiorari denied 444 U.S. 1076, 100 S.Ct. 1024 (1980), a "private" attorney. Gertz himself, of course, was a "private" attorney.

[7] Greenberg v. CBS et al., 69 A.D.2d 693, 419 N.Y.S.2d 988 (1979), 5 Med.L.Rptr. 1470, 1473.

* * *. This is significant because there is nothing in the record to suggest that the use of amphetamines or their substitute to combat obesity was a source of public debate during the course of Goldstein's treatment.

It is the lack of controversy which defeats the argument made by the media defendants * * *.

Moreover, * * * [in the program's portrayal of nationwide drug abuse] it is clear that the act of prescribing that which may lawfully be prescribed, without more, cannot be deemed significant participation in a nationwide controversy.

The court also found that Greenberg (like Gertz) had written widely but only for research publications for the medical profession; he did not publish in mass media or seek media attention. The audience was not broad and the topic not one of wide appeal.

Shifting from professional people to the realm of business and commerce, corporations and business firms are intensely "public" in their reliance on the public's custom. That may or may not be enough to make them public figures in libel actions. A San Francisco department store, City of Paris, advertised a close-out sale, and media reported widely its going-out-of-business. The store's agent in the sale, Vegod Corp., was said by KGO–TV to have brought inferior goods in during the sale, the story relying on the Better Business Bureau as its source for charges which included the "deceiving" of the public. Vegod sued, and claimed to be "private." The California Supreme Court agreed in a decision that said of the "public controversy test": [8]

Criticism of commercial conduct does not deserve the special protection of the actual malice test. Balancing one individual's limited First Amendment interest against another's reputation interest * * *, we conclude that a person in the business world advertising his wares does not necessarily become part of an existing public controversy.

In mid-1985, the United States Supreme Court ruled in a case where it found a plaintiff to be a private person involved in a matter of *private* concern. Greenmoss Builders sought punitive damages from Dun & Bradstreet's false, confidential report, sent to five subscribers to its credit-reporting service, that Greenmoss had declared bankruptcy. Presumed and punitive damages had been barred to private plaintiffs in Gertz v. Robert Welch unless they could show actual malice. But, Justice Lewis Powell wrote in a 5–4 decision, the *Gertz* rule applied only where the subject was a

---

[8] Vegod Corp. v. ABC, 25 Cal.3d 763, 160 Cal.Rptr. 97, 603 P.2d 14 (1979), 5 Med. L.Rptr. 2043, 2045. And see Robert E. Drechul and Moon, D., Corporate Libel Plaintiffs and the News Media * * *, 21 Am. Business L.Journ. 127, Summer 1983.

matter of public concern, and this credit report was "solely in the individual interest of the speaker and its specific business audience."[8.5] The special protection to speech of the *Gertz* rule and of *Sullivan*—to further robust debate on public issues—was not applicable here. The Court upheld a jury award to Greenmoss of $50,000 presumed (compensatory) damages and $300,000 punitive damages.

SEC. 26. ENDING STRICT LIABILITY IN LIBEL

The law may no longer presume injury to persons as a result of false defamation even though it is libelous on its face.

Gertz v. Robert Welch, Inc. told private people they would not have to meet the constitutional demand of proving actual malice against publishers in bringing libel suits. What, then, would be required of them? Justice Powell wrote for the majority that the states might set their own standards of liability for private people to prove, except that the Constitution would not permit states to impose "liability without fault."[9] Powell was saying that state standards could not include an ancient rule in libel *per se*—that for those words which are damaging on their face, the law presumes injury to reputation and liability for libel by the publisher; the only question is the amount of damages that may be recovered.[10] This was the long-standing rule of "strict liability" in libel, and the Court was saying that the media must be shielded from strict liability. The standard of fault for private people to prove, Powell said, need be no more than "negligence," instead of the "actual malice" of *Sullivan*. The Powell opinion therewith returned to the states much of the jurisdiction in libel cases that had been lost to them through the sweep of *Sullivan* and the temporary sway of Rosenbloom v. Metromedia, even as it made it plain that there must not be a return to "automatic" liability for defamation.

Apart from the change respecting liability, the Court added, there would be other new restrictions on states, these in respect to compensation for persons libeled. The states have a "strong and legitimate * * * interest in compensating private individuals for injury to reputation," but compensation may not be limitless. The Court said that state laws would not be permitted to provide "recovery of presumed or punitive damages" but only "compensa-

---

[8.5] Dun & Bradstreet, Inc. v. Greenmoss Builders, Inc., __ U.S. __, 105 S.Ct. 2939, 2947.

[9] Gertz v. Robert Welch, Inc., 418 U.S. 323, 94 S.Ct. 2997, 3010 (1974). Emphasis added.

[10] Prosser, 780–781.

tion for actual injury."[11]   An exception could occur where the plaintiff could show the knowing or reckless falsehood of the *Sullivan* standard.   It found that awarding presumed damages ("compensatory" or "general" damages) given where there is no demonstrated loss, "unnecessarily compounds the potential of any system of liability for defamatory falsehood to inhibit the vigorous exercise of First Amendment freedoms."[12]   It found that punitive damages do the same, and also are "wholly irrelevant to the state interest that justifies a negligence standard for private defamation actions. * * * they are private fines levied by civil juries to punish reprehensible conduct and to deter its future occurrence."[13]

Precisely what the Court meant by the permitted "compensation for actual injury" was not spelled out, but Justice Powell made it plain that he was not speaking strictly of compensation for proved dollar losses flowing from false defamation: [14]

> We need not define "actual injury," as trial courts have wide experience in framing appropriate jury instructions in tort action.   Suffice it to say that actual injury is not limited to out-of-pocket loss.   Indeed, the more customary types of actual harm inflicted by defamatory falsehood include impairment of reputation and standing in the community, personal humiliation, and mental anguish and suffering. * * * all awards must be supported by competent evidence concerning the injury, although there need be no evidence which assigns an actual dollar value to the injury.

The new rules, approved by five of the justices, represented major change from the elevated position of the public principle (Chap. 4) for libel in its ultimate expression by the plurality in *Rosenbloom*.   Dissenting, Justice Brennan, joined by Justice Douglas, reaffirmed his attachment to the requirement that private people involved in "matters of general or public interest" prove actual malice, as he had written for the plurality in *Rosenbloom*. He viewed the majority decision in *Gertz* as requiring media to observe a "reasonable care" standard (i.e., the "negligence" standard), and said it would lead to self-censorship because publishers would weigh carefully, under it, "a myriad of uncertain factors before publication."   The majority's examples of the "actual injury" for which states might provide compensation, he thought, were wide-ranging, and would give a jury bent on punishing expression of unpopular views a "formidable weapon for doing so."   Finally,

---

[11] Gertz v. Robert Welch, Inc., 418 U.S. 323, 94 S.Ct. 2997, 3011 (1974). This was close to Justice Marshall's position in Rosenbloom v. Metromedia, Inc., 403 U.S. 29, 91 S.Ct. 1811, 1836–38 (1971), above.

[12] Gertz v. Robert Welch, Inc., 418 U.S. 323, 94 S.Ct. 2997, 3011–12 (1974).

[13] Ibid., 3012.

[14] Ibid.

even if recovery were limited under "actual injury" rules, that
would not stop the self-censorship arising from the fear of having
to defend one's publication in an expensive and drawn-out libel
suit.   Brennan believed that the "general or public interest"
concept of *Rosenbloom* would lead to far less self-censorship by
publishers than would state laws imposing liability for negligent
falsehood.[15]

While Brennan and Douglas feared that the decision would
damage the media's protection, and Chief Justice Burger thought
it could inhibit some editors,[16] to Justice Byron White the decision
endangered quite the opposite party: the ordinary citizen who
might be defamed. White's opinion, the longest in the case, placed
his central objections to the majority in its "scuttling the libel
laws of the States in *   *   * wholesale fashion."[17]

The majority accomplished this, he said: [18]

• By requiring the plaintiff in defamation actions to
prove the defendant's culpability beyond his act of publishing defamation (i.e., the plaintiff could no longer have
an actionable case by merely showing "libel *per se;*" he
would also have to prove "fault" on the part of the
publisher—variously referred to in the Gertz opinions as
"negligence" or lack of "reasonable care");

• By requiring the plaintiff to prove actual damage
to reputation resulting from the publication (i.e., no longer would harm be presumed and general damages automatic as under the libel *per se* rule);

In addition, White deplored the fact that it would no longer be
possible to recover punitive damages by showing malice in the
traditional (tort-related) sense of ill will; now the *Sullivan* malice—knowing falsehood or reckless disregard of truth—would be
required.

White found that all this deprived the private citizen of his
"historic recourse" under libel *per se* as recognized by all 50 states,
to redress damaging falsehoods; he made no reference to the fact
that libel under the old tort rules had had almost no role since
Sullivan in 1964 had brought the offense under the Constitution,
and that hardly a handful of judgments under the old rules had
been won by plaintiffs during the decade.

It remains, then, to examine the standards of fault amounting
at least to negligence that the states have adopted since *Gertz*
ordained it in designing major changes in old and recent libel law.
It should be stressed that this level of fault, just as actual malice,

[15] Ibid., 3020.
[16] Ibid., 3014.
[17] Ibid., 3022.
[18] Ibid., 3024–25.

is to be pleaded by the plaintiff and scrutinized by the judge before a libel trial starts, for the possibility of summary judgment exists here as with cases brought by public people (Chap. 4, p. 145).

Most states have designated their standard as the "negligence" of which Justice Powell spoke in *Gertz*. But states were not restricted to this standard, and some have chosen others, more difficult for plaintiffs to prove than negligence. One is known by the shorthand of "gross irresponsibility" on the part of the news medium, the standard chosen by the State of New York. A few states have made the actual malice of Times v. Sullivan their standard: All persons, private as well as public, must prove knowing or reckless falsehood by the publisher—which of course means that these states are providing more protection to media than the First Amendment requires.[19]

In no part of journalism law have the courts more clearly and consistently entered the realm of setting journalistic standards than where they judge the level of "fault"—whether the fault of actual malice or the fault of negligence or gross irresponsibility. Courts examine carefully the reporting and writing process at least as much where a plaintiff is private as where he is public.

In Tennessee, the state Supreme Court decided that it was up to the jury to say whether there had been negligence in a reporter's reliance on a single police record to suggest mistakenly that a woman was an adulterer. Using the "arrest report" of the Memphis police, a Press-Scimitar reporter wrote a story saying that Mrs. Nichols had been shot. The suspect, said the story, was a woman who went to the Nichols home and found her own husband there with Mrs. Nichols. The story used "police said" and "police reported" in attribution, the reporter testifying that these were common terms used to indicate that a source was either a written police record or a policeman's spoken words.

Had the reporter gone to the police record called the "offense report," he would have learned that not only Mrs. Nichols was with the suspect's husband (named Newton), but also Mr. Nichols and two neighbors. There would thus have been no suggestion that Mrs. Nichols was having an adulterous affair and had been "caught" by Mrs. Newton. Almost a month later, the newspaper printed a story correcting the implication of the first story. But Mrs. Nichols sued for libel, and testified at trial that the article had torn up her home, children, and reputation, that the family had had to move, that she had had telephone calls asking how much it cost to get the newspaper to run the correcting account. A friend testified that, after the initial story, people gossipped

---

[19] Pruneyard Shopping Center v. Robbins, 447 U.S. 74, 100 S.Ct. 2035 (1980), 6 Med.L.Rptr. 1311, 1312. Libel Defense Resource Center reported that as of 1983, 24 states had chosen a negligence standard and five a higher standard: LDRC Bulletin # 10, Spring 1984, 21.

about Mrs. Nichols and "said that she was a whore." Before the
case went to the jury for decision, the trial court granted the
newspaper a directed verdict: While "no fault had been shown" on
the part of the reporter, the trial court said, it also noted its
uncertainty as to what standard of fault was required on the basis
of *Gertz.* The Tennessee Court of Appeals, which reversed the
trial court decision on several grounds, said that the standard of
liability was "ordinary care." The case then went to the Tennessee Supreme Court, which in upholding the Court of Appeals and
sending the case back for trial, laid down Tennessee's requirement
upon private libel plaintiffs: negligence.[20]

> In determining the issue of liability the conduct of
> defendant is to be measured against what a reasonably
> prudent person would, or would not, have done under the
> same or similar circumstances. This is the ordinary
> negligence test that we adopt, not a "journalistic malprac-
> tice" test whereby liability is based upon a departure
> from supposed standards of care set by publishers them-
> selves *   *   *.

> In our opinion, the appropriate question to be deter-
> mined from a preponderance of the evidence is whether
> the defendant exercised reasonable care and caution in
> checking on the truth or falsity and the defamatory
> character of the communication before publishing it. In
> answering the question, the jury may rely on its own
> experience and instincts to determine whether an ordina-
> rily prudent person would have behaved as the defendant
> did.

In General Products v. Meredith, an article on wood stoves in
Better Homes and Gardens Home Plan Ideas Magazine warned
against fire danger with the use of triple-walled chimneys in
certain stoves. The manufacturer (found to be "private") of one
type, not subject to the hazards of creosote buildup warned
against, brought suit. The federal District Court denied part of
the magazine's motion for summary judgment, saying that there
was evidence of possible negligence by the reporter in his fact
gathering: [21]

> *   *   * he relied on an earlier book and article and
> did not examine them directly, but drew on his general
> recall of their content. He did not contact the author of
> either source for an update, was not aware that the

---

[20] Memphis Pub. Co. v. Nichols, 569 S.W.2d 412, 418 (Tenn.1978), 4 Med.L.Rptr.
1573.

[21] General Products v. Meredith, 526 F.Supp. 546 (D.C.Va.1981), 7 Med.L.Rptr.
2257, 2261.

information in the magazine article had been repudiated by a subsequent article in another publication, and did not contact anyone in the industry on testing relevant to his subject.

A KARK–TV reporter who happened to be near the scene of police activity in a shopping center store was alerted to the fact, and a camera crew from the station was sent. The crew filmed the scene of police handcuffing two men and placing them in a squad car. Reporter Long questioned the police but got no comment, and interviewed a store clerk from whom she received vague responses. Her story accompanying the broadcast film called the event a "robbery attempt," and said that the two men "allegedly held a store clerk hostage." But the handcuffed men were never arrested, merely detained until police determined that the "tip" on which they acted was false and there had been no robbery attempt. On libel trial, each plaintiff was awarded $12,500.[22]

The Arkansas Supreme Court said there was enough evidence of reporting negligence for the trial court to send that issue to the jury:[23]

> The initial information about a robbery in progress and possible hostage situation was relayed to the television station by way of reports heard on a police scanner. That information was put together with a reporter's eye-witness account of the police taking the appellees into custody. The reporter could get no information from the officers at the scene nor could the producer of the news get any information verified by police headquarters * * *. We cannot say that a news report with its sources consisting of information from a police scanner, uncorroborated by police on the scene, in conjunction with an eye-witness account by a news reporter who did not know the surrounding circumstances of what she observed, will be found to be due care * * *.

If reports from a police "scanner" were suspect in that case, a news story about a gunshot death, based on a written report to media by police "hot line" established to eliminate the need for personal interviews by police, was not negligent. The reporter, who had often used the "hot line" before and found it reliable, accurately quoted the report's statement that the shooting occurred during an argument between husband and wife. Later, the

---

[22] KARK–TV v. Simon, 280 Ark. 228, 656 S.W.2d 702 (1983), 10 Med.L.Rptr. 1049. The Arkansas Supreme Court reversed and remanded the case because of the trial court's error in permitting the jury to consider punitive damages, even though it granted none.

[23] Ibid., 1051.

shooting was ruled accidental. The husband sued the newspaper for implying that he intentionally shot his wife, saying the reporter should have waited for a more "official" report. The Court found no negligence.[24] Nor, in another case, was there negligence in a reporter's failure to interview all eight persons arrested on drug charges, before publishing a story in which a father and son of the same name were confused. The court said that the reporter "undoubtedly could have taken additional steps to insure the accuracy of his facts." But he had talked with several officials, with an attorney, and with neighbors of the raided house, and had listened to a tape of a news conference about the event. His "procedures were well within the bounds of professionalism in the news gathering business." The court found no negligence.[25]

Illinois' Supreme Court adopted negligence as its standard, saying recovery might be had on proof that the defendant knew the statement to be false, or "believing it to be true, lacked reasonable grounds for that belief." It added that a journalist's "failure to make a reasonable investigation into the truth of the statement is obviously a relevant factor." [26] And it quoted the Kansas Supreme Court with approval as further elaboration of what "negligence" means: " * * * the lack of ordinary care either in the doing of an act or in the failure to do something. * * * The norm usually is the conduct of the reasonably careful person under the circumstances." [27]

If it's any help to the reporter, it may be noted that the word "care" is used in various courts' discussions of negligence: simply the "care" of the reasonably prudent person in the Arizona and Tennessee cases above; "ordinary care" in the Illinois/Kansas wording above; "reasonable care" (Washington),[28] "due care" (Ohio).[29]

One analyst has found that a decade's use of the negligence standard demonstrated high uncertainty and severe contradictions in results, and a likelihood that it produces self-censorship by media. He feels that the *Gertz* approach has failed.[30]

In New York, the fault of negligence is not serious enough for a private individual to maintain a libel suit. The New York Court

---

[24] Phillips v. Washington Post, (D.C.Sup.Ct.1982) 8 Med.L.Rptr. 1835.

[25] Horvath v. Ashtabula Telegraph, (Ohio App.1982) 8 Med.L.Rptr. 1657, 1662.

[26] Troman v. Wood, 62 Ill.2d 184, 340 N.E.2d 292, 298–9 (1975).

[27] Ibid., 299; Gobin v. Globe Pub. Co., 216 Kan. 223, 531 P.2d 76 (1975).

[28] Taskett v. King Broadcasting Co., 86 Wash.2d 439, 546 P.2d 81, 85 (1976).

[29] Thomas H. Maloney and Sons, Inc. v. E.W. Scripps Co., 43 Ohio App.2d 105, 334 N.E.2d 494 (1974).

[30] Marc Franklin, What Does Negligence Mean in Defamation Cases?, 6 Comm/ Ent 259, 276–281 (Winter, 1984), and see pp. 266–271 for an excellent analysis of journalistic practices as examined by courts under the negligence standard.

of Appeals has specified that, where the subject matter is of public concern, recovery for the private individual depends on his establishing "that the publisher acted in a grossly irresponsible manner without due consideration for the standards of information gathering and dissemination ordinarily followed by responsible parties." [31]   The Utica *Observer-Dispatch* had reported two different episodes involving drug-charge arrests in a single story.   At one point, it incorrectly brought together school teacher Chapadeau and two other men at a drug-and-beer party, referring to "the trio."   Chapadeau was not there, and he brought a libel action. The Court of Appeals noted the error but also pointed out that the story was written only after two authoritative agencies had been consulted, and that the story was checked by two desk hands at the newspaper.   "This is hardly indicative of gross irresponsibility," said the court.   "Rather it appears that the publisher exercised reasonable methods to insure accuracy." [32]   Summary judgment for the newspaper was upheld.   It was denied, however, where a television reporter who had broadcast an account of fraudulent practices concerning burial expenses could recall little or nothing about his sources and how he obtained the information, and made little or no effort to authenticate his report.   A jury, said the appeals court, would have to decide whether that was gross irresponsibility.[33]

A sterner test faces the private-person plaintiff in Alaska, Michigan, Indiana, Colorado and Wisconsin.   The courts in these states have chosen to apply the Rosenbloom v. Metromedia plurality position as the fault standard: All persons—including private individuals—involved in matters of general or public interest must plead and prove Times v. Sullivan actual malice.   In addition, a federal judge of the District of Columbia has ruled that where a corporation, as distinct from a "natural person", brings a libel suit, it must expect to do the same.[34]

Indiana's Court of Appeals ruled only six months after *Gertz*. It said that Indiana's own constitution called for this rigorous barrier to recovery for libel, rather than for a negligence standard. Differentiating requirements for public and private persons' libel suits, it said, "makes no sense in terms of our constitutional

[31] Chapadeau v. Utica Observer-Dispatch, Inc., 38 N.Y.2d 196, 379 N.Y.S.2d 61, 341 N.E.2d 569, 571 (1975). The similarity to U.S. Supreme Court Justice Harlan's recommended standard for public figures to meet, in Curtis Pub. Co. v. Butts, 388 U.S. 130, 87 S.Ct. 1975 (1967), above, p. 117, is too striking to avoid a connection.

[32] Ibid., 572. See also Goldman v. New York Post, 58 A.D.2d 769, 396 N.Y.S.2d 399 (1977).

[33] Meadows v. Taft Broadcasting Co., 98 A.D.2d 959, 470 N.Y.S.2d 205 (1983), 10 Med.L.Rptr. 1363.

[34] Martin Marietta Corp. v. Evening Star Newspaper Co., 417 F.Supp. 947 (D.D.C.1976). But see Drechsel & Moon, op. cit., for cases contra.

guarantees of free speech and press." [35]   As for Colorado's Supreme Court, it denied libel plaintiffs the use of *Gertz* negligence and said liability would issue "if, and only if, [the publisher] knew the statement to be false or made the statement with reckless disregard for whether it was true or not." [36]   The court felt that freedom of speech and press would be damaged with a lesser standard of fault than Times v. Sullivan actual malice.

Having proved fault at some level—actual malice, negligence, gross irresponsibility—the plaintiff next, as we saw in Justice Powell's majority opinion in the landmark *Gertz* case, must go on to prove actual injury.   No longer, as under old tort rules, will injury be presumed in libel cases except where the plaintiff shows *Sullivan* malice.   Powell said that this could include various injuries—"impairment of reputation and standing in the community, personal humiliation, and mental anguish and suffering," as well as actual out-of-pocket loss (above, p. 158).   Attorney Paul Littlefield, in a case treated above,[37] was not successful in showing injury.   Littlefield had been prohibited from the practice of law for three years, after he had been convicted of attempting to commit a felony.   Further, he was found to have resumed practicing in violation of his probation.   He brought a libel suit against the Fort Dodge Messenger for an erroneous report (it said he had pleaded guilty to a felony, a more serious offense than "attempting to commit a felony").   His injury, he testified, was that he was dismissed from his employment with the federal government after his superviser made a trip to Fort Dodge, Ia., where he learned of Littlefield's disbarment.   The court denied that there was injury: [38]

> Littlefield failed to prove either (1) that his superviser ever believed him to be a felon, or (2) that such belief, rather than knowledge of his disbarment, was the motivating factor in his termination.   Moreover, Littlefield failed to prove any link between the article of which he complains, published in 1974, and his superviser's 1976 discovery of his disbarment.   Thus, Littlefield failed to prove any actual damage resulting from the article.

[35] Aafco Heating and Air Conditioning Co. v. Northwest Publications, Inc., 162 Ind.App. 671, 321 N.E.2d 580 (1975), certiorari denied 424 U.S. 913, 96 S.Ct. 1112 (1976).   Another Indiana Appeals Court has questioned the propriety of this standard: Cochran v. Indianapolis Newspapers, 175 Ind.App. 548, 372 N.E.2d 1211 (1978).

[36] Walker v. Colorado Springs Sun, Inc., 188 Colo. 86, 538 P.2d 450 (1975), certiorari denied 423 U.S. 1025, 96 S.Ct. 469 (1976).   The court reserved judgment on precisely what "reckless disregard" should mean in Colorado.

[37] Littlefield v. Fort Dodge Messenger, 614 F.2d 581 (8th Cir.1980), certiorari denied 445 U.S. 945, 100 S.Ct. 1342, 5 Med.L.Rptr. 2325.

[38] Ibid., 584, 2327.

SEC. 27.   QUALIFIED PRIVILEGE AS A DEFENSE

News media may publish defamation from legislative, judicial or other public and official proceedings without fear of successful libel or slander action; fair and accurate reports of these statements are privileged.

Since long before the landmark year 1964 and the constitutional defense developed in and after New York Times Co. v. Sullivan, libel suits have been defended under statutory and common law provisions termed *qualified privilege, fair comment and criticism,* and *truth.* As noted earlier, the theory that free expression contributes to the public good in a self-governing society underlies the older defenses as well as the constitutional defense.

In some circumstances it is so important to society that people be allowed to speak without fear of a suit for defamation as a result, that their words are given immunity from a finding of libel or slander. The immunity is called privilege. For purposes of the mass media, it is applicable especially in connection with government activity.[39] The paramount importance of full freedom for participants in court, legislative or executive proceedings to say whatever bears on the matter, gives all the participants a full immunity from successful libel action. The immunity for the participant in official proceedings is called "absolute" privilege. No words relevant to the business of the proceeding will support a suit for defamation. If a person is defamed in these proceedings, he cannot recover damages.

Public policy also demands, in an open society, that people know to the fullest what goes on in the proceedings; for this reason, anyone who reports proceedings is given an immunity from successful suit for defamation. For the public at large, "anyone" ordinarily means the mass media. The protection is ordinarily more limited for the reporter of a proceeding than for the participant in the proceeding. It is thus called "qualified" (or "conditional") privilege.[40]

It may be argued that the mere fact of a person's participation in an official proceeding makes him a "public figure," and so puts him under the rigorous requirements of proving *Sullivan's* actual malice in a libel suit. The response, of course, is that neither

---

[39] For other circumstances where it applies, see Prosser, pp. 804–805.

[40] A few states give absolute privilege to press reports of official proceedings, e.g. Thompson's Laws of New York, 1939, Civ.P. § 337, Wis.Stats.1931, § 331.05(1). And as we have seen in Ch. 3, Sec. 14, broadcasters are immune from defamation suits brought for the words of politicians in campaign broadcasts: FECUA v. WDAY, Inc., 360 U.S. 525, 79 S.Ct. 1302 (1959).

Attorney Gertz nor Mrs. Firestone became a public figure through taking part in official court proceedings that resulted in news stories about them.   Both received damages for libel.   (Ch. 4).

It has been held that any citizen has *absolute* immunity in any criticism he makes of government.   The City of Chicago brought a libel suit against the *Chicago Tribune,* claiming damages of $10,000,000 through the *Tribune's* campaign coverage in 1920.   The stories had said that the city was broke, that its credit "is shot to pieces," that it "is hurrying on to bankruptcy and is threatened with a receivership for its revenue."   As a result, the city said, competitive bidding on materials used by the city was stifled, and it was unable to conduct business on an economical basis because of injury to its credit.

The court denied the city's claim.   It said that in any libelous publication concerning a municipal corporation, the citizen and the newspaper possess absolute privilege.[41]

> Every citizen has a right to criticize an inefficient government without fear of civil as well as criminal prosecution.   This absolute privilege is founded on the principle that it is advantageous for the public interest that the citizen should not be in any way fettered in his statements, and where the public service or due administration of justice is involved he shall have the right to speak his mind freely.

It has been said that "no American court which has considered the question has reached a result contrary" to that decision.[42]

Qualified privilege in reporting official proceedings is the heart of the concern here.   The privilege arose in the law of England, the basic rationale having been developed before the start of the nineteenth century in connection with newspaper reports of court proceedings.[43]   While American courts relied on English decisions, America was ahead of England in expanding the protection for press reports.   The immunity was broadened to cover the reporting of legislative and other public official proceedings by the New York legislature in 1854, 14 years before privilege for reporting legislative bodies was recognized in England.[44]   Other states readily adopted the New York rule.

[41] City of Chicago v. Tribune Co., 307 Ill. 595, 139 N.E. 86, 90 (1923).

[42] Grafton v. ABC, 70 Ohio App.2d 205, 435 N.E.2d 1131 (1980), 7 Med.L.Rptr. 1134, 1136, quoting Capital District Regional Off-Track Betting Corp. v. Northeastern Harness Horsemen's Ass'n, 92 Misc.2d 232, 399 N.Y.S.2d 597, 598 (1977).

[43] Curry v. Walter, 170 Eng.Rep. 419 (1796); King v. Wright, 101 Eng.Rep. 1396 (1799).

[44] New York Laws, 1854, Chap. 130; Wason v. Walter, L.R. 4 Q.B. 73 (1868).

For America a famous figure in jurisprudence stated the heart of the rationale for qualified privilege in an early case that has been relied upon by American courts countless times since. Judge Oliver Wendell Holmes, Jr., then of the Massachusetts bench and later a justice of the United States Supreme Court, wrote the words in Cowley v. Pulsifer, 1884.[45] Publisher Royal Pulsifer's *Boston Herald* had printed the content of a petition seeking Charles Cowley's removal from the bar, and Cowley sued. Judge Holmes wrote that the public must have knowledge of judicial proceedings, not because one citizen's quarrels with another are important to public concern,[46]

> * * * but because it is of the highest moment that those who administer justice should always act under the sense of public responsibility, and that every citizen should be able to satisfy himself with his own eyes as to the mode in which a public duty is performed.

The advantage to the nation in granting the privilege of press report, he stressed, is "the security which publicity gives for the proper administration of justice." [47]

While the privilege is "qualified" in the sense that it will not hold if the report of the proceeding is made with malice, it also requires that the story be a fair and accurate account of the proceeding, and not engage in comment. And, most states hold, the story must be one of a "public and official proceeding," not a report of related material that emerges before, after, or in some way outside the proceeding.

Fair and Accurate Reports

Errors can destroy qualified privilege: careless note-taking by a reporter at a court trial, the constant danger of a misspelled name, the arcane and technical jargon and findings of law courts, and all the slip-ups of life with tight deadlines. Further, if the report of an official proceeding is not fair to people involved in it, the reporter can be in trouble. We have seen in the previous chapter how Mrs. Firestone won a libel judgment for $100,000 from Time, Inc., for its error in reporting that her husband's divorce was granted on grounds of adultery.

In the case of Anthony Liquori of Agawam, Mass., a newspaper reporter made an error in an address after extracting other materials from a court record about a "breaking" case in which a man of the same name from Springfield pleaded guilty and was convicted. The reporter took an address from a phone book; the

[45] 137 Mass. 392 (1884).

[46] Ibid., 394.

[47] Ibid.

innocent Liquori was wrongly identified and sued the Republican Company, publisher of the Springfield papers which carried separate stories, both erroneous. The Republican defended with a plea of qualified privilege, arguing that the defense should hold "because the newspaper articles were a substantially accurate report of a judicial proceeding." [48] It asserted that since only the address of the accused was inaccurate, it had published an article which was "substantially true and accurate and entirely fair," and that no more was required. But citing several previous cases about fair and accurate press reports of official proceedings, the Massachusetts Appeals Court said: [49] " * * * an article which labels an innocent man as a criminal because it refers erroneously to his street address, which the reporter gained from a source outside the court records, is neither substantially accurate nor fair." It denied qualified privilege for the Republican. A wrong name, taken accurately from official police records, on the other hand, is privileged.[50]

A newsman who relied on second-hand information from persons in a courtroom following a judge's charge to a grand jury wrote this story:

(Special Dispatch to the News)

ANNAPOLIS, Oct. 20—Corruption in official circles of Annapolis and Anne Arundel County was strongly hinted at by Judge Robert Moss of the Circuit Court in his charge to the grand jury this morning. The judge's charge also included a stinging rebuke to Sheriff Bowie of the county. After declaring the increase of bootlegging was a disgrace to the county, Judge Moss said a clean up of conditions was in order. He referred to Garfield Chase * * * who was employed as a stool pigeon by the sheriff's office in running down bootlegs and said repeated attempts to tamper with Chase and make him useless as a state's witness had been made. He blamed Sheriff Bowie for permitting these attempts * * *.

Taking a chance on the hearsay picked up from persons to whom he talked, and not checking with Judge Moss, the newsman had made major blunders. Sheriff Bowie sued for libel, and as the suit unfolded, it turned out that there was no evidence that Judge Moss had blamed the sheriff for increasing illegal liquor sales, for

[48] Liquori v. Republican Co., 8 Mass.App.Ct. 671, 396 N.E.2d 726, 728 (1979), 5 Med.L.Rptr. 2180.

[49] Ibid., 728–29; 2181.

[50] Biermann v. Pulitzer Pub. Co., 627 S.W.2d 87 (Mo.App.1981), 7 Med.L.Rptr. 2601.

lax conditions in the county jail nor for permitting inmates at the jail to be influenced or tampered with. It was by no means a fair and accurate report of a proceeding, and qualified privilege as a defense failed.[51]

Not every inaccuracy in reporting proceedings is fatal, however. Privilege did not fail in Mitchell v. Peoria Journal-Star,[52] merely because the news story of a court action for liquor ordinance violation got the violators' place of arrest wrong. In Josephs v. News Syndicate Co., Inc.,[53] the newspaper did not lose privilege because somehow the reporter incorrectly slipped into his story of a burglary arrest the statement that the accused had been found under a bed at the scene of the burglary.

The story that is not "fair" often comes from an error of omission rather than one of commission. Given the complexity of some court proceedings, avoiding this is far from easy in many situations. An omission from the following story, rich in human interest and the kind that delights city editors, turned out later to be fatal to a newspaper's plea of privilege.

Ninety-nine-year-old twin sisters, perhaps the oldest twins in the United States, Saturday had won their suit for 13 acres of oil-rich land in Starr County.

The sisters, Inez Garcia Ruiz, and Aniceta Garcia Barrera, had alleged that the land was fraudulently taken from them by a nephew, Benigno Barrera, and Enrique G. Gonzalez, both of Starr County.

The women said they signed a deed to the land when Barrera represented it as a document permitting him to erect a corral fence there. The sisters cannot read or write Spanish or English.

Judge C.K. Quinn in 45th District Court last year returned the sisters the land, which had been in their family since a Spanish grant.

Saturday it was announced the appeals court had ruled against Barrera and Gonzalez.

But the story did not carry the fact that the sisters' original charge against both men had been amended to leave Gonzalez out of it. Gonzalez brought suit for libel against the newspaper and won. The appeals court said that the story implied that Gonzalez had been found guilty of fraud, and that the newspaper could not

[51] Evening News v. Bowie, 154 Md. 604, 141 A. 416 (1928).

[52] 76 Ill.App.2d 154, 221 N.E.2d 516 (1966).

[53] 5 Misc.2d 184, 159 N.Y.S.2d 537 (1957).

successfully plead privilege.[54] It upheld an award of $12,500 to Gonzalez.

Opinion and Extraneous Material

One way to destroy immunity for a news story is to add opinion or material extraneous to the proceeding. It is necessary for reporters to stick to the facts of what comes to light under officials' surveillance. Radio station KYW in Philadelphia broadcast a "documentary" on car-towing rackets, and Austin Purcell sued for defamation. The broadcast had used a judicial proceeding as a basis—a magistrate's hearing at which Purcell was convicted of violating the car-tow ordinance. (Purcell later was exonerated, on appeal.) But the producer of the documentary wove into his script all sorts of material that he had gathered from other sources—the voices of a man and a woman telling how they had been cheated, a conversation with detectives, and something from the district attorney. He added comment of his own to the effect that "the sentencing of a few racketeers is not enough." Said the court: [55]

> Thus through this manipulation of the audio tape and the employment of anonymous voices, the public was made to believe that Purcell was a "mug," a "thug," a "racketeer," one who "gypped" others, and one who "terrified" his victims who were afraid of "reprisals."
>
> * * * All the derogatory phrases and attacks on character employed in the broadcast were funneled by Taylor into a blunderbuss which was fired point-blank at Purcell * * *.

That was defamation, the court said, and it was not protected by qualified privilege. The documentary lost the protection because it contained "exaggerated additions": [56]

> The fault lay in breaking the egg of the extra-judicial "investigation" and the egg of judicial hearing into one omelet and seasoning it with comment and observations which made the parentage of either egg impossible of ascertainment * * *.

[54] Express Pub. Co. v. Gonzalez, 326 S.W.2d 544 (Tex.Civ.App.1959); 350 S.W.2d 589 (Tex.Civ.App.1961).

[55] Purcell v. Westinghouse Broadcasting Co., 411 Pa. 167, 191 A.2d 662, 666 (1963).

[56] Ibid., 668. See also Jones v. Pulitzer Pub. Co., 240 Mo. 200, 144 S.W. 441 (1912); Robinson v. Johnson, 152 C.C.A. 505, 239 F. 671 (1917); Embers Supper Club v. Scripps-Howard, 9 Ohio St.3d 22, 457 N.E.2d 1164 (1984), 10 Med.L.Rptr. 1729.

Malice

New York Times Co. v. Sullivan gave the term "malice" a restricted meaning and one increased in rigor and precision, where public officials and figures are concerned. This malice means that the publisher knew his words were false, or had reckless disregard for whether they were false or not. Malice before that decision was defined in many ways—as ill will toward another, hatred, intent to harm, bad motive, lack of good faith, reckless disregard for the rights of others, for example. People who claimed that news stories of government proceedings libeled them, often charged "malice" in the stories, in terms such as these. Such definitions are still alive for libel that does not proceed under the constitutional protection. One case shows a court's feeling its way in dealing with the question.

A news story in the *St. Paul Dispatch* told of a complaint filed in district court, which accused William and Frank Hurley of depleting almost the entire fortune of an aged woman during her last years of life when she was in an impaired state of mind. Some $200,000 was involved. The complaint had been filed at the order of the Probate Court, where the dead woman's estate was in process. The Hurleys sued for libel, saying among other things that the news report was malicious and thus not privileged.

But the court did not agree. It spoke of two malice rules: *New York Times* and *Restatement of Torts*. The court felt that the Restatement standard, which while it does not use the word malice, "states in effect * * * that actual malice will be present only if a publication was either an inaccurate report of the proceedings or 'made solely for the purpose of causing harm to the person defamed'." [57] This, it said, seemed more difficult to prove than the *Times* rule, but "whichever standard is adopted, plaintiffs in this case must prove actual malice or its equivalent in order to remove the cloak of privilege." And under either standard, the court said, it could find no malice: the news story reporter did not know the Hurleys and the Hurleys could produce no evidence of malice at the trial.

Other courts are using old definitions of malice, where qualified privilege is pleaded, alongside knowing or reckless falsehood. Thus one says there is no malice in that which "the publisher reasonably believed to be true"; another speaks of malice as "intent to injure," and another of malice as "ill will." [58]

---

[57] Hurley v. Northwest Pub. Inc., 273 F.Supp. 967, 972, 974 (D.C.Minn.1967).

[58] Bannach v. Field Enterprises, Inc., 5 Ill.App.3d 692, 284 N.E.2d 31, 32 (1972); and Brunn v. Weiss, 32 Mich.App. 428, 188 N.W.2d 904, 905 (1971). See, also, Orrison v. Vance, 262 Md. 285, 277 A.2d 573, 578 (1971), 3 Med.L.Rptr. 1170.

Official Proceedings

Reports of official activity outside the proceeding—the trial, the hearing, the legislative debate or committee—may not be protected. Some official activity has the color of official proceeding but not the reality.

To start with the courts: Any trial including that of a lesser court "not of record" such as a police magistrate's furnishes the basis for privilege.[59] The ex parte proceeding in which only one party to a legal controversy is represented affords privilege to reporting.[60] So does the grand jury report published in open court.[61]

In most states, the attorneys' pleadings filed with the clerk of court as the basic documents for joining issue are not proceedings that furnish protection. The judge must be involved; an early decision stated the rule that for the immunity to attach, the pleadings must have been submitted "to the judicial mind with a view to judicial action," [62] even if only in pretrial hearings on motions.

A New York decision, as so often in defamation, led the way for several states' rejecting this position and granting protection to reports of pleadings. Newspapers had carried a story based on a complaint filed by Mrs. Elizabeth Nichols against Mrs. Anne Campbell, claiming the latter had defrauded her of $16,000. After the news stories had appeared, Mrs. Nichols withdrew her suit. Mrs. Campbell filed libel suit. Acknowledging that nearly all courts had refused qualified privilege to stories based on pleadings not seen by a judge, the New York Court of Appeals said it would no longer follow this rule. It acknowledged that it is easy for a malicious person to file pleadings in order to air his spleen against another in news stories, and then withdraw the suit. But it said that this can happen also after judges are in the proceeding; suits have been dropped before verdicts. It added that newspapers had so long and often printed stories about actions brought before they reached a judge, that "the public has learned that accusation is not proof and that such actions are at times brought in malice to result in failure." [63] The newspapers won.

[59] McBee v. Fulton, 47 Md. 403 (1878); Flues v. New Nonpareil Co., 155 Iowa 290, 135 N.W. 1083 (1912).

[60] Metcalf v. Times Pub. Co., 20 R.I. 674, 40 A. 864 (1898).

[61] Sweet v. Post Pub. Co., 215 Mass. 450, 102 N.E. 660 (1913).

[62] Barber v. St. Louis Post-Dispatch Co., 3 Mo.App. 377 (1877); Finnegan v. Eagle Printing Co., 173 Wis. 5, 179 N.W. 788 (1920).

[63] Campbell v. New York Evening Post, 245 N.Y. 320, 327, 157 N.E. 153, 155 (1927).

At least a dozen jurisdictions follow this rule today; the filing of a pleading is a public and official act in the course of judicial proceedings in Alabama, California, District of Columbia, Georgia, Kentucky, Nevada, New York, Ohio, Pennsylvania, South Carolina, Tennessee, Washington, and Wyoming.

But other states have not chosen to follow this rule. Massachusetts specifically rejected it in 1945. *The Boston Herald-Traveler* had published a story based on pleadings filed in an alienation of affections case, had been sued for libel, and had lost. The state Supreme Court said: [64]

> * * * the publication of accusations made by one party against another is neither a legal nor a moral duty of newspapers. Enterprise in that matter ought to be at the risk of paying damages if the accusations prove false. To be safe, a newspaper has only to send its reporters to listen to hearings rather than to search the files of cases not yet brought before the court.

Stories based on the following situations were outside "official proceedings" of courts and did not furnish news media the protection of qualified privilege: A newsman's interview of ("conversation with") a United States commissioner, concerning an earlier arraignment before the commissioner; [65] the words of a judge [66] and of an attorney [67] in courtrooms, just before trials were convened formally; the taking by a judge of a deposition in his courtroom, where he was acting in a "ministerial capacity" only, not as a judge.[68] In Bufalino v. Associated Press,[69] the wire service did not actually demonstrate that it relied on FBI records, nor did it identify "officials" upon whom it relied, and did not, thus, show that it was within the scope of privilege. In a Louisiana case,[70] a reporter was outside the privilege by relying on another newspaper's story even though the latter was based on a sheriff's press release.

To shift now to news stories about the executive and administrative sphere of government, where the officer in a government holds a hearing or issues a report or even a press release, absolute privilege usually protects him. And where absolute privilege

---

[64] Sanford v. Boston Herald-Traveler Corp., 318 Mass. 156, 61 N.E.2d 5 (1945): But see Sibley v. Holyoke Transcript-Telegram Pub. Co., 391 Mass. 468, 461 N.E.2d 823 (1982), 8 Med.L.Rptr. 2497.

[65] Wood v. Constitution Pub. Co., 57 Ga.App. 123, 194 S.E. 760 (1937).

[66] Douglas v. Collins, 243 App.Div. 546, 276 N.Y.S. 87 (1935).

[67] Rogers v. Courier Post Co., 2 N.J. 393, 66 A.2d 869 (1949).

[68] Mannix v. Portland Telegram, 144 Or. 172, 23 P.2d 138 (1933).

[69] 692 F.2d 266 (2d Cir.1982), 8 Med.L.Rptr. 2384.

[70] Melon v. Capital City Press, 407 So.2d 85 (La.App.1981), 8 Med.L.Rptr. 1165.

leads, qualified privilege for press reports ordinarily follows. Yet while major and minor federal officials enjoy the privilege under federal decisions, state courts have not been unanimous in granting it.[71]

The formalized hearings of many administrative bodies have a quasi-judicial character, in which testimony is taken, interrogation is performed, deliberation is engaged in, and findings are reported in writing. The reporter can have confidence in such proceedings as "safe" to report. The minutes of a meeting and audits of a city water commission were the basis for a successful plea of privilege by a newspaper whose story reflected on an engineer.[72] The Federal Trade Commission investigated a firm and an account based on the investigation told that the firm had engaged in false branding and labeling; the account was privileged.[73] A news story reporting that an attorney had charged another with perjury was taken from a governor's extradition hearing, a quasi-judicial proceeding, and was privileged.[74]

Also, investigations carried out by executive-administrative officers or bodies without the dignity of hearing-chambers and the gavel that calls a hearing to order ordinarily furnish privilege. For example, a state tax commissioner audited a city's books and reported irregularities in the city council's handling of funds. A story based on the report caused a suit for libel, and the court held that the story was protected by privilege.[75]

Yet not every investigation provides a basis for the defense of qualified privilege; reporters and city editors especially need to know what the judicial precedent of their state is. In a Texas case, a district attorney investigated a plot to rob a bank, and obtained confessions. He made them available to the press. A libel suit brought on the basis of a news story that resulted was won; the confessions were held insufficient executive proceedings to provide the protection.[76]

"Proceedings" that need especially careful attention by the reporter alert to libel possibilities are the activities of police. Police blotters, the record of arrests and charges made, are the source for many news stories. Their status as a basis for a plea of

---

[71] Barr v. Matteo, 360 U.S. 564, 79 S.Ct. 1335 (1959); Prosser, pp. 802–803.

[72] Holway v. World Pub. Co., 171 Okl. 306, 44 P.2d 881 (1935).

[73] Mack, Miller Candle Co. v. Macmillan Co., 239 App.Div. 738, 269 N.Y.S. 33 (1934).

[74] Brown v. Globe Printing Co., 213 Mo. 611, 112 S.W. 462 (1908).

[75] Swearingen v. Parkersburg Sentinel Co., 125 W.Va. 731, 26 S.E.2d 209 (1943).

[76] Caller-Times Pub.Co. v. Chandler, 134 Tex. 1, 130 S.W.2d 853 (1939). But see Woolbright v. Sun Communications, Inc., 480 S.W.2d 864 (Mo.1972).

privilege varies from state to state.[77] The *Washington Star* based a story on an item from a police "hot line," a device for serving news media. The story erroneously reported that a man shot his wife during a quarrel and the man sued for libel. (The jury granted him $1.00 in damages.) So far as qualified privilege for a news story based on the police "hot line" was concerned, the court denied it. A police log of "hot line" reports, the court held, is only an informal arrangement between police and media and is not an official record to which privilege attaches.[78]

Oral reports of preliminary investigations by policemen do not support a plea of privilege in some states. The *Rutland Herald* published a story about two brothers arrested on charges of robbery, and included this paragraph:

> Arthur was arrested on information given to police by the younger brother, it is said. According to authorities, Floyd in his alleged confession, stated that Arthur waited outside the window in the rear of the clothing store while Floyd climbed through a broken window the second time to destroy possible clues left behind.

A suit for libel was brought, and the court denied qualified privilege to the story. It reviewed other states' decisions on whether statements attributed to police were a basis for privilege in news, and held that "a preliminary police investigation" is not a proper basis.[79]

The State of New Jersey has provided by statute that "official statements issued by police department heads" protect news stories, and Georgia has a similar law.[80] In other states, courts have provided the protection through decisions in libel suits. In Kilgore v. Koen,[81] privilege was granted to a story in which deputy sheriffs' statements about the evidence and arrest in a case involving a school principal were the newspaper's source.

As for the legislative branch, the third general sphere of government, state statutes have long declared that the immunity holds in stories of the legislative setting. A New York law led the way in this declaration even before the privilege was recognized in

[77] Sherwood v. Evening News Ass'n, 256 Mich. 318, 239 N.W. 305 (1931); M.J. Petrick, "The Press, the Police Blotter and Public Policy," 46 Journalism Quarterly 475, 1969.

[78] Phillips v. Evening Star, (D.C.Cir.1980) 6 Med.L.Rptr. 2191.

[79] Lancour v. Herald & Globe Ass'n, 111 Vt. 371, 17 A.2d 253 (1941); Burrows v. Pulitzer Pub. Co., 255 S.W. 925 (1923); Pittsburgh Courier Pub.Co. v. Lubore, 91 U.S.App.D.C. 311, 200 F.2d 355 (1952).

[80] Charles Angoff, Handbook of Libel (N.Y. 1946), p. 134; Rogers v. Courier Post, 2 N.J. 393, 66 A.2d 869 (1949); Code of Ga.1933 § 105–704.

[81] 133 Or. 1, 288 P. 192 (1930).

England.[82]   For debates on the floor of Congress or of a state legislature, there has been no question that protection would apply to news stories.   A few early cases indicated that stories of petty legislative bodies such as a town council [83] would not be privileged; but today's reporter need have little fear on this count.

In news stories about a New Jersey municipal council meeting, the city manager was quoted as saying that he was planning to bypass two policemen from promotion because they were insubordinate and "I should have fired them."   There was some question as to whether the meeting was the regular one, or a session held in a conference room later.   The New Jersey Supreme Court said that that didn't matter.   It was not only an official but also a public meeting, at which motions were made by councilmen, sharp discussion was held, and the city manager was queried by councilmen.   Privilege held for the newspaper.[84]

A series of "chain" libel suits in the 1920's against several major newspapers settled any question about immunity in news reporting of committees of legislative bodies: Immunity holds for press reports of committees.[85]

Legislative committees have a long history of operating under loose procedural rules.[86]   Irregular procedures raise the question whether committee activity always meets the requirements of a "legislative proceeding" that gives the basis for immunity in news reports.[87]   In reporting committee activity, the reporter may sense danger signals if the committee:

Holds hearings without a quorum;

Publishes material that its clerks have collected, without itself first investigating charges in the material;

Has not authorized the work of its subcommittees;

Has a chairman given to issuing "reports" or holding press conferences on matters that the committee itself has not investigated.

When state and congressional investigating committees relentlessly hunted "subversion" in the 1940s and 1950s, thousands of persons were tainted with the charge of "communist" during the committee proceedings.   High procedural irregularity was

---

[82] New York Laws, 1854, Chap. 130; Wason v. Walter, L.R. 4 Q.B. 73 (1868).

[83] Buckstaff v. Hicks, 94 Wis. 34, 68 N.W. 403 (1896).

[84] Swede v. Passaic Daily News, 30 N.J. 320, 153 A.2d 36 (1959).

[85] Cresson v. Louisville Courier-Journal, 299 F. 487 (6th Cir.1924).

[86] Walter Gelhorn (ed.), The States and Subversion (Ithaca: Cornell Univ.Press, 1952); Ernst J. Eberling, Congressional Investigations (New York: Columbia Univ. Press, 1928).

[87] H.L. Nelson, Libel in News of Congressional Investigating Committees (Minneapolis: Univ. of Minn.Press, 1961), Chs. 1, 2.

common.   Yet only one libel case growing out of these irregular proceedings reached the highest court of a state, and the newspaper successfully defended with a plea of privilege.[88]

Public Proceedings

The laws of at least ten states provide that qualified privilege applies to news reports of "public" proceedings.[89]   In some other states the same rule has been applied under common law principles.[90]   The word "public" has in almost all cases meant "not secret" rather than proceedings which have a strong element of "public interest" or "public concern." [91]   In several cases, immunity has been lost where a newspaper obtained access to secret proceedings of government bodies and reported libelous stories based on these proceedings.   In McCurdy v. Hughes,[92] a newspaper reported on the secret meeting of a state bar board in which a complaint against an attorney was considered.   The attorney brought a libel suit for derogatory statements in the story and won.

The state of New York denied privilege to news reports of secret proceedings repeatedly, under its ground-breaking statute of 1854.   The statute provided privilege to a "fair and true report * * * of any judicial, legislative, or other public official proceeding." [93]   But, in 1956, after 102 years under the "public" provision of the statute, New York changed its law and eliminated the word "public."   Editor & Publisher, trade publication of the American daily newspaper world, reported that the legislature made this change "at the behest of newspaper interests." [94]   The change was "drafted as the aftermath to two successful libel suits against New York City newspapers," the magazine said, and added that with the change, it had become possible for a newspaper to publish with immunity news of an official proceeding even though the proceeding was not public.

[88] Coleman v. Newark Morning Ledger Co., 29 N.J. 357, 149 A.2d 193 (1959).

[89] Angoff, passim, shows Arizona, California, Idaho, Louisiana, Minnesota, North Dakota, Oklahoma, South Dakota, Utah and Wisconsin besides New York which in 1956 deleted the word "public" from its statute.

[90] Parsons v. Age-Herald Pub. Co., 181 Ala. 439, 61 So. 345 (1913); Switzer v. Anthony, 71 Colo. 291, 206 P. 391 (1922).

[91] A rare exception is Farrell v. New York Evening Post, 167 Misc. 412, 3 N.Y.S.2d 1018, 1022 (1938) where the word "public" was held to mean "of general interest or concern," and a story based on the report by an executive officer of his secret proceeding was held privileged.

[92] McCurdy v. Hughes, 63 N.D. 435, 248 N.W. 512 (1933).

[93] New York Laws, 1854, Chap. 130: McCabe v. Cauldwell, 18 Abb Pr. 377 (N.Y.1865); Danziger v. Hearst Corp., 304 N.Y. 244, 107 N.E.2d 62 (1952); Stevenson v. News Syndicate Co., 276 App.Div. 614, 96 N.Y.S.2d 751 (1950).

[94] May 5, 1956, p. 52. See New York State Legislative Annual, 1956, pp. 494–495.

But the New York Court of Appeals ruled in a 4–3 decision in 1970 that elimination of the word "public" from that statute does not mean that news stories of matrimonial proceedings—secret under New York law—are protected by qualified privilege. Matrimonial proceedings are "inherently personal," the Court held, and "the public interest is served not by publicizing but by sealing them and prohibiting their examination by the public." [95]

With the New York law, there is the New Jersey decision mentioned above, Coleman v. Newark Morning Ledger Co.[96] In 1953, the late Senator Joseph McCarthy of Wisconsin was investigating the Army Signal Corps laboratory at Fort Monmouth, N.J. Sitting as a one-man subcommittee of the Senate permanent Subcommittee on Investigations, McCarthy repeatedly held secret executive-session hearings. Occasionally he emerged from them to give oral "reports" to waiting newsmen, portraying a sensational "spy ring" in operation at Fort Monmouth, associated with Julius Rosenberg who had been executed for espionage.

On October 23, 1953, the *Newark Star-Ledger* ran a story saying McCarthy orally reported that his secret investigation had learned that an ex-Marine officer, suspended from his Fort Monmouth job in 1949 after military intelligence found classified documents in his apartment, had once roomed with Rosenberg. Keys to the apartment were in the possession of known Communists, McCarthy said. Then on December 9, 1953, the Star-Ledger identified the ex-Marine as Coleman, in reporting a public hearing held by McCarthy.

Coleman sued the Star-Ledger for libel. He said that the statements were false and were unprotected because they were spoken outside the proceeding. McCarthy was among the witnesses at the libel trial. He said that the newspaper story was an accurate report of his report of the secret proceeding. He also said that he had been authorized by the subcommittee, in executive session, to make reports to the press as to what transpired during executive sessions.

The court accepted McCarthy's testimony, and held that the newspaper's plea of qualified privilege was good. It denied that the secret nature of McCarthy's subcommittee session destroyed qualified privilege for McCarthy as a reporter or for the newspaper as a reporter. Secret sessions often are indispensable, it said, and "this does not preclude the publication of such information as

---

[95] Shiles v. News Syndicate Co., 27 N.Y.2d 9, 313 N.Y.S.2d 104, 107, 261 N.E.2d 251 (1970).

[96] 29 N.J. 357, 149 A.2d 193 (1959).

the committee may in its discretion deem fit and proper for the general good." [97]

Chief Justice Joseph Weintraub of the New Jersey Supreme Court was the only dissenter in the 5-to-1 decision for the newspaper. He said that qualified privilege depends everywhere on a "fair and accurate report" of the proceedings; but who could say whether McCarthy gave the fair and accurate report required? In his words, "There is no way to measure a report against this standard when the proceedings are secret," and "The secret nature of the hearing negates the reason for the privilege." [98]

A final note about the word "public" in connection with qualified privilege: The immunity has been held to apply for news reports of the "public meeting" or "public gathering" where people are free to attend for discussion of matters of public concern. This is the general rule in England. The reasons for it are similar to those protecting reports of official proceedings: It is important for the community to know what is happening in matters where the public welfare and concern are involved. The protection in this situation has been granted by a few courts in America. [99] As for private gatherings of stockholders, directors, or members of an association or organization, they are no basis for privilege in news reports.

SEC. 28.   TRUTH AS A DEFENSE

Most state laws provide that truth is a complete defense in libel cases, but some require that the publisher show "good motives and justifiable ends." The United States Supreme Court has not ruled on whether truth may ever be subjected to civil or criminal liability.

The defense of truth (often called "justification") in civil libel has ancient roots developed in the common law of England. It was taken up by American courts as they employed the common law in the colonial and early national periods, and was transferred from the common law to many state statutes. Its basis appeals to common sense and ordinary ideas of justice: Why, indeed, should an individual be awarded damages for harm to his reputation when the truth of the matter is that his record does not merit a

---

[97] Ibid., 205–206. See also Ingenere v. ABC, (D.C.Mass.1984) 11 Med.L.Rptr. 1227, where Massachusetts' privilege was held applicable to news reports based on internal investigative documents of the federal General Services Administration not intended for distribution to the public; Medico v. Time, Inc., 643 F.2d 134 (3d Cir.1981), 6 Med.L.Rptr. 2529, 2535 certiorari denied 454 U.S. 836, 102 S.Ct. 139 (1981), secret FBI records.

[98] Ibid., 209.

[99] Phoenix Newspapers, Inc. v. Choisser, 82 Ariz. 271, 312 P.2d 150 (1957); Pulverman v. A.S. Abell Co., 228 F.2d 797 (4th Cir.1956).

good reputation? To print or broadcast the truth about a person is no more than he should expect; and in addition the social good may be served by bringing to light the truth about people whose work involves them in the public interest.

It is held by some courts that truth alone is a complete defense, regardless of the motives behind its publication, and this squares with the libel statutes in most states. Some state laws continue to qualify, and provide that truth is a defense if it is published "with good motives and justifiable ends." [1] The qualifying term goes back to 1804, when Alexander Hamilton used it in his defense of newspaperman Harry Croswell in a celebrated New York criminal libel case.[2] So far as the comatose *criminal* libel offense is concerned, however, the United States Supreme Court has ruled that the Hamiltonian qualification is unconstitutional, and may not be required of a defendant.[3]

The Supreme Court has shied away from ruling that truth is always a defense in libel. Justice White wrote in Cox Broadcasting Co. v. Cohn that the Court had not decided the question "whether truthful publications may ever be subjected to civil or criminal liability." Earlier cases, he said, had "carefully left open the question" whether the First Amendment requires "that truth be recognized as a defense in a defamation action brought by a private person * * *." [4]

Since the Supreme Court rules of *Sullivan* and *Gertz* have made it plain that some level of fault on the part of the media must be shown—from knowing falsity to negligence—the burden of pleading and showing falsity has largely been on the plaintiff where he is a public person. Yet the *Restatement of Torts* takes the position that it cannot yet be said that the burden is inescapably on the plaintiff: [5]

> Placing the burden on the party asserting the negative necessarily creates difficulties, and the problem is accentuated when the defamatory charge is not specific in its terms but quite general in nature. Suppose, for example, that a newspaper published a charge that a storekeeper short-changes his customers when he gets a chance. How

[1] State statutes and constitutional provisions are collected in Angoff, op cit. See also Note, 56 N.W.Univ.L.Rev. 547 (1961); Garrison v. Louisiana, 379 U.S. 64, 85 S.Ct. 209 (1964), footnote 7.

[2] 3 Johns.Cas. 337 (N.Y.1818).

[3] Garrison v. Lousianna, 379 U.S. 64, 85 S.Ct. 209 (1964).

[4] 420 U.S. 469, 490, 95 S.Ct. 1029, 1043–44 (1975). But see Restatement, Second, Torts, § 581A, p. 235, which says "There can be no recovery in defamation for a statement of fact that is true * * *."

[5] Ibid., § 613, p. 310. And see Robert Sack, Libel, Slander, and Related Problems (N.Y., 1980), 135–136.

is he expected to prove that he has not short-changed customers when no specific occasions are pointed to by the defendant?

One court has said that the burden of proof rests on the plaintiff to show defamation and to prove damages. "He need not show, however, that the statement is false. There is a legal presumption of falsity which the defendant may rebut by proving truth as a defense." [6] It is clear that defendants in libel suits frequently are at pains to prove that the alleged libel is true.

Not every detail of an allegedly libelous story must be proved accurate in order to rebut a charge of "falsity," but rather, that the story is "substantially" true.[7] But no formula can measure just what inaccuracy will be tolerated by a particular court.

The *New York World-Telegram and Sun* tried to establish truth of the following statement from its pages, but failed:

> John Crane, former president of the UFA now under indictment, isn't waiting for his own legal developments. Meanwhile, his lawyers are launching a $$$$$$ defamation suit.

Focusing on the word "indictment," Crane brought a libel suit against the newspaper and the columnist who wrote the item. He said that the defendant knew or could have learned the falsity of the charge by using reasonable care.

The defendants chose to try to establish the truth of the charge. They did not try to show that there had been a legal indictment by a grand jury. Instead, they said that the facts were widely published and commented upon by the press of the city. They claimed that Crane was "under indictment" in a nonlegal sense, that he had been accused of various crimes by others.

But you cannot prove the truth of one charge against a man by showing that he was suspected or guilty in connection with another.[8] The court held that "indictment" means the legal action, ordinarily carried out by a grand jury, and that use of the term to mean accusation by private persons is rare. No reader, it said, would accept the looser usage as the intended one.[9]

[6] Memphis Pub. Co. v. Nichols, 569 S.W.2d 412, 420 (Tenn.1978), 4 Med.L.Rptr. 1573, 1579.

[7] Hein v. Lacy, 228 Kan. 249, 616 P.2d 277 (1980), 6 Med.L.Rptr. 1662, 1666; Prosser, 825.

[8] Sun Printing and Pub. Ass'n v. Schenck, 40 C.C.A. 163, 98 F. 925 (1900); Kilian v. Doubleday & Co., 367 Pa. 117, 79 A.2d 657 (1951); Yarmove v. Retail Credit Co., 18 A.D.2d 790, 236 N.Y.S.2d 836 (1963).

[9] Crane v. New York World Telegram Corp., 308 N.Y. 470, 126 N.E.2d 753 (1955); Friday v. Official Detective Stories, 233 F.Supp. 1021 (D.C.Pa.1964).

The same term—"indictment"—was used by another newspaper in an incorrect way, but was held *not* to be libelous. The word appeared in connection with conflict-of-interest findings discussed in an editorial. A councilman was never truly indicted, but rather was charged by delivery of a summons, and convicted. The court held that "indictment" was substantially accurate, and although technically incorrect, did not constitute defamation.[10]

Thus loose usage of certain technical terms does not always destroy a plea of truth. This is what a court ruled when a Massachusetts newspaper said that a man named Joyce had been "committed" to a mental hospital when actually he had been "admitted" to the hospital at the request of a physician as the state law provided. The newspaper's words that caused the man to bring a libel suit were that the man "charges * * * that his constitutional rights were violated when he was committed to the hospital last November." In ruling for the newspaper which pleaded truth, the court said: [11]

> Strictly * * * "commitment" means a placing in the hospital by judicial order * * *. But the words [of the news story] are to be used in their "natural sense with the meaning which they could convey to mankind in general." This meaning of the word "commitment" was placing in the hospital pursuant to proceedings provided by law. In so stating as to the plaintiff * * * the defendant reported correctly.

Of course, the newsman who is highly attuned to nuances in word meanings may save his newspaper the expense and trouble of even a successful libel defense by avoiding gaffes such as confusing "commit" with "admit." While news media continue to be staffed in part by writers insensitive to shades of meaning, however, they may take some comfort in the law's willingness to bend as in the Joyce case.

Courts frequently hold that truth will not be destroyed by a story's minor inaccuracies. Thus truth succeeded although a newspaper had printed that the plaintiff was in police custody on August 16, whereas he had been released on August 15; [12] and it was not fatal to truth to report in a news story that an arrest, which in fact took place at the Shelly Tap tavern, occurred at the Men's Social Club.[13]

---

10 Schaefer v. Hearst Corp., (Md.Super.Ct.1979) 5 Med.L.Rptr. 1734.

11 Joyce v. George W. Prescott Pub. Co., 348 Mass. 790, 205 N.E.2d 207 (1965).

12 Piracci v. Hearst Corp., 263 F.Supp. 511 (D.C.Md.1966), affirmed 371 F.2d 1016 (4th Cir.1967).

13 Mitchell v. Peoria Journal-Star, 76 Ill.App.2d 154, 221 N.E.2d 516 (1966).

In accord with the maxim that "tale bearers are as bad as tale tellers," it is no defense for a news medium to argue that it reported accurately and truthfully someone else's false and defamatory statements. The broadcaster or newspaper reporter writes at the employer's peril; the words "it is reported by police" or "according to a reliable source" do not remove from the news medium faced with a libel suit the job of proving that the allegation or rumor itself is true.[14] Liability under the "republication" rule persists.[15]

Even though every fact in a story is truthful, an error of omission can result in libel. Recall, now, the *Memphis Press-Scimitar's* accurate facts about the shooting of Mrs. Nichols. A woman had gone to the home of Mrs. Nichols, and there, the newspaper said on the basis of a police arrest report, found her own husband (Newton) with Mrs. Nichols. The implication of an adulterous affair between the two was plain in the story, all of whose facts were accurate. Mrs. Nichols brought libel suits. The Press-Scimitar had omitted much from the story, as shown by a separate police document (the "offense report"): Not only were Mrs. Nichols and Mr. Newton at the home, but also Mr. Nichols and two other people. Had these facts been in the news story, there would have been no suggestion of an affair. The Press-Scimitar pleaded truth of its words, but the Tennessee Supreme Court said: [16]

> In our opinion, the defendant's reliance on the truth of the facts stated in the article in question is misplaced. The proper question is whether the *meaning* reasonably conveyed by the published words is defamatory * * *. The publication of the complete facts could not conceivably have led the reader to conclude that Mrs. Nichols and Mr. Newton had an adulterous relationship. The published statement, therefore, so distorted the truth as to make the entire article false and defamatory. It is no defense whatever that individual statements within the article were literally true.

Even ill will and an intent to harm will not affect truth where it is said of a public person; knowing or reckless falsehood must be shown.[17] As we have seen, however, against a *private* person's suit, some states provide that truth is a good defense only if made

---

[14] Miller, Smith & Champagne v. Capital City Press, 142 So.2d 462 (La.App.1962); Dun & Bradstreet, Inc. v. Robinson, 233 Ark. 168, 345 S.W.2d 34 (1961).

[15] Cianci v. New Times, (2d Cir. 7/11/80) 6 Med.L.Rptr. 1625, 1629–30.

[16] Memphis Pub. Co. v. Nichols, 569 S.W.2d 412, 420 (Tenn.1978), 4 Med.L.Rptr. 1573, 1579. See also for true facts but false implication, Dunlap v. Philadelphia Newspapers, 301 Pa.Super. 475, 448 A.2d 6 (1982), 8 Med.L.Rptr. 1974.

[17] Schaefer v. Lynch, 406 So.2d 185 (La.1981), 7 Med.L.Rptr. 2302.

with good motives and for justifiable ends—that ill will (the "malice" of tort law) may defeat the defense.[18] Belief in the truth of the charge may be useful in holding down damages, if it can be established to the satisfaction of the court. Showing honest belief indicates good faith and absence of malice, important to the mitigation of general damages and the denial or lessening of punitive damages to the successful suit-bringer in a libel case.

An article about a public official's criminal conviction failed to state that, upon retrial, the official was acquitted, and the defense of truth was denied the magazine.[19] Also, courts have refused to accept the plea of truth where news media would not identify anonymous sources upon whom defamatory stories were based.[20]

The plea of truth always presents an uncomfortable possibility to the defendant in a libel case: If the proof fails, the attempt to prove it may be considered a republication of the libel and become evidence of malice.[21] And malice, as indicated earlier, may be reason for assessing punitive damages. There is a tendency in recent decades, however, to examine the manner and spirit with which the defense of truth is made. If the plea of truth appears to have as its real object the defense of the case, rather than to repeat the defamation, evidence of malice is not necessarily concluded.

The *Las Vegas* (Nev.) *Sun* pleaded the truth of this charge which it made in a headline concerning one Franklin: "Babies for Sale. Franklin Black Market Trade of Child Told." The judge instructed the jury that "Failure to prove a plea of truth may be considered as evidence of express and continued malice." The jury decided that the Sun had not proved truth, and awarded Franklin damages. The Sun appealed, and the Nevada Supreme Court ruled that the judge's instruction to the jury was in error. It said that although there is authority to support the judge's instruction,[22]

> * * * the better rule is that failure of proof of truth is not itself evidence of malice. Where malice appears a plea of truth may be considered in aggravation of damages as an unprivileged republication of the original libel. However, to constitute such aggravation it should appear

[18] Sack, 130–131.

[19] Torres v. Playboy Enterprises, (D.S.Tex.1980) 7 Med.L.Rptr. 1182.

[20] Dowd v. Calabrese, 577 F.Supp. 238 (D.D.C.1983), 10 Med.L.Rptr. 1208, 1213.

[21] Hall v. Edwards, 138 Me. 231, 23 A.2d 889 (1942); Coffin v. Brown, 94 Md. 190, 50 A. 567 (1901).

[22] Las Vegas Sun, Inc. v. Franklin, 74 Nev. 282, 329 P.2d 867 (1958). See also Mitchell v. Peoria Journal-Star, Inc., 76 Ill.App.2d 154, 221 N.E.2d 516 (1966).

that the defense of truth was not pleaded in good faith. When the defendant actually believes his plea to be true and offers evidence in support of it in good faith, the rule should not apply to penalize him * * *.

SEC. 29. OPINION AND FAIR COMMENT AS DEFENSES

State statutes and the common law provide the doctrine of fair comment and criticism as a defense against libel suits brought by people and institutions who offer their work to the public for its approval or disapproval, or where matters of public interest are concerned. Despite a view that it has become obsolete under recent constitutional protection for opinion, media and courts continue to use it.

For most of two centuries, English and American courts have held that statements of opinion are to be differentiated from statements of fact and given special protection in defamation. Called the defense of "fair comment" under the common law, the protection persists today but lives a clouded life: For one thing, courts disagree whether constitutional doctrine of 1974 (in dictum from Gertz v. Robert Welch, Inc.) [23] has replaced the defense; for another, short of replacing the defense, *Gertz* has been interpreted in differing ways with confusing results. As one court wrote in a case involving comment, "Few areas of the law are as analytically difficult as that of libel and slander where courts attempt to mesh modern, first amendment principles with common law precedents." [24] First let us examine major outlines of fair comment under common law and state statutes, and second some developments under the Constitution since *Gertz*.

Fair Comment Under Common Law and State Statutes

Opinion embraces comment and criticism. The defense of fair comment was shaped to protect the public stake in the scrutinizing of important public matters; comment and criticism have permeated news and editorial pages and broadcasts, explaining, drawing inferences, reacting, evaluating. The law protects even scathing criticism of the public work of persons and institutions who offer their work for public judgment: public officials and figures; those whose performance affects public taste in such realms as music, art, literature, theater, and sports; and institutions whose activities affect the public interest such as hospitals,

[23] 418 U.S. 323, 94 S.Ct. 2997 (1974).

[24] Orr v. Argus-Press, 586 F.2d 1108 (6th Cir.1978), 4 Med.L.Rptr. 1593, 1595, certiorari denied 440 U.S. 960, 99 S.Ct. 1502 (1979).

schools, processors of food, public utilities, drug manufacturers. Under fair comment legal immunity against a defamation action is given for the honest expression of opinion on public persons and/or matters of public concern.[25]   New York Times Co. v. Sullivan quoted an earlier decision: [26]

> In the realm of religious faith, and in that of political belief, sharp differences arise. In both fields the tenets of one may seem the rankest error to his neighbor.   To persuade others to his own point of view, the pleader, as we know, at times resorts to exaggeration, to vilification of men who have been, or are, prominent in church or state, and even to false statement. But the people of this nation have ordained in the light of history, that, in spite of the probability of excesses and abuses, these liberties are, in the long view, essential to enlightened opinion and right conduct on the part of the citizens of a democracy.

Even the most public persons have some small sphere of private life. Although one's private character of course can deeply affect one's public acts, there are circumstances in which comment on private acts and personal character is not embraced by the protection of fair comment.[27] The wide sweep of *Sullivan,* it will be remembered, protects only statements about public persons' *public* acts; and courts continue to hold that public persons retain a private sphere.[28]

"*FACTS.*" States have varied in their fair comment rules. Most have said that the protection for comment does not extend to that which is falsely given out as "fact". This presents at the outset the often difficult problem of separating facts—which are susceptible of proof—and opinion—which cannot be proved true or false. Prof. Robert Sack writes that nothing in the law of defamation "is any more elusive than distinguishing between the two." [29] But beyond the problem of making that often cloudy distinction is the diversity of rules from state to state. The majority have insisted on the rule of "no protection for misstatement of fact." Oregon's Supreme Court, for example, held "it is one thing to comment upon or criticize * * * the acknowledged or proved act

[25] Prosser, 812–816; Harper and James, Law of Torts (Boston, 1956).

[26] 376 U.S. 254, 271, 84 S.Ct. 710, 721 quoting Cantwell v. Connecticut, 310 U.S. 296, 310, 60 S.Ct. 900, 906 (1940).

[27] Post Pub. Co. v. Moloney, 50 Ohio St. 71, 89, 33 N.E. 921 (1893); Harper and James, 461.

[28] Zeck v. Spiro, 52 Misc.2d 629, 276 N.Y.S.2d 395 (1966); Stearn v. MacLean-Hunter Ltd., 46 F.R.D. 76 (D.C.N.Y.1969); Standke v. B.E. Darby & Sons, Inc., 291 Minn. 468, 193 N.E.2d 139, 144 (1971). Note, Fact and Opinion after Gertz v. Robert Welch, Inc., 34 Rutgers L.Rev. 81, 88–89 (Fall 1981).

[29] Sack, 155. See also Gregory v. McDonnell Douglas Corp., 17 Cal.3d 596, 131 Cal.Rptr. 641, 644–645, 552 P.2d 425, 428–429 (1976).

of a public man, and quite another to assert that he has been guilty of particular acts of misconduct." [30] Under this interpretation, "charges of specific criminal misconduct are not protected as 'opinions'." [31]

But a minority of states provide protection for false statement of fact, the variation being illustrated by Snively v. Record Pub. Co.,[32] a California decision. The Los Angeles police chief brought a libel action against the *Los Angeles Record* for a cartoon which, he said, suggested he was receiving money secretly for illegal purposes. The California Supreme Court held that even if the charge of criminality were false, the cartoon was protected by fair comment: [33]

> The right of the publisher to speak or write is complete and unqualified under the Code, except that he must speak or write "without malice." When under these conditions he honestly believes that the person of whom he speaks or writes is guilty of a crime of a nature that makes the fact material to the interests of those whom he addresses, it is as much his right and duty to declare to them that fact as it would be to tell them any other fact pertinent to the occasion and material to their interests.
>
> * * * he is not liable for damages * * *.

Michigan's fair comment statute likewise has been held to protect false statements of fact such as a charge of "fraud" against a real estate developer. The Sixth Circuit Court of Appeals said in Orr v. Argus-Press [34] that the state's statute protected both opinion and fact about matters of public interest if the statement "be honestly believed to be true, and published in good faith" (i.e., without the "ill-will" malice of the common law).

The protection in states such as the above two—California and Michigan—is broad and deep. It applies to *any story on a matter of public concern or interest*. In such, whether the plaintiff is private or public does not matter. If there is honest belief and no ill-will malice on the part of the news medium, false statements of fact are protected. Could private citizens Hutchinson and Wol-

---

[30] Marr v. Putnam, 196 Or. 1, 246 P.2d 509, 524 (1952); Otero v. Ewing, 162 La. 453, 110 So. 648 (1926).

[31] Cianci v. New Times Pub. Co., 639 F.2d 54 (2d Cir.1980), 6 Med.L.Rptr. 1625, 1635, 639 F.2d 54; Restatement (Second) of Torts, # 571.

[32] 185 Cal. 565, 198 P. 1 (1921).

[33] Ibid., 571.

[34] 586 F.2d 1108, 1113–14 (6th Cir.1978), 4 Med.L.Rptr. 1594, 1696–97; Schultz v. Newsweek, 688 F.2d 911 (6th Cir.1982), 7 Med.L.Rptr. 2552, 2558. For a case whose facts were *not* matters deserving "robust public debate," and which denied protection, see Rouch v. Enquirer and News, 137 Mich.App. 39, 357 N.W.2d 794 (1984).

ston (above, pp. 130–132) have won their suits under such rules? Suing under Gertz v. Robert Welch,[35] it will be recalled, both could win by showing "negligence" on the part of the news medium. But negligence does not destroy the protection of fair comment under California and Michigan laws.

In point is the case of private citizen Rollenhagen of Orange, Calif., an auto mechanic about whom CBS aired a television story. After one of his customers had complained to police about his charges for repairs, they arrested him for failure to give a written estimate in advance of auto repairs as required by law, handcuffed him, and led him past a CBS camera crew. CBS interviewed Rollenhagen and police—who said the customer had been victimized—and then ran the story. Rollenhagen sued charging false defamation, and the California Court of Appeal ruled that the story was protected by the state law of fair comment on matters of public interest. It said that while *Gertz* had recently permitted states to let private persons recover where there was negligence in a story of public concern, California had not adopted that rule, but rather had stuck with its half-century-old fair comment law: [36] The subject of auto repair was a matter of general public interest (there had been "rather extensive legislative coverage in an attempt to protect the public from fraudulent and dishonest practices," the court noted), and there was no hatred or ill will (malice, under California tort law) on the part of CBS.

> The California standard [for fair comment] is codified in Civil Code section 47, subdivision 3, as granting a qualified privilege to all publications which concern a matter of legitimate public interest. This standard of liability predates *Gertz* by over 50 years and the only impact the *Gertz* decision has on the standard is to decree it a constitutionally acceptable one.
>
> Absent evidence of malice, the Civil Code ∗ ∗ ∗ privilege governs and the defendants are entitled to judgment as a matter of law.

Another question of "fact" (besides the foregoing differences over protection for factual falsity) faces the writer under some states' rules of fair comment: the comment must be based on facts—facts stated with the comment, or facts that are known or readily available to the reader. The Fisher Galleries asked art critic Leslie Ahlander of the *Washington Post* to review an exhibition of paintings by artist Irving Amen. Later, Mrs. Ahlander's column carried this comment:

[35] 418 U.S. 323, 94 S.Ct. 2997 (1974).

[36] Rollenhagen v. Orange, 116 Cal.App.3d 414, 172 Cal.Rptr. 49 (1981), 6 Med.L. Rptr. 2561, 2564.

The Fisher Galleries are showing about 20 oils by the noted printmaker, Irving Amen. The paintings are warm in color and expressionist in tendency, but lack the distinction of the prints. They are so badly hung among many commercial paintings that what quality they might have is completely destroyed. The Fisher Galleries should decide whether they are a fine arts gallery or a commercial outlet for genuine "hand-painted" pictures. The two do not mix.

Fisher sued for libel, and the *Post* defended on the grounds of fair comment and criticism. Fisher argued that in order for opinion to be protected by the fair comment doctrine, the facts upon which it is based must be stated or referred to so that the reader may draw his own conclusions. The court acknowledged that this is the rule in some jurisdictions.[37] But it followed instead the view adopted by the *Restatement of Torts*[38] that the facts do not necessarily have to be stated in the article, but may be facts "known or readily available to the persons to whom the comment or criticism is addressed * * *." The court said:[39]

> We believe that this is the better view, for criticism in the art world may be based on such intangibles as experience, taste, and feeling. It is often impossible for the critic to explain the basis for his opinion; to require him to do so would tend to discourage public discussion of artistic matters. So long as the facts are available to the public, the criticism is within the doctrine of fair comment. The Amen show was open to the public both before and after publication, and the facts upon which Mrs. Ahlander based her conclusions were readily accessible to any who wanted to test them.

Besides the problem of "fact," the ancient question of what constituted "malice" entered the picture and had much to do with what was "fair." Malice would destroy the protection of fair comment; and malice for centuries before New York Times Co. v. Sullivan had been defined in various ways. Furthermore, various characteristics of "unfair" expression were sometimes treated as suggesting malice. Thus from state to state and jurisdiction to jurisdiction, malice could be pretty much what the court felt it ought to be: ill-will, enmity, spite, hatred, intent to harm; "excessive publication,"[40] vehemence,[41] words that were not the honest

---

[37] A.S. Abell Co. v. Kirby, 227 Md. 267, 176 A.2d 340 (1961); Cohalan v. New York Tribune, 172 Misc. 20, 15 N.Y.S.2d 58 (1939).

[38] # 606.

[39] Fisher v. Washington Post Co., 212 A.2d 335, 338 (D.C.App.1965).

[40] Pulliam v. Bond, 406 S.W.2d 635, 643 (Mo.1966).

[41] England v. Daily Gazette Co., 143 W.Va. 700, 104 S.E.2d 306 (1958).

opinion of the writer,[42] words which there was no "probable cause to believe true," [43] words showing reckless disregard for the rights of others,[44] words which a reasonable man would not consider fair.[45] Malice still can be "adduced" [46] from such qualities of expression in some jurisdictions where qualified privilege or fair comment is at issue.

Thus the West Virginia Supreme Court held in denying fair comment's protection against the *Charleston Gazette* which had tongue-lashed several legislators who sued it for saying, among other things, that they had sold their votes: [47]

> While it is very generally held that fair comment as to matter of public affairs is not actionable, * * * it appears to be definitely settled if such comment is unfair or unreasonably violent or vehement, immunity from liability is denied. "Matters of public interest must be discussed temperately. Wicked and corrupt motive should never be wantonly assigned. And it will be no defense that the writer, at the time he wrote, honestly believed in the truth of the charges he was making, if such charges be made recklessly, unreasonably, and without any foundation in fact * * *. [T]he writer must bring to his task some degree of moderation and judgment." Newell, Slander and Libel * * *.

But in another state—Iowa—there was no suggestion in a Supreme Court decision that "matters of public interest must be discussed temperately." Journalists everywhere know the case of the Cherry sisters, one of the most famous in the annals of libel in America. The *Des Moines Leader* successfully defended itself in their libel suit, using the defense of fair comment. It started when the Leader printed this:

> Billy Hamilton, of the *Odebolt Chronicle* gives the Cherry Sisters the following graphic write-up on their late appearance in his town: "Effie is an old jade of 50 summers, Jessie a frisky-filly of 40, and Addie, the flower of the family, a capering monstrosity of 35. Their long skinny arms, equipped with talons at the extremities, swung mechanically, and anon waved frantically at the suffering audience. The mouths of their rancid features

---

[42] Russell v. Geis, 251 Cal.App.2d 560, 59 Cal.Rptr. 569 (1967).

[43] Taylor v. Lewis, 132 Cal.App. 381, 22 P.2d 569 (1933).

[44] Campbell v. Spottiswoode, 32 L.J.Q.B. 185 (1863).

[45] James v. Haymes, 160 Va. 253, 168 S.E. 333 (1933).

[46] Goldwater v. Ginzburg, 414 F.2d 324, 342 (2d Cir.1969).

[47] England v. Daily Gazette Co., 143 W.Va. 700, 104 S.E.2d 306, 316 (1958).

opened like caverns, and sounds like the wailing of damned souls issued therefrom. They pranced around the stage with a motion that suggested a cross between the *danse du ventre* and fox trot,—strange creatures with painted faces and hideous mien. Effie is spavined, Addie is stringhalt, and Jessie, the only one who showed her stockings, has legs and calves as classic in their outlines as the curves of a broom handle."

There was nothing moderate about Billy Hamilton's criticism of these three graces, but the Iowa Supreme Court said that that did not matter. What Hamilton wrote about the three sisters, and the Leader reprinted, was fair comment and criticism: [48]

One who goes upon the stage to exhibit himself to the public, or who gives any kind of a performance to which the public is invited, may be freely criticized. He may be held up to ridicule, and entire freedom of expression is guaranteed to dramatic critics, provided they are not actuated by malice or evil purpose in what they write. * * * Ridicule is often the strongest weapon in the hands of a public writer; and, if fairly used, the presumption of malice which would otherwise arise is rebutted * * *.

Opinion Under the Constitution

We have already seen in Chap. 3 (Sec. 12) that the First Amendment protects exaggerated, extravagant expression in the give-and-take of political controversy and labor dispute, often treated as if it were opinion that is not actionable. Deeply felt differences in these settings give rise to epithets, "rhetorical hyperbole" that is not to be construed literally. A union publication that charged "scabs" and "traitors" against non-union people was employing the words, a Supreme Court said, in a "loose, figurative sense to demonstrate the union's strong disagreement with the views of those workers who oppose unionization." Such an opinion was protected.[49] A newspaper's report of citizens' indignant charges against a real estate developer at a city council meeting—that he was engaging in "blackmail" and "unethical trade" in land negotiations with the city—could not be taken by readers to mean these accusations were charges of crime. Even careless readers, the Supreme Court said, would recognize the word "blackmail" to be rhetorical hyperbole—an epithet in the

[48] Cherry v. Des Moines Leader, 114 Iowa 298, 86 N.W. 323 (1901).

[49] Old Dominion Branch No. 496, Nat'l Ass'n of Letter Carriers, AFL–CIO v. Austin, 418 U.S. 264, 94 S.Ct. 2770 (1974).

realm of opinion.[50]   Another court held that "fellow traveler of the fascists", and contributor to "openly fascist journals" were "loosely definable, variously interpretable statements of opinion * * * made inextricably in the context of political, social, or philosophical debate." [51]   This was opinion, defined as such considerably by the *context in which it occurred*—political and labor dispute.[52]

Courts distinguish hyperbole from specific charges of crime and wrongdoing, and we have seen that charging one with "a SS [Nazi] background" and being associated with the Gestapo are not opinion or hyperbole, nor is "outright extortion" spoken of a councilman.[53]

In addition to the protection given rhetorical hyperbole, another constitutional immunity for opinion has been deduced by many courts from dictum written by United States Supreme Court Justice Powell in Gertz v. Robert Welch, Inc: [54]

> Under the First Amendment there is no such thing as a false idea.   However pernicious an opinion may seem, we depend for its correction not on the conscience of judges and juries but on the competition of other ideas.   But there is no constitutional value in false statements of fact.

Under this statement apparently giving an absolute protection for opinion, the Second Restatement of Torts has said that common-law fair comment has been obliterated.   It holds that only where a statement in the form of opinion implies the allegation of undisclosed defamatory facts as the basis for the opinion is the statement actionable.   Such a statement is "mixed" opinion, and not protected as "pure" opinion is.[55]   Some courts and legal commentators accept the general view and the qualification; others do not. While the United States Supreme Court has not chosen to give further interpretation to Powell's dictum in Gertz, Justice Rehnquist, supported by Justice White, has argued that it should do so. He said in objecting to the Court's denial of certiorari to an Oklahoma case of 1982, in which the state Supreme Court had held words to be protected opinion,[56] that the Oklahoma court apparently was relying on the *Gertz* dictum, and continued:

[50] Greenbelt Cooperative Pub. Ass'n v. Bresler, 398 U.S. 6, 90 S.Ct. 1537 (1970).

[51] Cianci v. New Times Pub. Co., 639 F.2d 54 (2d Cir.1980), 6 Med.L.Rptr. 1625, 1631, quoting Buckley v. Littell, 539 F.2d 882 (2d Cir.1976).

[52] Sack, 157–58, 160–61.

[53] Good Government Group of Seal Beach v. Superior Court, 22 Cal.3d 672, 150 Cal.Rptr. 258, 586 P.2d 572 (1978).

[54] 418 U.S. 323, 339–40, 94 S.Ct. 2997, 3007 (1974).

[55] Restatement (Second) Torts, # 566.

[56] Miskovsky v. Oklahoma Pub. Co., 654 P.2d 587 (Okl.1982), certiorari denied 459 U.S. 923, 103 S.Ct. 235, 7 Med.L.Rptr. 2607 (1982).

A respected commentator on the subject has stated with respect to this quotation that "[t]he problem of defamatory opinion was not remotely an issue in *Gertz,* and there is no evidence that the Court was speaking with an awareness of the rich and complex history of the struggle of the common law to deal with this problem." Hill, Defamation and Privacy Under the First Amendment, 76 Colum.L.Rev. 1205 (1976). * * * I am confident this Court did not intend to wipe out this "rich and complex history" with the two sentences of dicta in *Gertz* quoted above.

The Massachusetts Supreme Judicial Court decided a 1982 case with reliance on both the *Gertz* dictum and the Restatement of Torts pronouncement, and on strong elements of rhetorical hyperbole. In doing so, it illustrated the Gordian difficulty in distinguishing between fact and opinion. Reporter Cole was fired from television station WBZ–TV for "reasons of misconduct and insubordination," an official statement from the station's general manager said. Newspapers reported the firing and the reasons, and added that station spokeswoman Konowitz elaborated by telephone to them that "unofficially" the firing was also based on "sloppy and irresponsible reporting" and Cole's "history of bad reporting techniques." Cole sued for libel and her "unofficial" words. The Court held that Konowitz' words could only be viewed as expressions of opinion regarding Cole's reporting abilities. It said: [57]

> Whether a reporter is sloppy and irresponsible with bad techniques is a matter of opinion. The meaning of these statements is imprecise and open to speculation. They cannot be characterized as assertions of fact. They cannot be proved false. "An assertion that cannot be proved false cannot be held libelous." Hotchner v. Castillo-Puche, 55 F.2d 910, 913 * * *.

It may puzzle journalists that one cannot prove such charges false. After all, the United States Supreme Court and other courts often have canvassed reporters' techniques, finding them acceptable at times despite angry charges by plaintiffs, flawed and faulty at other times, and on the basis of the latter sometimes have granted libel judgments.[58]

---

[57] Cole v. Westinghouse Broadcasting, 386 Mass. 303, 435 N.E.2d 1021 (1982), 8 Med.L.Rptr. 1828, 1832–33. And see Marc A. Franklin, "The Plaintiff's Burden in Defamation * * *," 25 William & Mary L.Rev. 825, 868 (1983–84), saying that "goodness" and "badness" of anything are evaluative statements, "simply not concepts that can be judicially characterized as being either true or false."

[58] Curtis Pub. Co. v. Butts, 388 U.S. 130, 87 S.Ct. 1975 (1967), finding the Associated Press reporter's techniques blameless and the Saturday Evening Post's

But the Massachusetts Court found precedent for its judgment: One writer, for example, had called a judge one of the ten worst judges in New York, said he had made a sufficient pattern of incompetent decisions and should be removed from office. The New York court denied recovery for these "opinions," saying that the defendants had simply expressed "their opinion of his judicial performance," and the judge could not recover "no matter how unreasonable, extreme or erroneous these opinions might be." [59] (The statement that the judge was "probably corrupt," on the other hand, was an accusation of crime that could be proved true or false.) In another case, "liar" merely expressed an opinion and could not be libelous however mistaken the opinion might be.[60] In another, "fascist" and fellow traveller of fascism were matters of opinion and protected ideas—but in this case,[61] the assertion that the plaintiff had lied about people in his work as a journalist was ruled to be an assertion of fact.

In Cole's case, the Massachusetts Court said, "context was a significant factor. It was not exactly like a heated labor dispute or political controversy that produces epithets and hyperbole; but there was difference over why public figure Cole was fired, and the newspaper reporters' inquiries of Konowitz and their understandings that her own version was "unofficial" "lend support to our view that the statements were matters of opinion *   *   *." [62] The Court quoted a California case holding that "what constitutes a statement of fact in one context may be treated as a statement of opinion in another, in light of the nature and content of the communication taken as a whole." [63]

Employing the Restatement of Torts pronouncement, the Court went to the matter of whether "undisclosed, defamatory facts" might be said to underlie Konowitz' accusations of "sloppy, irresponsible reporting," and "history of bad reporting techniques." If so, libel might be found. It noted one instance, in the trial record, of Cole's failure to report "both sides" in a story about investigating fund-raising by the mayor of Boston and said:

constituting "reckless disregard." Where reckless disregard is found, it is commonly for bad reporting techniques.

[59] Citing Rinaldi v. Holt, Rinehart & Winston, Inc., 42 N.Y.2d 369, 376, 380–82, 397 N.Y.S.2d 943, 950–51, 366 N.E.2d 1299 (1977).

[60] Citing Edwards v. National Audubon Soc'y, Inc., 556 F.2d 113, 131 (2d Cir. 1977).

[61] Buckley v. Littell, 539 F.2d 882, 884–85 (2d Cir.1976).

[62] Cole v. Westinghouse Broadcasting, 386 Mass. 303, 435 N.E.2d 1021 (1982), 8 Med.L.Rptr. 1828, 1832.

[63] Ibid. (quoting Gregory v. McDonnell Douglas Corp., 17 Cal.3d 596, 601, 131 Cal.Rptr. 641, 644, 552 P.2d 425 (1976).)

These are the "facts" underlying the opinion. While Konowitz's statement may also imply that she had knowledge of other instances of Cole's alleged shortcomings as reporter, this possibility does not meet the requirements of [Restatement of Torts] # 566. * * * the undisclosed facts must be defamatory.

In the present case, it is not clear that any undisclosed facts are implied, or if any are implied, it is unclear what they are. Finally, it is entirely unclear (even assuming that facts are implied) that they are defamatory facts.[64]

The unsettled nature of the law as to opinion and comment under the Constitution is strikingly illustrated in Evans v. Ollman, a 1984 decision of the Court of Appeals, District of Columbia Circuit. Eleven judges sitting *en banc* delivered seven opinions. The majority found for two defendant newspaper columnists, and the U.S. Supreme Court refused to accept the plaintiff's appeal, in effect upholding the decision.[65] Bertell Ollman, a Marxist professor of political science at New York University under appointment procedures to head the department of government at the University of Maryland, sued syndicated newspaper columnists Evans and Novak. Their column stated that Ollman "is widely viewed in his profession as a political activist," whose "candid writings avow his desire to use the classroom as an instrument for preparing what he calls 'the revolution'." It also reported that an unnamed political scientist said that Ollman "has no status within the profession, but is a pure and simple activist."

Writing for himself and three others, Judge Kenneth W. Starr found this to be opinion protected under the First Amendment and the *Gertz* dictum. Judge Robert Bork, joined by three others, considered the statements in the column to be rhetorical hyperbole, and as such a category of words different from either "fact" or "opinion," but protected by the First Amendment. Judge Antonin Scalia, writing as one of five who dissented in part from the judgment, called the statement as to Ollman's status in the profes-

---

[64] Ibid., 1833. Decisions that have found indications of "undisclosed defamatory facts" and denied protection include: Braig v. Field Communications, 310 Pa. Super. 569, 456 A.2d 1366 (1983), 9 Med.L.Repr. 1057, allegation that "Judge Braig is no friend of the Police Brutality Unit"; Nevada Broadcasting Corp. v. Allen, 664 P.2d 337 (Nev.1983), 9 Med.L.Rptr. 1770, in a statement questioning whether a political candidate was "honorable"; Grass v. News Group Pubs., 570 F.Supp. 178 (D.C.S.D.N.Y.1983), 9 Med.L.Rptr. 2129, saying that Lew made the business a great success, while "Alex minded the store back home" and "was always in the shade when Lew was around."

[65] Ollman v. Evans, 750 F.2d 970 (D.C.Cir.1984), 11 Med.L.Rptr. 1433; appeal refused by Supreme Court, L. Greenhouse, "Supreme Court Roundup," New York Times, 5/29/85, 8.

sion "a classic and cooly crafted libel," and treated it as an unprotected statement of fact.[66]

Judge Starr noted the difficulty and the "dilemma" that courts often face in distinguishing between fact and opinion. For doing so, he shaped a four-part test which may be expected to find a part in future decisions that grapple with this deeply perplexing realm of libel law: [67]

1.   The inquiry must analyze the common usage or meaning of the words. Do they have a precise meaning such as a direct charge of crime, or are they only loosely definable?

2.   Is the statement verifiable—"objectively capable of proof or disproof?"

3.   What is the "linguistic" context in which the statement occurs? Here the article or column needs to be taken "as a whole": "The language of the entire column may signal that a specific statement which, standing alone, would appear to be factual, is in actuality a statement of opinion."

4.   What is the "broader social context into which the statement fits?" Here there are signals to readers or listeners that what is being read or heard is likely to be opinion, not fact. An example would be the labor dispute of *Letters Carriers* (above, p. 83), with its exaggerated rhetoric common in such circumstances. Another signal would be whether the article appeared on an editorial page—where opinion is expected—or in a front-page news story.

More than a few courts and legal analysts have questioned the Restatement of Torts pronouncement, and suggested doubts, as did the Rehnquist dissent in *Miskovsky* (above, p. 194), about the *Gertz* dictum.[68] And in agreement or not, some courts continue to use common-law fair comment, with or without *Gertz* and Restatement of Torts.[69]

The Illinois Appellate Court, Fifth District, in 1982 held that repeated charges of "liar" against a county official in a newspaper editorial, and warning of two more years of his "lying leadership," were not protected opinion. For while a single charge of "liar" about a single event had been held not actionable in Illinois, the

[66] Ibid., 1491.

[67] Ibid., 1440–1444.

[68] Sack, 178–82; Note, Fact and Opinion after Gertz v. Robert Welch, Inc., 34 Rutgers L.Rev. 81, 126 (Fall 1981); Jerry Chaney, Opinion Dicta New Law of Libel? 10 Med.Law Notes # 2, 5 (Feb., 1983); 10 Med.L.Rptr. # 15, 4/10/84, News Notes; Prosser & Keetan, Law of Torts, 5th ed. (1984), 831; Cianci v. New Times, 639 F.2d 54 (2d Cir.1980), 6 Med.L.Rptr. 1625, 1634.

[69] Goodrich v. Waterbury Republican-American, 188 Conn. 107, 448 A.2d 1317 (1982), 8 Med.L.Rptr. 2329; Orr v. Argus-Press, 586 F.2d 1108 (6th Cir.1978); Tawfik v. Lloyd, (D.C.N.D.Tex.1979), 5 Med.L.Rptr. 2067.

cumulative force of several such charges was "an actionable assault on the plaintiff's character in general, not mere criticism of his conduct in a particular instance." [70]   Without relying on the *Gertz* dictum, and without using the Restatement of Torts pronouncement, the Court found that these were factual assertions, not expressions of opinion and not rhetorical hyperbole as argued by the defendant.   Once more, the charge of "liar" had been found to be unprotected.   It is unsafe, like accusations of criminal activity even in the form of "In my *opinion,* he is a rapist." [71]

SEC. 30.   RETRACTION

A full and prompt apology following the publication of a libel will serve to mitigate damages awarded to the injured.

The news medium that has libeled a person may retract its statement, and in doing so, hope to lessen the chances that large damages will be awarded to the injured.   The retraction must be full and without reservation, it should be no attempt to justify the libel, and it must be given the prominence in space or time that the original charge received.   But while a full and timely apology may go to mitigate damages, it is in no sense a complete defense. The law reasons that many persons who saw the original story may not see the retraction.

In spite of a fulsome retraction in one case, it was estimated that the broadcaster involved agreed to an out-of-court settlement in the range of one-fourth to one-half of a million dollars.[72]   Under state statutes, a full and prompt retraction serves to negate punitive damages, for it is considered evidence that the libel was not published with common-law malice (ill will).   Under the constitutional (*Sullivan*) doctrine, however, retraction is in a somewhat ambiguous condition, jurisdictions varying in whether it negates actual malice (knowing or reckless falsehood) or not.[73]

Many states have had retraction statutes, some providing that punitive damages may not be awarded if retraction is made properly and the publisher shows that he did not publish with malice.   Others have gone further, providing that only special damages may be awarded following a retraction and demonstration of good faith on the part of the publisher.   California has the

[70] Costello v. Capital Cities Media, 111 Ill.App.3d 1009, 67 Ill.Dec. 721, 445 N.E.2d 13 (1982), 9 Med.L.Rptr. 1434.

[71] Cianci v. New Times, 639 F.2d 54 (2d Cir.1980), 6 Med.L.Rptr. 1625, 1631; Ollman v. Evans, 750 F.2d 970 (D.C.Cir.1984), 11 Med.L.Rptr. 1433, 1443.

[72] Green v. WCAU–TV, 8 Med.L.Rptr. # 35, 11/2/82, News Notes.

[73] Donna L. Dickerson, Retraction's Role Under the Actual Malice Rule, 6 Communications and the Law # 4, 39 (Aug. 1984).

statute most favorable to publishers. It provides that a proper retraction limits recovery to special damages, no matter what the motives of the publisher.[74]

Some retraction statutes have been attacked as unconstitutional, one reason being that they sometimes are applicable only to newspapers and as such are discriminatory. Many persons may publish libel in non-newspaper form, but not have the advantage of retraction statutes in these states. In Park v. Detroit Free Press, a Michigan retraction statute was held unconstitutional, the Court holding that "It is not competent for the legislature to give one class of citizens legal exemptions from liability for wrongs not granted to others." [75] The Supreme Court of Kansas held that state's retraction provision unconstitutional. The decision went to the law's preventing recovery of general damages, and said: [76]

> The injuries for which this class of damages is allowed are something more than merely speculative * * *. In short, they are such injuries to the reputation as were contemplated in the bill of rights * * *.

Where punitive damages only are barred to the defamed, however, the constitutionality of the statute ordinarily has been upheld.[77]

[74] T.M. Newell and Albert Pickerell, California's Retraction Statute: License to Libel?, 28 Journ.Quar. 474, 1951. For State retraction statutes, see Sack, App. IV, 589.

[75] 72 Mich. 560, 40 N.W. 731 (1888). See also Madison v. Yunker, 180 Mont. 54, 589 P.2d 126 (1978).

[76] Hanson v. Krehbiel, 68 Kan. 670, 75 P. 1041 (1904).

[77] Comer v. Age Herald Pub. Co., 151 Ala. 613, 44 So. 673 (1907); Meyerle v. Pioneer Pub. Co., 45 N.D. 568, 178 N.W. 792 (1920).

Chapter 6

THE LAW OF PRIVACY
AND THE MEDIA

SEC. 31. DEVELOPMENT OF PRIVACY LAW

Privacy—"the right to be let alone"—is protected by an evolving area of tort law and has been recognized as a constitutional right by the Supreme Court of the United States.

Privacy—roughly defined as "the right to be let alone" [1]—is one of the nation's hottest issues in the 1980s. It is often said that the United States has become "The Information Society." Increasingly, it is difficult for individuals to keep information about themselves from indiscriminate use by government agencies or business interests. The worry of the 1970s—when privacy was seen to be in peril by politicians, legal scholars, anthropologists, and citizen activists—now seems to have become the nightmare of the 1980s. [2] George Orwell's novel discussing a tortured future in which "Big Brother" was always watching everyone was titled *1984,* after all. [3]

[1] Thomas M. Cooley, A Treatise on the Law of Torts, 2d ed. (Chicago: Callaghan and Co., 1888) p. 29.

[2] See, e.g., Arthur R. Miller, The Assault on Privacy (Ann Arbor: University of Michigan Press, 1971); Don R. Pember, Privacy and the Press (Seattle: University of Washington Press, 1972); Alan Westin, Privacy and Freedom (New York: Atheneum, 1967); Subcommittee on Constitutional Rights of the Committee on the Judiciary, United States Senate, Ninety Second Congress, First Session ("The Ervin Subcommittee"), February 23–25, March 2–4, 9–11, 15 and 17, Parts 1 and 2, pp. 1–2164, *passim;* Final Recommendations of the Privacy Study Commission, and P. Allan Dionisopoulos and Craig R. Ducat, The Right to Privacy (St. Paul, Minn.: West Publishing Co., 1976).

[3] George Orwell, 1984.

It can't happen here? Don't bet your life on it. Remember that government's stake in information about individuals has implications for *control*. Knowledge is power. Also, there is an enormous financial stake in information about individuals. Consider the implications of this Christmas-time letter from a nationally known [4] life insurance company.

> Your son * * * will be celebrating that special family day—his birthday—on January 9th. Birthdays are for now and the future. But before that happy day, we at * * * [a life insurance company] would like to show you, and your son, how to help build toward his financial security with a birthday gift he will remember for a lifetime.
>
> * * *

The letter goes on, with computerized sincerity, to offer an opportunity to apply for "* * * this $10,000.00 Whole Life Insurance Plan and give him a birthday headstart on his financial security for future years."

This offer makes good financial sense, and it comes from a reputable company. Even so, why should an insurance company know the birthdate of the younger son of a journalism professor, without that family's knowledge or consent, and attempt to profit from that knowledge? This sort of thing, which happens to everyone who receives mail, is only the tip of the tail of a very large snake of the boa constrictor family.

Think about cable television. We are moving steadily toward a nation interconnected, by satellite transmission if not by wire, to interactive (two-way) in-the-home cable television systems. The cornucopia of services offered by cable television is dazzling.[5] The technology is now here for use of cable TV for shopping, mail delivery, consulting with physicians, communicating with one's elected representatives, answering polls, and on and on. Think also about the price which may be paid for such a cornucopia.

Consider a mythical American, Mr. I. Ben Hadd. Mr. Hadd, in 1989, is using his cable TV system to purchase groceries (special fat-free diet), and to consult with his physician about an occasional problem with an irregular heartbeat. He also gets some mild prescription medication for his "cardiac arrhythmia," ordering it via cable TV. Will that be the end of it for Mr. Hadd? Or will his employer begin to inquire into the state of his health? Will his

---

[4] Letter received from a life insurance company, December 29, 1980.

[5] J.D. McNamara, "Capital Cable and Franchise Strategy," unpublished paper, The University of Texas at Austin, Nov. 5, 1980; Douglas Ginsburg, Regulation of Broadcasting: Law and Policy Toward Radio, Television and Cable Communications. (St. Paul, Minn., West Publishing Co., 1979).

health insurance or auto insurance rates suddenly increase? Will the state driver's license bureau suddenly ask that Mr. Hadd submit to a physical exam? Will the motto of the 1990s become "Don't tell it to your TV set unless you'd put it on a billboard?"

So it is that the technology which serves us may also ensnare us. Infrared telephoto lenses "see in the dark." Super-sensitive directional microphones can hear across sizable distances. Dossiers are compiled by credit bureaus, and by myriad government agencies. All of these things were continuing phenomena, parts of what Vance Packard called "The Naked Society" back in 1964.[6] Arthur Miller of the Harvard School of Law produced an all-too prophetic study, The Assault on Privacy, investigating credit bureau abuses and use of systems for data collection and information storage and retrieval. Acknowledging the helpful uses of such technology, Professor Miller then warned: "we must be concerned about the axiom . . . that man must shape his tools lest they shape him."[7]

In the early 1970s, misconduct reaching into the Oval Office of the White House helped popularize the privacy issue. The term "Watergate" became a symbol of political dirty-dealing and invasion of privacy by bugging and wiretapping. Persons highly placed in then-President Richard M. Nixon's "law and order" administration not only got involved in such electronic attempts to "listen in," but also were connected with a break-in into the office of the psychiatrist of Pentagon Papers case defendant Daniel Ellsberg. The privacy issue helped lead to President Nixon's resignation. While some Congressmen moved to impeach Nixon, one cartoonist suggested a new version of the Presidential Seal: an eagle clutching a camera and a (presumably tapped) telephone in its talons.[8]

Privacy is worth fighting for, against governmental stupidity or arrogance, or against the prying of businesses or private individuals. Louis D. Brandeis, one of the Supreme Court's greatest justices, once wrote that the makers of the American Constitution "sought to protect Americans in their beliefs, their thoughts, their emotions and their sensations. They [the Constitution's framers] conferred, as against the Government, the right to be let alone— the most comprehensive of rights and the right most valued by civilized man."[9]

Privacy is a problem for each citizen, a desired right to be fought for and zealously guarded. Privacy is also a communica-

[6] Vance Packard, The Naked Society (New York: David McKay and Co., 1964).

[7] Miller, op. cit., pp. 7–8.

[8] Newsweek, April 30, 1973; Time, April 16, May 14, 1973.

[9] Olmstead v. United States, 277 U.S. 438, 48 S.Ct. 564 (1928).

tions media problem, one to be reported upon. And finally, privacy is a media problem in another sense because missteps by newspapers, magazines and radio and television stations have resulted in all too many of those privacy cases.

What, then, is privacy? *Black's Law Dictionary* says, in pertinent part: [10]

> **Privacy, right of.** The right to be let alone; the right of a person to be free from unwarranted publicity. Term "right of privacy" is generic term encompassing various rights recognized to be inherent in concept of ordered liberty, and such right prevents governmental interference in intimate personal relationships or activities, freedoms of individual to make fundamental choices involving himself, his family, and his relationship with others. * * * The right of an individual (or corporation) to withhold himself and his property from public scrutiny, if he so chooses.

Many of the more humorous—or tragicomic—American court decisions have come from settings involving privacy. When a landlord plants a microphone in the bedroom of a newly married couple, is that an invasion of privacy? [11] When a tavern owner takes a picture of a woman customer against her will—and in the women's restroom, later displaying the photograph to patrons at the bar—is that an invasion of privacy? [12]

Such cases, in their rather comical aspects, indicate growing pains in an area of law which is remarkably young. Privacy is nowhere mentioned in the Constitution, and its absence is understandable. In America during the Revolutionary generation, most people lived on farms. Urban residents made up not much more than 10 per cent of the new nation's population. When the Constitution was ratified, Philadelphia, then the nation's largest city, had little more than 40,000 residents. When people were out-of-doors, there was little real need for any specific Constitutional statement of a right to privacy. Indoors, privacy was another matter. In 18th Century America, homes often had living, eating and sleeping accommodations for an entire family in the same

---

[10] Black's Law Dictionary, 5th ed. (St. Paul, Minn., West Publishing Co.), 1979 p. 1075.

[11] Such "bugging" was held to be an invasion of privacy. See Hamberger v. Eastman, 106 N.H. 107, 206 A.2d 239, 11 A.L.R.3d 1288 (1964).

[12] Yoeckel v. Samonig, 272 Wis. 430, 75 N.W.2d 925 (1956) said this was not an invasion of privacy because Wisconsin's Legislature had twice refused to enact a statute creating the tort. In 1977, Wisconsin Statute § 895.50 recognized all four torts.

room.   In public inns, travelers often had to share rooms—and sometimes beds—with other wayfarers.[13]

Although privacy was not mentioned in the Constitution by name, its first eight amendments, plus the Fourteenth Amendment, include the right to be secure against unreasonable search and seizure and the principle of due process of law.   Taken together with the Declaration of Independence's demands for the right to "life, liberty and the pursuit of happiness," it can be seen that the founders of the nation had a lively concern for something akin to a "right to be let alone."

Since 1960, the Supreme Court of the United States has recognized privacy as a constitutional right, a right which to some extent protects citizens from intrusions by government or police agencies.[14]

Here, a useful distinction may be made between the *right* of privacy and the *law* of privacy.   As Professor James Willard Hurst of the University of Wisconsin Law School has written, American legal history is full of concern for a broad *right* to privacy, represented by interests protected in the Constitution's Bill of Rights.   (The Constitution, of course, protects citizens only against *government* actions.)   Of this broad *right* to privacy, only small slivers have been hammered into the narrower tort *law* of privacy as enunciated by judges and legislatures.[15]

The tort *law* of privacy is quite new.   It has been traced to an 1890 *Harvard Law Review* article written by two young Boston law partners, Samuel D. Warren and future Supreme Court Justice Louis D. Brandeis.   The article, often named as the best example of the influence of law journals on the development of the law, was titled "The Right to Privacy."

If this law journal article was the start of a law of privacy in America, it should also be noted that the newspaper press may have been involved too.   Standard accounts of the origins of the Warren-Brandeis article have it that Warren and his wife had been greatly annoyed by newspaper stories about parties which they gave.   This irritation, so the story goes, led to the drafting of the article, now thought to have been written primarily by Brandeis.   The co-authors asserted that an independent action for privacy could be found within then-established areas of the law

---

[13] Pember, Privacy and the Press, p. 5.

[14] See Mapp v. Ohio, 367 U.S. 643, 81 S.Ct. 1684 (1961): Griswold v. Connecticut, 381 U.S. 479, 85 S.Ct. 1678 (1965).

[15] James Willard Hurst, Law and Conditions of Freedom (Madison, Wis.: University of Wisconsin Press, 1956) p. 8.

such as defamation and trespass to property. Warren and Brandeis wrote: [16]

> The press is overstepping in every direction the obvious bounds of propriety and of decency. Gossip is no longer the resource of the idle and of the vicious, but has become a trade which is pursued with industry as well as effrontery. To satisfy a prurient taste the details of sexual relations are spread broadcast in the columns of the daily papers. To occupy the indolent, column upon column is filled with idle gossip, which can only be procured by intrusion upon the domestic circle. The intensity and complexity of life, attendant upon advancing civilization, have rendered necessary some retreat from the world, and man, under the refining influence of culture, has become more sensitive to publicity, so that solitude and privacy have become more essential to the individual; but modern enterprise and invention have, through invasions upon his privacy, subjected him to mental pain and distress, far greater than could be inflicted by mere bodily injury.

While this law journal article was indeed a catalyst toward the development of a law of privacy, the article's evidence, at some points, left something to be desired. As Justice Peters of the California Supreme Court noted in 1971,[17]

> [t]ry as they might, Warren and Brandeis had a difficult time tracing a right of privacy to the common law. In many respects a person had less privacy in the small community of the 18th century than he did in the urbanizing late 19th century or he does today in the modern metropolis. Extended family networks, primary group relationships, and rigid communal mores served to expose an individual's every deviation from the norm and to straitjacket him in a vise of backyard gossip, which threatened to deprive men of the right of "scratching where it itches."

And as a judge in a Missouri appeals court noted in 1911, the concept of a right of privacy was not new at all. Privacy, the judge wrote, "is spoken of as a new right, when in fact it is an old

---

[16] Samuel Warren and Louis D. Brandeis, "The Right to Privacy," 4 Harvard Law Review (1890) p. 196.

[17] Briscoe v. Reader's Digest Ass'n, 4 Cal.3d 529, 93 Cal.Rptr. 866, 483 P.2d 34, 36–37 (1971). Justice Peters cited Alan Westin, "Science, Privacy and Freedom: Issues and Proposals for the 1970's," 66 Columbia Law Review 1003, at 1025. See, also, John P. Roche's essay, "American Liberty: An Examination of the Tradition of Freedom," in Shadow and Substance (New York: Macmillan, 1964) pp. 3–38.

right with a new name. Life, liberty, and the pursuit of happiness are rights of all men." [18]

More than a century before 1890, when Warren and Brandeis added the word "privacy" to the vocabulary of the law, England's William Pitt gave ringing affirmation to the idea that "a man's home is his castle." Pitt said: "The poorest man may in his cottage bid defiance to all the forces of the Crown. It may be frail; its roof may shake; the winds may blow through it; the storms may enter,—but the King of England cannot enter; all his forces dare not cross the threshold of the ruined tenement!"

From such beginnings an expanding law of privacy has emerged. Although Warren and Brandeis complained about the excesses of the news media, the first privacy cases involved other settings. In his pathbreaking study, *Privacy and the Press,* Professor Don R. Pember argued that the first privacy case appeared in 1881—nine years before the Warren and Brandeis article was published. In that case, Demay v. Roberts, a woman sued a doctor when she discovered that the doctor's "assistant," who had been present when the woman gave birth to a baby, had no medical training. The Supreme Court of Michigan held that the woman could collect damages from the doctor. The court declared that the moment of a child's birth was sacred and that the mother's privacy had been invaded.[19]

Eleven years later, a package of flour led to an early—and famous—privacy case in New York: Roberson v. Rochester Folding Box Co. The judges of two New York courts were evidently readers of the Harvard Law Review, because they would have allowed recovery in a privacy lawsuit brought by Miss Abigail M. Roberson. She had sued for $15,000 because her likeness was used to decorate posters advertising Franklin Mills flour without her consent. But in 1902, New York's highest court—the Court of Appeals—ruled that she could not collect because there was no precedent which established a "right of privacy." Despite Miss Roberson's unwilling inclusion in an advertising campaign featuring the slogan of "The Flour of the Family," the Court of Appeals held that if her claim were allowed, a flood of litigation would result, and that it was too difficult to distinguish between public and private persons.[20]

The *Roberson* decision, however, hinted broadly that if the New York legislature wished to enact a law of privacy, it could do so. Considerable public outcry and a number of outraged newspaper editorials greeted the outcome of the *Roberson* case. The next

[18] Munden v. Harris, 153 Mo.App. 652, 659–660, 134 S.W. 1076, 1078 (1911).

[19] Pember, op. cit., pp. 50–51; 46 Mich. 160 (1881).

[20] 171 N.Y. 538, 64 N.E. 442, 447 (1902).

year, in 1903, the New York legislature passed a statute which made it both a misdemeanor and a tort to use the name, portrait, or picture of any person for advertising or "trade purposes" without that person's consent.   Note that this was narrowly drawn legislation, limited to the kind of fact situation which had arisen in *Roberson.*[21]

The New York statute, an amendment to the Civil Rights Law of the State of New York, has turned out to be a great generator of privacy law, and is responsible for perhaps one quarter of all reported privacy decisions in the United States since 1903.[22]   New York is a natural birthplace for such lawsuits: it is highly populous, and it is also the center of America's publishing and broadcasting industries.

In 1905, two years after the New York privacy statute was passed, the Georgia Supreme Court provided the first major judicial recognition of a law of privacy.   An unauthorized photograph of Paolo Pavesich and a bogus testimonial attributed to him appeared in a newspaper advertisement for a life insurance company.   The Georgia court ruled that there is a law of privacy which prevents unauthorized use of pictures and testimonials for advertising purposes.[23]

Since the 1905 *Pavesich* decision, the tort of privacy has grown mightily.   The late William L. Prosser, for many years America's foremost torts scholar, suggested that there are four kinds of torts included under the broad label of "invasion of privacy." [24]

1.   Intrusion on the plaintiff's physical solitude.

2.   Publication of private matters violating the ordinary decencies.

3.   Putting plaintiff in a false position in the public eye, as by signing that person's name to a letter or petition, attributing views not held by that person.

4.   Appropriation of some element of plaintiff's personality— his or her name or likeness—for commercial use.

---

[21] New York Session Laws 1903, Ch. 132, §§ 1–2, now known as §§ 50–51, New York Civil Rights Law.

[22] Pember, op. cit., p. 67.

[23] Pavesich v. New England Life Ins. Co., 122 Ga. 190, 50 S.E. 68, 79 (1905).

[24] Barbieri v. News-Journal Co., 189 A.2d 773, 774 (Del.1963).   The Delaware Supreme Court summarized Dean Prosser's analysis of the kinds of actions to be included by the law of privacy.   For fuller treatment, see Prosser's much-quoted "Privacy," 48 California Law Review (1960), pp. 383–423, and his Handbook of the Law of Torts, 4th Ed. (St. Paul, Minn., West Publishing Co., 1971, pp. 802–818).

It should be noted that these are not mutually exclusive categories; more than one of these four kinds of privacy actions may be present in the same case.

Some or all of those privacy areas have been recognized in nearly every state. The law of privacy—or one of its four sub-tort areas as listed above—has now been recognized by federal courts, in the District of Columbia, and 49 states.[25]   Court ("common law") recognition had come in most states, and statutes recognizing the law of privacy have been passed in seven states: California, Nebraska, New York, Oklahoma, Utah, Virginia, and Wisconsin.   Even in those states which were slow to recognize the law of privacy, privacy interests were apt to be protected under other legal actions such as libel or trespass.[26]

Professor Prosser noted that an action for invasion of privacy is much like the old concept *"libel per se:"* a plaintiff does not have to plead or prove actual monetary loss ("special damages") in order to have a cause of action.   In addition, a court may award punitive damages.   But while actions for defamation and for invasion of privacy have points of similarity, there are also major differences.   As a Massachusetts court said, "The fundamental difference between a right to privacy and a right to freedom from defamation is that the former directly concerns one's own peace of mind, while the latter concerns primarily one's reputation." [27]

While such a distinction may exist in theory, in practice the distinction between defamation and invasion of privacy is blurred. As noted previously, in 1890 Warren and Brandeis drew upon a number of old defamation cases on the way to extracting what they called a right to privacy.   Privacy, it would seem, may often

[25] Victor A. Kovner, "Recent Developments In Intrusion, Private Facts, False Light, and Commercialization Claims," in James C. Goodale, chairman, Communications Law 1984 (New York: Practising Law Institute, 1984); see especially his sampling of recent authorities for the four sub-torts which make up the law of privacy, "State Recognition of the Four Torts," pp. 509–538.   Minnesota appears to be the last holdout in 1985.

[26] State privacy statutes include California Civil Code, Section 3344, which is similar to the New York privacy statute, New York Civil Rights Law §§ 50–51. Wisconsin Statute § 895.50 recognized all four torts, thus overruling the notorious intrusion case, Yoeckel v. Samonig, 272 Wis. 430, 75 N.W.2d 925 (1956).   A woman brought suit, alleging that her picture had been taken in the restroom of Sad Sam's Tavern.   The Wisconsin Supreme Court decided that in the absence of statutory enactment, there was no right to privacy in Wisconsin.   For a similar statute, see Nebraska Civil Rights Rev.Stat. § 2–201–211.   Utah Code Annotated §§ 76–9–401– 403, 406 deals with intrusion, and U.S.A. § 76–9–401, 406 covers misappropriation (right of publicity).   Virginia Code § 8.01–40 covers right of publicity; Kovner, op. cit.

[27] Themo v. New England Newspaper Pub. Co., 306 Mass. 54, 27 N.E.2d 753, 755 (1940).   Note that Professor Prosser could not have forecast the U.S. Supreme Court decision in the libel case of Gertz v. Welch, 418 U.S. 323, 94 S.Ct. 2997 (1974), which demolished the old *libel per se* standard in rejecting the concept of liability without fault.

be regarded as a close cousin of defamation. Some publications, indeed, may be both defamatory and an invasion of privacy, and shrewd attorneys often sued for both libel and invasion of privacy on the basis of a single publication.[28]

Privacy actions also resemble defamation lawsuits in that the right to sue belongs only to the affronted individual. As a rule, relatives or friends cannot sue because the privacy of someone close to them was invaded, unless their own privacy was also invaded. In general, the right to sue for invasion of privacy dies with the individual.[29]

When considering privacy law, two things should be kept in mind:

First, the law of privacy is not uniform. In fact, one judge once compared the state of the law to a haystack in a hurricane. There is great conflict of laws from state to state and from jurisdiction to jurisdiction.

Second, when courts or legislatures become involved with the law of privacy, they are attempting to balance interests. On one side of the scale, you have the public interest in freedom of the press and the right to publish. On the other side, you have the individual's right to privacy.

SEC. 32. "INTRUSION" AS INVASION OF PRIVACY

Invading a person's solitude, including the use of microphones or cameras, has been held to be actionable.

Journalists are often seen as invaders of privacy *par excellence,* but they are rank amateurs compared to governmental units, including police and intelligence-gathering agencies. In times such as these, journalists are in an anomalous position where privacy is concerned. The federal Privacy and Freedom of Information Acts perhaps are somewhat at cross purposes.[30] Obviously, journalists using federal and state Freedom of Information legislation to pry information out of government are at times

---

[28] In general, although invasion of privacy and defamation are often included as elements of the same lawsuit, usually courts have not allowed a plaintiff to collect for both actions in one suit. "Duplication of Damages: Invasion of Privacy and Defamation," 41 Washington Law Review (1966), pp. 370–377; see, also, Brink v. Griffith, 65 Wash.2d 253, 396 P.2d 793 (1964), and Donald Elliott Brown, "The Invasion of Defamation by Privacy," Stanford Law Review 23 (Feb., 1971), pp. 547–568.

[29] Bremmer v. Journal-Tribune Pub. Co., 247 Iowa 817, 76 N.W.2d 762 (1956); Wyatt v. Hall's Portrait Studios, 71 Misc. 199, 128 N.Y.S. 247 (1911). In at least one state, heirs can sue for invasion of privacy. For example, see the Utah intrusion statute, U.C.A. §§ 76–9–401–403, 406.

[30] See Chap. 10, Sec. 62.

going to dig up facts which persons involved will feel to be an invasion of their privacy.

Because privacy was a hot issue in the mid-1970s and into the 1980s it accentuated the collision between individual rights to be let alone and the continuing struggle for access to information. [See Chapter 10 for further discussion of problems of access to information.]   Writer Paul Clancy asserted: [31]

> The trouble was, it [privacy] was already too hot, and freedom of information considerations were being largely ignored.   Draft versions of the Privacy Act of 1974— which was to open government files so that individuals might see and correct dossiers which various government agencies have—would have also shut the press away from much information.   *   *   * and from many records previously believed to be public.   After re-drafting, in response to press complaints, the Privacy Act of 1974 said that matters which may be disclosed in the Freedom of Information Act, as amended [discussed in Chapter 10] are exempted from the sweep of the Privacy Act.   And under the Freedom of Information Act, the public—and thus the press—has a right to all information but that which "would constitute a clearly unwarranted invasion of privacy."

In the area called "intrusion on the plaintiff's physical solitude," the media must beware of the modern technology which they call upon increasingly to gather and to broadcast news. Microphones—some of which can pick up quiet conversations hundreds of feet away—and telephoto lenses on cameras should be used with care.

More than 200 years ago, Sir William Blackstone's *Commentaries* (1765) considered a form of intrusion, calling eavesdropping one of a list of nuisances which law could punish.   Eavesdroppers were termed "people who listen under windows, or the eaves of a house, to conversation, from which they frame slanderous and mischievous tales." [32]   Now, the tort subdivision of intrusion includes matters from illegal entry into a house to surreptitious tape recording (in some instances) to window-peeping.

The camera has been something of a troublemaker.   Courts have held that it is not an invasion of privacy to take someone's photograph in a public place.   Here, photographers are protected on the theory that they "stand in" for the public, taking pictures

[31] Paul Clancy, Privacy and the First Amendment (Columbia, Mo.: Freedom of Information Foundation Series), No. 5 (March 1976).

[32] Sir William Blackstone's Commentaries on the Law, ed. by Bernard C. Gavit (Washington, D.C., Washington Book Co., 1892) p. 823.

of what any persons could see if they were there. It follows, of course, that photographers should beware of taking photos in private places. When journalists or photographers invade private territory, they and their employer could be in trouble.

Barber v. Time provides a classic example. In 1939, Mrs. Dorothy Barber was a patient in a Kansas City hospital, being treated for a disease which caused her to eat constantly but still lose weight. A wire service (International News Service) photographer invaded her hospital room and took her picture despite her protests. This resulted in stories about Mrs. Barber's illness appearing in Kansas City-area newspapers for several days. Time Magazine then purchased the picture from the wire service, and published it along with a 150-word story taken largely from an original wire-service story. The cutline under the picture said "Insatiable-Eater Barber; She Eats for Ten." Mrs. Barber won $3,000 in damages from Time, Inc.[33]

More recently, a television film crew's intrusion onto private property caused a CBS-owned station huge legal costs, although it wound up paying a minor damage award of only $1,200. Minor award or not, the case of LeMistral v. Columbia Broadcasting System underlines the principle that journalists must ask themselves whether they are attempting to report from a private place. In the LeMistral case, WCBS–TV reporter Lucille Rich and a camera crew charged unannounced into the famous and fashionable LeMistral Restaurant in New York City. The reporter-camera team was doing a series on restaurants cited for health-code irregularities. The arrival of the camera crew—with lights on and cameras rolling—caused a scene of confusion which a slapstick comedian would relish. (Persons lunching with persons other than their spouses were reported to have slid hastily under tables to try to avoid the camera.) The restaurant's suit for invasion of privacy and trespass resulted in a jury award against CBS of $1,200 in compensatory damages and $250,000 in punitive damages. On appeal, the case was sent back to the trial judge for reconsideration and, ultimately, cancellation of the punitive damages award.[34]

If you can see something in a public place, you can photograph it. However, photographs can go too far even in public places if their behavior becomes annoyingly intrusive. Ron Galella, a self-styled "paparazzo," was making a career out of taking pictures of Jacqueline Kennedy Onassis and her children.

[33] Barber v. Time, Inc., 348 Mo. 1199, 159 S.W.2d 291, 295 (1948). Time purchased the picture from "International," a syndicate dealing in news pictures, and mainly followed the wording of an account furnished by United Press.

[34] Le Mistral, Inc. v. Columbia Broadcasting System, 61 A.D.2d 491, 402 N.Y.S.2d 815 (1st Dept.1978); TV Guide, May 3, 1980, p. 6.

Paparazzi, in the words of U.S. Circuit Judge J. Joseph Smith, "make themselves as visible to the public and obnoxious to their photographic subjects as possible to aid in the advertisement and wide sale of their works."

Galella's posturing and gesturing while taking pictures of Mrs. Onassis and children ultimately led to issuance of an injunction against the photographer. He was forbidden to approach within 25 feet of Mrs. Onassis or within 30 feet of her children.[35] Temptation proved too strong for Galella, however. In 1981, on four different occasions, Galella was again too close and too obnoxious in his photographic shadowing of Mrs. Onassis (attending a mid-day film in New York City, attempting to board a boat at Martha's Vineyard, going to see a dance performance at New York City's Winter Garden) and Caroline Kennedy (bicycling with a friend on Martha's Vineyard). U.S. District Judge Cooper found Galella to be in contempt of the court's 1975 order, subjecting the persistent photographer to liability for a heavy fine and/or imprisonment.[36]

If photographers can see their quarry from a public spot, without going through strange gyrations or trespassing onto private property, no liability should result. The *Crowley* (La.) *Post-Signal* was sued for invasion of privacy by Mr. and Mrs. James Jaubert. The Jauberts returned from a trip to discover that a photograph of their home had been published on the *Post-Signal's* front page, with this caption: "One of Crowley's stately homes, a bit weatherworn and unkempt, stands in the shadow of a spreading oak." The Jauberts sought $15,000 for invasion of privacy, including mental suffering and humiliation; they were awarded a total of $1,000 by the trial court.

The Louisiana Supreme Court ruled that because the photograph was taken from the middle of the street in front of the Jaubert house, and because passers-by were presented with an identical view, there was no invasion of privacy.[37]

Ethical as well as legal considerations get involved in most privacy cases. In the case known as Cape Publications v. Bridges, Hilda Bridges Pate sued for invasion of privacy for a photograph published by the Florida newspaper, Cocoa Today. During the summer of 1977, Hilda Bridges Pate was abducted by her estranged husband. He went to her place of employment and—at gunpoint—forced her to go with him to their former apartment.[38]

---

[35] 487 F.2d 986 (2d Cir.1973).

[36] 533 F.Supp. 1076 (S.D.N.Y.1982), 8 Med.L.Rptr. 1321–1325.

[37] Jaubert v. Crowley Post-Signal, 375 So.2d 1386 (La.1979), 5 Med.L.Rptr. 2185.

[38] Cape Publications v. Bridges, 423 So.2d 426 (Fla.App. 5th Dist.1982), 8 Med.L. Rptr. 2535. See discussion in The News Media & The Law, Jan./Feb. 1984, at p.

Police were summoned and were surrounding the apartment. The husband forced her to undress in an effort to prevent her from trying to escape. As Judge Dauksch wrote for the Florida Court of Appeal, Fifth District: "This is a typical exciting emotion-packed drama to which newspeople, and others are attracted." He said, in short, it was a newsworthy story.[39]

The husband shot himself to death. Police heard the gunshot, stormed the apartment, and rushed the partially clad Ms. Pate to safety across a public parking lot as she clutched a dishtowel to her body, trying to conceal her nudity. Judge Dauksch said, "The photograph revealed little more than could be seen had ＊ ＊ ＊ (Ms. Pate) been wearing a bikini, and somewhat less than some bathing suits seen on the beaches." At the trial, a Florida jury awarded Ms. Pate $1 million in compensatory damages and $9 million in punitive damages.

In erasing the damage awards, Florida appeals court said, "The published photograph is more a depiction of grief, fright, emotional tension and flight than it is an appeal to other sensual appetites." Judge Dauksch added: [40]

> Although publication of the photograph, which won industry awards, could be considered by some to be in bad taste, the law in Florida seems settled that where one becomes an actor in an occurrence of public interest, it is not an invasion of her right to privacy to publish her photograph with an account of such an occurrence.

＊ ＊ ＊

> Courts should be reluctant to interfere with a newspaper's privilege to publish news in the public interest.

Dietemann v. Time, Inc.

Over the years, there have been few cases of "intrusion" privacy lawsuits against the news media. Life Magazine—a Time, Inc., publication—bit the privacy bullet, however, in the 1971 decision in Dietemann v. Time, Inc. In that case, reporters from Life, cooperating with the Los Angeles, California district attorney and the State Board of Health, did some role-playing to entrap a

41, noting that the Florida Supreme Court and the Supreme Court of the United States refused to review this decision in fall, 1983.

[39] Cape Publications v. Bridges, 423 So.2d 426 (Fla.App. 5th Dist.1982), 8 Med.L. Rptr. 2535, 2536. In footnote no. 2, Judge Dauksch quoted the Restatement (Second) of Torts, S652D, Comment G, on the definition of news: " 'Authorized publicity, customarily regarded as 'news,' includes publications concerning crimes, arrests, police raids, suicides, marriages, divorces, accidents, fires, catastrophes of nature, narcotics-related deaths, rare diseases, etc., and many other matters of genuine popular appeal.' "

[40] 423 So.2d 426 (Fla.App. 5th Dist.1982), 8 Med.L.Rptr. 2535, 2536.

medical quack. Reporter Jackie Metcalf and photographer William Ray went to the home of journeyman plumber A.A. Dietemann, a man who was suspected of performing medical services without a diploma or state license. Mrs. Metcalf and Mr. Ray gained admittance to Dietemann's house by claiming that they had been sent by (if you'll pardon the expression) the plumber's friends.

Mrs. Metcalf complained that she had a lump in her breast, and while Dietemann conducted his "examination," Ray was secretly taking pictures. Life later published pictures from Dietemann's home, and also reported on his "diagnosis." He said Mrs. Metcalf's difficulty was caused by eating some rancid butter 11 years, 9 months and 7 days prior to her visit to his home.[41]

Mrs. Metcalf, meanwhile, had a transmitter in her purse, and was relaying her conversations with Dietemann to a receiver/tape recorder in an auto parked nearby. That auto contained the following eavesdroppers: another Life reporter, a representative of the DA's office, and an investigator from the California State Department of Public Health. This detective work resulted in a conviction of Dietemann for practicing medicine without a license.[42] Although the record does not show whether the plumber was flushed with anger, he nonetheless sued for damages totaling $300,000 for invasion of his privacy. A jury, recognizing that Dietemann was not suing from a position of great strength as a convicted medical man-sans-license, nevertheless awarded Dietemann $1,000 for invasion of privacy.

In an opinion by Judge Shirley Hufstedler, a United States Court of Appeals upheld the damage award, disagreeing with Life magazine attorneys' arguments that concealed electronic instruments were "indispensable tools of investigative reporting." Judge Hufstedler wrote: [43]

> Investigative reporting is an ancient art; its successful practice long antecedes the invention of miniature cameras and electronic devices. The First Amendment has never been construed to accord newsmen immunity from torts or crimes committed during the course of newsgathering. The First Amendment is not a license to trespass, to steal, or to intrude by electronic means into the precincts of another's home or office. It does not become such a license simply because the person subjected to the intrusion is reasonably suspected of committing a crime.

[41] Dietemann v. Time, Inc., 449 F.2d 245, 246 (9th Cir.1971).

[42] Ibid.

[43] Ibid., pp. 249–250.

*   *   *

No interest protected by the First Amendment is adversely affected by permitting damages for intrusion to be enhanced by the fact of later publication of the information that the publisher improperly acquired. Assessing damages for the additional emotional distress suffered by a plaintiff when the wrongfully acquired data are purveyed to the multitude chills intrusive acts. It does not chill freedom of expression guaranteed by the First Amendment.

McCall v. Courier-Journal & Times

This case is discussed under the general heading of "Intrusion," and that certainly is an element here. Like a number of other privacy cases, however, it involves a number of issues. In this case, there was a libel suit, plus privacy law claims which are labeled "false light;" the false light tort area is discussed later in this chapter. McCall v. Courier-Journal and Times arose when Louisville Times reporters outfitted drug suspect Kristie Frazier's purse with a tape recorder. She had told them that attorney Tim McCall had said that if she would pay him $10,000, he could keep her out of jail. Ms. Frazier then returned to McCall's law office with tape recorder running and had another conversation with him. As the fact situation was summarized by The Reporters Committee for Freedom of the Press: [44]

> The transcript of the conversation revealed that McCall said that the case could not be "fixed" and warned Frazier not to speak in such terms. But he did say that he was going fishing with one of the judges involved, and that once the prosecutor knew McCall had elicited a substantial fee, he would be more sympathetic to her cause.

While Ms. Frazier was in McCall's office taping their conversation, he asked her several times whether she was using a recording device. She denied doing so. Once Ms. Frazier handed the tape over to Louisville Times reporters Richard Krantz and Tom Van Howe, it was used as the basis for an article. The article said, in part, "The Times requested that Miss Frazier tape-record the conversation because the newspaper was attempting to investigate her allegations that McCall offered to 'fix' her case for $10,000. However, the Times found no indication of any 'fix.'" The Times, even so, repeated Frazier's allegations.[45]

[44] News Media & the Law, Oct.-Nov. 1980, p. 31.

[45] News Media & the Law, Oct.-Nov. 1980, p. 31.

Attorney McCall sued for invasion of privacy and libel. He declared that the secret taping was a wrongful act, and that he had been libeled because the article implied that he had offered to fix the case and was published in reckless disregard of his rights. McCall asked $6 million in damages. The Louisville Times published a story about McCall's lawsuit, summarizing its first article. McCall then amended his complaint, adding the contention that the Times' second article was libelous, too.[46]

The trial court dismissed McCall's suit, finding no libel. The article, the court said, merely "brought into focus a question of ethics, and * * * itself disclaimed dishonesty (on McCall's part) by stating there was no evidence of a fix." The trial court did not reach the issue of whether McCall was a public figure for libel suit purposes. Also, the trial court found no invasion of privacy, in part because Ms. Frazier was not in McCall's office as a trespasser but because she had been invited.[47]

The Kentucky Court of Appeals in 1980 affirmed the trial court's decision, saying that McCall was not a public figure but that he could not collect for libel because the article was truthful. The Court of Appeals complained that McCall's reputation had been damaged and criticized the Louisville Times. If the newspaper " * * * sincerely believed a breach of legal ethics or professional conduct had occurred, various remedies were available other than a public spanking by the newspaper."[48]

The Kentucky Supreme Court, however, ruled that the lower courts had erred in allowing a summary judgment. The state's Supreme Court said finding in favor of the newspaper without allowing the matter to go to trial was improper, and that McCall's libel and privacy actions should not have been dismissed.

In terms of the privacy aspects of this case, the Kentucky Supreme Court did not focus on "intrusion." Instead, that court concentrated on the "false light" category of privacy law. Noting that the trial court had rejected McCall's claims that his privacy had been invaded by the intrusion by the sneaky tape recording— and by the newspaper article's implication that he might be an unethical and dishonest attorney. The Kentucky Supreme Court wrote:[49]

[46] Ibid.; see also McCall v. Courier-Journal & Times, 623 S.W.2d 882 (Ky.App. 1980), 8 Med.L.Rptr. 1112.

[47] McCall v. Courier-Journal & Times, 623 S.W.2d 882 (Ky.App.1980), 6 Med.L.Rptr. 1112.

[48] 623 S.W.2d 882 (Ky.App.1980), 6 Med.L.Rptr. 1112, 1114.

[49] McCall v. Courier-Journal and Times, 623 S.W.2d 882 (Ky.Supreme Court, 1981), 7 Med.L.Rptr. 2118, 2122–2123.

In affirming the trial court the Court of Appeals did not consider the "false light" ruling but addressed only the problem of the use of the concealed tape recorder. Because we decide the issue on the basis of "false light," we do not deem it necessary to discuss the other aspect of the right of privacy claim.

* * *

The article clearly indicates that there was a probability that McCall was guilty of unethical conduct, and would be read by a lay person as having stated that he intended to "fix" a case or bribe a judge. We believe that the issue of false light should have been submitted to a jury.

The Kentucky Supreme Court then sent the case back to the trial court for reconsideration. Before that jury trial could begin, the Courier-Journal and Louisville Times Co. agreed to pay attorney McCall $75,000 to settle the $6 million libel and invasion of privacy lawsuit. Paul Janensch, executive editor of the Louisville newspapers, said the settlement was agreed to rather than face the prospect of an expensive and time-consuming trial. On the other hand, McCall's attorney, Edward M. Post, told the Associated Press that the newspaper " 'did not want to face a jury in this community which would call it to account for both the wrongful invasion of McCall's privacy and improper reporting.' " [50]

Cassidy v. ABC

If people don't like hidden tape recorders, they may be even more hostile toward hidden television cameras. Sometimes, as Chicago policeman Arlyn Cassidy found out, TV cameras can show up at—from his viewpoint—an inopportune moment. Cassidy was working as an undercover vice squad agent assigned to investigate a massage parlor.

Policeman Cassidy stated in court that he had paid a $30 admission fee to see "de-luxe" lingerie modeling. He was then taken to a small cubicle, "Room No. 1," by one of the models. As the Illinois Appellate Court, First Division, reported: [51]

Upon entering the room he [Cassidy] noticed "camera lights" on each side of the bed. He remarked to the model that the lights had made the room quite warm. Plaintiff [Cassidy] stated he then reclined on the bed and watched the model change her lingerie several times. He made several suggestive remarks and physical advances

---

[50] The Associated Press, "Louisville Times, attorney settle suit," story published in The Kentucky Kernel, newspaper of the University of Kentucky, November 24, 1982, p. 5.

[51] Cassidy v. ABC, 60 Ill.App.3d 831, 17 Ill.Dec. 936, 377 N.E.2d 126 (1978).

to her. He arrested the model for solicitation after she established "sufficient" physical contact with him. Three of the other undercover agents joined plaintiff [Cassidy] and asked if anyone was in the room adjacent * * * (Room No. 2).

At that moment, someone rushed out of Room No. 2, yelling "Channel 7 News." That's right, a camera crew from Chicago's American Broadcasting Company television outlet had been in the adjoining room, filming Officer Cassidy and the model through a two-way mirror. The television station personnel testified that they had received complaints from the massage parlor's manager that his establishment was the subject of police harassment.

The whole television situation rubbed Officer Cassidy the wrong way. He complained that the camera crew's activities violated Illinois' anti-eavesdropping statute [52] and that his common law right to privacy was violated.[53] The Illinois Appellate Court had difficulty in terming a television camera "an eavesdropping device," the more so because the noise of the camera's operation drowned out sounds from the other room. Furthermore, Cassidy had noticed the lights and asked the model whether they were "on TV." She replied, "Sure, we're making movies." Under such circumstances, Officer Cassidy was believed by the court not to have much of an expectation of privacy.

In addition, Cassidy's effort to assert a cause of action under the "intrusion" theory of privacy failed, on grounds that Cassidy was a public official on duty at the time he heard those stirring words, "Channel 7 News." [54] The Illinois Appellate Court said:

> * * * the conduct of a policeman on duty is legitimately and necessarily an area upon which public interest may and should be focused. * * * In our opinion, the very status of a public official * * * is tantamount to an implied consent to informing the general public by all legitimate means regarding his activities in discharge of his public duties. There is no allegation in any of the pleadings charging defendants or any of them with actual malice or with any wilful attempt to impede police work. The motives of the defendants [the members of the television camera crew] are not impugned by the record before us.

[52] Ibid., p. 127; see § 14–2, Oh. 38, Ill.Rev.Stat. (1975).

[53] Ibid., p. 127.

[54] Ibid., pp. 128, 132.

Use of Tape Recorders

The Dietemann and Cassidy cases should inspire journalists to think carefully about their use of cameras, tape recorders, and electronic listening and transmitting gear. Professor Kent R. Middleton, in an important article on journalists' use of tape recorders, concluded: "Reporters may record or transmit conversations they overhear, they participate in, or they record with permission of one party." Recording with the permission of one party—that's called "consensual monitoring" in legal jargon—is what is involved here for the press.[55]

Does one-party consent sound confusing, or merely ludicrous? What would one-party consent do to the law of burglary or of rape? What "consensual monitoring" does as a legal concept is forbid an unauthorized third party from intercepting a conversation, as in the case of an illegal (not-authorized-by-a-court) tap on a telephone line, listening in on two other parties.

Please note that this section is discussing what is legal, and not necessarily what is ethical. The authors of this text know that many reporters often record conversations—particularly telephone conversations—without giving notice that a tape recorder is running. It is legal in a majority of states for a reporter to conceal a tape recorder in a pocket or purse, for example, while talking to news sources.

It is legal in most states for a reporter to conceal a tape recorder in pocket or purse while talking to news sources. Note, however, that roughly one-quarter of the states have statutes outlawing such use of recorders. Professor Middleton reported that such participant monitoring was forbidden by statute in 13 states: California, Delaware, Florida, Georgia, Illinois, Maryland, Massachusetts, Michigan, Montana, New Hampshire, Oregon, Pennsylvania, and Washington.[56] Furthermore, in Shevin v. Sunbeam Television Corporation, the Florida Supreme Court ruled that the Florida statute forbidding interception of telephone messages without consent of all parties involved did not violate a reporter's First Amendment rights.[57]

Many reporters routinely record telephone conversations without telling the party on the other end of the line, or without a

---

[55] Kent R. Middleton, "Journalists and Tape Recorders: Does Participant Monitoring Invade Privacy?", 2 COMM/ENT Law Journal (1980) at pp. 299–300.

[56] Ibid., pp. 304–309.

[57] Shevin v. Sunbeam Television Corp., 351 So.2d 723 (Fla.1977), rehearing denied 435 U.S. 1018, 98 S.Ct. 1892 (1978). See also Victor A. Kovner, "Recent Developments in Intrusion, Private Facts, False Light, and Commercialization Claims," in James C. Goodale, chairman, Communications Law, 1984, Vol. II (New York: Practising Law Institute, 1984), pp. 428–431.

warning "beep" signal as required by the Federal Communications Commission.[58] This kind of surreptitious recording may not violate specific state or federal law, but it is forbidden by telephone company tariffs, as Middleton has written. If a person is somehow caught while secretly recording phone conversations, the telephone company could cut off phone service. That, however, seems to be only a remote possibility.[59] Furthermore, as privacy expert Victor A. Kovner has noted, the FCC in 1983 advanced a "Notice of Proposed Rule-Making" to get rid of the "beep-tone" rule. The FCC argued that technology of recent years made the rule in effect unenforceable. Early in 1985, the FCC had taken no action on the proposal.[60]

Boddie v. ABC (1984)

In addition to state provisions and telephone company "tariffs" [rules] as overseen by the Federal Communications Commission (FCC), there is also the Federal Wiretap Statute. That statute was involved in Sandra Boddie's suit alleging defamation, invasion of privacy, and violation of the Federal Wiretap Statute by an American Broadcasting Co. report on its "20/20" program. That report investigated allegations that Judge James Barbuto of Akron, Ohio, had frequently granted leniency to criminal defendants in exchange for sex.

Co-defendants with the ABC Network were television personality Geraldo Rivera, senior producer and correspondent for the report, and Charles C. Thompson, executive producer and investigative reporter. While investigating the allegations about Judge Barbuto, Rivera and Thompson interviewed Sandra Boddie. She agreed to be interviewed by the journalists, but refused to appear on camera. Unknown to Ms. Boddie, Rivera, Thompson and some other journalists recorded the interview by using hidden microphones and a hidden videotape camera. A part of that surreptitiously taped interview was televised by ABC in its broadcast report titled "Injustice for All." [61]

Ms. Boddie also claimed that the defendants' actions violated rules of the FCC prohibiting use of electronic devices for eavesdropping, for "listening in" without the consent of the parties in the conversation.[62] Boddie's lawsuit pointed to a federal statute, 47 U.S.C.A. § 502, which provides civil penalties (monetary dam-

---

[58] Middleton, pp. 304–309.

[59] Ibid., pp. 319–320; Kovner, p. 429, citing 47 C.F.R. Sec. 64.501; Sec. 73.1206. FCC Rules.

[60] Kovner, p. 430, citing FCC Docket No. 20840.

[61] Boddie v. ABC, 731 F.2d 333 (6th Cir.1984), 10 Med.L.Rptr. 1923, 1924–1925.

[62] 731 F.2d 333 (6th Cir.1984), 10 Med.L.Rptr. 1923, 1924.

ages) for violation of FCC regulations against electronic eavesdropping.[63]   At the trial court level, the judge dismissed this complaint, claiming plaintiff Boddie had failed to state a cause of action.

The U.S. Court of Appeals for the Sixth Circuit disagreed, saying the lower court was "clearly incorrect."   Circuit Judge Brown said, "In the third count of her complaint, Boddie cited 18 U.S.C.A. § 2520 which authorizes a civil cause of action for any person 'whose wire or oral communication is intercepted, disclosed or used in violation of this chapter.' " [64]   The Court of Appeals also italicized a key phrase in another section of the Federal Wiretap Statute on "injurious acts" to indicate its view of how it should be read.[65]

Ms. Boddie did not succeed in her lawsuit for defamation and for invasion of privacy by placing her in a false light.   After a seven-week trial, a jury returned a verdict in favor of the defendant broadcasters.   The trial court judge, however, had—on his own volition—rejected Ms. Boddie's claim that the defendants' surreptitious recording of the interview violated the Federal Wiretap Statute, which provides: [66]

(1) Except as otherwise specifically provided in this chapter any person who—

(a) willfully intercepts, endeavors to intercept, or procures any other person to intercept or endeavor to intercept, any wire or oral communication [violates this section];

* * *

(c) willfully discloses, or endeavors to disclose, to any other person the contents of any wire or oral communication, knowing or having reason to know that the information was obtained through the interception of a wire or oral communication in violation of this subsection; or

(d) willfully uses, or endeavors to use, the contents of any wire or oral communication, knowing or having reason to know that the information was obtained through the interception of a wire or oral communication in violation of this subsection shall be fined not more than $10,000 or imprisoned not more than five years, or both.

[63] 731 F.2d 333, 335–336 (6th Cir.1984), 10 Med.L.Rptr. 1923, 1924.

[64] 731 F.2d 333, 336 (6th Cir.1984), 10 Med.L.Rptr. 1923, 1924–1925.

[65] 731 F.2d 333, 337 (6th Cir.1984), 10 Med.L.Rptr. 1923, 1925.

[66] 731 F.2d 333, 335–336 (6th Cir.1984), 10 Med.L.Rptr. at 1924, quoting Federal Wiretap Statute, 18 U.S.C.A. § 2511(1)(a), (c), and (d).

It shall not be unlawful under this chapter for a person not acting under color of law [e.g. with a valid court-issued warrant] to intercept a wire or oral communication where such person is a party to the communication or where one of the parties to the communication has given prior consent to such interception *unless such communication is intercepted* for the purpose of committing any criminal or tortious act in violation of the Constitution or laws of the United States or of any State or *for the purpose of committing any other injurious act.*

The Sixth Circuit, however, concluded that Ms. Boddie had a cause of action under the Federal Wiretap Statute which should be heard at the trial court level, and sent the case back to the lower court for further proceedings. In a concurring opinion, Judge Wellford said there are three guidelines in applying the Federal Wiretap Statute where use of hidden recorders is involved and should be considered as exceptions in applying the law: [67]

(1) A desire to make an accurate record of a conversation to which you are a party is a lawful purpose under the statute even if you want to use the recording in evidence. [Citing By-Prod Corp. v. Armen-Berry Co., 668 F.2d 956, 959 (7th Cir.1982).]

(2) "Congress, we believe, intended to permit one party to record conversation with another when the recorder is acting 'out of a legitimate desire to protect himself.'" [Citing Moore v. Telfon Communications Corp., 589 F.2d 959, 965–66 (9th Cir.1978).]

(3) "The provision would not, however, prohibit any such activity [intercepting a wire or oral communication] when the party records information of criminal activity by the other party with the purpose of taking such information to the police as evidence." [Citing United States v. Phillips, 540 F.2d 319, 325 (8th Cir.1976), cert. denied 429 U.S. 1000, 97 S.Ct. 530, (1976), quoting 114 Cong.Rec. 14694).]

Pearson v. Dodd

In a case which raises the question of the extent of reportorial involvement in removing documents from the office of a public official, Senator Thomas Dodd of Connecticut failed to collect in an intrusion-invasion of privacy lawsuit against muckraking columnists Drew Pearson and Jack Anderson. Pearson and Anderson had done great harm to Dodd's reputation and career. They had

---

[67] 731 F.2d 333, 340 (6th Cir.1984), 10 Med.L.Rptr. 1924, 1927–1928, quoting 18 U.S.C.A. § 2511(2)(d). Emphasis the court's.

published papers taken from Dodd's office files which showed an appropriation of campaign funds for personal purposes.

The exposé of Dodd began during the summer of 1965 when two employees and two former employees of Senator Dodd removed documents from his files, photocopied them, and then replaced the originals in their filing cabinets. The copies were turned over to Anderson, who knew how they had been obtained. The Pearson-Anderson "Washington Merry-Go-Round" column then ran six stories about the Senator, dealing—among other matters—with his relationship with lobbyists for foreign interests.

Dodd argued that the manner in which the information for the columns was obtained was an invasion of his privacy. After hearing Pearson and Anderson's appeal from a lower court judgment,[68] Court of Appeals Judge J. Skelly Wright said that Dodd's employees and former employees had committed improper intrusion when they removed confidential files to show them to outsiders. And what of the journalists?[69]

* * *

If we were to hold appellants [Pearson and Anderson] liable for invasion of privacy on these facts, we would establish the proposition that one who receives information from an intruder, knowing it has been obtained by improper intrusion, is guilty of a tort. In an untried and developing area of tort law, we are not prepared to go so far.

* * *

But in analyzing the claimed breach of privacy, injuries from intrusion and injuries from publication should be kept clearly separate. Where there is intrusion, the intruder should generally be liable whatever the content of what he learns. An eavesdropper to the marital bedroom may hear marital intimacies, or he may hear statements of fact or opinion of legitimate interest to the public; for purposes of liability, that should make no difference. On the other hand, where the claim is that private information concerning the plaintiff has been published, the question of whether that information is

[68] 279 F.Supp. 101 (D.C.D.C.1968).

[69] 133 U.S.App.D.C. 279, 410 F.2d 701, 704–705 (D.C.Cir.1969). See also Bilney v. Evening Star, 43 Md.App. 560, 406 A.2d 652 (1980), 5 Med.L.Rptr. 1931, in which a newspaper was sued for intrusion because it had published confidential academic records of members of the University of Maryland basketball team. The records involved were held to be newsworthy, and the lawsuit against the paper was dismissed because it was not demonstrated that reporters had solicited or encouraged reading of confidential records. The material involved came unasked for, from an unnamed source. See also Victor A. Kovner, op. cit. pp. 255–256.

genuinely private or is of public interest should not turn on the manner in which it has been obtained.

Florida Publishing Co. v. Fletcher

In 1972, 17-year-old Cindy Fletcher was alone one afternoon at her Jacksonville, Fla., home when a fire of undetermined origin did severe damage to the house. She died in the blaze. When the Fire Marshal and a police sergeant arrived at the house to make their investigation, they invited news media representatives to join them as was their standard practice.

The Fire Marshal desired a clear picture of the "silhouette" left on the floor after the removal of Cindy Fletcher's body to show that the body was already on the floor before the fire's heat damaged the room. The marshal took one Polaroid photograph of the outline, but that picture was unclear and he had no more film. A photographer for the Florida *Times-Union* was then asked to take the silhouette picture, which was made part of the official investigation files of both the fire and police departments.

This picture was not only part of the investigative record, it was also published—along with other pictures from the fire scene—in a Times-Union story on September 16, 1972. Cindy's mother, Mrs. Klenna Ann Fletcher, first learned of the facts surrounding the death of her daughter by reading the newspaper story and by seeing the published photographs.

Mrs. Fletcher sued the newspaper ["Florida Publishing Company"] and alleged three things: "(1) trespass and invasion of privacy, (2) invasion of privacy, and (3) wrongful intentional infliction of emotional distress—seeking punitive damages.[70] The trial court dismissed Count 2 and granted summary judgments in favor of the newspaper on counts 1 and 3. Speaking to the question of trespass, the trial judge said: [71]

"The question raised is whether the trespass alleged in Count I of the complaint was consented to by the doctrine of common custom and usage.

"The law is well settled in Florida that there is no unlawful trespass when peaceable entry is made, without objection, under common custom and usage."

[70] Florida Pub. Co. v. Fletcher, 340 So.2d 914, 915–916 (Fla.1977).

[71] Quoted at Ibid., p. 916.

Numerous affidavits had been filed by the news media saying that "common custom and usage" permitted the news media to enter the scene of a disaster.[72]

Mrs. Fletcher appealed from the trial court to Florida District Court of Appeal, First District, which held that she should have been able to go to trial on the issue of trespass.[73] The Florida Supreme Court, however, ruled that no actionable trespass or invasion of privacy had occurred. The Florida Supreme Court quoted approvingly from a dissenting opinion by Florida District Court of Appeal Judge McCord: [74]

> *"It is my view that the entry in this case was by implied consent.*
>
> "It is not questioned that this tragic fire and death were being investigated by the fire department and the sheriff's office and that arson was suspected. The fire was a disaster of great public interest and it is clear that the photographer and other members of the news media entered the burned home at the invitation of the investigating officers.
>
> "   *   *   *
>
> "The affidavits as to custom and practice do not delineate between various kinds of property where a tragedy occurs. They apply to any such place. If an entry is or is not a trespass, its character would not change depending upon whether or not the place of the tragedy is a burned out home (as here), an office or other building or place. An analysis of the cases on implied consent *   *   * indicates that they do not rest upon the previous nonobjection to the entry by the property owner in question but rest upon custom and practice generally. Implied consent would, of course, vanish if one were informed not to enter at that time by the owner or possessor or by their direction. But here there was not only no objection to the entry, but *there was an invitation to enter by the officers investigating the fire."*

Therefore, there was no trespass by the news media in this case.

---

[72] Ibid. Affidavits came from such sources as the Chicago Tribune; ABC–TV News, New York; the Associated Press; the Miami Hearld; United Press International; the Milwaukee Journal, and the Washington Post.

[73] Ibid., pp. 917–918.

[74] Ibid., pp. 918–919. See also Higbee v. Times–Advocate, (U.S.D.C., S.D.Cal., 1980), 5 Med.L.Rptr. 2372, dismissing a federal violation of civil rights claim but ruling that a photo taken inside plaintiffs' home was a matter of state tort law. Escondido, Calif., law enforcement officers had invited the press to be present during the execution of a search warrant.

When a reporter does not have permission to be on private property, however, the result could be troublesome. That's one message of a 1980 case, Oklahoma v. Bernstein, as decided by an Oklahoma District Court (Rogers County). Benjamin Bernstein and a number of other reporters had been arrested for trespassing onto private property. In hot pursuit of a newsworthy event, they followed protesting demonstrators onto the construction site of a Public Service Company of Oklahoma (PSO) nuclear power plant, Black Fox Station.

Despite showings of extensive governmental support (e.g. use of eminent domain to acquire part of the site for PSO, government-guaranteed loans, and close continuing supervision from the Nuclear Regulatory Commission), the Black Fox site was held to be private property. Although the Oklahoma court held that protests at the construction site were newsworthy—and although PSO was trying to minimize news coverage of an important public controversy, the reporters were found guilty of trespass.[75]

Similarly, consider the decision in Anderson v. WROC–TV (1981). Two Rochester, New York, television stations accepted the invitation of Humane Society investigator Ronald Storm to accompany him as he served a search warrant. The warrant authorized Storm to enter the house occupied by Barbara P. Anderson and Joy E. Brenon, to seize animals which might be found confined in an overcrowded, unhealthy situation or not properly cared for.

When investigator Storm served the search warrant, television photographers and reporters accompanied him into the home of Ms. Anderson and Ms. Brenon, and filmed the interior. Ms. Brenon asked the television people to stay outside her home, but they entered anyway. Stories about the search were broadcast that evening on news shows of WROC–TV and WOKR–TV.[76]

Citing Dietemann v. Time, Inc.,[77] the New York Supreme Court, Monroe County, held that the First Amendment right to gather news does not allow members of the press to get away with committing crimes or torts in the course of newsgathering. Reporters are not above the law. In this case, a resident of the house told television station employees to stay out of her house, and they did not do so. In addition, the New York Court distinguished this

[75] Oklahoma v. Bernstein, 5 Med.L.Rptr. 2313, 2323–2324 (Okla.D.C., Rogers County, Jan. 21, 1980).

[76] Anderson v. WROC–TV, 109 Misc.2d 904; 441 N.Y.S.2d 220, (N.Y.Sup.Ct.1981), 7 Med.L.Rptr. 1987, 1988.

[77] 109 Misc.2d 904, 441 N.Y.S. 220, (N.Y.Sup.Ct.1981), 7 Med.L.Rptr. 1997, 1990, discussing Dietemann v. Time, Inc., 449 F.2d 245 (9th Cir.1971).

case from Florida Publishing Company v. Fletcher,[78] discussed earlier at footnote 78.[79]

> Even were it necessary to decide this * * * solely upon the factual differences between * * * [this] case and Fletcher the same result would obtain. In Fletcher the Florida court characterized the fire as "a disaster of great public interest." (340 So.2d at 918). The entry here by the Humane Society investigator can hardly be compared to a fire which took the life of a young person.
>
> * * *
>
> As the plaintiffs correctly argue, one may not create an implied consent by asserting that it exists and without evidence to support it. In passing, and as previously noted, it also appears * * * that the entry was made in disregard of plaintiff Joy Brenon's express instructions to stay out.

SEC. 33. PUBLICATION OF PRIVATE MATTERS

With the law of privacy, "truth can hurt." Unlike the law of defamation, truth is not necessarily a defense to a lawsuit for invasion of privacy.

The case of Dorothy Barber discussed in the last section was not only an incident of "intrusion," but also involved a second sub-area of privacy law: "publication of private matters violating the ordinary decencies." In this area of law, missteps by the mass media have led to a substantial number of lawsuits. In publishing details of private matters, the media may make scrupulously accurate reports and yet—at least on some occasions—be found liable for damages. A suit for defamation would not stand where the press has accurately reported the truth, but the press could nevertheless lose an action for invasion of privacy based on the same fact situation. Here, the truth sometimes hurts.

In most cases, the existence of a public record has usually precluded recovery for invasion of privacy. Even if persons are embarrassed by publication of dates of a marriage or birth,[80] or information which is a matter of public record,[81] publication accurately based on such records have escaped successful lawsuits. Where there is a legitimate public record—and where the media's use of that record is not forbidden by law—the material generally

---

[78] 340 So.2d 914 (Fla.1977).

[79] 109 Misc.2d 904, 441 N.Y.S.2d 220, (N.Y.Sup.Ct.1981), 7 Med.L.Rptr. 1987, 1992.

[80] Meetze v. Associated Press, 230 S.C. 330, 95 S.E.2d 606 (1956).

[81] Stryker v. Republic Pictures Corp., 108 Cal.App.2d 191, 238 P.2d 670 (1951).

may be used for publication. In 1960, the Albuquerque (N.M.) *Journal* published a story which said:[82]

> Richard Hubbard, 16, son of Mrs. Ann Hubbard, 532 Ponderosa, NW, was charged with running away from home, also prior to date, several times endangered the physical and moral health of himself and others by sexually assaulting his younger sister.   *   *   *

The younger sister, Delores Hubbard, sued for invasion of privacy, asserting that she had suffered extreme humiliation and distress and that the story "caused her to be regarded as unchaste, and that her prospects of marriage have been adversely affected thereby." Attorneys for the newspaper, however, brought proof that the *Albuquerque Journal's* story was an exact copy of an official court record. In upholding a lower court's judgment for the newspaper, the New Mexico Supreme Court ruled that because this was a public record, the newspaper enjoyed privilege. Although the plaintiff complained that the article was not newsworthy, the court held that the story was accurate, newsworthy and exercised in a reasonable manner and for a proper purpose." The court added that the girl, although an unwilling participant who did not seek publicity, was in the unfortunate position of being a person who might come to the notice of the public and have her misfortunes told to the world.[83]

It should be apparent that much in the law of privacy is unpredictable, and the "private facts" area is no exception. Consider the lawsuits brought by Oliver Sipple, the ex-Marine who saved President Gerald Ford's life in 1975 by deflecting the aim of a would-be assassin, Sarah Jane Moore. Two days after the incident, the San Francisco Chronicle's famed columnist Herb Caen wrote some words strongly implying that Sipple was a homosexual. Caen wrote that San Francisco's gay community was proud of Sipple's action, and that it might dispel stereotypes about homosexuals.[84]

Sipple objected that his sexual preference had nothing to do with saving the President's life, and filed suit against *The* San Francisco Chronicle, Herb Caen, The Los Angeles Times, and several other newspapers, seeking $15 million in damages. Sipple argued that printing facts about his sexual orientation without his consent exposed him to ridicule. The Los Angeles Times countered that Sipple, as a person thrust into the "vortex of publicity" of an event of worldwide importance had become a newsworthy figure. "[M]any aspects of his life became matters of legitimate

---

[82] Hubbard v. Journal Pub. Co., 69 N.M. 473, 474, 368 P.2d 147 (1962).

[83] 69 N.M. 473, 474–475, 368 P.2d 147, 148–149 (1962).

[84] The News Media & The Law, Oct./Nov. 1980, p. 27.

public interest." Individuals who become public persons give up part of their right of privacy, the *Times* contended. Finally, in April, 1980, a California trial court—without giving any reasons— dismissed the invasion of privacy suit against the San Francisco Chronicle and other newspapers.[85]

Sipple appealed against the dismissal, asking the California Court of Appeal, First District, to reinstate his privacy lawsuit. The appellate court held, however, that Sipple's case was correctly terminated by the lower court. The Court of Appeal said that the facts about Sipple as a member of San Francisco's gay community were already quite widely known: "in the public domain." In addition, the Court of Appeal held that Sipple was indeed news- worthy after saving President Ford's life.

Sipple, of course, was involved in an event of international importance. When the newsworthiness is less, the privacy protec- tion for individuals may be correspondingly greater. Toni Ann Diaz, for example, had achieved a limited newsworthiness as the first woman student body president at a northern California school, the College of Alameda.

In 1978, Oakland Tribune columnist Sidney Jones published truthful—yet highly private—information about Ms. Diaz.[86]

> "More Education Stuff: The students at the College of Alameda will be surprised to learn their student body president Toni Diaz is no lady, but is in fact a man whose real name is Antonio.

> "Now I realize, that in these times, such a matter is no big deal, but I suspect his female classmates in P.E. 97 may wish to make other showering arrangements."

The trial court jury awarded Ms. Diaz a total of $775,000, finding that the information about the sex change was not news- worthy and would be offensive to ordinary readers.[87]

In January of 1983, although obviously in sympathy with Ms. Diaz, the California Court of Appeal, First District, sent the matter back to the lower court for a new trial. The appellate court held that the trial judge had committed reversible error in not emphasizing to the jury that a newspaper has a right to publish newsworthy information. Also, it was held that jury instructions should have made it clear that plaintiff Diaz had to

[85] Sipple v. Chronicle Publishing Company, 154 Cal.App.3d 1040, 201 Cal.Rptr. 665 (1st Dist.1984), 10 Med.L.Rptr. 1690, 1693–1694.

[86] Diaz v. Oakland Tribune, 139 Cal.App.3d 118, 188 Cal.Rptr. 762 (1983), 9 Med. L.Rptr. 1121, 1122.

[87] The News Media and the Law, Oct./Nov. 1980, p. 28.

carry the burden of proof in trying to show that the article she complained of was not newsworthy.[88]

The court held that there was little evidence that the gender-corrective surgery was part of the public record. It did not consider Diaz's Puerto Rican birth certificate to be a public record in this instance." [89] Given Diaz's efforts to conceal the operation, and considering Diaz's needs for privacy and the notoriety received as the first woman student body president at that college, the question of the story's newsworthiness—the judge said—should have been left to a jury.[90] The court added that there was no merit in the Oakland Tribune's claim that the story was made newsworthy by the changing roles of women in society. Judge Barry-Deal wrote:[91]

> This assertion rings hollow. The tenor of the article was by no means an attempt to enlighten the public on a contemporary social issue. Rather, as [columnist Sidney] Jones himself admitted, the article was directed to the students at the College about their newly elected president. Moreover, Jones' attempt at humor at Diaz's expense removes all pretense that the article was meant to educate the public. The social utility of the information must be viewed in context, and not based upon some arguably meritorious and unintended purpose.

The appellate court then sent the case back to the trial level, but a second jury never heard the Diaz case. After the decision by the California Court of Appeal, First District, the case was reported settled out of court for between $200,000 and $300,000. Marc Franklin has written that this is a record amount for money paid for an invasion of privacy in the "publication of private matters" category.[1]

The case of Howard v. Des Moines Register and Tribune Co. also raised both legal and ethical concerns. *Register* reporter Margaret Engel did an investigative story on a county home, and published the name of a young woman who had undergone forced sterilization. The article included this passage: "He [Dr. Roy C. Sloan, the home's psychiatrist] said the decision to sterilize the

---

[88] 139 Cal.App.3d 118, 188 Cal.Rptr. 762 (1983); 9 Med.L.Rptr. 1121.

[89] 139 Cal.App.3d 118, 188 Cal.Rptr. 762, 763 (1983), 9 Med.L.Rptr. 1121, 1127.

[90] Ibid.

[91] Ibid.

[1] Marc Franklin, 1985 Supplement for use with Cases and Materials on Mass Media Law, Second Edition (Mineola, N.Y., Foundation Press, 1985). Confirmed by Teeter's conversation with attorneys in the case. Ms. Diaz had received a jury award of $250,000 compensatory damages for emotional and psychological injury, plus punitive damages of $525,000 ($25,000 against columnist Jones and $500,000 against the Oakland Tribune).

resident Robin Woody was made by her parents and himself."
The article, based on public records, also noted that the woman
was 18 years old in 1970 at the time of her sterilization, and was
not mentally retarded or disabled, but an " 'impulsive, hair-trig-
gered, young girl' in the words of Dr. *   *   * Sloan." [2]

The *Register* defended itself successfully against a private
facts lawsuit, with the court concluding that in this context, use of
the defendant's name was justified. In granting the *Register* a
summary judgment, an Iowa District Court said that the relationship between the disclosure and a story's newsworthiness should
be considered. In this case, use of Robin Woody's name was said
to lend personal detail, specificity and credibility to a story on a
newsworthy topic, care of residents in a county home.[3]

In at least four states, statutes prohibited publishing the
identity of a rape victim. Those states are Wisconsin, Florida,
South Carolina, and Georgia.[4] A case based upon the South
Carolina statute resulted in a 1963 Federal District Court ruling
indicating that such statutes were valid. However, a 1975 Supreme Court of the United States decision held otherwise when
publication of a rape victim's name was based on a public record.[5]

Cox Broadcasting Corp. v. Cohn (1975)

Cox Broadcasting v. Cohn grew out of tragic circumstances.
In August, 1971, 17-year-old Cynthia Cohn was gang-raped and
died, and six youths were soon indicted for the crimes against her.
There was considerable coverage of the event, but the identity of
the victim was not disclosed until one defendant's trial began.
Some eight months later, in April of 1972, five of the six youths
entered pleas of guilty to rape or attempted rape, the charge of
murder having been dropped. Those guilty pleas were accepted,
and the trial of the defendant who pleaded not guilty was set for a
later date.[6]

Georgia had a statute forbidding publication of the identity of
a rape victim. Despite this, a television reporter employed by
WSB–TV—a Cox Broadcasting Corporation station—learned
Cynthia Cohn's name from indictments which were open to public
inspection. Later that day, the reporter broadcast her identity as

---

[2] Howard v. Des Moines Register and Tribune Co., 283 N.W.2d 289, 302 (Iowa
1979).

[3] Ibid., p. 303.

[4] Wis.Stat.Ann. 348.412; West's Fla.Stat.Ann., § 794.03; S.C.Ann.Code, § 16–81,
and Ga.Stat., § 26–9901.

[5] Cox Broadcasting Corp. v. Cohn, 420 U.S. 469, 95 S.Ct. 1029 (1975); Nappier v.
Jefferson Standard Life Ins. Co., 213 F.Supp. 174 (D.C.S.C.1968).

[6] Cox Broadcasting Corp. v. Cohn, 420 U.S. 469, 471, 95 S.Ct. 1029, 1034–1035
(1975).

part of his story on the court proceedings, and the report was repeated the next day.[7]

Martin Cohn sued Cox Broadcasting, claiming that the broadcasts which had identified his daughter invaded his own privacy by reason of the publication of his daughter's name. After hearing the Cohn case twice, the Georgia Supreme Court ruled that the statute forbidding publication of the name of a rape victim was constitutional * * * " 'a legitimate limitation on the right of freedom of expression contained in the First Amendment.' " [8]

The Supreme Court of the United States disagreed by a vote of 8–1. Writing for the Court, Mr. Justice White said:[9]

> The version of the privacy tort now before us— termed in Georgia the "tort of public disclosure" * * * is that in which the plaintiff claims the right to be free from unwanted publicity about his private affairs, which, although wholly true, would be offensive to a person of ordinary sensibilities. Because the gravamen [gist] of the claimed injury is the publication of information, whether true or not, the dissemination of which is embarrassing or otherwise painful to an individual, it is here that claims of privacy most directly confront the constitutional freedoms of speech and press.

Justice White wrote that truth may not always be a defense in either defamation or privacy actions. First, concerning defamation: "The Court has * * * carefully left open the question whether the First and Fourteenth Amendments require that truth be recognized as a defense in a defamation action brought by a private person as distinguished from a public official or a public figure." Writing about privacy, he continued, "In similar fashion, Time v. Hill, supra, [385 U.S. 374 at 383 n. 7, 87 S.Ct. 534 at 539 (1967)] expressly saved [reserved] the question whether truthful publication of very private matters unrelated to public affairs could be constitutionally proscribed." [10] Thus the Supreme Court recognized—but backed away—from a troubling constitutional question: may a state ever define and protect an area of privacy free from unwanted *truthful* publicity in the press? If so, then truth would not be a defense in such privacy areas, as still seems to be the case in the "embarrassing private facts" area of the privacy tort.

---

[7] 420 U.S. 469, 471, 95 S.Ct. 1029, 1034–1035 (1975).

[8] 420 U.S. 469, 475, 95 S.Ct. 1029, 1036 (1975). Justices Powell and Douglas filed concurring opinions, and Justice Rehnquist dissented, stating that the Supreme Court did not have jurisdiction in this case for want of a final decree or judgment from a lower court.

[9] 420 U.S. 469, 489, 95 S.Ct. 1029, 1043 (1975).

[10] 420 U.S. 469, 490, 95 S.Ct. 1029, 1044 (1975).

Having recognized this problem, Justice White then turned his majority opinion to narrower and safer ground. In *Cox Broadcasting,* the key question was whether Georgia might impose sanctions against the accurate publication of the name of a rape victim, when that name had been obtained from public records. "[M]ore specifically," White wrote, the issue arose when the rape victim's name was obtained "from judicial records which are maintained in connection with a public prosecution and which themselves are open to public inspection. We are convinced that the State may not do so." [11]

He wrote that the news media have a great responsibility to report fully and accurately the proceedings of government, "and official records and documents open to the public are the basic data of governmental operations." The function of the news media reporting of judicial proceedings "serves to guarantee the fairness of trials and to bring to bear the beneficial effects of public scrutiny upon the administration of justice.[12] White declared: [13]

> The special protected nature of accurate reports of judicial proceedings has repeatedly been recognized. This Court, in an opinion written by Mr. Justice Douglas, has said: "A trial is a public event. What transpires in the court room is public property. If a transcript of the court proceedings had been published, we suppose none would claim that the judge could punish the publisher for contempt. And we can see no difference though the conduct of the attorneys, of the jury, or even of the judge himself, may have reflected on the court. *Those who see and hear what transpired can report it with impunity.* There is no special perquisite of the judiciary which enables it, as distinguished from other institutions of democratic government, to suppress, edit, or censor events which transpire in events before it." Craig v. Harney, 331 U.S. 367, 374, 67 S.Ct. 1249, 1254 (1947).

The general rule for a journalist, then, is that if the material is part of a public record—in this case, of a judicial proceeding—it can be reported.

In 1979, the Supreme Court of the United States followed its reasoning from *Cox Broadcasting* in deciding Smith v. Daily Mail Publishing Co. *Smith* was a case which cut across areas of constitutional limitations on prior restraint, privacy, and free

[11] 420 U.S. 469, 491, 95 S.Ct. 1029, 1044 (1975).

[12] 420 U.S. 469, 492, 95 S.Ct. 1029, 1044–1045 (1975), citing Sheppard v. Maxwell, 384 U.S. 333, 350, 86 S.Ct. 1507, 1515 (1966).

[13] 420 U.S. 469, 492–493, 95 S.Ct. 1029, 1045 (1975). Emphasis Justice White's.

press-fair trial considerations. It arose in February, 1978, when a 14-year-old junior high school student in St. Albans, W.Va., shot and killed a 15-year-old fellow student. Reporters for nearby Charleston newspapers learned the identity of the youth accused of the shooting by their routine monitoring of the police radio. The Charleston *Daily Gazette* —and later, the *Daily Mail* —used the youth's name in their stories, in violation of a West Virginia statute forbidding newspapers' use of names of juveniles accused of crimes without a written court order.[14]

The state of West Virginia contended that even though this statute amounted to a prior restraint on speech, the state's interest in protecting the identity of juveniles caught up in the legal process overcame the presumption against the constitutional validity of prior restraints. In declaring the West Virginia statute unconstitutional by a vote of 8–0, Chief Justice Burger wrote: "At issue is simply the power of a state to punish the truthful publication of an alleged juvenile delinquent's name lawfully obtained by a newspaper. The asserted state interest cannot justify the statute's imposition of criminal sanctions on this type of publication."[15]

The "Social Value" Test: A California Aberration?

In decisions separated by 40 years, California courts added an element to privacy law: the existence of a public record did not necessarily serve as a defense to a lawsuit for invasion of privacy. One of the most famous—and wrong-headed—cases involving the disclosure of embarrassing private facts came in the 1931 case of Melvin v. Reid, which for many years was regarded as a leading decision in the law of privacy. Gabrielle Darley Melvin sued when a motion picture—"The Red Kimono"—was made about her life as a prostitute and her trial for murder in 1918. But Gabrielle Darley had been acquitted of the murder charge, and thereafter led a changed life: she got married, found many friends who were not aware of her tawdry past, and became an accepted member of society.[16]

Although the court found that a movie could be made about Mrs. Melvin's life without penalty—because the facts were part of a public record—it was found that damages could be recovered for

[14] West Virginia Statute § 49–7–3; Smith v. Daily Mail Pub. Co., 443 U.S. 97, 99 S.Ct. 2667 (1979).

[15] 443 U.S. 97, 99 S.Ct. 2667, 2672 (1979). See also the key prior restraint cases as discussed in Chapter 1: Near v. Minnesota, 283 U.S. 697, 51 S.Ct. 625 (1931); Organization for a Better Austin v. Keefe, 402 U.S. 415, 91 S.Ct. 1575 (1971): New York Times Co. v. U.S. 402 U.S. 713, 91 S.Ct. 2140 (1971), and Nebraska Press Ass'n v. Stuart, 427 U.S. 539, 96 S.Ct. 2791 (1976).

[16] Melvin v. Reid, 112 Cal.App. 285, 297 P. 91 (1931).

the use of her name, both in the motion picture and in advertisements for it.   Strangely, the California Supreme Court—via a decision written by Justice Emerson J. Marks—said that privacy as a tort action did not then (in 1931) exist in California.   However, Justice Marks found provisions in the California state constitution, such as Section 1, Article I: "men are by nature free *   *   * and have certain inalienable rights, among which are pursuing and obtaining safety and happiness."[17]

So it was that Mrs. Melvin won her lawsuit, even though Justice Marks denied the existence of the tort of invasion of privacy in California.   One especially curious thing about Melvin v. Reid is that the California Supreme Court gave little heed to the qualified privilege attached to reports made from public records. But then, in 1931, a movie such as "The Red Kimono" was not believed to be a defensible part of "the press" which is protected by the First Amendment.[18]   The court suggested strongly that if the motion picture company had used only those aspects of Gabrielle Darley's life which were in the trial record or public record of her case, then the film would have been privileged. Even so, Gabrielle Darley's name surely was part of the public record and it would seem that using it should have been "privileged."

In 1968, *Readers Digest* magazine published an article titled "The Big Business of Hijacking," describing various truck thefts and the efforts being made to stop such thefts.   Dates ranging from 1965 to the time of publication were mentioned throughout the article, but none of the hijackings mentioned had a date attached to it in the text.[19]

One sentence in the article said: "Typical of many beginners, Marvin Briscoe and [another man] stole a 'valuable-looking' truck in Danville, Ky. and then fought a gun battle with the local police, only to learn that they had hijacked four bowling-pin spotters."

There was nothing in the article to indicate that the hijacking had occurred in 1956, some 11 years before the publication of the *Reader's Digest* article.   In the words of the California Supreme Court, "As a result of defendant's [Reader's Digest's] publication,

---

[17] This was indeed a curious reading of the state's constitution. Usually, constitutions or bills of rights are seen as protecting individuals from the actions and powers of governments, rather than establishing protection against the actions of other individuals. See Pember, Privacy and the Press, p. 98.

[18] For years, courts were reluctant to accord First Amendment protection to motion pictures. See, e.g., Mutual Film Corp. v. Industrial Commission of Ohio, 236 U.S. 230, 35 S.Ct. 387 (1915); Burstyn, Inc. v. Wilson, 343 U.S. 495, 72 S.Ct. 777 (1952) was the case which first termed movies a significant medium for the expression of ideas.

[19] Briscoe v. Readers Digest Ass'n, 4 Cal.3d 529, 93 Cal.Rptr. 866, 483 P.2d 34, 36 (1971).

plaintiff's 11-year-old daughter, as well as his friends, for the first time learned of the incident. They thereafter scorned and abandoned him."[20] Briscoe argued that he had since "gone straight" and that he had become entirely rehabilitated, and led an exemplary and honorable life, making many friends in respectable society who were not aware of the hijacking incident in his earlier life.

Briscoe conceded the truth of the facts published in the *Reader's Digest* article, but claimed that the public disclosure of such private facts humiliated him and exposed him to contempt and ridicule. He conceded that the *subject* of the article might have been "newsworthy," but contended that the use of his *name* was not, and that *Reader's Digest* had therefore invaded his privacy.

Writing for a unanimous California Supreme Court, Justice Raymond E. Peters agreed with Briscoe's arguments, saying:[21]

> Plaintiff is a man whose last offense took place 11 years before, who has paid his debt to society, who has friends and an 11-year-old daughter who were unaware of his early life—a man who has assumed a position in "respectable society." Ideally, his neighbors should recognize his present worth and forget his past life of shame. But men are not so divine as to forgive the past trespasses of others, and plaintiff therefore endeavored to reveal as little as possible of his past life. Yet, as if in some bizarre canyon of echoes, petitioner's past life pursues him through the pages of Reader's Digest, now published in 13 languages and distributed in 100 nations, with a circulation in California alone of almost 2,000,000 copies.

> In a nation built upon the free dissemination of ideas, it is always difficult to declare that something may not be published. But the great general interest in an unfettered press may at times be outweighed by other societal interests. * * * But the rights guaranteed by the First Amendment do not require total abrogation of the right to privacy. The goals sought by each may be achieved with a minimum of intrusion on the other.

Although the California Supreme Court was not in a position to award damages to Mr. Briscoe, it did send his case back to a lower court for trial. Justice Peters declared that although there was good reason to discuss the crime of truck hijacking in the media, there was no reason to use Briscoe's name. A jury, in the view of the California Supreme Court, could certainly find that

[20] Ibid.

[21] 4 Cal.3d 529, 93 Cal.Rptr. 866, 483 P.2d 34, 41–42 (1971).

Mr. Briscoe had once again become an anonymous member of the community.[22]

Once legal proceedings have concluded, and particularly once the individual has reverted to the lawful and unexciting life led by the rest of the community, the public's interest in knowing is less compelling.

Second, a jury might find that revealing one's criminal past for all to see is grossly offensive to most people in America. Certainly a criminal background is kept even more hidden from others than is a humiliating disease * * *.

Third, in no way can plaintiff be said to have voluntarily consented to the publicity accorded him here. He committed a crime. He was punished. He was rehabilitated. And he became, for 11 years, an obscure and law-abiding citizen. His every effort was to forget and to have others forget that he had once hijacked a truck.

Despite such sweeping language, Briscoe did not win his lawsuit. The case was removed to the U.S. District Court, Central District of California, where Judge Lawrence T. Lydick granted a summary judgment to the *Reader's Digest*. Judge Lydick concluded that the article complained of by Briscoe was newsworthy and published without [actual] malice or recklessness. Further, the judge concluded that the article disclosed no private facts about Marvin Briscoe and that it did not invade his privacy.[23]

The language of the California Supreme Court in Briscoe lingered on. Take the case of Milo Conklin, who brought suit for invasion of privacy because the *Modoc County Record* published this item under the caption, "Twenty Years Ago Today in Modoc County: MILO CONKLIN has been charged with the murder of his brother-in-law, Louis Blodgett, in Cedarville Sunday."

The statement was true. Conklin had been tried for, and convicted of, Blodgett's murder. He served a prison sentence, completed parole, remarried, fathered two children, and rehabilitated himself. Conklin, at all material times, was a resident of Cedarville, California, a hamlet of 800 in the northeast corner of California. It strains credulity to believe that a town of 800 could forget that it had a convicted murderer in its midst, but the California Court of Appeal, Third District, evidently believed that

---

[22] 4 Cal.3d 529, 93 Cal.Rptr. 866, 483 P.2d 34, 43 (1971).

[23] Briscoe v. Reader's Digest Ass'n, (C.D.Cal. July 18, 1972) 1 Med.L.Rptr. 1852–1854. This decision, which was not reported in Federal Supplement, was a kind of "best kept secret;" the finding here—evidently unknown—other than in the media law reporting service, Media Law Reporter, was either unnoticed or ignored by courts in deciding Forsher v. Bugliosi, 26 Cal.3d 792, 163 Cal.Rptr. 628, 608 P.2d 716 (1980) and Conklin v. Sloss, (Cal.Ct. of Appeal 3d Dist.1978) 4 Med.L.Rptr. 1998.

Conklin's misdeed had been, if not forgotten, at least forgiven. In any case, that court accepted Conklin's argument that his friends and acquaintances for the first time learned of his unsavory past and abandoned him.[24]

The defendant newspaper replied that the statement was privileged under a California statute which says that a privileged publication is made by [25]

> * * * a fair and true report in a public journal, of (1) a judicial, (2) legislative, or (3) other public official proceeding, or (4) of anything said in the course thereof, or (5) of a verified charge or complaint made by any person to a public official, upon which complaint a warrant shall have issued.

Although this statutory language evidently conferred a privilege to protect the *Modoc County Record* from successful suit, the *Briscoe* case surfaced again to haunt the press.[26]

> To the extent that *Briscoe* may be said to have articulated California public policy * * * it would appear that questions concerning the scope of * * * the privilege should be resolved in favor of limiting it to publication of newsworthy items.
>
> * * *
>
> We therefore hold that the absolute privilege conferred by the Civil Code section 47, subdivision 4, applies only to publication of items that are "newsworthy" as defined in Briscoe v. Reader's Digest Association * * *.

As a result, the court held that Conklin's case should be taken to trial on the issue of whether or not publication of items of public record from 20 years before were "newsworthy," leaving the potential for a jury to tell a newspaper its business.

Some of the sting of *Briscoe* may have been lessened, however, by the California Supreme Court's 1980 decision in Forsher v. Bugliosi. Bugliosi, at one time a prosecuting attorney in the trial of Charles Manson and his "Family" for the "Tate-Labianca killings." Bugliosi was co-author of Helter-Skelter, a book purporting to be an inside view of the killings, the trial, and the Manson Family. James Forsher, who was mentioned in the book as having been on the periphery of the Manson Family's activities in a minor and non-criminal way, sued for invasion of privacy and libel. In his privacy claim, Forsher contended that there was no

[24] Conklin v. Sloss, (Cal.Ct. of App.3d Dist.1978) 4 Med.L.Rptr. 1998, 1999.

[25] West's Ann.Calif.Civil Code, § 47, subs. 4.

[26] 4 Med.L.Rptr. 1998, 2001 (Cal.Ct. of App.3rd Dist.1978). See also Restatement of Torts, § 857, comment c, quoted with approval by the court.

informational or social value in using his name in connection with retelling of past events.[27] Justice Manual's opinion in *Forsher* limited the impact of the *Briscoe* decision to cases involving rehabilitated criminals who were harmed by publication of their criminal records.[28]

> California courts have refrained from extending the Briscoe rule to other fact situations. * * * *Briscoe* * * * [held] that "where the plaintiff is a past criminal and his name is used in a publication, the mere lapse of time may provide a basis for an invasion of privacy suit."
>
>   *   *   *

Time Lapse

One of the problems referred to in Briscoe v. Reader's Digest involved the so-called time lapse problem.[29] How much time must pass before a person recovers from unwanted publicity, loses his or her newsworthiness, and again can be said to have regained anonymity? Take the case of William James Sidis, a person who did not seek publicity but who was found by it. In 1910, Sidis was an 11-year-old mathematical prodigy who lectured to famed mathematicians. He was graduated from Harvard at 16, and received a great deal of publicity. More than 20 years after his graduation, the New Yorker Magazine—in its August 14, 1937 issue—ran a feature story about Sidis plus a cartoon, with the captions "Where Are They Now?" and "April Fool." The article told how Sidis lived in a "hall bedroom of Boston's shabby south end," working at a routine clerical job, collecting streetcar transfers and studying the history of American Indians. Sidis sued for invasion of privacy, but a United States Court of Appeals ultimately held that he could not collect damages.

The court admitted that the New Yorker had perpetrated "a ruthless exposure of a once public character, who has since sought and has now been deprived of the seclusion of private life." Even so, the lawsuit did not succeed.[30]

> * * * [W]e are not yet disposed to afford to all of the intimate details of private life an absolute immunity from the prying of the press. Everyone will agree that at some point the individual interest in obtaining information becomes dominant over the individual's desire for

---

[27] Forsher v. Bugliosi, 26 Cal.3d 792, 163 Cal.Rptr. 628, 636–7, 608 P.2d 716, 724 (1980).

[28] Ibid., p. 726.

[29] See Chief Justice Raymond E. Peters opinion, 4 Cal.3d 529, 93 Cal.Rptr. 866, 483 P.2d 34, 41–42 (1971).

[30] Sidis v. F–R Pub. Corp., 113 F.2d 806 (2d Cir.1940).

privacy. * * * At least we would permit limited scrutiny of the "private" life of any person who has achieved, or
has had thrust upon him, the questionable and indefinable status of a "public figure." * * *

* * *

The article in the *New Yorker* sketched the life of an
unusual personality, and it possessed considerable popular news interest.

We express no comment on whether or not the newsworthiness of the matter printed will always constitute a
complete defense. Revelations may be so intimate and so
unwarranted in view of the victim's position as to outrage
the community's notions of decency. But when focused
upon public characters, truthful comments upon dress,
speech, habits, and the ordinary aspects of personality
will usually not transgress this line. Regrettably or not,
the misfortunes and frailties of neighbors and "public
figures" are subjects of considerable interest and discussion to the rest of the population. And when such are the
mores of the community, it would be unwise for a court to
bar their expression in the newspapers, books, and
magazines of the day.

The court implied that the invasion of privacy must be so
severe that it would cause more than minor annoyance to an
hypothetical "average" or "reasonable" man of "ordinary sensibilities." William James Sidis was an unusually sensitive man, and
it has been speculated that the *New Yorker* article was in large
measure responsible for his early death.[31]

The outcome of the Sidis case represents a general pattern.
American courts usually have ruled against "time lapse" privacy
lawsuits. Two post-1980 cases support that view: Underwood v.
First National Bank [32] and Roshto v. Hebert.[33] In the Underwood
case, Thomas G. Underwood sued the First National Bank of
Blooming Prairie, Minn. In 1980, the bank published a history of
its community. That history included a short summary of the
first degree murder trial—and conviction—of Underwood for
shooting a policeman to death. Underwood claimed that the
version in the book was defamatory (that he had killed the
policeman in a running gunfight, not—as said in the book—
shooting him when he was down on the ground). Additionally, he
argued that the "Hot News" that made him a public figure in 1952

[31] Prosser, "Privacy," California Law Review, Vol. 48 (1960) at p. 397.

[32] Underwood v. First National Bank (Minn.Dist.Ct., 3d Jud.Dist., Steele County,
1982), 8 Med.L.Rptr. 1278.

[33] Roshto v. Hebert, 439 So.2d 428 (La.1983), 9 Med.L.Rptr. 2417.

was now "Old News," and that appropriating Underwood's name for such an old story invaded his privacy.[34]   The Minnesota District Court, assuming for the sake of argument that the law of privacy has been adopted in Minnesota, nevertheless granted the bank's motion for summary judgment, halting Underwood's libel and privacy suit.[35]

In Roshto v. Hebert, the Heberts' newspaper—The Iberville South—found itself sued for invasion of privacy because of its regular "Page from our Past" feature.   In 1973, this weekly newspaper reproduced the entire front page from its April 4, 1952, edition, which included an article about the cattle theft trial of three brothers, Carlysle, Alfred, and E.R. Roshto.   Four years later, in 1977, the newspaper reproduced the front page of the November 14, 1952, edition, containing another article about the Roshto brothers—this time discussing their sentencing to prison after their sentences were affirmed on appeal.[36]

The Louisiana Supreme Court ruled in favor of the defendant newspapers, although giving some indications of reluctance: [37]

> The intermediate court was apparently concerned that newspapers are possibly being accorded a tremendous amount of freedom without being required to exercise a corresponding degree of responsibility, and arguably a balancing is required.   When the published information is accurate and true and a matter of public record, this fact weighs heavily in such a balancing process, but a newspaper cannot be allowed unrestricted freedom to publish any true statement of public record, regardless of the purpose or manner of publication or of the temporal and proximal relationship of the published fact to the present situation.   This case, however, does not reveal any abuse in the purpose or manner of publication.

> Defendants were arguably insensitive or careless in reproducing a former front page for publication without checking for information that might be currently offensive to some members of the community.   However, more than insensitivity or simple carelessness is required for the imposition of liability for damages when the publication is truthful, accurate and non-malicious.   Plaintiffs in the present case simply did not establish additional fac-

[34] 8 Med.L.Rptr. 1278, 1279, 1280.

[35] Ibid., 1281.   The judge noted that historically, the Minnesota Supreme Court has been reluctant to recognize the tort of invasion of privacy; it is the last holdout among the 50 states.

[36] Roshto v. Hebert, 439 So.2d 428 (La.1983), 9 Med.L.Rptr. 2417, 2418.

[37] 439 So.2d 428 (La.1983), 9 Med.L.Rptr. 2417, 2420.

tors and circumstances to warrant the imposition of damages.

Finally, consider the 1983 case of Doe v. Sarasota-Bradenton Television. "Jane Doe" was raped, and agreed to testify against her assailant at his upcoming trial. It was important to her that her name and photograph would not be displayed or photographed in connection with this trial.

In March, 1982, "Jane Doe" testified at the rape trial. A news team from the Sarasota-Bradenton Television Company was present in the courtroom. (As noted in Chapter 11, Section 67, below, under Florida law, news cameras are allowed in that state's courtrooms.) That night, the TV station ran a video tape of the trial featuring "Jane Doe's" testimony. As the video tape ran, a newscaster identified "Jane Doe" by name to the viewing audience.[38]

"Jane Doe" sued the TV station, seeking damages under a Florida statute [39] and for common-law invasion of privacy and for intentional infliction of emotional distress. The trial court found in favor of the television station, dismissing the woman's complaint.[40]

A Florida Court of Appeal agreed that the lawsuit must be dismissed, as under Cox Broadcasting v. Cohn,[41] a case discussed in Section 33 of this book.[42] As the Florida District Court of Appeal said:

> In Cox Broadcasting, the Supreme Court [of the U.S.] concluded that the State of Georgia could not punish a reporter and his employer for accurately publishing the name of a deceased rape victim where the information had been obtained from otherwise public judicial records. We agree with the trial court here that Cox Broadcasting controls. We conclude that the fact that the plaintiff in Cox Broadcasting was the deceased victim's father and the appellant here ["Jane Doe"] is the victim herself does not distinguish [differentiate between] the cases.

[38] Doe v. Sarasota-Bradenton Television, 436 So.2d 328 (Fla.App.2d Dist.1983), 9 Med.L.Rptr. 2074.

[39] Ibid., quoting Florida Statute section 794.03: "Unlawful to publish or broadcast information identifying sexual offense victims.—No person shall print, publish, or broadcast, or cause to be printed or broadcast, in any instrument of mass communication the name, address, or other identifying fact or information of the victim of any sexual offense within this chapter * * *."

[40] Ibid., at p. 2075.

[41] 420 U.S. 469, 95 S.Ct. 1029 (1975).

[42] Doe v. Sarasota-Bradenton Television Company, 436 So.2d 328 (Fla.App. 2d Dist.1983), 9 Med.L.Rptr. 2074.

The District Court of Appeal noted that in both the Cox Broadcasting and the "Jane Doe" cases, the broadcasts complained of contained completely accurate but pain-inflicting information. The Florida court said: [43]

> We deplore the lack of sensitivity to the rights of others that is sometimes displayed by such an unfettered exercise of first amendment rights. While we shall remain ever attentive to protect inviolate these first amendment rights, we do so with the admonition that those rights should not be arbitrarily exercised when unnecessary and detrimental to rights of others.
>
> * * *
>
> The publication added little or nothing to the sordid and unhappy story; yet, that brief little-or-nothing addition may well affect appellant's [Jane Doe's] well-being for years to come.

The court chastised the prosecution—representatives of the State of Florida—"for not having sought a protective order regarding cameras in the courtroom or other proper steps to support its alleged assurance" to Jane Doe that she could testify in the rape trial without her name and picture being used. Further, the court said that it recognized the frequent conflict between freedom of the press and the right of privacy. It then urged "compassionate discretion" by the media in such situations, saying:[44]

> Because we are no nearer to solving this dilemma * * * and because we are prohibited by Cox Broadcasting from balancing the competing interests at stake here, "reliance must rest on those who decide what to publish or broadcast." 420 U.S. at 496, 95 S.Ct. at ——, 43 L.Ed.2d at 350. Therefore, we believe that in the future it would behoove the media to engage in their own balancing test with an eye to avoiding harm such as may have occurred here.

Virgil v. Time, Inc. (1975)

Another case encouraging recovery in a privacy lawsuit *even when a truthful report is made by the news media* is Virgil v. Time, Inc. Sports Illustrated, a Time, Inc. publication, published an article on body surfing in February, 1971. The article devoted much attention to Mike Virgil, a surfer who was well known at "The Wedge," a dangerous beach near Newport Beach, California. Sports Illustrated staff writer Curry Kirkpatrick had interviewed Virgil at length—which obviously required a kind of consent from

43 Ibid., 2075–2076.
44 Ibid., 2076, 2077.

Virgil—and Virgil had also consented to the taking of pictures by a free-lance photographer working with Kirkpatrick.[45]

Before the article was published, another Sports Illustrated employee called Virgil's home and verified some of the information with his wife. At this point, Virgil "revoked all consent" for publication of the article and photographs and indicated that he did not want his name used in the story. Circuit Judge Merrill summarized Virgil's attempt to revoke his consent.[46]

> While not disputing the truth of the article or the accuracy of the statements about him which it contained, and while admitting that he had known that his picture was being taken, the plaintiff indicated that he thought the article was going to be limited to his prominence as a surfer at The Wedge, and that he did not know that it would contain references to some rather bizarre incidents in his life that were not directly related to surfing.

It can be objected that Judge Merrill was placing himself in the editor's chair: is it for a *judge* to say whether some of the "bizarre incidents" in Virgil's life are "not directly related to surfing?" If a person persists in body-surfing at a place known as one of earth's most dangerous beaches, might not some of his other actions—such as extinguishing a cigarette in his mouth, or diving down a flight of stairs because "there were all these chicks around"—unusually reckless (and therefore newsworthy?) approach to life? Or, consider this passage from Kirkpatrick's *Sports Illustrated* article, the accuracy of which is unchallenged: [47]

> "Every summer I'd work construction and dive off billboards to hurt myself or drop loads of lumber on myself to collect unemployment compensation so I could surf at The Wedge. Would I fake injuries? No, I wouldn't fake them. I'd be damn injured. But I would recover. I guess I used to live a pretty reckless life. I think I might have been drunk most of the time."

It was argued for the magazine—which had proceeded, on advice of counsel, to publish the article even after Virgil "revoked" his consent—that Virgil had voluntarily made public the facts he complained about. Judge Merrill disagreed, in words which frightened reporters and editors: [48]

> Talking freely to a member of the press, knowing the listener to be a member of the press, is not then in itself

[45] Virgil v. Time, Inc., 527 F.2d 1122, 1124 (9th Cir.1975).

[46] Ibid.

[47] Ibid., p. 1125n, quoting the Sports Illustrated article.

[48] Ibid., p. 1127.

making public. Such communication can be said to anticipate that what is said will be made public since making public is the function of the press, and accordingly such communication can be construed as a consent to publicize. Thus if publicity results it can be said to have been consented to. However, if consent is withdrawn prior to the act of publicization, the consequent publicity is without consent.

We conclude that the voluntary disclosure to Kirkpatrick did not in itself constitute a making public of the facts disclosed.

Judge Merrill paid particular attention to the Restatement, Second, Torts § 652D (Tentative Draft No. 21, 1975), saying that unless a subject is newsworthy, the publicizing of private facts is not protected by the First Amendment.[49] He then quoted a comment from the Restatement: [50]

> "In determining what is a matter of legitimate public interest, account must be taken of the customs and conventions of the community; and in the last analysis what is proper becomes a matter of the community mores. The line is to be drawn when the publicity ceases to be the giving of information to which the public is entitled, and becomes a morbid and sensational prying into public lives for its own sake, with which a reasonable member of the public, with decent standards, would say that he had no concern. * * *"

The prestigious Restatement of Torts, Second described the elements of a lawsuit for publication of embarrassing private facts in a way which has encouraged judges to "play editor." [51]

> One who gives publicity to a matter concerning the private life of another is subject to liability to the other for invasion of privacy, if the matter publicized is of a kind that
>
> > (a) would be highly offensive to a reasonable person and
> >
> > (b) is not of legitimate concern to the public.

In an action which startled constitutional lawyers, the Supreme Court refused to review the Court of Appeals decision in

[49] Ibid., p. 1128.

[50] Restatement quoted in Ibid., pp. 1129, 1129n.

[51] Restatement, Second, Torts, § 652D.

Virgil.[52] This meant that the *Virgil* case went back to the District [trial] Court, which decided—fortunately for Sports Illustrated— that the article about Virgil was "newsworthy." [53] But was this a victory for the magazine? Constitutional law specialists Alan U. Schwartz and Floyd Abrams say otherwise. Schwartz complained, "Under this formula truth becomes immaterial. The test is whether community mores (and *what* community? one may ask) have been offended. The peril to the journalist is extreme." [54] Abrams declared, "the test set forth by the Court in the Virgil case contains language so broad ('morbid and sensational prying'), so open-ended ('a reasonable member of the public') and so subjective ('decent standards') that it makes it all but impossible to determine in advance what may be published and what not." [55]

Campbell v. Seabury Press (1980)

Private facts—sometimes termed the "truthful tort" area— were also at issue in Campbell v. Seabury Press. Civil rights leader Will D. Campbell wrote his autobiography, Brother to a Dragonfly, which included an account of his now-deceased brother, Joe. Campbell wrote about his brother's addiction to drugs and the effects of that addiction on his personality, his family life, and on Will Campbell himself. Carlyne Campbell, Joe's first wife, sued for defamation and invasion of privacy, complaining about the book's portrayal of her marital relationship with Joe Campbell. Seabury Press was granted a summary judgment by the U.S. District Court on grounds that a public interest privilege under the first Amendment protected such disclosures.[56]

Carlyne Campbell appealed, arguing that her lawsuit should not be dismissed because there was no logical connection between the matters of legitimate public interest and her home life with Joe Campbell. The Court of Appeals for the Fifth Circuit upheld the dismissal of her case, and articulated a constitutional rationale favorable to the news media. In a per curiam opinion, Circuit Judges Charles Clark, Robert S. Vance, and Sam D. Johnson wrote: [57]

---

[52] Virgil v. Time, Inc., 527 F.2d 1122, 1130–1132 (9th Cir.1975), certiorari denied 425 U.S. 998, 96 S.Ct. 2215 (1976). Justices Brennan and Stewart said they would have granted certiorari.

[53] Floyd Abrams, "The Press, Privacy and the Constitution," New York Times Magazine, August 21, 1977, pp. 11ff, at p. 13; Virgil v. Sports Illustrated, 424 F.Supp. (S.D.Cal.1976).

[54] Schwartz, op.cit., p. 32.

[55] Abrams, op.cit., pp. 13, 65.

[56] Campbell v. Seabury Press, 614 F.2d 395 (5th Cir.1980), 5 Med.L.Rptr. 1829.

[57] 614 F.2d 395, 396 (5th Cir.1980), 5 Med.L.Rptr. 1829, 1803.

The first amendment mandates a constitutional privilege applicable to those torts of invasion of privacy that involve publicity. See Cox Broadcasting Corp. v. Cohn, 420 U.S. 469, 95 S.Ct. 1029 (1975) * * * This broad constitutional privilege recognizes two closely related yet analytically distinct privileges. First is the privilege to publish or broadcast facts, events, and information relating to public figures. Second is the privilege to publish or broadcast news or other matters of public interest. See Smith v. Doss, 251 Ala. 250, 253, 37 So.2d 118, 120 (1948). The inquiry in determining the applicability of the first privilege focuses on the person to whom the publicity relates and asks whether the individual either by assuming a role of special prominence in the affairs of society or by thrusting himself into the forefront of a particular public controversy in order to influence the resolution of the issues involved has become a public figure. In contrast, the inquiry in determining the applicability of the second privilege focuses on the information disclosed by publication and asks whether truthful information of legitimate concern to the public is publicized in a manner that is not merely limited to the dissemination of news either in the sense of current events or commentary upon public affairs. Rather, the privilege extends to information concerning interesting phases of human activity and embraces all issues about which information is needed or appropriate so that individuals may cope with the exigencies of their period.

As privacy and media law expert Harvey Zuckman has noted, because of the Fifth Circuit's "liberal outlook on the newsworthiness or public interest privilege, counsel for your newspapers may wish to consider attempting removal of private fact and even 'false light' cases from state courts where they are usually filed to the local United States District Court. If that court is located in Florida, Georgia, Alabama, Mississippi, Louisiana or Texas, it will be governed by the law of the *Campbell* case." [58]

[58] It should be noted that this third area of privacy overlaps a fourth area discussed later in this chapter, "appropriation of some element of plaintiff's personality for commercial use." This overlapping is especially apparent in cases involving spurious testimonials in advertisements. See, e.g., Flake v. Greensboro News Co., 212 N.C. 780, 195 S.E. 55 (1938) where a woman's picture was placed, by mistake, in an advertisement; Fairfield v. American Photocopy Equipment Co., 138 Cal.App.2d 82, 291 P.2d 194 (1955), where a plaintiff was labeled one of a number of law firms which used a certain brand of photocopying machine.

SEC. 34. FALSE PUBLICATIONS WHICH INVADE PRIVACY

Putting a person in a false position before the public has proven costly for many publications.

A third sub-area of privacy law, "putting plaintiff in a false position in the public eye," is one which holds great dangers of lawsuits for the mass media.[59] The first invasion of privacy case dealing with the mass media to be decided by the Supreme Court of the United States involved a "false position in the public eye." [60]

This branch of privacy law has roots which go back to an outraged English poet, Lord Byron, who successfully sued to prevent the publication of inferior poems under Lord Byron's name.[61] In more recent years, the press—or people who use the press— have misrepresented the views of other people at their peril. For example, the New York *Herald* published a fake story on "stopping a congo cannibal feast"—ostensibly written in a self-praising autobiographical style—which made fun of Antonio B. D'Altomonte, a well-known explorer. D'Altomonte collected damages as a result of this playfulness by the newspaper.[62] And in 1960, Rabbi Julius Goldberg received a judgment against a "romance" magazine. This publication had attributed to Rabbi Goldberg views on sex which he did not hold.[63]

The old saying that "photographs don't lie" is perhaps true most of the time, but photos—and especially their captions—must be carefully watched by editors. Pictures which would give, or are used in such a way that they give, a misleading impression of a person's character are especially dangerous. The *Saturday Evening Post* was stung by a privacy lawsuit in Peay v. Curtis Publishing Co. The magazine published an article about Washington, D.C., taxicab drivers titled "Never Give a Passenger an Even Break." The court noted that this article painted the city's drivers as "ill mannered, brazen, and contemptuous of their patrons * * * dishonest and cheating when opportunity arises." [64] The *Saturday Evening Post's* article was worth money to cab-

---

[59] Harvey Zuckman, "The Right of Privacy and the Press," presentation at Southern Newspaper Publishers Association law symposium, The University of Texas at Austin, October 13, 1980.

[60] Time, Inc. v. Hill, 385 U.S. 374, 87 S.Ct. 534 (1967).

[61] Lord Byron v. Johnston, 2 Mer. 29, 35 Eng.Rep. 851 (Chancery 1816).

[62] D'Altomonte v. New York Herald, 154 App.Div. 453, 139 N.Y.S. 200 (1913).

[63] Goldberg v. Ideal Pub. Corp., 210 N.Y.S.2d 928 (Sup.1960).

[64] Peay v. Curtis Pub. Co., 78 F.Supp. 305 (D.C.D.C.1948); Fowler v. Curtis Pub. Co., 78 F.Supp. 303, 304 (D.C.D.C.1948).

driver Muriel Peay, whose picture had been used, without her permission, to illustrate the article.

The Curtis Publishing Company lost another invasion of privacy lawsuit only three years later, and the cause was again careless use of a picture. Back in 1947, ten-year-old Eleanor Sue Leverton was knocked down by a careless motorist. A news photographer snapped a picture of a woman helping the little girl to her feet. This photo was published in a Birmingham, Ala., newspaper. To this point, there was no action for invasion of privacy possible for young Miss Leverton.

But 20 months after the little girl was hit by the car, the *Saturday Evening Post* used her picture to illustrate an article headlined "They Ask to Be Killed." The little girl's picture was captioned, "Safety education in schools has reduced child accidents measurably, but unpredictable darting through traffic still takes its sobering toll." In a box next to the headline, these words appeared: "Do you invite massacre by your own carelessness? Here's how to keep them alive." A Federal Court of Appeals said.[65]

> The sum total of all this is that this particular plaintiff, the legitimate subject for publicity for one particular accident, now becomes a pictorial, frightful example of pedestrian carelessness. This, we think, exceeds the bounds of privilege.

The lesson for photo-editors should be plain: if a picture is not taken in a public place or if that picture—or its caption—places someone in a false light, don't use it. The exception, of course, would be when you have received permission, in the form of a signed release, from the persons pictured. Two invasion of privacy lawsuits by Mr. and Mrs. John W. Gill, one successful and one not, illustrate the point rather neatly.

Mr. and Mrs. Gill were seated on stools at a confectionery stand which they operated at the Farmer's Market in Los Angeles. Famed photographer Henri Cartier-Bresson took a picture of the Gills, as Mr. Gill sat with his arm around his wife. The photograph was used in *Harper's Bazaar* to illustrate an article titled "And So the World Goes Around," a brief commentary having to do with the poetic notion that love makes the world go 'round. Although the Gills sued, they failed to collect from the Hearst Corporation, publisher of the magazine. The court held that the Gills had no right to collect since they took that voluntary pose in public and because there was nothing uncomplimentary about the photograph itself.[66]

[65] Leverton v. Curtis Pub. Co., 192 F.2d 974 (3d Cir.1951).
[66] Gill v. Hearst Pub. Co., 40 Cal.2d 224, 253 P.2d 441 (1952).

Although they couldn't collect from the Hearst Corporation for invasion of privacy, Mr. and Mrs. Gill had already won damages from the Curtis Publishing Company. The *Ladies Home Journal,* a Curtis publication, had printed the very same photograph taken at the Farmer's Market but had made that photo an invasion of privacy by using faulty captions. The *Journal* used the Gills' picture to illustrate an article titled "Love." Underneath the picture was this caption "Publicized as glamourous, desirable, 'love at first sight' is a bad risk." The story termed such love "100% sex attraction" and the "wrong" kind. The court held that the article implied that this husband and wife were "persons whose only interest in each other is sex, a characterization that may be said to impinge seriously upon their sensibilities." [67]

Context Providing a "False Light"

A 1984 Texas case suggests that the context in which something is published can cause lawsuits for defamation or for invasion of privacy. Jeannie Braun, trainer of "Ralph the Diving Pig" at Aquarena Springs Resort, San Marcos, Texas, took violent exception to having her picture displayed in Chic, a Larry Flynt-published magazine specializing in female nudity and photos and cartoons of an overtly sexual nature.

Part of Mrs. Braun's job at Aquarena Springs was to tread water while holding out a baby bottle of milk. Ralph the pig would then dive into the pool and feed from the bottle. Pictures and postcards were made of Ralph diving toward Mrs. Braun. Mrs. Braun had signed a release saying the picture could be used for advertising and publicity as long as the photo was used in good taste, without embarrassment to her and her family.

Once the picture appeared in Chic—surrounded by pictures and cartoons full of sexual content (captions on other items included "Lust Rock Rules" and "Chinese Organ Grinder")—Mrs. Braun sued for a total of $1.1 million for defamation and invasion of privacy. After ruling that Mrs. Braun was a private individual, the Court of Appeals for the Fifth Circuit took issue with the trial court's damage awards totaling $95,000. That figure represented defamation damages ($5,000 actual and $25,000 punitive) and false light privacy damages ($15,000 actual and $25,000 punitive). The appeals court said that as a matter of public policy, punitive damages should not be awarded in one case for both defamation and false-light privacy invasion. Therefore, the appeals court said

---

[67] Gill v. Curtis Pub. Co., 38 Cal.2d 273, 239 P.2d 636 (1952).

that only the damages assessed for invasion of privacy—$65,000—should be awarded.[68]

Duncan v. WJLA–TV

The "false light" area of law is so close to libel that—with evidently increasing frequency—people sue for both invasion of privacy and defamation. Take the case of Duncan v. WJLA–TV (1984), which illustrated, once again, that incautious picture captioning (or the television equivalent, "voice-overs") has its perils. A young woman named Linda K. Duncan was standing on a street corner in Washington, D.C. Meanwhile, WJLA–TV was shooting a "journalist-in-the-street" format story featuring reporter Betsy Ashton.

WJLA–TV broadcast two versions of a news story based on this videotaping of Ms. Ashton. For the 6 p.m. newscast, the camera was aimed down K street and focused on pedestrians on the corner behind reporter Ashton. The camera zeroed in on Linda Duncan, as she faced toward the camera and could be seen clearly. Then, the camera shifted back to reporter Ashton, who talked about her story, a new treatment for genital herpes.[69]

For the 11 p.m. newscast, a substantial amount of editing was done. Instead of the street scene including reporter Betsy Ashton in the foreground, reliance was placed on a "voice-over" as spoken by news anchor David Schoumacher. For the 11 p.m. version, Ms. Duncan was seen turning into the camera, and then pausing. As she did so, Schoumacher intoned: "For the twenty million Americans who have herpes, it's not a cure." The 11 p.m. version of the story concluded with Ms. Duncan turning away and walking off down the street.[70]

A United States District Court ruled that the 6 p.m. broadcast was neither defamatory nor a false light invasion of privacy—as far as the 6 p.m. broadcast was concerned. The earlier broadcast was said to provide sufficient context for viewers not to associate the subject matter of the news story with Ms. Duncan. The court said, however, that the 11 p.m. newscast presented different questions and should be submitted to a jury for consideration.[71] Ms. Duncan won a small damage award from WJLA–TV.

[68] Braun v. Flynt, 726 F.2d 245 (5th Cir.1984), 10 Med.L.Rptr. 1497, 1498, 1499, 1507–1508.

[69] Duncan v. WJLA–TV, 106 F.R.D. 4 (D.D.C.1984), 10 Med.L.Rptr. 1395, 1398.

[70] Ibid.

[71] Ibid.

New York's Privacy Statute and "False Light"

Construction worker Carl DeGregorio and a woman co-worker walked along New York City's Madison Avenue holding hands one fine spring day. A CBS–TV camera crew filming a story about romance in the Big Apple watched with interest; it's not every day you see two hard-hats holding hands.

DeGregorio and friend were then approached by a woman from the CBS crew telling about the photographic survey they had unwittingly joined, and wondering whether Mr. DeGregorio wanted to make any comments for the show. DeGregorio angrily declined, telling the CBS production manager that he was married and that his co-worker was engaged to be married. Nevertheless, the filmed segment showing DeGregorio and the female co-worker was aired on May 10–11, 1982 CBS–TV news broadcast, "Couples in Love in New York." [72]

DeGregorio sued CBS, claiming invasion of privacy, intentional infliction of mental distress, and defamation. The New York Supreme Court said that this documentary, exploring prevailing attitudes and showing people behaving in a "romantic" fashion, was indeed newsworthy. Also, DeGregorio was shown for only five seconds; this "incidental, minor use" was held not to violate the New York statute defining invasion of privacy.[73]

Photos of an actress—one showing her "topless" and the other depicting her in an orgy scene—were published in *Adelina* magazine. These black-and-white pictures were printed from movie film taken from that deathless epic, "The World is Full of Married Men." This anonymous actress was misidentified as Jackie Collins Lerman. (Ms. Lerman and her husband, Ocar Lerman, were the writer and director of "The World is Full of Married Men." Ms. Lerman did not appear in the film, nude or clad.)

Ms. Lerman, who had been alerted about the forthcoming pictures in *Adelina* by a former agent, sued for an injunction to halt distribution of the film and also asked damages for invasion of privacy. Meanwhile, Flynt Distributing Company—publishers of *Hustler*—bought rights to distribute *Adelina*. Ms. Lerman sued Flynt too, and again asked for similar legal relief.

Suing under New York's Civil Rights Law, Sections 50–51— which defines invasion of privacy in that state—Ms. Lerman found

---

[72] DeGregorio v. CBS, 123 Misc.2d 491, 473 N.Y.S.2d 922 (N.Y.Sup.Ct.1984), 10 Med.L.Rptr. 1799, 1800.

[73] 10 Med.L.Rptr. at 1801, 1803. Invasion of privacy is defined under Sections 50 and 51 of the New York Civil Rights Law; there is no common law right of privacy in New York.

a sympathetic jury which awarded $7 million in compensatory and $33 million in punitive damages against Flynt Distributing.[74]

On appeal, however, the U.S. Court of Appeals for the Second Circuit overturned the damage award to Ms. Lerman. Interpreting New York Civil Rights Law Section 51, the appeals court noted that the statute was narrowly drawn, dealing only with publications which made use of a person's name or likeness "for purposes of trade," generally translated into "advertising purposes."

Furthermore, since Ms. Lerman wrote the book from which the movie script for "The World is Full of Married Men" resulted, that "is a matter in which the public plainly has a legitimate public interest." The court added, "Further, plaintiff's status as an author and screenwriter of a film in the erotic genre makes her claim of 'no connection' with these particular photographs unpersuasive." [75]

It is emphasized that Sections 50 and 51 of the New York Civil Rights Act are narrowly written, based on commercial use of someone's name or picture—as befits a statute passed in reaction to the historic 1902 privacy case discussed earlier, in Section 31, Roberson v. Rochester Folding Box Co.[76] In other states, with a more sweeping common-law approach to privacy—or with less restrictive statutes—Ms. Lerman might well have won a false light or private facts judgment.

Fictionalization

The misuse of pictures or photographs is one way to get involved in a privacy lawsuit. So is *fictionalization*. Fictionalization, as used by the courts, involves more than mere incidental falsity. Fictionalization appears to mean the deliberate or reckless addition of untrue material, perhaps for entertainment purposes or to make a good story better. Although the courts' rules for determining fictionalization are by no means clear, journalists should be warned to look to their ethics and accuracy. Jazzing up or "sensationalizing" a story by adding untrue materials so that a false impression is created concerning the subject of the story may be actionable.

Triangle Publications, which produced magazines such as *Timely Detective Cases* and *Uncensored Detective*, lost a privacy suit because of fictionalization. Robert H. Garner and Grace M. Smith had become legitimate objects of news interest because they were on trial for the murder of her husband. Mr. Garner and

---

[74] Lerman v. Flynt Distributing, 745 F.2d 123 (2d Cir.1984), 10 Med.L.Rptr. 2497, 2498.

[75] Ibid., p. 2502.

[76] Roberson v. Rochester Folding Box Co., see supra at p. 206.

Mrs. Smith were convicted of the murder. Meanwhile, magazines published by Triangle carried numerous articles about the crime, adding some untrue elements to their stories. The magazines claimed that Mr. Garner and Mrs. Smith had had "improper relations with each other." However, after the detective magazines had published their stories, the convictions of Mr. Garner and Mrs. Smith were reversed.

A Federal District Court held that there could be no liability for presenting news about a matter of public interest such as a murder trial. However, Triangle Publications could be liable for a privacy lawsuit because when the magazines [77]

> enlarged upon the facts so as to go beyond the bounds of propriety and decency, they should not be cloaked with and shielded by the public interest in dissemination of "information." * * * It is no answer to say, as defendants do, that such interests, if they exist, can be adequately compensated for under the libel laws. If the articles violate rights of privacy, plaintiffs may bring their action under the privacy laws also.

It appears, however, that minor errors in fact will not be sufficient to defeat the defense of newsworthiness, which will be discussed later. In the first media-related privacy case to reach the Supreme Court of the United States, it was held that Constitutional protections for speech and press forbid recovery for false reports "in the absence of proof that the defendant published the report with knowledge of its falsity or in reckless disregard of the truth." [78]

A more recent lawsuit for fictionalization involved the famed Warren Spahn, the left-handed pitcher who won more than 300 games during a long career with the Boston—and later the Milwaukee—Braves. Spahn was a hero to many baseball card collectors in the 1950s and early 1960s, and some people wanted to cash in on "Spahnie's" success. Writer Milton J. Shapiro and publisher Julian Messner, Inc., brought out a book titled *The Warren Spahn Story.* This book was aimed at a juvenile audience, and was assembled from the author's vivid imagination and a collection of secondary sources—newspaper and magazine articles, for example—about Spahn. Throughout this book, Spahn's feats were exaggerated. For one thing, Spahn was portrayed as a war hero, which he was not. An elbow injury finally brought an end to

---

[77] Garner v. Triangle Publications, Inc., 97 F.Supp. 546, 550 (D.C.N.Y.1951). For similar holdings, see Hazlitt v. Fawcett Publications, Inc., 116 F.Supp. 538 (D.C. Conn.1953); Reed v. Real Detective Pub. Co., 63 Ariz. 294, 162 P.2d 133 (1945).

[78] Time, Inc. v. Hill, 385 U.S. 374, 388, 87 S.Ct. 534, 542 (1967). See also Binns v. Vitagraph Corp. of America, 210 N.Y. 51, 103 N.E. 1108 (1913); Stryker v. Republic Pictures Corp., 108 Cal.App.2d 191, 238 P.2d 670 (1951).

Spahn's career; author Shapiro consistently wrote about Spahn's "shoulder injury." Such inaccuracies were topped off by page after page of fictional dialogue—words attributed to Spahn and his associates but which had been invented by author Shapiro.[79]

Shapiro and Julian Messner, Inc., argued strenuously that Spahn was a public figure who enjoyed no right to privacy.[80] Spahn v. Julian Messner worked its way through the courts of New York from 1964 to 1967. Justice Charles Breitel of the Appellate Division, New York Supreme Court disagreed with contentions that Spahn no longer possessed a right of privacy. Justice Breitel said: [81]

> It is true * * * that a public figure is subject to being exposed in a factual biography, even one which contains inadvertent or superficial inaccuracies. But surely, he should not be exposed, without his control, to biographies not limited substantially to the truth. The fact that the fictionalization is laudatory is immaterial.

If, indeed, writers cannot down the impulse to fictionalize, they would be more likely to avoid a lawsuit if they do not use the names of actual people involved in an event upon which he bases his fictionalization. Where there is no identification, courts will not be able to find for the plaintiffs.[82] But where there is both identification and fictionalization, the publisher is in danger of losing a suit.[83]

Cantrell v. Forest City Publishing Co. (1974)

Major fact errors—or large swatches of fictionalizing—in something purporting to be a news story—can mean serious difficulty for the news media. Consider the case known as Cantrell v. Forest City Publishing Company. Mrs. Margaret Mae Cantrell and her son sued the company for an article which appeared in the Cleveland Plain Dealer in August of 1968, claiming that the article placed her and her family in a false light.

[79] Spahn v. Julian Messner, Inc., 43 Misc.2d 219, 230–232, 250 N.Y.S.2d 529, 540–542 (1964).

[80] See Time, Inc. v. Hill, 385 U.S. 374, 87 S.Ct. 534 (1967).

[81] 23 A.D.2d 216, 221, 260 N.Y.S.2d 451, 456 (1965).

[82] Bernstein v. NBC, 129 F.Supp. 817 (D.C.D.C.) affirmed 98 U.S.App.D.C. 112, 232 F.2d 369 (1955); Smith v. NBC, 138 Cal.App.2d 807, 292 P.2d 600 (1956).

[83] Mau v. Rio Grande Oil Co., 28 F.Supp. 845 (D.C.Cal.1939); Garner v. Triangle Publications, Inc., 97 F.Supp. 546 (D.C.N.Y.1951). But see Leopold v. Levin, 45 Ill. 2d 434, 259 N.E.2d 250 (1970), where a fictional treatment of Nathan Leopold's participation in the famed 1924 murder of Bobby Franks was declared to be protected by the First Amendment despite the addition of fictional embellishments. See Mayer, op. cit., p. 151.

The facts underlying the lawsuit were these: In December, 1967, Mrs. Cantrell's husband was killed—along with 43 other persons—when the Silver Bridge across the Ohio River at Point Pleasant, W.Va., collapsed. Cleveland *Plain Dealer* reporter Joseph Eszterhas had covered the disaster and he wrote a news feature on Mr. Cantrell's funeral. Five months later, Eszterhas and photographer Richard Conway returned to Point Pleasant and went to the Cantrell residence. Mrs. Cantrell was not there, so Eszterhas talked to the Cantrell children and photographer Conway took 50 pictures. Eszterhas' story appeared as the lead article in the August 4, 1968, edition of the *Plain Dealer's* Sunday magazine.

The article emphasized the children's old, ill-fitting clothes and the poor condition of the Cantrell home. The Cantrell family was used in the story to sum up the impact of the bridge collapse on the lives of people in the Point Pleasant area. Even though Mrs. Cantrell had not been present during Eszterhas' visit to her home, he wrote: [84]

> "Margaret Cantrell will talk neither about what happened nor about how they are doing. She wears the same mask of non-expression she wore at the funeral. She is a proud woman. She says that after it happened, the people in town offered to help them out with money and they refused to take it."

In a ruling that Mrs. Cantrell should be allowed to collect the $60,000 awarded by a U.S. District Court jury, the Supreme Court said: [85]

> * * * the District Judge was clearly correct in believing that the evidence introduced at trial was sufficient to support a jury finding that the respondents Joseph Eszterhas and Forest City Publishing Company had published knowing or reckless falsehoods about the Cantrells. There was no dispute during the trial that Eszterhas, who did not testify, must have known that a number of the statements in the feature story were untrue. In particular, his article plainly implied that Mrs. Cantrell had been present during his visit to her home and that Eszterhas had observed her "wear[ing] the same mask of non-expression she wore [at her husband's] funeral." These were "calculated falsehoods," and the jury was plainly justified in finding that Eszterhas had por-

---

[84] 419 U.S. 245, at 248, 95 S.Ct. 465 at 468 (1974), quoting Eszterhas, "Legacy of the Silver Bridge," The Plain Dealer Sunday Magazine, Aug. 4, 1968, p. 32, col. 1.

[85] 419 U.S. 245, 253, 95 S.Ct. 465, 470–471 (1974).

trayed the Cantrells in a false light through knowing or reckless untruth.

Bindrim v. Mitchell

The flip side of a journalist lapsing into fiction is a person who purports to write a novel with a story line which parallels too closely to actual persons and events. In point here is the case of Bindrim v. Mitchell. Although it was a libel action, the plaintiff—Paul Bindrim, Ph.D., a licensed clinical psychologist—could just as well have sued for invasion of privacy under the false light theory. Dr. Bindrim used the so-called "Nude Marathon" in group therapy in order to help people shed their psychological inhibitions along with the removal of their clothes. And then a novelist showed up and wanted to join his nude encounter group.[86]

Gwen Davis Mitchell had written a best-selling novel in 1969, and then set about writing a novel about women of the leisure class. When she asked to register in Dr. Bindrim's therapy group, he told her she could not come into the group if she planned to write about it in a novel. Bare-facedly, she said she would attend the sessions for therapeutic reasons and had no intention of writing about the group. Dr. Bindrim then brought to her attention a written contract, which included this language: [87]

> "The participant agrees that he will not take photographs, write articles, or in any manner disclose who has attended the workshop or what has transpired. If he fails to do so he releases all parties from this contract, but remains legally liable for damages sustained by the leaders and participants."

Ms. Mitchell reassured Dr. Bindrim that she would not write about the session, paid her money, signed the contract, and attended the nude marathon. Two months later, she entered into a contract with Doubleday publishers and was to receive $150,000 in advance royalties for her novel, which was subsequently published under the name "Touching." It depicted a nude encounter session in Southern California led by "Dr. Simon Herford." The fictional Dr. Herford was described in the novel a *psychiatrist,* as " 'a fat Santa Claus type with long white hair, white sideburns, a cherubic rosy face and rosy forearms.' "

Dr. Bindrim, on the other hand, a psychologist, was clean shaven and had short hair. He alleged that he had been libeled, because dialogue in the novel set in encounter groups included some sexually explicit language which tapes of actual sessions run

---

[86] Bindrim v. Mitchell, 92 Cal.App.3d 61, 69, 155 Cal.Rptr. 29, 33 (1979), 5 Med.L. Rptr. 1113, certiorari denied 444 U.S. 984, 100 S.Ct. 490 (1979).

[87] 92 Cal.App.3d 61, 69, 155 Cal.Rptr. 29, 33 (1979).

by Dr. Bindrim did not contain. As a therapist, the psychologist did not use such insulting and vulgar language.[88]

Despite these differences—and perhaps in part because author Mitchell had actually attended Dr. Bindrim's therapy group—it was held that there were sufficient similarities between the fictional Dr. Herford and the real Dr. Bindrim for identification to have taken place. Also, the situation was not improved for the author because she had signed the contract not to write about the sessions. Doubleday and Ms. Mitchell were ordered to pay damages totaling $75,000. This case thus hangs out a warning against slipshod disguising of fictional characters who are based on real, live persons.[89]

In dissent, Judge Files of the California Court of Appeals declared that this decision was a threat to freedom of expression:

> From an analytical standpoint, the chief vice of the majority opinion is that it brands a novel as libelous because it is "false," i.e. fiction; and infers "actual malice" from the fact that the author and publisher knew it was not a true representation of plaintiff. From a constitutional standpoint the vice is the chilling effect upon the publisher of any novel critical of any occupational practice, inviting litigation on the theory "when you criticize my occupation, you libel me."

SEC. 35. APPROPRIATION OF PLAINTIFF'S NAME OR LIKENESS

The appropriation or "taking" of some element of a person's personality for commercial or other advantage has been a source of many privacy lawsuits.

Often, careless use of a person's name or likeness will be the misstep which results in a privacy action. The first widely known privacy cases, Roberson v. Rochester Folding Box Co.[90] and Pavesich v. New England Life Ins. Co.,[91] both discussed earlier in this chapter, turned on taking a person's name or picture for advertising purposes.

The use of a name, by itself, is not enough to bring about a successful lawsuit. For example, a company could publish an advertisement for its breakfast cereal and say that the cereal "gave Fred Brown his tennis-playing energy." There are, of

---

[88] 92 Cal.App.3d 61, 70, 75, 155 Cal.Rptr. 29, 34, 37 (1979).

[89] 92 Cal.App.3d 61, 82–83, 155 Cal.Rptr. 29, 41 (1979).

[90] 171 N.Y. 538, 64 N.E. 442 (1902).

[91] 122 Ga. 190, 50 S.E. 68 (1905).

course, many Fred Browns in the nation. However, should the cereal company, without explicit permission, identify a *particular* individual—such as "Olympic High Hurdle Champion Fred Brown"—then Mr. Brown, the hurdler, would have an action for invasion of privacy. Thus a *name* can be used, as long as a person's *identity* is not somehow appropriated.

A good example of this point is a suit which was brought by a Joseph Angelo Maggio, who claimed that the use of a name— "Angelo Maggio"—in James Jones' best-selling novel, *From Here to Eternity,* invaded his privacy. The court ruled, however, that although the name was the same as that of the plaintiff, the plaintiff's *identity* had not been taken. The fictional "Angelo Maggio" was held not to be the same individual as Joseph Angelo Maggio.[92]

Where the media are concerned, however, the great bulk of the trouble has come in cases involving advertising. There have been successful lawsuits, time and time again, when a person's identity or picture is used in an ad.[93] Even the fact that a person's name or likeness appears in an advertisement through an innocent mistake will not provide a defense. For example, the Greensboro, N.C., *News* advertised the appearance of Mademoiselle Sally Payne at the Folies de Paree Theatre through a joint advertising agreement with a bakery. The published advertisement was intended to show a picture of Miss Payne in a bathing suit, but instead was printed with a picture of Miss Nancy Flake in a bathing suit. The court held that Miss Flake had a property right in her name and likeness. However, punitive damages were not allowed because the advertisement was a mistake made without malice and because the newspaper printed an apology.[94]

Persons who use the media should develop a kind of self-protective pessimism: it should always be assumed that if something could go wrong and result in a lawsuit, it might indeed go wrong. This is, of course, an almost paranoid approach, but it can help to avoid much grief. Take, for example, the case of Kerby v. Hal Roach Studios, Inc., where a simple failure to check as obvious a reference as a telephone directory led to a lost lawsuit. A publicity gimmick boosting one of the *Topper* movies involved the

---

[92] People on Complaint of Maggio v. Charles Scribner's Sons, 205 Misc. 818, 130 N.Y.S.2d 514 (1954). See also, Uproar Co. v. National Broadcasting Co., 8 F.Supp. 358 (D.C.Mass.1934), affirmed 81 F.2d 373 (1st Cir.1936); Nebb v. Bell Syndicate, 41 F.Supp. 929 (D.C.N.Y.1941).

[93] See, e.g., Flores v. Mosler Safe Co., 7 N.Y.2d 276, 196 N.Y.S. 975, 164 N.E.2d 853 (1959); Colgate Palmolive Co. v. Tullos, 219 F.2d 617 (5th Cir.1955).

[94] Flake v. Greensboro News Co., 212 N.C. 780, 195 S.E. 55 (1938).

studio's sending out 100 perfumed letters to men in the Los Angeles area. These letters gushed: [95]

Dearest:

Don't breathe it to a soul, but I'm back in Los Angeles and more curious than ever to see you. Remember how I cut up about a year ago? Well, I'm raring to go again, and believe me I'm in the mood for fun.

Let's renew our acquaintanceship and I promise you an evening you won't forget. Meet me in front of Warner's Downtown Theatre at 7th and Hill on Thursday. Just look for a girl with a gleam in her eye, a smile on her lips, and mischief on her mind!

Fondly,

Your ectoplasmic playmate,

Marion Kerby.

Marion Kerby was the name of one of the characters—a lady ghost—portrayed in the movie. Unfortunately for the Hal Roach Studios, there was a real-life Marion Kerby in Los Angeles, an actress and public speaker. She was the only one listed in the Los Angeles telephone directory. Miss Kerby, after being annoyed by numerous phone calls and a personal visit, sued for invasion of privacy, and ultimately collected.[96]

Sometimes the out-and-out use of a person's name or likeness *is* permissible in an advertisement—*if* a court decides that the use of the name or likeness is "incidental." Take Academy Award and Emmy Award-winning actress Shirley Booth, who was vacationing in Jamaica some years ago. A *Holiday* magazine photographer asked, and received, permission to take her picture, and that picture was later used in a *Holiday* feature story about Jamaica's Round Hill resort. Several months later, however, the same picture appeared in full-page promotional advertisements for *Holiday* in *Advertising Age* and *New Yorker* magazines. Beneath the picture of the actress were the words "Shirley Booth and Chapeau, from a recent issue of *Holiday*." [97]

Miss Booth sued *Holiday's* publisher, the Curtis Publishing Co., in New York, claiming invasion of privacy on the ground that *Holiday's* advertising use of that picture was impermissible. New York's privacy statute, after all, prohibits use of a person's name or likeness "for purposes of trade" unless the person involved has

[95] Kerby v. Hal Roach Studios, Inc., 53 Cal.App.2d 207, 127 P.2d 577, 578 (1942).

[96] Ibid., at 578. It should be noted that this case is also a good example of the privacy tort category called "false position in the public eye."

[97] Booth v. Curtis Pub. Co., 15 A.D.2d 343, 223 N.Y.S.2d 737 (1962).

given consent.[98] Curtis Publishing responded that this sort of promotional advertising was needed to help magazine sales, thus supporting the public's interest in news.[99]

Miss Booth won $17,500 at the trial level, but that finding was reversed on appeal. Finding for the Curtis Publishing Co., Justice Charles D. Breitel termed *Holiday's* advertising use of the picture "incidental," and therefore not prohibited by New York's privacy statute.[1]

As Victor A. Kovner has pointed out, there has been a growing number of misappropriation claims founded on unauthorized use of a person's photograph or likeness, in articles and on covers of magazines and books. "[T]he general rule," Kovner said, "is that a picture reasonably related to an article or book on a matter of public interest will not be actionable." [2]

A case in point is Arrington v. New York Times, where the newspaper—without permission—ran a photograph of a young black man on the cover of its Sunday magazine section. The man's likeness was recognizable, but his name was not used. The newspaper argued that it had taken his picture to illustrate an article titled "The Black Middle Class: Making It," using his picture to illustrate upward mobility of blacks.

Use of Arrington's photo in those circumstances was held not to violate New York's Civil Rights Act, §§ 50–51, dealing with appropriation of a person's name or likeness for commercial purposes.[3]

On the other hand, unauthorized use of a black student's photograph on the cover of a book aimed at students hoping to go to college was ruled to be a violation of the New York Civil Rights Statute. Valerie Spellman was initially awarded $120,000 in compensatory damages and $250,000 in punitive damages, but an appellate court threw out all but $1,500 in compensatory damages. Note that she had given verbal consent to having her picture taken, but never gave the written consent required by the statute.[4]

The Arrington and Spellman cases are "mild" fact situations. Sexy photos or pictures which are published without permission

[98] Sections 50–51, New York Civil Rights Law, McKinney's Consolidated Laws, Ch. 6. See 15 A.D.2d 343, 223 N.Y.S.2d 737, at 739 (1962).

[99] Booth v. Curtis Pub. Co., 15 App.Div.2d 343, 349, 223 N.Y.S.2d 737, 743–744 (1962).

[1] 11 N.Y.S.2d 907 (1962). See also, University of Notre Dame Du Lac v. Twentieth Century Fox, 22 A.D.2d 452, 256 N.Y.S.2d 301 (1965).

[2] Victor A. Kovner, "Privacy," in James C. Goodale, chairman, Communications Law 1980 (New York: Practising Law Institute, 1980) p. 282.

[3] (New York Supreme Court 1980), 5 Med.L.Rptr. 2581, 2584.

[4] (New York County Civil Court 1978), 3 Med.L.Rptr. 2407, 2408.

are apt to lead to being sued and, perhaps, to being sued successfully. In Hansen v. High Society, model Patti Hansen sought a preliminary injunction to halt publication of nude photos which had been taken of her on a beach. In the initial court, the injunction was granted: "If plaintiff's right of privacy has not been violated, certainly her right of publicity (i.e. the property right to exploit commercially her name, photographs and image) has."[5] However, the Appellate Division of New York Supreme Court, as Victor A. Kovner has reported, "found the injunction unwarranted for lack of irreparable harm and in view of the numerous substantial disputes as to matters of law and fact."[6]

The gasp-and-giggle genre of magazines continues to make problems for itself. Take, for example, the fact situations in Ali v. Playgirl. A frontally nude black boxer, his hands taped, was pictured—in something "between representational art and a cartoon"—sitting in the corner of a boxing ring. The features on the black male resembled former heavyweight boxing champion Muhammad Ali. Ali's name was not used, but the drawing was accompanied by some doggerel referring to the figure as "the Greatest." Ali, of course, made a career out of calling himself "the Greatest" and came to be so identified in the public mind. Ali was granted a preliminary injunction to halt further circulation of the February, 1978 issue of Playgirl which contained the offensive picture.[7]

Author-playwright A.E. Hotchner's attempt to write an intimate biography of American literary giant Ernest Hemingway led to a privacy suit under the New York statute. Hemingway had died in 1961, and his widow, Mary Hemingway, sued to enjoin Random House from publishing Hotchner's manuscript. Hotchner's biography covered the Nobel laureate's life from 1948, when Hemingway and Hotchner first met in a bar in Havana, Cuba, up to the time of Hemingway's death. New York Supreme Court Judge Harry B. Frank wrote of Hotchner's book:[8]

> The format and narrative style of the work make immediately apparent that it is intended as a subjective presentation from the vantage of the friendship, camaraderie, and personal experiences that the younger author shared with the literary giant. Their adventures, their travels, their meetings are all set forth in detail and the portrait of Hemingway that emerges is shaded in terms of

[5] Hansen v. High Society, (N.Y.Sup.Ct.N.Y. County, 1980), 5 Med.L.Rptr. 2398.

[6] Kovner, op. cit., p. 283.

[7] Ali v. Playgirl, 447 F.Supp. 723 (S.D.N.Y.1978), 3 Med.L.Rptr. 2541, 2546.

[8] Estate of Hemingway v. Random House, Inc., 49 Misc.2d 726, 268 N.Y.S.2d 531, 534 (1966).

the unique self that he manifested and revealed in the course of his particular relationship with Hotchner.

Mary Hemingway's suit for an injunction complained, among other things, that the Hotchner manuscript violated her statutory right of privacy under Section 51 of the New York Civil Rights Law. Mrs. Hemingway was mentioned in various places throughout the book, and she charged that those references to her amounted to an invasion of her privacy. Judge Frank rejected Mrs. Hemingway's privacy contentions and allowed Random House to publish the book: [9]

> The individual's security has fared best when pitted against naked commercial assault, and protection is afforded under the statute where the invasion has been solely for "advertising purposes, or for the purpose of trade." A book of biographical import such as is here involved, however, has been held not to fall within such category. Compelling public interest in the free flow of ideas and dissemination of factual information has outweighed considerations of individuals privacy in conjunction with factual publications of such type * * *.

In other lawsuits dealing with "appropriation," it has been held that the taking or appropriation need not be for a financial gain in those jurisdictions where the common-law right of privacy is recognized. Just as long as someone's identity or likeness is used for some advantage, an action for invasion of privacy may succeed. An example of this occurred when a political party used a man's name as a candidate when he had not given his consent.[10] However, a number of states—including New York, Oklahoma, Virginia, Utah and California—have privacy statutes requiring proof of monetary advantage gained by the publication.[11] It has often been urged that everything published by the mass media is done "for purposes of trade." [12] If such a construction were allowed, the press might be greatly threatened by privacy suits brought by persons who objected to the use of their names, even in news stories. In defense of press freedom, however, courts have repeatedly held that just because a newspaper, magazine, or broadcasting station makes a profit does not mean that everything published is "for purposes of trade."[13]

[9] 49 Misc.2d 726, 268 N.Y.S.2d 531, 534 (1966).

[10] State ex rel. LaFollette v. Hinkle, 131 Wash. 86, 229 P. 317 (1924).

[11] McKinney's N.Y. Civil Rights Law §§ 50–51; Virginia Code 1950, § 8–650; 15 Oklahoma Statutes Anno. § 839.1; Utah Code Ann. 1953, 76–4–8, and § 3344, California Civil Code.

[12] See Joseph Burstyn, Inc. v. Wilson, 343 U.S. 495, 501, 72 S.Ct. 777, 780 (1952); New York Times Co. v. Sullivan, 376 U.S. 254 at 266, 84 S.Ct. 710 at 718 (1964).

[13] See, e.g., Time, Inc. v. Hill, 385 U.S. 374, 87 S.Ct. 534, 546 (1967).

Actress Ann-Margret brought an invasion of privacy action under Section 51 of the New York Civil Rights Law, asking damages from *High Society* magazine. She contended that including her photograph, nude to the waist, in a publication known as *High Society Celebrity Skin* amounted to use of her likeness, without her consent, for purposes of trade, and also invaded her right of publicity. Although he dismissed her suit, a sympathetic federal judge wrote: [14]

> * * * Ann-Margret is a woman of beauty, talent, and courage. It would appear, from her reaction to her inclusion in defendants' magazine, that she is also a woman of taste.
>
> In 1978 the plaintiff appeared in the motion picture "Magic," a film in which, for the second time in her screen career, she appeared in one scene unclothed from the waist up. She states that the decision to disrobe was an "artistic" one, made in light of the script necessities.
>
> * * *
>
> The defendants * * * publish a magazine * * * which specializes in printing photographs of well-known women caught in the most revealing situations and positions that the defendants are able to obtain. In view of such content, the plaintiff has attempted to characterize Celebrity Skin as hard-core pornography. That description, however, by contemporary standards, appears inappropriate. A more apt description would be simply "tacky."

Judge Goettel's sympathies might have been with Ann-Margret, but he ruled that she could not collect for invasion of privacy. The actress, "who has occupied the fantasies of many moviegoers over the years," chose to perform unclad in one of her films; that is a matter of public interest.

The judge then expressed a liberal, non-authoritarian view of what constitutes newsworthiness, a view which seems to be losing favor in some other courts.[15] Judge Goettel wrote: [16]

> And while such an event may not appear overly important, the scope of what constitutes a newsworthy event has been afforded a broad definition and held to include even matters of "entertainment and amusement, concern-

[14] Ann-Margret v. High Society, 498 F.Supp. 401 (S.D.N.Y.1980), 5 Med.L.Rptr. 1774, 1775.

[15] See, e.g., Briscoe v. Reader's Digest, 4 Cal.3d 529, 93 Cal.Rptr. 866, 483 P.2d 34 (1971); Virgil v. Time, Inc., 527 F.2d 1122 (9th Cir.1975).

[16] Ann-Margret v. High Society, 498 F.Supp. 401 (S.D.N.Y.1980) 6 Med.L.Rptr. 1774, 1776.

ing interesting phases of human activity in general."
Paulsen v. Personality Posters, Inc., 59 Misc.2d 444 at
448, 299 N.Y.S.2d 501 and 506. See Sidis v. F–R Pub.
Corp., *   *   * 113 F.2d 806 at 809. As has been noted, it
is not for the courts to decide what matters are of interest
to the general public. See Goelet v. Confidential, Inc.
*   *   * 5 A.D.2d 226 at 229–30, 171 N.Y.S.2d 223 at 226.

SEC. 36. THE RIGHT OF PUBLICITY

**From Bela Lugosi to a "Human Cannonball," the right to
profit from one's own efforts or fame is emerging as a
spin-off from the privacy sub-tort of "appropriation."**

As a general rule, the right of privacy dies with the individual. As tort scholar William L. Prosser noted, "there is no common
law right of action for a publication concerning one who is already
dead." However, as with most general rules, there are exceptions.
A viable lawsuit for invasion of privacy may exist after a person's
death, "according to the survival rules of the particular state." [17]

Similarly, there is a general rule that relatives have no right
of action for an invasion of the privacy of a deceased person. A
satirical national television show, "That Was the Week that Was,"
included this statement in a broadcast over the National Broadcasting Company network: "Mrs. Katherine Young of Syracuse,
New York, who died at 99 leaving five sons, five daughters, 67
grandchildren, 72 great grandchildren, and 73 great-great
grandchildren—gets our First Annual Booby Prize in the Birth
Control Sweepstakes." Two of Mrs. Young's sons sued for invasion of privacy, but failed because there is no relative's right to sue
for invasion of the privacy of a deceased person.[18]

But what about famous people? What about performers, even
those as wildly different as Bela Lugosi or Elvis Presley? Their
likenesses, their personas, are still valuable commercial properties
long after their deaths. For example, the legal ghost of the late
horror-film star Bela Lugosi came back in the courtrooms to haunt
Universal Pictures Company, although Universal eventually won
its case after a series of lengthy court battles. Lugosi, famed for
his portrayal of Count Dracula, died in 1956. In 1960, however,
Universal began to capitalize on his fame, entering into licensing
agreements to allow manufacturing of a number of items, includ-

[17] William L. Prosser, Handbook of the Law of Torts, 4th ed., St. Paul, Minn.:
West Publishing Co., 1971, at p. 815, citing the highly confusing decision in Reed v.
Real Detective Pub. Co., 63 Ariz. 294, 162 P.2d 133 (1945).

[18] Young v. That Was the Week that Was, 423 F.2d 265 (6th Cir.1970); accord:
see Maritote v. Desilu Productions, Inc., 345 F.2d 418 (7th Cir.1965); Ravellette v.
Smith, 300 F.2d 854 (7th Cir.1962).

ing shirts, cards, games, kites, bar accessories and masks—all with the likeness of Count Dracula as played by Bela Lugosi.[19]

Lugosi's son and widow sued to recover profits made by Universal Pictures in its licensing arrangements, claiming a "right of property or right of contract which, upon Bela Lugosi's death, descended to his heirs." [20]   Although the Lugosis won their suit at the trial court level, the California Supreme Court ultimately voted 4–3 that the exclusive right to profit from his name and likeness did not survive the actor's death.   The California Supreme Court said, in adopting California Court of Appeal Presiding Justice Roth's opinion as its own:

> "Such '*   *   * a right of value' to create a business, product or service of value is embraced in the law of privacy and is protectable during one's lifetime but it does not survive the death of Lugosi.
>
> *   *   *
>
> "We hold that the right to exploit name and likeness is personal to the artist and must be exercised, if at all, by him during his lifetime."

More is likely to be heard, however, in the area of law involving profiting from celebrities' names or likenesses after their deaths.   Courts in different regions of the nation give contradictory signals.   Cases involving the legendary Elvis Presley are illustrative:

(1)   In Factors, Etc. v. Pro Arts, Inc., the Court of Appeals for the Second Circuit held in 1978 that there *was* a property right in Presley's name and likeness which continued on for his heirs after Presley's death.[21]

(2)   On the other hand, the Court of Appeals for the Sixth Circuit concluded in Memphis Development Foundation v. Factors, Etc. that Presley's heirs could *not* assign exclusive rights to use Presley's name and likeness.   Thus, a Memphis firm which was selling—without authorization—statuettes of Elvis was allowed to go right on doing just that.[22]

---

[19] Bela George Lugosi v. Universal Pictures, No. 877875, Memorandum Opinion, Superior Court of the State of California for the County of Los Angeles, published in full in Performing Arts Review, Vol. 3, No. 1 (1972), pp. 19–62.

[20] Ibid., pp. 21, 27–28.

[21] Factors, Etc. v. Pro Arts, Inc., 579 F.2d (2d Cir.1978).

[22] Memphis Development Foundation v. Factors, Etc., 616 F.2d 956 (6th Cir.1980).

As Victor Kovner has written, there is great disagreement among a number of courts [23] on "survivability" of name and likeness.

> Since it is universally agreed that any person can assign his right to commercially develop his own name and likeness, the principal ramifications of this current dispute are conflicting decisions on whether this right is descendible [that is, whether it survives the death of a person] (e.g. New Jersey, Georgia, federal courts in New York, Second Circuit) or is not (e.g. California, Ohio and Sixth Circuit).

Beyond that, actors imitating the famed late comedians, Stan Laurel and Oliver Hardy lost a suit to heirs of Laurel and Hardy.[24] Similarly, the right of publicity was recognized in a case involving the late mystery author, Agatha Christie. In this case, heirs of Miss Christie failed to collect, however, because the account was so obviously a fiction.[25] However, privacy law expert Victor A. Kovner has wondered whether the court would have ruled in that way if Miss Christie were alive, "since a living person would presumably assert false light and private facts claims, along with the right of publicity." [26]

Other cases have held that there is a kind of a property right in a person's picture or likeness. Bubble-gum "trading cards" offer cases in point. Beginning with Judge Jerome D. Frank's 1953 decision in Haelan Laboratories, Inc., v. Topps Chewing Gum, several cases involved players' photographs. Judge Frank wrote of a "right of publicity" apart from a right of privacy which compensates a person for mental suffering because that person has received unwanted publicity. Judge Frank said: "We think that in addition to an independent right of privacy * * * a man has a right in the publicity value of his photograph, i.e., the right

[23] Kovner, 1984 op. cit., at p. 501, citing six states with commercialization statutes providing for a property right to publicity surviving death: West's Fla. Stat.Ann. § 540.08; Neb.Rev.Stats. §§ 20–202, 20–208; Okla.Stat.Ann. tit. 2, § 839.2; Utah Code Ann. 76–9–406, and Va.Code § 8.01–40. Kovner added that Tennessee adopted the "Personal Rights Protection Act of 1984—protecting a property right in name, etc., 10 years after death, on June 5, 1984.

See also the remarkably useful LDRC [Libel Defense Resource Center] 50-State Survey 1984: Current Developments in Media Libel and Invasion of Privacy Law, ed. by Henry R. Kaufman. See state-by-state listings on court decisions and relevant statutes.

[24] Price v. Worldvision Enterprises, Inc., 455 F.Supp. 252 (S.D.N.Y.1978), aff'd 603 F.2d 214 (2d Cir.1979).

[25] Hicks v. Casablanca Records, 464 F.Supp. 426 (S.D.N.Y.1978).

[26] Victor A. Kovner, "Privacy," chapter in James C. Goodale, ed., Communications Law 1980 (New York: Practising Law Institute, 1980).

to grant the exclusive privilege of publishing his picture * * *. This right might be called a 'right of publicity.' " [27]

Consider "right of publicity" cases involving outfielder Ted Uhlaender and slugging first baseman Orlando Cepeda. Both sued for compensation for the unauthorized use of their names for advertising or promotional purposes. In the *Uhlaender* case, a court decided that a public figure such as a baseball player has a property or proprietary interest in his public personality. This included his identity, as embodied in his name, likeness, or other personal characteristics. This property interest—in effect the "right of publicity" of which Judge Frank wrote in 1953 in the *Haelan Laboratories* case—was held in *Uhlaender* to be sufficient to support an injunction against unauthorized appropriation.[28]

As if celebrities such as Bela Lugosi, Elvis Presley, and baseball players didn't add enough flair to the law of privacy, what about Hugo "Human Cannonball" Zacchini? Zacchini was doing his thing at the Geauga County Fair in Burton, Ohio—being shot out of a cannon into a net 200 feet away. This high-calibre entertainer, however, took exception to being filmed by a free-lancer working for Scripps-Howard Broadcasting. Zacchini noted the free-lancer and asked him not to film the performance, which took place in a fenced area, surrounded by grandstands.

The television station broadcast the film of the 15-second flight by Zacchini, with the newscaster saying this: [29]

> "This * * * now * * * is the story of a *true spectator* sport * * * the sport of human cannonballing * * * in fact, the great *Zacchini* is about the only human cannonball around these days * * * just happens that, *where* he is, is the Great Geauga County Fair, in Burton * * * and believe me, although it's not a *long* act, it's a thriller * * * and you really need to see it *in person* to appreciate it. * * *"

Zacchini sued for infringement of his "right of publicity," claiming that he was engaged in the entertainment business, following after his father, who had invented this act. He claimed that the television station had "showed and commercialized the film of his act without his consent," and that this was "an unlawful appropriation of plaintiff's professional property."

[27] Haelan Laboratories, Inc. v. Topps Chewing Gum, Inc., 202 F.2d 866 (2d Cir. 1953).

[28] Uhlaender v. Henricksen, 316 F.Supp. 1277 (D.C.Minn.1970); Cepeda v. Swift & Co., 415 F.2d 1205 (8th Cir.1969).

[29] Zacchini v. Scripps-Howard Broadcasting Co., 433 U.S. 562, 97 S.Ct. 2849 (1977).

The Ohio Supreme Court rejected Zacchini's claims, saying that a TV station has a privilege to report in its newscasts "matters of legitimate public interest which would otherwise be protected by an individual's right of publicity." The TV station could be held liable, but only when the actual intent of the station was to appropriate the benefit of the publicity for some non-privileged private use, or unless the actual intent was to injure the individual involved.[30]

The Supreme Court of the United States disagreed, saying that Zacchini was not contending that his act could not be reported as a newsworthy item.[31]

> His complaint is that respondent filmed his entire act and displayed the film on television for the public to see and enjoy.
>
> *   *   *
>
> It is evident, and there is no claim here to the contrary, that petitioner's state-law right of publicity would not serve to prevent respondent from reporting the newsworthy facts about petitioner's act. Wherever the line in particular situations is to be drawn between media reports that are protected and those that are not, we are quite sure that the First and Fourteenth Amendments do not immunize the media when they broadcast a performer's entire act without his consent.
>
> *   *   *
>
> The broadcast of a film of petitioner's entire act poses a substantial threat to the economic value of that performance.
>
> *   *   *
>
> We conclude that although the State of Ohio may as a matter of its own law privilege the press in the circumstances of this case, the First and Fourteenth Amendments do not require it to do so.

A five-member majority of the Supreme Court then sent the Zacchini case back to the Ohio courts for a decision on whether the Human Cannonball should recover damages. In dissent, Justice Powell—who was joined by Justices Brennan and Marshall—wondered just what constituted "an entire act."[32]   As attorney Floyd Abrams has asked—following Justice Powell's question—

---

[30] Ibid., 2091–2092.

[31] Ibid., 2093–2094, 2095.

[32] Ibid., p. 2096.

does the "entire act" include the fanfare and getting into the cannon, possibly lasting for several minutes? [33]

Justice Powell expressed concern that this decision might lead to media self-censorship when television news editors are unsure when their camera crews might be held to depict "an entire act." The public is then the loser," Powell said. "This is hardly the kind of news reportage that the First Amendment is meant to foster." [34]

SEC. 37. DEFENSES: NEWSWORTHINESS

Traditionally, the media's most useful defense against an invasion of privacy lawsuit has been the concept of "newsworthiness."

Newsworthiness, for many years, was a splendid defense in "private facts" invasion of privacy lawsuits. It is still a major factor, and in some cases may be *the* prime factor in a successful defense against an invasion of privacy lawsuit. However, a number of cases and the oft-quoted discussion of privacy in the Restatement of Torts, Second, suggest that this defense is undergoing erosion. [35]

Somewhat as Pontius Pilate asked "What is truth?," we must ask, "What is news?" No two journalists ever seem to be able to agree on a clear-cut definition of the term, but presumably, they know it when they see it. Courts, in numerous privacy cases, have tried to define news and newsworthiness. Even though many attorneys and judges act as if they were waiters/waitresses at the Last Supper, news has proved hard for courts to define, too. One court has even called news "that indefinable quality of information which arouses public attention."

Editors and reporters assert that "news is what we say it is" or that news is "whatever interests people." For years, many judges confronted with privacy cases tended to accept journalists' definitions. [36] Two cases discussed at some length in Section 33 of this chapter—Virgil v. Time, Inc. (1975) [37] and Campbell v. Seabury Press (1980) [38]—illustrate the tension between two ways of

[33] Floyd Abrams, "The Press, Privacy, and the Constitution," New York Times Magazine, August 21, 1977, at pp. 11ff.

[34] Zacchini v. Scripps-Howard, at p. 2096.

[35] Restatement, Second, Torts, § 652D.

[36] Sweenek v. Pathe News Co., 16 F.Supp. 746, 747 (D.C.N.Y.1939); Sidis v. F–R Pub. Co., 113 F.2d 806, 809 (2d Cir.1940); Associated Press v. International News Service, 245 F. 244, 248 (2d Cir.1917), aff'd 248 U.S. 215, 39 S.Ct. 68 (1918); Jenkins v. Dell Pub. Co., 251 F.2d 447, 451 (3d Cir.1958).

[37] Virgil v. Time, Inc., 527 F.2d 1122 (9th Cir.1975).

[38] Campbell v. Seabury Press, 614 F.2d 395 (5th Cir.1980).

defining news. In *Virgil,* the Circuit Court judge evidently believed that courts (and juries) should set standards of newsworthiness. Using the Restatement's formulation, judges and juries are to work out a kind of "community standard" in a privacy case, determining whether the matter publicized would be "highly offensive to a reasonable person" and whether it is "of legitimate concern to the public." [39]

In *Campbell,* however, the judge viewed newsworthiness in a way far more favorable to the press. The court there said that the First Amendment commands a newsworthiness privilege. As Harvey Zuckman has pointed out, *Campbell* held that the information publicized need not be limited to news dissemination or commentary on public affairs. The privilege "extends to 'information concerning interesting phases of human activity and embraces all issues about which information is needed or appropriate for coping with the exigencies of their period.'" [40] And that can include information about persons who have not sought out—or who have actively tried to avoid—publicity.

Often, of course, people are caught up in the news when they would much rather retain the anonymity of private persons. But when an event is news, the courts have uniformly forbidden recovery for substantially accurate accounts of an event which is of public interest. A rather extreme case in point here involved the unfortunate John Jacova, who had bought a newspaper at a Miami Beach hotel's cigar counter. As Jacova innocently stood at the counter, police rushed into the hotel in a raid and mistook Jacova for a gambler. Jacova was taken into custody, but was released after he showed identification. Mr. Jacova was understandably annoyed later in the day to see himself on television being questioned by policemen. He sued the television stations for invasion of privacy. He was not allowed to collect, however, because the court ruled that Jacova had become an "unwilling actor" in a news event.[41]

Mrs. Lillian Jones—much against her will—originated the "unwilling public figure" rule in a famous privacy case decided in 1929. Her husband was stabbed to death on a Louisville street in her presence. The Louisville *Herald-Post* published a picture of Mrs. Jones, and quoted her as saying of her husband's attackers:

[39] Restatement, Second, Torts, § 652D.

[40] Zuckman, "The Right of Privacy and the Press," presentation at Southern Newspaper Publishers Association law symposium, Austin, Texas, October 13, 1980.

[41] Jacova v. Southern Radio Television Co., 83 So.2d 34 (Fla.1955); see, also, Hubbard v. Journal Pub. Co., 69 N.M. 473, 368 P.2d 147 (1962); Elmhurst v. Pearson, 80 U.S.App.D.C. 372, 153 F.2d 467 (1946).

"I would have killed them." The court expressed sympathy and acknowledged the existence of a right to privacy, but added:[42]

> There are times, however, when one, whether willing or not, becomes an actor in an occurrence of public or general interest. When this takes place, he emerges from his seclusion and it is not an invasion of his right to privacy to publish his photograph with an account of such occurrence.

Even in the early 1980s there appeared to be an "involuntary public figure" category in privacy law. But that appears to fly in the face of developments in the law of libel. As discussed fully in Chapter 4, Section 21, the "involuntary public figure" category has been virtually killed off in libel law by the Supreme Court of the United States.[43] Will the Supreme Court shove the libel rule into the law of privacy, further weakening newsworthiness as a defense? Developments in this area need to be watched carefully by journalists and by their attorneys.

What of people who seek fame, public office, or otherwise *willingly* bring themselves to public notice? Public figures have been held to have given up, to some extent their right to be "let alone." Persons who have sought publicity—actors, explorers, or politicians to give a few examples—have made themselves "news" and have parted with some of their privacy. In one case, a suit by a former husband of movie star Janet Leigh was unsuccessful despite his protestations that he had done everything he could to avoid publicity. Her fame rubbed off on him.[44]

Even so, when the media go "too far," celebrities can bring successful privacy lawsuits. The taking of a name of a public figure, for example, to advertise a commercial product without his consent would be actionable. Also, even newsworthy public figures can collect damages when fictionalized statements are published about them. Some areas of life are sufficiently personal and private that the media may intrude only at their peril. Private sexual relationships, homes, bank accounts, and private letters of an individual would all seem to be in a danger zone for the press.[45]

One way in which the privilege of newsworthiness is sometimes attacked in court involves the passage of time since an event

[42] Jones v. Herald-Post Co., 230 Ky. 227, 18 S.W.2d 972 (1929).

[43] See also Time, Inc. v. Firestone, 424 U.S. 448, 96 S.Ct. 958 (1976), and Wolston v. Reader's Digest Ass'n, 443 U.S. 157, 99 S.Ct. 2701 (1979).

[44] Carlisle v. Fawcett Publications, 201 Cal.App.2d 733, 20 Cal.Rptr. 405 (1962).

[45] See Garner v. Triangle Publications, 97 F.Supp. 546 (D.C.N.Y.1951); Bazemore v. Savannah Hospital, 171 Ga. 257, 155 S.E. 194 (1930); Baker v. Libbie, 210 Mass. 599, 97 N.E. 109 (1912); Pope v. Curll, 2 Atk., 341, 26 Eng.Rep. 608 (1741).

was first reported. This argument runs that although an event may have been legitimate news when it occurred, say five years ago, the story is now out of the public eye and cannot be legitimately revived. A case in which a time lapse of seven years was crucial was the famed "Red Kimono" case discussed earlier in this chapter, Melvin v. Reid. Gabrielle Darley Melvin, the reformed prostitute, had been acquitted of a murder charge in 1918, and the movie based upon her involvement in the "Red Kimono" murder trial, was brought out in 1925.[46] The time lapse argument, however, used by itself, almost uniformly has failed to rebut a defense of newsworthiness. But when a time lapse argument is coupled with a publication's dredging up a reformed ex-convicts 11-year-old misadventure as a truck hijacker, as in Briscoe v. Reader's Digest—discussed earlier in this chapter—time lapse was part of an invasion of privacy lawsuit.[47]

Unwilling subjects of photographs or motion pictures have caused considerable activity in the law of privacy. Consider the case of Frank Man, a professional musician who made the scene at the Woodstock Festival in Bethel, N.Y., in August of 1969. At someone's request, Man clambered onto the stage and played "Mess Call" on his flugelhorn to an audience of movie cameras and 400,000 people. Subsequently, Warner Bros., Inc. produced and exhibited a movie under the title of "Woodstock." Man claimed that the producers and distributors of the film included his performance without his consent, and brought suit in New York against Warner Bros.

A United States District Court said:[48]

The film depicts, without the addition of any fictional material, actual events which happened at the festival. Nothing is staged and nothing is false. * * *

There can be no question that the Woodstock festival was and is a matter of valid public interest.

Man argued that a movie depicting Woodstock could no longer be treated as news because of the lapse of time. The court replied that "the bizarre happenings of the festival were not mere fleeting news but sensational events of deep and lasting public interest."

---

[46] 112 Cal. 285, 297 P. 91 (1931). However, more than mere time-lapse was involved in this decision. This case suggested that re-creating events might have been permissible, but that the unnecessary use of the name "Gabrielle Darley" in advertising and in the movie itself was not to be tolerated. More innocuous subject matter, however, has since been dealt with more leniently by the courts. See, e.g., Sidis v. F–R Pub. Corp., 113 F.2d 806 (2d Cir.1940); Smith v. Doss, 251 Ala. 250, 37 So.2d 118 (1948); Smith v. NBC, 138 Cal.App.2d 807, 292 P.2d 600 (1956).

[47] Briscoe v. Reader's Digest Ass'n, 4 Cal.3d 529, 93 Cal.Rptr. 866, 483 P.2d 34 (1971); see also Wolston v. Reader's Digest, 443 U.S. 157, 99 S.Ct. 2701 (1979).

[48] 317 F.Supp. 51, 53 (D.C.N.Y.1970).

The court concluded that Frank Man, by his own volition had placed himself in the spotlight at a sensational event. He had made himself newsworthy, and thus deprived himself of any right to collect for invasion of privacy.[49]

It should not, however, be inferred that all factual reports of current events have been—or will be—held absolutely privileged. Film Producer Wiseman produced a film—"The Titicut Follies"—which showed conditions in a mental hospital, with individuals identifiable. The film showed naked inmates, forced feeding, masturbation and sadism, and the court concluded that Wiseman's film had—by identifying individuals—gone beyond the consent which mental hospital authorities had given him to make the film. The film was taken out of commercial distribution, but was not destroyed. The court ruled that the film was of educational value, and that it could be shown to special audiences such as groups of social workers, or others who might be moved to work toward improving conditions in mental hospitals.[50]

The protection of newsworthiness may vanish suddenly if a careless or misleading caption is placed on a picture. Consider the case of Holmes v. Curtis Publishing Company.

"MAFIA: SHADOW OF EVIL ON AN ISLAND IN THE SUN" screamed the headline on a feature story in the February 25, 1967 issue of the *Saturday Evening Post.* Published along with the article was a picture of James Holmes and four other persons at a gambling table, evidently playing blackjack. This picture was captioned, "High-Rollers at Monte Carlo have dropped as much as $20,000 in a single night. The U.S. Department of Justice estimates that the Casino grosses $20 million a year, and that one-third is skimmed off for American Mafia 'families.' "

Holmes objected to publication of this article, and sued for libel and invasion of privacy, arguing that the picture and caption had placed him in a false light. Holmes was not mentioned by name in the article, but he was, however, the focal point of the photograph. A United States district court in South Carolina noted that the article dealt with subjects of great public interest—organized crime, the growth of tourism in the Bahama Islands, and legalized gambling.

The court refused to grant the Curtis Publishing Company's motions that the libel and privacy lawsuits by Holmes could not stand because of precedents such as New York Times Co. v.

---

[49] Ibid.

[50] Commonwealth v. Wiseman, 356 Mass. 251, 249 N.E.2d 610 (1969). See, also Daily Times Democrat v. Graham, 276 Ala. 380, 162 So.2d 474 (1964), where a woman collected for invasion of privacy after a newspaper used her identifiable picture as she emerged from a "fun house" where a jet of air blew her dress above her waist.

Sullivan [51] and Time, Inc. v. Hill.[52]   Instead, the court declared that the libel and privacy issues would have to go to trial:[53]

> Certainly defendant's caption is reasonably capable of amounting to a defamation, for one identified as a high-stakes gambler of having a connection with the Mafia would certainly be injured in his business, occupation, and/or reputation.

> As to plaintiff's action for privacy, there appears no question that if it were not for defendant's caption beneath plaintiff's photograph, this court would be justified in dismissing plaintiff's invasion of privacy cause of action.   But such is not the case.   Conflicting inferences also arise from the record as it stands today which preclude disposition of this cause of action summarily.

SEC. 38.   DEFENSES: TIME, INC. v. HILL AND THE CONSTITUTION

The "malice rule" from the libel landmark case, New York Times v. Sullivan, was stirred into privacy law in Time, Inc. v. Hill.

The law of privacy is much like a jigsaw puzzle with some pieces missing: it is sometimes hard to discern a meaningful pattern.   Just as the defense of newsworthiness—discussed in the preceding section—is in flux, the Constitution-based defense growing out of the 1967 Supreme Court decision in Time, Inc. v. Hill also is undergoing change.   After discussing this case in detail, this section will offer some discussion of the present importance of privacy-suit defenses based on *Hill*.

When the Supreme Court weighed the right to privacy against the First Amendment freedom to publish, the freedom to publish was given preference.   Time, Inc. v. Hill was noteworthy in one respect because the losing attorney was Richard Milhous Nixon, more recently known as sometime President of the United States. This decision is important because it represents the first time that the Supreme Court decided a privacy case dealing with the mass media.

In 1952, the James J. Hill family was minding its own business, living in the suburban Philadelphia town of Whitemarsh. On September 11, 1952, however, the Hills' anonymity was taken away from them by three escaped prisoners.   The convicts held Mr. and Mrs. Hill and their five children hostage in their own

---

[51] 376 U.S. 254, 84 S.Ct. 710 (1964).

[52] 385 U.S. 374, 87 S.Ct. 534 (1967), discussed in Section 39, this chapter.

[53] Holmes v. Curtis Pub. Co., 303 F.Supp. 522, 527 (D.C.S.C.1969).

home for 19 hours. The family was not harmed, but the Hills—much against their wishes—were in the news.[54] Their story became even more sensational when two of the three convicts who had held them hostage were killed in a shoot-out with police.[55]

In 1953, Random House published Joseph Hayes' novel, The Desperate Hours, a story about a family which was taken hostage by escaped convicts. The novel was later made into a successful play and, subsequently, a motion picture.

The publicity which led the Hills to sue for invasion of their privacy was an article published in 1955 by *Life* magazine. The article, titled "True Crime Inspires Tense Play," described the "true crime" suffered by the James Hill family of Whitemarsh, Pennsylvania.[56] The article said:[57]

> "Three years ago Americans all over the country read about the desperate ordeal of the James Hill family, who were held prisoners in their home outside Philadelphia by three escaped convicts. Later they read about it in Joseph Hayes's novel, *The Desperate Hours*, inspired by the family's experience. Now they can see the story reenacted in Hayes's Broadway play based on the book, and next year will see it in his movie, which has been filmed but is being held up until the play has a chance to pay off.

> "The play, directed by Robert Montgomery and expertly acted, is a heart-stopping account of how a family rose to heroism in a crisis. LIFE photographed the play during its Philadelphia tryout, transported some of the actors to the actual house where the Hills were besieged. On the next page scenes from the play are re-enacted on the site of the crime."

Life's pages of photographs included actors' depiction of the son being "roughed up" by one of the escaped convicts. This picture was captioned "brutish convict." Also, a picture titled "daring daughter" showed the daughter biting the hand of a convict, trying to make him drop the gun.[58]

The Joseph Hayes novel and play, however, did not altogether match up with *Life's* assertion that Hayes' writings were based on the ordeal of the Hill family. For one thing, Hayes' family was named "Hilliard," not Hill. Also, the Hills had not been harmed by the convicts in any way, while in the Hayes novel and play the

---

[54] 385 U.S. 374, 377, 87 S.Ct. 534, 536 (1967).

[55] Pember, Privacy and the Press, p. 210.

[56] Life, Feb. 28, 1955.

[57] 385 U.S. 374, 377, 87 S.Ct. 534, 536–537 (1967).

[58] Ibid.

father and son were beaten and the daughter was "subjected to a verbal sexual insult."

Hill sued for invasion of privacy under the privacy sections of New York's Civil Rights Law, which provides that a person whose name or picture was so used "for purposes of trade" without his consent could "sue and recover damages for any injuries sustained by reason of such use.[59]

The Hills sought damages on grounds that the *Life* article "was intended to, and did, give the impression that the play mirrored the Hill family's experience, which, to the knowledge of defendant ＊ ＊ ＊ was false and untrue." In its defense, Time, Inc., argued that "the subject of the article was 'a subject of legitimate news interest,' 'a subject of general interest and of value and concern to the public' at the time of publication, and that it was 'published in good faith without any malice whatsoever ＊ ＊ ＊.' "[60]

The trial court jury awarded the Hills $50,000 compensatory and $25,000 punitive damages. On appeal, the Appellate Division of the Supreme Court of New York ordered a new the question of damages, but upheld the jury's finding that *Life* magazine had invaded the Hill's privacy. The Appellate Division bore down hard on the issue of fictionalization.[61]

At the new trial on the issue of damages, a jury was waived and the court awarded $30,000 compensatory damages with no punitive damages.

When the *Hill* case reached the Supreme Court, issues of freedom of speech and press raised in the appeal by Time, Inc. were considered. Justice Brennan's majority opinion first dealt with the issue of whether truth could be a defense to a charge of invasion of privacy. Quoting a recent New York Court of Appeals decision, Brennan said it had been made "crystal clear" in construing the New York Civil Rights Statute, "that truth is a complete defense in actions under the statute based upon reports of newsworthy people or event."[62] Brennan added, "Constitutional questions which might arise if truth were not a defense are therefore no concern."[63]

[59] Sections 50–51, New York Civil Rights Law, McKinney's Consolidated Laws, Ch. 6.

[60] 385 U.S. 374, 378, 87 S.Ct. 534, 537 (1967).

[61] 385 U.S. 374, 379, 87 S.Ct. 534, 537 (1967), quoting Hill v. Hayes, 18 A.D.2d 485, 489, 240 N.Y.S.2d 286, 290 (1963).

[62] At the outset of his opinion, Justice Brennan relied heavily upon Spahn v. Julian Messner, Inc., 18 N.Y.2d 324, 274 N.Y.S. 877, 221 N.E.2d 543 (1966).

[63] 385 U.S. 374, 383–384, 87 S.Ct. 534, 539–540 (1967).

Justice Brennan then wrestled with the issue of fictionalization. He noted that James Hill was a newsworthy person " 'substantially without a right to privacy' insofar as his hostage experience was involved." Hill, however, was entitled to sue to the extent that *Life* magazine "fictionalized" and "exploited for the defendant's commercial benefit." Brennan then turned to a libel case, New York Times v. Sulivan, for guidance.[64]

Material and substantial falsification is the test. However, it is not clear whether proof of knowledge of the falsity or that the article was prepared with reckless disregard for the truth is also required. In New York Times Co. v. Sullivan * * * we held that the Constitution delimits a State's power to award damages for libel in actions brought by public officials against critics of their official conduct. Factual error, content defamatory of official reputation, or both, are insufficient to an award of damages for false statements unless actual malice—knowledge that the statements are false or in reckless disregard of the truth—is alleged and proved. * * *

* * *

We hold that the Constitutional protections for speech and press precluded the application of the New York statute to redress false reports of matters of public interest in the absence of proof that the defendant published the report with knowledge of its falsity or in reckless disregard of the truth.

The Supreme Court, however, did not appear to wish to tie all future privacy holdings to the "Times Rule" cited above. Justice Brennan carefully emphasized that the actual malice rule from New York Times v. Sullivan—"knowledge that it was false, or reckless disregard of whether it was false or not"—was here being applied only in the "discrete context" of the facts of the *Hill* case.[65]

It should be emphasized that Justice Brennan's opinion in Time v. Hill has not made truth an entirely dependable defense against a lawsuit for invasion of privacy. For one thing, the Supreme Court's adoption of the malice rule from New York Times v. Sullivan applies only to those privacy cases involving falsity. Furthermore, the Supreme Court was badly split in Time v. Hill; a five-Justice majority did vote in favor of *Life* magazine, but only two justices—Potter Stewart and Byron White—agreed with Brennan's use of the "Sullivan rule." Justices Hugo L. Black

---

[64] New York Times v. Sullivan, 376 U.S. 254, 84 S.Ct. 710 (1964), used in Time, Inc. v. Hill, 385 U.S. 374, 386–388, 87 S.Ct. 534, 541–542 (1967).

[65] 385 U.S. 374, 390–391, 87 S.Ct. 534, 543 (1967).

and William O. Douglas concurred in the decision, but on other grounds.

Brennan appeared to prize press freedom's benefits to society more than the individual's right to privacy.[66] If incidental, non-malicious error crept into a story, that was part of the risk of freedom, for which a publication should not be held responsible. Justice Brennan wrote:[67]

> Exposure of the self to others in varying degrees is a concomitant of life in a civilized community. The risk of exposure is an essential incident of life in a society which places a primary value on freedom of speech and press.
>
>   *   *   *
>
> Erroneous statement is no less inevitable in * * * [a case such as discussion of a new play] than in the case of comment upon public affairs, and in both, if innocent or merely negligent, * * * it must be protected if the freedoms of expression are to have the "breathing space" that they "need * * * to survive."

The "breathing space" mentioned by Justice Brennan—a phrase borrowed from New York Times v. Sullivan—indicated that the Court was giving the press a healthy "benefit of the doubt." Press freedom, Brennan declared, is essential to "the maintenance of our political system and an open society." Yet this freedom, he argued, could be dangerously invaded by lawsuits for libel or invasion of privacy.[68]

"We have no doubt," Brennan wrote, "that the subject of the *Life* article, the opening of a new play linked to an actual incident, is a matter of public interest. 'The line between the informing and the entertaining is too elusive for the protection of * * * [freedom of the press].' "[69]

The concurring opinions of Justices Black and Douglas contained stinging assertions that Brennan had undervalued the liberty of the press. Black repeated his bitter disagreement with the "Sullivan rule:" "The words 'malicious' and particularly 'reckless disregard' can never serve as effective substitutes for the First Amendment words: ' * * * make no law * * * abridging the

---

[66] See the dissent by Mr. Justice Abe Fortas, which was joined by Chief Justice Earl Warren and by Justice Tom C. Clark, 385 U.S. 374, 411, 416, 87 S.Ct. 534, 554, 556 (1967).

[67] 385 U.S. 374, 388–389, 87 S.Ct. 534, 542–543 (1967).

[68] 385 U.S. 374, 389, 87 S.Ct. 534, 543 (1967).

[69] 385 U.S. 374, 388, 87 S.Ct. 534, 542 (1967), quoting Winters v. New York, 333 U.S. 507, 510, 68 S.Ct. 665, 667 (1948).

freedom of speech, or of the press * * *.' "[70] And Justice Douglas dismissed discussions of privacy as "irrelevant" in the context of Time v. Hill; the Hills' activities, he maintained, were fully in the public domain.[71]

Justice Brennan's opinion is important on several counts. First, this was the first case on the law of privacy involving the communications media which was decided by the Supreme Court. Second, the use of the malice rule from New York Times v. Sullivan requiring proof that the defendant published material "with knowledge of its falsity or in reckless disregard of the truth" [72] was highly significant. True, the Times v. Sullivan malice formula was to be applied "only in this discrete context." But the context involved publications "of public interest," and not just political comment:[73]

> The guarantees for speech and press are not the preserve of political expression or comment upon public affairs, essential as those are to healthy government. One need only to pick up any newspaper or magazine to comprehend the vast range of published matter which exposes persons to public view, both private citizens and public officials.

Time, Inc. v. Hill thus erected an important constitutional shield in false-light privacy cases. If persons caught up in the news—as an "involuntary public figure" are to recover damages for falsity, they must prove "actual malice" as borrowed from the lore of libel: publication of knowing falsehoods or with reckless disregard for whether a statement was false or not. As noted earlier, the developments in the law of libel have virtually annihilated the "involuntary public person" category, and the question remains whether the "public interest" consideration in privacy law will continue to be a worthwhile defense.[74]

Cantrell v. Forest City Pub. Co.,[75] discussed in Section 34 of this chapter, allowed the widow of the victim of the famed collapse of the Point Pleasant Bridge to collect $60,000. The jury found

[70] 385 U.S. 374, 398, 87 S.Ct. 534, 547 (1967). See also Justice Black's concurring opinion in New York Times v. Sullivan, 376 U.S. 254 at 293m, 84 S.Ct. 710 at 773 (1964).

[71] 385 U.S. 374, 401–402, 87 S.Ct. 534, 549 (1967).

[72] 385 U.S. 374, 393, 87 S.Ct. 534, 545 (1967). In a footnote, Justice Brennan said that it was for a jury, not for the Supreme Court, to determine whether there had been "knowing or reckless falsehood." Cf. New York Times Co. v. Sullivan, 376 U.S. 254, 284–285, 84 S.Ct. 710, 728–729 (1964).

[73] 385 U.S. 374, 388, 87 S.Ct. 534, 542 (1967).

[74] See Chapter 4, Section 21; see also Time, Inc. v. Firestone, 424 U.S. 448, 96 S.Ct. 958 (1976), and Wolston v. Reader's Digest Ass'n, 443 U.S. 157, 99 S.Ct. 2701 (1979).

[75] 419 U.S. 245, 95 S.Ct. 465 (1974).

fictionalization amounting to "actual malice" in the sense of a knowing falsehood. However, as noted by Sallie Martin Sharp in a 1981 study, the *Cantrell* majority "∗   ∗   ∗ invited challenges to the [Time v.] *Hill* opinion when it said:"[76]

> "[T]his case presents no occasion to consider whether a State may constitutionally apply a more relaxed standard of liability for a publisher or broadcaster for false statements injurious to a private person under a false-light theory of invasion of privacy or whether the constitutional standard announced in Time, Inc. v. Hill applies to all false-light cases."

Dr. Sharp found that the Constitution-based defenses growing out of Time, Inc. v. Hill have become increasingly important. Since *Hill* was decided in 1967, she wrote, lower federal and state courts began considering private facts in terms of First Amendment limits ∗   ∗   ∗ "even though the *Hill* case involved false light invasion of privacy."[77] She concluded: "In fact, since 1967, almost every reported federal case which could have been evaluated solely on the basis of the newsworthiness defense at common law was evaluated as a First Amendment case."[78]

Beyond that, Victor A. Kovner has asked whether the important libel case of Gertz v. Robert Welch, Incorporated [79]—discussed at length in Section 22 of Chapter 4 "limits the actual malice standard to false light claims asserted by a public figure."[80]

In Wood v. Hustler, one of the frequent lawsuits against this magazine, the Fifth Circuit Court of Appeals took what seems to be the predominating approach to applying a constitutional standard in a false-light privacy suit by a private person. (Wood v. Hustler involved Hustler Magazine's publishing a stolen nude photo of a woman after carelessly accepting a faked consent form.) Circuit Judge Jolly wrote for the court:[81]

[76] Sallie Martin Sharp, "The Evolution of the Invasion of Privacy Tort and Its Newsworthiness Limitations," Ph.D. dissertation, The University of Texas at Austin, 1981. See also Don R. Pember and Dwight L. Teeter, Jr., "Privacy and the Press Since Time, Inc. v. Hill, 50 Washington Law Review (1974) at p. 77.

[77] Sallie Martin Sharp, "The Evolution of the Invasion of Privacy Tort and Its Newsworthiness Limitations," Ph.D. dissertation, The University of Texas at Austin, 1981.

[78] Ibid., p. 166.

[79] 418 U.S. 323, 94 S.Ct. 2997 (1974).

[80] Victor A. Kovner, "Recent Developments in Intrusion, Private Facts, False Light, and Commercialization Claims," pp. 419–606, in James C. Goodale, Chairman, Communications Law 1984 (New York: Practising Law Institute, 1984) at p. 466.

[81] Wood v. Hustler, 736 F.2d 1084 (5th Cir.1984), 10 Med.L.Rptr. 2113, at 2117–2118.

The Supreme Court first enunciated the actual malice standard in New York Times v. Sullivan * * * (1964), a defamation case. The Court held that, to comply with the First and Fourteenth Amendments, states could not impose liability on a defendant who published defamatory matter concerning a public official unless the publisher knew of the falsity of the matter or acted in reckless disregard for its truth or falsity. The Court later applied the prevailing constitutional standard to false light privacy actions in Time, Inc. v. Hill * * * (1967). The Court noted that it applied the *New York Times* actual malice requirement in the discrete context of a statutory privacy action brought by a private individual who was involved in a matter of public interest. [In Rosenbloom v. Metromedia (1974), in a] * * * divided opinion, the Court later required private figures in defamation actions to prove actual malice if the published material was matter of public or general concern. * * *

The Court substantially altered the direction of First Amendment law in Gertz v. Robert Welch, Inc., 418 U.S. 323, 94 S.Ct. 2997 * * * (1974) * * * Abandoning *Rosenbloom's* focus on whether defamatory matter was a matter of public concern, the *Gertz* court established a public figure-private figure dichotomy. See Braun v. Flynt, 726 F.2d at 249 & n. 6. * * * [S]tates had a greater interest in protecting private figures who had not "invite[d] attention and comment" and who generally lack effective opportunities for rebuttal." * * * After *Gertz,* states were permitted to establish negligence as a standard of care in defamation actions by private plaintiffs so long as the recovery was limited to actual damages. To recover punitive damages, however, private plaintiffs were required to satisfy the *New York Times* actual malice standard.

* * *

On the particular issue of standard of care under false light [privacy law], the Restatement (Second) of Torts § 652E Caveat & Comments d (1976) leaves open the possibility that liability may be based on a showing of negligence as to truth or falsity. "If Time v. Hill is modified along the lines of Gertz v. Robert Welch, then the reckless-disregard rule would apparently apply if the plaintiff is a public official or public figure and the negligence rule will apply to other plaintiffs." Restatement (Second) of Torts § 652E comment d at 399.

SEC. 39. DEFENSES: CONSENT

If a person has consented to have his privacy invaded, that individual cannot later sue to collect damages.

In addition to *newsworthiness,* another important defense to a lawsuit for invasion of privacy is *consent.* Logically enough, if a person has consented to have his privacy invaded, he should not be allowed to sue for the invasion. As Warren and Brandeis wrote in their 1890 *Harvard Law Review* article, "The right to privacy ceases upon the publication of the facts by the individual or with his consent." [82]

The defense of consent, however, poses some difficulties. To make this defense stand up, it must be *pleaded* and *proved* by the defendant. An important rule here is that the *consent* must be as broad as the invasion.

A young man had consented to have his picture taken in the doorway of a shop, supposedly discussing the World Series. But the youth was understandably chagrined when *Front Page Detective* used this photograph to illustrate a story titled "Gang Boy." The Supreme Court of New York allowed the young man to recover damages, holding that consent to one thing is not consent to another. In other words, when a photograph is used for a purpose not intended by the person who consented, that person may be able to collect damages for invasion of privacy.[83]

In the case of Russell v. Marboro Books, a professional model was held to have a suit for invasion of privacy despite the fact that she had signed a release. (In the states which have privacy statutes—California, New York, Oklahoma, Utah, Wisconsin and Virginia—prior consent in writing is required before a person's name or picture can be used in advertising or "for purposes of trade.") Miss Russell, at a picture-taking session had signed a printed release form: [84]

Model release

> The undersigned hereby irrevocably consents to the unrestricted use by * * * [photographer's name], advertisers, customers, successors and assigns of my name, portrait, or picture, for advertising purposes or purposes of trade, and I waive the right to inspect or approve such completed portraits, pictures or advertising matter used in connection therewith * * *.

[82] Warren and Brandeis, op. cit., p. 218.

[83] Metzger v. Dell Pub. Co., 207 Misc.2d 182, 136 N.Y.S.2d 888 (1955).

[84] Russell v. Marboro Books, Inc., 18 Misc.2d 166, 183 N.Y.S.2d 8 (1955).

Miss Russell maintained that her job as a model involved portraying an "intelligent, refined, well-bred, pulchritudinous, ideal young wife and mother in artistic settings and socially approved situations." Her understanding was that the picture was to depict a wife in bed with her "husband"—also a model—in bed beside her, reading. Marboro books did use the pictures in an advertisement, with the caption "For People Who Take Their Reading Seriously." Thus far, there was no invasion of privacy to which Miss Russell had not consented.

Marboro Books, however, sold the photograph to Springs Mills, Inc., a manufacturer of bed sheets which enjoyed a reputation for publishing spicy ads. The photo was retouched so that the title of the book Miss Russell was reading appeared to be *Clothes Make the Man,* a book which had been banned as pornographic. The advertisement suggested that the book should be consulted for suitable captions, and also suggested captions such as "Lost Weekend" and "Lost Between the Covers." The court held that Miss Russell had an action for invasion of privacy despite the unlimited release that she had signed. Such a release, the court reasoned, would not stand up "if the picture were altered sufficiently in situation, emphasis, background, or context * * * liability would accrue where the content of the picture had been so changed that it is substantially unlike the original."[85]

Even if a signed release is in one's possession, it would be well to make sure that the release is still valid. In a Louisiana case, a man had taken a body-building course in a health studio. This man had agreed to have "before" and "after" photos taken of his physique, showing the plaintiff's body in trunks. Ten years later, the health studio used the pictures in an ad. The court held that privacy had been invaded.[86]

Also, it would be well to make sure that you have explicit consent. On occasion, courts have found that the circumstances of a publication were such that there was *implied consent.* One such instance was when a person published a personal letter himself, and then sued to prevent further publication of the letter. The court held that the man had forfeited his right to prevent the letter's appearing in another publication.[87]

The best rule is this: make sure that the consent or release is broad and explicit enough to cover any invasion of privacy which might be claimed. A casual, offhand consent may be taken back at any time before publication actually takes place. Even celebri-

[85] Ibid.

[86] McAndrews v. Roy, 131 So.2d 256 (La.App.1964).

[87] Widdemer v. Hubbard, 19 Phil. 263 (Pa.1887), cited in Hofstadter and Horowitz, op.cit., p. 75.

ties such as movie stars have brought suit when they felt that their performances had been put to uses which they did not intend. Comedienne Beatrice Lillie, for example, sued Warner Bros. Pictures, contending that her contract with the company did not include the use of her performances in "short subjects." However, the court held that Miss Lillie's consent to such use of the film was included in her contract.[88]

If the topic of consent in media law does not make for wary publishers, it should. Hustler magazine was hoaxed by a snapshot and an un-neighborly neighbor, and lost a $150,000 invasion-of-privacy case as a result. Billy and LaJuan Wood, husband and wife, went for a skinny-dip swim at a secluded spot at a wilderness area in a state park. After swimming, they playfully took several photos of each other in the nude. Billy had the film developed by a business using a mechanical developing process, and they treated the snapshots as private, not showing them to others and keeping them out of sight in a drawer in their bedroom.

One Steve Simpson, a neighbor living in the other side of the Woods' duplex, broke into the Woods' home and stole some of the photos. Simpson and Kelly Rhoades, who was then his wife, submitted the nude photo of LaJuan to Hustler magazine for publication in its "Beaver Hunt" section.

Simpson and Rhoades filled out a consent form that requested personal information. They gave some true information about LaJuan Wood (her identity, and her hobby of collecting arrowheads), but also gave some false information such as LaJuan's age and a lurid sex fantasy attributed to her. Kelley Rhoades forged LaJuan's signature and the photograph and consent form were mailed to Hustler in California. The faked consent form did not list a phone number but gave Kelley Rhoades' address as the place where Hustler was to send the $50 it was to pay for each photo used in the "Beaver Hunt" section.[89]

After Hustler selected LaJuan's photo, Kelley Rhoades received and answered a mailgram addressed to LaJuan and phoned Hustler. A Hustler staff member then had about a two-minute conversation with Rhoades; that was the extent of the magazine's checking for consent.[90]

Hustler magazine urged that the action should fail under the one-year statute of limitations applying to defamation in Texas. The Court of Appeals, however, chose to keep the privacy action

---

[88] Lillie v. Warner Bros. Pictures, 139 Cal.App. 724, 728, 34 P.2d 835 (1934), see also Fairbanks v. Winik, 119 Misc. 809, 198 N.Y.S.2d 299, 301 (1922).

[89] Wood v. Hustler, 736 F.2d 1084, 1085–1086 (5th Cir.1984), 10 Med.L.Rptr. 2113–2114.

[90] 736 F.2d 1084 (5th Cir.1984), 10 Med.L.Rptr. at 2114.

alive under a two-year statute of limitations.[91]   Hustler further argued that it should not be held liable for placing LaJuan Wood in a false light because it did not publish in reckless disregard of the truth, having no serious doubts about the falsity of the consent form.[92]   However, the U.S. Court of Appeals for the Fifth Circuit held that since LaJuan Wood was a private figure [93] who need prove only negligent behavior in order to collect damages.   In upholding the trial court damage award to her of $150,000, the Court of Appeals said: [94]

> Hustler carelessly administered a slipshod procedure that allowed LaJuan be placed in a false light in the pages of Hustler Magazine.   The nature of material published in the Beaver Hunt section would obviously warn a reasonably prudent editor or publisher of the potential for defamation or privacy invasion if a consent form was forged.   The wanton and debauched sexual fantasies and the intimate photos of nude models were of such a nature that great care was required in verifying the model's consent.

Cher v. Forum International

Or, consider the famed entertainer "Cher."   Evidently she is determined to control as much of her performer's image as possible.   She willingly consented to and taped an interview with radio talk show host Fred Robbins, a writer who sells celebrity interviews to magazines.   Cher said she had consented to the interview believing she had an agreement that the resulting article was to appear in *US* magazine.   *US* did not run the interview, but instead returned it to Robbins with a "kill" fee.   Robbins then sold the interview to the sensational tabloid *Star* and to a pocket-sized magazine called *Forum*.   That publication was owned by Forum International, of which Penthouse International owned 80% of the stock.[95]

Cher sued, bringing a legal action which had—among other things—aspects of the "false light" branch of privacy law.   She did

---

[91] 736 F.2d 1084 (5th Cir.1984), 10 Med.L.Rptr. at 2114.   The Woods had sued for both libel and invasion of privacy; the libel action was ruled out because of the one-year statute of limitations on defamation, Tex.Civ.Stat.Ann.Art. 5524; however, the two-year limitations period of Art. 5526 was held to apply to false-light privacy cases.   Billy Woods' invasion of privacy action was disallowed because the publication of the photo did not invade his privacy.

[92] 736 F.2d 1084 (5th Cir.1984), 10 Med.L.Rptr. at 2116.

[93] See discussion of public figures in defamation law, Chapter 4, Sections 21 and 22.

[94] 736 F.2d 1084 (5th Cir.1984), 10 Med.L.Rptr. at 2119.

[95] Cher v. Forum International, et al., 692 F.2d 634, (9th Cir.1982), 8 Med.L.Rptr. 2484, 2485.

not claim that the interview was defamatory, nor did she complain that private facts had been published without her consent. Instead, her complaint charged breach of contract, unfair competition, and *misappropriation* of her name and likeness and of her *right to publicity.* Beyond the legal labels, Cher was complaining about the appearance she consented to for a much "tamer" kind of magazine, *US,* only to have it appear in the juicy tabloid *Star* and the generally salacious *Forum,* creating misleading impressions.[96]

Cher accused *The Star* of having falsely represented that she had given that publication an exclusive interview, which would be degrading to her as a celebrity, given the nature of that tabloid. The Court of Appeals held, however, that *The Star's* promotional claim of an "Exclusive Interview" did not constitute knowing or reckless falsity under the doctrine of Time, Inc. v. Hill.[97] Therefore, the judgment against *The Star* was reversed.[98]

Forum magazine, however, after identifying Fred Robbins as the interviewer, made it appear that *Forum* itself was the poser of the questions put to Cher. Cher complained through her attorneys that this created the false impression that she had given an interview directly to *Forum.* She argued that this exploited her celebrity value by implying that she endorsed *Forum.* Her name and likeness were used in promotional subscription "tear out" ads: "There are certain things that Cher won't tell *People* and would never tell *US.* She tells *Forum.*" [99]

The Court of Appeals ruled that publishers can use promotional ads or literature so long as there is no false claim that a celebrity endorsed the publication involved. Court of Appeals Judge Goodwin wrote, "* * * [T]he advertising staff [of Forum] engaged in the kind of knowing falsity that strips away the protection of the First Amendment."[1] The Court of Appeals cut the original damage award to Cher from the trial court's figure of more than $600,000 to roughly $200,000.[2]

When a defendant does not have consent and does invade someone's privacy, good intentions are not a defense. It may be pleaded that the defendant honestly believed that he had consent, but this can do no more than to mitigate punitive damages. Some

[96] 692 F.2d at 638 (9th Cir.1982), 8 Med.L.Rptr. 2484, 2485.

[97] 385 U.S. 374, 87 S.Ct. 534 (1967); this key privacy decision is discussed in Section 38.

[98] 692 F.2d at 638 (9th Cir.1982), 8 Med.L.Rptr. 2484, 2486.

[99] Ibid. The U.S. Court of Appeals, 9th Circuit, found that Robbins did not participate in the publishing, advertising, or marketing of the articles, and the trial court judgment against him was vacated. Also, it was stipulated at the trial court level that there was no contract between Cher and Robbins.

[1] 692 F.2d at 640 (9th Cir.1982), 8 Med.L.Rptr. 2484, 2487.

[2] Ibid.; see also News Media & The Law, Sept./Oct. 1983, pp. 17–18.

of the consequences of a publication's not getting a clear and specific consent from persons whose pictures were used in a magazine article may be seen in the case of Raible v. Newsweek. According to Eugene L. Raible, a Newsweek photographer visited his home in 1969, and asked to take a picture of Mr. Raible and his children in their yard for use in "a patriotic article." Then, the October 6, 1969, issue of that magazine featured an article which was headlined on the cover, "The Troubled American—A Special Report on the White Majority." [3] Newsweek did use Mr. Raible's picture (with his children cropped out of it); he was wearing an open sport shirt and standing next to a large American flag mounted on a pole on his lawn. The article ran for many pages thereafter, with such marginal headlines as "You'd better watch out, the common man is standing up," and "Many think the blacks live by their own set of rules." [4] Mr. Raible sued for libel and for invasion of privacy.

Although Raible's name was not used in the story, the court said it was readily understandable that his friends and neighbors in Wilkinsburg, Pa., might consider him to be typical of the "square Americans" discussed in the article. Raible argued that his association with the article meant that he was being portrayed as a "* * * typical 'Troubled American,' a person considered 'angry, uncultured, crude, violence prone, hostile to both rich and poor, and racially prejudiced.' " [5]

District Judge William W. Knox granted *Newsweek* a summary judgment, thus dismissing Mr. Raible's libel claims. Judge Knox declared that since the article indicated that the views expressed are those of the white majority of the United States—of whom Mr. Raible was one—"then we would have to conclude that the article, if libelous, libels more than half of the people in the United States and not plaintiff in particular." [6]

Judge Knox declared, however, that Mr. Raible's invasion of privacy lawsuit appeared to stand on firmer ground. Directing that Raible's privacy lawsuit go to trial, Judge Knox wrote: [7]

> It is true that if plaintiff [Raible] consented to the use of his photograph in connection with *this article,* he would have waived his right of action for invasion of privacy. However, it would appear to the court that the burden of proof is upon the defendant to show just what

[3] Raible v. Newsweek, Inc., 341 F.Supp. 804, 806, 809 (1972).

[4] Ibid., p. 805.

[5] Ibid., p. 806. See also De Salvo v. Twentieth Century Fox Film Corp., 300 F.Supp. 742 (D.C.Mass.1969).

[6] Ibid., p. 807.

[7] Ibid., p. 809.

plaintiff consented to and the varying inferences from this testimony will have to be resolved by the trier of facts.

SEC. 40. DEFENSES: LIMITATIONS AND PROBLEMS

Privacy is a relatively new region of law which has had much unplanned growth. Complexities and confusions affect defenses to privacy lawsuits.

Journalists should not take much comfort in the defenses available for use against suits for invasion of privacy. As noted in Section 37 of this chapter, the concept of "newsworthiness" can prove to be so elastic that it is dangerously subject to the whims of a judge or jury. Also, some courts now seem to be becoming more restrictive in their definitions of "news" and "public interest." Beyond that, being able to defend successfully against a privacy-invasion suit is only part of the equation: even for winners, the costs in dollars and time expended can be enormous.

As may be seen from reading this chapter, the "privacy" concept is many things: a generalized feeling about a "right to be let alone;" it is a constitutional right against some kinds of *governmental* interference in our lives, and it is a growing and increasingly complex body of tort law. As Victor A. Kovner has suggested, perhaps the privacy area must now receive some drastic rethinking and reworking.[8]

> Since "privacy" seems next to motherhood in the minds of many public officials, and apparently to some members of the judiciary as well, perhaps the time has come to abandon the term, at least as applied to these kinds of claims. The torts might simply be referred to as intrusion claims, embarrassing facts or "intimacy" claims, false light claims, misappropriation claims, and right of publicity claims. Privacy has little to do with many of these claims. * * * [O]veruse of the term "invasion of privacy" may only contribute to further misunderstanding of the field and further infringement of First Amendment rights.

Privacy is a new area of law, and has not had the centuries of trial-and-error development that attended the law of defamation. This relative newness is a great source of privacy law's danger for the media. Over time, defenses to defamation were built up: for one thing, truth was made a defense. And where slander is concerned, "special damages"—actual monetary loss—must gener-

---

[8] Kovner, op. cit., p. 251.

ally be proved before a plaintiff can collect. Where retraction statutes are in force, a plaintiff must prove special damages once a fair and full apology for the defamation has been published.[9] But with the law of privacy, the media do not have such shields. In only one of the privacy tort sub-groups discussed above—"putting plaintiff in a false position in the public eye"—is truth be a defense to a privacy action. Also, a publication need not be defamatory to invade someone's privacy.

Small wonder, then, that some eminent scholars have viewed the law of privacy as a threat to freedom of the press. Professor William L. Prosser has suggested that the law of privacy, in many respects, comes "into head-on collision with the constitutional guaranty of freedom of the press." He said privacy law may be "capable of swallowing up and engulfing the whole law of public dafamation."[10]

If, for example, a newspaper were to be sued for *both* libel and invasion of privacy for the same article, difficulties in making a defense hold up might well arise. If the publication were defamatory, the newspaper might be able to plead and prove truth as a defense. But proving truth would not halt the privacy suit unless the article had to do with "putting plaintiff in a false position in the public eye." It could be possible, if a plaintiff *alleged* that a newspaper printed "embarrassing private facts," that proving the truth of an article might encourage a sympathetic jury to find against the newspaper for invasion of privacy.

This means that an article containing no defamation, based on true facts, and published with the best of intentions or through an innocent mistake could be the basis for a successful invasion of privacy lawsuit. If, indeed, it becomes easier to collect for an invasion of privacy suit than for a defamation action, it has been suggested that privacy suits may supplant libel actions.[11]

The foregoing discussion has concentrated on invasion of privacy as a tort. Privacy, however, is protected not only by tort law—in which individuals may sue for damage if their privacy is invaded. Since 1960, privacy has become a constitutional right, a

---

[9] When the fact situation giving rise to a privacy action also involves defamation, retraction statutes have been held to apply. Werner v. Times-Mirror Co., 193 Cal. App.2d 111, 14 Cal.Rptr. 208 (1961).

[10] Prosser, Handbook of the Law of Torts, 3rd ed., p. 844; 4th ed. (1971), pp. 815–816; "Privacy," 48 California Law Review 383, 401 (1960).

[11] Zuckman, op. cit., citing I Prentice-Hall Government Disclosure Service, p. 30,001 (1980), and Biweekly Comparison of Key Statutes, National Law Journal, February 11, 1980, pp. 12–14.

right which to some extent protects citizens from intrusions by government or police agencies.[12]

Precisely because privacy is a hot political issue, it needs to be watched carefully lest it do great damage to First Amendment concerns. The Freedom of Information Act of the federal government was passed in 1966, and was amended in 1975. And while that was dedicated to disclosure of information, it was accompanied by a measure dedicated to non-disclosure of information (at least where the press is concerned). The Privacy Act of 1974 was passed in an effort to give citizens some control over the government's enormous system of dosiers, and to let individuals see and correct files about themselves. The Privacy Act also limited disclosure of individually identifiable information by federal agencies.

Some observers have contended that the federal Privacy Act is not in conflict with the Freedom of Information Act. Others, including Supreme Court reporter Lyle Denniston, disagree, arguing that the emphasis on privacy is likely to damage newsgathering through the loss of "inside" sources of information often vital to covering sensitive stories about government. His point is that when bureaucrats are torn between disclosure of information and retention of information, the safest course will seem to be against disclosure.

As Professor Harvey Zuckman has noted: [13]

> The idea behind the federal statute has spread to the states and as of May [1980] * * * 16 states had enacted some kind of privacy act * * * and 17 states have legislation providing for expungement [erasure] of non-conviction arrest records. * * *

But why shouldn't arrest records be sealed? After all, not all persons arrested—and thereby shown to be suspected of committing a crime—*have* committed a crime. Even when an innocent person is arrested, a so-called "criminal record" is created. Why shouldn't such records be sealed—hidden away for all time—or expunged, wiped off the record? Alan Westin has written that there are many instances of suicides and nervous breakdowns resulting from exposures by government investigations, press stories about such situations, and even published research. Westin said this should " 'constantly remind a free society that only grave social need can ever justify destruction of the privacy which

---

[12] John W. Wade, "Defamation and the Right of Privacy," 15 Vanderbilt Law Review 1093, 1121 (1962); Prosser, "Privacy" loc. cit.

[13] See, e.g., Mapp v. Ohio, 367 U.S. 643, 81 S.Ct. 1684 (1961); Griswold v. Connecticut, 381 U.S. 479, 85 S.Ct. 1678 (1965).

guards the individual's ultimate autonomy [over dissemination of information about oneself].' "[14]

On the other hand, in Minnesota, a teen-aged girl was placed in a foster home with a convicted sex offender. The Welfare Department that placed her there did not know about the sex offender because the agency was not allowed access to criminal records. Also, it is—or should be—a truism among journalists that the police and the jails and the courts need the closest scrutiny possible if this society is to retain its key freedoms. In order to preserve due process of law, information about police and judicial activities must be kept public and published in the press. As W.H. Hornby, editor of *The Denver Post,* has declared: [15]

> We still need to know who is in jail and what the charges are against him. We still need to know who has been indicted. If we don't insist on this knowledge, we are in the same position as the Germans who, in their privacy, wondered about the sighing cargoes of those long freight trains that passed in the night.

Infliction of Mental Distress

If there's a wild card or joker in an area of law related to privacy or defamation, some scholars will tell you it is called "infliction of mental distress." It is sometimes called "intentional infliction," sometimes "negligent infliction." And sometimes, it is talked about as "outrage."

This "infliction of mental distress" area, like other tort areas does not apply merely to the mass media. Nevertheless, a late-1984 case involving the Rev. Jerry Falwell certainly got the attention of media law specialists. Larry Flynt's raunchy Hustler magazine, in a would-be parody of a well known liquor advertisement, suggested that Moral Majority leader Falwell's behavior included drunkenness and incest.

On December 8, 1984, a Federal district court jury in Roanoke, Virginia, declined to find that the phony ad libeled Falwell. The ad was simply too farfetched to be believed. And if it could not be believed, it could not libel the evangelist.

The jury, however, found that Larry Flynt and Hustler should pay Falwell $200,000 in damages for emotional injury or distress. Flynt's own testimony did not help the publisher's case: he said he thought the ad was hilarious and that he was out to "assassinate" Falwell. Evidently believing Flynt's word that he intended to

---

[14] Alan F. Westin, Privacy and Freedom (New York: Atheneum, 1970), pp. 33–34, quoted in Wright, op. cit.

[15] W.H. Hornby, "Secrecy, Privacy and Publicity," Columbia Journalism Review, March-April, 1975, p. 11, quoted in Clancy, op. cit.

harm Falwell, the jury awarded damages for intentional infliction of emotional distress.[16]

First Amendment lawyer Floyd Abrams viewed this case with a jaundiced eye. He told The New York Times that the infliction of mental distress theory could create "an end run around constitutional protections for people who want to being libel suits but know they can't win them." Abrams added that every case involving Larry Flynt tests the First Amendment's outer limits, which may result in creating case law "which affords fewer constitutional protections to all our citizens." [17]

In any case, this theory of mental injury or outrage is abroad among lawyers, and—as privacy expert Victor Kovner has suggested at sessions of the Practising Law Institute, there are cases showing that theory is becoming practice.[18]

[16] Falwell v. Flynt, No. 830155–4, D.C.Va., Dec. 8, 1985, appeal docketed No. 83–0155 (4th Cir., April 22, 1985); discussed in News Media and the Law, Spring, 1985, p. 3, and in David Margolick, "Some See Threat in Non-Libel Verdict of Falwell," The New York Times, December 10, 1984, p. 15.

[17] Quoted in The New York Times, Ibid.

[18] See Victor Kovner, "Recent Developments in Intrusion, False Light, and Commercialization Claims," in James C. Goodale, chairman, Communications Law 1984, Volume II (New York: Practising Law Institute, 1984), pp. 455–461.

SEC. 41. DEVELOPMENT OF COPYRIGHT LAW

Copyright is the right to control or profit from a literary, artistic or intellectual production.

A furious Mark Twain once declared that every time copyright law was to be made, then all the idiots assembled. That was back around the turn of the century, and his anger was fueled by his helplessness to prevent unscrupulous individuals from making unauthorized use of his writings. In fact, Twain lobbied for passage of the Copyright Act of 1909, which was to remain the basic law for almost 70 years.

By the mid-1970s, that horse-and-buggy-era statute was pathetically out-of-date. Over the years, amendments to the 1909 statute were not sweeping, and were analogous to re-arranging the deck chairs on the Titanic. Copyright law was a prime example of an area where technology ran off and left efforts to regulate it. Think about 1909. The photocopying machine was unknown, and so were computers and communications satellites. Radio ("wireless") was a scientific curiosity and movies were little beyond the "magic lantern" stage.

The first major change in copyright statutes since 1909 was signed into law October 19, 1976, by President Gerald R. Ford, and went into effect January 1, 1978.[1] Passage of that law was a remarkable event. Copyright revision had been underway in Congress since 1961, with massive snags lurking all about. Where onrushing technology did not cause problems, vigorously competing special interest groups did. Take photocopying. Teachers and librarians wanted few if any restraints on photocopying, while

---

[1] One of the more useful sources in studying these changes in House of Representatives Report No. 94–1476, "Copyright Law Revision." Title 17, United States Code, "Copyrights," was amended in its entirety by Public Law 94–553, 94th Congress, 94 Stat. 2541 (1976). Also essential for study of this field is Melville B. Nimmer, Nimmer on Copyright, 4 vols. (New York: Matthew Bender, 1963–1985).

authors and publishers wanted to halt any copying which could cut into the sale of so much as one book or magazine.[2]

Copyright Defined

Black's Law Dictionary defines copyright as: [3]

> The right of literary property as recognized and sanctioned by positive law. An intangible, incorporeal right granted by statute to the author or originator of certain literary or artistic productions, whereby he is invested, for a limited period, with the sole and exclusive privilege of multiplying copies of the same and publishing and selling them.

Such definitions aside, journalists must have a basic understanding of this complicated, frustrating area of law. Perhaps this area of law is so complex because it draws authority from a number of bases: Anglo-American literary history and common law, state and federal laws, court decisions, plus Article I, Section 8 of the Constitution of the United States: [4]

> The Congress shall have power * * * to promote the Progress of Science and useful Arts by securing for limited Times to Authors and Inventors the exclusive Right to their respective Writings and Discoveries.

Passage of the first federal copyright statute as early as 1790 indicates that America's Revolutionary generation had a lively concern about the need for copyright protection. Additional copyright statutes were enacted during the 19th century.[5]

History of Copyright

Underlying the words of Article I, Section 8 of the Constitution was the principle of copyright, which had been known since ancient times. It is known that the Republic of Venice in 1469 granted John of Speyer the exclusive right to print the letters of Pliny and Cicero for a period of five years.[6]

The development of printing increased the need for some form of copyright. Although printing from movable type began in 1451 and although Caxton introduced printing into England in about

---

[2] For a view of efforts to resolve such disputes, see H.R. Report No. 94–1476, "Copyright Law Revision," pp. 66–70. The guidelines there were later approved by the Senate-House conference committee which hammered out the final bill.

[3] Black's Law Dictionary, 5th ed. (St. Paul, Minn., West Publishing Co.) p. 304.

[4] Benjamin Kaplan and Ralph S. Brown, Jr., Cases on Copyright (Brooklyn, Foundation Press, 1960) pp. 22–52.

[5] Thorvald Solberg, Copyright Enactments of the United States, 1783–1906. Washington, 1906.

[6] R.C. DeWolf, Outline of Copyright Law (Boston: John W. Luce, 1925) p. 2.

1476, the first copyright law was not passed in England until 1790 in the "Statute of 8 Anne." Before this time, the printing business was influenced in two distinct ways. First, printing gave royalty and government in England the opportunity to reward favored individuals with exclusive printing monopolies. Second, those in power recognized that printing, unless strictly controlled, tended to endanger their rule.

Hoping to control the output of the printing presses, Queen Mary I granted a charter to the Stationers Company in 1556. The Stationers Company, a guild of printers, thus was given a monopoly on book printing. Simultaneously these printers were given the authority to burn prohibited books and to jail the persons who published them.[7] The Stationers Company acted zealously against printers of unauthorized works, making use of terrifying powers of search and seizure. Tactics paralleling those of the Inquisition were used defending the doctrines of the Catholic Church against the burgeoning Reformation movement.[8]

The Stationers Company remained powerful into the seventeenth century, with its authority augmented by licensing statutes. The Act of 1662, for example, confined printing to 59 master printer members of the Stationers Company then practicing in London, and to the printers at Oxford and Cambridge Universities. The privileged position of the Stationers Company in England during the sixteenth and seventeenth centuries underlies the development of the law of copyright of more recent times. Printers who were officially sanctioned to print by virtue of membership in the Stationers Company complained when their works were issued in pirated editions by unauthorized printers.[9]

In time, the guild printers who belonged to the Stationers Company began to recognize a principle now known as "common law copyright." They began to assume that there was a common law right, *in perpetuity*, to literary property. That is, if a man printed a book, duly approved by government authority, the right to profit from its distribution remained with that man, or his heirs, forever.[10]

Authors, like England's printers, came to believe that they also had some rights to profit from their works. Authors joined printers in the latter half of the seventeenth century in seeking Parliamentary legislation to establish the existence of copyright.

[7] Philip Wittenberg, The Law of Literary Property (New York: World Publishing Co., 1957), pp. 25–26; Fredrick S. Siebert, Freedom of the Press in England, 1476–1776 (Urbana: University of Illinois Press, 1952) pp. 22, 65, 249.

[8] Siebert, op. cit., pp. 82–86; Mrs. Edward S. Lazowska, "Photocopying, Copyright, and the Librarian," American Documentation (April, 1968) pp. 123–130.

[9] Siebert, pp. 74–77, 239.

[10] Wittenberg, op. cit., pp. 45–46.

In 1709, Parliament passed the Statute of 8 Anne, believed to have been drafted, in part, by two famed authors, Joseph Addison and Jonathan Swift. This statute recognized the authors' rights, giving them—or their heirs or persons to whom they might sell their rights—exclusive powers to publish the book for 14 years after its first printing. If the author were still alive after those 14 years, that person could renew copyright for an additional 14 years.[11]

This limitation of copyright to a total of 28 years displeased both authors and printers. They complained for many years that they should have copyright in perpetuity, forever, under the common law. In 1774, the House of Lords, acting in its capacity of a court of the highest appeal, decided the case of Donaldson v. Beckett.

This 1774 decision was of enormous importance to the history of American law, because it outlined the two categories of copyrights, *statutory copyright* and *common law copyright*. The House of Lords ruled that the Statute of 8 Anne, providing a limited 28 year term of copyright protection, had superseded the common law protection for *published* works. Only *unpublished* works, therefore, could receive common law copyright protection in perpetuity. An author was to have automatic, limitless common law copyright protection for his creations only as long as they remained unpublished. But once publication occurred, the author or publisher could have exclusive right to publish and profit from his works for only a limited period of time as decreed by legislative authority. The Statute 8 Anne, as upheld by the House of Lords in Donaldson v. Beckett, is the ancestor of modern copyright legislation in the United States.[12]

When the first federal copyright statute was adopted in the United States in 1790, implementing Article I, Section 8 of the Constitution, it gave the federal government *statutory* authority to administer copyrights. Since there was no common law authority for federal courts, questions involving *common law* copyright remained to be adjudicated in state courts.[13] In the 1834 case of Wheaton v. Peters, the Supreme Court of the United States enunciated the doctrine of common law copyright in America: [14]

> That an author at common law has a property right in his manuscript, and may obtain redress against any one who endeavors to realize a profit by its publication,

[11] Siebert, op. cit., p. 249; Wittenberg, Ibid., pp. 47–48.

[12] Burr. 2408 (1774); Lazowska, op. cit., p. 124.

[13] Wheaton v. Peters, 33 U.S. (8 Peters) 591 8 L.Ed. 1055 (1834); W.W. Willoughby, Constitutional Law of the United States, p. 446.

[14] 8 Pet. 561, 657, 8 L.Ed. 1055 (1834); Hirsh v. Twentieth-Century Fox Films Corp., 207 Misc. 750, 144 N.Y.S.2d 38, 105 U.S.P.Q. 253 (1955).

cannot be doubted; but this is a very different right from that which asserts a perpetual and exclusive property in the future publication of the work, after the author shall have published it to the world.

Congress seemingly tried to do away with common law copyrights, phasing them out of existence with Sec. 301 of the Copyright Act of 1976. Of course, there would have to be a transitional period: Sec. 301 specifically preserved common law copyrights which were in effect before January 1, 1978—the effective date of the 1976 Copyright Act.

Common law copyright had both advantages and disadvantages. Its advantages were that it was automatic and perpetual so long as a manuscript or creation was not published. An author could circulate a manuscript among friends, could use it in class for experimental teaching materials, or, perhaps, could send it to several publishing houses without publication in the technical, legal sense. In general, as long as the manuscript was not offered to the general public, common law copyright protection remained intact.

Published works, however, had to have a copyright notice—for example, © John Steinbeck, 1941—in a specified place on a book or manuscript or other copyrightable item or the work would fall into the public domain. That meant that once "in the public domain" the work lacked copyright protection, and that anyone who wished to do so could republish the work for his or her own profit.[15]

The Copyright Act of 1976 was intended to allow the federal government to supersede entirely the states' authority to deal with copyright. The federal statute's language certainly sounds preemptive: " * * * no person is entitled to any such [copy] right or equivalent right in any such work under the common law or statutes of any State." [16] Confusingly and annoyingly for persons looking for uniformity in copyright law, state power impinging on copyright has not gone away.

As Howard B. Abrams has pointed out, the vaguely defined tort of "misappropriation" as dealt with in state courts has led to a chaotic situation in conflict with Sec. 301 of the 1976 Copyright Act. So, is copying to continue to be both a misappropriation ("wrongful taking") under the laws of various states or is it to be equivalent to an action for copyright infringement under the federal Copyright Act of 1976? Howard B. Abrams has written: [17]

---

[15] 17 U.S.C.A. § 102.

[16] H.R. Report No. 94–1476, pp. 146–149.

[17] Howard B. Abrams, "Copyright, Misappropriation, and Preemption: Constitutional and Statutory Limits of State Law Protection," pp. 75–147 in David Gold-

If anything, S301 [of the 1976 Copyright Act] has frustrated congressional intent to create "a single Federal system" and proliferated the "vague borderline areas between State and Federal protection" which Congress so sincerely yet so artlessly sought to avoid.

The Nature of Copyright

Copyright is an exclusive, legally recognizable claim to literary or pictorial property. It is a right, extended by federal statute, to entitle originators to ownership of the literary or artistic products of their minds. Before launching into more detailed discussion of provisions of the copyright statute now in force, consider the following three principles:

(1) *Facts or ideas cannot be copyrighted.* Copyright applies only to the literary style of an article, news story, book, or other intellectual creation. It does *not* apply to the themes, ideas, or facts contained in the copyrighted material. Anyone may write about any subject. Copyright's protection extends only to the particular manner or style of expression. What is "copyrightable" in the print media, for example, is the order and selection of words, phrases, clauses, sentences, and the arrangement of paragraphs.[18]

(2) *Copyright is both a protection for and a restriction of the communications media.* Copyright protects the media by preventing the wholesale taking of the form of materials, without permission, from one person or unit of the media for publication by another person or unit of the media. Despite the guaranty of freedom of the press, newspapers and other communications media must acquire permission to publish material that is protected by copyright.[19]

(3) *As a form of literary property, copyright belongs to that class of personal property including patents, trade-marks, trade names, trade secrets, good will, unpublished lectures, musical compositions, and letters.*

    (a) Copyright, it must be emphasized, is quite different from a patent. Copyright covers purely composition, style of expression or rhetoric, while a patent is the

berg, Chairman, Current Developments in Copyright Law, 1985 (New York: Practising Law Institute), at p. 147, quoting H.R. Report No. 94–1476 (1976), at p. 130. See also Abrams' pp. 83ff, for discussion of state cases endeavoring to deal with copying of sound recordings.

[18] Kaeser & Blair, Inc. v. Merchants Ass'n, 64 F.2d 575, 577 (6th Cir.1933); Eisenshiml v. Fawcett, 246 F.2d 598 (7th Cir.1957).

[19] Cf. Chicago Record-Herald Co. v. Tribute Ass'n, 275 F. 797 (7th Cir.1921).

right given to protect a novel idea which may be expressed physically in a machine, a design, or a process.

(b) Copyright may be distinguished from a trademark in that copyright protects a particular literary style while a trade-mark protects the sign or brand under which a particular product is made or distributed.

(c) When someone sends you a letter, you do not have the right to publish that letter. You may keep the letter, or throw it away; indeed, you can do anything you wish with the letter but publish it. Although the recipient of a letter gets physical possession of it—of the paper it is written upon—the copyright ownership remains with the sender.[20]

SEC. 42. SECURING A COPYRIGHT

Essentials in acquiring a copyright include notice of copyright, application, deposit of copies in the Library of Congress, and payment of the required fee.

What May Be Copyrighted

Reflecting awareness that new technologies will emerge and that human ingenuity will devise new forms of expression, the language of the new copyright statute is sweeping in defining what may be copyrighted. Section 102 says: [21]

(a) Copyright protection subsists * * * in original works of authorship fixed in any tangible medium of expression, now known or later developed, from which they can be perceived, reproduced, or otherwise communicated, either directly or with the aid of a machine or device. Works of authorship include the following categories:

(1) literary works;

(2) musical works, including any accompanying words;

(3) dramatic works, including any accompanying music;

(4) pantomimes and choreographic works;

(5) pictorial, graphic, and sculptural works;

(6) motion pictures and other audiovisual works; and

(7) sound recordings.

---

[20] Baker v. Libbie, 97 N.E. 109, 210 Mass. 599 (1912); Ipswich Mills v. Dillon, 157 N.E. 604, 260 Mass. 453 (1927). See also Alan Lee Zegas, "Personal Letters: A Dilemma for Copyright and Privacy Law," 33 Rutgers Law Review (1980) pp. 134–164. Writers who seek relief for unauthorized publication may sue for recovery under both copyright and privacy theories, although the author suggests that those areas of law offer writers inadequate protection.

[21] 17 U.S.C.A. § 102.

(b)   In no case does copyright protection for an original work of authorship extend to any idea, procedure, process, system, method of operation, concept, principle, or discovery, regardless of the form in which it is described, explained, illustrated, or embodied in such work.

The Copyright Notice

Under the 1976 statute, once something has been published the omission of a copyright notice or an error in that notice does not destroy the author or creator's protection.[22] Section 405 gives a copyright owner up to five years to register a work with the Register of Copyrights, Library of Congress, Washington, D.C., even if that work has been published without notice. (Formerly, under the 1909 statute, publication without notice could mean that the authors lost any copyrights in their works if a defective notice—or no notice at all—was used.)[23] The copyright owner, however, must make a reasonable effort to add a copyright notice to all copies or phonorecords distributed in the United States after the omission has been discovered.[24]

Section 401 makes the following general requirement about placing copyright notices on "visually perceptible copies."[25]

Whenever a work protected under this title [Title 17, United States Code, the copyright statute] is published in the United States or elsewhere by authority of the copyright owner, a notice of copyright in this section shall be placed on all publicly distributed copies from which the work can be visually perceived, either directly or with the aid of a machine or device.

The copyright notice shall consist of these three elements: [26]

(1)   the symbol © (the letter C in a circle), or the word "Copyright" or the abbreviation "Copr."; and

(2)   the year of first publication of the work; in the case of compilations or derivative works incorporating previously published material, the year date of the first publication of the compilation or derivative work is sufficient. The year date may be omitted where a pictorial, graphic, or sculptural work, with accompanying text matter, if any, is

[22] 17 U.S.C.A. §§ 405, 406.

[23] Leon H. Amdur, Copyright Law and Practice (New York: Clark Boardman Co., 1936), pp. 64–65; Holmes v. Hurst, 174 U.S. 82, 19 S.Ct. 606 (1899).

[24] 17 U.S.C.A. § 405.

[25] 17 U.S.C.A. § 401(a).

[26] 17 U.S.C.A. § 401(b).

reproduced in or on greeting cards, postcards, stationery, jewelry, dolls, toys, or any useful articles; and

(3)   the name of the owner of copyright abbreviation by which the name can be recognized or a generally known alternative designation of the owner.

If a sound recording is being copyrighted, the notice takes a different form. The notice shall consist of the following three elements: [27]

(1)   The symbol P (the letter P in a circle); and

(2)   the year of first publication of the sound recording; and

(3)   the name of the owner of copyright in the sound recording, or an abbreviation by which the name can be recognized, or a generally known alternative designation of the owner; if the producer of the sound recording is named on the phonorecord labels or containers, and if no other name appears in conjunction with the notice, the producer's name shall be considered a part of the notice.

The copyright statute adopts one of the former law's basic principles: in the case of works made for hire, the employer is considered the author of the work (and therefore the initial copyright owner) unless there has been an agreement to the contrary. The statute requires that any agreement under which the employee will own rights be in writing and signed by both the employee and the employer.[28]

The copyright notice shall be placed on the copies "in such manner and location as to give reasonable notice of the claim of copyright." Special methods of this "affixation" of the copyright notice and positions for notices on various kinds of works will be prescribed by regulations to be issued by the Register of Copyrights.[29]

Duration of Copyright

A most welcome change under the new statute sets copyright duration at the life of the owner plus 50 years. This replaced the fouled-up and complicated system of the 1909 statute of an initial period of 28 years plus a renewal period of another 28 years. Renewals had to be applied for, and if unwary copyright owners waited a full 28 years to apply for their second term, they had waited too long and their works became part of the public domain—everybody's property. Also, the U.S. system was badly out

[27] 17 U.S.C.A. § 402(b), (c).

[28] 17 U.S.C.A. § 201(b); see discussion of this section in House of Representatives Report No. 94–1476, "Copyright Law Revision."

[29] 17 U.S.C.A. § 401(c).

of step with a great majority of the world's nations which had adopted a copyright term of the author's life plus 50 years. As noted in the legislative commentary accompanying the 1976 statute,[30]

> * * * American authors are frequently protected longer in foreign countries than in the United States . . . [This] disparity in the duration of copyright has provoked * * * some proposals of retaliatory legislation. * * * The need to conform the duration of U.S. copyright to that prevalent throughout the rest of the world is increasingly pressing in order to provide certainty and simplicity in international business dealings. Even more important, a change in the basis of our copyright term would place the United States in the forefront of the international copyright community. Without this change, the possibility of future United States adherence to the Berne Copyright Union would evaporate, but with it would come a great and immediate improvement in our copyright relations.

Existing works already under statutory copyright protection at the time of passage of the new copyright statute have had their copyright duration increased to 75 years. Works now in their first 28-year copyright under the old system must be renewed if they are in their 28th year, but the second term will be expanded to 47 years to provide a total of 75 years' protection. For copyrighted works in their renewal term, 19 years will be added so that copyright on such works will exist for a total of 75 years.[31] Congress repeatedly extended the terms of expiring copyrights from 1964 to 1975, in anticipation of the enactment of copyright revision.[32]

Copyright Registration and Deposit

As in the past, copyright registration will be accomplished by filling out a form obtainable from:

> Register of Copyrights
> Library of Congress
> Washington, D.C. 20559

(In addition, corresponding with the Publications Division, Copyright Office, Library of Congress 20559 can yield much helpful information. See, for example, Copyright Office R–1, Copyright Basics. Also, in 1983 a Copyright Hotline was made availa-

---

[30] H.R. Report No. 94–1476, p. 135, discussing 17 U.S.C.A. § 302.

[31] 17 U.S.C.A. § 304.

[32] See H.R. Report No. 94–1476, p. 140.

ble to provide information on kinds of forms needed for various kinds of registration: (202) 287–8700, weekdays between 8:30 and 5 p.m.)

The Register of Copyrights will require (with some exceptions specified by the Copyright Office), that material deposited for registration shall include two complete copies of the best edition.[33] (The deposit of two copies of each work being copyrighted has built the collections of the Library of Congress.) These copies are to be deposited within three months after publication, along with a completed form as prescribed by the Register of Copyrights.[34] A fee of $10 must be paid for most items being copyrighted.[35] It should be noted that registration is required before any action for copyright infringement can be started.[36]

If an individual carries out a "bluff copyright"—that is, places a copyright notice on a work at the time of publication without bothering to register it and deposit copies as outlined above, that person could have some difficulties with the Register of Copyrights. The Register of Copyrights may demand deposit of such unregistered works. Unless deposit is made within three months, an individual may be liable to pay a fine of up to $250. If a person "willfully or repeatedly" refuses to comply with such demand, a fine of $2,500 may be imposed.[37]

Authors and the Copyright Act of 1976

The sweeping copyright revision which went into effect in 1978—compared to its 1909 predecessor—is truly the author's friend. As Professor Kent R. Middleton has pointed out, authors' ownership of rights under the old statute was precarious indeed. "One change," Middleton wrote, "which makes copyright divisible, gives the author greater flexibility in selling his work to different media. The other, vesting initial ownership with the creator of a work, makes the author's title more secure." [38]

Under the 1909 statute, a single legal title was held by a "proprietor" to any writing or artistic creation. Typically if an author sold the right to publish a work, he sold *all* rights to his

---

[33] 17 U.S.C.A. § 407. Other useful circulars available late in 1985 from the Publications Division of the Copyright include Circular Ric, Copyright Registration Procedures; Circular R22, How to Investigate the Copyright Status of a Work, and Circular R21, Reproduction of Copyrighted Works by Educators and Librarians.

[34] 17 U.S.C.A. § 407.

[35] Payment of fees is specified by 17 U.S.C.A. § 708.

[36] 17 U.S.C.A. § 411; see also 17 U.S.C.A. § 205.

[37] 17 U.S.C.A. § 407(d).

[38] Kent R. Middleton, "Copyright and the Journalist: New Powers for the Free-Lancer," Journalism Quarterly 56:1 (Spring, 1979), p. 39.

creation.[39]　Under the revised statute, authors can sell *some* rights or *all* rights as they wish.　In that way, a writer may sell "one-time rights"—for use of his work only once—and then will keep other rights to re-sell the same work.　For example, a magazine article—such as "The Urban Cowboy," published in *Esquire Magazine* —became the basis for a smash motion picture of the same name.　Under § 201 of the revised copyright act, an author retains ownership in anything he does unless he or she *expressly* signs away all rights to a publisher.[40]

Free-lance journalists should beware of the phrase "work made for hire."　Under both the old and new laws, a work produced while working for an employer constituted a "work made for hire," and all rights in that work belong to the employer.　As Professor Middleton has warned, "a free-lancer's commissioned work may also be considered a work made for hire if a publisher can get a free lancer to agree." [41]

Journalists should also pay attention to what kinds of rights they are selling.　If you sell "all rights," your financial stake in a piece of work is at an end.　Perhaps it would be better for you to sell "first serial rights"—which will allow, for example, a magazine to publish your writing one time anywhere in the world.　Then, the rights to that work revert to you, the author.　Or, you might sell first North American rights, which would allow publication of your work one time in this part of the world, but not anywhere else.[42]

SEC. 43.　ORIGINALITY

The concept of originality means that authors or artists have done their own work, and that their work is not copied from or grossly imitative of others' literary or artistic property.

Originality is a fundamental principle of copyright;　originality implies that the author or artist created the work through his own skill, labor, and judgment.[43]　The concept of originality means that the particular work must be firsthand, pristine, not copied or imitated.　Originality, however, does not mean that the work must be necessarily novel or clever, or that it have any value as literature or art.　What constitutes originality was explained in

[39] Harry G. Henn, "Ownership of Copyright, Transfer of Ownership," in James C. Goodale, chairman, Communications Law 1979 (New York: Practising Law Institute, 1979) pp. 709–711.

[40] 17 U.S.C.A. § 201.

[41] Middleton, op. cit., p. 40.

[42] The Writer's Market.

[43] American Code Co. v. Bensinger, et al., 282 F. 829 (2d Cir.1922).

an old but frequently quoted case, Emerson v. Davis. The famous Justice Joseph Story of Massachusetts wrote in 1845: [44]

> In truth, in literature, in science and in art, there are, and can be, few, if any, things, which, in an abstract sense, are strictly new and original throughout. Every book in literature, science, and art, borrows, and must necessarily borrow, and use much which was well known and used before. No man creates a new language for himself, at least if he be a wise man, in writing a book. He contents himself with the use of language already known and used and understood by others. No man writes exclusively from his own thoughts, unaided and uninstructed by the thoughts of others. The thoughts of every man are, more or less, a combination of what other men have thought and expressed, although they may be modified, exalted, or improved by his own genius or reflection. If no book could be the subject of copyright which was not new and original in the elements of which it is composed, there could be no ground for any copyright in modern times, and we should be obliged to ascend very high, even in antiquity, to find a work entitled to such eminence. * * *

> An author has as much right in his plan, and in his arrangements, and in the combination of his materials, as he has in his thoughts, sentiments, opinions, and in his modes of expressing them. The former as well as the latter may be more useful or less useful than those of another author; but that, although it may diminish or increase the relative values of their works in the market, is no ground to entitle either to appropriate to himself the labor or skill of the other, as embodied in his own work.

> It is a great mistake to suppose, because all the materials of a work or some parts of its plan and arrangements and modes of illustration may be found separately, or in a different form, or in a different arrangement, in other distinct works, that therefore, if the plan or arrangement or combination of these materials in another work is new, or for the first time made, the author, or compiler, or framer of it (call him what you please), is not entitled to a copyright.

The question of originality seems clear in concept but this quality of composition is not always easy to separate and identify in particular cases. This is true especially when different authors have conceived like expressions or based their compositions upon

[44] 8 Fed.Cas. 615, No. 4,436 (C.C.Mass.1845).

commonly accepted ideas, terms, or descriptions in sequence. It must be borne in mind that an idea as such cannot be the subject of copyright; to be eligible for copyright, ideas must have particular physical expressions, as signs, symbols, or words. As was stated in Kaeser & Blair, Inc. v. Merchants' Association, Inc., "copyright law does not afford protection against the use of an idea, but only as to the means by which the idea is expressed." [45]

Artistic treatment is one element in the consideration of copyright but not an absolutely necessary element. One might compile a directory of residents of a city, giving names, occupations, places of business and residence; information about the names and addresses of individuals cannot be subject to copyright. But when thousands of citizens' names are compiled, together with directory information about them, that creates an item which may be copyrighted. In Jewelers' Circular Publishing Co. v. Keystone, a court stated: [46]

> The right to copyright a book upon which one has expended labor in its preparation does not depend upon whether the materials which he has collected consist or not of matters which are *publici juris* [news of the day], or whether such materials show literary skill or originality, either in thought or language, or anything more than industrious collection. The man who goes through the streets of a town and puts down the names of each of the inhabitants, with their occupations and their street number, acquires material of which he is the author.

While such a compiler would have no right to copyright information on a mere listing of one man and his address and occupation, he would have a right to copyright a compilation of a large number of such names, their addresses, and occupations.

In sum, then, the best advice is this: do your own work. You may keep it in mind that the law does not copyright ideas or facts; only the manner in which these ideas or facts are expressed is protected by the law of literary property. As the Supreme Court of the United States said in 1899, "the right secured by copyright is not the right to forbid the use of certain words or facts or ideas by others; it is a right to that arrangement of words which the author has selected to express his ideas which the law protects." [47] Or, as a Circuit Court of Appeals said so aptly in 1951, " 'Original'

[45] 64 F.2d 575, 577 (6th Cir.1944). See also, Holmes v. Hurst, 174 U.S. 82, 19 S.Ct. 606 (1899); Eisenshiml v. Fawcett Publications, Inc., 246 F.2d 598, 114 U.S. P.Q. 199 (7th Cir.1957).

[46] Jewelers' Circular Pub. Co. v. Keystone Pub. Co., 281 F. 83, 88, 26 A.L.R. 571 (2d Cir.1922).

[47] Holmes v. Hurst, 174 U.S. 82, S.Ct. 606 (1899); Van Renssalaer v. General Motors, 324 F.2d 354 (6th Cir.1963).

in reference to a copyrighted work means that the particular work 'owes its origin' to the author. No large measure of novelty is necessary." [48] Thus, if care is taken to express ideas in one's own words—and to do one's own research or creative work—you are not likely to run afoul of copyright law.

SEC. 44. INFRINGEMENT AND REMEDIES

Violation of copyright includes such use or copying of an author's work that his possibility of profit is lessened.

Anyone who violates any of the exclusive rights spelled out by Sections 106 through 108 of the copyright statute is an infringer. Section 106 provides that copyright owners have the exclusive rights to do and to authorize any of the following: [49]

(1) to reproduce the copyrighted work in copies or phono records;

(2) to prepare derivative works based upon the copyrighted work;

(3) to distribute copies or phonorecords of the copyrighted work to the public by sale or other transfer of ownership, or by rental, lease or lending;

(4) in the case of literary, musical, dramatic, and choreographic works, to perform the copyrighted work publicly, and

(5) in the case of literary, musical, dramatic and choreographic works, pantomimes, and motion pictures and other audiovisual works, including the individual images of a motion picture or other audiovisual work, to display the copyrighted work publicly.

The next section of the statute—Section 107—inserted sizable limitations on the above-enumerated "exclusive rights" by sketching—in broad terms—the judicially created doctrine of fair use. Fair use is discussed in some detail in Section 46 later in this chapter.

[48] Lin-Brook Builders Hardware v. Gertler, 352 F.2d 298, 301 (9th Cir.1965) quoting Alfred Bell & Co., Ltd. v. Catalda Fine Arts, Inc., 191 F.2d 99, 102 (2d Cir. 1951). See also Runge v. Lee, 441 F.2d 579 (9th Cir.1971), certiorari denied 404 U.S., 887, 92 S.Ct. 197 (1971).

[49] 17 U.S.C.A. § 106. Note, however, that these "exclusive rights" are subject to limitations as spelled out in §§ 107 ("Fair Use"), 108 ("Reproduction by Libraries and Archives,"), 109 ("Effect of transfer of a particular copy or phonorecord"), and 110 ("Exemption of certain performances and displays," as by instructors or pupils in teaching activities in non-profit educational institutions.) See, also, §§ 111–118, dealing with secondary transmissions by cable TV systems, ephemeral recordings, pictorial, sculptural and graphic works, sound recordings, plays, juke boxes, computers and information systems, and certain works' use in non-commercial broadcasting.

It should be kept in mind that copyright law is now analogous to old wine in a new bottle. The "bottle" which holds this area of law together, so to speak, is the new statute. But its provisions, by and large, will be interpreted to a considerable extent in terms of copyright cases—some decided many years ago.

In order to win a lawsuit for copyright infringement, a plaintiff must establish two separate facts, as the late Circuit Judge Jerome N. Frank wrote some years ago: "(a) that the alleged infringer copied from plaintiff's work, and (b) that, if copying is proved, it was so 'material' or substantial as to constitute unlawful appropriation." [50] Even so, the material copied need not be extensive or "lengthy" in order to be infringement. "In an appropriate case," Judge Frank noted, "copyright infringement might be demonstrated, with no proof or weak proof of access, by showing that a simple brief phrase, contained in both pieces, was so idiosyncratic in its treatment as to preclude coincidence.[51] Judge Frank also noted that even a great, famous author or artist might be found guilty of copyright infringement. He wrote, "we do not accept the aphorism, when a great composer steals, he is 'influenced'; when an unknown steals, he is 'infringing.' "[52]

Copyright protection continues even though a usurper gives away the copyrighted material or obtains his profit on some associated activity. The old case of Herbert v. Shanley (1917) is relevant here. Shanley's restaurant employed musicians to play at mealtimes. Victor Herbert's song "Sweethearts," was performed, but no arrangement had been made with Herbert or his representatives to use the song. Defendant Shanley argued that he had not infringed upon Herbert's copyright because no profit came from music which was played merely to lend atmosphere to his restaurant. The Supreme Court of the United States, however, held that Shanley had benefited from the playing of the music.[53]

As under the former statute, a court may, in its discretion, award full court costs plus a "reasonable attorney's fee" to the winning party in a copyright lawsuit.[54] A plaintiff in an infringement suit also may opt to ask for "statutory damages" rather than actual damage and profits: [55]

> (1)   *   *   * the copyright owner may elect, at any time before final judgment is rendered, to recover, instead of actual

[50] Heim v. Universal Pictures Co., 154 F.2d 480, 487 (2d Cir.1946).

[51] Ibid., p. 488.

[52] Ibid.

[53] 242 U.S. 591, 37 S.Ct. 232 (1917).

[54] 17 U.S.C.A. § 505.

[55] 17 U.S.C.A. § 504(c)(1), (2).

damages and profits, an award of statutory damages for all infringements involved in the action, with respect to any one work, for which any one infringer is liable individually, or for which any two or more infringers are liable jointly and severally, in a sum of not less than $250 or more than $10,000 as the court considers just. * * *

(2) In a case where the copyright owner sustains the burden of proving, and the court finds, that infringement was committed willfully, the court in its discretion may increase the award of statutory damages to a sum of not more than $50,000. In a case where the infringer sustains the burden of proving, and the court finds, that such infringer was not aware and had no reason to believe that his or her acts constituted an infringement of copyright, the court in its discretion may reduce the award of statutory damages to a sum of not less than $100.

If you own a copyright and it is infringed upon, you have an impressive arsenal of remedies or weapons under the 1976 copyright statute.

For openers, if you know that someone is infringing on your copyright or can prove is about to do so, a federal court has the power to issue temporary and final injunctions "on such terms as it may deem reasonable to prevent or restrain injunctions." [56] Furthermore, this injunction may be served on the suspected copyright infringer anywhere in the United States.[57] That's a form, in other words, of prior restraint at the disposal of an affronted copyright owner.

A copyright owner may also apply to a federal court to get an order to impound "on such terms as it may deem reasonable, * * * all copies or phonorecords claimed to have been made or used in violation of the copyright owner's exclusive rights."[58] And, if a court orders it as part of a final judgment or decree, the articles made in violation of the copyright owner's exclusive rights may be destroyed or otherwise disposed of.[59]

A copyright infringer, generally speaking, is liable for either of two things: (1) the copyright owner's actual damages and any

[56] 17 U.S.C.A. § 502(a). For an example of an unsuccessful attempt to get an injunction, see Belushi v. Woodward, 598 F.Supp. 36 (D.D.C.1984), 10 Med.L.Rptr. 1870. Case involved widow of actor John Belushi asking that author Bob Woodward and publisher Simon & Schuster be enjoined from publishing book because of allegedly unauthorized use of her copyrighted photo.

[57] 17 U.S.C.A. § 502(b).

[58] 17 U.S.C.A. § 503(a).

[59] 17 U.S.C.A. § 503(b).

additional profits of the infringer * * * or (2) statutory damages.[60]

Actual Damages and Profits

Consider the statute's language on "actual damages and profits": [61]

> The copyright owner is entitled to recover the actual damages suffered by him or her as a result of the infringement, and any profits of the infringer that are attributable to the infringement and are not taken into account in computing actual damages. In establishing the infringer's profits, the copyright owner is required to present proof only of the infringer's gross revenue, and the infringer is required to prove his or her deductible expenses and the elements of profit attributable to factors other than the copyrighted work.

"Damages are awarded to compensate the copyright owner for losses from the infringement, and profits are awarded to prevent the infringer from unfairly benefiting from a wrongful act."[62]

In seeking to recover profits from a copyright infringer, the burden of proof falls upon the plaintiff to show the gross sales or profits arising from the infringement. The copyright infringer is permitted to deduct any legitimate costs or expenses which he can prove were incurred during publication of the stolen work. The winner of a suit to recover profits under copyright law can receive only the *net profits* resulting from an infringement. As the Supreme Court of the United States has declared, " 'The infringer is liable for actual, not for possible, gains.' "[63]

Net profits can run to a great deal of money, especially when the work is a commercial success as a book or motion picture. Edward Sheldon sued Metro-Goldwyn Pictures Corp. and others for infringing on his play, "Dishonored Lady" through the production of the Metro-Goldwyn film, "Letty Lynton." A federal district court, after an accounting had been ordered, found that Metro-Goldwyn had received net profits of $585,604.37 from their exhibitions of the motion picture.[64]

Mr. Sheldon did not get *all* of Metro-Goldwyn's net profits from the movie, however. On appeal, it was held that Sheldon

[60] 17 U.S.C.A. § 504(a).

[61] 17 U.S.C.A. § 504(b).

[62] H.R.Rep. No. 94–1476 (Sept. 3, 1976), "Copyright Law Revision," p. 161.

[63] Sheldon v. Metro-Goldwyn Pictures Corp., 309 U.S. 390, 400–401, 60 S.Ct. 681, 683 (1940); Golding v. R.K.O. Radio Pictures, Inc., 35 Cal.2d 690, 221 P.2d 95 (1950).

[64] Sheldon v. Metro-Goldwyn Pictures Corp., 26 F.Supp. 134, 136 (D.C.N.Y.1938), 81 F.2d 49 (2d Cir.1936).

should not benefit from the profits that motion picture stars had made for the picture by their talent and box-office appeal. Sheldon, after his case had been heard by both a United States Court of Appeals and the Supreme Court of the United States, came out with "only" 20 per cent of the net profits, or roughly $118,000. It still would have been much cheaper for Metro-Goldwyn simply to have bought Sheldon's script. Negotiations with Sheldon for his play had been started by Metro-Goldwyn, but were never completed. The price for movie rights to the Sheldon play was evidently to be about $30,000, or slightly more than one-fourth of the amount the courts awarded to the playwright.[65]

Copyright cases involving music have proved to be difficult. The evidence in such cases is largely circumstantial, resting upon similarities between songs. The issue in such a case, as one court expressed it, is whether "so much of what is pleasing to the ears of lay listeners, who comprise the audience for whom such popular music is composed, that defendant wrongfully appropriated something which belongs to the plaintiff."[66]

More than "lay listeners" often get involved in such cases, however. Expert witnesses sometimes testify in copyright infringement cases involving music. But it can happen that the plaintiff who feels that his musical composition has been stolen, and the defendant as well, will *both* bring their own expert witnesses into court, where these witnesses expertly disagree with each other.[67]

In proving a case of copyright infringement—and not just for those cases dealing with music—it is often useful if plaintiffs can show that the alleged infringement had "access" to the original work from which the copy was supposed to have been made. Such "access" needs to be proved by the plaintiff, if only by the circumstantial evidence of similarity between two works.

During the 1940s, songwriter Ira B. Arnstein tried to show that the noted composer, Cole Porter, not only had access to his work, but that Porter had plagiarized freely from Arnstein. The courts declared that Porter had not infringed upon any common law or statutory copyrights held by Arnstein. Porter's victory in the courts was hard-won, however.

Arnstein began a copyright infringement lawsuit against Cole Porter in a federal district court. Arnstein charged that Porter's "Begin the Beguine" was a plagiarism from Arnstein's "the Lord is My Shepherd" and "A Mother's Prayer." He also claimed that

[65] 309 U.S. 390, 398, 407, 60 S.Ct. 681, 683, 687 (1940).

[66] Arnstein v. Porter, 154 F.2d 464, 473 (2d Cir.1946).

[67] Ibid.

Porter's "My Heart Belongs to Daddy" had been lifted from Arnstein's "A Mother's Prayer."

On the question of access, plaintiff Arnstein testified that 2,000 copies of "The Lord is My Shepherd" had been published, and sold, and that over one million copies of "A Mother's Prayer" had been published and sold. Furthermore, Arnstein complained that his apartment had been burglarized and accused Porter of receiving the stolen manuscripts from the burglars. Arnstein declared that Porter's "Night and Day" had been stolen from Arnstein's "I Love You Madly," which had never been published but which had been performed once over the radio. Technically, this meant that Arnstein's "I Love You Madly" had never been published.

In reply, Porter swore that he had never seen or heard any of Arnstein's compositions, and that he did not know the persons said to have stolen them. Even so, Arnstein's lawsuit asked for a judgment against Porter of "at least one million dollars out of the millions this defendant has earned and is earning out of all the plagiarism."[68]

At the original trial, the district court directed the jury to bring in a summary verdict in favor of Porter. Arnstein then appealed to the Circuit Court of Appeals, where Judge Jerome Frank explained what the appellate court had done. The Circuit Court of Appeals had listened to phonograph records of Cole Porter's songs and compared them to records of Arnstein's songs. As he sent the case back to a district court, jury, Judge Frank wrote:

> * * * we find similarities, but we hold that unquestionably, standing alone, they do not compel the conclusion, or permit the inference, that defendant copied. The similarities, however, are sufficient so that, if there is enough evidence of access to permit the case to go to the jury, the jury may properly infer that the similarities did not result from coincidence.

The jury then found that Cole Porter's "Begin the Beguine" had indeed been written by Cole Porter.

Similarly, the U.S. Court of Appeals, Second Circuit ruled that A.A. Hoehling could not collect damages from Universal City Studios in a dispute involving the motion picture, *The Hindenburg*. Back in 1962, Hoehling—after substantial research—published a copyrighted book, *Who Destroyed the Hindenburg?* That book advanced the theory that a disgruntled crew member of The Graf Zeppelin had planted a crude bomb in one of its gas cells.

---

[68] Ibid., 474.

Ten years later, after consulting Hoehling's book plus many other sources, Michael MacDonald Mooney published his own book, *The Hindenburg.* Mooney's book put forward a similar cause for the airship's destruction, but there was also evidence that authors pre-dating Hoehling had suggested the same cause for the explosion. Circuit Judge Kaufman said for the court: [69]

All of Hoehling's allegations of copying, therefore, encompass material that is non-copyrightable as a matter of law * * *.

* * *

* * * in granting * * * summary judgment for defendants, courts should assure themselves that the works before them are not virtually identical. In this case, it is clear that all three authors relate the story of the Hindenburg differently.

In works devoted to historical subjects, it is our view that a second author may make significant use of prior work, so long as he does not bodily appropriate the expression of another. *Rosemont Enterprises, Inc.,* 366 F.2d at 310. This principle is justified by the fundamental policy undergirding the copyright laws—the encouragement of contributions to recorded knowledge * * * Knowledge is expanded as well, by granting new authors of historical works a relatively free hand to build upon the work of their predecessors.

In Litchfield v. Spielberg, the U.S. Court of Appeals for the Ninth Circuit decided in 1984 that a copyright infringement/unfair competition lawsuit involving the movie *E.T.—The Extraterrestrial* was—if not out of this world—at least legally insupportable. Lisa Litchfield claimed that her copyrighted one-act musical play, Lokey from Maldemar, had been infringed upon by *E.T.,* the box-office smash hit. As the appeals court put it, the issue, in addition to that of infringement, was whether the lower court had acted properly in granting defendants a summary judgment.[70]

After independently reviewing the facts, the Court of Appeals held: [71]

There is no substantial similarity * * * between the sequences of events, mood, dialogue and characters of the two works. Any similarities in plot exist only at the

[69] Hoehling v. Universal City Studios, 618 F.2d 972, 979–980 (2d Cir.1980), 6 Med. L.Rptr. 1053, 1057–1058.

[70] Lisa Litchfield v. Steven Spielberg; MCA, Inc.; Universal City Studios, Inc.; Extraterrestrial Productions; Kathleen Kennedy; Ned Tanen, and Melissa Mathison, 736 F.2d 1352 (9th Cir.1984) 10 Med.L.Rptr. 2102–2103.

[71] 736 F.2d 1352 (9th Cir.1984), 10 Med.L.Rptr at 2105–2106.

general level for which plaintiff cannot claim copyright protection.　*　*　*

There is even less similarity of expression. To constitute infringement of expression, the total concept and feel of the works must be substantially similar. *Sid & Marty Krofft*, 562 F.2d at 1164. The concept and feel of the works here are completely different.

Whereas *E.T.* concentrates on the development of the characters and the relationship between a boy and an extraterrestrial, *Lokey* uses caricatures to develop its theme of mankind divided by fear and hate. No lay observer would recognize *E.T.* as a dramatization or picturization of *Lokey*.

*　*　*

As is too often the case, Litchfield's action was premised "partly upon a wholly erroneous understanding of the extent of copyright protection; and partly upon that obsessive conviction, so common among authors and composers, that all similarities between their works and any others to appear later must be ascribed to plagiarism." *Dellar v. Samuel Goldwyn, Inc.,* 150 F.2d 612 (2d Cir. 1945).

As noted in Section 41 of this chapter, facts or ideas are not copyrightable, only the style in which they are expressed.[72] An additional gloss was put on this by a 1978 case, Miller v. Universal City Studios, which raised the question whether the research effort put into gathering facts is copyrightable.

Pulitzer Prize-winning reporter Gene Miller of The Miami Herald collaborated on writing a book with Barbara Mackle about her ordeal in a famous kidnapping incident. Ms. Mackle was held for ransom while literally buried alive in a box with seven days' life-sustaining capacity. She was rescued from the box on the fifth day. Miller worked an estimated 2500 hours in researching and writing this book.

A Universal Studios executive, William Frye, then offered Miller $15,000 for rights to use the Miller-Mackle account in a television "docudrama." Miller refused, asking for $200,000. At this point, negotiations between Miller and the studio collapsed, but the studio—unwisely, as it turned out—proceeded to produce and air a docudrama titled "The Longest Night." This production had obvious similarities to the Miller-Mackle book, and Miller sued for copyright infringement.[73]

---

[72] See Section 41 at footnote 18, and 17 U.S.C.A. § 102.

[73] Miller v. Universal City Studios, 460 F.Supp. 984, 985–986 (S.D.Fla.1977).

The script writer had proceeded to write "The Longest Night" on the assumption that his studios had closed a deal with Miller for rights to the book and that he could proceed to write the script on that basis.[74] Even so, Universal City Studios argued that no matter how hard Miller had worked to research the facts in the Mackle kidnapping case, he "may not monopolize those facts because they are historical facts and everyone has the right to write about them and communicate them to the public." The court disagreed with Universal City Studios' argument, saying: [75]

> To this court it doesn't square with reason or common sense to believe that Gene Miller would have undertaken the research involved in writing of *83 Hours Till Dawn* (or to cite a more famous example, that Truman Capote would have undertaken the research required to write *In Cold Blood*) if the author thought that upon completion of the book a movie producer or television network could simply come along and take the profits of the books and his research from him. In the age of television "docudrama" to hold other than research is copyrightable is to violate the spirit of the copyright law and to provide to those persons and corporations lacking in requisite diligence and ingenuity a license to steal.

On appeal, however, Universal City Studios won a reversal of the judgment. The U.S. Court of Appeals, Fifth Circuit, ruled that Universal should have a new trial "* * * because the case was presented and argued to the jury on a false premise: that the labor of research by an author is protected by copyright." The Court of Appeals added that its decision was difficult to reach because there was "* * * sufficient evidence to support a finding of infringement * * * under correct theories of copyright law." In sum, the Court of Appeals did not believe that *research* is copyrightable, only the manner in which it is *presented.* "It is well settled that copyright protection extends only to an author's expression of facts and not to the facts themselves." [76]

Alex Haley, author of the smash best-seller *Roots,* was sued for both copyright infringement and unfair competition by Margaret Walker Alexander. Ms. Alexander claimed that Haley's book, published in 1976, was drawn substantially from her novel, *Jubilee,* published in 1966, and a pamphlet, *How I Wrote Jubilee,* published in 1972. A federal district court granted Haley a

---

[74] Ibid., p. 986.

[75] Ibid., p. 987n, 988.

[76] Miller v. Universal City Studios (U.S.Ct. of App., 5th Cir., July 23, 1981), 7 Med.L.Rptr. 1785, 1736.

summary judgment, finding that no copyright infringement had occurred. The court said: [77]

> Many of the claimed similarities are based on matters of historical or contemporary fact. No claim of copyright protection can arise from the fact that plaintiff has written about such historical and factual items, even if we were to assume that Haley was alerted to the facts in question by reading *Jubilee.*   *   *   *

> Another major category of items consists of material traceable to common sources, the public domain, or folk custom. Thus, a number of claimed infringements are embodiments of the cultural history of black Americans, or of both black and white Americans planning out the cruel tragedy of white-imposed slavery. Where common sources exist for the alleged similarities, or the material that is similar is otherwise not original with the plaintiff, there is no infringement.   *   *   * This group of asserted infringements can no more be the subject of copyright protection than the cause of a date or the name of a president or a more conventional piece of historical information.

Also, there can be *criminal* penalties for copyright infringement. The new statute ups the ante where phonorecord or movie pirates are concerned. Section 506 provides: [78]

> (a) CRIMINAL INFRINGEMENT.—Any person who infringes a copyright willfully and for purposes of commercial advantage or private financial gain shall be fined not more than $10,000 or imprisoned for not more than one year, or both: *Provided, however,* That any person who infringes willfully and for purposes of commercial advantage or private financial gain the copyright in a sound recording shall be fined not more than $25,000 or imprisoned for not more than one year, or both, for the first such offense and shall be fined not more than $50,000 or imprisoned for not more than two years, or both, for any subsequent offense.

Criminal penalties—fines of up to $2,500—await any person who, "with fraudulent intent," places on any article a notice of copyright that is known to be false. Similar fines may be levied against individuals who fraudulently remove a copyright notice, or

---

[77] Alexander v. Haley, 460 F.Supp. 40, 44–45 (S.D.N.Y.1978).

[78] 17 U.S.C.A. § 506. See also § 507, which orders a three-year statute of limitations for both criminal prosecutions and civil proceedings under the Copyright Statute.

who knowingly make misstatements in copyright applications or related written statements.[79]

SEC. 45. COPYRIGHT, UNFAIR COMPETITION, AND THE NEWS

The news element of a story is not subject to copyright, although the style in which an individual story is written may be protected from infringement. Reporters, in short, should do their own reporting.

Any unauthorized and unfair use of a copyrighted news story constitutes an infringement which will support either lawsuits for damages or an action in equity to get an injunction against further publication. Although a news story—or even an entire issue of a newspaper—may be copyrighted, the *news element* in a newspaper story is not subject to copyright. News is *publici juris*—the history of the day—as was well said by Justice Mahlon Pitney in the important 1918 case of International News Service v. Associated Press. Justice Pitney wrote: [80]

> A News article, as a literary production, is the subject of copyright. But the news element—the information respecting current events in the literary production, is not the creation of the writer, but is a report of matters that ordinarily are publici juris; it is the history of the day. It is not to be supposed that the framers of the Constitution, when they empowered Congress to promote the progress of science and useful arts, by securing for limited times to authors and inventors the exclusive rights to their respective writings and discoveries (Const. Art. 1, § 8, par. 8), intended to confer upon one who might happen to be first to report an historic event the exclusive right for any period to spread the knowledge of it.

The Associated Press had complained of news pirating by a rival news-gathering agency, International News Service. The Supreme Court granted the Associated Press an injunction against the appropriation, by INS, of AP stories while the news was still fresh enough to be salable. "The peculiar value of news," Justice Pitney declared, "is in the spreading of it while it is fresh; and it is evident that a valuable property interest in the news, as news, cannot be maintained by keeping it secret."

Justice Pitney also denounced the taking, by INS, of AP stories, either by quoting or paraphrasing. Justice Pitney wrote that INS, "in appropriating * * * news and selling it as its own is endeavoring to reap where it has not sown, and by disposing of

---

[79] 17 U.S.C.A. § 506(c), (d) and (e).

[80] 248 U.S. 215, 39 S.Ct. 68, 71 (1918).

it to newspapers that are competitors * * * of AP members is appropriating to itself the harvest of those who have sown."[81]

What, then, can a newspaper or other communications medium do when it has been "beaten" to a story by its competition? It must be emphasized that the historic case of International News Service v. Associated Press did *not* say that the "beaten" news medium must sit idly by. "Pirating" news, of course, is to be avoided: pirating has been defined as "the bodily appropriation of a statement of fact or a news article, with or without rewriting, but without independent investigation or expense."[82] However, first-published news items may be used as "tips." When one newspaper discovers an event, such as the arrest of a kidnaper, its particular news presentation of the facts may be protected by copyright. Even so, such a first story may serve as a tip for other newspapers or press associations. After the first edition by the copyrighting news organization, other organizations may independently investigate and present their own stories about the arrest of the kidnaper. In such a case, the time element between the appearance of the first edition of the copyrighting newspaper and the appearance of a second or third edition by a competing newspaper might be negligible as far as the general public is concerned; only a few hours. If other newspapers or press associations make their own investigations and obtain their own stories, they do not violate copyright.

However, to copy a copyrighted news story—or to copy or paraphrase substantially from the original story—may lead to court action, as shown in the 1921 case of Chicago Record-Herald Co. v. Tribune Association. This case arose when the *New York Tribune* copyrighted a special news story on Germany's reliance upon submarines. This story, printed in the *New York Tribune* on Feb. 3, 1917, was offered for exclusive publication in the *Chicago Herald*. The *Herald* declined this opportunity, and the *Chicago Daily News* then purchased the Chicago rights to the story.

With full knowledge that the *Tribune's* story on the German submarine campaign was fully copyrighted, the *Herald* nevertheless ran a rewrite of the same story on the morning of Feb. 3.

A comparison of the stories follows:

Chicago Herald

Germany Pins Hope of Fleet on 300 Fast Supersubmarines

New York, Feb. 3—3 a.m. (special.—The Tribune this morning in a copyrighted article by Louis Durant Ed-

[81] 248 U.S. 215, 239–240, 39 S.Ct. 68, 71–72 (1918).

[82] 248 U.S. 215, 243, 39 S.Ct. 68, 74 (1918).

wards, a correspondent in Germany, says that Germany to make the final effort against Great Britain has plunged 300 or more submersibles into the North Sea. These, according to this writer, were mobilized from Kiel, Hamburg, Wilhemshaven, and Bremerhaven where for months picked crews were trained.

"They form the world's first diving battle fleet," he says, "a navy equally prepared to fight above or beneath the waves."

There are two types of these new boats now in commission, one of 2,400 tons and one of 5,000 tons displacement.

They dive beneath the water in a fraction of the time that it takes the older types to submerge. They mount powerful guns, are capable of great surface speeds, and are protected by a heavy armor of tough steel plate.

The motors develop 7,000 horsepower and drive the boats under the surface at 22 knots an hour. These smaller cruisers carry a crew of from 60 to 80 men.

The submersibles have a radius of action of 8,000 miles.

New York Tribune

By Louis Durant Edwards. Copyright, 1917, by The Tribune Association (New York Tribune).

Germany plays her trumps. Three hundred or more submersibles have plunged into the waters of the North Sea to make the final effort against Great Britain. They mobilized from Kiel, Hamburg, Wilhemshaven, Bremerhaven, where, for months, picked crews have trained.

* * *

They form the world's first diving battle fleet, a navy equally prepared to fight above or beneath the waves.

* * *

There are two types of these new boats now in commission, one of 2,400 tons and one of 5,000 tons displacement.

* * *

They dive beneath the water in a fraction of the time that it took the older types to submerge. They mount powerful guns, are capable of great surface speeds, and are protected by a heavy armor of tough steel plate.

* * *

The motors develop 7,000 horsepower, and drive the boats over the surface at a speed of 22 knots an hour. These smaller cruisers carry a crew of from 60 to 80 men.

* * *

They have a radius of action of 8,000 miles.[83]

* * *

The *Chicago Daily News* then refused to publish the story or to pay the *New York Tribune* for it. The *Daily News,* having agreed to purchase an exclusive story, had the right to refuse a story already published in its market. The publishers of the *New York Tribune* successfully sued the *Chicago Herald* for infringement.

The judge declared that the *New York Tribune's* original story "involves authorship and literary quality and style, apart from the bare recital of the facts or statement of news." So, although facts are not copyrightable, the style in which they are expressed is protected by law.[84]

In International News Service v. Associated Press (1918), the AP won its case despite the fact that the news stories it telegraphed to its members were not copyrighted. There, the Supreme Court of the United States held that the AP had a "quasi property" right in the news stories it produced, even after their publication. Once the Supreme Court found that such a "quasi property" right existed, it then declared that appropriation of such stories by INS amounted to unfair competition and could be stopped by a court-issued injunction against INS.[85]

Far more recently, a newspaper—the Pottstown, Pa., *Mercury*—won an unfair competition suit against a Pottstown radio station, WPAZ, getting an injunction of which prevented WPAZ " 'from any further appropriation of the newspaper's local news without its permission or authorization.' "[86] The court noted that businesses, radio, television, and newspapers were "competing with each other for advertising which has become a giant in our economy." This court viewed the Pottstown *Mercury's* news as "a commercial package of news items to service its advertising business." In the rather jaundiced view of the Pennsylvania Supreme Court, advertising has become virtually all-important, with "the presentation of news and entertainment almost a subsidiary function of newspapers, radio and television stations." Although copy-

---

[83] 275 F. 797 (7th Cir.1921).

[84] Ibid.

[85] The case of International News Service v. Associated Press was cited as important by the more recent case of Pottstown Daily News Pub. Co. v. Pottstown Broadcasting Co., 411 Pa. 383, 192 A.2d 657, 662 (1963).

[86] Ibid.

right infringement was not the precise issue here, the Pennsylvania Supreme Court found itself able to punish the radio station for appropriating news stories under the area of law dealing with unfair competition. The court said:[87]

> * * * for the purpose of an action of unfair competition the specialized treatment of news items as a service the newspaper provides for advertisers gives the News Company [publishers of the Pottstown *Mercury*] a limited property right which the law will guard and protect against wrongful invasion by a competitor whereas, for the purpose of an action for the infringement of copyright, the specialized treatment of news is protected because the law seeks to encourage creative minds."

The limited property right in news is to some extent waived by member organizations of the Associated Press. All A.P. members are entitled to all *spontaneous* news from areas served by other A.P. member newspapers or broadcasting stations. Membership in the Associated Press includes agreement to follow this condition as stated in Article VII of the A.P. bylaws:

> Sec. 3. Each member shall promptly furnish to the [A.P.] Corporation all the news of such member's district, the area of which shall be determined by the Board of Directors. No news furnished to the Corporation by a member shall be furnished by the Corporation to any other member within such member's district.

> Sec. 4. The news which a member shall furnish to the Corporation shall be all news that is spontaneous in origin, but shall not include news that is not spontaneous in its origin, or which has originated through deliberate and individual enterprise on the part of such member.

A.P. member newspapers or broadcasting stations are expected to furnish spontaneous or "spot" news stories to the Associated Press for dissemination to other members throughout the nation. However, Section 3 of the A.P. By-Laws (above) will protect the news medium originating such a story within its district. If a newspaper copyrights a spot news story about the shooting of a deputy sheriff by a gambler, other A.P. members could use the story despite the copyright. By signing the A.P. By-Laws, the originating newspaper has given its consent in advance for all A.P. members to use news stories of *spontaneous* origin. On the other hand, if a newspaper copyrights an exposé of gambling in a city based on that newspaper's individual enterprise and initiative, the other A.P. members could not use the story without permission from the copyrighting newspaper.

[87] 411 Pa. 383, 192 A.2d 657, 663–664 (1963).

Roy Export Company v. CBS

Eagerness to present the news as effectively as possible in pressure situations may sometimes lead to disregard of ownership rights. Evident lack of concern about such rights cost the Columbia Broadcasting System $717,000 [88] in copyright and unfair competition damages for missteps making a documentary on the occasion of the death of film legend Charlie Chaplin. In 1977, CBS broadcast a film biography of Chaplin, including film clips from six Chaplin-motion pictures. Exclusive rights in those films were held by several parties, including the first-named plaintiff in this case, Roy Export Company Establishment of Vaduz, Liechtenstein.[89]

The events leading to this lawsuit are traceable to 1972, when the Academy of Motion Picture Arts and Sciences (AMPAS) arranged to have a film tribute made from highlights of Chaplin's films. This tribute was broadcast by NBC-TV in connection with an appearance by Chaplin at the 1972 Academy Awards ceremonies. It was understood that excerpts compiled in that tribute were to be used only on that one occasion.[90]

In 1973, CBS started work on a retrospective of Chaplin's life, to be used as a broadcast obituary when Chaplin died. CBS made repeated requests for permission to use excerpts from Chaplin's films, but was rebuffed. CBS was told that the copyright owners were involved in producing their own film biography of Chaplin titled "The Gentleman Tramp." That production used some of the same footage used in the Academy Awards show compilation, but did not use that compilation itself. CBS, meanwhile, made a "rough cut" of a Chaplin obituary/biography. The network was offered a chance to purchase rights to show "The Gentleman Tramp" in 1976 and 1977, but did not do so.

Chaplin died on Christmas day, 1977. CBS had its "rough cut" biography ready to use, but instead used a copy of the 1972 Academy Award show compilation which CBS had obtained from

[88] Roy Export Co. Estab. v. CBS, 672 F.2d 1095, 1097 (2d Cir.1982), 8 Med.L.Rptr. 1637, 1639. See footnote 6: "Of the compensatory total, $7,280 was for statutory copyright infringement, $1 was for common-law copyright infringement, and $300,000 was for unfair competition. The punitive damages were divided between the common-law claims: $300,000 for common-law copyright infringement and $110,000 for unfair competition.

[89] 672 F.2d 1095 (2d Cir.1982), 8 Med.L.Rptr. 1637, cert. denied 459 U.S. 826, 103 S.Ct. 60 (1983). This case was complicated, Circuit Judge Newman said, by troublesome questions coming from pre-1978 common law protection for intellectual property, plus challenges to statutory copyrights, "on the ground that the work lost its common copyright prior to January 1, 1978, entered the public domain, and therefore was not eligible for statutory copyright." Judge Newman cited M. Nimmer, Nimmer on Copyright, Sec. 4.01 [B].

[90] 672 F.2d at 1098 (2d Cir.1982), 10 Med.L.Rptr. at 1639.

NBC. CBS put together a new biography, depending heavily "on what CBS knew to be copyrighted material." This hastily assembled new biography was broadcast on December 26, 1977.[91]

Roy Export Company and other copyright owners of Chaplin films then sued CBS for copyright infringement and for unfair competition. The latter claim said the CBS broadcast competed unfairly with the copyright owners' own Chaplin retrospective, "The Gentleman Tramp." A jury trial in a U.S. district court found CBS liable to the plaintiffs for $307,281 compensatory and $410,000 punitive damages.

In its appeal, CBS asserted that the First Amendment provides a general privilege to report newsworthy events such as Chaplin's death, and that this privilege shielded the network from liability. CBS claimed that the main reason for Chaplin's fame was his films, and that it would be meaningless to try to provide a full account of his life without making use of his films. Circuit Judge Newman summed up the network's First Amendment argument:[92]

> In CBS's view, the 1972 Academy Awards ceremony, at which the Compilation received its single public showing, was an "irreducible single news event" to which the showing of the Compilation was integral. The significance of the ceremony, CBS contends, was not simply that Chaplin appeared after a twenty-year exile provoked by Senator [Joseph] McCarthy's investigations, but that a collection of his work was shown, thereby bringing home to the American people both what they had been deprived of by McCarthyism and how ludicrous had been the attempt to find subversion and political innuendo in Chaplin's films. CBS concludes that the plaintiff's claims for infringement of the copyright in the films and the compilation must give way to an asserted First Amendment news-reporting privilege.

The Court of Appeals found CBS's First Amendment arguments "unpersuasive," resting on a theory that someday, some way, there might be an inseparability of news value and copyrighted work to the extent that copyright would have to yield. Judge Newman wrote, however: "No Circuit that has considered the question * * * has ever held that the First Amendment provides a privilege in the copyright field distinct from the accommodation embodied in the 'fair use' doctrine." And in a footnote he added,[93]

---

[91] Ibid.

[92] 672 F.2d 1095, 1099 (2d Cir.1982), 10 Med.L.Rptr. 1095.

[93] 672 F.2d 1095, 1099 (2d Cir.1982), 10 Med.L.Rptr. 1637, 1640.

Fair use balances the public interest in the free flow of ideas and information with the copyright holder's interest in exclusive proprietary control of his work. It permits use of the copyrighted matter " 'in a reasonable manner without [the copyright owner's] consent, notwithstanding the monopoly granted to the owner.' " Rosemont Enterprises, Inc., v. Random House, Inc., 366 F.2d 303 (2d Cir.1966), cert. denied 385 U.S. 1009, 87 S.Ct. 714 * * * (1967) * * *.

The Roy Export case and Unfair Competition

CBS also argued that the plaintiffs could not maintain a claim that the network's December 26, 1977, broadcast unfairly competed with the plaintiffs' rights in "The Gentleman Tramp." CBS asserted the unfair competition claim rested on "misappropriation" of films under New York state law, " * * * and that a state law claim based on misappropriation of federally copyrighted materials is pre-empted * * * " [94] The Court of Appeals replied:

An unfair competition claim involving misappropriation usually concerns the taking and use of the plaintiff's property to compete against the plaintiff's use of the same property, e.g. International News Service v. Associated Press * * * [248 U.S. 215, 39 S.Ct. 68 (1918)] By contrast, in this case the Compilation was taken and used to compete unfairly with a different property, "The Gentleman Tramp." Despite the unusual facts, we are satisfied that the plaintiffs have established an unfair competition tort under New York law.

* * *

CBS unquestionably appropriated the "skill, expenditures and labor" of the plaintiffs to its own commercial advantage. Its actions, in apparent violation of its own and the industry's guidelines, were arguably a form of "commercial immorality." We are confident that the New York courts would call that conduct unfair competition.

The Court of Appeals ruled that the damages of more than $700,000 against CBS should stand, including the punitive damage awards totaling $410,000. Judge Newman wrote, "The deterrent potential of an award of $410,000 must be measured by its likely effect on a national television network with 1977 earnings of some $217,000,000 * * * " [95]

We now turn to a discussion of a major defense against claims of copyright infringement: the doctrine of "fair use."

[94] 697 F.2d at 1104–1105, (2d Cir.1982), 10 Med.L.Rptr. at 1644–1645.
[95] 697 F.2d at 1107 (2d Cir.1982), 10 Med.L.Rptr. at 1646.

SEC. 46.   THE DEFENSE OF FAIR USE

The fair use doctrine—invented by courts to allow some use of others' works—was made explicit by the Copyright Act of 1976.   Major cases—such as Sony and The Nation magazine—continue to add to the definition of fair use in a piecemeal fashion.

The copyright law phrase "fair use" made a good deal of news during the mid-1980s.   Its growth in importance is quite remarkable, stemming as it does from judicial wriggling many years ago. Its growth may be understood as being fueled, in a major way, by onrushing technological changes.   Recent examples of important fair use cases decided by the Supreme Court—and which are taken up later in this Section—are Sony Corporation of America v. Universal City Studios,[96] and Harper & Row v. Nation Enterprises.[97]

The old 1909 copyright statute gave each copyright holder an exclusive right to "print, reprint, publish, copy and vend the copyrighted * * *."   As stated in that Act, it was an *absolute* right; the wording was put in terms so absolute that even pencil-and-paper copying was a violation of the U.S. Copyright Act.[98] Because the 1909 statute's terms were so stringent, if enforced to the letter, it could have prevented anyone except the copyright holder from making any copy of any copyrighted work.   Such a statute was clearly against public policy favoring dissemination of information and knowledge and was plainly unenforceable.   As a result, courts responded by developing the doctrine called "fair use."

American courts assumed—in creating a judge-made exception to the absolute language of the 1909 copyright statute—that "the law implies the consent of the copyright owner to a fair use of his publication for the advancement of science or art." [99]   The fair use doctrine, although a rather elastic yardstick, was a needed improvement.   The 1976 copyright statute has distilled the old common law copyright doctrine into some statutory guidelines. Factors to be considered by courts in determining whether the use made of a work in any particular case is a fair use include: [1]

[96] 464 U.S. 417, 104 S.Ct. 774 (1984).

[97] __ U.S. __, 105 S.Ct. 2218 (1985).

[98] See 17 U.S.C.A. § 10 of the statute which preceded the Copyright Statute of 1976: Verner W. Clapp, "Library Photocopying and Copyright: Recent Developments," Law Library Journal 55:1 (Feb., 1962) p. 12.

[99] Wittenberg, op. cit., p. 148, offers a good non-technical description of fair use before it was expanded in 1967.   See section 44 in this chapter.

[1] 17 U.S.C.A. § 107.

(1) the purpose and character of the use, including whether such use is of a commercial nature or is for nonprofit educational purposes;

(2) the nature of the copyrighted work;

(3) the amount and substantiality of the portion used in relation to the copyrighted work as a whole; and

(4) the effect of the use upon the potential market for or value of the copyrighted work.

What, then, is fair use? In 1964, one expert asserted that fair use of someone's copyrightable materials exists "somewhere in the hinterlands between the broad avenue of independent creation and the jungle of unmitigated plagiarism."[2] No easy or automatic formula can be presented which will draw a safe line between fair use and infringement. Fifty words taken from a magazine article might be held to be fair use, while taking one line from a short poem might be labeled infringement by a court. The House of Representatives Committee on the Judiciary said this in its report on the 1976 copyright statute:[3]

General intention behind the provision

The statement of the fair use doctrine in section 107 offers some guidance to users in determining when the principles of the doctrine apply. However, the endless variety of situations and combinations of circumstances that can rise in particular cases precludes the formulation of exact rules in the statute. The bill endorses the purpose and general scope of the judicial doctrine of fair use, but there is no disposition to freeze the doctrine in the statute, especially during a period of rapid technological change. Beyond a very broad statutory explanation of what fair use is and some of the criteria applicable to it, the courts must be free to adapt the doctrine to particular situations on a case-by-case basis. Section 107 is intended to restate the present judicial doctrine of fair use, not to change, narrow, or enlarge it in any way.

Generally speaking, courts have been quite lenient with quotations used in scholarly works or critical reviews. However, courts have been less friendly toward use of copyrighted materials for commercial or non-scholarly purposes, or in works which are competitive with the original copyrighted piece.[4] The problems

[2] Arthur N. Bishop, "Fair Use of Copyrighted Books," Houston Law Review, 2:2 (Fall, 1964) at p. 207.

[3] H.R. Report No. 94–1476, discussing the fair use provisions of 17 U.S.C.A. § 107.

[4] Eisenshiml v. Fawcett Publications, Inc., 246 F.2d 598 (7th Cir.1957); Benny v. Loew's, Inc., 239 F.2d 532 (9th Cir.1956), affirmed 356 U.S. 43, 78 S.Ct. 667,

surrounding the phrase "fair use" have often arisen in connection with scientific, legal, or scholarly materials. With such works, it is to be expected that there will be similar treatment given to similar subject matters.[5] A crucial question, obviously, is whether the writer makes use of an earlier writer's work without doing substantial independent work. Wholesale copying is *not* fair use.[6] Even if a writer had no intention of making unfair use of someone else's work, that writer still could be found liable for copyright infringement.[7] The idea of independent investigation is of great importance here. Copyrighted materials may be used as a *guide* for the purpose of gathering information, provided that the researcher or writer then performs an original investigation and expresses the results of such work in his or her own language.[8]

Fair Use and Public Interest

Although many earlier cases expressed a narrow, restrictive view of the doctrine of fair use, some important decisions since the mid-1960s have emphasized the idea of *public* interest. This changed approach is of great importance to journalists and scholars, for where there are matters which are newsworthy or otherwise of interest to the public, courts will consider such factors in determining whether a fair use was made of copyrighted materials. A key case here is the 1967 decision known as Rosemont Enterprises, Inc. v. Random House, Inc. and John Keats. This case arose because Howard Hughes, a giant in America's aviation, oil and motion picture industries had a passionate desire to remain anonymously out of the public eye. A brief chronology will illustrate how this copyright infringement action came about:

• January and February, 1954: *Look* magazine, owned by Cowles Communications, Inc., published a series of three articles by Stanley White, titled "The Howard Hughes Story."

• In 1962, Random House, Inc., hired Thomas Thompson, a journalist employed by *Life* magazine, to prepare a book-length biography of Hughes. Later, either Hughes or his attorneys learned of the forthcoming Random House book. An attorney employed by Hughes warned Random House that Hughes did not want this biography and "would make trouble if the book was

rehearing denied 356 U.S. 934, 78 S.Ct. 770 (1958); Pilpel and Zavin, op. cit., pp. 160–161.

[5] Eisenshiml v. Fawcett Publications, Inc., 246 F.2d 598 (7th Cir.1957), certiorari denied 355 U.S. 907, 78 S.Ct. 334 (1957).

[6] Benny v. Loew's Inc., 239 F.2d 532 (9th Cir.1956), affirmed 356 U.S. 43, 78 S.Ct. 667, rehearing denied 356 U.S. 934, 78 S.Ct. 770 (1958).

[7] Wihtol v. Crow, 309 F.2d 777 (8th Cir.1962).

[8] Jeweler's Circular Pub. Co. v. Keystone Pub. Co., 281 F. 83 (2d Cir.1922), certiorari denied 259 U.S. 581, 42 S.Ct. 464 (1922).

published." Thompson resigned from the project, and Random House then hired John Keats to complete the biography.

• Rosemont Enterprises, Inc., was organized in September, 1965 by Hughes' attorney and by two officers of his wholly-owned Hughes Tool Company.

• On May 20, 1966, Rosemont Enterprises purchased copyrights to the *Look* articles, advised Random House of this, and five days later brought a copyright infringement suit in New York. Attorneys for Rosemont somehow had gained possession of Random House galley proofs of the Random House biography of Hughes then being published: "Howard Hughes: a Biography by John Keats." [9]

Rosemont Enterprises sought an injunction to restrain Random House from selling, publishing, or distributing copies of its biography of Hughes because the book amounted to a prima facie case of copyright infringement. With his five-day-old ownership of the copyrights for the 1954 Look magazine articles, Hughes was indeed in a position to "cause trouble" for Random House.

The trial court agreed with the Rosemont Enterprises argument that infringement had occurred, and granted the injunction against Random House, holding up distribution of the book. The trial court rejected Random House's claims of fair use of the Look articles, saying that the privilege of fair use was confined to "materials used for purposes of criticism or comment or in scholarly works of scientific or educational value." This district court took the view that if something was published "for commercial purposes"—that is, if it was designed for the popular market—the doctrine of fair use could not be employed to lessen the severity of the copyright law.[10] The district court found that the Hughes biography by Keats was for the popular market and therefore the fair use privilege could not be invoked by Random House.[11]

Circuit Judge Leonard P. Moore, speaking for the Circuit Court of Appeals, took another view. First of all, he noted that the three *Look* articles, taken together, totalled only 13,500 words, or between 35 and 39 pages if published in book form. Keats' 1966 biography on the other hand, had 166,000 words, or 304 pages in book form. Furthermore, Judge Moore stated that the *Look* articles did not purport to be a biography, but were merely accounts of a number of interesting incidents in Hughes' life. Judge Moore declared: [12]

[9] Rosemont Enterprises, Inc. v. Random House, Inc. and John Keats, 366 F.2d 303, 304–305 (2d Cir.1966).

[10] Ibid., p. 304, citing the trial court, 256 F.Supp. 55 (D.C.N.Y.1966).

[11] Ibid.

[12] Ibid., pp. 306–307, certiorari denied 385 U.S. 1009, 87 S.Ct. 714 (1967).

* * * there can be little doubt that portions of the *Look* article were copied. Two direct quotations and one eight-line paraphrase were attributed to Stephen White, the author of the articles. A mere reading of the *Look* articles, however, indicates that there is considerable doubt as to whether the copied and paraphrased matter constitutes a material and substantial portion of those articles.

Furthermore, while the mode of expression employed by White is entitled to copyright protection, he could not acquire by copyright a monopoly in the narration of historical events.

In any case, the Keats book should fall within the doctrine of fair use. Quoting a treatise on copyright, Judge Moore stated: "Fair use is a privilege in others than the owner of a copyright to use the copyrighted material in a reasonable manner without his consent, notwithstanding the monopoly granted to the owner * * *." [13]

Judge Moore demanded that public interest considerations— the public's interest in knowing about prominent and powerful men—be taken into account. He wrote that "public interest should prevail over possible damage to the copyright owner." He complained that the district court's preliminary injunction against Random House deprived the public of the opportunity to become acquainted with the life of a man of extraordinary talents in a number of fields: "A narration of Hughes' initiative, ingenuity, determination and tireless work to achieve his concept of perfection in whatever he did ought to be available to a reading public." [14]

The Zapruder Case

A stunning event—the assassination of President John F. Kennedy—gave rise to a copyright case which added luster to the defense of fair use in infringement actions. On November 22, 1963, dress manufacturer Abraham Zapruder of Dallas stationed himself along the route of the President's motorcade, planning to take home movie pictures with his 8 millimeter camera. As the procession came into sight, Zapruder started his camera. Seconds later, the assassin's shots fatally wounded the President and Zapruder's color film caught the reactions of those in the President's car.

[13] Ibid., p. 306, quoting Ball, Copyright and Literary Property, p. 260 (1944).

[14] Ibid., p. 309. And, at p. 311, Judge Moore discussed Rosemont's claim that it was planning to publish a book: "One can only speculate when, if ever, Rosemont will produce Hughes' authorized biography."

On that same day, Zapruder had his film developed and three color copies were made from the original film. He turned over two copies to the Secret Service, stipulating that these were strictly for governmental use and not to be shown to newspapers or magazines because Zapruder expected to sell the film. Three days later, Zapruder negotiated a written agreement with *Life* magazine, which bought the original and all three copies of the film (including the two in possession of the Secret Service). Under that agreement, Zapruder was to be paid $150,000, in yearly installments of $25,000. *Life,* in its November 29, 1963, issue then featured thirty of Zapruder's frames. *Life* subsequently ran more of the Zapruder pictures. *Life* gave the Commission appointed by President Lyndon B. Johnson to investigate the killing of President Kennedy permission to use the Zapruder film and to reproduce it in the report.[15]

In May of 1967, *Life* registered the entire Zapruder film in the Copyright office as an unpublished "motion picture other than a photoplay." Three issues of *Life* magazine in which the Zapruder frames had been published had earlier been registered in the Copyright office as periodicals.[16] This meant that *Life* had a valid copyright in the Zapruder pictures when Bernard Geis Associates sought permission from *Life* magazine to publish the pictures in Josiah Thompson's book, Six Seconds in Dallas, a serious, thoughtful study of the assassination. The firm of Bernard Geis Associates offered to pay *Life* a royalty equal to the profits from publication of the book in return for permission to use specified Zapruder frames in the book. *Life* refused this offer.

Having failed to secure permission from *Life* to use the Zapruder pictures, author Josiah Thompson and his publisher decided to copy certain frames anyway. They did not reproduce the Zapruder frames photographically, but instead paid an artist $1,550 to make charcoal sketch copies. Thompson's book was then published, relying heavily on the sketches, in mid-November of 1967. Significant parts of 22 copyrighted frames were reproduced in the book.[17]

The court ruled that *Life* had a valid copyright in the Zapruder film, and added that "the so-called 'sketches' in the book are in fact copies of the copyrighted film. That they were done by an

---

[15] Time, Inc. v. Bernard Geis Associates, 293 F.Supp. 130, 131–134 (S.D.N.Y.1968). Although the Commission received permission from Time, Inc. to reproduce the photos, the Commission was told that it was expected to give the usual copyright notice. That proviso evidently was disregarded by the Commission.

[16] Ibid., p. 137.

[17] Ibid., pp. 138–139.

'artist' is of no moment." The Court then quoted copyright expert Melville B. Nimmer: [18]

> "It is of course, fundamental, that copyright in a work protects against unauthorized copying not only in the original medium in which the work was produced, but also in any other medium as well. Thus copyright in a photograph will preclude unauthorized copying by drawing or in any other form, as well as by photographic reproduction."

The court then ruled that the use of the photos in Thompson's book was a copyright infringement, "unless the use of the copyrighted material in the Book is a 'fair use' outside the limits of copyright protection." [19] This led the court to a consideration of fair use, the issue which is " 'the most troublesome in the whole law of copyright.' " [20] The court then found in favor of Bernard Geis Associates and author Thompson, holding that the utilization of the Zapruder pictures was a "fair use." [21]

> There is an initial reluctance to find any fair use by defendants because of the conduct of Thompson in making his copies and because of the deliberate appropriation in the Book, in defiance of the copyright owner. Fair use presupposes "good faith and fair dealing." * * * On the other hand, it was not the nighttime activities of Thompson which enabled defendants to reproduce copies of Zapruder frames in the Book. They could have secured such frames from the National Archives, or they could have used the reproductions in the Warren Report [on the assassination of President Kennedy] or in the issues of *Life* itself. Moreover, while hope by a defendant for commercial gain is not a significant factor in this Circuit, there is a strong point for defendants in their offer to surrender to *Life* all profits of Associates from the Book as royalty payment for a license to use the copyrighted Zapruder frames. It is also a fair inference from the facts that defendants acted with the advice of counsel.

> In determining the issue of fair use, the balance seems to be in favor of defendants.

> There is a public interest in having the fullest information available on the murder of President Kennedy. Thompson did serious work on the subject and has a theory entitled to public consideration. While doubtless

---

[18] Ibid., p. 144, citing Nimmer on Copyright, p. 98.

[19] Ibid., p. 144.

[20] Ibid., quoting from Dellar v. Samuel Goldwyn, Inc., 104 F.2d 661 (2d Cir.1939).

[21] Ibid., p. 146.

the theory could be explained with sketches * * * [not copied from copyrighted pictures] * * * the explanation actually made in the Book with copies [of the Zapruder pictures] is easier to understand. The Book is not bought because it contained the Zapruder pictures; the Book is bought because of the theory of Thompson and its explanation, supported by the Zapruder pictures.

There seems little, if any, injury to plaintiff, the copyright owner. There is no competition between plaintiff and defendants. Plaintiff does not sell the Zapruder pictures as such and no market for the copyrighted work appears to be affected. Defendants do not publish a magazine. There are projects for use by plaintiff of the film in the future as a motion picture or in books, but the effect of the use of certain frames in the Book on such projects is speculative. It seems more reasonable to speculate that the Book would, if anything, enhance the value of the copyrighted work; it is difficult to see any decrease in its value.

Copyright and a Comparative Ad

The publishers of TV Guide magazine were piqued by The Miami Herald's using pictures of TV Guide covers in an advertising campaign. The Miami Herald was indulging in "comparative advertising," whimsically suggesting that the newspaper's Sunday television listing supplement was a better product. In one television ad for the Miami Herald supplement, a Goldilocks and the Three Bears skit suggested that the newspaper's TV guide was "just right" for humans.[22]

TV Guide complained about the use of its name and cover picture in the *Herald's* advertisements, charging copyright violation and asking an injunction against the paper. However, a U.S. Court of Appeals upheld dismissal of the copyright lawsuit, on fair use grounds: [33]

We are simply unable to find any effect—other than possibly *de minimis*—on the commercial value of the copyright. To be sure, the Herald's advertisements may have had the effect of drawing customers away from TV Guide. But this results from the nature of advertising itself and in no way stems from the fact that TV Guide covers were used.

[22] Triangle Publications v. Knight-Ridder Newspapers, 445 F.Supp. 875, 876 (D.C. Fla.1978).

[33] 626 F.2d 1171 (5th Cir.1980).

Harper & Row v. Nation Enterprises (1985)

The defense of fair use, often helpful in fending off lawsuits for copyright infringement, can be pushed too far. The Supreme Court of the United States served notice in 1985 that the fair use doctrine at times may not prevent liability for unauthorized publishing, even the material involved is highly newsworthy. Nation Magazine—reputedly America's longest continuously published weekly magazine—in 1979 received an unauthorized copy of former President Gerald R. Ford's memoirs. Nation Editor Victor Navasky received the draft from an undisclosed source; this writing was the result of a collaboration between Ford and Trevor Armbrister, a senior editor of Reader's Digest.[24]

Nation Magazine carried an article developed by Navasky from the unauthorized copy, published in its issue of April 3, 1979, and was just over 2,000 words long. Harper & Row and The Reader's Digest Association, Inc., sued for copyright infringement. At the trial court level, U.S. District Judge Owen found that Navasky knew that the memoirs were soon to be published in book form by Harper & Row and Reader's Digest, with some advance publication rights assigned to Time Magazine. Judge Owen wrote: [25]

> However, believing that the draft contained "a real hot news story" concerning Ford's pardon of President Nixon * * * Navasky spent overnight or perhaps the next twenty-four hour period quoting and paraphrasing from a number of sections of the memoirs. Navasky added no comment of his own. He did not check the material. As he later testified, "I wasn't reporting on the truth or falsity of the account; I was reporting the fact that Ford reported this * * * " Part of Navasky's rush apparently was caused by the fact that he had to get the draft back to his "source" with some speed.

The Nation's article was about 2,250 words long, of which 300 to 400 words were taken from the Ford memoirs manuscript. Nation's publication may be said to have skimmed some of the more newsworthy aspects from the manuscript, which Harper & Row and Reader's Digest Association, as copyright holders, were preparing to market. For one thing, the copyright owners had negotiated a pre-publication agreement in which Time Magazine agreed to pay $25,000 ($12,500 in advance and the balance at the

---

[24] Harper & Row and The Reader's Digest Ass'n v. Nation Enterprises and The Nation Associates, 557 F.Supp. 1067, 1069 (S.D.N.Y.1983), 9 Med.L.Rptr. 1229.

[25] Ibid.

time of publication) for rights to excerpt 7,500 words from Mr. Ford's story of his pardon of President Nixon.

The Supreme Court of the United States said that The Nation had timed its publication to "scoop" Time Magazine's planned article. As a result of Nation's publication, Time cancelled its article and refused to pay the remaining $12,500 to Harper & Row and to Reader's Digest Association.[26] Writing for the Court, Justice Sandra Day O'Connor found that Nation's publication was not covered by the fair use defense: [27]

> * * * The Nation has admitted to lifting verbatim quotes of the author's original language totalling between 300 and 400 words and constituting some 13% of The Nation article. In using generous verbatim excerpts of Mr. Ford's unpublished manuscript to lend authenticity to its account of the forthcoming memoirs, The Nation effectively arrogated to itself the right of first publication, an important marketable subsidiary right. * * * [W]e find that use of the copyrighted manuscript, even stripped to the verbatim quotes conceded by The Nation to be copyrightable expression, was not a fair use within the meaning of the Copyright Act.

Justice O'Connor examined the tension between racing to publish news first and copyright: [28]

> In our haste to disseminate news, it should not be forgotten that the Framers intended copyright itself to be the engine of free expression. By establishing a marketable right to the use of one's expression, copyright supplies the economic incentive to create and disseminate ideas.

Further, she held that a writer's public figure status did not create a waiver of the copyright laws: [29]

> In view of the First Amendment protections already embodied in the Copyright Act's distinction between copyrightable expression and uncopyrightable facts and ideas, and the latitude for scholarship and comment traditionally afforded by fair use, we see no warrant for expanding the doctrine of fair use to create what amounts to a public figure exception to copyright. Whether verbatim copying from a public figure's manuscript in a given case is or is not fair must be judged according to the traditional equities of fair use.

[26] Harper & Row v. Nation Enterprises, ___ U.S. ___, 105 S.Ct. 2218 (1985), 11 Med.L.Rptr. 1969, 1971.

[27] ___ U.S. ___, 105 S.Ct. 2218, 2225 (1985), 11 Med.L.Rptr. 1969, 1973.

[28] ___ U.S. ___, 105 S.Ct. 2218, 2230 (1985), 11 Med.L.Rptr. 1969, 1978.

[29] ___ U.S. ___, 105 S.Ct. 2218, 2230–2231 (1985), 11 Med.L.Rptr. 1969, 1978.

The Court's majority opinion marched through the Copyright Statute's list of four factors to be considered in determining whether a use is "fair:"

(1) *The Nature and Purpose of the Use*—Justice Connor said the general purpose of The Nation's use was "general reporting." Part of this, however, was The Nation's stated purpose of scooping the forthcoming hardcover books and the excerpts to be published in Time Magazine. This, Justice O'Connor said, had " * * * the intended purpose of supplanting the copyright holder's commercially valuable right of first publication." [30]

(2) *Nature of the Copyrighted Work*—Justice O'Connor wrote that President Ford's narrative, "A Time to Heal" was "an unpublished historical narrative or autobiography." She said the unpublished nature of the work was critical to considering whether use of it by The Nation was fair. Although substantial quotes might qualify as fair use in a review or discussion of a published work, "the author's right to control the first public appearance of his expression weighs against such use of the work before its release." [31]

(3) *Amount and Substantiality of the Copying*—"Stripped of the verbatim quotes, the direct takings from the unpublished manuscript constitute at least 13% of the infringing article. * * * The Nation article is structured around the quoted excerpts which serve as its dramatic focal points."

(4) *Effect on the Market*—Noting that Time Magazine had cancelled its projected serialization of the Ford memoirs and had refused to pay $12,500, Justice O'Connor said those occurrences were direct results from the infringement. "Rarely will a case of copyright infringement present such clear cut evidence of damage." [32]

Thus a six-member majority concluded that The Nation's use of the Ford memoirs was not a fair use. This meant that a Court of Appeals finding that The Nation's publication was overturned, and that The Nation was liable to pay the $12,500 in damages, matching the amount which Time Magazine had refused to pay the copyright holders after the unauthorized publication.

Justice William J. Brennan, Jr.—who was joined by Justices Byron White and Thurgood Marshall—dissented. "The Court

[30] __ U.S. __, 105 S.Ct. 2218, 2232 (1985), 11 Med.L.Rptr. 1969, 1978.

[31] __ U.S. __, 105 S.Ct. 2218, 2232 (1985), 11 Med.L.Rptr. 1969, 1980.

[32] __ U.S. __, 105 S.Ct. 2218, 2233 (1985), 11 Med.L.Rptr. 1969, 1981.

holds that The Nation's quotation of 300 words from the unpublished 200,000-word manuscript of President Gerald R. Ford infringed the copyright," wrote Brennan. He said the Court's majority reached this finding even though the quotations related to a historical event of undoubted significance—the resignation and pardon of President Richard M. Nixon. Brennan added that "this zealous defense of the copyright owner's prerogative will, I fear, stifle the broad dissemination of ideas and information copyright is intended to nurture." [33]

Brennan concluded,[34]

> The Court's exceedingly narrow approach to fair use permits Harper & Row to monopolize information. This holding "effect[s] an important extension of property rights and a corresponding curtailment in the free use of knowledge and of ideas." International News Service v. Associated Press, 248 U.S. at 263 (Brandeis, J., dissenting). The Court has perhaps advanced the ability of the historian—or at least the public official who has recently left office—to capture the full economic value of information in his or her possession. But the Court does so only by risking the robust debate of public issues. * * *"

Technology and Fair Use: The Sony "Betamax" Decision (1984)

The Supreme Court of the United States seemed to squirm on the issue of whether or not home taping of television programs was legal. The Court even postponed its decision, evidently in hopes that Congress would act, taking the Court off the hook.[35] Finally, in January, 1984, the Court said by 5–4 vote that video recorders are legal for sale and home use under the Copyright Statute and the doctrine of fair use.[36]

The case of Sony Corporation v. Universal City Studios is an excellent symbol of a basic and continuing problem in the history of copyright law. Technological advances outrun legislative and judicial efforts to contain them. As Professor David Lange of Duke Law School said after the Betamax decision that the new technologies have caused copyright problems because it " 'is possible for people to duplicate copyrighted works in their private homes more frequently than ever before.' " And Professor Arthur

---

[33] ___ U.S. ___, 105 S.Ct. 2218, 2240 (1985), 11 Med.L.Rptr. 1969, 1983.

[34] ___ U.S. ___, 105 S.Ct. 2218, 2254 (1985), 11 Med.L.Rptr. 1969, 1994–1995.

[35] Stephen Wermeil "Taping of TV Programs at Home Is Approved 5–4 by Supreme Court," Wall Street Journal, Jan. 18, 1984, p. 3.

[36] Sony Corporation of America v. Universal City Studios, 464 U.S. 417, 104 S.Ct. 774 (1984).

R. Miller of Harvard Law School said the Copyright Act of 1976—which became operational on January 1, 1978—" 'was obsolete from the day it went into effect, at least in terms of technology.' " [37]

With its decision in the "Betamax Case," the Supreme Court produced great economic news for the Sony Corporation and others who make and sell video tape recorders (VTRs). This case arose when Universal City Studios and Walt Disney productions sued, claiming that use of Sony Betamax VTRs in homes by private individuals constituted copyright infringement.

In 1979, a federal district court held off-the-air copying for private, non-commercial use to be a "fair use." Plaintiffs had not proved to the court's satisfaction that harm to copyrighted properties was being done by such taping.[38] But in 1981, the United States Court of Appeals for the Ninth Circuit overturned that ruling, holding that makers and distributors of home video recorders were liable for damages if the machines were used to tape programs broadcast over-the-air.[39]

The Supreme Court, after granting certiorari, agreed in mid-1982 to hear Sony's appeal from the Court of Appeals holding. The Court, however, held the case over into a second term, and had it argued a second time in October, 1983.[40]

Writing for a five-Justice majority, Justice John Paul Stevens said that an average member of the public uses a VTR principally to record a program he or she cannot see as it is being telecast, and then use the home recording to watch the program at another time. This "time-shifting" practice, Justice Stevens said, enlarges the viewing audience: [41]

> * * * [A] significant amount of television programming may be used in this manner without objection from the owners of the copyrights on the programs. For the same reason, even the two respondents in this case, who do assert objections to time-shifting * * * were unable to prove that the practice has impaired the commercial value of their copyrights * * *

Justice Stevens noted that Universal and Disney studios were not seeking damages from individual Betamax users whom they claimed infringed their copyrights. Instead, they charge Sony with "contributory infringement. To prevail, they have the bur-

---

[37] Stuart Taylor, Jr., "Decision a Basis for Further Action," The New York Times, Jan. 18, 1984, p. 43.

[38] 480 F.Supp. 429, 452–453 (D.C.Cal.1979).

[39] 659 F.2d 963 (9th Cir.1981)

[40] 464 U.S. 417, 104 S.Ct. 774, 777 (1984); Wermeil, loc. cit.

[41] 464 U.S. 417, 104 S.Ct. 774, 778 (1984).

den of proving that users of Betamax have infringed their copyrights and that Sony should be held responsible for that infringement." [42]   Justice Stevens added,[43]

> If vicarious liability is to be imposed on * * *
> [Sony] * * *, it must rest on the fact that they have sold
> equipment with constructive knowledge of the fact that
> their consumers may use that equipment to make unauthorized copies of copyrighted material.   There is no
> precedent in the law of copyright for the imposition of
> vicarious liability on such a theory.

The Betamax decision was limited to noncommercial home uses. "If the Betamax were used to make copies for a commercial or profit-making purpose, such use would be presumptively unfair," Justice Stevens said.[44]   Thus the Sony case is clearly distinguishable from a situation where off-the-air taping is being done for commercial reasons.[45]

Importantly, Justice Stevens concluded that the home use of VTRs for noncommercial purposes was a fair use.[46]

> * * * [To] the extent that time-shifting expands
> public access to freely broadcast television programs, it
> yields societal benefits.   Earlier this year, in Community
> Television of Southern California v. Gottfried, __ U.S.
> __, __, n. 12, 103 S.Ct. 885, 891–892, 74 L.Ed.2d 705
> (1983), we acknowledged the public interest in making
> television broadcasting more available.   Concededly, that
> interest is not unlimited.   But it supports an interpretation of the concept of "fair use" that requires the copyright holder to demonstrate some likelihood of harm
> before he may condemn a private act of time-shifting as a
> violation of federal law.

Justice Stevens concluded the opinion of the Court with a summary of findings and with an invitation to Congress to provide legislative guidance in this case: [47]

> In summary, the record and findings of the District
> Court lead us to two conclusions.   First, Sony demonstrat-

[42] 464 U.S. 417, 104 S.Ct. 774, at 785 (1984).

[43] 464 U.S. 417, 104 S.Ct. 774, at 787 (1984).

[44] 464 U.S. 417, 104 S.Ct. 774, 792 (1984).

[45] Melville B. Nimmer, Nimmer on Copyright, Vol. 3, § 13.5[F] (New York: Matthew Bender, 1963, 1980), citing Elektra Records Co. v. Gem Electronic Distributors, Inc., 360 F.Supp. 821 (E.D.N.Y.1973) (taping of copyrighted records for commercial redistribution ruled infringing) and Walt Disney Productions v. Alaska Television Network, 310 F.Supp. 1073 (W.D.Wash.1969) (videotaping for commercial use).

[46] 464 U.S. 417, 104 S.Ct. 774, 795 (1984).

[47] 464 U.S. 417, 104 S.Ct. 774, 796 (1984).

ed a significant likelihood that substantial numbers of copyright holders who license their works for broadcast on free television would not object to having their broadcasts time-shifted by private viewers. And second, respondents failed to demonstrate that time-shifting would cause any likelihood of nominal harm to the potential market for, or the value of, their copyrighted works. The Betamax is, therefore, capable of substantial noninfringing uses. Sony's sale of such equipment to the general public does not constitute contributory infringement of respondent's copyrights.

V.

* * *

One may search the copyright act in vain for any sign that the elected representatives of the millions of people who watch television every day have made it unlawful to copy a program for later viewing at home, or have enacted a flat prohibition against the sale of machines that make such copying possible.

It may well be that Congress will take a fresh look at this new technology, just as it so often has examined other innovations in the past. But it is not our job to apply laws that have not yet been written. Applying the copyright statute, as it now reads, to the facts as they have been developed in this case, the judgment of the Court of Appeals must be reversed.

Justice Blackmun, joined by Justices Marshall, Powell, and Rehnquist, dissented.[48]

It is apparent from the record and from the findings of the District Court that time-shifting does have a substantial adverse effect upon the "potential market for" the Studios' copyrighted works. Accordingly, even under the formulation of the fair use doctrine advanced by Sony, time-shifting cannot be deemed a fair use.

Justice Blackmun added that the case should have been sent back to District Court for additional findings of fact on the matter of infringement and contributory infringement.[49]

Parody and Fair Use

Can a parody be fair use? The "Saturday Night Live" television program did a skit poking fun at New York City's public

[48] 464 U.S. 417, 104 S.Ct. 774, 811 (1984).

[49] 464 U.S. 417, 104 S.Ct. 774, 815 (1984).

relations campaign and its theme song. In this four-minute skit, the town fathers of Sodom discussed a plan to improve their city's image. This satire ended with the singing of "I Love Sodom" to the tune of "I Love New York." In a per curiam opinion, the U.S. Court of Appeals, Second Circuit rejected the complaint of Elsmere Record Co., owner of copyright to "I Love New York." "Believing that, in today's world of often unrelieved solemnity, copyright law should be hospitable to the humor of parody," the Court of Appeals approved District Judge Goettel's decision granting the defendant National Broadcasting Company a summary judgment on ground that the parody was a fair use.[50]

Judge Goettel's opinion said, in words useful for understanding both the concept of fair use and its application to parodies charged with copyright infringement: [51]

> In its entirety, the original song "I Love New York" is composed of a 45 word lyric and 100 measures. Of this only four notes, D C D E (in that sequence), and the words "I Love" were taken in the Saturday Night Live sketch (although they were repeated 3 or 4 times). As a result, the defendant now argues that the use it made was insufficient to constitute copyright infringement.

> This court does not agree. Although it is clear that, on its face, the taking involved in this action is relatively slight, on closer examination it becomes apparent that this portion of the piece, the musical phrase that the lyrics "I Love New York" accompanies, is the heart of the composition. * * * Accordingly, such taking is capable of rising to the level of a copyright infringement.

> Having so determined, the Court must next address the question of whether the defendant's copying of the plaintiff's jingle constituted a fair use which would exempt it from liability under the Copyright Act. Fair use has been defined as a "privilege in others than the owner of the copyright to use the copyrighted material in a reasonable manner without his consent, notwithstanding the monopoly granted to the owner of the copyright.

Judge Goettel then reviewed the four criteria set out by the 1976 copyright revision, 17 U.S.C.A. § 107 [quoted at the beginning of this Section], and compared those criteria to relevant cases on the fair use doctrine. He quoted copyright specialist Melville B. Nimmer, who has said, " 'short of * * * [a] complete identity of content, the disparity of functions between a serious work and a

[50] Elsmere Music v. NBC, 623 F.2d 252 (2d Cir.1980), 6 Med.L.Rptr. 1457.

[51] Elsmere Music v. NBC, 482 F.Supp. 741 (D.C.S.D.N.Y.1980), 5 Med.L.Rptr. 2455, 2456.

satire based upon it, may justify the defense of fair use even where substantial similarity exists.' " [52]

Plaintiff Elsmere Records argued that "I Love Sodom" was not a valid parody of "I Love New York." Elsmere pointed to two raunchy cases in which copyright infringement was found because use of copyrighted material was not parodying the material itself, but was instead using someone's intellectual property, without permission, to make statements essentially irrelevant to the original work.[53] Elsmere Records cited MCA, Inc. v. Wilson, in which the song "Cunnilingus Champion of Company C" was held to infringe the copyright of "Boogie Woogie Bugle Boy of Company B." [54] And in Walt Disney Productions v. Mature Pictures Corporation, the court held that while the defendants may have been displaying bestiality intended to parody life, but did not validly parody the Mickey Mouse March and sought only to use improperly copyrighted material.[55]

However, Judge Goettel found that the Saturday Night Live sketch validly parodied the plaintiff's jingle and the "I Love New York" ad campaign. Also, he ruled that the parody did not interfere with the marketability of a copyrighted work. Therefore, he held that the sketch was a fair use, and that no copyright violation had occurred.

[52] Nimmer on Copyright, § 13.05[C], at 13–60–61 (1979), quoted by Judge Goettel at 482 F.Supp. 741 at 745 (D.C.N.Y.1980), 5 Med.L.Rptr. 2455, 2457.

[53] 482 F.Supp. 741 (D.C.S.D.N.Y.1980), 5 Med.L.Rptr. 2455, 2457.

[54] MCA, Inc. v. Wilson, 425 F.Supp. 443 (S.D.N.Y.1976).

[55] 389 F.Supp. 1397 (S.D.N.Y.1975).

Chapter 8

OBSCENITY AND BLASPHEMY

SEC. 47. OBSCENITY: THE FREEDOM TO READ *VERSUS* CONCEPTS OF CONTROL

American courts and legislatures have long been searching for a "dim and uncertain line" which separates obscenity from constitutionally protected expression.

One of the nation's most literate and articulate judges—United States Court of Appeals Judge Leonard P. Moore—once wrote obscenity law with sour resignation. "It is unfortunate," said Judge Moore, " * * * that these matters have to come before the courts." [1] He was talking about the enormous amounts of time and effort courts—especially the Supreme Court of the United States—have spent grappling with what Justice John Marshall Harlan once termed "the intractable obscenity problem." [2] From the mid-1950s through the 1970s, every term brought dozens of obscenity cases in "the Court's annual non-climactic arousal." [3] Small wonder that Justice Robert H. Jackson fretted, years ago, that the Court would become the High Court of Obscenity.[4]

Jackson was prophetic. For years, aging, dignified members of the Supreme Court have spent endless hours looking at raunchy renditions of sexual activities in print and on film. The wording

[1] U.S. v. Various Articles of Obscene Merchandise, 562 F.2d 185, 190 (2d Cir. 1977).

[2] Interstate Circuit, Inc. v. Dallas, 390 U.S. 676, 704, 88 S.Ct. 1298, 1313 (1968).

[3] Nathan Lewin, "What's Happening to Free Speech," New Republic Vol. 171: Nos. 4 and 5 (July 27–Aug. 3, 1974) p. 14.

[4] Statement made in 1948 by Justice Jackson, quoted by Anthony Lewis, "Sex and the Supreme Court," Esquire Vol. 59 (June, 1963) p. 82.

of the Justices' opinions about obscenity has shown unease. They are judges, not literary historians or philosophers, after all. One person's obscenity may be another's art. As former Justice Potter Stewart noted, the Court keeps trying to define what may be indefinable. He added that he could not define obscenity, but that he knew it when he saw it.[5] Trying to define the obscene, the Supreme Court, along with other courts, has looked for a dim, uncertain, and non-existent line which separates "obscenity" from constitutionally protected expression.

In searching for such an elusive line, American courts have been left floundering by a society which makes enormous financial successes of literature, motion pictures, art and advertising which celebrate (or at least suggest) all manner of sexual exploits. As discussed in Section 52 of this Chapter, the Supreme Court in 1973 attempted to shift much of the burden of judging what is and is not obscene from the Court to states and localities. The obscenity problem, however, refuses to stay away. The Court finds itself in a position much like that of a child trying to throw away an unwanted boomerang.

Dictionary Definition

A key problem in the law of obscenity is in defining what is so offensive in describing or picturing sexual functions that it lawfully may be prohibited or punished. Excerpts from Black's Law Dictionary may outline the problem, but do not really provide much in the way of specificity.[6]

> Obscenity. The character of quality of being obscene; conduct tending to corrupt the public morals by its indecency or lewdness.
>
> Material is obscene if, taken as a whole, its predominant appeal is to prurient interest, that is, a shameful or morbid interest, in nudity, sex or excretion, and if in addition it goes substantially beyond customary limits of candor in describing or representing such matters. Predominant appeal shall be judged with reference to ordinary adults unless it appears from the character of the material or the circumstances of its dissemination to be designed for children or other specially susceptible audience. * * * Model Penal Code, § 251.4.

---

[5] Concurring opinion in Jacobellis v. Ohio, 378 U.S. 184, 197, 84 S.Ct. 1676, 1683 (1964).

[6] Black's Law Dictionary, 5th ed. (St. Paul, Minn., West Publishing Co., 1979) p. 971.

The Freedom to Read

The freedom to read is implicit in the First and Fourteenth Amendments to the Constitution.[7] But the freedom to read, as part of our freedoms of speech and press, is not absolute.[8] For the most part, however, we are free to read what we wish. It may not occur to most Americans that many books they enjoy reading today might have been banned as obscene and held out of circulation in another time or place.

The late Jake Ehrlich, one of America's leading criminal lawyers, once said that "every book that is worthwhile was condemned somewhere by someone."[9] Ehrlich's statement is accurate, for such works as Keats' Endymion, Shelley's Queen Mab, Whitman's Leaves of Grass, DeFoe's Moll Flanders, Dreiser's An American Tragedy and various editions of the Bible have at some time been condemned as obscene.[10]

That list of classic titles which have been banned indicates that the freedom to read cannot be taken for granted. Statutes which make it a criminal offense to distribute or to possess obscene literature are one way in which that freedom may be diminished. Such statutes, which will be discussed later in this chapter, draw no lines between obscenity and art. Obscenity is never defined in a workable fashion. Instead, various synonyms are used by statutes and by court decisions interpreting those statutes. The statutes and court decisions say only that writings, pictures, statutes, and substances which are obscene, lewd, immoral, lascivious, lecherous, libidinous, licentious, and so forth, may not be circulated in or imported into this nation.[11]

The roots of the freedom to read may be traced to what has been called the Democratic Creed, which has been expressed in the

---

[7] See, e.g., Near v. Minnesota, 283 U.S. 697, 713–717, 51 S.Ct. 625, 630–631 (1931); Ex Parte Jackson, 96 U.S. 727, 733 (1897).

[8] See, e.g., Near v. Minnesota, 283 U.S. 697, 51 S.Ct. 625 (1931); Schenck v. United States, 249 U.S. 47, 39 S.Ct. 247 (1919).

[9] David Perlman, " 'Howl' Not Obscene, Judge Rules," San Francisco Chronicle, Oct. 4, 1957, p. 1. See also People of the State of California v. Lawrence Ferlinghetti (Municipal Court, Dept. 10, San Francisco, Calif., Oct. 3, 1957).

[10] Stanley Fleishman et al., Brief for Appellant in the Supreme Court of the United States (in the case of David S. Alberts v. State of California, No. 61, Oct. Term, 1956) p. 78.

[11] See, e.g., cases interpreting such statutes such as Roth v. United States, 354 U.S. 476, 493–494, 77 S.Ct. 1304, 1314 (1957); United States v. Bennett, 24 Fed.Cas. 1093, 1104, No. 14,571 (S.D.N.Y.1879); United States v. One Book Entitled "Ulysses," 5 F.Supp. 182, 184 (S.D.N.Y.1933); Besig v. United States, 208 F.2d 142, 146 (9th Cir.1953); William B. Lockhart and Robert C. McClure, "Literature, the Law of Obscenity, and the Constitution," Minnesota Law Review 38:4 (March, 1954) p. 324.

writings of John Milton, Thomas Jefferson, John Stuart Mill and many others. As Milton wrote in his *Areopagitica* in 1644: [12]

> Since * * * the knowledge and survey of vice is in this world so necessary to the constituting of human virtue, and the scanning of error to the confirmation of truth, how can we more safely, and with less danger, scout into the regions of sin and falsity than by reading all manner of tractates and hearing all manner of reason?

Milton, who later in life served as a censor himself, clearly had a rather limited view of freedom. His ringing words have risen above his own frailties, however, and the idea that knowledge of any kind will make people better able to cope with life is basic to the freedom to read.

Concepts of Control

Concepts of control, to the contrary, have as their premise the notion that human beings are inherently weak and can be further weakened or even destroyed by reading improper literature. Attempts to censor literature regarded as obscene—or to legislate against obscene literature—are grounded on the assumption that if persons read such material, antisocial thoughts or actions will occur.

The roots of the various concepts of control may be traced to such varying personalities as Plato, St. Thomas Acquinas, and Anthony Comstock. This wildly differing trio had at least one thing in common: all approved state control of moral virtue. Plato asserted that poets should be censored lest their subtleties corrupt children. St. Thomas believed that the aim of laws should be to make people good, and it followed that the control of the arts as part of education was within the sphere of human laws.[13]

Anthony Comstock was a Victorian American who played a major and sexually preoccupied part in the passage of federal and state obscenity statutes in the United States. These statutes were intended to protect the young and the weak from being defiled by impure literature. Comstock was not without legal precedents to trot out in his attacks on literature, although the extent to which "obscenity" was a crime under English Common Law is by no means clear.[14]

[12] John Milton, The Student's Milton, ed. by Frank Allen Patterson (Rev. ed., Appleton-Century-Crofts, Inc., New York, 1933), p. 738.

[13] Mortimer Adler, Art & Prudence, 1st ed., (New York, Longmans, Green & Co., 1937), p. 103.

[14] H. Montgomery Hyde, A History of Pornography (New York: Farrar, Straus and Girous, 1965) pp. 165, 174.

An early case in the Anglo-American legal tradition which involved obscene conduct was that The King v. Sir Charles Sedley. In 1663, Sir Charles—nude, drunk and noisily talkative—appeared on a London balcony and delivered a lengthy harangue to the crowd which gathered below him. He hurled bottles filled with an "offensive liquor" upon the crowd.[15]

Hurling flasks, however, was not the same as publishing. Perhaps the first *recorded* prosecution for publication of obscene literature was Curll's case, circa 1727. Curll had published a nastily anti-Catholic writing called "Venus in the Cloister or the Nun in Her Smock," which was suppressed as a threat to morals.[16] This decision apparently had little effect on the flourishing sale of lusty literature, and by the 19th Century, England had entered into what has been called its pornographic period.

In America, meanwhile, the Tariff Act of 1842 forbade the "importation of all indecent and obscene prints, paintings, lithographs, engravings, and transparencies." [17] In 1865, in response to complaints about the reading materials of soldiers in the Civil War (including Cleland's *Memoirs of a Woman of Pleasure*), Congress for the first time outlawed mailing obscene matter.[18]

The Comstock Law

Anthony Comstock began his decency campaign shortly after the Civil War, and fervently denounced anyone who spoke up against him as lechers and defilers of American Womanhood.

"MORALS, not Art or Literature!" was the Comstockian battle cry.[19] In 1873, censorious pressure groups who favored what has come to be called "Comstockery" helped to force an obscenity bill through both houses of Congress. This law now provides a maximum criminal punishment of a $5,000 fine or a five-year penitentiary term, or both for anyone who sent obscene matter through the mail. Anyone convicted of a second such offense, may be fined $10,000 or imprisoned for 10 years, or both.[20] Although amended several times to broaden the definition of "obscene

[15] Noted in the concurring opinion of Mr. Justice Douglas in the "Fanny Hill" case, 383 U.S. 413, 428n., 86 S.Ct. 975, 983n. (1966).

[16] Hyde, op. cit., p. 165; 2 Strange 788, 93 Eng.Rep. 849 (N.D.1727).

[17] U.S. Public Statutes at Large, Vol. 5, Ch. 270, Sec. 28, pp. 566–567.

[18] James C. N. Paul and Murray L. Schwartz, Federal Censorship: Obscenity in the Mail (New York: Free Press of Glencoe, 1961) p. 244, citing Congressional Globe, 38th Congress, 2nd Sess., pp. 660–662 (1865).

[19] Alpert, loc. cit.

[20] 18 U.S.C.A. § 1461. See Historical and Revision Notes, p. 491.

matter," the law is still on the books. The law now provides, in part, that: [21]

> Every obscene, lewd, lascivious, indecent, filthy or vile article, matter, thing, device or substance; and
>
> * * *
>
>   * * *
>
> Every written or printed card, letter, circular, book, pamphlet, advertisement, or notice of any kind giving information, directly or indirectly, where, or how, or from whom, or by what means any of such mentioned matters * * * may be obtained * * *
>
>   * * *
>
> Is declared to be nonmailable matter and shall not be conveyed in the mails or delivered from any post office or by any letter carrier.

The 1873 Comstock Law was the forerunner of many other obscenity laws and ordinances which were soon thereafter enacted at the federal, state and local government levels. In California, for example, an obscenity law was put on the books within a year after the passage of the first Comstock law.[22]

The Hicklin Rule

Once the laws were passed, it was up to the American courts to decide how the laws should be applied. When obscenity cases reached the American courts, there was little American precedent to follow. So, American courts found a decision which was to lay a chilling hand on the circulation of literature for years to come: the 1868 decision, in England, in the case of Regina v. Hicklin.

In *Hicklin,* Lord Chief Justice Cockburn ruled that an anti-Catholic pamphlet, The Confessional Unmasked, was obscene. Lord Cockburn set down this test for obscenity: [23]

> Whether the tendency of the matter charged as obscene is to deprave and corrupt those whose minds are open to such immoral influences and into whose hands a publication of this sort might fall.

This "Hicklin rule" was readily accepted by American courts.[24] It can be seen that this test of obscenity echoed the concepts of control voiced by Plato and St. Thomas Acquinas and seconded, with more fervor and far less intellect, by America's

---

[21] Ibid.

[22] See West's Ann.Cal.Pen.Code, §§ 311–314.

[23] L.R. 3 Q.B. 360, 370 (1868).

[24] See United States v. Bennett, 24 Fed.Cas. 1093, 1103–1104, No. 14,571 (S.D. N.Y.1879); Commonwealth v. Friede, 271 Mass. 318, 320, 171 N.E. 472, 473 (1930).

own Anthony Comstock. Under such a test, a book did not have to offend or harm a normal adult. If it could be assumed that a book might have a bad effect on children or abnormal adults— "those whose minds are open to such immoral influences"—such a book could be suppressed.

American law added the so-called "partly obscene" test to the *Hicklin* rule. This was the practice of judging a book by passages pulled out of context. If a book had an obscenity in it, the entire book was obscene.[25] Perhaps the most troublesome portion of the *Hicklin* rule, for Americans who tried to defend their freedom to read, was the statement that a book was obscene if it suggested "thoughts of a most impure and libidinous character."[26] This judicial preoccupation with *thoughts* induced by the reading of literature—with no requirement that antisocial actions be tied to the reading matter—has continued to this time. In the law of obscenity, no harm or even likelihood of harm to readers need be shown in order to suppress a book as obscene.[27]

In 1913, Judge Learned Hand wrote an often quoted protest against the *Hicklin* rule, which he termed "mid-Victorian precedent." Although Judge Hand felt compelled to uphold the condemnation as obscene of Daniel Goodman's novel *Hagar Revelley,* the judge wrote:[28]

> I question whether in the end men will regard that as obscene which is honestly relevant to the adequate expression of innocent ideas, and whether they will not believe that truth and beauty are too precious to be mutilated in the interests of those most likely to pervert them to base uses. * * *

Despite such moving protests, the *Hicklin* rule remained the leading test of obscenity in America until the 1930s.[29]

The Ulysses Decision

About this time, however, other American courts began to relax enforcement of the *Hicklin* rule to some extent. A mother who wrote a book to help her children learn about sex—and who later published the book at the suggestion of friends—successfully defended herself against charges that the book *(Sex Side of Life)*

[25] Lockhart & McClure, op. cit., p. 343.

[26] Ibid.

[27] See Roth v. United States, 354 U.S. 476, 490, 77 S.Ct. 1304, 1312 (1957); see also dictum by Mr. Justice Frankfurter, Beauharnais v. Illinois, 343 U.S. 250, 266, 72 S.Ct. 725, 735 (1952).

[28] United States v. Kennerley, 209 F. 119 (S.D.N.Y.1913).

[29] See, e.g., Commonwealth v. Friede, 271 Mass. 318, 320, 171 N.E. 472, 473 (1930).

was obscene.[30]   And in 1933, James Joyce's famed stream-of-consciousness novel *Ulysses,* now an acknowledged classic, was the target of an obscenity prosecution under the Tariff Act of 1930.[31]

Customs officers had prevented an actress from bringing *Ulysses* into this country.   When *Ulysses* reached trial, Judge John Woolsey—a literate man acquainted with far more than law books—did read the entire book.   He attacked the *Hicklin* test head-on and ruled that *Ulysses* was art, not obscenity.   His decision has become one of the most noted in the law of criminal words, even though it by no means brought the end of the *Hicklin* rule, which continued to appear, in varying degrees, in the decisions of some other courts.[32]   Overrated or not, the *Ulysses* decision represents an often-cited step toward nullifying some of the most obnoxious aspects of the old *Hicklin* yardstick.

The *Ulysses* decision provided a new definition of obscenity for other courts to consider: that a book is obscene if it [33]

> tends to stir the sex impulses or to lead to sexually
> impure and lustful thoughts.   Whether a particular book
> would tend to excite such impulses must be the test by the
> court's opinion as to its effect (when judged as a whole) on
> a person with average sex instincts.

Four principles of law came from the *Ulysses* decision which had not then been accepted by most other courts:

(1)   The purpose of the author in writing his book was taken into account.   This was one way of giving a book a kind of judicial benefit of the doubt, because a court could disregard "impure" words if purity of purpose was found.

(2)   The opinion rejected the isolated passages ("partly obscene") standard for judging whether a book was obscene. Instead, a book was considered as a whole, by its dominant effect.

(3)   A book was judged by its effect on reasonable persons, not children or abnormal adults.

(4)   Finally, literary or artistic merit was weighed against any incidental obscenity in the book.[34]

[30] United States v. Dennett, 39 F.2d 564, 76 American Law Reports 1092 (2d Cir. 1931).

[31] United States v. One Book Called "Ulysses," 5 F.Supp. 182 (S.D.N.Y.1933); Paul and Schwartz, op. cit., p. 66.

[32] See e.g., United States v. Two Obscene Books, 99 F.Supp. 760 (N.D.Cal.1951), affirmed as Besig v. United States, 208 F.2d 142 (9th Cir.1953).

[33] United States v. One Book Called "Ulysses," 5 F.Supp. 182, 184 (S.D.N.Y.1933).

[34] Ibid., pp. 182–184.

Only one portion of the old *Hicklin* rule appeared in Judge Woolsey's *Ulysses* opinion: the emphasis on thoughts produced by a book as an indicator of a book's obscene effect on a reader. This judicial preoccupation with thoughts—and the tests outlined by Judge Woolsey in 1933—are markedly similar to rules for judging obscenity laid down in the Supreme Court's landmark decision in the 1957 case of Roth v. United States.[35]

SEC. 48. THE *ROTH* LANDMARK

In Roth v. United States, the Supreme Court held that obscenity is not constitutionally protected expression and set down its most influential standard for judging what is—or is not—obscene.

Even though efforts to control obscenity have a long history in this nation, it was not until the reasonably recent date of 1957—in the case of Roth v. United States—that the Supreme Court directly upheld the constitutionality of obscenity statutes.[36] This decision remains the most influential case in the law of obscenity because it declared that both state and federal anti-obscenity laws are valid exercises of government's police power.

Although this decision is called *Roth,* it actually included two cases. The Court simultaneously decided a case under the federal obscenity statute [37] (*Roth*) and under a state statute [38] (People v. Alberts). Taken together, the *Roth* and *Alberts,* cases thus raised the question of the constitutionality of both federal and state anti-obscenity laws.

In the federal prosecution, Roth was convicted of violating the statute by mailing various circulars plus a book, *American Aphrodite.* He was sentenced to what was then the maximum sentence: a $5,000 fine *plus* a five-year penitentiary term. His conviction was affirmed by the United States Court of Appeals, Second Circuit, although the great Judge Jerome M. Frank questioned the constitutionality of obscenity laws in a powerful concurring opinion. In words which have been called the beginning of the modern law of obscenity, Judge Frank declared that obscenity laws are unconstitutionally vague. He noted that Benjamin Franklin, named Postmaster General by the First Continental Congress, had written books—including The Speech of Polly Baker—which a 20th Century jury might find obscene. Judge Frank added: [39]

---

[35] 354 U.S. 476, 77 S.Ct. 1304 (1957).

[36] Ibid.

[37] United States v. Roth, 237 F.2d 796 (2d Cir.1956).

[38] West's Ann.Cal.Pen.Code, § 311; 138 Cal.App.2d Supp. 909, 292 P.2d 90 (1956).

[39] 237 F.2d 796, 825 826–827 (2d Cir.1965). See Stanley Fleishman, "Witchcraft and Obscenity: Twin Superstitions," Wilson Library Bulletin, April, 1965, p. 4.

To vest a few fallible men—prosecutors, judges, jurors—with vast powers of literary or artistic censorship, to convert them into what J.S. Mill called a 'moral police,' is to make them despotic arbiters of literary products. If one day they ban mediocre books as obscene, another day they may do likewise to a work of genius. Originality, not too plentiful, should be cherished, not stifled. An author's imagination may be cramped if he must write with one eye on prosecutors or juries; authors must cope with publishers who, fearful about the judgments of governmental censors, may refuse to accept the manuscripts of contemporary Shelleys or Mark Twains or Whitmans.

* * *

The troublesome aspect of the federal obscenity statute * * * is that (a) no one can now show that with any reasonable probability obscene publications tend to have any effects on the behavior of normal, average adults, and (b) that under the [federal] statute * * * punishment is apparently inflicted for provoking, in such adults, undesirable sexual thoughts, feelings or desire—not overt dangerous or anti-social conduct, either actual or probable.

Despite Judge Frank's denunciation of the "exquisite vagueness" of obscenity laws, Roth's conviction was upheld, with the Court of Appeals refusing to consider the contention that obscenity statutes are unconstitutionally vague curbs on speech and press. The Supreme Court then granted certiorari, taking jurisdiction of the case.[40]

Alberts v. California

The State of California prosecution against David S. Alberts went after his mail-order business in Los Angeles. In 1955, he was served with a warrant and his business office, warehouse and residence were searched. Hundreds—maybe thousands—of books and pictures were seized.[41] Such books as "Witch on Wheels," "She Made It Pay," and "Sword of Desire"—plus some mail circulars—were found to be obscene. In discussing "Sword of Desire," the trial judge [42] did not read the book in its entirety, showing that the *Ulysses* decision's 1933 holding [43] that a book should be judged as a whole was not always followed. He wrote, "This book is about a psychiatrist who is using his ability in the

[40] 352 U.S. 964, 77 S.Ct. 361 (1957).

[41] Fleishman, op. cit., p. 10.

[42] Ibid., Alberts was tried by a judge sitting alone since Alberts had waived jury trial.

[43] United States v. One Book Entitled "Ulysses," 5 F.Supp. 182 (S.D.N.Y.1933).

touching of certain nerve centers * * * to develop a sexual desire in any woman." The judge noted that he read up to a point where the psychiatrist had used that technique twice. "I did not go beyond p. 49," the judge added.[44]

Alberts' conviction was upheld by an appellate court. That court concluded that the words "obscene" and "indecent" were not unconstitutionally vague. The Supreme Court then noted probable jurisdiction.[45]

In jointly considering the *Roth* and *Alberts* cases, the Court did not rule on whether the books sold by the two men were in fact obscene. The only issue reviewed in each case was the validity of an obscenity law on its face.[46] Alberts argued that this mail-order business could not be punished under California law because a state cannot regulate an area pre-empted by the federal obscenity laws. The majority opinion replied that the federal statute deals only with actual mailing and does not prevent a state from punishing the advertising or keeping for sale of obscene literature.[47]

Roth contended, on the other hand, that the power to punish speech and press offensive to morality belongs to the states alone under the powers of the First, Ninth, and Tenth Amendments to the Constitution. The majority opinion discarded this argument, saying that obscenity is not speech or expression protected by the First Amendment.[48] Justice Brennan added, in language which was to greatly affect later decisions in the law of obscenity:[49]

> All ideas having even the slightest redeeming social importance—unorthodox ideas, controversial ideas, even ideas hateful to the prevailing climate of opinion—have the full protection of the guaranties [of free speech and press], unless excludable because they encroach upon the limited area of more important interests. But implicit in the area of more important interests. But implicit in the history of the First Amendment is the rejection of obscenity as utterly without redeeming social importance.

This passage had within it elements of freeing literature. Later cases would make much of the phrase "redeeming social importance" to protect sexy materials, because most literature

---

[44] Fleishman brief, loc. cit.

[45] Alberts v. California, 352 U.S. 962, 77 S.Ct. 349 (1956).

[46] 354 U.S. 476, 77 S.Ct. 1304, 1307 (1957).

[47] 354 U.S. 476, 493–494, 77 S.Ct. 1304, 1314 (1957).

[48] 354 U.S. 476, 492, 77 S.Ct. 1304, 1313 (1957).

[49] 354 U.S. 476, 484, 77 S.Ct. 1304, 1309 (1957).

must have something good you can say about it.[50] Justice Brennan's majority opinion set the stage for obscenity law developments in two ways. First, obscenity laws may be used to punish *thoughts;* overt sexual actions are not needed to bring a conviction.[51] Second—and more important—obscenity is expression *not* protected by the First Amendment.[52] Those are the two main strands in the law of obscenity. Other strands woven in by concurring and dissenting Justices in Roth v. United States forecast other themes which would crescendo and diminish for the next 20 years in the strange symphony of obscenity law.[53]

The Roth Test

Writing for the Court, Justice Brennan set down this try at defining the undefinable: "Obscene material is material which deals with sex in a manner appealing to prurient interest." [54] "Prurient interest," of course, refers to sexually oriented thoughts. Brennan then articulated "the Roth test" for judging whether or not material is obscene: [55]

> * * * whether to the average person, applying contemporary community standards, the dominant theme of the material taken as a whole appeals to prurient interest.

Subsequent decisions have returned for guidance to these words again and again. This "*Roth* test" rejected some features of the American rendition of the *Hicklin* rule. The practice of judging books by the presumed effect of isolated passages upon the most susceptible persons was rejected because it "might well encompass material legitimately dealing with sex." [56]

Although the language of the *Roth* test, as will be shown, was used in later decisions to uphold the freedom to read, Mr. Justice Brennan's words were not wholly libertarian. The *Roth* test,

[50] See, e.g., A Book Named John Cleland's "Memoirs of a Woman of Pleasure" v. Massachusetts, 383 U.S. 413, 419–420, 86 S.Ct. 975, 977–978 (1966).

[51] 354 U.S. 476, 486–487, 77 S.Ct. 1304, 1309–1310 (1957).

[52] 354 U.S. 476, 482, 77 S.Ct. 1304, 1307 (1957).

[53] For example, Chief Justice Earl Warren's concurrence in Roth argued that the conduct of a defendant was the key point in an obscenity prosecution. For a case which turned on the defendant's conduct, see Ginzburg v. United States, 383 U.S. 463, 86 S.Ct. 942 (1966).

[54] U.S. 476, 487, 77 S.Ct. 1304, 1310 (1957). The terms used in the three "tests" approved in Roth—"lustful desire," "lustful thoughts," and "appeal to prurient interest"—all imply that if a book can be assumed to cause or induce "improper" sexual thoughts, that book can be "banned." The "appeal to prurient interest" test was drawn from the American Law Institute's Model Penal Code, Tentative Draft No. 6 (Philadelphia, American Law Institute, May 6, 1957).

[55] 354 U.S. 476, 489, 77 S.Ct. 1304, 1311 (1957).

[56] 354 U.S. 476, 489, 77 S.Ct. 1304, 1311 (1957).

instead, is a "deprave and corrupt" test. Under *Roth,* a book
could be declared obscene if it could be assumed that it might
induce obscene thoughts in an hypothetical average person.[57]
There is no need for the prosecution to prove that there is a "clear
and present danger" [58] or even a "clear and possible danger" [59]
that a book will lead to antisocial conduct.

Roth: Concurrences and Dissents

Chief Justice Earl Warren was evidently puzzled by the idea
that *books* rather than persons were defendants in obscenity
prosecutions. His brief concurring opinion in *Roth* has proved to
be remarkably predictive since 1957. Chief Justice Warren stated
that in an obscenity trial, the conduct of the defendant rather
than the obscenity of a book should be the central issue: [60]

He concluded that both Roth and Alberts had engaged in "the
commercial exploitation of the morbid and shameful craving for
materials with prurient effect" and said that the state and federal
governments could constitutionally punish such conduct.[61] Justice
Brennan's majority opinion in *Roth* has influenced the course of
the law of obscenity. So, in an increasing degree in recent years,
has Chief Justice Warren's concurring opinion, which insisted that
the behavior of the defendant, rather than the nature of the book
itself, was the "central issue" in an obscenity case.[62] The impact
of the legal formulations in *Roth* by Justice Brennan and Chief
Justice Warren will be discussed later in this chapter.

Justice Harlan also disagreed with the majority opinion's
conclusion that obscenity laws are constitutional because an earlier Supreme Court had found that obscenity is "utterly without
redeeming social importance": [63]

> This sweeping formula appears to me to beg the very
> question before us. The Court seems to assume that
> "obscenity" is a particular *genus* of speech and press,
> which is as distinct, recognizable and classifiable as
> poison ivy is among plants. On this basis, the *constitu-
> tional* question before us becomes, as the Court says,
> whether "obscenity," as an abstraction, is protected by
> the First and Fourteenth Amendments, and the question

57 354 U.S. 476, 486, 77 S.Ct. 1304, 1310 (1957).

58 354 U.S. 476, 489, 77 S.Ct. 1304, 1310 (1957).

59 U.S. 476, 489, 77 S.Ct. 1304, 1310 (1957), citing Dennis v. United States, 341
U.S. 494, 71 S.Ct. 857 (1952).

60 354 U.S. 476, 495, 77 S.Ct. 1304, 1315 (1957).

61 354 U.S. 476, 496, 77 S.Ct. 1304, 1315 (1957).

62 354 U.S. 476, 495, 77 S.Ct. 1304, 1314–1315 (1957).

63 354 U.S. 476, 497, 77 S.Ct. 1304, 1315 (1957).

whether a *particular* book may be suppressed becomes a mere matter of classification, of "fact" to be entrusted to a fact-finder and insulated from independent judgment.

Justice Harlan thus told his fellow justices that the vital question was "what is obscenity?", not "is obscenity good or bad?"

While Harlan asked this challenging question of his brethren on the Court, Justice William O. Douglas was joined by Justice Hugo L. Black in a scathing attack on obscenity laws and obscenity prosecutions. This dissent foreshadowed arguments these Justices would advance in obscenity cases which subsequently followed *Roth* to the Supreme Court: [64]

> When we sustain these convictions, we make the legality of a publication turn on the purity of thought which a book or tract instills in the mind of the reader. I do not think we can approve that standard and be faithful to the command of the First Amendment which by its terms is a restraint on Congress and which by the Fourteenth Amendment is a restraint on the States.

Douglas wrote that Roth and Alberts were punished "for thoughts provoked, not for overt acts nor antisocial conduct." He was unimpressed by the possibility that the books involved might produce sexual thoughts: "The arousing of sexual thoughts and desires happens every day in normal life in dozens of ways." [65]

Problems involving freedom of speech and press, it was argued, must not be solved by "weighing against the values of free expression, the judgment of a court that a particular form of expression has 'no redeeming social importance.'" Justice Douglas warned: [66]

> For the test that suppresses a cheap tract today can suppress a literary gem tomorrow. All it need do is incite a lascivious thought or arouse a lustful desire. The list of books that judges or juries can place in that category is endless.

SEC. 49. PATENT OFFENSIVENESS

In the Manual Enterprises case, the Supreme Court added a new element—"patent offensiveness"—to its attempts to define obscenity.

Although *Roth* remains the leading decision on obscenity and said much, later court decisions showed that it had settled little.

---

[64] 354 U.S. 476, 508, 77 S.Ct. 1304, 1321 (1957).

[65] 354 U.S. 476, 509, 77 S.Ct. 1304, 1322 (1957).

[66] 354 U.S. 476, 514, 77 S.Ct. 1304, 1324 (1957).

Five years after *Roth* the Supreme Court attempted to refine its definition of obscenity in Manual Enterprises, Inc. v. J. Edward Day, Postmaster General of the United States. In writing for the Court, Justice Harlan termed *MANual* [sic], *Trim,* and *Grecian Pictorial* "dismally unpleasant, uncouth and tawdry" magazines which were published "primarily, if not exclusively, for homosexuals." [67]

Despite this, a majority of the Supreme Court held that these magazines which presented pictures of nude males were not obscene and unmailable because they were not "patently offensive." Harlan wrote: [68]

> Obscenity under the federal statute * * * requires proof of two distinct elements: (1) patent offensiveness; and (2) "prurient interest" appeal. Both must conjoin before challenged material can be found obscene under § 1461. In most obscenity cases to be sure, the two elements tend to coalesce, for that which is patently offensive will also usually carry the requisite "prurient interest" appeal.

Harlan reaffirmed the Supreme Court's long-held position that mere nudity was not enough to support a conviction for obscenity. [69]

After adding the "patent offensiveness" qualification to its definition of obscenity, the Court then turned to the tricky problem of giving meaning to the "contemporary community standards" phrase used in *Roth.* This time, a movie—the French film called *"Les Amants"* ("The Lovers") was the vehicle of expression which confronted the Court. Nico Jacobellis, manager of a Cleveland, Ohio, motion picture theater, had been convicted under Ohio law on two counts of possessing and exhibiting an obscene film. Jacobellis had been fined a total of $2,500 and his conviction was upheld by the Ohio Supreme Court. [70]

Writing for the Supreme Court in reversing Jacobellis' conviction, Mr. Justice Brennan ruled that the film was not obscene. He rejected the argument that the "contemporary community standards" aspect of the *Roth* test implied "a determination of the constitutional question of obscenity in each case by the standards of the particular local community from which the case arises." Brennan declared that no " 'local' definition of the 'community' could properly be employed by the Federal Constitution." [71]

[67] 370 U.S. 478, 481, S.Ct. 1432, 1434 (1962).

[68] 370 U.S. 478, 482–486, 82 S.Ct. 1432, 1434–1436 (1962).

[69] 370 U.S. 478, 490, 82 S.Ct. 1432, 1438 (1962).

[70] 378 U.S. 184, 84 S.Ct. 1676 (1964).

[71] 378 U.S. 184, 84 S.Ct. 1676, 1677 (1964).

Despite these brave words, a majority of the Court failed to agree with Justice Brennan that there should be a national standard for judging obscenity. In 1973, in Miller v. California, the Court—casting about for a way of shrugging off the burden of judging so many obscenity cases—said that states and localities could set their individual (if contradictory) standards for judging what is permissible for expression about sex.[72] But—as will be discussed in Sections 51 and 52, some subsequent state and local prosecutions were so censoriously wrongheaded that the Court was forced to continue its role as the "High Court of Obscenity." [73]

Back in 1966, however, the Court did not know what tortured obscenity cases it would face. Following—or at least echoing—the words of Chief Justice Warren in Roth v. United States,[74] the Court moved in 1966 toward judging the *conduct* of the distributor rather than the *content* of the communication which was being distributed. Cases involved here were "Fanny Hill," [75] Mishkin v. State of New York,[76] and Ginzburg v. United States.[77]

SEC. 50. FROM CONTENT TO CONDUCT

In 1966, the Supreme Court shifted—at least in part—from judging the *content* of a publication to judging the character of a bookseller's or distributor's *conduct*.

In 1966, the Supreme Court again tackled the tough problem of defining obscenity as decisions were announced in three cases, the "Fanny Hill" case,[78] Mishkin v. New York,[79] and Ginzburg v. United States.[80] First announced was the decision in the *Fanny Hill* case, in which the Court had to deal with one of the most durable wenches in Anglo-American literary history. *Fanny Hill,* or as the book is also known, *Memoirs of a Woman of Pleasure,* was written in England about 1749 by John Cleland. The book was well known in the American colonies and was first published in the United States around 1800 by Isaiah Thomas of Worcester, Massachusetts, one of the foremost printers of the American

[72] 413 U.S. 15, 93 S.Ct. 2607 (1973).

[73] See, e.g. Jenkins v. Georgia, 418 U.S. 153, 94 S.Ct. 2750 (1974).

[74] See Chief Justice Warren's dissent in Roth v. United States, 354 U.S. 476, at 495–496, 77 S.Ct. 1304, at 1315 (1957).

[75] 383 U.S. 413, 86 S.Ct. 975 (1966).

[76] 383 U.S. 502, 86 S.Ct. 958 (1966).

[77] 383 U.S. 463, 86 S.Ct. 942 (1966).

[78] 383 U.S. 413, 86 S.Ct. 975 (1966).

[79] 383 U.S. 502, 86 S.Ct. 958 (1966).

[80] 383 U.S. 463, 86 S.Ct. 942 (1966).

Revolution.[81] *Fanny Hill,* was also one of the first books in America to be the subject of an obscenity trial: in Massachusetts in 1821.[82] More than 140 years later, Fanny Hill was back in the courts of Massachusetts, as well as in New York, New Jersey and Illinois.[83]

In Fanny Hill, there is not one of the "four letter words" which have so often put more modern literature before the courts. But although the language was quite sanitary, author Cleland's descriptions of Fanny's sexual gyrations left little to the imagination. Even so, some experts—including poet and critic Louis Untermeyer—testified that *Fanny Hill* was a work of art and was not pornographic. The experts, however, were asked by a cross-examining prosecuting attorney if they realized that the book contained "20 acts of sexual intercourse, four of them in the presence of others; four acts of lesbianism, two acts of male homosexuality, two acts of flagellation and one of female masturbation." [84]

Fanny Hill, then, is a frankly erotic novel. Justice Brennan summed up the tests for obscenity which the highest court had approved: [85]

> We defined obscenity in *Roth* in the following terms: "[W]hether to the average person, applying contemporary community standards, the dominant theme of the material taken as a whole appeals to prurient interest." 354 U.S. at 489, 77 S.Ct. at 1311. Under this definition, as elaborated in subsequent cases, three elements must coalesce: it must be established that (a) the dominant theme of the materials taken as a whole appeals to a prurient interest in sex; (b) the material is patently offensive because it affronts contemporary community standards relating to the description or representation of sexual matters; and (c) the material is utterly without redeeming social value.

The Supreme Court of the United States held that the Massachusetts courts had erred in finding that a book didn't have to be "unqualifiedly worthless" before it could be deemed obscene. Justice Brennan, writing for the Court, stated that a book "can not be

[81] Peter Quennell, introduction to John Cleland's Memoirs of a Woman of Pleasure (New York: Putnam, 1963) p. xv.

[82] Commonwealth v. Peter Holmes, 17 Mass. 336 (1821).

[83] These prosecutions, as Justice Douglas pointed out, seemed a bit ironic in view of the fact that the Library of Congress had asked permission to translate the book into braille. 383 U.S. 413, 425–426, 86 S.Ct. 975, 981 (1966).

[84] Cf. the outraged dissent by Justice Tom C. Clark, 383 U.S. 413, 445–446, 86 S.Ct. 975, 990–991 (1966).

[85] 383 U.S. 413, 418, 86 S.Ct. 975, 977 (1966).

proscribed unless it is found to be *utterly* without redeeming social value." [86]

Second, Justice Brennan announced the Court's decision in the *Mishkin* case. Edward Mishkin, who operated a bookstore near New York City's Times Square, was appealing a sentence of three years and $12,500 in fines. Mishkin's publishing speciality was sadism and masochism, and he had been found guilty by New York courts of producing and selling more than 50 different paperbacks. Titles involved included *Dance With the Dominant Whip, Cult of the Spankers, Swish Bottom, Mrs. Tyrant's Finishing School* and *Stud Broad.*[87]

Mishkin had instructed one author working for him that the books should be " 'full of sex scenes and lesbian scenes * * *. [T]he sex had to be very strong, it had to be rough, it had to be clearly spelled out.' " [88] Mishkin's defense, however, was based on the notion that the books he published and sold did not appeal to the prurient interest of an average person. The average person, it was argued, would be disgusted and sickened by such books.[89]

Justice Brennan's majority opinion, however, dismissed Mishkin's argument.[90]

> Where the material is designed primarily for and primarily disseminated to a clearly defined deviant sexual group, rather than the public at large, the prurient-appeal requirement of the *Roth* test is satisfied if the dominant theme of the material taken as a whole appeals to the prurient interest of the members of that group.

After upholding Mishkin's conviction, Mr. Justice Brennan then turned to the *Ginzburg* case. With this opinion, the Supreme Court brought another element to the adjudication of obscenity disputes: the manner in which the matter charged with obscenity was sold.[91]

The *Ginzburg* case involved three publication: "EROS, a hardcover magazine of expensive format; Liaison, a bi-weekly newsletter; and The Housewife's Handbook on Selective Promiscuity, * * * a short book." Justice Brennan took notice of "abundant evidence" from Ralph Ginzburg's federal district court trial "that each of the accused publications was originated or sold as stock in trade of the sordid business of pandering—'the business

[86] 383 U.S. 413, 419, 86 S.Ct. 975, 978 (1966).

[87] 383 U.S. 502, 514–515, 86, S.Ct. 975, 978 (1966).

[88] 383 U.S. 502, 505, 86 S.Ct. 958, 961 (1966).

[89] 383 U.S. 502, 508, 86 S.Ct. 958, 963 (1966).

[90] 383 U.S. 502, 508–509, 86 S.Ct. 958, 963–964 (1966).

[91] 383 U.S. 463, 465–466, 86 S.Ct. 942, 944–945 (1966).

of purveying textual or graphic matter openly advertised to appeal to the erotic interest of their customers.' " [92]

Included as evidence of this "pandering" were EROS magazine's attempts to get mailing privileges from the whimsically named hamlets of Intercourse and Blue Ball, Pa. Mailing privileges were finally obtained in Middlesex, N.J.[93]

Also, Justice Brennan found " 'the leer of the sensualist' " permeating the advertising for the three publications. *Liaison,* for example, was extolled as "Cupid's Chronicle," and the advertising circulars asked, "Are you a member of the sexual elite?" [94] It is likely, however, that publisher Ginzburg believed that the *Roth* test had left him on safe ground, for his advertising proclaimed: [95]

> "EROS handles the subject of Love and Sex with complete candor. The publication of this magazine— which is frankly and avowedly concerned with erotica— has been enabled by recent court decisions ruling that a literary piece of painting, though explicitly sexual in content, has a right to be published if it is a genuine work of art."

> "EROS is genuine work of art."

The Court was severely split of the *Ginzburg* case, however, with Justices Black, Douglas, Harlan and Stewart all registering bitter dissents. Justice Black set the tone for his dissenting brethren, declaring: [96]

> Only one stark fact emerges with clarity out of the confusing welter of opinions and thousands of words written in this and two other cases today. * * * That fact is that Ginzburg, petitioner here, is now finally and authoritatively condemned to serve five years in prison for distributing printed matter about sex which neither Ginzburg nor anyone else could possibly have known to be criminal.

Justice Harlan accused the court's majority of rewriting the federal obscenity statute in order to convict Ginzburg, and called the new "pandering" test unconstitutionally vague.[97] And Justice Stewart asserted in his dissent that Ginzburg "was not charged with 'commercial exploitation'; he was not charged with 'pandering'; he was not charged with 'titillation.' " Convicting Ginzburg

[92] 383 U.S. 463, 467, 86 S.Ct. 942, 945 (1966).

[93] 383 U.S. 463, 467, 86 S.Ct. 942, 945 (1966).

[94] 383 U.S. 463, 469n 86 S.Ct. 942, 946n (1966).

[95] Ibid.

[96] 383 U.S. 463, 476, 86 S.Ct. 942, 954 (1966).

[97] 383 U.S. 463, 476, 86 S.Ct. 942, 954 (1966).

on such grounds, Stewart added, was to deny him due process of law.[98]

Justice Douglas added his denunciation of the condemnation of materials as obscene not because of their content, but because of the way they were advertised.[99]

Protecting the Young: The Ginsberg Case and the "Variable Obscenity" Concept

As if to confound careless spellers, it has happened that one of the most important cases after the Ralph *Ginzburg* case involved a man named *Ginsberg:* Sam Ginsberg. In the 1968 *Ginsberg* case, the Supreme Court held by a 6–3 vote that a New York statute which defined obscenity on the basis of its appeal to minors under 17 was not unconstitutionally vague.

Sam Ginsberg and his wife operated "Sam's Stationery and Luncheonette" in Bellmore, Long Island. In 1965, a mother sent her 16-year-old son to the luncheonette to by some "girlie" magazines. The boy purchased two magazines—apparently *Sir* and *Gent* or similar publications—and walked out of the luncheonette. On the basis of this sale, Sam Ginsberg was convicted of violation of a New York law making it a misdemeanor "knowingly to sell * * * to a minor" under 17 "any picture * * * which depicts nudity * * * and which is harmful to minors" and "any * * * magazine * * * which contains * * * [such pictures] and which, taken as a whole, is harmful to minors." [1]

It should be noted that magazines such as the 16-year-old boy purchased from Sam Ginsberg's luncheonette in 1967 had been held *not* obscene for adults by the Supreme Court.[2] However the judge at Sam Ginsberg's obscenity trial found pictures in the two magazines which depicted nudity in a manner that was in violation of the New York statute which forbids [3]

> "the showing of * * * female * * * buttocks with less than a full opaque covering, or the showing of the female breast with less than a fully opaque covering of any portion thereof below the top of the nipple * * *"

[98] 383 U.S. 463, 494, 86 S.Ct. 942, 954 (1966).

[99] 383 U.S. 463, 494, 497, 86 S.Ct. 942, 954, 956 (1966).

[1] Ginsberg v. New York, 390 U.S. 629, 634, 88 S.Ct. 1274, 1277 (1968). The statute is Article 484–H of the New York Penal Law, McKinney's Consol Laws c. 40.

[2] Redrup v. New York, 386 U.S. 767, 87 S.Ct. 1414 (1967).

[3] Ginsberg v. New York, 390 U.S. 629, 632, 88 S.Ct. 1274, 1276 (1968), quoting New York Penal Law Article 484–h as enacted by L.1965, c. 327, subsections (b) and (f).

The trial judge found that the pictures were "harmful to minors" under the terms of the New York law.[4]

In affirming Ginsberg's conviction, Justice Brennan approved the concept of "variable obscenity."[5] Brennan noted that the magazines involved in the *Ginsberg* case were not obscene for sale to adults. However, the New York statute forbidding their sale to minors "does not bar the appellant from stocking the magazines and selling them to persons 17 years of age or older." Brennan repeated the holding that obscenity is not within the area of protected speech or press.[6] It was permissible for the state of New York to "accord to minors under 17 a more restricted right than that assured to adults to judge and determine for themselves what sex material they may read or see."

In the case which resulted in the fining and jailing of *Eros* publisher Ralph Ginzburg, the Supreme Court served notice that not only *what* was sold but *how* it was sold would be taken into account.[7] The *how* of selling or distributing literature can include a legitimate public concern over the materials which minor children see. That is the lesson of the case of Ginsberg v. New York, and that lesson is wrapped up in the concept of "variable obscenity." That is, some materials are not obscene for adults but are obscene when children are involved.[8]

SEC. 51.   INDECISIVENESS ON OBSCENITY: *REDRUP* AND *STANLEY*

From 1967 until 1973, many convictions were reversed by the Supreme Court of the United States because a majority could not agree upon a definition of obscenity.

In the spring of 1967, the Supreme Court of the United States openly admitted its confusion over obscenity law in a case known as Redrup v. New York.[9] This decision did not *look* important: it took up only six pages in United States Reports and only about four pages were devoted to its unsigned *per curiam* ["by the court"] majority opinion. The other two pages were given over to a dissent by the late Justice John Marshall Harlan, with whom the

---

[4] Ginsberg v. New York, 390 U.S. 629, 633, 88 S.Ct. 1274, 1276 (1968).

[5] Ginsberg v. New York, 390 U.S. 629, 635n, 88 S.Ct. 1274, 1278n (1968), quoting Lockhart and McClure, "Censorship of Obsenity: The Developing Constitutional Standards," 45 Minnesota Law Review 5, 85 (1960).

[6] Ginsberg v. New York, 390 U.S. 629, 635, 88 S.Ct. 1274, 1277–1278 (1968); see Butler v. Michigan, 352 U.S. 380, 77 S.Ct. 524 (1957); Roth v. United States, 354 U.S. 476, 77 S.Ct. 1304, 1309 (1957).

[7] Ginzburg v. United States, 383 U.S. 463, 86 S.Ct. 942 (1966).

[8] Ginsberg v. New York, 390 U.S. 629, 88 S.Ct. 1274 (1968).

[9] 386 U.S. 767, 87 S.Ct. 1414 (1967).

now-retired Justice Tom C. Clark joined.[10] *Redrup* was an important case simply because the Court said that a majority of its members could not agree on a standard which could declare so-called "girlie magazines" and similar publications to be obscene.

Redrup seemed for a time to be the most important obscenity case since Roth v. United States because it was used by both state and federal courts for several years to avoid many of the complexities of judging whether works of art or literature are obscene. On June 12, 1967, the date the Court's term ended that year and less than two months after *Redrup* was decided, the Court reversed 11 obscenity convictions by merely referring to Redrup v. New York.[11] Another dozen state or federal obscenity convictions were reversed during the next year, with *Redrup* being listed as an important factor in each reversal.[12]

Redrup's unsigned majority opinion was merely a sketchy review of the varying—and sometimes contradictory—attempts made by the Court to define obscenity. After reviewing the justices' differing views on the subject, the *Redrup* majority opinion took a new tack. The Court ruled that no matter what test was applied to the sexy paperback novels (*Lust Pool* and *Shame Agent*) or girlie magazines (*Gent, High Heels, Spree*) before the Court, the convictions for obscenity reviewed in *Redrup* simply could not be upheld. The unsigned majority opinion concluded, "Whichever of these constitutional views [definitions of obscenity listed sketchily in the *Redrup* opinion] are brought to bear upon the cases before us, it is clear that the judgments [obscenity convictions in the lower courts] before us cannot stand." [13]

The majority opinion in *Redrup* placed significant reliance upon the Court's 1966 decision in Ginzburg v. United States. In *Ginzburg,* discussed earlier in this chapter, it will be recalled that the Court took special notice of the *manner* in which magazines or books were sold.[14] *Redrup* echoed this concern, but also took into account the *recipients* of materials charged with obscenity. The Court suggested that convictions for selling or mailing obscenity should be upheld in three kinds of situations:

> (1) Where there is evidence of "pandering" sales as in Ginzburg v. United States.

---

[10] 386 U.S. 767, 771, 87 S.Ct. 1414, 1416 (1967).

[11] Dwight L. Teeter, Jr., and Don R. Pember, "The Retreat from Obscenity: Redrup v. New York," Hastings Law Journal Vol. 21 (Nov., 1969) pp. 175–189.

[12] 386 U.S. 767, 771–772, 87 S.Ct. 1414, 1416–1417 (1967).

[13] 386 U.S. 767, 87 S.Ct. 1414, 1416 (1967).

[14] 383 U.S. 463, 86 S.Ct. 942 (1966).

(2) Where there is a statute reflecting "a specific and limited state concern for juveniles." [15]

(3) Where there is "an assault upon individual privacy by publication in a manner so obtrusive as to make it impossible for the unwilling individual to avoid exposure to it."[16]

Beyond these kinds of forbidden conduct *Redrup* gave little guidance. Perhaps, however, it may be guessed that *Redrup* meant this: If the *conduct* of the seller did not fit the three kinds of prohibited actions listed above, and if the *contents* were not so wretched that they would be held to be "hardcore pornography," [17] then the materials involved were constitutionally protected.[18]

Stanley v. Georgia (1969)

In 1969, there was hope that the Supreme Court of the United States—clearly irritated by obscenity cases which amounted to perhaps five per cent of its total workload—would bring order to that troublesome area of law. The Court's resolution of Stanley v. Georgia added to that hope.[19] The *Stanley* case arose when a Georgia state investigator and three federal agents, operating under a federal search warrant, searched the home of Robert E. Stanley, looking for bookmaking records. Evidence of bookmaking was not found, but the searchers found three reels of 8 millimeter film and—handily—a projector. They treated themselves to a showing and decided—as did a couple of courts—that the films were obscene. When Stanley's appeal reached the Supreme Court, Mr. Justice Thurgood Marshall—writing for a unanimous Court—named two constitutional rights.[20]

---

[15] Redrup v. New York, 386 U.S. 767, 769, 87 S.Ct. 1414, 1415 (1967). Note that (2) above, announced in Redrup on May 8, 1967, forecast with considerable precision the Court's decision in Ginsberg v. New York, 390 U.S. 629, 88 S.Ct. 1274 (1968).

[16] Ibid., citing Breard v. Alexandria, 341 U.S. 622, 71 S.Ct. 920 (1951), and Public Utilities Commission v. Pollak, 343 U.S. 415, 72 S.Ct. 813 (1952).

[17] 386 U.S. 767, 771n, 87 S.Ct. 1414, 1416n, referring to Justice Potter Stewart's quotation, in his dissent in Ginzburg v. United States, of this definition of hardcore pornography, including writings and "photographs, both still and motion picture, with no pretense of artistic value, graphically depicting acts of sexual intercourse, including various acts of sodomy and sadism, and sometimes involving several participants in scenes of orgy-like character. * * * verbally describing such activities in a bizarre manner with no attempt whatsoever to afford portrayals of character or situation and with no pretense to literary value." See Ginzburg v. United States, 383 U.S. 463, 499n, 86 S.Ct. 942, 956n (1966).

[18] 386 U.S. 767, 87 S.Ct. 1414, 1416 (1967).

[19] Stanley v. Georgia, 394 U.S. 557, 89 S.Ct. 1243 (1969).

[20] Black, J., concurred in the decision.

(1) A right growing out of the First Amendment, a "right to receive information and ideas, regardless of their social worth." [21]

(2) A constitutional right to privacy tied to the right to receive information and ideas: [22]

> * * * [F]undamental is the right to be free, except in very limited circumstances, from unwanted governmental intrusions into one's privacy. * * * These are the rights that appellant [Stanley] is asserting. * * * the right to satisfy his intellectual and emotional needs in the privacy of his own home.

Because Stanley v. Georgia involved no dangers of either injuring minors or invading the privacy of the general public, the Supreme Court concluded: [23]

> We hold that the First and Fourteenth Amendments prohibit making mere private possession of obscene material a crime. Roth and the cases following that decision are not impaired by today's holding. As we have said, the States retain broad power to regulate obscenity; that power simply does not extend to mere possession by the individual in the privacy of his own home.

Taken together, *Redrup* and *Stanley* suggested to some judges that the strictures of obscenity law had been loosened by the Supreme Court. *Redrup* said that the Court could not define anything but hard-core porn, the grossest of the gross. And *Stanley* seemed to say that people had a right to possess sexually explicit literature and films at home. This meant, to some judges, that if you got the stuff home, somebody, somewhere, had to have at least a limited right to sell it to you. Right? [24] Or, what if you wanted to go into a Triple-X rated film such as "Naked Came the Professor?" Couldn't you be somehow "publicly private"—sitting there in anonymous darkness in a theater? And you, in such a case, would be in effect a consenting adult whose privacy or other sensibilities were not being intruded upon. [25] Couldn't it be said that you have a right to receive such information and ideas? [26]

[21] 394 U.S. 557, 89 S.Ct. 1243 (1969), citing Winters v. New York, 333 U.S. 507, 510, 68 S.Ct. 665 (1948).

[22] 394 U.S. 557, 564–564, 89 S.Ct. 1243, 1247–1248 (1969).

[23] 394 U.S. 557, 568–569, 89 S.Ct. 1243, 1249–1250 (1969).

[24] See, e.g., Dyson v. Stein, 401 U.S. 200, 91 S.Ct. 769 (1971).

[25] See, e.g., United States v. Articles of "Obscene" Merchandise, 315 F.Supp. 191 (D.C.N.Y.1970), and Paris Adult Theatre I v. Slaton, 413 U.S. 49, 93 S.Ct. 2628 (1973).

[26] Stanley v. Georgia, 394 U.S. 557, 89 S.Ct. 1243 (1969).

No to all questions. Take, for example, the case of Byrne v. Karalexis.[27] Owners and operators of a theater sued in U.S. District Court for a declaration that a Massachusetts obscenity statute was unconstitutional and to enjoin the state from further prosecutions for exhibiting the film "I Am Curious (Yellow)." The three-judge court, with one judge dissenting, granted a preliminary injunction forbidding carrying out of sentence in the state prosecution or the starting of any future prosecutions.[28]

Ruling for the theater, Circuit Judge Bailey Aldrich wondered whether Stanley v. Georgia should be limited to "mere private possession of obscene material." He asked whether the *Stanley* case should be read as "the high water mark of a past flood, or is it the precursor of a new one?" Judge Aldrich then decided that the Stanley decision overturned the Roth v. United States ruling that "obscenity is not within the area of constitutionally protected speech or press." Instead, he argued that [29]

> * * * Roth remains intact only with respect to public distribution in the full sense * * * restricted distribution, adequately controlled, is no longer to be condemned. It is difficult to think that if Stanley has a constitutional right to view obscene films, the Court would intend its exercise to be only at the expense of a criminal act on behalf of the only logical source, the professional supplier. A constitutional right to receive a communication would seem meaningless if there were not a coextensive right to make it * * *. If a rich Stanley can view a film, or read a book, a poorer Stanley should be free to visit a protected theatre or library. We see no reason for saying he must go alone.

But in an unsigned *per curiam* decision, the Supreme Court of the United States showed that it was not impressed by the logic of Circuit Judge Aldrich's arguments. The Supreme Court erased the injunction and sent the case back for further prosecution at the state level.[30]

---

[27] 401 U.S. 200, 216, 91 S.Ct. 769, 777 (1971), reversing and remanding 306 F.Supp. 1363 (D.C.Mass.1969).

[28] 306 F.Supp. 1363 (D.C.Mass.1969), probable jurisdiction noted 397 U.S. 985, 90 S.Ct. 1123 (1970).

[29] Ibid. 1366–1367 (citations omitted).

[30] 401 U.S. 200, 216, 91 S.Ct. 769, 777 (1971).

SEC. 52. *MILLER v. CALIFORNIA:* ENCOURAGING STATE AND LOCAL CONTROL

In 1973, a new majority emerged on the Supreme Court in obscenity cases, and ruled that "community standards" used in judging literature or films need not be national.

Censors—or would-be censors—cheered when the Supreme Court decided Miller v. California in 1973.[31] This case, and four companion cases decided at the same time, said that a national standard was not required to judge obscenity.[32] Censorship boards began forming in numerous locales across the nation, and many adult movie houses and book stores shut down or "cleaned up"— however temporarily.[33]

Miller v. California

The most important of the five obscenity cases decided by the Supreme Court on June 21, 1973—and indeed the most important such case since Roth v. United States (1957)—was Miller v. California.[34] In that case, as in the four others of that date, the Court split 5–4, revealing a new coalition among the Justices where obscenity and pornography were concerned. This coalition included Justice Byron R. White (appointed by President John F. Kennedy) and four justices appointed by President Richard M. Nixon (Chief Justice Warren Burger, plus justices Harry Blackmun, William Rehnquist, and Lewis Powell). Dissenting in all five of those obscenity cases were Justices Thurgood Marshall, Potter Stewart, William O. Douglas, and the author of the *Roth* test of 1957 and of many of the obscenity decisions thereafter, Justice William J. Brennan, Jr.

Miller v. California arose when Marvin Miller mailed five unsolicited—and graphic—brochures to a restaurant in Newport Beach. The envelope was opened by the restaurant's manager, with his mother looking on, and they complained to police. The brochures advertised four books, Intercourse, Man-Woman, Sex Orgies Illustrated, and An Illustrated History of Pornography, plus a film titled Marital Intercourse. After a jury trial, Miller

[31] Miller v. California, 413 U.S. 15, 93 S.Ct. 2607 (1973).

[32] Paris Adult Theatre I v. Slaton, 413 U.S. 49, 93 S.Ct. 2628 (1973); U.S. v. Orito, 413 U.S. 139, 93 S.Ct. 2674 (1973); Kaplan v. California, 413 U.S. 115, 93 S.Ct. 2680 (1973), and U.S. v. Twelve 200-ft. Reels of Super 8 mm Film, 413 U.S. 123, 93 S.Ct. 2665 (1973).

[33] "Smut Peddlers Closing Doors—or Cleaning Up," Associated Press dispatch in St. Louis Globe-Democrat, June 23, 1973, Section A, pp. 1, 12.

[34] 413 U.S. 15, 93 S.Ct. 2607 (1973).

was convicted of a misdemeanor under the California Penal Code.[35]

Writing for the majority in *Miller*, Chief Justice Burger ruled that California could punish such conduct. He noted that the case involved "a situation in which sexually explicit materials have been thrust by aggressive sales action upon unwilling recipients who had in no way indicated any desire to receive such materials. He added: [36]

> This Court has recognized that the States have a legitimate interest in prohibiting dissemination of obscene material when the mode of dissemination carries with it a significant danger of offending the sensibilities of unwilling recipients or of exposure to juveniles. * * * It is in this context that we are called on to define the standards which must be used to identify obscene material that a State may regulate without infringing on the First Amendment as applicable to the States through the Fourteenth Amendment.

Endeavoring to formulate a new standard, Chief Justice Burger first returned to *Roth's* assurance that obscene materials were not protected by the First Amendment.[37] Then, he denounced the test of obscenity suggested in the Fanny Hill (*Memoirs of a Woman of Pleasure*) case nine years after *Roth*, in 1966. In that case, three justices, in a plurality opinion, held that material could not be judged obscene unless it were proven to be "utterly without redeeming social importance." Burger added: [38]

> While *Roth* presumed "obscenity" to be "utterly without redeeming social value," *Memoirs* required that to prove obscenity it must be affirmatively established that the material is "*utterly* without redeeming social value." Thus, even as they repeated the words of *Roth*, the *Memoirs* plurality produced a drastically altered test that called on the prosecution to prove a negative, i.e., that the

[35] West's Ann. California Pen. Code, § 312.2(a) makes it a misdemeanor to knowingly distribute obscene matter. After the jury trial, the Appellate Department, Superior Court of California, Orange County, summarily affirmed the conviction without offering an opinion.

[36] Miller v. State of California, 413 U.S. 15, 93 S.Ct. 2607, 2612 (1973). Relevant cases cited included Stanley v. Georgia, 394 U.S. 557, 89 S.Ct. 1243 (1969); Ginsberg v. New York, 390 U.S. 629, 88 S.Ct. 1274 (1968); Interstate Circuit, Inc. v. Dallas, 390 U.S. 676, 88 S.Ct. 1298 (1968); Redrup v. New York, 386 U.S. 767, 87 S.Ct. 1414 (1967); Jacobellis v. Ohio, 378 U.S. 184, 84 S.Ct. 1676 (1964), and Rabe v. Washington, 405 U.S. 313, 92 S.Ct. 993 (1972).

[37] 413 U.S. 15, 20, 93 S.Ct. 2607, 2613 (1973), citing Roth v. United States, 354 U.S. 476, 77 S.Ct. 1304 (1957).

[38] 413 U.S. 15, 22, 93 S.Ct. 2607, 2613–2614 (1973), citing Memoirs of a Woman of Pleasure v. Massachusetts, 383 U.S. 413, 86 S.Ct. 975 (1966). Emphasis the Court's.

material was *"utterly* without redeeming social value"—a burden virtually impossible to discharge under our criminal standards of proof.

The Chief Justice said that since the 1957 decision in *Roth,* the Court had not been able to muster a majority to agree to a standard of what constitutes "obscene, pornographic material subject to regulation under the States' police power." [39]   In 1973, however, Burger found himself in substantial agreement with four other Justices.   He made the most of it, setting out general rules on what States could regulate ("hard-core pornography") and rewording the *Roth* and *Memoirs* tests into a standard more congenial to convicting persons for distribution or possession of sexually explicit materials.[40]

> * * * [W]e now confine the permissible scope of such regulation to works which depict or describe sexual conduct. That conduct must be specifically defined by the applicable state law, as written or authoritatively construed. A state offense must also be limited to works which, taken as whole, appeal to the prurient interest in sex, which portray sexual conduct in a patently offensive way, and which, taken as a whole, do not have serious literary, artistic, political, or scientific value.

> The basic guidelines for the trier of fact must be: (a) whether "the average person, applying contemporary community standards" would find that the work, taken as a whole, appeals to the prurient interest * * * (b) whether the work depicts or describes, in a patently offensive way, sexual conduct specifically defined by the applicable state law, and (c) whether the work, taken as a whole, lacks serious literary, artistic, political or scientific value. We do not adopt as a constitutional standard the *"utterly* without redeeming social value" test of Memoirs v. Massachusetts * * *: that concept has never commanded the adherence of more than three Justices at one time.

[39] 413 U.S. 15, 22, 93 S.Ct. 2607, 2614 (1973).

[40] 413 U.S. 15, 23–24, 93 S.Ct. 2607, 2614, 2615 (1973).   Emphasis the Court's. Chief Justice Burger wrote that a State could, through statute, forbid:

"(a) Patently offensive representations or descriptions of ultimate sexual acts, normal or perverted, actual or simulated.

"(b) Patently offensive representations or descriptions of masturbation, excretory functions, and lewd exhibition of the genitals.

"Sex and nudity may not be exploited without limit by films or pictures exhibited or sold in places of public accommodation any more than live sex and nudity can be exhibited or sold without limit in such public places.   At a minimum, prurient, patently offensive depiction or description of sexual conduct must have serious literary, artistic, political or scientific value to merit First Amendment protection."

The majority opinion then declared that there can be no uniform national standard for judging obscenity or what appeals to "prurient interest" or what is "patently offensive." "[O]ur nation is simply too big and diverse for this Court to reasonably expect that such standards could be articulated for all 50 States in a single formulation * * *" [41] The First Amendment, Burger said, did not require the people of Maine or Mississippi to put up with public depiction of conduct tolerated in Las Vegas or New York City.

Deep disagreement with Justice Brennan sounded throughout the Chief Justice's opinion, providing a rather shrill counterpoint to Burger's main arguments. Brennan, the author of the majority opinion in *Roth* and long considered the Court's obscenity specialist, drew fire because Brennan had experienced a profound change of mind. Because of Justice Brennan's long study of this area of law—and because the problems he pointed to in 1973 are underlined every time the Court decides an obscenity case—he will be quoted at some length. [42]

Brennan's final rejection of the *Roth* test—and its modifications as expressed in *Memoirs* [43] and in Miller v. California [44]—was based in large measure upon his growing belief that obscenity statutes are unconstitutionally vague. That is, there are *"scienter"* problems: obscenity laws are so formless that defendants often do not have fair notice as to whether publications or films they distribute or exhibit are obscene. Without fair notice, there may occur a "chilling effect" upon protected speech. [45]

Brennan wrote: [46]

> I am convinced that the approach initiated 15 years
> ago in Roth v. United States * * * culminating in the
> Court's decision today, cannot bring stability to this area
> of the law without jeopardizing First Amendment values,

[41] 413 U.S. 15, 30, 93 S.Ct. 2607, 2618 (1973).

[42] Brennan, in company with Marshall and Stewart, dissented in all five of the obscenity decisions of the Court on June 21, 1973. Douglas dissented separately in all five cases. Brennan's dissent in Miller was brief, and referred to the major statement of his views in his dissent in the accompanying case of Paris Adult Theatre I v. Slaton, 413 U.S. 49, 93 S.Ct. 2607, 2627–2628 (1973), at pp. 2642–2663. Justice Brennan wrote opinions of the Court (or plurality opinions of the Court) in Roth v. United States, 354 U.S. 476, 77 S.Ct. 1304 (1957); Jacobellis v. Ohio, 378 U.S. 184, 84 S.Ct. 1676 (1964); Ginzburg v. United States, 383 U.S. 463, 86 S.Ct. 942 (1966); Mishkin v. New York, 383 U.S. 502, 86 S.Ct. 958 (1966), and Memoirs v. Massachusetts, 383 U.S. 413, 86 S.Ct. 975 (1966).

[43] 386 U.S. 767, 87 S.Ct. 1414 (1967).

[44] Memoirs of a Woman of Pleasure v. Massachusetts, 383 U.S. 413, 86 S.Ct. 975 (1966).

[45] Miller v. State of California, 413 U.S. 15, 93 S.Ct. 2607 (1973).

[46] Brennan dissent in Paris Adult Theatre I v. Slaton, 413 U.S. 49, 93 S.Ct. 2628, 2651 (1973).

and I have concluded that the time has come to make a significant departure from that approach.

*   *   *

Our experience with the *Roth* approach has certainly taught us that the outright suppression of obscenity cannot be reconciled with the fundamental principles of the First and Fourteenth Amendments. For we have failed to formulate a standard that sharply distinguishes protected from unprotected speech, and out of necessity we have resorted to the *Redrup* approach, which resolves cases as between parties, but offers only the most obscure guidance to legislation, adjudication by other courts, and primary conduct.

*   *   *

It comes as no surprise that judicial attempts to follow our lead conscientiously have often ended in hopeless confusion.

*   *   *

*   *   * These considerations suggest that no one definition, no matter how precisely or narrowly drawn, can positively suffice for all situations, or carve out fully suppressible expression for all media without also creating a substantial risk of encroachment upon the guarantees of the Due Process Clause and the First Amendment.

Our experience since *Roth* requires us not only to abandon the effort to pick out obscene materials on a case-by-case basis, but also to reconsider a fundamental postulate of *Roth:* That there exists a definable class of sexually oriented expression that may be totally suppressed by the Federal and State governments. Assuming that such a class of expression does in fact exist, I am forced to conclude that the concept of "obscenity" cannot be defined with sufficient specificity and clarity to provide fair notice to persons who create and distribute sexually oriented materials, to prevent substantial erosion of protected speech as a by-product of the attempt to suppress unprotected speech, and to avoid very costly institutional harms.

*   *   *

I would hold, therefore, that at least in the absence of distribution to juveniles or obtrusive exposure to unconsenting adults, the First and Fourteenth Amendments prohibit the state and federal governments from attempting wholly to suppress sexually oriented materials on the basis of their allegedly "obscene" contents. Nothing in this approach precludes those governments from taking action to serve what may be strong and legitimate interests through regulation of the manner of distribution of sexually oriented material.

From the *Miller* decision of 1973 well into the 1980s, the Court split 5–4 in most of the obscenity cases it has decided. The majority followed *Miller,* and favored stringent regulation of sexually explicit material. The split is profound, and may be traced to Justice Brennan's dissent which was quoted in the paragraphs immediately preceding this one. Time and time again, including many *per curiam* decisions in which the Court upheld obscenity prosecutions without an explanatory opinion, Brennan has dissented. He has said, repeatedly, that he does not believe that obscenity can be described with sufficient clarity to give defendants fair notice. Unless sexually explicit materials are distributed to juveniles or obtrusively presented to unconsenting adults, said Brennan, then the First and Fourteenth Amendments forbid states or the federal governments from suppressing such materials.[47]

"Refinements" of Miller: *Jenkins* and *Hamling*

To prosecutors and would-be censors, the decisions in *Miller* and its companion cases appeared to allow a kind of local-option in setting the limits of candor or disclosure in sexy books, magazines or films. As a result, Mike Nichols' serious film, *Carnal Knowledge,* became the target of an obscenity prosecution in Albany, Georgia in a case known as Jenkins v. Georgia. The prosecution took place even though it contained no frontal nudity or explicit depictions of sexual acts. The manager of a theater, Billy Jenkins, was convicted under a Georgia statute[48] forbidding distribution of obscene material and was fined $750 and sentenced to 12 months in jail.[49] His conviction was affirmed by the Georgia Supreme Court.[50]

Although agreeing with the Georgia Supreme Court that the U.S. Constitution does not require juries in obscenity cases to be instructed according to a hypothetical statewide standard,[51] the Supreme Court of the United States unanimously reversed Jen-

[47] See, e.g., Trinkler v. Alabama, 414 U.S. 955, 94 S.Ct. 265 (1973); Raymond Roth v. New Jersey, 414 U.S. 962, 94 S.Ct. 271 (1973); Jim Sharp v. Texas, 414 U.S. 1118, 94 S.Ct. 854 (1974); J–R Distributors, Inc. v. Washington, 418 U.S. 949, 94 S.Ct. 3217 (1974). See also Hamling v. U.S., 418 U.S. 87, 94 S.Ct. 2887, 2919–2924 (1974).

[48] Jenkins v. Georgia, 418 U.S. 153, 94 S.Ct. 2750, 2753 (1974) citing Ga.Code §§ 26–2011, 26–2105.

[49] 418 U.S. 153, 94 S.Ct. 2750, 2753 (1974).

[50] Ibid.

[51] Ibid.

kins' conviction. Writing for the Court, Justice William H. Rehnquist ruled that *Carnal Knowledge* was not patently offensive. He referred to Miller v. California, which said that a state statute could forbid patently offensive materials, including [52]

> "representations or descriptions of ultimate sexual acts, normal or perverted, actual or simulated," and "representations or descriptions of masturbation, excretory functions, and lewd exhibition of the genitals."

Because *Carnal Knowledge* did not contain such representations as described in *Miller,* the conviction of Jenkins could not stand.[53]

Hamling v. United States

If the film *Carnal Knowledge* was not "patently offensive," *The Illustrated Presidential Report of The Commission on Obscenity and Pornography* was exceptionally offensive and obscene in the eyes of five members of the Court. The case which *The Illustrated Presidential Report* inspired—Hamling v. United States—was indeed ironic, because the book in question used excruciatingly explicit photos to illustrate a text provided by a sobersided U.S. government report on obscenity and pornography.[54]

William L. Hamling and several co-defendants were indicted on 21 counts of using the mails to carry an obscene book. They had mailed approximately 55,000 copies of a single sheet advertising brochure to various parts of the U.S. One side contained a collage of photographs from the Illustrated Report portraying heterosexual and homosexual intercourse, fellatio, a group-sex arrangement involving nine persons, cunnilingus, and bestiality.[55] After a jury trial, the defendants were convicted on 12 counts of mailing and conspiring to mail an obscene advertisement.[56]

The book they advertised had taken the text from the actual report of the Commission on Obscenity and Pornography, but illustrations had been added. The publishers of the Illustrated Report said the pictures were included "as examples of the type of subject matter discussed and the type of the material shown to persons who were part of the research projects engaged in for the Commission as the basis for their [sic] Report." [57]

[52] 418 U.S. 153, 94 S.Ct. 2750, 2755 (1974).

[53] Ibid.

[54] Hamling v. United States, 418 U.S. 87, 94 S.Ct. 2887 (1974).

[55] 418 U.S. 87, 94 S.Ct. 2887, 2895 (1974).

[56] Ibid.

[57] 418 U.S. 87, 94 S.Ct. 1887, 2896 (1974).

The Court's majority opinion, delivered by Justice William H. Rehnquist, concluded that the advertising brochure was hard-core pornography.[58] That meant, of course, that circulating the brochure through the U.S. Mail was a crime. Hamling had been convicted in March, 1971, at a time when the question of whether national standards or state/local standards should be applied in judging obscenity was in limbo. Subsequently, the Court announced—in Miller v. California (1973)—that state or local standards and *not* national standards were to be used in evaluating allegedly obscene material. The trial judge had instructed the jury that obscenity was to be weighed according to a national standard. That judge ruled inadmissible the results of a survey of 718 San Diego, California, residents which indicated that a substantial majority of the respondents believed that the brochure should be available to the public. This survey was excluded on the ground that it dealt with a local standard, and that the proper rule to be used was a national standard.[59]

Even though the Supreme Court had ruled in 1973 *(Miller)* that the appropriate standard was state or local, Justice Rehnquist upheld the trial judge's ruling. He wrote that a trial court "retains considerable latitude even with admittedly relevant evidence * * * ".[60]

Hamling and his co-defendants had been convicted under a test rejected in *Miller,* a formulation drawn from Memoirs of a Woman of Pleasure v. Massachusetts (the *Fanny Hill* case of 1966).[61] The *Memoirs* test, it may be recalled, said that to be obscene, something had to be "utterly without redeeming social importance." In *Miller,* however, the Court complained that such a test required "proving a negative," and instead held that material could be found obscene if "the work, taken as a whole, lacks serious literary, artistic, political or scientific value." [62]

The Court also affirmed some earlier pronouncements on the law of obscenity. The federal statute forbidding mailing of obscene material—Title 18 U.S.C.A. § 1461—again was said to provide adequate notice of what is prohibited by law.[63] Furthermore, in line with Mishkin v. New York (1966),[64] the Court held that in deciding whether the brochure appealed to a prurient interest in

[58] 418 U.S. 87, 94 S.Ct. 2887, 2906 (1974).

[59] 418 U.S. 87, 94 S.Ct. 2887, 2903; see also dissent of Justice Brennan, 418 U.S. 87, 94 S.Ct. 2887, at pp. 2922–2923.

[60] 418 U.S. 87, 94 S.Ct. 2887, 2903 (1974).

[61] 383 U.S. 413, 86 S.Ct. 975, 977 (1966).

[62] 413 U.S. 15, 93 S.Ct. 2607, 2615 (1973).

[63] 418 U.S. 87, 94 S.Ct. 2887, 2898 (1974).

[64] 383 U.S. 463, 86 S.Ct. 942 (1966).

sex, the jury could consider whether some portions appealed to a specially defined deviant group as well as to average individuals.[65] Also, the Court approved the approach taken in Ginzburg v. New York (1966), saying that evidence of pandering sales can be relevant in determining obscenity [66]—as long as a correct constitutional definition of obscenity is applied.[67]

Justice Brennan, joined by Justices Stewart and Marshall, dissented vigorously. He again contended that material should not be suppressed unless there is distribution to juveniles or obtrusive exposure to unconsenting adults.[68] Brennan also drew dead aim on the dangers he saw in the local standards-let's-let-each-jury-call-the-shots approach to judging obscenity.[69]

Brennan's dissent termed this situation one which must lead to a debilitating self-censorship. National distributors, facing "variegated standards * * * impossible to discern," will be wary of what might be done according to the community standards will inevitably grow cautious, and distribution of sexually oriented materials, both obscene and not obscene, would be impeded.[70] He concluded that Hamling and friends had been charged with one crime—violating national obscenity standards—and their convictions were affirmed on another—violating local standards. He added: "Under standards long settled * * * treating a conviction as a conviction upon a charge not made is a denial of due process of law." [71]

SEC. 53. CUSTOMS AND POSTAL CENSORSHIP

Customs censorship continues to be a major activity, but postal censorship—after a disgraceful record throughout much of the nation's history—appears to have abated somewhat.

There is a ripple effect in obscenity decisions of the Supreme Court. Standards laid down in Roth v. United States (1957) and Miller v. California (1973) sometimes surface in some rather unusual ways. Take, for example, the area of customs censorship. The U.S. Customs Service has a long and rather checkered history of stopping materials suspected of being obscene—including, during the 1930s, some nude drawings. Those drawings were by

[65] 418 U.S. 87, 94 S.Ct. 2887, 2914 (1974).

[66] 383 U.S. 463, 86 S.Ct. 942 (1966).

[67] 418 U.S. 87, 94 S.Ct. 2887, 2914 (1974).

[68] 418 U.S. 87, 94 S.Ct. 2887, 2919 (1974).

[69] 418 U.S. 87, 94 S.Ct. 2887, 2920–2921 (1974).

[70] 418 U.S. 87, 94 S.Ct. 2887, 2921 (1974).

[71] 418 U.S. 87, 94 S.Ct. 2887, 2924 (1974).

Italian artist named Michelangelo, and the sketches were his preliminary work for what turned out to be the ceiling in the Sistine Chapel.[72] In the 1980s, the Customs Service is still operating under Title 19 U.S.C.A. § 1305, "Immoral articles; importation prohibited." As the literate if gently acerbic Circuit Judge Leonard P. Moore has said, this statute contains "a curious assortment of immoral articles, e.g., those writings 'advocating or urging treason or insurrection against the United States,' obscene publications, drugs for causing unlawful abortions, and lottery tickets." Such articles may not be allowed to enter the United States.[73] Judge Moore then described the procedure which will be followed to seize materials suspected of dealing impermissibly with sex. He wrote: [74]

> The customs employee is directed to seize the in-his-opinion offending article to wait the judgment of a district court thereon. To this end, the customs employee must transmit the article "to the district attorney of the district in which is situated the office at which such seizure has taken place", and he, undoubtedly through one of his assistants, "shall institute proceedings in the district court" for the confiscation and destruction of the matter seized.

> Some Assistant United States Attorney prepares a complaint whereby he demands judgment that the article is obscene and declares that he wants it destroyed. He attaches a schedule of all seized items (usually a week's collection) and prays that all interested persons be duly cited to answer. To all addresses he then sends a notice, giving them 20 days in which to file a claim, together with a form for such claim and answer. Upon receipt of such claims, if any, the matter is set for a so-called hearing before a District Judge. * * *

> The institution of court proceedings adds to the two primary censors, the customs employee and the Assistant United States Attorney, a District Judge and, potentially, three Court of Appeals Judges and nine Supreme Court Justices.

[72] Anne Lyon Haight, Banned Books, 2nd ed., (New York, R.R. Bowker, 1955) p. 12.

[73] United States v. Various Articles of Obscene Merchandise, 562 F.2d 185–186 (2d Cir.1977).

See also United States v. Twelve 200-ft. Reels of Super-8 mm Film, 413 U.S. 123, 93 S.Ct. 2665, 2667–2668 (1973). See 19 U.S.C.A. § 1305(a).

[74] United States v. Various Articles of Obscene Merchandise, 562 F.2d 185, 186 (2d Cir.1977).

A young man from Lancaster, Pa. was sent a pamphlet by a friend in Germany. The customs service, however, seized that pamphlet, which showed a young man and two women in varying combinations of close encounters of the sexual kind. The pamphlet was one of more than 500 printed articles seized that week by New York City customs employees. Circuit Judge Moore, writing for the court in this case which is rather coyly known as U.S. v. Various Articles of Obscene Merchandise, Schedule No. 1303, noted: [75]

> Schedule 1303, attached to the complaint and listing articles seized as well as the mailing destinations, includes some 573 addresses located in some 48 states. Of the 50 states, only 2, Colorado and North Dakota, failed to have residents exhibiting some "prurient interest" or at least curiosity. Most of the items seized were listed only as "Illustrated Advertising." The titles of the other so-called magazines were "Weekend Sex", "Nympho", "Children Love", "Anal Sex", "Sexual Positions", and similar designations.

Of the 573 addresses, only 14 filed claims asking that the materials which had been shipped to them be released by the government. And only one individual—the young man from Lancaster, Pa., showed up to try to get his pamphlet. Circuit Judge Moore quoted what he called the young man's wise comment "that it seems unusual for the United States Government to spend an awful lot of time and money and effort for one small mail article * * * when there is obviously better use for that money to be spent in the judicial system * * *" [76]

The U.S. District Court in this case—having trouble with the state and local standards aspects of Miller v. California [77]—said that the obscenity (or lack thereof) of an imported article should not be judged at the port of entry, but at the place where the addressee was to receive it. For example, Lancaster, Pa. The Circuit Court disagreed. In order to get the forfeiture and destruction of allegedly obscene imported material, the government must show that the material is obscene in the district where it was seized by customs agents. "Import" implies entry into the country at those places which have customs officers—ports of entry, in other words. Therefore, inspection would have to take place at the port of entry. Circuit Judge Moore added: [78]

[75] Ibid., 186–187.

[76] Ibid., p. 187.

[77] See the discussion of Miller v. California, 413 U.S. 15, 93 S.Ct. 2607 (1973), in Section 66 of this chapter.

[78] U.S. v. Various Articles of Obscene Merchandise, 562 F.2d 185, 188 (2d Cir. 1977).

The District Court [here sitting without a jury] will have to serve as a composite for the Southern District [of New York] jury—possibly representing the rural areas of Rockland and Dutchess Counties together with the urban sections of Manhattan and the Bronx. The Court will have to decide the question of obscenity "according to the average person in the community, rather than the most prudish or the most tolerant." Smith v. United States, 45 U.S.L.W. 4495, 4498 (May 23, 1977). Thus, the "average person" takes his or her stand beside the hypothetical and court-created mythical character "the reasonably prudent man". See id. Hamling v. United States, 418 U.S. 87, 104–105, 94 S.Ct. 2887 (1974). Again, there is probably no better way.

Shades of Anthony Comstock still hover over our obscenity statutes. But as long as they remain on the books it is the duty of Government to enforce them within constitutional limits.

Postal Censorship

Postal censorship appears to be in retreat, but that mechanism for hampering freedom of expression has such a sorry history in this nation that constant vigilance is needed. George Clinton of New York, governor throughout the Confederation period, complained in 1788 that the mail service was poor and that someone had tampered with letters addressed to him.[79] Strange things happened to Abolitionist mail sent to the southward during the Presidency of Andrew Jackson.[80] In time of war, of course, many people other than the addressees were reading the mail.[81]

Where obscenity is concerned, the Post Office was very frisky during the 1930s and 1940s. Over the years, the Post Office had slowly developed a method of administrative censorship, denying the mails to publications suspected of obscenity even if prosecution was not actually intended. Postal censors thus became something of a law unto themselves. A publisher who wanted to fight the Post Office would have to hire an attorney to sue to enjoin the censor's activities.[82] Among books excluded from the mails in the 1930s and early 1940s were Erskine Caldwell's *Tobacco Road* and

---

[79] Jackson Turner Main, The Antifederalists: Critics of the Constitution (Chaptel Hill: University of North Carolina Press, 1961) p. 250.

[80] Harold L. Nelson, ed., Freedom of the Press from Hamilton to the Warren Court, pp. 212–220.

[81] Peterson, H.C. and Gilbert Fite, Opponents of the War, 1917–1918 (Seattle: University of Washington Press, 1957) *passim.*

[82] James C.N. Paul and Murray L. Schwartz, Federal Censorship: Obscenity in the Mail (New York: Free Press of Glencoe, 1961) pp. 68–69.

God's Little Acre. John O'Hara's *Appointment in Samarra* and Ernest Hemingway's *For Whom the Bell Tolls* were confiscated when found in the mails even though they were sold freely in bookstores. John Steinbeck's *The Grapes of Wrath* was cleared for mailing, although a Post Office lawyer complained that it contained obscene passages.[83]

During World War II, however, the Post Office department overreached itself in trying to discipline *Esquire* magazine. In 1943, the Department attempted to withdraw second-class mailing rates in order to punish the magazine for its "smoking car" humor. Without that mail-rate classification, the magazine would have had to pay higher amounts to go through the mails. *Esquire's* publishers, fully realizing that the higher rates might cost an additional $500,000 and put them out of business, took the Post Office to court.[84]

Speaking for a unanimous Supreme Court, Justice William O. Douglas demolished the Post Office's contentions that if a publication did not meet some postal employees' concepts of being published for the "public good" they would have to pay higher mailing rates. He wrote: "[A] requirement that literature or art conform to some norm prescribed by an official smacks of an ideology foreign to our system." [85]

Despite the *Esquire* decision, the Post Office department retained the power to withdraw the second-class privilege if a publisher mails a series of "non-mailable" issues. (Increases in recent years in the costs of mailing magazines by Congress have symbolized a retreat from the nationalizing Postal Act of 1872. That act, in a nation sprawling toward its western frontier, provided subsidized mailing rates which made it as inexpensive to mail a magazine across the continent as across town.) In practice, the *Esquire* decision has meant that the Post Office department largely gave up the practice of revoking second-class permits to suppress materials which an administrator deemed obscene.[86]

As noted earlier, the basic federal anti-obscenity statute forbids mailing obscene literature or materials, and this kept the Post Office Department very much involved in efforts to control obscene literature.[87]

In 1970, Congress enacted the Postal Reorganization Act, the most comprehensive revision of postal legislation. It abolished the Post Office Department as a cabinet-level agency. The Postal

[83] Ibid., pp. 72–73.

[84] Hannegan v. Esquire, 327 U.S. 146, 151n., 66 S.Ct. 456, 459n. (1946).

[85] 327 U.S. 146, 157–158, 66 S.Ct. 456, 462 (1946).

[86] Paul and Schwartz, op. cit., pp. 76–77.

[87] 18 U.S.C.A. § 1461.

Service was established in its place as an independent establishment in the Executive Branch to own and operate the U.S. Postal Service.[88] Keep in mind, however, that basic legislation to prohibit the mailing of obscene materials remained in force.[89]

Also in 1970, Congress passed an "antipandering" statute which has allowed the Postal Service to concentrate upon dealers who mail "pandering advertisements" to persons who do not wish to receive them. If recipients request that no more such materials be sent to them by a specific sender, the Postal Service will order discontinuation of the mailings. Also, the Postal Service can order that the recipient's name be deleted from all mailing lists which the sender owns or controls. If the deletion is not made and another complaint occurs, the Postal Service can ask the Justice Department to halt such mailings. If a court order is ignored, the court will punish violations as contempt of court.[90]

In 1971, another weapon was created for mail recipients to use against mailers of sexually explicit materials. Recipients can fill out a form at their local Postal Service branch, asking that their names be removed from any lists used by mailers of material objectionable to the recipients.[91]

SEC. 54. MOTION PICTURE AND BROADCAST CENSORSHIP

While problems arising out of attempts to censor allegedly obscene printed materials have presented an apparently insoluble dilemma for American courts and legislatures, motion pictures and broadcast media have had difficulties of their own. With motion picture censorship, the assumption is similar to that in attempts to censor the printed word: the depiction of sexual scenes—if the sex is sufficiently blatant or explicit—is socially harmful and should be suppressed. As noted later in this section, there are signs that motion picture censorship is waning.

In recent years, the movies have been granted some of the protections of the First Amendment, yet they have also been subjected to censorship. And, in some instances, the courts have upheld systems of prior censorship over motion pictures. In 1915, when the film industry was in its infancy and the movies scarcely were out of the magic-lantern stage, the Supreme Court ruled that exhibiting films was a business which was not part of the press of

[88] See 39 U.S.C.A., "Explanation," at pp. v–vi (1980).

[89] See, e.g., 18 U.S.C.A. § 1461, and 30 U.S.C.A. §§ 3001–3010 (1980).

[90] 39 U.S.C.A. § 3008. Constitutionality of this statute section was upheld in Rowan v. United States Post Office Department, 397 U.S. 728, 90 S.Ct. 1484 (1970).

[91] 39 U.S.C.A. § 3010. This section was held constitutional in Pent-R-Books, 328 F.Supp. 297 (D.C.N.Y.1971).

the nation and therefore not deserving of constitutional protection.[92] In 1952, finally, the Supreme Court ruled that motion pictures are a "significant medium for the communication of ideas," important for the expression of political or social views and thus an important organ of public opinion.[93]

This case—Burstyn v. Wilson—involved Roberto Rossellini's film, "The Miracle." This was a story about a simple-minded goatherd who had been raped by a bearded stranger whom she believed to be St. Joseph. The film was accused not of obscenity but of "sacrilege." The New York Education Department had issued a license to allow showing of "The Miracle," but the Education Department's governing body, the New York Regents, ordered the license withdrawn after the regents had received protests that the film was "sacrilegious." [94] Burstyn appealed the license's withdrawal to the New York Courts, claiming that the state's licensing statute was unconstitutional. New York's courts, however, rejected the argument that the New York law abridged freedom of speech and press and approved the Regents' ruling. The Supreme Court of the United States, however, ruled unanimously that the New York statute and the term "sacrilegious" were so vague that they abridged freedom of expression.

Clark declared that the fact that motion pictures are produced by a large, profitable industry does not remove the protection of Constitutional guarantees. Although the Court said in *dicta* that a clearly drawn obscenity statute to regulate motion pictures might be upheld, the main thrust of the *Burstyn* decision was toward greater freedom. Not only were films given protection under the First and Fourteenth Amendments, movies which offended a particular religious group need not, for that reason alone, be banned. Thus "sacrilege" can no longer be a ground for censoring movies.[95]

Seven years after the *Burstyn* decision, the Supreme Court—in Kingsley International Pictures Corp. v. New York—again upheld the idea that films are within the protection of the First Amendment. The *Kingsley* decision, however, had within it the possibilities for once again expanding controls over films. The Court specifically refused to decide whether "the controls which a State may impose upon this medium of expression are precisely co-

---

[92] Mutual Film Corp. v. Industrial Commission of Ohio, 236 U.S. 230, 244, 35 S.Ct. 387, 391 (1915).

[93] Joseph Burstyn, Inc. v. Wilson, 343 U.S. 495, 72 S.Ct. 777 (1952).

[94] Ibid. Wilson was chairman of the New York Board of Regents.

[95] 343 U.S. 495, 502, 72 S.Ct. 777, 781 (1952).

extensive with those allowable for newspapers, books, or individual speech." [96]

Despite the veiled warning in the *Kingsley* opinion that the Supreme Court might once again strengthen controls over motion pictures, a bold attempt was made to get a prior censorship ordinance declared unconstitutional. This was the 1961 case of Times Film Corp. v. City of Chicago, which involved a film with a spicy name: "Don Juan." However, this film was merely a motion picture version of Mozart's opera, "Don Giovanni," obviously not obscene.

The Times Film Corporation paid the license fee for "Don Juan," but refused to submit the film to Chicago's Board of Censors for a license. Although the film was quite sedate, the company never argued that "Don Juan" was not obscene. Instead, the only question presented by the film company's lawyers was whether the Chicago ordinance which provided for pre-screening and licensing of motion pictures *before* public exhibition was constitutional. Thus the constitutionality of *prior restraint* was the sole issue in this film censorship case. Perhaps officials of the Times Film Corporation were irked by the Big-Brotherish overtones of Chicago's film censorship ordinance, which said: [97]

> It shall be unlawful for any person to show or exhibit in a public place * * * any * * * motion picture * * * without first having secured a permit therefore from the superintendent of police.

After a Federal District Court had dismissed the Times Film Corporation's complaint—and after a Court of Appeals had affirmed that decision—the Supreme Court of the United States granted certiorari.[98]

The Supreme Court, by a 5–4 decision, held that Chicago's censorship ordinance was constitutional. Mr. Justice Clark, writing for the majority, said the question presented by this case was whether a film exhibitor has "complete and absolute freedom to exhibit, at least once, any and every kind of motion picture." Clark replied, however, "it has never been held that liberty of speech is absolute. Nor has it been suggested that all previous restraints on speech are invalid." [99]

---

[96] 360 U.S. 684, 689–690, 79 S.Ct. 1362, 1366 (1959).

[97] Municipal Code of Chicago, Chapter 155, Section 1. However, Section 2 provided that newsreels do not have to be previewed. Films were to be approved before public showing by either the superintendent of police or by the "Film Review Section," six persons appointed by the superintendent of police.

[98] 362 U.S. 917, 80 S.Ct. 672 (1960).

[99] Times Film Corp. v. Chicago, 365 U.S. 43, 47, 81 S.Ct. 391, 393 (1961), citing Near v. Minnesota, 283 U.S. 697, 51 S.Ct. 625 (1931).

Clark noted that the content of the motion picture had not been raised as an issue. Instead, the Times Film Corporation challenged the censor's basic authority. By raising such a challenge to prior restraint, Times Film Corporation simply aimed too high. It might have helped the corporation's case had its attorneys shown that the film involved was not objectionable. But this was not done. As a result, a majority of the Supreme Court upheld the Chicago ordinance, drawing on language first used in the Burstyn case and echoed in the Kingsley Films decision. Motion pictures are not "necessarily subject to the precise rules governing any other particular method of expression." [1]

In 1965, the Supreme Court moved to take a bit of the sting out of its 1961 holding in Times Film Corporation v. City of Chicago.[2] The *Times Film* decision had upheld Chicago's movie censorship ordinance, and the 1965 case of Freedman v. Maryland presented a challenge to the constitutionality of a similar law. Freedman had shown the film "Revenge at Daybreak" in his Baltimore theater without first submitting the picture to the State Board of Censors as required by Maryland law.[3]

However, Freedman's challenge to the Maryland film censorship statute was much more focused and precise than the Times Film Corporation's attack on the Chicago censorship ordinance. Writing for the Court, Mr. Justice Brennan noted that [4]

> [u]nlike the petitioner in Times Film, appellant does not argue that Article 2 [of the Maryland statute] is unconstitutional simply because it may prevent even the first showing of a film whose exhibition may legitimately be the subject of an obscenity prosecution. He presents a question quite distinct from that passed on in Times Film; accepting the rule in Times Film, he argues that Article 2 constitutes an invalid prior restraint because, in the context of the remainder of the statute, it presents a danger of unduly suppressing protected expression.

Brennan added that the Maryland law made it possible for the state's Censorship Board to halt the showing of any film it disapproved, unless and until the film exhibitor started a time-consuming appeal procedure through Maryland Courts and got the Censorship Board's ruling overturned. So in the Freedman case, prior

---

[1] 365 U.S. 43, 46, 49, 81 S.Ct. 391, 393–394 (1961); Burstyn v. Wilson, 343 U.S. 495, 72 S.Ct. 777 (1952); Kingsley International Pictures v. Board of Regents, 360 U.S. 684, 79 S.Ct. 1362 (1959).

[2] 365 U.S. 43, 81 S.Ct. 391 (1961).

[3] Article 66A of the 1957 Maryland Statutes made it unlawful to sell, lease, lend or exhibit a motion picture unless the film had first been submitted to and approved by the Maryland State Board of Censors.

[4] Freedman v. Maryland, 380 U.S. 51, 54, 85 S.Ct. 734, 737 (1965).

restraint of movies was disallowed because of insufficient procedural safeguards in the Maryland law for the protection of the film exhibitor.

Nevertheless, the Court maintained that the "requirement of prior submission to a censor sustained in Times Film is consistent with our recognition that films differ from other forms of expression." Justice Brennan suggested that an orderly, speedy procedure for prescreening films could be constitutional.

Similarly, in Interstate Circuit, Inc. v. Dallas (1968), the Court declared an ordinance setting up a city's censorship board to be unconstitutionally vague. The Dallas ordinance had set up complicated procedures for exhibitors to follow in order to get Motion Picture Classification Board approval to show a film. In sticky instances, it could take three weeks or more before an exhibitor could get a definitive ruling. The Supreme Court, however, directed its scrutiny at the operation of the ordinance. Under that ordinance, the Board could declare a film "not suitable for young people" [5]

> if, in the judgment of the Board, there is a substantial probability that * * * [the film] will create the impression on young persons that * * * [crime, delinquency or sexual promiscuity] is profitable, desirable, acceptable, respectable, praiseworthy, or commonly accepted.

Justice Marshall's majority opinion ruled that this wording in the ordinance was so nebulous that the film industry might be intimidated into showing only totally inane films.[6] What, then, does an acceptable film censorship system have to do? This question was answered in the Supreme Court's affirmance of a three-judge district court action approving the wording of Maryland's censorship statute. That law includes these features: [7]

— Speedy procedures are required by the statute. Within five days after a film's submission, the Censor Board must decide whether it will grant a license to that film.

— Within three days of a license denial, the Board must initiate proceedings in the Circuit Court of Baltimore City for *de novo* review of the Board's decision.

— Prompt determination of obscenity (or lack thereof) by that court of equity after an adversary hearing *before* the Censor Board can make a final denial of a license.

— The Board must bear the burden of proof at all stages of the proceeding.

[5] 390 U.S. 676, 688, 88 S.Ct. 1298, 1305 (1968).

[6] 390 U.S. 676, 682, 88 S.Ct. 1298, 1305 (1968).

[7] Star v. Preller, 419 U.S. 956, 95 S.Ct. 217 (1974).

Times do change. *The New York Times* reported on June 29, 1981, that the Maryland State Board of Censors had viewed its last picture show. The Maryland board, which was founded in 1916, was allowed to expire under the state's "sunset law" which is designed to kill off useless state agencies. Jack Valenti, president of the Motion Picture Association of America, told *The Times:* " 'This removes a staining blot on the First Amendment. * * * It makes Maryland, the fabled Free State, a free state at last, along with the other 49.' " Even so, there is no assurance that the last has been seen of censorship boards. Censorship of all media—including films—has always run in cycles, and it is possible that a new wave agitated by decency groups of another time might lead to a flourishing of such boards. Prior restraint of film is not now unconstitutional, provided that strict procedural safeguards are followed.

In addition to—and in part because of—public and legal pressures, the American motion picture industry has long had systems of self-regulation. The industry decided to regulate itself, lest states and cities do it entirely by laws and censorship boards. By 1922, the Motion Picture Producers and Distributors of America (MPPDA) was formed, and former Postmaster General Will Hays was hired to apply a code to preserve decency on the screen.[8] During the 1930s, the industry developed a Motion Picture Code which made it mandatory that each motion picture company submit its films to a committee of the MPPDA before public showings. If the committee found code violations (nudity, profanity, or obscenity, to give three examples), a producer could not release the picture until its offending scenes had been snipped out.[9]

The Motion Picture Code, although it underwent minor changes, continued in force well into the 1960s. This code, despite its drawbacks,[10] apparently played a role in reducing the number of state and local censorship groups and may have helped avoid creation of a federal motion picture censorship organization.

[8] Raymond Moley, The Hays Office (New York: Bobbs-Merrill, 1945); Morris L. Ernst and Alexander Lindey, The Censor Marches on (New York: Doubleday, Doran, 1940) p. 80.

[9] Howard T. Lewis, The Motion Picture Industry (New York: Van Nostrand, 1933) p. 376.

[10] Two of the code's chief critics have charged that it creates a "viciously false picture of life" and that its mandates are too general. See Morris Ernst and Alexander Lindey, op. cit., p. 89. The code was amended in 1956, in order that films could deal with narcotics after a critically praised film. "The Man With the Golden Arm," had been denied an MPPDA seal for depicting a narcotic addict's problems. In 1961, the code was altered to "permit restrained, discreet treatment of sexual aberration in movies."

In the wake of the Supreme Court's decision in Interstate Circuit, Inc. v. Dallas, a case discussed earlier in this section, the motion picture industry adopted a film rating system reflecting the Court's interest in protecting minors.[11] This rating system, which went into effect late in 1968, has become familiar to movie-goers. "G" means suggested for general audiences, and "PG" means that a film is intended for all ages, and that parental guidance is advised. "PG–13" says "Parents Strongly Cautioned: Some Material May Be Improper for Children Under 13." "R" means restricted, and persons under the age of 17 are not admitted unless accompanied by a parent or an adult guardian. "X" means that persons under 17 are not admitted, and this age restriction may be higher in some areas.

Problems of "Vagueness" and *Scienter*

The law of obscenity is exquisitely vague, as Judge Jerome Frank once said. Many obscenity convictions have been reversed on appeal because the statute under which conviction was had suffered from "overbreadth"—that is, it prohibited constitutionally protected behavior as well as that which courts say is not subject to constitutional protection.[12] At stake here, of course, is fair play. A person should not be convicted of a crime unless he or she had some reasonable chance of knowing that a specific sort of behavior will result in a prosecution.

One of the most perplexing problems involves what lawyers call the question of *scienter* or "guilty knowledge." If the obscenity statutes are so all-fired vague, how—and when—does a bookseller or distributor know when something illegal has been done? In a leading case discussing the element of *scienter* in obscenity prosecutions, Smith v. California, the Supreme Court declared a Los Angeles ordinance unconstitutional because it made a book-seller liable to punishment even when he did not know the contents of a book. A unanimous court said that if booksellers can sell only those materials which they have inspected, "the State will have imposed a restriction upon the distribution of constitutionally protected as well as obscene literature."[13]

[11] Vincent Canby, "Movie Ratings for Children Grown Up," New York Times, Oct. 8, 1968, p. 1 ff.

[12] Scienter questions have been raised in many obscenity cases. Notable examples include Ginzburg v. United States, 383 U.S. 463, 86 S.Ct. 942 (1966), and Ginsberg v. New York, 390 U.S. 629, 88 S.Ct. 1274 (1968). See also Justice Brennan's dissent in Paris Adult Theater v. Slaton, 413 U.S. 49, 96 S.Ct. 2628–2662 (1973).

[13] Smith v. California, 361 U.S. 147, 149, 153, 80 S.Ct. 215, 216 (1959); see also Winters v. New York, 333 U.S. 507, 68 S.Ct. 665 (1948). For a more recent case dealing with *scienter,* see Miller v. California, 413 U.S. 15, 93 S.Ct. 2607 (1973).

Even that assumes, somehow, that booksellers or distributors will be able to do something that judges and lawyers have been unable to do: adequately define obscenity. Remember the case of Sam Ginsberg?[14] He got nailed under a New York obscenity statute for selling a so-called girlie magazine to a 16-year-old, not knowing that his state had a statute forbidding the sale of such materials to individuals under the age of 17.[15] Those materials had been declared not obscene in other jurisdictions,[16] and it is often difficult to discern someone's age. Should Sam Ginsberg have asked for an I.D.? Evidently so, if he had known enough of the law of New York to do so. And what of Ralph Ginzburg? He was convicted under a federal obscenity statute not for *what* he sold, but for *how* he sold it—and the element of pandering sale was written into the obscenity law by the Supreme Court, not by Congress.[17]

The element of pandering sales in obscenity prosecutions was still with us in 1977. Roy Splawn, for example, was convicted back in 1971 of selling an obscene film, a misdemeanor under California law. The California trial judge's jury instructions said that not only the content of the film but also the manner in which it was advertised should be taken into account in judging whether or not the film was obscene. Writing for a 5–4 majority in Splawn v. California (1977) Justice Rehnquist upheld Splawn's conviction,[18] citing Ginzburg v. United States (1966)[19] Hamling v. United States (1973).[20] Rehnquist declared that there "is no doubt that as a matter of First Amendment obscenity law, evidence of pandering to prurient interests in the creation, promotion, or dissemination of material is relevant in determining whether the material is obscene."[21] Justice Stevens—then a newcomer to the Court—showed himself to be a "quick study" on obscenity problems, and registered the following dissent in *Splawn:*

> Even if the social importance of the films themselves is dubious, there is a definite social interest in permitting them to be accurately described. Only an accurate description can enable a potential viewer to decide whether or not he wants to see them. Signs which identify the

[14] Ginsberg v. New York, 390 U.S. 629, 88 S.Ct. 1274 (1968).

[15] See discussion of Ginsberg v. New York, 390 U.S. 629, 88 S.Ct. 1274 (1968), in Sec. 64, this chapter.

[16] Redrup v. New York, 386 U.S. 767, 87 S.Ct. 1414 (1967).

[17] See discussion of Ginzburg v. United States, 383 U.S. 463, 86 S.Ct. 942 (1966), in Sec. 64, this chapter.

[18] Splawn v. California, 431 U.S. 595, 97 S.Ct. 1987 (1977).

[19] 383 U.S. 463, 86 S.Ct. 942 (1966).

[20] 418 U.S. 87, 94 S.Ct. 2887 (1974).

[21] Splawn v. California, 431 U.S. 595, 97 S.Ct. 1987 (1977).

"adult" character of a motion picture theater or of a
bookstore convey the message that sexually provocative
entertainment is to be found within; under the jury
instructions which the Court today finds acceptable, these
signs may deprive otherwise nonobscene matter of its
constitutional protection. Such signs, however, also provide a warning to those who find erotic materials offensive that they should shop elsewhere for other kinds of
books, magazines or entertainment. Under any sensible
regulatory scheme, truthful description of subject matter
that is pleasing to some and offensive to others ought to
be encouraged, not punished.

I would not send Mr. Splawn to jail for telling the
truth about his shabby business.

Juries

Closely related to *scienter* and "vagueness" problems in obscenity law is the reliance placed on juries as final arbiters of
what is and is not obscene. As Circuit Judge Leonard Moore has
said.[22]

In reality, no judge or jury can be expected to determine "community standards" * * *. The best that
anyone can do is to give his or her personal reaction
* * *. No juror or judge armed with a copy * * * [of
an allegedly obscene work] will have the opportunity to
rush up and down the streets of his community asking
friends and neighbors how they feel about it. Nor should
they rudely seek insights into community *mores* by asking
others what their intimate sexual practices may be. Yet
the fiction remains that a jury is somehow capable of
reflecting or determining "community standards". This
is so probably because there is simply no better method
for applying this test.

If judges, philosophers, and Presidential commissions can't
make sense out of the law of obscenity, then what chance does a
jury have? Relying on local juries has added even more variety to
obscenity law, but it has not removed the Supreme Court of the
United States from spending much of its valuable time and effort
in obscenity cases. And all too many of these cases have aspects
of damfoolishness. A Jacksonville, Fla., ordinance forbade drive-
in theaters from exhibiting motion pictures showing "human male
or female bare buttocks, human female bare breasts, or human
bare pubic areas * * *" if the movies could be seen from a

22 United States v. Various Articles of Obscene Merchandise, 562 F.2d 185, 189–
190 (2d Cir.1977).

public street or public place. Did this ordinance forbid too much?
Yes, said the Supreme Court in Erznoznik v. City of Jacksonville
(1975). Writing for a court split 6–3, Justice Lewis Powell held
that the ordinance was overbroad. The ordinance "would bar a
film containing a picture of a baby's buttocks, the nude body of a
war victim, or scenes from a culture in which nudity is indige-
nous." [23] But if that ordinance was overbroad, at least one ordinance was too specific. Consider this comment from a 1968 issue
of *The Saturday Review:* "The Fort Lauderdale (Florida) City
Commission just passed an ordinance banning obscenity in books,
magazines, and records. The law is so specific that it is obscene in
itself and cannot be made public." [24]

A cartoon by Lichty published some years ago did better than
most judges have done in making sense of the law of obscenity.
The cartoon showed one judge saying to another: "I know it's
obscenity if it makes my Adam's apple bobble." Meanwhile, the
Supreme Court—and other courts as well—wish to get out of the
obscenity-judging business.

Two additional cases will be mentioned here—the Detroit
zoning case and the prosecution of Larry C. Flynt and his raunchy
magazine, *Hustler.* In Coleman A. Young, Mayor of Detroit v.
American Mini Theatres,[25] the Supreme Court's 5–4 decision gave
rise to some sniggering that the Court thinks an erogenous zone
may be measured in city blocks. The Court, with Justice Stevens
delivering its judgment, upheld a Detroit ordinance which prohibits adult theaters or bookstores from being located within 500 feet
of a residential area or within 1,000 feet of each other. Justice
Stevens said that the city's interest "in the present and future
character of its neighborhoods adequately supports its classification of motion pictures. We hold that the zoning ordinances
* * * do not violate the Equal Protection Clause of the Fourteenth Amendment." [26] In dissent, Justice Stewart said that he
viewed the outcome of this case as an aberration: [27]

> By refusing to invalidate Detroit's ordinance the
> Court rides roughshod over cardinal principles of First
> Amendment law, which require that time, place and
> manner regulations that affect protected expression be
> content-neutral except in the limited context of a captive
> or juvenile audience.

[23] 422 U.S. 205, 95 S.Ct. 2268, 2271, 2274–2275 (1975).

[24] Jerome Beatty, Jr., "Trade winds," Saturday Review, November 23, 1968, p.
23.

[25] 44 U.S. Law Week 4999 (June 24, 1976)

[26] Ibid., p. 5006.

[27] Ibid., p. 5009, citing Erznoznik v. City of Jacksonville, 422 U.S. 205, 95 S.Ct.
2268 (1975).

It is often the people whom you would least like to invite home to dinner who make First Amendment law. Larry C. Flynt, when publisher and editor of Hustler magazine, was convicted in Cincinnati early in 1977 on some rather ingenious charges. A jury of seven men and five women found him guilty of pandering obscenity and participating in organized crime. This case suggested that through local prosecutions, communities can dictate their own obscenity standards and indirectly set standards which are nationwide.[28]

Flynt, who was freed on $55,000 bond after six days behind bars, then faced up to 25 years in prison if convicted. As the Louisville Courier-Journal said in an editorial.[29]

> [I]f any local community can toss a book or magazine publisher into the slammer, even if the offender lives and operates hundreds or thousands of miles away, then that community is able to impose its standards upon the nation, and the Supreme Court's 1973 ruling is turned upside-down. That's precisely what may happen because of the Cincinnati case. Hustler is published in Columbus, printed in Dayton, and distributed nationwide. Yet the decision of the Cincinnati jury, if it is not reversed on appeal, may shut down the whole operation.

The Courier-Journal added that the danger of the criminal conspiracy—community standards two-pronged attack on alleged pornography is obvious. Conspiracy laws won't stick unless the accused individuals have conspired to do something illegal. But if a local jury decides that the materials people are distributing are obscene and therefore illegal (according to the standards of that community as supposedly represented by a jury) then the conspiracy would be complete in law if not in fact. And local juries could be able to call the tune nationwide.

Broadcast Obscenity

Obscenity, variously defined, has never received constitutional protection from the Supreme Court of the United States. Where broadcasting is involved, moreover, explicitly sexy language or "dirty words" can bring down the wrath of the Federal Communications Commission and may even cause difficulties at license renewal time for the broadcaster who has allowed such stuff to be broadcast or televised.

[28] "We'll Sell More Copies Now," AP story in The Lexington Leader, Lexington, Ky., Feb. 9, 1977, p. A–8, G.G. LaBelle, "What Is Obscene?", AP story in the Louisville Courier-Journal, p. A–3, Feb. 10, 1977; FOI Digest, January-February, 1977 (Vol. 19, No. 1), p. 1.

[29] Louisville Courier-Journal, editorial from February, 1977, reprinted in The Kentucky Press, March, 1977, p. 4.

For openers, the Federal Communications Act of 1934's Section 326 contained a prohibition against censorship but also included language outlawing obscene or indecent speech over the airwaves. In 1948, the proscription against obscenity was removed from Section 326 but reappeared in the United States Criminal Code. Title 18 U.S.C.A. Section 1464 says:

> Whoever utters any obscene, indecent, or profane language by means of radio communication shall be fined not more than $10,000 or imprisoned not more than two years, or both.

Obscenity became a real problem for the FCC in the early 1960s. The now-legendary Charley Walker disc jockey programs broadcast by WDKD, Kingstree, S.C., foretold some of the difficulties for the Commission. The WDKD case—usually called the Palmetto Broadcasting Company case—came about as the result of good old Charley's "bucolic humor" and ultimately resulted in the FCC's refusal to renew the station's license. His jibes were sufficiently ribald to the FCC of the early 1960s that the Commission did not quote examples. Instead, the Commission merely repeated an FCC examiner's conclusion that Walker's material was " 'obscene and indecent and [certainly] coarse, vulgar and susceptible of indecent double meaning.' " [30]

Station owner Edward G. Robinson, Jr. had argued that he was not aware of extensive listener complaints, but the FCC found that many witnesses contradicted Robinson's claims.[31] The Walker programs were not isolated instances, the FCC said, being broadcast four hours a day from 1949 to 1952 and from 1954 to June, 1960.[32]

The FCC declared—and this was upheld by a Circuit Court of Appeals—that Palmetto licensee Robinson's misrepresentations to the Commission about the program contents formed sufficient grounds for the denial of a broadcast license. "[A]s the Supreme Court has stated '[t]he fact of concealment may be even more significant than the facts concealed. The willingness to deceive a regulating body may be disclosed by unmaterial and useless deceptions as well as by material and persuasive ones.' " [33]

Other matters, such as the likelihood that "listeners in the home or car (including children) might be subjected to such

---

[30] Palmetto Broadcasting Co. (WDKD), Kingstree, S.C., 33 FCC 250, 255 (July 25, 1962); 34 FCC 101 Jan. 3, 1963), affirmed in E.G. Robinson, Jr., t/a Palmetto Broadcasting Company (WDKD) v. Federal Communications Commission, 334 F.2d 534 (D.C.Cir.1964), certiorari denied 379 U.S. 843, 85 S.Ct. 84 (1964).

[31] 334 F.2d 534, 536 (D.C.Cir.1964).

[32] 34 FCC 101, 104 (Jan. 3, 1963).

[33] 33 FCC 250, 253 (July 25, 1962), quoting FCC v. WOKO, 329 U.S. 223, 67 S.Ct. 213 (1939); 334 F.2d 534, 536 (D.C.Cir.1964).

materials * * * " simply by having the set turned to a particular
frequency or station were not pivotal in the Palmetto case although such matters were discussed. The mention of the problem
of *who* might be listening or viewing, however, forecast later
difficulties.

Although the *Palmetto* case turned, in part, upon the misrepresentations of the broadcaster and upon a "substantial period of
operations of the broadcaster and upon a "substantial period of
operation inconsistent with the public-interest standard," the
Pacifica case dealt with only "a few isolated programs, presented
over a four-year period." FM radio stations owned by the Pacifica
Foundation—KPFK, Los Angeles, Calif., and KPFA, Berkeley,
Calif.—had broadcast a number of programs which drew listeners'
gripes. Poet Lawrence Ferlinghetti had read some of his own
poems over KPFK during a 1959 program, and playwright Edward
Albee, poet Robert Creeley, and novelist Edward Pomerantz read
from their own works in three separate programs broadcast by
KPFA during 1963. In addition, eight homosexuals discussed
their attitudes and problems in a program called "Live and Let
Live" broadcast at 10:15 p.m. over KPFK on January 15, 1963.[34]

The Commission's response to complaints that such programs
were "offensive or 'filthy' " gave little comfort to the complainers.
The FCC ruled that the broadcasts lay well within the licensee's
judgment under the public-interest standard.[35]

> The situation here stands on an entirely different
> footing than *Palmetto* * * * where the licensee had
> devoted a substantial period of his broadcast day to mate-
> rial which we found to be patently offensive * * * and
> as to which programing the licensee himself never assert-
> ed that it was not offensive or vulgar, *or that it served the
> needs of his area or had any redeeming features.* In this
> case, Pacifica has stated its judgment that the above-cited
> programs served * * * the needs and interests of its
> listening public. * * * Finally, as to the program "Live
> and Let Live," Pacifica states that "so long as the pro-
> gram is handled in good taste, there is no reason why
> subjects like homosexuality should not be discussed on the
> air" * * *.

> 5. We recognize that as shown by the complaints
> here, such provocative programing as here involved may
> offend some listeners. But this does not mean that those
> offended have the right, through the Commission's licens-
> ing power, to rule such programing off the airwaves.

[34] In re Pacifica Foundation, 36 FCC 147 (Jan. 22, 1964).

[35] 36 FCC 148–149 (Jan. 22, 1964).

Were this the case, only the wholly inoffensive, the bland, could gain access to the radio microphone or TV camera.

The Commission, however, was not grateful for the words which Jerry Garcia, leader of the California rock group called "The Grateful Dead," uttered over WUHY—FM in Philadelphia. On January 4, 1970, WUHY—FM broadcast its weekly "Cycle II" from 10 to 11 p.m., featuring an interview with Garcia. The licensee later told the Commission that this was a one-hour weekly broadcast which was " 'underground' " in its orientation and " 'is concerned with the avant-garde movement in music, publications, art, film, personalities, and other forms of social and artistic experimentation.' "

Garcia's interview ran 50 minutes, and his comments were intermixed frequently with the words "fuck" and "shit"—words which were used as adjectives or as an introductory expletive or a substitute for "et cetera." [36]   For example:

Shit.

Shit. I gotta get down there, man.

All that shit.

Readily available every fucking where.

Any of that shit either.

Political change is so fucking slow.

Thus Mr. Garcia used his capacious vocabulary to express "his views on ecology, music, philosophy, and interpersonal relations." [37]   WUHY's problem was complicated because a visitor to the station, who called himself "Crazy Max," whose real identity was not known to the licensee, had asked to be allowed to make some remarks about computers. Put on the air, Max had his say and also used the word "fuck." The FCC noted in its report of the Eastern Education Radio case: "The licensee states that Mr. Hill did not know what 'Crazy Max' was going to say in detail or how he was going to say it. It adds that 'Crazy Max' will not be allowed access to the microphone again." [38]

The Jerry Garcia-Crazy Max show had been taped five hours before it was aired, so there was ample time for the producer to consult with the station manager to allow review of controversial subject matter or language before it was aired. Because such consultation did not take place, the producer was fired for that infraction of station policy. [39]

[36] Eastern Educational Radio, WUHY—FM, 18 R.R.2d 860, 861 (April 1, 1970).

[37] Ibid., p. 861.

[38] Ibid., p. 862.

[39] Ibid.

Citing an obscenity statute [40] and the public interest standard of the Communications Act,[41] the Commission imposed a forfeiture of $100, adding: "This case was one of the first impression and court review would be welcomed." The licensee, however, paid the $100 fine and the FCC did not get the review it wished. The Commission action drew a typically heated dissent from Commissioner Nicholas Johnson, who complained that the FCC was condemning not words, but a culture—"a lifestyle it fears because it does not understand." He added: "To call The Grateful Dead a 'rock and roll musical group' is like calling the Los Angeles Philharmonic a 'jug band.' And that about shows 'where this Commission's at.'" Johnson also contended that when the FCC goes after broadcasters, it always seems to pick on small community service stations "that can scarcely afford the postage to answer our letters, let alone hire lawyers." [42]

The Jerry Garcia-Crazy Max incident took up only an hour of air time. Consider, then "Femme Forum," which ran five hours a day, 10 a.m. to 3 p.m. over WGLD–FM, Oak Park, Illinois. This station, licensed to the Sonderling Broadcasting Corporation, was one of a number of stations using a format nicknamed "topless radio." An announcer took calls from the audience and discussed topics, usually sexual ones. On February 23, 1973, the topic was "oral sex," and female callers talked explicitly about their oral sex experiences. Some recommended where to do it ("when you're driving") or and the discussions included suggestions for helpful substances (peanut butter, whipped cream, marshmallow * * *).[43]

The FCC concluded that these broadcasts called for imposition of a $2,000 forfeiture under Section 503(b)(1)(E) of the Communications Act. That section authorizes penalizing broadcasters who violate the federal obscenity statute by airing "obscene or indecent matter." [44] The FCC said that many basic concepts relevant to *Sonderling* had been set forth in *Eastern Educational Radio* (WUHY–FM).[45] The Commission's majority said that sex is not a forbidden subject on the broadcast medium. It added: [46]

> In this area as in others, we recognize the licensee's right to present provocative or unpopular programming

[40] 18 U.S.C.A. § 1464, at Ibid., 867.

[41] Section 503(b)(1)(A)(B), at Ibid., 867.

[42] 18 R.R.2d 860, 872d (April 1, 1970).

[43] Sonderling Broadcasting Corporation, Station WGLD–FM, Oak Park, Illinois, 27 R.R.2d 285 (April 11, 1973).

[44] Ibid., p. 287, citing 18 U.S.C.A. § 1464.

[45] 24 F.C.C.2d 408, R.R.2d 860 (1970).

[46] Sonderling Broadcasting Corporation, Station WGLD–FM, 27 R.R.2d 285, 287 (April 11, 1973).

which may offend some listeners, Pacifica Foundation, 36 FCC 147, 149 (1964).   Second, we note that we are not dealing with works of dramatic or literary art as we were in Pacifica.   We are rather confronted with the talk or interview show where clearly the interviewer can readily moderate his handling of the subject matter so as to conform to the basic statutory standards—standards which, as we point out, allow much leeway for provocative material.[47]

The Commission turned to obscenity decisions by the Supreme Court, particularly the "Fanny Hill" case and the *Ginzburg* case.[48] The nature of radio, however, led the FCC to some observations on the "pervasive and intrusive nature of broadcast radio."   The presence of children in the broadcast audience—for there is always a significant number of school-age children out of school on any given day—was important to the Commission.   "Many listen to radio; indeed it is almost the constant companion of the teenager." [49]   In *Sonderling,* the FCC again asked for a court review of its forfeiture order, but the broadcaster paid the fine.   A citizens' group and a civil liberties group asked the FCC to return the $2,000 forfeiture and to reconsider the Commission's notice of apparent liability against Sonderling Broadcasting.   The Commission refused, and the Court of Appeals for the District of Columbia held that the FCC was within its authority when it found the talk shows under consideration to be obscene.[50]

Considerations of *who* is listening were also important in a 1973 case involving yet another Pacifica Foundation station, WBAI–FM in New York City.   That station broadcast—on October 30, 1973—a monologue by comedian George Carlin.   This monologue, "Filthy Words," amounted to a discussion of "Seven Words You Can't Say on Radio," was a cut from the album, "George Carlin, Occupation: FOOLE."   Indeed, it turned out that Carlin was correct—the seven words he used did cause WBAI–FM trouble.   On December 3, 1973, the Commission received a complaint from the New Yorker saying that on October 30, he had been driving in his car and had heard offensive language on his car

---

[47] Ibid., p. 287n.   "In order to assure compliance with the law and their own programming policies, many licensees interpose a 'tape delay' in telephone interview programs, enabling the licensee to delete certain material before it is broadcast."

[48] See Section 64 of this chapter for a discussion of the "Fanny Hill" case, 383 U.S. 413, 86 S.Ct. 975 (1966), and the *Ginzburg* case, 383 U.S. 463, 86 S.Ct. 942 (1966).

[49] Sonderling Broadcasting Corporation, 27 R.R.2d 285, 289 (1973).

[50] Illinois Citizens Committee for Broadcasting v. Federal Communications Commission, 515 F.2d 397, 404 (D.C.Cir.1975).   The civil liberties group involved in this litigation was the Illinois Division of the American Civil Liberties Union.

radio. The man said that any child could have been turning the dial, and added: "Incidentally, my young son was with me when I heard the above *   *   *." [51]

The station argued that the Carlin routine had been broadcast as part of a discussion of the use of language in American society. Just before the monologue was put on the air, listeners were warned that it contained language which might be offensive to some. Persons who might be offended were advised to change the station and to return to WBAI in 15 minutes.

The FCC noted that broadcasting comes directly into the home.[52]

> Broadcasting requires special treatment because of four important considerations: (1) children have access to radios and in many cases are unsupervised by parents; (2) radio receivers are in the home, a place where people's privacy interest is entitled to extra defense, see Rowan v. Post Office Dept., 397 U.S. 728, 90 S.Ct. 1484 (1970); (3) unconsenting adults may tune in a station without any warning that offensive language is being or will be broadcast; and (4) there is a scarcity of spectrum space, the use of which the government must therefore license in the public interest.

The Commission attempted to distinguish "indecent" language from "obscene" words. Indecent language was defined as that which "describes, in terms patently offensive as measured by contemporary community standards for the broadcast medium, sexual or excretory activities and organs, at times of the day when there is a reasonable risk that children may be in the audience. To the Commission, the most important characteristic of the broadcast medium is its intrusive nature—"the television or radio broadcast comes directly into the home without any significant affirmative activity on the part of the listener."

The Commission's ruling against WBAI was overturned by a U.S. Court of Appeals, with Circuit Judge Tamm discussing the FCC in scathing terms: [53]

> *   *   *[T]he Commission felt that questions concerning the broadcast of patently offensive language should be dealt with in a public nuisance context.[54] As a result, the Commission determined that the principle of channeling

[51] Pacifica Foundation v. F.C.C., 556 F.2d 9 (D.C.Cir.1977).

[52] Ibid., p. 11.

[53] Ibid., pp. 11, 13–14.

[54] Ibid., at p. 12n. "The law of nuisance does not say, for example, that no one shall maintain a cement plant; it simply says that no one shall maintain a cement plant in an inappropriate place, such as a residential neighborhood."

should be borrowed from nuisance law and applied to the broadcasting medium. Rather than prohibit the broadcast of indecent language altogether, the Commission sought to channel it to times of the day when it would offend the fewest number of listeners.

* * *

Despite the Commission's professed intentions, the direct effect of the *Order* is to inhibit the free and robust exchange of ideas on a wide range of issues and subjects * * *. In promulgating the *Order* the Commission has ignored both the statute which forbids it to censor radio communications [47 U.S.C.A. § 326 (1970)] and its own previous decisions which leave the question of programming content to the discretion of the licensee.

* * *

As the study cited by the amicus curiae * * * illustrates, large numbers of children are in the broadcast audience until 1:30 a.m. The number of children does not fall below one million until 1 a.m. As long as such large numbers of children are in the audience the seven words noted in the *Order* may not be broadcast. Whether the broadcast containing such words may have serious artistic, literary, political or scientific value has no bearing. * * *. The Commission's action proscribes the uncensored broadcast of many of the great works of literature including Shakespearian plays which have won critical acclaim, the works of renowned classical and contemporary poets and writers, the passages from the *Bible*.

The Supreme Court of the United States, however, granted certiorari and reversed the Court of Appeals. It voted 5–4 that the FCC could forbid the use of the seven "filthy words" over the airwaves at times when children may be listening. Writing for the Court, Mr. Justice Stevens declared that offensive language need not be legally obscene to be excluded from broadcasts by the FCC.[55]

In summary, the Commission stated "We therefore hold that the language as broadcast was indecent and prohibited by 18 U.S.C.A. § 1464."

* * *

Entirely apart from the fact that the subsequent review of program content is not the sort of censorship at which the statute was directed, its history makes it perfectly clear that it was not intended to limit the Commis-

---

[55] Federal Communications Comm'n v. Pacifica Foundation, 438 U.S. 726, 98 S.Ct. 3026 (1978), rehearing denied, 439 U.S. 883, 99 S.Ct. 227 (1979).

sion's power to regulate the broadcast of obscene, indecent, or profane language.

*   *   *

The Commission identified several words that referred to excretory or sexual activities or organs, stated
that the repetitive deliberate use of those words in an
afternoon broadcast when children are in the audience
was patently offensive, and held that the broadcast was
indecent.   Pacifica takes issue with the Commission's
definition of indecency, but does not dispute the Commission's preliminary determination that each of the components of its definition was present.   Specifically, Pacifica
does not quarrel with the conclusion that this afternoon
broadcast was patently offensive.   Pacifica's claim that
the broadcast was not indecent within the meaning of the
statute rests entirely on the absence of prurient appeal.

*   *   *

The plain language of the statute does not support
Pacifica's argument.   The words "obscene, indecent or
profane" are written in the disjunctive, implying that
each has a separate meaning.   Prurient interest appeal is
an element of the obscene, but the normal definition of
"indecent" merely refers to non-conformance with accepted standards of morality.

Because the First Amendment is not an absolute prohibition
on governmental regulation of the content of speech, Carlin's
"seven words" could be barred from the air.   Justice Stevens
conceded, however, that even though those words "ordinarily lack
literary, political, or scientific value, they are not entirely outside
the protection of the First Amendment."   In some contexts, use of
even the most offensive words may be protected.   Justice Stevens
paraphrased Justice John Marshall Harlan: "one occasion's lyric
is another's vulgarity." [56]

But in this *Pacifica* case, a situation was presented which
called for keeping Carlin's language lesson off the air.   First,
broadcasting is a pervasive presence in American homes, and
second, it is uniquely accessible to children.   "Pacifica's broadcast," Stevens wrote, "could have enlarged a child's vocabulary in
an instant." [57]

It is appropriate *   *   * to emphasize the narrowness
of our holding.   This does not involve a two-way radio
conversation between one cab driver and a dispatcher, or

[56] 438 U.S. 726, 747, 98 S.Ct. 3026, 3039 (1978); cf. Cohen v. California, 403 U.S.
15, 25, 91 S.Ct. 1780, 1788 (1971).

[57] 438 U.S. 726, 749, 98 S.Ct. 3026, 3040 (1978).

a telecast of an Elizabethan comedy. We have not decided that an occasional expletive in either setting would justify any sanction * * *. The Commission's decision rested entirely on a nuisance rationale under which context is all-important. * * * As Mr. Justice Sutherland wrote, a nuisance may be merely a right thing in the wrong place—like a pig in the parlor instead of the barnyard. * * * We simply hold that when the Commission finds that a pig has entered the parlor, the exercise of its regulatory power does not depend on proof that the pig is obscene.

Four members of the Court—Brennan, Stewart, White and Marshall—dissented, arguing that the intent of Congress in passing the statute [58] had intended the word "indecent" to prohibit nothing more than obscene speech. Given that reading of the statute, the Commission's order was not authorized.[59]

SEC. 55. OBSCENITY: WOMEN'S AND CHILDREN'S RIGHTS

In a sexually fixated society, the law of obscenity is likely to remain an intractable problem area.

One common emotion after studying the law of obscenity is not lust or titillation but a kind of resignation. And, yes, some sympathy, too, for authors or artists who run afoul of benighted prosecutors/censors. (It often seems that there are more obscenity cases in the months shortly before prosecuting attorneys' elections than during the remainder of their elective terms. Prosecutors should be in favor of God, Mother, and Apple Pie, and against pornography.) Sympathy for members of the decency groups who protect thee and me (whether we want protection or not) but who don't have anyone to protect them. (Who will watch the watchdogs while the watchdogs watch us?)

Although some aspects of obscenity law are laughable, this section briefly will explore two deadly serious topics: child pornography and the growing pressure by some women's organizations to treat pornography as an atack on women's rights.

Child Pornography

Some of the seamier kinds of sexually explicit writings and films are produced by some pretty slimy individuals—people you would not invite home to dinner. Even so, their basic rights of expression must be upheld. Our language is so clumsy an instru-

---

[58] 18 U.S.C.A. § 1464.

[59] 438 U.S. 726, 780, 98 S.Ct. 3026, 3056 (1978).

ment that the verbal formulation which does away with repellant trash may also be used—when the dogs of censorship bay most loudly—to silence and punish politically and socially important expression. So runs one point of view. Another, exemplified by Chief Justice Burger, would have states or localities control certain kinds of sexually explicit matter as long as that material does not have literary, artistic, scientific, or political importance. By and large, however, expression tends to be the rule, with censorship its exception.

Child pornography is a different matter. It might be defined as the unspeakable done by the inhuman to cater to the sexual appetites of the ill. Strong legislative measures have been taken to halt something far more dangerous than distributing pornography—however defined—to children. Legislation has been created to outlaw using minors to perform or act in the creation of films, books, or magazine articles or other items depicting the sexual exploitation of children.[60] This might put a stop to magazines which could be purchased in 1977 such as "Chicken Delight," "Lust for Children," "Lollitots," and "Child Discipline." Dr. Judianne Densen-Gerber, president of the Odyssey Institute, made this outraged statement to the Subcommittee on Crime of Congress' Committee on the Judiciary: [61]

> There comes a point where we can no longer defend by intellectualization or forensic debate. We must simply say "I know the difference between right and wrong and I am not afraid to say 'no' or demand that limits be imposed".

> Common sense and maternal instinct tell me that this [child pornography which she found in New York, Philadelphia, Boston, Washington, New Orleans, Chicago, San Francisco, and Los Angeles] goes way beyond free speech. Such conduct mutilates children's spirits; they aren't consenting adults, they're victims. The First Amendment isn't absolute. Furthermore, even if I had to give up a portion of my First Amendment rights to stop this stuff, then I'd be willing to do it. When the Constitution and Bill of Rights were written, Franklin, Jefferson, Adams and Washington were interested in guaranteeing the right to religious, political and philosophical debate— not to publish a primer instructing a sex molester on how

---

[60] Senate Bill 1585, 95th Congress, 1st Session, No. 95–438, "Protection of Children Against Sexual Exploitation Act of 1977; Report of the Committee on the Judiciary, United States Senate, on S. 1585.

[61] Prepared Statement of Judianne Densen-Gerber, J.D., M.D., F.C.L.M., President, Odyssey Institute, for submission to The U.S. House of Representatives, Committee on the Judiciary, Subcommittee on Crime, May 23, 1977.

to pick up a child in the park and subsequently sexually assault her ("Lust for Children") or a booklet advocating that a father have incest with his daughter and illustrating positions to be used if she, at nine, is too small for normal penetration ("Schoolgirls", Los Angeles, and "Preteen Sexuality", Philadelphia). If we use constitutional rights to justify intercourse with children * * *! In summary, sadly, there is many a scoundrel wrapped in the American Flag.

This legislation, formerly known as Senate Bill No. 1585 before it was signed into law on Feb. 6, 1978 by President James Earl Carter, was formally called the "Protection of Children Against Sexual Exploitation Act of 1977." This legislation, in the words of U.S. Senators John C. Culver of Iowa and Charles McC. Mathias of Maryland, is intended to do the following: [62]

— Make it a Federal crime to use children in the production of pornographic materials.

— Prohibit the interstate transportation of children for the purpose of engaging in prostitution, and

— Increase the penalty provisions of the current Federal obscenity laws if the materials adjudged obscene involve the use of children engaging in sexually explicit conduct.

This measure corrects loopholes in existing federal obscenity statutes. Before this legislation, there was no federal statute prohibiting use of children in production of materials that depict explicit sexual conduct. This statute defines "minor" as any person under the age of 16 years. "Sexually explicit conduct" is defined as actual or simulated sexual intercourse, including genital-genital, oral-genital, anal-genital, or oral-anal, whether between people of the same or opposite sexes. Also forbidden are depiction of actual or simulated masturbation, bestiality, sadomasochistic abuse for purposes of sexual stimulation, or lewd exhibition of the genitals or pubic area of any person. Penalties for violation of this statutory provision are two–ten years imprisonment and/or a fine of up to $10,000 on first offense, or five–fifteen years imprisonment and/or a fine of up to $15,000 for subsequent offenses. [63]

Committees of the U.S. Senate and House of Representatives found a close connection between child pornography and the use of

---

[62] Form letter sent to the author by Senators Culver and Mathias, circa September 1977; letter to the author of October 19, 1977, by Rep. John Conyers, Jr. of Michigan's First District. See Public Law 95–225.

[63] 18 U.S.C.A. § 2251, Chapter 110—Sexual Exploitation of Children. The Mann Act, 18 U.S.C.A. § 2423, prohibits the interstate transportation of minor females for purposes of prostitution and did not include young males until amended in 1977.

young children as prostitutes. For example, a 17-year-old Chicago youth who had sold himself on the streets for two years, could often earn close to $500 a week by selling himself two or three times a night to have various sex acts with "chicken hawks" or pose for pornographic pictures or both.[64]

Kidporn and New York v. Ferber (1982)

In 1982, the Supreme Court of the United States made one thing clear about the murky law of obscenity: it will uphold state efforts to punish individuals for the production or sale of "kidporn." In New York v. Ferber, the Court declared valid a New York criminal statute prohibiting persons from knowingly authorizing or inducing a child less than 16 years old to engage in a sexual performance.[65] "Sexual performance" is defined by the New York statute as " 'any performance or part thereof which includes sexual performance or part thereof which includes sexual conduct by a child less than sixteen years of age.' " The specific statutory provision tested said: [66]

> A person is guilty [of a class D felony, which carries punishment of up to seven years imprisonment for persons and a fine of up to $10,000 for corporations] of promoting a sexual performance by a child when, knowing the character and content thereof, he produces, directs, or promotes any performance which includes sexual conduct by a child less than sixteen years of age.

The case began when Paul Ira Ferber, proprietor of a Manhattan bookstore specializing in sexually oriented materials, sold two films to undercover police officers. The two films dealt almost exclusively with depictions of boys masturbating. A jury trial convicted Ferber of two counts of promoting a sexual performance and Ferber was sentenced to 45 days in prison. Ferber's convictions were upheld on first appeal, but the New York Court of Appeals said that the statute section under which Ferber was convicted was too sweeping. The New York Court of Appeals held that Section 263.15 might be used to punish sale or promotion of

---

[64] Report of the Committee on the Judiciary, United States Senate on S.1585, Protection of Children Against Sexual Exploitation Act of 1977 (Washington, D.C., 1977), p. 7. See also Robin Lloyd, For Money or Love: Boy Prostitution in America (New York: Vanguard Press, 1976).

[65] 458 U.S. 747, 102 S.Ct. 3348 (1982), 8 Med.L.Rptr. 1809.

[66] McKinney's, New York Penal Law, § 263.1. In addition, as noted by the Court, the New York statute defines a performance as " 'any play, motion picture, photograph or dance' or 'any other visual presentation exhibited before an audience.' " See McKinney's, N.Y.Penal Law, § 263.4. "Sexual conduct" is defined as " 'actual or simulated sexual intercourse, deviate; sexual intercourse, sexual bestiality, masturbation, sado-masochistic abuse, or lewd exhibition of the genitals.' " McKinney's, N.Y.Penal Law, § 263.3.

material protected by the First Amendment. Protected material which seemed to come under the New York statute, the appeals court said, included " 'medical books and educational sources, which "deal with adolescent sex in a realistic but nonobscene manner." ' " [67]

The Supreme Court of the United States granted certiorari. In deciding the case, the Court said that that it presented just one question: [68]

> To prevent the abuse of children who are made to engage in sexual conduct for commercial purposes, could the New York State Legislature, consistent with the First Amendment, prohibit the dissemination of material which shows children engaged in sexual conduct, regardless of whether such material is obscene?

Writing for the Court, Justice Byron White said: [69]

> Like obscenity statutes, laws directed at the dissemination of child pornography run the risk of suppressing protected expression by allowing the hand of the censor to become unduly heavy. For the following reasons, however, we are persuaded that the States are entitled to greater leeway in the regulation of pornographic depictions of children.
>
> *First.* It is evident beyond the need for elaboration that a state's interest in "safeguarding the physical and psychological well being of a minor" is "compelling." Globe Newspapers v. Superior Court, 457 U.S. 596, 607, 102 S.Ct. 2613, 2620 (1982), 8 Med.L.Rptr. 1689. * * * In Ginsberg v. New York, supra, we sustained a New York law protecting children from exposure to nonobscene literature. Most recently, we held that the government's interest in the "well-being of its youth" justified special treatment of indecent broadcasting received by adults as well as children. FCC v. Pacifica Foundation, 438 U.S. 726, 98 S.Ct. 3026, (1978), 8 Med.L.Rptr. 2553.
>
> The prevention of sexual exploitation and abuse of children constitutes a government objective of surpassing importance.
>
> *   *   *
>
> *Second.* The distribution of photographs and films depicting sexual activity by juveniles is intrinsically related to the sexual abuse of children in at least two ways.

---

[67] 458 U.S. 747, 102 S.Ct. 3348, 3352 (1982), 8 Med.L.Rptr. at 1811–1812.

[68] 458 U.S. 747, 102 S.Ct. 3348, 3352 (1982), 8 Med.L.Rptr. at 1812.

[69] 458 U.S. 747, 102 S.Ct. 3348 (1982), 8 Med.L.Rptr. at 1813–1815.

First, the materials produced are a permanent record of
the children's participation and the harm to the child is
exacerbated by their circulation. Second, the distribution
network for child pornography must be closed if the
production of material which requires the sexual exploitation of children is to be effectively controlled. Indeed,
there is no serious contention that the legislature was
unjustified in believing that it is difficult, if not impossible, to halt the exploitation of children by pursuing only
those who produce the photographs and movies. While
the production of pornographic materials is a low-profile,
clandestine industry, the need to market the resulting
products requires a visible apparatus of distribution. The
most expeditous if not the only practical method of law
enforcement may be to dry up the market for this material by imposing severe criminal penalties on persons selling, advertising, or otherwise promoting the product.
Thirty-five States and Congress have concluded that restraints on the distribution of pornographic materials are
required in order to effectively combat the problem, and
there is a body of literature to support these legislative
conclusions.

Justice White noted the economic motive involved in the
production of such materials. " 'It rarely has been suggested that
the constitutional freedom for speech and press extends immunity
to speech or writing used as an integral part of conduct in
violation of a valid criminal statute.' " [70] Further, the value of
children depicted as engaged in lewd sexual conduct "is exceedingly modest, if not de minimis * * *. We consider it unlikely that
visual depictions of children performing sexual acts * * * would
often constitute an important and necessary part of a literary
performance or scientific or educational work." [71] Further, classifying child pornography as a category outside protection of the
First Amendment is compatible with the Supreme Court's earlier
rulings.[72] Finally, the Court concluded that the New York statute
was not unconstitutionally overbroad: "We consider this the para-
digmatic case of a statute whose legitimate reach dwarfs its
arguably impermissible applications." The statute is directed at
"the hard core of child pornography," not at protected expression
"ranging from medical textbooks to pictorials in National Geo-
graphic." [73]

[70] 458 U.S. 747, 102 S.Ct. 3348, 3357 (1982), 8 Med.L.Rptr. 1815–1816, quoting
Giboney v. Empire Storage, 336 U.S. 490, 498, 69 S.Ct. 684 (1949).

[71] 458 U.S. 747, 102 S.Ct. 3348, 3357 (1982), 8 Med.L.Rptr. at 1816.

[72] 458 U.S. 747, 102 S.Ct. 3348, 3357–3358 (1982), 8 Med.L.Rptr. 1820–1821.

[73] 458 U.S. 747, 102 S.Ct. 3348, 3363 (1982), 8 Med.L.Rptr. at 1821.

Justice O'Connor concurred, stressing that in her view, the New York statute "permits discussion of child sexuality, forbidding only attempts to render the "portrayal(s) somewhat more 'realistic' by utilizing or photographing children." Justice O'Connor emphasized children's welfare, suggesting that even material with serious literary or scientific value could be forbidden if its depictions would, by involving children, do them psychological harm.[74] Justice Brennan, with Justice Marshall joining him, contended that the statute could not constitutionally be applied to materials with serious literary, scientific, or educational value. Finally, Brennan reiterated his familiar position: "I, of course, adhere to my view that, in the absence of exposure, or particular harm, to juveniles or unconsenting adults the State lacks power to suppress sexually oriented materials." [75]

Women's Rights, Pornography and the First Amendment

Sex sells, and erotic movies make up a startlingly large amount of the trade of video stores. As Newsweek magazine noted in 1985, "Combat Zones" in cities—the sleazy areas with massage parlors and video peep shows are shrinking in some cities. "But home porn is booming: wherever VCR's go, porn is sure to follow." The owner of a chain of video stores told Newsweek that one-fifth of his video sales are of the X-rated variety. A Newsweek poll said that nearly 40 percent of VCR owners bought or rented an X-rated cassette during 1984.[76] Beyond that, the sick "kicks" portrayed seem to be escalating, growing increasingly inventive and unusual, as if some jaded entrepreneurs are trying to dream up things truly on the outer frontiers of S & M (sadomasochism).

The mid-1980s scrapping over pornography is causing new divisions, new emotional and political line-ups. " 'It's one of those issues where you just can't predict how your friends are going to line up,' " said Minneapolis writer Karen Branan.[77]

Some feminists decided during the 1970's that pornography "expresses the ideology of male supremacy."[78] And feminist and attorney Wendy Kaminer has written, "Pornography is speech that legitimizes and fosters the physical abuse and sexual repres-

[74] 458 U.S. 747, 102 S.Ct. 3348 (1982), 8 Med.L.Rptr. 1821.

[75] 458 U.S. 747, 102 S.Ct. 3348 (1982), 8 Med.L.Rptr. 1822.

[76] Newsweek (cover story), "The War Against Pornography," March 18, 1985, pp. 58, 61.

[77] Mary Kay Blakely, "Is One Woman's Sexuality Another Woman's Pornography?", Ms. magazine, April, 1985, p. 37.

[78] David Bryden, "Between Two Constitutions: Feminism and Pornography," 2 Constitutional Commentary (1985), p. 147.

sion of women."[79] Two kinds of counter-attacks on pornography emerged during the mid-1980s, and they will be discussed in turn.

(1) The "Indianapolis Ordinance," involving government action to try to control pornography.

(2) One version of a "Minneapolis Ordinance," involving private action, with one citizen suing another, to try to control pornography.

The Indianapolis Ordinance: Prior Restraint

In the spring of 1984, the Indianapolis-Marion County City-County Council ("Council") passed and then amended an ordinance to define, prevent, and prohibit "all discriminatory practices of sexual subordination or inequality through pornography." Mayor Richard Hudnut signed them into law.[80] The ordinance said, in part: [81]

16. "Pornography" is defined in the Ordinance as follows:

"(q) Pornography shall mean the graphic sex—sexually explicit subordination of women, whether in pictures or in words, that also includes one or more of the following:

"(1) Women who are presented as sexual objects or who enjoy pain or humiliation; or

"(2) Women are presented as sexual objects who experience sexual pleasure in being raped; or

"(3) Women are presented as sexual objects tied up or cut or mutilated or bruised or physically hurt, or as dismembered or truncated or fragmented or severed into body parts; or

"(4) Women are presented being penetrated by objects or animals; or

"(5) Women are presented in scenarios of degradation, injury, abasement, torture, shown as filthy or inferior, bleeding, bruised, or hurt in a context that makes these conditions sexual, and

"(6) Women are presented as sexual objects for domination, conquest, violation, exploitation, possession, or

[79] Wendy Kaminer, "Pornography and the First Amendment: Prior Restraints and Private Action," in Take Back the Night, p. 241.

[80] American Booksellers Association v. Hudnut, 598 F.Supp. 1316 (S.D.Ind.1984), 11 Med.L.Rptr. 1105, 1106.

[81] 598 F.Supp. at 1320 (S.D.Ind.1984), 11 Med.L.Rptr. at 1106, quoting Indianapolis ordinance.

use, or through postures or positions of sevility or submission or display.

"The use of men, children, or transsexuals in the place of women in paragraphs (1) through (6) above shall also constitute pornography under this section."

Another part of the ordinance said, "Trafficking in pornography: The production, sale, exhibition, or distribution of pornography" was made unlawful. In addition, the ordinance had a provision saying "any woman may file a complaint as a woman acting against the subordination of women."[82] Men and transsexuals could file similar complaints "but must prove injury in the same way that a woman is injured in order to obtain relief under this chapter."

In response, the American Booksellers Association—an organization of some 5,200 members, plus other groups and individuals including the Association of American Publishers and the Freedom to Read Foundation of the American Library Association challenged the constitutionality of the ordinance.[83]

The American Booksellers Association and other plaintiffs contended that the ordinance "severely restricts the availability, display and distribution of constitutionally protected, non-obscene materials in violation of the First and Fourteenth Amendments." More specifically, plaintiffs complained that the sweep of the ordinance took in more than materials which are constitutionally unprotected speech (such as obscenity). [84]

Further, the plaintiffs said the ordinance was unconstitutionally vague in not giving notice of what might be a crime. And, in District Judge Barker's words,[85]

> Plaintiffs furthermore charge that the Ordinance, by providing for "cease and desist" orders to enforce its proscriptions, constitutes a prior restraint which impermissibly allows a governmental Board to act as censor in determining what is and is not protected material under the First Amendment, and to control what materials may be written, distributed, sold, viewed or read in Indianapolis.

Judge Barker's lengthy opinion found multiple defects in the Indianapolis ordinance: it sought to control speech without reference to applicable constitutional requirements;[86] and the expres-

---

[82] 598 F.Supp. at 1320 (S.D.Ind.1984), 11 Med.L.Rptr. at 1108.

[83] 598 F.Supp. at 1319 (S.D.Ind.1984), 11 Med.L.Rptr. at 1107.

[84] 598 F.Supp. at 1327 (S.D.Ind.1984), 11 Med.L.Rptr. at 1113.

[85] 598 F.Supp. at 1328 (S.D.Ind.1984), 11 Med.L.Rptr. at 1114.

[86] 598 F.Supp. at 1331 (S.D.Ind.1984), 11 Med.L.Rptr. at 1117.

sion sought to be controlled may not meet the test for obscenity as spelled out in Miller v. California: [87]

> "(a) whether 'the average person, applying contemporary community standards,' would find that the work, taken as a whole, appeals to the prurient interest, * * *; (b) whether the work depicts or describes, in a patently offensive way, sexual conduct specifically defined by the applicable state law; and (c) whether the work, taken as a whole, lacks serious literary, artistic, political, or scientific value."

Additionally, the broad language of the ordinance extended over into broadcasting, but "was not written to protect children from the distribution of pornography." In addition, the language of the ordinance was, Judge Barker said, "impermissibly vague." In sum, although government has a recognized interest in prohibiting sex discrimination, Judge Barker said "that interest does not outweigh the constitutionally protected interest in free speech."

On appeal, a three-judge panel of the U.S. Court of Appeals, Seventh Circuit, affirmed the district court's judgment that the Indianapolis anti-pornography ordinance was unconstitutional. Circuit Judge Easterbrook said the ordinance did not refer, as in Miller v. California (1973), to prurient interest, offensiveness, or community standards. Further, it concentrated on particular depictions, not judging a work as a whole, and made it irrelevant whether a work had literary, artistic, political, or scientific value. Judge Easterbrook added,

> The ordinance contains four prohibitions. People may not "traffic" in pornography, "coerce" others into performing in pornographic works, or "force" pornography on anyone. Anyone injured by someone who has seen or read pornography has a right of action against the maker or seller.

Judge Easterbrook accepted the premises of the city's ordinance that that depictions of subordination tend to perpetuate subordination. "The subordinate status of women," he wrote, "leads to affront and lower pay at work, insult and injury at home, battery and rape on the battery." Even so, the ordinance's definition of pornography was unconstitutional.[88]

> A law awarding damages for assaults caused by speech * * * has the power to muzzle the press, and again courts (as in the law of libel) would place careful

[87] 598 F.Supp. at 1332 (S.D.Ind.1984), 11 Med.L.Rptr. at 1123.

[88] American Booksellers Association, Inc. v. William Hudnut, III, Mayor of Indianapolis, 771 F.2d 323 (7th Cir.1985), 11 Med.L.Rptr. 2465, 2466, 2469, 2473–2474.

limits on the scope of the right. Certainly no damages could be awarded unless the harm flowed directly from the speech and there was an element of intent on the part of the speaker * * *

Much speech is dangerous. Chemists whose work might help someone build a bomb, political theorists whose papers might start political movements that lead to riots, speakers whose ideas attract violent protesters, all these and more leave loss in their wake. Unless the remedy is very closely confined, it could be more dangerous to speech than all the libel judgments in history. The constitutional requirements for a valid recovery for assault caused by speech might turn out to be too rigorous for any plaintiff to meet.

The Minneapolis Approach

In Minneapolis, on the other hand, a different approach was sought. Wendy Kaminer has argued, it is possible to protect First Amendment values while moving effectively against pornography. "Feminists need not and should not advocate censorship, but we have every right to organize politically and to protest material that is degrading and dangerous to women. Her solution, as that of Andrea Dworkin and Catharine MacKinnon—driving forces behind the Minnesota ordinance—is to sue for violation of rights.[89] Since in their view, pornography is sex-based discrimination—"the sexually explicit subordination of women, graphically depicted"— then persons offended by such materials should have the right to sue for damages. This ordinance, however, was twice vetoed by Minneapolis Mayor Fraser.[90]

Constitutional scholar Robert O'Neil has written down a disquieting thought. He sees growing problem in a mounting tension between "freedom of expression on the one hand, and freedom from discrimination on grounds of race, religion, sex or nationality on the other." He predicts that this tension will "increasingly become one of the deepest and most trying dilemmas of our time."[91] If so, the contests in Indianapolis, and in Minneapolis, and in other places such as Suffolk, New York, too, may be bearing out his prophecy.

[89] Kaminer, loc. cit.

[90] Bryden, op. cit.

[91] Robert O'Neil, "Second Thoughts on the First Amendment," New Mexico Law Review Vol. 13, Summer, 1983, pp. 577ff.

SEC. 56. BLASPHEMY

Publications which revile the Deity were long held to be blasphemous; in 20th Century America, the crime has all but disappeared.

The law of blasphemy, as it remains in the United States, is little more than an historical artifact. But blasphemy statutes—although not enforced recently in the United States—are still on the books of some 15 states. The ancient crime of blasphemy (technically, a form of criminal libel) was first a common-law offense, although the crime was later codified into statutory form in both England and America. Blackstone defined blasphemy as "denying [God's] being, or providence; or by contumelious reproaches of our Savior Christ." [92] Black's Law Dictionary defines blasphemy as "[a]ny oral or written reproach maliciously cast upon God, His name, attributes, or religion." [93]

Blasphemy should be distinguished from several other allied offenses:

Sacrilege: "The crime of breaking a church or chapel, and stealing therein. * * * The desecration of anything considered holy * * *".[94]

Heresy: "An offense against religion, consisting not in a total denial of Christianity, but of some of its essential doctrines [such as the Trinity], publicly and obstinately avowed." [95]

Apostacy: "The total renunciation of Christianity, by embracing either a false religion or no religion at all."[96]

Profanity: "Irreverance toward sacred things; particularly, an irreverant or blasphemous use of the name of god." [97] Public swearing and cursing—variously defined—seems to be treated as "disturbing the peace" or a related offense in many jurisdictions today.

Witchcraft: This old and nearly forgotten crime doubtless has the bloodiest history of any offense listed in this brief catalog. Witchcraft—sometimes called sorcery, enchantment, or conjuration—has been called supposed communication with evil spirits. This offense was punishable by death, on the theory, evidently,

[92] William Blackstone, Commentaries on the Laws of England, Vol. IV, adapted by Robert Malcolm Kerr (Boston: Beacon Press, 1952) p. 55.

[93] Henry Campbell Black, Black's Law Dictionary, 4th ed. (St. Paul, Minn., West Publishing Co., 1951) p. 216.

[94] Ibid., 1501.

[95] Ibid., 859.

[96] Ibid., 122.

[97] Ibid., 1375.

that witches (female) and warlocks (male) revered the Devil more than God. Once people rejected the picturesque theology of the supernatural power of evil, prosecutions for witchcraft ceased. But in Salem Village, Massachusetts, in 1692, belief in witches and warlocks was in full flower. Twenty persons were killed for witchcraft in that enlightened village.[98]

Note that the early beginnings of the Anglo-American law of blasphemy were shot through with fervent, right-minded attachment to the idea that there was only one true religion: Christianity. Violent advocates of such a view, in the 17th Century, were all too readily to kill, maim, or imprison nonconformists who questioned their views. Over time, however, severity of punishment for blasphemy and related offenses in the United States decreased enormously. It should be noted, nevertheless, that as recently as 1937, a man was convicted in Connecticut for violating that state's blasphemy statute.[99] There is now grave doubt whether any statute serving as the basis for a conviction for blasphemy could be upheld as constitutional.[1]

Even so, if only for crassly political "let's us legislators act like Good Christians for our constituents" reasons, the Massachusetts Senate voted late in 1977 *against* repeal of a 280-year-old anti-blasphemy statute. The statute forbids profane remarks involving God or "things divine." Violators of the statute could spend up to a year in jail (if the statute's constitutionality were to be upheld) and could pay a fine of up to $300. Massachusetts Senator William H. Wall piously said, supporting the statute, " 'We are opening the doors to destroying one of the Ten Commandments'." Senator Wall's political platitudes were answered rather acidly by Senator Alan D. Sisitsky, co-chairman of the Massachusetts Senate's Judiciary Committee: " 'I would hate to hear one of my colleagues make a slip and swear * * * and then have to go to jail.' "[2]

[98] Ibid., 1776.

[99] "Fined as Blasphemer," New York Times, Oct. 14, 1937, p. 29, col. 1.

[1] See, e.g., Burstyn v. Wilson, 343 U.S. 495, 72 S.Ct. 777 (1952).

[2] United Press International dispatch datelined Boston, November 30, 1977.

Part III

FACT GATHERING AND CITIZENS' RIGHTS

Chapter 9

SHIELDING INFORMATION FROM DISCLOSURE

SEC. 57. THE GOVERNMENT CONTEMPT POWER

Persons who disobey the orders of courts may be cited, tried and convicted for contempt of court, the coercive power that underlies the courts' authority. The legislative branch has similar power. Journalists most often have come in conflict with the contempt power when they have refused court orders to disclose confidential information.

The common law has long provided that relationships between certain people are so personal and intimate that their confidences deserve protection against legally compelled disclosure. The clergyman and penitent, the physician and patient, the attorney and client, the husband and wife all share information that in some circumstances warrants unbroken confidentiality. The law has resisted expanding the protection to other interpersonal relationships, and even in the few listed above it has carefully avoided establishing any never-failing or absolute protection against the general rule: When government requires a citizen's testimony in furthering its legitimate ends such as ensuring fair judicial process or making laws, it is the citizen's duty to appear and testify.[1]

Printers of the American colonial period universally provided many contributors with anonymity, and occasionally resisted demands of the legislative branch to reveal their names. Early in nationhood, journalists continued to refuse demands of Congress and legislatures to break confidences, and as the Nineteenth

---

[1] 8 J. Wigmore, Evidence, 2286, 2290, 2394 (J. McNaughton Rev.Ed.1961).

413

Century progressed, sought expansion of the common law's protection to their own setting. They argued that journalistic ethics and their own professional livelihood required that they keep confidences; especially in reporting malfeasance or corruption in government, they added, the public interest required that the news be told and that sometimes the news could be told only if they promised their source confidentiality. Their success was modest indeed, but by the end of the century, a start was made toward legal protection when the State of Maryland passed the nation's first "shield law" for journalists—a law that recognized a journalist's privilege to not reveal confidential sources. Within the next three or four decades, a few more states joined Maryland in establishing journalists' privilege by statute.[2] Broad protection, however, was to await the decade of the 1970s, when the First Amendment, increased numbers of state statutes, and the federal common law were brought to bear.

The authority of government to compel testimony and to respond to journalists' refusal to break confidences is its contempt power—to declare that refusals to testify are contempt of authority, and to punish the person in contempt with imprisonment. The clash between the demand and refusal comes to resolution in the exercise of this power.

Annette Buchanan wrote a story for her college newspaper, the University of Oregon *Daily Emerald,* about the use of marijuana among students at the University. She said that seven students, whom she did not name, gave her information. And when the district attorney asked her to name the sources of information to a grand jury that was investigating drug use, and subsequently a judge directed her to do so, she refused. A reporter should be privileged not to reveal her sources, she said, and not to break confidences. To betray a pledge of secrecy to a source, Buchanan added, would be a signal to many sources to "dry up." The judge, and upon appeal the Oregon Supreme Court, found her in contempt of court for refusing to obey the judge's order, and she was sentenced to a brief jail term.[3]

Buchanan's was a case of "direct" contempt: it took place in the presence of the judge. Goss, a television personality, was not

---

[2] The history of journalists' privilege not to reveal information is best told by A. David Gordon, "Protection of News Sources: the History and Legal Status of the Newsman's Privilege," Ph.D. dissertation, unpublished (Univ. of Wis., 1970). See also Thomas H. Kaminski, "Congress, Correspondents and Confidentiality in the 19th Century: a Preliminary Study," Journalism History, 4:3, Autumn 1977, pp. 83–87. For an overview of the current status, see Anon., "Privilege of the Newsgatherer Against Disclosure of Confidential Sources of Information," 99 A.L.R.2d 37–114 (1980).

[3] State v. Buchanan, 250 Or. 244, 436 P.2d 729 (1968), certiorari denied 392 U.S. 905, 88 S.Ct. 2055 (1968).

within shouting distance of the court when on his program he attacked witnesses in a divorce case in which he was accused of adultery with the wife. For his attempt to prevent witnesses from giving testimony unfavorable to him by vilifying them, he was convicted of contempt which takes place away from the court, by publication, called indirect or "constructive" contempt.[4] On appeal, his conviction was overruled, the court holding that his broadcasts were no real danger to justice because while the targets might have been angered by his words, they had no reason to feel threatened in their testimony by them.[5]

In the *Goss* case of contempt by publication as in the *Buchanan* case of direct contempt, a judge ruled initially that the reporter's acts interfered with the administration of justice—that the acts were contemptuous of court. In each case, the judge convicted the reporter under his inherent power to punish for the interference, punishment for contempt being the basis of all legal procedure and the means of courts' enforcing their judgments and orders.[6]

The cases diverged in their outcomes, Buchanan failing in her appeal, Goss succeeding in his; and, indeed, the outcomes illustrate the fortunes of reporters in recent years in similar circumstances. Direct contempt is a current, serious problem for the press; constructive contempt has almost vanished, as we saw in Chapter 2, Sec. 9, and needs no further treatment in this chapter.

Summary procedure is the ordinary procedure in contempt. In it, the judge accuses, tries, and sentences in his own case without resort to trial by jury. It is often justified by reference to the British legal writer of the 18th Century, Sir William Blackstone, who wrote: [7]

> Some * * * contempts may arise in the face of the court; as by rude and contumelious behavior; by obstinacy, perverseness, or prevarication; by breach of the peace; or any wilful disturbance whatever; others, in the absence of the party; as by disobeying or treating with disrespect the king's writ, or the rules of process of the court; by perverting such writ or process to the purposes of private malice, extortion, or injustice; by speaking or writing contemptuously of the court or judges, acting in their judicial capacity; by printing false accounts (or even

[4] People v. Goss, 10 Ill.2d 533, 141 N.E.2d 385, 390 (1957).

[5] Goss v. State of Illinois, 204 F.Supp. 268 (N.D.Ill.1962), reversed on other grounds, 312 F.2d 257 (7th Cir.1963).

[6] Sir John C. Fox, History of Contempt of Court (Oxford, 1927), p. 1.

[7] Blackstone, pp. 284, 285.

true ones, without proper permission) of causes then depending in judgment * * *.

The process of attachment for these and the like contempts must necessarily be as ancient as the laws themselves * * *. A power therefore in the supreme courts of justice to suppress such contempts by an immediate attachment of the offender results from the first principles of judicial establishments and must be an inseparable attendant upon every superior tribunal.

For the United States, an act declaratory of the law of contempt in the federal courts, passed in 1831, is the basis of contempt proceedings before federal judges. State courts likewise possess the power to punish for contempt, under authority of inherent power or statute, or both.[8] State courts have ignored or denied acts by state legislatures to limit this power. Many followed the early lead of State v. Morrill,[9] an influential Arkansas case of 1855. In it, a charge published in a newspaper that an alleged murderer had bribed the state supreme court was the basis for summary contempt proceedings. The court was faced with a state statute limiting contempt proceedings to specified acts not including out-of-court publications. The court ruled that the statute was not binding upon the judiciary, for it must have power to enforce its own process, and the contempt power which provides this springs into existence upon the creation of the courts.[10] Without this authority, courts would be powerless to enforce their orders.

Attempts by Congress and state legislatures to limit contempt to certain specific classifications have not been universally successful. The legislative and judicial branches of government are coordinate under the "separation of powers" doctrine that gives each branch of government autonomy in its own sphere. While the legislative branch of any governmental unit has the power to make the law, the judicial branch has inherent rights to enforce its orders, rules, writs, or decrees. Even in states where there is a strict definition of what constitutes contempt, under special circumstances there is precedent for the courts' considering their inherent power above the legislative enactment.[11]

Some headway has been made by those who pose a more general challenge to the contempt power of courts, and who assert that jury trials should be substituted for a judge's summary proceeding. It is sometimes objected by these that American

---

[8] Act of Mar. 2, 1831, c. 99, 4 Stat. 487.

[9] 16 Ark. 384 (1855).

[10] Ibid., 384, 407.

[11] Farr v. Superior Court, 22 Cal.App.3d 60, 99 Cal.Rptr. 342, 348 (1972).

traditions are violated where a judge may sit as accuser, prosecutor, and judge in his own or a fellow judge's case: "It is abhorrent to Anglo-Saxon justice as applied in this country that one man, however lofty his station or venerated his vestments, should have the power of taking another man's liberty from him." [12] There are flaws in the Blackstonian position that summary procedure is an "immemorial power" of judges in all contempt cases; [13] and the United States Supreme Court in 1968 addressed itself to the problem and said that the old rule did not justify denying a jury trial in serious contempt cases. It ruled in Bloom v. Illinois [14] that "If the right to jury trial is a fundamental matter in other criminal cases, * * * it must also be extended to criminal contempt cases." The length of the sentence imposed was used by the Court as the test of "seriousness," which it found in a two-year jail term given Bloom.

In addition to courts, legislative bodies are jealous of their power to cite for contempt. Congressional and state legislative investigating committees sometimes seek the testimony of reporters who have special knowledge about subjects under the committees' official inquiry. Citations for contempt have occurred when reporters have refused to answer lawmakers' questions, and occasionally, over the last two centuries, convictions have been had.

The legislative power to cite for contempt derives its force from the power possessed by the English Parliament, on which both the legislatures and the Congress were modeled.[15] No limitations are imposed upon Congress in its punishment for either disorderly conduct or contempt, but in Marshall v. Gordon,[16] it was held that the punishment imposed could not be extended beyond the session in which the contempt occurs.

The Supreme Court has conceded to Congress the power to punish nonmembers for contempt when there occurs "either physical obstruction of the legislative body in the discharge of its duties, or physical assault upon its members, for action taken or words spoken in the body, or obstruction of its officers in the performance of their official duties, or the prevention of members from attending so that their duties might be performed, or finally,

[12] Ballantyne v. U.S., 237 F.2d 657, 667 (5th Cir.1956); J. Edward Gerald, The Press and the Constitution, pp. 30–31.

[13] W. Nelles and C.W. King, "Contempt by Publication in the United States," 28 Col.L.Rev. 408 (1928).

[14] 391 U.S. 194, 88 S.Ct. 1477, 1485 (1968).

[15] Max Radin, Anglo American Legal History, pp. 63, 64.

[16] 243 U.S. 521, 37 S.Ct. 448, 61 L.Ed. 881, L.R.A.1917F, 279, Ann.Cas.1918B, 371 (1917).

for refusing with contumacy to obey orders, to produce documents or to give testimony which there was a right to compel." [17]

Seldom has a reporter gone to jail for refusing to reveal to Congress a source of information. One of the cases involved Z.L. White and Hiram J. Ramsdell, Washington correspondents of the *New York Tribune.* They published what they claimed was the "Treaty of Washington," a document being studied by the Senate in executive meeting. They refused to say from whom they got the copy, were tried and convicted of contempt by the Senate, and were committed to the custody of the Sergeant at Arms until the end of the Session.[18]

Congress has not in many decades chosen to try and convict for contempt. Instead, it has cited for contempt and certified the persons cited to the district attorney of the District of Columbia for prosecution under a law that gives the courts power to try such cases.[19]

It is uncertain how far the principles of freedom of the press protect a reporter from contempt charges if he refuses to answer the questions of a Congressional Committee. Journalists have argued that the First Amendment sharply limits Congress in questioning and investigating the press: Congress may investigate only the matters on which it may legislate, they point out, and the First Amendment says that "Congress shall make no law * * * abridging freedom of * * * the press."

In 1971, a prize-winning television documentary by CBS, "The Selling of the Pentagon," raised a storm of protest against alleged bias in the film's portrayal of the American military's public information programs. Selective editing for the documentary, the military charged, distorted the intent, management and messages of the military. The House of Representatives Commerce Committee, under its chairman Rep. Harley O. Staggers, undertook an investigation of the matter, and CBS president Frank Stanton refused to furnish the committee parts of film edited out of the final version. In response to the subpoena ordering him to appear with the materials, he appeared but declared that furnishing materials would amount to a violation of freedom of the press. The Committee voted 25 to 13 to recommend to Congress a contempt citation. The House, however, turned down the recommendation, Rep. Emanuel Celler declaring that "The First Amendment towers over these proceedings like a colossus. No tender-

[17] Ibid.

[18] U.S. Senate, Subcommittee on Administrative Practice and Procedure of Committee on the Judiciary, The Newsman's Privilege, 89 Cong., 2 Sess., Oct. 1966, pp. 57–61. Nineteenth century investigations of news media and reporters were not rare according to Kaminski, op.cit., p. 85.

[19] 2 U.S.C.A. §§ 192, 194.

ness of one member for another should cause us to topple over this monument to our liberties." [20]

More recently, newsman Daniel Schorr, then of CBS, came under protracted investigation by Congress, and heavy fire from a segment of the media, for his refusal to testify. Schorr had obtained a copy of the Pike Committee (House Intelligence Committee) report on operations of the Central Intelligence Agency, which the House of Representatives had voted should be kept secret after heavy pressure not to disclose it from the federal administration. National security, the administration said, was at stake. Schorr broadcast some of the contents; passed the report to the *Village Voice* which published much of it; was investigated for several months during which he was suspended by CBS; and finally came before the House Ethics Committee.[21] Under a congressman's solemn admonition against publishers' taking it "upon themselves to publish secret and classified information against the will of Congress and the people," [22] Schorr illuminated the rationale for a journalist's refusing to reveal sources, saying in part: [23]

> We all build our lives around certain principles, without which our careers lose their meaning.
>
> For some of us—doctors, lawyers, clergymen, and journalists—it is an article of faith that we must keep confidential those matters entrusted to us only because of the assurance that they would remain confidential.
>
> For a journalist, the most crucial kind of confidence is the identity of a source of information. To betray a confidential source would mean to dry up many future sources for many future reporters. The reporter and the news organization would be the immediate losers. The ultimate losers would be the American people and their free institutions.
>
> But, beyond all that, to betray a source would be to betray myself, my career, and my life. It is not as simple as saying that I refuse to do it. I cannot do it.

Unlike the committee that recommended on Stanton, the Ethics Committee did not recommend to the full House that

[20] Congressional Record, 117:107, July 13, 1971, p. 6643.

[21] See Daniel Schorr, Clearing the Air (New York: Houghton Mifflin, 1977), passim; "The Daniel Schorr Investigation," Freedom of Information Center Report, # 361, Oct. 1976.

[22] Anthony Lewis, "Congress Shall Make No Law * * *," New York Times, Sept. 16, 1976, p. 39.

[23] I. William Hill, "Schorr Sticks to His Refusal to Name Source," Editor & Publisher, Sept. 25, 1976, p. 14.

Schorr be cited for contempt. He was released from subpoena
without revealing his source.

The courts have not decided contempt of Congress cases on
First Amendment grounds, one of them saying, "We shrink from
this awesome task" of drawing lines between the investigative
power of Congress and the First Amendment rights of a member
of the press.[24] Instead, the courts have found other reasons for
reversing convictions of newsmen who were found in contempt of
Congress for refusing to answer questions. In 1956, William Price
of the *New York Daily News* and Robert Shelton and Alden
Whitman of the *New York Times* refused to answer certain questions put by committees of Congress that were investigating communism. All three were indicted for contempt and convicted.
The Supreme Court overturned the convictions, not on press
freedom grounds, but because the indictments that put the newsmen before the grand jury were faulty. They failed to state the
subject of the investigation, the Court held, and without knowing
that, Price, Shelton and Whitman could not know just what they
were accused of. "Price was put to trial and convicted upon an
indictment which did not even purport to inform him in any way
of the identity of the topic under subcommittee inquiry. * * *
Far from informing Price of the nature of the accusation against
him, the indictment instead left the prosecution free to roam at
large—to shift its theory of ciminality so as to take advantage of
each passing vicissitude of the trial and appeal."[25]

SEC. 58. REFUSING TO TESTIFY ABOUT SOURCES AND INFORMATION

**Journalists' clashes with courts for refusing to testify as to
sources and information were infrequent until the 1970s
when the incidence multiplied manyfold. Protection has
developed under the First Amendment, the common law,
and state statutes.**

The refusal to testify before grand juries and courts about
confidential sources has become a familiar phenomenon of the
1970s and 1980s. Subpoenas to appear and testify were for
decades only an occasional problem for journalists whose stories
suggested to officialdom that the reporters had information of use
to government; there are probably fewer than 40 reported contempt cases before 1965 for refusal to testify when subpoenaed.
But in 1969 and 1970 the sometime problem of subpoenas changed
to a burst, and across the nation reporters faced demands that

[24] Shelton v. U.S., 117 U.S.App.D.C. 155, 327 F.2d 601 (1963); 89 Editor &
Publisher 12, July 7, 1956.

[25] Russell v. U.S., 369 U.S. 749, 82 S.Ct. 1038, 1049 (1962).

they appear and testify. No one was able to track down every subpoena issued during these years and in 1971 and 1972. In a two-and-one-half-year segment of this period, 121 subpoenas for news material were said to have gone to CBS and NBC alone, and in three years, more than 30 to Field Enterprises newspapers.[26] A high level persisted, the U.S. attorney general reporting that his office had approved 42 requests to him for subpoenas of reporters between May 1975 and November 1976.[27]

In particular demand were reporters who had been reporting widespread social and political turmoil. Grand juries wanted these journalists to reveal their confidential sources as well as to surrender their unpublished notes and records, unused photographs, tape recordings and television film "outtakes." To much of this, reporters responded "no" with intensity and solidarity.[28] Their unwritten code of ethics stood in the way of breaking confidences, they said; but more important, if they broke confidences they would become known as untrustworthy and their sources would dry up, thereby harming or destroying their usefulness as news gatherers for the public, and their own status as professionals would be damaged. Moreover, some argued, compelling them to disclose their news sources was tantamount to making them agents of government investigation.

As for turning over unused film, files, photos and notes, some media adopted the policy of early destruction of unpublished materials after *Time, Life, Newsweek,* the *Chicago Sun-Times,* CBS, NBC and others were called by subpoena, or in the name of cooperation with government, to deliver large quantities of news materials.[29] According to Attorney General John Mitchell, journalists' willingness to accept contempt convictions and jail terms rather than reveal confidences, along with their unyielding protests to government, made the controversy "one of the most difficult issues I have faced * * *."[30] The storm of objection to subpoenas issuing from the Department of Justice led attorneys general to issue "Guidelines for Subpoenas to the News Media"—a set of instructions to Justice Department attorneys over the na-

[26] House of Rep. Committee on the Judiciary, Subcommittee No. 3, 92 Cong., 2d sess., "Newsmen's Privilege," Hearings, Oct. 4, 1972, p. 204; Sept. 27, 1972, p. 134.

[27] "Justice Department Subpoenas Fewer Reporters," News Media and the Law 1:1 (Oct.1977), p. 30.

[28] S.Res. 3552, 91 Cong., 2d Sess., 116 Cong.Rec. 4123–31, 1970; Noyes & Newbold, "The Subpoena Problem Today," Am.Soc. Newspaper Editors Bull., Sept. 1970, pp. 7–8; Editor & Publisher, Feb. 7, 1970, p. 12. For several journalists' positions, see U.S. Congress, Senate, Committee on the Judiciary, Newsmen's Privilege Hearings Before the Subcommittee on Constitutional Rights, 93rd Cong., 1st Sess., 1973, passim.

[29] Columbia Journalism Rev., Spring 1970, pp. 2–3.

[30] Editor & Publisher, Aug. 15, 1970, pp. 9–10.

tion—that sought to resolve testimonial questions with reporters through negotiating rather than through subpoenas except in the last resort.[31]

The Constitutional Protection

Journalists who have assumed or asserted that the First Amendment guarantee of freedom of the press has protected the craft historically against compelling testimony have not reckoned with the course of court decisions. Privilege cases were adjudicated for most of a century under the common law or state statutes without the Constitution's even entering the picture. Not until 1958, in Garland v. Torre,[32] was the first claim to First Amendment protection an issue in the reported cases.

Here, Marie Torre, columnist for the *New York Herald Tribune,* attributed to an unnamed executive of a broadcasting company, certain statements which actress Judy Garland said libeled her. In the libel suit, Torre refused to name the executive, asserting privilege under the First Amendment. She was cited for contempt and convicted, and the appeals court upheld the conviction. "The concept that it is the duty of a witness to testify in a court of law," the Second Circuit Court of Appeals said, "has roots fully as deep in our history as does the guarantee of a free press." It added that if freedom of the press was involved here, "we do not hesitate to conclude that it too must give place under the Constitution to a paramount public interest in the fair administration of justice."[33] Subsequent claims to constitutional protection were likewise denied in other cases.[34]

The United States Supreme Court in 1972 ruled for the first time on whether the First Amendment protects journalists from testifying about their confidential sources and information. The cases of three newsmen who had refused to testify before grand juries during 1970 and 1971 were decided together in Branzburg v. Hayes.[35] Paul Branzburg, a reporter for the *Louisville Courier-Journal,* had observed two people synthesizing hashish from marijuana and written about that and drug use, and had refused to answer the grand jury's questions about the matters. Paul Pap-

[31] Department of Justice, Memo No. 692, Sept. 2, 1970. The guidelines were adjusted and developed by subsequent attorneys general. See "Guidelines on News Media Subpoenas," 6 Med.L.Rptr. 2153 (11/5/80) for the most recent.

[32] 259 F.2d 545 (2d Cir.1958), certiorari denied 358 U.S. 910, 79 S.Ct. 237.

[33] Ibid., at 548–549.

[34] In re Goodfader's Appeal, 45 Hawaii 317, 367 P.2d 472 (1961); In re Taylor, 412 Pa. 32, 193 A.2d 181 (1963); State v. Buchanan, 250 Or. 244, 436 P.2d 729 (1968), certiorari denied 392 U.S. 905, 88 S.Ct. 2055 (1968); Murphy v. Colorado, (Colo. Supreme Court), certiorari denied 365 U.S. 843, 81 S.Ct. 802 (1961).

[35] Branzburg v. Hayes, 408 U.S. 665, 92 S.Ct. 2646 (1972).

pas, a television reporter of New Bedford, Mass., had visited Black Panther headquarters during civil turmoil in July 1970, and refused to tell a grand jury what he had seen there.   Earl Caldwell, a black reporter for the *New York Times* in San Francisco, who had covered Black Panther activities regularly for some years, was called by a federal grand jury and had refused to appear or testify.

Only Caldwell received protection from the lower courts.   The federal district court of California and the Ninth Circuit Court of Appeals ruled that the First Amendment provided a qualified privilege to newsmen and that it applied to Caldwell.[36]   The Kentucky Court of Appeals refused Branzburg protection under either the Kentucky privilege statute, or the First Amendment interpretation of the Caldwell case.[37]   And the Supreme Judicial Court of Massachusetts, where no privilege statute existed, rejected the idea of a First Amendment privilege.[38]

The Supreme Court of the United States found that none of the three men warranted First Amendment protection.   It reversed the Caldwell decision of the lower federal court and upheld the Kentucky and Massachusetts decisions, in a 5–4 decision.[39]   It said that the First Amendment would protect a reporter if grand jury investigations were not conducted in good faith, or if there were harassment of the press by officials who sought to disrupt a reporter's relationship with his news sources.[40]   But it found neither of these conditions present here.   The journalist's obligation is to respond to grand jury subpoenas as other citizens do and to answer questions relevant to commission of crime, it said.

The Caldwell decisions in lower courts had focused on the need of recognition for First Amendment protection for the news gathering process; the Supreme Court said "It has generally been held that the first Amendment does not guarantee the press a constitutional right of special access to information not available to the public generally * * *," and "Despite the fact that news gathering may be hampered, the press is regularly excluded from grand jury proceedings, our own conferences, the meetings of other official bodies gathered in executive session * * *."[41]

[36] Application of Caldwell, 311 F.Supp. 358 (N.D.Cal.1970); Caldwell v. U.S., 434 F.2d 1081 (9th Cir.1970).

[37] Branzburg v. Pound, 461 S.W.2d 345 (Ky.1971); Branzburg v. Hayes, 408 U.S. 665, 92 S.Ct. 2646 (1972).

[38] In re Pappas, 358 Mass. 604, 266 N.E.2d 297 (1971).

[39] Branzburg v. Hayes, 408 U.S. 665, 92 S.Ct. 2646 (1972).

[40] Ibid., at 2669–2670.

[41] Ibid., at 2657, 2658.

The reporters had asserted that the First Amendment should take precedence over the grand jury's power of inquiry. The Supreme Court said that at common law, courts consistently refused to recognize a privilege in journalists to refuse to reveal confidential information, and that the First Amendment claim to privilege had been turned down uniformly in earlier cases, the courts having concluded "that the First Amendment interest asserted by the newsman was outweighed by the general obligation of a citizen to appear before a grand jury or at trial, pursuant to a subpoena, and give what information he possesses."[42] It said that the only constitutional privilege for unofficial witnesses before grand juries is the Fifth Amendment privilege against compelled self-incrimination, and the Court declined to create another.

The reporters argued that the flow of news would be diminished by compelling testimony from them; the Supreme Court said it was unconvinced, and "the evidence fails to demonstrate that there would be a significant constriction of the flow of news to the public if the Court reaffirms the prior common law and constitutional rule regarding the testimonial obligations of newsmen."[43]

The reporters said the freedom of the press would be undermined; the Court said this is not the lesson that history teaches, for the press had operated and thrived without common law or constitutional privilege since the beginning of the nation.[44]

The Supreme Court said that while the Constitution did not provide the privilege sought, Congress and the state legislatures were free to fashion standards and rules protecting journalists from testifying by passing legislation.

Concurring, Justice Lewis F. Powell, Jr., expanded, in general terms, the possibilities for first Amendment protection for journalists subpoenaed to testify. "The Court," he said, "does not hold that newsmen * * * are without constitutional rights with respect to the gathering of news or in safe-guarding their sources. * * * the courts will be available to newsmen under circumstances where legitimate First Amendment interests require protection." And where they claim protection, Powell said, "The asserted claim to privilege should be judged on its facts by the striking of a proper balance between freedom of the press and the obligation of all citizens to give relevant testimony * * *."[45] His opinion was to become central to many subsequent cases.

The dissenting justices wrote two opinions. One was that of Justice William O. Douglas, who said that a reporter's immunity

[42] Ibid., at 2658, 2659.

[43] Ibid., at 2662.

[44] Ibid., at 2665.

[45] Ibid., at 2670, 2671.

from testifying is "quite complete" under the First Amendment and a journalist "has an absolute right not to appear before a grand jury * * *."[46]

Writing for himself and two others, Justice Potter Stewart argued for a qualified privilege. He called the majority's opinion a "crabbed view of the First Amendment" that reflected a disturbing insensitivity to the critical role of an independent press. And he said that in denying the protection, "The Court * * * invites state and federal authorities to undermine the historic independence of the press by attempting to annex the journalistic profession as an investigative arm of government." Justice Stewart said the protection was essential, not "for the purely private interests of the newsman or his informant, nor even, at bottom, for the First Amendment interests of either partner in the newsgathering relationship."[47]

> Rather it functions to insure nothing less than democratic decisionmaking through the free flow of information to the public, and it serves, thereby, to honor the "profound national commitment to the principle that debate on public issues should be uninhibited, robust, and wide-open."

Stewart indicated what he felt the government should be required to do in overriding a constitutional privilege for the reporter:[48]

> * * * it is an essential prerequisite to the validity of an investigation which intrudes into the area of constitutionally protected rights of speech, press, association and petition that the State *show a substantial relation between the information sought and a subject of overriding and compelling state interest.*
>
> * * *
>
> Government officials must, therefore, demonstrate that the information sought is *clearly* relevant to a *precisely* defined subject of governmental inquiry. * * * They must demonstrate that it is reasonable to think the witness in question has that information. * * * And they must show that there is not any means of obtaining the information less destructive of First Amendment liberties.

These were essentially the requirements placed upon government by the lower courts in holding that Caldwell had been protected by

[46] U.S. v. Caldwell, 408 U.S. 665, 92 S.Ct. 2686, 2691 (1972).

[47] Branzburg v. Hayes, 408 U.S. 665, 92 S.Ct. 2646, 2678 (1972).

[48] Ibid., at 2679–2680.

the First Amendment, and Stewart endorsed that decision. He would have upheld the protection for Caldwell, and vacated and remanded the Branzburg and Pappas judgments.

Largely innocent of the history of the shield, reporters and editors expressed shock and dismay that the First Amendment did not protect the reporters in the Supreme Court's *Branzburg* decision.[49] Still innocent several years later, one wrote that the decision had "beclouded what American newsmen had come to assume was a traditional privilege—to refuse to testify either as to the source or the content of information received under confidential circumstances."[50] Predictions of doom for press freedom, on the heels of *Branzburg,* scouted the several statements in that decision which said that the First Amendment was still around and might well see service in future confidentiality cases: Justice White's plurality opinion, assuring journalists that the First Amendment would protect them against bad faith investigations of grand juries and against harassment by officials; Justice Powell's concurring opinion, asserting that this decision didn't strip journalists of "constitutional rights with respect to the gathering of news," and that the courts would protect them "where legitimate First Amendment interests require protection"; Justice Stewart's dissent containing concepts that courts quickly were to employ in support of journalists in subsequent cases.

Within months after the cold application of *Branzburg* to the sensitive skin of American journalists, the U.S. Court of Appeals, Second Circuit, presented the doom-sayers with a new shock: Magazine journalist Alfred Balk, it said, was *protected* by the First Amendment in his refusal to reveal a source. Balk had once written an article for the *Saturday Evening Post* on Chicago "block busting"—real estate practices including racially discriminatory activities by landlords and speculators. Now civil rights proponents sought, in a court action, the identity of one of Balk's sources ("Vitcheck," a pseudonym). Balk refused, on grounds that Vitchek gave him the information in confidence. The trial court ruled for Balk; the appeals court affirmed.[51]

The court found that the identity of Vitchek did not go to the heart of the appellants' case, and that, anyway, there were other available sources that the appellants could have tried to reach and that might have disclosed Vitchek's identity (*vide* Stewart, dissent

---

[49] See generally Columbia Journalism Review, 10:3, Sept.–Oct. 1972, for articles by Norman E. Isaacs, Benno C. Schmidt, Jr., and Fred W. Friendly. The only extensive history of journalists' privilege is Gordon, op.cit.

[50] William Hornby, "Journalists Split in Shield Law Imbroglio," IPI Report, 25:3, March 1976, p. 8.

[51] Baker v. F & F Investment Co., 470 F.2d 778 (2d Cir.1972), certiorari denied 411 U.S. 966, 93 S.Ct. 2147 (1973).

in *Branzburg*).   It said that the majority in *Branzburg* had applied
traditional First Amendment doctrine, which teaches that First
Amendment rights cannot be infringed absent a "compelling" or
"paramount" state interest (once more, Stewart); that the
Branzburg majority had indeed found that overriding interest in
the investigation of crime by grand juries; but that:[52]

> *   *   * though a journalist's right to protect confi-
> dential sources may not take precedence over that rare
> overriding and compelling interest, we are of the view
> that there are circumstances, at the very least in civil
> cases, in which the public interest in non-disclosure of a
> journalist's confidential sources outweighs the public and
> private interest in compelled testimony. The case before
> us is one where the First Amendment protection does not
> yield.
>
> *   *   *
>
> Manifestly, the [Supreme] Court's concern with the
> integrity of the grand jury as an investigating arm of the
> criminal justice system distinguishes *Branzburg* from the
> case presently before us.   If, as Mr. Justice Powell noted
> in that case, instances will arise in which First Amend-
> ment values outweigh the duty of a journalist to testify
> even in the context of a criminal investigation, surely in
> civil cases, courts must recognize that the public interest
> in non-disclosure of journalists' confidential news sources
> will often be weightier than the private interest in com-
> pelled disclosure.

Here was a line of reasoning (one which took its departure
from the widely damned *Branzburg* decision) that was to prove a
protection for the journalist in the court-room faceup in which his
testimony was demanded, disturbingly frequent as such was becoming.   In civil cases, the public's interest was likely to weigh
with the journalist's refusal to name his sources, and thus the
journalist's position would outweigh the private litigant's demand
for disclosure.   It was the start of courts' using *Branzburg* to
establish a qualified privilege under the First Amendment for
journalists who claimed protection not to reveal sources.

Quickly other courts brought the privilege into play.[53]   In a
case decided in 1973, the District Court for the District of Columbia ruled on a demand of the Committee for the Re-Election of the
President (Nixon) for news materials.[54]   The Committee was party

[52] Ibid., 783–85.   See also U.S. v. Orsini, 424 F.Supp. 229 (E.D.N.Y.1976).

[53] See Press Censorship Newsletter, IX, April–May 1976, pp. 46, 48–9; Loadholtz
v. Fields, 389 F.Supp. 1299 (D.Fla.1975).

[54] Democratic National Committee v. McCord, 356 F.Supp. 1394 (D.D.C.1973).

to civil actions arising out of the break-in at the Watergate offices of the Democratic National Committee. It had obtained subpoenas for reporters or management of the *New York Times,* the *Washington Post,* the *Washington Star-News,* and *Time* magazine to appear and bring all papers and documents they had relating to the break-in. The media ("movants") asked the court to quash the subpoenas.

Judge Richey defined the issue: Were the subpoenas valid under the First Amendment? He distinguished this case from Branzburg, noting that the re-election committee was not involved in criminal cases, but civil. He felt, furthermore, that the cases were of staggering moment: " * * * unprecedented in the annals of legal history." "What is ultimately involved in these cases * * * is the very integrity of the judicial and executive branches of our Government and our political processes in this country."[55]

Not only did the civil nature of the cases involving the re-election committee weigh for the media in Richey's opinion. He saw a chilling effect in the enforcement of the subpoenas upon the flow of information about Watergate to the press and thus to the public:[56]

> This court stands convinced that if it allows the discouragement of investigative reporting into the highest levels of Government no amount of legal theorizing could allay the public suspicions engendered by its actions and by the matters alleged in these lawsuits.

Then Richey balanced; as Justice Powell had instructed in *Branzburg,* a reporter's claim to privilege should be judged " * * * 'on its facts by the striking of a proper balance between freedom of the press and the obligation of all citizens to give relevant testimony'." Richey said that here, "The scales are heavily weighted in the Movants' [media's] favor." For the Committee for the Re-Election of the President had made no showing that "alternative sources of information have been exhausted or even approached. Nor has there been any positive showing of the materiality of the documents and other materials sought by the subpoenas [i.e., that the materials sought "go to the heart of the claim"]." [57]

Even the legal proceeding which the Supreme Court plurality was so concerned to elevate above reporter's privilege—namely,

---

[55] Ibid., 1395–1397.

[56] Ibid., 1397.

[57] Ibid., 1398. On exhausting the sources of information, see also Conn. Labor Relations Board v. Fagin, 33 C.S. 204 (Conn.Super.Ct.1976), 2 Med.L.Rptr. 1765, 1766; Altemose Constr. Co. v. Building Trades Council of Phila., 443 F.Supp. 492 (E.D.Pa.1977), 2 Med.L.Rptr. 1878.

the grand jury investigation—could in some circumstances give way to the journalist's claim. This happened in the case of Lucy Ware Morgan, who for three years fought a 90-day contempt sentence for refusing to disclose her source, and finally won.[58] Her story in the St. Petersburg, Fla., *Times* brought two actions against her to compel her to say who told her of a grand jury's secret criticism of Police Chief Nixon. The Florida Supreme Court found the story innocuous. It overruled the lower court which had found that the mere preservation of secrecy in grand jury proceedings outweighed any First Amendment considerations. The high state court said "A nonspecific interest, even in keeping the inner workings of the Pentagon secret, has been held insufficient to override certain First Amendment values."[59] It found further that the proceedings against Morgan had an improper purpose—namely, "to force a newspaper reporter to disclose the source of published information, so that the authorities could silence the source." Then it called on the leading case in precedent:[60]

> The present case falls squarely within this language in the *Branzburg* plurality opinion: "Official harassment of the press undertaken not for purposes of law enforcement but to disrupt a reporter's relationship with his news sources would have no justification."

Thus *Branzburg* supporting, First Amendment protection for the reporter's shield was being discovered. As ACLU attorney Joel M. Gora said about the prospects, "In short, the situation is far from bleak."[61]

No court conceded that the privilege under the First Amendment was an "absolute" protective shield for the journalist in all conceivable circumstances. In applying the First Amendment, courts widely started with Justice Powell's instruction in *Branzburg* ("striking a proper balance between freedom of the press and the obligation of all citizens to give relevant testimony"), and then used criteria such as those advocated by Justice Stewart in his *Branzburg* dissent (whether the testimony sought from reporters was clearly relevant, whether the subject was one of overriding state interest, whether all other means of obtaining the sought-after information had first been exhausted). They followed, thus, the Second Circuit in the *Baker* case and Judge

---

[58] Morgan v. State, 337 So.2d 951 (Fla.1976).

[59] Ibid., 955.

[60] Ibid., 956.

[61] Gora, p. 28. Gora's handbook, prepared for the American Civil Liberties Union, despite being dated, should be available to every reporter and editor. It covers true-to-life, practical problems in several fields of law that involve journalists, using a "Q" and "A" approach.

Richey in *McCord* (above, pp. 427–428. In most cases in which the First Amendment was employed, the procedure worked out to provide protection.[62]

But the First Amendment shield sometimes dropped. For one thing, in balancing the journalist's right to a shield against the need of the state or a plaintiff, as Powell instructed, courts sometimes found that the hurdles such as Stewart's criteria were surmounted by those seeking testimony, and the balance tipped against the journalist. This could happen at trial, or in pre-trial discovery procedure (see Chap. 4, Sec. 24) in which plaintiffs were attempting to obtain from journalists certain facts that would help them establish their cases. Also, as we shall see below, some courts interpreted *Branzburg* to deny a First Amendment shield of any kind.

To go first to the hurdles which the state in criminal cases, or the plaintiff in civil cases, would have to clear before overcoming the journalist's First Amendment qualified privilege, these have been expressed in several ways. The most-used rules [63] are that the party seeking the information from the journalist must show:

• That the information sought can be obtained from no other source or by means less destructive of First Amendment interests:

• That the information is centrally relevant to the party's case ("goes to the heart of the claim," or is information for which the party has a "compelling need").

• That the subject is one of "overriding and compelling state interest."

While, as we have seen above in *Baker* and in *McCord,* the journalist won because the plaintiffs failed to show that the materials sought "went to the heart of their claim," or that the information might not be available from an alternative source, other parties seeking information have been more successful in piercing the shield of the First Amendment. That was the case in

---

[62] U.S. v. Hubbard, 493 F.Supp. 202, 206, 209 (D.C.D.C.1979), 5 Med.L.Rptr. 1719; Montezuma Realty Corp. v. Occidental Petroleum Corp., 494 F.Supp. 780 (D.C.N.Y. 1980), 6 Med.L.Rptr. 1571; In re Consumers Union of United States, Inc., 495 F.Supp. 582 (D.C.N.Y.1980), 6 Med.L.Rptr. 1681; Hart v. Playboy Enterprises, (D.C. Kans.9/22/78), 4 Med.L.Rptr. 1616; U.S. v. DePalma, 466 F.Supp. 917 (D.C.N.Y. 1979), 4 Med.L.Rptr. 2499; Zelenka v. State, 83 Wis.2d 601, 266 N.W.2d 279 (1978).

[63] Others have included: Plaintiff must show that the information "is necessary to prevent a miscarriage of justice" Florida v. Taylor, (Fla.Cir.Ct.1982), 9 Med.L. Rptr. 1551; there is "reasonable possibility that information sought would affect the verdict" Washington v. Rinaldo, 36 Wash.App. 86, 673 P.2d 614 (1983), 9 Med.L. Rptr. 1419; the action is not "facially frivolous or patently without merit" Winegard v. Oxberger, 258 N.W.2d 847, 852 (Iowa 1977).

Winegard v. Oxberger,[64] decided by the Iowa Supreme Court in 1977.

Diane Graham, reporter for the *Des Moines Register,* wrote articles about legal proceedings brought by Sally Ann Winegard to dissolve her claimed common-law marriage to John Winegard. The articles quoted Sally's attorney extensively. John, who denied that there had been a marriage, brought a libel suit and invasion of privacy action against the attorney, who had told John that he had spoken with reporter Graham, but who denied saying the alleged libel. Then John sought, through discovery proceedings before the trial, to obtain from Graham or the Register any information they had in connection with the preparation of the articles. Graham was subpoenaed, and refused to answer questions about conversations with her sources or their identity, and about preparation and editing of the articles. She said that the First Amendment and the Iowa Constitution protected her. She and the Register applied to the court for an order quashing the subpoena; John Winegard moved to compel discovery; and Judge Oxberger ruled for Graham and the Register, saying that a qualified privilege under the First Amendment protected Graham.

Winegard appealed to the Iowa Supreme Court, which reversed the trial court and said that Judge Oxberger had erred in denying John's motion to compel discovery by reporter Graham. The Supreme Court said that a First Amendment qualified privilege existed, but was lost to Graham upon the application of the Court's "three-pronged standard." [65] First, it said that John's basic discovery objective "is necessary and critical to his cause of action" against the attorney; John "needs to know what was said to Graham and by whom." Second, the Court said, John's questioning of Sally's attorney resulted in the attorney's denying "having made statements attributed to him by Graham's articles. Under these circumstances we find Winegard did reasonably exercise and exhaust other plausible avenues of information," and that "Graham is apparently the only remaining person who could conceivably provide the information essential to Winegard's invasion of privacy and defamation action." And as for the last of the "three-prong standard," the Court said there was nothing in the record to suggest that John's action against the attorney "is facially frivolous or patently without merit." For good measure, the unanimous opinion said that the Court found no cause to hold that John was abusing judicial process to force a "wholesale disclosure of a newspaper's confidential sources of news," nor that

[64] 258 N.W.2d 847 (Iowa 1977), certiorari denied 436 U.S. 905, 98 S.Ct. 2234 (1978), 3 Med.L.Rptr. 1326. See also Goldfeld v. Post Pub. Co., (Conn.Sup.Ct.7/11/78) 4 Med.L.Rptr. 1167; In re Powers (Vt.Dist.Ct.10/19/78), 4 Med.L.Rptr. 1600.

[65] Winegard v. Oxberger, 258 N.W.2d 847, 852 (Iowa 1977).

John was embarked upon a course "designed to annoy, embarrass or oppress Graham.[66] John won the case for compelled disclosure.

Some courts have denied or doubted that any First Amendment protection exists. The Massachusetts Supreme Judicial Court did so in the case of Peter Pappas,[67] and reaffirmed that position in 1982.[68] A Connecticut Superior Court has said that the First Amendment gives no greater protection to the electronic media "than the same action by any other citizen," nor "any privilege to refuse to reveal information solely because the writers deem it confidential."[69] Idaho's Supreme Court has read Branzburg v. Hayes, the leading case,[70] to mean that "no newsman's privilege against disclosure of confidential sources exists * * *."[71]

A shield case which arose in New Jersey cost its media principals more than any other in the 1970s. It was the famous In re Farber.[72] Before it had run its course, in fines alone it had cost the *New York Times* approximately $265,000, at the rate of $5,000 per day and including a flat $101,000 and had sent reporter Myron Farber to jail for 40 days.[73] Farber had written lengthy articles about deaths at a New Jersey hospital, and their possible connection with drugs. A grand jury probe of the matter resulted in the indictment of Dr. Mario Jascalevich for murder, and after he went to trial, Farber and the Times were subpoenaed to bring thousands of documents to the court for *in camera* inspection. The Times and Farber demanded a hearing before turning over materials.

[66] The Iowa Court relied directly on the first of the shield cases in which a reporter claimed a First Amendment protection—Garland v. Torre, 259 F.2d 545 (2d Cir.1958), which continues to carry weight with courts in frequent citations. An example is Silkwood v. Kerr-McGee, 563 F.2d 433 (10th Cir.1977), 3 Med.L.Rptr. 1087, 1091.

[67] In the Matter of Peter Pappas, 358 Mass. 604, 266 N.E.2d 297 (1971).

[68] Mass. v. Corsetti, 458 U.S. 1306, 103 S.Ct. 3 (1982), 8 Med.L.Rptr. 2113 and reporter's jail term for contempt commuted in 1982, 8 Med.L.Rptr. # 28, 9/14/82, News Notes. In 1984, the Massachusetts Supreme Judicial Court was asked by a governor's task force to promulgate rules about journalists' privilege, and recommended details for protection of journalists asserting such, the Court having denied until then any recognition of privilege: 10 Med.L.Rptr. # 41, 10/16/84, News Notes.

[69] Rubera v. Post-Newsweek, 8 Med.L.Rptr. 2293, 2295 (1982).

[70] 408 U.S. 665, 92 S.Ct. 2646 (1972), 1 Med.L.Rptr. 2617.

[71] Caldero v. Tribune Pub. Co., 98 Idaho 288, 562 P.2d 791 (1977), 2 Med.L.Rptr. 1490, 1495.

[72] In re Farber, 78 N.J. 259, 394 A.2d 330 (1978), 4 Med.L.Rptr. 1360, 1362.

[73] Anon., "Lets Stand Contempts Against New York Times," News Media & the Law, Jan. 1979, 4–5. For a step-by-step account of the complex process applied to the Times and Farber, see Anon., "Reporter Jailed; N.Y.Times Fined," Ibid., Oct. 1978, 2–4. Farber and the Times were ultimately pardoned of the contempt conviction by the Governor of New Jersey, and the $101,000 criminal contempt fine was returned: 7 Med.L.Rptr. # 42, 2/2/82, News Notes.

But the trial judge refused a hearing, saying he would have to examine the documents before deciding whether the shield law would protect them against disclosure to Jascalevich.   Facing contempt citations, the Times and Farber appealed unsuccessfully; the contempt findings went into effect, with jail for Farber and the $5,000-a-day fine against the Times pending its bringing forth the materials.

Appealing once more, the newspaper and reporter reached the New Jersey Supreme Court.   That court denied that the First Amendment provided any privilege to remain silent, interpreting Branzburg v. Hayes to be a flat rejection of that notion.   In response to the journalists' claim to privilege, the New Jersey court said that U.S. Supreme Court Justice White, had "stated the issue and gave the Court's answer in the first paragraph of his opinion":[74]

> "The issue in these cases is whether requiring newsmen to appear and testify before state or federal grand juries abridges the freedom of speech and press guaranteed by the First Amendment.   We hold that it does not."
>
> *   *   *
>
> Thus we do no weighing or balancing of societal interests in reaching our determination that the First Amendment does not afford appellants the privilege they claim.   The weighing and balancing has been done by a higher court.   Our conclusion that appellants cannot derive the protection they seek from the First Amendment rests upon the fact that the ruling in *Branzburg* is binding upon us and we interpret it as applicable to, and clearly including, the particular issue framed here.   It follows that the obligation to appear at a criminal trial on behalf of a defendant who is enforcing his Sixth Amendment rights is at least as compelling as the duty to appear before a grand jury.

Having settled the First Amendment issue for New Jersey, the court went on to say that the Times and Farber of course deserved a hearing such as they sought, but that they had aborted it by refusing to submit the material subpoenaed for the court to examine in private—and that such an examination is no invasion of the New Jersey shield statute.   "Rather, it is a preliminary step to determine whether, and if so to what extent, the statutory privilege must yield to the defendant's constitutional rights."

It added, however, that in future similar cases there should be a preliminary determination before being compelled to submit materials to a trial judge—in which the party seeking the materi-

---

[74] In re Farber, 78 N.J. 259, 394 A.2d 330 (1978), 4 Med.L.Rptr. 1360, 1362.

als would show the relevancy of them to his defense, and that the information could not be obtained from any less intrusive source. This, it said, did not stem from any First Amendment right, but rather, it would seem necessary from the legislature's "very positively expressed" intent, in passing the shield law, to protect confidentiality and secrecy of media sources.

Dissenting, Judge Pashman expressed in legal terms what much of the world of news media considered sound, good sense, fairness, and due process—Farber and the Times should have had a hearing:[75]

> At no point prior to the rendition of the contempt judgments were appellants accorded an opportunity to marshal legal arguments against *in camera* production of the subpoenaed materials. Their claims that the subpoena is impermissibly overbroad and that compelled *in camera* disclosure is forbidden by the First Amendment and the New Jersey Shield Law * * * were denied consideration * * *. In effect, appellants were to be afforded an opportunity to contest the legality of *in camera* disclosure *only after* the materials had been so disclosed. Such a result not only turns logic on its head, but, more importantly, makes a mockery of "due process" * * *. Mr. Farber probably assumed, as did I, that hearings were supposed to be held and findings made *before* a person went to jail and *not afterwards.*

Wrote First Amendment attorney James C. Goodale about the outcome and the persistent ineffectiveness of the New Jersey shield law—sometimes, ironically, considered the most protective of all the states' shield laws:[76]

> I defy anyone to study the *Farber* record and conclude that procedural due process was applied. * * * While reasonable men may disagree as to the precise nature of the journalist's privilege, one would have thought everyone would agree that reporters are entitled to a hearing before being shipped off to jail—particularly when there is a statute that states they are totally protected and when there are scores of decisions upholding the claim of privilege even where there is no such statute.

Farber was released from jail in October 1978, following the acquittal of Jascalevich by a jury at the end of an eight-month trial. The judge suspended penalties against him and the Times. The New Jersey legislature began work on a bill to prevent a recurrence of the Farber incident, and on Feb. 28, 1981, Governor

---

[75] Ibid., 343; 1369–70.

[76] "Reporters Have Rights Too," *The Nation,* Nov. 3, 1979, 435–36.

Byrne signed a law saying that a criminal defendant would have to prove at a subpoenaed journalist's hearing that the material sought was relevant and unavailable elsewhere, and that the hearing would be held before the start of the criminal trial.[77] The new law substantially strengthened various protections in reporters' privilege.[78]

Confidentiality Under the Federal Common Law

Even as journalists' successes in asserting a First Amendment privilege not to testify were proving about as frequent as were their failures, in 1979 the United States Third Circuit Court of Appeals discovered and applied an added basis of privilege for journalists to rely on in refusing to divulge sources: the federal common law. Was there a ghostly cheer from Nineteenth-Century journalists, vindicated in their plea at last when on Dec. 14, 1979, Judge Sloviter wrote that the Court of Appeals, Third Circuit, had concluded "that journalists have a federal common law privilege, albeit qualified, to refuse to divulge their sources."?

The case began when Policeman Riley of Chester, Pa., a candidate for mayor, alleged that Mayor Battle and Police Chief Owens had violated his constitutional right to freedom to conduct his campaign, by surveillance of his activity, by conducting investigations of his performance as a policeman, and by public announcements of the investigations. He sought a preliminary injunction from federal court to restrain them from continued activities of this kind. Reporter Geraldine Oliver was called as a witness concerning her news story which reported that Riley had been suspended as a policeman, docked, and officially reprimanded, and that he had been investigated on several occasions during his 13 years as a policeman. She refused to give the source of her information and under an order by the trial judge was cited for civil contempt. She appealed, and the Third Circuit Court reversed the contempt citation.[79]

The Court found that Riley had not first exhausted other sources of information that might have "leaked," including other reporters, Battle, and Owens. Nor had Riley shown that the information sought to be disclosed was more than marginally relevant to his case—a matter "of most significance." Criteria such as these were applicable to the case of anyone seeking disclosure, the Court said, under any standard. And with that, it

---

[77] New York Times, Feb. 28, 1981, p. 25.

[78] Maressa v. N.J. Monthly, 89 N.J. 176, 445 A.2d 376 (1982), 8 Med.L.Rptr. 1473, 1475–76.

[79] Riley v. Chester, 612 F.2d 708 (3d Cir.1979). For a state decision bottomed explicitly on common law as providing privilege, see Senear v. Daily Journal-American, 97 Wash.2d 148, 641 P.2d 1180 (1982), 8 Med.L.Rptr. 1151, 1152.

applied the standard of the federal common law, emerging from
Rule 501 of the Federal Rules of Evidence and the legislative
history of the Rule. The importance of the decision for journalists' privilege emerges not so much in the finding for Oliver as for
the general matter of journalists' privilege, addressed in part by
the Court in the following excerpts: [80]

> Rule 501 of the Federal Rules of Evidence provides:
> " * * * the privilege of a witness, person, government,
> State, or political subdivision thereof shall be governed by
> the principles of the common law as they may be inter-
> preted by the courts of the United States in the light of
> reason and experience * * *."

> * * * The legislative history of Rule 501 manifests
> that its flexible language was designed to encompass,
> *inter alia,* a reporter's privilege not to disclose a source.
> The original draft of the Rule defined nine specific non-
> constitutional privileges, but failed to include among the
> enumerated privileges one for a reporter or journalist.
> The Advisory Committee gave no reason for the omission.
> This was one of the primary focuses of the congressional
> review of the proposed evidentiary rules, stemming in
> part from the "nationwide discussions of the newspaper-
> man's privilege." Following testimony on behalf of
> groups such as The Reporters Committee for Freedom of
> the Press, the privilege rule was revised to eliminate the
> proposed specific rules on privileges and to leave the law
> of privilege in its current state to be developed by the
> federal courts.

Then, in a footnote, the Court referred to the intent of the rule, as
expressed by Congressman Hungate, the principal draftsman of
the Federal Rules of Evidence:

> "For example, the Supreme Court's rule of evidence con-
> tained no rule of privilege for a newspaperperson. The
> language of Rule 501 permits the courts to develop a
> privilege for newspaperpersons on a case-by-case basis."

The Court then added:

> The strong public policy which supports the unfet-
> tered communication to the public of information, com-
> ment and opinion and the Constitutional dimension of
> that policy, expressly recognized in Branzburg v. Hayes,
> lead us to conclude that journalists have a federal com-
> mon law privilege, albeit qualified, to refuse to divulge
> their sources.

[80] Ibid., 713, 714.

In two subsequent cases under the federal common law in the Third Circuit, the reporter's shield has been denied. One of them, concerning a newspaper reporter's refusal to say whether she had conversations with a U.S. attorney in connection with "Abscam" prosecutions, ruled that the defendant had shown that the information sought was crucial to its case, and that the information could be obtained only from the reporter.[81] In the other, a television network was ordered by the Court to disclose in a pre-trial, *in camera* proceeding, film, audio tapes, and written transcripts concerning persons whom the government intended to call as witnesses in a trial. It refused and appealed the Court's order. The order was upheld so far as it applied to the named persons whom the government intended to call, but was overturned so far as it applied to other people, whose testimony was not relevant.[82]

An important point was made by the Court in its decision in the former case to apply the common law instead of a First Amendment standard: "If a case may be decided on either non-constitutional or constitutional grounds, a federal court will inquire first into the non-constitutional question. The practice reflects the deeply rooted doctrine 'that we ought not to pass on questions of constitutionality * * * unless such adjudication is unavoidable * * *.' " [83]

Confidentiality Under State Statutes and in State Courts

The mixed results for confidentiality under the First Amendment and the federal common law, meanwhile, were characteristic of developments under state shield statutes and state court decisions. Media Attorney Robert Sack has said that shield laws are like insurance policies, in that "they cover absolutely everything except what happens to you."[84] If, as attorney Joel Gora had said in the journalistic climate of discouragement under *Branzburg,* "the situation is far from bleak," there were nonetheless more than enough jailings to warrant confusion and anger among journalists. Probably more reporters were going to jail in the 1970s for refusal to reveal sources, than for any offense since 1798–1800 and the Alien and Sedition Acts.[85] The interpretations of the legitimacy of journalists' privilege under state laws and rulings contributed heavily to this unlovely fact. Yet it was plain by the 1980s that the large majority of state (and federal) jurisdictions had recognized qualified shield protection. Further, the

[81] U.S. v. Criden, 633 F.2d 346, 349 (3d Cir.1980).

[82] U.S. v. Cuthbertson, 630 F.2d 139 (3d Cir.1980), 6 Med.L.Rptr. 1545.

[83] U.S. v. Criden, 633 F.2d 346, 353 (3d Cir.1980).

[84] 9 Med.L.Rptr. # 7, 3/15/83, News Notes.

[85] Quill, 61:1, Jan. 1973, p. 28.

number of actions by mid-decade was declining; media Attorney James C. Goodale found state shield laws increasingly effective.[86]

The Supreme Court in *Branzburg* made it plain that either Congress or the states or both might pass laws providing a shield. Attempts in state legislatures to adopt shield laws (15 antedated *Branzburg*) were sometimes successful in following years, the total of old and new having reached 26 in number by 1975. In addition, 16 other states' courts had adopted a qualified privilege in case decisions by that year, while a few rejected the privilege.[87] Some statutes provided a privilege that appeared "absolute," while others qualified the protection in various ways. Alabama's, passed in 1935 and amended in 1949, was one of those that, on the surface, seemed absolute:[88]

> No person engaged in, connected with, or employed on any newspaper (or radio broadcasting station or television station) while engaged in a news gathering capacity shall be compelled to disclose, in any legal proceeding or trial, before any court or before a grand jury of any court, or before the presiding officer of any tribunal or his agent or agents, or before any committee of the legislature, or elsewhere, the sources of any information procured or obtained by him and published in the newspaper (or broadcast by any broadcasting station or televised by any television station) on which he is engaged, connected with, or employed.

Among states that hedged the privilege, Illinois, for example, said that a person seeking the reporter's information could apply for an order divesting the reporter of the privilege. The application would have to state the specific information sought, its relevancy to the proceedings, and a specific public interest which would be adversely affected if the information sought were not disclosed. And the court would have to find, before granting divestiture of the privilege, that all other available sources of information had been exhausted and that disclosure of the infor-

[86] Note, "Developments in the News Media Privilege: the Qualified Constitutional Approach Becoming Common Law," 33 Maine L.Rev. 372, 441 (1981); 10 Med.L. Rptr. # 47, 11/27/84, News Notes.

[87] Don Woodman, "State by State Press Shield Laws," National Law Journal, Dec. 14, 1979, p. 14, following J.C. Goodale's "Review of Privilege Cases," Communication Law Handbook (Practicing Law Institute, 1979). States that rejected a shield in case decisions included Colorado, Idaho, and Massachusetts. Of the 11 federal circuit courts, all adopted a shield by 1979 except the First Circuit, which rejected it, and the Fifth Circuit: Ibid. The state statutes are collected in Sack, op. cit., App. V, 621.

[88] Ala.Code, Tit. 7, # 370, 1960. See Jacqueline L. Jackson, "Shield Laws Vary Widely," Presstime, May 1981, p. 14; See also New Jersey's, Maressa v. N.J. Monthly, 89 N.J. 176; 445 A.2d 376 (1982); 8 Med.L.Rptr. 1473.

mation was essential to the protection of the public interest involved.[89]

But absolute or qualified, state laws might contain loopholes through which under certain conditions, journalists could lose the privilege. Branzburg, before seeking constitutional protection, had failed to receive protection under Kentucky's statute. The statute gave him a firm shield, as a newspaper employee, against disclosing before a court or grand jury, the source of information procured by him and published in a newspaper. But the Kentucky court held that he himself was the source of information for a story reporting his observation of the manufacture of hashish by others. He would have to give the identity of the manufacturer— to identify those whom he saw breaking the law. It was contempt for him to refuse to do so.[90]

New York's shield law is termed "absolute" in its protection, and even protects a journalist against testifying before a grand jury.[91] But it applies only to information obtained under the "cloak of confidentiality," and did not protect CBS against producing, under subpoena, video and audio takes and outtakes not made under promises of confidentiality.[92] California's constitution immunizes against contempt convictions for refusing to testify, but not against various other sanctions[93] nor does it protect certain free-lance authors.[94] Ohio's shield law protects against disclosure only of the source of the information, not against disclosure of information in notes, tapes, and records from the source.[95]

A case whose permutations enmeshed its principal for eight years was that of William Farr, reporter for the *Los Angeles Herald Examiner* and later the *Los Angeles Times*. Reporting the murder trial of Charles Manson, Farr learned that a Mrs. Virginia Graham had given a statement to a district attorney in the case, claiming that a Manson "family" member, Susan Atkins, had confessed taking part in the multiple crimes and told of the group's plans for other murders. The judge in the case had

---

[89] Ill.Legis.H.Bill 1756, 1971, Gen. Assembly.

[90] Branzburg v. Pound, 461 S.W.2d 345 (Ky.1970). For a similar position under New York's statute, see People v. Dupree, 88 Misc.2d 791, 388 N.Y.S.2d 1000 (1976); for Texas, Ex parte Grothe, 687 S.W.2d 736 (Tex.Cr.App.1984); 10 Med.L.Rptr. 2009.

[91] Beach v. Shanley, 62 N.Y.2d 241, 476 N.Y.S.2d 765, 465 N.E.2d 304 (1984), 10 Med.L.Rptr. 1753.

[92] New York v. Korkala, 99 A.D.2d 161, 472 N.Y.S.2d 310 (1984), 10 Med.L.Rptr. 1355.

[93] KSDO v. Riverside Sup.Ct., 136 Cal.App.3d 375, 186 Cal.Rptr. 211 (1982), 8 Med.L.Rptr. 2360. Also New York: Oak Beach Inn v. Babylon Beacon, 62 N.Y.2d 158, 476 N.Y.S.2d 269, 464 N.E.2d 967 (1984), 10 Med.L.Rptr. 1761.

[94] In re Van Ness, (Cal.3d 1982) 8 Med.L.Rptr. 2563.

[95] Ohio v. Geis, 2 Ohio App.3d 258, 441 N.E.2d 803 (1981), 7 Med.L.Rptr. 1675.

ordered attorneys, witnesses and court employees not to release for public dissemination, any content or nature of testimony that might be given at the trial; but Farr obtained copies of the Graham statement, according to him from two attorneys in the case. The court learned that he had the statement. Farr refused to tell the court the names of the sources, and published a story carrying sensational details. Later, he identified a group of six attorneys as including the two. The judge queried them, and all denied being the source. Once more the court asked Farr for his sources, and he continued to refuse under the California reporters' privilege law.[96] The court denied him protection under the statute and he appealed.

The appeals court upheld the conviction for contempt, essentially under the doctrine of the "inherent power" of courts to regulate judicial proceedings without interference from other government branches—a principle, as we have seen, reaching far back in the history of contempt. It said that courts' power of contempt is inherent in their constitutional status, and no legislative act could declare that certain acts do not constitute a contempt. If Farr were immunized from liability, it would violate the principle of separation of powers among the three branches of government; it would mean that the legislative branch could interfere with the judicial branch's power to control its own officers:[97]

> Without the ability to compel petitioner to reveal which of the six attorney officers of the court leaked the Graham statement to him, the court is without power to discipline the two attorneys who did so, both for their violations of the court order [concerning no publicity] and for their misstatement to the court that they were not the source of the leak.

Farr served 46 days in jail before he was released pending a further appeal, and in his uncertain freedom lived with the possibility of indeterminate, unlimited imprisonment if his appeal failed and he persisted in refusing to reveal his sources. That "coercive" sentence was later ruled by the courts to have no further purpose, as there was no likelihood that continuing it would induce Farr to testify. It was still possible, however, that he might have to serve a further "punitive" sentence for his contempt. Five years after the opening of the case against Farr— on Dec. 6, 1976—he was finally freed from the latter possibility by

---

[96] West's Ann.Cal.Evidence Code § 1070 (1966).

[97] Farr v. Superior Court of California, 22 Cal.App.3d 60, 99 Cal.Rptr. 342, 348, (1971). New Mexico's Supreme Court ruled similarly that that state's shield law was without effect where testimony before courts was concerned: Ammerman v. Hubbard Broadcasting, Inc., 89 N.M. 307, 551 P.2d 1354 (1976).

ruling of the California Court of Appeal, Second District.[98] He had served the longest jail term on record in the United States for refusing to reveal news sources, and his case had lasted longer than any other.

But his ordeal was not over. Two of the six attorneys whom he had identified brought a libel suit for $24 million against him. The trial court and the California Appellate Court ruled that the shield law did not protect him from answering questions in the case.[99] The long contest ended in April 1979. The libel plaintiffs had missed the five-year statute of limitations for bringing an action, and Farr's attorney convinced the trial court that their failure was a result of insufficient effort to bring the case to trial. The judge dismissed the suit.[1] The adhesive web of process had finally dissolved.

Sixteen months later, Californians voted to elevate the state's shield for journalists to a better-fortified position than that of a statute; they passed Proposition 5, which placed the shield directly into the State Constitution.[2]

In 1982, one test demonstrating the limitation of the new shield came when Riverside (Calif.) policemen brought a libel suit against KSDO radio and its reporter, Hal Brown, for a story that implicated police in drug traffic. They demanded Brown's notes and memoranda.[3] And while the journalists won in their refusal to yield the material, they did so under *First Amendment* protection, said the court of appeal: the police had failed to show that the information was not available from any other source, or that the desired material went to the heart of their case.[4]

But so far as California's constitutional shield was concerned, said the court, decades of assumptions about its protective reach were mistaken: All it does is protect a journalist from contempt conviction. It does not stop courts from taking other actions in a libel case, as here, where journalists themselves are defendants: Their refusal to testify about information needed by the plaintiff could result in the court's striking their defense, or even awarding

[98] In re William T. Farr, 64 Cal.App.3d 605, 134 Cal.Rptr. 595 (1976); Milwaukee Journal, Dec. 7, 1976.

[99] 64 Cal.App.3d 605, 134 Cal.Rptr. 595 (1976). See also Quill, Nov. 1977, p. 14.

[1] Anon., "William Farr's Seven [sic] Year Fight to Protect Sources Is Victorious," News Media & the Law, Aug./Sept. 1979, 22.

[2] Anon., "Californians Vote to Include a Newsmen's Shield in the State Constitution," Quill, July/August 1980, 9.

[3] KSDO v. Riverside Superior Court, 136 Cal.App.3d 375, 186 Cal.Rptr. 211 (1982), 8 Med.L.Rptr. 2360.

[4] Ibid., 2366.

the plaintiff a default judgment. The court said that the shield law [5]

> * * * does not create a privilege for newspeople, rather, it provides an immunity from being adjudged in contempt. This rather basic distinction has been misstated and apparently misunderstood by members of the news media and our courts as well.

Though vulnerable under any law journalists occasionally got more protection from their states' courts than the statutes suggested might be available. One loophole in several "absolute" statutes was the lack of provision protecting the reporter from revealing *information* that he had gathered, even though it protected him from revealing the *source* of that information. Robert L. Taylor, president and general manager, and Earl Selby, city editor of the *Philadelphia Bulletin,* were convicted of contempt of court for refusing to produce documents in a grand jury investigation of possible corruption in city government. Both were fined $1,000 and given five-day prison terms. They appealed, relying on the Pennsylvania statute stating that no newsman could be "required to disclose the source of any information" that he had obtained. "Source" they said, means "documents" as well as "personal informants." The Pennsylvania Supreme Court, reversing the conviction, agreed. The court said that the legislature, in passing the act, declared the gathering of news and protection of the source of news as of greater importance to the public interest than the disclosure of the alleged crime or criminal.[6]

Finally, there is the frequent case of whether a shield against testifying is justified where a newspaper and reporter are sued for libel. If a reporter refuses to reveal an unnamed source who had allegedly libeled the plaintiff, may the plaintiff be foreclosed from discovering and confronting his accuser? Who, besides the reporter, can identify the accuser? Conversely, if the sources must be revealed, then is it not possible "for someone to file a libel suit as a pretext to discover the reporters' sources and subject them to harassment"? [7] This line of actions, of course, produced the suit which, perhaps more than any other, alerted the news world to the possibilities of danger in required testimony—Garland v. Torre, of 1958. As Marie Torre in that case, most other reporters since then who have been sued for libel have argued fruitlessly that they should not be required to name the source.

Shield statutes of Oregon, Rhode Island, and Tennessee provide expressly that the privilege is not available to persons sued

[5] Ibid., 2362.

[6] In re Taylor, 412 Pa. 32, 193 A.2d 181, 185 (1963).

[7] Gora, p. 40.

for libel.[8] Supreme Courts of Massachusetts [9] and Idaho, which have no shield statutes, reject reporters' claims that there is an alternative First Amendment protection against the requiring of testimony—including testimony about sources of alleged libel. An Idaho decision, in which certiorari was denied by the United States Supreme Court, confirmed a 30-day jail sentence for reporter-editor Jay Shelledy.[10] He had quoted a "police expert" as criticizing state narcotics agent Michael Caldero who had been involved in a shooting incident. He was sued for libel by the agent, and, refusing to reveal the name of the expert, was held in contempt. The trial judge decided not to press the contempt citation, however, finding that another course of action would be more helpful to Caldero: The court would treat Shelledy's failure to identify the police expert "as an admission by the defendant Shelledy that no such 'police expert' exists, and the jury shall be so instructed." [11] The trial proceeded; the jury was instructed, and in place of the shield that his now-spent effort had hoped to raise, the jury served as armor: It brought in the verdict that Shelledy's article was not libelous.

The Caldero trial judge's ruling that Shelledy "had no source" was unusual but not unique. Only months before, one case in precedent had used the move—a decision by the New Hampshire Supreme Court. A former police chief sued for libel after a newspaper cast doubt on his truthfulness, alleging that he had failed polygraph tests. Its staff refused to reveal the sources of the accusation. The court, after determining that the sought-after testimony was "essential to the material issue in dispute," and "not available from any source other than the press," granted the chief's motion to compel disclosure. The newspaper appealed, and the New Hampshire Supreme Court felt that there was a better way to enforce the trial court's order than by holding the newspaper in contempt.[12]

> We are aware * * * that most media personnel have refused to obey court orders to disclose, electing to go to jail instead. Confining newsmen to jail in no way aids the plaintiff in proving his case. Although we do not say that contempt power should not be exercised, we do say

[8] Gora, p. 247. And see Ibid., pp. 243–48, for a summary of 25 states' shield laws.

[9] Dow Jones & Co., Inc. v. Superior Court, 364 Mass. 317, 303 N.E.2d 847 (1973).

[10] Caldero v. Tribune Pub. Co., 98 Idaho 288, 562 P.2d 791 certiorari denied 434 U.S. 930, 98 S.Ct. 418 (1977).

[11] Anon., "Lewiston reporter Wins Jury Verdict in Libel Case," News Media & the Law, Oct./Nov.1980, 10–11, Downing v. Monitor Pub. Co., 120 N.H. 383, 415 A.2d 683 (1980), 6 Med.L.Rptr. 1193.

[12] Downing v. Monitor Pub. Co., 120 N.H. 383, 415 A.2d 683, 686 (1980), 6 Med.L. Rptr. 1193, 1195.

that something more is required to protect the rights of a libel plaintiff. Therefore, we hold that when a defendant in a libel action, brought by a plaintiff who is required to prove actual malice under *New York Times,* refuses to disclose his sources of information upon a valid order of the court, there shall arise a presumption that the defendant had no source. The presumption may be removed by a disclosure of the sources a reasonable time before trial.

Nonetheless, the frequent success of the claim to the shield (usually where plaintiffs fail to show necessity, relevancy, and unavailability of the information) occasionally can extend to the libel situation, where the reporter is so likely to be vulnerable because he is the only source of the information sought. Before Marie Torre ever pleaded for protection in a libel case, a decision under the shield law of Alabama had furnished it to a reporter who refused to reveal sources of a story on prison conditions.[13] New York, New Jersey, and Pennsylvania protect, in varying degree, confidentiality in libel cases.[14] Even in Idaho (which has no shield law and whose Supreme Court has interpreted *Branzburg* to provide no First Amendment protection), the appeal process has brought relief to journalists who fruitlessly sought a shield in discovery proceedings in a libel case. Sierra Life Insurance Co. demanded the names of confidential sources for a series of stories about the firm's financial difficulties, written by reporters for the *Twin Falls Times-News.*[15] Through complex legal processes, the reporters and the newspaper alleged that their stories were true and refused to name sources. In response, the trial judge ruled that Idaho provided no protection for them, struck all their defenses, and entered a "default" judgment against them for $1.9 million. But the Idaho Supreme Court reversed the trial court. It did not feel that the refusal to testify should stand in the way of the newspaper's employing defenses— truth and lack of a connection between the stories and the damages suffered. Striking defenses in this case, it agreed, amounted to unwarranted punishment of the newspaper. And it said that Sierra had failed to show that its inability to discover the sources damaged its ability to prove the news stories false, which would be

---

[13] Ex parte Sparrow, 14 F.R.D. 351 (N.D.Ala.1953). Federal courts have provided protection in some libel cases also: Mize v. McGraw-Hill, Inc., 82 F.R.D. 475, 86 F.R.D. 1 (D.C.S.Tex.1979), 5 Med.L.Rptr. 1156; Bruno & Stillman, Inc. v. Globe Newspaper Co., 633 F.2d 583 (1st Cir.1980), 6 Med.L.Rptr. 2057.

[14] Respectively, Oak Beach Inn v. Babylon Beacon, 62 N.Y.2d 158, 476 N.Y.S.2d 269, 464 N.E.2d 967 (1984), 10 Med.L.Rptr. 1761; Maressa v. N.J. Monthly, 89 N.J. 176, 445 A.2d 376 (1982), 8 Med.L.Rptr. 1473; D'Alfonso v. A.S. Abell Co., 765 F.2d 138 (4th Cir.1985), 9 Med.L.Rptr. 1015.

[15] Sierra Life Insurance Co. v. Magic Valley Newspapers, 101 Idaho 795, 623 P.2d 103, (1980), 6 Med.L.Rptr. 1769.

necessary to its case. It remanded the case, with "guidance" to the trial judge which included the Supreme Court's suggestion that the confidential sources' identity might not be relevant.[16]

Summarizing Issues in Confidentiality

The Branzburg decision having hedged the constitutional protection that the news world sought, the media turned to lobbying for statutes at the state and federal levels, and to strengthening existing state statutes. The number of states with statutes reached 26 by 1975,[17] about half of them passed during the 1960s and 1970s. At the federal level, the major news organizations turned their leaders and lawyers to work in appearances before congressional committees. They found strong support and strong opposition among congressmen. It was estimated in early 1973 that more than 50 bills offering a shield had been introduced,[18] and more appeared in subsequent years. Whatever the level of government, the issues were similar.

(1) What are the competing social values in granting or denying journalists an immunity from testifying? The reporter's ethic of not betraying sources, and his property right in not losing his effectiveness and value as a reporter through losing his sources, had long been asserted unsuccessfully in cases under the common law. Now he was grounding his claim in society's loss of his service if he lost his sources through betraying them.

Earl Caldwell was one of a corporal's guard of reporters who had gained the confidence of the Black Panthers at a time when society had a real need to know about this alienated group. The Ninth Circuit Court of Appeals accepted Caldwell's argument that he would lose the Panthers' confidence if he even entered the secret grand jury chambers, for this extremely sensitive group would not know what he might say under the compulsion of the legal agency.[19] And if Caldwell could not report the Panthers, society was the real loser. This situation illustrated the difference between the values served in the case of privilege for the journalist and that for the doctor, lawyer, or clergyman:[20]

> " * * * the doctor-patient privilege is there to make it possible for patients to get better medical care. A journalist's privilege should be there not only to make it

[16] Ibid., 109; 1773.

[17] Press Censorship Newsletter No. VIII, Oct.-Nov.1975, p. 29.

[18] Thomas Collins, "Congress Grapples with Press Bill," Milwaukee Journal, March 25, 1973, p. 16.

[19] Caldwell v. U.S., 434 F.2d 1081, 1088 (9th Cir.1970).

[20] House of Rep. Committee on the Judiciary, Subcommittee No. 3, 92 Cong., 2d Sess., "Newsmen's Privilege," Hearings, Testimony of Victor Navasky, Oct. 5, 1972, p. 236.

possible for a journalist to get better stories, but to contribute to the public's right to know. So in that sense it is a more critical privilege than some of these other privileges, which are based primarily on the relationship between two people."

Asserting an equal service in the cause of the "public's right to know" was the position that in many circumstances, government-as-the-public sought information vital to the public weal, from reporters. In State v. Knops,[21] an "underground" newspaper editor refused to tell a grand jury the names of people to whom he had talked about the bombing of a university building that killed a researcher, and about alleged arson of another university building. "[T]he appellant's information could lead to the apprehension and conviction of the person or persons who committed a major criminal offense resulting in the death of an innocent person," said the Wisconsin Supreme Court in denying privilege to editor Mark Knops.[22] Here government was saying that the journalist was practicing secrecy similar to that which he so often criticized in government, and that government was trying to serve the public's right to know about a major crime.

A few reporters, meanwhile, rejected the notion that the privilege was either needed by or appropriate to the journalist. They said that most journalists of the nation had done their work for decades without a shield. And they worried about unethical reporters' using a shield law to hide behind in dishonest reporting.

In point was the episode—dismaying to journalists everywhere—of the fabricated story of tyro reporter Janet Cooke of the *Washington Post* in 1981. Her account of an unnamed eight-year-old heroin addict, whose identity she refused to disclose to her editors out of alleged fear of death from the child's "supplier," was awarded a Pulitzer Prize. But the award was scarcely announced when a standing challenge to the story's accuracy by city officials (resisted by Post editors who had insisted on shielding their reporter from disclosure of her sources), took strength from the revelation that Cooke had falsified her biographical resumé in applying for a position at the Post. Faced with the dual challenge, she confessed that the story was of whole cloth and resigned, and the Post returned the Pulitzer Award with agonized apologies to readers, the city, and the field of journalism. No law court, no threat of contempt was involved, but the parallels were too close for cavil. The integrity of a shield claimed by a reporter and afforded by editors had been shattered; and so, too, in some

---

[21] State v. Knops, 49 Wis.2d 647, 183 N.W.2d 93 (1971).

[22] Ibid., at 99.

measure, had that of a great newspaper, and the fact-gathering principle of special treatment—privilege—for the journalist.[23]

(2) Can the news gathering function be protected by a qualified immunity, or must it be absolute? Hard positions for absolute shields were taken by many journalists and their organizations including the directors of the American Newspaper Publishers Association and those of the American Society of Newspaper Editors.[24] U.S. Sen. Alan Cranston of California, a former reporter, introduced a bill in Congress that was sweeping, simple and unconditional, saying that [25]

> * * * a person connected with or employed by the news media or press cannot be required by a court, a legislature, or any administrative body to disclose before the Congress or any federal court or agency any information or the source of any information procured for publication or broadcast.

Many taking the absolutist view argued from the position that government in the early 1970's—and especially the federal executive branch—was actively seeking ways to curb the press, trying to "prevent the press from performing its duties." [26] From this vantage point, qualifications in a shield bill often were seen as loopholes through which government could fire at the mass media. A qualified protection was no shield to these. They rejected the minority opinion in Branzburg v. Hayes that urged a shield unless the government could show a compelling and overriding interest in the information. The absolutists felt that courts would find "compelling and overriding interest" readily (although the fact was, of course, that the federal trial and appeals courts had protected Earl Caldwell under that principle the first time that it had appeared in a shield case).[27]

Yet "absolute" protection was a chimera, however much some states' statutes might be labeled with that word, as we have seen in the previous section.[28] And a federal statute of any kind

---

[23] Jerry Chaney, "Level With Us, Just How Sacred Is Your Source?", Quill, March 1979, 28; Quill, 61:4, April 1973, 38. Paul Magnusson, "Reporter's Lies Undermine Paper, Profession," Wisconsin State Journal, April 19, 1981, Sec. 4, p. 6; Robert H. Spiegel, "Notes from Pulitzer Juror," Wisconsin State Journal, April 21, 1981, Sec. 1, p. 6.

[24] Quill, 61:1, Jan. 1973, 29.

[25] Editor & Publisher, Aug. 19, 1972, p. 9.

[26] A.M. Rosenthal, "Press Government Conflict Escalates," Milwaukee Journal, Feb. 11, 1973, p. 1; N.E. Isaacs, "Beyond the 'Caldwell' Decision: 1," Columbia Journalism Rev., Sept./Oct. 1972, p. 18; P.J. Bridge, "Absolute Immunity, Absolutely," Quill 61:1, Jan. 1973, p. 8.

[27] Caldwell v. U.S., 434 F.2d 1081, 1089 (9th Cir.1970).

[28] AP Log, Sept. 3–9, 1973, pp. 1, 4.

became a more and more remote possibility as years of drafting, committee work, and lobbying failed.[29]

(3) Also at issue was the question: Who deserves the shield? and following that: Would not defining "reporter" in effect be to license journalists and thus bring them under state control? The United States Supreme Court in denying Paul Branzburg protection summarized the question and found that deciding it would bring practical and conceptual difficulties of a high order:[30]

> Sooner or later, it would be necessary to define those categories of newsmen who qualified for the privilege, a questionable procedure in light of the traditional doctrine that liberty of the press is the right of the lonely pamphleteer who uses carbon paper or a mimeograph just as much as of the large metropolitan publisher who utilizes the latest photo-composition methods * * *. Freedom of the press is a "fundamental personal right" which "is not confined to newpapers and periodicals. It necessarily embraces pamphlets and leaflets * * *. Almost any author may quite accurately assert that he is contributing to the flow of information to the public, that he relies on confidential sources of information, and that these sources will be silenced if he is forced to make disclosures before a grand jury.

Troubling as the question was, it did not deter states as they adopted statutes from 1970 onward. New York's 1970 law defined "professional journalist" and "newscaster" in its law that protected only those agencies normally considered "mass media"—newspaper, magazine, news agency, press association, wire service, radio or television transmission station or network.[31] Illinois, in its 1971 statute, defined "reporter" as one who worked for similar media.[32] Neither included books among the media immunized; neither included scholars and researchers among the persons immunized. In two cases, courts have ruled that state statutes which gave protection specifically to newspapers did not protect magazines.[33] But in late 1977, the U.S. Court of Appeals, Tenth Circuit, ruled that Arthur Buzz Hirsch, a film maker engaged in preparing a documentary on Karen Silkwood who had died myste-

---

[29] Press Censorship Newsletter No. IX, April–May 1976, p. 53.

[30] Branzburg v. Hayes, 408 U.S. 665, 92 S.Ct. 2646, 2668 (1972).

[31] McKinney's N.Y.Civ.Rights Law § 79–h (Supp.1971). In New York v. LeGrand, 67 A.D.2d 446 (N.Y.Sup.Ct.App.Div.1979), 4 Med.L.Rptr. 2524, the law was held not to apply to a book author, because the law specifies that only professional journalists and newscasters are shielded.

[32] Ill.Legis.H.Bill 1756, 1971 Gen.Assembly.

[33] Application of Cepeda, 233 F.Supp. 465 (S.D.N.Y.1964); Deltec, Inc. v. Dun and Bradstreet, Inc., 187 F.Supp. 788 (N.D.Ohio 1960).

riously in a puzzling auto accident in Oklahoma, was indeed protected by the First Amendment in refusing to disclose confidential information concerning his investigation. This was the case despite the fact that the Oklahoma shield law gave protection only to those "regularly engaged in obtaining, writing, reviewing, editing or otherwise preparing news." [34]

These issues and questions run deep. They are not likely to be resolved for all sides soon. For the young journalist who will live with them and who may find them coming to bear personally in his professional work, the veteran investigative reporter Clark R. Mollenhoff has some rules of thumb for guidance. Winner of a Pulitzer Prize, Sigma Delta Chi Distinguished Service Awards, and various professional citations, Mollenhoff writes that "You'd better know what you're getting into".[35]

SEC. 59. PROTECTING NEWSROOMS FROM SEARCH AND TELEPHONE RECORDS FROM DISCLOSURE

Courts have not granted First Amendment protection against officials' searches of newsrooms, but Congress and several states have passed laws providing protection. Confidentiality of journalists' telephone-call records that are on file at telephone companies has not been recognized.

When the United States Supreme Court rejects a claim to First Amendment protection, Congress and state legislatures may be able to furnish protection by passing laws. The news world's drive for a statutory privilege against revealing sources—after the Supreme Court in Branzburg v. Hayes seemed to journalists to restrict protection under the First Amendment to a shadow—succeeded in a few states by dint of long, hard work, and failed in others. The effort to get a law through Congress, despite extended and steady application by the House Committee on the Judiciary, ground to a frustrated halt in 1976 and 1977 as we saw above.

But another aspect of confidentiality denied First Amendment protection by the Supreme Court—shielding news rooms and offices against official searches and seizures of news material—got an early remedy in the form of state legislation and a national law—the Privacy Protection Act of 1980.[36] It was passed less than three years after a Supreme Court decision of May 1978 sent the

---

[34] Silkwood v. Kerr-McGee, see "Court Protects Film Maker's Sources," News Media & the Law, 1:1 (Oct.1977), p. 26.

[35] Quill, March 1979, p. 27, for Mollenhoff's rules.

[36] Pub.Law # 96–440, 94 Stat. 1879, approved Oct. 13, 1980, 6 Med.L.Rptr. 2255. For summary and discussion of the law and the state actions, see Anon., "Newsroom Searches," News Media & the Law, Oct./Nov. 1980, 3–5.

news media into a reaction of alarm and denunciation; the very security of their news rooms and files was at stake. Their outrage over the decision was widespread, at what they saw as the Court's approval of a "right to rummage" in their offices, a breach of custom and understanding.

By a 5–3 margin, the Court said in Zurcher v. Stanford Daily that newspapers (and all citizens, for that matter) may be the subjects of unannounced searches as long as those searches are approved beforehand by a court's issuance of a search warrant.[37] They need not be suspected of any crime themselves; but as "third parties" who may hold information helpful to law enforcement, their property may be searched. A particular issue in this case was a question of how to interpret the words of the Fourth Amendment to the Constitution. That amendment says:

> The right of the people to be secure in their persons, houses, papers, and effects, against unreasonable searches and seizures, shall not be violated, and no Warrants shall issue, but upon probable cause, supported by Oath or affirmation, and particularly describing the place to be searched, and the persons or things to be seized.

The Zurcher case arose during violent demonstrations at Stanford University on April 9, 1971. Two days later, the *Stanford Daily* carried articles and photographs about the clash between demonstrators and police. It appeared to authorities from that coverage that a Daily photographer had been in a position to photograph fighting between students and police. As a result, a search warrant was secured from a municipal court. The warrant was issued [38]

> on a finding of "just, probable and reasonable cause for believing that: Negatives and photographs and films, evidence material and relevant to the identification of the perpetrators of felonies, to wit, Battery on a Peace Officer, and Assault with a Deadly Weapon, will be located [on the premises of the Daily]."

Later that day, the newspaper office was searched by four police officers, with some newspaper staffers present. The search turned up only the photographs already published in the Daily, so no materials were removed from the newspaper's office. In May of 1971, the Daily and some of its staffers sued James Zurcher, the Palo Alto chief of police, the officers who conducted the search, and the county's district attorney.

[37] 436 U.S. 547, 98 S.Ct. 1970 (1978).

[38] Ibid., 551; 1974.

A federal district court held that the search was illegal. It declared that the Fourth and Fourteenth Amendments forbade the issuance of a warrant to search for materials in possession of a person not suspected of a crime unless there was probable cause to believe, based on a sworn affidavit, that a subpoena *duces tecum* would be impractical.

Some translation is needed here. As *New York Times* reporter Warren Weaver, Jr. noted, a subpoena *duces tecum* (that's Latin for "bring it with you") "can be enforced by a judge only after a hearing in which the holder of the evidence has the opportunity to present arguments why the material should not be given to the government." That process means, of course, that the holder of the documents sought would have some warning and a chance to "clean up" files. If investigators have a search warrant, on the other hand, the holder of the documents "has no more warning than a knock on the door." [39] In finding in favor of the Stanford Daily, District Judge Robert F. Peckham wrote:[40]

> It should be apparent that means less drastic than a search warrant do exist for obtaining materials from a third party. A subpoena duces tecum, obviously, is much less intrusive than a search warrant: the police do not go rummaging through one's house, office, or desk armed only with a subpoena. And, perhaps equally important, there is no opportunity to challenge the search warrant prior to the intrusion, whereas one can always move to quash the subpoena before producing the sought-after materials. * * * In view of the difference in degree of intrusion and the opportunity to challenge possible mistakes, the subpoena should always be preferred to the search warrant, for non-suspects.

The Daily's lawsuit thus was upheld by a U.S. district court and, five years later, by a U.S. Court of Appeals.[41] The Supreme Court of the United States, however, in a decision announced by Justice White, declared that newspapers are subject to such unannounced "third party" searches as the one involving the *Stanford Daily.* Justice White's majority opinion said:[42]

> It is an understatement to say that there is no direct authority in this or any other federal court for the District Court's sweeping revision of the Fourth Amendment. Under existing law, valid warrants may be issued to

[39] Warren Weaver, Jr., "High Court Bars Newspaper Plea Against Search," New York Times, June 1, 1978, pp. Al ff, at p. B6

[40] Stanford Daily v. Zurcher, 353 F.Supp. 124, 130 (N.D.Cal.1972).

[41] 550 F.2d 464 (9th Cir.1977).

[42] Zurcher v. Stanford Daily, 436 U.S. 547, 554–56, 98 S.Ct. 1970, 1975–77 (1978).

search *any* property, whether or not occupied by a third party, at which there is probable reason to believe that fruits, instrumentalities, or evidence of a crime will be found.

* * *

As the Fourth Amendment has been construed and applied by this Court, "when the State's reason to believe incriminating evidence will be found becomes sufficiently great, the invasion of privacy is justified and a warrant to search and seize will issue." Fisher v. United States, 425 U.S. 391, 96 S.Ct. 1569, 1576 (1976).

* * *

The critical element in a reasonable search is not that the owner of the property is suspected of a crime but that there is reasonable cause to believe that the specific "things" to be searched for and seized are located on the property to which entry is sought.

The Court enumerated—and rejected—the following arguments that additional First Amendment factors would forbid use of search warrants and permit only the subpoena *duces tecum*— arguments which held that searches of newspaper offices for evidence of crime would threaten the ability of the press to do its job.[43]

This is said to be true for several reasons: first, searches will be physically disruptive to such an extent that timely publication will be impeded. Second, confidential sources of information will dry up, and the press will also lose opportunities to cover various events because of fears of the participants that press files will be readily available to the authorities. Third, reporters will be deterred from recording and preserving their recollections for future use if such information is subject to seizure. Fourth, the processing of news and its dissemination will be chilled by the prospects that searches will disclose internal editorial deliberations. Fifth, the press will resort to self-censorship to conceal its possession of information of potential interest to the police.

Justice White's majority opinion brushed aside such arguments and expressed confidence that judges could guard against searches which would be so intrusive as to interfere with publishing newspapers.

Justice Potter Stewart, joined by Justice Thurgood Marshall, dissented, arguing that in place of the unannounced "knock-on-the-door" intrusion, "a subpoena would afford the newspaper itself

---

[43] Ibid., 561–66, 1977–1982.

an opportunity to locate whatever material might be requested and produce it." Then, as did his dissent in Branzburg v. Hayes, his argument hammered at society's need for confidentiality of the journalist's information, and for constitutional protection.[44]

Today, the Court does not question the existence of this constitutional protection, but says only that it is not "convinced * * * that confidential sources will disappear and that the press will suppress news because of fears of warranted searches." This facile conclusion seems to me to ignore common experience. It requires no blind leap of faith to understand that a person who gives information to a journalist only on condition that his identity will not be revealed will be less likely to give that information if he knows that, despite the journalist's assurance, his identity may in fact be disclosed. And it cannot be denied that confidential information may be exposed to the eyes of police officers who execute a search warrant by rummaging through the files, cabinets, desks and wastebaskets of a newsroom. Since the indisputable effect of such searches will thus be to prevent a newsman from being able to promise confidentiality to his potential sources, it seems obvious to me that a journalist's access to information, and thus the public's, will thereby be impaired.

* * *

Perhaps as a matter of abstract policy a newspaper office should receive no more protection from unannounced police searches than, say, the office of a doctor or the office of a bank. But we are here to uphold a Constitution. And our Constitution does not explicitly protect the practice of medicine or the business of banking from all abridgment by government. It does explicitly protect the freedom of the press.

Justice John Paul Stevens' dissent focused not on First Amendment matters, but on the justification needed to issue a search warrant without running afoul of the Fourth Amendment. Stevens wrote that every private citizen—not only the media— shall be protected.[45]

The only conceivable justification for an unannounced search of an innocent citizen is the fear that if notice were given, he would conceal or destroy the object of the search. Probable cause to believe that the custodian is a criminal, or that he holds a criminal's weapons,

---

[44] Ibid., 572, 576; 1985, 1987.

[45] Ibid., 582–83; 1990.

spoils, or the like, justifies that fear, and therefore such a showing complies with the clause [of the Fourth Amendment saying that warrants shall issue only upon "probable cause, supported by Oath or affirmation"]. But if nothing said under oath in the warrant application demonstrates the need for an unannounced search by force, the probable cause requirement is not satisfied. In the absence of some other showing of reasonableness, the ensuing search violates the Fourth Amendment.

Students of the problem questioned Justice White's reliance on "neutral magistrates" to protect media from harassment, and to issue warrants only upon reasonable requests whose propriety they could gauge on the basis of probable cause to believe that evidence would be found on the premises to be searched. For one thing, between the 1971 raid on the *Stanford Daily* offices and the Supreme Court decision in 1978, there were at least 14 other searches of media properties. And beyond that:[46]

> Journalists should perhaps be forgiven if they regard the protection of "neutral magistrates" as illusory. First, most, if not all, journalists tend to believe the folklore item about police walking around with fill-in-the-blank search warrants already signed by a complacent magistrate. Even if that is rankest slander of the judiciary, statistics on the issuance of search warrants compel the belief that the preconditions for warrant issuance are often improperly administered. "From 1969 through 1976, police sought 5,563 applications for search warrants under the 1968 Omnibus Crime Control Act. Only 15 of these applications were denied." Bluntly, the general rule seems to be that a search warrant sought equals a search warrant granted.

> Beyond that, the term "neutral magistrate" puts an all too flattering gloss on some persons who are empowered to issue search warrants. The House Committee on Government Operations has noted that the Court's implications that "magistrates * * * have at least a working knowledge of constitutional law" is in error. By one estimate of the National Center for State Courts, 8,800 of the 14,900 judges and comparable officials in states are not attorneys, and "a number of states appear not to require that warrant issuers be lawyers."

The legislation that Congress passed in 1980 in reaction to the *Zurcher* decision took effect in 1981. It provides a subpoena

[46] Dwight L. Teeter and Singer, S.G., Search Warrants in Newsrooms, 67 Ky.L. Journ. 847, 858 (1978–79).

procedure, and a hearing for those subpoenaed. It prohibits "knock-on-the-door," search-warrant raids of news media offices and those of authors and researchers, by federal, state, and local law enforcement agencies, except in three unusual circumstances. These are: where there is cause to believe that the reporter himself is involved in a crime, where the information sought relates to the national defense or classified information, or where there is reason to believe that immediate action through search warrant is needed to prevent bodily harm or death to a human being.[47] *News Media & the Law* found that, by late 1980, nine states had adopted their own laws along the same lines, some extending the protection to all private citizens, not only those in the field of writing. While the federal bill avoids that reach, it requires the Justice Department to work out guidelines for federal searches that will take into account personal privacy interests of the person to be searched.[48] Searches of media after *Zurcher* and before passage of the new law seemed to retreat; one compiler of actions found only a single search-warrant raid in the nation from the announcement of *Zurcher* in May 1978 to May 1980.[49]

As recent a problem in confidentiality as searches of the *Zurcher* kind—and an even rarer one—is that which arises in officials' subpoenaing of journalists' telephone records from telephone companies. In 1976, the Reporters Committee for Freedom of the Press and other journalists lost a case in federal district court to compel AT & T to inform media when government subpoenas were issued for media phone records. The court of appeals also turned down the media, saying that no right of privacy under the First Amendment existed because the records belonged to the telephone company and not the media.[50] In an unsuccessful appeal to the United States Supreme Court to review the decision, the journalists stated the heart of their case for protection of their telephone records:[51]

> The impact of the ruling below cannot be minimized * * *. When government investigators obtain a reporter's toll records * * * they learn the identity of (his) sources. And they also learn * * * much about the

[47] Pub.Law 96–440, 94 Stat. 1879; 6 Med.L.Rptr. 2255, 2256 (1981). And see "Carter Signs Newsroom Raid Ban," News Media & the Law, Oct./Nov. 1980, 3–5.

[48] Attorney General's Guidelines for Litigation to Enforce Obligations to Submit Materials for Predissemination Review, 6 Med.L.Rptr. 2261 (1981), dated 12/9/80, and published 1/2/81.

[49] "Police Raid Newspaper Printing Office," News Media & the Law, Aug./Sept. 1980, 25.

[50] Reporters Committee for Freedom of the Press v. American Tel. & Tel. Co., 593 F.2d 1030 (D.C.Cir.1978), certiorari denied, 440 U.S. 949, 99 S.Ct. 1431 (1979), 4 Med.L.Rptr. 1177.

[51] News Media & the Law, Oct./Nov. 1980, 6.

pattern of his investigative activities—whom he called, when and in what order he makes calls to develop his leads, what subjects he is looking into and how actively he is exploring these subjects.

In the fall of 1980, it was reported that phone records of the Atlanta bureau of the *New York Times,* as well as those of its bureau chief, Howell Raines, had been subpoenaed in June by the Justice Department. The telephone company had waited 90 days, at the request of the Justice Department, before telling the Times. Shortly thereafter, attorney General Benjamin Civiletti announced new rules for issuing subpoenas for phone records— essentially, that no subpoena is to be issued to media people for their toll phone records without "express authorization" of the Attorney General.[52]   This was the extent of protection that the media found.

Thus in one more setting, journalists were asserting that secrecy—anathema when employed by the government—was essential to the highest performance of their own craft.   And once again, it was clear that deep values in the journalist's work—the "watchdogging" of government and other powerful institutions, and informing the members of an open society about their world— would continue to adjust in some of the contests where other cherished values sometimes would take precedence.

[52] New York Times, Nov. 13, 1980, A30.

Chapter 10

LEGAL PROBLEMS IN REPORTING LEGISLATIVE AND EXECUTIVE BRANCHES OF GOVERNMENT

Sec.
60. The Problem of Secrecy in Government.
61. Access and the Constitution.
62. Records and Meetings of Federal Government.
63. Records and Meetings in the States.
64. Access to Judicial Proceedings.

SEC. 60. THE PROBLEM OF SECRECY IN GOVERNMENT

Following World War II, obtaining access to information at various levels of government became an acute problem in American journalism.

A self-governing people needs to know what its public officials are up to. The proposition seems plain to reporters who work from day to day in the offices and chambers of government, as they gather information for publication to the people of a democracy. If officials in any branch of government, at any level, may do their work in secret, they may shield themselves from accountability. Ancient words like "tyranny" and "oppression" take on reality for modern man where secrecy pervades government; unfairness, unchecked power, unconcern for human rights and needs, and inefficiency and corruption can thrive in seclusion. The democratic public has every reason to assume that the great bulk of the work of government will be open and available for inspection.

The assumption has honorable origins. Colonial courts had been generally open, following Britain's practice since the mid-Seventeenth Century, and the new America accepted the practice as a matter of course. The Revolutionary Continental Congresses had, indeed, been highly secret bodies, as the colonial legislatures before them had generally been. But with the 1780s and 1790s, first the House of Representatives and then the Senate had opened its doors to the public and press. Granting access had been hard for some congressmen to concede; both Houses wrote rules under which they might operate behind closed doors if the need arose.[1]

---

[1] Secret Journal of Congress, 1775–1788, Introduction; Lewis Deschler, Constitution, Jefferson's Manual, and Rules of the House of Representatives, 82 Cong.2d

457

But the policy was plain and was to be rarely breached during the decades to come: Legislative debates and halls were the domain of people and press as they were of the elected representatives.

No segment of the American public has been more concerned about tendencies to secrecy in government than journalists. Some feel that it is the central threat to freedom of expression in mid-Twentieth Century America. Accepting, during World War II, the need for extensive secrecy for an enormous war machine in a government bureaucracy grown gigantic, journalists after the war soon detected a broad pattern of continued secrecy in government operations. Access to meetings was denied; reports, papers, documents at all levels of government seemed less available than before officialdom's habits of secrecy developed in the passion for security during World War II. An intense, insistent campaign for access to government information was launched in the 1950's by editors, publishers, reporters, and news organizations. It went under a banner labeled "Freedom of Information," and under the claim that the press was fighting for the "people's right to know." [2]

To combat what they viewed as a severe increase in denial of access to the public's business, journalists took organized action. "Freedom of Information" committees were established by the American Society of Newspaper Editors (ASNE) and by the Society of Professional Journalists—Sigma Delta Chi. The ASNE commissioned newspaper attorney Harold L. Cross to perform a major study on the law of access to government activity. His book, *The People's Right to Know,* was published in 1953 and served as a central source of information. State and local chapters of professional groups worked for the adoption of state access laws. In 1958, a Freedom of Information Center was opened at the University of Missouri School of Journalism, as a clearing house and research facility for those concerned with the subject. Meanwhile, an early and vigorous ally was found in the House Subcommittee on Government Information under Rep. John E. Moss of California, created to investigate charges of excessive secrecy in the Executive branch of government.[3]

Journalism had powerful allies also in the scientific community. It found that the advance of knowledge in vast areas of

Sess., House Doc. 564 (1953), Rule 29. For a powerful statement of the Mid-Nineteenth Century, see Francis Lieber, On Civil Liberty and Self-Government (Phila., 1853), I, 149–157.

[2] See Annual Reports, Sigma Delta Chi Advancement of Freedom of Information Committee (Chicago, Sigma Delta Chi).

[3] Rep. John E. Moss, Preface to Replies from Federal Agencies to Questionnaire Submitted by the Special Subcommittee on Government Information of the Committee on Government Operations, 84 Cong. 1 Sess. (Nov. 1, 1955), p. iii.

government-sponsored science was being slowed, sometimes crippled for years, in the blockage of the flow of research information between and even within agencies of the federal government. Fear of "leakage" of secrets important to defense in the Cold War with the Soviet Union brought administrative orders that were contrary to the tenets of scientists and researchers. A snarl of regulations, rules, and red tape, besides official policy that fostered sequestering, prevented scientists from sharing their findings with others. Their concern about the damage to the advance of knowledge in science paralleled the news fraternity's alarm about damage to the democratic assumption that free institutions rest on an informed public.[4]

Public understanding of the dangers of official secrecy broadened in the exposé of the Executive's abuse of power in the Watergate episode of the mid-1970's. Earl Warren, retired Chief Justice of the United States, crediting the news media with a share in exposing the fraud and deceit, said if we are to learn from "the debacle we are in, we should first strike at secrecy in government wherever it exists, because it is the incubator for corruption."[5] New recruits entered the battle against official secrecy—Common Cause, the Center for National Security Studies, and Ralph Nader among them.

SEC. 61. ACCESS AND THE CONSTITUTION

Courts have given little support to the position that the First Amendment includes a right of access to government information.

In many journalists' view, freedom of speech and press and the First Amendment encompass a right to gather government information as much as they encompass the right to publish and distribute it. Constitutional protection against denial of access seems to them only reasonable. Madison said that "A popular government without popular information or the means of acquiring it, is but a prologue to a farce or a tragedy, or perhaps both."[6] For their own time, the legal scholar Harold Cross argued that "Freedom of information is the very foundation for all those freedoms that the First Amendment of our Constitution was intended to guarantee."[7]

---

[4] Science, Education and Communications, 12 Bulletin of Atomic Scientists, 333 (Nov.1956); Walter Gellhorn, Security, Loyalty, and Science (Ithaca: Cornell Univ. Press, 1950).

[5] Governmental Secrecy: Corruption's Ally, 60 ABA Journal 550 (May, 1974).

[6] James Madison to W.T. Barry, 1822, quoted in Saul Padover, ed., The Complete Madison (New York: Harper & Brothers, 1953), p. 337.

[7] Harold L. Cross, The People's Right to Know (Morningside Heights: Columbia Univ. Press, 1953), pp. xiii–xiv.

First Amendment legal scholar Thomas I. Emerson holds that "we ought to consider the right to know as an integral part of the system of freedom of expression, embodied in the first amendment and entitled to support by legislation or other affirmative government action." He finds the argument for "starting from this point * * overwhelming," and further, that the Supreme Court has in some respects recognized a constitutional right to know.[8]

But the courts have provided scant acknowledgement of a "right of access" under the First Amendment, except for access to public, criminal court trials, declared open as a First Amendment right in a major case of 1980, Richmond Newspapers v. Virginia (detailed in Chap. 11, below). Our concern here is news-gathering problems in the legislative and executive/administrative branches.

Reporter William Worthy of the *Baltimore Afro-American* in 1956 ignored an order of Secretary of State John Foster Dulles which barred American newsmen from going to Red China to report. When Worthy returned to the United States, the State Department revoked his passport and refused to give him another. Worthy went to court to attempt to regain his passport. The trial court held, without elaborating, that Dulles' refusal to issue the passport did not violate Worthy's rights to travel under the First Amendment. Worthy appealed, but his argument for First Amendment protection failed, the Court of Appeals holding:[9]

> * * * the right here involved is not a right to think or speak; it is a right to be physically present in a certain place * * *.
>
> The right to travel is a part of the right to liberty, and a newspaperman's right to travel is a part of freedom of the press. But these valid generalizations do not support unrestrained conclusions. * * *
>
> Freedom of the press bears restrictions * * *. Merely because a newsman has a right to travel does not mean he can go anywhere he wishes. He cannot attend conferences of the Supreme Court, or meetings of the President's Cabinet or executive sessions of the Committees of Congress. He cannot come into my house without permission or enter a ball park without a ticket of admission from the management * * *.

In another case, Zemel argued that a State Department travel ban was a direct interference with the First Amendment rights of

[8] Legal Foundations of the Right To Know, 1976 Wash.U.L.Quar. 1–3. See also Jacob Scher, "Access to Information: Recent Legal Problems," Journalism Quarterly, 37:1 (1960), p. 41.

[9] Worthy v. Herter, 270 F.2d 905 (D.C.Cir.1959), certiorari denied 361 U.S. 918, 80 S.Ct. 255.

citizens to inform themselves at first hand of events abroad. The United States Supreme Court agreed that the Secretary's denial rendered "less than wholly free the flow of information concerning that country," but denied that a First Amendment right was involved. "The right to speak and publish does not carry with it the unrestrained right to gather information," [10] the Court said. It drew parallels with other situations where access is restricted, such as the prohibition of unauthorized entry to the White House.

While an occasional lower court or a dissenting judge has found reason for the First Amendment to protect a right of access to government information,[11] the United States Supreme Court has done so only in the setting of public, criminal trials. Justice Potter Stewart delivered a rationale for the denial of a constitutional right of access to government, in a 1975 speech:[12]

> So far as the Constitution goes, the autonomous press may publish what it knows, and may seek to learn what it can.
>
> But this autonomy cuts both ways. The press is free to do battle against secrecy and deception in government. But the press cannot expect from the Constitution any guarantee that it will succeed. There is no constitutional right to have access to particular government information, or to require openness from the bureaucracy. The public's interest in knowing about its government is protected by the guarantee of a Free Press, but the protection is indirect. The Constitution itself is neither a Freedom of Information Act nor an Official Secrets Act.
>
> The Constitution, in other words, establishes the contest, not its resolution. Congress may provide a resolution, at least in some instances, through carefully drawn legislation. For the rest, we must rely, as so often in our system we must, on the tug and pull of the political forces in American society.

Stewart's speech spelled out in fresh formulation views which he had expressed in writing the majority opinion in Pell v. Procunier.[13] Here, journalists Eve Pell, Betty Segal, and Paul

[10] Zemel v. Rusk, 381 U.S. 1, 17–18, 85 S.Ct. 1271, 1281 (1965). See also Trimble v. Johnston, 173 F.Supp. 651 (D.D.C.1953); In re Mack, 386 Pa. 251, 126 A.2d 679 (1956).

[11] Providence Journal Co. et al. v. McCoy et al., 94 F.Supp. 186 (D.C.R.I.1950); In re Mack, 386 Pa. 251, 126 A.2d 679, 689 (1956); Lyles v. Oklahoma, 330 P.2d 734 (Okl.Cr.1958).

[12] Potter Stewart, Or of the Press, 26 Hastings L.Journ. 631 (1975).

[13] 417 U.S. 817, 94 S.Ct. 2800 (1974). At least 11 states have statutes permitting reporters to interview inmates in confidential settings: Press Censorship Newsletter VII, April–May 1975, p. 61.

Jacobs challenged a California prison regulation which barred press and other media interviews with specific, individual inmates. Denied their requests to interview prison inmates Apsin, Bly and Guild, they asserted that the rule limited their news-gathering activity and thus infringed freedom of the press under the First and Fourteenth Amendments. They lost in District Court and appealed to the U.S. Supreme Court. Stewart wrote for the majority that the press and public are afforded full opportunities to observe minimum security sections of prisons, to speak about any subject to any inmates they might encounter, to interview inmates selected at random by the corrections officials, to sit in on group meetings of inmates. "The sole limitations on news-gathering in California prisons is the prohibition in [regulation] # 415.071 of interviews with individual inmates specifically designated by representatives of the press." [14]

Before the regulation was adopted, Stewart continued, unrestrained press access to individual prisoners resulted in concentration of press attention on a few inmates, who became virtual "public figures" in prison society and gained great influence. One inmate who advocated non-cooperation with prison regulations had extensive press attention, encouraged other inmates in his purpose, and eroded the institution's ability to deal effectively with inmates in general. San Quentin prison authorities concluded that an escape attempt there, resulting in deaths of three staff members and two inmates, flowed in part from an unrestricted press access policy, and regulation # 415.071 was adopted as a result. Stewart wrote:[15]

> The Constitution does not * * * require government to accord the press special access to information not shared by members of the public generally. It is one thing to say that a journalist is free to seek out sources of information not available to members of the general public * * *.
>
> It is quite another thing to suggest that the Constitution imposes upon government the affirmative duty to make available to journalists sources of information not available to members of the public generally. The proposition finds no support in the words of the Constitution or in any decision of this Court.

Dissenting in this case and in a companion case, Saxbe v. Washington Post Co.[16] which involved an unsuccessful challenge to a Federal Bureau of Prisons rule similar to California's, was

[14] Pell v. Procunier, 417 U.S. 817, 94 S.Ct. 2800, 2808 (1974).

[15] Ibid., 2810.

[16] 417 U.S. 843, 94 S.Ct. 2811 (1974). Powell's statements are at 2820–2826.

Justice Powell. He said that "sweeping prohibition of prisoner-press interviews substantially impairs a core value of the First Amendment." In these cases, he argued, society's interest "in preserving free public discussion of governmental affairs" was great and was the value at stake. Since the public is unable to know most news at first hand, "In seeking out the news the press * * * acts as an agent of the public at large. * * * By enabling the public to assert meaningful control over the political process, the press performs a critical function in effecting the societal purpose of the First Amendment."

Much more restrictive access to a jail was at issue when Sheriff Houchins of Alameda Co., Calif., was ordered by injunction to open up his facility to reporters and their cameras and recorders. His rules had limited journalists to regular, once-a-month tours open to the public in general. No cameras or recorders were allowed, nor was access to a part of the jail where violence had reportedly broken out earlier. KQED, which made a practice of covering prisons in the area and wanted access to shoot film and interview prisoners, took Houchins to court, saying its journalistic usefulness was reduced by his tour rules. The sheriff objected that the access sought would infringe the privacy of inmates, create jail "celebrities" and cause attendant difficulties, and disrupt jail operations. He told of other forms of access by which information about the jail could reach the public. The district court agreed with KQED's contentions, and enjoined the sheriff from further blocking of media access "at reasonable times," cameras and recorders included.[17] The California Court of Appeals upheld the injunction, saying that the U.S. Supreme Court's *Pell* and *Saxbe* decisions were not controlling.

Houchins appealed to the Supreme Court, and it reversed the lower courts, Chief Justice Warren Burger writing that neither of the earlier cases, nor indeed Branzburg v. Hayes (Chapter 9, above), provided a constitutional right to gather news, or a constitutional right of access to government.[18] He agreed that news of prisons is important for the public to have, and that media serve as "eyes and ears" for the public. He said, however, that the Supreme Court had never held that the First Amendment compels anyone, private or public, to supply information. He discussed various ways in which information about prisons reaches the public, and said the legislative branch was free to pass laws opening penal institutions if it wished. But the press, Burger said, enjoys no special privilege of access beyond that which officials grant to the public in general. *Pell* and *Saxbe* would hold, and

---

[17] Houchins v. KQED, Inc., 438 U.S. 1, 98 S.Ct. 2588 (1978), 3 Med.L.Rptr. 2521.

[18] Ibid., 2523–24.

Houchins' access rules also. Separately, Justice Stewart joined in the decision, differing only to the extent of saying that reporters on tour with the public should be allowed to carry and use their tools of the trade, including cameras and recorders.

Justice Powell, who as we have seen had dissented in *Pell* and *Saxbe*, joined two others in dissenting again, on similar grounds. He and the other dissenters in *Pell* had totaled four, the greatest support that the Supreme Court has furnished for "access to government" as a constitutionally protected principle outside the judicial branch.[19]

SEC. 62. RECORDS AND MEETINGS OF FEDERAL GOVERNMENT

Access to records and meetings of federal executive and administrative agencies is provided under the "Freedom of Information" and the "Sunshine in Government" Acts; the Privacy Act provides for secrecy of records.

Freedom of Information Act

On July 4, 1966, Pres. Lyndon B. Johnson signed the Federal Public Records Law, shortly to be known as the federal Freedom of Information (FOI) Act.[20] Providing for the public availability of records of executive and administrative agencies of the government, it sprang, President Johnson said, "from one of our most essential principles: a democracy works best when the people have all the information that the security of the Nation permits." He expressed a "deep sense of pride that the United States is an open society in which the people's right to know is cherished and guarded." [21]

The FOI Act replaced section 3 of the Administrative Procedure Act of 1946, which had permitted secrecy if it was required in the public interest or for "good cause." [22] The new law expressed neither this limitation nor another which had said disclosure was necessary only to "persons properly and directly concerned" with

---

[19] Richmond Newspapers v. Virginia, 448 U.S. 555, 100 S.Ct. 2814 (1980), 6 Med. L.Rptr. 1833. For a view that sees the approach of a broad constitutional right of access to government, see Roy V. Leeper, Richmond Newspapers, Inc. v. Virginia and the Emerging Right of Access, 61 Journ.Quar. 615 (Autumn 1984).

[20] 5 U.S.C.A. § 552, amended by Pub.Law 93–502, 88 Stat. 1561–1564. For history, text, and extensive judicial interpretation of this act, and information on the federal Privacy Act, see Allan Adler and Halperin, M.H., Litigation under the Federal Freedom of Information Act and Privacy Act, 1984 (Washington, 1983).

[21] Public Papers of the Presidents, Lyndon B. Johnson, 1966 II, p. 699.

[22] 5 U.S.C.A. § 1002 (1946).

the subject at hand.   In the words of Attorney General Ramsey Clark, the FOI Act [23]

> imposes on the executive branch an affirmative obligation to adopt new standards and practices for publication and availability of information. It leaves no doubt that disclosure is a transcendent goal, yielding only to such compelling considerations as those provided for in the exemptions of the act.

Every federal executive branch agency is required under the FOI Act to publish in the Federal Register its organization plan, and the agency personnel and methods through which the public can get information.   Every agency's procedural rules and general policies are to be published.   Every agency's manuals and instructions are to be made available for public inspection and copying, as are final opinions in adjudicated cases.   Current indexes are to be made available to the public.   If records are improperly withheld, the U.S. district court can enjoin the agency from the withholding and order disclosure.   And if agency officials fail to comply with the court order, they may be punished for contempt.

Exceptions to that which must be made public are called "exemptions."   There are nine of them, some of them revised and tightened against abuse by agencies after a three-year congressional study which brought about amendments effective Feb. 19, 1975:

1. Records "specifically authorized under criteria established by an Executive order to be kept secret in the interest of national defense or foreign policy" and which are properly classified.

2. Matters related only to "internal personnel rules and practices" of an agency.

3. Matters exempt from disclosure by statute.

4. Trade secrets and commercial or financial information obtained from a person and that are privileged or confidential.

5. Inter-agency or intra-agency communications, such as memoranda showing how policy-makers within an agency feel about various policy options.

6. Personnel and medical files which could not be disclosed without a "clearly unwarranted invasion" of someone's privacy.

7. Investigatory files compiled for law enforcement purposes, if the production of such records would interfere with law enforcement, deprive one of a fair trial, constitute an

[23] Foreward, Attorney General's Memorandum on the Public Information Section of the Administrative Procedure Act (1967).

unwarranted invasion of personal privacy, disclose the identity of a confidential source, disclose investigative techniques, or endanger the life or safety of law enforcement personnel.

8.   Reports prepared by or for an agency responsible for the regulation or supervision of financial institutions.

9.   Geological and geophysical information and data, including maps, concerning wells—particularly explorations by gas and oil companies.

Long delays, high costs for searching and copying documents, and widespread agency reluctance to comply with the original act's provisions characterized its early history.[24] Not only were several exemptions tightened by the amendments; also, rules were passed requiring agencies to inform persons making requests for information within ten days whether or not access would be granted, and to decide upon requests for appeals within 20 days. Uniform schedules of fees—limited to reasonable standard charges for document search and copying—were also mandated in the amendments.[25]

The amendments brought a flood of requests for information, primarily from persons who asked the FBI, the CIA, and the IRS, whether files were kept on them, and, if so, what the files contained. The Justice Department was receiving 2,000 requests per month by August 1975.[26] Media requests mounted under the amendments. One study found more than 400 between 1972 and 1984, but said that was far fewer than the actual total. Another study found that almost 50% of its list came from "public interest" groups, and about one-fourth from media.[27]

Court cases decided under the Act as of mid-1976 totaled 295, half of them less than two years old.[28] The increase suggested the

[24] Wallis McClain, "Implementing the Amended FOI Act," Freedom of Information Center Report No. 343, Sept. 1975, p. 1; U.S. Congress, Freedom of Information Act and Amendments of 1974 (P.L. 93–502) Source Book: Legislative History, Texts, and Other Documents. Joint Committee Print (94th Cong., 1 Sess.), Washington: U.S. Government Printing Office, March 1975.

[25] Anon., "FOI Act Amendments Summarized," FOI Digest, 17:1, Jan.-Feb. 1975, p. 5.

[26] Anon., "FOI Act: Access Increases, Some Nagging Problems Remain," FOI Digest, 17:4, July-Aug. 1975, p. 5, citing Wall Street Journal, June 27, 1975; John A. Jenkins, "Ask, and You Shall Receive," Quill, July-Aug. 1975, pp. 22, 24.

[27] Ibid., quoting Attorney Ronald Plesser, 22; Anon., Media Use of FOIA Documented in New Study, 10 Med.L.Rptr. # 34, 8/21/84, News Notes, quoting a study done for the House Subcommittee on Government Information, Justice, and Agriculture; Sam Archibald, Use of the FOIA, Freedom of Information Report # 457, May 1982, 3 (Univ. of Mo.).

[28] Anon., "Justice Dept. Indexes Decided FOIA Cases," FOI Digest, 18:5, Sept.-Oct. 1976, p. 5, citing Congressional Record, Senate, Aug. 2, 1976, p. S13028. Reprinted in Marwick, App. p. 72.

impact of the 1975 amendments. Actions concerning investigatory files (exemption 7) outstripped the pre-amendments leaders, agency memoranda and trade secrets (exemptions 5 and 4). One important change provided for *in camera* review by judges of documents which the Executive Branch might refuse to open on grounds of national defense or foreign policy (exemption 1). Under the original FOI Act, Congress had not provided this, but rather, said Justice Stewart in an acid concurring opinion, had simply chosen "to decree blind acceptance of Executive fiat" that secrecy was called for.[29]

With the deluge of requests for information came growing complaints by all government agencies that it was too costly and too time-consuming to process FOI Act requests. Costs to the Treasury Department in 1978 alone totalled more than $6 million, and CIA Director William Casey said that FOIA and Privacy Act (below) requests of the agency required 257,420 man-hours of service at a cost of about $2 million.[30] Agencies complained that the act was used by law firms and commercial competitors to learn trade secrets and government enforcement policies, by foreign agents to gain national security information, and by organized crime to discover and thwart criminal investigations.[31]

Congressional efforts to restrict access to various agencies by amending the FOI Act never stop. The 1980s saw several. With President Ronald Reagan's support, the Central Intelligence Agency was authorized by law in 1984 to exempt its operational files on sources and methods from disclosure. In 1983, the 97th Congress passed six measures authorizing withholding by agencies that deal with trade, consumer product safety, income tax, energy, and health. New restrictions aimed especially at trade-secret rules were provided, again with President Reagan's support, in the Hatch Bill of 1984, but after passage by the Senate, were unsuccessful in the House.[32]

Exemption 1, the national security exemption, was clarified in an executive order, effective in 1978, which imposed stricter minimum standards on classification of material. If the disclosure "reasonably could be expected to cause *identifiable* damage to

[29] Environmental Protection Agency v. Mink, 410 U.S. 73, 136, 93 S.Ct. 827 (1973).

[30] "Diverse Legislative Efforts To Amend the FOIA Increase," FOI Digest, Jan.-Feb. 1980, 22:1, p. 5. Rod Perlmutter, Proposed FOIA Amendments—2, Freedom of Information Report # 451, Jan. 1982 (Univ. of Mo.).

[31] "Congress, Courts Mutilate FOI Act," News Media & The Law, Aug.-Sept. 1980, 4:3, p. 16.

[32] Anon., CIA Exemption Bill Passed, News Media & the Law, Nov./Dec. 1984; 8 Med.L.Rptr. # 46, 1/25/83, News Notes; Anon., Note, Developments under the Freedom of Information Act 1983, 1984 Duke Law J. 377, 382; News Media & the Law, Sept./Oct. 1983, 24.

national security," the information was confidential. However, any reasonable doubt should be resolved in favor of declassification, if the public interest in disclosure outweighed the damage to national security that "might be reasonably expected from disclosure." [33]

The exemption was also the target of suits involving the definition of "possession" of records. In Forsham v. Harris, a 1980 Supreme Court decision, Justice Rehnquist stated that written data held by a private research firm receiving federal grant money from HEW were not "agency records" if the agency providing the funds had not yet obtained possession of the data. The FOI Act provided no direct access to such data; therefore, HEW had not improperly "withheld" the data. The Act applied not to records that could exist, but only to records that did exist.[34]

In Kissinger v. Reporters Committee for Freedom of the Press, the Supreme Court held that the State Department had not "withheld" records of former Secretary of State Henry Kissinger's phone calls by failing to file a lawsuit to recover documents which Kissinger had improperly donated to the Library of Congress, and which would be unavailable to the public for 25 years.[35] A Justice Department suit was considered, and Kissinger later agreed to a new review of documents to determine whether they are needed for departmental files.[36]

In other developments related to national security, a federal district court judge ruled in Hayden v. National Security Agency/ Central Security Service that disclosure of the existence of particular records, obtained through NSA monitoring of foreign electromagnetic signals, could be withheld, since the existence of such records might be more sensitive than their substance.[37]

Attempts by media to open records through court cases commonly run afoul of exemptions 7 and 5—investigatory files and agency memoranda—source materials which are often expected by media to be relevant to criminal activity. National Public Radio, for example, sought disclosure of records compiled by the Justice Department and the FBI about the perplexing death of Karen Silkwood. An employee of a manufacturer of plutonium and

[33] Alan S. Madens, "Developments Under the Freedom of Information Act— 1979," 1980 Duke L.J. 139, 146–147.

[34] "The Supreme Court 1979 Term," 94 Harv.L.Rev. 1, 232–237 (1980); Forsham v. Harris, 445 U.S. 169, 100 S.Ct. 978 (1980).

[35] "The Supreme Court 1979 Term," Harv.L.Rev. 1, 232–235; Kissinger v. Reporters Committee for Freedom of the Press, 445 U.S. 136, 100 S.Ct. 960 (1980), 6 Med. L.Rptr. 1001.

[36] "Nixon Tapes Available to Public: Archives Requests More Materials," FOI Digest, May-June 1980, 22:3, p. 1.

[37] Madens, op. cit., 148.

uranium fuels for nuclear reactors, Silkwood was reportedly driving to attend a meeting with a union official and a newspaper reporter when she was killed in an auto crash. Uncertain evidence suggested that her car might have been driven off the road by another car, and that a file of documents she was supposedly carrying was not recovered. NPR also sought the record of the agency's investigation of the contamination of Silkwood by plutonium.

The Justice Department furnished NPR with some of the requested materials, but refused others. The parts of the death investigation file withheld were the "closing memoranda"—agency materials prepared during its final deliberations—and about 15 pages of notes and working papers of Justice Department attorneys. The Justice Department said that exemption 5 of the FOI Act—intra-agency memoranda or letters—protected these materials from disclosure. The Federal district court agreed,[38] saying the agency memoranda are protected as "papers which reflect the agency's group thinking in the process of working out its policy and determining what its law shall be." [39] The court rejected NPR's argument that the memoranda were "final" opinions, which under the Supreme Court's interpretation of the FOI Act would have been subject to disclosure.[40]

As for exemption 7 of the FOI Act, protecting from disclosure matters which are "investigatory records compiled for law enforcement purposes" whose release would "interfere with enforcement proceedings * * *.": This applied to the Justice Department investigation of Silkwood's contamination by plutonium, and the court said that the records of the case suggested law-violation in materials-handling by personnel. It said that Congress' intent in writing exemption 7 was plainly to prevent harm to a "concrete prospective law enforcement proceeding" that might result from disclosure of information. And though the department's leads in the investigation had currently run out, and want of finances for the moment precluded assignment of an investigator to the case, the case was "active." Disclosure would present "the very real possibility of a criminal learning in alarming detail of the government's investigation of his crime before the government has had the opportunity to bring him to justice," said the court in rejecting NPR's request.[41]

[38] National Public Radio et al. v. Bell, 431 F.Supp. 509 (D.D.C.1977), 2 Med.L. Rptr. 1808.

[39] Ibid.

[40] N.L.R.B. v. Sears, Roebuck & Co., 421 U.S. 132, 95 S.Ct. 1504 (1975).

[41] National Public Radio et al. v. Bell, 431 F.Supp. 509 (D.D.C.1977). The investigatory exemption was tightened in lower court cases. Records must be both investigatory *and* compiled for law enforcement purposes: Pope v. United States,

Exemption 5 was expanded in Federal Open Market Committee v. Merrill, in which the Supreme Court upheld an agency's refusal to release monthly policy directives while they were in effect, if they contained sensitive information not otherwise available, and if release of the directive would significantly harm the government's monetary functions or commercial interests.[42]

A power of withholding has always been asserted by the President and his Executive Department heads. This is the power exercised under the doctrine of "executive privilege." President George Washington was asked by Congress to make available documents relating to General St. Clair's defeat by Indians. He responded that "the Executive ought to communicate such papers as the public good would permit, and ought to refuse those, the disclosure of which would injure the public * * *."[43] In this case the records were made available to Congress, but many presidents since have refused to yield records, as have the heads of executive departments. Their power to do so was upheld early in the nation's history by the United States Supreme Court. The famous decision written by Chief Justice John Marshall was delivered in 1803 in Marbury v. Madison, where Marshall said that the Attorney General (a presidential appointee) did not have to reveal matters which had been communicated to him in confidence.[44]

> By the Constitution of the United States, the president is invested with certain important political powers, in the exercise of which he is to use his own discretion, and is accountable only to the country in his political character and to his own conscience.

Justice Marshall elaborated the principle in the trial of Aaron Burr, accused of treason, saying that "The propriety of withholding * * * must be decided by [the President] himself, not by another for him. Of the weight of the reasons for and against producing it he himself is the judge."[45]

Executive privilege came to be asserted and used increasingly during the government's efforts to maintain security in the cold

---

599 F.2d 1383 (5th Cir.1979). The information must be originally gathered for law enforcement purposes: Gregory v. Federal Deposit Insurance Corp., 470 F.Supp. 1329 (D.D.C.1979). Courts have given mixed reactions to records for "improper" investigations. See Lamont v. Department of Justice, 475 F.Supp. 761 (S.D.N.Y. 1979), and Irons v. Bell, 596 F.2d 468 (1st Cir.1979). See also Madens, op. cit., at 162–163.

[42] Madens, op. cit., 155.

[43] Francis E. Rourke, Secrecy and Publicity (Baltimore: Johns Hopkins Press, 1961), p. 65. And see Ibid., pp. 64–69, for general discussion of executive privilege.

[44] 5 U.S. (1 Cranch.) 137 (1803).

[45] 1 Burr's Trial 182.

war with the U.S.S.R. following World War II. Presidents Truman and Eisenhower used the power to issue orders detailing what might and might not be released from the executive departments; both came under heavy attack from Congress and the news media.[46] President Nixon's Executive Order No. 11–652 of March 8, 1972, replaced and modified rules set by President Eisenhower.

One of the most far-reaching directives of this period was issued by President Eisenhower in 1954. A senate subcommittee was investigating a controversy between the Army and Senator Joseph McCarthy of Wisconsin. President Eisenhower sent to Secretary of the Army Robert Stevens a message telling him that his departmental employees were to say nothing about internal communications of the Department.[47]

> Because it is essential to efficient and effective administration that employees of the executive branch be in a position to be completely candid in advising with each other on official matters, and because it is not in the public interest that any of their conversations or communications, or any documents or reproductions, concerning such advice be disclosed, you will instruct employees of your Department that in all of their appearances before the subcommittee of the Senate Committee on Government Operations regarding the inquiry now before it they are not to testify to any such conversations or communications or to produce any such documents or reproductions.

While the directive was aimed at a single situation and a single Executive Department, it soon became used by many other executive and administrative agencies as justification for their own withholding of records concerning internal affairs.[48] While journalists protested the spread of the practice, and while Congressional allies joined them, there was not much legal recourse then apparent.

The President's powers to restrict access are substantial, used extensively by some and little by others. Journalists have widely asserted that President Ronald Reagan employed these powers more vigorously than his predecessors of many terms. We have seen (Chap. 1, p. 28) that his directive placed a "lifelong" nondisclosure restriction on many government employees, although it

[46] Rourke, pp. 75–83.

[47] House Report, No. 2947, 84 Cong., 2 Sess., July 27, 1956. Availability of Information from Federal Departments and Agencies. Dwight D. Eisenhower to Sec. of Defense, May 17, 1954, pp. 64–65.

[48] Rourke, p. 74.

was partially withdrawn. In his 1982 Executive Order 12,356, he tightened declassification rules set by President Jimmy Carter, permitting permanent exemption from disclosure of documents in the realm of national security and foreign policy. In 1981, he submitted proposals to the Senate to give the Attorney General power to exempt some kinds of intelligence files from disclosure. In 1983, the Justice Department, with his support, notably tightened the rules for waiving fees charged to those who seek information from government agencies. Under him as Commander in Chief, journalists were kept uninformed and were excluded from the armed forces' invasion of the Caribbean island of Grenada. Journalists found him and his administration much less accessible than his predecessor, and expert at frustrating reporters, one analyst declaring that "bureaucrats have largely succeeded in undermining the FOI Act at will." [49]

A head-on confrontation emerged in the Watergate investigations, as President Richard M. Nixon refused to turn over to a grand jury, tape recordings of conversations with his White House aides. Federal Judge John J. Sirica ruled that the tapes must be submitted to him for *in camera* scrutiny and possible forwarding to the grand jury. The President refused, asserting executive privilege, and said he was protecting "the right of himself and his successors to preserve the confidentiality of discussions in which they participate in the course of their constitutional duties." Special prosecutor Archibald Cox argued it was intolerable that "the President would invoke executive privilege to keep the tape recordings from the grand jury but permit his aides to testify fully as to their recollections of the same conversations." The President fired Cox, and the Attorney General resigned and his deputy was fired before the President yielded the tapes (which of course were to prove central to the discrediting of him and his aides) amid a public cry for his impeachment.[50]

The Supreme Court ruled that executive privilege is not absolute, but qualified. The *in camera* court inspection of the tapes that Sirica ordered, it said, would be a minimal intrusion on the President's confidential communications. The President's claim was not based on grounds of national security—that milita-

---

[49] Floyd Abrams, The New Effort to Control Information, New York Times Magazine, Sept. 25, 1983, 23; Government Shuts Up, Columbia Journalism Rev., July/Aug. 1982, 31; Executive Order No. 12356 on National Security Information, April 2, 1982, 8 Med.L.Rptr. 1306; 1984 Duke L.Journ. 377, 387, op. cit.; Anon., Reagan Signs New Secrecy Order to Seal More Public Documents, News Media & the Law, June/July 1982, 22; 8 Med.L.Rptr. # 46, 1/25/83, News Notes; Anon., Coverage Efforts Thwarted, News Media & the Law, Jan.-Feb. 1984, 6; Carl Stepp, Grenada Skirmish over Access Goes On, SPJ/SDX, Freedom of Information 84–'85, Report, 5; Steve Weinberg, Trashing the FOIA, Columbia Journalism Rev., Jan./Feb. 1985, 21, 22; Donna A. Demac, Keeping America Uninformed (N.Y., 1984).

[50] New York Times, Sept. 11, 1973, p. 36; Oct. 24, 1973, p. 1.

ry or diplomatic secrets were threatened—but only on the ground of his "generalized interest in confidentiality." That could not prevail over "the fundamental demands of due process of law in the fair administration of justice." It would have to yield to the "demonstrated, specific need for evidence in a pending criminal trial." [51]

Subsequent assertions of executive privilege by Nixon involved his post-resignation claim to custody of presidential papers from his term in office—millions of pages of documents and almost 900 tapes—and also his denial of the rights of record companies and networks to copy, sell, and broadcast tapes that had been played at one of the trials arising from Watergate. The Supreme Court ruled in one case that the government should have custody of all but Nixon's private and personal papers,[52] and in the other it granted Nixon's plea to deny networks and record companies the right to copy, sell, or broadcast the tapes.[53]

On July 24, 1979, a U.S. District Court ruled that Nixon's dictabelt "diaries" were not personal and would not be screened for use by archivists. Also, the court ruled that the public should have access to the actual tapes, instead of synopses or transcripts.[54] As of June 1980, National Archives had released 31, or about 12½ hours of conversation, of the 950 tapes, and Nixon was fighting release of another 6,000 hours.[55] Usage of the tapes is restricted: no more than 24 persons may listen at a time, for 45 to 90 minutes depending on the length of the tape played; and listeners are forbidden to make their own recordings of the tapes.[56]

Access to federal officials' papers and claims of executive privilege were active issues during the latter half of the seventies. The Nixon papers cases and the Kissinger "phone calls" case both involved dispute about ownership of executive papers. President Carter signed the Presidential Records Act of 1978, effective January 1981, which clarified ownership of executive branch papers. The National Archives assumes control of presidential papers at the end of a president's last term. Records related to defense and foreign policy, plus presidential appointment records

[51] U.S. v. Nixon, 418 U.S. 683, 684–5, 713, 94 S.Ct. 3090–3095–6, 3110 (1974).

[52] Nixon v. General Services Administrator, 433 U.S. 425, 97 S.Ct. 2777 (1977).

[53] Nixon v. Warner Communications, Inc., News Media and the Law, 1:1 (Oct. 1977), p. 14. Anon., "High Court Bars Networks' Right To Nixon Tapes," New York Times, April 19, 1978, p. 1.

[54] "Nixon Documents Litigation Reaches Court Settlement," News Media & The Law, March-April 1980, 4:2, p. 50.

[55] "Nixon Tapes Available to Public; Archives Requests More Materials," op. cit. See also, "Anyone Can Hear Nixon Tapes," Wisconsin State Journal, May 29, 1980, p. 12, sec. 1.

[56] Ibid.

involving trade secrets, may be restricted for 12 years. Papers not restricted become available to the public under the FOI Act as soon as the Archives processes them.[57]

The recorded word, in literally billions of pages of government documents, is the focus of the FOI Act, dedicated to dissemination of this record. But developments during 1979 and 1980 included two Supreme Court decisions involving "reverse-FOI Act" suits, in which persons or organizations submitting information to a federal agency sought to prevent disclosure in response to FOI Act requests.[58] In Chrysler Corp. v. Brown, the Court banned such suits under the FOI Act, stating that while exempt records could be withheld, the Act did not *require* nondisclosure.[59] However, in GTE Sylvania, Inc. v. Consumers Union, the Consumer Product Safety Act was used successfully to exempt information from release unless its accuracy is verified first.[60]

Privacy Act of 1974

"After long years of debate, a comprehensive federal privacy law passed the Congress * * * as a solid legislative decision in favor of individual privacy and the 'right to be let alone',," writes attorney James T. O'Reilly.[61] It is a statute shaped to deal with the federal government's gargantuan systems of secret dossiers on citizens, to give citizens access to the content of files that may be kept on them, and to provide citizens with a means for correcting inaccurate content of these files. If agencies are not responsive in making changes, civil suits may be brought against them. A crucial element in the law is that no file may be transferred from one agency to another without the individual's consent, except where the purpose squares with the purpose for which the information was collected.

Under the law, a supposedly exhaustive index to all federal government "data banks" or personal information systems on individuals has been published. Also published in the Federal Register are the categories of individuals on whom records are maintained, and where one can learn whether a particular govern-

---

[57] Robert Schwaller, "Access to Federal Officials' Papers," FOI Center Report No. 411, October 1979, pp. 7, 8.

[58] Madens, op. cit., p. 141.

[59] Ibid., p. 142; See also Chrysler Corp. v. Brown, 441 U.S. 281, 99 S.Ct. 1705 (1979).

[60] "Safety Data Release Depends On Who Reaches Courtroom First," News Media & The Law," Feb.-March 1981, 5:1, p. 49; GTE Sylvania, Inc. v. Consumers Union, 445 U.S. 375, 100 S.Ct. 1194 (1980); Consumers Product Safety Commission v. GTE Sylvania, Inc., 447 U.S. 102, 100 S.Ct. 2051 (1980).

[61] "The Privacy Act of 1974," Freedom of Information Report No. 342, Sept. 1975, p. 1.

ment agency has information about him.[62]   No citizen who inquires about himself need give any reason for a request to examine the record, and may obtain a copy.   Some exceptions to citizen access are provided, mostly dealing with law enforcement agencies' records, and including, notably, the CIA and the Secret Service.[63]   However, foreign nationals working for the government have no access rights to personnel records about themselves under either the FOI Act or the Privacy Act, according to a U.S. Court of Appeals.[64]

Privacy issues increased during 1977 and 1978.   Individuals made greater use of the Privacy Act to gain access to personal records maintained about them, and they used the act to amend or correct inaccuracies.[65]   States were active also in protecting privacy of financial, medical, and criminal records.[66]   However, the Reagan administration proposed in 1981 a national data bank listing names of some 25 million people on public assistance to help detect fraud, abuse, and waste in public assistance programs. The American Civil Liberties Union, calling the data bank an invasion of privacy, plans to take the matter to court.[67]

The Privacy Act's controls on the flow of personal information presents little or no conflict with the public's right to know proclaimed in the FOI Act, according to one analysis.   "The Privacy Act * * * simply does not affect the release of information that *must be released* under the FOIA.   In other words, information not exempt [from disclosure] under the FOIA * * * is still not exempt." [68]

Journalists see looming dangers to the "right to know" in the Privacy Act.   Loss of "inside" sources of information in federal

[62] Anon., "Citizens' Guide to Privacy Act Available," FOI Digest, 18:2 (March-April 1976), p. 2.   For an editor's struggle of more than a year to get a file kept on him by the FBI, see John Seigenthaler, "Publisher Finally Gets His FBI Files, or Some of Them," (Memphis) Tennessean, July 10, 1977.   False accusations of immoral conduct, the FBI said after finally releasing content of the file, would be purged.

[63] Anon., "Government Information and the Rights of Citizens," 73 Mich.L.Rev. 971, 1317.   This study of more than 370 pages describes, analyzes, and criticizes the FOI Act, state open records and meetings laws, and the Privacy Act of 1974.

[64] Raven v. Panama Canal Co., 583 F.2d 169 (5th Cir.), certiorari denied 440 U.S. 980, 99 S.Ct. 1787 (1978).   See also, "Allows Personnel Files to be Kept From Alien," News Media & The Law, March-April 1980, 4:2, p. 31.

[65] In 1977, of 1,417,214 requests, 1,355,515 were granted either entirely or in part: "Privacy Roundup: Report Shows Increasing Use of Privacy Act by Individuals," FOI Digest, July-Aug. 1978, 20:4, p. 2.

[66] "Poll Shows Privacy Concerns Rising," FOI Digest, May-June 1979, 21:3, p. 2.

[67] "National Welfare Listing Proposed," The Milwaukee Journal, April 10, 1981, p. 1.

[68] William H. Harader, "Interface of FOI and Privacy Acts," FOI Center Report # 371, May 1977, pp. 2, 4.   And see Greentree v. Customs Service, 674 F.2d 74 (D.C.Cir.1982), 8 Med.L.Rptr. 1510.

government is one, and the possibility of tracing "leaks" through the agencies' records of disseminations of files.[69] One reporter specialized in covering courts and law warns that the long partnership of journalists with civil rights lawyers may be damaged under growing privacy protection, for the lawyers "are keener on the protection of privacy."[70]

Government in the Sunshine Act

As the FOI Act of 1975 is to federal government records, so the "Sunshine Act"[71] is to federal government meetings. The Act mandates open meetings for regular sessions and quorum gatherings of approximately 50 agencies—all those headed by boards of two or more persons named by the President and confirmed by the Senate. Included are the major regulatory agencies such as the Securities Exchange Commission and the Interstate Commerce Commission—whose meetings always had been secret—and such little-known entities as the National Council on Educational Research and the National Homeownership Foundation board of directors.[72]

All meetings of the named agencies are to be open—with at least one week's public notice—unless agendas take up matters in 10 categories which permit closed sessions. Either a verbatim transcript or detailed minutes of all matters covered in closed sessions is to be kept. And as for the record of open meetings, it is to be kept as minutes and made available to the public at minimal copying cost.

Closed-to-the-public meetings will hardly be rare, whatever strength the Sunshine Act may prove to generate. The ten categories of subject-matter whose discussion warrants closed doors for meetings of the boards and commissions are much like the exemptions to disclosure under the FOI Act. Abbreviated, the ten are:[73]

1. National defense or foreign policy matters which are properly classified;

2. Internal agency personnel matters;

---

[69] O'Reilly, p. 4.

[70] Lyle Denniston, "A Citizen's Right to Privacy," Quill, 63:4, April 1975, p. 16. See also Editor & Publisher, Jan. 31, 1976, p. 9.

[71] 5 U.S.C.A. § 552b. The FOI Act and the Privacy Act of 1974 are in the federal statutes under the same number, as 5 U.S.C.A. § 552a and 5 U.S.C.A. § 552c respectively.

[72] Editor & Publisher, Feb. 26, 1977, p. 32. This account's details of the Sunshine Act are taken largely from James T. O'Reilly, "Government in the Sunshine," Freedom of Information Center Report 366, Jan. 1977.

[73] O'Reilly, p. 2.

3. Matters expressly required by law to be held confidential;

4. Confidential commercial or financial information, and trade secrets;

5. Accusations of criminal activity, or of censure, against a person;

6. Matters which if disclosed would be clearly unwarranted invasions of a person's privacy;

7. Law enforcement and criminal investigatory records, subject to the same categories as FOI Act exemption (b)(7);

8. Bank examiners' records;

9. Matters which if disclosed would generate financial speculation (included to protect the Federal Reserve Board Open Market Committee) or which would frustrate agency action which has not been announced;

10. Matters which involve the agency's issuance of a subpoena or participation in hearings or other adjudication-related proceedings.

It may prove significant that the ten exemptions of the Sunshine Act apply to the some 1,300 Advisory Committees spread throughout the Executive Branch of government. These committees of private citizens contribute expertise, advice, and recommendations to government policy making. The members tend to be prominent persons from industries which deal with the agencies they advise. By one account, the Advisory Committees have "never been more powerful than they are now."[74]

Ways exist for attacking illegal secrecy under the Sunshine Act. One may seek an injunction in advance to force a pending meeting to be open, and having found one illegal closing of an agency, a court may enjoin the agency from further illegal closings. One may sue, within 60 days after the secret meeting, to require that a transcript be furnished. No financial penalty for illegal meetings may be levied against members themselves, but courts may assign costs or fees against the United States—or against a plaintiff whose suit is found to be "dilatory or frivolous." The range of possibilities for future secrecy or openness is large, and the crystal balls of various observers offer varied forecasts of cheer and gloom.[75]

---

[74] FOI Digest, 19:1, Jan.-Feb. 1977, p. 4.

[75] Ibid., 19:2, March-April 1977, p. 1; O'Reilly, "Government in the Sunshine," pp. 4–5.

SEC. 63.   RECORDS AND MEETINGS
IN THE STATES

The extent of access in the states varies under statutes providing what shall be open and what closed in the meetings and records of executive, administrative, and legislative agencies.

Many states have laws declaring that public policy demands maximum disclosure of official business, both meetings and records. Rarely, however, is it conceded that every act or every document of officialdom must be open to public scrutiny. Every branch of government within the states performs some of its work or maintains some of its records in secret. There are situations here as in the federal government's domain which favor secrecy as protection for the individual's private rights and for government's carrying out its work. But the principle of disclosure and openness is as central to the democratic spirit at the state and local level as it is at the federal. A 1977 study found that all states had open records laws, and a 1974 study found that 48 states had open meetings laws.[76] Much of this legislation was enacted in the 1960s and 1970s.

The diversity among these statutes prohibits detailed treatment here.[77] Every reporter of government needs to know the peculiarities and special provisions of his own state's access laws. Even among those newspapers or broadcast stations that rely more on their own power than on access laws to penetrate the offices and meetings of government, ignorance of the law's provisions leaves the reporter at the mercy of officials leery of disclosure.

To start with records kept by government offices, the fact that many may be termed "public" records does not necessarily mean that they are open to inspection by the public or the press. The common law definition of "public records" referred to the need of government to preserve the documents that told of the activities of its officers. Thus the definition of public record under the com-

[76] All except Miss. and W. Va.: John B. Adams, "State Open Meetings Laws: an Overview," Freedom of Information Foundation Series No. 3, July 1974, pp. 1, 14; William Randolph Henrick, Public Inspection of State and Municipal Executive Documents, 45 Fordham L.Rev. 1105, 1106 (1977). Adams provides "model" open meetings statutes at pp. 22–29, and Henrick a model records statute at pp. 1143–50.

[77] Tables indicating presence or absence of various provisions of records and meetings laws of all the states are in Henrick, pp. 1151–53, and Adams, pp. 14–15. For a useful state-by-state digest of all states' meetings and records laws, see "Gaining Access '84," pullout section of 1985 Report of the Society of Professional Journalists, Sigma Delta Chi, Freedom of Information '84–'85; for one of records laws, see Burt Braverman and Heppler, W.R., A Practical Review of State Open Records Laws, 49 Geo.Wash.L.Rev. 720 (1981).

mon law is that it is a written memorial by an authorized public officer in discharge of a legal duty to make such a memorial to serve as evidence of something written, said, or done.[78]

In that, of course, the word "public" does not imply a general right of inspection; and in the statutes, various qualifications in the public's right to inspect "public" records exist:[79]

> Some documents which constitute public records un-
> der * * * an open records statute have been exempted
> from disclosure. These may be available to specified
> individuals [e.g., licensing examination data available on-
> ly to individual examinee, or reports of mental examina-
> tions of school children available only to their parents]
> * * *. [Also] not all state-affiliated organizations will
> meet the definition of "agency" within an open records
> act [e.g., consulting firms and quasi-public corporations
> are frequently outside the terms of an open records act.]

Statutes may define records in extensive detail, or they may do so in brief and general terms. The latter kind may be so general as to give no guide to judges, leaving them to employ, in decisions, common law definition. On the other hand, open records statutes may be specific and limiting, as Pennsylvania's which goes to documents related to state funds and money trans-actions and state property, and to actions by state agencies that affect citizens' property rights and duties. The statute has been construed to deny public record status and thus access, to person-nel files. The statute specifically excludes from public records, "any record * * * access to * * * which would operate to the prejudice or impairment of a person's reputation or personal security * * *."[80]

All the statutes acknowledge and approve the fact that cer-tain state laws specifically provide for secrecy, for example income tax laws that include clauses protecting the individual's income tax returns from disclosure. Frequent exemptions that appear in state open records statutes have much the character of the federal Freedom of Information Act exemptions (above, p. 465), such as intra- or inter-agency memoranda or preliminary draft documents, investigatory information, and trade secrets. And in addition, many exempt various health department records, juvenile and adoption records, licensing examination data, and public assis-

---

[78] Amos v. Gunn, 84 Fla. 285, 287, 94 So. 615, 616 (1922).

[79] Henrick, p. 1112. A qualified right of inspection does exist under common law: Cross, p. 35.

[80] Henrick, pp. 1114–20, includes the laws of Illinois, Michigan, Nebraska, and New York, with Pennsylvania's, as "strict" definers of public records, and the "most liberal" laws as those of Alabama, Alaska, Idaho, Iowa, Kentucky, Massa-chusetts, and Montana.

tance records,[81] lawmakers having determined that injury to individuals concerned may result from disclosure. Not seldom, journalists disagree.

While the common law right to inspect public records depends ordinarily on the citizen's having a proper purpose in seeing or copying the record, relatively few statutes speak to this. One study finds that Louisiana and Texas permit no inquiry by the keeper of the record into the applicant's motives; Michigan says that access may be had "for any lawful purpose"; and Washington prohibits its agencies from giving access to lists of persons wanted for commercial purposes.[82] Courts have held in some cases that "idle curiosity" is not a sufficient purpose for access to records, but in other cases have approved the same.[83]

Most open records laws provide legal instruments for the seeker to use in attempting to pierce denial of access. Most common is appeal to a court for an order to disclose, but administrative avenues are available in other states, including appeal to the state's attorney general, and in Connecticut and New York, appeal to a special freedom of information body. Penalties for illegal denial of access are provided in many statutes, ranging from the rare impeachment or removal from office, to the more common imprisonment and fines.[84]

Henrick finds a trend toward "liberality" developing in statutes and amendments, particularly in definitions that expand the scope of "what is a public record." As an example, he cites the California statute of 1968:[85]

> This was the first statute to encompass "all writings containing information relating to the conduct of the public's business," in its definition of public records. This is * * * the second broadest of the [states' various] definitional categories in as much as it does not require "official" or "public" business of the agency as an essential factor. Other states adopted this definition * * *.

---

[81] Ibid., pp. 1129–30.

[82] Ibid., p. 1131. See also Anon., Government Information and the Rights of Citizens, 73 Mich.L.Rev. 971, at 1179 (1975). See also, for state records in general, Ibid., pp., 1163–86.

[83] Bend Pub. Co. v. Haner, 118 Or. 105, 244 P. 868 (1926); Hardman v. Collector of Taxes of North Adams, 317 Mass. 439, 58 N.E.2d 845 (1945), both holding it insufficient; contra., State ex rel. Holloran v. McGrath, 104 Mont. 490, 67 P.2d 838 (1937). For common law and records in general, see Cross, pp. 36, 55–56, passim.

[84] Henrick, pp. 1135–36. For the New York statute providing a Freedom of Information Committee to review, see "New York's Access to Records Law," FOI Center Report # 340, Aug. 1975.

[85] Henrick, p. 1137.

In some statutes, "general exclusion" clauses permit custodians of records to refuse access if they find that opening the records would in some way damage the public interest. Then it is up to the applicant to bring an action to override the custodian's refusal. To illustrate, before Wisconsin's records statute had such a provision, the State placed a similar procedure in effect by way of state Supreme Court decision.[86] Here, city officials refused to release to the *Waukesha Freeman* a report that concerned alleged mistreatment of citizens by police. In the first reported case brought by a newspaper to force access to Wisconsin government records, the *Freeman* obtained a court order requiring the release of the report under the state records law, and the city appealed to the State Supreme Court. The high court, in a preliminary decision, ordered the Circuit Court to read the secret document before deciding whether it should be made public. The Circuit Judge read it and again ordered that it be made public. Once more the city appealed, and the State Supreme Court in 1965 upheld the Circuit Court's order.

The Supreme Court of Wisconsin placed real responsibility upon the officer withholding documents, in determining whether a request to disclose would be proper:[87]

> The duty of first determining that the harmful effect upon the public interest of permitting inspection outweighs the benefit to be gained by granting inspection rests upon the public officer having custody of the record or document sought to be inspected. If he determines that permitting inspection would result in harm to the public interest which outweighs any benefit that would result from granting inspection, it is incumbent upon him to refuse the demand for inspection and state specifically the reasons for this refusal.

And once the officer states the reasons for the refusal, if the person seeking inspection takes the action to court, then the trial court has responsibilities:[88]

> * * * the proper procedure is for the trial judge to examine *in camera* the record or document sought to be inspected. Upon making such *in camera* examination, the trial judge should then make his determination of whether or not the harm likely to result to the public interest by permitting the inspection outweighs the benefit to be gained by granting inspection.

---

[86] State ex rel. Youmans v. Owens, 28 Wis.2d 672, 137 N.W.2d 470 (1965).

[87] Ibid., 682. See also Beckon v. Emery, 36 Wis.2d 510, 153 N.W.2d 501 (1967).

[88] State ex rel. Youmans v. Owens, 28 Wis.2d 672, 682–83, 137 N.W.2d 470 (1965).

In reaching a determination so based upon a balancing of the interests involved, the trial judge must ever bear in mind that public policy favors the right of inspection of public records and documents, and, it is only in the exceptional case that inspection should be denied.

Access to certain personnel records, under the widespread recognition of claims to "privacy," was denied the Gannett Company under New York's Public Officers Law # 85, its "Freedom of Information Law." Gannett wanted the names, titles and salaries of 276 Monroe County employees laid off as the result of budget cuts in early 1977.[89] The county's regulations provided that each of its agencies should make such information on "every officer or employee" available to news media. The court held that the 276 discharged persons were no longer public "employees," but private citizens. The state FOI Law specifically provides that its command to release information should not apply to information that is "an unwarranted invasion of personal privacy," the court pointed out, and the discharged people feared that their chances for new jobs would be harmed by announcing their discharge. The court denied Gannett's request, saying the invasions of privacy and the "resultant economic or personal hardships" from disclosure were obvious.

The rules of states and municipalities about disclosure of police records vary widely. The most exhaustive study of the general picture of access—that by the late Harold L. Cross—found that press and public have no enforceable legal right to inspect police records, "using that term broadly, as such, as a whole, or without exceptions."[90] Unless statutes provide specifically for access to investigatory, arrest, and law enforcement records of police, there is long precedent for denying access to this most-requested of all classes of records.[91] Developing friendships and good working relations with police is probably as valuable an avenue to their records, for reporters, as relying on statutes about access.

The power of state law to overrule local ordinances is illustrated in State v. Mayo.[92] Here the city of Hartford, Conn., had exercised its local option powers to pass its own building code, instead of adopting the state code. Part of the Hartford code

---

[89] Gannett Co. v. Monroe County, 90 Misc.2d 76, 393 N.Y.S.2d 676, 678 (1977). Not all personnel records in all jurisdictions are closed: News-Press Pub. Co. v. Wisher, 345 So.2d 646 (Fla.1977); Ayers v. Lee Enterprises, 277 Or. 527, 561 P.2d 998 (1977).

[90] Cross, Ch. 8 and p. 118.

[91] Anon., "Access to Police Blotters and Reports," Freedom of Information Center Report # 27, Jan. 1969 (mimeo).

[92] 4 Conn.Cir. 511, 236 A.2d 342 (1967).

provided that documents in support of applications for building permits were not public records. Two state agencies dealing with engineering and architecture wanted to review the documents, but Glendon R. Mayo, Hartford's Director of Licenses and Inspections, refused to disclose them on the basis of the city code. The state petitioned for a disclosure order, and won it. The court held that the Connecticut "right to know" statute should be construed broadly. The "exception" clauses of the statute did not cover the documents in question, it said, and no city ordinance in conflict with a state statute can stand, since the city's powers to legislate are conferred by the state.

In turning from laws on state government records to laws on meetings of executive/administrative and legislative bodies, the diversity of provisions from state to state is no less than with records. The publications of the University of Missouri Freedom of Information Center are of first importance to obtaining an understanding of the laws of 50 states. Adams, Higginbotham, and Thompson spread wide nets to capture similarities and differences among the statutes or decisions as they stood in the mid-1970s, and their accounts are central to this discussion.[93]

As of 1977, Keefe found that all states had open meetings laws,[94] many of them adopted in the 1970s and many others under state legislatures' ongoing scrutiny for possible change. Adams studied all meetings laws and ranked them on a scale reaching from maximum to minimum openness. Taking maximum openness to be desirable in a democracy, he identified 11 characteristics that would go into an "ideal" open meetings law, as follows:[95]

(1) Include a statement of public policy in support of openness.

(2) Provide for an open legislature.

(3) Provide for open legislative committees.

(4) Provide for open meetings of state agencies or bodies.

(5) Provide for open meetings of state agencies and bodies of the political subdivisions of the state.

(6) Provide for open County boards.

(7) Provide for open city councils (or their equivalent).

(8) Forbid closed executive sessions.

---

[93] Adams, op. cit.; Robert Higginbotham, "The Case Law of Open Meetings Laws," Freedom of Information [FOI] Center Report No. 354, May 1976; William Thompson, "FOI and State Attorneys General," Ibid., No. 307, July 1973. See also Jack Clarke, "Open Meeting Laws: an Analysis," Ibid., No. 338, June 1975.

[94] Pat Keefe, "State Open Meetings Activity," FOI Center Report # 378, Sept. 1977, p. 7.

[95] Adams, p. 4.

(9) Provide legal recourse to halt secrecy.

(10) Declare actions taken in meetings which violate the law to be null and void.

(11) Provide for penalties for those who violate the law.

A single state—Tennessee—scored the maximum of 11 points on Adams' scale, while three—Arizona, Colorado, and Kentucky—each scored 10, lacking in each instance a provision that would forbid closed executive sessions. Florida, the state which perhaps originated the term "Sunshine Law" as a popular name for open meetings acts, and which is perhaps the best-known to journalists as a model of openness, actually scored no more than "good" on the Adams scale—8. Major gaps in its law are those notable in many states: there is no provision for open legislative or legislative committee meetings. Here, of course, the legislative will is at work, permitting secrecy for itself (as in about half the states), forbidding it for others.[96]

Of all the 11 provisions, those which most states include are 4 through 7, those applying to state agencies and political subdivisions of states including county boards and city councils. Frequently, Adams found, exceptions were made for judicial and quasi-judicial bodies. The rarest of all provisions, on the other end of the spectrum, is the forbidding of closed executive sessions of some or all agencies, found only in the states of Colorado, Florida, Maine, Minnesota, North Dakota, and Tennessee. Adams notes, however, that in 15 states, *final* action may not be taken in executive sessions.

A 1984 study covering all state "sunshine" laws was conducted by the Hubert H. Humphrey Public Affairs Institute at the University of Minnesota. Using 23 indicators of "openness," it found that Tennessee (21), Florida (20), and Alabama (19) were most open, and Pennsylvania (4), Idaho, Wisconsin, and Wyoming—all at 8—were least open.[97]

A survey of state press associations in 1980 showed that state sunshine struggles continued. Nearly every state complained of annual attempts by groups to exempt themselves from open meetings and open records laws. However, in 24 states, there were no current attempts to weaken the laws and no media attempts to strengthen them. Many states passed or amended their laws to be more specific in what types of meetings were covered.[98] However, some laws were mixed blessing. Pennsylvania, for instance, passed a stronger open meetings law, but two amendments—

[96] Ibid., pp. 14–15.

[97] Anon., Trustees' Group Weighs Plan to Press for Closed Meetings, Chronicle of Higher Education, Oct. 10, 1984, 18.

[98] "States' Sunshine Struggle Continues," FOI Digest, Nov.-Dec. 1980, 22:6, p. 6.

requiring newspapers to publish legal notices free and to give corrections and retractions the same play and same type as the original erroneous articles—were deemed "unpalatable" to the press.[99]

Newspapers and news groups have opposed a proposal by the American Bar Association for a model state law governing access. The Uniform Information Practices Code would shield from disclosure many records already routinely available to the public. In the case of "individually identifiable" documents, the record would be presumed to be exempt from disclosure unless the person requesting disclosure showed that "the public interest in disclosure outweighs the privacy interest of the individual" named in the record. Thus, the standard for disclosure would be the public interest, not the special need of the individual requesting disclosure. Reporters Committee for Freedom of the Press told ABA's Board of Governors the act amounted to a "government secrecy act."[1]

A noteworthy feature of these laws is that they stimulate few news media to bring actions against alleged offenders. Higginbotham noted that "comparative dearth of cases involving the media" in his study of legal actions in eight of the 16 states Adams rates most open.[2] News media usually leave the instrument of legal actions for forcing admission, to other agencies and persons. The latter, of course, seldom have immediate access to the levers of publicity that media have at instant command: publicizing in columns or broadcasts the fact of closed meetings, cultivating sources who will talk on condition their names are not given in news stories, editorializing against those who apparently offend, and carrying a copy of the state open-meeting statute at all times, to show to door-closers.

The scaling of state statutes performed by Adams assigns equal weight to each of the 11 desirable characteristics. It is of course likely that some should outweigh the others in importance; but in the laws' and decisions' present state, it would be difficult indeed to suggest that number 1 is more important than, say, number 6, or 11 more important than 9. Number 11 was long absent from most laws; its absence was widely thought to render the laws "toothless" and a matter of no concern to those who wanted closed meetings, and its addition was much sought in states without it. Yet a high incidence of cases under Arkansas' 1968 open meetings law has taken place despite the presence of

[99] Ibid. See also, "Courts Rebuke Federal Agencies for Skirting Sunshine Act," FOI Digest, Nov.-Dec.1980, 22:6, p. 4.

[1] "Press Groups Challenge Model Law on Records Access at ABA Convention," FOI Digest, Jan.-Feb.1981, 23:1, p. 1.

[2] Higginbotham, p. 9.

number 11. And Florida, whose law includes number 11, according to the Higginbotham study "has perhaps the most extensive record of litigation of any state considered in this report."[3] Plainly, secret meetings are not ended because those who are responsible for the secrecy may be penalized for violation.

After reviewing the Arkansas cases, Higginbotham concludes they reveal "that a statute may seem to be weak or strong on its face," but the crucial fact is that the "interpretation of the statute by the courts can add or detract and cure an apparent weakness or hopelessly cripple an otherwise strong statute."[4] He illustrated with Arkansas Gazette Co. v. Pickens,[5] which he says "shows that a court's interpretation can read a word into the statute that the legislature did not put there." Here, a board of trustees committee of the University of Arkansas had met with university legal counsel and executives on the matter of possessing or using alcoholic beverages on university property. It asked a Gazette reporter to leave the meeting. The Gazette took the action to court under the state Freedom of Information Law, and the trial court ruled that since the definition section of the act did not include committees or other subdivisions of governing bodies, the committees were not subject to the act's requirement of openness. But the State Supreme Court overturned the decision, saying it attached "no particular significance to the fact that the word 'committees' is not specifically enumerated" in the law itself. It elaborated:[6]

> * * * it was the intent of the legislature, as so emphatically set forth in its statement of policy, that *"public business* be performed in an open and public manner. * * * it appears to us somewhat incongruous that a parent body cannot go into executive session * * * but its component parts (the committees) which actually investigate the complaints, and act on those complaints by making recommendations to the board, are at liberty to bar the public from their deliberations. Surely a part (of a board) is not possessed of a prerogative greater than the whole.

Higginbotham concluded, on the basis of his study of the eight states, that the courts' refusal to permit attempted evasions of the state freedom of information laws "was the predominant pattern," although some cases clearly illustrated successful evading methods.[7]

[3] Ibid., pp. 4–7.

[4] Ibid., p. 4.

[5] 258 Ark. 69, 522 S.W.2d 350 (1975).

[6] Ibid., at 353–4.

[7] Higginbotham, p. 9.

Attorneys general have been called on to interpret meetings and records laws in many states. As for meetings, it is occasionally feasible for a reporter to seek "instant action" in the form of an attorney general's opinion even while a secret meeting is in session, and through such an opinion, force a meeting open. More likely, however, before an opinion can be had, the meeting will have adjourned. Nevertheless, either a formal opinion delivered at the request of a state government agency, or an informal one delivered at the request of a non-official person or entity—such as a reporter or newspaper—can have future impact on the behavior of the sequestering committee or group. For many reasons, "The opinions of an attorney general are followed by their recipients."[8] The attorney general interprets the law of a state; his opinion does not carry the force of a court opinion, of course, but it is authoritative until a court has passed on the question.

A study of more than 250 attorneys general opinions in "right to know" cases of all states, covering the years 1930 to 1970, found that 43 concerned meetings and 216 concerned records. About 80% of the opinions on meetings favored openness, as did about 55% of those on records—for a total score of 59.8% favoring openness and 40.2% secrecy.[9] The governmental subject-matter that most often won the attorneys general ruling in favor of secrecy was predictably public safety—generally, law enforcement, in which only 26% of the opinions supported access. At the other end of the scale, where the subject-matter was education, 70% of the opinions ruled for openness. Between were welfare (45% for openness) and health (43%). The attorney general of a state, of course, is often centrally involved with the police and is especially sensitized to the secrecy employed in investigating criminal activity.

Thompson points out that law enforcement and health and welfare often involve personal records of individuals, and that here principles and notions of privacy may forestall access. He found that among the opinions that specifically went to records of individuals, 42% held for openness, while of all other cases, 68% did.[10]

Other findings of Thompson:

• Over time, the ratio of attorneys general rulings on the side of granting access has increased: before 1950, 47%; decade of the 1950s, 61%; decade of the 1960s, 67%.

• Characteristics of attorneys general that seem to be indicators of how they will rule: *age,* with the youngest attorneys

[8] Thompson, p. 1.

[9] Ibid., pp. 1, 10.

[10] Ibid., pp. 10–12.

general (under 35) the most likely to support access; *tenure in office,* with those in office longer less likely to support access; *political party,* with no difference between Democrats and Republicans; *political ambition,* with more support for access among those attorneys general who retired from politics without seeking other office after they served as attorneys general, than from those who sought other offices.

The news medium that wants legal action on an agency's proposal to close a government meeting, or on one in session, may find a court order far too slow to meet the needs of the moment. As an alternative, it may wish to consider getting an attorney general's opinion, which may or may not come down on the side of opening the meeting but which in any event should give guidance for the future.

SEC. 64.   ACCESS TO JUDICIAL PROCEEDINGS

The problems of obtaining access to judicial proceedings present questions substantially different from those of access to legislative and executive/administrative activities, and are taken up in the next chapter, devoted to reporting the courts and the legal questions involved.

Chapter 11

LEGAL PROBLEMS IN REPORTING COURTS

Sec.

65. Free Press *Versus* Fair Trial.
66. Pre-Trial Publicity.
67. Publicity During Trial: Cameras in the Courtroom.
68. Publicity Before and During Trial.
69. The Judge's Role.
70. External Guidelines and Self-Regulatory Efforts.
71. Restrictive Orders and Reporting the Judicial Process.
72. Closing Pre-Trial Hearings, Opening Trials.

SEC. 65. FREE PRESS *VERSUS* FAIR TRIAL

Attorneys, judges and members of the press continue to try to settle long-standing issues in the "free press—fair trial" dispute.

Like death and taxes, controversy over journalistic coverage of the judicial process never seems to go away. Perhaps conflict is guaranteed by tensions between the First and Sixth Amendments to the Constitution of the United States. The First Amendment says that Congress (and by extension, state and local governments) shall make no law abridging freedom of the press. The Sixth Amendment declares that "in all criminal prosecutions, the accused shall enjoy the right to a speedy and public trial by an impartial jury * * *."

These two constitutional provisions outline a continuing dispute between the news media and the judiciary. This dispute—the "free press-fair trial" problem—has a lengthy and nasty history in this country, and heated up remarkably in 1979 and 1980. At issue in the cases of Gannett v. DePasquale (1979)[1] and Richmond Newspapers, Inc. v. Virginia (1980)[2] was the question of the basic right to report on the criminal justice process.

Back in the 1960s, "trial by newspaper" or "trial by mass media" were phrases which were often heard as the bar-press controversy steamed up. Some attorneys blamed the mass media for many of the shortcomings of the American court system.[3] In

---

[1] 443 U.S. 368, 99 S.Ct. 2898 (1979).

[2] 448 U.S. 555, 100 S.Ct. 2814 (1980).

[3] See, e.g., Advisory Committee on Fair Trial and Free Press, Standards Relating to Fair Trial and Free Press (New York, 1966); see also draft approved Feb. 19,

reply, many journalists went to great lengths in trying to justify questionable actions of the news media in covering criminal trials.[4]

Many of the lawyers' arguments contained the assertion that the media were destroying the rights of defendants by publicizing cases before they got to court.[5] Such publicity, it was said, prejudiced potential jurors to such an extent that a fair trial was not possible. Editors and publishers—and some attorneys, too— retorted that the media were not harmful, and contended that the First Amendment's free press guarantees took precedence over other Constitutional provisions, including the Sixth Amendment.[6]

What about prejudicing jurors by media accounts? More than 100 years ago, Mark Twain questioned whether an impartial—in the sense of know-nothing—jury was not a perversion of justice. He wrote that the first 26 graves in Virginia City, Nevada, were occupied by murdered men, and their murderers were never punished. Why? Let Mark Twain tell it.

Twain asserted that when Alfred the Great invented trial by jury, news could not travel fast. Therefore, he could easily find a jury of honest, intelligent men who had not heard of the case they were to try. But in Twain's day—with newspapers and the telegraph—the jury system "compels us to swear in juries composed of fools and rascals, because the system rigidly excludes honest men and men of brains." Twain wrote about a trial in 19th Century Nevada: [7]

> When the peremptory challenges were all exhausted, a jury of twelve men was empanelled—a jury who swore they had neither heard, read, talked about, nor expressed an opinion concerning a murder which the very cattle in the corrals, the Indians in the sagebrush, and the stones in the streets were cognizant of! It was a jury composed of two desperadoes, two low beerhouse politicians, three barkeepers, two ranchmen who could not read, and three dull, stupid human donkeys! It actually came out afterward that one of these latter thought that incest and arson were the same thing.

1968, by delegates to the American Bar Association convention as published in March, 1968.

[4] See, e.g., American Newspaper Publishers Association, Free Press and Fair Trial (New York): American Newspaper Publishers Association, 1967, p. 1 and passim.

[5] See footnote 3, above.

[6] American Newspaper Publishers Association, op. cit., p. 1.

[7] Mark Twain, Roughing It (New York: New American Library, Signet Paperback, 1962) pp. 256–257.

Actually, Mark Twain had the history of the jury system a bit wrong. The jury began in 11th Century England, utilizing a defendant's neighbors who were called to serve as both witnesses and as arbiters of fact. It was not until several centuries later that juries stopped serving as witnesses and served only as triers of fact. In addition, Twain's 19th Century exaggeration does not apply to jury selection procedures in the last quarter of the 20th Century. Jurors need not be absolutely ignorant of—or completely unbiased about—a case which is to go to trial. If jurors can set aside their prejudices and biases, and keep an open mind, that is sufficient.[8]

During the past four decades, the free press-fair trial controversy took place against a backdrop of several sensational, nationally publicized trials and the assassinations of President John F. Kennedy in 1963 and Senator Robert Kennedy and Martin Luther King in 1968. Resultant disputes arrayed the media's right to report against defendants' rights to a fair trial, generated new law in the form of several important Supreme Court decisions, and brought forth efforts to make rules to regularize dealings between the media and law enforcement officials.[9]

The assassination of President Kennedy brought problems of "trial by mass media" dramatically to public consciousness. That fact was underscored by the report of a Presidential Commission headed by Chief Justice Earl Warren. The Warren Commission was intensely critical of both the Dallas police and the news media for the reports of the news of that event. The accused assassin, Lee Harvey Oswald, never lived to stand trial, because he himself was assassinated by Jack Ruby in a hallway of Dallas police headquarters. The hallway was a scene of confusion, clogged with reporters, cameramen, and the curious.[10]

The month after Kennedy's slaying, the American Bar Association charged that "widespread publicizing of Lee Harvey Oswald's alleged guilt, involving statements by officials and public disclosures of the details of 'evidence' would have made it extremely difficult to impanel an unprejudiced jury and afford the accused a fair trial." [11] Indeed, had Oswald survived to stand trial, he might not have been convicted. This was so even though the

---

[8] Rita J. Simon, The Jury: Its Role in American Society (Lexington, Mass. D.C. Health and Company, 1980), p. 5; Murphy v. Florida, 421 U.S. 794, 95 S.Ct. 2031 (1975).

[9] See Advisory Committee on Fair Trial and Free Press, op. cit., passim; see also Irvin v. Dowd, 366 U.S. 717, 81 S.Ct. 1639 (1961); Rideau v. Louisiana, 373 U.S. 723, 83 S.Ct. 1417 (1963); Sheppard v. Maxwell, 384 U.S. 333, 86 S.Ct. 1507 (1966).

[10] Report of the President's Commission on the Assassination of President John F. Kennedy (Washington: Government Printing Office, 1964), p. 241.

[11] William A. Hachten, The Supreme Court on Freedom of the Press: Decisions and Dissents (Ames, Iowa: Iowa State University Press, 1968), p. 106.

Warren Commission—after the fact—declared that Oswald was in all likelihood Kennedy's killer. Under American judicial procedures, it seems possible that Oswald could not have received a fair and unprejudiced trial, and that any conviction of him might have been upset on appeal.[12]

The Warren Commission placed first blame on police and prosecutors, but additionally criticized the media for their part in the events following the President's death. The Commission said that "part of the responsibility for the unfortunate circumstances following the President's death must be borne by the news media * * *." Journalists were excoriated by Commission members for showing a lack of self-discipline, and a code of professional conduct was called for as evidence that the press was willing to support the Sixth Amendment right to a fair and impartial trial as well as the right of the public to be informed.[13]

If the reporters behaved badly in Dallas, so did the Dallas law enforcement officials, who displayed "evidence" in crowded corridors and released statements about other evidence. Conduct of police and other law enforcement officials, however, has by no means been the only source of prejudicial materials which later appeared in the press to the detriment of defendants' rights. All too often, both defense and prosecution attorneys have released statements to reporters which were clearly at odds with the American Bar Association's Canons of Professional Ethics. Canon 20, adopted more than 50 years ago, advised lawyers to avoid statements to the press which might prejudice the administration of justice or interfere with a fair trial. In any case, lawyers were not to go beyond quotation from the records and papers on file in courts in making statements about litigation.[14]

Canon 20, in theory, could be used as a weapon to punish lawyers who released statements to the press which harmed a defendant's chances for a fair trial. Although this Canon was adopted by the bar associations of most states, there was rarely a case brought to disbar or discipline an attorney or judge who made prejudicial remarks to the press.[15]

The ABA's Code of Professional Responsibility—which has superseded the old ABA Canons—outlines standards of trial conduct for attorneys. Disciplinary Rule DR 7–107 deals with "Trial Publicity." It says that lawyers who are involved in a criminal

[12] Ibid.

[13] Report of the President's Commission on the Assassination of President John F. Kennedy, p. 241.

[14] Canons of Professional and Judicial Ethics of the American Bar Association, Canon 20.

[15] Donald M. Gillmor, Free Press and Fair Trial (Washington, D.C., Public Affairs Press, 1966) p. 110.

matter shall not make "extra-judicial statements" to the news media which go beyond unadorned factual statements including.[16]

(1) Information contained in the public record.

(2) That the investigation is in progress.

(3) The general scope of the investigation including a description of the offense and, if permitted by law, the identity of the victim.

(4) A request for assistance in apprehending a suspect or assistance in other matters and the information necessary thereto.

(5) A warning to the public of any dangers.

Reporters are not the only offenders in disrupting trials. A quick skimming of the General Index of a legal encyclopedia, *American Jurisprudence,* adds support for such a generalization. The General Index of "Amjur" contains nearly 1,000 categories under the topic, "New Trial." New trials may be granted because something went awry in the original trial, somehow depriving a defendant of the right to a fair trial under the Sixth Amendment. These categories include such things as persons fainting in the courtroom, hissing, technical mistakes by attorneys, prejudice of judges, and misconduct by jurors: jurors who read newspapers.[17]

Findings of social scientists lend some support to assumptions about jurors being prejudiced by the mass media.[18] Much more research, however, remains to be done before assertions can be made confidently that what a juror reads or learns from the mass media will affect the juror's subsequent behavior. On the other hand, it has been argued that lawyers, before casting aspersions at the press, might consider the question of whether their own legal house is in order. Consider what psychologists can tell lawyers about a fair trial. Consider the rules of procedure in a criminal trial in many states as attorneys make their final arguments to a jury. First, the prosecution sums up its case. Then the defense attorney makes the final argument. And last, the prosecuting attorney makes the final statement to the jury. For years, psychologists have been arguing about order of presentation in persuasion. Some evidence has been found that having the first say is most persuasive; there is other evidence that having the last

[16] American Bar Association, Code of Professional Responsibility and Code of Judicial Conduct (Chicago, ABA, 1976) p. 37C.

[17] 3 Am.Jur., Gen.Index, New Trial.

[18] See, e.g., Mary Dee Tans and Steven H. Chaffee, "Pretrial Publicity and Juror Prejudice," Journalism Quarterly Vol. 43:4 (Winter, 1966) pp. 647–654, and a list of juror prejudice studies on p. 647, notes 4, 5 and 6.

word might be best.[19] But in many jurisdictions, who gets neither
the first say nor the last word during the final arguments before a
jury? The defendant.[20]

SEC. 66. PRE-TRIAL PUBLICITY

**Pre-trial publicity which makes it difficult—if not impossi-
ble—for a defendant to receive a fair trial was summed
up in the Supreme Court cases of Irvin v. Dowd (1961)
and Rideau v. Louisiana (1963).**

"Pre-trial publicity" is a phrase which is a kind of shorthand
expression meaning strain between the press and the courts. The
kind of publicity which "tries" a defendant in print or over the air
before the real courthouse trial starts—that's the issue here. This
section discusses two classic instances of pre-trial publicity, instances in which the news media did not cover themselves with
glory: Irvin v. Dowd and Rideau v. Louisiana.

Irvin v. Dowd (1961)

The Irvin case presents the first time that the Supreme Court
overturned a state criminal conviction because publicity before the
trial had prevented a fair trial before an impartial jury.[21]

The defendant in this murder case, Leslie Irvin, was subjected
to a barrage of prejudicial news items in the hysterical wake of six
murders which had been committed in the vicinity of Evansville,
Indiana. Two of the murders were committed in December, 1954,
and four in March, 1955. These crimes were covered extensively
by news media in the locality, and created great agitation in
Vanderburgh County, where Evansville is located, and in adjoining Gibson County.[22]

Leslie Irvin, a parolee, was arrested in April, 1955, on suspicion of burglary and writing bad checks. Within a few days, the
Evansville police and the Vanderburgh County prosecutor issued
press releases asserting that "Mad Dog Irvin" had confessed to all
six murders, including three members of one family. The news
media had what can conservatively be described as a field day
with the Irvin case, and were aided in this by law enforcement
officials. Many of the accounts published or broadcast before
Irvin's trial referred to him as the "confessed slayer of six."

---

[19] See, e.g., Carl I. Hovland, et al., The Order of Presentation in Persuasion, (New
Haven: Yale, 1957) passim.

[20] The authors are grateful to Professors Jack M. McLeod and Steven H. Chaffee,
of the University of Wisconsin Mass Communications Research Center for this
insight.

[21] Gillmor, op. cit., pp. 116–117.

[22] Irvin v. Dowd, 366 U.S. 717, 719, 81 S.Ct. 1639, 1641 (1961).

Irvin's court-appointed attorney was quoted as saying he had received much criticism for representing Irvin. The media, by way of excusing the attorney, noted that he faced disbarment if he refused to represent the suspect.[23]

Irvin was soon indicted by the Vanderburgh County Grand Jury for one of the six murders. Irvin's court-appointed counsel sought—and was granted—a change of venue. However, the venue change was made only from Vanderburgh County to adjoining Gibson County, which had received similar prejudicial accounts about "Mad Dog Irvin" from the news media in the Evansville vicinity. Irvin's attorney then sought to have the trial removed from Gibson County to a location which had not received such widespread and inflammatory publicity. This motion was denied on grounds that Indiana law allowed only one change of venue.[24]

The trial began in November of 1955. Of 430 prospective jurors examined by the prosecution and defense attorneys, 370—nearly 90 per cent—had formed some opinion about Irvin's guilt. These opinions ranged from mere suspicion to absolute certainty.[25] Irvin's attorney had used up all of his 20 peremptory challenges. When 12 jurors were finally seated by the court, the attorney then unsuccessfully challenged all jurors on grounds that they were biased. He complained bitterly that four of the seated jurors had stated that Irvin was guilty.[26] Even so, the trial was held, Irvin was found guilty, and the jury sentenced him to death. Irvin's conviction was upheld by the Indiana Supreme Court, which denied his motions for a new trial.[27] Protracted appeals brought Irvin's case to the Supreme Court of the United States twice,[28] but his case was not decided on its merits by the nation's highest court until 1961.

Then, in 1961, all nine members of the Supreme Court agreed that Irvin had not received a fair trial. The upshot of this was that Irvin received a new trial, although he was ultimately con-

---

[23] 366 U.S. 717, 725–726, 81 S.Ct. 1639, 1641, 1645 (1961); Gillmor, op. cit., p. 11.

[24] 366 U.S. 717, 720, 81 S.Ct. 1639, 1641 (1961).

[25] 366 U.S. 717, 727, 81 S.Ct. 1639, 1945 (1961).

[26] 359 U.S. 394, 398, 79 S.Ct. 825, 828 (1959).

[27] 236 Ind. 384, 139 N.E.2d 898 (1957).

[28] Irvin's appeal for a writ of *habeas corpus* to a Federal District Court was denied on the basis that he had not exhausted his opportunities to appeal through the Indiana courts. 153 F.Supp. 531 (D.C.Ind.1957). A United States Court of Appeals affirmed the dismissal of the writ, 251 F.2d 548 (7th Cir.1958). In a 5–4 decision in 1959, the Supreme Court of the United States sent Irvin's case back to the Federal Court of Appeals for reconsideration. 359 U.S. 394, 79 S.Ct. 825 (1959). The Court of Appeals again refused to grant a writ of *habeas corpus* to Irvin, 271 F.2d 552 (7th Cir.1959). Irvin's case was then appealed to the Supreme Court for the second time.

victed. This time, however, his sentence was set at life imprisonment.[29]

In his majority opinion, Justice Tom C. Clark—a former attorney general of the United States—concentrated on the effect of prejudicial publicity on a defendant's rights. Clark noted that courts do not require that jurors be totally ignorant of the facts and issues involved in a criminal trial. It is sufficient if a juror can render a verdict based on the evidence presented in court.[30]

Justice Clark then considered the publicity Irvin had received, and concluded: "Here the build-up of prejudice is clear and convincing." He noted that arguments for Irvin presented evidence that "a barrage of newspaper headlines, articles, cartoons and pictures was unleashed against him during the six or seven months before his trial" in Gibson County, Indiana. Furthermore, that evidence indicated that the newspapers in which the stories appeared were delivered regularly to 95 per cent of the residences in that county. Furthermore, "Evansville radio and TV stations, which likewise blanketed the county, also carried extensive newscasts covering the same incidents."

After noting the difficulty in finding impartial jurors, Justice Clark emphasized that eight of the 12 jurors finally placed in the jury box believed Irvin to be guilty. One juror announced that he "could not * * * give the defendant the benefit of the doubt that he is innocent." Another said that he had " 'somewhat' certain fixed opinions about Irvin's guilt." [31]

In a concurring opinion, Justice Frankfurter unleashed a bitter denunciation of "trial by newspapers instead of trial in court before a jury." He stated that the Irvin case was not an isolated incident or an atypical miscarriage of justice. Frankfurter wrote: [32]

> Not a term passes without this Court being importuned to review convictions, had in State throughout the country, in which substantial claims are made that a jury trial has been distorted because of inflammatory newspaper accounts—too often, as in this case, with the prosecutor's collaboration—exerting pressures upon potential jurors before trial and even during the course of trial * * *.
>
> * * *
>
> This Court has not yet decided that the fair administration of criminal justice must be subordinated to anoth-

[29] Gillmor, op. cit., pp. 11–12.

[30] Irvin v. Dowd, 366 U.S. 717, 723, 81 S.Ct. 1639, 1642–1643 (1961).

[31] 366 U.S. 717, 728, 81 S.Ct. 1939, 1645 (1961).

[32] 366 U.S. 717, 730, 81 S.Ct. 1639, 1646–1647 (1961).

er safeguard of our constitutional system—freedom of the press, properly conceived. The Court has not yet decided that, while convictions must be reversed and miscarriages of justice result because the minds of jurors were poisoned, the poisoner is constitutionally protected in plying his trade.

Trial by Television: Rideau v. Louisiana (1963)

If Leslie Irvin was mistreated primarily by newspapers during the period before his trial, Wilbert Rideau found that television was the major offender in interfering with his right to a fair trial. Early in 1961, a Lake Charles, La., bank was robbed. The robber kidnaped three of the bank's employees and killed one of them. Several hours later, Wilbert Rideau was arrested by police and held in the Calcasieu Parish jail in Lake Charles. The next morning, a moving picture film—complete with a sound track— was made of a 20-minute "interview" between Rideau and the Sheriff of Calcasieu Parish. The Sheriff interrogated the prisoner and elicited admissions that Rideau had committed the bank robbery, the kidnaping, and the murder. Later in the day, this filmed interview was broadcast over television station KLPC in Lake Charles. Over three days' time, the film was televised on three occasions to an estimated total audience of 97,000 persons, as compared to the approximately 150,000 persons then living in Calcasieu Parish.[33]

Rideau's attorneys subsequently sought a change of venue away from Calcasieu Parish. It was argued that it would take away Rideau's right to a fair trial if he were tried there after the three television broadcasts of Rideau's "interview" with the sheriff. The motion for change of venue was denied, and Rideau was convicted and sentenced to death on the murder charge in the Calcasieu Parish trial court. The conviction was affirmed by the Louisiana Supreme Court,[34] but the Supreme Court of the United States granted *certiorari*.[35]

Justice Potter Stewart's majority opinion noted that three of the 12 jurors had stated during *voir dire* examination before the trial that they had seen and heard Rideau's "interview" with the Sheriff. Also, two members of the jury were Calcasieu Parish deputy sheriffs. Although Rideau's attorney challenged the deputies, asking that they be removed "for cause," the trial judge denied this request. Since Rideau's lawyers had exhausted his

[33] Rideau v. Louisiana, 373 U.S. 723, 724, 83 S.Ct. 1417, 1419 (1963).

[34] 242 La. 431, 137 So.2d 283 (1962).

[35] 371 U.S. 919, 83 S.Ct. 294 (1962).

"peremptory challenges"—those for which no reason need be given—the deputies remained on the jury.[36]

Justice Stewart noted that the *Rideau* case did not involve physical brutality. However, he declared that the "kangaroo court proceedings in this case involved a more subtle but no less real deprivation of due process of law." Justice Stewart added: [37]

> Under our Constitution's guarantee of due process, a person accused of committing a crime is vouchsafed basic minimal rights. Among these are the right to counsel, the right to plead not guilty, and the right to be tried in a courtroom presided over by a judge. Yet in this case the people of Calcasieu Parish saw and heard, not once but three times, a "trial" of Rideau in a jail, presided over by a sheriff, where there was no lawyer to advise Rideau of his right to stand mute.

Rideau's conviction was reversed, and a new trial was ordered by the Supreme Court.

SEC. 67. PUBLICITY DURING TRIAL: CAMERAS IN THE COURTROOM

The notorious Lindbergh kidnaping trial of the 1930s and the Estes case of 1965 severely limited still and television cameras in the courtroom. Cameras are returning now in some states, under the Supreme Court's 1981 decision in Chandler v. Florida.

"The Lindbergh Case" and "the trial of Bruno Hauptmann" are phrases heard whenever the free press—fair trial debate heats up. These phrases, of course, refer to the kidnaping in 1932 of the 19-month-old son of the aviator famed for the first solo crossing of the Atlantic. The child's kidnaping was front-page news for weeks, long after the child's body was found in a shallow grave not far from the Lindbergh home in New Jersey.

More than two years later, in September, 1934, Bruno Richard Hauptmann was arrested. His trial for the kidnap-murder of the Lindbergh child did not begin until January, 1935. The courtroom where Hauptmann was tried had a press section jammed with 150 reporters. During the Hauptmann trial, which lasted more than a month, there were sometimes more than 700 newsmen in Flemington, N.J., the site of the trial.[38]

Much of the publicity of the Hauptmann trial was prejudicial, and lawyers and newsmen authored statements which were clearly

[36] 373 U.S. 723, 725, 83 S.Ct. 1417, 1418 (1963).

[37] 373 U.S. 723, 727, 83 S.Ct. 1417, 1419 (1963).

[38] John Lofton, Justice and the Press (Boston: Beacon Press, 1966), pp. 103–104.

inflammatory. Hauptmann was described in the press, for example, as a "thing lacking in human characteristics." [39]   After the trial—and after Hauptmann's execution—a Special Committee on Cooperation Between the Press, Radio, and Bar was established to search for "standards of publicity in judicial proceedings and methods of obtaining an observance of them."   In a grim report issued in 1937, the 18-man committee—including lawyers, editors, and publishers—termed Hauptmann's trial "the most spectacular and depressing example of improper publicity and professional misconduct ever presented to the people of the United States in a criminal trial." [40]

One result of the committee's investigation of the Hauptmann trial was the American Bar Association's adoption in 1937 of Canon 35 of its Canons of Professional Ethics.   Canon 35 forbade taking photographs in the courtroom, including both actual court sessions and recesses.   As updated, Canon 35 declared that broadcasting or televising court proceedings "detract from the essential dignity of the proceedings, distract the participants and witnesses in giving testimony, and create misconceptions * * * and should not be permitted."   This was replaced by ABA Canon of Judicial Conduct 3(7): [41]

> A judge should prohibit broadcasting, televising, recording, or taking photographs in the courtroom and areas immediately thereto during sessions of court or recesses between sessions, except that a judge may authorize:
>
> (a) the use of electronic or photographic means for the presentation of evidence, for the perpetuation of a record, or for other purposes of judicial administration;
>
> (b) the broadcasting, televising, recording, or photographing of investitive, ceremonial, or naturalization proceedings;
>
> (c) the photographic or electronic recording and reproduction of appropriate court proceedings under the following conditions:
>
> > (i) the means of recording will not distract participants or impair the dignity of the proceedings;

[39] Lofton, op. cit., p. 124.

[40] American Bar Association, "Report of Special Committee on Cooperation between Press, Radio and Bar," Annual Report, Volume 62, pp. 851–866 (1937), at p. 861.   See, also, New Jersey v. Hauptmann, 115 N.J.L. 412, 180 A. 809 (Ct.Err. & App.1935), certiorari denied 296 U.S. 649, 56 S.Ct. 310 (1935).

[41] American Bar Association, Code of Professional Responsibility and Code of Judicial Conduct, p. 59C.   For Canon 35, see ABA, Annual Report, Vol. 62, at p. 1134; see it as updated by Justice John Marshall Harlan in his concurring opinion in Estes v. Texas, 381 U.S. 532, 601n, 85 S.Ct. 1628, 1699n (1965).

(ii) the parties have consented, and the consent to being depicted or recorded has been obtained from each witness appearing in the recording and reproduction.

(iii) the reproduction will not be exhibited until after the proceeding has been concluded and all direct appeals have been exhausted; and

(iv) the reproduction will be exhibited only for instructional purposes in educational institutions.

Commentary: Temperate conduct of judicial proceedings is essential to the fair administration of justice. The recording and reproduction of a proceeding should not distort or dramatize the proceeding.

Estes v. Texas

Excesses in televising a trial in Texas during the 1960s meant the end of televising virtually all criminal trials for a period of more than a decade. As is discussed later in this section, however, developments in the late 1970s—capped by the January, 1981 decision of the Supreme Court of the United States in Chandler v. Florida [42]—have seen a substantial movement toward getting both television and still cameras back into state courtrooms. At this writing, however, federal courtrooms are still off limits.

The crucial case of the 1960s involved the swindling trial of flamboyant Texas financier Billie Sol Estes. Estes was ultimately convicted, but not until he had received a new trial as a result of the manner in which a judge allowed his original trial to be photographed and televised. Fallout from the U.S. Supreme Court decision which granted Estes a new trial seemed to rule out cameras in the courtroom.[43] As William A. Hachten wrote in 1968, the *Estes* decision did not kill television in the courtroom, but it left it in a critical condition.[44]

Estes came before a judicial hearing in Smith County, Texas, in 1962, after a change of venue from Reeves County, some 500 miles west. The courtroom was packed and about 30 persons stood in the aisles. A New York Times story described the setting for the pre-trial hearing in this way: [45]

[42] Chandler v. Florida, 449 U.S. 560, 101 S.Ct. 802 (1981).

[43] Estes v. Texas, 381 U.S. 532, 85 S.Ct. 1628 (1965).

[44] Hachten, op. cit., p. 273.

[45] Estes v. Texas, 381 U.S. 532, 553, 85 S.Ct. 1628, 1638 (1965), from Chief Justice Warren's concurring opinion, with which Justices Douglas and Goldberg concurred.

A television motor van, big as an intercontinental bus, was parked outside the courthouse and the second-floor courtroom was a forest of equipment. Two television cameras have been set up inside the bar and four more marked cameras were aligned just outside the gates.

* * *

Cables and wires snaked over the floor.

With photographers roaming unchecked about the courtroom, Estes' attorney moved that all cameras be excluded from the courtroom. As the attorney spoke, a cameraman walked behind the judge's bench and took a picture.[46]

After the two-day hearing was completed on September 25, 1962, the judge granted a continuance (delay) to the defense, with the trial to begin on October 22. Meanwhile, the judge established ground rules for television and still photographers. Televising of the trial was allowed, with the exception of live coverage of the interrogation of prospective jurors or the testimony of witnesses. The major television networks, CBS, NBC, and ABC, plus local television station KLTV were each allowed to install one television camera (without sound recording equipment) and film was made available to other television stations on a pooled basis. In addition, through another pool arrangement, only still photographers for the Associated Press, United Press, and from the local newspaper would be permitted in the courtroom.

At its own expense, and with the permission of the court, KLTV built a booth at the back of the courtroom, painted the same color as the courtroom. An opening in the booth permitted all four television cameras to view the proceedings. However, in this small courtroom, the cameras were visible to all.[47]

Despite these limitations the judge placed on television and still photographers, a majority of the Supreme Court held that Estes had been deprived of a fair trial in violation of the due process clause of the Fourteenth Amendment. Chief Justice Warren and Justices Douglas, Goldberg, and Clark asserted that a fair trial could not be had when television is allowed in any criminal trial. Justice Harlan, the fifth member of the majority in this 5–4 decision, voted to overturn Estes' conviction because the case was one of "great notoriety." Even so, it should be noted that Harlan reserved judgment on the televising of more routine cases.

---

[46] 381 U.S. 532, 553, 85 S.Ct. 1628, 1638 (1965). From concurring opinion by Chief Justice Warren.

[47] 381 U.S. 532, 554–555, 85 S.Ct. 1628, 1638–1639 (1965), from Chief Justice Warren's concurring opinion.

In delivering the opinion of the Court, Mr. Justice Clark wrote: [48]

> We start with the proposition that it is a "public trial" that the Sixth Amendment guarantees to the "accused." The purpose of the requirement of a public trial was to guarantee that the accused would be fairly dealt with and not unjustly condemned. His story had proven that secret tribunals were effective instruments of oppression * * *.
>
> It is said, however, that the freedoms granted in the First Amendment extend a right to news media to televise from the courtroom, and that to refuse to honor this privilege is to discriminate between the newspapers and television. This is a misconception of the rights of the press.

Justice Clark then took aim on the assertion that if courts exclude television cameras or microphones, they are discriminating in favor of the print media. Clark retorted, "[t]he news reporter is not permitted to bring his typewriter or printing press." Clark did concede that technical advances might someday make television equipment and cameras quieter and less obtrusive.[49]

Justice Clark wrote that televising and photographing criminal trials did not aid the courts' solemn purpose of endeavoring to ascertain the truth. Instead, he argued, television injects an irrelevant factor into court proceedings which might not only be distracted by the presence of cameras, with their "telltale red lights," but by an awareness of the fact of televising felt by jurors throughout an entire trial. Also, if a new trial be ordered, prospective jurors for the second trial might be prejudiced by what they had seen over television of the first trial, and televising a trial court impair the quality of witnesses' testimony.[50]

In addition, televising a trial could simply make a judge's task of attempting to insure fairness in the proceedings that much more difficult. And finally, the presence of the television cameras in a courtroom was termed by Clark a form of mental if not physical harassment, "resembling a police line-up or the third degree." [51]

Chief Justice Warren was joined by Justices Douglas and Goldberg in his concurring opinion. Warren agreed with Clark

[48] 381 U.S. 532, 538–539, 85 S.Ct. 1628, 1631 (1965).

[49] 381 U.S. 532, 540, 85 S.Ct. 1628, 1631 (1965).

[50] 381 U.S. 532, 544–547, 85 S.Ct. 1628, 1634–1636 (1965).

[51] 381 U.S. 532, 549, 85 S.Ct. 1628, 1636 (1965).

that televising criminal trials is a denial of due process of law. Warren argued that televising diverts a trial from its proper purpose by having an inevitable impact on all the trial participants.[52]

Chief Justice Warren rejected contentions that excluding cameras and microphones from court unfairly or unconstitutionally discriminated against the electronic media. Warren wrote: [53]

> So long as the television industry, like the other communications media, is free to send representatives to trials and to report on those trials to its viewers, there is no abridgment of the freedom of the press. The right of the communications media to comment on court proceedings does not bring with it the right to inject themselves into the fabric of the trial process to alter the purpose of that process.

In his concurring opinion, Justice John Marshall Harlan agreed that in the notorious *Estes* case, the use of television was made in such a way that the right to a fair trial assured by the Due Process Clause of the Fourteenth Amendment was infringed. But even so, Harlan suggested that [54]

> * * * the day may come when television will have become so commonplace an affair in the daily life of the average person as to dissipate all reasonable likelihood that its use in courtrooms may disparage the judicial process.

In a strongly worded dissent, Justices Stewart, Black, Brennan and White raised constitutional arguments in objecting to the ban on television from courtrooms, at least at that stage of television's development. Justice Stewart wrote: [55]

> I think that the introduction of television into a courtroom is, at least in the recent state of the art, an extremely unwise policy. It invites many constitutional risks, and it detracts from the inherent dignity of a courtroom. But I am unable to escalate this personal view into a *per se* constitutional rule. And I am unable to find, on the specific record of this case, that the circumstances attending the limited televising of the petitioner's trial resulted in the denial of any right guaranteed to him by the United States Constitution.

[52] 381 U.S. 532, 565, 85 S.Ct. 1628, 1644 (1965).

[53] 381 U.S. 532, 585–586, 85 S.Ct. 1628, 1654 (1965).

[54] 381 U.S. 532, 595–596, 85 S.Ct. 1628, 1662 (1965).

[55] 381 U.S. 532, 601–602, 85 S.Ct. 1628, 1669 (1965).

Brennan argued that the *Estes* decision was "*not* a blanket constitutional prohibition against the televising of state criminal trials." [56] Television, said Brennan, was barred by the majority side of *Estes* only from "notorious trials." Nevertheless, from 1965 to 1975, cameras—including television cameras—were kept out of virtually *all* courtrooms.

Cameras in the Courtroom

After 1975, cautious efforts to get cameras back in the courtroom became evident in a number of states. In 1977, the Associated Press Managing Editors Association published a report titled "Cameras in the Courtroom: How to Get 'Em There." The report noted that if "you're going to get your Nikon into that courtroom you've got to have more tools than just a camera. For one thing, you've got to have the clout of your State Supreme Court." The report added: [57]

> That the highest court must give the "go ahead" is testified to by the experience of editors in three states that allow cameras in the courtroom—Colorado, Washington and Alabama—and the two states that are allowing it on an experimental basis—Florida and Georgia.

> Without that approval, forget it, they'll tell you.

> * * * [H]ere are the additional tools used to attain photography of trial proceedings (with the states that utilized each particular one listed):

> 1. A committee of the bench and the press, either a new one or an existing bench-bar-press group that has been dealing with fair trial and free press. It is here that initial discussion of the objective takes place (Washington, Georgia, Alabama and Florida).

> 2. Still and TV coverage of actual trials, the result either to be confined to a review by a committee or by the courts, or also to be shown by the press or on television (Washington and Florida).

> 3. A hearing conducted by the State Supreme Court at which the pros and cons of the proposed change in court rules is fully aired (Colorado and Alabama).

> 4. Production of a film of the trial coverage experiment, to be used in making a sales pitch, particu-

---

[56] 381 U.S. 532, 615–616, 85 S.Ct. 1628, 1676–1677 (1965).

[57] Freedom of Information Committee, APME, "Cameras in the Courtroom: How to Get 'Em There," 1977 Freedom of Information Report, p. 2.

larly before lower court and bar associations which are generally opposed to courtroom photography (Washington, which loaned it to Florida).

5. Writing of guidelines for the courtroom coverage for review and adoption by the State Supreme Court (Colorado, Washington, Alabama, Florida and Georgia).

Rather tentatively a number of states began to allow television, radio and photographic coverage of judicial proceedings. Modern cameras, available-light photography, smaller and quieter television and camera gear: technological advances have helped get cameras back into many courtrooms. More important, however, has been intelligent negotiation by thoughtful members of bench, bar and press who realize that photography in the courtroom, properly used, can be a valuable tool for educating and informing the public.

By 1979, six states allowed some form of television, radio or photographic coverage on a permanent basis.[58] Twelve other states permitted some coverage on an experimental basis, and several others were considering allowing coverage. By 1985, there were about 40 states permitting at least some camera access to state judicial proceedings.[59]

Chandler v. Florida: The Lower Courts

A key case testing admission of cameras to courtrooms is Chandler v. Florida.[60] It raised the issue of whether admitting television cameras to a courtroom, over the objection of a participant in a criminal case, made a fair trial impossible.[61]

The *Chandler* case stated the issue in rather extreme form, because in jurisdictions where coverage is permitted, consent of parties is required in most instances.[62] The Supreme Court of the

---

[58] Petition of Post-Newsweek Stations, Florida, Inc., 370 So.2d 764 (Fla.1979), Appendix 2.

[59] News Media & The Law, Jan.-Feb. 1984, p. 56. States having no courts allowing or entertaining proposals for camera coverage were Indiana, Michigan, Mississippi, Missouri, South Carolina, Texas, Utah, Vermont and Virginia.

[60] Chandler v. Florida, 366 So.2d 64 (Fla.App.1978), certiorari denied 376 So.2d 1157 (Fla.1979); probable juris. noted, Supreme Court of the United States, April 21, 1980, 48 USLW 3677.

[61] 366 So.2d 64, 69 (Fla.App.1978).

[62] See Appendix 2, "Television in the Courtroom—Recent Developments," National Center for State Courts, quoted in entirety in Petition of Post-Newsweek Stations, Florida, Inc., 370 So.2d 764 (Fla.1979).

United States held early in 1981 that television coverage had not denied Chandler a fair trial.[63]

Chandler v. Florida also is important because of its interrelationship with another Florida matter, In re Petition of Post-Newsweek Stations, Florida, Inc., for Change in Code of Judicial Conduct.[64] In that proceeding, the Supreme Court of Florida ruled that electronic media coverage of courtroom proceedings is not in itself a denial of due process of law. However, the court also held that the First and Sixth Amendments do not mandate the electronic media be allowed to cover courtroom proceedings. The Florida Supreme Court then issued a rule to amend 3 A(7) of Florida's Code of Judicial Conduct to allow still photography and electronic media coverage of public judicial proceedings in the appellate and trial courts, subject at all time to the authority of the presiding judge.[65]

The *Post-Newsweek Stations* ruling, with its lengthy appendices spelling out the deployment of equipment and personnel, the kind of equipment to be used, and pooling arrangements for coverage to cut down on in court distractions, has been used elsewhere as a primer for drafting petitions to seek changes in state judicial rules.

Petition of Post-Newsweek Stations, Florida, Inc.

After careful testing procedures, the Supreme Court of Florida on April 12, 1979, amended Canon 3 A(7) of the Florida Code of Judicial Conduct to read: [66]

> Subject at all times to the authority of the presiding judge to (i) control the conduct of proceedings before the court, (ii) ensure decorum and prevent distractions, and (iii) ensure the fair administration of justice in the pending case, electronic media and still photography coverage of public judicial proceedings in the appellate and trial courts of this state shall be allowed with standards of conduct and technology promulgated by the Supreme Court of Florida.

Note that this canon relies on the judge's discretion; the consent of participants to coverage is not required. Appendix 3 to this ruling is titled "STANDARDS OF CONDUCT AND TECHNOLOGY GOVERNING ELECTRONIC MEDIA AND STILL PHOTOGRAPHY COVERAGE OF JUDICIAL PROCEEDINGS."

[63] 449 U.S. 560, 101 S.Ct. 802 (1981).

[64] 370 So.2d 764 (Fla.1979).

[65] Ibid., p. 781.

[66] Ibid., Appendix 3, pp. 792–794.

That appendix stipulates that not more than one portable television camera ["film camera—16mm sound-on-film (self-blimped) or video tape electronic camera"] which is operated by not more than one camera person, shall be permitted in any trial court proceeding. No more than "two television cameras, with no more than two camera operators, shall be permitted in any appellate court proceeding. No more than one still photographer, with not more than two still cameras (with no more than two lenses for each camera) shall be permitted in any proceeding in a trial or appellate court. And no more than one audio system for radio broadcast purposes shall be allowed in any proceeding in trial or appellate court. Personnel pooling for coverage purposes is to be the responsibility of the media.

Furthermore, equipment used must not produce distracting sound and light. News media personnel are not to be placed in or removed from courtrooms except before a proceeding begins, or ends, or during a recess. No audio pickup or broadcast of attorney-client or counsel-judge conferences is allowed.

Chandler v. Florida involved the burglary trial of two Miami Beach policemen, Noel Chandler and Robert Granger. During their trial, the defendants raised various objections to Florida's [then] Experimental Canon 3 A(7). Under that canon, despite requests from the defendants that live television coverage be excluded, cameras were allowed to televise parts of the trial.[67]

The Supreme Court of Florida denied a petition for a writ of certiorari, asserting a lack of jurisdiction. That court said, "No conflict has been demonstrated, and the question of great public interest has been rendered moot by the decisions in Petition of Post-Newsweek Stations, Florida, Inc., 370 So.2d 764 (Fla.1979)."

The Supreme Court of the United States, however, noted probable jurisdiction in Chandler v. Florida on April 21, 1980.[68]

Chandler v. Florida: The Supreme Court

On January 26, 1981, the Supreme Court of the United States decided *Chandler* by an 8–0 vote, thus upholding the conviction of two Miami Beach police officers for burglarizing Piccolo's Restaurant. This case—regardless of its outcome—would have been memorable for its fact situation. Officers Noel Chandler and Robert Grander were chatting with each other via walkie-talkies as they broke into the restaurant; they were overheard by an insomniac ham radio operator who recorded their conversations.[69]

---

[67] Chandler v. Florida, 366 So.2d 64, 69 (Fla.App.1978).

[68] 48 USLW 3677 (April 21, 1980).

[69] Chandler v. Florida, 449 U.S. 560, 101 S.Ct. 802 (1981).

Writing for that unanimous Court, Chief Justice Burger based his decision on the principle of federalism. States may work out their own approaches to allowing photographic and broadcast coverage of trials, as long as the Constitution of the United States is not violated.

Chandler and Granger had argued that the very presence of television cameras violated their rights to a fair trial because cameras were psychologically disruptive.[70] Chief Justice Burger, long known for his opposition to cameras in the courtroom, wrote for the Court. (Keep in mind that in 1981, and in 1985, for that matter, federal courtrooms were still off-limits for cameras and broadcast gear; the ban was set by the Judicial Conference of the United States). Burger said: [71]

> An absolute Constitutional ban on broadcast coverage of trials cannot be justified simply because there is a danger in some cases that prejudicial broadcast accounts of pretrial and trial proceedings may impair the ability of jurors to decide the issue of guilt or innocence. * * * [T]he risk of juror prejudice does not warrant an absolute Constitutional ban on all broadcast coverage. * * *
>
> * * *
>
> If it could be demonstrated that the mere presence of photographic and recording equipment and the knowledge that the event would be broadcast invariably and uniformly affected the conduct of participants so as to impair fundamental fairness, our task would be simple; prohibition of broadcast coverage of trials would be required.
>
> * * *
>
> The [appellants] have offered nothing to demonstrate that their trial was subtly tainted by broadcast coverage—let alone that all broadcast trials would be so tainted.

Note that states do not have to admit cameras or broadcast equipment: they *may* do so according to rules which the states develop themselves. Although Florida, unlike most other states which allow cameras in the courtrooms, does not require the permission of the participants in a trial, there are still careful regulations imposed. As noted earlier in this Section,[72] only one television camera and only one still photographer are allowed in the courtroom at one time. Equipment must be put in one place; photographers/camerapersons cannot come and go in the middle

[70] The News Media & The Law, 5:1 (Feb./Mar.1981) p. 5.

[71] Chandler v. Florida, 449 U.S. 560, 101 S.Ct. 802, 810 (1981).

[72] Section 67, at footnote 449.

of a proceeding, and no artificial light is allowed. Further, if the judge finds cameras disruptive, he can exclude them.[73]

As Florida media attorneys James D. Spaniolo and Talbot D'Alemberte have said, it is likely that the Court will deal with questions of cameras in the courtroom on a case-by-case basis. Although defendants Chandler and Granger could not show any prejudice, other defendants in more sensational trials are sure to try that tack. As the Court said in *Chandler*, [74]

> Dangers lurk in this, as in most, experiments, but unless we are to conclude that television coverage under all conditions is prohibited by the Constitution, the states must be free to experiment. * * * The risk of prejudice to particular defendants is ever present and must be examined carefully as cases arise.

Although access of television cameras, microphones, and still cameras increased mightily in the decade after 1975, there were—in 1985—highly uneven patterns of broadcast and camera access to judicial proceedings. Although some kind of television/camera coverage was allowed in some 40 states in 1985, a 1984 survey by the Radio-Television News Directors Association characterized 16 states' camera/microphone access plans as "experimental," with 25 listed as "permanent" and two as "pending." [75]

The camera coverage plans vary widely from state to state. Some states (e.g. Wyoming, Idaho) allow such coverage only of the states' Supreme Courts. Others—and this is by far the most common pattern—allow at least some coverage by cameras in both trial and appellate courts. Within such categories, further variation exists: some courts (e.g. Utah) allow still photography but not television cameras in the courtroom. And in Texas, cameras of any kind were not allowed as of 1985, but audio taping of appellate proceedings was permissible.[76]

Even though remarkable gains have been made in getting television and still cameras into state courtrooms, the federal court picture remained unchanged: nothing doing. Sometimes it doesn't pay to ask a question: the Judicial Conference Ad Hoc Committee on Cameras in the Courtroom considered a request to liberalize Canon 3A(7) and Rule 53 of the Federal Rules of Criminal Procedure to allow coverage by still cameras, radio and television. The Ad Hoc Committee responded with a firm "No," con-

[73] For a good contemporaneous discussion of *Chandler*, see James D. Spaniolo and Talbot D'Alemberte, "Despite 'cameras' ruling, some questions persist," Press-time, March, 1981, p. 16.

[74] 449 U.S. 560, 101 S.Ct. 802, 813 (1981).

[75] The News Media & The Law, Jan.-Feb. 1984, p. 40.

[76] Ibid.

cluding that potential harm to the administration of justice was greater than any benefits to be derived from the proposed coverage. As attorney Dan Paul and co-authors noted in 1984, the Committee's report showed that 78% of federal judges and 84% of the American College of Trial Lawyers members who answered a survey were against cameras in the courtroom.[77]

SEC. 68. PUBLICITY BEFORE AND DURING TRIAL

The long ordeal of Dr. Samuel Sheppard ended with the reversal of his murder conviction on grounds that pretrial and during-trial publicity had impaired his ability to get a fair trial.

The Trial of Dr. Sam Sheppard

When the free press—fair trial controversy is raised, the case most likely to be mentioned is that *cause celebre* of American jurisprudence, Sheppard v. Maxwell.[78] This case was one of the most notorious—and most sensationally reported—trials in American history. With perhaps the exception of the Lindbergh kidnaping case of the 1930s, the ordeal of Dr. Sam Sheppard may well have been the most notorious case of the Twentieth Century.

This case began in the early morning hours of July 4, 1954, when Dr. Sheppard's pregnant wife, Marilyn, was found dead in the upstairs bedroom of their home. She had been beaten to death. Dr. Sheppard, who told authorities he had found his wife dead, called a neighbor, Bay Village Mayor Spence Houk. Dr. Sheppard appeared to have been injured, suffering from severe neck pains, a swollen eye, and shock.

Dr. Sheppard, a Bay Village, Ohio, osteopath, told a rambling and unconvincing story to officials: that he had dozed off on a downstairs couch after his wife had gone upstairs to bed. He said that he heard his wife cry out and ran upstairs. In the dim light from the hall, he saw a "form" which he later described as a bushy haired man standing next to his wife's bed. Sheppard said he grappled with the man and was knocked unconscious by a blow to the back of his neck.

He said he then went to his young son's room, and found him unharmed. Hearing a noise, Sheppard then ran downstairs. He saw a "form" leaving the house and chased it to the lake shore. Dr. Sheppard declared that he had grappled with the intruder on the beach, and had been again knocked unconscious.[79]

---

[77] Dan Paul, Richard J. Ovelmen, James D. Spaniolo, and Steven M. Kamp, "Access After Press-Enterprise," p. 67 in James C. Goodale, chairman, Communications Law 1984 (New York: Practising Law Institute, 1984).

[78] 384 S.Ct. 333, 86 S.Ct. 1507 (1966).

[79] 384 U.S. 333, 335–336, 86 S.Ct. 1507, 1508–1509 (1966).

From the outset, Dr. Sheppard was treated as the prime suspect in the case. The coroner was reported to have told his men, "Well, it is evident the doctor did this, so let's go get the confession out of him.'" Sheppard, meanwhile, had been removed to a nearby clinic operated by his family. While under sedation, Sheppard was interrogated in his hospital room by the coroner. Later, on the afternoon of July 4, he was also questioned by Bay Village police, with one policeman telling Sheppard that lie detector tests were "infallible." This same policeman told Dr. Sheppard, "'I think you killed your wife.'" Later that same afternoon, a physician sent by the coroner was permitted to make a careful examination of Sheppard.[80]

As early as July 7—the date of Marilyn Sheppard's funeral—a newspaper story appeared quoting a prosecuting attorney's criticism of the Sheppard family for refusing to permit his immediate questioning. On July 9, Sheppard re-enacted his recollection of the crime at his home at the request of the coroner. This re-enactment was covered by a group of newsmen which had apparently been invited by the coroner. Sheppard's performance was reported at length by the news media, including photographs. Front-page headlines also emphasized Sheppard's refusal to take a lie-detector test.[81]

On July 20, 1954, newspapers began a campaign of front-page editorials. One such editorial charged that someone was "getting away with murder." The next day, another front-page editorial asked, "Why No Inquest?" A coroner's inquest was indeed held on that day in a school gymnasium. The inquest was attended by many newsmen and photographers, and was broadcast with live microphones stationed at the coroner's chair and at the witness stand. Sheppard had attorneys present during the three-day inquest, but they were not permitted to participate.[82]

The news media also quoted authorities' versions of the evidence before trial. Some of this "evidence"—such as a detective's assertion that "'the killer washed off a trail of blood from the murder bedroom to the downstairs section'"—was never produced at the trial. Such a story, of course, contradicted Sheppard's version of what had happened in the early morning hours of July 4, 1954.[83]

The news media's activities also included playing up stories about Sheppard's extramarital love life, suggesting that these affairs were a motive for the murder of his wife. Although the

[80] 384 U.S. 333, 337–338, 86 S.Ct. 1507, 1509–1510 (1966).

[81] 384 U.S. 333, 338, 86 S.Ct. 1507, 1510 (1966).

[82] 384 U.S. 333, 339, 86 S.Ct. 1507, 1510 (1966).

[83] 384 U.S. 333, 340, 86 S.Ct. 1507, 1511 (1966).

news media repeatedly mentioned his relationship with a number of women, testimony taken at Sheppard's trial never showed that Sheppard had any affairs except the one with Susan Hayes.[84]

Late in July, newspaper editorials appeared bearing titles such as "Why Don't Police Quiz Top Suspect?" and "Why Isn't Sam Sheppard in Jail?" Another headline shrilled: "Quit Stalling—Bring Him In." The night that headline appeared—July 30—Sheppard was arrested at 10 p.m. at his father's home on a murder charge. He was then taken to the Bay Village City Hall where hundreds of spectators, including many reporters, photographers, and newscasters, awaited his arrival. The Supreme Court of the United States, in Justice Tom C. Clark's majority opinion in the Sheppard case in 1966, summed up the news accounts in this way: [85]

> The publicity then grew in intensity until his indictment on August 17. Typical of the coverage during this period is a front-page interview entitled: "Dr. Sam: 'I Wish There Was Something I Could Get Off My Chest—but There Isn't.'" Unfavorable publicity included items such as a cartoon of the body of a sphinx with Sheppard's head and the legend below: "'I Will Do Everything In My Power to Help Solve This Terrible Murder.'—Dr. Sam Sheppard." Headlines announced, *inter alia* [among other things], that: "Doctor Evidence is Ready for Jury," "Corrigan Tactics Stall Quizzing," "Sheppard 'Gay Set' Is Revealed by [Bay Village Mayor Spence] Houk," "Blood Is Found in Garage," "New Murder Evidence Is Found, Police Claim," "Dr. Sam Faces Quiz At Jail on Marilyn's Fear Of Him."

Justice Clark indicated that there were many other newspaper articles which appeared before and during the trial: "five volumes filled with similar clippings from each of the three Cleveland newspapers covering the period from the murder until Sheppard's conviction in December, 1954." Although the record of Sheppard's trial included no excerpts from radio and television broadcasts, the Court assumed that coverage by the electronic media was equally extensive since space was reserved in the courtroom for representatives of those media.

Justice Clark also noted that the chief prosecutor of Sheppard was a candidate for common pleas judge and that the trial judge, Herbert Blythin, was a candidate to succeed himself. Furthermore, when 75 persons were called as prospective jurors, all three Cleveland newspapers published their names and addresses. All

[84] 384 U.S. 333, 340–341, 86 S.Ct. 1507, 1511 (1966).

[85] 384 U.S. 333, 341–342, 86 S.Ct. 1507, 1511–1512 (1966).

of the prospective jurors received anonymous letters and telephone calls, plus calls from friends, about the impending Sheppard trial.[86]

Even the physical arrangements made in the courtroom to accommodate the newsmen and photographers seemed to work to Dr. Sheppard's disadvantage. The courtroom where the trial was held measured only 26 by 48 feet. In back of the single counsel table, inside the bar, a long temporary table stretching the width of the courtroom was set up, accommodating about 20 reporters who were assigned seats for the duration of the trial. One end of this table was less than three feet from the jury box. Behind the bar railing were four rows of benches, with seats likewise assigned by the court for the entire trial. The first row behind the bar was assigned to representatives of the television and radio stations, with the second and third rows being occupied by reporters from out-of-town newspapers and magazines. Thus the great majority of the seats in the courtroom were occupied by reporters. Private telephone lines were installed in other rooms on the same floor with the courtroom, and one radio station was allowed to make broadcasts from the room next to the jury room throughout the trial, and while the jury reached its verdict. Photographs could be taken in court during recesses. All of these arrangements, and the massive coverage by the media, continued during the nine weeks of the trial. Reporters moving in and out of the courtroom during times when the court was in session caused so much confusion that it was difficult for witnesses and lawyers to be heard despite a loudspeaker system.[87]

During the trial, pictures of the jury appeared more than 40 times in the Cleveland newspapers. And the day before the jury rendered its verdict of guilty against Dr. Sam Sheppard, while the jurors were at lunch in the company of two bailiffs, the jury was separated into two groups to pose for pictures which were published in the newspapers. The jurors, unlike those in the Estes case, were not sequestered ["locked up" under the close supervision of bailiffs]. Instead, the jurors were allowed to do what they pleased outside the courtroom while not taking part in the proceedings.[88]

The intense publicity given the Sheppard case in the news media continued unabated while the trial was actually in progress. Sheppard's attorneys took a "random poll" of persons of the streets asking their opinion about the osteopath's guilt or innocence in an effort to gain evidence for a change of venue. This

[86] 384 U.S. 333, 342, 86 S.Ct. 1507, 1512 (1966).

[87] 384 U.S. 333, 343–344, 86 S.Ct. 1507, 1512–1513 (1966).

[88] 384 U.S. 333, 345, 353, 86 S.Ct. 1507, 1513, 1517 (1966).

poll was denounced in one newspaper editorial as smacking of "mass jury tampering" and stated that the bar association should do something about it.

A debate among newspaper reporters broadcast over radio station WHK in Cleveland contained assertions that Sheppard had admitted his guilt by hiring a prominent criminal lawyer. In another broadcast heard over WHK, columnist and radio-TV personality Robert Considine likened Sheppard to a perjuror. When Sheppard's attorneys asked Judge Blythin to question the jurors as to how many had heard the broadcast, Judge Blythin refused to do this. And when the trial was in its seventh week, a Walter Winchell broadcast available in Cleveland over both radio and television asserted that a woman under arrest in New York City for robbery had stated that she had been Sam Sheppard's mistress and had borne him a child. Two jurors admitted in open court that they had heard the broadcast. However, Judge Blythin merely accepted the jurors' statements that the broadcast would have no effect on their judgment and the judge accepted the replies as sufficient.[89]

When the case was submitted to the jury, the jurors were sequestered for their deliberations, which took five days and four nights. But this "sequestration" was not complete. The jurors had been allowed to call their homes every day while they stayed at a hotel during their deliberations. Telephones had been removed from the jurors' hotel rooms, but they were allowed to use phones in the bailiffs' rooms. The calls were placed by the jurors themselves, and no record was kept of the jurors who made calls or of the telephone numbers or of the persons called. The bailiffs could hear only the jurors' end of the telephone conversations.[90]

When Sheppard's case was decided by the Supreme Court of the United States in 1966, Justice Tom C. Clark's majority opinion included this ringing statement of the importance of the news media to the administration of justice.[91]

> The principle that justice cannot survive behind walls of silence has long been reflected in the "Anglo-American distrust for secret trials." A responsible press has always been regarded as the handmaiden of effective judicial administration, especially in the criminal field. Its function in this regard is documented by an impressive record of service over several centuries. The press does not simply publish information about trials but guards against the miscarriage of justice by subjecting the police,

[89] 384 U.S. 333, 346, 348, 86 S.Ct. 1507, 1514–1515 (1966).
[90] 384 U.S. 333, 349, 86 S.Ct. 1507, 1515 (1966).
[91] 384 U.S. 333, 349–350, 86 S.Ct. 1507, 1515–1516 (1966).

prosecutors, and judicial processes to extensive public scrutiny and criticism.

Implicit in some of Justice Clark's other statements in his opinion was deep disapproval of the news media's conduct before and during the Sheppard trial. But the news media were by no means the only culprits who made it impossible for Sheppard to get a fair trial. There was more than enough blame to go around, and Justice Clark distributed that blame among the deserving: news media, police, the coroner, and the trial court. The trial judge, Herbert Blythin, had died in 1960, but Justice Clark nevertheless spelled out what Judge Blythin should have done to protect the defendant.

At the outset of Sheppard's trial, Judge Blythin stated that he did not have the power to control publicity about the trial. Justice Clark declared that Judge Blythin's arrangements with the news media "caused Sheppard to be deprived of that 'judicial serenity and calm to which [he] was entitled.'" Justice Clark added that "bedlam reigned at the courthouse during the trial and newsmen took over practically the entire courtroom hounding most of the participants in the trial, especially Sheppard."[92] Justice Clark asserted: [93]

> The carnival atmosphere at trial could easily have been avoided since the courtroom and courthouse premises are subject to the control of the court. As we stressed in *Estes,* the presence of the press at judicial proceedings must be limited when it is apparent that the accused might otherwise be prejudiced or disadvantaged. Bearing in mind the massive pre-trial publicity, the judge should have adopted stricter rules governing the use of the courtroom by newsmen, as Sheppard's counsel requested. The number of reporters in the courtroom itself could have been limited at the first sign that their presence would disrupt the trial. They certainly should have not been placed inside the bar. Furthermore, the judge should have more closely regulated the conduct of newsmen in the courtroom. For instance, the judge belatedly asked them not to handle and photograph trial exhibits lying on the counsel table during recesses.

In addition, the trial judge should have insulated the jurors and witnesses from the news media, and "should have made some effort to control the release of leads, information, and gossip to the press by police officers, witnesses, and the counsel for both sides." [94]

[92] 384 U.S. 333, 355, 86 S.Ct. 1507, 1518 (1966).

[93] 384 U.S. 333, 358, 86 S.Ct. 1507, 1520 (1966).

[94] 384 U.S. 333, 359, 361, 86 S.Ct. 1507, 1521–1522 (1966).

SEC. 69. THE JUDGE'S ROLE

It is the judge's responsibility to see that each defendant receives a fair trial.

The decision in the Sheppard case left its mark in the recommendations of the American Bar Association's "Reardon Report" discussed later in this chapter. The cases discussed in this chapter—*Irvin, Rideau, Estes,* and *Sheppard*—generated new law and suggested strongly that American courts may insist more and more on tighter controls over the information released to the news media in criminal trials by police, prosecution and defense attorneys, and by other employees under the control of the courts. The primary responsibility, however, for seeing to it that a defendant receives a fair trial, rests with the courts. Judges are expected to remain in control of trials in their courts.

A judge with great respect for the press, Frank W. Wilson of a U.S. District Court in Nashville, Tenn., wrote: "Certain it is that the press coverage of crimes and criminal proceedings make more difficult the job that a judge has of assuring a fair trial. But no one has yet shown that it renders the job impossible. In fact, no one has yet shown, to the satisfaction of any court, an identifiable instance of miscarriage of justice due to press coverage of a trial where the error was not remedied." [95] Note that Judge Wilson said that it is the *judge's* job to assure a fair trial. Judge Wilson declared, "show me an unfair trial that goes uncorrected and I will show you a judge who has failed in his duty." [96]

Judge Wilson thus placed great—some would argue *too great*— [97] reliance upon the remedies which a judge can use to attempt to set things right for the defendant once he has received what the judge considers to be an undue amount of prejudicial publicity. Some of the most important of these trial-level "remedies" are outlined below:

(1) *Change of venue,* moving the trial to another area in hopes that jurors not prejudiced by mass media publicity or outraged community sentiment can be found. This "remedy," however, requires that a defendant give up his Sixth Amendment right to a trial in the "State and *district* wherein the crime shall have been committed

---

[95] Frank A. Wilson, "A Fair Trial and a Free Press," presented at 33rd Annual convention of the Ohio Newspaper Association, Columbus, Ohio, Feb. 11, 1966.

[96] Ibid.

[97] Don R. Pember, Pretrial Newspaper Publicity in Criminal Proceedings: A Case Study (unpublished M.A. thesis, Michigan State University, East Lansing, Mich.) pp. 12–16.

* * *." [98] Change of venue may have been a relatively
effective remedy, say, in 1900, before radio and television
blanketed the nation so effectively with instantaneous
communication. Also, one locality's sensational trial, after it is moved, will become another locality's sensational
trial, largely defeating the change of venue.

(2) *Continuance or postponement.* This is simply a matter
of postponing a trial until the publicity or public clamor
abates. A problem with this "remedy" is that there is
no guarantee that the publicity will not begin anew. It
might be well to remember the axiom, "justice delayed
is justice denied." A continuance in a case involving a
major crime might mean that a defendant—even an
innocent defendant—might thus be imprisoned for a
lengthy time before his trial. A continuance means that
a defendant gives up his Sixth amendment right to a
speedy trial.

(3) *Voir dire* examination of potential jurors. This refers to
the procedure by which each potential juror is questioned
by opposing attorneys and may be dismissed "for cause" if
the juror is shown to be prejudiced. (In addition, attorneys have a limited number of "peremptory challenges"
which they can use to remove jurors whose prejudice
cannot be sufficiently demonstrated but who may give
hints that they favor the other side in the impending
legal battle.) Professor Don R. Pember of the University
of Washington says that the voir dire examination is an
effective tool and one of the best available trial-level
remedies.

(4) *Sequestration,* or "locking up" the jury. Judges have the
power to isolate a jury, to make sure that community
prejudices—either published or broadcast in the mass
media or of the person-to-person variety—do not infect a
jury with information which might harm a defendant's
chances for a fair trial by an impartial jury. This remedy, of course, could not halt the pre-trial publicity which
jurors might have seen or heard before the trial. As
Professor Pember has said, judges are reluctant to do this
today because of the complexities in the life of the average person. [99]

[98] Constitution, Sixth Amendment, emphasis added; Lawrence E. Edenhofer,
"The Impartial Jury—Twentieth Century Dilemma: Some Solutions to the Conflict
Between Free Press and Fair Trial," Cornell Law Quarterly Vol. 51 (Winter, 1966)
pp. 306, 314.

[99] Another trial-level remedy which is more infrequently used is the blue-ribbon
jury. When a case has received massive prejudicial publicity, a court may

(5) *Contempt of Court.* This punitive "remedy" is discussed
at length in Chapter 9. Courts have the power to cite for
contempt those actions—either in court or out of court—
which interfere with the orderly administration of justice.
American courts—until the "gag order" controversies of
recent years—have been reluctant to use the contempt
remedy to punish pre-trial or during-trial publications.
(See Section 71 of this chapter, on "restrictive" or "gag"
orders.) Some critics of the American mass media would
go even further: they would like to see the British system
imported. That would mean using contempt of court
citations as a weapon to control media coverage of criminal cases.

The British system of contempt citations to regulate media
activities has worked well, according to some observers. The
British press—knowing that the threat of a contempt citation
hangs over it for a misstep—cannot quote from a confession (or
even reveal its existence); nor can the British publish material—
including previous criminal records—which would not be admissi-
ble evidence. One of the things about the British system which is
most offensive to American journalists is the prohibition of a
newspaper's making its own investigation and printing the results
of it. After the trial is concluded, *then* British newspapers can
cover the trial.[1]

As distinguished American journalists have pointed out, however, America is not Britain. The *New York Times'* Anthony
Lewis has suggested that the British system of using contempt
citations to preclude virtually all comment on criminal cases
simply could not work in the United States. While some criminal
trials in the United States drag on for years, even trials involving
major crimes—including appeals—are usually completed in Britain in less than two months' time.[2] Anthony Lewis has also
argued that Britain is a small, homogeneous nation where police
or judicial corruption is virtually unknown. America has not
been so fortunate: occasionally corrupt policemen or judges are
discovered, and perhaps the media's watchdog function is more
needed in reporting on police and courts in this nation than it is in
Britain.[3]

empower either the prosecution or the defense to impanel a special, so-called "blue
ribbon" jury. Intelligent jurors are selected through the use of questionnaires and
interviews, under the assumption that a more intelligent jury will be more likely to
withstand pressures and remain impartial.

[1] Harold W. Sullivan, Trial by Newspaper (Hyannis, Mass., Patriot Press, 1961).

[2] New York Times, June 20, 1965.

[3] Ibid.

SEC. 70.   EXTERNAL GUIDELINES AND SELF-REGULATORY EFFORTS

An external regulatory threat—the fair trial reporting guidelines of the "Reardon Committee"—led to press-bar-bench efforts to agree to rules for covering the criminal justice process.

During the middle 1960s, the American Bar Association again got into the act in attempting to regulate prejudicial publicity.[4] As should be evident from preceding sections, there was plenty of pressure on the ABA to do something.   First, as noted earlier in Section 65, the Warren Commission investigating the assassination of President Kennedy had some harsh things to say about media coverage of the arrest of suspect Lee Harvey Oswald.[5] Then, there had been a chain of cases involving prejudicial publicity—Irvin v. Dowd (1961),[6] Rideau v. Louisiana (1963),[7] Estes v. Texas (1965)[8] and Sheppard v. Maxwell (1966).[9]   Although the [Attorney General Nicholas DeB.] Katzenbach Guidelines for federal courts and law enforcement officers had met with considerable approval, the ABA's concern continued.   Early in 1968, the ABA Convention meeting in Chicago approved the "Standards Relating to Fair Trial and Free Press" recommended by the Advisory Committee headed by Massachusetts Supreme Court Justice Paul C. Reardon.[10]   The "Reardon Report," as the document came to be known, was greeted with outraged concern by a large segment of the American media.[11]   This report dealt primarily with things that attorneys and judges were *not* to say lest the rights of defendants be prejudiced.   For example, if a defendant in a murder case had confessed before trial, that confession should not be revealed until duly submitted as evidence during an actual trial.   What was most frightening to the media, however, were

---

[4] Advisory Commitee on Fair Trial and Free Press, Standards Relating to Fair Trial and Free Press (New York, 1966); see also draft approved Feb. 19, 1968, by delegates to the ABA Convention as published in March, 1968.   For earlier ABA involvement in trying to come to terms with prejudicial publicity see ABA, "Report of Special Committee on Cooperation Between [sic] Press, Radio and Bar," Annual Report, Volume 62, pp. 851–866 (1937).

[5] Report of the President's Commission on the Association of President John F. Kennedy (Washington: Government Printing Office, 1964) p. 241.

[6] 366 U.S. 717, 81 S.Ct. 1639 (1961).

[7] 373 U.S. 723, 83 S.Ct. 1417 (1963).

[8] 381 U.S. 532, 85 S.Ct. 1628 (1965).

[9] 384 U.S. 333, 86 S.Ct. 1507 (1966).

[10] Advisory Committee on Fair Trial and Free Press (of the ABA), Approved Draft, op. cit.

[11] See, e.g., American Newspaper Publishers Association, Free Press and Fair Trial (New York: ANPA, 1967) p. 1 and passim.

suggestions that contempt powers be used against the media if it were to publish a statement which could affect the outcome of a trial.

Replies from representatives of the news media were not long in coming after the ABA House of Delegates adopted the "Reardon Report" on February 19, 1968. J. Edward Murray, managing editor of *The Arizona Republic,* said: "Fortunately, neither the ABA nor the House of Delegates makes the law." Murray emphasized that the ABA action was merely advisory, and had no force of law unless adopted by statutes or as rules of courts at the state and local levels.[12] The Reardon Report touched off many press-bar meetings, seeking to reach voluntary guidelines on coverage of the criminal arrest, arraignment, hearing and trial process. More than two dozen states adopted voluntary agreements based on conferences among judges, lawyers, and members of the media. States with such guidelines include Colorado, Kentucky, Massachusetts, Minnesota, New York, Oregon, Texas, Washington, and Wisconsin.

In such a setting—in the aftermath of the Warren Commission Report on the Kennedy assassination (which called for curtailment of pretrial news)—the *Sheppard* case came along to illustrate once again just how wretchedly prejudicial news coverage of a criminal trial could become. In that setting, the ABA Advisory Committee on Fair Trial—Free Press (Reardon Committee) was formed.[13]

In many places, a press-bar agreement occurred, leading to construction, by joint press-bar committees in roughly half of the states, of guidelines for the coverage of criminal trials. In Wisconsin, for example, the following guidelines were adopted: [14]

WISCONSIN FAIR TRIAL AND FREE PRESS PRINCIPLES AND GUIDELINES

Introduction

Nearly ten years ago, in the wake of the Reardon Report and the Sam Sheppard case, a committee was formed under the aegis

[12] Advisory Committee on Fair Trial and Free Press, op. cit., 1966 and 1968; "Bar Votes to Strengthen Code on Crime Publicity," Editor & Publisher, Vol. 101 (Feb. 24, 1968) p. 9.

[13] J. Edward Gerald, "Press-Bar Relationships: Progress Since *Sheppard* and Reardon," Journalism Quarterly 47: 2 (Summer, 1970), p. 223. See, also, the Report of the President's Commission on the Association of President John F. Kennedy (1964), and Judicial Conference of the United States Committee on the Jury System, Report of the Committee on the Operation of the Jury Systems on the Free Press—Fair Trial Issue 1-3 (1968).

[14] Reprinted from A Wisconsin News Reporter's Legal Handbook, prepared by the Media-Law Relations Committee in cooperation with the State Bar of Wisconsin, the Wisconsin Broadcasters Association, and the Wisconsin Newspaper Association, 1979.

of the Wisconsin attorney general to draft some guidelines designed to reconcile the fundamental constitutional precepts of freedom of the press (as protected in the First Amendment) and the right of a criminal defendant to a fair trial (guaranteed in the Sixth Amendment). This joint committee published its "Statement of Principles" in early 1969 for the guidance of those involved in the criminal and juvenile justice systems in Wisconsin—participants, observers and reporters. Although the guidelines appear to have served well in the intervening years, disputes have arisen under them and the course of legal events have left them somewhat dated.

The American Bar Association's adoption in 1977 of "Recommended Court Procedures to Accommodate Rights of Fair Trial and Free Press," and the United States Supreme Court's decision in Nebraska Press Association v. Stuart, 427 U.S. 539 (1977), led the Wisconsin Journalists/Lawyers Joint Interests Committee to conclude that the time had come to review and update the 1969 "Statement of Principles" in the hope that these voluntary professional standards will avoid the need for gag orders in Wisconsin judicial proceedings. To accomplish this, the Committee appointed a special task force of persons with direct and working knowledge of the problems, equally representative of media personnel and participants in the legal system. Professor Mary Ann Yodelis Smith, of the University of Wisconsin School of Journalism, chaired the group. In addition to Professor Smith, the Committee consisted of Attorney Robert H. Friebert of Milwaukee; Dane County District Attorney James E. Doyle, Jr.; Attorney James P. Brody of Milwaukee; Portage County Sheriff Nick Check; Eau Claire County Circuit Judge Thomas H. Barland; Mr. Thomas Bolger, President and General Manager of WMTV, Madison; Mr. Robert H. Wills, Editor of the Milwaukee Sentinel; Ms. Patricia Simms, reporter, Wisconsin State Journal; Mr. David Block, Assignments Editor, FRV, Green Bay; and Mr. John M. Lavine, Publisher/Editor, Chippewa Falls.

The following principles and guidelines on fair trial and free press are offered to members of the bar, judiciary, law enforcement agencies and news media as a standards of professional conduct the Committee believes will protect the constitutional liberties involved and promote harmony among the professions.

Purpose

The right to a fair and prompt trial and the right of freedom of the press are fundamental liberties guaranteed by the United States and Wisconsin constitutions. These basic rights must be rigidly preserved and responsibly practiced according to highest professional standards.

Nearly always, a court's performance of its responsibility (in cooperation with the bar and law enforcement agencies) to dispense justice with respect to the parties before it, is entirely consistent with the media's responsibility to apprise the public regarding the proceedings. However, it is important that the judiciary, bar, media and law enforcement agencies appreciate that in performing their respective duties they can jeopardize one or another of the constitutional precepts of fair trial and free press.

To promote understanding toward recounciling the constitutional guarantees of freedom of the press and the right to a fair, impartial trial, the following principles and guidelines, submitted for voluntary compliance, are recommended to all members of the judiciary, bar, news media, and law enforcement agencies in Wisconsin.

It is further recommended that annually, representatives of the judiciary, bar, law enforcement agencies, and the news media meet to review those principles and guidelines to promote understanding of these principles by the public and by all directly involved persons, agencies, and organizations.

Principles to Insure Free Press and Fair Trial

1. The judiciary, bar, news media, and law enforcement agencies are obliged to preserve the principle that any person suspected or accused of a crime is innocent until found guilty in a court under competent evidence fairly presented. Parties to civil court proceedings likewise are entitled to have their rights adjudicated in court according to due process.

2. Access to legitimate information involving the administration of justice in criminal or civil cases and guaranteeing the defendants and plaintiffs a fair trial, free of prejudicial information and conduct, are both vital rights which should be carefully protected. Within their canons of ethics, members of the bar, judiciary, and law enforcement agencies should cooperate with the news media in reporting the administration of justice.

3. The bar, judiciary, news media, and law enforcement agencies share the responsibility to assure that the outcome of a trial not be influenced by publicity or by the police.

4. Freedom for news media to report proceedings in open court is recognized. However, all concerned should cooperate with the court to insure that a jury's deliberations are based only on evidence presented to the jury in court. News media should use

care in reporting portions of jury trials which take place in the absence of the jury. Publicizing court rulings made or evidence rejected in the absence of a jury may cause prejudice. There may be other specific cases where cooperation between the court and news media is appropriate.

5. All news media should strive for accuracy, balance, fairness, and objectivity. They should remember that readers, listeners, and viewers are potential jurors. They should fairly report both sides of court proceedings; reporting only one side of a case may give the public a distorted view.

6. A court of law is intended to serve as a forum in which questions of guilt or innocence, rights and liabilities, are determined pursuant to procedures relating to the admissibility of evidence, burden of proof, and other established principles of law. The procedures are designed to provide fairness to the parties and permit the court to reach a just verdict. The judge has a responsibility to see that the court serves this intended purpose and to provide timely, accurate information consistent with the law and these guidelines.

7. Law enforcement agencies have the responsibility to provide timely, accurate information consistent with the law and these guidelines.

8. Lawyers should observe the code of professional responsibility and these guidelines. Lawyers should not use publicity to promote their sides of pending cases. Public prosecutors should not take unfair advantage of their positions as an important source of news. These cautions shall not be construed to limit a lawyer's obligation to make available information to which the public is entitled.

9. Journalistic, law enforcement, and legal training should include instruction in the meaning of constitutional rights to a fair trial, freedom of the press, and their roles in guarding these rights.

Guidelines for Criminal Proceedings

10. Subject to professional codes of ethics, there should be no restraint on making public in the investigation of a criminal matter information that:

a.   Is contained in a public record;

b.   Indicates an investigation is in progress;

c.   Presents the general scope of the investigation, including a description of the offense, and, if permitted by law, the identity of the victim;

    d.   Is a request for assistance in apprehending a suspect, or assistance in other matters, and the information necessary thereto;

    e.   Is a warning to the public of any dangers.

    11.   Subject to professional codes of ethics, there should be no restraint on making public the following information concerning a defendant:

    a.   The defendant's name, age, residence, employment, marital status, and other non-prejudicial factual background information.

    b.   The identity of the investigating and arresting officers or agencies, and the status of the investigation where appropriate.

    c.   The circumstances surrounding an arrest, including the time and place of arrest, resistance, pursuit, possession and use of weapons, and a description of the physical evidence seized at the time of arrest. Concerning crimes against property, an officer can factually report the property destroyed, damaged or stolen and release a general description of the items recovered.

    d.   The nature, substance or text of the charge, such as complaint indictment and information, or other matters of public record.

    e.   The scheduling or result of any step in the judicial proceedings.

    f.   Information that the accused denies the charges made against him.

    12.   The release to news media of certain types of information, or its publication, may create dangers of prejudice to the defense or prosecution without serving a significant law enforcement or public interest function. Lawyers are prohibited by their code of professional responsibility from releasing the following information until the commencement of the trial or disposition without trial:

    a.   Comments on the character, reputation, or prior criminal record (including arrests, indictments, or other charges of crime) of the accused.

    b.   The possibility of a plea of guilty of the offense charged, or to a lesser offense.

    c.   The existence or contents of any confession, admission, or statement given by the accused, or a refusal or failure to make a statement.

    d.   The performance or results of any examination or tests, or the refusal of the accused to submit to examinations or tests.

    e.   The identity, testimony, or credibility of a prospective witness.

    f.   Any opinion as to the guilt or innocence of the accused, the evidence, or the merits of the case.

Law enforcement agencies and news media should be aware of the dangers of prejudice in making pre-trial disclosures concerning these matters.

    13.   Prior criminal charges and conviction are matters of public record, available through police agencies or court clerks. Law enforcement agencies should make such information available upon legitimate inquiry, but the public disclosure of it may be highly prejudicial without benefit to the public's need to be informed. When there has been a disclosure of a prior arrest or charges, the news media and law enforcement agencies have a special duty to report the disposition or status of the arrest or prior charges.

    14.   Law enforcement and court personnel should not prevent the photographing of defendants, or suspects, when they are in public places outside the courtroom. The Wisconsin Supreme Court standards for use of cameras and recorders for news coverage of judicial proceedings should be followed in the courtroom. Law enforcement agencies should, if possible, make available a suitable, non-prejudicial photograph of a defendant or a person in custody.

    15.   Information about a suspect not in custody may be released by law enforcement personnel, provided it serves a valid law enforcement function. To that end, it is proper to disclose information necessary to enlist public assistance in apprehending suspects, including photographs and records of prior arrests and convictions.

Guidelines for Juvenile Proceedings

    16.   When news media attend sessions of the juvenile court, they may not disclose names or identifying data of the juvenile or the juvenile's family unless it is a public fact-finding hearing. News media should make every effort to observe and report fully such sessions, and the disposition by the court, with regard for the juvenile's rights and the public interest. When a juvenile is regarded as an adult under criminal law, the foregoing guidelines for criminal proceedings apply.

17. Whenever non-public records are reviewed by the news media, the identity of the juvenile should not be reported.

Guidelines for Civil and Administrative Proceedings

18. Except where prohibited by law, records in civil and administrative proceedings, including pleadings, depositions, interrogatories, verdicts, orders, and judgments, are public record available to the news media. The media should be mindful that reporting on a deposition or written interrogatories prior to presentation at trial may prejudice jurors and one or more of the litigants. Prematurely reporting such matters may be unfair if, on the presentation of the deposition or interrogatory in open court, portions are not admitted into evidence. Also, only one side of the issue may be presented in a deposition or answers to interrogatories.

19. Pleadings are only allegations. Bar and news media should be mindful of possible injustice that may result from one-sided publication of such allegations.

20. Adoption, mental illness, paternity, and certain family court proceedings, by their nature and by law, deserve special treatments as to public disclosure. Investigative reports in such proceedings are usually confidential. In certain circumstances, statutes provide that the court may grant the news media access to such records.

21. Personal and financial data often must be revealed to the court. The public's need to know such information should be balanced against the potential negative effects on persons involved.

22. Lawyers are prohibited by their code of professional responsibility from releasing the following information, other than a quotation from or reference to public records:

    a. Evidence regarding the occurrence or transaction involved;

    b. The character, credibility, or criminal record of a party, witness, or prospective witness;

    c. Physical evidence, or the performance or results of any examinations or tests, or the refusal or failure of a party to submit to such;

    d. An opinion as to the merits of the claims or defense of a party except as required by law or administrative rule;

    e. Any other matter reasonably likely to interfere with a fair trial of the action.

News media should be aware of the dangers of prejudice in making pre-trial disclosures concerning the above matters.

Keep in mind that such guidelines do not have the force of law; they are merely suggested standards of conduct. Also, such guidelines are often unknown to journalists or disregarded when a "hot story" comes along. Perhaps over time, however, these guidelines will have a cumulative effect to the good, encouraging a fair press which covers the courts fully but which runs less risk of prejudicing defendants' rights to a fair trial.

Federated Publications v. Swedberg (1981)

On the other hand, voluntary guidelines may become a two-edged sword. In fact, some states reworked their guidelines after the harsh lesson of Federated Publications v. Swedberg as decided by the Supreme Court of the State of Washington. Reworkings of the state guidelines were to re-emphasize their VOLUNTARY nature.

Judge Byron L. Swedberg presided over a trial involving charges of attempted murder. The case, in Whatcom County, north of Seattle, had great notoriety. It involved Veronica Lynn Compton, a woman reputedly the girlfriend of Kenneth Bianchi. Bianchi was known regionally and even nationally as the "Hillside Strangler."

Judge Swedberg refused to grant a defense motion in the case of State v. Compton which would have closed a pretrial hearing to the public. However, the judge conditioned media attendance at the trial upon reporters' signing an agreement to abide by the Washington Bench-Bar-Press Guidelines. Federated Publications, publishers of the Bellingham Herald, challenged Judge Swedberg's order.

The Washington guidelines were created as a voluntary document and had no legal force until Judge Swedberg incorporated them in his order. In that situation, the guidelines—if enforced—would, for example, have stopped the media from reporting on the defendant's previous criminal record or on the existence of a pre-trial confession. In most cases, journalists will agree that pre-trial confessions should not be reported until officially accepted as evidence in court. However, situations could conceivably arise where the best judgment of journalists would be to include information about the existence of such a confession in pre-trial stories. As journalist Tony Mauro said in a Society of Professional Journalists Freedom of Information report in 1982,

> *   *   * [I]n a single stroke, Swedberg made suspect all the guidelines, developed in many instances only after years of delicate negotiations. Editors who were wary in

the first place of sitting down with judges and lawyers were given new reasons to be suspicious—if we agree to talk about guidelines, the thinking went, someday they'll be used against us, as with Swedberg.

In upholding Judge Swedberg's ruling that members of the press must agree to abide by the Washington guidelines if so ordered by a judge, Justice Rosellini of the State of Washington's Supreme Court concluded that Swedberg's limitation was "reasonable." He compared the Swedberg situation to the Washington Supreme Court's holding in Federated Publications v. Kurtz. In the Kurtz case, the court held that the public has a right under the state and federal constitutions to have access to judicial proceedings, including pretrial hearings.

Justice Rosellini listed alternatives to closing a courtroom (see discussion of a similar list in Sec. 69 of this Chapter: continuance (delay), change of venue, change of venire, voir dire, and so forth). Those alternatives, Justice Rosellini wrote, "all involved some compromise of a right or interest of the accused or the State. None of the suggested alternatives involved the exercise of some restraint on the part of the media." He concluded that since his court had the power to exclude all of the public, including the media, he also had the power to impose reasonable conditions upon the media's attendance at a trial.[15]

SEC. 71.   RESTRICTIVE ORDERS AND REPORTING THE JUDICIAL PROCESS

After "gag orders" became a nationwide problem, Nebraska Press Association v. Stuart (1976) halted such prior restraints on the news media.

Bar-press guidelines such as those disclosed in the preceding sections tried to honor both the public's right to know about the judicial process and a defendant's right to a fair trial. Not all was well, however, despite the various meeting-of-minds between press and bar. Another disturbing counter-current was perceived during the late 1960s, starting mainly in California and involving judges issuing "restrictive" or "gag" orders in some cases.[16] In a Los Angeles County Superior Court in 1966, for example, a judge ordered the attorneys in a case, the defendants, the sheriff, chief

[15] Federated Publications v. Swedberg, 96 Wash.2d 13, 633 P.2d 74, 75 (1981), 7 Med.L.Rptr. 1865, 1871, citing Federated Publications v. Kurtz, 94 Wash.2d 51, 615 P.2d 440 (1980), 6 Med.L.Rptr. 1577. See also Tony Mauro, "Bench-media misunderstanding threatens press access to courts," FOI '82: A Report from the Society of Professional Journalists, p. 3.

[16] Robert S. Warren and Jeffrey M. Abell, "Free Press—Fair Trial: The 'Gag Order,' A California Aberration," Southern California Law Review 45:1 (Winter, 1972) pp. 51–99, at pp. 52–53.

of police, and members of the Board of Police Commissioners not to talk to the news media about the case in question. The order forbade "[r]eleasing or authorizing the release of any extrajudicial statements for dissemination by any means of public communication relating to the alleged charge or the Accused."

All that could be reported under such an order were the facts and circumstances of the arrest, the substance of the charge against the defendant, and the defendant's name, age, residence, occupation, and family status. If such an arrangement were to be worked out on a voluntary basis between press and bar, that might be one thing. However, the fact of a judge's *order*—a "gag rule"—worried some legal scholars, and with good reason.

Such fears about the so-called gag rules have substance, in light of a number of orders from judges that reporters curtail various aspects of their reporting of criminal trials. One kind of "gag rule" deals with judges telling reporters that they should confine themselves to reporting only those events which take place in front of a jury, in open court. Judge Thomas D. McCrea of the Snohomish County, Washington, Superior Court issued such an order to reporters just before a jury trial for first-degree murder was about to begin in his courtroom. Reporters Sam Sperry and Dee Norton of the Seattle times ignored the order, and wrote a story about an evidence hearing which occurred while the jury was outside of the courtroom.

After they were cited for contempt, Sperry and Norton appealed to the Washington Supreme Court, claiming that the judge's order was prior restraint in violation of the First Amendment.

The Washington Supreme Court overturned the contempt citation, saying that the trial court's earnest efforts to provide a fair and impartial jury had taken away the reporters' constitutional right to report to the public what happened in the open trial.[17]

In a New York case during 1971, Manhattan Supreme Court Justice George Postel, concerned about possibly prejudicial news accounts, called reporters into his chambers and laid down what he called "Postel's Law." The trial involved Carmine J. Persico, who had been charged with extortion, coercion, criminal usury ("loan sharking") and conspiracy. Justice Postel admonished the reporters not to use Persico's nickname ("The Snake") in their accounts and not to mention Persico's supposed connections with Joseph A. Columbo, Sr., a person said to be a leader of organized crime. The reporters, irked by Postel's declarations, reported

---

[17] State ex rel. Superior Court of Snohomish County v. Sperry, 79 Wash.2d 69, 483 P.2d 608, 613 (1971).

what the judge had told them, including references to "The Snake" and to Columbo.

Persico's defense attorney then asked that the trial be closed to the press and to the public, and Judge Postel so ordered. However, the prosecutor—Assistant District Attorney Samuel Yasgur—complained that the order would set an unfortunate and dangerous precedent. For one thing, Yasgur declared, the absence of press coverage might mean that possible witnesses who could become aware of the trial through the media would remain ignorant of the trial and thus could not come forward to testify: Prosecutor Yasgur added.[18]

> But most importantly, Your Honor, as the Court has noted, the purpose of having press and the public allowed and present during the trial of a criminal case is to insure that defendants do receive an honest and a fair trial.

Newsmen appealed Judge Postel's order closing the trial to New York's highest court, the Court of Appeals. Chief Judge Stanley H. Fuld then ruled that the trial should not have been closed.[19]

> "Because of the vital function served by the news media in guarding against the miscarriage of justice by subjecting the police, prosecutors, and the judicial processes to extensive public scrutiny and criticism," the Supreme Court has emphasized that it has been "unwilling to place any direct limitations on the freedom traditionally exercised by the news media for '[w]hat transpires in the court room is public property.'"

Chief Judge Fuld added that courts should meet problems of prejudicial publicity not by declaring mistrials, but by taking careful preventive steps to protect their courts from outside interferences. In most cases, Judge Fuld suggested, a judge's cautioning jurors to avoid exposure to prejudicial publicity, or to disregard prejudicial material they had already seen or heard, would be effective. In extreme situations, he said, a court might find it necessary to sequester ("lock up") a jury for the duration of a trial.[20]

Although reporters were ultimately vindicated in the *Postel*, and *Sperry* cases, a Louisiana case went against the press. This case, United States v. Dickinson, arose when reporters Larry

[18] *New York Times*, "Trial of Persico Closed to Public," pp. 1, 40, November 16, 1971.

[19] Oliver v. Postel, 30 N.Y.2d 171, 331 N.Y.S.2d 407, 282 N.E.2d 306, 311 (1972).

[20] Ibid. See, also, People of the State of New York v. Holder, 70 Misc.2d 31, 332 N.Y.S.2d 933 (1972), and Phoenix Newspapers, Inc. v. Jennings, Justice of the Peace, 107 Ariz. 557, 490 P.2d 563, 566–567 (1971).

Dickinson and Gibbs Adams of the Baton Rouge *Star Times* and the *Morning Advocate* tried to report on a U.S. District Court hearing involving a VISTA worker who had been indicted by a Louisiana state grand jury on suspicion of conspiring to murder a state official. The District Court hearing was to ascertain whether the state's prosecution was legitimate. In the course of this hearing, District Court Judge E. Gordon West issued this order:

"And, at this time, I do want to enter an order in the case, and that is in accordance with this Court's rule in connection with Fair Trial—Free Press provisions, the Rules of this Court.

"It is ordered that no * * * report of the testimony taken in this case today shall be made in any newspaper or by radio or television, or by any other news media."

Reporters Dickinson and Adams ignored that order, and wrote articles for their newspapers summarizing the day's testimony in detail. After a hearing, Dickinson and Adams were found guilty of criminal contempt and were sentenced to pay fines of $300 each. Appealing to the Court of Appeals for the Fifth Circuit, the reporters were told that the District Court judge's gag order was unconstitutional.[21] They were not in the clear, however. The Court of Appeals sent their case back to the District Court so that the judge could reconsider the $300 fines. The judge again fined the reporters $300 apiece, and they again appealed to the Court of Appeals. This time, the contempt fines were upheld. The Fifth Circuit Court declared that the reporters could have asked for a rehearing or appealed against the judge's order not to publish. Once the appeal was decided in their favor, the court evidently reasoned, *then* they could publish.[22]

Attorney James C. Goodale—then vice president of the *New York Times*—was indignant.

It doesn't take much analysis to see that what the Court has sanctioned is the right of prior restraint subject to later appeal. * * * What this case means, in effect, is that when a judge is disposed to order a newspaper not to report matters that are transpiring in public he may do so, and a newsman's only remedy is to appeal or decide to pay the contempt penalty, be it a fine or imprisonment.

In the fall of 1973, the Supreme Court—evidently not seeing a major issue requiring its attention—refused to grant certiorari,

[21] United States v. Dickinson, 465 F.2d 496, 514 (5th Cir.1972).

[22] 476 F.2d 373, 374 (5th Cir.1973); 349 F.S. 227 (1972). See also James C. Goodale's "The Press 'Gag' Order Epidemic," Columbia Journalism Review, Sept./ Oct. 1973, pp. 49–50.

thereby allowing the lower court decision to stand.[23] By 1976, however, the gag issue was an obvious problem. Attorney Jack C. Landau, Supreme Court reporter for the Newhouse News Service and a trustee of the Reporters Committee for Freedom of the Press, came up with some agonizing statistics. From 1966 to 1976, at least 174 restrictive orders were issued by courts against the news media.[24]

Nebraska Press Ass'n v. Stuart (1976)

Although the Supreme Court refused to hear the reporters' appeal in the Dickinson case [25]—thus allowing contempt fines against two reporters to stand—a virtual nationwide epidemic of restrictive orders quickly showed that the Baton Rouge case was no rarity.[26] A ghastly 1976 multiple-murder case in the hamlet of Sutherland, Neb. (population 840) was reported avidly by the mass media. This provided the Supreme Court with the factual setting which led to the Court's clamping down on the indiscriminate issuance of gag orders. The issue was stated succinctly by E. Barrett Prettyman, the attorney who represented the news media in Nebraska Press Association v. Stuart.[27]

> The basic question before the Court is whether it is permissible under the First Amendment for a court to issue direct prior restraint against the press, prohibiting in advance of publication the reporting of information revealed in public court proceedings, in public court records, and from other sources about pending judicial proceedings.

The nightmarish Nebraska case involved the murder of six members of one family, and necrophilia was involved. Police released the description of a suspect, 29-year-old Erwin Charles Simants, an unemployed handyman, to reporters who arrived at the scene of the crime. After a night of hiding, Simants walked into the house where he lived—next door to the residence where six had been slain—and was arrested.

Three days after the crime, the prosecuting attorney and Simants' attorney jointly asked the Lincoln County Court to enter a restrictive order. On October 22, 1975, the County Court grant-

[23] 414 U.S. 979, 94 S.Ct. 270 (1973), refusing certiorari in 465 F.2d 496 (5th Cir. 1972).

[24] Jack C. Landau, "The Challenge of the Communications Media," 62 American Bar Association Journal 55 (January, 1976).

[25] 414 U.S. 979, 94 S.Ct. 270 (1973).

[26] Landau, p. 57.

[27] "Excerpts from the Gag Order Arguments," Editor & Publisher, May 1, 1976, p. 46A.

ed a sweeping order prohibiting the release or publication of any "testimony given or evidence adduced * * * ".[28] On October 23, Simants' preliminary hearing was open to the public, but the press was subject to the restrictive order.   On that same day, the Nebraska Press Association intervened in the District Court of Lincoln County and asked Judge Hugh Stuart to set aside the County Court's restrictive order. Judge Stuart conducted a hearing and on October 27 issued his own restrictive order, prohibiting the Nebraska Press Association and other organizations and reporters from reporting on five subjects: [29]

> (1) the existence or contents of a confession Simants had made to law enforcement officers, which has been introduced in open court at arraignment; (2) the fact or nature of statements Simants had made to other persons; (3) the contents of a note he had written the night of the crime; (4) certain aspects of the medical testimony at the preliminary hearing; (5) the identity of the victims of the alleged sexual assault and the nature of the assault.

This order also prohibited reporting the exact nature of the restrictive order itself, and—like the County Court's order—incorporated the Nebraska Bar-Press Guidelines.[30]

The Nebraska Press Association and its co-petitioners on October 31 asked the District Court to suspend its restrictive order and also asked that the Nebraska Supreme Court stop the gag order. Early in December, the state's Supreme Court issued a modification of the restrictive order "to accommodate the defendant's right to a fair trial and the petitioners' [i.e., the Nebraska Press Association, other press associations, and individual journalists'] interest in reporting pretrial events." This modified order prohibited reporting of three matters: [31]

> (a) the existence and nature of any confessions or admissions made by the defendant to law enforcement officers; (b) any confessions or admissions made to any third parties, except members of the press, and (c) other facts "strongly implicative" of the accused.

The Nebraska Supreme Court did not reply on the Nebraska Bar-Press Guidelines. After interpreting state law to permit closing of court proceedings to reporters in certain circumstances, the Nebraska Supreme Court sent the case back to District Judge Hugh Stuart for reconsideration of whether pretrial hearings in the

[28] 427 U.S. 539, 542, 96 S.Ct. 2791, 2795 (1976).

[29] 427 U.S. 539, 543–544, 96 S.Ct. 2791, 2795 (1976).

[30] 427 U.S. 539, 545, 96 S.Ct. 2791, 2796 (1976).

[31] 427 U.S. 539, 545, 96 S.Ct. 2791, 2796 (1976).

Simants case should be closed to the press and public. The Supreme Court of the United States granted certiorari.[32]

Writing for a unanimous Supreme Court, Chief Justice Burger reviewed free press-fair trial cases and prior restraint cases. He wrote: "None of our decided cases on prior restraint involved restrictive orders entered to protect a defendant's right to a fair and impartial jury, but the opinions on prior restraint have a common thread relevant to this case." The Chief Justice then quoted from Organization for a Better Austin v. Keefe: [33]

> "Any prior restraint on expression comes to this Court with a 'heavy presumption' against its constitutional validity. ＊ ＊ ＊ Respondent [Keefe] thus carries a heavy burden of showing justification for the imposition of such a restraint. He has not met that burden. ＊ ＊ ＊"

Chief Justice Burger noted that the restrictive order at issue in the Simants case did not prohibit publication but only postponed it. Some news, he said, can be delayed and often is when responsible editors call for more fact-checking. "But such delays," he added, "are normally slight and they are self-imposed. Delays imposed by governmental authority are a different matter." [34]

The Court then turned to an examination of whether the threat to a fair trial for Simants was so severe as to overcome the presumption of unconstitutionality which prior restraints carry with them. The Chief Justice borrowed Judge Learned Hand's language (oft criticized by libertarians) from a case involving the trial of Communists in 1950: whether the "gravity of the evil," discounted by its improbability, justifies such invasion of free speech as is necessary to avoid the danger.[35] The Court's review of the pretrial record in the Simants case indicated that Judge Stuart was justified in concluding that there would be intense and pervasive pretrial publicity. The judge could have concluded reasonably that the publicity might endanger Simants' right to a fair trial.

Even so, the restrictive order by the trial court judge was not justified in the view of the Supreme Court of the United States. Alternatives to prior restraint were not tried by the Nebraska trial court. Those alternatives included a change of venue; postponement of the trial to allow public furore to subside, and searching questioning of prospective jurors to screen out those who had already made up their minds about Simants' guilt or inno-

---

[32] 423 U.S. 1027, 96 S.Ct. 557 (1975).

[33] 427 U.S. 539, 96 S.Ct. 2791, 2802 (1976).

[34] 427 U.S. 539, 560, 96 S.Ct. 2791, 2803 (1976).

[35] 427 U.S. 539, 562, 96 S.Ct. 2791, 2804 (1976).

cence. Sequestration ("locking up") of jurors would insulate jurors from prejudicial publicity only after they were sworn, but
that measure "enhances the likelihood of dissipating the impact of
pretrial publicity and emphasizes the elements of the jurors'
oaths." The Chief Justice wrote: [36]

> * * * [P]retrial publicity, even if pervasive and
> concentrated, cannot be regarded as leading automatical-
> ly and in every kind of criminal case to an unfair trial.
>
> * * *
>
> We reaffirm that the guarantees of freedom of expres-
> sion are not an absolute prohibition under all circum-
> stances, but the barriers to prior restraint remain high
> and the presumption against its use continues intact. We
> hold that, with respect to the order entered in this case
> prohibiting reporting or commentary on judicial proceed-
> ings held in public, the barriers have not been overcome;
> to the extent that this order restrained publication of
> such material, it is clearly invalid. To the extent that it
> prohibited publication based on information gained from
> other sources, we conclude that the heavy burden imposed
> as a condition to securing prior restraint was not met and
> the judgment of the Nebraska Supreme Court is therefore
> *reversed.*

Nebraska Press Association v. Stuart was hailed as a sizable
victory for the news media. Nevertheless, some scholars were
fretful about that decision's ultimate impact. Columbia University law professor Benno C. Schmidt, for example, found some
"disturbing undertones." He expressed the fear that the [37]

> * * * Court may have invited severe controls on
> the press's access to information about criminal proceed-
> ings from principals, witnesses, lawyers, the police, and
> others; it is even possible that some legal proceedings
> may be closed completely to the press and public as an
> indirect result of *Nebraska.*

He also worried that the Supreme Court's decision might encourage trial judges to place increasing reliance on stipulations
that parties in a trial—lawyers, witnesses, police, etc.—not provide
information in the press.

Schmidt was correct in his gloomy assessment of the Simants
case; the so-called victory of the press in Nebraska Press Associa-

[36] 427 U.S. 539, 565, 570, 96 S.Ct. 2791, 2804, 2806 (1976).

[37] Schmidt, "The Nebraska Decision," Columbia Journalism Review, November/
December, 1976, p. 51.

tion was hollow. As former Washington Star editor Newbold Noyes has observed.[38]

> It was Star Chamber, not publicity, that the founding fathers worried about. Defendants were guaranteed a public trial, not a cleared courtroom. The whole thrust of these amendments was—and must remain—that what happens in the courts happens out in the open, in full view of the citizenry, and that therein lies the individual's protection against the possible tyranny of government. There is no possible conflict between this idea and the idea of a free press.

Gagging Everybody But the Press?

Back in 1978, a trend then was discernible: gag news sources related to a judicial proceeding while leaving the press alone. The net result, of course, was much the same: a diminished flow of information about the judicial process. As trial courts close various courtroom proceedings, seal certain records, and decree that witnesses, attorneys and participants in trials do not speak to reporters, all that can be done is for the news media to fight back by going to court themselves. Noted First Amendment attorneys Dan Paul, Richard Ovelmen, James Spaniolo and Steven Kamp wrote late in 1984: "The most troubling trend in the cases decided during the last twelve months has been the use of gag orders on litigants and trial participants in order to block at the source public access to information concerning judicial proceedings." [39] The leading case? Seattle Times v. Rhinehart.[40]

Seattle Times v. Rhinehart (1984)

Keith Milton Rhinehart, leader of a religious group—the Aquarian Foundation. The Seattle Times had published a number of stories about Rhinehart and the Foundation, a group with fewer than 1,000 members, believers in life after death and the ability to communicate with the dead. Rhinehart was the group's chief spiritual medium.[41] As Justice Powell described articles about Rhinehart in the Seattle Times and the Walla Walla Union-Bulletin: [42]

[38] Speech at the University of Oregon, Ruhl Symposium Lectures, November 21, 1975, reprinted in "The Responsibilities of Power," School of Journalism, University of Oregon, June, 1976, pp. 16–17.

[39] Dan Paul, et al., op. cit., pp. 57–58.

[40] Seattle Times v. Rhinehart, 467 U.S. 20, 104 S.Ct. 2199 (1984), 10 Med.L.Rptr. 1705.

[41] 467 U.S. 20, 104 S.Ct. 2199, 2202 (1984), 10 Med.L.Rptr. 1705, 1706.

[42] Ibid.

One article referred to Rhinehart's conviction, later vacated, for sodomy. The four articles that appeared in 1978 concentrated on an "extravaganza" sponsored by Rhinehart at the Walla Walla State Penitentiary. The articles stated that he had treated 1,100 inmates to a 6-hour-long show, during which he gave away between $35,000 and $50,000 in cash and prizes. One article described a "chorus line of girls [who] shed their gowns and bikinis and sang * * *" The two articles that appeared in 1959 referred to a purported connection between Rhinehart and Lou Ferrigno, star of the popular television program, "The Incredible Hulk."

Rhinehart and five of the female members of the Aquarian Society who had taken part in the presentation at the penitentiary sued for libel and invasion of privacy, claiming that the stories were "'fictional and untrue.'" They asked damages totalling $14.1 million.

As part of the pre-trial discovery proceedings, the defendant newspapers asked for information about the financial affairs of The Aquarian Foundation, including information on donors. The trial court judge issued a protective order [called a "gag order" by journalists] forbidding the Seattle Times from publishing pre-trial discovery information about the Aquarian Foundation's donors, members, and finances.[43]

A unanimous Supreme Court of the United States upheld the gag order preventing release and publication of deposition material. Writing for the Court, Justice Powell said:[44]

> * * * [I]t is necessary to consider whether the "practice in question [furthers] an important or substantial governmental interest unrelated to the suppression of expression" and whether "the limitation of First Amendment freedoms [is] no greater than necessary or essential to the protection of the particular governmental interest involved." Procunier v. Martinez, 415 U.S. 396, 413, 94 S.Ct. 1800, 1811 (1974) * * *.
>
> * * *
>
> A litigant has no First Amendment right of access to information made available only for purposes of trying his suit. * * * Moreover, pretrial depositions and interrogatories are not public components of a civil trial.

Attorney Dan Paul and co-authors were not unconvinced by that reasoning. They wrote:[45]

[43] 467 U.S. 20, 104 S.Ct. 2199, 2204 (1984), 10 Med.L.Rptr. at 1707.

[44] 467 U.S. 20, 104 S.Ct. 2199, 2207 (1984), 10 Med.L.Rptr. at 1711.

[45] Dan Paul et al., op. cit., p. 59.

None of these reasons is persuasive. First Amendment cases have uniformly recognized that once the press has information in hand, by whatever lawful means, any prohibition on publication is a prior restraint.

SEC. 72. CLOSING PRE–TRIAL HEARINGS, OPENING TRIALS

Gannett v. DePasquale (1979) declared that *pre-trial* matters could be closed to press and public; Richmond Newspapers v. Virginia (1980) held that there is a First Amendment right to attend *trials*.

The Supreme Court had some good news for the press in 1978, and it came in the decision in Landmark Communications, Inc. v. Virginia. The Virginian Pilot, a daily newspaper owned by Landmark, late in 1975 published an accurate article reporting on a pending investigation by the Virginia Judicial Inquiry and Review Commission. The article named a state judge whose conduct was being investigated. Because such proceedings were required to be confidential by the Constitution of Virginia and by related enabling statutes, a grand jury indicted Landmark for violating Virginia law.

The newspaper's managing editor, Joseph W. Dunn, Jr., testified that he had chosen to publish material about the Judicial Inquiry and Review Commission because he believed the subject was a matter of public importance. Dunn stated that although he knew it was a misdemeanor for participants in such an action to divulge information from that Commission's proceedings, he did not think that the statute applied to newspaper reports.[46]

Chief Justice Burger, writing for a unanimous Court, said the issue was whether the First Amendment allows criminal punishment of third persons—including news media representatives— who publish truthful information about proceedings of the Judicial Inquiry and Review Commission. The Court concluded that "the publication Virginia seeks to punish under its statute lies near the core of the First Amendment, and the Commonwealth's interests advanced by the imposition of criminal sanctions are insufficient to justify the actual and potential encroachments on freedom of speech and of the press."

Although the Commission was entitled to meet in secret, and could preserve confidentiality of its proceedings and working papers, the press could not be punished for publication of such information once it has obtained it.[47]

[46] Landmark Communications, Inc. v. Virginia, 435 U.S. 829, 98 S.Ct. 1535 (1978).

[47] 435 U.S. 829, 838, 98 S.Ct. 1535, 1541 (1978).

Obtaining information about judicial proceedings, of course, implies access by public and press to those proceedings. And then, after the "good news" of *Landmark Communications* (1978), along came one of the Supreme Court's unpleasant surprises for the press: Gannett v. DePasquale.

Gannett v. DePasquale (1979)

Journalists are taught that government should never be given the power of secret arrest, secret confinement, or secret trial. With its decision in Gannett v. DePasquale, the Supreme Court of the United States said, in effect, that two out of three aren't bad. In a badly fragmented 5–4 vote, with a total of five opinions written, the Court held that the public—including the press—has no right to attend pretrial hearings. The issue in *DePasquale* was narrow: the Gannett Company was seeking to overturn a ruling barring its reporter from a pretrial hearing and forbidding the immediate release of a transcript of a secret hearing.

The Court's majority, however, did not restrict itself to pretrial hearings. Justice Potter Stewart's majority opinion also declared that the rights guaranteed by the Sixth Amendment did not extend to the public or to the press. Instead, those rights "are personal to the accused. * * * We hold that members of the public [and thus the press] have no constitutional right to attend criminal trials." Joining Justice Stewart in that view were Justices William Rehnquist and John Paul Stevens. Chief Justice Warren E. Burger joined the opinion of the Court, but argued that by definition, a " * * *; hearing on a motion before trial is not a *trial:* it is a *pre* trial hearing." Mr. Justice Lewis Powell, like the Chief Justice, concurred separately. Justice Powell expressed the belief that the reporter had an interest protected by the First Amendment to attend the pretrial hearing. However, he added that this right of access to courtroom proceedings is not absolute and must be balanced against a defendant's Sixth Amendment fair trial rights. In his concurring opinion, Justice William Rehnquist said that so far as the Constitution is concerned, it is up to the lower courts, "by accommodating competing interests in a judicious manner," to decide whether to open or close a court proceeding.

In a 44-page dissent joined by Justices William Brennan, Byron White, and Thurgood Marshall, Justice Harry Blackmun contended that the Sixth Amendment guarantees the public's right to attend hearings and trials. Justice Blackmun wrote that the Court's majority overreacted to "placid, routine, and innocuous" coverage of a criminal prosecution.

Gannett v. DePasquale arose when 42-year-old former police-man Wayne Clapp did not return from a July, 1976, fishing trip on upstate New York's Lake Seneca. He had been fishing with two men, aged 16 and 21, and those men returned in the boat without Clapp and drove away in Clapp's pickup truck. They were later arrested in Michigan after Clapp's disappearance had been report-ed and after bullet holes were found in Clapp's boat.

Gannett newspapers, the morning *Democrat & Chronicle* and the evening *Times-Union,* published stories about Clapp's disap-pearance and reported on police speculations that Clapp had been shot on his own boat and his body dumped overboard. In one story, the *Democrat & Chronicle* reported that the 16-year-old suspect, Kyle Greathouse, had led Michigan police to a place where he had buried Clapp's .357 magnum revolver. Defense attorneys then began taking steps to try to suppress statements made to police, claiming that those statements had been given involuntarily. The defense also tried to suppress evidence turned up in relation to the allegedly involuntary confessions, including the pistol.

During a pretrial hearing, when defense attorneys requested that press and public be excluded, Justice Daniel DePasquale granted the motion, evidently fearing that reporting on the hear-ing might prejudice defendants' rights in a later trial. Neither the prosecution nor reporter Carol Ritter of the *Democrat & Chronicle* objected to the clearing of the courtroom. On the next day, however, Ritter wrote Judge DePasquale, asserting a right to cover the hearing and asking to be given access to the transcript. The judge, refused to rescind his exclusion order or to grant the press or public immediate access to a transcript of the pre-trial hearing. Judge DePasquale's orders were overturned by an inter-mediate-level New York appeals court, but were upheld by the state's highest court, the Court of Appeals.[48] The Supreme Court of the United States subsequently granted certiorari.[49]

Although the issue of covering a pretrial hearing on suppre-sion of evidence is technically narrow, it is important. As James C. Goodale, former vice president of *The New York Times,* has written: [50]

> Only a fraction of the criminal cases brought ever go to trial. The real courtroom for most criminal trials in the United States is the pre-trial hearing, where proceed-

[48] Gannett v. De Pasquale, 43 N.Y.2d 370, 372 N.E.2d 544 (1977), reversing the Supreme Court of the State of New York, Appellate Division, Fourth Department's decision in 55 A.D.2d 107, 389 N.Y.S.2d 719 (1976).

[49] 443 U.S. 368, 99 S.Ct. 2898 (1979).

[50] James C. Goodale, "Open Justice: The Threat of *Gannett*," Communications and the Law, Vol. 1, No. 1 (Winter, 1979) pp. 12–13.

ings of a vital public concern often take place. * * *
[A] successful suppression motion will probably mean that
an account of the improper methods the police have used
to extract a certain confession will be brought out only at
the pretrial hearing, and nowhere else. * * * [T]his is
information which the public needs to have if its public
officers are to be held accountable. Without multiplying
examples, we need only remember the shocking trials of
Ginzburg and Scharansky behind closed doors in Russia
in the summer of 1978 to realize that criminal trials in
this country must remain open.

Other constitutional scholars and a variety of publications
expressed both shock and outrage at the Supreme Court's decision
in *DePasquale*. Fear of secret trials is in the American grain.
Even though England's despised secret Court of the Star Chamber
was abolished in 1641, it has been remembered as a symbol of
persecution ever since. The assumption by both public and press
has long been that open trials are needed to make sure that justice
is done. Harvard Law Professor Lawrence Tribe, a leading scholar, said after *DePasquale* was decided that there " ' * * * will be
no need to gag the press if stories can be choked off at the
source.' " Allen Neuharth, chairman of The Gannett Co., Inc.,
declared that " ' * * * those judges who share the philosophy of
secret trials can now run Star Chamber justice.' " [51] In any event,
the *DePasquale* holding was far removed from Justice William O.
Douglas's words in a 1947 contempt of court case, Craig v. Harney:
"[w]hat transpires in the court room is public property." [52]

Justice Potter Stewart wrote for the Court: [53]

* * *

Publicity concerning pretrial suppression hearings
such as the one involved in the present case poses special
risks of unfairness. The whole purpose of such hearings
is to screen out unreliable or illegally obtained evidence
and insure that this evidence does not become known to
the jury. Cf. Jackson v. Denno, 378 U.S. 368, 84 S.Ct.
1774 (1964). Publicity concerning the proceedings at a
pretrial hearing, however, could influence public opinion
against a defendant and inform potential jurors of incul-
patory information wholly inadmissible at the actual
trial.

* * *

[51] "Slamming the Courtroom Doors," Time, July 16, 1979, p. 66.

[52] Craig v. Harney, 331 U.S. 367, 374, 67 S.Ct. 1249, 1254 (1947).

[53] Gannett v. DePasquale, 443 U.S. 368, 378–381, 99 S.Ct. 2898, 2905–2906 (1979).

The Sixth Amendment, applicable to the States through the Fourteenth, surrounds a criminal trial with guarantees such as the rights to notice, confrontation, and compulsory process that have as their overriding purpose the protection of the accused from prosecutorial and judicial abuses. Among the guarantees that the Amendment provides to a person charged with the commission of a criminal offense, and to him alone, is the "right to a speedy and public trial, by an impartial jury." The Constitution nowhere mentioned any right of access to a criminal trial on the part of the public; its guarantee, like the others enumerated, is personal to the accused. See Faretta v. California, 422 U.S. 806, 846, 95 S.Ct. 2525, 2546 (1975) ("[T]he specific guarantees of the Sixth Amendment are personal to the accused.") (Blackmun, J., dissenting).

Our cases have uniformly recognized the public trial guarantee as one created for the benefit of the defendant.

Chief Justice Burger's concurring opinion simply maintained that by definition, a hearing on a motion before trial to suppress evidence is not a *trial*, it is a *pre-trial* hearing. Trials should be open, but pre-trial proceedings are "private to the litigants" and could be closed.

Justice Powell's concurrence argued that the reporter had an interest protected by the First and Fourteenth Amendments in being present at the pretrial suppression hearing. He added: [54]

As I have argued in Saxbe v. Washington Post Co., 417 U.S. 843, 850, 94 S.Ct. 2811, 2815 (1974) (Powell, J., dissenting), this constitutional protection derives, not from any special status of members of the press as such, but rather because "[i]n seeking out the news the press * * * acts as an agent of the public at large," each individual member of which cannot obtain for himself "the information needed for the intelligent discharge of his political responsibilities." Id., at 863, 94 S.Ct., at 2821.

Justice Powell then swung into his balancing act, stating that the right of access to courtroom proceedings is not absolute. It is limited by both the right of defendants to a fair trial and by needs of governments to obtain convictions and to maintain the confidentiality of sensitive information and of the identity of informants. In his view, representatives of the public and the press must be given an opportunity to protest closure motions. Then it would be the defendant's burden to offer evidence that the fairness

[54] 443 U.S. 368, 397–398, 99 S.Ct. 2898, 2914 (1979).

of his trial would be jeopardized by public and press access to the proceedings. On the other hand, the press and public should have to show that alternative procedures are available which would take away dangers to the defendant's chances of receiving a fair trial.[55]

Justice Rehnquist's concurring opinion scoffed that Justice Powell was advancing the idea " * * * that the First Amendment is some sort of constitutional 'sunshine law' that requires notice, an opportunity to be heard and substantial reasons before a governmental proceeding may be closed to public and press." [56]

Justice Blackmun's lengthy dissent was joined by Justices Brennan, White, and Marshall. Blackmun termed the news coverage of this case "placid, routine, and innocuous" and, indeed, relatively infrequent. After a long review of Anglo-American historical and constitutional underpinnings for public trials, he pointed to dangers he saw in closing court proceedings.[57]

> I, for one, am unwilling to allow trials and suppression hearings to be closed with no way to ensure that the public interest is protected. Unlike the other provisions of the Sixth Amendment, the public trial interest cannot adequately be protected by the prosecutor and judge in conjunction, or connivance, with the defendant. The specter of a trial or suppression hearing where a defendant of the same political party as the prosecutor and the judge—both of whom are elected officials perhaps beholden to the very defendant they are to try—obtains closure of the proceeding without any consideration for the substantial public interest at stake is sufficiently real to cause me to reject the Court's suggestion that the parties be given complete discretion to dispose of the public's interest as they see fit. The decision of the parties to close a proceeding in such a circumstance, followed by suppression of vital evidence or acquittal by the bench, destroys the appearance of justice and undermines confidence in the judicial system in a way no subsequent provision of a transcript might remedy. * * *

III

> At the same time, I do not deny that the publication of information learned in an open proceeding may harm irreparably, under certain circumstances, the ability of a defendant to obtain a fair trial. This is especially true in

---

[55] 443 U.S. 368, 398–399, 99 S.Ct. 2898, 2915 (1979).

[56] 443 U.S. 368, 405, 99 S.Ct. 2898, 2918 (1979).

[57] 443 U.S. 368, 438–439, 448, 99 S.Ct. 2898, 2935–2936, 2940 (1979).

the context of a pretrial hearing, where disclosure of information, determined to be inadmissible at trial, may severely affect a defendant's rights. Although the Sixth Amendment's public trial provisions establishes a strong presumption in favor of open proceedings, it does not require that all proceedings be held in open court when to do so would deprive a defendant of a fair trial.

* * *

On this record, I cannot conclude, as a matter of law, that there was sufficient showing to establish the strict and inescapable necessity that supports an exclusion order. The circumstances also would not have justified a holding by the trial court that there was a substantial probability that alternatives to closure would not have sufficed to protect the rights of the accused.

It has been said that publicity "is the soul of justice." J. Bentham, A Treatise on Judicial Evidence, 67 (1825). And in many ways it is: open judicial processes, especially in the criminal field, protect against judicial, prosecutorial, and police abuse; provide a means for citizens to obtain information about the criminal justice system and the performance of public officials; and safeguard the integrity of the courts. Publicity is essential to the preservation of public confidence in the rule of law and in the operation of courts.

Richmond Newspapers v. Virginia (1980)

On July 2, 1980—exactly one year after the Supreme Court of the United States ruled in Gannett v. DePasquale [58] that pretrial hearings could be closed—the Court held 7–1 that the public and the press have a First Amendment right to attend criminal trials. The 1980 case, Richmond Newspapers, Inc. v. Virginia, brought joyous responses from the press.

Anthony Lewis of *The New York Times* wrote, "For once a Supreme Court decision deserves that overworked adjective, historic."[59] His newspaper editorialized: "Now the Supreme Court has reasserted the obvious, at least as it pertains to trials. 'A presumption of openness inheres in the very nature of a criminal trial under our system of justice.' "[60] Even though *Richmond Newspapers* did not overrule *Gannett* where pretrial matters are

[58] 443 U.S. 368, 99 S.Ct. 2098 (1979).

[59] Anthony Lewis, "A Right To Be Informed," The New York Times, July 3, 1980, p. A–19.

[60] Editorial, "Wiping the Graffiti Off the Courtroom," The New York Times, July 3, 1980, p. A–18.

concerned, the Court's 1980 reliance on the First Amendment—
and not on the Sixth Amendment as in *Gannett*—gave hope to
journalists.

In fact, if Justice John Paul Stevens was correct in his
concurring opinion in *Richmond Newspapers,* "This is a watershed
case." He continued,[61]

> Until today the Court has accorded virtually absolute
> protection to the dissemination of information or ideas,
> but never before has it squarely held that the acquisition
> of newsworthy matter is entitled to any constitutional
> protection whatsoever.

Lewis said " * * * the Court today established for the first
time that the Constitution gives the public a right to learn how
public institutions function: a crucial right in a democracy." [62]
Attorney James Goodale said the Richmond case will help reporters to see " 'prisons, small-town meetings, the police blotter' " and
other places and documents often closed to the news media in the
past.

Years ago, Judge Learned Hand described his career on the
bench as "shoveling smoke." In 1979, the Supreme Court un-
limbered its smoke generator in the infamous *Gannett* case, ruling
by a 5–4 margin that the public and the press did not have a right
to attend pre-trial proceedings in criminal cases. Some of the
Justices' language billowed beyond pre-trial matters. As noted,
Justice Potter Stewart's plurality opinion announcing the Court's
judgment in *Gannett* declared that rights guaranteed by the Sixth
Amendment did not reach to the public or to the press. Those
rights, said Stewart, " * * * are personal to the accused.
* * * We hold that members of the public [and thus the press]
have no constitutional right to attend criminal trials." [63]

Four members of the Court later made public statements
professing shock about the way *Gannett* had been "misinterpreted," and that wholesale closings had not been endorsed by a
majority of the Court. Howls of protest arose from the media.
Goodale, then executive vice president of *The New York Times,*
wrote in 1979 that only a small fraction—perhaps 10 per cent—of
all criminal cases reach the trial stage. The real courtroom for
most criminal proceedings is the pre-trial hearing.[64]

In the wake of *Gannett,* many pretrial *and* trial proceedings
were closed. As a study by The Reporters Committee for Freedom

[61] Opinion of Mr. Justice Stevens, 448 U.S. 555, 100 S.Ct. 2814, 2830 (1980).

[62] Lewis, loc. cit.

[63] Gannett v. DePasquale, 443 U.S. 368, 99 S.Ct. 2898 (1979).

[64] Goodale, loc. cit.

of the Press showed, in the 10 months between the *Gannett* decision of July 2, 1979 and April 30, 1980, there were at least 220 attempts to close criminal justice proceedings. More than half were successful. Jack C. Landau, director of The Reporters Committee, wrote that "[j]udges are closing pre-indictment, trial, and post-trial proceedings, in addition to pre-trial proceedings." [65] *Newsweek* reported that in the year after *Gannett*, 155 proceedings were closed, including 30 actual trials. Four hundred attempts were made to close courtrooms between July, 1979, and May, 1981.[66]

The Richmond case arose when Baltimore resident John Paul Stevenson was convicted of second-degree murder in the slaying of a Hanover County, Virginia, motel manager. In late 1977, however, the Virginia Supreme Court reversed Stevenson's conviction, concluding that a bloodstained shirt belonging to Stevenson had been admitted improperly as evidence.[67] Subsequently, two additional jury trials of Stevenson ended in mistrials, one when a juror had to be excused and the other because a prospective juror may have read about the defendant's previous trials and may have told other jurors about the case before the retrial began.

On September 11, 1978, the same court—for the fourth time—attempted to try Stevenson. Reporters Tim Wheeler of the *Richmond Times-Dispatch* and Kevin McCarthy of the *Richmond News-Leader,* along with all other members of the public, were barred from the courtroom by Hanover County Circuit Court Judge Richard H.C. Taylor, after defense counsel said.[68]

> "[T]here was this woman that was with the family of the deceased when we were here before. She had sat in the Courtroom. I would like to ask that everybody be excluded from the Courtroom because I don't want any information being shuffled back and forth when we have a recess as to what—who testified to what."

Trial judge Taylor had presided after two of the previous three trials of Stevenson. After hearing that the prosecution had no objection to the closure, excluded all parties from the trial except witnesses when they testified.[69] Since no one—including reporters Wheeler and McCarthy—had objected to closure, the

---

[65] The Reporters Committee for Freedom of the Press, Court Watch Summary, May, 1980; Southern Newspaper Publishers Association Bulletin, Aug. 10, 1981.

[66] Newsweek, July 14, 1980, p. 24.

[67] Stevenson v. Commonwealth, 218 Va. 462, 237 S.E.2d 779 (1977).

[68] Opinion of Chief Justice Burger, Richmond Newspapers, Inc. v. Virginia, 448 U.S. 555, 559, 100 S.Ct. 2814, 2818 (1980).

[69] Virginia Code § 19.2–2.66, which provided that courts may, in their discretion, exclude any persons from the trial whose presence would impair the trial's conduct, provided that the right of an accused to a fair trial shall not be violated.

order was made. Later that same day, however, the Richmond newspapers and their reporters asked for a hearing on a motion to vacate the closure order. Reporters were not allowed to attend the hearing on that order, however, since Judge Taylor ruled that it was a part of the trial. The closure order remained in force.

On the trial's second day, Judge Taylor—after excusing the jury—declared that Stevenson was not guilty of murder, and the defendant was allowed to leave. The Richmond Newspapers then appealed the court closing, unsuccessfully petitioning the Virginia Supreme Court for writs of mandamus and prohibition. The Supreme Court of the United States granted certiorari.

Chief Justice Burger's Opinion

Chief Justice Warren Burger reiterated his view, as stated in Gannett v. DePasquale, that while pre-trial hearings need not be open, trials should be open. In this case, he did not take the Sixth Amendment (right to fair trial) route of the majority in *DePasquale*. [70] Instead, he emphasized that the question in *Richmond Newspapers* [71] was whether the First and Fourteenth Amendments guarantee a right of the public (including the press) to attend trials.

He said that in prior cases, the Court has dealt with questions involving conflicts between publicity and defendants' rights to a fair trial, including Nebraska Press Association v. Stuart,[72] Sheppard v. Maxwell,[73] and Estes v. Texas.[74] But this case, in his view, was a "first:" the Court was asked to decide whether a criminal trial itself may be closed to the public on the defendant's request alone, with no showing that closure is required to protect the right to a fair trial.

After having thus stated the issue, the Chief Justice traced Anglo-American judicial history back to the days before the Norman Conquest and forward through the American colonial experience.[75] In addition to this historical ammunition, Burger quoted Dean Wigmore, who wrote long ago that " '[t]he publicity of a judicial proceeding is a requirement of much broader bearing than its mere effect on the quality of testimony.' " The Chief Justice

[70] Gannett v. DePasquale, 443 U.S. 368, 99 S.Ct. 2898 (1979).

[71] Richmond Newspapers, Inc. v. Virginia, 448 U.S. 555, 564, 100 S.Ct. 2814, 2821 (1980).

[72] 427 U.S. 539, 96 S.Ct. 2791 (1976).

[73] 384 U.S. 333, 86 S.Ct. 1507 (1966).

[74] 381 U.S. 532, 85 S.Ct. 1628 (1965). The Chief Justice also cited Murphy v. Florida, 421 U.S. 794, 95 S.Ct. 2031 (1975), in which Jack (Murph the Surf) Murphy, unsuccessfully pleaded that prejudicial pre-trial publicity had deprived him of a fair day in court.

[75] Richmond Newspapers, Inc. v. Virginia, 448 U.S. 555, 100 S.Ct. 2814 (1980).

also found a "significant community therapeutic value" in public trials. He then became expansive about the role of the press as a stand-in for the public, a role often claimed by the press but one which had received little judicial support.[76]

Looking back, we see that when the ancient "town meeting" form of trial became too cumbersome, twelve members of the community were delegated to act as surrogates, but the community did not surrender its right to observe the conduct of trials. The people retained a "right of visitation" which enabled them to satisfy themselves that justice was in fact being done.

People in an open society do not demand infallibility from their institutions, but it is difficult for them to accept what they are prohibited from observing.

* * *

In earlier times, both in England and America, attendance at court was a common mode of "passing the time." * * * With the press, cinema and electronic media now supplying the representations of reality of the real life drama once available only in the courtroom, attendance at court is no longer a widespread pastime. * * * Instead of acquiring information about trials by firsthand observation or by word of mouth from those who attended, people now acquire it chiefly through the print and electronic media. In a sense, this validates the media claim of functioning as surrogates for the public. While media representatives enjoy the same right of access as the public, they often are provided special seating and priority of entry so that they may report what people in attendance have seen and heard. This "contribute[s] to public understanding of the rule of law and to comprehension of the functioning of the entire criminal justice system. * * *" Nebraska Press Ass'n v. Stuart, 427 U.S. 539, 587, 96 S.Ct. 2791, 2816 (1976) (Brennan, J., concurring).

Burger than disposed of the State of Virginia's arguments that neither the constitution nor the Bill of Rights contains guarantees of a public right to attend trials. He responded that the Court has recognized that "certain unarticulated rights" are implicit in the Bill of Rights, including the rights of association, privacy, and the right to attend criminal trials. He then inserted footnote 17, which may become important in the future: "Whether the public has a right to attend trials of civil cases is a question

76 448 U.S. 555, 572–573, 100 S.Ct. 2814 (1980).

not by this case, but we note that historically both civil and criminal trials have been presumptively open." [77]

Despite the sweep of Burger's words, he was not saying that all criminal trials must be open to the press and public. Instead, he criticized the conduct of the court in the murder trial of John Paul Stevenson. There, despite its being the fourth trial of the defendant, the judge " * * * made no findings to support closure; no inquiry was made as to whether alternative solutions [such as sequestration of the jury] would have met the need to insure fairness; there was no recognition of any right under the Constitution for the public or press to attend the trial." He concluded: "Absent an overriding interest articulated in findings, the trial of a criminal case must be open to the public. Accordingly, the judgment under review is reversed." [78]

Note that Justice Powell took no part in the consideration or decision of this case. And remember that Powell declared, concurring in Gannett v. DePasquale, that reporters had a *limited* First Amendment right to attend pre-trial hearings. And Justices Blackmun, Brennan, White, and Marshall all agreed that public and press had a right, either under the First or the Sixth Amendment, to attend both pre-trial hearings and trials. Thus, although the First Amendment is not an absolute, it appears that the breadth of the language in *Richmond Newspapers* about *trials* has once again made attendance at *pre-trial* proceedings an open question.

In his concurring opinion, Justice Stevens said: [79]

> * * * I agree that the First Amendment protects the public and the press from abridgment of their rights of access to information about the operation of their government, including the judicial branch; given the total absence of any record justification for the closure order entered in this case, that order violated the First Amendment.

Justice Brennan, joined by Justice Marshall, presented a marvelously complex concurrence, speaking of the structural value of public access in various circumstances. "But the First Amendment embodies more than a commitment to free expression and communicative interchange for their own sakes; it has a *structural* role to play in securing and fostering our republican form of self-government." He added: [80]

[77] 448 U.S. 555, 581, 100 S.Ct. 2814, 2829 (1980), at footnote 17.

[78] 448 U.S. 555, 581, 100 S.Ct. 2814, 2830 (1980).

[79] 448 U.S. 555, 584, 100 S.Ct. 2814, 2830 (1980).

[80] 448 U.S. 555, 595, 100 S.Ct. 2814, 2833, 2837 (1980).

Open trials assure the public that procedural rights are respected, and that justice is afforded equally. Closed trials breed suspicion of prejudice and arbitrariness, which in turn spawns disrespect for the law. Public access is essential, therefore, if trial adjudication is to achieve the objective of maintaining public confidence in the administration of justice.

Note also that Justice Rehnquist, who seems unconcerned by possible threats of secret judicial proceedings to society, was the only member of the court in both the *Gannett* and *Richmond* cases who could find no support for a right of public and press to attend judicial proceedings under either a Sixth Amendment or First Amendment rationale.[81]

Access Rights Need Defense

Although *Richmond Newspapers* has a much nicer ring than Gannett v. DePasquale, it does leave unanswered questions about the right to cover pre-trial matters, the matters which make up the bulk of our criminal justice process. During the dark days of 1979 and 80, after Gannett v. DePasquale was decided, reporters covering the judicial process began carrying their "Gannett cards." Various organizations made up statements for reporters to read in court when they were about to be ousted from pre-trial or trial proceedings. In fact, a Gannett card—literally from the Gannett organization—said: [82]

"Your honor, I am _____, a reporter for _____, and I would like to object on behalf of my employer and the public to this proposed closing. Our attorney is prepared to make a number of arguments against closings such as this one, and we respectfully ask the Court for a hearing on those issues. I believe our attorney can be here relatively quickly for the Court's convenience and he will be able to demonstrate that closure in this case will violate the First Amendment, and possibly state statutory and constitutional provisions as well. I cannot make the arguments myself, but our attorney can point out several issues for your consideration. If it pleases the Court, we request the opportunity to be heard through counsel."

Reporters, then, should hang on to their "Gannett Cards" and be ready to read them should a judge decide—on application from counsel—to give them the heave-ho from a judicial (including pre-trial) proceedings. After all, as attorney James C. Goodale has

[81] 448 U.S. 555, 605, 100 S.Ct. 2814, 2843 (1980).

[82] Other news organizations, such as Knight-Ridder, had similar cards made for their reporters.

written, even the *Gannett* case required three conditions before closure of a pre-trial hearing: [83]

> (1) there would be irreparable damage to the defendant's fair trial rights,
>
> (2) there were no alternative means to deal with the publicity and
>
> (3) the closure would be effective, i.e. no leaks.

If judicial proceedings are to remain open, reporters will have to stand ready to speak up, to protest closures. And their employers, obviously, will have to stand ready to go to court—to expend the money and energy to try to keep court proceedings open. Without protests and court tests, closures will simply occur. And when contested, closures can often be reversed. Reporters in courts—whether they like it or not—must sometimes be a first line of defense against secret court proceedings.[84]

Access to Courts after *Richmond Newspapers*

During the first four years after Richmond Newspapers v. Virginia (1980), the Supreme Court of the United States filled in some of that decision's promising outlines where coverage of the judicial process is concerned. Three key cases are: [85]

1. Globe Newspapers v. Superior Court (1982).

2. Press-Enterprise Co. v. Superior Court (1984).

3. Waller v. Georgia (1984).

Globe Newspapers v. Superior Court (1982)

The Boston Globe challenged the constitutionality of a Massachusetts statute providing for the exclusion of the public from trials of certain sex offenses involving victims under the age of 18. Globe reporters had tried unsuccessfully to get access to a rape trial in the Superior Court for the County of Norfolk, Massachusetts. Charges against the defendant in the trial involved forcible rape and forced unnatural rape of three girls who were minors at the time of the trial—two were 16 and one was 17. Writing for

---

[83] James C. Goodale, "The Three-Part Open Door Test in Richmond Newspapers Case," The National Law Journal, Sept. 22, 1980, p. 26.

[84] See James D. Spaniolo, Dan Paul, Parker D. Thomson and Richard Ovemlen, "Access After *Richmond Newspapers*," in James C. Goodale, chairman, Communications Law 1980 (New York: Practising Law Institute, 1980), pp. 385–648, for an intensive discussion of and listing of recent cases involving access to judicial proceedings. See especially pp. 452–456, dealing with access to judicial records.

[85] Globe Newspapers v. Superior Court, 457 U.S. 596, 102 S.Ct. 2613 (1982), 8 Med.L.Rptr. 1689; Press-Enterprise v. Superior Court, 464 U.S. 501, 104 S.Ct. 819 (1984), 10 Med.L.Rptr. 1161; Waller v. Georgia, 467 U.S. ___, 104 S.Ct. 2210 (1984), 10 Med.L.Rptr. 1714.

the Court, Justice Brennan held that the Massachusetts statute providing for mandatory closure of such cases violated the First Amendment of access to criminal trials. He said: [86]

> The Court's recent decision in Richmond Newspapers firmly established for the first time that the press and the general public have a constitutional right of access to criminal trials. Although there was no opinion of the Court in that case, seven Justices recognized that this right of access is embodied in the First Amendment, and applied to the States through the Fourteenth Amendment.
>
> * * *
>
> * * * [T]he right of access to criminal trials plays a particularly significant role in the functioning of the judicial process and the government as a whole. Public scrutiny of a criminal trial enhances the quality and safeguards the integrity of the factfinding process, with benefits to both the defendant and to society as a whole.
>
> * * *
>
> We agree * * * that the first interest—safeguarding the physical and psychological wellbeing of a minor is a compelling one. But as compelling as that is, it does not justify a mandatory closure rule, for it is clear that the circumstances of the particular case may affect the significance of the interest. A trial court can determine on a case-by-case basis whether closure is necessary to protect the welfare of a minor victim.

Chief Justice Burger and Justice Rehnquist dissented, complaining that Justice Brennan had ignored " * * * a long history of exclusion of the public from trials involving sexual assaults, particularly those against minors." [87]

Press-Enterprise v. Superior Court (1984)

The Riverside (California) Press-Enterprise was trying to cover a rape trial, and wanted its reporters present during the *voir dire* proceedings, the in-depth questioning of prospective jurors. The newspaper moved that the *voir dire* be open to public and press. The State of California opposed the motion, arguing that with the public and press present, jurors' responses would not be candid, and that this would endanger the entire trial.

Writing for a unanimous Supreme Court, Chief Justice Burger wrote that the roots of open trials reach back to the days before

[86] Globe Newspapers v. Superior Court, 457 U.S. 596, 102 S.Ct. 2613, 2618–2620 (1984), 8 Med.L.Rptr. 1689, 1692–1694.

[87] 457 U.S. 596, 102 S.Ct. 2613, 2624 (1984), 8 Med.L.Rptr. at 1697.

the Norman Conquest in England, and related to that was a "presumptive openness" in the jury selection process.[88]   He added:

> For present purposes, how we allocate the "right" to openness as between the accused and the public, or whether we view it as a component inherent in the system benefitting both, is not crucial.   No right ranks higher than the right of the accused to a fair trial.   But the primacy of the accused's right is difficult to separate; from the right of everyone in the community to attend the *voir dire* which promotes fairness.

This fact situation was made harsher by the trial judge's keeping six weeks of the *voir dire* proceedings closed (although three days were open).   Media requests for transcripts of the *voir dire* were refused; the California court argued that Sixth Amendment (defendant's right to a fair trial) and juror privacy rights coalesced to support closure of the proceeding.   The Supreme Court disagreed.   Chief Justice Burger wrote: [89]

> The judge at this trial closed an incredible six weeks of *voir dire* without considering alternatives to closure. Later the court declined to release a transcript of the voir dire even while stating that most of the material in the transcript was "dull and boring." * * * Those parts of the transcript reasonably entitled to privacy could have been sealed without such a sweeping order; a trial judge should explain why the material is entitled to privacy.

Waller v. Georgia (1984)

Waller was a defendant charged with violation of Georgia's Racketeer Influenced and Corrupt Organizations (RICO) Act.   A pre-trial suppression hearing was held, in which Waller and other defendants asked that wiretap evidence and evidence seized during searches be suppressed—that is, disallowed or declared inadmissible.

The prosecuting attorney asked that the suppression hearing be closed, contending that if the evidence were presented in open court and published, it might become "tainted" and therefore unusable, especially in future prosecutions.   The court ordered the suppression hearing closed to all persons except witnesses, the defendants, and lawyers and court personnel.   The defendant, however, wanted the hearings to be open.

---

[88] Press-Enterprise v. Superior Court, 464 U.S. 501, 104 S.Ct. 819, 823 (1984), 10 Med.L.Rptr. 1161, 1164.

[89] 464 U.S. 501, 104 S.Ct. 819, 826 (1984), 10 Med.L.Rptr. 1161, 1166.

Writing for the Court, Justice Lewis Powell cited the *Press-Enterprise* case approvingly, noting that even though the suppression hearing had been closed for its seven days, there were less than two and one-half hours' worth of wiretap evidence tapes played in the court.[90]

As trial courts close various courtroom proceedings, seal certain records, and decree that witnesses, attorneys, and participants in trials do not speak to the press, all can be done is for news media to fight back by going to court themselves. At this point, decisions of judges and appellate courts on questions such as closing pretrial hearings and sealing records ride off in many directions.[91] However, it may be said that Richmond Newspapers v. Virginia's broad language seeming to endorse a First Amendment right to access to information has had some effect. Whether this right (if indeed it yet exists) will continue to grow depends on future decisions. Meanwhile, there will likely continue to be many situations in which the news media will be thwarted in efforts to cover the judicial process.

A case which Miami Herald attorney Dan Paul has called "a real high water mark showing just how far a judge can go and get away with it" [92] involved a criminal prosecution of former U.S. Senator Edward J. Gurney of Florida. During Gurney's 1975 trial, Federal District Judge Ben Krentzman would not allow the press access to exhibits which had been identified but were not yet received as evidence. The press could not see written communications between the judge and the jury. Reporters were also denied access to a list of jury members, and could not listen in on conferences at the bench between attorneys and the judge. The Miami Herald had argued that access to such exhibits and information was necessary for an understanding of the case. On appeal, the Circuit Court for the Fifth Circuit held that the trial court was within its rights in denying press access to the information it sought.[93]

[90] 467 U.S. 39, 104 S.Ct. 2210, 2213 (1984), 10 Med.L.Rptr. 1714, 1715–1716.

[91] See Dan Paul et al., op. cit., pp. 247–276.

[92] See Carmody, op. cit.; and Floyd Abrams, "Gathering the News, Rights and Restraints" in James C. Goodale, Chairman, Communications Law 1977, Volume One (New York City: Practising Law Institute, 1977), pp. 85–103; Paul quoted in Carmody, op. cit.

[93] United States v. Gurney, 562 F.2d 1257 (5th Cir.1977).

Part IV

MEDIA INSTITUTIONS AND THE ADMINISTRATIVE AGENCIES

Chapter 12

REGULATION OF BROADCASTING AND CABLE

SEC. 73. BROADCASTING AND FREE EXPRESSION

While government regulation of broadcasting has retreated sharply during the 1980s, major controls remain for radio, television, and cable.

The faint pulse of government regulation that greeted broadcasting's infancy swelled within a half century to a sometimes thundering if erratic beat, before subsiding under the doctrine of the deregulation of industry and commerce mandated by the federal administration of the 1980s. It would not go away, of course, for electronic devices and systems were multiplying inordinately. Their capacity for interfering with each other and confounding delivery of communication demanded continuing oversight.

Voice broadcasting had emerged in the 1920's under law that permitted anyone who applied for a broadcast license to get one. By 1926, the limited number of frequencies available for broadcasting was unable to carry the traffic without intolerable interference among stations. A dial-twirler's excursion across his radio set frequencies was a tour of Babel. At broadcasters' request and with full agreement from officials, Congress passed the Radio Act of 1927, establishing a Federal Radio Commission (FRC) as an administrative agency to regulate and control traffic and to see that broadcasting was carried out according to the "public interest, convenience, or necessity." The FRC was to choose among applicants for access to the air waves, and license the chosen. In 1934, Congress passed the Communications Act establishing the Federal Communications Commission (FCC), under which radio and television have been regulated since, and telephone and telegraph as well.[1] Seven Commissioners appointed by the President made up its membership until the number was cut to five as of 1983.

The nature of the physical universe had dictated that broadcasting somehow be controlled; there were not enough frequencies to permit everyone who wished to do so to broadcast. And the fact that individuals and corporations could scarcely lay claim to ownership of the air waves, which existed much more in the context of a public resource than of a private one, argued for government's controlling access to the air waves in the name of the public.

Yet this situation plainly raised questions about government's relation to free speech and press. No agency of government regulated newspapers, books and magazines. The government's choosing among applicants and subsequent licensing of the chosen was a process that was not tolerable under free press principles for the print media. The FCC was indeed barred by the Communications Act from censorship of the content of broadcasting, but the choosing and licensing process was upheld by the courts as constitutional. It was held in National Broadcasting Co. v. United States: [2]

> Freedom of utterance is abridged to many who wish to use the limited facilities of radio. Unlike other media of expression, radio inherently is not available to all. That is its unique characteristic; and that is why, unlike other modes of expression, it is subject to governmental regulation. Because it cannot be used by all, some who wish to use it must be denied * * *. The standard provided for the licensing of stations by the Communications Act of 1934 was the "public interest, convenience, or necessity." Denial of a station license on that ground, if valid under the Act, is not a denial of free speech.

Principles of free speech, then, did not stand in the way of denying a person a license. Furthermore, there were positive obligations upon the holder of a license to operate in the public interest, obligations which were not imposed upon the printed media. In a case involving complaints against a station for

---

[1] Sydney W. Head, Broadcasting in America (Boston: Houghton Mifflin Company, 1972) 2d ed., Chap. 8. The Act of 1927 is 44 Stat. 1162; of 1934, 48 Stat. 1064.

[2] 319 U.S. 190, 63 S.Ct. 997, 1014 (1943).

programming public affairs shows that had overtones of racial and religious discrimination, the Federal Court of Appeals spoke of the differences between newspapers and broadcasters: [3]

> A broadcaster has much in common with a newspaper publisher, but he is not in the same category in terms of public obligations imposed by law. A broadcaster seeks and is granted the free and exclusive use of a limited and valuable part of the public domain; when he accepts that franchise, it is burdened by enforceable obligations. A newspaper can be operated at the whim or caprice of its owners; a broadcasting station cannot. After nearly five decades of operation, the broadcasting industry does not seem to have grasped the simple fact that a broadcast license is a public trust subject to termination for breach of duty.

A striking example of expression that might result in the legal foreclosure of continued broadcasting, but not of newspaper publishing, appeared in a pair of court decisions in 1931 and 1932. The first was Near v. Minnesota; the second was Trinity Methodist Church, South v. FRC. In the first case, the United States Supreme Court ruled that government could not forbid a newspaper to publish because it had made scurrilous attacks on police and law enforcement officials, and on Jews. In the second, the Federal Appeals Court ruled that the Federal Radio Commission could deny a radio broadcaster a new license and thus access to the air waves because it had previously made scurrilous attacks on judges and the administration of justice and on Roman Catholics.

Near v. Minnesota [4] involved a scandal sheet published in Minneapolis by J.M. Near and a partner who ran afoul of an extraordinary Minnesota law. The famous "Gag law" provided that it was a public nuisance to engage in the regular, persistent publication of a "malicious, scandalous and defamatory" periodical. The state could step in, stop, and permanently suppress such a publication. If a publisher disobeyed an injunction against his publishing, and resumed it, he could be punished for contempt of court. Under the law, Near was enjoined from continuing to publish his *Saturday Press*. He challenged the constitutionality of the law, and the United States Supreme Court reversed his conviction.

Chief Justice Charles Evans Hughes said the question was whether a law authorizing such government action to restrain publication squared with freedom of the press as historically

---

[3] Office of Communications of United Church of Christ v. FCC, 123 U.S.App.D.C. 328, 359 F.2d 994, 1003 (1966).

[4] 283 U.S. 697, 51 S.Ct. 625 (1931).

conceived and guaranteed. What was done to Near was to restrain him in advance of publication—the "prior restraint" that was the licensing and censorship of old. Tracing the history of the guarantee of free press, he said that previous restraint is unconstitutional except in "exceptional cases" such as publication of troop movements in war time and incitements to acts of violence endangering the community. He said it was unavailing to the state to insist [5]

> * * * that the statute is designed to prevent the circulation of scandal which tends to disturb the public peace and to provoke assaults and the commission of crime. Charges of reprehensible conduct, and in particular of official malfeasance, unquestionably create a public scandal, but the theory of the constitutional guaranty is that even a more serious public evil would be caused by authority to prevent publication.

Hughes said that "reckless assaults upon public men * * * exert a baleful influence" and deserve condemnation by public opinion. But, he said, the growth of complexity in government, the opportunities for corruption in government, the rise in crime and the danger of its protection by unfaithful officials and official neglect, emphasize "the primary need of a vigilant and courageous press." He added: [6]

> The fact that the liberty of the press may be abused by miscreant purveyors of scandal does not make any the less necessary the immunity of the press from previous restraint in dealing with official misconduct.

Prosecutions and law suits for libel, said Justice Hughes, are the proper remedy for false and defamatory statements, not prohibition of publishing which is "the essence of censorship." The law was unconstitutional, and Near was free to publish.

But not so the Reverend Doctor Schuler, lessee and operator of radio station KGEF in Los Angeles. He filed for the renewal of his broadcast license in 1930, and numerous citizens protested to the FRC. It denied Schuler's request for re-licensing on grounds that his broadcasts attacked the Roman Catholic Church, were sensational rather than instructive, and obstructed the orderly administration of public justice (he had been convicted of contempt for attacking judges). The Reverend Schuler's church, Trinity Methodist South, took the decision to court on grounds that it violated free speech and due process. The Federal Appeals

[5] Ibid., 283 U.S. 697, 722, 51 S.Ct. 625, 633 (1931).

[6] Ibid., 720.

Court denied its appeal and upheld the denial of a license.[7] It said that Congress has the right to establish agencies to regulate the airwaves, and such agencies can refuse to renew licenses to one who has abused a license to broadcast defamatory and untrue matter. This denial of a permit, the Court held, is different from taking away property. Then it spoke of the kinds of materials and attacks that KGEF had broadcast, and gave its view as to their effect:[8]

> If it be considered that one in possession of a permit to broadcast in interstate commerce may, without let or hindrance from any source, use these facilities, reaching out, as they do, from one corner of the country to the other, to obstruct the administration of justice, offend the religious susceptibilities of thousands, inspire political distrust and civic discord, or offend youth and innocence by the use of words suggestive of sexual immorality, and be answerable for slander only at the instance of the one offended, then this great science, instead of a boon, will become a scourge, and the nation a theatre for the display of individual passions and collision of personal interests. This is neither censorship nor previous restraint, nor is it a whittling away of the rights guaranteed by the First Amendment, or an impairment of their free exercise
>
> * * *.

Taken together, the two decisions made it clear that a newspaper owner could not be stopped from publishing because of his attacks on officials and religious groups, but that a radio broadcaster could be stopped for similar attacks.

Yet the Trinity decision was not the end of the matter. As the FCC groped in its early decades for policies that would regulate without violating free expression, it reached a position which said that the airing of controversial topics—including religion—should be encouraged in broadcasting. Its famous fairness doctrine, first elaborated in its report of 1949,[9] offered the position that the "public interest requires ample play for the free and fair competition of opposing views." And in a case of 1968, where the Anti-Defamation League charged anti-Semitism in the broadcasts of station KTYM, Inglewood, Calif., the Commission did not refuse to renew the license. After noting that KTYM had offered the ADL free and equal time to respond to the anti-Semitism and that the ADL had refused, the Commission said:[10]

[7] Trinity Methodist Church, South v. FRC, 61 U.S.App.D.C. 311, 62 F.2d 850 (1932), certiorari denied 284 U.S. 685, 52 S.Ct. 204, 288 U.S. 599, 53 S.Ct. 317 (1933).

[8] Ibid., 61 U.S.App.D.C. 311, 62 F.2d 850, 852–3 (1932).

[9] Editorializing by Broadcast Licensees, Report, 13 F.C.C. 1246 (1949).

[10] Anti-Defamation League of B'Nai B'Rith v. FCC, 403 F.2d 169 (D.C.Cir.1968), certiorari denied 394 U.S. 930, 89 S.Ct. 1190 (1969).

The Commission has long held that its function is not to judge the merit, wisdom or accuracy of any broadcast discussion or commentary but to insure that all viewpoints are given fair and equal opportunity for expression and that controverted allegations are balanced by the presentation of opposing viewpoints. Any other position would stifle discussion and destroy broadcasting as a medium of free speech.

With the growth in stature and importance of non-commercial broadcasting stations in the 1970s and 1980s, decisions expanding autonomy were delivered by courts. One concerned the film "Death of a Princess," the account of the execution for adultery of a Saudi Arabian princess and her commoner lover. Alabama's Educational Television Commission publicly scheduled the film for its station, and so did the University of Houston (Texas) station, KUHT–TV. But both withdrew it from the schedule, reacting in Alabama to viewers who said they feared for friends and relatives in Saudi Arabia if the film were shown, and in Texas to the "strong and understandable objections by the government of Saudi Arabia" at a time when crisis in the Middle East and America's national interests were factors. Residents of both states sued to have the film reinstated, and the U.S. Court of Appeals, Fifth District, sitting *en banc* with 23 judges taking part, decided the cases—16 to 7—in favor of the stations.[11]

The Court held that it was not censorship or violation of the First Amendment rights of viewers for state-operated stations to cancel scheduled programs because of station officials' opposition to programs' political content. Stations, it said, are not "public forums" like parks, streets, and certain buildings where there is a right of public access and the government may impose only minimal restrictions on speech and press. What these stations were up to was exercising program authority under statutes; the plaintiffs had no right of access to airwaves or public stations—as they might have to public forums—to compel the broadcast of any particular program.[12]

The First Amendment, it said, does not hinder the government from exercising editorial control over its own medium of expression. The plaintiffs failed to recognize differences between state regulation of private expression and the exercise of editorial discretion by these state officials: [13]

[11] Muir v. Alabama Educational Television Commission, 688 F.2d 1033 (5th Cir. 1982) 8 Med.L.Rptr. 2305, certiorari denied 9 Med.L.Rptr. # 7, 3/15/83, News Notes.

[12] 8 Med.L.Rptr. 2312.

[13] Ibid., 2315, 2316.

As the Supreme Court pointed out in *CBS,* 412 U.S. at
124, 93 S.Ct. at 3097, "[f]or better or worse, editing is
what editors are for; and editing is selection and choice of
material." In exercising their editorial discretion state
officials will unavoidably make decisions which can be
characterized as "politically motivated." All television
broadcast licensees are required, under the public interest
standard, to cover political events and to provide news
and public affairs programs dealing with the political,
social, economic and other issues which concern their
community. * * *

While the plaintiffs agreed that it is proper for a licensee to
decide not to schedule a program at the outset, they argued that
it is unconstitutional for the licensee to decide to cancel a
scheduled program because of its political content. But the
Court of Appeals said that both decisions are editorial in nature,
and both require the licensee to determine what will best serve
the public interest.

Federal Communications Commission v. League of Women
Voters, a 1984 decision by the United States Supreme Court,
supported quite another kind of autonomy.[14] It ruled that a
federal law which prohibited editorializing by noncommercial stations that received monies from the Corporation for Public Broadcasting—a federal agency—was unconstitutional. The law—Sec.
399 of the Public Broadcasting Act of 1967—was a "substantial
abridgement of important journalistic freedoms which the First
Amendment jealously protects," Justice William Brennan wrote
for the majority in a 5–4 decision. The government argued that
Sec. 399 had been passed to prevent these stations from being
pressured to become government propaganda voices as a *quid pro
quo* for receiving federal funds. Brennan scoffed at that danger,
finding various protections against such an eventuality; but in
dissent, Justice John Paul Stevens found the law important as a
provision "designed to avoid the insidious evils of government
propaganda favoring particular points of view."[15] Also in dissent,
Justice Rehnquist wrote that, in passing Sec. 399, "Congress
simply * * * decided not to subsidize stations" of the noncommercial class which editorialize, and that nothing in the Constitution is at odds with that. Thus by the narrowest of margins,
Pacifica Foundation, owner of several noncommercial stations and
one of the challengers of Sec. 399, expanded (as it had in other
cases) the elbow-room in which noncommercial stations may operate.

[14] __ U.S. __, 104 S.Ct. 3106 (1984), 10 Med.L.Rptr. 1937.

[15] Ibid., 1948–49, 1958.

During decades of controversy over regulation as a dilution of free expression, the Federal Communications Commission never has been free from attacks by polar opposites. On the one hand are those who charge that the Commission is a "captive" of broadcasters whose pressure to keep hands off the industry prevents it from fulfilling proper regulatory duties. On the other hand are those who charge that it has limited or suppressed freedom of expression through an excess of regulatory zeal and bureaucratic red tape.

Not until the 1980s, however, did a combination of political, technological, and economic factors place the latter clearly in the ascendancy, and the former on the defensive. Deregulation of broadcasting, begun in the mid 1970s, leaped ahead in the Reagan administration of the 1980s, under a changed philosophy about government's role in the public life. But in addition, decades of insistence that airwave frequencies were no longer a "scarce resource" permitting only limited competition among broadcast voices, became ever more prominent and persuasive. President Reagan's FCC Chairman, Mark Fowler, stressed the theme that there was vastly greater head-to-head competition among broadcasters than among daily newspapers, a result of technological advances over decades, and that under 1984 FCC rulemaking, more than 1,000 new FM radio stations would soon be on the air, as well as hundreds of low-power television stations.[16]

In rejecting the "scarce resource" argument, proponents of deregulation were belaboring one of two underlying bases for deregulation long and widely relied upon. Above, we saw a Federal Appeals Court citing scarce resources.[17] A second basis cited by that Court was that "a broadcast license is a public trust subject to termination for breach of duty," [18] and this also was rejected by Fowler. Broadcasting, he held, should be viewed as a business, owned by an entrepreneuer and lost only through failure in the marketplace or through sale. He urged that the "public-trusteeship notion" be abandoned, and that the ultimate aim for broadcasting be the "print model" with all its superior First Amendment protections.[19] Section 79 below will detail some of the deregulation that has taken place under Fowler and others.

[16] Mark Fowler and Brenner, D.L., "A Marketplace Approach to Broadcast Regulation," 60 Tex.L.Rev. 207, Feb. 1982; Broadcasting, Sept. 24, 1984, 64.

[17] Text accompanying footnote 3.

[18] Office of Communication of United Church of Christ v. FCC, 359 F.2d 994, 1003 (D.C.Cir.1966).

[19] Fowler and Brenner, 209–211; Broadcasting, April 23, 1984, 37.

SEC. 74. LICENSING BROADCASTERS

Under the Communications Act of 1934, the FCC grants licenses where such will serve the public interest, convenience, or necessity. In mid-1981, Congress approved legislation extending the term of license (three years, renewable) to five years for television and seven for radio.[20] This was an early manifestation of sweeping changes (Sec. 79, below) such as the Communication Act had never faced. Congress, the President, and the FCC all were committed by fall 1981 to continue the process of change that had begun soon after the Reagan administration and the 1981 Congress came to office. Yet the proposed Telecommunications Competition and Deregulation Act, heavily influenced by amendments recommended by the FCC itself, had not reached Congress by the end of 1984, and prospects for passage were small.

Applicants for licenses provide the Commission with information as to "citizenship, character, and financial, technical and other qualifications * * * to operate the station. * * *" (# 308). An application may be challenged by other "parties in interest" on grounds that in granting it, the public convenience, interest and necessity would not be served (# 309(d)(1)). If the Commission finds, in the applicant's materials or through challenge, that "a substantial and material question of fact is presented," or that for any reason the public interest, convenience or necessity would not be served by granting the license, it must hold hearings on the matter (# 309(e)).

In its Policy Statement on Comparative Broadcast Hearings of 1965,[21] the Commission said its choosing among contestants would be based on two principal considerations: the "best practicable service to the public," and the "maximum diffusion of control of the media of mass communications," the latter often termed "diversification of ownership." Its decisions may be organized under these two concepts.

Best Practicable Service to the Public

The indicators of best service to the public are many. Congress furnishes the FCC some of them in the Communications Act. The Commission must take into account citizenship, character, and financial, technical and other qualifications of applicants for licenses (# 308(b)). The historical development of the FCC's decision-making brings other factors into the accounting, and some of these are formalized in the 1965 Policy Statement (above): full-

[20] 47 U.S.C.A. § 151 and following. Appropriate sections of the Act are noted in the text rather than footnotes in this chapter.

[21] 1 F.C.C.2d 393; 5 R.R.2d 1901.

time participation in station operation by owners, the proposed program service and the past broadcast record, the efficient use of the frequency, character, and the catchall "other factors."[22]

Problems of "character" may include misrepresentations by applicants when they file their plans for service with the Commission. The Faith Theological Seminary of Elkins Park, Pa., was approved for transfer of WXUR licenses after various groups of people had opposed it. They held that the Rev. Carl McIntyre, one of its directors, had established a record as radio commentator that was sufficient evidence that he could not bring about a fair and balanced presentation of controversial public issues. Less than a year after the transfer, WXUR's licenses came up for renewal. The FCC found that the station, very soon after receiving the license, had drastically altered its programming to present an offering nothing like that which it had proposed in its application. On the grounds of misrepresentation about its intent, as well as others, the FCC denied renewal of the license, and was upheld by the federal appeals court.[23]

Character questions may also be raised by improper business activities.[24] In 1980, RKO General, Inc., a wholly owned subsidiary of General Tire and Rubber Co., was denied license renewals for its television stations in Boston (WNAC), Los Angeles (KHJ), and New York (WOR) after the FCC examined records of financial misconduct by both corporations.[25] The Commission found that RKO had participated in reciprocal trade practices in which companies had been induced to advertise on RKO stations as a condition of receiving business from General Tire. RKO was also found to have knowingly filed false financial statements with the FCC and to have "demonstrated a persistent lack of candor with the Commission." The FCC majority said its concern was increased by the misconduct of RKO's parent corporation, General Tire, which exercised both legal and practical control over RKO operations. As part of a consent decree reached with the Securities and Exchange Commission in 1976, a committee of General Tire board members conducted an investigation and documented

---

[22] A total of 14 "best-service-to-the-public" factors that emerged before the 1965 policy statement was extracted from FCC decisions by William K. Jones, Cases and Materials on Electronic Mass Media (Mineola, N.Y.: Foundation Press, 1976), pp. 41–45.

[23] Brandywine-Main Line Radio, Inc. v. FCC, 25 R.R.2d 2010, affirmed 473 F.2d 16 (D.C.Cir.1972).

[24] For a discussion of character issues in general and business misconduct in particular, see Stephen A. Sharp and Don Lively, "Can the Broadcaster in the Black Hat Ride Again? 'Good Character' Requirement for Broadcast Licensees," 32 Fed.Comm.L.J. 173 (1980).

[25] RKO General, Inc. (WNAC-TV), 78 F.C.C.2d 1, 47 R.R.2d 921; RKO General, Inc. (KHJ-TV), 78 F.C.C.2d 355; RKO General, Inc. (WOR-TV), 78 F.C.C.2d 357.

company activities which included improper domestic political contributions, the use of secret funds to avoid foreign agents and officials, and the use of secret bank accounts to overbill foreign affiliates. In the FCC's decision, RKO and General Tire were thus found to have failed on each of the three questions the Commission says it asks in considering the impact of misconduct on character qualifications: [26]

(1) Does the misconduct relate to broadcast operations or to non-broadcast activities which indicate how the applicant will operate a broadcast station?

(2) Is the misconduct an isolated incident or does it reflect a pattern of misbehavior?

(3) How recently did the misconduct occur?

The denial of RKO's license renewal applications, the FCC maintained, was not to punish the company for past wrongs, but to obtain the "best practicable service for the public" in the future. In an effort to save its three television licenses and to prevent the eventual loss of 13 other broadcast stations it owned, RKO began an appeals process. Faced with the possibility of losing RKO broadcast properties worth an estimated $400 million, General Tire issued a statement calling the FCC action "the most unfair and discriminatory ever handed down by a government agency." M.G. O'Neil, president of the corporation, was quoted as saying that it "could result in the largest 'fine' ever levied against a company in the history of American free enterprise." [27]

Appealing to the U.S. Court of Appeals for the District of Columbia, RKO won at least a chance to retain two television stations out of the three—New York and Los Angeles. But the firm's persistent lack of candor ("egregious" and "conspicuous," the Court called it) with the FCC in applying for the re-licensing of Boston's WNAC–TV was another matter altogether, and sufficient to warrant the FCC's denial of a new license there.[28] Charged to service more than 10,000 broadcast stations, each requiring re-licensing every three years, the Court said, the FCC "must rely heavily on the completeness and accuracy" of the stations' applications, and the applying stations have an affirmative duty to inform the Commission of the facts it needs in order to fulfill its statutory mandate. "Their duty of candor is basic and well known."[29] But RKO withheld facts relevant to the Commission's

---

[26] Ibid., 27.

[27] Broadcasting, June 9, 1980, p. 34. For additional reactions, see ibid., January 28, 1980, pp. 27–28; March 24, 1980, pp. 67–68; October 6, 1980, pp. 25, 27; November 10, 1980, p. 82.

[28] RKO General v. FCC, 670 F.2d 215 (D.C.Cir.1982), 7 Med.L.Rptr. 2313.

[29] Ibid., 2326.

needs, "stonewalled" when pressed to deliver information, failed to concede that it had inaccurately reported certain revenues, failed to report to the FCC that a formal investigation of General Tire by the Securities and Exchange Commission was under way.

The Court said that other grounds used by the FCC to deny relicensing would not stand: The reciprocal trade practices had occurred during the early 1960s before it was clear that such were illegal; and concerning the charge of "financial misconduct," the FCC had never given RKO a hearing on the matter and so it was never determined whether RKO had knowingly submitted inaccurate reports with intent to mislead the Commission.

As for RKO's applications for re-licensing the Los Angeles and New York stations, the Court said that the Commission had improperly denied them. It had based its decision to do so not upon direct investigation of them, but rather upon its investigation of the Boston license application. The Court remanded the proceedings on the two former stations, saying, "These stations are entitled to an opportunity to appear directly before the Commission and to argue that they deserve different treatment than RKO's Boston station."[30] The U.S. Supreme Court denied RKO's request for review of the decision.[31]

By late 1984, RKO had obtained renewal of license for WOR–TV, after removing the station to Secaucus, N.J., from New York City, but still faced proceedings over the Los Angeles station. And the FCC had opened the 13 "other stations" of RKO to competing applications of which more than 160 were received.[32] Twenty years of litigation had not ended the matter.

Shortly after the RKO decision, the FCC granted a license renewal to Westinghouse Broadcasting Co., Inc., (Group W) while noting that its corporate parent, Westinghouse Electric Corporation, had pleaded guilty to 30 counts of making false statements to a government agency. The FCC explained that the character of Westinghouse Electric was not an issue because its Group W subsidiary was virtually autonomous in its operations.[33]

Denials of re-licensing by the FCC, such as those above, are rare. It has often spoken of the importance of providing security to licensees and stability to the industry.[34] While a challenger at renewal time is given a chance to show that granting his applica-

[30] Ibid., 2330.

[31] 8 Med.L.Rptr. # 9, 4/27/82, News Notes.

[32] Broadcasting, Nov. 12, 1984, 42.

[33] Westinghouse Broadcasting Co., Inc., 75 F.C.C.2d 736, 46 R.R.2d 1431 (1980).

[34] See FCC, Policy Statement on Comparative Hearings Involving Regular Renewal Applicants, 22 F.C.C.2d 424 (1970), for the FCC's detailing of its attitude in this regard. Fidelity Television, Inc. v. FCC, 515 F.2d 684 (D.C.Cir.1975).

tion will better serve the public interest than would re-licensing the incumbent, "a challenger is in a less favorable position * * * because he asks the Commission to speculate whether his untested proposal is *likely* to be superior to that of * * * incumbent."[35] Challenges are relatively few—only eight among approximately 250 television license renewals during the industry's troubled year following the opinion in the famous, protracted WHDH (Boston) case. This hinged upon what is termed the "comparative renewal proceeding," in which the FCC scrutinized past performance of WHDH in comparison to the promise of other applicants who sought its license at renewal time.[36]

That case labored through FCC proceedings and into and out of the courts for decades. It is known as Greater Boston Television Corp. v. FCC.[37] WHDH and its television station were owned by and were a principal financial support of the *Boston Herald-Traveler* newspaper. Recommended for renewal by the FCC Hearing Examiner in 1966, WHDH lost out to one of three contesting applicants when the FCC reversed its Hearing Examiner's decision and was upheld by the Federal Appeals Court.[38] How the FCC applies its criteria from the 1965 Policy Statement (above, p. 563) to weigh merits of competing applicants in comparative hearings emerges in a digest made by the court as it developed its opinion. The relative merits of WHDH, Boston Broadcasters, Inc., and Charles River were assayed on several scores:[39]

> On January 22, 1969, the Commission reversed the Hearing Examiner's decision, and entered an order denying the application of WHDH and granting that of BBI. 16 F.C.C.2d 1. Its Decision reviewed the comparative merits of the applications.
>
> *Past Performance of WHDH:* The Commission's decision stated that the principles of the 1965 Policy Statement would be applied to the proceedings. Specifically it invoked the provision of its 1965 Policy Statement that an applicant's past record was to be given an affirmative preference only if it were outside the bounds of average performance. It read the Examiner's findings of fact as showing that the record of WHDH–TV was "favorable" on the whole—except for its failure to editorialize—but concluded that it was only within the bounds of average

[35] Cowles Florida Broadcasting, Inc., 60 F.C.C.2d 372, 37 R.R.2d 1487 (1976); on reconsiderations, 39 R.R.2d 541 (1977).

[36] Citizens Communications Center v. FCC, 447 F.2d 1201, fn. 21 (D.C.Cir.1971).

[37] 444 F.2d 841 (D.C.Cir.1970).

[38] Ibid.; 16 F.C.C.2d 1, 15 R.R.2d 411; 17 F.C.C.2d 856 (1969).

[39] Greater Boston Television Corp. v. FCC, 444 F.2d 841, 847–48 (D.C.Cir.1970).

performance, and "does not demonstrate unusual attention to the public's needs or interests." 16 F.C.C.2d at 10.

Diversification of Media of Mass Communications: WHDH's ownership by the Herald-Traveler resulted in an adverse factor on the diversification criterion. The Commission stated that the desirability of maximizing the diffusion of control of the media of mass communications in Boston was highlighted by the incident wherein the Herald-Traveler prematurely published a preliminary draft of the report of the Massachusetts Crime Commission without also simultaneously publicizing the report over the broadcast station. It was brought out at the hearing that such a news broadcast would have impaired the story's "scoop" value for the Herald-Traveler.

The Commission further referred to the contention of WHDH that since it had never editorialized there existed a factor that minimized the charge of concentration of control. The Commission disagreed, stating that licensees have an obligation to devote reasonable broadcast time to controversial programs, and the failure to editorialize, if anything, demonstrated the wisdom of the Commission's policy for diversification of control of media of mass communications. On the factor of diversification, it concluded by awarding a substantial preference to both BBI and Charles River as against WHDH, and giving BBI a slight edge over Charles River (which also operates an FM radio station in Waltham, Massachusetts devoted to serious music).

Integration of Ownership with Management: The Commission affirmed the Examiner's conclusion that the applications of both Charles River and BBI reflect an integration—which in FCC parlance means integration of ownership with management—of substantially greater degree than WHDH, whose integration is small. It restated its view that the public interest is furthered through participation in operation by proprietors, as increasing the likelihood of greater sensitivity to an area's changing needs and programming to serve these needs. * * *.

Proposed Program Service: The Commission agreed that both BBI and Charles River proposed generally well-balanced program schedules, and concluded that neither proposal demonstrated such a substantial difference as to constitute a "superior devotion to public service." * * *.

The slight demerits assessed against BBI and Charles River on proposed program service, were deemed to offset each other.

Other Factors: The Commission assessed a demerit against WHDH because of a failure to obtain the approval of the Commission on the transfer of de facto control when Choate was selected as president following the death of his predecessor, and when his death was followed by the accession of Akerson. However, since there was no attempt at misrepresentation or concealment it was concluded that the circumstances did not reflect so adversely on character qualifications as to warrant the absolute disqualification of WHDH.

Cries of pain from the television industry followed the refusal to renew WHDH licenses. Broadcasters interpreted the action as unsettling patterns of stability and foreclosing reasonable predictions that licenses would be renewed. It was the first time that the Commission, "in applying comparative criteria in a renewal proceeding deposed the incumbent and awarded the frequency to a challenger."[40] Settled doctrine of earlier decisions had given the incumbent "a virtually insuperable advantage on the basis of his past broadcast record *per se*";[41] it seemed that the doctrine now was being abandoned. WHDH programming service had been only "within the bounds of the average," the FCC found, and that performance entitled it to no preference in competition with the other applicants. Among the latter was at least one superior to WHDH on various criteria—especially integration of ownership and management, and diversification of control over mass media in Boston.

In a policy statement of 1970 the following year, the FCC tried to reassure the industry.[42] It said that, in a renewal proceeding where another applicant seeks the license of the incumbent, if the incumbent demonstrates substantial past performance without serious deficiencies, it shall have a controlling preference. And if the incumbent showed that, all other applicants would be dismissed without a hearing as to their own merits though they might, indeed, be heard for the purpose of calling attention to the incumbent's failings.

The Federal Appeals Court ruled that this policy violated the Communication Act of 1934.[43] The Act promises (Sec. 309(e)) a

[40] Citizens Communications Center v. FCC, 447 F.2d 1201, 1208 (D.C.Cir.1971).

[41] Ibid.

[42] Policy Statement on Comparative Hearings Involving Regular Renewal Applicants, 22 F.C.C.2d 424 (1970).

[43] Citizens Communications Center v. FCC, 447 F.2d 1201 (D.C.Cir.1971).

"full hearing" for contestants for a license and the FCC's 1970 policy statement short-changed challenging applicants in promising them only limited hearings. Revising according to the court's finding, the Commission issued a new statement accepting the hearing requirement, and stressing that a "plus of major significance" should be awarded to a renewal applicant whose past record is outstanding.[44]

Beleaguered, the Commission struggled to administer the comparative renewal process. Angry attacks of broadcasters demanded at least an expectation of renewals; the U.S. Court of Appeals, District of Columbia Circuit—the tribunal for appeals of Commission findings—found the Commission likely to give renewals that were close to "automatic." In a 1978 case, the Court vacated the Commission's renewal of the television license of Cowles Florida Broadcasting at Daytona Beach, and returned the case to the Commission for re-examining. The Court found the FCC's rationale for renewing "thoroughly unsatisfying" and its conclusion based on administrative "feel" to be intuitional and thus arbitrary as a form of decision-making. It said:[45]

> * * * the Commission's handling of the facts of this case makes embarrassingly clear that the FCC has practically erected a presumption of renewal that is inconsistent with the full hearing requirement. * * *

The FCC had found that the Cowles television station performance up to renewal time had been "a substantial performance—i.e., sound, favorable"; and as such, had warranted "legitimate renewal expectancies"; and that this consideration was "decisive." True, Central Enterprises, which challenged Cowles for the license, had shown certain advantages over Cowles, but the FCC discounted these: a "merit" for its plan for minority group participation in ownership, another for management, and a "preference" on diversification of ownership. True also that the FCC gave Cowles a minor downcheck for making plans to move its main studio without Commission approval. But all such factors supporting Central, the Commission said, nevertheless "do not outweigh the substantial service Cowles rendered to the public during the last license period."[46] Cowles's license was renewed.

The Court found the Commission's "belittling" of Central's advantages unacceptable. In diversification of ownership, the Commission had awarded Central a "clear advantage" that gave it

[44] Formulation of Policies Relating to the Broadcast Renewal Applicant Stemming from the Comparative Hearing Process, 2 R.R. Current Service 53:442 (Aug. 20, 1971).

[45] Central Florida Enterprises v. FCC, 598 F.2d 37 (D.C.Cir.1978) 4 Med.L.Rptr. 1502, 1509–10.

[46] Ibid., 1509.

a "clear preference"—but reduced its weight and said the preference was "of little significance." To the Court, the Commission was ignoring its own prior rule that diversification was a matter of "primary significance." It said that it was unreasonable for the Commission to find Central's advantage in diversification "clear," and yet to give that factor "little decisional significance."[47]

Besides that factor in diversification, "best practicable service" factors as handled by the FCC were "puzzling" and "bizarre" to the Court. The FCC had found Central superior to Cowles on management integration and minority participation in ownership. For determining "best practicable service," these matters constituted *"the only evidence comparing the applicants and also the only evidence whatsoever pertaining to the challenger."* Yet Central's superiority here was found by the FCC not to "outweigh" a rather unexceptional record made by Cowles.

Under order of the Court, then, the Commission took the Cowles-Central face-up back to the drawing board, re-examined it in detail, and under new procedures, renewed the Cowles license again. This time the Appeals Court found the FCC methods and conclusions acceptable, and approved.[48]

The Commission has long been caught between the broadcasters' hammer and the courts' anvil as it undertakes comparative renewals, and it is plain that the D.C. Court of Appeals was right in saying that "the Commission dislikes the idea of comparative renewal proceedings altogether."[49] The process of deregulation may, indeed, bring an end to comparative renewal, but it will have to be done by Congress because statute requires the proceedings.

The challenge to license renewal may be made by "parties at interest" who are not themselves seeking the frequency but rather saying that the renewal applicant is not qualified to hold a license. It has been recognized by the courts since the mid-1960s. In *Office of Communication of the United Church of Christ v. FCC*,[50] the federal appeals court had granted standing to the United Church of Christ and to segments of the listening audience of WLBT, Jackson, Miss., to intervene in a station's application for renewal. The church had objected to renewal on grounds that the station's news and public affairs programming displayed racial and religious discrimination. The FCC twice found for WLBT, but the court found for the church and ordered the FCC to vacate its renewal of the license. The FCC's hearings at which the church

---

[47] Ibid., 1513.

[48] Central Florida Enterprises, Inc. v. FCC, 683 F.2d 503 (D.C.Cir.1982).

[49] Central Florida Enterprises, Inc. v. FCC, 598 F.2d 37 (D.C.Cir.1978), 4 Med.L. Rptr. 1502, 1510.

[50] 359 F.2d 994 (D.C.Cir.1966).

and other intervenors had appeared were ruled by the court to have been hopelessly biased against the intervenors; the FCC had exhibited, in the hearing and in its opinions and rulings, "a profound hostility to the participation of the Public Intervenors and their efforts."[51] Henceforth, "parties in interest" was to be understood to include representatives of the station's audience or any segment of the audience, as well as contestants for licenses.[52]

Maximum Diffusion of Control of Broadcasting

Analyzing and testing as in the foregoing to gauge the "best practicable service to the public" in awarding licenses, the Commission decides only after it is satisfied as to a second major consideration as well: maximum diffusion of control of the media of mass communications. This criterion flows not from conclusive empirical research that multiple station ownerships in a community will usually or always provide better broadcast fare than will fewer ownerships. It flows, rather, from faith in the tenet of the self-governing society that truth emerges from the clash of differing ideas and opinions. Borrowing heavily from judicial formulations developed over a half century, the Commission expresses the principle this way:[53]

> Basic to our form of government is the belief that "the widest possible dissemination of information from diverse and antagonistic sources is essential to the welfare of the public." (Associated Press v. United States, 326 U.S. 1, 20, 65 S.Ct. 1416 (1945).) Thus, our Constitution rests upon the ground that "the ultimate good desired is better reached by free trade in ideas—that the best test of truth is the power of the thought to get itself accepted in the competition of the market." Justice Holmes dissenting in Abrams v. United States, 250 U.S. 616, 630, 40 S.Ct. 17 (1919).

> These principles, upon which Judge Learned Hand observed that we had staked our all, are the wellspring, together with a concomitant desire to prevent undue economic concentration, of the Commission's policy of diversifying control of the powerful medium of broadcasting. For, centralization of control over the media of mass

[51] Office of Communication of United Church of Christ v. FCC, 425 F.2d 543, 550 (D.C.Cir.1969).

[52] For the history and growth of the citizen movement in broadcasting, see Joseph A. Grundfest, Citizen Participation in Broadcast Licensing Before the FCC (Santa Monica: Rand, 1976). A recapitulation of several local citizens'-group petitions against renewal of licenses to broadcast-newspaper combination owners is in Editor & Publisher, Jan. 29, 1977, p. 44.

[53] Multiple Ownership of Standard, FM and TV Broadcast Stations, 18 R.R.2d 1735, 1740–41; 22 F.C.C.2d 306 (1970).

communications is, like monopolization of economic power, per se undesirable. The power to control what the public hears and sees over the airways matters, whatever the degree of self-restraint which may withhold its arbitrary use.

It is accordingly firmly established that in licensing the use of the radio spectrum for broadcasting, we are to be guided by the sound public policy of placing into many, rather than a few hands, the control of this powerful medium of public communication * * *.

Application of the principles set forth above dictates that one person should not be licensed to operate more than one broadcast station in the same place, and serving substantially the same public, unless some other relevant public interest consideration is found to outweigh the importance of diversifying control. It is elementary that the number of frequencies available for licensing is limited. In any particular area there may be many voices that would like to be heard, but not all can be licensed. A proper objective is the maximum diversity of ownership that technology permits in each area.

Such principles and policies have led to rules governing patterns of ownership of stations. The long-standing "duopoly rule" first prohibited one party from owning, operating or controlling more than one station in the same "broadcast service" (AM radio, FM radio, or television) in the same area. The "one-to-a-market" restriction was extended by rules of 1970 to prevent common ownership of a VHF television station and a radio station (AM or FM) in the same market. For single ownership or control of both a UHF station and a radio station, the FCC said it would review each application on a case-by-case basis. It did not bar the formation of new AM–FM combinations.[54]

Meanwhile, the Commission evolved rules for maximum number of stations that might be owned or controlled, nationwide, by a single person or entity. The "concentration of control" rule long permitted common ownership of no more than seven AM stations, seven FM stations, and seven television stations not more than five of which might be VHF.[55]

The rule of "sevens" was changed to "twelves" for AM and FM radio in 1984, but the same change for television was delayed.

With diversity not concentration of control of the broadcasting media standing as a first principle of the Commission, it was also

[54] Ibid.; On reconsideration, 28 F.C.C.2d 662, 21 R.R.2d 1551 (1971).

[55] Amendment of Multiple Ownership Rules, 18 Fed.Reg. 7796, 9 R.R. 1563 (1953).

troubled for years about concentration of control over mass media more generally. The implications of common ownership of a broadcast station and a newspaper in the same location were raised in 1970 by the Commission.[56] It began the formal process of considering rules about the matter. There were 94 ownership combinations of television and newspapers in the nation at the time, and many more radio-newspaper combinations.

By 1975, pros and cons of the matter had been canvassed and hearings and oral arguments had been held by the Commission. It issued a report and order.[57] It said that no future applicant would be permitted to own both a daily newspaper and a broadcast station in the same community. But it "grandfathered" all existing crossownerships except for 16 in small cities. The 16, is said, must within five years divest themselves of their broadcast holdings. Seven were television-newspaper combinations and nine were radio-newspaper.

The FCC said that in the early days of radio and television, it looked upon ownership of stations by newspapers favorably, for newspapers had then brought a pioneering spirit to broadcasting. But now, "the broadcast medium has matured * * *. [T]he special reason for encouraging newspaper ownership, even at the cost of a lessened diversity, is no longer generally operative in the way it once was * * *." Diversity would not, under changed conditions of the present, be enhanced by cross-ownership, and "We think that any new licensing should be expected to add to local diversity. Accordingly, the rules will bar combinations that would not do so." The rules would apply to radio as well as television.

The Commission worked deliberately at the touchy matter of requiring divestiture of present combinations, noting that it had been urged to do so wherever "the two entities are co-located." But contrary to these urgings, it found "public interest consequences" of an undesirable kind, which it had not previously weighed enough:[58]

> We remain no less convinced than before of the importance of diversity, but this is not the only point to consider. Our examination of the situation leads us to conclude that we may have given too little weight [in previous analyses and statements of intent] to the consequences which could be expected to attend a focus on the

[56] Notice of Proposed Rule Making, 22 F.C.C.2d 349 (1970).

[57] FCC, Amendment of Multiple Ownership Rules (Newspapers), Second Report and Order, 50 F.C.C.2d 1046, 32 R.R.2d 954, 40 Fed.Reg. 6449 (1975); On reconsideration 53 F.C.C.2d 589, 33 R.R.2d 1603 (1975).

[58] Second Report and Order, paragraphs 108 and 109.

abstract goal alone. There are a number of public interest consequences which form the basis of our concern. Requiring divestiture could reduce local ownership as well as the involvement of owners in management as many sales would have to be to outside interests. The continuity of operation would be broken as the new owner would lack the long knowledge of the community * * *. Local economic dislocations are also possible as a result of the vast demand for equity capital * * *.

In our view, stability and continuity of ownership do serve important public purposes. Traditions of service were established and have been continued. Entrance and exit from broadest ownership by these parties are determined by factors other than just profit maximization. Many began operation long before there was hope of profit * * *. There is a long record of service to the public * * *. We have concluded that a mere hoped for gain in diversity is not enough [to warrant disturbing such ownerships] * * *.

The Commission said that as a result of the disruption and losses which could be expected to attend divestiture, and the loss of service to the public that would follow, divestiture would be required only in the "most egregious cases." At the heart of the matter was obtaining for communities the mass communication service that would bring "a real diversity on vital issues of local concern. In fact, it is local issues on which so much decision making by the electorate is required." The "egregious cases" in which diversity on local issues seemed most threatened were those where a single ownership controlled the only local television station and the only local daily newspaper (regardless of number of local radio stations); or, if no television station existed, where a single ownership held the only local radio station and the newspaper. Finding 16 such combinations, it ordered them to divest themselves of either station or newspaper by Jan. 1, 1980.[59] This "limited divestiture" order left scores of television-newspaper combinations unaffected, "grandfathered" by the FCC to protect them from the new rule.

At once, attacks were launched at this new level of divestiture, some declaring it unwarranted to break up newspaper-broadcast combinations, others incensed at divestiture rules that would break up fewer than a score of combinations out of a total estimated at anywhere from 150 to 475.[60] Among the latter was a media "reform" group called the National Citizens Committee for

[59] Ibid., paragraphs 115–117.

[60] Editor & Publisher, Feb. 1, 1975, p. 26; March 5, 1977, p. 8.

Broadcasting.[61] Among the former were the American Newspaper Publishers Association, the National Association of Broadcasters, and various "combination" owners. Both sides brought a challenge to the federal courts.

With Chief Judge David Bazelon writing, the District of Columbia Circuit Court of Appeals[62] found the FCC order banning cross-ownership unwarrantedly narrow and limited in its effect— breaking up fewer than a score of the combinations. The Court focused its critique largely on the desirability of diversity of ownership (diffusion of control of broadcasting) as the great good to be sought and achieved. It found that the Commission's decision not to order wide-scale divestiture, despite its oft-expressed dedication to diversity of ownership, was unexplained. It quoted heavily from the Commission's 1975 report and order which exalted the principle of diversity. The Commission had said:[63]

> The premise is that a democratic society cannot function without the clash of divergent views. It is clear to us that the idea of diversity of viewpoints from antagonistic sources is at the heart of the Commission's licensing responsibility. If our democratic society is to function, nothing can be more important than insuring that there is a free flow of information from as many divergent sources as possible. This * * * is a recognition that it is unrealistic to expect true diversity from a commonly owned station-newspaper combination. The divergency of their viewpoints cannot be expected to be the same as if they were antagonistically run.

In that context of FCC dedication to diversity, the Court of Appeals examined the Commission's concern that sweeping divestiture would nevertheless have undesirable public interest consequences: shrunken local ownership and management of stations, loss of stability and continuity of operation in new "outside" owners' ignorance of the locality, and local economic dislocations. The Court saw no merit in such worries of the FCC, which, it said, were far less compelling than "The gains * * * from divestiture * * *, the most promising method for increasing diversity that does not entail governmental supervision of speech * * *."[64] It said that divestiture should be required except in cases where the

---

[61] Headed by former FCC Commissioner Nicholas Johnson, famed for his vigorous minority views favoring sterner regulation of broadcasting.

[62] National Citizens Committee for Broadcasting v. FCC, 555 F.2d 938 (D.C.Cir. 1977), 39 R.R.2d 1463, certiorari granted FCC v. National Citizens Committee for Broadcasting, 434 U.S. 815, 98 S.Ct. 52 (1977).

[63] FCC, Amendment of Multiple Ownership Rules (Newspapers), 50 F.C.C.2d 1046, 32 R.R.2d 954 at paragraph 111.

[64] Ibid., 965.

evidence clearly discloses that cross-ownership is in the public interest, and reversed the Commission, telling it to make new rules. The Commission appealed, and the United States Supreme Court reversed the Appeals Court, upholding the FCC "grandfathering" of most stations:[65]

> The Commission was well aware that separating existing newspaper-broadcast combinations would promote diversification of ownership. It concluded, however, that ordering widespread divestiture would not result in "the best practicable service to the American public." * * * The FCC Order identified several specific respects in which the public interest would or might be harmed if a sweeping divestiture were imposed: the stability and continuity of meritorious service provided by the newspaper owners as a group would be lost; owners who had provided meritorious service would unfairly be denied the opportunity to continue in operation; "economic dislocations" might prevent new owners from obtaining sufficient working capital to maintain the quality of local programming; and local ownership of broadcast stations would probably decrease * * *. We cannot say that the Commission acted irrationally in concluding that these public interest harms outweighed the potential gains that would follow from increasing diversification of ownership.

> * * *

> * * * we cannot agree with the Court of Appeals that it was arbitrary and capricious for the Commission to "grandfather" most existing combinations * * *. [W]e are unable to find anything in the Communications Act, the First Amendment, or the Commission's past or present practices that would require the Commission to "presume" that its diversification policy should be given controlling weight in all circumstances.

> Such a "presumption" would seem to be inconsistent with the Commission's long-standing and judicially approved practice of giving controlling weight in some circumstances to its more general goal of achieving "the best practicable service to the public."

The FCC issued a Policy Statement about another aspect of providing diversity in radio programming in 1976. It said that market forces and competition among broadcasters provide diversity in radio entertainment formats more reliably than do regulation and review of format changes by the FCC. The Communica-

[65] FCC v. National Citizens Committee for Broadcasting, 434 U.S. 815, 98 S.Ct. 52 (1978), 3 Med.L.Rptr. 2409.

tion Act, it said, does not compel Commission review of a station when it changes its entertainment format; that such review does not advance the radio listening public's welfare; and that review can deter innovation in broadcasting. Several citizens groups interested in preserving and fostering particular entertainment formats challenged the Policy Statement.

They won at the Court of Appeals, District of Columbia Circuit,[66] which held that the FCC's reliance on market forces was an unreasonable interpretation of the Act's public-interest standard. The appeals court said that its own format doctrine, developed in decisions since 1970 and requiring the FCC to hold hearings over some format changes, was compelled by the Communication Act. It ruled that the FCC's 1976 Policy Statement was of no force.

But the Supreme Court reversed.[67] It said the FCC Policy Statement was a permissible means of implementing the Act's public interest standard. It was unconvinced that the Court of Appeals format doctrine was compelled by the Act. The Supreme Court had long since found that Congress gave the FCC broad discretion in determining how best to achieve the public interest goal, and had recognized that the Commission decisions must rest often on judgment and prediction rather than complete factual support.[68]

The FCC's decision, the Supreme Court found, came after it had weighed benefits and harm likely to flow from a government hearing and review on one hand, and from reliance on market forces on the other:[69]

> The Commission concluded that "even after all relevant facts had been fully explored in an evidentiary hearing, [the Commission] would have no assurance that a decision finally reached * * * would contribute more to listener satisfaction than the result favored by station management." It recognized that either mechanism would not bring perfect correlation between listener preferences and available entertainment programming, and it concluded that the marketplace alone could best accommodate the varied and changing tastes of the listening public. These predictions are within the institutional competence of the Commission.

[66] WNCN Listeners Guild v. FCC, 610 F.2d 838 (D.C.Cir.1979), 5 Med.L.Rptr. 1449.

[67] FCC v. WNCN Listeners Guild et al., 450 U.S. 582, 101 S.Ct. 1266 (1981).

[68] Ibid., 595, 1274.

[69] Ibid., 596, 1274.

SEC. 75.   THE EQUAL OPPORTUNITY
REQUIREMENT

If a broadcaster furnishes air time to one candidate for public office, he must offer equal opportunity to opposing candidates.

The Communications Act of 1934 under which the FCC holds its powers to regulate broadcasting carries a specific provision that shows Congress' concern over possible damage to the political process that unregulated broadcasting could cause.   This is Section 315 of the Act, known to every radio and television journalist as the "equal time" or "equal opportunities" provision.   It says, broadly, that if a station provides time for one political candidate, it must do so for his opponents.   Under the aggressive "deregulation" drive of FCC Chairman Mark Fowler in 1981, the FCC has recommended that Congress kill "equal time," and also "reasonable access" (p. 580) and the fairness doctrine (Sec. 76 below). Section 315 of the Act reads: [70]

> If any licensee shall permit any person who is a legally qualified candidate for any public office to use a broadcasting station, he shall afford equal opportunities to all other such candidates for that office in the use of such broadcasting station: *provided,* that such licensee shall have no power of censorship over the material broadcast under the provisions of this section.   No obligation is imposed upon any licensee to allow the use of its station by any such candidate.

This said to a broadcaster: Refuse time to all qualified candidates for a political position, or accept all.   While refusing access was thus legal, it hardly squared with the great potentialities of the medium for contributing to public information about candidates.   Both politicians and citizens had legitimate questions to put to broadcasters who did not make air time available during campaign periods.   Yet for the broadcaster, it could cause real problems, especially in contests where a great many candidates were running.   Who could furnish "equal opportunities"—either on a free basis or on a "paid time" basis—to every candidate if 15 were running for mayor?   Many broadcasters found the requirement a perilous one, and some were willing to accept the opprobrium that might go with refusing all candidates.

In 1972, the option of refusing all candidates was restricted by Congress where candidates for federal elective office were concerned, through an amendment (47 U.S.C.A. § 312(a)(7)) providing

---

[70] 47 U.S.C.A. §§ 151, 315, 1934.

that "reasonable access" must be provided these people. It did not affect access for state and local candidates.

Within the terms of Section 315, the FCC had power to make rules as to what could constitute "equal opportunities." Through rules, letters, hearings, opinions and decisions of the FCC on various practices, as well as through stations' appeals to the courts, the details of "equal opportunities" were gradually described: The term "equal time" does not cover the entire consideration that must be given a candidate whose opponent has preceded him. The candidate must receive not only as much time, but also just as desirable a time of day or week as his opponent; a half hour on Sunday morning at 9 o'clock is not an "equal opportunity" for a candidate if his opponent has had prime evening time.[71] This does not mean, however, that all candidates must be given exactly the same opportunity, such as appearance on a regularly scheduled discussion program.

Equal opportunities do not extend to campaign managers or other spokesmen for candidates; Section 315 refers only to the candidates themselves. In Felix v. Westinghouse Radio Stations,[72] the court ruled that political parties, as such, did not have claim to "equal opportunities"; the law extends the claim only to candidates. This case also held that the "no-censorship" provision of Section 315 applies only to the candidates themselves, and not to their spokesmen.

"Equal opportunities" rules take hold after a legally qualified candidate has announced for office. Just who is the "legally qualified candidate" emerges in technical definition by the FCC and by the candidate's own electoral jurisdiction. Condensing the detailed and qualified definition to workable prose is important if perilous: The candidate may be said, for working purposes, to be one who has announced that he is running for nomination or election; who is qualified under his local laws so that people may vote for him; who can get his name on the ballot or else has promised to run as a write-in candidate; and who makes a convincing case that he is a real candidate.[73]

In nominating or primary elections, equal opportunities must be afforded the candidates for an office within a single party. But the fact that all Democrats running for nomination as sheriff are given equal opportunities does not mean that equal time must be

---

[71] Roscoe L. Barrow, The Equal Opportunities and Fairness Doctrines in Broadcasting; Pillars in the Forum of Democracy, 37 Cincinnati L.Rev. 447, 452–459 (1969); 31 Fed.Reg. 6660, 6661, 6669 (1966).

[72] 186 F.2d 1 (3d Cir.1950), certiorari denied 341 U.S. 909, 71 S.Ct. 622 (1951).

[73] For exact wording, see William K. Jones, Electronic Mass Media 1977 Supplement (Mineola, N.Y.: Foundation Press, 1977), p. 35. Hereinafter referred to as Jones, 1977 Supplement.

made available to all Republicans seeking nomination for the same post.[74]

Section 315 talks of equal opportunities for candidates in the "use" of broadcasting stations. The word "use" has caused many problems of interpretation. It has been held by the FCC that "use" includes air time employed by a candidate who did not speak directly to his candidacy; a station was not to evaluate whether the original user was furthering his campaign in his talk.[75] Also, the FCC held that a candidate who went on the air to broadcast in a capacity other than as a candidate, gave the basis for his opponent to claim equal opportunity. A Congressman's weekly broadcast to his constituents, made after he became a candidate for re-election, might have no content dealing with his campaign, but it would furnish the ground for his opponent to claim equal time.[76]

In 1959, Congress amended § 315 of the Communications Act to provide that four kinds of broadcast news programs were exempt from the equal opportunities rule: bona fide newscasts, bona fide news interviews, bona fide news documentaries, and spot coverage of bona fide news events.[77] The FCC ruled that none of these (the last was the most pertinent) exempted news conferences of presidential candidates from the equal opportunities rule.[78] And it ruled also that the bona fide news event exemption did not apply to broadcasts of debates between candidates in two gubernatorial campaigns, effectively excluding all campaign debates from the exemption.[79] The only debates between candidates for political office that escaped the equal opportunities rule were those for which Congress itself made an exception—those of the 1960 presidential campaign, which featured the so-called "Great Debates" between John F. Kennedy and Richard M. Nixon. Congress made no further exceptions in following years, and the FCC would not change its rule. Campaign year after campaign year echoed with denunciations of these FCC positions by broadcasters and concerned citizens. Networks worked on edge for fear that the equal

[74] KWFT, Inc., 4 R.R. 885 (1948).

[75] WMCA, Inc., 7 R.R. 1132 (1952).

[76] KNGS, 7 R.R. 1130 (1952).

[77] 47 U.S.C.A. § 315(a)(1)–(4). The amendments were a response to the alarm of broadcasters that was voiced after the FCC ruled in the famous Lar Daly case. Daly, running in a Chicago primary election for mayor on both the Republican and Democratic tickets in his typically quixotic form, declared he deserved equal time on regularly scheduled newscasts, following appearances of other candidates on these newscasts. The FCC ruled for him. Columbia Broadcasting System, 18 R.R. 238 (1959).

[78] Columbia Broadcasting System, Inc., 40 F.C.C. 395, 3 R.R.2d 623, 627 (1964).

[79] The Goodwill Station, Inc., 40 F.C.C. 362, 24 R.R. 413 (1962); National Broadcasting Co., 40 F.C.C. 370, 24 R.R. 401 (1962).

opportunities rule would be triggered. CBS pointed out that Pres. Gerald Ford became a formally declared candidate for the presidency 15 months before the election; and had other Republicans qualified as "candidates" for the presidency at any time during this period, Ford's press conferences would have constituted a trigger.

Until 1975, the FCC stood firm on both points. In *Aspen,*[80] it reversed the long-standing position. It ruled that presidential press conferences and press conferences of other candidates for political office, broadcast "live and in their entirety," could be exempt under the "bona fide news events" provision. Broadcasters must make a good-faith judgment that the conferences were newsworthy; there must be no evidence of broadcaster favoritism.

Closing out its long-standing refusal to recognize campaign debates as exempt, it held further that the new rule would embrace "Debates between candidates for public office, not encompassing all candidates for the office, where such debates were arranged by organizations other than the broadcaster and were considered news worthy by the broadcaster."[81] Re-examination of its position, upon petition of the Aspen Institute and CBS, it said, led it to realize that its non-exemption rules for press conferences and debates rested on its own faulty reading of the legislative history surrounding Congress's 1959 amendments. The Commission's reversal was challenged in the courts by the Democratic National Committee, the National Organization for Women, and Rep. Shirley Chisholm. The U.S. Court of Appeals, District of Columbia, upheld the Commission.[82] And under the ruling, the 1976 televised debates between Pres. Gerald Ford and Jimmy Carter were held—and arranged, as the ruling required, not by the broadcasters but by an outside agency—in this case, the League of Women Voters of the United States. The broadcasters were constrained, according to the FCC position in *Aspen,* to being observer and reporter of others' event. In 1980, debates between Pres. Jimmy Carter and Ronald Reagan went ahead under the same rules.

In 1983, however, the FCC ruled that broadcasters might themselves conduct political debates without triggering the equal time rule. The U.S. Court of Appeals, District of Columbia Circuit, upheld the Commission's new rule, over the objection of the League of Women Voters. In March of 1984, the first national

[80] Aspen Institute Program on Communications and Society Petition, 35 R.R.2d 49 (1975).

[81] William K. Jones, Electronic Mass Media (Mineola, N.Y.: Foundation Press, 1976), p. 195. And see Michael J. Petrick, "Equal Opportunities" and "Fairness" in Broadcast Coverage of Politics, Annals, AAPSS, 472, Sept., 1976, pp. 73–83.

[82] Chisholm v. FCC, 538 F.2d 349 (D.C.Cir.1976).

network-sponsored debate among presidential candidates since 1960 was staged by CBS, with Walter Mondale, Gary Hart, and Jesse Jackson.[83]

Congress made a law in 1971 giving elective federal candidates access to broadcasting stations.[84] It empowered the FCC to revoke any station license for "willful or repeated failure to allow reasonable access to or to permit purchase of reasonable amounts of time by a legally qualified candidate for federal elective office on behalf of his candidacy." In 1979, all three major networks turned down the Carter-Mondale Presidential Committee's request for a half-hour program between 8 p.m. and 10:30 p.m. on a day between the 4th and 7th of December. They felt December was too early to start campaigning, fearing the snarling of their schedules by demands for time from many candidates. The Committee complained to the FCC, which ordered the networks to accede to the Committee's request for such "reasonable access"; the Court of Appeals and the U.S. Supreme Court upheld the Commission.[85]

Chief Justice Burger, writing for the majority, said that the Commission had consistently interpreted the new law as a specific command to provide a certain group of officials with special access. And Congress, which wrote the law, had been abundantly aware of the FCC interpretation over several years and found no fault with it.

The Court rejected the networks' argument that December 1979 was too early before 1980 elections to consider that a "campaign" had really started (12 candidates had formally announced and were on the hustings, endorsements were being made, states had begun selecting delegates to conventions). It said also that broadcasters' editorial discretion as a First Amendment right was not unduly hedged by requiring "reasonable access" in this case. It quoted from the famous *Red Lion* decision making the public's First Amendment right paramount in broadcasting, said that the law furthers the public need for news of candidates, and found that the statutory right of access as defined by the Commission and applied here "properly balances the First Amendment rights of federal candidates, the public, and broadcasters." [86]

Justice White, with Justices Rehnquist and Stevens concurring, dissented. He wrote that the networks' judgments as to what was "reasonable access" were slighted. The FCC, he said, misconstrued the statute "when it assumed that it had been given

[83] News Media and the Law, Nov./Dec. 1984, 32.

[84] Sec. 312(a)(7), Communications Act of 1934.

[85] CBS et al. v. FCC, 453 U.S. 367, 101 S.Ct. 2813 (1981), 7 Med.L.Rptr. 1563.

[86] Ibid., 1576.

authority to insist on its own views as to reasonable access" in the face of media dissent.[87]

SEC. 76. THE FAIRNESS DOCTRINE:
CONTROVERSIAL ISSUES OF
PUBLIC IMPORTANCE

Broadcasters are charged by the Federal Communications Commission with the affirmative duty to seek out and broadcast contrasting viewpoints on controversial issues of public importance.

Recognition of the public interest in wide ventilation of important public issues by broadcasting does not stop with the law requiring equal opportunities for political candidates. The principle has been recognized by FCC decisions and documents for decades in respect to the general airing of viewpoints on significant public issues. Under its "fairness doctrine" the Commission takes the position that "public interest requires ample play for the free and fair competition of opposing views * * *" and it long considered "strict adherence to the fairness doctrine as the single most important requirement of operation in the public interest— the 'sine qua non' for grant of a renewal of license." [88]

As noted above (p. 562), FCC Chairman Mark Fowler and other commissioners as early as 1981 urged Congress to repeal the fairness doctrine as part of a sweeping policy of deregulation of broadcasting.[89] They are supported by the position that such a special limitation on broadcasting is chilling to First Amendment freedom. They add that broadcast outlets have multiplied in number so strongly as to deny that "scarcity of frequencies" limits the diversity of broadcast voices. Shelving the fairness doctrine while driving for other deregulation, Fowler returned to it in February of 1985, holding hearings for one more airing of the controversy.[90]

Fowler's power and support are formidable, dedicated and vocal though the fairness doctrine advocates are. No aspect of broadcast regulation has come under heavier fire than the fairness doctrine. Simmons' studies lead him to conclude that the instrument has become an "Unfairness Doctrine"—unfair "to the public, to broadcasters, to parties seeking access to the media, and,

---

[87] Ibid., 1577.

[88] Great Lakes Broadcasting Co., 3 F.R.C. 32 (1929); Committee for the Fair Broadcasting of Controversial Issues, 25 F.C.C.2d 283, 292 (1970).

[89] 7 Med.L.Rptr. # 25, 9/29/81, News Notes.

[90] 11 Med.L.Rptr. # 11, 2/19/85, News Notes.

ironically, to the Federal Communications Commission itself." [91]
As for broadcasters, their argument runs that government's compelling "fairness", with failure to be fair a possible ground for
losing a license, flies in the face of the First Amendment, and
demonstrates that freedom of expression is a weak freedom as
applied to broadcasting. For the print media, of course "freedom
to be unfair" is broadly protected under the First Amendment.
The controversy mounted with a huge increase in complaints of
fairness violations, largely following the 1966 court recognition of
the public's standing to intervene in licensing and re-licensing.[92]

The doctrine applies in any case in which broadcast facilities
are used for discussion of a controversial issue of public importance; when one position has been broadcast, there must be an
opportunity for opposing views to be heard. Furthermore, the
doctrine holds, the licensee must devote a reasonable percentage
of its broadcast time to the airing of controversial issues of public
importance, although as we shall see below, there has been little
enforcement of this provision by the FCC.

Starting with the obligation to be fair in presenting opposing
views on issues, then, the position was laid out broadly in the FCC
report of 1949, Editorializing by Broadcast Licensee.[93] The station's part and the FCC's part in applying the doctrine are
described thus: [94]

> [T]he licensee, in applying the fairness doctrine, is
> called upon to make reasonable judgments in good faith
> on the facts of each situation—as to whether a controver-
> sial issue of public importance is involved, as to what
> viewpoints have been or should be presented, as to the
> format and spokesmen to present the viewpoints, and all
> the other facets of such programing * * *.
>
> In passing on any complaint in this area, the Commis-
> sion's role is not to substitute its judgment for that of the
> licensee as to any of the above programming decisions,

[91] Steven J. Simmons, The Fairness Doctrine and the Media (Berkeley, 1978), p.
189.

[92] Radio Television News Directors Ass'n v. U.S., 400 F.2d 1002, 1010, 1012 (7 Cir.
1969), reversed Red Lion Broadcasting Co. v. FCC, 395 U.S. 367, 89 S.Ct. 1794
(1969). For a major journalist's detailed account of major cases involving the
fairness doctrine, see Fred. W. Friendly, The Good Guys, the Bad Guys and the
First Amendment (N.Y.: Vintage Books, 1977). For public standing: Office of
Communications of United Church of Christ v. FCC, 359 F.2d 944 (D.C.Cir.1966).
The number rose to 2,400 for the year 1973: Fairness Report, 30 R.R.2d 1261
(1974).

[93] 13 F.C.C. 1246 (1949).

[94] Applicability of the Fairness Doctrine in the Handling of Controversial Issues
of Public Importance, 40 F.C.C. 598, 599, 29 Fed.Reg. 10415, 10416 (1964). This is
the so-called "Fairness Primer."

but rather to determine whether the licensee can be said to have acted reasonably and in good faith. There is thus room for considerably more discretion on the part of the licensee under the fairness doctrine than under the "equal opportunities" requirement.

The doctrine applies broadly to news, comment, and entertainment.[95] The Commission has not stated specific rules for its interpretation. Broadcasters receive guidance through such means as compilations of important FCC rulings of the past, occasional statements elaborating its stance and the scope of the doctrine,[96] and court decisions.

Repeatedly, the Commission has returned to its 1949 report Editorializing by Broadcast Licensees, for explaining what is called for in the fairness doctrine. In the case of John J. Dempsey,[97] it held that the broadcaster's obligations in the public interest are not met simply by a general policy of not refusing to broadcast opposing views where a demand is made upon it for air time. More positive attention to the public interest in hearing various positions is needed from broadcasters; the FCC 1949 Report said that [98]

> * * * broadcast licensees have an affirmative duty generally to encourage and implement the broadcast of all sides of controversial public issues over their facilities, over and beyond their obligation to make available on demand opportunities for the expression of opposing views. It is clear that any approximation of fairness in the presentation of any controversy will be difficult if not impossible of achievement unless the licensee plays a conscious and positive role in bringing about balanced presentation of the opposing viewpoints.

This is sometimes referred to as the "seek out" rule, in that the broadcaster is told it is his duty to take the initiative in encouraging those with varying viewpoints on an issue to broadcast. The "seek out" process is not finished if no opponent of an aired view shows up in response to an over-the-air invitation to do so; the licensee as a community expert on controversy should notify persons with contrasting viewpoints of their opportunity to be heard.

---

[95] Steven J. Simmons, The Problem of "Issue" in the Administration of the Fairness Doctrine, 65 Calif.L.Rev. 546, 554 (May, 1977).

[96] An extended re-examination of the Fairness Doctrine by the FCC resulted in its most recent comprehensive statement, Fairness Doctrine and Public Interest Standards, Fairness Report Regarding Handling of Public Issues, 39 Fed.Reg. 26372, 48 F.C.C.2d 1, 30 R.R.2d 1261 (1974). The short title, "Fairness Report," is used hereinafter.

[97] 6 R.R. 615 (1950).

[98] 13 F.C.C. 1246, 1251 (1949).

Determining what is a "controversial issue of public importance" is a matter of judgment, not defined by the Commission. It is considerably up to the broadcaster. As stated above, he is to "make reasonable judgments in good faith on the facts of each situation—as to whether a controversial issue of public importance is involved, as to what viewpoints have been or should be presented, as to the format and spokesmen to present the viewpoints * * *." [99] Opposing positions do not need to be made on the same show or in the same programming format as that which gave rise to the claim of fairness violation.[1]

Difficult determinations are involved in many cases reaching the FCC, starting often with the question: What issue is raised by the program complained of? [2] In Green v. FCC [3] the appeals court found uncertainty as to what issues could invoke the fairness doctrine. It considered five possible issues that seemed to be involved in spot announcements that appealed for enlistment in the armed forces. Discarding two, it found that the other three could be equated: the "desirability" of military service, the draft, and the Vietnam War. It found that the *un*desirable features of the Vietnam War had been aired for years, and that prior coverage by the stations involved was sufficient to negate any fairness doctrine violation.

A further question is whether the issue is controversial and a matter of public importance. In its Fairness Report of 1964, the Commission says it relies heavily on the "reasonable, good faith judgments of our licensees" in determining these matters. It also, however, identifies three factors that are involved in the determination of whether a matter is of "public importance," and is "controversial": the amount of media attention; the degree of attention given the issue by leaders, including government officials; and the principal test—a "subjective evaluation [by the broadcaster] of the impact that the issue is likely to have on the community at large." [4]

The famous "Pensions" case [5] illustrated the elusive nature of pinning down just what the issues are and whether they are controversial. NBC presented a one-hour documentary titled

[99] Supra, text at footnote 72.

[1] Accuracy in Media, Inc., 39 F.C.C.2d 416, 421 (1973); 521 F.2d 288 (D.C.Cir. 1975); Diocesan Union of Holy Name Societies, 41 F.C.C.2d 297, 298–99 (D.C.Cir. 1973).

[2] Simmons, op. cit.

[3] 447 F.2d 323 (D.C.Cir.1971).

[4] Fairness Report, 30 R.R.2d 1262, 48 F.C.C.2d 1, 11–12 (1974).

[5] Accuracy in Media, Inc., 40 F.C.C.2d 958 (1973). When NBC appealed the decision of the FCC to federal court, the name of the case became National Broadcasting Co. v. FCC, 516 F.2d 1101 (D.C.Cir.1973).

"Pensions; the Broken Promise." Edwin Newman narrated it. It told of private pension plans that, for a variety of reasons, failed to provide retired workers with the pensions they had expected. Newman spoke of empty hopes, shattered dreams, and false promises that—experience showed—would visit many persons as they entered retirement. Case histories of workers to whom such had happened were prominent in the documentary. Before closing, Newman said " * * * we don't want to give the impression that there are no good private pension plans. There are many good ones, and there are many people for whom the promise has become reality." But, he finished:[6] "Our own conclusion about all this, is that it is almost inconceivable that this enormous thing has been allowed to grow up with so little understanding of it and with so little protection and such uneven results for those involved. The situation, as we've seen it, is deplorable."

Accuracy in Media brought a complaint of violating the fairness doctrine to the FCC. It charged that NBC's program was a one-sided presentation of the controversial issue of the performance and regulation of private pension plans. The network's response was that no controversial issue of public importance inhered in the program: NBC had sought to inform viewers of some of the problems that exist in some private pension plans and that "deserve a closer look." It said there was no question—no controversy—over the fact that some private pension plans present problems.[7]

The FCC ruled for Accuracy in Media. "Pensions," it said, had indeed gone to the general performance and proposed regulation of private pension plans; this was a controversial issue of public importance; and the program had been overwhelmingly anti-pensions despite a few comments on successful plans.[8]

NBC took the case to the court of appeals. The court reversed the FCC, again with the matter of "controversial issue" prominent. It said that the case histories of hardships did not constitute a controversial issue because there was no questioning that such existed; that criticisms of private plans on the program were balanced by general comments that were pro-private pension plans; and that while specific proposals for remedial legislation were controversial, these were not raised in the documentary in detail, and the more general point of a need for legislation was not controversial.[9]

[6] Accuracy in Media, Inc., 40 F.C.C.2d 958, 963 (1973).

[7] Ibid., at 959–60.

[8] Ibid., at 967.

[9] National Broadcasting Co. v. FCC, 516 F.2d 1101 (D.C.Cir.1973). For a penetrating critique of the divided court's decision, see Simmons, pp. 573–576.

The Commission has said that "a fairness response is not required as a result of offhand or insubstantial statements." [10] Within this context, it ruled in National Broadcasting Co. [11] that dangers caused by private pilots over congested airports, brought up during a segment on congestion by the Huntley-Brinkley news show, did not require a fairness response. It said that the "thrust of the program" was congestion at large airports. And, it added, "If every statement, or inference from statements or presentations, could be made the subject of a separate and distinct fairness requirement, the doctrine would be unworkable." [12] The matter of private pilots was a subissue within the larger concern and danger in airport congestion in general.

Yet relying on *NBC* as it has in subsequent cases, the FCC has not produced consistent results on what is a "subissue" that requires a fairness response. Nor has it produced a clear-cut line between subissues and "passing references," the latter more "offhand" or "insubstantial" than the former.

Not only politics and government are included in the realm of public controversial issues. As early as 1962, the FCC rejected several stations' contention that a program conducted by a nutritionalist on health and diet did not belong in the realm of controversial issues of public importance. The fairness doctrine, it said, applied in the broadcasting of such subjects.[13] More recently, it has said that entertainment programs can include issues subject to the fairness doctrine, although it "has always found licensees to have been reasonable in concluding that fairness doctrine issues were not raised by entertainment programming.[14] The Commission says, for example, that there is a difference between a fictional program's *depicting* an issue and the program's *discussing* an issue. Thus National Organization for Women, in challenging a television license renewal, said that the licensee was given to showing stereotyped women—sex objects, dependent creatures—without balancing that view with others. The FCC found no discussion of the matter, only depiction, and ruled against NOW.[15]

Besides exercising judgment and "good sense" in deciding what constitutes a public controversial issue, the licensee must gauge what is "reasonable opportunity" for an opposing viewpoint to be heard. The Democratic National Committee (DNC) complained to the FCC that the television networks in the fall of 1981

[10] Fairness Report, 39 Fed.Reg. at 26376.

[11] 19 R.R.2d 137 (1970), on reconsideration 25 F.C.C.2d 735 (1970).

[12] Ibid., p. 736.

[13] "Living Should Be Fun" Inquiry, 33 F.C.C. 101, 23 R.R. 1599 (1962).

[14] Simmons, p. 557.

[15] American Broadcasting Co., 52 F.C.C.2d 385 (1975).

violated the fairness doctrine by failing to provide adequate coverage to critics of the Reagan administration's economic policies. It provided figures from monitoring services indicating that evening news programs and two weekly interview programs—"Meet the Press" and "Face the Nation"—showed imbalances of coverage favoring the Reagan administration viewpoint of 2 to 1 or 3 to 1 or more. It provided no data on other parts of the networks' news programming.[16]

The FCC ruled against the DNC. It said that even if there were ratios of 3 to 1 or 4 to 1, "Such imbalance could hardly be considered a 'glaring disparity' calling for further investigation." The complaint's evidence was insufficient to warrant an inquiry by the FCC into network programming.[17]

The District of Columbia Appeals Court agreed with the FCC. It emphasized the large discretion given to broadcasters in deciding what is a "reasonable opportunity" for opposition views to be heard. It agreed that it is not practicable to require equality for each of the great number of issues aired daily, and that for the Commission to try to do this would inject it deeply and intrusively into the editorial process of broadcasting. The Court then emphasized a major difference between the fairness doctrine and equal time: [18]

> Behind DNC's argument is an implicit attempt to have this court erect an equal time standard under which compliance with the fairness doctrine would be determined by rough approximations of equality rather than by reference to broadcaster good faith and reasonableness. * * * Reasonableness was the guidepost that the Commission correctly used in reaching its decision. * * *

Also unlike the equal opportunities rule, under the fairness doctrine the FCC gives the broadcaster discretion to choose a person to speak for the contrasting views, and discretion to designate the techniques or formats of the program for contrasting views. There is "no single group or person entitled as a matter of right to present a viewpoint differing from that previously expressed on the station." [19] More recently, however, the Commission has ruled that: [20]

> Where a spokesman for, or supporter of candidate A, buys time and broadcasts a discussion of the candidates or

[16] Democratic National Committee v. FCC, 717 F.2d 1471 (D.C.Cir.1983), 9 Med.L. Rptr. 2272.

[17] Ibid., 2274–5.

[18] Ibid., 2277.

[19] Letter to Cullman Broadcasting Co., Inc., 25 R.R. 895 (1963).

[20] Nicholas Zapple, 23 F.C.C.2d 707, 19 R.R.2d 421, 422 (1970).

the campaign issues, there has clearly been the presentation of one side of a controversial issue of public importance. It is equally clear that spokesmen or supporters of opposing candidate B are not only appropriate, but the logical spokesmen for presenting contrasting views. Therefore, barring unusual circumstances, it would not be reasonable for a licensee to refuse to sell time to spokesmen for or supporters of candidate B comparable to that previously bought on behalf of candidate A.

Another difference between the equal opportunities rule regarding political candidates and the fairness doctrine applying to controversial issues: Under the former, the broadcaster who has charged the first candidate for air time, does not have to grant equal opportunity to an opponent who is not willing or able to pay. But under the fairness doctrine, the broadcaster who has aired one view on a controversial issue supported by a sponsor, may not ordinarily refuse to air another view on the issue on grounds that a sponsor for the second view cannot be found. The FCC held in *Cullman* that "the public's paramount right to hear opposing views on controversial issues * * * cannot be nullified by * * * the inability of the licensee to obtain paid sponsorship of the broadcast time." [21] Yet again, there are exceptions, at least in the "direct political arena." The *Zapple* decision said: [22]

> When spokesmen or supporters of candidate A have purchased time, it is our view that it would be inappropriate to require licensees to in effect subsidize the campaign of an opposing candidate by providing candidate B's spokesmen or supporters with free time.

Also in contrast with the equal opportunities rule, the fairness doctrine places "an affirmative duty" on the broadcaster to see to it that opposing views are presented. Equal opportunities requires only that the candidate who wishes to reply has the chance to do so.

Early in this section, attention was called to a part of the fairness doctrine that long went unenforced by the FCC. Not until 1976 did it say that licensees must air issues—not merely seek out responses to issues that happen to be aired. In the words of its 1949 Editorializing by Broadcast Licensees, it recognized "the necessity for licensees to devote a reasonable percentage of their broadcast time to the presentation of news and programs devoted to the consideration and discussion of public issues of interest in the community served by the particular station." [23]

[21] Letter to Cullman Broadcasting Co., Inc., 25 R.R. 895 (1963).

[22] Nicholas Zapple, 23 F.C.C.2d 707, 19 R.R.2d 421–423 (1970).

[23] New Broadcasting Co. (WLIB), 6 R.R. 258, 259 (1950).

The Commission has long felt that requiring a station to air any particular issue placed the Commission in the position of arbiter of programming, and that programming was the station's function. Nevertheless, it had said that "some issues are so critical or of such public importance that it would be unreasonable for a licensee to ignore them completely * * *." [24]

And that seemed to be its finding in Representative Pasty Mink.[25] The FCC ruled that a radio station which had simply ignored a controversy of central importance and interest to its area would have to provide coverage of the issue. Station WHAR of Clarksburg, W.Va., was one of several asked by Rep. Patsy Mink to broadcast a tape of her views on strip-mining legislation. WHAR responded that it did no programming on strip mining. Mink made a case of it before the FCC, presenting heavy documentation that Clarksburg was in the heart of the West Virginia strip-mining area, that the issue occupied newspapers and community and government leaders of the Clarksburg region intensely, that environment and people's welfare were directly affected and that the legislation was involved in the future condition of the area. The Commission declared that it had "no intention of intruding on licensees' day-to-day editorial decision making," and that its intrusion in this case was one rarely to be followed. But the strip-mining issue was of such magnitude in Clarksburg, that it could be considered to have a "significant and possibly unique impact on the licensee's service area." [26] WHAR would have to program the strip-mining issue.

The limited enforcement of the Fairness Doctrine's coverage requirement that the FCC insisted on in the Representative Patsy Mink decision has been criticized both for effectively allowing broadcasters to neglect subjects of importance and for sometimes placing the Commission in the position of making programming decisions.[27] During the 1970s the FCC considered and rejected a number of proposals for establishing additional or alternative approaches to its policies on the handling of public issues.[28] In a ruling issued in 1977, however, the U.S. Court of Appeals for the District of Columbia Circuit required that further attention be given to two of the rejected proposals—the petitions of the Com-

[24] Fairness Report, 48 F.C.C.2d 1, 25 (1974).

[25] 59 F.C.C.2d 987 (1976).

[26] Ibid., p. 997. For a critique and warning in the FCC's enforcement of this so-called "Fairness Doctrine Part One" obligation of licensees, see Simmons, pp. 582–586.

[27] Bill F. Chamberlin, "The FCC and the First Principle of the Fairness Doctrine: A History of Neglect and Distortion," 31 Fed.Comm.L.J. 361 (1979).

[28] The central work on the Fairness Doctrine from its inception to the latter part of the 1970s is Simmons, op. cit.

mittee for Open Media and of Henry Geller, former general counsel to the FCC.[29] The Committee for Open Media suggested that licensees could be deemed in compliance with the Fairness Doctrine if they voluntarily instituted local right of access systems which would set aside time for statements by members of the public.[30] The Geller proposal called for television stations to list annually the ten issues they had chosen for the most coverage in the prior year and to report on the programming efforts made on each issue outside of "routine" news coverage. After reconsideration, the FCC again denied the two petitions. Both were questioned with regard to their potential interference with journalistic discretion. In addition, the Committee for Open Media plan was said to be an inadequate substitute for the Fairness Doctrine since it did not provide assurances that the topics discussed would be important and timely or that a variety of viewpoints would be presented in an informative and comprehensible way. The Geller "Ten Issue" proposal was characterized as an additional record-keeping requirement which would "impose an undue administrative burden on the licensee and the Commission" without necessarily enhancing coverage of controversial issues.[31]

The Commission relies almost entirely on the warning force of its opinions and rulings to get stations to change their ways under the fairness doctrine. It has power to deny re-licensing, to issue cease and desist orders, to give "short-term" license renewals (e.g., one year instead of the customary five), or even to revoke a license in mid-term. It has often come under heavy attack for not using these powers, its critics arguing that it is a "captive" of the industry it supposedly regulates. One study found that the FCC had used a sanction of this kind in only one fairness doctrine case until 1965.[32]

In this case, Lamar Life Broadcasting Co. was granted a conditional one-year renewal of its license for WLBT in Jackson, Miss. The United Church of Christ objected to any renewal, on grounds that the station's news and public affairs programming displayed racial and religious discrimination. The Church asked that it be granted the license instead. The FCC granted a one-year renewal of Lamar's license (instead of the usual three), provided that it

[29] National Citizens Committee for Broadcasting v. FCC, 567 F.2d 1095, certiorari denied 436 U.S. 926, 98 S.Ct. 2820 (1978).

[30] For a discussion of the philosophical basis for the Committee's point of view by one of its members, see Phil Jacklin, "Representative Diversity," 28 Journal of Communication, (Spring 1978), pp. 85–88.

[31] In the Matter of the Handling of Public Issues Under the Fairness Doctrine and the Public Interest Standards of the Communications Act, 74 F.C.C.2d 163, 46 R.R.2d 999 (1979).

[32] Barrow, p. 469. For a case decided in 1977, involving a $1,000 forfeiture for violation of the personal attack rule (see below, next section): Pleasant Broadcasting v. FCC, (D.C.Cir.1977), 2 Med.L.Rptr. 2277, 2279.

comply strictly with the fairness doctrine and cease discriminatory programming patterns.   It held no hearing in the matter.

The United Church of Christ took the case to federal court. There the FCC was told that renewal of the WLBT license was erroneous, for hearings should have been held and segments of WLBT's listening public allowed to intervene and participate. The church had standing to be heard as public intervenors.[33]

The FCC conducted the hearings, the church giving testimony about racial slurs, the cutting off of a network program and the results of its monitoring of the station for a week.   The Commission then reconsidered the probationary license of one year, and decided it was in the public interest to remove the probationary status and grant WLBT a three-year renewal.   Again the church appealed; the federal appeals court found for the church, and ordered the FCC to vacate its renewal of the license.   The court said that the FCC examiner and the Commission itself incorrectly treated the intervenors like plaintiffs who must carry the burden of proof.   They exhibited, in the hearing and in their opinions and rulings: [34]

> * * * at best a reluctant tolerance of this court's mandate [in the earlier decision granting the church standing to intervene] and at worst a profound hostility to the participation of the Public Intervenors and their efforts.

The court said the hearing and the decision to renew were so faulty that "it will serve no useful purpose to ask the Commission to reconsider the Examiner's actions and its own Decision and Order * * *.   The administrative conduct in this record is beyond repair." [35]   It directed the Commission to invite applications to be filed for the license held by WLBT.

SEC. 77.   THE FAIRNESS DOCTRINE: PERSONAL ATTACKS AND POLITICAL EDITORIALS

When a broadcast attacks the integrity or character of a person or group, or an editorial supports or opposes a political candidate, the station must promptly notify the person attacked or opposed, furnish him with the content of the attack, and offer him air time to respond.

An attack on the character, honesty, or integrity of a person or group during a broadcast of a controversial issue of public

[33] Office of Communication of United Church of Christ v. F.C.C., 123 U.S.App. D.C. 328, 359 F.2d 994 (1966).

[34] Office of Communication of United Church of Christ v. F.C.C., 138 U.S.App. D.C. 112, 425 F.2d 543, 550 (1969).

[35] Ibid.

importance, calls for the application of special rules under the fairness doctrine. So does a station's editorial support for or opposition to a political candidate. In both cases, the FCC reasons that the public interest in full debate and airing of issues, rather than the interest of the one attacked, is the factor of first concern.

The Commission's policies developed in cases over the years were formalized in rules in 1967 and 1968. One is that the broadcaster must notify the target of the attack promptly, and furnish him with a transcript, tape, or summary of the attack. Also, an offer of time to reply must be given. Where the licensee has broadcast an editorial endorsing or opposing a political candidate, the opposing candidates are supposed to be notified within 24 hours after the attack, and furnished with the transcript and an offer of time.[36]

A second rule refers to the kinds of programs that are exempt from the special provisions. A bona fide newscast, a broadcast of a bona fide news event, and news interviews and commentaries are not within the requirements.[37] This leaves editorials and documentaries among the kinds of programs that remain under the special requirements. The Commission recognizes, in the exceptions to the requirements, the broadcasters' strongly argued point that the rules calling for notice, transcript, and offer of time may have the effect of discouraging stations from airing important controversial issues.

One case involved the complaint of the general manager of a rural electric cooperative association. For five days, a station broadcast a series of editorials attacking him in connection with a public controversial issue. He learned of the attacks upon his arrival in town the fourth day. On the fifth day, he tried to get copies of the editorials, and on the same day, the station offered him a broadcast interview to answer the attacks. His total stay in town was for only two days, and he rejected the offer because he would not have time to prepare an adequate reply. In ruling that the station "had not fully met the requirements of the Commission's fairness doctrine," the FCC said that [38]

> [T]he fairness doctrine requires that a copy of the specific editorial or editorials shall be communicated to the person attacked either prior to or at the time of the broadcast * * * so that a reasonable opportunity is afforded that person to reply. This duty on the part of the station is greater where, as here, interest in the editorials was consciously built up over a period of days

[36] Barrow, pp. 472–476; 32 Fed.Reg. 10303–ff. (1967).

[37] 32 Fed.Reg. 11531 (1967).

[38] Billings Bctg. Co., 23 R.R. 951 (1962).

and the time within which the person attacked would have an opportunity to reply was known to be so limited.

Another case involved attacks on county and state officials, accusing them of using their offices for personal gain and charging that their administration employed procedures similar to political methods of dictators. The persons attacked were invited several times to use the station to discuss the matter. At license-renewal time, those attacked in the broadcasts said that the station was used for selfish purposes, and to vent personal spite. But the Commission renewed the license, saying that although the broadcast attacks were highly personal and impugned the character and honesty of named individuals, those attacked were told of the attacks and were aware of the opportunities afforded them to reply.[39]

Another case involving repeated attacks by a commentator on California's Governor Pat Brown, a candidate for reelection, illustrates a further rule in personal attack on political candidates under the fairness doctrine. This rule is that in affording the opportunity for response, the station may insist that an appropriate spokesman for the attacked candidate deliver the response rather than the candidate himself. If the candidate were permitted to respond, this would bring into operation the "equal opportunities" provision of Section 315 of the Communications Act, and the candidate's opponents could then insist on equal time. In the case involving Governor Brown, the FCC held that while the station could require that a spokesman rather than Brown make the response, "The candidate should * * * be given a substantial voice in the selection of the spokesman * * *." [40]

The strength and reach of the fairness doctrine are great. Broadcasters' attacks upon it as burdensome and unconstitutional have been rejected by the Supreme Court. And the application of the principle has been expanded, in decisions since 1969, to certain kinds of advertising.[41]

Red Lion Broadcasting Co. v. FCC [42] produced a unanimous endorsement of the doctrine's personal attack rule by the court, and the flat declaration that the central First Amendment interest in free speech by broadcasting is the public's, not the broadcaster's. The case rose in Red Lion, Pa., after the company refused Fred J. Cook free time to answer attacks on him by the

---

[39] Clayton W. Mapoles, 23 R.R. 586 (1962).

[40] Times-Mirror Bctg. Co., 24 R.R. 404, 406 (1962).

[41] Steven J. Simmons, "The FCC's Personal Attack and Political Editorial Rules Reconsidered," 125 Pa.Law Rev. 990, 1002–1006 (Fall, 1977) for refinements in the fairness doctrine during the 1970's. Hereinafter cited as Simmons, Personal Attack Rules.

[42] 395 U.S. 367, 80 S.Ct. 1794 (1969).

Rev. Billy James Hargis, a program moderator for its station, who associated Cook with left-wing activities. Cook took the case to the FCC which directed Red Lion to provide free time for Cook to reply, and Red Lion went to the courts, claiming the fairness doctrine unconstitutional. Meanwhile, Radio-Television News Directors Ass'n. (RTNDA), Columbia Broadcasting System and National Broadcasting Co. were bringing a separate action on constitutional ground, claiming that the notification process of the personal attack—political editorial rules was expensive and burdensome, discouraging broadcasters from airing controversial issues.[43] The Supreme Court decided the two cases together in a decision since known as *Red Lion.*

Congress had ratified the long-standing fairness requirement of the FCC in positive legislation of 1959, when in amending Sec. 315 it said specifically that stations must "operate in the public interest and * * * afford reasonable opportunity for the discussion of conflicting views on issues of public importance." While Congress had not spoken precisely to the personal attack—political editorial rules, the Court found no reason to consider that these rules were out of joint with the "controversial issues of public importance" rule. As implementation of the statutory "public interest, convenience or necessity" provision, the fairness doctrine was within the FCC's function and not an unconstitutional exercise of power delegated by Congress.[44]

Then the Supreme Court considered the broadcasters' contention that the First Amendment protects their wish to use their allotted frequencies to broadcast whatever they choose and to exclude from the frequency whomever they choose. As other "new media," it said, broadcasting had to live with certain special standards under the First Amendment: Not everyone who wanted to could broadcast, or each would drown the other out because of the limited number of frequencies. "[I]t is idle to posit an unabridgeable First Amendment right to broadcast comparable to the right of every individual to speak, write or publish." [45]

The Court laid out its interpretation of whose First Amendment right is primarily at stake in free speech by broadcasting: the public's, not the licensee's.[46]

> But the people as a whole retain their interest in free
> speech by radio and their collective right to have the
> medium function consistently with the ends and purposes
> of the First Amendment. It is the right of the viewers

[43] Ibid.

[44] Ibid., 385.

[45] Ibid., 388.

[46] Ibid., 390.

and listeners, not the right of the broadcasters, which is paramount. * * * It is the purpose of the First Amendment to preserve an uninhibited marketplace of ideas in which truth will ultimately prevail, rather than to countenance monopolization of that market, whether it be by the Government itself or a private licensee. * * * It is the right of the public to receive suitable access to social, political, esthetic, moral, and other ideas and experiences which is crucial here.

Yet endorsed though they are by the Supreme Court in *Red Lion,* the fairness doctrine and its personal attack rule live under barrage. One attack says that consistent results are not to be had in the FCC's adjudication of fairness doctrine cases. When " * * * the rulings are read together, the decisions seem haphazard, and they hopelessly confuse any effort to figure out what general principles delineate the scope of the personal attack rules." [47] This is the case, says Attorney Benno C. Schmidt, Jr., even though when the single FCC personal attack decision is studied, it may not seem unreasonable.

There is also the position that the personal attack rules do not serve the claimed FCC objectives of the airing of issues in the crucial work of informing the public. Instead, the reasoning goes, it is precisely when issues retreat and name-calling comes to the fore that the personal attack rules require reply opportunity. "To a large extent, the personal attack rules generate name calling exercises, allowing those parties whose personalities are criticized to rebut the charges without requiring rebuttal opportunities on the more substantive issues." [48]

The constitutional question, furthermore, dies hard among journalists, for many of whom the Seventh Circuit Court of Appeals stated a simple truth in RTNDA v. FCC: The personal attack and political editorial rules "collide with the free speech and free press guarantees contained in the First Amendment * * *." [49]

On one occasion since *Red Lion,* the FCC has relied on the fairness doctrine to refuse to renew a license and found its reliance rejected by the District of Columbia Court of Appeals. The case involved Faith Theological Seminary of Elkins Park, Pa., and the Rev. Carl McIntire, one of its directors.[50] The Seminary was approved for transfer of WXUR (Brandywine-Main Line Ra-

---

[47] Benno C. Schmidt, Jr., Freedom of the Press vs. Public Access (N.Y.: Praeger, 1976), p. 171.

[48] Simmons, Personal Attack Rules, p. 1016.

[49] 400 F.2d 1002, 1021 (7th Cir.1968).

[50] Brandywine-Main Line Radio, Inc., 24 F.C.C.2d 18 (1970).

dio) licenses after the FCC had carefully stressed to it the requirements of balance under the fairness doctrine; many groups had
opposed the transfer on grounds that McIntire's previous record as
radio commentator was evidence that he could not bring about a
fair and balanced presentation of controversial public issues. Less
than a year after the transfer, WXUR's licenses came up for
renewal. The FCC found that the company had plunged into
controversial-issue programming immediately after the transfer,
had not provided opposing views a reasonable chance, and had
engaged in much personal attack without observing the notification rules. All this was violation of the fairness doctrine so
flagrant that license renewal was not warranted, the Commission
ruled; and furthermore, the licensee had misrepresented its real
programming intent when it had applied for the transfer of
license.

Brandywine appealed to the courts. Of three judges at the
Court of Appeals, one favored refusal to renew on grounds of both
misrepresentation and violating the fairness doctrine, and one
joined him only on the ground of misrepresentation. The third
judge dissented, finding the misrepresentation grounds infected
with aspects and overtones of the fairness doctrine, which, he said,
while unquestioned for 50 years, now needed its values, purposes
and effects re-examined. In silencing WXUR, Judge David
Bazelon said, the Commission had dealt a death blow to the
licensee's freedom of speech and press, and also denied the public
access to many controversial issues. Bazelon said that licensing
and regulating radio and television come down in the end to an
assumption of technical scarcity—limited frequencies to which all
cannot have access; but the viewer now has the prospect in a few
years of 400 television channels, and the enormous capacity of
cable television to carry communication is now a technical reality.
"I fear that ancient assumptions and crystallized rules have blind-
ed all of us to the depth of the First Amendment issues involved
here,"[51] he said. Does silencing WXUR in the name of the
fairness doctrine violate the First Amendment? he asked.

SEC. 78.   THE FAIRNESS DOCTRINE: ADVERTISING

**The fairness doctrine applies to commercials devoted in an
obvious and meaningful way to the discussion of public
issues, but not to ordinary product commercials.**

While the fairness doctrine was receiving its test in *Red Lion*
and *RTNDA,* a new application of its reach was being asserted—to

[51] Brandywine-Main Radio, Inc., 25 R.R.2d 2010, 2076; Brandywine-Main Line
Radio v. FCC, 473 F.2d 16, 63–4 (D.C.Cir.1972).

advertising. This is treated in detail herein in Chapter 14. Crusaders against tobacco looked with anger at the flood of cigarette ads on television for years. Finally an action was brought, and the Commission required response time under the fairness doctrine to commercials for cigarettes, and for that product only.[52] Reasoning that Congress had urged people to stop smoking and that the health question was uncomplicated in the case of cigarettes, it later refused to extend the requirement to cars, although it agreed that health problems inhered in exhaust. It was overruled, in its refusal to extend the doctrine, by the District of Columbia Court of Appeals.[53] Knowing a hornet's nest when it saw one, the FCC beat a retreat from the confrontation that thus lay ahead in the unbounded world of product commercials that might warrant fairness responses. In its 1974 Fairness Report, the Commission simply reversed its cigarette ruling, and said that henceforth no product ads would generate fairness doctrine treatment, because they merely discuss the desirability of the product and make no meaningful contribution to public debate. It said that in the future it would apply the fairness doctrine to commercials "which are devoted in an obvious and meaningful way to the discussion of public issues." [54]

"Editorial advertisements," however, have been found by the Supreme Court to be outside the reach of the fairness doctrine. Business Executives' Move for Vietnam Peace (BEM), a nationwide group of 2,700 owners and executives, prepared radio spot ads urging immediate withdrawal of American forces from overseas military installations. WTOP, Washington, refused to sell time to BEM. The Station said its long-established policy was not to sell time for spot announcements to groups or individuals who wished to set forth their views on controversial issues. The FCC upheld WTOP's policy of rejecting all editorial advertisements, saying that stations have wide leeway in the format they choose for airing controversial issues.[55] The Supreme Court, in a decision joining BEM to Columbia Broadcasting System, Inc. v. Democratic National Committee, upheld the FCC.[56]

---

[52] WCBS–TV, 8 F.C.C.2d 381 (1967); sustained Banzhaf v. FCC, 405 F.2d 1082 (D.C.Cir.1968), certiorari denied 396 U.S. 842, 90 S.Ct. 50 (1969).

[53] Friends of the Earth, 24 F.C.C.2d 743 (1970); Friends of the Earth v. FCC, 449 F.2d 1164 (D.C.Cir.1971).

[54] 48 F.C.C.2d 1, 26 (1974); Complaint of Energy Action Committee, Inc., 2 Med.L. Rptr. 1623 (Apr. 26, 1977).

[55] Business Executives' Move for Vietnam Peace, 25 F.C.C.2d 242 (1971).

[56] 412 U.S. 94, 93 S.Ct. 2080 (1973).

SEC. 79.   DEREGULATION

In dropping long-standing regulatory measures, Congress and the FCC have attempted to let "marketplace forces" decide the issues.

In 1976, plans to begin a "basement to penthouse" remodeling of the Communications Act of 1934 were announced by Representative Lionel Van Deerlin, then chairman of the House Communications Subcommittee. The California Congressman, a former broadcast reporter, suggested the 40-year-old law had become antiquated in an age of cable television, communication satellites, computers and fiber optics. Three years later, after hearing more than 1,200 witnesses and drafting several sweeping documents aimed at replacing government regulation with "marketplace forces," Van Deerlin and his subcommittee watched their project collapse under a weight of negative criticisms. Broadcasters welcomed provisions for granting licenses for indefinite periods and for relaxing or eliminating fairness doctrine and equal-time rules, but they expressed fears at the prospect of increased competition resulting from the removal of FCC regulations affecting other suppliers or potential suppliers of communication services—notably cable television operators and telephone companies. An additional concern was that licensees were expected to pay annually a new spectrum-use fee (ranging from a few hundred dollars to several million depending on the size of the station) which would have provided support for public broadcasting, minority ownership of stations, rural telecommunications services, and the administrative costs of a five-member Communications Regulatory Commission designed to replace the seven-member FCC. Citizens groups, meanwhile, protested the loss of virtually all their legal weapons as well as the elimination of the "public interest" standard itself. They criticized the draft legislation as a give-away of public rights and property that would have the ultimate effect of changing regulated monopolies into unregulated monopolies.[57]

What remained of the arduous Van Deerlin effort was especially the elevation of "market forces" as a guiding principle to substantially replace government regulation in obtaining satisfactory broadcast service. Under Chairman Charles Ferris, the FCC picked up that banner in the early 1980's and began a deregulation program that would reach major proportions. In its Second Computer Inquiry decision issued on May 2, 1980, the Commission helped to clear the way for the American Telephone and Tele-

---

[57] Manny Lucoff, "The Rise and Fall of the Third Rewrite," 30 Journal of Communication 47 (1980). Florence Heffron, The Federal Communications Commission and Broadcast Deregulation, in John J. Havick (ed.), Communications Policy and the Political Process (1983), Chap. 3, 39.

graph Co. to provide electronic communication services and thereby compete with print and broadcast media in news and advertising.[58]   The decision distinguished between basic transmission services that simply move information and "enhanced" transmission services which use computers to process and present information—the former being subject to common carrier rules and the latter being regulated only on occasions when the FCC would consider it necessary.   The Commission said that it would permit AT & T to offer enhanced services as long as the company did so through a subsidiary.   In the wake of the decision, newspaper publishers and other potential rivals of "Ma Bell" sought a law to prevent AT & T from generating an "enhanced report."   Success seemed likely, but in the event, no law was needed.   An antitrust suit brought by the government resulted in a decision by Federal Judge Harold Greene of the D.C. District Court that largely gave the media what they wanted.

Greene approved, with modifications, a "consent decree"—an agreement reached between the government and AT & T.[59]   (His decision and the consent decree provided much beyond the immediate concern of news media, including the requirement that AT & T divest itself of all its 22 local Bell operating companies, which supply local telephone service.)   The Court told AT & T it must stay out of the business of electronic publishing—controlling the content of the information being transmitted—for a period of at least seven years.   The U.S. Supreme Court affirmed.[60]   The entry of the world's largest corporation into the news field, by means of advanced computer technology, was barred by the judge because of the threat it posed both to competition in the infant electronic publishing industry and to First Amendment values.

The prospect that the computer had enabled AT & T—the agency that long had dominated the information "pipeline" (the transmission facilities)—to gather, organize, and furnish any kind of news report to the news-consuming audience had haunted the media world for years.   AT & T's minor entry into the field was already a fact.   An example was its "Dial-It" mass calling service, which provided that customers could call a number and get information such as stock prices, sports reports, and other news, available in AT & T's computer storage for retrieval by subscribers over the telephone.   Such were the "enhanced services" of AT &

---

[58] 77 F.C.C.2d 384 (1980).   The decision was later modified and clarified in some of its details.   79 F.C.C.2d 953 (1980); 46 Fed.Reg. 5984 (1980).   FCC's rulemaking was upheld in Computer and Communications Industry Ass'n v. FCC, 693 F.2d 198 (D.C.Cir.1982), 8 Med.L.Rptr. 2457.

[59] United States v. AT & T, 552 F.Supp. 131 (D.C.D.C.1982), 8 Med.L.Rptr. 2118.

[60] 9 Med.L.Rptr. # 6, 3/8/83, News Notes.

T.[61]   Was AT & T to be permitted to gather, write, edit, and make available any sort of news whatsoever?

Judge Greene ruled "no" to AT & T's engaging in such electronic publishing.[62]   Permitting AT & T to provide enhanced services would present real danger to the development of competition from other electronic publishers, the Court found.   Against small firms' attempts to enter the field, AT & T's combination of "financial, technological, manufacturing, and marketing resources would dwarf any efforts of its competitors," discouraging or effectively blocking them.[63]   On competitive considerations alone, Judge Greene reasoned, the Court might be justified in barring AT & T from electronic publishing.

But beyond such considerations lay the danger to the First Amendment value of the public's need for a diversity of sources and information.   Supreme Court decisions such as that in Associated Press v. United States [64] had recognized, he said, that "in promoting diversity in sources of information, the values underlying the First Amendment coincide with the policy of the antitrust laws."

For years, Greene noted, concentration of ownership among daily newspapers, presumably brought about by impersonal economic and technological forces, has increasingly restricted the diversity of sources of control of the news.   "Diversity has disappeared in many areas," he said, and "unless care is taken, both the concentration and the attendant dangers will be significantly increased by the new technologies." [65]

> Indeed, it is not at all inconceivable that electronic publishing, with its speed and convenience will eventually overshadow the more traditional news media, and that a single electronic publisher would acquire substantial control over the provision of news in parts of the United States. . . .   AT & T's ability to use its control of the interexchange network to reduce or eliminate competition in the electronic publishing industry is the source of this threat to the First Amendment principle of diversity.

[61] Federal Communications Commission, Second Computer Inquiry, Amendment, 84 F.C.C.2d 50, 51, 54 (1980).

[62] United States v. AT & T, 552 F.Supp. 131 (D.C.D.C.1982), 8 Med.L.Rptr. 2118, 2120.

[63] Ibid., 2121.

[64] 326 U.S. 1, 20, 65 S.Ct. 1416, 1424 (1945), 1 Med.L.Rptr. 2269.

[65] United States v. AT & T, 552 F.Supp. 131 (D.C.D.C.1982), 8 Med.L.Rptr. 2118, 2123.

Greene made the restriction effective only for a period he thought necessary to establish conditions conducive to free and fair competition in electronic publishing—seven years.

The Court placed similar restrictions upon the seven new operating companies that would replace the 22 former Bell System companies. It permitted them, however, to produce, publish, and distribute printed directories containing advertisements—the "Yellow Pages"—and told AT & T itself that it could continue to provide electronic directory (advertising data), time, and weather service as it had done previously.

The FCC took steps to liberalize its channel allocations system in order to allow the creation of hundreds or possibly thousands of stations offering low-power television service (LPTV).[66] Under rules proposed by the Commission on September 9, 1980, LPTV signals would typically be limited to something less than 15 miles in any direction, but the stations themselves would operate under simpler and more flexible rules than regular television broadcasters. The FCC, for example, would not require formal ascertainment, studio facilities, or local program origination. LPTV stations would, however, have to comply with Fairness Doctrine and equal-time provisions to the extent their facilities would allow.

Within six months of issuing its low-power proposal, the FCC had received more than 3,500 interim applications from individuals and groups ready to try their luck in LPTV once it became available.[67] Few obstacles appeared to be in the way of the eventual adoption of the low-power rulemaking. What was less clear was LPTV's economic feasibility and its possible impact on existing broadcasters and cable operators. Start-up costs to put an LPTV station on the air were understood to be a fraction of what would otherwise be required for a television facility, but it was anticipated that low-power broadcasters would establish themselves in areas with small populations or else in larger markets where they would have to compete with "full-service" stations. A number of groups—some interested in particular themes ranging from a country-western format to religious programming—made plans for low-power networks fed by satellite.[68]

On January 14, 1981, the FCC attacked its own regulations on another front by terminating some of its policies and record-

---

[66] Notice of Proposed Rulemaking, 82 F.C.C.2d 47 (1980). For a brief summary of the Commission's proposal, see Anon., "FCC Opens Pandora's Box of Low Power," Broadcasting, September 15, 1980, pp. 29–30. Final rules were adopted by the FCC on March 4, 1982: 8 Med.L.Rptr. # 3, 3/16/82, News Notes.

[67] Anon., "FCC Begins to Weed LPTV Field," Broadcasting, March 23, 1981, pp. 29–30.

[68] Anon., "LPTV," Broadcasting, February 23, 1981, pp. 39, 43, 46, 50, 54, 58.

keeping requirements affecting radio.[69] The commissioners, who voted 6-to-1 in favor of the deregulation, abandoned guidelines that had limited advertising to 18 minutes per hour and had a minimum portion of airtime for news and public affairs (eight percent for AM and six percent for FM). They said they were taking action in four principal areas: [70]

A. *Nonentertainment Programming Guideline* —We are eliminating the guideline and retaining only a generalized obligation for commercial radio stations to offer programming responsive to public issues. Under certain circumstances, the issues may focus upon those of concern to the station's listenership as opposed to the community as a whole. This meant that FCC guidelines, prescribing news/public affairs levels of 8% for AM stations and 6% for FM stations were abandoned.

B. *Ascertainment* —We are eliminating both the 1971 Ascertainment Primer and the Renewal Primer. New applicants must file programming proposals with their application and licensees seeking renewal are only obligated to determine the issues facing their community. They may do so by any means reasonably calculated to apprise them of the issues. This meant that stations no longer would have to undertake detailed, formal surveys of listeners and community leaders to ascertain audience needs in programming, when seeking re-licensing.

C. *Commercial Guidelines* —We are eliminating the commercial guidelines leaving it to marketplace forces to determine the appropriate level of commercialization. This meant that FCC guidelines, prescribing a maximum of 18 minutes of advertising per hour, were abandoned.

D. *Program Logs* —We are eliminating programming logging requirements. The only record of programming that will be required will be an annual listing of five to ten issues that the licensee covered together with examples of programming offered in response thereto. This record must be placed in the public file. This meant that the detailed logs of all programming, kept for public inspection and for official use, were no longer required.

The FCC also noted that it had received complaints charging that its action was replacing the public interest standard with a marketplace concept. The commissioners responded by saying the issue for them was whether marketplace forces or federal regula-

[69] 46 Fed.Reg. 13888 (1981). See Anon., "Freer At Last," Broadcasting, January 19, 1981, pp. 31–34.

[70] 46 Fed.Reg. 13888, 13889.

tion would best serve the public interest in the future. Radio stations, the FCC maintained, had proliferated and specialized to such an extent that "unnecessarily burdensome regulations of uniform applicability" were no longer appropriate. The commissioners observed that the public interest standard as well as the Fairness Doctrine, the Petition to Deny process and periodic license renewals were statutory requirements of the Communications Act that could be removed by Congress but not by the FCC.[71]

By spring of 1984, *Broadcasting* magazine had assembled a list of 42 deregulatory acts by the Fowler Commission.[72] In June of 1984, furthermore, the major deregulations that had been applied to radio in 1981 (above, p. 605) were extended by the FCC to television. Guidelines for amounts of nonentertainment programming and advertising limits went out the window, the Commission being of the view that very few stations shaved the first or nudged the second, kept pure by competition. Also abandoned were ascertainment and program logging requirements, not only for commercial television but also for noncommercial television and radio.[73]

National Broadcasting Co., which owned five stations, said it would make no changes because its stations always had been within the FCC's news and advertising limits, and that the network believed in ascertainment and in program logging. Media watchdogs were fearful, Andrew Schwartzman of Media Access Project calling the measure "a cynical fraud on the American public." Citizen complaints against broadcasters, he reasoned, could hardly be expected to arise now that program logs open to the public were no longer kept. Eddie Fritts, National Association of Broadcasters President, had only praise, and brimmed with confidence that television would attain new levels of diversity and would show fewer commercials as competition increased. As for the FCC, its people said the result would partly be the elimination of millions of government-required paperwork hours per year for licensees.[74]

Still on the deregulation docket in Fowler's and other's views: Elimination of the fairness doctrine and equal time rules, narrowing of the FCC's purview over the "character" of licensees, streamlining of comparative renewal criteria, and removing the FCC from all content regulation not required by the Communications Act. Meanwhile, the deregulation theme was loud in debates over

---

[71] Ibid., 13888, 13890.

[72] April 30, 1984, 122. For aspects of the controversy and analysis of FCC rules gone or going, see Channels of Communication, Sept.–Oct., 1984, 52–70.

[73] Deregulation Comes to Television, Broadcasting, July 2, 1984, 31–32.

[74] Ibid.

a proposed act by Congress under which cable television would operate.

SEC. 80.   CABLE TELEVISION

Authority over cable television is partly in the FCC, partly in municipalities and states, the Cable Communications Policy Act of 1984 providing much of the framework.

A new technology burst from its small-town setting in the late 1950s and swept the Federal Communications Commission into an unmapped sphere of regulation of communications systems. Known as CATV (Community Antenna Television), the system picked up distant and near-by television stations' signals with a powerful antenna, and fed them by cable into the sets of people in towns where television reception was weak or absent. It could be done for a $20 installation fee and $5.00 a month; and "the cable," as delighted set owners named it, had the capacity to carry multiple channels—five in early years, then 12, 20 and on up. Systems spread in the 1950s through small-town America, and in the 1960s began moving into major cities with programs from afar to supplement the several television channels already operating. By 1976, there were approximately 3,450 operating systems with 10,800,000 subscribers, and by 1982, some 4,500 systems entered more than 38,000,000 homes with the basic, advertiser-supported service.[75]

It was plain by the early 1960s that cable was in direct competition with existing television stations, and was entering FCC ground. Moreover, cable's capacity to carry a vast variety of non-broadcasting communication suggested that its reach would transcend television considerations in the future.

The potential for profit spurred businessmen, financiers, and investors, many of them innocent of experience with television. The concept of the "wired nation" in which the cable would be strung in city after city to scores of millions of households, and service sold, frequently in situations without competition, was as awesome to the beholder as exciting to the entrepreneur.

And the potential for a new public service that would link people, groups, and communities in new ways was equally challenging. It spurred the public-spirited to the possibilities of moving information in quantities never dreamed of by television; of two-way communication that would some day bring the traditional "receiver" of media messages into an interchange with the traditional "source"; of establishing some of the many available chan-

---

[75] 8 Med.L.Rptr. # 9, 4/27/82, News Notes; Jones, Electronic Mass Media, 319, 320.

nels as "common carrier" services by which anyone who had the money and some who did not could claim time on a channel to say his say, speak his piece, reach his group.

The FCC confirmed its basic authority over cable by 1968, when the Supreme Court of the United States ruled in its favor in United States v. Southwestern Cable Co.[76] By 1972, the Commission adopted an extensive set of Rules and Regulations,[77] shaped in a context of preventing unfair competition to television, a service available to the public without charge in contrast to cable. Quickly, the document saw change, but the broad outline provided a system of shared control that would last, with states and primarily municipalities deeply involved. The FCC called this a program of "deliberately structured dualism": Local authorities would have the responsibility for granting cable companies franchises to operate and overseeing construction of cable facilities;[78] the FCC retained for itself exclusive jurisdiction over technical standards for cable systems, and the signals that cable systems would carry.[79]

What First Amendment protection would apply to cable? We have already seen that broadcasting's First Amendment rights are hedged in ways that printed media's are not. As "new media" appear, the Supreme Court ruled in 1952 in a case involving motion pictures,[80] their different characteristics justify different application to them of First Amendment standards. Reaffirming this in 1969 in a case involving radio, the Court said that the scarcity of available frequencies required government regulation of broadcasting,[81] including choosing among applicants for licenses, the fairness doctrine and equal opportunities.

Whether cable is to be treated more like broadcasting than like printed media in relation to the First Amendment in the long run remains to be seen. The commands of the fairness doctrine and equal opportunities do indeed apply to cable.[82] The Circuit Court of Appeals, Tenth District, ruled in 1981 that the "nearly absolute strictures" against regulating newspaper dissemination of information cannot be applied "in wholesale fashion" to cable.[83] It was inappropriate for a trial court to apply to cable operators the First Amendment principles applying to newspapers, the

[76] 392 U.S. 157, 88 S.Ct. 1994 (1968).

[77] 37 Fed.Reg. 3252, 24 R.R.2d 1501 (1972).

[78] Cable Television Report and Order, 36 F.C.C.2d 143 (1972).

[79] Clarification of the Cable Television Rules, 46 F.C.C.2d 175, 178 (1975).

[80] Burstyn v. Wilson, 343 U.S. 495, 503, 72 S.Ct. 777, 781 (1952).

[81] Red Lion Broadcasting Co. v. FCC, 395 U.S. 367, 89 S.Ct. 1794 (1969).

[82] 47 C.F.R. §§ 76.205, 76.209.

[83] Community Communications Co. v. Boulder, 660 F.2d 1370 (10th Cir.1981), 7 Med.L.Rptr. 1993, 1998.

Court ruled. Government and cable are tied in ways that government and newspapers are not: cable's use of public property, for example in laying underground wires, with disruption to public streets. Further, cable represents "medium scarcity," with both physical and economic limitations on the feasible number of systems in a community. The Court said that government must have some authority to see that optimum use of the cable is made "in the public interest." It remanded the case to the district court to make a "particularized inquiry into the unique attributes of the cable broadcasting medium," and to "fashion the First Amendment standards to be applied to this new medium." [84]

Predictably, the Commission's 1972 Cable Television Report and Order aroused storms of controversy in the world of broadcasting and cable. Much of it stemmed from the Commission's determination to protect television broadcasting from damage in the rise of cable, with regulations that satisfied neither medium. Quality and cost of service were left with local authorities in the franchising of cable, and resulting stories of bribery, shoddy service, and broken promises prompted *Newsweek* to declare in 1980 that the wiring of America was becoming a "national scandal," and a "mammoth mess." [85]

Regulating content ("signal carriage") of cable was relaxed as the FCC gained experience and analyzed the "television damage" factor. "Origination cablecasting"—programming provided by and subject to the exclusive control of the cable operator, rather than television signals received and transmitted by cable—was first required but in 1974 abandoned, the Commission finding the results "disappointing" in terms of quality and cost.[86] Also eliminated were the requirements in the 1972 rules that new cable systems include the technical capacity for return communication from the subscriber, and have access channels and production equipment for public use.

Another major deregulatory move came on July 22, 1980, when the FCC lifted two of its restrictions on cable television operators. In a 4–to–3 vote, the Commission adopted an order which removed both its limits on the number of television signals a cable system could provide and its protection against cable duplication of non-network programming purchased by local sta-

[84] Ibid., 1998–2000. For the position that the First Amendment should protect cable in these and other circumstances, see William E. Lee, Cable Franchising and the First Amendment, 36 Vanderbilt L.Rev. 867 (May 1983).

[85] Aug. 4, 1980, 44. For the Commission's policy of protecting television, see Heffron, 59–61.

[86] By Supreme Court decision: FCC v. Midwest Video Corp., 440 U.S. 689, 99 S.Ct. 1435 (1979).

tions for exclusive area distribution.[87] Arguing that the elimination of these distant signal and syndicated program exclusivity rules would not significantly harm broadcasters, the FCC thus retreated to a position where it would retain little regulatory power over cable TV beyond protecting stations against simultaneous cable importation of network programming and requiring that cable systems carry local television signals.[88] Broadcasters immediately challenged the action, but the FCC was upheld by the Second Circuit Court of Appeals.[89]

The Commission refused to relax a certain set of requirements in signal carriage. Its "must carry" rules said that cable operators would transmit the broadcast signals of any local television station located within a specified 35-mile zone of the cable operator or that is "significantly viewed" in the community served by the operator. The rules were intended to maintain availability of local television service to cable subscribers as well as to those without cable. And in mid-1985, the United States Court of Appeals found them impermissible under the First Amendment.[90] It said that the rules had never been closely examined by the FCC, which had not adequately demonstrated that an unregulated cable industry would seriously threaten local broadcasting, or that the rules actually serve to modify a threat. FCC assumptions were unsupported—that absent protective rules, cable subscribers would stop viewing local television, and in sufficient numbers to adversely affect the economic vitality of local broadcasting. The First Amendment tolerates far more government intrusion into broadcasting under the "channel scarcity" rationale than it does into various other media, including cable with its scores or hundreds of channels. The "must-carry" rules in their long-standing form were unconstitutional burdens on cable companies.

Persistent, acrimonious controversy that focused first in battles between cable companies and municipalities over the franchise umbrellas under which both sides operated, had much to do with the coming of a new framework for cable in 1984. Congress passed the Cable Communications Act of 1984.[91] Principals on

---

[87] 79 F.C.C.2d 663. The number of signals allowed was based on the number of subscribers, the number of local television stations, and the size of the market.

[88] Anon., "FCC Now All But Out of Cable Business," Broadcasting, July 28, 1980, pp. 25–27. The FCC also continued to administer a rule preventing cable systems from carrying sports events when a local blackout is in effect. See Eric B. Yeldell, "Copyright Protection for Live Sports Broadcasts: New Statutory Weapons with Constitutional Problems," 31 Fed.Comm.L.J. 277 (1979).

[89] Malrite TV of New York, Inc. v. FCC et al., 652 F.2d 1140 (2d Cir.1981), 7 Med. L.Rptr. 1649.

[90] Quincy Cable Co. v. F.C.C., 768 F.2d 1434 (D.C.Cir.1985), 12 Med.L.Rptr. 1001).

[91] 98th Cong., 98 Stat. 2779, Public Law 98–549, Oct. 30, 1984.

both sides expressed satisfaction. James Mooney, president of the National Cable Television Ass'n., said that the bill "takes the heart out of municipal regulation of cable. * * * With the elimination of rate regulation and with sharp restrictions placed on cities' [franchise] renewal decisions, you are going to take away much of the reason for being of cable regulatory bureaucracies." Cynthia Pols, legislative counsel for the National League of Cities, said, "You can't believe how badly the cities wanted this bill. They dread the FCC." The law, she added, "takes the FCC out of our hair," and "it establishes for us a clear regulatory authority." [92]

Authorizing municipalities to regulate cable systems by way of franchises, and establishing standards for giving franchises, the law provided, among many other rules:

- Annual franchise fees charged by municipalities may not exceed 5% of the cable operator's gross revenue from the operation of the cable system. The cable operator may pass on to the subscribers the amount of any increase in franchise fees, and must pass on to subscribers the amount of decrease in franchise fees.

- Cable companies' rates to customers may be regulated by franchising municipalities for two years only after the effective date of the law, after which rates will not be regulated.

- Crossownership of cable systems by local television stations is prohibited, but crossownership by newspapers is permitted.

- Cable operators may shift a particular service from one "tier" to another (a "tier" meaning a category of provided service for which a separate rate is charged by the cable operator).

- Franchising authorities have no control over the content of cable's messages.

- Franchises may include certain requirements with respect to the designation of channels for public, educational, or government use.

- The FCC is to rule annually as to a cable system's compliance with equal employment opportunity standards. Each system is to file an annual report on the matter. No specific level of minority or female employment is required.

On Oct. 15, 1984, *Broadcasting* magazine shouted in a headline: "Free at Last: Cable Gets Its Bill." [93]

[92] Broadcasting, Oct. 15, 1984, 38.
[93] 38.

Chapter 13

REGULATION OF ADVERTISING

SEC. 81. FROM *CAVEAT EMPTOR* TO CONSUMER PROTECTION

The history of advertising in the United States has seen a gradual change away from the motto of *caveat emptor* ("let the buyer beware").

It is hardly news that advertising is both a necessity and a nuisance in American society. It encourages and advances the nation's economy by providing information to the public about goods and services. Although its economic role in supporting the news media has been criticized, advertising has paid the bills for most of the news and vicarious entertainment which we receive. Historically, we owe advertising another debt. The rise of advertising in the 19th Century did much to free the press from excessive reliance on political parties or government printing contracts which tended to color news columns with their bias.

Despite advertising's undeniably worthwhile contributions, this chapter unavoidably must emphasize the seamy side of American salesmanship. We will concentrate to a great extent upon issues raised by cheats and rascals. There can be little question that all too much advertising has been—and is—inexact, if not spurious and deceitful. Better units of the communications media now operate their advertising as a business with a definite obligation to the public. The realization evidently has dawned that unless advertising is both truthful and useful, the public may react unfavorably.

612

Advertising in the United States has a colorful if sometimes sordid past. From the first days of the nation throughout the Nineteenth Century, the philosophy motivating advertising was largely *laissez faire*. Too much advertising, in spirit if not to the letter, resembled this 1777 plug for "Dr. RYAN's *incomparable* WORM *destroying* SUGAR PLUMBS, *Necessary to be kept in all* FAMILIES:" [1]

The plumb is a great diurectic, cleaning the veins of slime; it expels wind, and is a sovereign medicine in the cholic and griping of the guts. It allays and carries off vapours which occasion many disorders of the head. It opens all obstructions in the stomach, lungs, liver, veins, and bladder; causes a good appetite, and helps digestion.

About two years later, some new advertising copy made claims for Dr. Ryan's Sugar Plumbs which were even more graphic. The plumbs were said to be a remedy for [2]

PALENESS of the Face, Itching of the Nose, Hollowness of the Eyes, Grating of the teeth when asleep, Dullness, Pains, and Heaviness in the Head, a dry Cough, an Itching in the Fundament, white and thick Urine, unquiet Sleep, often starting, lost appetite, swell'd Belly, Gnawing and Biting about the Stomach, frightful Dreams, extreme Thirsts, the Body decay'd lean, Fits, often Vomiting, stinking Breath.

Such exploitation of the *laissez faire* philosophy went unpunished for more than a century of this nation's existence. There was little or no regulation; what would be termed unreliable or even fraudulent advertising was published by some of the most respectable newspapers and periodicals. The general principle seemed to be that advertising columns were an open business forum with space for sale to all who applied.

Before 1900, advertising had little established ethical basis. The liar and the cheat capitalized on glorious claims for dishonest, shoddy merchandise. The faker lured the ill and suffering to build hopes on pills and tonics of questionable composition. Cures were promised by the bottle. Fortunes were painted for those who invested in mining companies of dubious reliability. Foods were frequently adulterated. Fifteen dollar suits were offered as being worth $25. Faked testimonials praised dishonest or unproved wares. Manufacturers of these products were able to buy advertising space in reputable journals.

Exposés of frauds and fraud promoters who were using advertising to ensnare new prospects were important early in the

---

[1] Pennsylvania Gazette, March 12, 1777.

[2] Ibid., March 31, 1779.

Twentieth Century. Mark Sullivan exposed medical fakes and frauds in the *Ladies Home Journal* in 1904. Upton Sinclair's novel, *The Jungle,* revolted readers with its description of filthy conditions in meat-packing plants. Spurred by such exposés, Congress passed the Pure Food and Drug Act in 1906. Despite being a truth-in-labeling measure the 1906 statute did nothing to insure truth in advertising.[3]

Campaigning against advertising and promotional chicanery, many magazines and newspapers exposed fraudulent practices.[4] Some newspapers of this period, including the Cleveland Press and other Scripps-McRae League papers, monitored advertisements, refusing those which appeared to be fraudulent or misleading. A Scripps-McRae official asserted that the newspaper group turned away approximately $500,000 in advertising revenue in one year by rejecting advertisements.

Such self-regulation has grown considerably over the years, but legal restraints and constraints have grown even more. People working in advertising come under all the laws which affect other branches of mass communications, including libel, invasion of privacy, copyright infringement, and obscenity. In addition, there are batteries of statutes and regulatory powers aimed at advertising *in addition to* the legal bonds which affect, for example, the editorial side of a newspaper. There's the Food and Drug Administration (FDA), the Securities Exchange Commission (SEC), the Federal Communications Commission (FCC), and quite an alphabet soup of other federal agencies which gets into the advertising regulation act. Beyond that, there is increasing activity at the state level to attempt to control false or deceptive advertising. This chapter, then, can be only a sparse survey of advertising regulation.

SEC. 82. FEDERAL ADMINISTRATIVE CONTROLS: THE FEDERAL TRADE COMMISSION

The most important governmental controls over advertising are exercised by the Federal Trade Commission, which has experienced considerable controversy in recent years.

The Federal Trade Commission

For many years, the Federal Trade Commission has been more important than most other official controls over advertising combined. The FTC Act was passed in 1914 to supplement sanc-

---

[3] Ibid.

[4] H.J. Kenner, The Fight for Truth in Advertising (1936) pp. 13–14; Alfred McClung Lee, The Daily Newspaper in America (1937), p. 328.

tions against unfair competition which had been provided by the Sherman Anti-Trust Act of 1890 and by the Clayton Act of 1914.[5] Gradually, the FTC grew in power and assumed an increasingly important place in regulating advertising.

By the 1960s, as will be discussed later in this section, there was increasing criticism that the FTC was a do-nothing agency, and efforts were made to reorganize [6] and to strengthen [7] the commission. Ironically, when the FTC became really assertive during the late 1970s, that set about a backlash which weakened its efforts to regulate advertising. The future of the Federal Trade Commission as a serious regulator of advertising is now in doubt.[8]

The question may also be raised whether American society—as represented by Congress—*really* wishes to regulate advertising. After all, only part of the FTC's budget ($69.1 million in 1985)—only $2.85 million—is used to regulate (or *try* to regulate) deceptive advertising. And advertising was more than a $90 billion dollar industry in 1985. When some advertisers—e.g. Bayer Aspirin, Anacin, and Bufferin—spend more on television advertising each year than the FTC has in its annual budget to attend to the regulation of all products which are advertised in interstate commerce, one senses something of a mismatch. In terms of size, asking the FTC to regulate the advertising industry is analogous to asking a ground squirrel to whip a rhinoceros. While the FTC Act was conceived to prevent monopoly and restraint of trade, checking dishonest advertising was long regarded as a principal activity of the Commission.

This change of emphasis, created partly by criticisms of advertising, has not been without major opposition on the part of American business. There was—and is—fear that the govern-

[5] Sherman Act, 26 Stat. 209 (1890), 15 U.S.C.A. § 1; Clayton Act, 38 Stat. 730 (1914), 15 U.S.C.A. § 12.

[6] See Report of "Nader's Raiders," The Consumer and the Federal Trade Commission—A Critique of the Consumer Protection Record of the FTC, published in 115 Congressional Record 1539 (1969); William F. Lemke, Jr., "Souped Up Affirmative Disclosure Orders of the Federal Trade Commission," 4 University of Michigan Journal of Law Reform (Winter, 1970), p. 193. See also Charles McCarry, Citizen Nader (New York: Saturday Review Press, 1972); American Bar Association, Report of the ABA Commission to Study the Federal Trade Commission, reprinted as Appendix II, pp. 123–244, "Federal Trade Commission Procedures," Hearings Before the Subcommittee on Administrative Practice and Procedures of the Committee on the Judiciary, United States Senate, First Session, Ninety-First Congress, Part I (Washington, D.C.: Government Printing Office, 1970).

[7] See, e.g., Consumer Product Warranties and Federal Trade Commission Improvements Act ("Moss-Magnuson Act"), Pub.L. 93–637, 88 Stat. 2183 (1975).

[8] Susan Bartlett Foote and Robert H. Mnookin, "The 'kid vid' crusade," The Public Interest, Vol. 61 (Fall, 1980), pp. 90–91.

ment would so shackle advertising and sales efforts that business enterprise and even freedom of the press would be hampered.

The Federal Trade Commission is a major example of administrative rule and law-making authority delegated by Congress. Five Federal Trade Commissioners are appointed by the President and confirmed by the Senate. No more than three of the five commissioners may be from the same political party.

The Federal Trade Commission came under increasing attack in recent years as the tides of "consumerism" mounted. The FTC's critics, to borrow adman Stan Freberg's phrase, could be counted on the fingers of the Mormon Tabernacle Choir. One of the persons who led the charge against the FTC was consumer advocate Ralph Nader. Such critics have not only denigrated its effectiveness, they have even questioned its right to continue to exist. In addition to such "self-appointed" critics, the American Bar Association weighed in in 1969 with a harshly critical evaluation of FTC performance. The ABA study concluded that FTC activity had been declining while FTC staff and budget increased. The report contended that the FTC had mismanaged its resources, and that it had failed to set goals and provide necessary guidance for its staff.[9]

Extensive reorganizations of the FTC were carried out after the ABA study. A Bureau of Consumer Protection was created to handle consumer protection activities. The Bureau's responsibility extends not only to the enforcement of consumer protection statutes but also to the development of Trade Regulation Rules (with the force of law), of industry guidelines, and of consumer protection programs.[10]

The Bureau of Consumer Protection is responsible for enforcing the FTC Act where deceptive or unfair marketing practices of national or interstate scope are concerned. A sub-unit of the Bureau, the Division of Advertising Practices, is said by the FTC to have as its goal "* * * the promotion of the free flow of truthful information in the marketplace. Its law enforcement activities focus on:" [11]

- Advertising claims, particularly those relating to safety or effectiveness, for food and drugs sold over the counter.

- Performance and energy-savings claims for solar products, furnaces, storm windows, residential siding, wood-burning products, gas-saving products, motor oils, and

---

[9] See footnote 6, above.

[10] George Eric Rosden and Peter Eric Rosden, The Law of Advertising (New York Matthew Bender, 1973, 1985, 2 vols.) Vol. 2, § 32.05; see also Gerry Thain, "Advertising Regulation," 1 Fordham Urban Law Journal (1973), pp. 367–381.

[11] "A Guide to the Federal Trade Commission," FTC pamphlet, 1984, pp. 7–8.

other products that are marketed by emphasizing their energy conservation features.

• Advertising directed at children.

• Cigarette advertising, which includes monitoring for deceptive claims; operating a tobacco-testing laboratory to measure tar, nicotine, and carbon monoxide content of cigarettes; and reporting to Congress annually on cigarette labeling, advertising, and promotion.

The FTC, long expected to help enforce a crazy quilt of statutes, gets involved with the FTC Act, the Truth-in-Lending Act, the Fair Credit Reporting Act, the Wool Products Labeling Act, the Textile Fiber Products Identification Act, and the Fur Products Labeling Act, plus other statutes for which the FTC has enforcement responsibilities. Regional offices in Atlanta, Boston, Chicago, Cleveland, Dallas, Denver, Los Angeles, New York, San Francisco and Seattle have handled compliance matters in cases begun in the offices' respective geographical areas.

This complicated bureaucratic structure is part of the FTC machinery which tries to enforce Section 5 of the Federal Trade Commission Act, which says: "Unfair methods of competition in commerce, and unfair or deceptive practices in commerce, are declared unlawful." [12]

Early FTC cases which came before the courts cast doubt on the Commission's powers over advertising.[13] However, in 1921, something as mundane as partly wool underwear masquerading as real woolies gave the FTC the case it needed to establish its authority. For many years the Winsted Hosiery Company had been selling its underwear in cartons branded with labels such as "Natural Merino," "Natural Wool," or "Australian Wool." In fact, none of this company's underwear was all wool, and, some of its products had as little as 10 per cent wool.

The FTC complaint against Winsted Hosiery asked the company to show cause why the use of its brands and labels which seemed deceptive should not be discontinued. After hearings, the FTC issued a cease and desist order against the company. On appeal, the FTC lost, with a United States Circuit Court saying: "Conscientious manufacturers may prefer not to use a label which is capable of misleading, and it may be that it will be desirable to prevent the use of the particular labels, but it is in our opinion not within the province of the Federal Trade Commission to do so." [14]

---

[12] 15 U.S.C.A. § 45(a)(1).

[13] Federal Trade Commission v. Gratz, 253 U.S. 421, 40 S.Ct. 572 (1920); L.B. Silver Co. v. Federal Trade Commission, 289 F. 985 (6th Cir.1923).

[14] Winsted Hosiery Co. v. Federal Trade Commission, 272 F. 957, 961 (2d Cir. 1921).

In 1922, the Supreme Court of the United States upheld the FTC in language broad enough to support the Commission's power to control false labeling and advertising as unfair methods of competition. Speaking for the Court, Justice Brandeis declared that the Commission was justified in its conclusions that the hosiery company's practices were unfair methods of competition. He authorized the Commission to halt such practices. Brandeis said, "when misbranded goods attract customers by means of the fraud which they perpetrate, trade is diverted from the producer of truthfully marked goods."[15]

Despite the efforts of the Federal Trade Commission, the idea of consumer protection had little support from the Courts during the early 1930s. In 1931, the *Raladam* case, for example, cut sharply into the FTC's attempts to defeat the ancient, amoral doctrine of caveat emptor, "let the buyer beware." The Raladam Company manufactured an "obesity cure" containing "dessicated thyroid." This preparation, sold under the name of "Marmola," was advertised in newspapers and on printed labels as being the result of scientific research. It was claimed that "Marmola" was "safe and effective and may be used without discomfort, inconvenience, or danger of harmful results to health."

The FTC complaint focused upon the likelihood of actual physical harm to consumers who used Marmola believing it safe as claimed. The Supreme Court, however, disallowed the FTC's order that the Raladam Corporation cease such advertising. Speaking for the Court, Justice George Sutherland ruled that Section 5 of the FTC Act did not forbid the deception of consumers unless the advertising injured competing business in some way. Accordingly, the FTC was not allowed to work directly for consumer protection.[16]

The FTC's authority over advertising grew slowly. As late as 1936—when the FTC had been in operation for some 22 years—the famed Judge Learned Hand of a U.S. Circuit Court decided a case against the FTC and in favor of an advertising scheme for encyclopedias which involved false representation. The publisher of the encyclopedias tried to lure customers into believing that the company gave them a set of encyclopedias "free," and that the customer's payment of $69.50 was only for a loose leaf supplement to the encyclopedia. The $69.50 was actually the combined regular price for both books and supplements. Despite this, Judge Hand could declare:[17] "Such trivial niceties are too impalpable for

[15] Federal Trade Commission v. Winsted Hosiery Co., 258 U.S. 483, 493–494, 42 S.Ct. 384, 385–386 (1922).

[16] Federal Trade Commission v. Raladam Co., 284 U.S. 643, 51 S.Ct. 587, 589 (1931).

[17] 2 U.S. 112, 116, 58 S.Ct. 113, 115 (1937), quoting Judge Hand's opinion in the same case in the Circuit Court, 86 F.2d 692, 695 (2d Cir.1936).

practical affairs, they are will-o'-the-wisps, which divert attention from substantial evils."

When this case reached the Supreme Court, Justice Hugo L. Black reacted indignantly, saying the sales method used to peddle the encyclopedia "successfully deceived and deluded its victims."[18] In overturning Judge Hand's "let the buyer beware" ruling in the lower court, Justice Black added:[19]

> The fact that a false statement may be obviously false to those who are trained and experienced does not change its character, nor take away its power to deceive others less experienced. There is no duty resting upon a citizen to suspect the honesty of those with whom he transacts business. Laws are made to protect the trusting as well as the suspicious. The best element of business has long since decided that honesty should govern competitive enterprises, and that the rule of caveat emptor [let the buyer beware] should not be relied upon to reward fraud and deception.

In 1938, the year after the Supreme Court endorsed the concept of consumer protection from advertising excesses, Congress acted to give the FTC greater authority over deceptive advertising. The 1938 Wheeler-Lea Amendment changed Section 5 of the Federal Trade Commission Act to read: "Unfair methods of competition in commerce, and *unfair or deceptive acts or practices* in commerce, are hereby declared unlawful.[20] Note the italicized phrase. These words were added by the Wheeler-Lea Amendment, and this seemingly minor change in phrasing proved to be of great importance. The italicized words removed the limits on FTC authority imposed by the *Raladam* decision. No longer would the FTC have to prove that a misleading advertisement harmed a competing business. Now, if an advertisement deceived consumers, the FTC's enforcement powers could be put into effect.[21]

Aiming at false advertising, the Wheeler-Lea Amendment also inserted Sections 12 and 15(a) into the Federal Trade Commission Act. Section 12 provides:[22]

[18] 302 U.S. 112, 117, 58 S.Ct. 113, 115 (1937).

[19] 302 U.S. 112, 116, 58 S.Ct. 113, 115 (1937).

[20] 52 Stat. 111 (1938); 15 U.S.C.A. § 45. Italics added.

[21] Ibid.; Earl W. Kinter, "Federal Trade Commission Regulation of Advertising," Michigan Law Review Vol. 64:7 (May, 1966) pp. 1269–1284, at pp. 1275–1276, 1276n.

[22] Section 12, 52 Stat. 114 (1938), 15 U.S.C.A. § 52; Section 15(a), 52 Stat. 114 (1938), 15 U.S.C.A. § 55(a).

It shall be unlawful for any person, partnership, or corporation to disseminate, or cause to be disseminated, any false advertisement—(1) by United States mails, or in [interstate] commerce by any means, for the purpose of inducing, or which is likely to induce, directly or indirectly, the purchase in commerce of food, drugs, devices or cosmetics.

Section 15(a) of the FTC Act says:

The term 'false advertising' means an advertisement, other than labeling, which is misleading in a material respect; and in determining whether any advertisement is misleading, there shall be taken into account (among other things) not only representations made or suggested by statement, word, design, device, sound, or any combination thereof, but also the extent to which the advertisement fails to reveal facts material in the light of such representations or material with respect to consequences which may result from the use of the commodity *   *   *.

Such statutory changes gave the FTC some of the power it sought to protect consumers. As FTC Commissioners Everett MacIntyre and Paul Rand Dixon wrote in the 1960s, the Wheeler-Lea "amendment put the consumer on a par with the businessman from the standpoint of deceptive practices."[23]

Some observers people contended—back in the 1960s—that the FTC had compiled an impressive record. Professor Glenn E. Weston wrote in 1964, on the 50th anniversary of the establishment of the FTC, that the Commission's accomplishments "probably dwarf that of any other administrative agency, state or federal." Up to 1964, the FTC had accepted more than 12,000 stipulations from advertisers that they would halt certain practices, and had also obtained "countless" promises to discontinue false advertising claims. At a more formal level of enforcement, the FTC has issued "several thousand" complaints and cease-and-desist orders against advertisers, and had inspected millions of ads.[24]

Not everyone took such a cheery view of the FTC. This commission was often called "toothless" and other less flattering things. The delays which have attended FTC enforcement procedures—especially those involved in lengthy court battles—became legendary. An often cited example was the famed "Carter's Little Liver Pills" case. In 1943, the FTC decided that the word "liver"

[23] Everette MacIntyre and Paul Rand Dixon, "The Federal Trade Commission After 50 Years," Federal Bar Journal Vol.24:4 (Fall,1964) pp. 377–424, at p. 416.

[24] Glenn E. Weston, "Deceptive Advertising and the Federal Trade Commission," Federal Bar Journal 24:4 (Fall, 1964) pp. 548–578, at p. 548.

was misleading, and a classic and lengthy battle was on. Carter's Little Liver Pills had been a well known laxative product for 75 years. It took the FTC a total of 16 years—from 1943 to 1959—to win its point before the courts and get "liver" deleted.[25]

In addition, the FTC could not hope to regulate all advertising in interstate commerce—it could merely regulate by example, by pursuing a relatively small number of advertisers who appeared to operate in a deceptive fashion, in hopes that this would encourage others to tone down their advertising claims. It has been objected that during most of the FTC's history, it had tended to go after "little guys" or unimportant issues, too often ignoring misdeeds by big and powerful corporations which tied into important issues.

Beyond that, the FTC's enforcement machinery, for the most part, was creaky and slow. If an advertising campaign on television is deemed "deceptive" or "false and misleading" by the FTC, the ad campaign might have run its course (generally three months, six months, or nine months) before the FTC could have any impact. In lawyer's jargon, such cases are moot, essentially.

The FTC has several weapons to use against misleading advertising:

(1) *Assurance of Voluntary Compliance (Non-Adjudicative)*— If the FTC believes the public interest is served, it may halt an investigation by accepting a promise that a questioned practice will be stopped. The Commission accepts such a promise only in rare cases, and then after considering the seriousness of the advertising practice complained of and the prior record and good faith of the party involved.

(2) *Consent Orders*—Instead of litigating an FTC complaint, a respondent may enter into an agreement amounting to a cease and desist order for consideration by the Commission. If this agreement is approved by the FTC, the order is placed in the public record for 60 days. During that period, interested persons may file comments concerning the order. If a consent order is approved by the FTC, it will have the force of adjudicative orders (discussed below). Respondents in consent order proceedings do not admit violations of the law.[26]

(3) *Adjudicative Orders*—These are based on evidence from a record developed during a proceeding that starts when the FTC issues a complaint. The proceeding is conducted

---

[25] Carter Products v. Federal Trade Commission, 268 F.2d 461 (9th Cir.1959), certiorari denied 361 U.S. 884, 80 S.Ct. 155 (1959).

[26] Federal Trade Commission, Your FTC: What It Is and What It Does (U.S. Government Printing Office, 1977), p. 26.

before an Administrative Law Judge who serves as the initial trier of facts. After hearings, the judge will issue a decision within 90 days. That decision may be reviewed by the FTC, and if not appealed or if upheld, a cease and desist order will issue. Appeals from a final FTC decision may be made to a U.S. Court of Appeals, and ultimately, to the Supreme Court of the United States. Unless a cease and desist order is appealed within 60 days, it becomes self-executing. Violation of such an order is punishable by a civil penalty of $10,000 a day for each offense.[27]

(4) *Publicity*—The FTC publicizes complaints and cease-and-desist orders which it promulgates. News releases on such subjects are regularly issued to the media, and publicity has proven to be a strong weapon at the Commission's disposal.[28]

It can be seen from the foregoing list of FTC activities that the Commission is not dependent solely on harsh actions such as cease and desist orders or court procedures. The Commission also takes positive steps to attempt to clarify its view of fair advertising practices. The Commission has three major programs which attempt to secure voluntary compliance. These are:

1. INDUSTRY GUIDES. This program involved issuing interpretations of the rules of the Commission to its staff. These guides are made available to the public, and are aimed at certain significant practices of a particular industry, especially those involved in advertising and labeling. The guides can be issued by the Commission as its interpretation of the law without a conference or hearings, and, therefore, in a minimum of time.

2. ADVISORY OPINIONS. In 1962, the FTC began giving advisory opinions in response to industry questions about the legality of a proposed industry action. Advisory opinions generally predict the FTC's response, although the Commission reserves the right to reconsider its advice if the public interest so requires.[29]

3. TRADE REGULATION RULES. The FTC publishes a notice before issuing a Trade Regulation Rule on a specific practice. Industry representatives may then comment on the proposed Trade Regulation before the rule is adopted and put into effect.[30]

---

[27] Ibid.; Rosden & Rosden, op. cit., Vol. II, § 25.06, p. 35–16.

[28] Federal Trade Commission, Your FTC: What It Is and What It Does, p. 19.

[29] Rosden and Rosden, Vol. II, § 32.04, pp. 32–37 and 32–38.

[30] Ibid.

Voluntary compliance with laws and FTC rules is not always forthcoming. The FTC sometimes is compelled to begin a case against an advertiser. Cases sometimes open after a complaint from an aggrieved citizen or a competitor who has suffered a loss because of what he believes to be illegal activity. The FTC also screens advertisements, looking for false or misleading statements. When a suspicious advertisement is found, a questionnaire is sent to the advertiser. The FTC may also request samples of the product advertised, if practicable. If the product is a compound, its formula may be requested. Copies of all advertisements published or broadcast during a specified period are requested, together with copies of supplementary information such as booklets, folders, or form letters.

Product samples may be inspected by the FTC or referred to another appropriate government agency for scientific analysis. If false or misleading advertising claims are indicated by such an examination, the advertiser is advised of the scientific opinions of the Commission's experts. The advertiser is allowed to submit evidence in support of his advertisement.

Strengthening of the FTC's regulatory powers came in 1973 in a stealthy fashion. While an energy crisis absorbed attention of Congress and of the public in 1973, a rider to the Trans-Alaska Pipeline Authorization Act gave the FTC powers which it had sought for years.[31] Thanks to that rider, the FTC was given the power to go to a federal court and ask for an injunction against an advertisement which is—in the eyes of the Commission—clearly in violation of federal law prohibiting false or misleading advertising. This injunctive sanction is not likely to be much used because it is so drastic. However, an injunction could—in critical instances— put a stop to ads which might otherwise continue to run through their campaign cycle, be it three months or six months or nine months, before the FTC could act.

More help was on the way for the FTC. In January, 1975, the "Consumer Product Warranties and Federal Trade Commission Improvements Act"—hereafter referred to as the Moss-Magnuson Act—was signed into law by President Gerald R. Ford.[32] One part of this measure was designed to provide minimum disclosure standards for written consumer product warranties. The standards of disclosure provide a challenge for those writing warranty statements analogous to trying to make a hit musical out of the

---

[31] 15 U.S.C.A. § 53. See Note, " 'Corrective Advertising' Orders of the Federal Trade Commission," 85 Harvard Law Review (Dec.1971), pp. 485–486. The FTC already has injunctive powers to deal with advertising for products which could pose an immediate health threat to consumers: medical devices, foods, drugs, and cosmetics.

[32] Pub. L. 93–637, 88 Stat. 2183 (1975).

instructions for filling out I.R.S. Form 1040. More important for this discussion is the FTC Improvements portion of this legislation.

Before the Moss-Magnuson Act, jurisdiction of the FTC was limited to advertising *in* interstate commerce. In 1941, the Supreme Court held that an Illinois company which limited its sales to wholesalers located only in Illinois was not "in [interstate] commerce,"[33] and was thus beyond the reach of FTC control. Now, under the new statute, the FTC can regulate advertising *affecting* commerce. A small change, on the surface, but not in actuality. This wording change gives the FTC the power, in effect, to say that *all* commerce affects interstate commerce, and therefore is under FTC jurisdiction.[34]

Also, the Moss-Magnuson Act gave the power to the Commission to get beyond of "regulation by example"—that is, to do more than let a shave cream manufacturer know with a cease-and-desist order that an advertising campaign was considered misleading by the FTC. The FTC was enabled to issue Trade Regulation Rules which can apply to an entire product type or industry. Trade Regulation Rules—when formally issued by the FTC—have the force of law. Fines for violation of a Trade Regulation Rule through misleading advertising can draw fines of up to $10,000 a day, so the FTC was given the clout to get advertisers to pay attention.[35]

Although the Magnuson-Moss Act strengthened FTC powers, the activist stance of the FTC during the late 1970s brought a counter-attack from the business community plus 1980 legislation to weaken the FTC. Although the Great Sugar Imbroglio was by no means the only source of the FTC's troubles, it may be used as an example of Commission behavior that horrified business and industry. In 1977 and 1978,[36]

> [t]he FTC staff proposed rules that would have resulted in a ban of most children's television advertising. The FTC primarily premised its far-reaching rulemaking proceeding on "unfairness," a standard with few legal precedents, rather than on "deception," a well-established standard with more confining limits.

Issues involved in the regulation of children's advertising—including FTC hearing on whether some sugary foods should be banned—provided a sticky situation for the commission. In 1977

---

[33] Federal Trade Commission v. Bunte Bros., 312 U.S. 349, 61 S.Ct. 580 (1941).

[34] Moss-Magnuson Act, Pub.L. 93–637, 88 Stat. 2183 (1975).

[35] Ibid.

[36] Foote and Mnookin, op. cit., p. 90.

and 1978, FTC Chairman Michael Pertschuk made a variety of statements critical of techniques used in children's advertising.

The FTC soon began a major trade regulation relemaking procedure on "Children's Advertising," under Section 18 of the Magnuson-Moss Act.[37] The Association of National Advertisers and the Kellogg Company, after asking without success that Pertschuk disqualify himself from hearings on the subject, then went to court for an order to restrain Pertschuk from further involvement. It was contended that the chairman had prejudged fact issues and would not be able to participate fairly in the rulemaking procedure.[38] Pertschuk, in fact, had said: " 'Advertisers seize on the child's trust and exploit it as a weakness for their gain. * * *' " and " 'Cumulatively, commercials directed at children tend to distort the role of food. * * * Rarely is their emphasis on good nutrition.' "[39]

U.S. District Court Judge Gerhard Gesell disqualified Chairman Pertschuk from the hearings after declaring that in an adjudicative proceeding, an FTC Commissioner must meet this test: [40]

> " * * * whether 'a disinterested observer may conclude that [the agency] has in some measure adjudged the facts as well as the law of a particular case in advance of hearing it.' "

> * * *

> "[A]n administrative hearing 'must be attended, not only with every element of fairness but with the very appearance of complete fairness,' " * * *

Judge Gesell concluded for the Court of Appeals for the District of Columbia Circuit that Chairman Pertschuk did not pass that test.

Late in 1979, however, the U.S. Court of Appeals, District of Columbia Circuit, overturned the District Court ruling disqualifying FTC Chairman Michael Pertschuk from the Commission's rulemaking proceeding on children's advertising. Circuit Judge Tamm announced the decision of the Court of Appeals, talking at length about the different hats an FTC commissioner must wear. When wearing his legislative or rulemaking hat, Pertschuk and his colleagues "must have the ability to exchange views with

[37] 15 U.S.C.A. § 57a (1976).

[38] Med.L.Rptr. 1716 (1979).

[39] The News Media & The Law, Vol. 3: No. 2 (May/June 1979), p. 18.

[40] Judge Gesell quoting Cinderella Career and Finishing Schools, Inc. v. FTC, 425 F.2d 583, 591 (D.C.Cir.1970).

constituents and to suggest public policy that is dependent upon factual assumptions." Judge Tamm continued: [41]

> Chairman Pertschuk's remarks, considered as a whole, represent discussion, and perhaps advocacy, of the legal theory that might support exercise of the Commission's jurisdiction over children's advertising. The mere discussion of policy or advocacy on a legal question, however, is not sufficient to disqualify an administrator.

Because the Association of National Advertisers had not made a clear and convincing showing that Chairman Pertschuk had an "unalterably closed mind on matters critical to the children's television proceeding," the Court of Appeals chose not to disqualify him.

Although that Court of Appeals supported the FTC's activism, Congress in 1980 passed the whimsically named Federal Trade Commission Improvements Act of 1980.[42] A few more such "improvements" and the FTC can pack it in. This legislation removed "unfairness"[43] as a basis for regulation of commercial advertising. Instead of being able to forbid "unfair" ads the FTC will have to show out-and-out *deception,* which is harder to prove. Also, the 1980 act removed FTC powers to make rules on children's advertising and the funeral industry. In addition, the FTC now has Congress breathing down its neck. Under the 1980 "Improvements Act," there is established a 90-day review period for any FTC Trade Regulation Rules. If both Houses of Congress pass a resolution objecting to the rule, the rule is overturned. This procedure has been called the "two-House legislative veto." [44]

As advertising law experts Earl W. Kintner, Christopher Smith, and David B. Goldston have said: [45]

> Although the Federal Trade Commission Improvements Act of 1980 restrains some of the Commission's

---

[41] 5 Med.L.Rptr. 2233, 2236, Ibid., pp. 2245–2246, 2247. Despite this ruling, Pertschuk withdrew from the rulemaking procedure. See P. Cameron DeVore and Robert D. Sack, "Advertising and Commercial Speech," in James C. Goodale, chairman, Communications Law 1980, Vol. II (New York: Practising Law Institute, 1980) p. 487.

[42] Pub.L.No. 96–252, 94 Stat. 374 (1980).

[43] Foote and Mnookin, op. cit., pp. 90–91; see also discussion in text in preceding footnote number 36.

[44] Pub.L.No. 96–252, 94 Stat. 374 (1980), § 21, discussed in Earl W. Kintner, Christopher Smith, and David B. Goldston, "The Effect of the Federal Trade Commission Improvements Act of 1980 on the FTC's Rulemaking and Enforcement Authority," 58 Washington University Law Quarterly No. 4 (Winter, 1980) pp. 847–859, at 853. This legislative veto provision stays in effect until September 30, 1982, and contains a provision for expedited judicial review should this provision's constitutionality be attacked through a lawsuit.

[45] Kintner, Smith and Goldston, op. cit., pp. 858–859.

more controversial initiatives, the legislation does not alter the Commission's basic enforcement authority. Congressional criticism of the Commission, however, already has and will likely continue to cause the Commission to enter new frontiers of trade regulation law much more cautiously.

SEC. 83.   LITERAL TRUTH IS NOT ENOUGH

Even literally true statements may cause an advertiser difficulty if those statements are part of a misleading advertisement.

Sometimes even the *literal truth* can be misleading. When truth misleads in an advertisement, the FTC is able to issue a "cease and desist" order and make it stick. A photo album sales scheme offers a case in point. Door-to-door salesmen told customers that for $39.95, they could take advantage of a "once in a lifetime combination offer" and receive a "free" album by purchasing 10 photographic portraits at the "regular price" of the photographs alone.

The FTC ordered the company selling the photo albums to stop suggesting that its albums were given away free, when in fact the albums were part of a $39.95 package deal. The company was also ordered to stop claiming that it sold only to "selected persons" and that a special price was involved. The photo album company retorted that its sales pitch was the literal truth, and that the FTC's cease and desist order should, therefore, be set aside by the courts.[46] The company argued that its customers actually were "selected;" that the word "few" is a relative term which is very elastic, and that the $39.95 price was in fact "promotional" because it tended to support the sale of the albums.

A U.S. Court of Appeals upheld the FTC's cease and desist order. The Circuit Court announced that there should be a presumption of validity when courts reviewed FTC orders involving advertising. Tendencies of advertisements to mislead or deceive were held to be factual questions which would be determined by the FTC. Finally, the Circuit Court vigorously upheld the idea that even literal truthfulness of statement cannot protect an advertisement if it is misleading. A statement may be deceptive even if the constituent words may be literally or technically construed so as not to constitute a misrepresentation.[47]

Other courts' decisions have supported FTC contentions that literal truth of an advertisement is not enough to prevent it from

---

[46] Kalwajtys v. Federal Trade Commission, 237 F.2d 654, 655–656 (7th Cir.1957).

[47] 237 F.2d 654, 656 (7th Cir.1957).

being misleading, as illustrated in the case of P. Lorillard Co. v. Federal Trade Commission (1950). An advertisement for Old Gold cigarettes during the late 1940s urged readers to see an issue of *Reader's Digest* magazine which reported tests on the tar and nicotine content of various brands of cigarettes. True, Old Golds, among six leading cigarette brands, had been found by scientific tests to have less—infinitesimally less—nicotine and tar than the other brands. This led to advertising blurbs that Old Golds were "lowest in throat-irritating tars and resins."

The FTC issued a cease and desist order, saying that it was false and misleading advertising. In upholding the FTC order, a United States Court of Appeals quoted from the *Reader's Digest* article: " 'The laboratory's general conclusion will be bad news for the advertising copy writers but good news for the smoker, who need no longer worry as to which cigarette can most effectively nail down his coffin. For one nail is just about as good as another.' " [48] The court denounced the advertisement saying:[49]

> An examination of the advertisements * * * shows a perversion of the meaning of the *Readers Digest* article which does little credit to the company's advertising department,—a perversion which results in the use of the truth in such a way as to cause the reader to believe the exact opposite of what was intended by the writer of the article * * *.

In a 1981 deceptive advertising case, the Federal Trade Commission pursued Reader's Digest Association, claiming that a sweepstakes mail solicitation campaign was unfair and deceptive. The solicitation involved a direct mass mailing, "promising money or merchandize to a small percentage of those who returned the sweepstakes entry forms." [50] The United States Court of Appeals, Third Circuit, ruled that Reader's Digest had violated an earlier consent order promising to cease distributing confusing simulated checks. The court assessed Reader's Digest a whopping $1.75 million penalty for violation of the consent order.[51]

[48] P. Lorillard Co. v. Federal Trade Commission, 186 F.2d 52, 57 (4th Cir.1950).

[49] Ibid. If an ad's statement is sufficiently sweeping so that no one should reasonably believe it, it becomes "puffery," a form of legalized lying so whopping that successful prosecutions cannot result. See Ivan L. Preston, "The FTC's Handling of Puffery," 5 Journal of Business Research (June, 1977) pp. 155–181.

[50] United States v. Reader's Digest Association, 662 F.2d 955 (3d Cir.1981) 7 Med. L.Rptr. 1921, 1922.

[51] United States v. Reader's Digest Association, 621 F.2d 955 (3d Cir.1981) 7 Med. L.Rptr. at 1924.

SEC. 84. THE "SANDPAPER SHAVE" CASE
AND "MOCKUPS"

In the famed 1965 decision in Federal Trade Commission v. Colgate Palmolive Company, the Supreme Court attempted to define which kinds of "mock-up" demonstrations were permissible in television commercials.

Advertising—especially television advertising—can be frivolous even if not amusing. There were some entertaining features behind a 1965 decision of the U.S. Supreme Court sometimes termed "The Great Sandpaper Shave" case.[52] Kyle Rote and Frank Gifford—both professional football players more recently known as sports commentators—figured prominently in this story. In 1959 Rote and Gifford, both rugged males with heavy "sandpaper beards," appeared in advertisements for a Colgate-Palmolive Co. product, Rapid Shave aerosol shaving cream.

The televised commercial showed both Rote and Gifford shaving easily and unconcernedly with Rapid Shave.[53] The advertising firm of Ted Bates & Company, Inc. prepared commercials to demonstrate that "Rapid Shave out-shaves them all." The commercials showed that Rapid Shave not only worked well on heavy beards, but could soften even coarse sandpaper. An announcer smoothly told the audience that, " 'To prove RAPID SHAVE'S super-moisturizing power, we put it right from the can onto this tough, dry sandpaper. It was apply * * * soak * * * and off in a stroke.' " As the announcer spoke, Rapid Shave was applied to a substance that appeared to be sandpaper, and immediately thereafter a razor was shown shaving the substance clean, removing every abrasive grain in its path.[54]

By the time the Federal Trade Commission issued a complaint against Colgate and Bates, the "sandpaper shave" commercial was old-hat to television viewers. An FTC hearing examiner took testimony after the FTC's complaint that the commercial was deceptive. Evidence showed that sandpaper of the kind used in the commercial could not be "shaved" immediately after the Rapid Shave had been applied, but needed a lengthy soaking period of about 80 minutes. The FTC examiner also found that the substance shaved in the Ted Bates-produced commercial was in fact a simulated prop or "mock-up" made of plexiglas to which sand had

[52] Federal Trade Commission v. Colgate-Palmolive Co., 380 U.S. 374, 85 S.Ct. 1035 (1965). For an amusing account of this case, see Daniel Seligman, "The Great Sandpaper Shave: A Real-Life Story of Truth in Advertising," Fortune (Dec.1964) pp. 131–133ff.

[53] Seligman, ibid., p. 131.

[54] 380 U.S. 374, 376, 85 S.Ct. 1035, 1038 (1965).

been applied. The examiner *did* find, however, that Rapid Shave could shave sandpaper, even if a much longer time was needed than represented by the commercials. As a result, the examiner dismissed the FTC complaint, because in his opinion there had been no material deception that would mislead the public.[55]

The Federal Trade Commission was of a different mind and overturned the ruling of the hearing examiner late in 1961. The Commission reasoned that the undisclosed use of plexiglas as a substitute for sandpaper—plus the fact that Rapid Shave could not shave sandpaper within the time depicted in commercials— amounted to materially deceptive acts. Furthermore, even if sandpaper could be shaved just as the commercials showed, the Commission decided that viewers had been tricked into believing that they had seen, with their own eyes, the actual shaving being done. The Commission issued a cease-and-desist order against Colgate and Bates, forbidding them from: [56]

> Representing, directly or by implication, *in describing, explaining,* or purporting to prove the quality or merits of any products, that pictures, depictions, or demonstrations * * * *are genuine or accurate representations * * * of,* or prove the *quality or merits of, any product,* when such pictures, depictions, or demonstrations are *not in fact genuine or accurate representations * * * of,* or do not prove the quality or merits of, *any such product.*

This inclusive Federal Trade Commission order of December 29, 1961, set off lengthy litigation. When a Court of Appeals considered the FTC order, it expressed concern that the flexible Article 5 of the FTC Act was being used in a new area. Article 5 provides:

> Unfair methods of competition in commerce, and unfair or deceptive acts or practices in commerce, are declared unlawful.[57]

The Circuit Court of Appeals concluded that the FTC was going too far in declaring all mock-ups illegal. The court declared, "where the only untruth is that the substance [the viewer] sees on the screen is artificial, and the visual appearance is otherwise a correct and accurate representation of the product itself, he is not injured.[58]

[55] 380 U.S. 374, 376–377, 85 S.Ct. 1035, 1038 (1965).

[56] 380 U.S. 374, 380, 85 S.Ct. 1035, 1040 (1965), quoting 59 F.T.C. 1452, 1477–1478. Emphasis the Court's.

[57] 380 U.S. 374, 376n, 85 S.Ct. 1035, 1038n, quoting 38 Stat. 719, as amended, 52 Stat. 111, 15 U.S.C.A. § 45(a)(1).

[58] 380 U.S. 374, 381, 85 S.Ct. 1035, 1040 (1968), quoting 310 F.2d 89, 94 (1st Cir. 1962).

Following this ruling by the Circuit Court, the FTC entered a new "proposed final order" on February 18, 1963, attempting to answer the court's criticisms of its earlier order to Colgate and Bates. The Commission explained that it did not intend to prohibit all undisclosed simulated props in commercials, but merely wanted to prohibit Colgate and Bates from misrepresenting to the public that it was actually seeing for itself a test, experiment or demonstration which purportedly proved a product claim. The Commission argued that the "sandpaper shave" commercial's demonstration left a misleading impression that a demonstration or experiment had actually been performed. On May 7, 1963, the Commission issued its final order that Colgate and Bates cease and desist from: [59]

> Unfairly or deceptively advertising any ＊ ＊ ＊ product by presenting a test, experiment or demonstration that (1) is represented to the public as actual proof of a claim made for the product which is material to inducing a sale, and (2) is not in fact a genuine test, experiment or demonstration being conducted as represented and does not in fact constitute actual proof of the claim ＊ ＊ ＊.

Although Colgate and Bates also challenged the 1963 FTC order, the Supreme Court of the United States made the order stick. Note that the use of *all* mock-ups in televised commercials was not forbidden as deceptive. The Court found that "the undisclosed use of plexiglas" in the Rapid Shave commercials was "a material deceptive practice." But there is a fine line between the forbidden kind of "demonstration" in the Rapid Shave commercial and an acceptable "commercial which extolled the goodness of ice cream while giving viewers a picture of a scoop of mashed potatoes appearing to be ice cream." The Court was able to draw such a distinction, stating: [60]

> In the ice cream case the mashed potato prop is not being used for additional proof of the product claim, while the purpose of the Rapid Shave commercial is to give the viewer objective proof of the claims made. If in the ice cream hypothetical the focus of the commercial becomes the undisclosed potato prop and the viewer is invited, explicitly or by implication, to see for himself the truth of the claims about the ice cream's rich texture and full

[59] 380 U.S. 374, 382, 85 S.Ct. 1035, 1041 (1965), quoting Colgate Palmolive Co., No. 7736, FTC May 7, 1963. This clause was added by the FTC for the benefit of Ted Bates & Co., because advertising agencies do not always have all the information about a product that a manufacturer has. The clause said, " 'provided, however, that respondent [Bates] neither knew nor had reason to know that the product, article or substance used in the test, experiment, or demonstration was a mock-up or a prop.' "

[60] 380 U.S. 374, 390, 85 S.Ct. 1035, 1045, 1047 (1965).

color, and perhaps compare it to a "rival product," then the commercial has become similar * * * [to the Rapid Shave commercial.]   Clearly, however, a commercial which depicts happy actors delightedly eating ice cream that is in fact mashed potatoes or drinking a product appearing to be coffee but which is in fact some other substance is not covered by the present order.

Marbles In The Soup

The Campbell Soup Company, however, slipped over the fine line between "demonstration" and "deception," at least in the eyes of the Federal Trade Commission.   Campbell Soup consented to stop the practice of putting marbles in bowls of soup to force solid chunks of meat and vegetables to the surface, making them visible to viewers of television ads.[61]

SEC. 85.   CORRECTIVE ADVERTISING ORDERS OF THE FTC

The Federal Trade Commission has attempted to enforce truth in advertising by requiring some advertisers to correct past misstatements.

After being roughly handled by critics ranging from Ralph Nader to the American Bar Association during the late 1960s, the Federal Trade Commission of the 1970s became much more active than in previous years.   Symptomatic of this increased activity was an FTC complaint against Standard Oil Company of California.   The company's advertising had been claiming that its Chevron gasoline, thanks to an additive called F–310, could significantly decrease harmful substances in auto exhaust emissions, thus helping to reduce air pollution.   This sort of "we're good for the environment" advertising has been termed "Eco-Porn" (ecological pornography) by cynical critics of advertising.

The FTC issued a cease and desist order to halt allegedly misleading F–310 advertising claims, but the matter did not end there.   The FTC also demanded that the Standard Oil Company run "corrective" ads for a year, disclosing that its earlier advertising campaign had included false and deceptive statements.   The Commission said that 25 per cent of the advertising for Chevron— either published space or broadcast time—should be devoted to

---

[61] Campbell Soup Co., 3 Trade Reg.Rep. Para. 19,261 (FTC, 1970); the Campbell Soup Co. consented to stop the practice of putting marbles in soup bowls to force solid chunks of meat and vegetables to the surface of the soup so as to be visible to viewers of television ads.

making "affirmative disclosures" about the earlier advertising.[62] An FTC administrative judge dismissed charges against the F–310 ads, but he was then overruled by the Commission. The FTC then re-instituted its cease-and-desist order. The U.S. Court of Appeals for the Ninth Circuit held that the FTC was correct in concluding that the F–310 commercials had a tendency to mislead consumers. However, the FTC was held to have erred in having issued an order against Standard Oil Company asking the company to refrain from making certain representations about F–310 "or any other product in commerce" unless every statement is true and completely substantiated. The court said that order was too broad, and had to be narrowed to deal only with gasoline additive F–310.[63]

Other corporate defendants in cases where the FTC has sought to obtain corrective advertising include Coca Cola, for claims made about nutrient and vitamin content of its Hi-C fruit drinks,[64] and ITT Continental Baking Company, for ads implying that eating Profile Bread could help people to lose weight. The FTC charged that Profile was different from other bread only in being more thinly sliced, meaning that there were seven fewer calories per slice. ITT Continental Baking Company consented to a cease and desist order which does two things: first, it prohibits all further claims of weight-reducing attributes for Profile Bread, and second, the company has to devote 25 per cent of its Profile advertising for one year to disclosing that the bread is not effective for weight reduction.[65] Television commercials indeed appeared, with an actress saying sweetly: [66]

> I'd like to clear up any misunderstandings you may have about Profile Bread from its advertising or even its name. Does Profile have fewer calories than other breads? No, Profile has about the same per ounce as other breads. To be exact Profile has 7 fewer calories per slice. That's because it's sliced thinner. But eating Profile will not cause you to lose weight. A reduction of 7 calories is insignificant. * * *

[62] 3 Trade Reg.Rep.Para. 19,420 (FTC Complaint issued, Dec. 29, 1970). See also William F. Lemke, Jr., "Souped Up Affirmative Disclosure Orders of the Federal Trade Commission," 4 University of Michigan Journal of Law Reform (Winter, 1970) pp. 180–181; Note, " 'Corrective Advertising' Orders of the Federal Trade Commission," 85 Harvard Law Review (December, 1971) pp. 477–478.

[63] Standard Oil Co. v. FTC, 377 F.2d 653, 658 (9th Cir.1978).

[64] 3 Trade Reg.Rep. Para. 19,351 (FTC, 1970).

[65] 3 Trade Reg.Rep. Para. 19,780 (FTC, Aug. 17, 1971); Note, " 'Corrective Advertising' Orders of the Federal Trade Commission," 85 Harvard Law Review (December, 1971), p. 478.

[66] *Newsweek,* Sept. 27, 1971, p. 98.

Law Professor William F. Lemke, Jr. contended that such "affirmative disclosure" orders as parts of cease and desist orders mean that the FTC is exceeding its authority. He suggested that courts reviewing the appropriateness of such orders may regard them as punitive rather than regulatory.[67] Other legal scholars, however, regarded "corrective advertising" orders of the FTC as legitimate and potentially useful additions to the regulation of advertising.[68]

Such orders, however, were mere palliatives, and did nothing to solve the FTC's great problems with delays. Delays of from three to five years between issuance of an FTC complaint and final issuance of a cease and desist order were commonplace. Meanwhile, the advertiser was free to continue his advertising campaign: "By the time the order has become final, the particular campaign has probably been squeezed dry, if not already discarded in favor of a fresh one."[69]

The FTC—as if to confound some of its earlier critics—showed increasing willingness to move against advertising campaigns by big-name firms or products. "Listerine Antiseptic Mouthwash," a product of the Warner-Lambert Company had advertised its product for years as preventing or alleviating the common cold. The FTC ordered in 1972 that Warner-Lambert disclose in future advertisements that: "Contrary to prior advertising, Listerine will not help prevent colds or sore throats or lessen their severity." Hearing the case on appeal, the Court of Appeals for the Fifth Circuit affirmed the order, but dropped the phrase "Contrary to Prior Advertising."[70] Writing for the court in 1977, Circuit Judge J. Skelly Wright found persuasive scientific testimony that gargling Listerine could not help a sore throat because its active ingredients could not penetrate tissue cells to reach viruses. "[T]he Commission found that the ability of Listerine to kill germs by millions on contact is of no medical significance in the treatment of colds or sore throats. Expert testimony showed the bacteria in the oral cavity, the 'germs' which Listerine purports to kill, do not cause colds and play no role in cold symptoms."[71]

The makers of Listerine had told an FTC Administrative Law Judge that the FTC evidence against the mouthwash was contradicted by a study done by the Food and Drug Administration (FDA) which had termed Listerine "likely to be effective" as an

[67] Lemke, op. cit., pp. 180, 191.

[68] Note, " 'Corrective Advertising' Orders of the Federal Trade Commission," 85 Harvard Law Review (December, 1971), p. 506.

[69] Ibid., pp. 482–483.

[70] Warner-Lambert Co. v. FTC, 562 F.2d 749, 762 (C.A.D.C.1977).

[71] Ibid., p. 754.

over-the-counter cold remedy. Circuit Judge Wright, however said that the "likely to be effective" language did not accurately reflect the FDA study, which, in any case, was based on less extensive data than the FTC study.[72] In this case the Warner-Lambert Company was not playing for small monetary stakes. The FTC required the corrective advertising statement to appear in Listerine advertising until about $10 million had been spent on touting the mouthwash.

The Warner-Lambert Company also played for high legal stakes in this suit, challenging the very authority of the FTC to issue "corrective advertising" orders. The Commission contended, on the other hand, that the affirmative disclosure that Listerine will not prevent colds or lessen their severity is needed to give effect to a cease and desist order which would remove the misleading claim from the mouthwash's ads.[73]

Delving into the legislative history of the 1914 Federal Trade Commission Act, the Wheeler-Lea amendments of 1938, and the 1975 amendments to the FTC Act, the court held that corrective advertising had not been removed from the Commission's remedies. The Circuit Court also rejected arguments that mandatory corrective advertising is unconstitutional as a violation of the First Amendment: [74]

> A careful reading of Virginia State Board of Pharmacy v. Virginia Citizens Consumer Council compels rejection of this argument. For the Supreme Court expressly noted that the First Amendment presents "no obstacle" to government regulation of false or misleading advertising. The First Amendment, the Court said,
>
>> as we construe it today, does not prohibit the State from insuring that the stream of commercial information flow[s] cleanly as well as freely.[75]
>
> In a footnote the Court went on to delineate several differences between commercial speech and other forms which may suggest "that a different degree of protection is necessary * * *." For example, the court said, the FTC may
>
>> make it appropriate to require that a commercial message appear in such a form, or include such

[72] Ibid., p. 755.

[73] Ibid., p. 756.

[74] Ibid., pp. 758–759.

[75] 425 U.S. 748, 96 S.Ct. 1817 (1976). This case is discussed at length in Section 92 of this chapter.

additional information, warnings, and disclaimers, as are necessary to prevent its being deceptive.[76]

Having concluded that the First Amendment did not preclude corrective advertising orders and that the FTC has the power to issue such orders, the Court then turned to the question whether the remedy used against Listerine was warranted and equitable.[77]

Our role in reviewing the remedy is limited. The Supreme Court has set forth the standard:

> The Commission is the expert body to determine what remedy is necessary to eliminate the unfair or deceptive trade practices which have been disclosed. It has wide latitude for judgment and the courts will not interfere except where the remedy selected has no reasonable relation to the unlawful practices found to exist.[78]

The Commission has adopted the following standard for the imposition of corrective advertising:

> [I]f a deceptive advertisement has played a substantial role in creating or reinforcing in the public's mind a false and material belief which lives on after the false advertising ceases, there is clear and continuing injury to competition and to the consuming public as consumers continue to make purchasing decisions based on the false belief. Since this injury cannot be averted by merely requiring respondent to cease disseminating the advertisement, we may appropriately order respondent to take affirmative action designed to terminate the otherwise continuing ill effects of the advertisement.

We think this standard is entirely reasonable. It dictates two factual inquiries: (1) did Listerine's advertisements play a substantial role in creating or reinforcing in the public's mind a false belief about the product? and (2) would this belief linger on after the false advertising ceases? It strikes us that if the answer to both questions is not yes, companies everywhere may be wasting their massive advertising budgets. Indeed, it is more than a little peculiar to hear petitioner assert that its commercials really have no effect on consumer belief.

---

[76] 425 U.S. 748, 772, 96 S.Ct. 1817, 1831 (1976). See also Bates v. State Bar of Arizona, 431 U.S. 350, 97 S.Ct. 2691 (1977).

[77] Ibid., p. 762.

[78] Ibid., quoting Jacob Siegel Co. v. FTC, 327 U.S. 608, 612–613, 66 S.Ct. 758, 760 (1946).

The court next turned to the specific disclosure required ("Listerine will not help prevent colds or sore throats or lessen their severity.") and the duration of the FTC's disclosure requirement. The disclosure "must be displayed in type size at least as large as that in which the principal portion of the text of the advertisement appears and it must be separated from the text so that it can be readily noticed." On television, the disclosure must be presented via both audio and video. Those specifications, the court said, "are well calculated to assure that the disclosure will reach the public." [79] As for the duration of the corrective disclosure—which would amount to about one year if Listerine continued to advertise at its 1977 rate—the Court said it was not an unreasonably long time in which to correct a hundred years of cold claims. Therefore, the corrective order of the FTC against Listerine was upheld.

Comparative Advertising

People reading or viewing advertising sometimes see claims made that Product A is "better," "more effective," etc. than Product B. This is what is known as "comparative advertising" and has been encouraged by the Federal Trade Commission in the belief that this will assist consumers in getting more needed information about products. This comparative advertising, however, must be susceptible of substantiation; false and misleading comparative statements will draw legal consequences.

For example, consider American Home Products [makers of Anacin] v. Johnson and Johnson [makers of Tylenol]. Anacin ads based on the theme "Your Body Knows" contended that Anacin was superior to Tylenol, that it was more effective in reducing inflammation, and that it worked faster than Tylenol. Johnson and Johnson [Tylenol] complained to the three television networks that the Anacin advertising was deceptive and misleading. American Home Products [Anacin] countered by suing Johnson and Johnson, claiming that the makers of Tylenol violated the Lanham Trademark Act by disparaging a competitor's product,[80] and seeking an injunction against the Tylenol folks.[81]

This lawsuit backfired, however, because a federal district court dismissed the American Home Products [Anacin] suit and instead slapped a permanent injunction on American Home Prod-

[79] Ibid., pp. 673–764.

[80] Lanham Trademark Act, 44 Fed.Reg. 4738 § 43(a), cited in DeVore and Sack, op. cit., p. 475.

[81] American Home Products Corp. v. Johnson and Johnson, 436 F.Supp. 785 (S.D. N.Y.1977), affirmed 577 F.2d 160 (2d Cir.1978).

ucts forbidding them from publishing a misleading advertisement.[82]

In a comparative advertising case that involved both advertising regulation and copyright law, Triangle Publications—publishers of *TV Guide* magazine—sued Knight-Ridder Newspapers, publishers of *The Miami Herald.* The *Herald* developed a new supplement for its Sunday edition; a guide to television programs. *The Herald* began a campaign of newspaper and television ads late in 1977, promoting its own new TV listing supplement. For example, one such ad used a "Goldilocks and the Three Bears" theme, emphasizing that *The Herald*'s supplement was bigger than *TV Guide* and smaller than another magazine * * * and therefore presumably "just right."

The *TV Guide* complaint stemmed from *The Miami Herald*'s use of a photograph of a copyrighted *TV Guide* cover in a *Herald* promotional ad. Even though it was held that the defendant *Miami Herald* had exceeded "fair use"—see Section 46 of Chapter 7, discussing fair use in copyright law. Ultimately, it was held that *The Herald*'s use of the *TV Guide* cover in the context of a truthful comparative advertisement was indeed a fair use.[83]

Advertising Substantiation

Since the early 1970s, the FTC has set down requirements that advertisers keep available proof—"substantiation," in FTC terminology—to back up their claims. At the start of its substantiation efforts, the Commission demanded of entire industries—e.g. soap and detergents, air conditioners, deodorant manufacturers—that they come forward to back up their claims. An early case in the substantiation area was the FTC proceeding, In re Pfizer, Inc., decided in 1972. Pfizer, a chemical/drug manufacturing concern, had advertised its "Un-Burn" product with claims that its application would stop the discomfort of sunburn by tuning out nerve endings. The FTC told Pfizer that unless it could prove such a claim, that would be considered an unfair (and therefore illegal) trade practice. That meant an advertiser should have "a reasonable basis [for its claims] before disseminating an ad." [84] As Associate Director for Advertising Practices Wallace S. Snyder wrote in 1984, " * * * ads for objective claims imply that the advertiser has a prior reasonable basis for making the claim. In light of the

[82] Ibid.

[83] 621 F.2d 1318 (5th Cir.1980), affirming 445 F.Supp. 875 (S.D.Fla.1978), 3 Med. L.Rptr. 2086; see also DeVore and Sack, op. cit., p. 476.

[84] Wallace S. Snyder, "Advertising Substantiation Program," in Christopher Smith and Christian S. White, chairmen, The FTC 1984 (New York: Practising Law Institute, 1984), p. 121; In re Pfizer, Inc., 81 FTC 23 (1981).

implied representation of substantiation, therefore, a performance claim that lacks a reasonable basis is deceptive." [85]

SEC. 86.   OTHER FEDERAL ADMINISTRATIVE CONTROLS

In addition to the Federal Trade Commission, many other federal agencies—including the Food and Drug Administration, the Federal Communications Commission, and the United States Postal Service—exert controls over advertising in interstate commerce.

Although of paramount importance as a control over advertising, the FTC does not stand alone among federal agencies in its fight against suspect advertising.   Federal agencies which have powers over advertising include:

(1)   The Food and Drug Administration

(2)   The Federal Communications Commission

(3)   The United States Postal Service

(4)   The Securities and Exchange Commission

(5)   The Alcohol and Tobacco Tax Division of the Internal Revenue Service

Such a list by no means exhausts the number of federal agencies which, tangentially at least, can exert some form of control over advertising.   Bodies such as the Civil Aeronautics Board and perhaps the Interstate Commerce Commission and the Federal Power Commission have power to curtail advertising abuses connected with matters under each agency's jurisdiction.[86]

1.   Food and Drug Administration

The Food and Drug Administration's (FDA) activities in controlling labelling and misbranding overlap the powers of the FTC to a considerable degree.   The Pure Food and Drug Act gives the FDA jurisdiction over misbranding and mislabeling of foods, drugs, and cosmetics.[87]   The FTC, however, was likewise given jurisdiction over foods, drugs, and cosmetics by the Wheeler-Act

---

[85] Snyder, loc. cit., citing General Dynamics Corp., 82 FTC 488 (1973), and also Firestone Tire & Rubber Co., 81 FTC 398 (1972), affirmed 481 F.2d 246 (6th Cir. 1972), certiorari denied 414 U.S. 1112, 94 S.Ct. 841 (1973).

[86] See Note, "The Regulation of Advertising," Columbia Law Review Vol. 56:7 (Nov. 1956) pp. 1019–1111, at p. 1054, citing 24 Stat. 378 (1887), 49 U.S.C.A. § 1 (ICC); 41 Stat. 1063 (1920), 16 U.S.C.A. § 791(a) (FTC); 52 Stat. 1003 (1938), as amended, 49 U.S.C.A. § 491.

[87] 52 Stat. 1040 (1938), 21 U.S.C.A. § 301.

Amendment.[88]   The FTC and the FDA have agreed upon a division of labor whereby FTC concentrates on false advertising and the FDA focuses attention on false labelling.[89]   However, this division of labor is quite inexact.   Pamphlets or literature distributed with a product have been held to be "labels" for purposes of FDA enforcement.[90]

2. The Federal Communications Commission

The Federal Communications Commission has been endowed by Congress with licensing and regulatory powers over broadcasting.[91]   Although prohibited from exercising censorship over broadcasting stations, the FCC does have the power to judge overall performance when considering renewal of a station's license every three years.   According to the Communications Act of 1934, broadcast licenses are granted or renewed if it is judged that a station operating in "the public interest, convenience, and necessity."[92] Occasionally, the FCC has looked at the merits and demerits of advertising broadcast by a station as it considered license renewal.[93]

FCC powers over advertising, however, were long regarded as potential and indirect rather than actual and direct.[94]

The FCC became more directly concerned with advertising in the mid-1960s.   The Commission was drawn more heavily into this area by the troubled interrelationship between advertising and the issues which surfaced during the controversy over cigarette smoking and its harmful effects.   The FCC's involvement began, with a letter in 1966 from John F. Banzhaf III, a young New York lawyer.   Banzhaf complained that a network-owned station in New York, WCBS–TV had broadcast many cigarette commercials without time for spokesmen to rebut the ads with information about smoking's harmful effects.   WCBS–TV replied that it had

[88] See "The Wheeler Lea Amendment" to the Federal Trade Commission Act, 52 Stat. 111 (1938), as amended, 15 U.S.C.A. § 45(a)(1).

[89] See, for example, 2 CCH Trade Reg.Rep. (10th ed.), Paragraph 8540, p. 17,081 (1954).

[90] See U.S. v. Kordel, 164 F.2d 913 (7th Cir.1947); U.S. v. Article of Device Labeled in Part "110 V Vapozone," 194 F.Supp. 332 (D.C.Cal.1961).

[91] Communications Act of 1934, 48 Stat. 1064, 47 U.S.C.A. § 151.

[92] 48 Stat. 1083, 1091 (1934), 47 U.S.C.A. §§ 307, 326.

[93] See, e.g., a case involving advertisements by a physician, Farmers & Bankers Life Insurance Co., 2 F.C.C. 455 (1936); for a case involving a lottery, WRBL Radio Station, Inc., 2 F.C.C. 687 (1936).

[94] See Note, "The Regulation of Advertising," Columbia Law Review Vol. 56 (1956) pp. 1019–1111, at pp. 1045–1046.

telecast numerous programs, from 1962 to 1966, about the hazards cigarette present to health.[95]

In his letter, Banzhaf urged that the FCC's long-standing "Fairness Doctrine" be invoked to allow replies to the many cigarette advertisements broadcast every day. The Fairness Doctrine, in the past, has dealt primarily with the presentation of news or editorial matter. As articulated by the FCC in its 1949 report, *Editorializing by Broadcast Licensees,* the Fairness Doctrine—before Banzhaf—meant this: Issues of public significance should be broadcast in such a manner that the public will hear important—if not all—sides of such matters.[96] This FCC doctrine became a United States statute in a 1959 amendment to the Communications Act.[97] The 1959 amendment said:[98]

> Nothing in the foregoing sentence shall be as relieving broadcasters, in connection with the presentation of newscasts, news interviews, news documentaries, and on-the-spot coverage of news events, from the obligation imposed upon them under this chapter to operate in the public interest and to afford a reasonable opportunity for the discussion of conflicting views on issues of public importance.

On June 2, 1967, the FCC sent a letter to WCBS–TV, holding that the Fairness Doctrine was applicable to cigarette advertising, and that a station broadcasting cigarette advertising must give responsible voices opposing smoking an opportunity to be heard.[99]

That decision of the FCC—and the viability of the entire Fairness Doctrine as well—were in doubt for some time: the Fairness Doctrine was under attack in a case in the federal court system.[1] In the spring of 1969, however, the Supreme Court, in

[95] "Fairness, Freedom, and Cigarette Advertising, A Defense of the Federal Communications Commission," Columbia Law Review Vol. 67 (1967) pp. 1470–1489; Norman P. Leventhal, "Caution: Cigarette Commercials May be Hazardous to Your License—The New Aspect of Fairness," Federal Communications Bar Journal Vol. 22:1 (1968), pp. 55–124, at pp. 92–93.

[96] 13 F.C.C. 1246 (1949), also published in 25 Pike & Fischer Radio Regulations 1901 (1963).

[97] 48 Stat. 1088 (1934), as amended, 47 U.S.C.A. § 315(a); see also Note, "Administrative Law—FCC Fairness Doctrine—Applicability to Advertising," Iowa Law Review Vol. 53:2 (Oct.1967) pp. 480–491, at pp. 481–482.

[98] 47 U.S.C.A. § 315(a).

[99] WCBS–TV Case, 9 Pike & Fischer Radio Regulations 2d 1423 (1967); Leventhal, op. cit., p. 92.

[1] See Red Lion Broadcasting Co. v. FCC, 127 U.S.App.D.C. 129, 381 F.2d 908 (D.C. Cir.1967), which upheld the Fairness Doctrine as 1) a constitutional delegation of Congress' legislative power; 2) sufficiently explicit to avoid being unconstitutionally vague; 3) not in violation of the 9th and 10th amendments to the Constitution, and 4) not an abrogation of broadcasting station licensees' rights under the 1st and 5th amendment.

deciding two cases which did not involve advertising, upheld the Fairness Doctrine. The Court's language was broad enough to include not only the right to answer personal attacks and political editorializing but also seemed to have enough scope to provide opportunity for answers to be broadcast to advertising which dealt with controversial political or social issues.[2] The Court declared:[3]

> Because of the scarcity of radio frequencies, the Government is permitted to put restraints on licensees in favor of others whose views should be expressed on this unique medium. But the people as a whole retain their interest in free speech by radio and their collective right to have the medium function consistently with the ends and purposes of the First Amendment. It is the right of the viewers and listeners, not the right of the broadcasters, which is paramount. * * * "It is the purpose of the First Amendment to preserve an uninhibited marketplace of ideas in which truth will ultimately prevail, rather than to countenance monopolization of that market, whether it be by the Government itself or a private license. * * * [S]peech concerning public affairs is more than self-expression, it is the essence of self government. * * * It is the right of the public to receive suitable access to social, political, esthetic, moral, and other ideas and experiences which is crucial here. That right may not constitutionally be abridged either by Congress or by the FCC.

> *   *   *

> In view of the scarcity of broadcast frequencies, the Government's role in allocating those frequencies, and the legitimate claims of those unable without governmental assistance to gain access to those frequencies for expression of their views, we hold the regulations and ruling at issue are both authorized by statute and constitutional.

3. The U.S. Postal Service

Postal controls over advertising can be severe. Congress was provided with lawmaking power to operate the postal system under Article I, Section 8 of the Constitution. This power was long delegated by Congress to a Postmaster General and his Post Office Department. It has long been established that the mails could not be used to carry things which, in the judgment of

[2] See Red Lion Broadcasting Co. v. FCC, 395 U.S. 367, 89 S.Ct. 1794 (1969), discussed in Chapter 12, in Section 77.

[3] 395 U.S. 367, 390, 89 S.Ct. 1794, 1806, 1812 (1969).

Congress, were socially harmful.[4] The Postmaster General had the power to exclude articles or substances which Congress has proscribed as non-mailable. With the passage of the Postal Reorganization Act of 1970, the Post Office Department was abolished as a Cabinet-level agency, and was replaced by the United States Postal Service, a subdivision of the Executive branch.[5]

Perhaps the Postal Service's greatest deterrent to false advertising is contained in the power to halt delivery of materials suspected of being designed to defraud mail recipients.[6] The Postal Service can order nondelivery of mail, and can impound suspected mail matter.[7]

The administrative fraud order is not the only kind of mail fraud action available to the Postal Service. Instead of administrative procedure through the Service, a *criminal* mail fraud case may be started. Criminal cases are prosecuted by a U.S. attorney in a United States District Court. Conviction under the federal mail fraud statute can result in a fine of up to $1,000, imprisonment for up to 5 years, or both.[8] Criminal fraud orders are used when the U.S. Postal Service wishes to operate in a punitive fashion. The administrative fraud orders, on the other hand, are more preventive in nature.

4. The Securities and Exchange Commission

Securities markets are attractive to fast-buck artists, so the sale and publicizing of securities are kept under a watchful governmental eye. Most states have "Blue Sky" laws which enable a state agency to halt the circulation of false or misleading information about the sale of stocks, bonds or the like.[9] The work of the Securities and Exchange Commission, however, is far more important in protecting the public.

After the stock market debacle of 1929, strong regulations were instituted at the federal level to prevent deceptive statements about securities. Taken together, the Securities Act of 1933 [10] and the Securities Exchange Act of 1934 [11] gave the S.E.C. great power over the sale and issuance of securities.

[4] See, for example, early federal tax laws on obscenity discussed in Chapter 11, or see Public Clearing House v. Coyne, 194 U.S. 497, 24 S.Ct. 789 (1904).

[5] 39 U.S.C.A. § 3003.

[6] Ibid.

[7] Ibid.

[8] 18 U.S.C.A. § 1341; Ague, ibid., p. 61.

[9] See Note, "The Regulation of Advertising," Columbia Law Review op. cit. p. 1065.

[10] 48 Stat. 74 (1933), 15 U.S.C.A. § 77.

[11] 48 Stat. 881 (1934), as amended, 15 U.S.C.A. §§ 78(a)–78(jj).

Sale of securities to investors cannot proceed until complete and accurate information has been given, registering the certificates with the S.E.C.[12] A briefer version of the registration statement is used in the "prospectus" circulated among prospective investors before the stock or bond can be offered for sale.[13] If misleading statements have been made about a security "in any material respect" in either registration documents or in the prospectus, the Commission may issue a "stop order" which removes the right to sell the security.[14] Furthermore, unless a security is properly registered and its prospectus accurate, it is a criminal offense to use the mails to sell it or to advertise it for sale.[15]

An unscrupulous seller of securities has more to fear than just the S.E.C. Under a provision of the United States Code, a person who has lost money because he was tricked by a misleading prospectus may sue a number of individuals, including persons who signed the S.E.C. registration statement and every director, officer, or partner in the firm issuing the security.[16]

The mid-1980s brought two cases underlining the reach of SEC efforts to try to control the circulation of investment information. The case of Securities and Exchange Commission v. Lowe saw the SEC's effort to enjoin Christopher Lowe and Lowe Management Corporation from circulating a newsletter. Lowe, who was convicted in New York in 1977 for appropriating the funds of an investment client and for failure to register as an investment adviser with New York's Department of Law, and in 1978 and 1979, respectively, for stealing from a bank and for deception by issuing worthless checks.[17] Lowe nevertheless continued to offer investment advice, including "The Lowe Investment and Financial Letter," a market newsletter, and "The Lowe Stock Chart Service."

The SEC asked for an injunction to halt Lowe's publications, urging—among other things—that Lowe had failed to register under the federal Investment Advisers Act.[18] A U.S. Court of Appeal allowed the injunction: because there was great government interest in trying to insure trustworthy stock market information, the prior restraint on Lowe's publications was justified.

[12] 48 Stat. 77 (1933), as amended, 15 U.S.C.A. § 77(f).

[13] 48 Stat. 78 (1933), 15 U.S.C.A. § 77(j).

[14] 48 Stat. 79 (1933), as amended, 15 U.S.C.A. § 77(h)(b) and (d).

[15] 48 Stat. 84 (1933), as amended, 15 U.S.C.A. § 77(e).

[16] 48 Stat. 82 (1933), 15 U.S.C.A. § 77(k).

[17] SEC v. Lowe, 725 F.2d 892 (2d Cir.1984), 10 Med.L.Rptr. 1225–1226; see also Investment Adviser's Act, 15 U.S.C. § 80b–3(e) and 3(f).

[18] Ibid., pp. 1232–1233.

Attorneys P. Cameron Devore and Robert Sack said in 1984: [19]

The *Lowe* case raises significant prior restraint issues. Lowe has been forbidden from publishing his newsletter essentially because of his previous convictions for misappropriating funds and passing bad checks. The SEC has not contended that Lowe published false or misleading reports.

The Supreme Court of the United States, however, reversed the S.E.C. order, holding that the S.E.C. had over-reached its authority as delegated by Congress. This outcome is discussed in Section 99 of Chapter 15, at footnotes 49–57.

5. The Alcohol and Tobacco Tax Division, Internal Revenue Service

Ever since this nation's unsuccessful experiment with prohibition, the federal government has kept a close eye on liquor advertising. The responsible agency is the Alcohol and Tobacco Tax Division of the Internal Revenue Service.[20] Liquor advertising may not include false or misleading statements, and may not disparage competing products. False statements may include misrepresenting the age of a liquor, or claiming that its alcoholic content is higher than it is in reality.[21]

The Alcohol and Tobacco Tax Division has harsh sanctions at its disposal. If an advertiser violates a regulation of the Division, he is subject to a fine, and could even be put out of business if his federal liquor license is revoked.[22]

The FTC and other federal agencies by no means provide the whole picture of controls over advertising. There are many state regulations affecting political advertising and legal advertising by government bodies, but they cannot be treated here. States also regulate the size and location of billboards, but space does not permit discussion of these statutes. We now turn to consideration of some of the ways in which states have regulated commercial advertising in the mass media.

SEC. 87. THE PRINTERS' INK STATUTE

Most states have adopted some version of the model statute which makes fraudulent and misleading advertising a misdemeanor.

One of the best known restraints upon advertising exists at the state level in the various forms of the Printers' Ink statute

---

[19] P. Cameron Devore and Robert Sack, "Advertising and Commercial Speech," in James C. Goodale, chairman, Communications Law 1984 (New York: Practising Law Institute, 1984), at p. 127.

[20] 49 Stat. 481 (1936), as amended, 27 U.S.C.A. § 205.

[21] Ibid.

[22] Ibid.

adopted in 48 states. *Printer's Ink* magazine, in 1911, advocated that states adopt a model statute which would make false advertising a misdemeanor. Leaders in the advertising and publishing world realized the difficulty in securing prosecutions for false advertising under the usual state fraud statutes. Considerable initiative in gaining state enactment of Printers' Ink statutes was generated through the Better Business Bureau and through various advertising clubs and associations.

The model statute, as revised in 1945 and approved by the National Association of Better Business Bureaus, says—in tangled prose: [23]

> Any person, firm, corporation or association or agent or employee thereof, who, with intent to sell, purchase or in any wise dispose of, or to contract with reference to merchandise, real estate, service, employment, or anything offered by such person, firm, corporation or association, or agent or employee thereof, directly or indirectly, to the public for sale, purchase, distribution, or the hire of personal services, or with intent to increase the consumption of or to contract with reference to any merchandise, real estate, securities, service, or employment, or to induce the public in any manner to enter into any obligation relating thereto, or to acquire title thereto, or an interest therein, or to make any loan, makes, publishes, disseminates, circulates, or places before the public, or causes, directly or indirectly, to be made, published, disseminated, circulated, or placed before the public, in this state, in a newspaper, magazine or other publication, or in the form of a book, notice, circular, pamphlet, letter, handbill, poster, bill, sign, placard, card, label, or over any radio or television station or other medium of wireless communication, or in any other way similar or dissimilar to the foregoing, an advertisement, announcement, or statement of any sort regarding merchandise, securities, service, employment, or anything so offered for use, purchase or sale, or the interest, terms or conditions upon which such loan will be made to the public, which advertisement contains any assertion, representation or statement of fact which is untrue, deceptive, or misleading, shall be guilty of a misdemeanor.

All but two states—Delaware and New Mexico—have some version of the Printers' Ink statute on their books.[24] Although the

---

[23] "Basis for State Laws on Truth in Publishing—The Printers' Ink Model Statute," Reprint, Printers' Ink Publishing Corp., 1959.

[24] Note, "Developments in the Law—Deceptive Advertising," Harvard Law Review, op. cit., p. 1122.

Printers' Ink statute is famous, its fame is perhaps greater than its present-day usefulness as a control over advertising. Relatively few relevant cases exist which indicate that the statute has seen little use in bringing cheating advertisers to court. The Printers' Ink statute may still be useful as a guideline, or in providing a sanction which local Better Business Bureaus may threaten to invoke even if they seldom do so.[25]

The Printers' Ink statute is aimed and enforced primarily against advertisers rather than against units of the mass media which may have no knowledge that an ad is false or misleading.[26] This statute was widely adopted, apparently because the common law simply did not provide adequate remedies against false advertising, especially in an economy which has grown so explosively.

The model statute is more flexible than common law prosecutions or fraud statutes. It does not make *scienter*, guilty knowledge or intent to publish false advertisements an element of the offense. A number of states, however, have variants of the Printers' Ink statute which are not as comprehensive as the model law in that some element of *scienter* must be shown for conviction.[27]

A major and obvious difficulty with the Printers' Ink statute—and with all attempts to control advertising—is that concepts of "truth" and "falsity" tend to elude definition. What is misleading, deceptive, or untrue is not defined in the model statute. The problem of making such a determination is left up to the jury. A state of Washington case in 1917 is in point. J.J. Massey had published this advertisement:

Pre-opening sale of Used Pianos

These pianos must be closed out to make room for carload of new pianos coming from the east. Every piano fully guaranteed two years; exchange privilege; unheard of easy terms. All look like new.

Smith & Barnes, oak case, was $400; now $200.

Schilling & Sons, beautiful case, was $375; now $167.

Brinkerhoff, art case, was $400; now $218.

Free delivery and stool.

[25] Note, "The Regulation of Advertising," op. cit. p. 1057.

[26] Ibid., pp. 1059–1060; State v. Beacon Publ. Co., 141 Kan. 734, 42 P.2d 960 (1935).

[27] Note, "Developments in the Law of Deceptive Advertising," Harvard Law Review loc. cit.

J.J. Massey.

It was charged that the Smith & Barnes and the Schilling pianos never had market values of $400 and $375. In the trial, the defendant was convicted of fraudulent advertising. A higher court reversed the conviction, saying that the advertisement referred to the retail selling price, not to the true market value of the pianos.[28]

SEC. 88. LOTTERIES

Advertising or publicizing of lotteries is prohibited by both federal and state laws.

Many journalists, whether in news or advertising, pay little attention to federal and state statutes which forbid publicizing of lotteries. The theory of such laws is that the public needs to be protected from gambling. In practice, many cities have church bingo socials or merchants' promotional lottery schemes which are rarely if ever prosecuted. As a result, journalists often ignore lottery laws because they are ignored by law enforcement officials at the state or local level.

When interstate commerce or use of the United States mails is involved, however, journalists should be especially careful to heed the laws forbidding lotteries. Advertising a lottery, for example, could result in having a publication's second-class mailing privilege lifted. Also, the persons responsible for publicizing or advertising the lottery could be prosecuted for committing a crime punishable by a fine of up to $1,000, imprisonment of up to two years, or both.

Often, journalists have difficulty in recognizing a lottery. There are three elements in a lottery:

(1) *Consideration*—Commonly, consideration means money paid to purchase a lottery ticket or a chance on a sewing machine or automobile which some service organization, for example, is "giving away" in a fund-raising effort. However, one should know the laws of his individual state concerning "consideration." In some states, the consideration need not be money paid. Instead, the effort required to enter a contest, such as having to go to a certain store to get an entry blank or having to mail a product's lable, might be deemed to be "consideration."[29]

[28] State v. Massey, 95 Wash. 1, 163 P. 7 (1917).

[29] Brooklyn Daily Eagle v. Voorhies, 181 F. 579 (D.C.N.Y.1910).

(2) *Prize*—A prize in a lottery is something of value, generally of greater value or worth than the consideration invested.[30]

(3) *Chance*—The element of chance—the gambling element— is what led Victorian-era Congressmen to pass the first federal statutes against lotteries in 1890.[31] There can, however, be an element of certainty accompanying the element of chance in a lottery. For example, if a person buys a newspaper subscription he is certain to receive the newspaper which includes a chance in a prize contest, this kind of promotion has been held to be a lottery.[32]

Similarly, a scheme for the sale of bonds in which the purchaser gets investments, and also participates in a prize drawing, is a lottery.[33]

Lotteries are forbidden in the electronic media as well as in the print media. Sections 1301 through 1305 of Title 18 of the United States Code all use identical terminology. Section 1301 forbids the importing or transporting of lottery tickets; Section 1302 forbids the mailing of lottery tickets or related materials; Section 1303 prohibits participation in lottery schemes by postmasters and postal employees, and Section 1304 forbids the broadcasting of lottery information. All four sections contain the same phrase forbidding " 'any lottery, gift, enterprise, or similar scheme, offering prizes dependent in whole or in part upon lot of chance.' " Section 1307, however, states that a station may broadcast information about lotteries in its circulation area—in an adjoining state, for example—as long as the station's own state has a legalized lottery scheme.

During the first half of the 1980s, Congress considered legislation to liberalize federal lottery statutes. For example, one proposal passed by the Senate Judiciary Committee in the summer of 1984 (S.B.1876) involved looser rules for federally regulated advertising of certain gambling activities including lotteries, and would allow advertising of state-run or state-allowed lotteries to be advertised. Cameron Devore and Robert P. Sack have also noted a U.S. district court case out of Illinois in which a publisher sued to enjoin what he called harassment of vendors of his publication. The vendors were being accused of possessing gambling materials because they were selling publications containing a coupon which would give a buyer a chance at winning a cash prize by naming

[30] United States v. Wallis, 58 F.2d 942, 943 (D.C.Idaho 1893).

[31] State ex inf. McKittrick v. Globe-Democrat Co., 341 Mo. 862, 110 S.W.2d 705 (1937).

[32] Stevens v. Cincinnati Times-Star, 72 Ohio St. 112, 73 N.E. 1058 (1905).

[33] Horner v. United States, 147 U.S. 449, 13 S.Ct. 409 (1893).

the winner in a horse race. The court held that the injunction should not be issued; government had an allowable stake in stopping the flow of illegal information which added up to an off-track betting scheme.[34]

More change is apt to occur in laws regulating lotters and other gambling, at both state and federal levels. Society seems to tolerate gambling more and more, and the scramble for government revenues no doubt provides impetus toward creation of more state-run or state-authorized lotteries.

SEC. 89. SELF–REGULATION

Leading communications companies have developed standards to govern their acceptance or rejection of advertising.

Publishers and broadcasters must know the legal status of advertising. If it can be proved that they knew that an advertisement is fraudulent, they may be held responsible for that ad along with the person or company who placed it in the publication. Advertising departments on many newspapers, moreover, often serve as a kind of advertising agency. In this capacity, the advertising staff must be able to give knowledgeable counsel and technical advice to advertisers.

In general, publishers are not liable to the individual consumer for advertising which causes financial loss or other damage unless the publisher or his employees knew that such advertising was fraudulent or misleading. The absence of liability for damage, however, does not mean that there is an absence of responsibility to the public generally and to individual readers of a publication.

The newspaper or broadcast station which permits dishonest or fraudulent advertising hurts its standing with both its readers and its advertisers. Publishers and broadcasters, who perceive psychological and economic advantages in refusing dishonest advertising, also appear to be becoming more cognizant that they have a moral duty to protect the public.

Responsible media units go to great lengths to ensure that advertising which they print is honest. An example of this is The Dallas Morning News' pamphlet, Advertising Standards of Acceptability, which is reprinted below.[35]

[34] Devore and Sack, in Communications Law 1984, p. 122, citing Ingram v. Chicago, 544 F.Supp. 654 (N.D.Ill.1982).

[35] Advertising Standards of Acceptability in The Dallas Morning News, pamphlet dated August, 1983. Reprinted by permission.

ADVERTISING STANDARDS OF ACCEPTABILITY IN *THE DALLAS MORNING NEWS*

FOREWORD

This pamphlet is published as a general guide to advertising standards of acceptability in *The Dallas Morning News*. The guidelines contained herein conform to generally accepted standards of good taste and business ethics.

The Advertising Code of American Business has been developed by the American Advertising Federation and the Association of Better Business Bureaus International. It has been endorsed by the National Association of Broadcasters, the International Newspaper Advertising Executives Association, the National Newspaper Association, the Magazine Publishers Association, the American Association of Advertising Agencies, and more than 70 national trade groups.

GENERAL PROVISIONS

Advertising standards of The Dallas Morning News have been formulated not only for the protection of the reader, but also the advertiser. The good names and reputations of honest businesses should not be jeopardized by those who ignore or bend the truth.

The Dallas Morning News works in cooperation with the Dallas Better Business Bureau and the Dallas Consumer Affairs Office in maintaining truth and integrity in advertising. It supports the Advertising Code of American Business.

We urge all advertisers to review these advertising guidelines and to make them part of their own advertising accountability standards.

Continued adherence to these standards contributes to Dallas' reputation for ethical advertising, marketing and selling standards.

Advertisers shall be classified as retailers doing retail business when they sell directly to consumers through one or more retail stores located in the Standard Metropolitan Statistical Area.

All advertising offering the sale of merchandise to the general public—to qualify as retail advertising—must contain the name of the person or firm making the offer, along with an address and/or telephone number.

The primary responsibility for truthful and nondeceptive advertising rests with the advertiser. Advertisers must—upon request and before publication—be prepared to substantiate any claims or offers made.

Advertisements which are untrue, misleading, deceptive, fraudulent, and/or disparaging of competitors shall not be used.

No advertisement—which as a whole may be misleading, although every sentence considered separately is literally true—will be considered for publication. The same applies to advertisements where misrepresentation may result not only from direct statements, but from omitting or obscuring material facts.

Any advertiser seeking investment capital for any business must be individually checked and fully investigated to establish the character and financial stability of the owners or principles involved. Financial advertising, to be accepted, must: (1) be submitted by firms registered with the Federal Securities and Exchange Commission and/or firms that are members of the National Association of Securities Dealers, National Association of Investment Companies or comparable organizations; (2) or be by private individuals offering for sale only those securities qualified with the state securities board (in such case, a name and address must be included in the advertisement); (3) and have financial statements to substantiate any promise or implication of exact returns.

UNACCEPTABLE ADVERTISING

No advertiser shall use the name of another retail business in any advertisement without providing The Dallas Morning News with written permission of said retailer.

Other unacceptable advertising includes—but is not limited to:

- Fraudulent advertisements or those that contain statements of doubtful honesty.
- Attacks on a person or company, or on the goods or services of another person or company.
- Advertisements in bad taste or offensive to any group on moral, religious or discriminatory grounds.
- Suggestive captions or illustrations.
- Headlines, copy or illustrations which state or imply conduct which—by normal standards—is considered morally or socially unacceptable.

- Advertisements describing goods not available and not intended to be sold on request, but used as "bait" to lure customers.
- Advertisements proposing marriage.
- Advertising that can be misinterpreted by the reader.
- Advertising likely to cause injury to the health or morals of the reader.
- Advertisements containing dubious or exaggerated claims.
- Advertisements that could be construed as an invasion of privacy (such as birthday greetings, missing spouse searches, et al.)
- Use of the word "wholesale" in retail advertisements.
- Advertising offering goods or services for sale and not containing the name of both advertiser and location.
- Advertising that is clearly obscene.
- Advertising soliciting contributions. (Accepted only at the discretion of the advertising director.)

The above lists some of the more common abuses found in retail advertising. It is not meant to cover all advertising unacceptable to The Dallas Morning News.

A STATEMENT OF ADVERTISING PRINCIPLES

Here is the creed of the American Advertising Federation * * * principles fully subscribed to by The Dallas Morning News

GOOD ADVERTISING aims to inform consumers and help them to buy more intelligently.

GOOD ADVERTISING tells the truth, avoiding misstatements of facts as well as possible deception through implication and omission. It makes no claims which cannot be met in full without further qualifications. It uses only testimonials of competent witnesses.

GOOD ADVERTISING conforms to generally accepted standards of good taste. It seeks public acceptance on the basis of the merits of products or services advertised, rather than by disparaging of competing goods. It tries to avoid practices that are offensive or annoying.

GOOD ADVERTISING recognizes both its economic responsibility to help reduce distribution costs and its social responsibility in serving the public interest.

THE ADVERTISING CODE OF AMERICAN BUSINESS

1. TRUTH * * * Advertising shall tell the truth, and shall reveal significant facts, the concealment of which would mislead the public.

2. RESPONSIBILITY * * * Advertising agencies and advertisers shall be willing to provide substantiation of claims made.

3. TASTE AND DECENCY * * * Advertising shall be free of statements, illustrations or implications which are offensive to good taste or public decency.

4. DISPARAGEMENT * * * Advertising shall offer merchandise or service on its merits and refrain from attacking competitors unfairly or disparaging their products, services or methods of doing business.

5. BAIT ADVERTISEMENTS * * * Advertising shall offer only merchandise or services which are really available for purchase at the advertised price.

6. GUARANTEES AND WARRANTIES * * * Advertising of guarantees and warranties shall be explicit. Advertising of any guarantee or warranty shall clearly and conspicuously disclose its nature and extent, the manner in which the guarantor or warrantor will perform, and the identity of the guarantor or warrantor.

7. PRICE CLAIMS * * * Advertising shall avoid price or savings claims which are false and misleading, or which do not offer provable bargains or savings.

8. UNPROVABLE CLAIMS * * * Advertising shall avoid the use of exaggerated or unprovable claims.

9. TESTIMONIALS * * * Advertising containing testimonials shall be limited to those of competent witnesses who are reflecting a real and honest choice.

SEC. 90. THE RIGHT TO REFUSE SERVICE

A newspaper or magazine is not a public utility and therefore may choose those with whom it cares to do business.

A newspaper or magazine is a private enterprise and as such may carry on business transactions with whom it pleases. If its managers so desire they may refuse to sell newspapers to individuals or news agents, or to publish news stories about any particular event or on any opinion. By weight of legal authority, a newspaper is not a public utility.

There is pressure to create a "right of access" to news and advertising columns of the media. Arguments heard with increasing frequency run something like this:[36]

> The free marketplace of ideas is not working at all well during the latter third of the 20th Century. Competition among newspapers, magazines, and the electronic media is so diminished that only ideas acceptable to the nation's establishment can gain a hearing. Laissez faire in the media has come to mean, as John P. Roche once said in another context, "Every man for himself—as the elephant said, dancing among the chickens." Government has an affirmative obligation to stop the discriminatory refusal of advertisements and notices in publications.

Such arguments, at this writing, have not succeeded. If a change does come which affects the right to refuse advertising, it would seem that advertising with a political or otherwise socially significant message might first be forced upon publishers before the right to refuse ordinary commercial advertising would be affected. An old but important case decided in 1931 declared:[37]

> The newspaper business is an ordinary business. It is a business essentially private in nature—as private as that of the baker, grocer, or milkman, all of whom perform a service on which, to a greater or less extent, the communities depend, but which bears no such relation to the public as to warrant its inclusion in the category of businesses charged with the public use. If a newspaper were required to accept an advertisement, it could be compelled to publish a news item. If some good lady gave a tea, and submitted to the newspaper a proper account of the tea, and the editor of the newspaper, believing that it had no news value, refused to publish it, she, it seems to us, would have as much right to compel the newspaper to publish the account as would a person engaged in busi-

---

[36] See, e.g., Jerome A. Barron, "Access to the Press—A New First Amendment Right," Harvard Law Review Vol. 80 (1967), p. 1641; Willard H. Pedrick, "Freedom of the Press and the Law of Libel," Cornell Law Quarterly Vol. 49 (1964) p. 581; Report of the 1968 Biennial Conference of the American Civil Liberties Union, New York, Sept., 1968; Gilbert Cranberg, "New Look at the First Amendment," Saturday Review, Sept. 14, 1968, pp. 136–137; Simon Lazarus, "The Right of Reply," New Republic, Oct. 5, 1968.

[37] Shuck v. Carroll Daily Herald, 215 Iowa 1276, 1281, 247 N.W. 813, 815, 87 A.L.R. 975 (193). See also Friedenberg v. Times Publishing Co., 170 La. 3, 127 So. 345 (1930); In re Wohl, Inc., 50 F.2d 254 (D.C.Mich.1931). See also Miami Herald v. Tornillo, 418 U.S. 241, 94 S.Ct. 2831 (1974).

ness to compel a newspaper to publish an advertisement of the business that the person is conducting.

Thus, as a newspaper is strictly a private enterprise, the publishers thereof have a right to publish whatever advertisements they desire and to refuse to publish whatever advertisements they do not desire to publish.

Non-private entities, however—such as transit authorities or state-owned publications—can not refuse advertising with impunity. Consider the 1967 case, Kissinger v. New York City Transit Authority, which originated from actions of members of Students for a Democratic Society (SDS). SDS attempted to buy space on subway walls and in subway trains for posters protesting the Vietnam War. The posters showed a little girl who was reported to have been burned by napalm. The SDS request was refused by an advertising agency which sold space for posters for the Transit Authority. Arguing that the poster copy was protected by the First and Fourteenth Amendments, and saying that the Transit Authority had to accept all advertisements submitted to it, SDS brought suit in a United States District Court. SDS sought a declaratory judgment which would force the Transit Authority to accept its posters.[38]

The U.S. District Court was sympathetic up to a point, ruling that the First and Fourteenth Amendments extended to the posters. Additionally, the advertising agency could not arbitrarily accept some posters and reject others. The posters were neither obscene nor profane, and expressed political opinions. The court said that the Transit Authority could not "refuse to accept the posters for display because they are 'entirely too controversial' and would be objectionable to large segments of our population." [39]

Although the court gave the above language to SDS, it gave the decision to the Transit Authority and its advertising agency. The court held that questions of whether the posters could be refused because they presented a "clear and present danger" or posed a "threat to public safety" could be determined only by a jury trial. Thus the court denied the SDS motion for a summary judgment which would have required the Transit Authority to accept the posters.[40]

A California case involved a group called Women for Peace. In 1964, Women for Peace sought to place advertising placards in buses owned by the Alameda-Contra Costa Transit District. The placards said:

[38] Kissinger v. New York City Transit Authority, 274 F.Supp. 438, 441 (D.C.N.Y. 1967).

[39] Ibid., p. 443.

[40] Ibid.

"Mankind must put an end to war or war will put an end to mankind."   President John F. Kennedy.

Write to President Johnson: Negotiate Vietnam. Women for Peace, P.O. Box 944, Berkeley.[41]

The private advertising agency which managed advertising for the transit district rejected the placards.   It was declared that "political advertising and advertising on controversial subjects are not acceptable unless approved by the [transit] district, and that advertising objectionable to the district shall be removed * * *." [42]

After a trial and two appeals, the Women for Peace finally won their case in 1967 before the California Supreme Court.   The court said that the ad was protected by the First Amendment and that once a public facility is opened for use of the general public, arbitrary conditions cannot be imposed upon the use of that facility.[43]

The California Supreme Court declared.[44]

We conclude that defendants, having opened a forum for the expression of ideas by providing facilities for advertisements on its buses, cannot for reasons of administrative convenience decline to accept advertising expressing opinions and beliefs within the ambit of First Amendment protection.

In 1969, a college newspaper was told it could not refuse political advertising.   A number of non-students wished to place political ads in the *Royal Purple,* the offical campus newspaper at Wisconsin State University-Whitewater.   Their requests for advertising space were denied on the ground that the newspaper had a policy against accepting "editorial advertisements"—those advertisements expressing political views.   Refusal of the advertisements led to suits charging that the plaintiffs' First and Fourteenth Amendment rights had been violated by Wisconsin, acting through the regents of the state colleges, and by the university itself.   This refusal, it was claimed, amounted to "state action" because the board of regents—a state agency—had delegated policy-setting powers to the president of the university and to the student publications board.[45]

[41] Wirta v. Alameda-Contra Costa Transit District, 64 Cal.Rptr. 430, 434 P.2d 982, 984 (1967).

[42] Ibid.

[43] 64 Cal.Rptr. 430, 434 P.2d 982, 985 (1967), citing Danskin v. San Diego Unified School District, 28 Cal.2d 536, 171 P.2d 885 (1946).

[44] 64 Cal.Rptr. 430, 432, 434 P.2d 982, 984 (1967).

[45] Lee v. Board of Regents of State Colleges, 306 F.Supp. 1097 (D.C.Wis.1969).

U.S. District Judge James Doyle ruled that the *Royal Purple* should have accepted the advertisements: [46]

> Defendant's acceptance of commercial advertisements and of those public service advertisements that do not "attack an institution, group, person or product" and their rejection of editorial advertisements constitutes an impermissible form of censorship.

> There can be no doubt that defendants' restrictive advertising policy—a policy enforced under color of state law—is a denial of free speech and expression.

En route to that holding Judge Doyle found that the *Royal Purple* was indeed a newspaper, and that letters to the editor—even if accepted for publication—would not be a proper substitute for a paid advertisement. Advertisements offered certain advantages in presentation, including options for large type, photographic display, and repeated publication as "some of the modes of expression available in an editorial advertisement that might not be available in a letter to the editor." [47]

Note that the theme of state action runs through all of the above cases in which courts have listened with sympathy to demands that advertisements be accepted. That is, the agency refusing to accept an advertisement was either a transit authority funded by public money [48] or an official campus newspaper on a tax-supported campus which had advertising acceptance rules set up under delegated state authority.[49] In the absence of a strong showing of state action, however, the general rule is that advertisements may be refused by the print media.

One possible exception to that rule—and a rare and hard to prove exception at that—might be if a newspaper, for example, refused ads in some sort of an anticompetitive scheme to injure another business. One example is offered by Home Placement Service v. Providence Journal Company, in 1982. The U.S. Court of Appeal for the First Circuit ruled that a newspaper's refusal to accept classified ads from a rental referral business was held to violate antitrust provisions of the Sherman Act.

This was a special case, however. On the one hand, it is understandable why the Providence Journal didn't want to carry Homefinders' ads. Homefinders would advertise a property with

[46] Ibid., 1101, affirmed 441 F.2d 1257 (7th Cir.1971).

[47] Ibid., p. 1101.

[48] Cf. Kissinger v. New York City Transit Authority, 274 F.Supp. 438, 441 (D.C. N.Y.1967); Wirta v. Alameda-Contra Costa Transit District, 68 Cal.2d 51, 64 Cal. Rptr. 430, 434 P.2d 982, 984 (1967).

[49] Lee v. Board of Regents, 441 F.2d 1257 (7th Cir.1971), affirming 306 F.Supp. 1097 (D.C.Wis.1969).

an untraceable location, and then—once someone called the phone number listed in the ad—the person was told that the listed property was " 'no longer available, but if the prospective tenant would merely come to Homefinders' office and pay the fee of $20, other listings would be made available.' " On the other hand, the newspaper's refusal of the ads appeared a bit strange because The Providence Journal, the only metro daily in the area, itself served as a rental referral agency through its advertising columns. The Court of Appeal said that the evidence in the case " * * * indicates the simplest form of attempted strangulation of a competitor by refusal to deal." The Court said this conduct violated both Sections 1 and 2 of the Sherman Act.[50]

One other situation where an ad refusal might bring legal trouble involves contract law. If a newspaper has entered into a contract to carry advertising, and then refuses to do so, that could be a problem. That's the message from a 1982 Indiana case, Herald-Telephone v. Fatouros, a case involving a political ad which was accepted—as was payment for the ad—and then the message was refused because it might be "inflammatory." The Indiana Court of Appeals, Fourth District, said:[51]

> * * * we agree * * * that a newspaper has a right to publish or reject advertising as its judgment dictates. However, once a newspaper forms a contract to publish an advertisement, it has given up the right to publish or not publish the ad unless that right is specifically reserved or an equitable defense to [refusing] publication exists.

In more usual cases, however, the media are free to refuse ads, as in Person v. New York Post Corp., 1977. The plaintiff asked a court order to prevent the newspaper from refusing to run a "tombstone" ad on a financial matter. Instead, the federal district court declared that it is a newspaper's prerogative to accept or reject ads as it sees fit.[52]

The *Resident Participation* Case

One of the most eloquent pleas for forced access to advertising space can be found in an air pollution dispute in Denver, Colorado. The setting in Denver should be idyllic—a city ringed by the

[50] Home Placement Service v. Providence Journal, 682 F.2d 274, 276, 279 (1st Cir. 1982), 8 Med.L.Rptr. 1881, 1884, reversed in part at 739 F.2d 671 (1st Cir.1984). Although lawyers' fees ran to over $35,000, the *treble damage* award was a mere $3.

[51] Herald Telephone v. Naomi Fatouros, 431 N.E.2d 171 (Ind.App. 4th Dist.1982), 8 Med.L.Rptr. 1230m, 1231.

[52] Person v. New York Post Corporation, 427 F.Supp. 1297, affirmed 573 F.2d 1294 (2d Cir.1977).

magnificent Rocky Mountains, close to some of the American continent's most spectacular scenery. But not all was well in Denver during the late 1960's: on some days, Denver residents suffered from an eyeburning smog which would seem more at home in Los Angeles, California, roughly 950 miles away.

When word got out that Pepcol, Inc.—a subsidiary of the giant conglomerate Beatrice Foods, Inc.—was going to build a rendering plant within the city limits of Denver, a protest resulted. A citizens group calling itself Resident Participation of Denver, spurred by visions of a malodorous plant processing "dead animals, guts, and blood" and producing "disgusting" garbage,[53] attempted to place advertisements in Denver's two competing daily newspapers, the *Denver Post* and the *Rocky Mountain News*. The newspapers rejected the ads on the ground that the proposed wording called for a boycott of Beatrice Foods products, and boycott advertising is forbidden by Colorado statute.[54]

Undaunted, the Resident Participation group re-worded its advertising copy to avoid any reference to boycott, but listed each Beatrice Foods products as Meadow Gold milk, cheese, and ice cream, and Zooper Dooper fruit drinks and ice cream. The advertisement, as rewritten, included suggested letters: readers were to be asked to clip out, sign, and mail the letters, thereby protesting the rendering plant project to city and state officials. Both newspapers again refused to print the advertisements.[55]

Resident Participation then sought a court order under the First Amendment to force the newspapers to punish the advertisements. The newspapers countered with arguments that the First Amendment forbids only official abridgments of free speech and press, not merely private ones, and this was an argument the ecology group was unable to overcome. Nevertheless, Resident Participation argued strenuously to have the court consider the newspapers refusals to publish the advertisements as a kind of official or state action. The citizens' group argued: [56]

> * * * state action is present in this case because defendant newspapers enjoy a special relationship with the State of Colorado and City of Denver which involves those governments in the newspaper business and because

---

[53] Plaintiffs Exhibit "A," Resident Participation, Inc. Newsletter quoted in brief in Resident Participation of Denver, Inc. v. Love, 322 F.Supp. 1100 (D.C.Colo.1971). The authors wish to thank Thomas A Stacey, graduate student in journalism at the University of Wisconsin-Madison, for his assistance.

[54] Colo.Rev.Stat.Ann. § 80–11–12.

[55] Resident Participation of Denver, Inc. v. Love, 322 F.Supp. 1100, 1101 (D.C. Colo.1971).

[56] Ibid., 1102.

the papers "enjoy monopoly control in an area of vital public concern."

Resident Participation also contended that the state and city are involved in the newspaper business because of sections of the Colorado Revised Statutes which require that legal notices be published in newspapers of general circulation.[57] Other provisions which were said to make newspapers a public business included a statute which exempts editors and reporters from jury service,[58] and a Denver ordinance which allows newspaper vending machines on public property, including sidewalks.[59]

A three-judge federal district court rejected these arguments with dispatch, saying it could find nothing "remotely suggesting that these measures are sufficient to justify labeling the newspapers conduct state action." [60] Chief Circuit Judge Alfred A. Arraj said that where private conduct is concerned, there has to be great justification for concluding that the private party serves as an alter ego for government, either because officialdom has in some important way become involved with the private party, or because the private party performs a function of a governmental nature. Circuit Judge Arraj discussed some problems of access to the media for advertisers, and how the law should be applied to such problems.[61]

> Plaintiffs have made no allegations which would suggest a marriage among these parties, and the historic function of newspapers, like the pamphlets of a prior day, has been to oppose government, to be its critic not its accomplice. While few newspapers may live up to that idea, plaintiffs do not allege that either the Rocky Mountain News or Denver Post is the lackey of a city or state administration or in any other way in the grip of official power.

> * * *

> Our conclusion that newspapers' conduct cannot be considered state action agrees with the conclusion arrived at by the Seventh Circuit Court of Appeals in Chicago Joint Board, Amalgamated Clothing Workers of America, AFL–CIO v. Chicago Tribune Co., 435 F.2d 470 (7th Cir. 1970), the only other case we have discovered which raises issues identical to those presented in this litigation.

[57] Colorado Rev.Stat.Ann. §§ 49–10–3, 49–8–1, 49–22–5, 49–22–11 (1963).

[58] Colo.Rev.Stat.Ann. § 7801–3 (1963).

[59] Denver Municipal Code, §§ 339G, 334.1–2.

[60] 322 F.Supp. 1100, 1103 (D.C.Colo.1971).

[61] 322 F.Supp. 1100, 1105 (D.C.Colo.1971).

As the Resident Participation case showed, general circulation newspapers cannot be compelled to accept and publish controversial advertisements. Some newspapers, however, publish controversial political advertisements as a matter of responsibility to the public. In the spring of 1972, for example, The New York Times published two advertisements which drew considerable protest from readers. The first advertisement, signed by a group of citizens calling themselves "The National Committee for Impeachment," demanded the removal from office of President Richard M. Nixon, alleging violations of law and the Constitution in his prosecution of the Vietnam war. A second advertisement, an open letter to President Nixon signed by Norman F. Dacey, inveighed against the President for a Middle East policy termed "blind support" for Israel.[62]

Readers responded to these advertisements with hundreds of letters, and many of those letters criticized *The Times* for publishing such emotionally loaded and politically heated ads, opinions with which neither *The Times*—nor a large part of its readership agreed. That criticism of *The Times* was expressed so frequently and with such obvious sincerity that *The Times* published an editorial, "Freedom to Advertise," stating the principles which guide The Times in accepting controversial advertising on topics of political or social importance. The editorial declared: [63]

* * *

As we see it, the issue goes to the very heart of the freedom and responsibility of the press. *The Times* believes it has an obligation to afford maximum reasonable opportunity to the public to express its views, however much opposed to our own, through various outlets in this newspaper including the advertising columns.

It has long been held by American courts that a newspaper or magazine is a private enterprise, and that it may choose to omit certain news items or to refuse certain advertising. In recent years, and in part because of the thrust given to a "new right of access" by Professor Jerome Barron, the old "right to refuse ads" has undergone considerable challenge. Nevertheless, this generalization may still be made: unless the publication or agency which is to carry an advertisement is clearly some sort of a public entity because of some kind of "state action," an advertisement lawfully may be refused.

Take the case of a film exhibitor who was angered because the *Los Angeles Times* altered advertising copy for a movie, The Killing of Sister George, slightly changing a drawing of a female

---

[62] See New York Times, May 31 and June 6, 1972.

[63] New York Times, June 16, 1972. © 1972 by The New York Times Company.

figure and omitting a reference to "deviate sexual conduct". *The Times,* by virtue of its enormous advertising revenues, was said by the film distributor to have attained a "substantial monopoly in Southern California." It was further argued that the *Times's* "semi-monopoly and quasi-public position" amounted to state action. The United States Court of Appeals for the 9th Circuit rejected the film distributors arguments, saying: "Unlike broadcasting, the publication of a newspaper is not a government conferred privilege. As we have said, the press and the government have had a history of disassociation." [64]

The right to refuse ads seems to be holding solidly into the late 1980s.

SEC. 91. BROADCAST ADVERTISING AND THE FAIRNESS DOCTRINE

The Supreme Court has limited the Fairness Doctrine, confirming in broadcasters a right to refuse editorial advertising on public issues such as war and politics. Product ads do not trigger the Fairness Doctrine.

Fred Friendly once referred to the Federal Communications Commission (FCC) as the "Leaning Tower of Jell-O." Whether or not one regards the FCC as being *that* wishy-washy, it has indeed had a curious career in attempting to apply (and at times, *not* to apply) the fairness doctrine to broadcast advertising. The origins and application of the fairness doctrine are discussed in general terms in Sections 76 and 77 and the preceding chapter. Also, as noted in Section 78, the fairness doctrine applies to commercials devoted in an obvious and meaningful way to the discussion of public issues, but not to ordinary product commercials.

To basics. A brief quote from Public Media Center v. FCC (1978) is offered as a "refresher" on the outlines of the fairness doctrine: [65]

> The fairness doctrine imposes two duties on a broadcaster: (1) it must present coverage of issues of public importance, and (2) such programming must fairly reflect differing viewpoints on controversial issues. Columbia Broadcasting System, Inc. v. Democratic National Committee, 412 U.S. 94, 111, 93 S.Ct. 2080, 2090 (1973); Red Lion Broadcasting Co. v. FCC, 395 U.S. 367, 377, 89 S.Ct. 1794, 1799–1800 (1969). A broadcaster has great editorial

---

[64] Associates and Aldrich Co. v. Times Mirror Co., 440 F.2d 133, 136 (9th Cir. 1971); see also Adult Film Ass'n of America v. Times Mirror Co., 3 Med.L.Rptr. 2292, Civil Action No. C217216 (L.A.Cty.Sup.Ct.1978), upholding a newspaper's right to refuse ads.

[65] Public Media Center v. FCC, 587 F.2d 1322, 1326 (D.C.Cir.1978).

freedom in implementing the fairness doctrine, and will violate it only when its actions and decisions have been unreasonable or in bad faith.

Until 1967, the Fairness Doctrine was applied only to the airing of major social and political issues. But then, as noted in Section 82 earlier in this chapter, attorney John Banzhaf III wrote a letter to the FCC urging extension of the Fairness Doctrine to cigarette commercials.[66] The FCC ruled that the Fairness Doctrine was applicable.[67] Thereafter, licensees who broadcast cigarette commercials were forced to make free time available for messages warning of the dangers of smoking.[68] However, a majority of the FCC wanted to view cigarettes as a unique product raising issues; the FCC did not want to stretch the Fairness Doctrine to open other commercial advertising channels.

A test case came when an environmental protection organization—Friends of the Earth—asked the FCC for time under the Fairness Doctrine to respond to commercials for cars with large engines, cars which created sizable air pollution problems. The FCC had wanted to ban cigarette advertising, but it was not similarly committed to curtailing advertising for large-engined automobiles, nor did it want "answers" being broadcast to such ads. A majority of the FCC ruled that the Fairness Doctrine did not apply to such auto advertising, but Friends of the Earth appealed. The Circuit Court of Appeals for the District of Columbia agreed with the environmentalists, finding an exact parallel between the dangers of cigarette advertising and the dangers of advertising big autos: [69]

The Court of Appeals then sent the *Friends of the Earth* case back to the FCC to determine whether the broadcasting station had met fairness doctrine obligations through other programming dealing with environmental concerns.

[66] "Fairness Freedom and Cigarette Advertising, A Defense of the Federal Trade Commission," Columbia Law Review (1967) pp. 1470–1489; Norman P. Leventhal, "Caution: Cigarette Commercials May Be Hazardous to Your License—the New Aspect of Fairness," Federal Communications Bar Journal 22:1 (1968) pp. 55–124, at pp. 92–93.

[67] CBS–TV Case, 9 Pike & Fischer Radio Regulations 2d 1423 (1967). Cigarette advertising was banned from television by Congress, effective January 2, 1971. See 15 U.S.C.A. Section 1335.

[68] Ira Mark Ellman, "And Now a Word Against Our Sponsor: Extending the Fairness Doctrine to Advertising," 60 California Law Review No. 4 (June, 1972), p. 1423.

[69] Friends of the Earth v. FCC, 146 U.S.App.D.C. 88, 449 F.2d 1164, 1169 (1971), reversing and remanding 24 F.C.C.2d 743 (1970). See also a case involving environmentalists' efforts to answer Standard Oil of New Jersey ads pushing construction of a pipeline across the Alaskan wilderness; In re Wilderness Society, 30 F.C.C.2d 643, 729 (1971). The FCC ruled that licensees must insure that such advertisements were countered or "balanced" by material opposing construction of the pipeline.

Knowing an impenetrable thicket when it saw one, the FCC veered away from treating commercials for *products* as matters which would trigger the fairness doctrine. To say that the FCC fled from the basic concept of the *Banzhaf* decision (see sec. 83) is entirely accurate. The Commission's retreat was spelled out in its 1974 Fairness Report, announcing a new direction in its policy on the fairness doctrine and commercial advertising.[70] This report, as Steven J. Simmons has noted, categorized commercials into three areas: (1) *editorial advertising* overtly stating a political or social issue; (2) *institutional advertising*—such as Esso Corporation's subtle advocacy of construction of the trans-Alaska Pipeline, and (3) *commercial advertising*—selling of products or services.[71]

Editorial Advertising

If a station airs an advertisement which is a " 'direct and substantial commentary on important public issues' " that is simply an editorial paid for by a sponsor. As such, under the FCC's 1974 Fairness Report, the political or social message aired in the commercial would have to be counter-balanced by differing viewpoints in a station's overall programming. Otherwise, a complaint for time to respond to that ad under the fairness doctrine would be successful.

On the other hand, a broadcast licensee is not compelled to sell time for editorial advertisements if it chooses not to do so. Back in 1973, the Supreme Court ruled that broadcasters are not obligated to accept paid ads dealing with controversial political or social issues. By a 7–2 vote, the Court constructed a right to refuse ads for broadcasters which is somewhat similar to the print media's "right to refuse service."[72] This case, Columbia Broadcasting System, Inc. v. Democratic National Committee, dealt with the efforts of a political party and of an anti-war group to get air time for their respective viewpoints.[73] This decision is important, because it blunted a number of efforts to have courts construct a "right of access" under the First Amendment and under the FCC's fairness doctrine. Under such a right of access, broadcasters could have been forced to accept paid commercials dealing with public issues.

This case started when Business Executives' Move for a Vietnam Peace (BEM) filed a complaint with the Federal Communica-

[70] 48 F.C.C.2d 1, 39 Fed.Reg. 26372 (1974).

[71] For a clear and thorough discussion of these matters, see Steven J. Simmons, The Fairness Doctrine and the Media (Berkeley: University of California Press, 1978), pp. 113–131.

[72] See Section 90 of this chapter, "The Right to Refuse Service."

[73] 412 U.S. 94, 93 S.Ct. 2080 (1973).

tions Commission in January, 1970. BEM argued that radio station WTOP, Washington, D.C., had violated the fairness doctrine by refusing to sell time to broadcast a series of one-minute spot announcements against the Vietnam conflict. WTOP refused, saying it already had presented full and fair coverage on important public issues, including the war and the viewpoints of U.S. policy in dealing with Southeast Asia.

Four months later, the Democratic National Committee (DNC) sought a declaratory ruling on this statement:[74]

> That under the First Amendment to the Constitution and the Communications Act, a broadcaster may not, as a general policy, refuse to sell time to responsible entities, such as DNC, for the solicitation of funds and for comment on public issues.

After reviewing the history of the fairness doctrine, and of the Communications Act of 1934—as well as the problems inherent in administering a right of access—the Commission rejected the demands of both DNC and BEM.[75] The Court of Appeals for the District of Columbia reversed the FCC and declared that BEM and DNC should not be rendered voiceless by a blanket prohibition against public interest advertising. Writing for a 2–1 court, Judge J. Skelly Wright said: [76]

> We hold specifically that a flat ban on paid public issue announcements is in violation of the First Amendment, at least when other sorts of paid announcements are accepted. We do not hold, however, that the planned announcements of the petitioners—or, for that matter, of any other particular applicant for air time—must necessarily be accepted by broadcast licensees. Rather, we confine ourselves to invalidating the flat ban alone, leaving it up to licensees and to the Commission to develop and administer reasonable procedures * * *.

Judge Wright's vigorous opinion, however, did not carry the day for BEM and DNC when the case reached the Supreme Court. That Court voted against the BEM–DNC position by a margin of 7 to 2. Chief Justice Burger's plurality opinion—he had Justices Rehnquist and Stewart with him—concluded that broadcast licensees were not common carriers. He compared a newspaper's freedom to that of a broadcast licensee, finding that a broadcaster has a large measure of freedom, but not as much as that exercised

---

[74] 412 U.S. 94, 93 S.Ct. 2080, 2084 (1973).

[75] 412 U.S. 94, 93 S.Ct. 2080, 2085 (1973).

[76] Business Executives Move for Vietnam Peace v. FCC, Democratic National Committee v. FCC, 450 F.2d 642 (D.C.Cir.1971), overturning Business Executives, 24 F.C.C.2d 242 (1970), and Democratic National Committee, 25 F.C.C.2d 216 (1970).

by a newspaper. Broadcasters are supervised—and periodically licensed—by the FCC, which must "oversee without censoring." [77] Even so, government control over licensees is not sufficiently close to make them "common carriers" or "public utilities." Burger wrote: [78]

> If the Fairness Doctrine were applied to editorial advertising, there is also the substantial danger that the effective operation of that doctrine would be jeopardized. To minimize financial hardship and to comply fully with its public responsibilities, a broadcaster might well be forced to make regular programming time available to those holding a view different from that expressed in an editorial advertisement * * *. The result would be a further erosion of the journalistic discretion of broadcasters * * *.
>
>   *   *   *
>
> For better or worse, editing is what editors are for, and editing is selection and choice of material. That editors—newspaper or broadcast—can and do abuse this power is beyond doubt, but that is not reason to deny the discretion Congress provided. Calculated risks of abuse are taken in order to preserve higher values.

The concurring and dissenting opinions galloped off in several directions. Justice William O. Douglas's concurrence declared that TV and radio stand in the same protected position under the First Amendment as newspapers and magazines.[79] And Douglas, along with Justice Stewart, had nasty things to say about the "right of access" to the media, arguing that if government can *require* publication, then freedom of the press would be gone. Justices Brennan and Marshall, on the other hand, dissented to the effect that if time could not be purchased for the airing of controversial political and social viewpoints, then broadcasting will continue to be filled with little but bland, noncontroversial mediocrities.

In sum, then, if a broadcast station accepts an editorial advertisement, that advertisement could trigger a successful fairness doctrine complaint. The point is, however, that a station does *not* have to accept such advertising or sell air time unless the request for time is made by candidates for Federal office.

In the "Carter-Mondale" case decided July 1, 1981, the Supreme Court voted 6–3 that television stations must sell "reasonable" amounts of air time when it is requested by candidates for

[77] 414 U.S. 94, 93 S.Ct. 2080, 2094 (1973).

[78] 412 U.S. 94, 93 S.Ct. 2080, 2096–2097 (1973).

[79] 412 U.S. 94, 93 S.Ct. 2080, 2109 (1973).

Federal office. This case arose in October, 1979, when the Carter-Mondale Presidential Committee requested the ABC, NBC and CBS networks to provide time for a 30-minute program between 8 p.m. and 10:30 p.m. on the 4th through the 7th of December, 1979. The Committee wished to present a documentary about the achievements of Carter's administration, plus a formal announcement of his candidacy. The networks refused this request.

The Federal Communications Commission, however, ruled 4–3 that this refusal violated Section 312(a)(7) of the Communications Act of 1934. That section provides that station licenses may be revoked for refusing to allow reasonable access to or permit purchase of reasonable amounts of time over a broadcasting station by a legally qualified candidate for Federal office.[80] This decision will increase the ability of Presidential candidates to try to set the themes of their campaigns early through television. In addition, as the New York Times noted this is the first time the Court has given any group an affirmative right of access to any medium.[81]

Institutional Advertising

As Steven J. Simmons has written in his important study of the fairness doctrine, "The Commission refers to *National Broadcasting* for an example of advertising that is not so overt. Esso's advertisements in that case 'did not explicitly mention that pipeline, but they did present what could be termed arguments in support of its construction.' "[82] The *National Broadcasting* case arose when two environmental groups contended to the FCC that ESSO ads broadcast by NBC spoke to the issue of a need for rapid development of Alaskan oil fields and the need for a pipeline to move the oil safely, without harming the Alaskan environment. Those commercials, being aired at a time when construction of the Alaskan pipeline was a hot issue, were held by the FCC to be more than noncontroversial institutional ads: they were grounds for a response under the fairness doctrine.[83]

Also, consider the case of Public Media Center v. FCC.[84] There, a public interest group filed a public interest complaint against sixteen California radio stations, claiming the stations

[80] CBS, Inc. v. Federal Communications Commission, 453 U.S. 367, 101 S.Ct. 2813 (1981), affirming 629 F.2d 1 (D.C.Cir.1980).

[81] The New York Times, July 2, 1981, p. 1. See also Miami Herald Pub. Co. v. Tornillo, 418 U.S. 241, 94 S.Ct. 2831 (1974), discussed at pp. 12–14 in Chapter 1.

[82] Simmons, op. cit., p. 114.

[83] 30 F.C.C.2d 643 (1971), discussed in Simmons, pp. 106–107, 114.

[84] 587 F.2d 1322 (D.C.Cir.1978).

were not meeting their obligations to present both sides of the controversy surrounding construction of nuclear power plants. Specifically, the Public Media Center charged that the stations were broadcasting advertisements for the Pacific Gas & Electric Co. (PG & E) which touted the benefits of nuclear energy but failed to present views of those opposed to such development.

The Commission held that eight of the radio stations had violated the Fairness Doctrine. A U.S. Court of Appeals, however, said that it could not affirm an FCC order which did not clearly and explicitly articulate the standards applied to decide which licensees violated the fairness doctrine and which did not. Therefore, the court sent the matter back to the FCC for clarification. The point here is that ads can express controversial issues of public importance, and that such ads should be counterbalanced by overall programming which gives citizens other points of view on such issues.[85]

Product Advertisements

The FCC's 1974 Fairness Report scrambled away from the implications of the Banzhaf matter discussed earlier in this section. The Commission simply changed its mind. It declared that in the future, product ads would not start fairness doctrine responses. Why? Because—the FCC decided in 1974—product ads are simple discussions of the good points of a commodity and do not make any significant contribution to public discourse. In the future, application of the fairness doctrine would run only to commercials involved meaningfully in "the discussion of public issues." [86]

SEC. 92. ADVERTISING AND THE CONSTITUTION

Beginning in 1975, some commercial advertising began to receive protection under the First Amendment.

Commercial speech customarily has been a poor stepchild where the First Amendment is concerned. Advertising, over the years, has been denied freedoms of speech and press which the courts have granted to unconventional religious minorities,[87] to persons accused of blasphemy,[88] to free-love advocates,[89] and to

[85] Ibid.

[86] 48 F.C.C.2d 1, 26 (1974).

[87] Minersville School District v. Gobitis, 310 U.S. 586, 60 S.Ct. 1010 (1940).

[88] Burstyn v. Wilson, 343 U.S. 495, 72 S.Ct. 777 (1952).

[89] Kingsley Pictures Corp. v. Regents, 360 U.S. 684, 688–689, 79 S.Ct. 1362, 1365 (1959).

persons sued for defaming a public official or public figure.[90] During the 1970s, however, a number of court rulings held that just because a message is disseminated in the form of commercial advertising does not withdraw First Amendment protection.[91]

The leading case in denying First Amendment protection to advertising is the 1942 Supreme Court decision in Valentine v. Chrestensen. F.J. Chrestensen was incensed when New York City officials refused to allow him to distribute handbills advertising the exhibit of a former U.S. submarine which Chrestensen owned. Police Commissioner Lewis J. Valentine told Chrestensen that he could not distribute handbills asking people to visit the submarine, where an admission fee would be charged. Meanwhile, Chrestensen's submarine was moored at a pier in the East River. No matter, said Police Commissioner Valentine. New York City's Sanitary Code forbade distribution of commercial and business advertising matter in the streets.[92]

Chrestensen then altered his handbill. One side consisted of commercial advertising (with the deletion of the statement about the admission fee). The other side was a protest against an action of the City Dock Department refusing Chrestensen wharfage for his submarine. Police officials told Chrestensen that he could distribute a handbill criticizing the City Dock Department, but that the commercial advertising would have to go. Two years later, in 1942, Mr. Justice Owen J. Roberts spoke for a unanimous Supreme Court in saying that Chrestensen's advertising was not entitled to Constitutional protection.[93]

> This court has unequivocally held that the streets are proper places for the exercises of the freedom of communicating information and disseminating opinion and that, though the states and municipalities may appropriately regulate the privilege in the public interest, they may not unduly burden or proscribe its employment in these public thoroughfares. We are equally clear that the Constitution imposes no such restraint on government as respects purely commercial advertising.

[90] See New York Times v. Sullivan, 376 U.S. 254, 84 S.Ct. 710 (1964) and subsequent cases, including Rosenblatt v. Baer, 383 U.S. 75, 86 S.Ct. 669 (1966); Curtis Publishing Co. v. Butts, Associated Press v. Edwin A. Walker, 388 U.S. 130, 87 S.Ct. 1975 (1967), and St. Amant v. Thompson, 390 U.S. 727, 88 S.Ct. 1323 (1968).

[91] See, e.g., Bigelow v. Virginia, 421 U.S. 809, 95 S.Ct. 2222 (1975); Virginia State Board of Pharmacy v. Virginia Citizens Council, Inc., 425 U.S. 748, 96 S.Ct. 1817 (1976).

[92] 316 U.S. 52, 62 S.Ct. 920 (1942).

[93] 316 U.S. 52, 54, 62 S.Ct. 920, 921 (1942).

The Court's decision in Valentine v. Chrestensen was brief, amounting to only five pages in the official *United States Reports.* Mr. Justice Roberts' statement that commercial advertising is not entitled to Constitutional protections was slipped into the opinion unsupported by a number of relevant cases which he might have cited.[94]

In 1959, Mr. Justice Douglas authored a concurring opinion in Cammarano v. United States in which he expressed concern over the rule laid down in Valentine v. Chrestensen. William R. Cammarano and his wife owned an interest in a beer distributorship in Washington state. They had paid nearly $900 into a trust fund which with other contributions, ultimately added up to over $50,000. This trust fund was being collected by persons opposed to a 1948 ballot measure which would have placed all wine and beer sales in Washington exclusively in the hands of the State. The trust fund was used for advertising which urged, and may well have helped secure, defeat of the ballot measure.

The Cammaranos sued the Department of Internal Revenue because they were not allowed to deduct their contribution to the trust fund as a "business expense." Writing for the Supreme Court, Justice John Marshall Harlan upheld a finding against the Cammaranos' contentions. He wrote: [95]

> Nondiscriminatory denial of deduction from gross income to sums expended to promote or defeat legislation is plainly not " 'aimed at the suppression of dangerous ideas.' " Rather, it appears to us that since purchased publicity can influence the fate of legislation which will affect, directly or indirectly, all in the community, everyone in the community should stand on the same footing as regards its purchase so far as the Treasury of the United States is concerned.

Although Mr. Justice Douglas concurred in the Court's decision, he expressed grave worries about the rule of Valentine v. Chrestensen that business advertisements and commercial matters do not enjoy the protection of the First Amendment as made applicable to the States by the Fourteenth. Douglas wrote: [96]

---

[94] See Mr. Justice William O. Douglas's concurring opinion in Cammarano v. United States, 358 U.S. 498, 513–515, 79 S.Ct. 524, 533–535 (1959), which listed two cases prior to the Chrestensen case which approved broad control over commercial advertising: Fifth Avenue Coach Co. v. New York, 221 U.S. 467, 31 S.Ct. 709 (1911), and Packer Corp. v. Utah, 285 U.S. 105, 52 S.Ct. 273 (1932). In the latter case, Justice Douglas noted, the First Amendment problem was never raised.

[95] 358 U.S. 498, 79 S.Ct. 533 (1959).

[96] 358 U.S. 498, 513–515, 79 S.Ct. 524, 533–535 (1959).

The ruling [in Valentine v. Chrestensen] was casual, almost offhand. And it has not survived reflection. That "freedom of speech or of the press," directly guaranteed against encroachment by the Federal Government and safeguarded against state action by the Due Process Clause of the Fourteenth Amendment, is not in terms or by implication confined to discourse of a particular kind of nature. It has often been stressed as essential to the exposition and exchange of political ideas, to the expression of philosophical attitudes, to the flowering of the letters. Important as the First Amendment is to all those cultural ends, it has not been restricted to them. Individual or group protests against actions which results in monetary injuries are certainly not beyond the reach of the First Amendment * * *. A protest against government action that affects a business occupies as high a place.

* * *

* * * I find it impossible to say that the owners of the present business who were fighting for their lives in opposing these initiative measures were not exercising First Amendment rights.

* * *

The landmark 1964 libel decision of the Supreme Court of the United States in New York Times v. Sullivan did not endorse completely Justice Douglas's demand for a governmental policy of "hands off" where expression is involved. Nevertheless, the Court did grant constitutional protection for advertisements which deal with important or social matters. The *Sullivan* case, discussed fully in libel chapters earlier in this book, carefully distinguished the kind of advertising involved in the Valentine v. Chrestensen case from the advertising involved in New York Times v. Sullivan. It had been contended in the *Sullivan* case that "the constitutional guarantees of freedom of speech and of the press are inapplicable * * * at least so far as the Times is concerned, because the allegedly libelous statements were published as part of a paid, 'commercial' advertisement." The Court rejected this argument, saying: [97]

The New York Court of Appeals has since declared unconstitutional the New York City ordinance which had been upheld by the Supreme Court in Valentine v. Chrestensen. See New York v. Remeny, 40 N.Y.2d 527, 387 N.Y.S.2d 415, 355 N.E.2d 375 (1976), citing Virginia State Board of Pharmacy v. Virginia Citizens Consumer Council, Inc., 425 U.S. 748, 96 S.Ct. 1817 (1976).

[97] New York Times Co. v. Sullivan, 376 U.S. 254, 265–266, 84 S.Ct. 710, 718 (1964).

The argument relies on Valentine v. Chrestensen * * * where the Court held that a city ordinance forbidding street distribution of commercial and business advertising matter did not abridge the First Amendment freedoms, even as applied to a handbill having a commercial message on one side but a protest against certain official action on the other. The reliance is wholly misplaced. * * *

The publication here [in New York Times v. Sullivan] was not a "commercial" advertisement in the sense in which the word was used in *Chrestensen.* It communicated information, expressed opinion, recited grievances, protested claimed abuses, and sought financial support on behalf of a [civil rights] movement whose existence and objectives are matters of the highest public interest and concern. * * * That the Times was paid for publishing the advertisement is as immaterial in this connection as is the fact that newspapers and books are sold. * * * Any other conclusion would discourage newspapers from carrying "editorial advertisements" of this type, and so might shut off an important outlet for the promulgation of information and ideas by persons who do not themselves have access to publishing facilities—who wish to exercise their freedom of speech even though they are not members of the press. * * * The effect would be to shackle the First Amendment in its attempt to secure "the widest possible dissemination of information from diverse and antagonistic sources." To avoid placing such a handicap upon the freedoms of expression, we hold that if the allegedly libelous statements would otherwise be constitutionally protected * * * they do not forfeit that protection because they were published in the form of a paid advertisement.

What advertising, then, was protected by the First Amendment after Times v. Sullivan (1964)? Not all advertising, said the Supreme Court in Pittsburgh Press Co. v. Pittsburgh Commission on Human Relations (1973). A Pittsburgh ordinance empowered the city's human relations commission to issue cease and desist orders against discriminatory hiring practices. The Pittsburgh Press ran "Help Wanted" ads in columns labeled "Jobs—Male Interest," and "Jobs—Female Interest." The city commission issued a cease and desist order.[98]

---

[98] 413 U.S. 376, 93 S.Ct. 2553, 2556 (1973).

Arguing for the Pittsburgh Press, attorneys contended that the order against the newspaper violated the First Amendment because it tampered with the newspaper's editorial judgment in accepting and placing ads. The newspaper, then, was told that it could not have greater protection than the firms placing advertisements; the firms were forbidden to discriminate, and the newspaper could not run discriminatory ads. Writing for the Court, Justice Lewis Powell said discrimination in employment is illegal commercial activity under the city's ordinance. "We have no doubt that a newspaper constitutionally could be forbidden to publish a want ad proposing a sale of narcotics or soliciting prostitutes." The Court's five-member majority added: [99]

> * * * [A]ny First Amendment interest which might be served by advertising an ordinary commercial proposal and which arguably might outweigh the governmental interest supporting the regulation is altogether absent when the commercial activity itself is illegal and the restriction on advertising is incidental to a valid limitation on economic activity.

Dissenting in *Pittsburgh Press,* Chief Justice Burger declared that the cease and desist order was in fact prior restraint on publication, and Justice Stewart said that no court has the power to tell a newspaper, before publication, what it can print and what it cannot.[1]

It should be remembered that the Court, in New York Times v. Sullivan, drew a distinction between "commercial" advertising which attempted to sell products or services and other kinds of expression.[2] This distinction, however, was too oversimplified for the mid-1970s. Some products or services—by their very nature—may be matters of public debate or controversy, and advertisements for those products or services may have the characteristics and importance of political speech. A 1975 Virginia case involving advertising about the availability and legality of abortions in New York—the case called Bigelow v. Virginia—has shown that "commercial speech" does have at least some constitutional protection.

An advertisement was published in The Virginia Weekly, a newspaper which focuses its coverage on the University of Virginia campus there. Jeffrey C. Bigelow was a director of and the managing editor of the newspaper which published the following advertisement on February 7, 1971: [3]

[99] 413 U.S. 376, 93 S.Ct. 2553, 2560 (1973).

[1] 413 U.S. 376, 93 S.Ct. 2553, 2563 (1973).

[2] New York Times Co. v. Sullivan, 376 U.S. 254, 84 S.Ct. 710 (1964).

[3] Bigelow v. Virginia, 421 U.S. 809, 95 S.Ct. 2222, 2227 (1975).

"UNWANTED PREGNANCY
LET US HELP YOU
Abortions are now legal in New York
There are no residency requirements.
FOR IMMEDIATE PLACEMENT IN
ACCREDITED HOSPITALS AND
CLINICS AT LOW COST
Contact
WOMAN'S PAVILION
515 Madison Avenue
New York, N.Y. 10022
or call any time
(212) 371–6670 or (212) 371–6550
AVAILABLE 7 DAYS A WEEK
STRICTLY CONFIDENTIAL. We will
make all arrangements for you and help
you with information and counseling."

On May 13, 1971, Bigelow was charged with violating a section of the Virginia Code which read: [4] "If any person, by publication, lecture, advertisement, or by the sale or circulation of any publication, or in any other manner, encourage or prompt the procuring of abortion or miscarriage, he shall be guilty of a misdemeanor."

Bigelow was tried and convicted by a Virginia Court, and was sentenced to pay a $500 fine, with $350 suspended "conditioned upon no further violation" of the statute.[5] The Supreme Court of Virginia affirmed Bigelow's conviction by a vote of 4–2,[6] declaring that because the advertisement involved was a "commercial advertisement," Bigelow's First Amendment claim was not valid. Such an advertisement, said the Virginia Supreme Court, " 'may be constitutionally prohibited by the state, particularly where, as here, the advertising relates to the medical-health field.' " [7]

Writing for the seven-member majority of the Court, Justice Blackmun distinguished the Virginia case from *Chrestensen*.[8] He said that the handbill advertisement involved in *Chrestensen* did

[4] Code Va.1950, § 18.1–63, quoted at 421 U.S. 809, 815, 95 S.Ct. 2222, 2228 (1975). That statute was amended by Va.Acts, 1972, c. 725, and the amended statute is quoted in Bigelow's majority opinion, at footnote 99. Justice Blackmun, writing for the Court, refused to take up the question of "overbreadth" of the statute in 1971, because the 1972 statutory amendment meant that "the issue of overbreadth has become moot for the future." 421 U.S. 809, 818, 95 S.Ct. 2222, 2230 (1975).

[5] 421 U.S. 809, 814, 95 S.Ct. 2222, 2228 (1975).

[6] 213 Va. 191, 191 S.E.2d 173 (1972).

[7] 421 U.S. 809, 814, 95 S.Ct. 2222, 2229 (1975), quoting 213 Va. 191, 193–195, 191 S.E.2d at 174–176 (1972).

[8] Valentine v. Chrestensen, 316 U.S. 52, 62 S.Ct. 920 (1942).

no more than propose a purely commercial transaction, while The Virginia Weekly's advertisement about abortions "contained factual material of clear 'public interest.'"   Justice Blackmun added: [9]

> Viewed in its entirety, the advertisement conveyed information of potential interest and value to a diverse audience—not only to readers possibly in need of the services offered, but also to those with a general curiosity about, or general interest in, the subject matter or the law of another State and its development, and to readers seeking reform in Virginia.

The very existence of the Women's Pavilion in New York City was "not unnewsworthy" and also pertained to constitutional privacy interests.[10]   Virginia, moreover, had no authority to regulate services offered in New York.   A State, Justice Blackmun wrote, "may not * * * bar a citizen of another State from disseminating information about an activity that is legal in that State."   Although advertising "may be subject to reasonable regulation that serves a legitimate public interest," some commercial speech is still worthy of constitutional protection.[11]   Advertising is not stripped of all First Amendment protection: "The relationship of speech to the marketplace of products or services does not make it valueless in the marketplace of ideas."   Justice Blackmun continued,[12]

> — a court may not escape the task of assessing the First Amendment interest at stake and weighing it against the public interest allegedly served by the regulation.   The diverse motives, means, and messages of advertising may make speech "commercial" in widely varying degrees. We need not decide here the extent to which constitutional protection is afforded commercial advertising under all circumstances and in the face of all kinds of regulation.

Justice Blackmun and a majority of the Court, concluded, however, that Virginia courts erred in assuming that advertising was entitled to no First Amendment protection.[13]   What Justice Blackmun's majority opinion called for, of course, is a balancing of interests—with the courts, and most especially the Supreme Court—to have final say in deciding what is "merely" commercial speech and what is advertising which is "newsworthy" or anointed

[9] 421 U.S. 809, 822, 95 S.Ct. 2222, 2233 (1975).

[10] 421 U.S. 809, 821, 95 S.Ct. 2222, 2233 (1975), citing Roe v. Wade, 410 U.S. 113, 95 S.Ct. 705 (1973), and Doe v. Bolton, 410 U.S. 179, 93 S.Ct. 739 (1973).

[11] 421 U.S. 809, 826, 95 S.Ct. 2222, 2234, 2235 (1975).

[12] 421 U.S. 809, 826, 95 S.Ct. 2222, 2235 (1975).

[13] 421 U.S. 809, 825, 95 S.Ct. 2222, 2234 (1975).

with the "public interest." More custard pies, in other words, to be nailed to more walls.

Virginia State Board of Pharmacy v. Virginia Citizens Consumer Council, Inc. (1976)

What Bigelow v. Virginia started, the Virginia State Board of Pharmacy case continued when it was decided in May of 1976.[14] A Virginia statute forbade the "advertising of the price for any prescription drug," and was challenged in a lawsuit.[15] The plaintiffs in *Pharmacy* were two non-profit organizations and a Virginia citizen who had to take prescription drugs on a daily basis. These people claimed that the First Amendment entitled users of prescription drugs to receive information from pharmacists—through advertisements or other promotional means—about the price of such drugs.[16]

Writing for a 7–1 majority of the Supreme Court Justice Blackmun said that information about drug prices may be of value to the public. He noted, for example, that the litigants on both sides of this lawsuit had stipulated that there was a striking variance in the price of prescription drugs: " * * * in the Newport News-Hampton area the cost of tetracycline ranges from $1.20 to $9.00, a difference of 650%." [17]

> Last term, in Bigelow v. Virginia, 421 U.S. 809, 95 S.Ct. 2222 (1975), the notion of unprotected "commercial speech" all but passed from the scene. * * * We rejected the contention that the publication was unprotected because it was commercial. *Chrestensen's* continued validity was questioned, and its holding was described as "distinctly a limited one" that merely upheld "a reasonable regulation of the manner in which commercial advertising could be distributed." * * * [W]e observed that the "relationship of speech to the marketplace of products or services does not make it valueless in the marketplace of ideas." 421 U.S. 809, 826–827, 95 S.Ct., at 2235 (1975). * * * We concluded that "the Virginia courts erred in their assumption that advertising, as such, was entitled to no First Amendment protection * * *".

* * *

[14] Virginia State Board of Pharmacy v. Virginia Citizens Council, Inc., 425 U.S. 748, 96 S.Ct. 1817 (1976).

[15] 425 U.S. 748, 752, 96 S.Ct. 1817, 1820–21 (1976), citing Code Va.1974, § 54–524.35.

[16] 425 U.S. 748, 754, 96 S.Ct. 1817, 1821 (1976).

[17] 425 U.S. 748, 754, 96 S.Ct. 1817, 1821 (1976).

Here, in contrast, the question whether there is a First Amendment exception for 'commercial speech' is squarely before us. Our pharmacist does not wish to editorialize on any subject, cultural, philosophical, or political. He does not wish to report any particularly newsworthy fact, or to make generalized observations even about commercial matters. The "idea" he wishes to communicate is simply this: "I will sell you the X prescription drug at the Y price." Our question, then, is whether this communication is wholly outside the protection of the First Amendment.[18]

The Supreme Court of the United States declared that the consumer had a great interest in the free flow of commercial information—perhaps a greater interest than in the day's most important political debate. The individuals hardest hit, said Blackmun, by the suppression of prescription drug price information are the poor, the sick and the old.[19] Therefore, despite the State of Virginia's admittedly valid interest in protection of professionalism among pharmacists, it was concluded that the Virginia statute was invalid.

Subsequent cases indicate that commercial speech now will often be protected by the Constitution. See, for example, *Horner-Rausch Optical Company,* decided in 1976 in Tennessee. There, a state administrative regulation forbidding price advertising of eyeglasses was declared unconstitutional. The Supreme Court of Tennessee said that a state can no longer " * * * completely suppress the dissemination of concededly truthful information about entirely lawful activity, fearful of the information's effect upon its disseminators and its recipients." [20] More recently, on June 27, 1977, the Supreme Court of the United States ruled—by a 5–4 margin—that lawyers have a constitutional right to advertise their prices for various services. Justice Blackmun's majority opinion said, "[I]t is entirely possible that advertising will serve to reduce, not advance, the cost of legal services to the consumer." In this case, the consumer's need for information about the cost of various legal services was held to outweigh the legal profession's interest in having a self-regulated restraint against virtually all kinds of advertising by attorneys. The opinion added that the time, place and manner of advertising may still be regulated, and

[18] 425 U.S. 748, 759–671, 96 S.Ct. 1817, 1824–1825 (1976).

[19] 425 U.S. 748, 763, 96 S.Ct. 1817, 1826 (1976).

[20] Horner-Rausch Optical Co. et al. v. R.A. Ashley et al., 547 S.W.2d 577, 580 (Tenn.1976), quoting Virginia State Board of Pharmacy v. Virginia Citizens Consumer Council, 425 U.S. 748, 96 S.Ct. 1817, 1831 (1976).

that false and misleading advertising by lawyers will be forbidden.[21]

In holding that advertising by attorneys may not be subjected to blanket suppression, and that the advertisement at issue is protected, we, of course, do not hold that advertising by attorneys may not be regulated in any way. We mention some of the clearly permissible limitations on advertising not foreclosed by our holding. Advertising that is false, deceptive, or misleading of course is subject to restraint. See Virginia Pharmacy Board v. Virginia Citizens Council, 425 U.S. at 771–772, and n. 24.

* * *

The constitutional issue in this case is only whether the State may prevent the publication in a newspaper of appellants' truthful advertisement concerning the availability and terms of routine legal services. We rule simply that the flow of such information may not be restrained, and we therefore hold the present application of the disciplinary rule against appellants to be violative of the First Amendment.

If abortion clinics, pharmacists, and lawyers have some First Amendment protection for their advertisements, what about corporations' right to exercise political speech? In First National Bank of Boston v. Bellotti,[22] the Supreme Court of the United States invalidated a Massachusetts statute forbidding business corporations from making contributions or expenditures " 'for the purpose of * * * influencing or affecting the vote on any question submitted to the voters, other than one materially affecting any of the property, business or assets of the corporation.' " [23] That statute had provided that a corporation which violated its provisions could be fined $50,000, and that corporate officers involved in such a violation could be fined up to $10,000, imprisoned for up to one year, or both.

The Bank wanted to spend money to publicize its views on a constitutional amendment which was to be submitted to voters as a ballot question. The amendment would have allowed the legislature to impose a graduated tax on the income of individuals.

---

[21] Bates v. State Bar of Arizona, 431 U.S. 350, 377, 383, 384, 97 S.Ct. 2691, 2706, 2708, 2709 (1977).

Advertising by attorneys can go too far, however, when it includes a lawyer's visiting the family of a person injured in an auto accident, and even visiting with the driver herself in her hospital room. Personal solicitation of that nature is "beyond the pale;" see Ohralik v. Ohio State Bar Ass'n, 436 U.S. 447, 98 S.Ct. 1912 (1978).

[22] 435 U.S. 765, 98 S.Ct. 1407 (1978).

[23] Massachusetts General Laws Ann. ch. 55, § 8.

Attorney General Francis X. Bellotti of Massachusetts informed the First National Bank of Boston that he would enforce the statute, and the bank brought an action asking that the statute be declared unconstitutional. The Supreme Judicial Court of Massachusetts held the statute valid.[24]

Writing for the Supreme Court, Justice Lewis Powell declared that the Massachusetts statute was unconstitutional. He said that the political argument which the bank wished to make "is at the heart of the First Amendment's protection." He added, "[t]he question in this case, simply put, is whether the corporate identity of the speaker deprives this proposed speech of what otherwise would be its clear entitlement to protection." [25]

Justice Powell cited the Court's recent commercial speech cases—including *Virginia State Board of Pharmacy*—as illustrating "that the First Amendment goes beyond protection of the press and the self-expression of individuals to prohibit government from limiting the stock of information from which members of the public may draw." Thus corporations' political speech was entitled to First Amendment protection.[26]

Justice Bryon White dissented, and was joined in that opinion by Justices Brennan and Marshall. He argued that the Massachusetts statute did not infringe on First Amendment interests, but instead protected them. Corporations which had amassed great wealth could thus be prevented from having "an unfair advantage in the political process." [27]

> Indeed, what some have considered to be the principal function for the First Amendment, the use of communication as a means of self-expression, self-realization and self-fulfillment, is not at all furthered by corporate speech. It is clear that the communications of profitmaking corporations are not "an integral part of the development of ideas, of mental exploration and of the affirmation of self."

Some scholars are expressing concern that the First Amendment is being stretched out of all recognition in recent years, and that—in a sense—the right of free speech is being trivialized. Attorney Charles Rembar has said: [28]

> Bringing commercial hawking within the fold of the First Amendment has resulted in rulings that can fairly

---

[24] 371 Mass. 773, 359 N.E.2d at 1268 (1976).

[25] 435 U.S. 765, 778, 98 S.Ct. 1407, 1416 (1978).

[26] 435 U.S. 765, 783, 98 S.Ct. 1407, 1409 (1978).

[27] 435 U.S. 765, 809, 98 S.Ct. 1407, 1433 (1978).

[28] Charles Rembar, "For Sale: Freedom of Speech," The Atlantic Monthly, March, 1981, pp. 25–32, at p. 28.

be called bizarre.   Last June the Supreme Court handed
down decisions in two cases involving power companies.
In each, the Court nullified efforts of the New York State
Public Service Commission to act in the public interest.

One case involved a commission order that the Central Hudson Gas & Electric Corporation cease promoting
consumption of electricity: a desirable measure, one
would think, when the nation is held hostage to imported
oil.

In *Central Hudson,* the Supreme Court of the United States
invalidated New York's ban on promotional advertising by electric
utilities.   Justice Powell—writing for an eight-to-one court—laid
out a four-part test: [29]

> In commercial speech cases, then, a four-part analysis has
> developed.   At the outset, we must determine whether
> the expression is protected by the First Amendment.   For
> commercial speech to come within that provision, it at
> least must concern lawful activity and not be misleading.
> Next, we ask whether the asserted governmental interest
> is substantial.   If both inquiries yield positive answers, we
> must determine whether the regulation directly advances
> the governmental interest asserted, and whether it is not
> more extensive than necessary to serve that interest.

Because advertising promoting use of electricity was seen as
protected by the First Amendment, and because the ad was
neither misleading nor "unlawful," the New York regulation was
overturned as unconstitutional.   Although the state did have a
substantial interest in terms of energy conservation, the state's
regulation was more extensive than necessary.   No demonstration
had been made that the state's interest in energy conservation
could not have been served adequately by a more limited restriction on the content of promotional advertisements.   Powell concluded,[30]

> To the extent that the Commission's order suppresses
> speech that in no way impairs the State's interest in
> energy conservation, the Commission's order violates the

[29] Central Hudson Gas & Electric Corp. v. Public Service Commission of New
York, 447 U.S. 557, 100 S.Ct. 2343 (1980).

[30] 447 U.S. 557, 100 S.Ct. 2343 (1980).   See also a related case, Consolidated
Edison Co. of New York v. Public Service Commission of New York, 447 U.S. 530,
100 S.Ct. 2326 (1980), 6 Med.L.Rptr. 1518.   In that case, the Supreme Court struck
down an order of the Commission forbidding the utility's including statements of
"Con Ed's" views on matters of public policy controversies.   Powell, quoting First
National Bank of Boston v. Bellotti, 435 U.S. 765, 98 S.Ct. 1407 (1978), wrote for the
Court that this ruling by the Commission "strikes at the heart of the freedom to
speak."

First and Fourteenth Amendments and must be invalidated.

These commercial speech decisions have a disquieting ring to some. Charles Rembar questioned the premise that use of wealth to amplify voices furthers freedom of speech. ("If I speak through a bullhorn while you speak through a kazoo, you have no freedom of speech.")

Like these decisions or not, there is evidence that the Supreme Court of the United States is concerned with freedom of advertising as well as with control of its abuses. A notable 18th Century Englishman, Dr. Samuel Johnson, considered advertising and delivered this neat phrase: "Promise, large promise is the soul of an advertisement." [31] To keep advertising's promises within socially manageable bounds is the task, worth of Sisyphus, which falls upon the Federal Trade Commission and other federal and state agencies, as well as upon the profession of advertising and the mass media.

It is a fearfully complex job, and the FTC even seems to have moments when it appears to be in danger of falling on its own sword. The FTC—the very agency charged with protecting consumers from deceptive advertising—in 1980 was itself accused of conducting an unfair advertising campaign. The FTC wanted to display a poster in 10,000 post offices across the land. The posters showed a large, unfriendly monster looking out of a package which just came in the mail. The poster said, "If something shows up in the mail that you didn't order, you can keep it for free." The Direct Mail Market Association griped that this poster gave a negative image of the mail-order industry.[32]

---

[31] Statement attributed to Dr. Johnson, quoted by Ira M. Millstein, "The Federal Trade Commission and False Advertising," Columbia Law Review, 64:3 (March, 1964) at p. 439, from David Ogilvy, Confessions of An Advertising Man (New York: Dell Publishing, 1963) p. 116.

[32] Caroline E. Mayer, Washington Star Service, "FTC accused of unfair advertising," Austin American Statesman, September 11, 1980, p. Cl.

Chapter 14

ANTITRUST LAW AND THE MASS MEDIA

Sec.
93. Concentration or Diversity?
94. Merger Mania and Takeover Tactics.
95. Newspaper Antitrust Law.
96. Consent Decrees.
97. Broadcasting, Cable and Antitrust Law.

SEC. 93. CONCENTRATION OR DIVERSITY?

Despite antitrust laws, the mass media have continued to become more and more concentrated in ownership patterns.

For the last two decades, concern over concentration of too much media power in too few hands has been expressed with frequency and fervor. The disappearance of many daily newspapers—particularly independent, locally owned newspapers—is part of the story. Phrases frequently heard include "concentration of newspaper ownership," "problems of bigness and fewness," and "fewer voices in the marketplace of ideas."[1]

Newspaper ownership patterns are by no means the only points of concern. Professor Ben H. Bagdikian of the University of California-Berkeley—one of the best-known media critics—is an important voice pointing out that media power is political, and that 50 corporations have real opportunities to control most of "what America sees, hears, and reads." Bagdikian wrote that finance capitalism and new technologies have forged[2]

> * * * a new kind of central authority over information—the national and multinational corporation. By the 1980s, the majority of all major American media—newspapers, magazines, radio, television, books, and movies—were controlled by fifty giant corporations. These corporations were interlocked in common financial interest with other massive industries and with a few dominant banks.

[1] Toby J. McIntosh, "Why the Government Can't Stop Press Mergers," Columbia Journalism Review, December, 1980, pp. 48–50; "America's Press: Too Much Power for Too Few?", U.S. News & World Report, Aug. 15, 1977, pp. 27ff; Kevin Phillips, "Busting the Media Trusts," Harper's Magazine, July 1977, pp. 23ff, and Neil Hickey, "Can the Networks Survive," TV Guide, March 21, 1981, pp. 7ff.

[2] Ben H. Bagdikian, The Media Monopoly (Boston: Beacon Press, 1983), book jacket copy, plus quote from p. xv.

Ironically, this chapter will discuss concentration of media power mostly from the perspective of federal antitrust law—an area of law largely in disuse where the media are concerned during the Presidency of Ronald Reagan. With Administration policies clearly favoring less regulation—including regulation of mergers—the Song of Goliath is heard, not the Song of David. Times do change, however, and antitrust concepts will be discussed here because they may be back in operation in another political climate.

So what is "antitrust?" Black's Law Dictionary says:[3]

Antitrust acts. Federal and state statutes to protect trade and commerce from unlawful restraints, price discriminations, price fixing, and monopolies. Most states have mini-antitrust acts patterned on the federal acts. The principal federal antitrust acts are: Sherman Act (1890); Clayton Act (1914); Federal Trade Commission Act (1914); Robinson-Patman Act (1936). See Boycott; Combination in restraint of trade; Price fixing; Restraint of trade; * * *

The nation's premier scholar of the law of mass communications—the late Professor Zechariah Chafee of Harvard University—knew back in 1947 that the problem of concentration of media ownership was of pivotal importance to American society. Chafee asked to what extent antitrust laws should be used to prevent concentration of media units from hindering the free interchange of ideas. Chafee also declared in 1947 that antitrust law problems were the most important facing the press and also the most difficult.[4]

Antitrust law is an area which from time to time causes considerable fright among publishers and broadcasters. For example, the Federal Communications Commission (FCC) proposed in 1970 that broadcast station owners should cut their mass media operations in any community to either broadcast properties or to newspaper ownership. That FCC "proposed rulemaking" was enough to cause a substantial number of cross-ownerships to be split up by their owners. The FCC backed down from its proposal in 1975, issuing a ruling which "grandfathered"—left in effect—most existing local cross-ownerships of broadcast and newspaper properties. A group calling itself The National Citizens Commission for Broadcasting sued the FCC, asking that such cross-ownerships be broken up unless positive showings could be made that

[3] Black's Law Dictionary, Fifth Edition (St. Paul, West Pub. Co., Minn., 1979) p. 86.

[4] Zechariah Chafee, Jr., Government and Mass Communications, 2 vols. (Chicago: University of Chicago Press, 1947) I, p. 537.

such patterns served the public interest.[5] In 1978, the Supreme Court of the United States held that it was within the FCC's authority to decide that existing cross-media ownerships were in the public interest. That upheld the FCC's grandfathering of existing ownership patterns.[6] The FCC, however, made clear it would approve no new local cross-media ownerships.

In certain circumstances, the power of antitrust law over the media can be awesome. The shock wave generated by the *RKO General* case provides one example. The Federal Communications Commission (FCC), claiming (among other things) antitrust law violations by RKO General and its parent company—General Tire and Rubber Company—refused to renew broadcast licenses for three television stations owned by RKO General. With that stroke, the FCC tried to lift the license of WNAC–TV, Boston; WOR–TV, New York City, and KHJ–TV, Los Angeles.[7] RKO General appealed the FCC's decision, setting off lengthy court battles described in Section 74 of Chapter 12. The antitrust/trade practices complaints were only part of the FCC's proceedings against RKO General. But as noted in Chapter 12, RKO got its license renewed for WOR–TV (after moving the station to New Jersey), but still faced proceedings on its Los Angeles station and saw the opening of 13 other broadcast stations to competing license applications.[8]

Also, it should be kept in mind that antitrust law is not exclusively a federal matter. Although this chapter concentrates on federal antitrust activity, state antitrust laws are a formidable thicket. Antitrust experts Conrad M. Shumadine and Michael S. Ives noted in 1980 that although state antitrust prosecutions have been relatively rare, state laws contain some scary provisions. Under the laws of many states, convictions for antitrust violations may result in forfeiture of a corporation's charter. That could add up to dissolving of a corporation based in an individual state or the ouster of a corporation from one state when it is chartered in another state.[9]

This chapter will not consider in any detail the entire range of antitrust activity affecting the media. It is aimed, instead, at the increasingly interrelated question of newspaper and broadcast/cable ownership situations. This chapter does not take up such

[5] National Citizens for Broadcasting v. FCC, 555 F.2d 938 (D.C.Cir.1977).

[6] FCC v. National Citizens Committee for Broadcasting, 436 U.S. 775, 98 S.Ct. 2096 (1978).

[7] In re RKO General, Inc., 78 F.C.C.2d 1.

[8] See discussion at footnotes 28–32, Section 74, in Chapter 12, above.

[9] Conrad M. Shumadine and Michael S. Ives, "Selected Antitrust Issues of Interest to the Media," in James C. Goodale, editor, Communications Law 1980, Vol. 2 (New York: Practising Law Institute, 1980) pp. 296–298.

matters as exclusive syndication or newspaper distribution problems, nor does it treat important related questions of ownership of magazines, film studios, community newspapers and billboards.[10]

Professor Ben H. Bagdikian of The University of California-Berkeley continues to keep track of the growth of media conglomerates. "The phenomenon of fewer and fewer people controlling more and more public intelligence affects every mass medium in the United States," Bagdikian wrote in 1980. His findings include these items:[11]

— Twenty corporations control 52 percent of all daily newspaper circulation.

— Twenty corporations control 50 percent of all periodical sales.

— Twenty corporations control 52 percent of all book sales.

He concluded that fewer than 100 corporations control the majority of newspaper, periodical, book, record and tape sales, plus two-thirds of the audience in television and radio, and 75 percent of movie distribution. Consider just one corporate example: CBS, Inc. CBS, along with NBC and ABC, controls roughly half of the nation's prime-time viewing audience, although cable television will cut into that percentage in the future. CBS also publishes some 20 magazines (including *World Tennis, Field & Stream, Woman's Day, Family Weekly* and *Road & Track*), the book publishing firms of Holt, Rinehart and Winston, W.B. Saunders Co. (the world's largest medical publisher), Praeger Publishers, and Fawcett paperbacks.[12]

Ben Bagdikian is no lonely alarmist. A 1977 study by The Washington Post concluded that by 1997, almost all newspapers in America will be owned by fewer than two dozen major communications conglomerates.[13] Of 52 dailies that were sold in 1980, 48 joined group ownerships.[14] Because of the structure of the newspaper business, the Antitrust Division of the Department of Jus-

[10] Exclusive syndication problems involve features such as columns or comic strips. Such features are offered to major newspapers under an agreement that no other newspapers within a certain region can publish those particular features. For a discussion of territorial exclusivity problems and distribution problems involving newspapers, see Marc A. Franklin, et al., The First Amendment and the Fourth Estate (Mineola, N.Y.; Foundation Press, 1977 and later editions).

[11] Ben H. Bagdikian, "Conglomeration, Concentration and the Media," Journal of Communication 30:2 (Spring, 1980), pp. 59–60.

[12] 1984 Annual Report to the Shareholders of CBS Inc., *passim.*

[13] William H. Jones and Laird Anderson, "Newspapers: Just Another Business?", Washington Post study reprinted in The Corpus Christi Caller, Section B, pp. 1ff, August 7, 1977.

[14] Editor & Publisher, January 3, 1981, pp. 9ff.

tice has been unable to make much of an impact on newspaper chains acquiring newspapers like charms for a charm bracelet. The federal government can do little, for example, to prevent a newspaper group from New York from acquiring newspapers far away—as in Texas or California.

The communications media are businesses, and as such, are ringed about by federal and state laws which regulate businesses. Congress has enacted several statutes—most commonly called antitrust laws—which attempt to preserve competition. The most important statements of national antitrust policy are found in the Sherman[15] and Clayton[16] Acts.

The Sherman Act of 1890 begins: "Every contract, combination in the form of a trust or otherwise, or conspiracy, in restraint of trade or commerce among the several states, or with foreign nations, is hereby declared to be illegal."[17] Every person who acts to restrain trade, as mentioned generally above, is guilty of a crime.   The Sherman Act prohibits "contracts, combinations * * * or conspiracies in restraint of trade or commerce" and makes it illegal to "monopolize, or attempt to monopolize, or combine or conspire * * * to monopolize * * * trade or commerce."

Criminal prosecution—with penalties of fines, imprisonment, or both—is provided for in the Sherman Act.   Fines may reach a maximum amount of $100,000 per individual, and imprisonment for up to three years may also be imposed.   A corporation may be fined up to $1 million for violating the Sherman Act.   The Act also enables the government to bring suits in equity to get injunctions against violations of the statute.   As Chafee observed in 1947, suits in equity are "preferred because it is not always easy for businessmen to know in advance whether their transactions are illegal or not."[20]   Also, a person (or business) who has suffered damages because a competitor has violated the Sherman Act may sue the competitor for *treble damages.*

Treble damages lawsuits work in this way: suppose that the Fluke Manufacturing Company has violated the Sherman Act. The United States Department of Justice takes Fluke Manufacturing to court and gets an order to make it stop monopolistic or trade-restraining practices.   An interested spectator, meanwhile, is Fluke's competitor, whom we shall call the Flimsy Manufacturing Company.   Flimsy Manufacturing then begins a treble damage antitrust suit, and is able to prove in court that Fluke Manufac-

[15] 26 Stat. 209, 15 U.S.C.A. §§ 1–7; P.L. No. 190, 51st Congress (1890).

[16] 38 Stat. 730, 15 U.S.C.A. §§ 12ff; P.L. No. 201, 63rd Congress (1914).

[17] 15 U.S.C.A. § 1.

[20] Chafee, op. cit., p. 538.

turing's illegal business practices cost Flimsy $100,000 in business. However, since this would be a *treble damage* lawsuit, Flimsy Manufacturing would actually collect $300,000 from the competing Fluke company.

The Clayton Act of 1914 added to the government's antitrust enforcement powers, enumerating many acts as illegal when "they tend to lessen competition or to create a monopoly in any line of commerce."[21] Section 7 of the Clayton Act—more commonly called the Celler-Kefauver Act of 1950—is the most important section of the Clayton Act where newspapers are concerned.[22] The "Celler-Kefauver Act" forbids corporations to acquire stock or assets of a competing corporation "where * * * the effect * * * may be substantially to lessen competition, or tend to create a monopoly."

Upon such vaguely worded provisions of the Sherman and Clayton Acts is built federal antitrust policy. The vagueness of the statutory provisions make antitrust one of the most perplexing branches of public law, especially where newspapers and other units of the communications media are involved.

SEC. 94. MERGER MANIA AND TAKEOVER TACTICS

Earning power of media units during the 1980s—coupled with hands-off deregulatory policies and Federal Communications Commission rule changes—aided concentration of media power.

The poet T.S. Eliot wrote that April is the cruelest month. Perhaps so, but March, 1985, was the most acquisitive month in the history of the communications media in the United States. Increasingly and perhaps inevitably, the business of media is more prominent—and often seems more highly valued—than the social roles of the media. Unfortunately, media theorists who talk about a free press or competition in the marketplace of ideas seem more and more out-of-date. Whatever else it was, the First Amendment rights of speech and press and religion and assembly were citizens' rights:

> Congress shall make no law respecting an establishment of religion, or prohibiting the free exercise thereof; or abridging the freedom of speech, or of the press; or the right of the people peaceably to assemble, and to petition the Government for a redress of grievances.

---

[21] 15 U.S.C.A. § 18.

[22] 64 Stat. 1125, 15 U.S.C.A. § 18; P.L. 899, 81st Congress (1950).

Although it may well be, as historian Leonard W. Levy has argued, that the First Amendment was merely a kind of fortunate political accident, freedom of speech and press are very much in the American grain. It is commonly accepted—or at least given lip service—that the news media provide incalculably valuable services to society.[23] The media, so the belief goes, create an informed public necessary for meaningful self-government. This is one key reason why the press is shielded by the First Amendment, so that citizens might be informed about government and speak out as necessary. Those are the kinds of assumptions ringed about the First Amendment.

Now, however, there is room for skepticism about the First Amendment as a citizens' right. Increasingly, it demands enormously large amounts of capital to own a newspaper or broadcast station, on the one hand, or to defend oneself against a libel or privacy lawsuit, on the other.

On March 18, 1985, Capital Cities Communications announced that it would buy a whole network—the American Broadcasting Company—for the untidy sum of $3.5 billion. On that date, this corporate wedding was called the largest merger in the nation's history outside of the oil industry.[24]

Other big-buck mergers taking place in March, 1985, included:

— News Corporation (Rupert Murdoch, chairman), bought half of 20th-Century Fox Film Corporation for $162 million. Two months later, and definitely linked to the 20th-Century purchase, Murdoch (along with Denver oil multimillionaire Marvin Davis) agreed to buy the nation's largest independent television station group from Metromedia, Inc. The price tag was $2 billion.[25]

Murdoch was seen as moving toward establishing another TV network with the combination of his 20th-Century Fox holdings (including its huge film library). The new owners of Metromedia quickly moved to sell Boston's Metromedia station WTVB–TV to the Hearst Corporation for $450 million.[26]

The other TV stations acquired in the Metromedia deal in 1985 reached more than 18 percent of all U.S.

[23] Leonard W. Levy, Emergence of a Free Press (New York: Oxford University Press, 1985), passim.

[24] Alex S. Jones, "And now, the Media Mega-Merger," The New York Times, Sec. 3, P. 11, March 24, 1985.

[25] Ibid.; Bill Abrams and Michael Cieply, "Metromedia, Inc. Agrees to Sell 7 TV Stations," The Wall Street Journal, May 7, 1985, p. 2.

[26] Abrams and Cieply, p. 27.

television homes. Those stations are WNEW–TV, New York; WTTG, Washington, D.C.; KRLD–TV, Dallas-Fort Worth; KRIV–TV, Houston; WFLD–TV, Chicago, and KTTV in Los Angeles.[27]

— Washington Post Co., bought 17 percent of Cowles Media. (The flagship enterprise of Cowles Media is the Minneapolis Star and Tribune.) [28]

— Advance Publications (S.I. Newhouse, chairman) bought New Yorker Magazine for $142 million.

— U.S. News & World Report sold to Mortimer Zuckerman for $164 million.[29]

Earlier in 84–85, Gannett Company purchased The Des Moines Register and Tribune, plus some smaller papers, for $200 million, and Time, Inc., the huge magazine and cable TV power, bought Southern Progress Corporation, publisher of Southern Living and other profitable magazines, for $480 million.[30] Westinghouse Electric Corporation bought cable television properties from Teleprompter Corporation for $647 million, and the A.H. Belo Corporation—publishers of the Dallas Morning News—acquired Corinthian Broadcasting Corporation's six television stations from Dun & Bradstreet for $606 million.[31] Small wonder that Newsweek Magazine termed this wave of acquisitiveness a "feeding frenzy." Newsweek added: [32]

> For the American news media, accustomed to thinking of themselves as a Fourth Estate, it has been something of a shock to be treated as Wall Street darlings instead. The pell-mell quest for media properties has bid up their sale prices to heady levels.

Many journalists (except for business writers, Wall Street Journal types, and the like) have long had the reputation for being financial illiterates. But when the media became such attractive properties in the 1980s, self-interest began to impel journalists to learn some new terms, such as:

—**"Leveraged Buyout."** This is a deal in which money is borrowed to buy a corporation. Then, the cash flow from the purchased company is put to work to pay off the interest and principal of the loan.

[27] Alex S. Jones, loc. cit.

[28] Ibid.

[29] Ibid.; see also Newsweek, "Big Media, Big Money," April 1, 1985, p. 52.

[30] Ibid.

[31] Newsweek, "Big Media, Big Money," April 1, 1985, p. 52.

[32] Ibid.

The purchase of the ABC Network by Capital Cities is a startling example of a leveraged buyout. A Nebraska financier—Warren Buffett—bought Capital Cities stock to provide $517.5 million of the $3.5 billion "Cap Cities" spent to get control of ABC. Note that Cap Cities was much smaller than ABC—its 1984 revenues amounted to $950 million, compared to $3.7 billion for ABC.[33] "It's a little like the canary eating the cat," said Roone Arledge, president of ABC News and Sports.[34]

But then, with media companies, cash flow is so great that enormous loans can be paid off. Alex S. Jones reported in The New York Times that "well-run television stations in major markets can generate pre-tax operating income of over 50 percent * * * cash flow can be 60 percent or more of revenues." Further, cash flow for the more profitable newspapers can range as high as 40 percent or more.[35]

"12–12–12 Rule"—A 1985 change in Federal Communications Commission (FCC) rules has shaken the structure of the United States mass communication industry. The new 12–12–12 rule was crucial to bringing about the Capital Cities Communications merger with ABC. Until April 1, 1985, a 7–7–7 rule in broadcast station ownership was in effect.

That 7–7–7 rule meant that one company could own no more than seven AM radio stations, seven FM stations, and seven TV stations. The FCC, however, pushed the limit up to 12–12–12. The major restriction (if one can call it that) beyond those numbers is that no one company can have TV stations with the reach to hit broadcast into more than 25 percent of the nation's homes.[36]

The ABC–Capital Cities merger pushed the new entity's holdings into more than 25 percent; that meant that some of the TV stations had to be sold. In mid-1985, ABC and Capital Cities were planning to sell 19 broadcasting stations in eight cities. For example, the merged company planned to keep WABC–TV, New York City, while selling off two AM stations and two FM stations in The Big Apple. Similarly, KABC–TV, Los Angeles, was to be

---

[33] "Omaha's Plain Dealer," Newsweek, April 1, 1985, p. 56.

[34] Peter W. Kaplan, "Takeover's Impact Is Uncertain," The New York Times, March 19, 1985, p. 54.

[35] Alex S. Jones, loc. cit.; see also Geraldine Fabrikant, "3 TV Stations High Margins," The New York Times, July 1, 1985, p. 25.

[36] David Clark Scott, "ABC Merger Likely to Generate Spinoff Sales," Christian Science Monitor, March 20, 1985, p. 19.

kept, while four radio stations—two AM, two FM, were to be sold. And in San Francisco, KGO–TV was to be kept, and KGO–AM was to be sold. In Dallas, KTKS–FM was to be sold, while WBAP–AM and KSCS–FM were to be sold.[37]

"Friendly Takeover"—As the term implies, it is an amicable merger between two corporations. The Capital Cities Communications-ABC merger again provides a good example. ABC's architect and Chairman, 79-year-old Leonard Goldenson, had for some years been the subject of speculation: who would replace him at the 214-station network? Cap Cities Chairman Thomas Murphy talked with the ABC Executive Vice President, and they agreed that if the FCC ever liberalized its "7–7–7 rule" [see above], the two companies would be a "natural fit." After the FCC changed to its "12–12–12" rule on April 1, 1985, the merger took place.[38]

"Hostile Takeover"—There had been rumors that ABC was being stalked for a hostile takeover—a situation in which entrepreneurs buy up a controlling interest in a company's stock, thus gaining effective ownership. The rumors mentioned potential takeover bidders as the Bass brothers of Fort Worth, Texas, and Ted Turner, the feisty and aggressive owner of Atlanta "super-station" WTBS, Cable News Network, the Atlanta Braves baseball team, and so on. But ABC Board Chairman Goldenson said that the network had found no evidence of investors buying up huge blocs of ABC stock, and added that the sale to Capital Cities was not put together to prevent someone less desirable from gaining control of the network.[39]

Some of the elements of a hostile takeover may be seen in the 1985 financial soap opera featuring Atlanta's Ted Turner, most often referred to as "the flamboyant Ted Turner," or, even as "Captain Outrageous" (from his yachting exploits) or as "The Mouth of the South."

Turner decided that he wanted to own the CBS network, and set about trying to do so. (CBS, the network the Political Right loves to hate, also had rumblings in 1985 of a hostile takeover from North Carolina Democratic Senator Jesse Helms and his supporters in a conservative

[37] Michael Weiss, "Companies to Sell Broadcast Outlets in Dallas, 7 Cities," The Dallas Morning News, April 14, 1985, p. D–1.

[38] Newsweek, April 1, 1985, p. 54.

[39] Ibid., p. 53; "Network Blockbuster," Time, April 1, 1985, p. 60.

group calling itself Fairness in Media). Turner tried—unsuccessfully by late summer of 1985—to raise $5.4 billion to buy out CBS.[40]

"Junk Bonds"—Turner tried to exchange some shares in his Turner Broadcast Company and $5.4 million in financial paper nicknamed "junk bonds" for the 67 percent share needed to control CBS under New York law. As reported in The Economist, "The bid contains not one cent of cash. Mr. Turner hopes instead to tempt CBS shareholders with an annual dividend" some seven times the 1985 CBS dividend rate. The term "junk bonds" is slang for "high yield, low quality bonds." [41]

As Fred R. Bleakley wrote in 1985, "Junk bond financing involves putting together a package of securities whose high rates of interest and dividends will be paid mostly by the target company once it is acquired." [42]

In mid-July, 1985, Turner withdrew his proposal to take control of the CBS network. Meanwhile, Turner shifted his attention to another venture, proposing in August, 1985—evidently successfully—to buy the MGM/UA film studio and its large film library (ever so useful to his Atlanta based "super-station" WTBS) for $1.03 billion.[43]

When all this merger activity is added up—and there is much more than could be included in this short summary—it appears that the trend toward consolidation will continue to gallop along. Edward J. Atorino, communications consultant for the Wall Street firm of Smith, Barney, told The New York Times that change will continue. " 'In 10 years, the current list of the top 20 communications companies may be smaller by a quarter to a third, and maybe more,' " Atorino said.[44]

SEC. 95. NEWSPAPER ANTITRUST LAW

Antitrust statutes, as applied to the press, are not in violation of the First Amendment guarantee of freedom of the press.

Although decided just after the end of World War II, the decision of the Supreme Court of the United States in Associated

---

[40] Newsweek, April 1, 1985, p. 57.

[41] "When the junketing has to stop," The Economist, April 27, 1985, p. 91.

[42] Newsweek, April 1, 1985, p. 57.

[43] Fred R. Bleakley, "The Power and Perils of Junk Bonds," The New York Times, Sec. 3, p. 1, April 14, 1985; "Turner Drops Trustee Plan," The New York Times, July 17, 1985, p. 32; Thomas C. Hayes, "New UA's Assets Are Not Yet Known," The New York Times, August 8, 1985, p. 28.

[44] Quoted in Alex S. Jones, op. cit., at page 10.

Press v. United States[45] still ranks as a leading case in antitrust law affecting the media. The Justice Department had brought suit under the Sherman Act[46] to get an injunction preventing the AP from continuing to operate under a restrictive clause in its by-laws. The Associated Press is a cooperative news-gathering organization. Its by-laws forbade AP member newspapers or broadcast stations from selling news to non-members. Other by-law provisions also gave a newspaper which had an AP membership virtual veto power over competing newspapers' attempts to gain AP membership.[47]

Associated Press v. United States (1945)

One of several cases combined under the case name of Associated Press v. United States involved Chicago publisher Marshall Field's efforts to get an AP membership for his Chicago Sun, a new newspaper trying to compete with crusty Col. Robert R. McCormick's Chicago Tribune. The Chicago Tribune protested against the upstart Chicago Sun's AP membership application, trying to prevent the competition from gaining the benefit of the premier news wire service. Once such a protest was made, the AP by-laws then required a majority vote of ALL members of the Associated Press before the new applicant could be admitted to the club.[48] That majority vote—from publisher members of AP, many of whom enjoyed exclusive use of that wire service in their own publication areas—was most unlikely to occur. Thus Marshall Field's Chicago Sun could not join the AP without Col. McCormick's consent, unless the federal government intervened—in the public interest, of course—to use antitrust laws to force a change in the AP bylaws.

In 1943, the Justice Department charged that the conduct of the AP and the Chicago Tribune constituted "(1) a combination and conspiracy of restraint of trade and commerce in news among the states, and (2) an attempt to monopolize part of that trade." [49] The Associated Press and the Chicago Tribune fought against the Justice Department charges, arguing that the application of the Sherman Act in this case would violate freedom of the press guaranteed by the First Amendment. A majority of the Supreme

[45] 326 U.S. 1, 65 S.Ct. 1416 (1945).

[46] See discussion of the Sherman Act, Section 93, supra, at footnote 15.

[47] Chafee, op. cit., pp. 542–543; Associated Press v. United States, 326 U.S. 1, 9–10, 65 S.Ct. 1416, 1419 (1945).

[48] Chafee, p. 543; Associated Press v. United States, loc. cit. Another newspaper which like the Chicago Sun had applied for AP membership and had been turned down by a 2–1 vote margin of AP members, was the Washington Times-Herald.

[49] 326 U.S. 1, 7, 65 S.Ct. 1416, 1418 (1945).

Court was not impressed by this argument. Writing for the Court, Justice Hugo L. Black said: [50]

> Member publishers of AP are engaged in business for profit exactly as are other businessmen who sell food, steel, aluminum, or anything else people need or want * * *. All are alike covered by the Sherman Act. The fact that the publisher handles news while others handle goods does not, as we shall later point out, afford the publisher a peculiar constitutional sanctuary in which he can with impunity violate laws regulating his business practices.

Finally, Justice Black answered the assertion that the Sherman Act's application to the Associated Press abridged the AP's First Amendment freedom. He declared that it would be strange if the concern for press freedom underlying the First Amendment should be read "as a command that the government was without power to protect that freedom." Black continued,[51]

> The First Amendment, far from providing an argument against application of the Sherman Act, here provides powerful reasons to the contrary.
>
> * * *
>
> Freedom to publish means freedom for all and not for some. Freedom to publish is guaranteed by the Commission, but freedom to combine to keep others from publishing is not. Freedom of the press from governmental interference under the First Amendment does not sanction repression of that freedom by private interests. The First Amendment affords not the slightest support for the contention that a combination to restrain trade in news and views has any constitutional immunity.

Justice Frankfurter added other arguments in favor of government action under the Sherman Act to attempt to control media activities which tended to restrain trade. To Frankfurter, the press was a business, but it was also much more: "in addition to being a commercial enterprise, it [the press] has a relation to the public interest unlike that of any other enterprise pursued for profit." Following this premise, Justice Frankfurter then quoted words written by America's most famous United States District Court judge. The oft-quoted words below came from Judge Learned Hand's lower-court opinion in this same case of Associated Press v. United States,[52]

[50] 326 U.S. 1, 8–10, 65 S.Ct. 1416, 1419 (1945).

[51] 326 U.S. 1, 20, 65 S.Ct. 1416, 1424–1425 (1945).

[52] 326 U.S. 1, 28, 65 S.Ct. 1416, 1428 (1945), quoting Judge Hand, Associated Press v. United States, 52 F.Supp. 362, 372 (D.C.N.Y.1943).

> *   *   * that [the newspaper] industry serves one of
> the most vital of all general interests: the dissemination
> of news from as many different sources, and with as many
> different facets and colors as is possible. That interest is
> closely akin to, if indeed it is not the same as, the interest
> protected by the First Amendment; it presupposes that
> right conclusions are more likely to be gathered out of a
> multitude of tongues than through any kind of authorita-
> tive selection. To many this is, and always will be, folly;
> but we have staked upon it our all.

To Frankfurter, the By-Laws of the Associated Press were a clear
restriction of commerce. Such a restriction was unreasonable
because it subverted the function of a constitutionally guaranteed
free press.

Dissents from Justices Owen J. Roberts and Frank Murphy
took a traditional libertarian view: in general, government should
leave the press alone. Justice Murphy wrote: [53]

> Today is *   *   * the first time that the Sherman Act
> has been used as a vehicle for affirmative intervention by
> the Government in the realm of dissemination of informa-
> tion. As the Government states, this is an attempt to
> remove "barriers erected by private combination against
> access to reports of world news." *   *   *. [The press
> associations] are engaged in collecting and distributing
> news and information rather than in manufacturing auto-
> mobiles, aluminum or gasoline. We cannot avoid that
> fact. Nor can we escape the fact that governmental
> action directly aimed at the methods or conditions of such
> collection or distribution is an interference with the press,
> however differing in degree it may be from governmental
> restraints on written or spoken utterances themselves
> *   *   *. We should therefore be particularly vigilant in
> reviewing a case of this nature, a vigilance that apparent-
> ly is not shared by the Court today.

Lorain Journal Company v. United States (1951)

The 1951 case of Lorain Journal Co. et al. v. United States [54]
dealt with a straightforward instance of a newspaper's attempting
to restrain trade by cutting into a radio station's advertising
revenues. It seems safe to say that the newspaper company
involved here placed its competitive practices in an even more
unfavorable light before the courts because it previously had

[53] 326 U.S. 1, 51–52, 65 S.Ct. 1416, 1439 (1945).

[54] 342 U.S. 143, 72 S.Ct. 181 (1951).

tried—and failed—to get a license to operate a radio station in *Lorain*.[55]

From 1933 until 1948, the publisher of the *Lorain Journal* in Lorain, Ohio, had enjoyed a "substantial monopoly in Lorain of the mass dissemination of news and advertising, both of a local and national character." This idyllic situation ended in 1948, however, when the Elyria-Lorain Broadcasting Company, a corporation independent of the newspaper publisher, was licensed by the Federal Communications Commission. The radio station— WEOL—was located in Elyria, just eight miles from Lorain, and also opened a branch studio in Lorain.[56]

The publishers of the *Lorain Journal* did not welcome this new competitor for advertising dollars, and set about trying to drive the radio station out of business. The newspaper refused to accept local advertising from Lorain merchants who also bought advertising time from the radio station. Because of the *Lorain Journal's* coverage of 99 per cent of Lorain's families this forced many advertisers to avoid buying time from WEOL.

The United States government brought a civil antitrust suit against the Lorain Journal Company, charging an attempt to monopolize commerce under the Sherman Antitrust Act. The government sought an injunction against the publisher's business practices. In reply, the newspaper company argued that it had the right to select its customers and to refuse or accept advertising from whomever it pleases. Furthermore, the Journal Company declared that an injunction which would prevent the newspaper from refusing to print advertisements of persons or businesses who advertised over WEOL would restrict freedom of the press. That is, the newspaper publisher argued that such an injunction would amount to a prior restraint on what a newspaper may publish.[57]

In a trial in a United States district court, the Lorain Journal Company was found to be attempting to monopolize commerce. The court issued an injunction to prevent the newspaper's continuing the attempt.[58] The Lorain Journal Company appealed to the Supreme Court of the United States but to no avail. By a 7–0 vote, the Court held that the District Court's injunction was justified.[59]

The Supreme Court, in fact, was quite unkind in its description of the Lorain Journal Company's business practices. It

[55] See 92 F.Supp. 794, 796 (D.C.Ohio 1950). See also Lorain Journal Co. v. Federal Communications Commission, 86 U.S.App.D.C. 102, 180 F.2d 28 (1950).

[56] 342 U.S. 143, 147, 72 S.Ct. 181, 183 (1951).

[57] 342 U.S. 143, 148–156, 72 S.Ct. 181, 184–187 (1951).

[58] 342 U.S. 143, 145, 72 S.Ct. 181, 182 (1951).

[59] 342 U.S. 143, 144, 72 S.Ct. 181, 182 (1951).

quoted the District Court's statement that the newspaper was guilty of "'bold, relentless, and predatory commercial behavior.'"[60] The Court, through Mr. Justice Harold H. Burton's opinion, turned aside the newspaper's defense arguments one by one.

First, on the newspaper's right to do business with whomever it wished, Justice Burton wrote:[61]

> The right claimed by the publisher is neither absolute nor exempt from regulation. [The refusal to accept advertising] * * * as a purposeful means of monopolizing interstate commerce is prohibited by the Sherman Act. The operator of the radio station, equally with the publisher of the newspaper, is entitled to the protection of that Act. *"In the absence of any purpose to create or maintain a monopoly,* the act does not restrict the long recognized right of trader or manufacturer engaged in an entirely private business, freely to exercise his own independent discretion as to parties with whom he will deal."

Second, the court rejected the argument that the injunction to force the newspaper to cease its policy of discriminatory refusal of advertising to merchants who bought time from WEOL was an infringement of the newspaper's First Amendment rights.[62] With this decision, the Supreme Court forced the Lorain Journal Company to conform its business policies with the rugged conditions set forth by the injunction issued in the case by the United States District Court. These conditions in the injunction were not only burdensome, they were downright embarrassing. The injunction ordered the *Lorain Journal* not to discriminatorily refuse advertisements—or to attach discriminatory conditions in accepting advertisements—against persons or businesses who advertised in other media.[63]

The District Court retained jurisdiction over the case so that any of the parties to the judgment could ask for further orders or directions. In this way, the pressure was kept on the newspaper, because the District Court left itself in a position to step in quickly

[60] 92 F.Supp. 794, 796 (1950), quoted at 342 U.S. 143, 72 S.Ct. 181, 184 (1951).

[61] 342 U.S. 143, 155, 72 S.Ct. 181, 187 (1951), quoting United States v. Colgate & Co., 250 U.S. 300, 307, 39 S.Ct. 465, 468 (1919). Emphasis the Court's.

[62] 342 U.S. 143, 156–157, 72 S.Ct. 181, 187–188 (1951).

[63] "Final Judgment," quoted at 342 U.S. 143, 157–159, 72 S.Ct. 181, 188–189 (1951). The newspaper was forbidden to discriminate as to acceptance for publication, plus "price, space, arrangement, location, commencement or period of insertion or any other terms or conditions of publication of advertisement or advertisements where the reason for such refusal or discrimination is in whole or in part, express or implied, that the person, firm or corporation submitting the advertisement or advertisements has advertised, advertises, has proposed or proposes to advertise in or through another medium."

to clarify or amend the injunction, to enforce compliance, or to punish violations of the order.

All of this was doubtless bad enough, from the newspaper's point of view. But the injunction also forced the newspaper to publish notices admitting its violation of the Sherman Act for 26 consecutive weeks.[64]

The Lorain Journal Company's troubles were not finished, however. In antitrust law, as noted earlier, the findings of fact in a civil or criminal suit brought by the government may be used as a springboard for a private *treble damage* lawsuit. In 1961 came the decision in the case of Elyria Lorain Broadcasting v. Lorain Journal. There it was held that the newspaper was liable to treble damages for lost revenue caused the radio station by the newspaper's illegal business practices.[65]

Times-Picayune v. United States (1953)

Where business practices do not produce a demonstrably harmful effect, the antitrust laws will not be enforced. Although the United States government won its antitrust case against the Lorain Journal in 1950, it was not successful in proving violation of the Sherman Act in Times-Picayune v. United States in 1953. From the outset, the government side of this case must have looked like a sure victory for the antitrust lawyers employed by the United States. It appeared simply that two New Orleans newspapers owned by one publisher were ganging up on an independent, competing newspaper, trying to drive it out of business through illegal advertising contracts. However, for reasons which will be described below, the Supreme Court held that the government had presented insufficient evidence to show a violation of the Sherman Act.

At issue was the legality under the Sherman Act of the Times-Picayune Company's contracts for the sale of newspaper classified and general display (national) advertising. The company owned and published two New Orleans newspapers: the morning Times-Picayune (188,402 daily average circulation in 1950) and the evening States (105,235 daily average circulation in 1950). The Times-Picayune Company's two newspapers were competing with the evening New Orleans Item (114,660 daily average circulation in 1950).

The United States government filed a civil antitrust suit against the Times-Picayune Company because of the company's "unit" or "forced combination" contracts with its advertisers.

[64] Quoted at 342 U.S. 143, 158, 72 S.Ct. 181, 189 (1951).

[65] 298 F.2d 356 (6th Cir.1961).

That is, anyone wishing to buy classified advertising or local display advertising in either the morning Times-Picayune or the evening States had to purchase space in *both* the morning and afternoon newspapers. The United States challenged these "forced combination" contracts with advertisers as unreasonable restraints of interstate trade and as part of an attempt to monopolize a segment of interstate commerce.[66] A United States District Court in Louisiana found violations of the Sherman Antitrust Act and issued an injunction against further use of the Times-Picayune Company's advertising contracts.

Involved here was the complicated notion of "illegal tying" under the anti-trust laws. "Tying" is unlawful when a business with a dominant position in its industry coerces its customers to buy an unwanted product along with the desired product.[67] The United States government case rested upon the belief that the morning Times-Picayune, with its circulation of 188,402, was such a "desired product" for advertisers. However, to be able to buy space in the Times-Picayune, the advertisers were forced to also buy space in its sister newspaper, the evening States, which had a circulation of only 105,235. This, of course, must have operated to take some advertising revenue away from the States' competitor, the afternoon Item, which had a circulation of 114,660. The government even contended that the Times-Picayune Company had deliberately operated its afternoon newspaper at a loss—with low advertising rates—in order to attract revenue away from the competing afternoon Item and drive it out of business.[68]

A majority of the Supreme Court of the United States, however, found that there had been no unlawful "tying." The Times-Picayune was not regarded as the "dominant" product, nor was the States seen as an "inferior" product. Instead, Justice Tom C. Clark's majority opinion held that the two newspapers—owned by one publisher—were selling identical products: advertising space in a newspaper.[69]

Although the Supreme Court's decision left the Times-Picayune Company's combined unit advertising contracts in operation, the Court may well have had some real misgivings. Many actions of the Times-Picayune Company which were charged by the government to be unlawful restraints of trade or monopolistic practices seemed to the Supreme Court to be defensible as legitimate business practices. The government's evidence was simply not

[66] 345 U.S. 594, 597, 73 S.Ct. 872, 874 (1953). See the Sherman Act, 15 U.S.C.A. §§ 1 and 2.

[67] 105 F.Supp. 670 (D.C.La.1952).

[68] 345 U.S. 594, 627, 73 S.Ct. 872, 890 (1953).

[69] 345 U.S. 594, 614, 73 S.Ct. 872, 883 (1953).

strong enough, according to a majority of the Court, to support a finding that the Sherman Act had been violated.

An important part of Justice Tom C. Clark's majority opinion was his discussion of the relationship between freedom of expression and the economics of the newspaper business in the middle of the 20th century: [70]

> The daily newspaper, though essential to the effective functioning of our political system, has in recent years suffered drastic economic decline. A vigorous and dauntless press is a chief source feeding the flow of democratic expression and controversy which maintains the institutions of a free society. * * * By interpreting to the citizen the policies of his government and vigilantly scrutinizing the official conduct of those who administer the state, an independent press stimulates free discussion and focuses public opinion on issues and officials as a potent check on arbitrary action or abuse. * * * Yet today, despite the vital task that in our society the press performs, the number of daily newspapers in the United States is at its lowest point since the century's turn: in 1951, 1,773 daily newspapers served 1,443 American cities, compared with 2,600 dailies published in 1,207 cities in the year 1909. Moreover, while 598 new dailies braved the field between 1929 and 1950, 373 of these suspended publication during that period—less than half of the new entrants survived. Concurrently, daily newspaper competition within individual cities has grown nearly extinct: in 1951, 81% of all daily newspaper cities had only one daily paper; 11% more had two or more publications, but a single publisher controlled both or all. In that year, therefore, only 8% of daily newspaper cities enjoyed the clash of opinion which competition among publishers of their daily press could provide.

Despite this statement by the Justice Clark, he later declared in his decision that the New Orleans Item—the newspaper in competition with the *Times-Picayune* and its sister paper, the States—was flourishing. He noted that between 1946 and 1950, the Item had increased its general display advertising volume by nearly 25 per cent. This local display linage, he added, was twice the equivalent linage in the States. Clark asserted: "The record in this case thus does not disclose evidence from which demonstrably deleterious effects on competition may be inferred." [71] One ironic footnote should be added: the only afternoon newspaper

[70] 345 U.S. 594, 602–604, 73 S.Ct. 872, 877–878 (1953).

[71] 345 U.S. 594, 73 S.Ct. 872, 887 (1953).

now published in New Orleans is published by the Times-Picayune Company. The name of this afternoon newspaper, thanks to a 1958 merger, is the *New Orleans States Item.*

United States v. Kansas City Star (1957)

After the setback in the *Times-Picayune* case, the federal government turned to a *criminal* antitrust prosecution against the powerful *Kansas City Star.* The criminal prosecution was only part of the story, however, because the Department of Justice also brought a concurrent *civil* antitrust action against the *Star,* which was later dropped when the *Star* signed a consent decree agreeing to halt certain business practices.[72] Thus the case of United States v. Kansas City Star cuts across many major aspects of antitrust activity, including a criminal prosecution, a civil antitrust action brought by the U.S., the signing of a consent decree, and, finally, a number of treble damage antitrust lawsuits brought against the *Star* by persons, publications and firms who claimed they had been injured by the newspaper's tough competitive practices.[73]

The Department of Justice brought the criminal antitrust prosecution against the *Kansas City Star* and its advertising manager, Emil Sees. The action began under the provision of the Sherman Antitrust Act saying that every person who monopolizes or attempts to monopolize interstate commerce shall be guilty of a misdemeanor.[74] The Kansas City Star had been making the best of a favorable competitive situation. The corporation had no daily newspaper competition, owning the morning *Kansas City Times,* a morning paper with more than 350,000 circulation, and the *Kansas City Star,* an afternoon publication with more than 360,000 circulation. The circulation of the *Sunday Star* amounted to more than 378,000. In addition, the Kansas City Star corporation owned WDAF radio and WDAF–TV.

The *Times* and *Star* were delivered to 96 per cent of all homes in Kansas City each day. In order to get one of the Star Company's three newspapers, residents of Kansas City had to subscribe to all three. Classified advertisers and general advertisers were required to run their ads in both the *Star* and the *Times,* regardless of the desire of some advertisers to use only one of the papers.

[72] Editor & Publisher, Nov. 23, 1957, p. 9.

[73] Consent decrees, discussed later in this chapter, are negotiated settlements reached between the Antitrust Division of the Justice Department and a defendant. In such a decree the defendant agrees to stop certain business or to divest himself of certain holdings, but without admitting violation of any law.

[74] United States v. Kansas City Star, 240 F.2d 643 (8th Cir.1957); 15 U.S.C.A. § 2.

The facts of the *Kansas City Star* operation differed markedly from that which faced Federal antitrust attorneys in the Times-Picayune case. First, unlike the New Orleans situation, the morning, afternoon, and Sunday newspapers were *forced* upon readers. Persons who wished to place general or classified advertising were forced to buy space in all three newspapers as a condition of having their advertising accepted. Second, and also unlike New Orleans, the *Star*'s daily competition, the Journal-Post, was bankrupt and had ceased publication. Third, the Kansas City Star Corporation, thanks to its newspaper-radio-television enterprises, accounted for nearly 85 per cent of all mass media income in the Kansas City area in 1952. On facts such as these, the government built a strong antitrust case.[75]

In prosecuting its case, the government showed that the *Star*'s dominant position in the Kansas City area gave it the power to exclude competition. The government also assembled evidence that the power had been used in rather ruthless fashion. For example, the manager of three Kansas City theatres testified that he had been told, several years earlier, to take his advertising out of the then-competing newspaper, the Kansas City Journal-Post. If not, he said, he was told that his advertisements would be left out of the *Kansas City Star* and *Times*.[76] Other evidence was found of threats and coercion by the Star Corporation to attempt to hamper competition. It was even charged that the dissemination of news was used to control advertising. Consider the instance of a big league baseball player who was a partner in a florist's shop in Kansas City.[77]

> The florist shop also advertised in the [competing newspaper, the] *Journal-Post*. A *Star* solicitor informed one of the partners that The *Star* would discontinue publicizing the baseball player if the florist shop continued using the *Journal-Post* for advertising, Sees [the *Star's* advertising manager] instructing a *Star* solicitor to tell them, "* * * to get out of the *Journal-Post* or he wouldn't get any sports, that he wouldn't get any cooperation from the sports desk on anything that he did in organized baseball."

Evidence was also presented that television and radio advertising on the stations owned by the Star Company went only to advertisers who were favored. In 1952, the *Star* refused time on its WDAF–TV station to a furniture company. A *Star* advertising salesman then called the furniture company's attention to the fact

[75] United States v. Kansas City Star, 240 F.2d 643, 648 (8th Cir.1957).

[76] Ibid., p. 654.

[77] Ibid., p. 655.

that the company did not advertise in the *Star* Company's newspapers. When the salesman was told that the furniture company had no need for newspaper advertising, the salesman replied that if that were the case, the furniture company likewise had no need for television.[78]

Also involved was the issue whether the *Kansas City Star* and the *Kansas City Times* were one and the same newspaper since they were published by the same firm. The Star corporation argued that the *Star* and *Times* were one newspaper, published in 13 different editions each week. The government retorted that the *Times* and *Star* were in fact two separate and distinct newspapers owned by the *Star* company, and that this was a "forced combination" perpetrated upon subscribers and advertisers to exclude competition. The District Court trial jury found the Times and the Star to be separate newspapers, illegally tied together to restrain trade.[79]

By upholding the District Court conviction of the Kansas City Star and its advertising manager, Emil Sees, the Circuit Court approved fines of $5,000 against the newspaper corporation and of $2,500 against Sees. But the Kansas City Star's problems, even after the lengthy trial and the criminal antitrust conviction, were just beginning. While the *criminal* antitrust prosecution was underway, the government had also brought a *civil* antitrust action against the Star company. On November 15, 1957, ten months after the Circuit Court affirmed the criminal conviction and fines, the Kansas City Corporation settled the civil suit by agreeing to the terms of a consent decree.[80]

This decree, like other consent decrees between an antitrust defendant and the government, was a negotiated settlement. In return for getting government agreement to drop the action, the Kansas City Company agreed to a tough settlement. The Star agreed to sell its television and radio stations, and was forever prohibited from buying any Kansas City broadcasting or publishing operation without first receiving government approval. Government approval of such a purchase could be secured only upon a showing that it would not tend to restrain competition. The consent decree also forbade forcing advertisers to buy advertising space in both the Star and the Times in order to get an ad published. Furthermore, the Star was forbidden to discriminate among advertisers.[81]

[78] Ibid., p. 656.

[79] Ibid., pp. 656–657.

[80] See Editor and Publisher, Nov. 23, 1957, p. 9.

[81] Ibid.

Even the consent decree did not end the Star's problems. The criminal antitrust conviction was used repeatedly as evidence by would-be competitors who brought treble-damage antitrust suits. Defending against such lawsuits is an expensive proposition, and a number of such actions apparently were settled out of court.[82]

United States v. Times-Mirror Corporation (1967)

Mergers which eliminate actual or potential competition in a newspaper market area were forbidden.

Mergers between newspapers which lessen competition in a region were forbidden by the 1967 decision in United States v. Times-Mirror Corporation. That decision rescinded the $15 million purchase of The San Bernardino [California] Sun by the Times-Mirror Corporation of Los Angeles, California. The San Bernardino *Sun* is a profitable daily located about 40 miles from Los Angeles. In 1964, the Pulitzer Corporation of St. Louis offered $15 million to buy the *Sun.* Instead of accepting Pulitzer's offer, *Sun* publisher James A. Guthrie offered to sell to a long-time friend, Norman Chandler, chief executive of the Times-Mirror Corporation, for the same amount.

Mr. Guthrie evidently believed that the Times-Mirror Corporation had a greater interest in the development of the West than would a Missouri-based company such as the Pulitzer Corporation. Mr. Chandler, was on the board of directors of three of the largest corporations in San Bernardino County, Kaiser Steel Corporation, The Atchison, Topeka and Santa Fe Railroad, and Safeway Stores, Inc. In any event, the Chandler family accepted Guthrie's offer and purchased the Sun in 1964.[83]

Acquisition of the *Sun* by the Times-Mirror Corporation was challenged by the Antitrust Division of the Justice Department in 1965. The government complained that the merger meant that the publisher of California's largest daily newspaper, The Los Angeles *Times,* had gained control of the largest independent daily publisher in Southern California. The government contended: [84]

---

[82] See, e.g., M. Robert Goodfriend and J.S. Levinson v. Kansas City Star Co., 158 F.Supp. 531 (D.C.Mo.1958); Ernie M. Duff v. Kansas City Star Co., 299 F.2d 320 (8th Cir.1962), and Craig Siegfried v. Kansas City Star Co., 193 F.Supp. 427 (D.C. Mo.1961).

[83] United States v. Times-Mirror Corp., 274 F.Supp. 606, 609–11 (D.C.Cal.1967), affirmed by the Supreme Court of the United States without opinion, 390 U.S. 712, 88 S.Ct. 1411 (1968).

[84] 274 F.Supp. 606, 609 (D.C.Cal.1967), Section 1 of the Sherman Act, 15 U.S.C.A. § 1, provides in pertinent part: "Every contract, combination in the form of trust or otherwise, or conspiracy, in restraint of [interstate] trade or commerce among the several states, or with foreign nations, is declared to be illegal ∗ ∗ ∗." Section 7 of the Clayton Act, 15 U.S.C.A. § 18, provides in pertinent part: "No corporation engaged in [interstate] commerce shall acquire, directly or indirectly,

Times-Mirror's acquisition and ownership of the stock of the Sun Company constitutes an unlawful control and combination which unreasonably restrains interstate trade and commerce in violation of Section 1 of the Sherman Act, 15 U.S.C.A. § 1, and that the effect of the acquisition may be to substantially lessen competition in violation of Section 7 of the Clayton Act, 15 U.S.C.A. § 18.

The Times-Mirror Corporation, indeed, is a financial power-house, and its holdings, by 1985, included *The Dallas Times-Herald* and *The Denver Post.* Just between 1960 and 1964, its total assets including newspaper publishing, book publishing, and commercial printing as well as other holdings—more than doubled, rising from $81 million to $165 million. Times-Mirror's principal enterprise, *The Los Angeles Times,* in 1964 had daily circulation figures of 790,255 and Sunday circulation of 1,122,143.

The Sun Company, less than one-twentieth the size of the Times-Mirror Corporation, was likewise financially healthy. The Sun Company had three newspapers: the morning Sun (1964 daily circulation, 53,802), the evening Telegram, and the Sunday Sun-Telegram (1964 circulation of 70,664). These newspapers were the only ones, other than the Los Angeles papers, offering home delivery throughout San Bernardino County.[85]

After hearing the Federal government's complaint against the merger, U.S. District Court Judge Warren J. Ferguson studied patterns of decreasing newspaper competition in San Bernardino County in particular and in the Southern California area—already dominated by the powerful Los Angeles Times—in general.[86] The judge noted, "In 1952, 59% of Southern California dailies were independent; in 1966, only 24% were independent."

Judge Ferguson declared the acquisition of The Sun Company by Times-Mirror to be particularly anticompetitive. That merger, he said, eliminated one of the few independent newspapers which had been able to operate successfully in the morning and Sunday fields in Southern California in the face of strong Los Angeles Times circulation. In addition, the judge said that the San Bernardino newspapers were in direct competition with the Times for advertising. The Sun's largest competitor for national advertising was the Times. The Times even ran promotional ads arguing to national advertisers that ads placed with the Los Angeles paper were "a better buy than a carefully selected group of Southern

the whole or any part of the stock or other share capital * * * of another corporation engaged in [interstate] commerce in any section of the country the effect of such acquisition may be substantially to lessen competition, or to tend to create a monoply."

[85] Ibid., p. 610.

[86] Ibid., p. 621.

California dailies." That group included the Sun papers of San Bernardino.[87]

For such reasons, Judge Ferguson ruled that the purchase of The Sun Company by Times-Mirror violated the antimerger provision of Section 7 of the Clayton Act. As a result, Times-Mirror was told to divest itself of Sun Company stock, and—within just 60 days—to present to the court "a plan for divestiture which shall provide for the continuation of The Sun Company as a strong and viable company." To make sure his orders would be followed, Judge Ferguson "retained jurisdiction" in the case, and also ruled that the Times-Mirror Company had to pay the government's costs in bringing the antitrust suit.[88]

The Antitrust Division of the Department of Justice held that its victory in the Times-Mirror case was a significant one. In 1968, the leading antitrust lawyer Charles D. Mahaffie, Jr. wrote that the Antitrust Division was "and will continue to be particularly concerned with mergers which may eliminate the actual and potential competition afforded by the suburban, small-city and community papers."[89]

Underlying such a statement was a basic philosophy of communication and freedom of expression filtered through antitrust law. The idea is that many voices in the marketplace of information and opinion—"diversified, quarrelsome, and competitive"— are; in the public interest.[90] After the Times-Mirror's acquisition of the San Bernardino Sun was voided, the Sun newspapers were acquired by the nation's largest newspaper group, The Gannett Company, then headquartered in Rochester, New York.

United States v. Citizen Publishing Co. (1968) and the "Newspaper Preservation Act" of 1970

In 1969, the Supreme Court of the United States decided a case of great importance to the daily newspaper industry: United States v. Citizen Publishing Company, often called "The Tucson Case." That decision declared "joint operating agreements to be illegal. Such agreements were and are important to the profit

[87] Ibid., p. 618.

[88] Ibid., p. 624.

[89] Charles D. Mahaffie, Jr., "Mergers and Diversification in the Newspaper, Broadcasting and Information Industries," The Antitrust Bulletin Vol. 13 (Fall 1968) pp. 927–935, at p. 928.

[90] See the classic statement by Judge Learned Hand in United States v. Associated Press, 52 F.Supp. 362, 372 (D.C.N.Y.1943), quoted at 326 U.S. 1, 28, 65 S.Ct. 1416, and printed in the text to footnote 52 earlier in this chapter.

margins if not to the very survival of competing newspapers in about two-dozen cities.[91]

The Supreme Court's judgment that joint operating agreements were illegal didn't last long. The ruling brought a wave of protests from publishers whose newspapers are involved in joint operating agreements. On March 12, 1969, just two days after the Court's Tucson decision, a number of bills were offered in both the U.S. House of Representatives and the Senate to legalize joint operating agreements between two newspapers. Those bills tied in with lengthy hearings held by the preceding Congress on the so-called "Failing Newspaper Act."[92]

After the Supreme Court's decision in the Tucson Case, the "Failing Newspaper Act" was given the euphemistic label "Newspaper Preservation Act" and was passed by both houses of Congress.[93] President Nixon signed the bill—called the Crybaby Publishers Bill by some unconvinced critics—into law on July 24, 1970. The text of the Newspaper Preservation Act is quoted at length in Appendix—at the end of this book.

Joint operating agreements work in this fashion. Two competing newspapers in one town combine their printing, advertising, circulation and business operations. The news and editorial operations of the two newspapers, however, retain their separate identities. Then, the two newspapers—one published in the morning and the other in the afternoon—can use the same publishing, business and distribution facilities, resulting in substantial economies in operation.

To say that the Tucson Case worried a number of publishers would be one hellacious understatement. Arguments filed before the Supreme Court in the Tucson Case early in 1969 included an amicus curiae brief filed on behalf of newspaper publishers in 16 cities. In that brief, attorney Robert L. Stern asserted that "a joint operating plant is the only feasible way to preserve competition in cities which cannot support two completely separate newspapers." [94]

The Antitrust Division of the Department of Justice, however, disagreed with the line of thinking argued by attorney Stern. So did a Federal district court, in deciding that the Tucson joint

[91] Editor & Publisher, Jan. 18, 1969, p. 9. Such cities include Tucson; San Francisco; Madison, Wisconsin, El Paso, Texas, and Honolulu.

[92] See Subcommittee on Antitrust and Monopoly of the Committee on the Judiciary, United States Senate, 90th Congress, First Session, on S. 1312, The Failing Newspaper Act, Part 1, July 12–14, 18–19, 25–26, 1967, at p. 2.

[93] 15 U.S.C.A. §§ 1801–1804.

[94] Editor & Publisher, Dec. 21, 1968, p. 9.

operating agreement was illegal.[95] That joint operating agreement had been in existence since 1940. Then, Citizen Publishing Company (publishers of The Tucson Daily Citizen, an evening paper) and The Star Publishing Company (publishers of The Arizona Daily Star, a morning and Sunday paper) joined forces to form a third corporation: Tucson Newspapers, Inc. Tucson Newspapers, Inc. took over all departments of the two newspapers except news/editorial.

This joint operating agreement was started because—the publishers of the two newspapers later said—they beleived there could not be successful operation of two competing dailies in a city with a population of less than 100,000.[96]

In the district court decision, Chief Justice James A. Walsh found that the joint operating agreement amounted to illegal "price fixing, profit pooling, and market allocations by the parties to the agreement,"[97] a violation of the Sherman Act.

In arguments to the Supreme Court of the United States, the Tucson newspapers contended that joint operating agreements were necessary in a number of cities to allow newspapers to survive while maintaining competing news and editorial voices. There were 22 cities with a total of 44 newspapers involved in joint operating agreements similar to the Tucson situation in the mid-1960s. Thus, it was feared that the Justice Department, should it succeed in the Tucson case, would begin antitrust actions against other newspapers' joint operating agreements. That would mean, to use the example of Arizona, that Tucson Newspapers, Inc., could no longer operate single advertising and circulation departments serving both newspapers.[98]

In March of 1969, the Supreme Court of the United States indeed did find the Tucson joint operating agreement illegal. Writing for the Court, Mr. Justice Douglas ruled that the agreement was for the purpose of ending competition between the two newspapers.

The Supreme Court thus affirmed the orders issued by the U.S. District Court in the Tucson case. This meant that the Tucson newspapers must "submit a plan for divestiture and re-establishment of the Star as an independent competitor and for modification of the joint operating agreement so as to eliminate the price-fixing, market control, and profit pooling provisions."

[95] United States v. Citizen Pub. Co., Tucson Newspapers, Inc., Arden Pub. Co. and William A. Small, Jr., 280 F.Supp. 978 (D.C.Ariz.1968).

[96] Ibid., at p. 981.

[97] Ibid., 993–994.

[98] Ibid. See also Editor & Publisher, Jan. 18, 1969, p. 9.

It should be noted that Douglas emphasized the "failing company doctrine" as he wrote the majority opinion in the Tucson case. Douglas declared the "only real defense of appellants [the Citizen Publishing Company and its co-defendants] was the failing company defense—a judicially created doctrine." The failing company doctrine means that acquisition of a company by a competitor does not illegally lessen competition if the firm which has been purchased is in grave danger of business failure. Justice Douglas, however, found that the Citizen had not been a failing newspaper in 1940 when it entered the joint operating agreement with the Star, despite the fact that the Citizen was then losing money.[99] The Supreme Court, as Justice Douglas put it, found that "beyond peradventure of doubt" the joint operating agreement between Tucson's two daily newspapers violated antitrust laws.

The Newspaper Preservation Act

As noted earlier, the Supreme Court's decision in the Citizen Publishing Company case was promptly legislated out of existence by the Newspaper Preservation Act.[1] This act's purpose was stated to be maintaining—in the public interest—"a newspaper press editorially and reportorially competitive in all parts of the United States" by legalizing such joint operating agreements. In one sense, this legislation might be viewed as "too little, too late" because by 1969 there were not many cities left with competing, independently owned daily newspapers. In another sense, there is also room for doubt about how truly "independent" newspapers bound together by common financial and business operations will be when a choice has to be made between serving the public interest and serving economic self-interest.[2] As a result, the Newspaper Preservation Act of 1970 approved all 22 joint operating agreements then in existence, involving 44 daily papers.[3]

---

[99] 394 U.S. 131, 89 S.Ct. 927 (1969); United States Law Week, Vol. 37, pp. 4208–4212 (March 11, 1969); Barry Schweid, "Newspapers Want Congress to Legalize Joint Operation," Associated Press dispatch in Madison, Wis., Capital Times, March 11, 1969; "Publishers seek relief in Congress," Editor & Publisher, March 15, 1969, p. 9ff. See also International Shoe Co. v. Federal Trade Commission, 280 U.S. 291, 302, 50 S.Ct. 89, 93 (1930).

[1] 15 U.S.C.A. §§ 1801–1804.

[2] See Ben H. Bagdikian, The Media Monopoly (Boston: Beacon Press, 1983, pp. 98–103.

[3] Cities with daily newspapers in joint operating agreements in 1970 included: Albuquerque, N.M.; Bristol, Tenn.; Charleston, W.Va.; Columbus, Ohio; El Paso, Texas; Evansville, Ind.; Fort Wayne, Ind; Franklin-Oil City, Pa.; Honolulu; Knoxville, Tenn.; Lincoln, Neb.; Madison, Wis.; Miami, Fla.; Nashville, Tenn.; Pittsburgh, Pa.; Saint Louis, Mo.; Salt Lake City; San Francisco; Shreveport, La.; Tucson, and Tulsa. Since then, Birmingham, Ala., Cincinnati, Ohio, Chattanooga, Tenn., and Seattle, Wn. have gone into joint operation. Dailies in Anchorage, Alaska, dissolved a joint operating agreement after a brief period, and The Derrick,

The Newspaper Preservation Act was passed despite strenuous objections from the Antitrust Division of the Department of Justice. The government's attorneys expressed fear that if profit pooling or price fixing laws were relaxed to aid newspapers, "many publishers will opt for that way [joint operating agreements] even though they might be capable of remaining fully independent, or of finding other solutions to the difficulties which preserve competition."[4] Weekly newspapers, small dailies, and the American Newspaper Guild strongly and repeatedly urged against passage of a failing newspaper act, often complaining that joint advertising rates provide newspapers in a joint operation situation with an advantage which competitors simply cannot overcome.[5] Senator Philip Hart of Michigan, chairman of the subcommittee which held hearings on the bill, declared that propping up a failing large or middle-sized newspaper might put competing small dailies or weeklies in the same area at an insuperable disadvantage.[6]

John H. Carlson, writing in the Indiana Law Journal, expressed dismay about the antitrust exemption for so-called failing newspapers.[7] Carlson declared that the Newspaper Preservation Act, which legalized the *Tucson* arrangement as well as similar operations elsewhere, allowed newspapers which were nowhere close to failing financially to dodge antitrust laws.[8]

> The Newspaper Preservation Act of 1970, while purporting to advance the public interest of "maintaining a newspaper press editorially and reportorially independent * * * is another step toward the disturbing trend of special legislation following governmental antitrust victories.

Just as Carlson's critique of the Newspaper Preservation Act first appeared in print in the spring of 1971, publisher Bruce Brugman of the *San Francisco Bay Guardian* offered his own critique in the form of a challenge to the Act's constitutionality. *The Bay Guardian,* a monthly with a circulation of 17,000, saw itself in a tough competitive situation. *San Francisco's Chronicle*

Oil City, Pa., ended its joint operating agreement in 1985 by buying its partner, the Franklin News-Herald.

[4] Statement of Donald F. Turner, assistant attorney general, Antitrust Division, Department of Justice, before the Senate Judiciary Committee, Subcommittee on Antitrust and Monopoly, on S. 1312, April 1968, p. 18.

[5] See, e.g., The Guild Reporter, Sept. 8, 1967, p. 8; "Failing Newspaper Bill Assailed," Associated Press dispatch in Wisconsin State Journal, Madison, Sec. 1, p. 8, April 17, 1968.

[6] Wisconsin State Journal, loc. cit.

[7] John H. Carlson, "Newspaper Preservation Act: A Critique," Indiana Law Journal 46:392 (Spring, 1971).

[8] Ibid., pp. 397–399, 400.

and Examiner had tied themselves into a joint newspaper operating agreement some years before, in September of 1965. Under that agreement, one newspaper—*The News-Call-Bulletin*—was put to death, and the two remaining dailies carved up the morning (*Chronicle*) and evening (*Examiner*) markets. Printing for the *Chronicle* and the *Examiner* is done by a jointly owned subsidiary, the San Francisco Newspaper Printing Company. The two remaining daily papers' editorial staffs are kept independent, although the two newspapers jointly published a unified Sunday edition. Profits from all operations are shared half-and-half. As a result, the *Chronicle* and *Examiner* have achieved a highly profitable position in San Francisco's daily newspaper market.[9]

Publisher Brugman and the *Bay Guardian* contended that the Newspaper Preservation Act is unconstitutional because it unfairly encourages such a journalistic monopoly. The effect of the Act, they contended, causes it to violate the press freedom guarantee of the First Amendment.

Chief Judge Oliver J. Carter summed up the *Bay Guardian's* arguments:[10]

> The plaintiffs are the owners and publishers of a small paper that has been a bimonthly paper and is now monthly. They contend that the defendants' monopoly position in the San Francisco market enables the defendants to destroy or weaken any potential competition. They contend that the profit sharing, joint ad rates, and other cooperative aspects of the joint operating agreement enable the defendants to establish and perpetuate a stranglehold on the San Francisco newspaper market. The plaintiffs contend that the Act is unconstitutional because it unfairly encourages this journalistic monopoly.

Judge Carter, however, was not persuaded by such arguments. He ruled that the simple answer to the plaintiffs' contention is that the Act does not authorize any conduct. He added that the Newspaper Preservation Act is a narrow exception to the antitrust laws for newspapers in danger of failing, and that the Act is "in many respects merely a codification of the judicially created

---

[9] Bay Guardian Co. v. Chronicle Publ. Co., 344 F.Supp. 1155, 1157 (D.C.Cal.1972). This court confrontation did not represent a full-dress trial. The plaintiffs originally sought a declaratory judgment that the Act was unconstitutional, but "such an action could not be maintained for technical jurisdictional reasons." See 340 F.Supp. 76 (Feb. 24, 1972). Then, the defendants—including the *Examiner* and the *Chronicle*—"answered the antitrust portions of the complaint by asserting the Act in two affirmative defenses to those claims." Plaintiff *Bay Guardian Co.* then moved to strike those defenses on grounds that the Newspaper Preservation Act is unconstitutional on its face.

[10] 344 F.Supp. 1155, 1157 (D.C.Cal.1972).

'failing company' doctrine." [11]   Although he upheld the Act's constitutionality, Judge Carter's words were not kind to the legislation: [12]

> * * * [T]he Act was designed to preserve independent editorial voices. Regardless of the economic or social wisdom of such a course, it does not violate the freedom of the press. Rather it is merely a selective repeal of the antitrust laws. It merely looses the same shady market forces which existed before the passage of the Sherman, Clayton and other antitrust laws.

The Bay Guardian Company lawsuit, however, contained another wrinkle. It was contended that the *Chronicle* and the *Examiner* were not truly "failing newspapers" and that the *News-Call-Bulletin* should not have been shut down as part of the merger. A $1,350,000 out-of-court settlement was awarded to a number of parties, including the Bay Guardian Company.

Such considerations aside, the importance of the Newspaper Preservation Act should not be overestimated. As Professor Paul Jess of the University of Kansas has noted, the Act did little more than legalize the 22 joint operating agreements already in existence at the time the Act was passed. There has been no great scramble to add to the number of joint operating agreements as such agreements are outlined by the act. The test of the Newspaper Preservation Act provides that to enter a joint operating agreement requires that at least one of the two newspapers must be "failing", or "in probable danger of financial failure." Any new joint operating agreement, furthermore, must be undertaken only after receiving written consent from the Attorney General of the United States. The Attorney General must determine that at least one of the newspapers applying for joint operation is "failing" or "in probable danger of financial failure."

At the 15th anniversary of the Newspaper Preservation Act in 1985, there were still 22 joint operating agreements in the nation, although the cast of newspapers had changed somewhat.[13]   As Margaret Genovese noted, further change was occurring. One paper in a "JOA"—The Derrick of Franklin-Oil City, Pennsylvania—had ended the partnership by buying out The News Herald of Franklin. In addition, the Columbus (Ohio) Dispatch was planning to end its JOA with a Scripps-Howard paper, the Columbus Citizen-Journal.[14]

[11] Ibid.

[12] Ibid., p. 1158.

[13] See cities listed in Footnote 3, above.

[14] Margaret Genovese, "JOA," Presstime, August, 1985, pp. 16–17.

One of the recent JOA partnerships—in Seattle, between the Post-Intelligencer (P–I) and the Times—is speaking of a " 'substantially improved' " financial picture.[15] The P–I had reported losses of averaging $1 a year from 1969 until 1983, but made a profit in 1984, the second year of the JOA—a JOA created despite employees of the P–I hiring an attorney to prevent its creation. Although opponents continue to be heard, the publishers of the Times and the P–I say that their editorial product has improved and that the two papers' news sides are competing briskly.[16]

Total Market Coverage ("TMC") and The Newspaper Preservation Act

A case involving the Tucson joint operating agreement papers—the Arizona Daily Star and the Tucson Citizen—illustrates an increasingly troublesome wrinkle in antitrust law for newspapers. Obviously trying to offer a more attractive package to advertisers, the Tucson papers—joined together in their business, production, and distribution sides to form the joint operator, Tucson Newspapers, Inc.—tried "Total Market Coverage." A TMC a product designed to keep advertisers from defecting to the local "shoppers," controlled or free-circulation publications. TMCs have often been added—as they were in Tucson—to newspapers, going to every house in an area, often in "zoned" editions tailored to particular locales.[17]

As lawyer George Freeman has written, "The shopper finds competition tougher than it used to be. It is about this time that the shopper realizes that its biggest asset may be an antitrust lawsuit against the [urban daily] newspaper publisher [who has started a TMC]."[18]

In the Tucson-area TMC case, Walter and Robert Wick— publishers of a biweekly newspaper, the Green Valley News & Sun—brought an antitrust action against the Tucson dailies. Green Valley is located about 25 miles from Tucson. The Wicks objected to the TMCs offered by the Tucson papers. The Arizona Star published a " * * * four-page newsprint jacket [which] appears in the Arizona Daily Star on a weekly basis. It is named THE ROUNDUP." It contains as filler advertising inserts called

---

[15] Genovese, pp. 18–19.

[16] Ibid.; see also Editor & Publisher, March 28, 1981, p. 15; April 26, 1981, p. 16.

[17] Wick v. Tucson Newspaper, Inc., 598 F.Supp. 1155 (D.C.Ariz.1984).

[18] George Freeman, "Antitrust Actions: At least 25 lawsuits in the last few years have focused on newspapers' total market coverage products," Presstime, January, 1985, p. 8.

inserts or preprints, and was distributed once a week as a part of the Arizona Daily Star.

As George Freeman explains the operation of a TMC product, the cost of its production is low. Therefore, "the publisher charges little for space (or inserts), offering bargain rates to clients already advertising in the daily."[19]

The Tucson Citizen, the other half of the JOA, was publishing its own TMC—the BULLETIN BOARD—in an identical way. In addition, in order to blanket the area with the TMC product, the Tucson daily newspapers mailed THE ROUNDUP and BULLETIN BOARD to all persons in the area—whether there were subscribing to the Tucson dailies or not.[20]

The court noted that the Tucson papers' joint operating agreement had been declared in violation of the antitrust laws, and that the Newspaper Preservation Act had exempted certain newspapers from the operation of antitrust statutes. The court initially concluded that the biweekly TMC products, THE ROUNDUP and BULLETIN BOARD were not parts of the Tucson Newspapers; they were not sections of daily newspapers. The content of THE ROUNDUP and BULLETIN BOARD was seen as primarily distributing advertising rather than editorial material. Why did this matter? The court said:[21]

> The Court * * * finds that these publications [THE ROUNDUP and BULLETIN BOARD] constitute "shopping newspapers" which were not intended to be included among those activities of a joint operating agreement exempt from the operation of anti-trust laws. The only thing exempted by the Newspaper Preservation Act from the operation of those laws is a newspaper publication * * *. That is a limited exemption and unless it is found to be applicable, the joint operation of these two daily newspapers constitutes a violation of the Sherman Act * * *.

The court then issued an injunction to prevent the Arizona Daily Star and the Tucson Citizen from distributing those portions of their papers referred to as ROUNDUP and BULLETIN BOARD to non-subscribers to the dailies. This distribution was forbidden whether by mail or otherwise, and included the "slick" advertising material that ROUNDUP and BULLETIN BOARD provided as

---

[19] Freeman, loc. cit.

[20] 598 F.Supp. 1155, 1157 (D.C.Ariz.1984).

[21] Wick v. Tucson Newspaper, Inc., 598 F.Supp. 1155, 1160 (D.C.Ariz.1984).

"jackets" (covers) for, to any non-subscribers in the Green Valley zip code area.

On reargument several months later, however, the court changed its ruling in part:[22]

> The Court is now advised by counsel that, contrary to the above [the earlier preliminary injunction order and accompanying language], the publication of ROUNDUP and BULLETIN BOARD is being distributed in Green Valley, almost uniformly, without any slick paper inserts.

> Therefore, the prior finding of the Court that there was a contemporary violation of the antitrust laws . . . which was likely to recur is inaccurate as there has been no violation to date. Further, the Court now finds, for reasons and on the authority set forth in the September 5, 1984 Order, that ROUNDUP and BULLETIN BOARD, as distributed in Green Valley, are not "shopping newspapers."

* * *

The Court finds that the portion of ROUNDUP and BULLETIN BOARD printed on newsprint and referred to in both this and the Court's prior opinion as a "jacket" is a "newspaper publication" within the meaning of 15 U.S.C. Sec. 1802(4), and is not a "shopping newspaper" in its present form. It is thus exempt from the antitrust laws.

Other TMC Activity

The TMC antitrust challenge to the Tucson joint operating agreement by no means shows the whole picture of TMC antitrust action. The joint operating agreement was merely a complicating factor. Most dailies, of course, are not parts of joint operating agreements.

Attorney George Freeman has noted that at least 15 lawsuits in the mid 1980s have zeroed in on daily newspapers efforts to provide total-market-coverage publications. And that's where the going gets sticky: if an antitrust suit is brought involving a TMC product, then it will be up to a court to discover what may be nearly indiscoverable: is the intent behind the TMC to compete better for ad revenues or is it to put competing publications out of business? One is good competition; the other is violative of antitrust laws.[23]

[22] Ibid., p. 1163.

[23] Freeman, loc. cit.

SEC. 96. CONSENT DECREES

Negotiated settlements, which settle antitrust proceedings without a formal trial, may be used in cases affecting the mass media.

Court decisions, however, are only a part of the antitrust story affecting the communications media. Also available in antitrust law is a court-adjudicated legal instrument known as a consent decree. Consent decrees—also sometimes called consent judgments—are negotiated final legal settlements between the government and a business. Consent decrees have the force of law once they have been approved by a judge. Such consent decree settlements can take place in civil, but not criminal, antitrust cases.[24]

Where a newspaper or broadcasting station is concerned, antitrust consent decrees have been used in the following fashion. First, civil antitrust suit is filed by the Antitrust Division of the Justice Department against the owners of a newspaper or broadcasting station. In the opinion of the Justice Department, the communications medium involved may have been engaging in anti-competitive business practices.

Second, the owners may decide that it will do them no good to fight the antitrust suit. The owners' attorneys may see that a court battle is almost certain to result in defeat. So, in order to avoid lengthy and expensive trial, attorneys for the owner will sit down with attorneys from the Antitrust Division of the Justice Department. Once a consent agreement is worked out, it means that the owners have promised to stop certain business practices or to divest themselves of certain media units. After the agreement is reached, it is made final by being formalized before a federal district judge.

Consent decrees have the advantage of allowing a defendant to settle a suit without admitting a violation of law. An example of this was the sale, late in 1968, of WREX–TV in Rockford, Ill., by the Gannett Company of Rochester, New York. In that year, the Antitrust Division of the Department of Justice has filed a civil antitrust suit against the Gannett Company, which owned, in addition to WREX–TV, also owned the Rockford Newspaper, the Morning Star and the Register-Republic. Gannett had acquired

[24] As Dr. Lorry Rytting, formerly of the University of Utah noted, the Justice Department is sensitive to charges that criminal antitrust suits might be filed, in effect, to force the signing of civil consent decrees. Department of Justice policy discourages the use of concurrent criminal and civil antitrust complaints. Rytting, "Antitrust Consent Decrees: A Threat to Freedom of the Press?", unpublished paper, School of Journalism, University of Wisconsin, 1967.

the two newspapers in 1967, and had purchased WREX–TV in 1962 for $3,500,000. Under the consent decree, the Gannett Company agreed to divest itself of the television station to James S. Gilmore, Jr., president of Gilmore Broadcasting Co., for $6,850,000.[25]

Earl A. Jinkinson, formerly chief of the Midwest Office of Chicago of the Department of Justice's Antitrust Division, has summarized some of the differing ways consent decrees are viewed.[26]

> To the Government attorneys the consent decree is an act of grace granted in order to give the attorneys and the entire staff more time to attend to other ever-pressing and sometimes more important matters. On the other hand, many defense counsel at least profess to believe, erroneously I might add, that the consent decree is a governmental device for winning cases, thrust upon an unwilling defendant which, to adopt the words of Seth Dabney, is like "Byron's maiden who strove and repented, but ultimately consented." To attorneys for private parties injured because of the violation [of antitrust statutes], the consent decree is an abrogation of the duty of the Department of Justice to protect their client's rights.

In 1947, Zechariah Chafee warned that consent decrees could increase the danger to press freedom through heavy use of the antitrust laws. Consent decrees are reached without trials, after secret proceedings. Evidence presented in reaching these decrees is not made public. Furthermore, such decrees are as legally binding as the decision of a federal court, and may be enforced with contempt-of-court sanctions if they are not obeyed.[27]

It has been suggested that the government, when it begins—or which has indicated that it soon may begin—an antitrust action is very much in the driver's seat against the defendant, which may feel compelled to "settle" by way of a consent decree. True, if an owner decides that the terms insisted on by the Antitrust Division violate his rights, he may halt the negotiations for a consent decree and demand a full trial. Trials, however, are expensive, lengthy, and may carry with them publicity which the media owners find damaging.[28]

Whether consent decrees are a threat to press freedom or a boon to media owners which allows them to avoid full-dress

---

[25] The Gannetteer, magazine of the Gannett Co., January 1969, p. 3.

[26] Earl A. Jinkinson, "Negotiation of Consent Decrees," Antitrust Bulletin, Vol. 9: Nos. 5–9 (Sept.-Dec., 1964), pp. 673–690, at pp. 676–677.

[27] Chafee, op. cit. Vol. 2, p. 670.

[28] Rytting, op. cit.

antitrust trials, the fact remains that such decrees affecting the mass media are a weapon in government's antitrust arsenal.

That kind of agreement is by no means a thing of the past. For example, in February of 1984, the Tribune Company—owners of the Orlando (Florida) Sentinel—agreed to a settlement with the Department of Justice to end an antitrust action. Back in 1980, the Sentinel had purchased five publications—two shoppers and three weeklies—for $4.1 million. The Justice Department brought suit, contending that those five acquired publications added up to 20 percent of the advertising in Osceola County, and that the Sentinel already had another 40 percent.

The Chicago-based Tribune Company settled with the Department of Justice, agreeing to sell off the five publications within a year. Also, the agreement forbids the Orlando Sentinel from buying any other publications in its main circulation area for 10 years.[29]

SEC. 97.   BROADCASTING, CABLE AND ANTITRUST LAW

New configurations of media ownership patterns, coupled with deregulation of broadcasting, may bring new roles for antitrust law.

In a thoughtful 1984 article, law professors Monroe E. Price and Mark S. Nadel examined possible roles for antitrust law, especially in the electronic media. They noted—as was also discussed in Section 79 of Chapter 12—that the Federal Communications Commission has eliminated many of its regulatory controls. The FCC, they said, relies increasingly on "what it views as a competitive market-place."[30] In the absence of regulation—and with the heightened reliance on competition—Professors Price and Nadel predict "that the antitrust laws will play a greater part * * * in establishing the rules * * *."[31]

Meanwhile, the antitrust laws did not and could not prevent the mid-1980s' remarkable surge in media mergers. In July, 1985, The New York Times noted that radio stations may not have the glamour of television stations or cable systems, but they are hot properties nevertheless. Geraldine Fabrikant reported in The Times that radio stations were changing hands at a record pace.

---

[29] SNPA Bulletin, Feb. 10, 1984.

[30] Monroe E. Price and Mark S. Nadel, "Antitrust Issues in the New Video Media," Cardozo Arts & Entertainment Law Journal, Vol. 3, No. 1 (1984), p. 27.

[31] Ibid., p. 52.

In fact, more than 1,000 radio stations were purchased in 1984, a jump of some 200 over 1983. Ms. Fabrikant added: [32]

> Deregulation has spurred much of the activity. The Federal Communications Commission no longer requires owners to hold on to stations for a minimum of three years. And it has pushed the limit on station ownership to 12 AM and 12 FM stations, from the previous limit of 7 each.

In addition, the new TV ownership rules mean that one individual or corporation may own 12 television stations. The prime limitation on ownership is that no one firm or person may own television stations that reach more than 25 percent of the population.

> While this financial carnival—described in part in Section 94, above—has continued and the mergers have mounted, some voices expressed concern. An English professor at the University of New Mexico named David K. Dunaway wrote to The New York Times complaining that public control of the airwaves is ebbing. He said that the 1985 sale of American Broadcasting Companies and the news-making efforts to take over CBS and other media giants will lead to less diversity in programming.

He contended: [33]

> The merger activity reflects a larger tendency—spurred by key decisions of the Federal Communications Commission—toward the greatest concentration of power in American history.

*   *   *

Should the nation's communications channels be left to the highest bidder?

[32] Geraldine Fabrikant, "Hot Market for Radio Stations," The New York Times, July 25, 1985, p. 27.

[33] David K. Dunaway, "A Threat to the Airwaves," The New York Times, June 1, 1985, p. 19.

Chapter 15

TAXATION AND LICENSING

SEC. 98. TAXATION

The mass media are constitutionally protected from discriminatory or punitive taxation.

Taxation has long been a fighting word to the press. Taxes on the press instituted in England in 1712 were called "taxes on knowledge," because they raised the purchase price of pamphlets or other printed materials beyond the means of most persons. In American history, taxation of the press has long been hated and feared. The Stamp Act of 1765 imposed great hardships on printers, taxing newspapers, advertisements, and pamphlets, as well as many legal documents [1] and became a great rallying cry for colonists who resisted British authority. Such a storm of protest arose in the colonies through both newspapers and pamphlets, to say nothing of mobs which forced British stamp agents to resign, that Parliament repealed the Stamp Act taxes as they affected printer-editors.

If American colonists hated the Stamp Act taxes because they infringed on "the liberty of the press" and "free inquiry," American memories were also very short. In 1785, only two short years after the War of Independence officially ended, the state of Massachusetts passed a newspaper stamp tax. If the Massachusetts legislature had a short memory, printers and publishers did not. Howls of protest reminiscent of the Stamp Act disturbances of 1765 soon echoed from the columns of Massachusetts newspapers. One writer who called himself "Lucius" declared that the tax on newspapers was a *"stab to the freedom of the people."* He acknowledged that Massachusetts newspapers were full of scurrilous articles, and admitted that the tax of a penny on each copy seemed small. But "Lucius" added that "tyranny begins small," and that the tax of even a half-penny on each newspaper copy could be a precedent for a tax of £100 on each issue.[2] Protests such as these led to the repeal of the Massachusetts stamp tax on newspapers

[1] Arthur M. Schlesinger, Prelude to Independence: The Newspaper War on Britain, 1763–1776 (New York: Knopf. 1958) p. 68.

[2] Massachusetts Centinel, May 28, 1735.

721

later in 1785, although the Massachusetts legislature shortly thereafter enacted a tax upon newspaper advertisements.[3] The tax on advertisements was not repealed until 1788.[4]

Newspapers and other units of the mass media of communications are businesses. As such, the media are not immune from taxation just like other business enterprises, as long as the taxes fall with a more or less even hand upon the press as well as other businesses. *Discriminatory* or *punitive* taxation, however, raises quite different issues. The classic case in United States constitutional law occurred during the 1930s and involved the flamboyant Huey "Kingfish" Long, the political boss and governor of Louisiana who entertained dreams of someday becoming President. The Supreme Court decision in Grosjean, Supervisor of Accounts of Louisiana, v. American Press Co., Inc.[5] effectively halted a Huey Long-instigated attempt to use a punitive tax to injure newspapers which opposed Long's political regime.

During the 1930s, Louisiana's larger daily newspapers were increasingly expressing opposition to Long's political machine. Louisiana's larger newspapers' sniping at Governor Long's dictatorial posturings soon brought about retaliation. The Louisiana legislature passed a special two per cent license tax on the gross receipts of all newspapers, magazines, or periodicals having a circulation of more than 20,000 copies per week.[6] Of Louisiana's 163 newspapers, only 13 had circulations of more than 20,000 per week. Of these 13 newspapers to which the tax applied, 12 were opponents of Long's political machine.[7] This transparent attempt to silence newspaper critics was challenged in the courts by nine Louisiana newspaper publishers who produced the 13 newspapers then appearing in the state which had circulations of more than 20,000 copies a week.

Newspapers subject to the gross receipts tax were required to file a report every three months showing the amount of the tax and the gross receipts. When such reports were filed, the tax for each three month period was to be due and payable. Failure to report or to pay the tax was made a misdemeanor, subject to a $500 fine. In addition, an officer of a publishing company which

[3] Ibid., July 6, July 30, 1785.

[4] Clyde Augustus Duniway, Freedom of the Press in Massachusetts (New York, 1906) P. 137.

[5] 297 U.S. 233, 56 S.Ct. 444 (1936).

[6] 297 U.S. 233, 240, 56 S.Ct. 444, 445 (1936).

[7] J. Edward Gerald, The Press and the Constitution 1931–1947 (Minneapolis, University of Minnesota Press, 1948) p. 100; William A. Hachten, The Supreme Court on Freedom of the Press: Decisions and Dissents (Ames, Iowa: Iowa State University Press 1968) p. 77; 297 U.S. 233, 56 S.Ct. 444, 445 (1936).

failed to file a report and pay the gross receipts tax could be sentenced to not more than six months in jail.

In declaring the Louisiana tax unconstitutional, a noted conservative—Justice George Sutherland—spoke for a unanimous Supreme Court. Justice Sutherland, a man not revered for his felicity of expression, may indeed have had some able assistance in writing what has come to be known as "Sutherland's great opinion in *Grosjean.*" It has been asserted that Sutherland's opinion included a proposed concurring opinion which had been drafted by the famed liberal Justice Benjamin Nathan Cardozo, and which the Court wished to add into Justice Sutherland's opinion.[8]

Whether assisted by Cardozo or not, the Sutherland opinion in Grosjean remains noteworthy. Justice Sutherland began with a historical overview of government-imposed dangers to freedom of expression, including reference to John Milton's 1644 "Appeal for the Liberty of Unlicensed Printing" and to the end of the licensing of the press in England in 1695. As Sutherland noted, "mere exemption from previous censorship was soon recognized as too narrow a view of the liberty of the press." Sutherland wrote.[9]

> In 1712, in response to a message from Queen Anne (Hansard's Parliamentary History of England, vol. 6, p. 1063), Parliament imposed a tax upon all newspapers and upon advertisements. * * * That the main purpose of these taxes was to suppress the publication of comments and criticisms objectionable to the Crown does not admit of doubt. * * * There followed more than a century of resistance to, and evasion of, the taxes, and of agitation for their repeal. * * * [T]hese taxes constituted one of the factors that aroused the American colonist to protest against taxation for the purposes of the home government; and that the revolution really began when, in 1765, that government sent stamps for newspaper duties to the American colonies.
>
> These duties were quite commonly characterized as "taxes on knowledge," a phrase used for the purpose of describing the effect of the exactions and at the same time condemning them. That the taxes had, and were intended to have, the effect of curtailing the circulation of newspapers, and particularly the cheaper ones whose readers were generally found among the masses of the people, went almost without question, even on the part of those who defended the act. May (Constitutional History

[8] Irving Brant, The Bill of Rights: Its Origin and Meaning (New York: Bobbs-Merrill, 1965) pp. 403–404.

[9] 297 U.S. 233, 249, 56 S.Ct. 444, 449 (1936).

of England, 7th ed., vol. 2, p. 245), after discussing the
control by "previous censure" [licensing and prior re-
straint], says: * * * a new restraint was devised in the
form of a stamp duty upon newspapers and advertisements,—avowedly for the purpose of repressing libels.
This policy, being found effectual in limiting the circulation of cheap papers, was improved upon in the two
following reigns, and continued in high esteem until our
own time. Collett [History of the Taxes on Knowledge]
(vol. I, p. 14), says: "Any man who carried on printing or
publishing for a livelihood was actually at the mercy of
the Commissioners of Stamps, when they chose to exert
their powers."

Sutherland quoted Thomas Erskine's great speech in defense
of Thomas Paine, when Erskine said: "The liberty of opinion
keeps governments themselves in due subjection to their duties."
The Justice asserted that if taxes had been the only issue, many of
England's best men would not have risked their careers and their
lives to fight against them. The issue in England for many years,
however, involved discriminatory taxation designed to control the
press and silence criticism of government. The *Grosjean* opinion
added: [10]

The framers of the First Amendment were familiar
with the English struggle, which had then continued for
nearly eighty years and was destined to go on for another
sixty-five years, at the end of which time it culminated in
a lasting abandonment of the obnoxious taxes. The framers were likewise familiar with the then recent [1785–
1788] Massachusetts [stamp tax] episode; and while that
occurrence did much to bring about the adoption of the
amendment, the predominant influence must have come
from the English experience.

Justice Sutherland rejected the State of Louisiana's argument
that the English common law in force when the Constitution was
adopted forbade only prior restraints on the press and said nothing about forbidding taxation.[11] In reply, Sutherland quoted from
a great 19th century American constitutional scholar, Judge
Thomas Cooley, and declared that Cooley had laid down the test to
be applied.[12]

The evils to be prevented were not the censorship of
the press merely, but any action of the government by

[10] 297 U.S. 233, 247–248, 56 S.Ct. 444, 448 (1936).

[11] 297 U.S. 233, 249, 56 S.Ct. 444, 449 (1936).

[12] 297 U.S. 233, 249, 56 S.Ct. 444, 449 (1936), quoting 2 Cooley's Constitutional
Limitations (8th ed.) p. 886.

means of which it might prevent such free and general discussion of public matters as seems absolutely essential to prepare the people for an intelligent exercise of their rights as citizens.

Application of this test led Justice Sutherland to rule that the Louisiana gross receipts tax on its larger newspapers was an unconstitutional abridgement of the First and Fourth Amendments. Sutherland declared: [13]

> It is not intended by anything we have said to suggest that the owners of newspapers are immune from any of the ordinary forms of taxation for support of the government. But this is not an ordinary form of tax, but one single in kind, with a long history of hostile misuse against the freedom of the press.
>
> The predominant purpose of the grant of immunity here invoked was to preserve an untrammeled press as a vital source of public information. The newspapers, magazines, and other journals of the country, it is safe to say, have shed and continue to shed, more light on the public and business affairs of the nation than any other instrumentality of publicity; and since informed public opinion is the most potent of all restraints upon misgovernment, the suppression or abridgement of the publicity afforded by a free press cannot be regarded otherwise than with grave concern. The tax here involved is bad not because it takes money from the pockets of the appellees. If that were all, a wholly different question would be presented. It is bad because, in the light of its history and of its present setting, it is seen to be a deliberate and calculated device in the guise of a tax to limit the circulation of information to which the public is entitled in virtue of the constitutional guaranties. A free press stands as one of the great interpreters between the government and the people. To allow it to be fettered is to fetter ourselves.
>
> In view of the persistent search for new subjects of taxation, it is not without significance that, with the single exception of the Louisiana statute, so far as we can discover no state during the one hundred fifty years of our national existence has undertaken to impose a tax like that now in question.

---

[13] 297 U.S. 233, 250–251, 56 S.Ct. 444, 449 (1936). Accord: See *City of Baltimore v. A.S. Abell Co.*, 218 Md. 273, 145 A.2d 111, 119 (1958). It was held that Baltimore city ordinances imposing taxes on advertising media were unconstitutional in that they discriminatorily taxed newspapers and radio and television stations. About 90 per cent of the impact of the taxes was on those businesses.

The form in which the tax is imposed is in itself suspicious. It is not measured or limited by the volume of advertisements. It is measured alone by the extent of the circulation of the publication in which the advertisements are carried, with the plain purpose of penalizing the publishers and curtailing the circulation of a selected group of newspapers.

Despite these ringing words, it should be noted again that the communications media are not exempt from paying non-discriminatory general business taxes. A case in point involved *The Corona Daily Independent,* a California newspaper which challenged a $32-a-year business license tax imposed by the City of Corona. The newspaper, which had paid the tax in a number of previous years, in 1951 refused to pay the tax. The newspaper went to court, arguing that the tax violated freedom of the press as guaranteed by the First and Fourteenth Amendments. However, the California Appellate Court ruled: [14]

There is ample authority to the effect that newspapers and the business of newspaper publication are not made exempt from the ordinary forms of taxes for the support of local government by the provisions of the First and Fourteenth Amendments.

* * *

In Tampa Times Co. v. City of Tampa * * * an ordinance imposed an annual business license tax upon newspapers, magazines, and other periodicals or publications, based upon gross receipts, with a minimum tax of $10 per annum upon receipts from all sales and advertising, both wholesale and retail. The tax was applied equally to all lines of business. There was no claim that the ordinance was arbitrary or harsh in nature. There the court held that the ordinance was one for revenue; that the question was one of whether or not a newspaper was immune from the burden of taxation to maintain government; and declared that it had no knowledge of any case where a newspaper had been held immune from all forms of taxation. The court states that a tax in any form is a burden, yet that alone does not impair freedom of the press any more than an *ad valorem* tax will destroy freedom of speech. On appeal to the Supreme Court of

[14] City of Corona v. Corona Daily Independent, 115 Cal.App.2d 382, 252 P.2d 56 (1953), certiorari denied 343 U.S. 833, 74 S.Ct. 2 (1953). See also Giragi v. Moore, 48 Ariz. 33, 64 P.2d 819 (1937) (general sales tax law placing a one per cent tax upon businesses' sales or gross income not unconstitutional as applied to newspapers); Arizona Publishing Co. v. O'Neil, 22 F.Supp. 117 (D.C.Ariz.1938), affirmed 304 U.S. 543, 58 S.Ct. 950 (1938).

the United States, the action was dismissed for want of a substantial Federal question.

The phrase "power to tax is the power to destroy" is without application to the issue here presented. There is no allegation or showing by defendant that the amount levied was arbitrary or harsh in nature, or oppressive or confiscatory, or that defendant's freedom to disseminate news and comment has been actually curtailed or abridged by the requirement that it shall pay a tax of $8 per quarter for publishing its newspaper. Nor is there any showing that the imposition of the tax was for the purpose of regulating defendant's business.

* * *

We conclude that a nondiscriminatory tax levied upon the doing of business, for the sole purpose of maintaining the municipal government, without whose municipal services and protection the press could neither exist nor function, must be sustained as being within the purview and necessary implications of the Constitution and its amendments.

The general rule to be drawn from cases such as Grosjean v. American Press Co. and Corona Daily Independent v. City of Corona seems to be this: the media are not exempt from nondiscriminatory taxation. More broadly, the media are businesses and are subject to general laws which regulate business. As it was said by the Supreme Court of the United States in 1939 in *Associated Press v. National Labor Relations Board:* [15]

The business of the Associated Press is not immune from regulation because it is an agency of the press. The publisher of a newspaper has no special immunity from

[15] Associated Press v. National Labor Relations Board, 301 U.S. 103, 132–133, 57 S.Ct. 650, 656 (1937). See Lee Enterprises v. Iowa State Tax Commission, 162 N.W.2d 730, 734, 754–755 (Iowa 1969). Ten corporations, including newspapers, radio and television broadcasters, advertising agencies and firms engaged in retail merchandising and in the auto business challenged an Iowa tax law known as Section 25 of Division VII, Iowa House File 702. With that measure, the Iowa General Assembly had amended the state's revenue statutes, including as taxable "the gross receipts of * * * directors, shoppers guides and newspapers whether or not circulated free or without charge to the public, magazine, radio and television advertising * * *." The Iowa Supreme Court held that the tax does not violate freedom of the press as guaranteed in either the United States or Iowa Constitutions because the law was of general application and not discriminatory.

A number of states, including Texas, Oklahoma, Kansas and Arkansas, exempt newspapers from paying taxes on consumable materials used in printing and processing operations. Interview with Lyndell Williams, executive vice president, Texas Press Association, May 16, 1978. In 1977, Texas passed a measure exempting newspapers from a sales tax on circulation income. See Vernon's Anno.Tex. Stat.Tax.Gen., Title 122A, § 20.04(BB)(1)(b) and § 20.04(BB)(4).

the application of general laws. He has no special privileges or immunities to invade the rights and liberties of others. He must answer for libel. He may be punished for contempt of court. He is subject to the anti-trust laws. Like others he must pay equitable and nondiscriminatory taxes on his business.

Grosjean v. American Press Co. is the leading case for the proposition that the mass media are constitutionally protected from discriminatory or punitive taxation. The *Grosjean* case, as seen on earlier pages, dealt with a garish fact situation, a transparent attempt by Louisiana Governor Huey "Kingfish" Long and his allies to silence newspaper critics.

Unlike the *Grosjean* situation, the State of Minnesota was operating out of more defensible motives during the 1970s when it enacted a "use tax" on paper and ink consumed applicable to newspapers. This apparently was only a revenue measure, not an attempt to control or to punish the press. Even so, the Supreme Court of the United States voided the tax by an 8–1 margin. The tax was held unconstitutional because it singled out the press for special treatment.

"Use taxes" are imposed by states to discourage their citizens from purchasing items in other states which have lower sales taxes. Minnesota's newspapers were exempted from use taxes until 1971, when the state began taxing the cost of paper and ink used in producing a publication.[16] In 1974, another change in the tax law exempted a publication's first $100,000 of ink and paper consumed from the 4% use tax.[17]

The $100,000 exemption meant that only the largest of Minnesota's publishers were liable to pay the tax. Only 11 publishers, producing 14 of the state's 388 paid-circulation newspapers, had to pay the tax in 1974. The Minneapolis Star and Tribune Company was the major revenue source from the tax. Of $893,355 collected in 1974, $608,634 was paid by the Star and Tribune.[18]

The Star and Tribune Company sued, asking a refund of the use taxes paid from January 1, 1974, to May 31, 1975. The company contended that the use tax violated freedom of the press and equal protection of the laws as guaranteed by the First and Fourteenth Amendments.[19] The Minnesota Supreme Court ruled

---

[16] Minn.Stat.Ann. §§ 297A.14, 287A.25i.

[17] Minn.Stat.Ann. § 297A.14.

[18] Minneapolis Star and Tribune v. Minnesota Commissioner of Revenue, 460 U.S. 575, 103 S.Ct. 1365, 1368 (1983), 9 Med.L.Rptr. 1369.

[19] Ibid.

the use tax constitutional,[20] and the Supreme Court of the United States then noted probable jurisdiction.[21]

Justice Sandra Day O'Connor wrote for an 8–1 Supreme Court in declaring the Minnesota tax unconstitutional. Baltimore Sun Supreme Court reporter Lyle Denniston commented: [22]

> The Court once more has used plenty of pro-press phrasing. The opinion is almost rhapsodic about the role of the press at the founding of the Republic, but it also establishes a firm precedent with no cleverly veiled qualifications. For added value, it comes as the work of Justice Sandra Day O'Connor, until now somewhat doubtful as a partisan of the press.

Justice O'Connor wrote that the tax was discriminatory on its face because it singled out publications for unique treatment under the state's law. She noted that the Minnesota use tax did not serve the function of protecting the sales tax. Also, it taxed " * * * an intermediate transaction rather than the ultimate retail sale. She added: [23]

> * * * [T]he ordinary rule in Minnesota * * * is to tax only the ultimate, or retail, sale rather than the use of components like ink and paper.
>
> * * *
>
> By creating this special use tax * * * Minnesota has singled out the press for special treatment. We must then determine whether the First Amendment permits such special taxation. A tax that burdens rights protected by the First Amendment cannot stand unless the burden is necessary to achieve an overriding governmental interest. * * * [T]his Court has long upheld governmental regulation of the Press. The cases approving such economic regulation, however, emphasized the general applicability of the challenged regulation to all businesses * * * suggesting that a regulation that singled out the press might place a heavier burden of justification on the State, and we now conclude that the special problems created by differential treatment do indeed impose such a burden.

Justice O'Connor declared that there is evidence that differential taxation of the press would have troubled the Framers of the First Amendment. "A power to tax differentially, as opposed to a

[20] 314 N.W.2d 201 (Minn.1981).

[21] 457 U.S. 1130, 102 S.Ct. 2955 (1982).

[22] Lyle Denniston, "Beware of Courts Bearing Gifts," Washington Journalism Review, June, 1983, p. 14.

[23] 460 U.S. 575, 103 S.Ct. 1365, 1370 (1983).

power to tax generally, gives government a powerful weapon against the taxpayer selected." [24] Here opinion also suggested the threat of burdensome taxes might operate as a form of censorship, making the press wary of publishing the critical comments which often allow it to serve as an important restraint on government. "Further, differential treatment, unless justified by some special characteristic of the press, suggests that the goal of the regulation is not unrelated to suppression of expression, and such a goal is presumptively unconstitutional." [25] The majority opinion concluded that Minnesota had offered not adequate justification for singling out the press with the use tax. Without that justification, the tax was held to violate the First Amendment.[26]

Justice William Rehnquist's dissenting opinion declared that the Supreme Court's concern " *   *   * seems very much akin to protecting something so much that in the end it is smothered." He expressed doubts that the Framers of the First Amendment would have seen such a use tax as an abridgment of the press. Furthermore: [27]

> The Court recognizes in several parts of its opinion that the State of Minnesota could avoid constitutional problems by imposing on newspapers the 4% sales tax that it imposes on other retailers.

Justice Rehnquist calculated that if a sales tax had been in effect in 1974 and 1975, the Star and Tribune's liability would have been more than $3.6 million, compared to less than $1.3 million paid in use taxes during those years. Such a differential treatment under the use taxes, Rehnquist concluded, actually benefited the press.[28]

> To collect from newspapers their fair share of taxes under the sales and use tax scheme and at the same time avoid abridging the freedom of speech and press, the Court holds today that Minnesota must subject newspapers to millions of dollars in sales tax liability. Certainly this hollow victory for the newspapers and I seriously doubt the Court's conclusion that this result would have been intended by the "Framers of the First Amendment."

The basic rule remains: the press may not be singled out for "differential treatment" when being taxed. That does not mean the press will pay less in taxes than other kinds of businesses.

[24] Ibid., p. 1372.

[25] Ibid., p. 1374.

[26] Ibid., p. 1376.

[27] Ibid., p. 1378.

[28] Ibid., p. 1382.

SEC. 99.   LICENSING

When licensing power over expression amounts to prior censorship, it is constitutionally forbidden.

Older than discriminatory taxation—although often closely related to it—is the control over the press called licensing. Licensing is one aspect of that most hated of all controls over the media: prior censorship. Licensing in England in the 16th and 17th centuries, for example, meant that only licensed printers—persons who had the approval of the government—were allowed to print. In the 1980s, of course, some forms of licensing are seen as permissible. For example, there is the Federal Communications Commission's system of allocating broadcast frequencies "in the public interest, convenience, and necessity." [29]

If licensing broadcasting stations is a rather benign form of that ancient control (although it has its critics), other kinds of licensing raise sharp-edged issues in our time. Consider the American Nazis decision to march—displaying swastikas—through a predominantly Jewish neighborhood in Skokie, Illinois, in 1977. Nazi leader Frank Collin asked a number of Chicago suburbs for permits (licenses) for demonstrations in their parks or on their streets. Skokie officials responded that the Nazis would have to post insurance of $350,000, a kind of bond against property damage resulting from a demonstration.[30]

The American Civil Liberties Union—which lost many of the Jews in its membership over Nazi-march-related issues—was cast in the ironic role of defending the Nazis' right to march and to demonstrate. The Illinois Supreme Court struck down the licensing attempts by the Village of Skokie, saying: [31]

> The display of the swastika, as offensive to the principles of a free nation or the memories it recalls may be, is symbolic political speech intended to convey to the public the beliefs of those who display it. It does not, in our opinion, fall within the doctrine of "fighting words," and that doctrine cannot be used here to overcome the heavy presumption against the constitutional validity of prior restraint.
>
> Nor can we find that the swastika * * * is * * * so offensive and peace threatening to the public that its display can be enjoined. We do not doubt that the sight

[29] See chapter on Broadcast Regulation.

[30] See Areyeh Neier, Defending My Enemy: American Nazis, the Skokie Case, and the Risks of Freedom (New York: E.P. Dutton, 1979).

[31] Skokie v. National Socialist Party of America, 69 Ill.2d 605, 14 Ill.Dec. 890, 373 N.E.2d 21 (1978).

of this symbol is abhorrent to the Jewish citizens of
Skokie, and that the survivors of the Nazi persecutions,
tormented by their recollections, may have strong feelings
regarding its display. Yet it is entirely clear that this
factor does not justify enjoining defendants' speech.

So it may be seen that licensing battles reoccur. England's
authoritarian licensing system was allowed to expire in 1695,[32] but
no battle for freedom ever seems to be won once and for all.
Major weapons in the battles against licensing in this century
were forged by Jehovah's Witnesses in their repeated battles for
free expression against city ordinances which involved license
taxes. The struggles of the Jehovah's Witnesses during the 1930s
and 1940s were noteworthy: time and again, they fought their
cases all the way to the Supreme Court of the United States and
ultimately succeeded. This religious sect, as Professor William A.
Hachten has noted, endured great suffering. The American Civil
Liberties Union reported, for example, that in one six-month
period of 1940, "1,488 men, women and children in the sect were
victims of mob violence in 355 communities in 44 states." [33] As
Professor J. Edward Gerald has pointed out, the Jehovah's Witnesses made themselves unpopular with their refusal to salute the
American flag; their contempt for most if not all organized
religion, and with their denunciations of the Catholic Church.
Likewise, their persistent street sales of literature and doorbell
ringings for their cause often raised hackles among non-believ-
ers.[34]

The Jehovah's Witness cases are useful reminders that the
right of freedom of expression belongs not only to media corporations but also to the people. Furthermore, the landmark case of
Lovell v. City of Griffin is crucially important, as Professor
Hachten has emphasized, because it explicitly gives constitutional
protection to distribution of literature as well as to publication.[35]

Alma Lovell, a Jehovah's Witness, was convicted in a municipal court in Griffin, Ga., and sentenced to 50 days in jail when she
refused to pay a $50 fine. Her crime? She had not received
written permission from the City Manager of Griffin to distribute
her religious tracts. The city ordinance provided:[36]

> That the practice of distributing, either by hand or
> otherwise, circulars, handbooks, advertisings, or literature

---

[32] Fredrick S. Siebert, Freedom of the Press in England, 1476–1776 (Urbana, Ill.:
University of Illinois Press, 1952) pp. 260–263.

[33] Hachten, op. cit., p. 73; see also Gerald, op. cit., pp. 136–137.

[34] Gerald, p. 137.

[35] 303 U.S. 444, 58 S.Ct. 666 (1938); Hachten, p. 74.

[36] Lovell v. Griffin, Ga., 303 U.S. 444, 447, 58 S.Ct. 668, 667 (1938).

of any kind, whether said articles are being delivered free, or whether same are being sold, within the limits of the City of Griffin, without first obtaining permission from the City Manager of the City of Griffin, such practice shall be deemed a nuisance, and punishable as an offense against the City of Griffin.

Alma Lovell simply could not be bothered with such "technicalities." She regarded herself as a messenger sent by Jehovah, and believed that applying to the City Manager for permission would have "been 'an act of disobedience to His commandments.'" The Supreme Court, however, regarded the City of Griffin's ordinance as far more than a mere technicality. Speaking for an undivided court, Chief Justice Charles Evans Hughes denounced the ordinance: [37]

> We think that the ordinance is invalid on its face. Whatever the motive which induced its adoption, its character is such that it strikes at the very foundation of the freedom of the press by subjecting it to license and censorship. The struggle for the freedom of the press was primarily directed against the power of the licensor. It was against that power that John Milton directed his assault by his "Appeal for the Liberty of Unlicensed Printing." And the liberty of the press became initially a right to publish "without a license what formerly could be published only *with* one." While this freedom from previous restraint upon publication cannot be regarded as exhausting the guaranty of liberty, the prevention of that restraint was a leading purpose in the adoption of the constitutional provisions. * * * Legislation of the type of the ordinance in question would restore the system of license and censorship in its baldest form.

> The liberty of the press is not confined to newspapers and periodicals. It necessarily embraces pamphlets and leaflets. These indeed have been historic weapons in the defense of liberty, as the pamphlets of Thomas Paine and others in our own history abundantly attest. The press in its historic connotation comprehends every sort of publication which affords a vehicle of information and opinion.
> * * *

> The ordinance cannot be saved because it relates to distribution and not to publication. "Liberty of circulating is as essential to that freedom as liberty of publishing; indeed, without circulation, the publication would be of

[37] 303 U.S. 444, 451–452, 58 S.Ct. 666, 669 (1938). Mr. Justice Cardozo took no part in this decision.

little value." Ex parte Jackson, 96 U.S. 727, 733, 24 L.Ed. 877.

Since the ordinance of the City of Griffin was not limited to " 'literature' that is obscene or offensive to public morals or that advocates unlawful conduct," the ordinance could not be upheld.[38] In Schneider v. New Jersey, the Supreme Court reviewed four cities' ordinances. Three of these anti-littering ordinances in effect punished distributors should the recipient of a leaflet throw it to the ground. The Supreme Court held that such ordinances were unconstitutional.

Referring to its opinion in Lovell v. Griffin, the Court handed down this ruling in Schneider: [39]

> [W]hatever the motive [behind the ordinance at issue in Lovell v. City of Griffin], the ordinance was bad because it imposed penalties for the distribution of pamphlets, which had become historical weapons in the defense of liberty, by subjecting such distribution to license and censorship; and that the ordinance was void on its face, because it abridged the freedom of the press. Similarly in Hague v. C.I.O., 307 U.S. 496, 59 S.Ct. 954 [1939], an ordinance was held void on its face because it provided for previous administrative censorship for the exercise of the right of speech and assembly in appropriate public places.

> The Los Angeles, the Milwaukee, and the Worcester ordinances under review do not purport to license distribution but all of them absolutely prohibit it in the streets, and, one of them, in other public places as well.

> * * *

> We are of the opinion that the purpose to keep the streets clean and of good appearance is insufficient to justify an ordinance which prohibits a person rightfully on a public street from handing literature to one willing to receive it. Any burden imposed upon the city authorities in cleaning and caring for the streets as an indirect consequence of such distribution results from the constitutional protection of the freedom of speech and press. This constitutional protection does not deprive a city of all power to prevent street littering. There are obvious methods of preventing littering. Amongst these is the punishment of those who actually throw papers on the streets.

[38] 303 U.S. 444, 58 S.Ct. 666, 668 (1938).

[39] Schneider v. State of New Jersey (Town of Irvington), 308 U.S. 147, 161–162, 60 S.Ct. 146, 151 (1939).

In this same decision, the Supreme Court also dealt with an ordinance of the Town of Irvington, New Jersey, which denied street distribution or house-to-house calls to anyone who did not have written permission from the chief of police. The Irvington ordinance also required that any person distributing circulars or seeking contributions had to restrict his canvassing to hours between 9 a.m. and 5 p.m. Also, the canvasser had to have with him a permit, including a photograph of himself, which had to be shown to a police officer or other person upon request.[40]

In declaring the Irvington ordinance unconstitutional, Mr. Justice Owen Roberts wrote:[41]

> If it [the ordinance] covers the petitioner's activities [in making house-to-house calls], it equally applies to one who wishes to present his views on political, social or economic questions. The ordinance is not limited to those who canvass for private profit; nor is it merely the common type of ordinance requiring some form of registration or license of hawkers, or peddlers. It is not a general ordinance to prohibit trespassing. It bans unlicensed communication of any views or the advocacy of any cause from door to door, and permits canvassing only subject to the power of a police officer to determine, as a censor, what literature may be distributed from house to house and who may distribute it. The applicant must submit to that officer's judgment evidence as to his good character and as to the absence of fraud in the "project" he proposes to promote or the literature he intends to distribute, and must undergo a burdensome and inquisitorial examination, including photographing and fingerprinting. In the end, his liberty to communicate with the residents of the town at their homes depends upon the exercise of the officer's discretion.
>
> As said in Lovell v. City of Griffin, supra, pamphlets have proved most effective instruments in the dissemination of opinion. And perhaps the most effective way of bringing them to the notice of individuals is their distribution at the homes of the people. On this method of communication the ordinance imposes censorship, abuse of which engendered the struggle in England which eventuated in the establishment of the doctrine of the freedom of the press embodies in our Constitution. To require a censorship through license which makes impossible the

---

[40] 308 U.S. 147, 157–158, 60 S.Ct. 146, 149 (1939).

[41] 308 U.S. 147, 163–165, 60 S.Ct. 146, 152 (1939).

free and unhampered distribution of pamphlets strikes at the very heart of the constitutional guarantees.

Conceding that fraudulent appeals may be made in the name of charity and religion, we hold a municipality cannot, for this reason, require all who wish to disseminate ideas to present them first to police authorities for their consideration and approval, with a discretion in the police to say some ideas may, while others may not, be carried to the homes of citizens; some persons may, while others may not, disseminate information from house to house. Frauds may be denounced as offenses and punished by law. Trespasses may similarly be forbidden. If it is said that these means are less efficient and convenient than bestowal of power on police authorities to decide what information may be disseminated from house to house, and who may impart the information the answer is that considerations of this sort do not empower a municipality to abridge freedom of speech and press. We are not to be taken as holding that commercial soliciting and canvassing may not be subjected to such regulation as the ordinance requires. Nor do we hold that the town may not fix reasonable hours when canvassing may be done by persons having such objects as the petitioner. Doubtless there are other features of such activities which may be regulated in the public interest without prior licensing or other invasion of constitutional liberty. We do hold, however, that the ordinance in question, as applied to the petitioner's conduct, is void, and she cannot be punished for acting without a permit.

Jehovah's Witnesses were to have many other days in court, defending the freedoms of religion, speech and press guaranteed by the First Amendment and protected from state encroachment by the Fourteenth Amendment. Even though the Court's 1938 Lovell v. Griffin decision had overturned a license tax, the case of Jones v. Opelika, Alabama, brought the issue back to the Court in slightly different form. In some respects, the Opelika ordinance looked quite innocuous: a $10 per annum license fee for engaging in business as a "Book Agent." [42] Although he gave some stirring judicial language to the concept of freedom of expression, Justice Stanley Reed, writing for the majority in this 5–4 decision, upheld the Opelika ordinance. Reed wrote: [43]

One man, with views contrary to the rest of his compatriots, is entitled to the privilege of expressing his

[42] Jones v. Opelika, 316 U.S. 584, 586, 62 S.Ct. 1231, 1234 (1942).

[43] 316 U.S. 584, 594–595, 62 S.Ct. 1231, 1238 (1942).

ideas by speech or broadside to anyone willing to listen or read. Too many settled beliefs have in time been rejected to justify this generation in refusing a hearing to its own dissentients. But that hearing may be limited by action of the proper legislative body to times, places and methods for the enlightment of the community which, in view of existing social and economic conditions, are not at odds with the preservation of peace and good order.

This means that the proponents of ideas cannot determine entirely for themselves the time and place and manner for the diffusion of knowledge or for their evangelism, any more than the civil authorities may hamper or suppress the public dissemination of facts and principles to the people. The ordinary requirements of civilized life compel this adjustment of interests.

In 1942, Justice Reed thus held that nothing in the collection of *nondiscriminatory* license fees—from persons selling Bibles, books, or papers—abridged freedom of worship, speech or press.[44] Justice Reed's opinion dismissed as unsubstantial the Jehovah's Witness complaint that the license tax of Opelika could be a dangerous weapon of censorship because the license could be revoked at will by city officials.[45]

Some eleven months later, however, after more Jehovah's Witness cases had been heard, the Supreme Court reversed itself and vacated its ruling that the Opelika ordinance was constitutional.[46] By this action, the Court adopted, as its majority position, the 1942 dissent in Jones v. Opelika written by Chief Justice Harlan Fiske Stone.[47] Stone's opinion held:

The ordinance in the Opelika case should be held invalid * * * the requirement of a license for dissemination of ideas, when as here the license is revocable at will without cause and in the unrestrained discretion of administrative officers, is likewise an unconstitutional restraint on those freedoms.

Chief Justice Stone insisted that speech and religion are freedoms which hold a "preferred position" in the framework of constitutional values. He wrote: [48]

[44] 316 U.S. 584, 598, 62 S.Ct. 1231, 1240 (1942).

[45] 316 U.S. 584, 599, 62 S.Ct. 1231, 1240 (1942).

[46] 319 U.S. 103, 62 S.Ct. 890 (1943). See also other Jehovah's Witness cases, Martin v. Struthers, 319 U.S. 141, 63 S.Ct. 862 (1943); Douglas v. Jeannette, 319 U.S. 157, 63 S.Ct. 877 (1943); Murdock v. Pennsylvania, 319 U.S. 105, 63 S.Ct. 870 (1943), all decided May 3, 1943.

[47] 316 U.S. 584, 600, 62 S.Ct. 1231, 1240–1241 (1942).

[48] 316 U.S. 584, 608, 62 S.Ct. 1231, 1244 (1942).

The First Amendment is not confined to safeguarding freedom of speech and freedom of religion against discriminatory attempts to wipe them out. On the contrary the Constitution, by virtue of the First and Fourteenth Amendments, has put those freedoms in a preferred position. Their commands are not restricted to cases where the protected privilege is sought out for attack. They extend at least to every form of taxation which, because it is a condition of the exercise of the privilege, is capable of being used to control or suppress it.

The victories of the Jehovah's Witnesses before the Supreme court in cases such as Lovell v. City of Griffin and Jones v. City of Opelika are still worth savoring. A relatively small—and often unpopular—religious sect fought hard to defend freedoms guaranteed to all Americans. In so doing, Jehovah's Witnesses helped greatly to fend off ancient threats to the press revived in modern times: licensing and taxation.

Lowe v. SEC (1985)

A more recent licensing effort—by the Securities and Exchange Commission (SEC)—was slapped down in the spring of 1985 by an 8–0 vote of the Supreme Court of the United States. The SEC, concerned about regulating many things affecting the health of the nation's financial communities, set about licensing financial news media.[49]

Take the case of Christopher Lowe, operator of the "Lowe Investment & Financial Letter." He ran afoul of SEC contentions that it had the power to require permission to publish, plus the power to get injunctions to stop publications if SEC dictates were not obeyed. Lowe had been a licensed investment adviser, operating within the provisions of the Investment Advisers Act of 1940, and founded his newsletter in 1974.[50]

Lowe, however, fell on hard times. He was convicted of stock fraud, of check kiting, and of tampering with evidence.[51]

Until 1981, he had been registered with the S.E.C., but that registration was withdrawn in 1981 after Lowe's convictions in New York for securities law violations, fraud, and bad checks. As News Media & the Law reported, "Lowe stopped giving individual advice on investments after his license was revoked, but continued

[49] "SEC Attacks Financial Press," The News Media & The Law, November/December 1984, p. 4

[50] Ibid.

[51] "Publisher Elated By S.E.C. Victory," The New York Times, June 12, 1985, p. 30.

to publish the newsletters.[52]   In 1981, the S.E.C. issued an order, revoking Lowe's registration as an investment adviser, and forbidding him to associate with any investment advisers.[53]   As the U.S. Court of Appeals reported as it upheld the S.E.C. action in trying to halt Lowe's newsletters,[54]

> No contention is made that any of the information published in the [Lowe] advisory services has been false or materially misleading.   Nor is it alleged that Lowe himself * * * has profited through personal or corporate investments from the investment advice offered.

Saying that it believed that the Lowe case added up to permissible regulation of economic activity, the court added: "we believe that the Investment Advisers Act withstands constitutional scrutiny under the First Amendment doctrine relating to commercial speech as well." [55]

The Supreme Court disagreed, finding—without reaching constitutional analysis—that the SEC had overreached its authority. Writing for the Court, Justice John Paul Stevens said that Congressional legislation creating the S.E.C. gave the regulatory body no jurisdiction over investment publications.[56]

The New York Times noted that the Supreme Court did not rule out all S.E.C. control over investment newsletters.   If a newsletter's publishers had an interest in some stock they were recommending—or if the publication contained information that was purposely misleading or false—then the S.E.C. could have sway over the situation under the Investment Advisers Act of 1940.[57]

[52] News Media & the Law, November/December, 1984, p. 4

[53] Ibid.; see also "Newsletter Setback for S.E.C.," The New York Times, June 11, 1985, p. 33.

[54] SEC v. Lowe, 725 F.2d 892 (2d Cir.1984), 10 Med.L.Rptr. 1225, 1226.

[55] Ibid., at p. 1231.

[56] Lowe v. SEC, ___ U.S. ___, 105 S.Ct. 2557 (1985).

[57] "Newsletter Setback for S.E.C.," The New York Times, June 11, 1985, p. 33.

*

Appendix A

ABBREVIATIONS

A.	Atlantic Reporter.
A.2d	Atlantic Reporter, Second Series.
A.C.	Appeal Cases.
A.L.R.	American Law Reports.
Aff.	Affirmed; affirming.
Ala.	Alabama;—Alabama Supreme Court Reports.
Am.Dec.	American Decisions.
Am.Jur.	American Jurisprudence, a legal encyclopedia.
Am.Rep.	American Reports.
Am.St.Rep.	American State Reports.
Ann.Cas.	American Annotated Cases.
App.D.C.	Court of Appeals, District of Columbia.
App.Div.	New York Supreme Court, Appellate Divisions, Reports.
Ariz.	Arizona; Arizona Supreme Court Reports.
Ark.	Arkansas; Arkansas Supreme Court Reports.
Bing.	Bingham, New Cases, Common Pleas (England).
C.D.	Copyright Decision.
C.J.	Corpus Juris, a legal encyclopedia.
C.J.S.	Corpus Juris Secundum, a legal encyclopedia.
Cal.	California; California Supreme Court Reports.
Can.Sup.Ct.	Canada Supreme Court Reports.
Cert.	Certiorari, a legal writ by which a cause is removed from an inferior to a superior court.
C.F.R.	Code of Federal Regulations.
Colo.	Colorado; Colorado Supreme Court Reports.
Conn.	Connecticut; Connecticut Supreme Court of Errors Reports.
Cranch	Cranch, United States Supreme Court Reports; United States Circuit Court Reports.
Cush.	Cushing (Massachusetts).
D.C.App.	District of Columbia Court of Appeals Reports.
Dall, Dal.	Dallas, United States Supreme Court Reports; Pennsylvania Reports.
Del.	Delaware; Delaware Supreme Court Reports.
Edw.	Edward; refers to a particular king of England; which king of that name is indicated by the date; used to identify an act of Parliament.
Eng.Rep.	English Reports (reprint).
F.	Federal Reporter.

741

F.2d .... Federal Reporter, Second Series.

F.C.C. .... Federal Communications Commission Reports.

F.R.D. .... Federal Rules Decisions.

F.Supp. .... Federal Supplement.

Fed.Cas. or F.Cas. Reports of United States Circuit and District Courts, 1789–1879.

Fla. .... Florida; Florida Supreme Court Reports.

Ga. .... Georgia; Georgia Supreme Court Reports.

Ga.App. .... Georgia Appeals Reports.

How.St.Tr. .... Howell's State Trials.

Hun .... Hun, New York Supreme Court Reports.

Ibid. .... Ibidem, the same, in the same volume, or on the same page.

Ill. .... Illinois; Illinois Supreme Court Reports.

Ill.App. .... Illinois Appellate Court Reports.

Ind. .... Indiana; Indiana Supreme Court Reports.

Ind.App. .... Indiana Appellate Court Reports.

Johns.Cas. .... Johnson's Cases (New York).

K.B. .... King's Bench Reports (England).

Kan. .... Kansas; Kansas Supreme Court Reports.

Ky. .... Kentucky; Kentucky Court of Appeals Reports.

L.J. .... Law Journal (England).

L.R.Q.B. .... Law Reports, Queen's Bench (England).

L.R.A. .... Lawyers Reports Annotated.

L.R.A.,N.S., ... Lawyers Reports Annotated, New Series.

L.R.Ex. .... Law Reports, Exchequer (England).

L.T. .... The Law Times (England).

La. .... Louisiana; Louisiana Supreme Court Reports.

La.Ann. .... Louisiana Annual Reports.

Mass. .... Massachusetts; Massachusetts Supreme Judicial Court Reports.

Md. .... Maryland; Maryland Court of Appeals Reports.

Me. .... Maine; Maine Supreme Judicial Court Reports.

Mich. .... Michigan; Michigan Supreme Court Reports.

Minn. .... Minnesota; Minnesota Supreme Court Reports.

Miss. .... Mississippi; Mississippi Supreme Court Reports.

Mo. .... Missouri; Missouri Supreme Court Reports.

Mo.App. .... Missouri Appeals Reports.

Mont. .... Montana; Montana Supreme Court Reports.

N.C. .... North Carolina; North Carolina Supreme Court Reports.

N.D. .... North Dakota; North Dakota Supreme Court Reports.

N.E. .... Northeastern Reporter.

N.E.2d .... Northeastern Reporter, Second Series.

N.H. .... New Hampshire; New Hampshire Supreme Court Reports.

N.J. .... New Jersey; New Jersey Court of Errors and Appeals Reports.

N.J.L. .... New Jersey Law Reports.

N.M. .... New Mexico; New Mexico Supreme Court Reports.

N.W. .... Northwestern Reporter.

N.W.2d .... Northwestern Reporter, Second Series.

N.Y. .... New York; New York Court of Appeals Reports.

N.Y.S. .... New York Supplement Reports.

Neb. .... Nebraska; Nebraska Supreme Court Reports.

Nev. .... Nevada; Nevada Supreme Court Reports.

Ohio App. .... Ohio Appeals Reports.

Ohio St. .... Ohio State Reports.

Okl. .... Oklahoma; Oklahoma Supreme Court Reports.

Ops. .... Opinions, as of Attorney General of the United States, or a state.

Or., Ore., Oreg. .. Oregon; Oregon Supreme Court Reports.

P. .... Pacific Reporter.

P.2d .... Pacific Reporter, Second Series.

P.L. & R. .... Postal Laws and Regulations (1948 ed.).

Pa. .... Pennsylvania District and County Court Reports.

Pa.D. & C. .... Pennsylvania District and County Court Reports.

Pa.Super. .... Pennsylvania Superior Court Reports.

Paige .... Paige, New York Chancery Reports.

per se .... In itself or by itself; used in connection with words actionable *per se,* libelous *per se,* or slanderous, *per se.*

Phila. (Pa). .... Philadelphia Reports.

Pick. .... Pickering, Massachusetts Reports.

Q.B. .... Queen's Bench.

R. .... Rex king; regina, queen.

R.C.L. .... Ruling Case Law.

R.C.P. .... Rules of Civil Procedure.

R.I. .... Rhode Island; Rhode Island Supreme Court Reports.

R.R. .... Pike & Fisher Radio Regulations.

S.C. .... South Carolina; South Carolina Supreme Court Reports.

S.D. .... South Dakota; South Dakota Supreme Court Reports.

S.E. .... Southeastern Reporter.

S.E.2d .... Southeastern Reporter, Second Series.
S.W. .... Southwestern Reporter.
S.W.2d .... Southwestern Reporter, Second Series.
Sandf. .... Sandford, New York Superior Court Reports.
Sec. .... Section.
So. .... Southern Reporter.
So.2d .... Southern Reporter, Second Series.
Stark. .... Starkie, English Reports.
S.Ct. .... Supreme Court Reporter.
T.L.R. .... Times Law Reports (England).
Tenn. .... Tennessee; Tennessee Supreme Court Reports.
Tex. .... Texas; Texas Supreme Court (and the Commission of Appeals) Reports.
Tex.Civ.App. .... Texas Civil Appeals Reports.
Tex.Cr.R. .... Texas Court of Criminal Appeals Reports.
U.S.C. .... United States Code.
U.S.C.A. .... United States Code Annotated.
U.S.P.Q. .... United States Patents Quarterly.
V. .... Volume.
Va. .... Virginia; Virginia Supreme Court of Appeals Reports.
Vt. .... Vermont; Vermont Supreme Court Reports.
W.Va. .... West Virginia; West Virginia Supreme Court of Appeals Reports.
Wash. .... Washington; Washington Supreme Court Reports.
Wash.L.Rep. .... Washington Law Reporter, Washington, D.C.
Whart. .... Wharton (Pa.).
Wheat. .... Wheaton (U.S.).
Wis. .... Wisconsin; Wisconsin Supreme Court Reports.
Wyo. .... Wyoming; Wyoming Supreme Court Reports.

Appendix B

SELECTED COURT AND PLEADING
TERMS

Action

A formal legal demand of one's rights made in a court of law.

Actionable per quod

Words not actionable in themselves may be defamatory when special damages are proved.

Actionable per se

Words that need no explanation in order to determine their defamatory effect.

Amicus curiae

A friend of the court or one who interposes and volunteers information upon some matter of law.

Answer

The pleading of a defendant against whom a complaint has been filed.

Appeal

An application by an appellant to a higher court to change the order or judgment of the court below.

Appellant

The person or party appealing a decision or judgment to a higher court.

Appellee

The party against whom an appeal is taken.

Bind over

To hold on bail for trial.

Brief

A written or printed document prepared by counsel to file in court, normally providing both facts and law in support of the case.

Cause of action

The particular facts on which an action is based.

Certiorari

A writ commanding judges of a lower court to transfer to a higher court records of a case so that judicial review may take place.

Change of venue

Removing a civil suit or criminal action from one county or district to another county or district for trial.

Civil action (suit, trial)

Court action brought to enforce, redress, or protect private rights, as distinguished from a Criminal action (q.v.).

Criminal action (trial)

An action undertaken to punish a violation of criminal laws, as distinguished from a Civil action (q.v.).

Code

A compilation or system of laws, arranged into chapters, and promulgated by legislative authority.

Common law

The law of the decided cases, derived from the judgments and decrees of courts. Also called "case law." Originally, meant law which derived its authority from the ancient usages or customs of England.

Complaint

The initial proceeding by a complainant, or plaintiff, in a civil action.

Contempt of court

Any act calculated to embarrass, hinder, or obstruct a court in the administration of justice, or calculated to lessen its dignity or authority.

Courts of record

Those whose proceedings are permanently recorded, and which have the power to fine or imprison for contempt. Courts not of record are those of lesser authority whose proceedings are not permanently recorded.

Damages

> Monetary compensation which may be recovered in court by a person who has suffered loss, detriment, or injury to his person, property, rights, or business, through the unlawful or negligent act of another person or party.

De novo

> Anew, afresh. A trial de novo is a retrial of a case.

Dictum (pl. Dicta; also, Obiter Dictum)

> An observation made by a judge, in an opinion on a case, that does not go to the main issue—a saying "by the way".

Discovery

> A party's pre-trial devices used, in preparation for trial, to obtain facts from the other party.

Due process

> Law in its regular course of administration through the courts of justice. The guarantee of due process requires that every man have the protection of a fair trial.

En banc

> A session where the entire membership of a court, instead of one or a few, participates in the decision of an important case. ("Banc" means the judge's "bench" or place to sit.)

Equity

> That system of jurisprudence which gives relief when there is no full, complete and adequate remedy at law; based originally upon the custom of appealing to the King or chancellor when the formality of the common law did not give means for relief.

Estoppel

> An admission which prevents a person from using evidence which proves or tends to prove the contrary.

Executive session

> A meeting of a board or governmental body that is closed to the public.

Ex parte

By or concerning only one party. This implies an examination in the presence of one party in a proceeding and the absence of the opposing party.

Ex post facto

After the fact.

Habeas corpus

Latin for "you have the body." A writ issued to an officer holding a person in detention or under arrest to bring that person before a court to determine the legality of the detention.

In camera

In the judge's private chambers or in a courtroom from which all spectators have been excluded.

Indictment

A written accusation of a crime prepared by a prosecuting attorney and presented for the consideration of a grand jury.

Information

A formal, written accusation of a crime prepared by a competent law officer of the government, such as a district or prosecuting attorney.

Injunction

A judicial order in equity directed against a person or organization directing that an act be performed or that the person or organization refrain from doing a particular act.

Judgment

The decision of a court of law.

Jury

A group of a certain number of persons, selected according to law and sworn to inquire into certain matters of fact, and to declare the truth from evidence brought before them. A *grand jury* hears complaints and accusations in criminal cases, and issues bills of indictment in cases where the jurors believe that there is enough evidence to bring a case to trial. A *petit jury* consists of 12 (or fewer) persons who hear the trial of a civil or criminal case.

Mandamus

An extraordinary legal writ issued from a court to a corporation or its officers, to a public official, or to an inferior court commanding the doing of an act which the person, corporation, or lower court is under a duty to perform.

Motion to dismiss

A formal application by a litigant or his counsel addressed to the court for an order to dismiss the case.

Nol pros, nolle prosequi

A formal notification of unwillingness to prosecute which is entered upon the court record.

N.O.V. ("non obstante veredicto")

A judgment by the court in favor of one party notwithstanding a verdict that has been given to the other party.

Plaintiff

The person (including an organization or business) who initiates a legal action.

Pleading

The process in which parties to a lawsuit or legal action alternately file with a court written statements of their contentions. By this process of statement and counter-statement, legal issues are framed and narrowed. These statements are often termed "pleadings."

Preliminary hearing, preliminary examination

A person charged with a crime is given a preliminary examination or hearing before a magistrate or judge to determine whether there is sufficient evidence to hold that person for trial.

Prima facie (pron.: prī ma fā shē)

"At first sight" or "on the face of it." So far as can be judged from the first disclosure.

Reply

The pleading of plaintiff in response to the "answer" of the defendant.

Res adjudicata or res judicata

> A thing decided.

Respondent

> A party who gives an answer to a bill in equity; also, one who opposes a party who has taken a case to a higher court.

Stare decisis

> To stand by the decisions, or to maintain precedent. This legal doctrine holds that settled points of law will not be disturbed.

Subpoena

> A command to appear at a place and time and to give testimony. "Subpoena-duces tecum" is a command to produce some document or paper at a trial.

Summary

> Connoting "without a full trial." A summary judgment is a judge's rule that one party in a lawsuit wins before the conclusion of a full trial.

Venue

> The particular county, city, or geographical area in which a court with jurisdiction may hear and decide a case.

Verdict

> The decision of a jury as reported to the court.

Voir dire

> Denotes the preliminary examination which the court may make of one presented as a witness or juror, where his competency or interest is objected to.

Writ

> A legal instrument in the judicial process to enforce compliance with orders and sentences of a court.

Appendix C

BIBLIOGRAPHY

American Law Institute, Restatement of the Law: Torts. 2d ed. St. Paul, 1977.

Adler, Allan, and M.H. Halperin, Litigation Under the Federal Freedom of Information Act and Privacy Act, 1984 Washington, D.C., 1984.

Angoff, Charles, Handbook of Libel. New York, 1946.

Bagdikian, Ben, The Media Monopoly. Boston, 1983.

Barnouw, Erk, A History of Broadcasting in the United States, 3 vols. (N.Y., 1966–1972).

Barron, Jerome, Freedom of the Press for Whom? Bloomington, Ind., 1973.

Beck, Carl, Contempt of Congress. New Orleans, 1959.

Berns, Walter, The First Amendment and the Future of American Democracy. New York, 1976.

Blackstone, William, Commentaries on the Law of England, IV, adapted by Robert Malcom Kerr, Boston, 1952.

Blasi, Vincent, The Checking Value in First Amendment Theory, Am. Bar Foundation Research Journal, 1977, # 3.

Center for National Security Studies, FOIA Handbook. Washington, D.C., 1979.

Chafee, Zechariah, Jr., Free Speech in the United States. Boston, 1941.

————, Government and Mass Communications, 2 vols. Chicago, 1947.

Chamberlin, Bill F., and Charlene Brown, The First Amendment Reconsidered. Chapel Hill, 1981.

Cooley, Thomas M., Constitutional Limitations (8th ed.). Boston, 1927.

Cooper, Thomas, The Law of Libel and the Liberty of the Press. New York, 1830.

Denniston, Lyle, The Reporter and the Law. New York, 1980.

Devol, Kenneth S., Mass Media and the Supreme Court, 2d ed. New York, 1976.

Duniway, Clyde A., The Development of Freedom of the Press in Massachusetts. Cambridge, 1906.

Emerson, Thomas I., The System of Freedom of Expression. New York, 1970.

Emery, Walter B., Broadcasting and Government: Responsibilities and Regulations. East Lansing, Mich., 1961.

Fox, Sir John C., The History of Contempt of Court. Oxford, 1927.

Franklin, Marc A., Mass Media Law Cases and Materials, Mineola, N.Y., 1977.

Friendly, Fred, Minnesota Rag. New York, 1981.

Gerald, J. Edward, The Press and the Constitution, 1931–1947. Minneapolis, 1948.

Gillmor, Donald M., Free Press and Fair Trial. Washington, D.C., 1966.

Ginsburg, Douglas H., Regulation of Broadcasting. St. Paul, 1979.

Goldfarb, Ronald L., The Contempt Power. New York, 1963.

Goodale, James, C., Communications Law 1984. New York, 1984.

Gora, Joel M., The Rights of Reporters. New York, 1974.

Grundfest, Joseph A., Citizen Participation in Broadcasting Licensing Before the FCC, Santa Monica, Cal., 1976.

Hachten, William A., The Supreme Court on Freedom of the Press: Decisions and Dissents. Ames, Iowa, 1968.

Haight, Anne Lyon, Banned Books (rev. 2d ed.). New York, 1955.

Havick, John J., Communications Policy and the Political Process. Westport, Conn., 1983.

Head, Sydney W., Broadcasting in America. (3d ed.). Boston, 1976.

Hentoff, Nat, History of Freedom of the Press in America. New York, 1980.

Hocking, William E., Freedom of the Press. Chicago, 1947.

Holmes, Oliver Wendell Jr., The Common Law. Boston, 1881.

Jolliffe, John, The Constitutional History of Medieval England (2d ed.). London, 1947.

Jones, William, Cases and Materials on Electronic Mass Media. Mineola, N.Y., 1977.

Kahn, F.J., ed., Documents of American Broadcasting. New York, 1968.

Kinsley, Philip, Liberty and the Press. Chicago, 1944.

Konvitz, Milton R., First Amendment Freedoms. Ithaca, 1963.

Kaufman, Henry R., ed., LDRC 50–State Survey 1984, III. New York, 1984.

Levy, Leonard W., Emergence of a Free Press. New York, 1985.

————, ed., Freedom of the Press from Zenger to Jefferson. Indianapolis, 1966.

————, Legacy of Suppression, Freedom of Speech and Press in Early American History. Cambridge, 1960.

Lockhart, William B., and Robert C. McClure, Censorship of Obscenity: the Developing Constitutional Standards, 45 Minnesota Law Review 5 (Nov. 1960).

————, Literature, the Law of Obscenity, and the Constitution, 38 Minnesota Law Review (March 1954).

Lofton, John, The Press as a Defender of the First Amendment. Columbia, S.C., 1980.

McCormick, Robert R., The Freedom of the Press. New York, 1936.

Meiklejohn, Alexander, Free Speech and Its Relation to Self Government. New York, 1948.

Miller, Arthur, The Assault on Privacy. Ann Arbor, 1971.

Murphy, Paul, World War I and the Origins of Civil Liberties in the United States. New York, 1979.

Nelson, Harold L., ed., Freedom of the Press from Hamilton to the Warren Court. Indianapolis, 1967.

Nimmer, Melville B., Nimmer on Copyright, 4 vols. New York, 1963, 1985.

Odgers, W. Blake, A Digest of the Law of Libel and Slander (6th ed.). London, 1929.

Owen, Bruce M., Economics and Freedom of Expression. Cambridge, 1975.

Paterson, James, Liberty of Press, Speech and Public Worship. London, 1880.

Patterson, Giles J., Free Speech and a Free Press. Boston, 1939.

Paul, James C.N., and Murray L. Schwartz, Federal Censorship: Obscenity in the Mail. New York, 1961.

Pember, Don R., Privacy and the Press. Seattle, 1972.

Peterson, H.C., and Gilbert C. Fite, Opponents of War, 1917–1918. Madison, 1957.

Pilpel, Harriet, and Theodora Zavin, Rights and Writers. New York, 1960.

Preston, Ivan, The Great American Blowup. Madison, 1975.

Preston, William, Jr., Aliens and Dissenters. Cambridge, 1963.

Prosser, William L., The Law of Torts. 4th ed. St. Paul, 1971.

Rohrer, Daniel M., Mass Media, Freedom of Speech, and Advertising. Dubuque, Ia., 1979.

Rosden, George Eric and Peter Eric, The Law of Advertising, 2 vols. (New York, 1963, 1976, 1985).

Rourke, Francis E., Secrecy and Publicity. Baltimore, 1961.

Sack, Robert D., Libel, Slander, and Related Problems. New York, 1980.

Sanford, Bruce, The Law of Libel and the Right of Privacy. New York, 1984.

Schmidt, Benno C., Jr., Freedom of the Press vs. Public Access. New York, 1976.

Seldes, George, Freedom of the Press. Cleveland, 1935.

Shapiro, Martin, Freedom of Speech: The Supreme Court and Judicial Review. Englewood Cliffs, N.J., 1966.

Siebert, Fredrick S., Freedom of the Press in England, 1476–1776. Urbana, 1952.

Simmons, Steven J., The Fairness Doctrine and the Media. Berkeley, 1978.

Simon, Morton J., Public Relations Law. New York, 1969.

Smith, James Morton, Freedom's Fetters: the Alien and Sedition Laws and American Civil Liberties. Ithaca, 1956.

Stansbury, Arthur J., Report of the Trial of James H. Peck. Boston, 1833.

Starkie, Thomas, The Law of Slander, Libel, Scandalum Magnatum and False Rumors, with the Practise and Pleadings. London, 1813; 4th ed. by Henry C. Folkard, with notes and references to American Cases by Horace G. Wood. New York, 1877.

Sullivan, Harold W., Contempts by Publication. New Haven, 1940.

Warren, Samuel D., and Louis D. Brandeis, The Right to Privacy, 4 Harvard Law Review 193 (1890).

Westin, Alan, Privacy and Freedom. New York, 1967.

Winfield, Richard N., New York Times v. Sullivan, the Next Twenty Years (New York, Practising Law Institute, 1984).

Wolff, Robert Paul, Barrington Moore and Herbert Marcuse, A Critique of Pure Tolerance. Boston, 1965.

Wortman, Tunis, Treatise Concerning Political Enquiry, and the Liberty of the Press. New York, 1800.

Yudof, Mark G., When Government Speaks. Berkeley, 1983.

Additional Resources

American Digest System, Decennial Digests, valuable for lists of cases and points adjudicated.

American Jurisprudence, a legal encyclopedia.

Annotated Report System, selected reports and annotations, with summaries of arguments of counsel.

Compilations of Laws Affecting Publications, particularly those put out by various states. Consult managers of various state press associations.

Corpus Juris Secundum, a legal encyclopedia.

Freedom of Information Center, University of Missouri, issues frequent Reports, the FOI Digest (bi-monthly newsletter), and occasional studies covering a wide variety of media-and-law-subjects. Invaluable for state laws on meetings and records.

Law Dictionaries, including Black's, Ballentine's, and Bouvier's.

Law Reviews. Among the outstanding law reviews published under the direction of law schools are Columbia Law Review, Cornell Law Quarterly, Harvard Law Review, Illinois Law Review, Michigan Law Review, Texas Law Review, Wisconsin Law Review, and Yale Law Journal.

Libel Defense Resource Center Bulletin. Reports studies and analyses by the Center, many of them wide-sweeping surveys of aspects of libel nationally.

Media Law Reporter. Bureau of National Affairs, Inc., Washington, D.C. This looseleaf service provides up-to-date coverage of court decisions (full texts) and news notes in communication law, beginning in 1976.

National Reporter System, giving texts of appellate court decisions in various jurisdictions of the nation.

News Media and the Law, publication of the Reporters Committee for Freedom of the Press (formerly Press Censorship Newsletter). Washington, D.C.

Words and Phrases, a legal encyclopedia based on definitions of terms as used in statutes and by the courts.

Appendix D

THE SIGMA DELTA CHI AND ASNE
CODES OF ETHICS

THE SOCIETY OF PROFESSIONAL JOURNALISTS, SIGMA DELTA CHI CODE OF ETHICS

The Society of Professional Journalists, Sigma Delta Chi, believes the duty of journalists is to serve the truth.

We believe the agencies of mass communication are carriers of public discussion and information, acting on their Constitutional mandate and freedom to learn and report the facts.

We believe in public enlightenment as the forerunner of justice, and in our Constitutional role to seek the truth as part of the public's right to know the truth.

We believe those responsibilities carry obligations that require journalists to perform with intelligence, objectivity, accuracy and fairness.

To these ends, we declare acceptance of the standards of practice here set forth:

• **Responsibility:** The public's right to know of events of public importance and interest is the overriding mission of the mass media. The purpose of distributing news and enlightened opinion is to serve the general welfare. Journalists who use their professional status as representatives of the public for selfish or other unworthy motives violate a high trust.

• **Freedom of the Press:** Freedom of the press is to be guarded as an inalienable right of people in a free society. It carries with it the freedom and the responsibility to discuss, question and challenge actions and utterances of our government and of our public and private institutions. Journalists uphold the right to speak unpopular opinions and the privilege to agree with the majority.

• **Ethics:** Journalists must be free of obligation to any interest other than the public's right to know the truth.

1. Gifts, favors, free travel, special treatment or privileges can compromise the integrity of journalists and their employers. Nothing of value should be accepted.

2. Secondary employment, political involvement, holding public office and service in community organizations should be avoided if it compromises the integrity of journalists and their

756

employers. Journalists and their employers should conduct their personal lives in a manner which protects them from conflict of interest, real or apparent. Their responsibilities to the public are paramount. That is the nature of their profession.

3. So-called news communications from private sources should not be published or broadcast without substantiation of their claims to news value.

4. Journalists will seek news that serves the public interest, despite the obstacles. They will make constant efforts to assure that the public's business is conducted in public and that public records are open to public inspection.

5. Journalists acknowledge the newsman's ethic of protecting confidential sources of information.

• **Accuracy and Objectivity:** Good faith with the public is the foundation of all worthy journalism.

1. Truth is our ultimate goal.

2. Objectivity in reporting the news is another goal, which serves as the mark of an experienced professional. It is a standard of performance toward which we strive. We honor those who achieve it.

3. There is no excuse for inaccuracies or lack of thoroughness.

4. Newspaper headlines should be fully warranted by the contents of the articles they accompany. Photographs and telecasts should give an accurate picture of an event and not highlight a minor incident out of context.

5. Sound practice makes clear distinction between news reports and expressions of opinion. News reports should be free of opinion or bias and represent all sides of an issue.

6. Partisanship in editorial comment which knowingly departs from the truth violates the spirit of American journalism.

7. Journalists recognize their responsibility for offering informed analysis, comment and editorial opinion on public events and issues. They accept the obligation to present such material by individuals whose competence, experience and judgment qualify them for it.

8. Special articles or presentations devoted to advocacy or the writer's own conclusions and interpretations should be labeled as such.

• **Fair Play:** Journalists at all times will show respect for the dignity, privacy, rights and well-being of people encountered in the course of gathering and presenting the news.

1.   The news media should not communicate unofficial charges affecting reputation or moral character without giving the accused a chance to reply.

2.   The news media must guard against invading a person's right to privacy.

3.   The media should not pander to morbid curiosity about details of vice and crime.

4.   It is the duty of news media to make prompt and complete correction of their errors.

5.   Journalists should be accountable to the public for their reports and the public should be encouraged to voice its grievances against the media. Open dialogue with our readers, viewers and listeners should be fostered.

• **Pledge:** Journalists should actively censure and try to prevent violations of these standards, and they should encourage their observance by all newspeople. Adherence to this code of ethics is intended to preserve the bond of mutual trust and respect between American journalists and the American people.

Adopted by the 1973 national convention.

ASNE STATEMENT OF PRINCIPLES

PREAMBLE

The First Amendment, protecting freedom of expression from abridgment by any law, guarantees to the people through their press a constitutional right, and thereby places on newspaper people a particular responsibility.

Thus journalism demands of its practitioners not only industry and knowledge but also the pursuit of a standard of integrity proportionate to the journalist's singular obligation.

To this end the American Society of Newspaper Editors sets forth this Statement of Principles as a standard encouraging the highest ethical and professional performance.

ARTICLE I: RESPONSIBILITY

The primary purpose of gathering and distributing news and opinion is to serve the general welfare by informing the people and enabling them to make judgments on the issues of the time. Newspapermen and women who abuse the power of their professional role for selfish motives or unworthy purposes are faithless to that public trust.

The American press was made free not just to inform or just to serve as a forum for debate but also to bring an independent scrutiny to bear on the forces of power in the society, including the conduct of official power at all levels of government.

ARTICLE II: FREEDOM OF THE PRESS

Freedom of the press belongs to the people. It must be defended against encroachment or assault from any quarter, public or private.

Journalists must be constantly alert to see that the public's business is conducted in public. They must be vigilant against all who would exploit the press for selfish purposes.

ARTICLE III: INDEPENDENCE

Journalists must avoid impropriety and the appearance of impropriety as well as any conflict of interest or the appearance of conflict. They should neither accept anything nor pursue any activity that might compromise or seem to compromise their integrity.

ARTICLE IV: TRUTH AND ACCURACY

Good faith with the reader is the foundation of good journalism. Every effort must be made to assure that the news content is accurate, free from bias and in context, and that all sides are presented fairly. Editorials, analytical articles and commentary should be held to the same standards of accuracy with respect to facts as news reports.

Significant errors of fact, as well as errors of omission, should be corrected promptly and prominently.

ARTICLE V: IMPARTIALITY

To be impartial does not require the press to be unquestioning or to refrain from editorial expression. Sound practice, however, demands a clear distinction for the reader between news reports and opinion. Articles that contain opinion or personal interpretation should be clearly identified.

ARTICLE VI: FAIR PLAY

Journalists should respect the rights of people involved in the news, observe the common standards of decency and stand accountable to the public for the fairness and accuracy of their news reports.

Persons publicly accused should be given the earliest opportunity to respond.

Pledges of confidentiality to news sources must be honored at all costs, and therefore should not be given lightly. Unless there is clear and pressing need to maintain confidences, sources of information should be identified.

These principles are intended to preserve, protect and strengthen the bond of trust and respect between American journalists and the American people, a bond that is essential to sustain the grant of freedom entrusted to both by the nation's founders.

This Statement of Principles was adopted by the ASNE Board of Directors, Oct. 23, 1975; it supplants the 1922 Code of Ethics ("Canons of Journalism").

Appendix E

NEWSPAPER PRESERVATION ACT

(15 U.S.C.A. Sections 1801–1804)

Section 1801. Congressional Declaration of Policy

In the public interest of maintaining a newspaper press editorially and reportorially independent and competitive in all parts of the United States to preserve the publication of newspapers in any city, community, or metropolitan area where a joint operating arrangement has been heretofore entered into because of economic distress or is hereafter effected in accordance with the provisions of this chapter.

Section 1802. Definitions

As used in this chapter—

(1) The term "antitrust law" means the Federal Trade Commission Act and each statute defined by section 44 of this title as "Antitrust Acts" and all amendments to such Act and such statutes and any other Acts in pari materia.[1]

(2) The term "joint newspaper operating arrangement" means any contract, agreement, joint venture (whether or not incorporated), or other arrangement entered into by two or more newspaper owners for the publication of two or more newspaper publications, pursuant to which joint or common production facilities are established or operated and joint or unified action is taken or agreed to be taken with respect to any one or more of the following: printing; time, method, and field of publication, allocation of production facilities; distribution; advertising solicitation; circulation solicitation; business department; establishment of advertising rates; establishment of circulation rates and revenue distribution: *Provided,* That there is no merger, combination, or amalgamation of editorial or reportorial staffs, and that editorial policies be independently determined.

(3) The term "newspaper owner" means any person who owns or controls directly, or indirectly through sepa-

---

[1] "In pari materia" means "upon the same matter or subject;" Black's Law Dictionary, 5th Rev.Ed., p. 1004. Statutes *in pari materia* are to be construed together.

rate or subsidiary corporations, one or more newspaper publications.

(4) The term "newspaper publication" means a publication produced on newsprint paper which is published in one or more issues weekly (including as one publication any daily newspaper and any Sunday newspaper published by the same owner in the same city, community, or metropolitan area), and in which a substantial portion of the content is devoted to the dissemination of news and editorial opinion.

(5) The term "failing newspaper" means a newspaper publication which, regardless of its ownership or affiliations, is in probable danger of financial failure.

(6) The term "person" means any individual, and any partnership, corporation, association, or other legal entity existing under or authorized by the law of the United States, any State or possession of the United States, the District of Columbia, the Commonwealth of Puerto Rico, or any foreign country.

Section 1803. Antitrust Exemption

(a) It shall not be unlawful under any antitrust law for any person to perform, enforce, renew, or amend any joint newspaper operating arrangement entered into prior to July 24, 1970, if at the time at which such arrangement was first entered into, regardless of ownership or affiliations, not more than one of the newspaper publications involved in the performance of such arrangement was likely to remain or become a financially sound publication: *Provided,* That the terms of a renewal or amendment to a joint operating arrangement must be filed with the Department of Justice and that the amendment does not add a newspaper publication or newspaper publications to such arrangement.

(b) It shall be unlawful for any person to enter into, perform, or enforce a joint operating arrangement, not already in effect, except with the prior written consent of the Attorney General of the United States. Prior to granting such approval, the Attorney General shall determine that not more than one of the newspaper publications involved in the arrangement is a publication other than a failing newspaper, and that approval of such arrangement would effectuate the policy and purpose of this chapter.

(c) Nothing contained in this chapter shall be construed to exempt from any antitrust law any predatory pricing, any predatory practice, or any other conduct in the otherwise lawful operations of a joint newspaper operating arrangement which would be unlawful under any antitrust law if engaged in by a single entity. Except as provided in this chapter, no joint newspaper operating arrangement or any part thereto shall be exempt from any antitrust law.

Section 1804. Reinstatement of Joint Operating Arrangement Previously Judged Unlawful Under Antitrust Laws

(a) Notwithstanding any final judgment rendered in any action brought by the United States under which a joint operating arrangement has been held to be unlawful under any antitrust law, any party to such final judgment may reinstate said joint newspaper operating arrangement to the extent permissible under section 1803(a) of this title.

(b) The provisions of section 1803 of this title shall apply to the determination of any civil or criminal action pending in any district court of the United States on July 24, 1970, in which it is alleged that any such joint operating agreement is unlawful under any antitrust law.

*

TABLE OF CASES

References are to Pages

*

INDEX

References are to Pages

†